THE COMPLETE
ILLUSTRATED WORKS OF
LEWIS
CARROLL

LEWIS CARROLL (CHARLES LUTWIDGE DODGSON) AT AGE TWENTY-FOUR

THE COMPLETE ILLUSTRATED WORKS OF
LEWIS CARROLL

Edited by Edward Guiliano

Alice's Adventures in Wonderland

Through the Looking-Glass
and What Alice Found There

The Hunting of the Snark

Rhyme? and Reason?

A Tangled Tale

Alice's Adventures Under Ground

Sylvie and Bruno

Sylvie and Bruno Concluded

Three Sunsets and Other Poems

*Illustrated by John Tenniel, Lewis Carroll, Arthur B. Frost,
Henry Holiday, Harry Furniss, and E. Gertrude Thomson*

AVENEL BOOKS · NEW YORK

This 1982 edition is published by Avenel Books,
distributed by Crown Publishers, Inc.

Manufactured in the United States of America

Library of Congress Cataloging in Publication Data

Carroll, Lewis, 1832–1898.
  The complete illustrated works of Lewis Carroll.

  Bibliography: p.
  Contents: Alice's adventures in Wonderland—
Through the looking-glass and what Alice found there—
The hunting of the snark—[etc.]
  I. Guiliano, Edward.   II. Tenniel, John, Sir, 1820–
1914.   III. Title.
PR4611.A4   1982   828'.809   82-13878
ISBN: 0-517-38566-X
ISBN: 0-517-37155-3 (lib. bdg.)
h g f e d c b a

Publisher's Note - Illustrations on the following pages have been
enlarged from their original sizes, but no more than five to ten
percent: 299, 301, 308, 312, 319, 331, and 797.

CONTENTS

Note: *The Hunting of the Snark* appears separately in its entirety, so it has not been repeated in this section.

Note: Two *Sylvie and Bruno* poems, "Far Away" and "A Song of Love," have not been repeated in this section.

INTRODUCTION

THE ILLUSTRATED WORLD OF LEWIS CARROLL AND HIS *ALICE*S

"and what is the use of a book," thought Alice, "without pictures or conversations?"—*Alice's Adventures in Wonderland*

AFTER lunch on July 4, 1862, Charles Lutwidge Dodgson, a thirty-year-old Oxford mathematics don and clergyman (later to become universally known as Lewis Carroll) met the three daughters of the dean of his college, Christ Church, for a boating excursion up the river Isis. The events of that "golden afternoon" when the shy, handsome bachelor first told the story of Alice's adventures have become famous and his dream-child immortal. *Alice in Wonderland* and its sequel, *Through the Looking-Glass,* are now classics, of course, with enormous and continuing appeal to children and adults alike. Today Carroll's works are widely quoted and enmeshed in the popular culture not only of English-speaking countries but of others elsewhere as well; in fact, *Alice in Wonderland* has become one of the world's most frequently translated works, now appearing in fifty-five languages. Carroll's indelible creations—the White Rabbit, the Cheshire Cat, the Caterpillar, the Mad Hatter, Humpty Dumpty, the White Knight—all now live lives of their own, and with Alice herself, Carroll created a character whose fame far exceeds that of her author.

On that memorable July day, there was nothing unusual about Dodgson taking the children out for the day; he loved children, had a special rapport with them, and at the time was in the habit of taking the dean's children for outings. About two weeks earlier, he and his friend Robinson Duckworth, then a Fellow at Trinity College, Oxford, had taken Lorina— "Ina"—(age thirteen), Alice (age ten), and Edith Liddell (age eight) downriver by boat to Nuneham, where they were caught in a rainstorm and had to return to Oxford by foot and carriage. For the outing on the fourth, which had been rescheduled from the previous day on account of rain, Dodgson again took Ina, Alice, and Edith (their brother Harry, a frequent companion, was away at school), and was again accompanied by Duckworth, who possessed a pleasant singing voice and was well liked by the children. The two dons exchanged their clerical black for white flannels for the excursion of some three miles to Godstow where they would take tea and cakes by a haystack with the young girls.

Twenty-five years later Dodgson, a bad stammerer who often lost his impediment in the company of children, could recall vividly "the three eager faces" that begged him that afternoon to "tell us a story, please," and that he sent his heroine "straight down the rabbit-hole, to begin with, without the least idea what was to happen afterwards. . . ." "I rowed *stroke* and he rowed *bow* in the famous Long Vacation voyage to Godstow," Duckworth wrote following Dodgson's death in 1898, "and the story was actually composed and spoken *over my shoulder* for the benefit of Alice Liddell, who was acting as 'cox' of our gig. I remember turning round and saying, 'Dodgson, is this an extempore romance of yours?' And he replied, 'Yes, I'm inventing as we go along.' I also well remember how, when we had conducted the three children back to the Deanery, Alice said, as she bade him good-night, 'Oh, Mr. Dodgson, I wish you would write down Alice's adventures for me.' " Many years later Alice reminisced that she pestered Dodgson about writing down the story for her and that "it was due to my 'going on, going on' an importunity [such] that, after saying he would think about it, he eventually gave the hesitating promise which started him writing it down at all."

Dodgson began carrying out Alice's charge to write it down the morning following the boat trip, and over the course of the next seven months he worked up a complete text of *Alice's Adventures Under Ground*. He then turned with an unskilled hand but soaring imagination to the task of illustrating the tale. Simultaneously he also showed his completed text to a few friends, notably the family of George MacDonald, a poet-novelist and author of children's books. Mrs. MacDonald read the story aloud to her children who loved it, and the MacDonalds urged Dodgson to have it published. Acting on the advice and enthusiasm of his friends, Dodgson arranged to have *Alice* published at his own expense by a leading publishing house, Macmillan & Company.

Dodgson did not finish his illustrations for the tale until fall 1864, and on November 26 presented Alice Liddell with the manuscript book, bound in green leather, of *Alice's Adventures Under Ground*. (Years later, in 1885, Dodgson borrowed the volume from Alice in order to produce a trade edition in facsimile; the original is now in the British Library, London.) When, in 1864, he presented Alice with her book he had already begun reworking the manuscript for publication. He had also come to the realization, again aided by the counsel of friends, that the book would benefit from drawings done by a professional illustrator. Earlier that year he had been successful in securing the services for that purpose of John Tenniel, *Punch*'s leading cartoonist and an established book illustrator.

In Tenniel, who excelled at drawing animals, Dodgson found the ideal illustrator for bringing his wild and fanciful creatures into view. Tenniel's illustrations are inextricably wedded to the text, and it is in his definitive portraits that Alice, the Cheshire Cat, the White Rabbit, the Mad Hatter, and all the other Wonderland characters have diffused into our popular culture. Although the Dodgson-Tenniel collaboration appears on paper to be flawless, their personal relationship was not without some tension. Much has been made of the fastidious young author bombarding his seasoned illustrator with suggestions, criticisms, and detailed analyses. But while Dodgson was exacting and hard to please, he was also sensitive to Tenniel's needs and temperament. Perhaps the best illustration of this appears in the final extraordinary twist in the story of how *Alice's Adventures in Wonderland* came into being.

Midyear in 1865, Macmillan printed two thousand copies of *Alice,* and Dodgson wrote to his publisher asking that fifty copies be bound so he could distribute them early to friends and that the remainder be bound at the publisher's leisure. When the bound copies arrived, Dodgson found them agreeable and signed and distributed twenty or so presentation copies. However, he soon received the shocking news from Tenniel that the printing of the pictures was not acceptable and would have to be redone. Dodgson contemplated his options and decided to honor his illustrator's request and to reprint *Alice* at considerable personal expense. He thought to sell off the printed sheets at Macmillan's as waste paper, but, in fact, the nearly two thousand sets of sheets were shipped to America where they were bound and sold in 1866 by D. Appleton & Company of New York. Dodgson also did his best to recover the forty-eight copies he had by then sent out. He divided the returns among five hospitals. Only twenty-three or so of the 1865 *Alices* are known for certain to survive, and each is an exceedingly prized and valuable rare book. A comparison today of the 1865 *Alice* with the subsequent edition that was approved by Tenniel demonstrates that while the later edition is clearly superior, the 1865 is by no means poor. The canceling of an entire run of a children's book by the young, unknown, and not wealthy Dodgson was an extraordinary action displaying courage and righteousness, and an exceptional sensitivity to the temperament and wishes of his illustrator.

An acceptable *Alice* was finally published in November 1865 (though dated 1866) in time for holiday giving. Its initial reviews were good, and as praise for the slim volume spread by word of mouth, the book sold and sold and has never stopped selling. Its sales quickly exceeded the wildest expectations of its author, Lewis Carroll. Rather than sign the book with his real name, Dodgson had opted for a pseudonym, thereby partitioning the serious Dodgson, the Oxford don and clergyman, from the humorous and playful Carroll. He had settled on Lewis Carroll as a pen name a decade earlier when the editor of a comic weekly to which he submitted some comic verses asked him for a pseudonym. Dodgson sent a list of potential names for the editor to choose from: Edgar Cuthwellis, Edgar U. C. Westhill, Louis Carroll, and, of course, Lewis Carroll.

The *Alice* that was published and that is now a classic is considerably different from the manuscript version Dodgson presented to Alice Liddell in 1864; in fact, it is twice as long. Three chapters were added, "Pig and Pepper," "A Mad Tea-Party," and "The Caucus Race," as was much of the Trial scene. In preparing *Alice's Adventures Under Ground* for publication, Carroll also introduced one of his most memorable characters, the Cheshire Cat. Furthermore, private jokes were excised, as were references to events in the real Alice's life, such as the outing to Nuneham when the party was drenched by rain. Many references to people, events, and other things familiar to the Liddells, however, remained woven into the text—perhaps most noticeably the identification of the Dodo with the stammering Do-Do Dodgson, the Duck with Duckworth, the Lory with Lorina, the Eaglet with Edith, and Alice with, well, Alice. The expanded version of *Alice* contains three new poems and is generally more tightly crafted than the initial version, and is also filled out to twelve chapters. It also bears a new title. Carroll considered his original title as well as such possibilities as "Alice among the Goblins" and "Alice's Hour in Elf-Land" before settling on *Alice's Adventures in Wonderland*.

Carroll followed *Alice* with *Through the Looking-Glass and What Alice Found There*, published in December 1871 (dated 1872). The second *Alice* book was illustrated reluctantly by John Tenniel, who thereafter never again drew for Carroll but whose reputation today rests most conspicuously on his *Alice* drawings. The *Alice* books, as they are widely known, share numerous though somewhat superficial similarities: They are both dream visions in twelve chapters, both are characterized by a quest motif, both contain comic poems, both are illustrated by Tenniel, both have always been produced as companion volumes in identical formats, both contain vivid and fanciful characters and more or less the same heroine. A deeper analysis reveals parallels in linguistic playfulness, in probings into the potential of play as escape, as well as darker probings into the nature of being, time, and death.

Despite these similarities, and the filmmakers and playwrights who cavalierly introduce characters from one book into the other, and also the literary critics who write about the *Alice* books as if they were one work and who select examples from one to support assertions about the other, they are distinct books. *Through the Looking-Glass,* which came six years after *Alice,* is one of those rare sequels in literature that lives up to the expectations established by the initial volume, but it is not a sequel in the sense of being a continuation of *Alice's Adventures in Wonderland*; rather, in *Through the Looking-Glass,* Alice (six months older) is delivered into a new land with new characters and new adventures. Moreover, the tone of the second *Alice* book is decidedly different from the first. There is a fatalism that tarnishes some of the humor in *Through the Looking-Glass.* While the world of *Alice in Wonderland* is seemingly random and nonsensical, a world where escape and individual possibility are appealingly present, the world of *Through the Looking-Glass* is determined and absurd, bound into a metaphor of life as a chessboard and all its people only pawns and pieces.

Carroll's next masterpiece was *The Hunting of the Snark,* a heroic nonsense poem written in eight episodes labeled "fits," and published in 1876. Although it has been overshadowed through the years by the *Alice* books, it clearly ranks with them as the finest of Carroll's literary achievements. The poem—the tale of the quest by boat of a snark, a unique monster, by an improbable and confused crew—was, in effect, composed backward. In 1874, while Dodgson was out walking, a line of pure nonsense came into his head, the line that would become the poem's final statement:

"For the Snark *was* a Boojum, you see." Over the next couple of years, Dodgson built the verses up to this final statement, and when three stanzas, or "fits," were complete, he engaged an acquaintance, Henry Holiday, a painter and sculptor (and later, accomplished designer of stained-glass windows), to draw the illustrations. This was despite the advice of John Ruskin, the distinguished art critic and fellow Oxford don, that Holiday would not be able to illustrate the *Snark* properly. While Holiday's work is not up to the standards of Tenniel, he was patient with Dodgson, listening to and following the writer's exacting comments, and he produced a series of woodcuts that more than satisfied the author.

Although lacking an Alice, *The Hunting of the Snark* is in many ways similar to the *Alice* books. It, too, is first and foremost a humorous and entertaining fantasy that appeals to children and adults alike, and it, too, is laced with philosophical depth, social satire, linguistic playfulness, mathematical and logical paradoxes, and a layer of subtle humor. As in the *Alice*s, there is a tension in the *Snark* between the comic tone and the underlying anxieties that readers today find immediate and compelling. And while Victorian readers would have dismissed the thought that the *Snark*, or the *Alice*s, were composed of inner layers dark with seriousness, critics today find dreams, death, probings into the nature of being, reminders of the inescapability of time, and a mythic quest motif figuring in all three works.

Looking back on Carroll's literary career, we can point to the *Alice* and *Snark* years, 1862–1876, as the years of his greatest literary creativity. However, he wrote all his life, from childhood up until his death, and if he never again reached the heights of genius evidenced in these three works, he was brilliantly creative throughout his life, occasionally reaching great heights for short periods in his literary works, regularly reaching them in his letters, and reaching them in quite a different way in his logical, mathematical, and political papers. Also, if Carroll had never written the *Alice*s or the *Snark*, he still would have earned a place in history as the most outstanding photographer of children in the nineteenth century, as well as a distinguished photographic portraitist who captured many artists and literary figures, Oxford dignitaries, and other celebrities on wetplate, the forerunner of film.

Largely because of the *Alice*s and the *Snark*, Carroll is remembered as a nonsense poet, although, strictly speaking, apart from "Jabberwocky" and a few other poems, he did not write nonsense literature but rather parodies and absurd poems and stories, works in which he took logic and pushed it too far. Carroll also wrote serious verse, and he collected some of his early comic and serious verse in *Phantasmagoria and Other Poems* (1869). Later in *Rhyme? and Reason?* (1883), he reprinted thirteen of the humorous verses from this book, with some changes and additions, along with *The Hunting of the Snark* and six additional poems, four of which appeared for the first time. For *Rhyme? and Reason?* he engaged an American artist, Arthur B. Frost, to provide sixty-five illustrations. Most of the serious poems from *Phantasmagoria* were reprinted with additions and emendations in *Three Sunsets and Other Poems,* which was in production when Dodgson died. It is illustrated with twelve "fairy-fancies" by his valued friend E. Gertrude Thompson. While Carroll's serious poems are dull poems, now dated period pieces, they are, nevertheless, worthy of reading and study. In these poems, with their recurrent themes of loss of innocence and of love, we come closer to Dodgson the man than in his other imaginative writing and are led to an understanding of the enigmatic Dodgson/Carroll personality.

Dodgson the mathematician and Carroll the storyteller can be seen working together in many of Carroll's imaginative works but never more directly than in a relatively late work, *A Tangled Tale* (1885). This book, comprised of ten "knots," each containing at least one mathematical problem or puzzle, originally appeared (beginning in 1880) in the *Monthly Packet* (a magazine chiefly read by women, edited by Charlotte Yonge). When the problems and puzzles were reprinted in book form, six new illustrations by Arthur B. Frost were added. Although Dodgson issued most of his serious and advanced work in mathematics and logic under his real name, *A Tangled Tale* was designed for a large audience of general readers and was issued as a work by Lewis Carroll.

Unquestionably the most ambitious literary undertaking of Dodgson's career was *Sylvie and Bruno* (1889) and *Sylvie and Bruno Concluded* (1893), a continuous novel published in two books. The idea for this work dated from the *Alice* period, when in 1867 Carroll published "Bruno's Revenge," the kernel of the *Sylvie and Bruno* books. In them Carroll partially returned late in his life to the *Alice* vein. Dreams, play, logic, and probings into the nature of language figure prominently in the architecture of the *Alices* and the *Sylvie and Bruno* books, and numerous minor similarities figure less prominently, some of which Carroll points out in his Preface to *Sylvie and Bruno*; but the *Sylvie and Bruno* books are markedly different from the *Alices*. In them Carroll strikes out a new course.

The *Sylvie and Bruno* books, a long and complex combination of fairy-tale and social novel, are the most pedantic of Carroll's works. They are filled with the Reverend Dodgson's preachings on love and religion. The continuous novel has two main settings and two main plots. Part of the novel takes place in the real world, in late Victorian England, and is about love and marriage, with the main characters overcoming various barriers and complications to happiness. Interlaced with this is the remainder of the novel set in a fairy world, the Outland country of Fairyland where the young Bruno and his sister Sylvie, children of the rightful ruler, live; this portion is about love, evil, and just reward in a country where a political order disrupted through subterfuge is set right. There are parallels between the two worlds, and the most overt connection between them is in the person of the unnamed narrator, a London lawyer or businessman, who is able to induce states of semiconsciousness, or "eeriness," in himself that enable him to visit the fairy world. To lesser degrees, other characters are able to achieve some state of "eeriness" and gain an awareness of another world. These books are laced with ethical discussions and a spectrum of Dodgson's ideas and personal attitudes which bring us close to a true portrait of the man.

Although portions of the *Sylvie and Bruno* books, such as the "Mad Gardener's Song," have become famous, the books generally are not well known. This has begun to change somewhat, and recently critics have turned to them with admiration, especially for Carroll's complex and modern method of storytelling. The books are being reprinted and have begun to be translated; there are already editions of the *Sylvie and Bruno* books in French, German, Japanese, and Spanish. The long-held reader preference for the fantasy sections over the realistic sections—the nonsense world of Outland and the antiutopia of Mein Herr's other world to *fin-de-siècle* England—is still evident, but more and more readers are becoming aware of the regular presence of a master of dialogue and narration at work in *Sylvie and Bruno* and *Sylvie and Bruno Concluded*.

For the drawings for *Sylvie and Bruno,* which at first was planned as a single volume but, due to its length, had to be split into two, Dodgson selected Harry Furniss, "a very clever illustrator in *Punch*." Their painstaking, intense collaboration of almost a decade yielded ninety-two illustrations. The collaboration between these somewhat eccentric men was filled with strain and compromise on both sides, but in the end they appear to have gotten on well and Dodgson was happy with Furniss's final illustrations. They are clearly good, well-drafted drawings. The illustrations to the realistic portions of the story are creditable renderings in the Victorian society-novel tradition, and the lively, clever drawings for the fairy-world portions, poems, and songs—many seemingly inspired by sketches Dodgson sent along to Furniss—are equally creditable.

The *Alice* books, *The Hunting of the Snark,* humorous and serious poetry, the *Sylvie and Bruno* books, *A Tangled Tale,* elementary and advanced works in logic and mathematics, letters, drawings, photographs—the artistic achievements of the multifaceted genius known as Lewis Carroll still flourish. Why? There are no simple solutions to the mystery of the *Alice*s' success or explanations for the continuing popularity of Carroll's works or for the interest in the life of their puzzle-loving and child-loving author, the paradoxical and proper Victorian, Charles Lutwidge Dodgson. Still, a few basic explanations can be readily advanced.

Carroll's skills as a writer and entertainer and the special understanding of children he brought to his works help to explain their popularity in the nineteenth century and to some extent, their continuing appeal in the twentieth. Although Carroll's works have always appealed to adults as well as children, they were written primarily to amuse children. They are successful as children's books in part because Dodgson brought to them a special respect for and an understanding and love of children. He knew children and their world well. He passed his happy childhood with ten sisters and brothers (he was the eldest boy) in relative isolation at rectories in northern England, where the Dodgson children, often led by Charles, devised their own entertainments. As an adult, Dodgson remembered well the sorts of things he and his family enjoyed as children. His understanding and appreciation of children also enabled Dodgson to see things from the child's point of view and to bring this point of view to his literary works.

Carroll's works are not only successful entertainments but are also good literature, particularly the *Alice*s. *Alice's Adventures in Wonderland* was Carroll's first book, but it was the work of a man who was thoroughly familiar with the practices nineteenth-century writers used to entertain their audiences. He was familiar with the way comic journalists and the creators of theatrical burlesques and pantomimes used puns, dialect, and parodies to entertain, how they drew upon creatures from folktales and fairy tales and mixed them with contemporary people and events and often ended up with grotesqueries like the fanciful ones that regularly appeared as cartoons in the comic weeklies. *Alice* may have been Carroll's first book, but it was the work of someone who had developed his skills as a storyteller and a comic entertainer for almost twenty years. As a boy, he edited a series of illustrated family magazines that were imitations of the popular comic weeklies and monthlies, and as a young man, he contributed verse and prose sketches to these popular Victorian magazines.

Perhaps the best criterion of good literature is not a close analysis of the many fine points of merit in a work but the work's longevity. The *Alice* books are more than a century old, and their appeal continues to be remarkable. They have made the passage into the twentieth century not only as literature but as plays and films. Carroll has been well served by adaptors. He helped bring *Alice* to the stage for the first time in 1886, and there have been countless stage versions since then performed all over the world. *Alice* was first brought to the screen in 1903 and has since been filmed dozens of times. In part, it is thanks to Disney and other filmmakers or stage directors that Carroll and his Alice are so enmeshed in our popular culture. Today politicians, journalists, ad men, teachers, and executives quote Carroll in full confidence of being understood.

Yet, what other reasons are there for Carroll's works transcending time while many other celebrated works of the nineteenth century have aged poorly and sunk into disregard? Why have filmmakers and stage directors invested in Carroll again and again? The profound impact of Carroll's art, like Shakespeare's and Dickens's, is in the areas of language and character. His characters are so fresh, clever, provocative, and bizarre that they are unforgettable. They speak to us in a language that is at once simple and profound, funny and serious. His metaphors and startling images appear timeless and especially revealing of the modern condition. "*Here,*" as the Red Queen noted of her culture, "it takes all the running *you* can do, to keep in the same place."

In addition to being a gifted writer and entertainer, an author of works that appeal to children and adults alike, and the creator of indelible characters and languages, Carroll is, at times, both a social critic of the highest order and a prophet. He is a Victorian modern who is the precursor of Joyce and Nabokov along an important road of literary history, a relative of the Surrealists, a revolutionizer of children's literature, and someone who speaks to us from a century past in ways we like to hear and about ideas that have become both fashionable and compelling. It is no wonder that, with twentieth-century hindsight, Freudians and Jungians, linguists and philosophers, critics and cultists of seemingly every persuasion, find Carroll's works exceedingly rich veins to mine. And while theories and readings abound—some far removed from the conscious world of Lewis Carroll—the *Alice*s and many of Carroll's other works remain fresh.

The essential plurality of Carroll's art is a key to his continuing appeal. The *Alice* books have been called "the most inexhaustible tales in the world," and Carroll's work, like all great literature, repays readers and rereaders with fresh insights and aesthetic rewards. Dodgson would have welcomed the continuing and diverse attention his creations have received and would have accepted that there are more than a few creditable ways of viewing his art. In fact, this man whose works have given pleasure to generations of readers essentially passed his blessings on to would-be interpreters when he wrote: "As to the meaning of the *Snark*? I'm very much afraid I didn't mean anything but nonsense! Still, you know, words mean more than we mean to express when we use them; so a whole book ought to mean a great deal more than the writer meant. So, whatever good meanings are in the book, I'm very glad to accept as the meaning of the book."

EDWARD GUILIANO
New York City, 1982

A NOTE ON THE TEXT

CHARLES LUTWIDGE DODGSON favored the idea of a moderately priced edition of his works. On February 15, 1869, less than four years after *Alice's Adventures in Wonderland* was first published, he proposed for the second time to his publisher, Alexander Macmillan, "bringing out a 'cheap edition' of *Alice,*" explaining in a letter "My feeling is that the present price puts the book entirely out of reach of many thousands of children of the middle classes, who might, I think, enjoy it." He held this wish until 1887 when Macmillan brought out a "People's Edition" of *Alice's Adventures in Wonderland* at a price less than half of the edition that had been selling well since 1865. At the same time, Macmillan also brought out a "People's Edition" of *Through the Looking-Glass* as well as a combined "People's Edition" of the *Alice* books. The precedent, then, for this relatively inexpensive edition of Lewis Carroll's illustrated works, featuring reliable texts, and with illustrations faithfully reproduced from the original editions, was established by the author himself.

Reprinted in this collection are all the illustrated works Lewis Carroll published in his lifetime. For *Alice's Adventures in Wonderland* the text selected is that of the 86th thousandth, the revised edition published in 1897, containing Carroll's final changes. Tenniel's illustrations are re-produced directly from that edition, published by Macmillan, London. The text and illustrations for *Through the Looking-Glass* are similarly taken from the 1897 Macmillan edition, the sixty-first thousandth, which contained the author's final revisions. The text of *The Hunting of the Snark* is taken from the first edition of *Rhyme? and Reason?* (1883) since Carroll made minor textual changes to his 1876 text for this edition. Henry Holiday's illustrations to the *Snark,* however, are reproduced directly from the first edition of 1876 (with the 1883 captions added). The texts of *Rhyme? and Reason?* (1883), *A Tangled Tale* (1885), *Sylvie and Bruno* (1889), *Sylvie and Bruno Concluded* (1893), and *Three Sunsets and Other Poems* (1898), with illustrations respectively by Arthur B. Frost, again Frost, Harry Furniss (with one by Alice Havers), again Furniss (with the same by Havers), and E. Gertrude Thompson are all reproduced from first editions published by Macmillan. *Three Sunsets* was published posthumously, but while Carroll was alive, he made the arrangements for its publication and checked galley proofs. The text and Carroll's illustrations to *Alice's Adventures Under Ground* are reproduced from the facsimile edition published under the author's supervision by Macmillan in 1886. For that edition of the manuscript volume presented to Alice, the pages were photographically reduced to fit the format of the new book; here that process has been reversed so that the text and illustrations in Carroll's hand more closely approximate those of the manuscript now in the British Library. Also, folio numbers have been made consistent with the rest of this new edition.

Not included in this collection are Carroll's juvenilia, his youthful writings principally in his family magazines, which have been published in this century. Although this material is interesting, Carroll never prepared it for publication, nor did he express any desire to do so during his lifetime. He did, however, collect and publish some of his early poems in *Phantasmagoria and Other Poems* (1869), although without illustrations. This book appears implicitly in this volume, since almost all of the poems in Part I were included in *Rhyme? and Reason?* and almost all in Part II in *Three Sunsets*. The Nursery *"Alice"* (1889), a simplified version with enlarged illustrations of *Alice's Adventures in Wonderland,* is not reprinted in this volume, since all the characters and events, and all Tenniel's illustrations, appear in the standard version of *Alice,* first published in 1865.

E.G.

ABOUT THE EDITOR

EDWARD GUILIANO, writer and editor, is a noted authority on the life and works of the Reverend Charles Lutwidge Dodgson—the eccentric, brilliant, paradoxical, proper, and fascinating Victorian who is universally known as Lewis Carroll. Dr. Guiliano has published numerous essays and several books on Carroll, including *Lewis Carroll Observed; Lewis Carroll: An Annotated International Bibliography; Lewis Carroll: A Celebration;* and *Soaring with the Dodo: Essays on Lewis Carroll's Life and Art,* which he co-edited. He currently teaches English at the New York Institute of Technology and lives with his wife in Greenwich Village, New York City.

ALICE'S ADVENTURES IN WONDERLAND

Illustrated by
JOHN TENNIEL

ALL in the golden afternoon
　Full leisurely we glide;
For both our oars, with little skill,
　By little arms are plied,
While little hands make vain pretence
　Our wanderings to guide.

Ah, cruel Three! In such an hour,
　Beneath such dreamy weather,
To beg a tale of breath too weak
　To stir the tiniest feather!
Yet what can one poor voice avail
　Against three tongues together?

Imperious Prima flashes forth
　Her edict "to begin it":
In gentler tones Secunda hopes
　"There will be nonsense in it!"
While Tertia interrupts the tale
　Not *more* than once a minute.

Anon, to sudden silence won,
　In fancy they pursue
The dream-child moving through a land
　Of wonders wild and new,
In friendly chat with bird or beast—
　And half believe it true.

And ever, as the story drained
　The wells of fancy dry,
And faintly strove that weary one
　To put the subject by,
"The rest next time—" "It *is* next time!"
　The happy voices cry.

Thus grew the tale of Wonderland:
　Thus slowly, one by one,
Its quaint events were hammered out—
　And now the tale is done,
And home we steer, a merry crew,
　Beneath the setting sun.

Alice! A childish story take,
　And, with a gentle hand,

Lay it where Childhood's dreams are twined
   In Memory's mystic band,
Like pilgrim's wither'd wreath of flowers
   Pluck'd in a far-off land.

CHAPTER I.

DOWN THE RABBIT-HOLE.

ALICE was beginning to get very tired of sitting by her sister on the bank, and of having nothing to do: once or twice she had peeped into the book her sister was reading, but it had no pictures or conversations in it, "and what is the use of a book," thought Alice, "without pictures or conversations?"

So she was considering, in her own mind (as well as she could, for the hot day made her feel very sleepy and stupid), whether the pleasure of making a daisy-chain would be worth the trouble of getting up and picking the daisies, when suddenly a White Rabbit with pink eyes ran close by her.

There was nothing so *very* remarkable in that; nor did Alice think it so *very* much out of the way to hear the Rabbit say to itself "Oh dear! Oh dear! I shall be too late!" (when she thought it over afterwards, it occurred to her that she ought to have wondered at this, but at the time it all seemed quite natural); but, when the Rabbit actually *took a watch out of its waistcoat-pocket*, and looked at it, and then hurried on, Alice started to her feet, for it flashed across her mind that she had never before seen a rabbit with either a waistcoat-pocket, or a watch to take out of it, and, burning with curiosity, she ran across the field after it, and was just in time to see it pop down a large rabbit-hole under the hedge.

5

In another moment down went Alice after it, never once considering how in the world she was to get out again.

The rabbit-hole went straight on like a tunnel for some way, and then dipped suddenly down, so suddenly that Alice had not a moment to think about stopping herself before she found herself falling down what seemed to be a very deep well.

Either the well was very deep, or she fell very slowly, for she had plenty of time as she went down to look about her, and to wonder what was going to happen next. First, she tried to look down and make out what she was coming to, but it was too dark to see anything: then she looked at the sides of the well, and noticed that they were filled with cupboards and book-shelves: here and there she saw maps and pictures hung upon pegs. She took down a jar from one of the shelves as she passed: it was labeled "ORANGE MARMALADE," but to her great disappointment it was empty: she did not like to drop the jar, for fear of killing somebody underneath, so managed to put it into one of the cupboards as she fell past it.

"Well!" thought Alice to herself. "After such a fall as this, I shall think nothing of tumbling down-stairs! How brave they'll all think me at home! Why, I wouldn't say anything about it, even if I fell off the top of the house!" (Which was very likely true.)

Down, down, down. Would the fall *never* come to an end? "I wonder how many miles I've fallen by this time?" she said aloud. "I must be getting somewhere near the centre of the earth. Let me see: that would be four thousand miles down, I think—" (for, you see, Alice had learnt several things of this sort in her lessons in the school-room, and though this was not a *very* good opportunity for showing off her knowledge, as there was no one to listen to her, still it was good practice to say it over) "—yes, that's about the right distance—but then I wonder what Latitude or Longitude I've got to?" (Alice had not the slightest idea what Latitude was, or Longitude either, but she thought they were nice grand words to say.)

Presently she began again. "I wonder if I shall fall right *through* the earth! How funny it'll seem to come out among the people that walk with their heads downwards! The antipathies, I think—" (she was rather glad there *was* no one listening, this time, as it didn't sound at all the right word) "—but I shall have to ask them what the name of the country is, you know. Please, Ma'am, is this New Zealand? Or Australia?" (and she tried to curtsey as she spoke—fancy, *curtseying* as you're falling through the air! Do you think you could manage it?) "And what an ignorant little girl she'll think me for asking! No, it'll never do to ask: perhaps I shall see it written up somewhere."

Down, down, down. There was nothing else to do, so Alice soon began talking again. "Dinah'll miss me very much to-night, I should think!" (Dinah was the cat.) "I hope they'll remember her saucer of milk at tea-time. Dinah, my dear! I wish you were down here with me! There are no mice in the air, I'm afraid, but you might catch a bat, and that's very like a mouse, you know. But do cats eat bats, I wonder?" And here Alice began to get rather sleepy, and went on saying to herself, in a dreamy sort of way, "Do cats eat bats? Do cats eat bats?" and sometimes "Do bats eat cats?", for, you see, as she couldn't answer either question, it didn't much matter which way she put it. She felt that she was dozing off, and had just begun to dream that she was walking hand in hand with Dinah, and was saying to her, very earnestly, "Now, Dinah, tell me the truth: did you ever eat a bat?", when suddenly, thump! thump! down she came upon a heap of sticks and dry leaves, and the fall was over.

Alice was not a bit hurt, and she jumped up on to her feet in a moment: she looked up, but it was all dark overhead: before her was another long passage, and the White Rabbit was still in sight, hurrying down it. There was not a moment to be lost: away went Alice like the wind, and was just in time to hear it say, as it turned a corner, "Oh my ears and whiskers, how late it's getting!" She was close behind it when she turned the corner, but the Rabbit was no longer to be seen: she found herself in a long, low hall, which was lit up by a row of lamps hanging from the roof.

There were doors all round the hall, but they were all locked; and when Alice had been all the way down one side and up the other, trying every door, she walked sadly down the middle, wondering how she was ever to get out again.

Suddenly she came upon a little three-legged table, all made of solid glass: there was nothing on it but a tiny golden key, and Alice's first idea was that this might belong to one of the doors of the hall; but, alas! either the locks were too large, or the key was too small, but at any rate it would not open any of them. However, on the second time round, she came upon a low curtain she had not noticed before, and behind it was a little door about fifteen inches high: she tried the little golden key in the lock, and to her great delight it fitted!

Alice opened the door and found that it led into a small passage, not much larger than a rat-hole: she knelt down and looked along the passage into the loveliest garden you ever saw. How she longed to get out of that dark hall, and wander about among those beds of bright flowers and those cool fountains, but she could not even get her head through the doorway; "and even if my head *would* go through," thought poor Alice, "it would be of very little use without my shoulders. Oh, how I wish I could shut up like a telescope! I think I could, if I only knew how to begin." For, you see, so many out-of-the-way things had happened lately, that Alice had begun to think that very few things indeed were really impossible.

There seemed to be no use in waiting by the little door, so she went back to the table, half hoping she might find another key on it, or at any rate a book of rules for shutting people up like telescopes: this time she found a little bottle on it ("which certainly was not here before," said Alice), and tied round the neck of the bottle was a paper label, with the words "DRINK ME" beautifully printed on it in large letters.

It was all very well to say "Drink me," but the wise little Alice was not going to do *that* in a hurry. "No, I'll look first," she said, "and see whether it's marked '*poison*' or not"; for she had read several nice little stories about children who had got burnt, and eaten up by wild beasts, and other unpleasant things, all because they *would* not remember the simple rules their friends had taught them: such as, that a red-hot poker will burn you if you hold it too long; and that, if you cut your finger *very* deeply with a knife, it usually bleeds; and she had never forgotten that, if you drink much from a bottle marked "poison," it is almost certain to disagree with you, sooner or later.

However, this bottle was *not* marked "poison," so Alice ventured to taste it, and, finding it very nice (it had, in fact, a sort of mixed flavour of cherry-tart, custard, pine-apple, roast turkey, toffy, and hot buttered toast), she very soon finished it off.

   *   *   *   *
     *   *   *
   *   *   *   *

"What a curious feeling!" said Alice. "I must be shutting up like a telescope!"

And so it was indeed: she was now only ten inches high, and her face brightened up at the thought that she was now the right size for going through the little door into that lovely garden. First, however, she waited for a few minutes to see if she was going to shrink any further: she felt a little nervous about this; "for it might end, you know," said Alice to herself, "in my going out altogether, like a candle. I wonder what I should be like then?" And she tried to fancy what the flame of a candle looks like after the candle is blown out, for she could not remember ever having seen such a thing.

After a while, finding that nothing more happened, she decided on going into the garden at once; but, alas for poor Alice! when she got to the door, she found she had forgotten the little golden key, and when she went back to the table for it, she found she could not possibly reach it: she could see it quite plainly through the glass, and she tried her best to climb up one of the legs of the table, but it was too slippery; and when she had tired herself out with trying, the poor little thing sat down and cried.

"Come, there's no use in crying like that!" said Alice to herself rather sharply. "I advise you to leave off this minute!" She generally gave herself very good advice (though she very seldom followed it), and sometimes she scolded herself so severely as to bring tears into her eyes; and once she remembered trying to box her own ears for having cheated herself in a game of croquet she was playing against herself, for this curious child was very fond of pretending to be two people. "But it's no use now," thought poor Alice, "to pretend to be two people! Why, there's hardly enough of me left to make *one* respectable person!"

Soon her eye fell on a little glass box that was lying under the table: she opened it, and found in it a very small cake, on which the words "EAT ME" were beautifully marked in currants. "Well, I'll eat it," said Alice, "and if it makes me grow larger, I can reach the key; and if it makes me grow smaller, I can creep under the door: so either way I'll get into the garden, and I don't care which happens!"

She ate a little bit, and said anxiously to herself "Which way? Which way?", holding her hand on the top of her head to feel which way it was growing; and she was quite surprised to find that she remained the same size. To be sure, this is what generally happens when one eats cake; but Alice had got so much into the way of expecting nothing but out-of-the-way things to happen, that it seemed quite dull and stupid for life to go on in the common way.

So she set to work, and very soon finished off the cake.

   *   *   *   *
     *   *   *
   *   *   *   *

CHAPTER II.

THE POOL OF TEARS.

"Curiouser and curiouser!" cried Alice (she was so much surprised, that for the moment she quite forgot how to speak good English). "Now I'm opening out like the largest telescope that ever was! Good-bye, feet!" (for when she looked down at her feet, they seemed to be almost out of sight, they were getting so far off). "Oh, my poor little feet, I wonder who will put on your shoes and stockings for you now, dears? I'm sure

I sha'n't be able! I shall be a great deal too far off to trouble myself about you: you must manage the best way you can—but I must be kind to them," thought Alice, "or perhaps they wo'n't walk the way I want to go! Let me see. I'll give them a new pair of boots every Christmas."

And she went on planning to herself how she would manage it. "They must go by the carrier," she thought; "and how funny it'll seem, sending presents to one's own feet! And how odd the directions will look!

> *Alice's Right Foot, Esq.*
> *Hearthrug,*
> *near the Fender,*
> *(with Alice's love).*

Oh dear, what nonsense I'm talking!"

Just at this moment her head struck against the roof of the hall: in fact she was now rather more than nine feet high, and she at once took up the little golden key and hurried off to the garden door.

Poor Alice! It was as much as she could do, lying down on one side, to look through into the garden with one eye; but to get through was more hopeless than ever: she sat down and began to cry again.

"You ought to be ashamed of yourself," said Alice, "a great girl like you," (she might well say this), "to go on crying in this way! Stop this moment, I tell you!" But she went on all the same, shedding gallons of tears, until there was a large pool around her, about four inches deep, and reaching half down the hall.

After a time she heard a little pattering of feet in the distance, and she hastily dried her eyes to see what was coming. It was the White Rabbit returning, splendidly dressed, with a pair of white kid-gloves in one hand and a large fan in the other: he came trotting along in a great hurry, muttering to himself, as he came, "Oh! The Duchess, the Duchess! Oh! *Wo'n't* she be savage if I've kept her waiting!" Alice felt so desperate that she was ready to ask help of any one: so, when the Rabbit came near her, she began, in a low, timid voice, "If you please, Sir——" The Rabbit started violently, dropped the white kid-gloves and the fan, and skurried away into the darkness as hard as he could go.

Alice took up the fan and gloves, and, as the hall was very hot, she kept fanning herself all the time she went on talking. "Dear, dear! How queer everything is to-day! And yesterday things went on just as usual. I wonder if I've been changed in the night? Let me think: *was* I the same when I got up this morning? I almost think I can remember feeling a little different. But if I'm not the same, the next question is 'Who in the world am I?' Ah, *that's* the great puzzle!" And she began thinking over all the children she knew that were of the same age as herself, to see if she could have been changed for any of them.

"I'm sure I'm not Ada," she said, "for her hair goes in such long ringlets, and mine doesn't go in ringlets at all; and I'm sure I ca'n't be Mabel, for I know all sorts of things, and she, oh, she knows such a very little! Besides, *she's* she, and *I'm* I, and—oh dear, how puzzling it all is! I'll try if I know all the things I used to know. Let me see: four times

five is twelve, and four times six is thirteen, and four times seven is—oh dear! I shall never get to twenty at that rate! However, the Multiplication-Table doesn't signify: let's try Geography. London is the capital of Paris, and Paris is the capital of Rome, and Rome—no, *that's* all wrong, I'm certain! I must have been changed for Mabel! I'll try and say '*How doth the little*—'," and she crossed her hands on her lap, as if she were saying lessons, and began to repeat it, but her voice sounded hoarse and strange, and the words did not come the same as they used to do:—

"How doth the little crocodile
Improve his shining tail,
And pour the waters of the Nile
On every golden scale!

"How cheerfully he seems to grin,
How neatly spreads his claws,
And welcomes little fishes in,
With gently smiling jaws!"

"I'm sure those are not the right words," said poor Alice, and her eyes filled with tears again as she went on, "I must be Mabel after all, and I shall have to go and live in that poky little house, and have next to no toys to play with, and oh, ever so many lessons to learn! No, I've made up my mind about it: if I'm Mabel, I'll stay down here! It'll be no use their putting their heads down and saying 'Come up again, dear!' I shall only look up and say 'Who am I, then? Tell me that first, and then, if I like being that person, I'll come up: if not, I'll stay down here till I'm somebody else'—but, oh dear!" cried Alice, with a sudden burst of tears, "I do wish they *would* put their heads down! I am so *very* tired of being all alone here!"

As she said this she looked down at her hands, and was surprised to see that she had put on one of the Rabbit's little white kid-gloves while she was talking. "How *can* I have done that?" she thought. "I must be growing small again." She got up and went to the table to measure herself by it, and found that, as nearly as she could guess, she was now about two feet high, and was going on shrinking rapidly: she soon found out that the cause of this was the fan she was holding, and she dropped it hastily, just in time to save herself from shrinking away altogether.

"That *was* a narrow escape!" said Alice, a good deal frightened at the sudden change, but very glad to find herself still in existence. "And now for the garden!" And she ran with all speed back to the little door; but, alas! the little door was shut again, and the little golden key was lying on the glass table as before, "and things are worse than ever," thought the poor child, "for I never was so small as this before, never! And I declare it's too bad, that it is!"

As she said these words her foot slipped, and in another moment, splash! she was up to her chin in salt-water. Her first idea was that she had somehow fallen into the sea, "and in that case I can go back by railway," she said to herself. (Alice had been to the seaside once in her life, and had come to the general conclusion that, wherever you go to on the English coast, you find a number of bathing-machines in the sea, some children digging in the sand with wooden spades, then a row of lodging-houses, and behind them a railway station.) However, she soon made out that she was in the pool of tears which she had wept when she was nine feet high.

"I wish I hadn't cried so much!" said Alice, as she swam about, trying to find her way out. "I shall be punished for it now, I suppose, by being drowned in my own tears! That *will* be a queer thing, to be sure! However, everything is queer to-day."

Just then she heard something splashing about in the pool a little way off, and she swam nearer to make out what it was: at first she thought it must be a walrus or hippopotamus, but then she remembered how small she was now, and she soon made out that it was only a mouse, that had slipped in like herself.

"Would it be of any use, now," thought Alice, "to speak to this mouse? Everything is so out-of-the-way down here, that I should think very likely it can talk: at any rate, there's no harm in trying." So she began: "O

Mouse, do you know the way out of this pool? I am very tired of swimming about here, O Mouse!" (Alice thought this must be the right way of speaking to a mouse: she had never done such a thing before, but she remembered having seen, in her brother's Latin Grammar, "A mouse— of a mouse—to a mouse—a mouse—O mouse!") The mouse looked at her rather inquisitively, and seemed to her to wink with one of its little eyes, but it said nothing.

"Perhaps it doesn't understand English," thought Alice. "I daresay it's a French mouse, come over with William the Conqueror." (For, with all her knowledge of history, Alice had no very clear notion how long ago anything had happened.) So she began again: "Où est ma chatte?", which was the first sentence in her French lesson-book. The Mouse gave a sudden leap out of the water, and seemed to quiver all over with fright. "Oh, I beg your pardon!" cried Alice hastily, afraid that she had hurt the poor animal's feelings. "I quite forgot you didn't like cats."

"Not like cats!" cried the Mouse in a shrill, passionate voice. "Would *you* like cats, if you were me?"

"Well, perhaps not," said Alice in a soothing tone: "don't be angry about it. And yet I wish I could show you our cat Dinah. I think you'd take a fancy to cats, if you could only see her. She is such a dear quiet thing," Alice went on, half to herself, as she swam lazily about in the pool, "and she sits purring so nicely by the fire, licking her paws and washing her face—and she is such a nice soft thing to nurse—and she's such a capital one for catching mice——oh, I beg your pardon!" cried Alice again, for this time the Mouse was bristling all over, and she felt certain it must be really offended. "We wo'n't talk about her any more, if you'd rather not."

"We, indeed!" cried the Mouse, who was trembling down to the end of its tail. "As if *I* would talk on such a subject! Our family always *hated* cats: nasty, low, vulgar things! Don't let me hear the name again!"

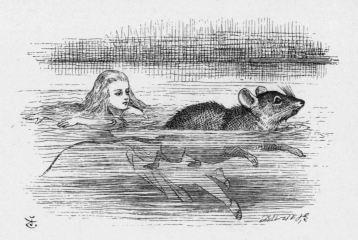

"I wo'n't indeed!" said Alice, in a great hurry to change the subject of conversation. "Are you—are you fond—of—of dogs?" The Mouse did not answer, so Alice went on eagerly: "There is such a nice little dog, near our house, I should like to show you! A little bright-eyed terrier, you know, with oh, such long curly brown hair! And it'll fetch things when you throw them, and it'll sit up and beg for its dinner, and all sorts of things—I ca'n't remember half of them—and it belongs to a farmer, you know, and he says it's so useful, it's worth a hundred pounds! He says it kills all the rats and—oh dear!" cried Alice in a sorrowful tone. "I'm afraid I've offended it again!" For the Mouse was swimming away from her as hard as it could go, and making quite a commotion in the pool as it went.

So she called softly after it, "Mouse dear! Do come back again, and we wo'n't talk about cats, or dogs either, if you don't like them!" When the Mouse heard this, it turned round and swam slowly back to her: its face was quite pale (with passion, Alice thought), and it said, in a low trembling voice, "Let us get to the shore, and then I'll tell you my history, and you'll understand why it is I hate cats and dogs."

It was high time to go, for the pool was getting quite crowded with the birds and animals that had fallen into it: there was a Duck and a Dodo, a Lory and an Eaglet, and several other curious creatures. Alice led the way, and the whole party swam to the shore.

CHAPTER III.

A CAUCUS-RACE AND A LONG TALE.

THEY were indeed a queer-looking party that assembled on the bank—the birds with draggled feathers, the animals with their fur clinging close to them, and all dripping wet, cross, and uncomfortable.

The first question of course was, how to get dry again: they had a consultation about this, and after a few minutes it seemed quite natural to Alice to find herself talking familiarly with them, as if she had known them all her life. Indeed, she had quite a long argument with the Lory, who at last turned sulky, and would only say, "I'm older than you, and must know better." And this Alice would not allow, without knowing how old it was, and, as the Lory positively refused to tell its age, there was no more to be said.

At last the Mouse, who seemed to be a person of some authority among them, called out "Sit down, all of you, and listen to me! *I'll* soon make you dry enough!" They all sat down at once, in a large ring, with the Mouse in the middle. Alice kept her eyes anxiously fixed on it, for she felt sure she would catch a bad cold if she did not get dry very soon.

"Ahem!" said the Mouse with an important air. "Are you all ready? This is the driest thing I know. Silence all round, if you please! 'William the Conqueror, whose cause was favoured by the pope, was soon submitted to by the English, who wanted leaders, and had been of late much accustomed to usurpation and conquest. Edwin and Morcar, the earls of Mercia and Northumbria——' "

"Ugh!" said the Lory, with a shiver.

"I beg your pardon!" said the Mouse, frowning, but very politely. "Did you speak?"

"Not I!" said the Lory, hastily.

"I thought you did," said the Mouse. "I proceed. 'Edwin and Morcar, the earls of Mercia and Northumbria, declared for him; and even Stigand, the patriotic archbishop of Canterbury, found it advisable——' "

"Found *what?*" said the Duck.

"Found *it,*" the Mouse replied rather crossly: "of course you know what 'it' means."

"I know what 'it' means well enough, when *I* find a thing," said the Duck: "it's generally a frog, or a worm. The question is, what did the archbishop find?"

The Mouse did not notice this question, but hurriedly went on, " '—found it advisable to go with Edgar Atheling to meet William and offer him the crown. William's conduct at first was moderate. But the insolence of his Normans——' How are you getting on now, my dear?" it continued, turning to Alice as it spoke.

"As wet as ever," said Alice in a melancholy tone: "it doesn't seem to dry me at all."

"In that case," said the Dodo solemnly, rising to its feet, "I move that the meeting adjourn, for the immediate adoption of more energetic remedies——"

"Speak English!" said the Eaglet. "I don't know the meaning of half those long words, and, what's more, I don't believe you do either!" And the Eaglet bent down its head to hide a smile: some of the other birds tittered audibly.

"What I was going to say," said the Dodo in an offended tone, "was, that the best thing to get us dry would be a Caucus-race."

"What *is* a Caucus-race?" said Alice; not that she much wanted to know, but the Dodo had paused as if it thought that *somebody* ought to speak, and no one else seemed inclined to say anything.

"Why," said the Dodo, "the best way to explain it is to do it." (And, as you might like to try the thing yourself, some winter-day, I will tell you how the Dodo managed it.)

First it marked out a race-course, in a sort of circle, ("the exact shape doesn't matter," it said,) and then all the party were placed along the course, here and there. There was no "One, two, three, and away!", but they began running when they liked, and left off when they liked, so that it was not easy to know when the race was over. However, when they had been running half an hour or so, and were quite dry again, the Dodo suddenly called out "The race is over!", and they all crowded round it, panting, and asking "But who has won?"

This question the Dodo could not answer without a great deal of thought, and it stood for a long time with one finger pressed upon its forehead (the position in which you usually see Shakespeare, in the pictures of him), while the rest waited in silence. At last the Dodo said "*Everybody* has won, and *all* must have prizes."

"But who is to give the prizes?" quite a chorus of voices asked.

"Why, *she*, of course," said the Dodo, pointing to Alice with one finger; and the whole party at once crowded round her, calling out, in a confused way, "Prizes! Prizes!"

Alice had no idea what to do, and in despair she put her hand in her pocket, and pulled out a box of comfits (luckily the salt water had not got into it), and handed them round as prizes. There was exactly one a-piece, all round.

"But she must have a prize herself, you know," said the Mouse.

"Of course," the Dodo replied very gravely. "What else have you got in your pocket?" it went on, turning to Alice.

"Only a thimble," said Alice sadly.

"Hand it over here," said the Dodo.

Then they all crowded round her once more, while the Dodo solemnly presented the thimble, saying "We beg your acceptance of this elegant thimble"; and, when it had finished this short speech, they all cheered.

Alice thought the whole thing very absurd, but they all looked so grave that she did not dare to laugh; and, as she could not think of anything to say, she simply bowed, and took the thimble, looking as solemn as she could.

The next thing was to eat the comfits: this caused some noise and confusion, as the large birds complained that they could not taste theirs, and the small ones choked and had to be patted on the back. However, it was over at last, and they sat down again in a ring, and begged the Mouse to tell them something more.

"You promised to tell me your history, you know," said Alice, "and why it is you hate—C and D," she added in a whisper, half afraid that it would be offended again.

"Mine is a long and a sad tale!"said the Mouse, turning to Alice, and sighing.

"It *is* a long tail, certainly," said Alice, looking down with wonder at the Mouse's tail; "but why do you call it sad?" And she kept on puzzling about it while the Mouse was speaking, so that her idea of the tale was something like this:

```
            " Fury said to
                a mouse, That
                    he  met  in  the
                        house, 'Let
                            us both go
                            to law: I
                            will prose-
                            cute you.—
                            Come, I'll
                        take no de-
                        nial: We
                    must have
                the trial;
            For really
          this morn-
        ing I've
        nothing
        to do.'
          Said the
            mouse to
                the cur,
              'Such a
                trial, dear
                  sir, With
                    no   jury
                      or judge,
                        would
                        be wast-
                        ing our
                      breath.'
              'I'll be
                judge,
            I'll be
          jury,'
        said
        cun-
        ning
        old
          Fury:
          'I'll
            try
              the
                whole
                  cause,
                    and
                    con-
                    demn
          death'." you to
```

"You are not attending!" said the Mouse to Alice, severely. "What are you thinking of ?"

"I beg your pardon," said Alice very humbly: "you had got to the fifth bend, I think?"

"I had *not!*" cried the Mouse, sharply and very angrily.

"A knot!" said Alice, always ready to make herself useful, and looking anxiously about her "Oh, do let me help to undo it!"

"I shall do nothing of the sort," said the Mouse, getting up and walking away. "You insult me by talking such nonsense!"

"I didn't mean it!" pleaded poor Alice. "But you're so easily offended, you know!"

The Mouse only growled in reply.

"Please come back, and finish your story!" Alice called after it. And the others all joined in chorus "Yes, please do!" But the Mouse only shook its head impatiently, and walked a little quicker.

"What a pity it wouldn't stay!" sighed the Lory, as soon as it was quite out of sight. And an old Crab took the opportunity of saying to her daughter "Ah, my dear! Let this be a lesson to you never to lose *your* temper!" "Hold your tongue, Ma!" said the young Crab, a little snappishly. "You're enough to try the patience of an oyster!"

"I wish I had our Dinah here, I know I do!" said Alice aloud, addressing nobody in particular. *"She'd* soon fetch it back!"

"And who is Dinah, if I might venture to ask the question?" said the Lory.

Alice replied eagerly, for she was always ready to talk about her pet: "Dinah's our cat. And she's such a capital one for catching mice, you ca'n't think! And oh, I wish you could see her after the birds! Why, she'll eat a little bird as soon as look at it!"

This speech caused a remarkable sensation among the party. Some of the birds hurried off at once: one old Magpie began wrapping itself up very carefully, remarking "I really must be getting home: the night-air doesn't suit my throat!" And a Canary called out in a trembling voice, to its children, "Come away, my dears! It's high time you were all in bed!" On various pretexts they all moved off, and Alice was soon left alone.

"I wish I hadn't mentioned Dinah!" she said to herself in a melancholy tone. "Nobody seems to like her, down here, and I'm sure she's the best cat in the world! Oh, my dear Dinah! I wonder if I shall ever see you any more!" And here poor Alice began to cry again, for she felt very lonely and low-spirited. In a little while, however, she again heard a little pattering of footsteps in the distance, and she looked up eagerly, half hoping that the Mouse had changed his mind, and was coming back to finish his story.

CHAPTER IV.

THE RABBIT SENDS IN A LITTLE BILL.

IT was the White Rabbit, trotting slowly back again, and looking anxiously about as it went, as if it had lost something; and she heard it muttering to itself, "The Duchess! The Duchess! Oh my dear paws! Oh my fur and whiskers! She'll get me executed, as sure as ferrets are ferrets! Where *can* I have dropped them, I wonder?" Alice guessed in a moment that it was looking for the fan and the pair of white kid-gloves, and she very good-naturedly began hunting about for them, but they were nowhere to be seen—everything seemed to have changed since her swim in the pool; and the great hall, with the glass table and the little door, had vanished completely.

Very soon the Rabbit noticed Alice, as she went hunting about, and called out to her, in an angry tone, "Why, Mary Ann, what *are* you doing out here? Run home this moment, and fetch me a pair of gloves and a fan! Quick, now!" And Alice was so much frightened that she ran off at once in the direction it pointed to, without trying to explain the mistake that it had made.

"He took me for his housemaid," she said to herself as she ran. "How surprised he'll be when he finds out who I am! But I'd better take him his fan and gloves—that is, if I can find them." As she said this, she came upon a neat little house, on the door of which was a bright brass plate with the name "W. RABBIT" engraved upon it. She went in without knocking, and hurried upstairs, in great fear lest she should meet the real Mary Ann, and be turned out of the house before she had found the fan and gloves.

"How queer it seems," Alice said to herself, "to be going messages for a rabbit! I suppose Dinah'll be sending me on messages next!" And she began fancying the sort of thing that would happen: " 'Miss Alice! Come here directly, and get ready for your walk!' 'Coming in a minute, nurse! But I've got to watch this mouse-hole till Dinah comes back, and see that the mouse doesn't get out.' Only I don't think," Alice went on, "that they'd let Dinah stop in the house if it began ordering people about like that!"

By this time she had found her way into a tidy little room with a table in the window, and on it (as she had hoped) a fan and two or three pairs of tiny white kid-gloves: she took up the fan and a pair of the gloves, and was just going to leave the room, when her eye fell upon a little bottle that stood near the looking-glass. There was no label this time with the words "DRINK ME," but nevertheless she uncorked it and put it to her lips. "I know *something* interesting is sure to happen," she said to herself, "whenever I eat or drink anything: so I'll just see what this bottle does. I do hope it'll make me grow large again, for really I'm quite tired of being such a tiny little thing!"

It did so indeed, and much sooner than she had expected: before she had drunk half the bottle, she found her head pressing against the ceiling, and had to stoop to save her neck from being broken. She hastily put down the bottle, saying to herself "That's quite enough—I hope I sha'n't grow any more—As it is, I ca'n't get out at the door—I do wish I hadn't drunk quite so much!"

Alas! It was too late to wish that! She went on growing, and growing, and very soon had to kneel down on the floor: in another minute there was not even room for this, and she tried the effect of lying down with one elbow against the door, and the other arm curled round her head. Still she went on growing, and, as a last resource, she put one arm out of the window, and one foot up the chimney, and said to herself "Now I can do no more, whatever happens. What *will* become of me?"

Luckily for Alice, the little magic bottle had now had its full effect, and she grew no larger: still it was very uncomfortable, and, as there seemed to be no sort of chance of her ever getting out of the room again, no wonder she felt unhappy.

"It was much pleasanter at home," thought poor Alice, "when one wasn't always growing larger and smaller, and being ordered about by mice and rabbits. I almost wish I hadn't gone down that rabbit-hole—and yet—and yet—it's rather curious, you know, this sort of life! I do wonder what *can* have happened to me! When I used to read fairy tales, I fancied that kind of thing never happened, and now here I am in the middle of one! There ought to be a book written about me, that there ought! And when I grow up, I'll write one—but I'm grown up now,"

she added in a sorrowful tone: "at least there's no room to grow up any more *here*."

"But then," thought Alice, "shall I *never* get any older than I am now? That'll be a comfort, one way—never to be an old woman—but then—always to have lessons to learn! Oh, I shouldn't like *that!*"

"Oh, you foolish Alice!" she answered herself. "How can you learn lessons in here? Why, there's hardly room for *you*, and no room at all for any lesson-books!"

And so she went on, taking first one side and then the other, and making quite a conversation of it altogether; but after a few minutes she heard a voice outside, and stopped to listen.

"Mary Ann! Mary Ann!" said the voice. "Fetch me my gloves this moment!" Then came a little pattering of feet on the stairs. Alice knew it was the Rabbit coming to look for her, and she trembled till she shook the house, quite forgetting that she was now about a thousand times as large as the Rabbit, and had no reason to be afraid of it.

Presently the Rabbit came up to the door, and tried to open it; but, as the door opened inwards, and Alice's elbow was pressed hard against it, that attempt proved a failure. Alice heard it say to itself "Then I'll go round and get in at the window."

"*That* you wo'n't!" thought Alice, and, after waiting till she fancied she heard the Rabbit just under the window, she suddenly spread out her hand, and made a snatch in the air. She did not get hold of anything, but she heard a little shriek and a fall, and a crash of broken glass, from which she concluded that it was just possible it had fallen into a cucumber-frame, or something of the sort.

Next came an angry voice—the Rabbit's—"Pat! Pat! Where are you?" And then a voice she had never heard before, "Sure then I'm here! Digging for apples, yer honour!"

"Digging for apples, indeed!" said the Rabbit angrily. "Here! Come help me out of *this!*" (Sounds of more broken glass.)

"Now tell me, Pat, what's that in the window?"

"Sure, it's an arm, yer honour!" (He pronounced it "arrum.")

"An arm, you goose! Who ever saw one that size? Why, it fills the whole window!"

"Sure, it does, yer honour: but it's an arm for all that."

"Well, it's got no business there, at any rate: go and take it away!"

There was a long silence after this, and Alice could only hear whispers now and then; such as "Sure, I don't like it, yer honour, at all, at all!" "Do as I tell you, you coward!", and at last she spread out her hand again, and made another snatch in the air. This time there were *two* little shrieks, and more sounds of broken glass. "What a number of cucumber-frames there must be!" thought Alice. "I wonder what they'll do next! As for pulling me out of the window, I only wish they *could!* I'm sure *I* don't want to stay in here any longer!"

She waited for some time without hearing anything more: at last came a rumbling of little cart-wheels, and the sound of a good many voices all talking together: she made out the words: "Where's the other ladder?—Why, I hadn't to bring but one. Bill's got the other—Bill! Fetch it here,

lad!—Here, put 'em up at this corner—No, tie 'em together first—they
don't reach half high enough yet—Oh, they'll do well enough. Don't be
particular—Here, Bill! Catch hold of this rope—Will the roof bear?—
Mind that loose slate—Oh, it's coming down! Heads below!" (a loud
crash)—"Now, who did that?—It was Bill, I fancy—Who's to go down
the chimney?—Nay, *I* sha'n't! *You* do it!—*That* I wo'n't, then!—Bill's got
to go down—Here, Bill! The master says you've got to go down the
chimney!"

"Oh! So Bill's got to come down the chimney, has he?" said Alice to
herself. "Why, they seem to put everything upon Bill! I wouldn't be in
Bill's place for a good deal: this fireplace is narrow, to be sure; but I
think I can kick a little!"

She drew her foot as far down the chimney as she could, and waited
till she heard a little animal (she couldn't guess of what sort it was)
scratching and scrambling about in the chimney close above her: then,
saying to herself "This is Bill", she gave one sharp kick, and waited to
see what would happen next.

The first thing she heard was a general chorus of "There goes Bill!"
then the Rabbit's voice alone—"Catch him, you by the hedge!" then
silence, and then another confusion of voices—"Hold up his head—
Brandy now—Don't choke him—How was it, old fellow? What happened
to you? Tell us all about it!"

Last came a little feeble, squeaking voice ("That's Bill," thought Alice),
"Well, I hardly know—No more, thank ye; I'm better now—but I'm a

deal too flustered to tell you—all I know is, something comes at me like a Jack-in-the-box, and up I goes like a sky-rocket!"

"So you did, old fellow!" said the others.

"We must burn the house down!" said the Rabbit's voice. And Alice called out, as loud as she could, "If you do, I'll set Dinah at you!"

There was a dead silence instantly, and Alice thought to herself "I wonder what they *will* do next! If they had any sense, they'd take the roof off." After a minute or two, they began moving about again, and Alice heard the Rabbit say "A barrowful will do, to begin with."

"A barrowful of *what?*" thought Alice. But she had not long to doubt, for the next moment a shower of little pebbles came rattling in at the window, and some of them hit her in the face. "I'll put a stop to this," she said to herself, and shouted out "You'd better not do that again!", which produced another dead silence.

Alice noticed, with some surprise, that the pebbles were all turning into little cakes as they lay on the floor, and a bright idea came into her head. "If I eat one of these cakes," she thought, "it's sure to make *some* change in my size; and, as it ca'n't possibly make me larger, it must make me smaller, I suppose."

So she swallowed one of the cakes, and was delighted to find that she began shrinking directly. As soon as she was small enough to get through the door, she ran out of the house, and found quite a crowd of little animals and birds waiting outside. The poor little Lizard, Bill, was in the middle, being held up by two guinea-pigs, who were giving it something out of a bottle. They all made a rush at Alice the moment she appeared; but she ran off as hard as she could, and soon found herself safe in a thick wood.

"The first thing I've got to do," said Alice to herself, as she wandered about in the wood, "is to grow to my right size again; and the second thing is to find my way into that lovely garden. I think that will be the best plan."

It sounded an excellent plan, no doubt, and very neatly and simply arranged: the only difficulty was, that she had not the smallest idea how to set about it; and, while she was peering about anxiously among the trees, a little sharp bark just over her head made her look up in a great hurry.

An enomous puppy was looking down at her with large round eyes, and feebly stretching out one paw, trying to touch her. "Poor little thing!" said Alice, in a coaxing tone, and she tried hard to whistle to it; but she was terribly frightened all the time at the thought that it might be hungry, in which case it would be very likely to eat her up in spite of all her coaxing.

Hardly knowing what she did, she picked up a little bit of stick, and held it out to the puppy: whereupon the puppy jumped into the air off all its feet at once, with a yelp of delight, and rushed at the stick, and made believe to worry it: then Alice dodged behind a great thistle, to keep herself from being run over; and, the moment she appeared on the other side, the puppy made another rush at the stick, and tumbled head over heels in its hurry to get hold of it: then Alice, thinking it was very like having a game of play with a cart-horse, and expecting every moment to be trampled under its feet, ran round the thistle again: then the puppy began a series of short charges at the stick, running a very little way forwards each time and a long way back, and barking hoarsely all the while, till at last it sat down a good way off, panting, with its tongue hanging out of its mouth, and its great eyes half shut.

This seemed to Alice a good opportunity for making her escape: so she set off at once, and ran till she was quite tired and out of breath, and till the puppy's bark sounded quite faint in the distance.

"And yet what a dear little puppy it was!" said Alice, as she leant against a buttercup to rest herself, and fanned herself with one of the leaves. "I should have liked teaching it tricks very much, if—if I'd only been the right size to do it! Oh dear! I'd nearly forgotten that I've got to grow up again! Let me see—how *is* it to be managed? I suppose I ought to eat or drink something or other; but the great question is 'What?' "

The great question certainly was "What?". Alice looked all round her at the flowers and the blades of grass, but she could not see anything that looked like the right thing to eat or drink under the circumstances. There was a large mushroom growing near her, about the same height as herself; and, when she had looked under it, and on both sides of it, and behind it, it occurred to her that she might as well look and see what was on top of it.

She stretched herself up on tiptoe, and peeped over the edge of the mushroom, and her eyes immediately met those of a large blue caterpillar, that was sitting on the top, with its arms folded, quietly smoking a long hookah, and taking not the smallest notice of her or of anything else.

CHAPTER V.

ADVICE FROM A CATERPILLAR.

THE Caterpillar and Alice looked at each other for some time in silence: at last the Caterpillar took the hookah out of its mouth, and addressed her in a languid, sleepy voice.

"Who are *you?*" said the Caterpillar.

This was not an encouraging opening for a conversation. Alice replied, rather shyly, "I—I hardly know, Sir, just at present—at least I know who I *was* when I got up this morning, but I think I must have been changed several times since then."

"What do you mean by that?" said the Caterpillar, sternly. "Explain yourself!"

"I ca'n't explain *myself*, I'm afraid, Sir," said Alice, "because I'm not myself, you see."

"I don't see," said the Caterpillar.

"I'm afraid I ca'n't put it more clearly," Alice replied, very politely, "for I ca'n't understand it myself, to begin with; and being so many different sizes in a day is very confusing."

"It isn't," said the Caterpillar.

"Well, perhaps you haven't found it so yet," said Alice; "but when you have to turn into a chrysalis—you will some day, you know—and then after that into a butterfly, I should think you'll feel it a little queer, wo'n't you?"

"Not a bit," said the Caterpillar.

"Well, perhaps *your* feelings may be diferent," said Alice: "all I know is, it would feel very queer to *me*."

"You!" said the Caterpillar contemptuously. "Who are *you?*"

Which brought them back again to the beginning of the conversation. Alice felt a little irritated at the Caterpillar's making such *very* short remarks, and she drew herself up and said, very gravely, "I think you ought to tell me who *you* are, first."

"Why?" said the Caterpillar.

Here was another puzzling question; and, as Alice could not think of any good reason, and the Caterpillar seemed to be in a *very* unpleasant state of mind, she turned away.

"Come back!" the Caterpillar called after her. "I've something important to say!"

This sounded promising, certainly. Alice turned and came back again.

"Keep your temper," said the Caterpillar.

"Is that all?" said Alice, swallowing down her anger as well as she could.

"No," said the Caterpillar.

Alice thought she might as well wait, as she had nothing else to do, and perhaps after all it might tell her something worth hearing. For some minutes it puffed away without speaking; but at last it unfolded its arms, took the hookah out of its mouth again, and said "So you think you're changed, do you?"

"I'm afraid I am, Sir," said Alice. "I ca'n't remember things as I used— and I don't keep the same size for ten minutes together!"

"Ca'n't remember *what* things?" said the Caterpillar.

"Well, I've tried to say '*How doth the little busy bee,*' but it all came different!" Alice replied in a very melancholy voice.

"Repeat '*You are old, Father William,*'" said the Caterpillar.

Alice folded her hands, and began:—

"*You are old, Father William,*" *the young man said,*
  "*And your hair has become very white;*
And yet you incessantly stand on your head—
  Do you think, at your age, it is right?"

"*In my youth,*" *Father William replied to his son,*
  "*I feared it might injure the brain;*
But, now that I'm perfectly sure I have none,
  Why, I do it again and again."

"*You are old,*" *said the youth,* "*as I mentioned before,*
  And have grown most uncommonly fat;
Yet you turned a back-somersault in at the door—
  Pray, what is the reason of that?"

"*In my youth,*" *said the sage, as he shook his grey locks,*
  "*I kept all my limbs very supple*

By the use of this ointment—one shilling the box—
  Allow me to sell you a couple?"

"You are old," said the youth, "and your jaws are too weak
  For anything tougher than suet;
Yet you finished the goose, with the bones and the beak—
  Pray, how did you manage to do it?"

"In my youth," said his father, "I took to the law,
  And argued each case with my wife;
And the muscular strength, which it gave to my jaw
  Has lasted the rest of my life."

"You are old," said the youth, "one would hardly suppose
  That your eye was as steady as ever;
Yet you balanced an eel on the end of your nose—
  What made you so awfully clever?"

"I have answered three questions, and that is enough,"
  Said his father, "Don't give yourself airs!
Do you think I can listen all day to such stuff?
  Be off, or I'll kick you down-stairs!"

"That is not said right," said the Caterpillar.

"Not *quite* right, I'm afraid," said Alice, timidly: "some of the words
have got altered."

"It is wrong from beginning to end," said the Caterpillar, decidedly; and there was silence for some minutes.

The Caterpillar was the first to speak.

"What size do you want to be?" it asked.

"Oh, I'm not particular as to size," Alice hastily replied; "only one doesn't like changing so often, you know."

"I *don't* know," said the Caterpillar.

Alice said nothing: she had never been so much contradicted in all her life before, and she felt that she was losing her temper.

"Are you content now?" said the Caterpillar.

"Well, I should like to be a *little* larger, Sir, if you wouldn't mind," said Alice: "three inches is such a wretched height to be."

"It is a very good height indeed!" said the Caterpillar angrily, rearing itself upright as it spoke (it was exactly three inches high).

"But I'm not used to it!" pleaded poor Alice in a piteous tone. And she thought to herself "I wish the creatures wouldn't be so easily offended!"

"You'll get used to it in time," said the Caterpillar; and it put the hookah into its mouth, and began smoking again.

This time Alice waited patiently until it chose to speak again. In a minute or two the Caterpillar took the hookah out of its mouth, and yawned once or twice, and shook itself. Then it got down off the mushroom, and crawled away into the grass, merely remarking, as it went, "One side will make you grow taller, and the other side will make you grow shorter."

"One side of *what*? The other side of *what*?" thought Alice to herself.

"Of the mushroom," said the Caterpillar, just as if she had asked it aloud; and in another moment it was out of sight.

Alice remained looking thoughtfully at the mushroom for a minute, trying to make out which were the two sides of it; and, as it was perfectly round, she found this a very difficult question. However, at last she stretched her arms round it as far as they would go, and broke off a bit of the edge with each hand.

"And now which is which?" she said to herself, and nibbled a little of the right-hand bit to try the effect. The next moment she felt a violent blow underneath her chin: it had struck her foot!

She was a good deal frightened by this very sudden change, but she felt that there was no time to be lost, as she was shrinking rapidly: so she set to work at once to eat some of the other bit. Her chin was pressed so closely against her foot, that there was hardly room to open her mouth; but she did it at last, and managed to swallow a morsel of the left-hand bit.

```
    *         *         *         *
        *         *         *
    *         *         *         *
```

"Come, my head's free at last!" said Alice in a tone of delight, which changed into alarm in another moment, when she found that her shoulders were nowhere to be found: all she could see, when she looked down, was an immense length of neck, which seemed to rise like a stalk out of a sea of green leaves that lay far below her.

"What *can* all that green stuff be?" said Alice. "And where *have* my shoulders got to? And oh, my poor hands, how is it I ca'n't see you?" She was moving them about, as she spoke, but no result seemed to follow, except a little shaking among the distant green leaves.

As there seemed to be no chance of getting her hands up to her head, she tried to get her head down to *them,* and was delighted to find that her neck would bend about easily in any direction, like a serpent. She had just succeeded in curving it down into a graceful zigzag, and was going to dive in among the leaves, which she found to be nothing but the tops of the trees under which she had been wandering, when a sharp hiss made her draw back in a hurry: a large pigeon had flown into her face, and was beating her violently with its wings.

"Serpent!" screamed the Pigeon.

"I'm *not* a serpent!" said Alice indignantly. "Let me alone!"

"Serpent, I say again!"repeated the Pigeon, but in a more subdued tone, and added, with a kind of sob, "I've tried every way, but nothing seems to suit them!"

"I haven't the least idea what you're talking about," said Alice.

"I've tried the roots of trees, and I've tried banks, and I've tried hedges," the Pigeon went on, without attending to her; "but those serpents! There's no pleasing them!"

Alice was more and more puzzled, but she thought there was no use in saying anything more till the Pigeon had finished.

"As if it wasn't trouble enough hatching the eggs," said the Pigeon; "but I must be on the look-out for serpents, night and day! Why, I haven't had a wink of sleep these three weeks!"

"I'm very sorry you've been annoyed," said Alice, who was beginning to see its meaning.

"And just as I'd taken the highest tree in the wood," continued the Pigeon, raising its voice to a shriek, "and just as I was thinking I should be free of them at last, they must needs come wriggling down from the sky! Ugh, Serpent!"

"But I'm *not* a serpent, I tell you!" said Alice. "I'm a——I'm a——"

"Well! *What* are you?" said the Pigeon. "I can see you're trying to invent something!"

"I—I'm a little girl," said Alice, rather doubtfully, as she remembered the number of changes she had gone through, that day.

"A likely story indeed!" said the Pigeon, in a tone of the deepest contempt. "I've seen a good many little girls in my time, but never *one* with such a neck as that! No, no! You're a serpent; and there's no use denying it. I suppose you'll be telling me next that you never tasted an egg!"

"I *have* tasted eggs, certainly," said Alice, who was a very truthful child; "but little girls eat eggs quite as much as serpents do, you know."

"I don't believe it," said the Pigeon; "but if they do, why, then they're a kind of serpent: that's all I can say."

This was such a new idea to Alice, that she was quite silent for a minute or two, which gave the Pigeon the opportunity of adding "You're looking for eggs, I know *that* well enough; and what does it matter to me whether you're a little girl or a serpent?"

"It matters a good deal to *me*," said Alice hastily; "but I'm not looking for eggs, as it happens; and, if I was, I shouldn't want *yours:* I don't like them raw."

"Well, be off, then!" said the Pigeon in a sulky tone, as it settled down again into its nest. Alice crouched down among the trees as well as she could, for her neck kept getting entangled among the branches, and every now and then she had to stop and untwist it. After a while she remembered that she still held the pieces of mushroom in her hands, and she set to work very carefully, nibbling first at one and then at the other, and growing sometimes taller, and sometimes shorter, until she had succeeded in bringing herself down to her usual height.

It was so long since she had been anything near the right size, that it felt quite strange at first; but she got used to it in a few minutes, and began talking to herself, as usual, "Come, there's half my plan done now! How puzzling all these changes are! I'm never sure what I'm going to be, from one minute to another! However, I've got back to my right size: the next thing is, to get into that beautiful garden—how *is* that to be done, I wonder?" As she said this, she came suddenly upon an open place, with a little house in it about four feet high. "Whoever lives there," thought Alice, "it'll never do to come upon them *this* size: why, I should frighten them out of their wits!" So she began nibbling at the right-hand bit again, and did not venture to go near the house till she had brought herself down to nine inches high.

CHAPTER VI.

PIG AND PEPPER.

FOR a minute or two she stood looking at the house, and wondering what to do next, when suddenly a footman in livery came running out of the wood—(she considered him to be a footman because he was in livery: otherwise, judging by his face only, she would have called him a fish)—and rapped loudly at the door with his knuckles. It was opened by another footman in livery, with a round face, and large eyes like a frog; and both footmen, Alice noticed, had powdered hair that curled all over their heads. She felt very curious to know what it was all about, and crept a little way out of the wood to listen.

The Fish-Footman began by producing from under his arm a great letter, nearly as large as himself, and this he handed over to the other,

saying, in a solemn tone, "For the Duchess. An invitation from the Queen to play croquet." The Frog-Footman repeated, in the same solemn tone, only changing the order of the words a little, "From the Queen. An invitation for the Duchess to play croquet."

Then they both bowed low, and their curls got entangled together.

Alice laughed so much at this, that she had to run back into the wood for fear of their hearing her; and, when she next peeped out, the Fish-Footman was gone, and the other was sitting on the ground near the door, staring stupidly up into the sky.

Alice went timidly up to the door, and knocked.

"There's no sort of use in knocking," said the Footman, "and that for two reasons. First, because I'm on the same side of the door as you are: secondly, because they're making such a noise inside, no one could possibly hear you." And certainly there *was* a most extraordinary noise going on within—a constant howling and sneezing, and every now and then a great crash, as if a dish or kettle had been broken to pieces.

"Please, then," said Alice, "how am I to get in?"

"There might be some sense in your knocking," the Footman went on, without attending to her, "if we had the door between us. For instance, if you were *inside,* you might knock, and I could let you out, you know." He was looking up into the sky all the time he was speaking, and this Alice thought decidedly uncivil. "But perhaps he ca'n't help it," she said to herself; "his eyes are so *very* nearly at the top of his head. But at any rate he might answer questions.—How am I to get in?" she repeated, aloud.

"I shall sit here," the Footman remarked, "till to-morrow——"

At this moment the door of the house opened, and a large plate came skimming out, straight at the Footman's head: it just grazed his nose, and broke to pieces against one of the trees behind him.

"——or next day, maybe," the Footman continued in the same tone, exactly as if nothing had happened.

"How am I to get in?" asked Alice again, in a louder tone.

"*Are* you to get in at all?" said the Footman. "That's the first question, you know."

It was, no doubt: only Alice did not like to be told so. "It's really dreadful," she muttered to herself, "the way all the creatures argue. It's enough to drive one crazy!"

The Footman seemed to think this a good opportunity for repeating his remark, with variations. "I shall sit here," he said, "on and off, for days and days."

"But what am *I* to do?" said Alice.

"Anything you like," said the Footman, and began whistling.

"Oh, there's no use in talking to him," said Alice desperately: "he's perfectly idiotic!" And she opened the door and went in.

The door led right into a large kitchen, which was full of smoke from one end to the other: the Duchess was sitting on a three-legged stool in the middle, nursing a baby: the cook was leaning over the fire, stirring a large cauldron which seemed to be full of soup.

"There's certainly too much pepper in that soup!" Alice said to herself, as well as she could for sneezing.

There was certainly too much of it in the *air*. Even the Duchess sneezed occasionally; and as for the baby, it was sneezing and howling alternately without a moment's pause. The only two creatures in the kitchen, that did *not* sneeze, were the cook, and a large cat, which was lying on the hearth and grinning from ear to ear.

"Please would you tell me," said Alice, a little timidly, for she was not quite sure whether it was good manners for her to speak first, "why your cat grins like that?"

"It's a Cheshire-Cat," said the Duchess, "and that's why. Pig!"

She said the last word with such sudden violence that Alice quite jumped; but she saw in another moment that it was addressed to the baby, and not to her, so she took courage, and went on again:—

"I didn't know that Cheshire-Cats always grinned; in fact, I didn't know that cats *could* grin."

"They all can," said the Duchess; "and most of 'em do."

"I don't know of any that do," Alice said very politely, feeling quite pleased to have got into a conversation.

"You don't know much," said the Duchess; "and that's a fact."

Alice did not at all like the tone of this remark, and thought it would be as well to introduce some other subject of conversation. While she was trying to fix on one, the cook took the cauldron of soup off the fire, and at once set to work throwing everything within her reach at the

Duchess and the baby—the fire-irons came first; then followed a shower of saucepans, plates, and dishes. The Duchess took no notice of them even when they hit her; and the baby was howling so much already, that it was quite impossible to say whether the blows hurt it or not.

"Oh, *please* mind what you're doing!" cried Alice, jumping up and down in an agony of terror. "Oh, there goes his *precious* nose!", as an unusually large saucepan flew close by it, and very nearly carried it off.

"If everybody minded their own business," the Duchess said, in a hoarse growl, "the world would go round a deal faster than it does."

"Which would *not* be an advantage," said Alice, who felt very glad to get an opportunity of showing off a little of her knowledge. "Just think what work it would make with the day and night! You see the earth takes twenty-four hours to turn round on its axis——"

"Talking of axes," said the Duchess, "chop off her head!"

Alice glanced rather anxiously at the cook, to see if she meant to take the hint; but the cook was busily stirring the soup, and seemed not to be listening, so she went on again: "Twenty-four hours, I *think;* or is it twelve? I——"

"Oh, don't bother *me!*" said the Duchess. "I never could abide figures!" And with that she began nursing her child again, singing a sort of lullaby to it as she did so, and giving it a violent shake at the end of every line:—

> *"Speak roughly to your little boy,*
> *And beat him when he sneezes:*
> *He only does it to annoy,*
> *Because he knows it teases."*

CHORUS

(in which the cook and the baby joined):—

> *"Wow! Wow! Wow!"*

While the Duchess sang the second verse of the song, she kept tossing the baby violently up and down, and the poor little thing howled so, that Alice could hardly hear the words:—

> *"I speak severely to my boy,*
> *I beat him when he sneezes;*
> *For he can thoroughly enjoy*
> *The pepper when he pleases!"*

CHORUS

> *"Wow! wow! wow!"*

"Here! You may nurse it a bit, if you like!" the Duchess said to Alice, flinging the baby at her as she spoke. "I must go and get ready to play croquet with the Queen," and she hurried out of the room. The cook threw a frying-pan after her as she went, but it just missed her.

Alice caught the baby with some difficulty, as it was a queer-shaped little creature, and held out its arms and legs in all directions, "just like a star-fish," thought Alice. The poor little thing was snorting like a steam-engine when she caught it, and kept doubling itself up and straightening itself out again, so that altogether, for the first minute or two, it was as much as she could do to hold it.

As soon as she had made out the proper way of nursing it (which was to twist it up into a sort of knot, and then keep tight hold of its right ear and left foot, so as to prevent its undoing itself), she carried it out into the open air. "If I don't take this child away with me," thought Alice, "they're sure to kill it in a day or two. Wouldn't it be murder to leave it behind?" She said the last words out loud, and the little thing grunted in reply (it had left off sneezing by this time). "Don't grunt," said Alice; "that's not at all a proper way of expressing yourself."

The baby grunted again, and Alice looked very anxiously into its face to see what was the matter with it. There could be no doubt that it had a *very* turn-up nose, much more like a snout than a real nose: also its eyes were getting extremely small for a baby: altogether Alice did not like the look of the thing at all. "But perhaps it was only sobbing," she thought, and looked into its eyes again, to see if there were any tears.

No, there were no tears. "If you're going to turn into a pig, my dear," said Alice, seriously, "I'll have nothing more to do with you. Mind now!" The poor little thing sobbed again (or grunted, it was impossible to say which), and they went on for some while in silence.

Alice was just beginning to think to herself, "Now, what am I to do with this creature, when I get it home?" when it grunted again, so violently, that she looked down into its face in some alarm. This time there could be *no* mistake about it: it was neither more nor less than a pig, and she felt that it would be quite absurd for her to carry it any further.

So she set the little creature down, and felt quite relieved to see it trot away quietly into the wood. "If it had grown up," she said to herself, "it would have made a dreadfully ugly child: but it makes rather a handsome pig, I think." And she began thinking over other children she knew, who might do very well as pigs, and was just saying to herself "if one only knew the right way to change them——" when she was a little startled by seeing the Cheshire-Cat sitting on a bough of a tree a few yards off.

The Cat only grinned when it saw Alice. It looked good-natured, she thought: still it had *very* long claws and a great many teeth, so she felt that it ought to be treated with respect.

"Cheshire-Puss," she began, rather timidly, as she did not at all know whether it would like the name: however, it only grinned a little wider. "Come, it's pleased so far," thought Alice, and she went on. "Would you tell me, please, which way I ought to go from here?"

"That depends a good deal on where you want to get to," said the Cat.

"I don't much care where——" said Alice.

"Then it doesn't matter which way you go," said the Cat.

"——so long as I get *somewhere*," Alice added as an explanation.

"Oh, you're sure to do that," said the Cat, "if you only walk long enough."

Alice felt that this could not be denied, so she tried another question. "What sort of people live about here?"

"In *that* direction," the Cat said, waving its right paw round, "lives a Hatter: and in *that* direction," waving the other paw, "lives a March Hare. Visit either you like: they're both mad."

"But I don't want to go among mad people," Alice remarked.

"Oh, you ca'n't help that," said the Cat: "we're all mad here. I'm mad. You're mad."

"How do you know I'm mad?" said Alice.

"You must be," said the Cat, "or you wouldn't have come here."

Alice didn't think that proved it at all: however, she went on: "And how do you know that you're mad?"

"To begin with," said the Cat, "a dog's not mad. You grant that?"

"I suppose so," said Alice.

"Well, then," the Cat went on, "you see a dog growls when it's angry, and wags its tail when it's pleased. Now *I* growl when I'm pleased, and wag my tail when I'm angry. Therefore I'm mad."

"*I* call it purring, not growling," said Alice.

"Call it what you like," said the Cat. "Do you play croquet with the Queen to-day?"

"I should like it very much," said Alice, "but I haven't been invited yet."

"You'll see me there," said the Cat, and vanished.

Alice was not much surprised at this, she was getting so well used to queer things happening. While she was still looking at the place where it had been, it suddenly appeared again.

"By-the-bye, what became of the baby?" said the Cat. "I'd nearly forgotten to ask."

"It turned into a pig," Alice answered very quietly, just as if the Cat had come back in a natural way.

"I thought it would," said the Cat, and vanished again.

Alice waited a little, half expecting to see it again, but it did not appear, and after a minute or two she walked on in the direction in which the March Hare was said to live. "I've seen hatters before," she said to herself: "the March Hare will be much the most interesting, and perhaps, as this is May, it wo'n't be raving mad—at least not so mad as it was in March." As she said this, she looked up, and there was the Cat again, sitting on a branch of a tree.

"Did you say 'pig', or 'fig'?" said the Cat.

"I said 'pig'," replied Alice; "and I wish you wouldn't keep appearing and vanishing so suddenly: you make one quite giddy!"

"All right," said the Cat; and this time it vanished quite slowly, beginning with the end of the tail, and ending with the grin, which remained some time after the rest of it had gone.

"Well! I've often seen a cat without a grin," thought Alice; "but a grin without a cat! It's the most curious thing I ever saw in all my life!"

She had not gone much farther before she came in sight of the house of the March Hare: she thought it must be the right house, because the chimneys were shaped like ears and the roof was thatched with fur. It was so large a house, that she did not like to go nearer till she had nibbled some more of the left-hand bit of mushroom, and raised herself to about two feet high: even then she walked up towards it rather timidly, saying to herself "Suppose it should be raving mad after all! I almost wish I'd gone to see the Hatter instead!"

CHAPTER VII.

A MAD TEA-PARTY.

THERE was a table set out under a tree in front of the house, and the March Hare and the Hatter were having tea at it: a Dormouse was sitting between them, fast asleep, and the other two were using it as a cushion, resting their elbows on it, and talking over its head. "Very uncomfortable for the Dormouse," thought Alice; "only as it's asleep, I suppose it doesn't mind."

The table was a large one, but the three were all crowded together at one corner of it. "No room! No room!" they cried out when they saw Alice coming. "There's *plenty* of room!" said Alice indignantly, and she sat down in a large arm-chair at one end of the table.

"Have some wine," the March Hare said in an encouraging tone.

Alice looked all round the table, but there was nothing on it but tea. "I don't see any wine," she remarked.

"There isn't any," said the March Hare.

"Then it wasn't very civil of you to offer it," said Alice angrily.

"It wasn't very civil of you to sit down without being invited," said the March Hare.

"I didn't know it was *your* table," said Alice: "it's laid for a great many more than three."

"Your hair wants cutting," said the Hatter. He had been looking at Alice for some time with great curiosity, and this was his first speech.

"You should learn not to make personal remarks," Alice said with some severity: "it's very rude."

The Hatter opened his eyes very wide on hearing this; but all he *said* was "Why is a raven like a writing-desk?"

"Come, we shall have some fun now!" thought Alice. "I'm glad they've begun asking riddles—I believe I can guess that," she added aloud.

"Do you mean that you think you can find out the answer to it?" said the March Hare.

"Exactly so," said Alice.

"Then you should say what you mean," the March Hare went on.

"I do," Alice hastily replied; "at least—at least I mean what I say—that's the same thing, you know."

"Not the same thing a bit!" said the Hatter. "Why, you might just as well say that 'I see what I eat' is the same thing as 'I eat what I see'!"

"You might just as well say," added the March Hare, "that 'I like what I get' is the same thing as 'I get what I like'!"

"You might just as well say," added the Dormouse, which seemed to be talking in its sleep, "that 'I breathe when I sleep' is the same thing as 'I sleep when I breathe'!"

"It *is* the same thing with you," said the Hatter, and here the conversation dropped, and the party sat silent for a minute, while Alice thought over all she could remember about ravens and writing-desks, which wasn't much.

The Hatter was the first to break the silence. "What day of the month is it?" he said, turning to Alice: he had taken his watch out of his pocket, and was looking at it uneasily, shaking it every now and then, and holding it to his ear.

Alice considered a little, and then said "The fourth."

"Two days wrong!" sighed the Hatter. "I told you butter wouldn't suit the works!" he added, looking angrily at the March Hare.

"It was the *best* butter," the March Hare meekly replied.

"Yes, but some crumbs must have got in as well," the Hatter grumbled: "you shouldn't have put it in with the bread-knife."

The March Hare took the watch and looked at it gloomily: then he dipped it into his cup of tea, and looked at it again: but he could think of nothing better to say than his first remark, "It was the *best* butter, you know."

Alice had been looking over his shoulder with some curiosity. "What a funny watch!" she remarked. "It tells the day of the month, and doesn't tell what o'clock it is!"

"Why should it?" muttered the Hatter. "Does *your* watch tell you what year it is?"

"Of course not," Alice replied very readily: "but that's because it stays the same year for such a long time together."

"Which is just the case with *mine*," said the Hatter.

Alice felt dreadfully puzzled. The Hatter's remark seemed to her to have no sort of meaning in it, and yet it was certainly English. "I don't quite understand you," she said, as politely as she could.

"The Dormouse is asleep again," said the Hatter, and he poured a little hot tea upon its nose.

The Dormouse shook its head impatiently, and said, without opening its eyes, "Of course, of course: just what I was going to remark myself."

"Have you guessed the riddle yet?" the Hatter said, turning to Alice again.

"No, I give it up," Alice replied. "What's the answer?"

"I haven't the slightest idea," said the Hatter.

"Nor I," said the March Hare.

Alice sighed wearily. "I think you might do something better with the time," she said, "than wasting it in asking riddles that have no answers."

"If you knew Time as well as I do," said the Hatter, "you wouldn't talk about wasting *it*. It's *him*."

"I don't know what you mean," said Alice.

"Of course you don't!" the Hatter said, tossing his head contemptuously. "I dare say you never even spoke to Time!"

"Perhaps not," Alice cautiously replied; "but I know I have to beat time when I learn music."

"Ah! That accounts for it," said the Hatter. "He wo'n't stand beating. Now, if you only kept on good terms with him, he'd do almost anything you liked with the clock. For instance, suppose it were nine o'clock in the morning, just time to begin lessons: you'd only have to whisper a hint to Time, and round goes the clock in a twinkling! Half-past one, time for dinner!"

("I only wish it was," the March Hare said to itself in a whisper.)

"That would be grand, certainly," said Alice thoughtfully; "but then— I shouldn't be hungry for it, you know."

"Not at first, perhaps," said the Hatter: "but you could keep it to half-past one as long as you liked."

"Is that the way *you* manage?" Alice asked.

The Hatter shook his head mournfully. "Not I!" he replied. "We quarreled last March——just before *he* went mad, you know——" (pointing with his teaspoon at the March Hare,) "——it was at the great concert given by the Queen of Hearts, and I had to sing

> 'Twinkle, twinkle, little bat!
> How I wonder what you're at!'

You know the song, perhaps?"

"I've heard something like it," said Alice.

"It goes on, you know," the Hatter continued, "in this way:—

> *'Up above the world you fly,*
> *Like a tea-tray in the sky.*
> *Twinkle, twinkle——'"*

Here the Dormouse shook itself, and began singing in its sleep *"Twinkle, twinkle, twinkle, twinkle——"* and went on so long that they had to pinch it to make it stop.

"Well, I'd hardly finished the first verse," said the Hatter, "when the Queen bawled out 'He's murdering the time! Off with his head!'"

"How dreadfully savage!" exclaimed Alice.

"And ever since that," the Hatter went on in a mournful tone, "he wo'n't do a thing I ask! It's always six o'clock now."

A bright idea came into Alice's head. "Is that the reason so many tea-things are put out here?" she asked.

"Yes, that's it," said the Hatter with a sigh: "it's always tea-time, and we've no time to wash the things between whiles."

"Then you keep moving round, I suppose?" said Alice.

"Exactly so," said the Hatter: "as the things get used up."

"But what happens when you come to the beginning again?" Alice ventured to ask.

"Suppose we change the subject," the March Hare interrupted, yawning. "I'm getting tired of this. I vote the young lady tells us a story."

"I'm afraid I don't know one," said Alice, rather alarmed at the proposal.

"Then the Dormouse shall!" they both cried. "Wake up, Dormouse!" And they pinched it on both sides at once.

The Dormouse slowly opened its eyes. "I wasn't asleep," it said in a hoarse, feeble voice, "I heard every word you fellows were saying."

"Tell us a story!" said the March Hare.

"Yes, please do!" pleaded Alice.

"And be quick about it," added the Hatter, "or you'll be asleep again before it's done."

"Once upon a time there were three little sisters," the Dormouse began in a great hurry; "and their names were Elsie, Lacie, and Tillie; and they lived at the bottom of a well——"

"What did they live on?" said Alice, who always took a great interest in questions of eating and drinking.

"They lived on treacle," said the Dormouse, after thinking a minute or two.

"They couldn't have done that, you know," Alice gently remarked. "They'd have been ill."

"So they were," said the Dormouse; *"very* ill."

Alice tried a little to fancy to herself what such an extraordinary way of living would be like, but it puzzled her too much: so she went on: "But why did they live at the bottom of a well?"

"Take some more tea," the March Hare said to Alice, very earnestly.

"I've had nothing yet," Alice replied in an offended tone: "so I ca'n't take more."

"You mean you ca'n't take *less*," said the Hatter: "it's very easy to take *more* than nothing."

"Nobody asked *your* opinion," said Alice.

"Who's making personal remarks now?" the Hatter asked triumphantly.

Alice did not quite know what to say to this: so she helped herself to some tea and bread-and-butter, and then turned to the Dormouse, and repeated her question. "Why did they live at the bottom of a well?"

The Dormouse again took a minute or two to think about it, and then said "It was a treacle-well."

"There's no such thing!" Alice was beginning very angrily, but the Hatter and the March Hare went "Sh! Sh!" and the Dormouse sulkily remarked "If you ca'n't be civil, you'd better finish the story for yourself."

"No, please go on!" Alice said very humbly. "I wo'n't interrupt you again. I dare say there may be *one*."

"One, indeed!" said the Dormouse indignantly. However, he consented to go on. "And so these three little sisters—they were learning to draw, you know——"

"What did they draw?" said Alice, quite forgetting her promise.

"Treacle," said the Dormouse, without considering at all, this time.

"I want a clean cup," interrupted the Hatter: "let's all move one place on."

He moved on as he spoke, and the Dormouse followed him: the March Hare moved into the Dormouse's place, and Alice rather unwillingly took the place of the March Hare. The Hatter was the only one who got any advantage from the change; and Alice was a good deal worse off than before, as the March Hare had just upset the milk-jug into his plate.

Alice did not wish to offend the Dormouse again, so she began very cautiously: "But I don't understand. Where did they draw the treacle from?"

"You can draw water out of a water-well," said the Hatter; "so I should think you could draw treacle out of a treacle-well—eh, stupid?"

"But they were *in* the well," Alice said to the Dormouse, not choosing to notice this last remark.

"Of course they were," said the Dormouse: "well in."

This answer so confused poor Alice, that she let the Dormouse go on for some time without interrupting it.

"They were learning to draw," the Dormouse went on, yawning and rubbing its eyes, for it was getting very sleepy; "and they drew all manner of things—everything that begins with an M——"

"Why with an M?" said Alice.

"Why not?" said the March Hare.

Alice was silent.

The Dormouse had closed its eyes by this time, and was going off into a doze; but, on being pinched by the Hatter, it woke up again with a little shriek, and went on: "——that begins with an M, such as mouse-traps, and the moon, and memory, and muchness—you know you say things are 'much of a muchness'—did you ever see such a thing as a drawing of a muchness!"

"Really, now you ask me," said Alice, very much confused, "I don't think——"

"Then you shouldn't talk," said the Hatter.

This piece of rudeness was more than Alice could bear: she got up in great disgust, and walked off: the Dormouse fell asleep instantly, and neither of the others took the least notice of her going, though she looked back once or twice, half hoping that they would call after her: the last time she saw them, they were trying to put the Dormouse into the teapot.

"At any rate I'll never go *there* again!" said Alice, as she picked her way through the wood. "It's the stupidest tea-party I ever was at in all my life!"

Just as she said this, she noticed that one of the trees had a door leading right into it. "That's very curious!" she thought. "But everything's curious to-day. I think I may as well go in at once." And in she went.

Once more she found herself in the long hall, and close to the little glass table. "Now, I'll manage better this time," she said to herself, and began by taking the little golden key, and unlocking the door that led into the garden. Then she set to work nibbling at the mushroom (she had kept a piece of it in her pocket) till she was about a foot high: then she walked down the little passage: and *then*—she found herself at last in the beautiful garden, among the bright flower-beds and the cool fountains.

CHAPTER VIII.

THE QUEEN'S CROQUET GROUND.

A LARGE rose-tree stood near the entrance of the garden: the roses growing on it were white, but there were three gardeners at it, busily painting them red. Alice thought this a very curious thing, and she went nearer to watch them, and, just as she came up to them, she heard one of them say "Look out now, Five! Don't go splashing paint over me like that!"

"I couldn't help it," said Five, in a sulky tone. "Seven jogged my elbow."

On which Seven looked up and said "That's right, Five! Always lay the blame on others!"

"*You'd* better not talk!" said Five. "I heard the Queen say only yesterday you deserved to be beheaded."

"What for?" said the one who had spoken first.

"That's none of *your* business, Two!" said Seven.

"Yes, it *is* his business!" said Five. "And I'll tell him—it was for bringing the cook tulip-roots instead of onions."

Seven flung down his brush, and had just begun "Well, of all the

unjust things——" when his eye chanced to fall upon Alice, as she stood watching them, and he checked himself suddenly: the others looked round also, and all of them bowed low.

"Would you tell me, please," said Alice, a little timidly, "why you are painting those roses?"

Five and Seven said nothing, but looked at Two. Two began, in a low voice, "Why, the fact is, you see, Miss, this here ought to have been a *red* rose-tree, and we put a white one in by mistake; and, if the Queen was to find it out, we should all have our heads cut off, you know. So you see, Miss, we're doing our best, afore she comes, to——" At this moment, Five, who had been anxiously looking across the garden, called out "The Queen! The Queen!", and the three gardeners instantly threw themselves flat upon their faces. There was a sound of many footsteps, and Alice looked round, eager to see the Queen.

First came ten soldiers carrying clubs: these were all shaped like the three gardeners, oblong and flat, with their hands and feet at the corners: next the ten courtiers: these were ornamented all over with diamonds, and walked two and two, as the soldiers did. After these came the royal children: there were ten of them, and the little dears came jumping merrily along, hand in hand, in couples: they were all ornamented with hearts. Next came the guests, mostly Kings and Queens, and among them Alice recognised the White Rabbit: it was talking in a hurried nervous manner, smiling at everything that was said, and went by without noticing her. Then followed the Knave of Hearts, carrying the King's crown on a crimson velvet cushion; and, last of all this grand procession, came THE KING AND THE QUEEN OF HEARTS.

Alice was rather doubtful whether she ought not to lie down on her face like the three gardeners, but she could not remember ever having heard of such a rule at processions; "and besides, what would be the use of a procession," thought she, "if people had all to lie down on their faces, so that they couldn't see it?" So she stood where she was, and waited.

When the procession came opposite to Alice, they all stopped and looked at her, and the Queen said, severely, "Who is this?". She said it to the Knave of Hearts, who only bowed and smiled in reply.

"Idiot!" said the Queen, tossing her head impatiently; and, turning to Alice, she went on: "What's your name, child?"

"My name is Alice, so please your Majesty," said Alice very politely; but she added, to herself, "Why, they're only a pack of cards, after all. I needn't be afraid of them!"

"And who are *these*?" said the Queen, pointing to the three gardeners who were lying round the rose-tree; for, you see, as they were lying on their faces, and the pattern on their backs was the same as the rest of the pack, she could not tell whether they were gardeners, or soldiers, or courtiers, or three of her own children.

"How should *I* know?" said Alice, surprised at her own courage. "It's no business of *mine*."

The Queen turned crimson with fury, and, after glaring at her for a moment like a wild beast, began screaming "Off with her head! Off with——"

"Nonsense!" said Alice, very loudly and decidedly, and the Queen was silent.

The King laid his hand upon her arm, and timidly said "Consider, my dear: she is only a child!"

The Queen turned angrily away from him, and said to the Knave "Turn them over!"

The Knave did so, very carefully, with one foot.

"Get up!" said the Queen in a shrill, loud voice, and the three gardeners instantly jumped up, and began bowing to the King, the Queen, the royal children, and everybody else.

"Leave off that!" screamed the Queen. "You make me giddy." And then, turning to the rose-tree, she went on "What *have* you been doing here?"

"May it please your Majesty," said Two, in a very humble tone, going down on one knee as he spoke, "we were trying—"

"*I* see!" said the Queen, who had meanwhile been examining the roses. "Off with their heads!" and the procession moved on, three of the soldiers remaining behind to execute the unfortunate gardeners, who ran to Alice for protection.

"You sha'n't be beheaded!" said Alice, and she put them into a large flower-pot that stood near. The three soldiers wandered about for a minute or two, looking for them, and then quietly marched off after the others.

"Are their heads off?" shouted the Queen.

"Their heads are gone, if it please your Majesty!" the soldiers shouted in reply.

"That's right!" shouted the Queen. "Can you play croquet?"

The soldiers were silent, and looked at Alice, as the question was evidently meant for her.

"Yes!" shouted Alice.

"Come on, then!" roared the Queen, and Alice joined the procession, wondering very much what would happen next.

"It's—it's a very fine day!" said a timid voice at her side. She was walking by the White Rabbit, who was peeping anxiously into her face.

"Very," said Alice. "Where's the Duchess?"

"Hush! Hush!" said the Rabbit in a low hurried tone. He looked anxiously over his shoulder as he spoke, and then raised himself upon tiptoe, put his mouth close to her ear, and whispered "She's under sentence of execution."

"What for?" said Alice.

"Did you say 'What a pity!'?" the Rabbit asked.

"No, I didn't," said Alice. "I don't think it's at all a pity. I said 'What for?'"

"She boxed the Queen's ears—" the Rabbit began. Alice gave a little scream of laughter. "Oh, hush!" the Rabbit whispered in a frightened tone. "The Queen will hear you! You see she came rather late, and the Queen said—"

"Get to your places!" shouted the Queen in a voice of thunder, and people began running about in all directions, tumbling up against each other: however, they got settled down in a minute or two, and the game began.

Alice thought she had never seen such a curious croquet-ground in her life: it was all ridges and furrows: the croquet balls were live hedgehogs, and the mallets live flamingoes, and the soldiers had to double themselves up and stand on their hands and feet, to make the arches.

The chief difficulty Alice found at first was in managing her flamingo: she succeeded in getting its body tucked away, comfortably enough, under her arm, with its legs hanging down, but generally, just as she had got its neck nicely straightened out, and was going to give the hedgehog a blow with its head, it *would* twist itself round and look up in her face, with such a puzzled expression that she could not help bursting out laughing; and, when she had got its head down, and was going to begin again, it was very provoking to find that the hedgehog had unrolled itself, and was in the act of crawling away: besides all this, there was

generally a ridge or a furrow in the way wherever she wanted to send the hedgehog to, and, as the doubled-up soldiers were always getting up and walking off to other parts of the ground, Alice soon came to the conclusion that it was a very difficult game indeed.

The players all played at once, without waiting for turns, quarreling all the while, and fighting for the hedgehogs; and in a very short time the Queen was in a furious passion, and went stamping about, and shouting "Off with his head!" or "Off with her head!" about once in a minute.

Alice began to feel very uneasy: to be sure, she had not as yet had any dispute with the Queen, but she knew that it might happen any minute, "and then," thought she, "what would become of me? They're dreadfully fond of beheading people here: the great wonder is, that there's any one left alive!"

She was looking about for some way of escape, and wondering whether she could get away without being seen, when she noticed a curious appearance in the air: it puzzled her very much at first, but after watching it a minute or two she made it out to be a grin, and she said to herself "It's the Cheshire-Cat: now I shall have somebody to talk to."

"How are you getting on?" said the Cat, as soon as there was mouth enough for it to speak with.

Alice waited till the eyes appeared, and then nodded. "It's no use speaking to it," she thought, "till its ears have come, or at least one of them." In another minute the whole head appeared, and then Alice put down her flamingo, and began an account of the game, feeling very glad she had some one to listen to her. The Cat seemed to think that there was enough of it now in sight, and no more of it appeared.

"I don't think they play at all fairly," Alice began, in rather a complaining tone, "and they all quarrel so dreadfully one ca'n't hear oneself speak— and they don't seem to have any rules in particular: at least, if there are, nobody attends to them—and you've no idea how confusing it is all the things being alive: for instance, there's the arch I've got to go through next walking about at the other end of the ground—and I should have croqueted the Queen's hedgehog just now, only it ran away when it saw mine coming!"

"How do you like the Queen?" said the Cat in a low voice.

"Not at all," said Alice: "she's so extremely—" Just then she noticed that the Queen was close behind her, listening: so she went on "—likely to win, that it's hardly worth while finishing the game."

The Queen smiled and passed on.

"Who *are* you talking to?" said the King, coming up to Alice, and looking at the Cat's head with great curiosity.

"It's a friend of mine—a Cheshire-Cat," said Alice: "allow me to introduce it."

"I don't like the look of it at all," said the King: "however, it may kiss my hand, if it likes."

"I'd rather not," the Cat remarked.

"Don't be impertinent," said the King, "and don't look at me like that!" He got behind Alice as he spoke.

"A cat may look at a king," said Alice. "I've read that in some book, but I don't remember where."

"Well, it must be removed," said the King very decidedly; and he called to the Queen, who was passing at the moment, "My dear! I wish you would have this cat removed!"

The Queen had only one way of settling all difficulties, great or small. "Off with his head!" she said without even looking round.

"I'll fetch the executioner myself," said the King eagerly, and he hurried off.

Alice thought she might as well go back and see how the game was going on, as she heard the Queen's voice in the distance, screaming with passion. She had already heard her sentence three of the players to be executed for having missed their turns, and she did not like the look of things at all, as the game was in such confusion that she never knew whether it was her turn or not. So she went off in search of her hedgehog.

The hedgehog was engaged in a fight with another hedgehog, which seemed to Alice an excellent opportunity for croqueting one of them with the other: the only difficulty was that her flamingo was gone across the other side of the garden, where Alice could see it trying in a helpless sort of way to fly up into a tree.

By the time she had caught the flamingo and brought it back, the fight was over, and both the hedgehogs were out of sight: "but it doesn't matter much," thought Alice, "as all the arches are gone from this side of the ground." So she tucked it away under her arm, that it might not escape again, and went back to have a little more conversation with her friend.

When she got back to the Cheshire-Cat, she was surprised to find quite a large crowd collected round it: there was a dispute going on between the executioner, the King, and the Queen, who were all talking at once, while all the rest were quite silent, and looked very uncomfortable.

The moment Alice appeared, she was appealed to by all three to settle the question, and they repeated their arguments to her, though, as they all spoke at once, she found it very hard to make out exactly what they said.

The executioner's argument was, that you couldn't cut off a head unless there was a body to cut it off from: that he had never had to do such a thing before, and he wasn't going to begin at *his* time of life.

The King's argument was that anything that had a head could be beheaded, and that you weren't to talk nonsense.

The Queen's argument was that, if something wasn't done about it in less than no time, she'd have everybody executed, all round. (It was this last remark that had made the whole party look so grave and anxious.)

Alice could think of nothing else to say but "It belongs to the Duchess: you'd better ask *her* about it."

"She's in prison," the Queen said to the executioner: "fetch her here." And the executioner went off like an arrow.

The Cat's head began fading away the moment he was gone, and, by the time he had come back with the Duchess, it had entirely disappeared: so the King and the executioner ran wildly up and down, looking for it, while the rest of the party went back to the game.

CHAPTER IX.

THE MOCK TURTLE'S STORY.

"YOU ca'n't think how glad I am to see you again, you dear old thing!" said the Duchess, as she tucked her arm affectionately into Alice's, and they walked off together.

Alice was very glad to find her in such a pleasant temper, and thought to herself that perhaps it was only the pepper that had made her so savage when they met in the kitchen.

"When *I'm* a Duchess," she said to herself (not in a very hopeful tone, though), "I wo'n't have any pepper in my kitchen *at all*. Soup does very well without—Maybe it's always pepper that makes people hot-tempered," she went on, very much pleased at having found out a new kind of rule, "and vinegar that makes them sour—and camomile that makes them bitter—and—and barley-sugar and such things that make children sweet-tempered. I only wish people knew *that*: then they wouldn't be so stingy about it, you know——"

She had quite forgotten the Duchess by this time, and was a little startled when she heard her voice close to her ear. "You're thinking about something, my dear, and that makes you forget to talk. I ca'n't tell you just now what the moral of that is, but I shall remember it in a bit."

"Perhaps it hasn't one," Alice ventured to remark.

"Tut, tut, child!" said the Duchess. "Everything's got a moral, if only you can find it." And she squeezed herself up closer to Alice's side as she spoke.

Alice did not much like her keeping so close to her: first, because the Duchess was *very* ugly; and secondly, because she was exactly the right height to rest her chin on Alice's shoulder, and it was an uncomfortably sharp chin. However, she did not like to be rude: so she bore it as well as she could.

"The game's going on rather better now," she said, by way of keeping up the conversation a little.

"'Tis so," said the Duchess: "and the moral of that is—'Oh, 'tis love, 'tis love, that makes the world go round!'"

"Somebody said," Alice whispered, "that it's done by everybody minding their own business!"

"Ah well! It means much the same thing," said the Duchess, digging her sharp little chin into Alice's shoulder as she added "and the moral of *that* is—'Take care of the sense, and the sounds will take care of themselves.'"

"How fond she is of finding morals in things!" Alice thought to herself.

"I dare say you're wondering why I don't put my arm round your waist," the Duchess said, after a pause: "the reason is, that I'm doubtful about the temper of your flamingo. Shall I try the experiment?"

"He might bite," Alice cautiously replied, not feeling at all anxious to have the experiment tried.

"Very true," said the Duchess: "flamingoes and mustard both bite. And the moral of that is—'Birds of a feather flock together.'"

"Only mustard isn't a bird," Alice remarked.

"Right, as usual," said the Duchess: "what a clear way you have of putting things!"

"It's a mineral, I *think*," said Alice.

"Of course it is," said the Duchess, who seemed ready to agree to everything that Alice said: "there's a large mustard-mine near here. And the moral of that is—'The more there is of mine, the less there is of yours.'"

"Oh, I know!" exclaimed Alice, who had not attended to this last remark. "It's a vegetable. It doesn't look like one, but it is."

"I quite agree with you," said the Duchess; "and the moral of that is—'Be what you would seem to be'—or, if you'd like it put more simply—'Never imagine yourself not to be otherwise than what it might appear to others that what you were or might have been was not otherwise than what you had been would have appeared to them to be otherwise.'"

"I think I should understand that better," Alice said very politely, "if I had it written down: but I ca'n't quite follow it as you say it."

"That's nothing to what I could say if I chose," the Duchess replied, in a pleased tone.

"Pray don't trouble yourself to say it any longer than that," said Alice.

"Oh, don't talk about trouble!" said the Duchess. "I make you a present of everything I've said as yet."

"A cheap sort of present!" thought Alice. "I'm glad people don't give birthday-presents like that!" But she did not venture to say it out loud.

"Thinking again?" the Duchess asked, with another dig of her sharp little chin.

"I've a right to think," said Alice sharply, for she was beginning to feel a little worried.

"Just about as much right," said the Duchess, "as pigs have to fly; and the m——"

But here, to Alice's great surprise, the Duchess's voice died away, even in the middle of her favourite word 'moral,' and the arm that was linked into hers began to tremble. Alice looked up, and there stood the Queen in front of them, with her arms folded, frowning like a thunderstorm.

"A fine day, your Majesty!" the Duchess began in a low, weak voice.

"Now, I give you fair warning," shouted the Queen, stamping on the ground as she spoke; "either you or your head must be off, and that in about half no time! Take your choice!"

The Duchess took her choice, and was gone in a moment.

"Let's go on with the game," the Queen said to Alice; and Alice was too much frightened to say a word, but slowly followed her back to the croquet-ground.

The other guests had taken advantage of the Queen's absence, and were resting in the shade: however, the moment they saw her, they hurried back to the game, the Queen merely remarking that a moment's delay would cost them their lives.

All the time they were playing the Queen never left off quarreling with the other players, and shouting "Off with his head!" or "Off with her head!" Those whom she sentenced were taken into custody by the soldiers, who of course had to leave off being arches to do this, so that, by the end of half an hour or so, there were no arches left, and all the players, except the King, the Queen, and Alice, were in custody and under sentence of execution.

Then the Queen left off, quite out of breath, and said to Alice, "Have you seen the Mock Turtle yet?"

"No," said Alice. "I don't even know what a Mock Turtle is."

"It's the thing Mock Turtle Soup is made from," said the Queen.

"I never saw one, or heard of one," said Alice.

"Come on, then," said the Queen, "and he shall tell you his history."

As they walked off together, Alice heard the King say in a low voice, to the company generally, "You are all pardoned." "Come, *that's* a good thing!" she said to herself, for she had felt quite unhappy at the number of executions the Queen had ordered.

They very soon came upon a Gryphon, lying fast asleep in the sun. (If you don't know what a Gryphon is, look at the picture.) "Up, lazy thing!" said the Queen, "and take this young lady to see the Mock Turtle, and to hear his history. I must go back and see after some executions I have ordered;" and she walked off, leaving Alice alone with the Gryphon. Alice did not quite like the look of the creature, but on the whole she thought it would be quite as safe to stay with it as to go after that savage Queen: so she waited.

The Gryphon sat up and rubbed its eyes: then it watched the Queen till she was out of sight: then it chuckled. "What fun!" said the Gryphon, half to itself, half to Alice.

"What *is* the fun?" said Alice.

"Why, *she*," said the Gryphon. "It's all her fancy, that: they never executes nobody, you know. Come on!"

"Everybody says 'come on!' here," thought Alice, as she went slowly after it: "I never was so ordered about before, in all my life, never!"

They had not gone far before they saw the Mock Turtle in the distance,

sitting sad and lonely on a little ledge of rock, and, as they came nearer, Alice could hear him sighing as if his heart would break. She pitied him deeply. "What is his sorrow?" she asked the Gryphon. And the Gryphon answered, very nearly in the same words as before, "It's all his fancy, that: he hasn't got no sorrow, you know. Come on!"

So they went up to the Mock Turtle, who looked at them with large eyes full of tears, but said nothing.

"This here young lady," said the Gryphon, "she wants for to know your history, she do."

"I'll tell it her," said the Mock Turtle in a deep, hollow tone. "Sit down, both of you, and don't speak a word till I've finished."

So they sat down, and nobody spoke for some minutes. Alice thought to herself "I don't see how he can *ever* finish, if he doesn't begin." But she waited patiently.

"Once," said the Mock Turtle at last, with a deep sigh, "I was a real Turtle."

These words were followed by a very long silence, broken only by an occasional exclamation of "Hjckrrh!" from the Gryphon, and the constant heavy sobbing of the Mock Turtle. Alice was very nearly getting up and saying, "Thank you, Sir, for your interesting story," but she could not help thinking there *must* be more to come, so she sat still and said nothing.

"When we were little," the Mock Turtle went on at last, more calmly, though still sobbing a little now and then, "we went to school in the sea. The master was an old Turtle—we used to call him Tortoise——"

"Why did you call him Tortoise, if he wasn't one?" Alice asked.

"We called him Tortoise because he taught us," said the Mock Turtle angrily. "Really you are very dull!"

"You ought to be ashamed of yourself for asking such a simple question," added the Gryphon; and then they both sat silent and looked at poor Alice, who felt ready to sink into the earth. At last the Gryphon said to the Mock Turtle "Drive on, old fellow! Don't be all day about it!", and he went on in these words:—

"Yes, we went to school in the sea, though you mayn't believe it——"

"I never said I didn't!" interrupted Alice.

"You did," said the Mock Turtle.

"Hold your tongue!" added the Gryphon, before Alice could speak again. The Mock Turtle went on.

"We had the best of educations—in fact, we went to school every day——"

"*I've* been to a day-school, too," said Alice. "You needn't be so proud as all that."

"With extras?" asked the Mock Turtle, a little anxiously.

"Yes," said Alice: "we learned French and music."

"And washing?" said the Mock Turtle.

"Certainly not!" said Alice indignantly.

"Ah! Then yours wasn't a really good school," said the Mock Turtle in a tone of great relief. "Now, at *ours*, they had, at the end of the bill, 'French, music, *and washing*—extra.'"

"You couldn't have wanted it much," said Alice; "living at the bottom of the sea."

"I couldn't afford to learn it," said the Mock Turtle with a sigh. "I only took the regular course."

"What was that?" inquired Alice.

"Reeling and Writhing, of course, to begin with," the Mock Turtle replied; "and then the different branches of Arithmetic—Ambition, Distraction, Uglification, and Derision."

"I never heard of 'Uglification,'" Alice ventured to say. "What is it?"

The Gryphon lifted up both its paws in surprise. "Never heard of uglifying!" it exclaimed. "You know what to beautify is, I suppose?"

"Yes," said Alice doubtfully: "it means—to—make—anything—prettier."

"Well, then," the Gryphon went on, "if you don't know what to uglify is, you *are* a simpleton."

Alice did not feel encouraged to ask any more questions about it: so she turned to the Mock Turtle, and said "What else had you to learn?"

"Well, there was Mystery," the Mock Turtle replied, counting off the subjects on his flappers,—"Mystery, ancient and modern, with Seaography: then Drawling—the Drawling-master was an old conger-eel, that used to come once a week: *he* taught us Drawling, Stretching, and Fainting in Coils."

"What was *that* like?" said Alice.

"Well, I ca'n't show it you, myself," the Mock Turtle said: "I'm too stiff. And the Gryphon never learnt it."

"Hadn't time," said the Gryphon: "I went to the Classical master, though. He was an old crab, *he* was."

"I never went to him," the Mock Turtle said with a sigh. "He taught Laughing and Grief, they used to say."

"So he did, so he did," said the Gryphon, sighing in his turn; and both creatures hid their faces in their paws.

"And how many hours a day did you do lessons?" said Alice, in a hurry to change the subject.

"Ten hours the first day," said the Mock Turtle: "nine the next, and so on."

"What a curious plan!" exclaimed Alice.

"That's the reason they're called lessons," the Gryphon remarked: "because they lessen from day to day."

This was quite a new idea to Alice, and she thought it over a little before she made her next remark. "Then the eleventh day must have been a holiday?"

"Of course it was," said the Mock Turtle.

"And how did you manage on the twelfth?" Alice went on eagerly.

"That's enough about lessons," the Gryphon interrupted in a very decided tone. "Tell her something about the games now."

CHAPTER X.

THE LOBSTER-QUADRILLE.

THE Mock Turtle sighed deeply, and drew the back of one flapper across his eyes. He looked at Alice and tried to speak, but, for a minute or two, sobs choked his voice. "Same as if he had a bone in his throat," said the Gryphon; and it set to work shaking him and punching him in the back. At last the Mock Turtle recovered his voice, and, with tears running down his cheeks, he went on again:—

"You may not have lived much under the sea—" ("I haven't," said Alice)—"and perhaps you were never even introduced to a lobster—"

(Alice began to say "I once tasted——" but checked herself hastily, and said "No, never") "——so you can have no idea what a delightful thing a Lobster-Quadrille is!"

"No, indeed," said Alice. "What sort of a dance is it?"

"Why," said the Gryphon, "you first form into a line along the sea-shore——"

"Two lines!" cried the Mock Turtle. "Seals, turtles, salmon, and so on: then, when you've cleared all the jelly-fish out of the way——"

"*That* generally takes some time," interrupted the Gryphon.

"——you advance twice——"

"Each with a lobster as a partner!" cried the Gryphon.

"Of course," the Mock Turtle said: "advance twice, set to partners——"

"——change lobsters, and retire in same order," continued the Gryphon.

"Then, you know," the Mock Turtle went on, "you throw the——"

"The lobsters!" shouted the Gryphon, with a bound into the air.

"——as far out to sea as you can——"

"Swim after them!" screamed the Gryphon.

"Turn a somersault in the sea!" cried the Mock Turtle, capering wildly about.

"Change lobsters again!" yelled the Gryphon at the top of its voice.

"Back to land again, and—that's all the first figure," said the Mock Turtle, suddenly dropping his voice; and the two creatures, who had been jumping about like mad things all this time, sat down again very sadly and quietly, and looked at Alice.

"It must be a very pretty dance," said Alice timidly.

"Would you like to see a little of it?" said the Mock Turtle.

"Very much indeed," said Alice.

"Come, let's try the first figure!" said the Mock Turtle to the Gryphon. "We can do it without lobsters, you know. Which shall sing?"

"Oh, *you* sing," said the Gryphon. "I've forgotten the words."

So they began solemnly dancing round and round Alice, every now and then treading on her toes when they passed too close, and waving their fore-paws to mark the time, while the Mock Turtle sang this, very slowly and sadly:—

"Will you walk a little faster?" said a whiting to a snail,
"There's a porpoise close behind us, and he's treading on my tail.
See how eagerly the lobsters and the turtles all advance!
They are waiting on the shingle—will you come and join the dance?
Will you, wo'n't you, will you, wo'n't you, will you join the dance?
Will you, wo'n't you, will you, wo'n't you, wo'n't you join the dance?

"You can really have no notion how delightful it will be
When they take us up and throw us, with the lobsters, out to sea!"
But the snail replied "Too far, too far!", and gave a look askance—
Said he thanked the whiting kindly, but he would not join the dance.
Would not, could not, would not, could not, would not join the dance.
Would not, could not, would not, could not, could not join the dance.

"What matters it how far we go?" his scaly friend replied.
"There is another shore, you know, upon the other side.
The further off from England the nearer is to France—
Then turn not pale, beloved snail, but come and join the dance.
   Will you, wo'n't you, will you, wo'n't you, will you join the dance?
   Will you, wo'n't you, will you, wo'n't you, wo'n't you join the dance?"

"Thank you, it's a very interesting dance to watch," said Alice, feeling very glad that it was over at last: "and I do so like that curious song about the whiting!"

"Oh, as to the whiting," said the Mock Turtle, "they—you've seen them, of course?"

"Yes," said Alice, "I've often seen them at dinn——" she checked herself hastily.

"I don't know where Dinn may be," said the Mock Turtle; "but, if you've seen them so often, of course you know what they're like?"

"I believe so," Alice replied thoughtfully. "They have their tails in their mouths—and they're all over crumbs."

"You're wrong about the crumbs," said the Mock Turtle: "crumbs would all wash off in the sea. But they *have* their tails in their mouths;

and the reason is——" here the Mock Turtle yawned and shut his eyes. "Tell her about the reason and all that," he said to the Gryphon.

"The reason is," said the Gryphon, "that they *would* go with the lobsters to the dance. So they got thrown out to sea. So they had to fall a long way. So they got their tails fast in their mouths. So they couldn't get them out again. That's all."

"Thank you," said Alice, "it's very interesting. I never knew so much about a whiting before."

"I can tell you more than that, if you like," said the Gryphon. "Do you know why it's called a whiting?"

"I never thought about it," said Alice. "Why?"

"*It does the boots and shoes,*" the Gryphon replied very solemnly.

Alice was thoroughly puzzled. "Does the boots and shoes!" she repeated in a wondering tone.

"Why, what are *your* shoes done with?" said the Gryphon. "I mean, what makes them so shiny?"

Alice looked down at them, and considered a little before she gave her answer. "They're done with blacking, I believe."

"Boots and shoes under the sea," the Gryphon went on in a deep voice, "are done with whiting. Now you know."

"And what are they made of?" Alice asked in a tone of great curiosity.

"Soles and eels, of course," the Gryphon replied, rather impatiently: "any shrimp could have told you that."

"If I'd been the whiting," said Alice, whose thoughts were still running on the song, "I'd have said to the porpoise 'Keep back, please! We don't want *you* with us!'"

"They were obliged to have him with them," the Mock Turtle said. "No wise fish would go anywhere without a porpoise."

"Wouldn't it, really?" said Alice, in a tone of great surprise.

"Of course not," said the Mock Turtle. "Why, if a fish came to *me*, and told me he was going a journey, I should say 'With what porpoise?'"

"Don't you mean 'purpose'?" said Alice.

"I mean what I say," the Mock Turtle replied, in an offended tone. And the Gryphon added "Come, let's hear some of *your* adventures."

"I could tell you my adventures—beginning from this morning," said Alice a little timidly; "but it's no use going back to yesterday, because I was a different person then."

"Explain all that," said the Mock Turtle.

"No, no! The adventures first," said the Gryphon in an impatient tone: "explanations take such a dreadful time."

So Alice began telling them her adventures from the time when she first saw the White Rabbit. She was a little nervous about it, just at first, the two creatures got so close to her, one on each side, and opened their eyes and mouths so *very* wide; but she gained courage as she went on. Her listeners were perfectly quiet till she got to the part about her repeating "*You are old, Father William,*" to the Caterpillar, and the words all coming different, and then the Mock Turtle drew a long breath, and said "That's very curious!"

"It's all about as curious as it can be," said the Gryphon.

"It all came different!" the Mock Turtle repeated thoughtfully. "I should like to hear her try and repeat something now. Tell her to begin." He looked at the Gryphon as if he thought it had some kind of authority over Alice.

"Stand up and repeat '*'Tis the voice of the sluggard,*'" said the Gryphon.

"How the creatures order one about, and make one repeat lessons!" thought Alice. "I might just as well be at school at once." However, she got up, and began to repeat it, but her head was so full of the Lobster-Quadrille, that she hardly knew what she was saying; and the words came very queer indeed:—

> "*'Tis the voice of the Lobster: I heard him declare*
> *'You have baked me too brown, I must sugar my hair.'*
> *As a duck with its eyelids, so he with his nose*
> *Trims his belt and his buttons, and turns out his toes.*
> *When the sands are all dry, he is gay as a lark,*
> *And will talk in contemptuous tones of the Shark:*
> *But, when the tide rises and sharks are around,*
> *His voice has a timid and tremulous sound.*"

"That's different from what *I* used to say when I was a child," said the Gryphon.

"Well, *I* never heard it before," said the Mock Turtle; "but it sounds uncommon nonsense."

Alice said nothing: she had sat down with her face in her hands, wondering if anything would *ever* happen in a natural way again.

"I should like to have it explained," said the Mock Turtle.

"She ca'n't explain it," said the Gryphon hastily. "Go on with the next verse."

"But about his toes?" the Mock Turtle persisted. "How *could* he turn them out with his nose, you know?"

"It's the first position in dancing," Alice said; but she was dreadfully puzzled by the whole thing, and longed to change the subject.

"Go on with the next verse," the Gryphon repeated: "it begins 'I *passed by his garden.*'"

Alice did not dare to disobey, though she felt sure it would all come wrong, and she went on in a trembling voice:—

> *"I passed by his garden, and marked, with one eye,*
> *How the Owl and the Panther were sharing a pie:*
> *The Panther took pie-crust, and gravy, and meat,*
> *While the Owl had the dish as its share of the treat.*
> *When the pie was all finished, the Owl, as a boon,*
> *Was kindly permitted to pocket the spoon:*
> *While the Panther received knife and fork with a growl,*
> *And concluded the banquet by——"*

"What *is* the use of repeating all that stuff?" the Mock Turtle interrupted, "if you don't explain it as you go on? It's by far the most confusing thing *I* ever heard!"

"Yes, I think you'd better leave off," said the Gryphon, and Alice was only too glad to do so.

"Shall we try another figure of the Lobster-Quadrille?" the Gryphon went on. "Or would you like the Mock Turtle to sing you another song?"

"Oh, a song, please, if the Mock Turtle would be so kind," Alice replied, so eagerly that the Gryphon said, in a rather offended tone, "Hm! No accounting for tastes! Sing her '*Turtle Soup*,' will you, old fellow?"

The Mock Turtle sighed deeply, and began, in a voice choked with sobs, to sing this:—

> *"Beautiful Soup, so rich and green,*
> *Waiting in a hot tureen!*
> *Who for such dainties would not stoop?*
> *Soup of the evening, beautiful Soup!*
> *Soup of the evening, beautiful Soup!*
> *   Beau—ootiful Soo—oop!*
> *   Beau—ootiful Soo—oop!*
> *Soo—oop of the e—e—evening,*
> *   Beautiful, beautiful Soup!*

> *"Beautiful Soup! Who cares for fish,*

> *Game, or any other dish?*
> *Who would not give all else for two p*
> *ennyworth only of beautiful Soup?*
> *Pennyworth only of beautiful soup?*
> *Beau—ootiful Soo—oop!*
> *Beau—ootiful Soo—oop!*
> *Soo—oop of the e—e—evening,*
> *Beautiful, beauti—FUL SOUP!"*

"Chorus again!" cried the Gryphon, and the Mock Turtle had just begun to repeat it, when a cry of "The trial's beginning!" was heard in the distance.

"Come on!" cried the Gryphon, and, taking Alice by the hand, it hurried off, without waiting for the end of the song.

"What trial is it?" Alice panted as she ran; but the Gryphon only answered "Come on!" and ran the faster, while more and more faintly came, carried on the breeze that followed them, the melancholy words:—

> *"Soo—oop of the e—e—evening,*
> *Beautiful, beautiful Soup!"*

CHAPTER XI.

WHO STOLE THE TARTS?

THE King and Queen of Hearts were seated on their throne when they arrived, with a great crowd assembled about them—all sorts of little birds and beasts, as well as the whole pack of cards: the Knave was standing before them, in chains, with a soldier on each side to guard him; and near the King was the White Rabbit, with a trumpet in one hand, and a scroll of parchment in the other. In the very middle of the court was a table, with a large dish of tarts upon it: they looked so good, that it made Alice quite hungry to look at them—"I wish they'd get the trial done," she thought, "and hand round the refreshments!" But there seemed to be no chance of this; so she began looking at everything about her to pass away the time.

Alice had never been in a court of justice before, but she had read about them in books, and she was quite pleased to find that she knew the name of nearly everything there. "That's the judge," she said to herself, "because of his great wig."

The judge, by the way, was the King; and, as he wore his crown over the wig (look at the frontispiece if you want to see how he did it), he did not look at all comfortable, and it was certainly not becoming.

"And that's the jury-box," thought Alice; "and those twelve creatures," (she was obliged to say "creatures," you see, because some of them were animals, and some were birds,) "I suppose they are the jurors." She said this last word two or three times over to herself, being rather proud of it: for she thought, and rightly too, that very few little girls of her age knew the meaning of it at all. However, "jurymen" would have done just as well.

The twelve jurors were all writing very busily on slates. "What are they doing?" Alice whispered to the Gryphon. "They ca'n't have anything to put down yet, before the trial's begun."

"They're putting down their names," the Gryphon whispered in reply, "for fear they should forget them before the end of the trial."

"Stupid things!" Alice began in a loud indignant voice; but she stopped herself hastily, for the White Rabbit cried out "Silence in the court!", and the King put on his spectacles and looked anxiously round, to make out who was talking.

Alice could see, as well as if she were looking over their shoulders, that all the jurors were writing down "Stupid things!" on their slates, and she could even make out that one of them didn't know how to spell "stupid," and that he had to ask his neighbour to tell him. "A nice muddle their slates'll be in, before the trial's over!" thought Alice.

One of the jurors had a pencil that squeaked. This, of course, Alice could *not* stand, and she went round the court and got behind him, and very soon found an opportunity of taking it away. She did it so quickly that the poor little juror (it was Bill, the Lizard) could not make out at all what had become of it; so, after hunting all about for it, he was obliged to write with one finger for the rest of the day; and this was of very little use, as it left no mark on the slate.

"Herald, read the accusation!" said the King.

On this the White Rabbit blew three blasts on the trumpet, and then unrolled the parchment-scroll, and read as follows:—

> "The Queen of Hearts, she made some tarts,
>   All on a summer day:
> The Knave of Hearts, he stole those tarts
>   And took them quite away!"

"Consider your verdict," the King said to the jury.

"Not yet, not yet!" the Rabbit hastily interrupted. "There's a great deal to come before that!"

"Call the first witness," said the King; and the White Rabbit blew three blasts on the trumpet, and called out "First witness!"

The first witness was the Hatter. He came in with a teacup in one hand and a piece of bread-and-butter in the other. "I beg pardon, your Majesty," he began, "for bringing these in; but I hadn't quite finished my tea when I was sent for."

"You ought to have finished," said the King. "When did you begin?"

The Hatter looked at the March Hare, who had followed him into the court, arm-in-arm with the Dormouse. "Fourteenth of March, I *think* it was," he said.

"Fifteenth," said the March Hare.

"Sixteenth," said the Dormouse.

"Write that down," the King said to the jury; and the jury eagerly wrote down all three dates on their slates, and then added them up, and reduced the answer to shillings and pence.

"Take off your hat," the King said to the Hatter.

"It isn't mine," said the Hatter.

"*Stolen!*" the King exclaimed, turning to the jury, who instantly made a memorandum of the fact.

"I keep them to sell," the Hatter added as an explanation. "I've none of my own. I'm a hatter."

Here the Queen put on her spectacles, and began staring hard at the Hatter, who turned pale and fidgeted.

"Give your evidence," said the King; "and don't be nervous, or I'll have you executed on the spot."

This did not seem to encourage the witness at all: he kept shifting from one foot to the other, looking uneasily at the Queen, and in his confusion he bit a large piece out of his teacup instead of the bread-and-butter.

Just at this moment Alice felt a very curious sensation, which puzzled her a good deal until she made out what it was: she was beginning to grow larger again, and she thought at first she would get up and leave the court; but on second thoughts she decided to remain where she was as long as there was room for her.

"I wish you wouldn't squeeze so," said the Dormouse, who was sitting next to her. "I can hardly breathe."

"I ca'n't help it," said Alice very meekly: "I'm growing."

"You've no right to grow *here*," said the Dormouse.

"Don't talk nonsense," said Alice more boldly: "you know you're growing too."

"Yes, but *I* grow at a reasonable pace," said the Dormouse: "not in that ridiculous fashion." And he got up very sulkily and crossed over to the other side of the court.

All this time the Queen had never left off staring at the Hatter, and, just as the Dormouse crossed the court, she said, to one of the officers of the court, "Bring me the list of the singers in the last concert!" on which the wretched Hatter trembled so, that he shook off both his shoes.

"Give your evidence," the King repeated angrily, "or I'll have you executed, whether you are nervous or not."

"I'm a poor man, your Majesty," the Hatter began, in a trembling voice, "and I hadn't begun my tea—not above a week or so—and what with the bread-and-butter getting so thin—and the twinkling of the tea——"

"The twinkling of *what?*" said the King.

"It *began* with the tea," the Hatter replied.

"Of course twinkling *begins* with a T!" said the King sharply. "Do you take me for a dunce? Go on!"

"I'm a poor man," the Hatter went on, "and most things twinkled after that—only the March Hare said——"

"I didn't!" the March Hare interrupted in a great hurry.

"You did!" said the Hatter.

"I deny it!" said the March Hare.

"He denies it," said the King: "leave out that part."

"Well, at any rate, the Dormouse said——" the Hatter went on, looking anxiously round to see if he would deny it too; but the Dormouse denied nothing, being fast asleep.

"After that," continued the Hatter, "I cut some more bread-and-butter——"

"But what did the Dormouse say?" one of the jury asked.

"That I ca'n't remember," said the Hatter.

"You *must* remember," remarked the King, "or I'll have you executed."

The miserable Hatter dropped his teacup and bread-and-butter, and went down on one knee. "I'm a poor man, your Majesty," he began.

"You're a *very* poor *speaker*," said the King.

Here one of the guinea-pigs cheered, and was immediately suppressed by the officers of the court. (As that is rather a hard word, I will just explain to you how it was done. They had a large canvas bag, which tied up at the mouth with strings: into this they slipped the guinea-pig, head first, and then sat upon it.)

"I'm glad I've seen that done," thought Alice. "I've so often read in the newspapers, at the end of trials, 'There was some attempt at applause, which was immediately suppressed by the officers of the court,' and I never understood what it meant till now."

"If that's all you know about it, you may stand down," continued the King.

"I ca'n't go no lower," said the Hatter: "I'm on the floor, as it is."

"Then you may *sit* down," the King replied.

Here the other guinea-pig cheered, and was suppressed.

"Come, that finishes the guinea-pigs!" thought Alice. "Now we shall get on better."

"I'd rather finish my tea," said the Hatter, with an anxious look at the Queen, who was reading the list of singers.

"You may go," said the King, and the Hatter hurriedly left the court, without even waiting to put his shoes on.

"——and just take his head off outside," the Queen added to one of the officers; but the Hatter was out of sight before the officer could get to the door.

"Call the next witness!" said the King.

The next witness was the Duchess's cook. She carried the pepper-box in her hand, and Alice guessed who it was, even before she got into the court, by the way the people near the door began sneezing all at once.

"Give your evidence," said the King.

"Sha'n't," said the cook.

The King looked anxiously at the White Rabbit, who said, in a low voice, "Your Majesty must cross-examine *this* witness."

"Well, if I must, I must," the King said with a melancholy air, and, after folding his arms and frowning at the cook till his eyes were nearly out of sight, he said, in a deep voice, "What are tarts made of?"

"Pepper, mostly," said the cook.

"Treacle," said a sleepy voice behind her.

"Collar that Dormouse!" the Queen shrieked out. "Behead that Dormouse! Turn that Dormouse out of court! Suppress him! Pinch him! Off with his whiskers!"

For some minutes the whole court was in confusion, getting the Dormouse turned out, and, by the time they had settled down again, the cook had disappeared.

"Never mind!" said the King, with an air of great relief. "Call the next witness." And, he added, in an under-tone to the Queen, "Really, my dear, *you* must cross-examine the next witness. It quite makes my forehead ache!"

Alice watched the White Rabbit as he fumbled over the list, feeling very curious to see what the next witness would be like, "—for they haven't got much evidence *yet*," she said to herself. Imagine her surprise, when the White Rabbit read out, at the top of his shrill little voice, the name "Alice!"

CHAPTER XII.

ALICE'S EVIDENCE.

"Here!" cried Alice, quite forgetting in the flurry of the moment how large she had grown in the last few minutes, and she jumped up in such a hurry that she tipped over the jury-box with the edge of her skirt, upsetting all the jurymen on to the heads of the crowd below, and there they lay sprawling about, reminding her very much of a globe of goldfish she had accidentally upset the week before.

"Oh, I *beg* your pardon!" she exclaimed in a tone of great dismay, and began picking them up again as quickly as she could, for the accident of the gold-fish kept running in her head, and she had a vague sort of idea that they must be collected at once and put back into the jury-box, or they would die.

"The trial cannot proceed," said the King, in a very grave voice, "until all the jurymen are back in their proper places—*all*," he repeated with great emphasis, looking hard at Alice as he said so.

Alice looked at the jury-box, and saw that, in her haste, she had put the Lizard in head downwards, and the poor little thing was waving its tail about in a melancholy way, being quite unable to move. She soon got it out again, and put it right; "not that it signifies much," she said to herself; "I should think it would be *quite* as much use in the trial one way up as the other."

As soon as the jury had a little recovered from the shock of being upset, and their slates and pencils had been found and handed back to them, they set to work very diligently to write out a history of the accident, all except the Lizard, who seemed too much overcome to do anything but sit with its mouth open, gazing up into the roof of the court.

"What do you know about this business?" the King said to Alice.

"Nothing," said Alice.

"Nothing *whatever*?" persisted the King.

"Nothing whatever," said Alice.

"That's very important," the King said, turning to the jury. They were just beginning to write this down on their slates, when the White Rabbit interrupted: "*Un*important, your Majesty means, of course," he said, in a very respectful tone, but frowning and making faces at him as he spoke.

"*Un*important, of course, I meant," the King hastily said, and went on to himself in an under-tone, "important—unimportant—unimportant—important——" as if he were trying which word sounded best.

Some of the jury wrote it down "important," and some "unimportant." Alice could see this, as she was near enough to look over their slates; "but it doesn't matter a bit," she thought to herself.

At this moment the King, who had been for some time busily writing

in his note-book, called out "Silence!", and read out from his book, "Rule Forty-two. *All persons more than a mile high to leave the court.*"

Everybody looked at Alice.

"*I'm* not a mile high," said Alice.

"You are," said the King.

"Nearly two miles high," added the Queen.

"Well, I sha'n't go, at any rate," said Alice: "besides, that's not a regular rule: you invented it just now."

"It's the oldest rule in the book," said the King.

"Then it ought to be Number One," said Alice.

The King turned pale, and shut his note-book hastily. "Consider your verdict," he said to the jury, in a low trembling voice.

"There's more evidence to come yet, please your Majesty," said the White Rabbit, jumping up in a great hurry: "this paper has just been picked up."

"What's in it?" said the Queen.

"I haven't opened it yet," said the White Rabbit; "but it seems to be a letter, written by the prisoner to—to somebody."

"It must have been that," said the King, "unless it was written to nobody, which isn't usual, you know."

"Who is it directed to?" said one of the jurymen.

"It isn't directed at all," said the White Rabbit: "in fact, there's nothing written on the *outside*." He unfolded the paper as he spoke, and added "It isn't a letter, after all: it's a set of verses."

"Are they in the prisoner's handwriting?" asked another of the jurymen.

"No, they're not," said the White Rabbit, "and that's the queerest thing about it." (The jury all looked puzzled.)

"He must have imitated somebody else's hand," said the King. (The jury all brightened up again.)

"Please your Majesty," said the Knave, "I didn't write it, and they ca'n't prove that I did: there's no name signed at the end."

"If you didn't sign it," said the King, "that only makes the matter worse. You *must* have meant some mischief, or else you'd have signed your name like an honest man."

There was a general clapping of hands at this: it was the first really clever thing the King had said that day.

"That *proves* his guilt, of course," said the Queen: "so, off with——."

"It doesn't prove anything of the sort!" said Alice. "Why, you don't even know what they're about!"

"Read them," said the King.

The White Rabbit put on his spectacles. "Where shall I begin, please your Majesty?" he asked.

"Begin at the beginning," the King said, very gravely, "and go on till you come to the end: then stop."

There was dead silence in the court, whilst the White Rabbit read out these verses:—

"They told me you had been to her,
And mentioned me to him:
She gave me a good character,
But said I could not swim.

He sent them word I had not gone
(We know it to be true):
If she should push the matter on,
What would become of you?

I gave her one, they gave him two,
You gave us three or more;
They all returned from him to you,
Though they were mine before.

If I or she should chance to be
Involved in this affair,
He trusts to you to set them free,
Exactly as they were.

My notion was that you had been
(Before she had this fit)
An obstacle that came between
Him, and ourselves, and it.

Don't let him know she liked them best,
For this must ever be
A secret, kept from all the rest,
Between yourself and me."

"That's the most important piece of evidence we've heard yet," said the King, rubbing his hands; "so now let the jury——"

"If any one of them can explain it," said Alice, (she had grown so large in the last few minutes that she wasn't a bit afraid of interrupting him,) "I'll give him sixpence. *I* don't believe there's an atom of meaning in it."

The jury all wrote down, on their slates, "*She* doesn't believe there's an atom of meaning in it," but none of them attempted to explain the paper.

"If there's no meaning in it," said the King, "that saves a world of trouble, you know, as we needn't try to find any. And yet I don't know," he went on, spreading out the verses on his knee, and looking at them with one eye; "I seem to see some meaning in them, after all. '*—said I could not*

swim—' you ca'n't swim, can you?" he added, turning to the Knave.

The Knave shook his head sadly. "Do I look like it?" he said. (Which he certainly did *not*, being made entirely of cardboard.)

"All right, so far," said the King; and he went on muttering over the verses to himself: "'*We know it to be true*'—that's the jury, of course—'*If she should push the matter on'*—that must be the Queen—*'What would become of you?'*—What, indeed!—*'I gave her one, they gave him two'*—why, that must be what he did with the tarts, you know——"

"But it goes on *'they all returned from him to you,'* " said Alice.

"Why, there they are!" said the King triumphantly, pointing to the tarts on the table. "Nothing can be clearer than *that*. Then again—*'before she had this fit'*—you never had *fits*, my dear, I think?" he said to the Queen.

"Never!" said the Queen, furiously, throwing an inkstand at the Lizard as she spoke. (The unfortunate little Bill had left off writing on his slate with one finger, as he found it made no mark; but he now hastily began again, using the ink, that was trickling down his face, as long as it lasted.)

"Then the words don't *fit* you," said the King, looking round the court with a smile. There was a dead silence.

"It's a pun!" the King added in an angry tone, and everybody laughed. "Let the jury consider their verdict," the King said, for about the twentieth time that day.

"No, no!" said the Queen. "Sentence first—verdict afterwards."

"Stuff and nonsense!" said Alice loudly. "The idea of having the sentence first!"

"Hold your tongue!" said the Queen, turning purple.

"I wo'n't!" said Alice.

"Off with her head!" the Queen shouted at the top of her voice. Nobody moved.

"Who cares for *you?*" said Alice (she had grown to her full size by this time). "You're nothing but a pack of cards!"

At this the whole pack rose up into the air, and came flying down upon her; she gave a little scream, half of fright and half of anger, and tried to beat them off, and found herself lying on the bank, with her head in the lap of her sister, who was gently brushing away some dead leaves that had fluttered down from the trees upon her face.

"Wake up, Alice dear!" said her sister. "Why, what a long sleep you've had!"

"Oh, I've had such a curious dream!" said Alice. And she told her sister, as well as she could remember them, all these strange Adventures of hers that you have just been reading about; and, when she had finished, her sister kissed her, and said "It *was* a curious dream, dear, certainly; but now run in to your tea: it's getting late." So Alice got up and ran off, thinking while she ran, as well she might, what a wonderful dream it had been.

But her sister sat still just as she left her, leaning her head on her hand, watching the setting sun, and thinking of little Alice and all her wonderful Adventures, till she too began dreaming after a fashion, and this was her dream:—

First, she dreamed about little Alice herself: once again the tiny hands

were clasped upon her knee, and the bright eager eyes were looking up into hers—she could hear the very tones of her voice, and see that queer little toss of her head to keep back the wandering hair that *would* always get into her eyes—and still as she listened, or seemed to listen, the whole place around her became alive with the strange creatures of her little sister's dream.

The long grass rustled at her feet as the White Rabbit hurried by— the frightened Mouse splashed his way through the neighbouring pool— she could hear the rattle of the teacups as the March Hare and his friends shared their never-ending meal, and the shrill voice of the Queen ordering off her unfortunate guests to execution—once more the pig-baby was sneezing on the Duchess's knee, while plates and dishes crashed around it—once more the shriek of the Gryphon, the squeaking of the Lizard's slate-pencil, and the choking of the suppressed guinea-pigs, filled the air, mixed up with the distant sob of the miserable Mock Turtle.

So she sat on, with closed eyes, and half believed herself in Wonderland, though she knew she had but to open them again, and all would change to dull reality—the grass would be only rustling in the wind, and the pool rippling to the waving of the reeds—the rattling teacups would change to tinkling sheep-bells, and the Queen's shrill cries to the voice of the shepherd-boy—and the sneeze of the baby, the shriek of the Gryphon, and all the other queer noises, would change (she knew) to the confused clamour of the busy farm-yard—while the lowing of the cattle in the distance would take the place of the Mock Turtle's heavy sobs.

Lastly, she pictured to herself how this same little sister of hers would, in the after-time, be herself a grown woman; and how she would keep, through all her riper years, the simple and loving heart of her childhood; and how she would gather about her other little children, and make *their* eyes bright and eager with many a strange tale, perhaps even with the dream of Wonderland of long ago; and how she would feel with all their simple sorrows, and find a pleasure in all their simple joys, remembering her own child-life, and the happy summer days.

THE END.

THROUGH
THE
LOOKING-GLASS

AND WHAT ALICE
FOUND THERE

Illustrated by
JOHN TENNIEL

DRAMATIS PERSONÆ.

(As arranged before commencement of game.)

	WHITE.			RED.	
PIECES.	**PAWNS.**	**PAWNS.**			**PIECES.**
Tweedledee	Daisy.	Daisy			Humpty Dumpty.
Unicorn	Haigha.	Messenger			Carpenter.
Sheep	Oyster.	Oyster			Walrus.
W. Queen	"Lily."	Tiger-lily			R. Queen.
W. King	Fawn.	Rose			R. King.
Aged man	Oyster.	Oyster			Crow.
W. Knight	Hatta.	Frog			R. Knight.
Tweedledum . . .	Daisy.	Daisy			Lion.

White Pawn (Alice) to play, and win in eleven moves.

CHILD of the pure unclouded brow
  And dreaming eyes of wonder!
Though time be fleet, and I and thou
  Are half a life asunder,
Thy loving smile will surely hail
The love-gift of a fairy-tale.

I have not seen thy sunny face,
  Nor heard thy silver laughter:
No thought of me shall find a place
  In thy young life's hereafter—
Enough that now thou wilt not fail
To listen to my fairy-tale.

A tale begun in other days,
  When summer suns were glowing—
A simple chime, that served to time
  The rhythm of our rowing—
Whose echoes live in memory yet,
Though envious years would say 'forget.'

Come, hearken then, ere voice of dread,
  With bitter tidings laden,
Shall summon to unwelcome bed
  A melancholy maiden!
We are but older children, dear,
Who fret to find our bedtime near.

Without, the frost, the blinding snow,
  The storm-wind's moody madness—
Within, the firelight's ruddy glow,
  And childhood's nest of gladness.
The magic words shall hold thee fast:
Thou shalt not heed the raving blast.

And, though the shadow of a sigh
  May tremble through the story,
For 'happy summer days' gone by,
  And vanish'd summer glory—
It shall not touch, with breath of bale,
The pleasance of our fairy-tale.

CHAPTER I.

LOOKING-GLASS HOUSE.

ONE thing was certain, that the *white* kitten had had nothing to do with it—it was the black kitten's fault entirely. For the white kitten had been having its face washed by the old cat for the last quarter of an hour (and bearing it pretty well, considering): so you see that it *couldn't* have had any hand in the mischief.

The way Dinah washed her children's faces was this: first she held the poor thing down by its ear with one paw, and then with the other paw she rubbed its face all over, the wrong way, beginning at the nose: and just now, as I said, she was hard at work on the white kitten, which was lying quite still and trying to purr—no doubt feeling that it was all meant for its good.

But the black kitten had been finished with earlier in the afternoon, and so, while Alice was sitting curled up in a corner of the great armchair, half talking to herself and half asleep, the kitten had been having a grand game of romps with the ball of worsted Alice had been trying to wind up, and had been rolling it up and down till it had all come undone again; and there it was, spread over the hearth-rug, all knots and tangles, with the kitten running after its own tail in the middle.

"Oh, you wicked wicked little thing!" cried Alice, catching up the kitten, and giving it a little kiss to make it understand that it was in disgrace. "Really, Dinah ought to have taught you better manners! You *ought*, Dinah, you know you ought!" she added, looking reproachfully at the old cat, and speaking in as cross a voice as she could manage—and then she scrambled back into the arm-chair, taking the kitten and the worsted with her, and began winding up the ball again. But she didn't get on very fast, as she was talking all the time, sometimes to the kitten, and sometimes to herself. Kitty sat very demurely on her knee, pretending to watch the progress of the winding, and now and then putting out one paw and gently touching the ball, as if it would be glad to help if it might.

"Do you know what to-morrow is, Kitty?" Alice began. "You'd have guessed if you'd been up in the window with me—only Dinah was making you tidy, so you couldn't. I was watching the boys getting in sticks for the bonfire—and it wants plenty of sticks, Kitty! Only it got so cold, and it snowed so, they had to leave off. Never mind, Kitty, we'll go and see the bonfire to-morrow." Here Alice wound two or three turns of the worsted round the kitten's neck, just to see how it would look: this led to a scramble, in which the ball rolled down upon the floor, and yards and yards of it got unwound again.

"Do you know, I was so angry, Kitty," Alice went on, as soon as they were comfortably settled again, "when I saw all the mischief you had been doing, I was very nearly opening the window, and putting you out into the snow! And you'd have deserved it, you little mischievous darling! What have you got to say for yourself? Now don't interrupt me!" she went on, holding up one finger. "I'm going to tell you all your faults. Number one: you squeaked twice while Dinah was washing your face this morning. Now you ca'n't deny it, Kitty: I heard you! What's that you say?" (pretending that the kitten was speaking). "Her paw went into your eye? Well, that's *your* fault, for keeping your eyes open—if you'd shut them tight up, it wouldn't have happened. Now don't make any more excuses, but listen! Number two: you pulled Snowdrop away by the tail just as I had put down the saucer of milk before her! What, you were thirsty, were you? How do you know she wasn't thirsty too? Now for number three: you unwound every bit of the worsted while I wasn't looking!

"That's three faults, Kitty, and you've not been punished for any of them yet. You know I'm saving up all your punishments for Wednesday week—Suppose they had saved up all *my* punishments?" she went on, talking more to herself than the kitten. "What *would* they do at the end of a year? I should be sent to prison, I suppose, when the day came. Or—let me see—suppose each punishment was to be going without a dinner: then, when the miserable day came, I should have to go without fifty dinners at once! Well, I shouldn't mind *that* much! I'd far rather go without them than eat them!

"Do you hear the snow against the window-panes, Kitty? How nice and soft it sounds! Just as if some one was kissing the window all over outside. I wonder if the snow *loves* the trees and fields, that it kisses them so gently? And then it covers them up snug, you know, with a white quilt; and perhaps it says 'Go to sleep, darlings, till the summer comes

again.' And when they wake up in the summer, Kitty, they dress themselves
all in green, and dance about—whenever the wind blows—oh, that's very
pretty!" cried Alice, dropping the ball of worsted to clap her hands.
"And I do so *wish* it was true! I'm sure the woods look sleepy in the
autumn, when the leaves are getting brown.

"Kitty, can you play chess? Now, don't smile, my dear, I'm asking it
seriously. Because, when we were playing just now, you watched just as
if you understood it: and when I said 'Check!' you purred! Well, it *was*
a nice check, Kitty, and really I might have won, if it hadn't been for
that nasty Knight, that came wriggling down among my pieces. Kitty,
dear, let's pretend——" And here I wish I could tell you half the things
Alice used to say, beginning with her favourite phrase "Let's pretend."
She had had quite a long argument with her sister only the day before—
all because Alice had begun with "Let's pretend we're kings and queens;"
and her sister, who liked being very exact, had argued that they couldn't,
because there were only two of them, and Alice had been reduced at
last to say "Well, *you* can be one of them, then, and *I'll* be all the rest."

And once she had really frightened her old nurse by shouting suddenly in her ear, "Nurse! Do let's pretend that I'm a hungry hyæna, and you're a bone!"

But this is taking us away from Alice's speech to the kitten. "Let's pretend that you're the Red Queen, Kitty! Do you know, I think if you sat up and folded your arms, you'd look exactly like her. Now do try, there's a dear!" And Alice got the Red Queen off the table, and set it up before the kitten as a model for it to imitate: however, the thing didn't succeed, principally, Alice said, because the kitten wouldn't fold its arms properly. So, to punish it, she held it up to the Looking-glass, that it might see how sulky it was, "—and if you're not good directly," she added, "I'll put you through into Looking-glass House. How would you like *that*?

"Now, if you'll only attend, Kitty, and not talk so much, I'll tell you all my ideas about Looking-glass House. First, there's the room you can see through the glass—that's just the same as our drawing-room, only the things go the other way. I can see all of it when I get upon a chair— all but the bit just behind the fireplace. Oh! I do so wish I could see *that* bit! I want so much to know whether they've a fire in the winter: you never *can* tell, you know, unless our fire smokes, and then smoke comes up in that room too—but that may be only pretence, just to make it look as if they had a fire. Well then, the books are something like our books, only the words go the wrong way: I know *that*, because I've held up one of our books to the glass, and then they hold up one in the other room.

"How would you like to live in Looking-glass House, Kitty? I wonder if they'd give you milk in there? Perhaps Looking-glass milk isn't good to drink—but oh, Kitty! now we come to the passage. You can just see a little *peep* of the passage in Looking-glass House, if you leave the door of our drawing-room wide open: and it's very like our passage as far as you can see, only you know it may be quite different on beyond. Oh, Kitty, how nice it would be if we could only get through into Looking-glass House! I'm sure it's got, oh! such beautiful things in it! Let's pretend there's a way of getting through into it, somehow, Kitty. Let's pretend the glass has got all soft like gauze, so that we can get through. Why, it's turning into a sort of mist now, I declare! It'll be easy enough to get through——" She was up on the chimney-piece while she said this, though she hardly knew how she had got there. And certainly the glass *was* beginning to melt away, just like a bright silvery mist.

In another moment Alice was through the glass, and had jumped lightly down into the Looking-glass room. The very first thing she did was to look whether there was a fire in the fireplace, and she was quite pleased to find that there was a real one, blazing away as brightly as the one she had left behind. "So I shall be as warm here as I was in the old room," thought Alice: "warmer, in fact, because there'll be no one here to scold me away from the fire. Oh, what fun it'll be, when they see me through the glass in here, and ca'n't get at me!"

Then she began looking about, and noticed that what could be seen from the old room was quite common and uninteresting, but that all the rest was as different as possible. For instance, the pictures on the wall

next the fire seemed to be all alive, and the very clock on the chimney-piece (you know you can only see the back of it in the Looking-glass) had got the face of a little old man, and grinned at her.

"They don't keep this room so tidy as the other," Alice thought to herself, as she noticed several of the chessmen down in the hearth among the cinders; but in another moment, with a little "Oh!" of surprise, she was down on her hands and knees watching them. The chessmen were walking about, two and two!

"Here are the Red King and the Red Queen," Alice said (in a whisper, for fear of frightening them), "and there are the White King and the White Queen sitting on the edge of the shovel—and here are two Castles walking arm in arm—I don't think they can hear me," she went on, as she put her head closer down, "and I'm nearly sure they ca'n't see me. I feel somehow as if I was getting invisible——"

Here something began squeaking on the table behind Alice, and made her turn her head just in time to see one of the White Pawns roll over

and begin kicking: she watched it with great curiosity to see what would happen next.

"It is the voice of my child!" the White Queen cried out, as she rushed past the King, so violently that she knocked him over among the cinders. "My precious Lily! My imperial kitten!" and she began scrambling wildly up the side of the fender.

"Imperial fiddlestick!" said the King, rubbing his nose, which had been hurt by the fall. He had a right to be a *little* annoyed with the Queen, for he was covered with ashes from head to foot.

Alice was very anxious to be of use, and, as the poor little Lily was nearly screaming herself into a fit, she hastily picked up the Queen and set her on the table by the side of her noisy little daughter.

The Queen gasped, and sat down: the rapid journey through the air had quite taken away her breath, and for a minute or two she could do nothing but hug the little Lily in silence. As soon as she had recovered her breath a little, she called out to the White King, who was sitting sulkily among the ashes, "Mind the volcano!"

"What volcano?" said the King, looking up anxiously into the fire, as if he thought that was the most likely place to find one.

"Blew—me—up," panted the Queen, who was still a little out of breath. "Mind you come up—the regular way—don't get blown up!"

Alice watched the White King as he slowly struggled up from bar to bar, till at last she said "Why, you'll be hours and hours getting to the table, at that rate. I'd far better help you, hadn't I?" But the King took no notice of the question: it was quite clear that he could neither hear her nor see her.

So Alice picked him up very gently, and lifted him across more slowly than she had lifted the Queen, that she mightn't take his breath away; but, before she put him on the table, she thought she might as well dust him a little, he was so covered with ashes.

She said afterwards that she had never seen in all her life such a face as the King made, when he found himself held in the air by an invisible hand, and being dusted: he was far too much astonished to cry out, but his eyes and his mouth went on getting larger and larger, and rounder and rounder, till her hand shook so with laughing that she nearly let him drop upon the floor.

"Oh! *please* don't make such faces, my dear!" she cried out, quite forgetting that the King couldn't hear her. "You make me laugh so that I can hardly hold you! And don't keep your mouth so wide open! All the ashes will get into it—there, now I think you're tidy enough!" she added, as she smoothed his hair, and set him upon the table near the Queen.

The King immediately fell flat on his back, and lay perfectly still; and Alice was a little alarmed at what she had done, and went round the

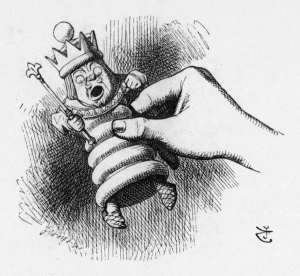

room to see if she could find any water to throw over him. However, she could find nothing but a bottle of ink, and when she got back with it she found he had recovered, and he and the Queen were talking together in a frightened whisper—so low, that Alice could hardly hear what they said.

The King was saying "I assure you, my dear, I turned cold to the very ends of my whiskers!"

To which the Queen replied "You haven't got any whiskers."

"The horror of that moment," the King went on, "I shall never, *never* forget!"

"You will, though," the Queen said, "if you don't make a memorandum of it."

Alice looked on with great interest as the King took an enormous memorandum-book out of his pocket, and began writing. A sudden thought struck her, and she took hold of the end of the pencil, which came some way over his shoulder, and began writing for him.

The poor King looked puzzled and unhappy, and struggled with the pencil for some time without saying anything; but Alice was too strong for him, and at last he panted out, "My dear! I really *must* get a thinner pencil. I ca'n't manage this one a bit; it writes all manner of things that I don't intend——"

"What manner of things?" said the Queen, looking over the book (in which Alice had put '*The White Knight is sliding down the poker. He balances very badly*'). "That's not a memorandum of *your* feelings!"

There was a book lying near Alice on the table, and while she sat watching the White King (for she was still a little anxious about him, and had the ink all ready to throw over him, in case he fainted again),

she turned over the leaves, to find some part that she could read,
"—for it's all in some language I don't know," she said to herself.
 It was like this.

JABBERWOCKY.

'Twas brillig, and the slithy toves
  Did gyre and gimble in the wabe;
All mimsy were the borogoves,
  And the mome raths outgrabe.

She puzzled over this for some time, but at last a bright thought struck
her. "Why, it's a Looking-glass book, of course! And, if I hold it up to
a glass, the words will all go the right way again."
 This was the poem that Alice read.

JABBERWOCKY.

'Twas brillig, and the slithy toves
  Did gyre and gimble in the wabe:
All mimsy were the borogoves,
  And the mome raths outgrabe.

"Beware the Jabberwock, my son!
The jaws that bite, the claws that catch!
Beware the Jubjub bird, and shun
The frumious Bandersnatch!"

He took his vorpal sword in hand:
Long time the manxome foe he sought—
So rested he by the Tumtum tree,
And stood awhile in thought.

And, as in uffish thought he stood,
  The Jabberwock, with eyes of flame,
Came whiffling through the tulgey wood,
  And burbled as it came!

One, two! One, two! And through and through
  The vorpal blade went snicker-snack!
He left it dead, and with its head
  He went galumphing back.

"And hast thou slain the Jabberwock?
  Come to my arms, my beamish boy!
O frabjous day! Callooh! Callay!"
  He chortled in his joy.

'Twas brillig, and the slithy toves
  Did gyre and gimble in the wabe:
All mimsy were the borogoves,
  And the mome raths outgrabe.

"It seems very pretty," she said when she had finished it, "but it's *rather* hard to understand!" (You see she didn't like to confess, even to herself, that she couldn't make it out at all.) "Somehow it seems to fill my head with ideas—only I don't exactly know what they are! However, *somebody* killed *something:* that's clear, at any rate——"

"But oh!" thought Alice, suddenly jumping up, "if I don't make haste, I shall have to go back through the Looking-glass, before I've seen what the rest of the house is like! Let's have a look at the garden first!" She was out of the room in a moment, and ran down stairs—or, at least, it wasn't exactly running, but a new invention for getting down stairs quickly and easily, as Alice said to herself. She just kept the tips of her fingers on the hand-rail, and floated gently down without even touching the stairs with her feet: then she floated on through the hall, and would have gone straight out at the door in the same way, if she hadn't caught hold of the door-post. She was getting a little giddy with so much floating in the air, and was rather glad to find herself walking again in the natural way.

CHAPTER II.

THE GARDEN OF LIVE FLOWERS.

"I SHOULD see the garden far better," said Alice to herself, "if I could get to the top of that hill: and here's a path that leads straight to it—at least, no, it doesn't do *that*——" (after going a few yards along the path, and turning several sharp corners), "but I suppose it will at last. But how curiously it twists! It's more like a corkscrew than a path! Well, *this* turn goes to the hill, I suppose—no, it doesn't! This goes straight back to the house! Well then, I'll try it the other way."

And so she did: wandering up and down, and trying turn after turn, but always coming back to the house, do what she would. Indeed, once, when she turned a corner rather more quickly than usual, she ran against it before she could stop herself.

"It's no use talking about it," Alice said, looking up at the house and pretending it was arguing with her. "I'm *not* going in again yet. I know I should have to get through the Looking-glass again—back into the old room—and there'd be an end of all my adventures!"

So, resolutely turning her back upon the house, she set out once more down the path, determined to keep straight on till she got to the hill. For a few minutes all went on well, and she was just saying "I really *shall* do it this time——" when the path gave a sudden twist and shook itself (as she described it afterwards), and the next moment she found herself actually walking in at the door.

"Oh, it's too bad!" she cried. "I never saw such a house for getting in the way! Never!"

However, there was the hill full in sight, so there was nothing to be done but start again. This time she came upon a large flower-bed, with a border of daisies, and a willow-tree growing in the middle.

"0 Tiger-lily!" said Alice, addressing herself to one that was waving gracefully about in the wind, "I *wish* you could talk!"

"We *can* talk," said the Tiger-lily, "when there's anybody worth talking to."

Alice was so astonished that she couldn't speak for a minute: it quite seemed to take her breath away. At length, as the Tiger-lily only went on waving about, she spoke again, in a timid voice—almost in a whisper. "And can *all* the flowers talk?"

"As well as *you* can," said the Tiger-lily. "And a great deal louder."

"It isn't manners for us to begin, you know," said the Rose, "and I really was wondering when you'd speak! Said I to myself, 'Her face has got *some* sense in it, though it's not a clever one!' Still, you're the right colour, and that goes a long way."

"I don't care about the colour," the Tiger-lily remarked. "If only her petals curled up a little more, she'd be all right."

Alice didn't like being criticized, so she began asking questions. "Aren't you sometimes frightened at being planted out here, with nobody to take care of you?"

"There's the tree in the middle," said the Rose. "What else is it good for?"

"But what could it do, if any danger came?" Alice asked.

"It could bark," said the Rose.

"It says 'Bough-wough!' " cried a Daisy. "That's why its branches are called boughs!"

"Didn't you know *that?*" cried another Daisy. And here they all began shouting together, till the air seemed quite full of little shrill voices. "Silence, every one of you!" cried the Tiger-lily, waving itself passionately from side to side, and trembling with excitement. "They know I ca'n't get at them!" it panted, bending its quivering head towards Alice, "or they wouldn't dare to do it!"

"Never mind!" Alice said in a soothing tone, and, stooping down to the daisies, who were just beginning again, she whispered "If you don't hold your tongues, I'll pick you!"

There was silence in a moment, and several of the pink daisies turned white.

"That's right!" said the Tiger-lily. "The daisies are worst of all. When one speaks, they all begin together, and it's enough to make one wither to hear the way they go on!"

"How is it you can all talk so nicely?" Alice said, hoping to get it into a better temper by a compliment. "I've been in many gardens before, but none of the flowers could talk."

"Put your hand down, and feel the ground," said the Tiger-lily. "Then you'll know why."

Alice did so. "It's very hard," she said; "but I don't see what that has to do with it."

"In most gardens," the Tiger-lily said, "they make the beds too soft—so that the flowers are always asleep."

This sounded a very good reason, and Alice was quite pleased to know it. "I never thought of that before!" she said.

"It's *my* opinion that you never think *at all*," the Rose said, in a rather severe tone.

"I never saw anybody that looked stupider," a Violet said, so suddenly, that Alice quite jumped; for it hadn't spoken before.

"Hold *your* tongue!" cried the Tiger-lily. "As if *you* ever saw anybody! You keep your head under the leaves, and snore away there, till you know no more what's going on in the world, than if you were a bud!"

"Are there any more people in the garden besides me?" Alice said, not choosing to notice the Rose's last remark.

"There's one other flower in the garden that can move about like you," said the Rose. "I wonder how you do it——" ("You're always wondering," said the Tiger-lily), "but she's more bushy than you are."

"Is she like me?" Alice asked eagerly, for the thought crossed her mind, "There's another little girl in the garden, somewhere!"

"Well, she has the same awkward shape as you," the Rose said: "but she's redder—and her petals are shorter, I think."

"They're done up close, like a dahlia," said the Tiger-lily: "not tumbled about, like yours."

"But that's not *your* fault," the Rose added kindly. "You're beginning to fade, you know—and then one ca'n't help one's petals getting a little untidy."

Alice didn't like this idea at all: so, to change the subject, she asked "Does she ever come out here?"

"I daresay you'll see her soon," said the Rose. "She's one of the kind that has nine spikes, you know."

"Where does she wear them?" Alice asked with some curiosity.

"Why, all round her head, of course," the Rose replied. "I was wondering *you* hadn't got some too. I thought it was the regular rule."

"She's coming!" cried the Larkspur. "I hear her footstep, thump, thump, along the gravel-walk!"

Alice looked round eagerly and found that it was the Red Queen. "She's grown a good deal!" was her first remark. She had indeed: when Alice first found her in the ashes, she had been only three inches high— and here she was, half a head taller than Alice herself!

"It's the fresh air that does it," said the Rose: "wonderfully fine air it is, out here."

"I think I'll go and meet her," said Alice, for, though the flowers were interesting enough, she felt that it would be far grander to have a talk with a real Queen.

"You ca'n't possibly do that," said the Rose: "*I* should advise you to walk the other way."

This sounded nonsense to Alice, so she said nothing, but set off at once towards the Red Queen. To her surprise she lost sight of her in a moment, and found herself walking in at the front-door again.

A little provoked, she drew back, and, after looking everywhere for the Queen (whom she spied out at last, a long way off), she thought she would try the plan, this time, of walking in the opposite direction.

It succeeded beautifully. She had not been walking a minute before she found herself face to face with the Red Queen, and full in sight of the hill she had been so long aiming at.

"Where do you come from?" said the Red Queen. "And where are you going? Look up, speak nicely, and don't twiddle your fingers all the time."

Alice attended to all these directions, and explained, as well as she could, that she had lost her way.

"I don't know what you mean by *your* way," said the Queen: "all the ways about here belong to *me*—but why did you come out here at all?" she added in a kinder tone. "Curtsey while you're thinking what to say. It saves time."

Alice wondered a little at this, but she was too much in awe of the Queen to disbelieve it. "I'll try it when I go home," she thought to herself, "the next time I'm a little late for dinner."

"It's time for you to answer now," the Queen said, looking at her watch: "open your mouth a *little* wider when you speak, and always say 'your Majesty.'"

"I only wanted to see what the garden was like, your Majesty——"

"That's right," said the Queen, patting her on the head, which Alice didn't like at all: "though, when you say 'garden'—*I've* seen gardens, compared with which this would be a wilderness."

Alice didn't dare to argue the point, but went on: "—and I thought I'd try and find my way to the top of that hill——"

"When you say 'hill,'" the Queen interrupted, "*I* could show you hills, in comparison with which you'd call that a valley."

"No, I shouldn't," said Alice, surprised into contradicting her at last: "a hill *ca'n't* be a valley, you know. That would be nonsense——"

The Red Queen shook her head. "You may call it 'nonsense' if you like," she said, "but *I've* heard nonsense, compared with which that would be as sensible as a dictionary!"

Alice curtseyed again, as she was afraid from the Queen's tone that she was a *little* offended: and they walked on in silence till they got to the top of the little hill.

For some minutes Alice stood without speaking, looking out in all directions over the country—and a most curious country it was. There were a number of tiny little brooks running straight across it from side to side, and the ground between was divided up into squares by a number of little green hedges, that reached from brook to brook.

"I declare it's marked out just like a large chess-board!" Alice said at last. "There ought to be some men moving about somewhere—and so there are!" she added in a tone of delight, and her heart began to beat quick with excitement as she went on. "It's a great huge game of chess that's being played—all over the world—if this *is* the world at all, you know. Oh, what fun it is! How I *wish* I was one of them! I wouldn't mind being a Pawn, if only I might join—though of course I should *like* to be a Queen, best."

She glanced rather shyly at the real Queen as she said this, but her companion only smiled pleasantly, and said "That's easily managed. You can be the White Queen's Pawn, if you like, as Lily's too young to play; and you're in the Second Square to begin with: when you get to the Eighth Square you'll be a Queen——" Just at this moment, somehow or other, they began to run.

Alice never could quite make out, in thinking it over afterwards, how it was that they began: all she remembers is, that they were running hand in hand, and the Queen went so fast that it was all she could do to keep up with her: and still the Queen kept crying "Faster! Faster!", but Alice felt she *could not* go faster, though she had no breath left to say so.

The most curious part of the thing was, that the trees and the other things round them never changed their places at all: however fast they went, they never seemed to pass anything. "I wonder if all the things move along with us?" thought poor puzzled Alice. And the Queen seemed to guess her thoughts, for she cried "Faster! Don't try to talk!"

Not that Alice had any idea of doing *that*. She felt as if she would never be able to talk again, she was getting so much out of breath: and still the Queen cried "Faster! Faster!", and dragged her along. "Are we nearly there?" Alice managed to pant out at last.

"Nearly there!" the Queen repeated. "Why, we passed it ten minutes ago! Faster!" And they ran on for a time in silence, with the wind whistling in Alice's ears, and almost blowing her hair off her head, she fancied.

"Now! Now!" cried the Queen. "Faster! Faster!" And they went so fast that at last they seemed to skim through the air, hardly touching the ground with their feet, till suddenly, just as Alice was getting quite exhausted, they stopped, and she found herself sitting on the ground, breathless and giddy.

The Queen propped her up against a tree, and said kindly, "You may rest a little, now."

Alice looked round her in great surprise. "Why, I do believe we've been under this tree the whole time! Everything's just as it was!"

"Of course it is," said the Queen. "What would you have it?"

"Well, in *our* country," said Alice, still panting a little, "you'd generally

get to somewhere else—if you ran very fast for a long time as we've been doing."

"A slow sort of country!" said the Queen. "Now, *here*, you see, it takes all the running *you* can do, to keep in the same place. If you want to get somewhere else, you must run at least twice as fast as that!"

"I'd rather not try, please!" said Alice. "I'm quite content to stay here— only I *am* so hot and thirsty!"

"I know what *you'd* like!" the Queen said good-naturedly, taking a little box out of her pocket. "Have a biscuit?"

Alice thought it would not be civil to say "No," though it wasn't at all what she wanted. She took it, and ate it as well as she could: and it was *very* dry: and she thought she had never been so nearly choked in all her life.

"While you're refreshing yourself," said the Queen, "I'll just take the measurements." And she took a ribbon out of her pocket, marked in inches, and began measuring the ground, and sticking little pegs in here and there.

"At the end of two yards," she said, putting in a peg to mark the distance, "I shall give you your directions—have another biscuit?"

"No, thank you," said Alice: "one's *quite* enough!"

"Thirst quenched, I hope?" said the Queen.

Alice did not know what to say to this, but luckily the Queen did not wait for an answer, but went on. "At the end of *three* yards I shall repeat them—for fear of your forgetting them. At the end of *four*, I shall say good-bye. And at the end of *five*, I shall go!"

She had got all the pegs put in by this time, and Alice looked on with great interest as she returned to the tree, and then began slowly walking down the row.

At the two-yard peg she faced round, and said "A pawn goes two squares in its first move, you know. So you'll go *very* quickly through the

Third Square—by railway, I should think—and you'll find yourself in the Fourth Square in no time. Well, *that* square belongs to Tweedledum and Tweedledee—the Fifth is mostly water—the Sixth belongs to Humpty Dumpty—But you make no remark?"

"I—I didn't know I had to make one—just then," Alice faltered out.

"You *should* have said," the Queen went on in a tone of grave reproof, " 'It's extremely kind of you to tell me all this'—however, we'll suppose it said—the Seventh Square is all forest—however, one of the Knights will show you the way—and in the Eighth Square we shall be Queens together, and it's all feasting and fun!" Alice got up and curtseyed, and sat down again.

At the next peg the Queen turned again, and this time she said "Speak in French when you ca'n't think of the English for a thing—turn out your toes as you walk—and remember who you are!" She did not wait for Alice to curtsey, this time, but walked on quickly to the next peg, where she turned for a moment to say "Good-bye," and then hurried on to the last.

How it happened, Alice never knew, but exactly as she came to the last peg, she was gone. Whether she vanished into the air, or whether she ran quickly into the wood ("and she *can* run very fast!" thought Alice), there was no way of guessing, but she was gone, and Alice began to remember that she was a Pawn, and that it would soon be time for her to move.

CHAPTER III.

LOOKING-GLASS INSECTS.

Of course the first thing to do was to make a grand survey of the country she was going to travel through. "It's something very like learning geography," thought Alice, as she stood on tiptoe in hopes of being able to see a little further. "Principal rivers—there *are* none. Principal mountains—I'm on the only one, but I don't think it's got any name. Principal towns—why, what *are* those creatures, making honey down there? They ca'n't be bees—nobody ever saw bees a mile off, you know——" and for some time she stood silent, watching one of them that was bustling about among the flowers, poking its proboscis into them, "just as if it was a regular bee," thought Alice.

However, this was anything but a regular bee: in fact, it was an elephant—as Alice soon found out, though the idea quite took her breath away at first. "And what enormous flowers they must be!" was her next idea. "Something like cottages with the roofs taken off, and stalks put to them—and what quantities of honey they must make! I think I'll go down and—no, I wo'n't go *just* yet," she went on, checking herself just as she was beginning to run down the hill, and trying to find some excuse for turning shy so suddenly. "It'll never do to go down among them without a good long branch to brush them away—and what fun it'll be when they ask me how I liked my walk. I shall say 'Oh, I liked it well enough——' (here came the favourite little toss of the head), 'only it *was* so dusty and hot, and the elephants *did* tease so!'

"I think I'll go down the other way," she said after a pause; "and perhaps I may visit the elephants later on. Besides, I *do* so want to get into the Third Square!"

So, with this excuse, she ran down the hill, and jumped over the first of the six little brooks.

*　　　　*　　　　*　　　　*　　　　*

*　　　　*　　　　*　　　　*　　　　*

*　　　　*　　　　*　　　　*　　　　*

"Tickets, please!" said the Guard, putting his head in at the window. In a moment everybody was holding out a ticket: they were about the same size as the people, and quite seemed to fill the carriage.

"Now then! Show your ticket, child!" the Guard went on, looking angrily at Alice. And a great many voices all said together ("like the chorus of a song," thought Alice) "Don't keep him waiting, child! Why, his time is worth a thousand pounds a minute!"

"I'm afraid I haven't got one," Alice said in a frightened tone: "there wasn't a ticket-office where I came from." And again the chorus of voices went on. "There wasn't room for one where she came from. The land there is worth a thousand pounds an inch!"

"Don't make excuses," said the Guard: "you should have bought one from the engine-driver." And once more the chorus of voices went on with "The man that drives the engine. Why, the smoke alone is worth a thousand pounds a puff!"

Alice thought to herself "Then there's no use in speaking." The voices didn't join in, *this* time, as she hadn't spoken, but, to her great surprise, they all *thought* in chorus (I hope you understand what *thinking in chorus* means—for I must confess that *I* don't), "Better say nothing at all. Language is worth a thousand pounds a word!"

"I shall dream about a thousand pounds to-night, I know I shall!" thought Alice.

All this time the Guard was looking at her, first through a telescope, then through a microscope, and then through an opera-glass. At last he said "You're traveling the wrong way," and shut up the window, and went away.

"So young a child," said the gentleman sitting opposite to her, (he was dressed in white paper,) "ought to know which way she's going, even if she doesn't know her own name!"

A Goat, that was sitting next to the gentleman in white, shut his eyes

and said in a loud voice, "She ought to know her way to the ticket-office, even if she doesn't know her alphabet!"

There was a Beetle sitting next the Goat (it was a very queer carriage-full of passengers altogether), and, as the rule seemed to be that they should all speak in turn, *he* went on with "She'll have to go back from here as luggage!"

Alice couldn't see who was sitting beyond the Beetle, but a hoarse voice spoke next. "Change engines——" it said, and there it choked and was obliged to leave off.

"It sounds like a horse," Alice thought to herself. And an extremely small voice, close to her ear, said "You might make a joke on that—something about 'horse' and 'hoarse,' you know."

Then a very gentle voice in the distance said, "She must be labeled 'Lass, with care,' you know——"

And after that other voices went on ("What a number of people there are in the carriage!" thought Alice), saying "She must go by post, as she's got a head on her——" "She must be sent as a message by the tele-graph——" "She must draw the train herself the rest of the way——," and so on.

But the gentleman dressed in white paper leaned forwards and whispered in her ear, "Never mind what they all say, my dear, but take a return-ticket every time the train stops."

"Indeed I sha'n't!" Alice said rather impatiently. "I don't belong to this railway journey at all—I was in a wood just now—and I wish I could get back there!"

"You might make a joke on *that*," said the little voice close to her ear: "something about 'you *would* if you could, you know."

"Don't tease so," said Alice, looking about in vain to see where the voice came from. "If you're so anxious to have a joke made, why don't you make one yourself?"

The little voice sighed deeply. It was *very* unhappy, evidently, and Alice would have said something pitying to comfort it, "if it would only sigh like other people!" she thought. But this was such a wonderfully small sigh, that she wouldn't have heard it at all, if it hadn't come *quite* close to her ear. The consequence of this was that it tickled her ear very much, and quite took off her thoughts from the unhappiness of the poor little creature.

"I know you are a friend," the little voice went on: "a dear friend, and an old friend. And you wo'n't hurt me, though I *am* an insect."

"What kind of insect?" Alice inquired, a little anxiously. What she really wanted to know was, whether it could sting or not, but she thought this wouldn't be quite a civil question to ask.

"What, then you don't——" the little voice began, when it was drowned by a shrill scream from the engine, and everybody jumped up in alarm, Alice among the rest.

The Horse, who had put his head out of the window, quietly drew it in and said "It's only a brook we have to jump over." Everybody seemed satisfied with this, though Alice felt a little nervous at the idea of trains jumping at all. "However, it'll take us into the Fourth Square, that's some comfort!" she said to herself. In another moment she felt the carriage rise straight up into the air, and in her fright she caught at the thing nearest to her hand, which happened to be the Goat's beard.

```
        *         *         *         *         *
             *         *         *         *
        *         *         *         *         *
```

But the beard seemed to melt away as she touched it, and she found herself sitting quietly under a tree—while the Gnat (for that was the insect she had been talking to) was balancing itself on a twig just over her head, and fanning her with its wings.

It certainly was a *very* large Gnat: "about the size of a chicken," Alice thought. Still, she couldn't feel nervous with it, after they had been talking together so long.

"—then you don't like *all* insects?" the Gnat went on, as quietly as if nothing had happened.

"I like them when they can talk," Alice said. "None of them ever talk, where *I* come from."

"What sort of insects do you rejoice in, where *you* come from?" the Gnat inquired.

"I don't *rejoice* in insects at all," Alice explained, "because I'm rather afraid of them—at least the large kinds. But I can tell you the names of some of them."

"Of course they answer to their names?" the Gnat remarked carelessly.

"I never knew them do it."

"What's the use of their having names," the Gnat said, "if they wo'n't answer to them?"

"No use to *them*," said Alice; "but it's useful to the people that name them, I suppose. If not, why do things have names at all?"

"I ca'n't say," the Gnat replied. "Further on, in the wood down there, they've got no names—however, go on with your list of insects: you're wasting time."

"Well, there's the Horse-fly," Alice began, counting off the names on her fingers.

"All right," said the Gnat. "Half way up that bush, you'll see a Rocking-horse-fly, if you look. It's made entirely of wood, and gets about by swinging itself from branch to branch."

"What does it live on?" Alice asked, with great curiosity.

"Sap and sawdust," said the Gnat. "Go on with the list."

Alice looked at the Rocking-horse-fly with great interest, and made up her mind that it must have been just repainted, it looked so bright and sticky; and then she went on.

"And there's the Dragon-fly."

"Look on the branch above your head," said the Gnat, "and there you'll find a Snap-dragon-fly. Its body is made of plum-pudding, its wings of holly-leaves, and its head is a raisin burning in brandy."

"And what does it live on?" Alice asked, as before.

"Frumenty and mince-pie," the Gnat replied; "and it makes its nest in a Christmas-box."

"And then there's the Butterfly," Alice went on, after she had taken a good look at the insect with its head on fire, and had thought to herself, "I wonder if that's the reason insects are so fond of flying into candles— because they want to turn into Snap-dragon-flies!"

"Crawling at your feet," said the Gnat (Alice drew her feet back in some alarm), "you may observe a Bread-and-butter-fly. Its wings are thin

slices of bread-and-butter, its body is a crust, and its head is a lump of sugar."

"And what does *it* live on?"

"Weak tea with cream in it."

A new difficulty came into Alice's head. "Supposing it couldn't find any?" she suggested.

"Then it would die, of course."

"But that must happen very often," Alice remarked thoughtfully.

"It always happens," said the Gnat.

After this, Alice was silent for a minute or two, pondering. The Gnat amused itself meanwhile by humming round and round her head: at last it settled again and remarked "I suppose you don't want to lose your name?"

"No, indeed," Alice said, a little anxiously.

"And yet I don't know," the Gnat went on in a careless tone: "only think how convenient it would be if you could manage to go home without it! For instance, if the governess wanted to call you to your lessons, she would call out 'Come here——,' and there she would have to leave off, because there wouldn't be any name for her to call, and of course you wouldn't have to go, you know."

"That would never do, I'm sure," said Alice: "the governess would never think of excusing me lessons for that. If she couldn't remember my name, she'd call me 'Miss,' as the servants do."

"Well, if she said 'Miss,' and didn't say anything more," the Gnat remarked, "of course you'd miss your lessons. That's a joke. I wish *you* had made it."

"Why do you wish *I* had made it?" Alice asked. "It's a very bad one."

But the Gnat only sighed deeply, while two large tears came rolling down its cheeks.

"You shouldn't make jokes," Alice said, "if it makes you so unhappy."

Then came another of those melancholy little sighs, and this time the poor Gnat really seemed to have sighed itself away, for, when Alice looked up, there was nothing whatever to be seen on the twig, and, as she was getting quite chilly with sitting still so long, she got up and walked on.

She very soon came to an open field, with a wood on the other side of it: it looked much darker than the last wood, and Alice felt a *little* timid about going into it. However, on second thoughts, she made up her mind to go on: "for I certainly wo'n't go *back*," she thought to herself, and this was the only way to the Eighth Square.

"This must be the wood," she said thoughtfully to herself, "where things have no names. I wonder what'll become of *my* name when I go in? I shouldn't like to lose it at all——because they'd have to give me another, and it would be almost certain to be an ugly one. But then the fun would be, trying to find the creature that had got my old name! That's just like the advertisements, you know, when people lose dogs—— '*answers to the name of "Dash": had on a brass collar*'——just fancy calling everything you met 'Alice,' till one of them answered! Only they wouldn't answer at all, if they were wise."

She was rambling on in this way when she reached the wood: it looked very cool and shady. "Well, at any rate it's a great comfort," she said as she stepped under the trees, "after being so hot, to get into the—into the—into *what*?" she went on, rather surprised at not being able to think of the word. "I mean to get under the—under the—under *this*, you know!" putting her hand on the trunk of the tree. "What *does* it call itself, I wonder? I do believe it's got no name—why, to be sure it hasn't!"

She stood silent for a minute, thinking: then she suddenly began again. "Then it really *has* happened, after all! And now, who am I? I *will* remember, if I can! I'm determined to do it!" But being determined didn't help her much, and all she could say, after a great deal of puzzling, was "L, I *know* it begins with L!"

Just then a Fawn came wandering by: it looked at Alice with its large gentle eyes, but didn't seem at all frightened. "Here then! Here then!" Alice said, as she held out her hand and tried to stroke it; but it only started back a little, and then stood looking at her again.

"What do you call yourself?" the Fawn said at last. Such a soft sweet voice it had!

"I wish I knew!" thought poor Alice. She answered, rather sadly, "Nothing just now."

"Think again," it said: "that wo'n't do."

Alice thought, but nothing came of it. "Please, would you tell me what *you* call yourself?" she said timidly. "I think that might help a little."

"I'll tell you, if you'll come a little further on," the Fawn said. "I ca'n't remember *here*."

So they walked on together through the wood, Alice with her arms clasped lovingly round the soft neck of the Fawn, till they came out into another open field, and here the Fawn gave a sudden bound into the air, and shook itself free from Alice's arm. "I'm a Fawn!" it cried out in a voice of delight. "And, dear me! you're a human child!" A sudden look of alarm came into its beautiful brown eyes, and in another moment it had darted away at full speed.

Alice stood looking after it, almost ready to cry with vexation at having lost her dear little fellow-traveler so suddenly. "However, I know my name now," she said: "that's *some* comfort. Alice—Alice—I wo'n't forget it again. And now, which of these finger-posts ought I to follow, I wonder?"

It was not a very difficult question to answer, as there was only one

road through the wood, and the two finger-posts both pointed along it. "I'll settle it," Alice said to herself, "when the road divides and they point different ways."

But this did not seem likely to happen. She went on and on, a long way, but, wherever the road divided, there were sure to be two finger-posts pointing the same way, one marked 'TO TWEEDLEDUM'S HOUSE,' and the other 'TO THE HOUSE OF TWEEDLEDEE.'

"I do believe," said Alice at last, "that they live in the *same* house! I wonder I never thought of that before—But I ca'n't stay there long. I'll just call and say 'How d'ye do?' and ask them the way out of the wood. If I could only get to the Eighth Square before it gets dark!" So she wandered on, talking to herself as she went, till, on turning a sharp corner, she came upon two fat little men, so suddenly that she could not help starting back, but in another moment she recovered herself, feeling sure that they must be.

CHAPTER IV.

TWEEDLEDUM AND TWEEDLEDEE.

THEY were standing under a tree, each with an arm round the other's neck, and Alice knew which was which in a moment, because one of them had 'DUM' embroidered on his collar, and the other 'DEE.' "I suppose they've each got 'TWEEDLE' round at the back of the collar," she said to herself.

They stood so still that she quite forgot they were alive, and she was just going round to see if the word 'TWEEDLE' was written at the back of each collar, when she was startled by a voice coming from the one marked 'DUM.'

"If you think we're wax-works," he said, "you ought to pay, you know. Wax-works weren't made to be looked at for nothing. Nohow!"

"Contrariwise," added the one marked 'DEE,' "if you think we're alive, you ought to speak."

"I'm sure I'm very sorry," was all Alice could say; for the words of the old song kept ringing through her head like the ticking of a clock, and she could hardly help saying them out loud:—

"Tweedledum and Tweedledee
Agreed to have a battle;
For Tweedledum said Tweedledee
Had spoiled his nice new rattle.

Just then flew down a monstrous crow,
As black as a tar-barrel;
Which frightened both the heroes so,
They quite forgot their quarrel."

"I know what you're thinking about," said Tweedledum: "but it isn't so, nohow."

"Contrariwise," continued Tweedledee, "if it was so, it might be; and if it were so, it would be; but as it isn't, it ain't. That's logic."

"I was thinking," Alice said politely, "which is the best way out of this wood: it's getting so dark. Would you tell me, please?"

But the fat little men only looked at each other and grinned.

They looked so exactly like a couple of great schoolboys, that Alice couldn't help pointing her finger at Tweedledum, and saying "First Boy!"

"Nohow!" Tweedledum cried out briskly, and shut his mouth up again with a snap.

"Next Boy!" said Alice, passing on to Tweedledee, though she felt quite certain he would only shout out "Contrariwise!" and so he did.

"You've begun wrong!" cried Tweedledum. "The first thing in a visit is to say 'How d'ye do?' and shake hands!" And here the two brothers gave each other a hug, and then they held out the two hands that were free, to shake hands with her.

Alice did not like shaking hands with either of them first, for fear of hurting the other one's feelings; so, as the best way out of the difficulty, she took hold of both hands at once: the next moment they were dancing round in a ring. This seemed quite natural (she remembered afterwards), and she was not even surprised to hear music playing: it seemed to come from the tree under which they were dancing, and it was done (as well as she could make it out) by the branches rubbing one across the other, like fiddles and fiddle-sticks.

"But it certainly *was* funny," (Alice said afterwards, when she was telling her sister the history of all this,) "to find myself singing '*Here we go round the mulberry bush.*' I don't know when I began it, but somehow I felt as if I'd been singing it a long long time!"

The other two dancers were fat, and very soon out of breath. "Four times round is enough for one dance," Tweedledum panted out, and they left off dancing as suddenly as they had begun: the music stopped at the same moment.

Then they let go of Alice's hands, and stood looking at her for a minute: there was a rather awkward pause, as Alice didn't know how to begin a conversation with people she had just been dancing with. "It would never do to say 'How d'ye do?' *now*," she said to herself: "we seem to have got beyond that, somehow!"

"I hope you're not much tired?" she said at last.

"Nohow. And thank you *very* much for asking," said Tweedledum.

"So *much* obliged!" added Tweedledee. "You like poetry?"

"Ye-es, pretty well—*some* poetry," Alice said doubtfully. "Would you tell me which road leads out of the wood?"

"What shall I repeat to her?" said Tweedledee, looking round at Tweedledum with great solemn eyes, and not noticing Alice's question.

" '*The Walrus and the Carpenter*' is the longest," Tweedledum replied, giving his brother an affectionate hug.

Tweedledee began instantly:

"The sun was shining——"

Here Alice ventured to interrupt him. "If it's *very* long," she said, as politely as she could, "would you please tell me first which road——"

Tweedledee smiled gently, and began again:

"The sun was shining on the sea,
Shining with all his might:
He did his very best to make
The billows smooth and bright—
And this was odd, because it was
The middle of the night.

The moon was shining sulkily,
　　Because she thought the sun
Had got no business to be there
　　After the day was done—
'It's very rude of him,' she said,
　　'To come and spoil the fun!'

The sea was wet as wet could be,
　　The sands were dry as dry.
You could not see a cloud, because
　　No cloud was in the sky:
No birds were flying overhead—
　　There were no birds to fly.

The Walrus and the Carpenter
　　Were walking close at hand:
They wept like anything to see
　　Such quantities of sand:
'If this were only cleared away,'
　　They said, 'it would be grand!'

'If seven maids with seven mops
　　Swept it for half a year,
Do you suppose,' the Walrus said,
　　'That they could get it clear?'
'I doubt it,' said the Carpenter,
　　And shed a bitter tear.

'O Oysters, come and walk with us!'
  The Walrus did beseech.
'A pleasant walk, a pleasant talk,
  Along the briny beach:
We cannot do with more than four,
  To give a hand to each.'

The eldest Oyster looked at him,
  But never a word he said:
The eldest Oyster winked his eye,
  And shook his heavy head—
Meaning to say he did not choose
  To leave the oyster-bed.

But four young Oysters hurried up,
  All eager for the treat:
Their coats were brushed, their faces washed,
  Their shoes were clean and neat—
And this was odd, because, you know,
  They hadn't any feet.

Four other Oysters followed them,
  And yet another four;
And thick and fast they came at last,
  And more, and more, and more—
All hopping through the frothy waves,
  And scrambling to the shore.

The Walrus and the Carpenter
  Walked on a mile or so,
And then they rested on a rock
  Conveniently low:
And all the little Oysters stood
  And waited in a row.

'The time has come,' the Walrus said,
  'To talk of many things:
Of shoes—and ships—and sealing-wax—
  Of cabbages—and kings—
And why the sea is boiling hot—
  And whether pigs have wings.'

'But wait a bit,' the Oysters cried,
  'Before we have our chat;
For some of us are out of breath,
  And all of us are fat!'
'No hurry!' said the Carpenter.
  They thanked him much for that.

'A loaf of bread,' the Walrus said,
　'Is what we chiefly need:
Pepper and vinegar besides
　Are very good indeed—
Now, if you're ready, Oysters dear,
　We can begin to feed.'

'But not on us!' the Oysters cried,
　Turning a little blue.
'After such kindness, that would be
　A dismal thing to do!'
'The night is fine,' the Walrus said.
　'Do you admire the view?

'It was so kind of you to come!
　And you are very nice!'
The Carpenter said nothing but
　'Cut us another slice.
I wish you were not quite so deaf—
　I've had to ask you twice!'

'It seems a shame,' the Walrus said,
　'To play them such a trick.
After we've brought them out so far,
　And made them trot so quick!'
The Carpenter said nothing but
　'The butter's spread too thick!'

'I weep for you,' the Walrus said:
'I deeply sympathize.'
With sobs and tears he sorted out
Those of the largest size,
Holding his pocket-handkerchief
Before his streaming eyes.

'O Oysters,' said the Carpenter,
'You've had a pleasant run!
Shall we be trotting home again?'
But answer came there none—
And this was scarcely odd, because
They'd eaten every one."

"I like the Walrus best," said Alice: "because he was a *little* sorry for the poor oysters."

"He ate more than the Carpenter, though," said Tweedledee. "You see he held his handkerchief in front, so that the Carpenter couldn't count how many he took: contrariwise."

"That was mean!" Alice said indignantly. "Then I like the Carpenter best—if he didn't eat so many as the Walrus."

"But he ate as many as he could get," said Tweedledum.

This was a puzzler. After a pause, Alice began, "Well! They were *both* very unpleasant characters——" Here she checked herself in some alarm, at hearing something that sounded to her like the puffing of a large steam-engine in the wood near them, though she feared it was more likely to be a wild beast. "Are there any lions or tigers about here?" she asked timidly.

"It's only the Red King snoring," said Tweedledee.

"Come and look at him!" the brothers cried, and they each took one of Alice's hands, and led her up to where the King was sleeping.

"Isn't he a *lovely* sight?" said Tweedledum.

Alice couldn't say honestly that he was. He had a tall red night-cap on, with a tassel, and he was lying crumpled up into a sort of untidy heap, and snoring loud——"fit to snore his head off!" as Tweedledum remarked.

"I'm afraid he'll catch cold with lying on the damp grass," said Alice, who was a very thoughtful little girl.

"He's dreaming now," said Tweedledee: "and what do you think he's dreaming about?"

Alice said "Nobody can guess that."

"Why, about *you!*" Tweedledee exclaimed, clapping his hands triumphantly. "And if he left off dreaming about you, where do you suppose you'd be?"

"Where I am now, of course," said Alice.

"Not you!" Tweedledee retorted contemptuously. "You'd be nowhere. Why, you're only a sort of thing in his dream!"

"If that there King was to wake," added Tweedledum, "you'd go out— bang!—just like a candle!"

"I shouldn't!" Alice exclaimed indignantly. "Besides, if *I'm* only a sort of thing in his dream, what are *you*, I should like to know?"

"Ditto," said Tweedledum.

"Ditto, ditto!" cried Tweedledee.

He shouted this so loud that Alice couldn't help saying "Hush! You'll be waking him, I'm afraid, if you make so much noise."

"Well, it's no use *your* talking about waking him," said Tweedledum, "when you're only one of the things in his dream. You know very well you're not real."

"I *am* real!" said Alice, and began to cry.

"You wo'n't make yourself a bit realler by crying," Tweedledee remarked: "there's nothing to cry about."

"If I wasn't real," Alice said—half-laughing through her tears, it all seemed so ridiculous—"I shouldn't be able to cry."

"I hope you don't suppose those are *real* tears?" Tweedledum interrupted in a tone of great contempt.

"I know they're talking nonsense," Alice thought to herself: "and it's foolish to cry about it." So she brushed away her tears, and went on as cheerfully as she could, "At any rate I'd better be getting out of the wood, for really it's coming on very dark. Do you think it's going to rain?"

Tweedledum spread a large umbrella over himself and his brother, and looked up into it. "No, I don't think it is," he said: "at least—not under *here*. Nohow."

"But it may rain *outside*?"

"It may—if it chooses," said Tweedledee: "we've no objection. Contrariwise."

"Selfish things!" thought Alice, and she was just going to say "Goodnight" and leave them, when Tweedledum sprang out from under the umbrella, and seized her by the wrist.

"Do you see *that*?" he said, in a voice choking with passion, and his eyes grew large and yellow all in a moment, as he pointed with a trembling finger at a small white thing lying under the tree.

"It's only a rattle," Alice said, after a careful examination of the little white thing. "Not a rattle-*snake*, you know," she added hastily, thinking that he was frightened: "only an old rattle—quite old and broken."

"I knew it was!" cried Tweedledum, beginning to stamp about wildly and tear his hair. "It's spoilt, of course!" Here he looked at Tweedledee,

who immediately sat down on the ground, and tried to hide himself under the umbrella.

Alice laid her hand upon his arm, and said, in a soothing tone, "You needn't be so angry about an old rattle."

"But it *isn't* old!" Tweedledum cried, in a greater fury than ever. "It's *new*, I tell you—I bought it yesterday-mmy nice new RATTLE!" and his voice rose to a perfect scream.

All this time Tweedledee was trying his best to fold up the umbrella, with himself in it: which was such an extraordinary thing to do, that it quite took off Alice's attention from the angry brother. But he couldn't quite succeed, and it ended in his rolling over, bundled up in the umbrella, with only his head out: and there he lay, opening and shutting his mouth and his large eyes——"looking more like a fish than anything else," Alice thought.

"Of course you agree to have a battle?" Tweedledum said in a calmer tone.

"I suppose so," the other sulkily replied, as he crawled out of the umbrella: "only *she* must help us to dress up, you know."

So the two brothers went off hand-in-hand into the wood, and returned in a minute with their arms full of things—such as bolsters, blankets, hearth-rugs, table-cloths, dish-covers, and coal-scuttles. "I hope you're a good hand at pinning and tying strings?" Tweedledum remarked. "Every one of these things has got to go on, somehow or other."

Alice said afterwards she had never seen such a fuss made about anything in all her life—the way those two bustled about—and the quantity of things they put on—and the trouble they gave her in tying strings and fastening buttons——"Really they'll be more like bundles of old clothes than anything else, by the time they're ready!" she said to herself, as she arranged a bolster round the neck of Tweedledee, "to keep his head from being cut off," as he said.

"You know," he added very gravely, "it's one of the most serious things that can possibly happen to one in a battle—to get one's head cut off."

Alice laughed loud: but she managed to turn it into a cough, for fear of hurting his feelings.

"Do I look very pale?" said Tweedledum, coming up to have his helmet tied on. (He *called* it a helmet, though it certainly looked much more like a saucepan.)

"Well—yes—a *little*," Alice replied gently.

"I'm very brave, generally," he went on in a low voice: "only to-day I happen to have a headache."

"And *I've* got a toothache!" said Tweedledee, who had overheard the remark. "I'm far worse than you!"

"Then you'd better not fight to-day," said Alice, thinking it a good opportunity to make peace.

"We *must* have a bit of a fight, but I don't care about going on long," said Tweedledum. "What's the time now?"

Tweedledee looked at his watch, and said "Half-past four."

"Let's fight till six, and then have dinner," said Tweedledum.

"Very well," the other said, rather sadly: "and *she* can watch us—only you'd better not come *very* close," he added: "I generally hit everything I can see—when I get really excited."

"And *I* hit every thing within reach," cried Tweedledum, "whether I can see it or not!"

Alice laughed. "You must hit the *trees* pretty often, I should think," she said.

Tweedledum looked round him with a satisfied smile. "I don't suppose," he said, "there'll be a tree left standing, for ever so far round, by the time we've finished!"

"And all about a rattle!" said Alice, still hoping to make them a *little* ashamed of fighting for such a trifle.

"I shouldn't have minded it so much," said Tweedledum, "if it hadn't been a new one."

"I wish the monstrous crow would come!" thought Alice.

"There's only one sword, you know," Tweedledum said to his brother: "but *you* can have the umbrella—it's quite as sharp. Only we must begin quick. It's getting as dark as it can."

"And darker," said Tweedledee.

It was getting dark so suddenly that Alice thought there must be a thunderstorm coming on. "What a thick black cloud that is!" she said. "And how fast it comes! Why, I do believe it's got wings!"

"It's the crow!" Tweedledum cried out in a shrill voice of alarm; and the two brothers took to their heels and were out of sight in a moment.

Alice ran a little way into the wood, and stopped under a large tree.

"It can never get at me *here*," she thought: "it's far too large to squeeze itself in among the trees. But I wish it wouldn't flap its wings so—it makes quite a hurricane in the wood—here's somebody's shawl being blown away!"

CHAPTER V.

WOOL AND WATER.

SHE caught the shawl as she spoke, and looked about for the owner: in another moment the White Queen came running wildly through the wood, with both arms stretched out wide, as if she were flying, and Alice very civilly went to meet her with the shawl.

"I'm very glad I happened to be in the way," Alice said, as she helped her to put on her shawl again.

The White Queen only looked at her in a helpless frightened sort of way, and kept repeating something in a whisper to herself that sounded like "Bread-and-butter, bread-and-butter," and Alice felt that if there was to be any conversation at all, she must manage it herself. So she began rather timidly: "Am I addressing the White Queen?"

"Well, yes, if you call that a-dressing," the Queen said. "It isn't *my* notion of the thing, at all."

Alice thought it woul never do to have an argument at the very beginning of their conversation, so she smiled and said "If your Majesty will only tell me the right way to begin, I'll do it as well as I can."

"But I don't want it done at all!" groaned the poor Queen. "I've been a-dressing myself for the last two hours."

It would have been all the better, as it seemed to Alice, if she had got some one else to dress her, she was so dreadfully untidy. "Every single thing's crooked," Alice thought to herself, "and she's all over pins!—— May I put your shawl straight for you?" she added aloud.

"I don't know what's the matter with it!" the Queen said, in a melancholy voice. "It's out of temper, I think. I've pinned it here, and I've pinned it there, but there's no pleasing it!"

"It *ca'n't* go straight, you know, if you pin it all on one side," Alice said as she gently put it right for her; "and, dear me, what a state your hair is in!"

"The brush has got entangled in it!" the Queen said with a sigh. "And I lost the comb yesterday."

Alice carefully released the brush, and did her best to get the hair

into order. "Come, you look rather better now!" she said, after altering most of the pins. "But really you should have a lady's-maid!"

"I'm sure I'll take you with pleasure!" the Queen said. "Two pence a week, and jam every other day."

Alice couldn't help laughing, as she said "I don't want you to hire *me*—and I don't care for jam."

"It's very good jam," said the Queen.

"Well, I don't want any *to-day*, at any rate."

"You couldn't have it if you *did* want it," the Queen said. "The rule is, jam to-morrow and jam yesterday—but never jam *to-day*."

"It *must* come sometimes to 'jam to-day,'" Alice objected.

"No, it ca'n't," said the Queen. "It's jam every *other* day: to-day isn't any other day, you know."

"I don't understand you," said Alice. "It's dreadfully confusing!"

"That's the effect of living backwards," the Queen said kindly: "it always makes one a little giddy at first——"

"Living backwards!" Alice repeated in great astonishment. "I never heard of such a thing!"

"—but there's one great advantage in it, that one's memory works both ways."

"I'm sure *mine* only works one way," Alice remarked. "I ca'n't remember things before they happen."

"It's a poor sort of memory that only works backwards," the Queen remarked.

"What sort of things do *you* remember best?" Alice ventured to ask.

"Oh, things that happened the week after next," the Queen replied in a careless tone. "For instance, now," she went on, sticking a large piece of plaster on her finger as she spoke, "there's the King's Messenger. He's in prison now, being punished: and the trial doesn't even begin till next Wednesday: and of course the crime comes last of all."

"Suppose he never commits the crime?" said Alice.

"That would be all the better, wouldn't it?" the Queen said, as she bound the plaster round her finger with a bit of ribbon.

Alice felt there was no denying *that*. "Of course it would be all the better," she said: "but it wouldn't be all the better his being punished."

"You're wrong *there*, at any rate," said the Queen. "Were *you* ever punished?"

"Only for faults," said Alice.

"And you were all the better for it, I know!" the Queen said triumphantly.

"Yes, but then I *had* done the things I was punished for," said Alice: "that makes all the difference."

"But if you *hadn't* done them," the Queen said, "that would have been better still; better, and better, and better!" Her voice went higher with each "better," till it got quite to a squeak at last.

Alice was just beginning to say "There's a mistake somewhere——," when the Queen began screaming, so loud that she had to leave the sentence unfinished. "Oh, oh, oh!" shouted the Queen, shaking her hand about as if she wanted to shake it off. "My finger's bleeding! Oh, oh, oh, oh!"

Her screams were so exactly like the whistle of a steam-engine, that Alice had to hold both her hands over her ears.

"What *is* the matter?" she said, as soon as there was a chance of making herself heard. "Have you pricked your finger?"

"I haven't pricked it *yet*," the Queen said, "but I soon shall—oh, oh, oh!"

"When do you expect to do it?" Alice asked, feeling very much inclined to laugh.

"When I fasten my shawl again," the poor Queen groaned out: "the brooch will come undone directly. Oh, oh!" As she said the words the brooch flew open, and the Queen clutched wildly at it, and tried to clasp it again.

"Take care!" cried Alice. "You're holding it all crooked!" And she caught at the brooch; but it was too late: the pin had slipped, and the Queen had pricked her finger.

"That accounts for the bleeding, you see," she said to Alice with a smile. "Now you understand the way things happen here."

"But why don't you scream *now*?" Alice asked, holding her hands ready to put over her ears again.

"Why, I've done all the screaming already," said the Queen. "What would be the good of having it all over again?"

By this time it was getting light. "The crow must have flown away, I think," said Alice: "I'm so glad it's gone. I thought it was the night coming on."

"I wish *I* could manage to be glad!" the Queen said. "Only I never can remember the rule. You must be very happy, living in this wood, and being glad whenever you like!"

"Only it is so *very* lonely here!" Alice said in a melancholy voice; and, at the thought of her loneliness, two large tears came rolling down her cheeks.

"Oh, don't go on like that!" cried the poor Queen, wringing her hands in despair. "Consider what a great girl you are. Consider what a long way you've come to-day. Consider what o'clock it is. Consider anything, only don't cry!"

Alice could not help laughing at this, even in the midst of her tears. "Can *you* keep from crying by considering things?" she asked.

"That's the way it's done," the Queen said with great decision: "nobody can do two things at once, you know. Let's consider your age to begin with—how old are you?"

"I'm seven and a half, exactly."

"You needn't say 'exactually,' the Queen remarked. "I can believe it without that. Now I'll give *you* something to believe. I'm just one hundred and one, five months and a day."

"I ca'n't believe *that!*"said Alice.

"Ca'n't you?" the Queen said in a pitying tone. "Try again: draw a long breath, and shut your eyes."

Alice laughed. "There's no use trying," she said: "one *ca'n't* believe impossible things."

"I daresay you haven't had much practice," said the Queen. "When I was your age, I always did it for half-an-hour a day. Why, sometimes

I've believed as many as six impossible things before breakfast. There goes the shawl again!"

The brooch had come undone as she spoke, and a sudden gust of wind blew the Queen's shawl across a little brook. The Queen spread out her arms again, and went flying after it, and this time she succeeded in catching it for herself. "I've got it!" she cried in a triumphant tone. "Now you shall see me pin it on again, all by myself!"

"Then I hope your finger is better now?" Alice said very politely, as she crossed the little brook after the Queen.

```
    *         *         *         *         *         *
        *         *         *         *         *
    *         *         *         *         *         *
```

"Oh, much better!" cried the Queen, her voice rising into a squeak as she went on. "Much be-etter! Be-etter! Be-e-e-etter! Be-e-ehh!" The last word ended in a long bleat, so like a sheep that Alice quite started.

She looked at the Queen, who seemed to have suddenly wrapped herself up in wool. Alice rubbed her eyes, and looked again. She couldn't make out what had happened at all. Was she in a shop? And was that really—was it really a *sheep* that was sitting on the other side of the counter? Rub as she would, she could make nothing more of it: she was in a little dark shop, leaning with her elbows on the counter, and opposite to her was an old Sheep, sitting in an arm-chair, knitting, and every now and then leaving off to look at her through a great pair of spectacles.

"What is it you want to buy?" the Sheep said at last, looking up for a moment from her knitting.

"I don't *quite* know yet," Alice said very gently. "I should like to look all round me first, if I might."

"You may look in front of you, and on both sides, if you like," said the Sheep; "but you ca'n't look *all* round you—unless you've got eyes at the back of your head."

But these, as it happened, Alice had *not* got: so she contented herself with turning round, looking at the shelves as she came to them.

The shop seemed to be full of all manner of curious things—but the oddest part of it all was that, whenever she looked hard at any shelf, to make out exactly what it had on it, that particular shelf was always quite empty, though the others round it were crowded as full as they could hold.

"Things flow about so here!" she said at last in a plaintive tone, after she had spent a minute or so in vainly pursuing a large bright thing, that looked sometimes like a doll and sometimes like a work-box, and was always in the shelf next above the one she was looking at. "And this one is the most provoking of all—but I'll tell you what——" she added, as a sudden thought struck her. "I'll follow it up to the very top shelf of all. It'll puzzle it to go through the ceiling, I expect!"

But even this plan failed: the 'thing' went through the ceiling as quietly as possible, as if it were quite used to it.

"Are you a child or a teetotum?" the Sheep said, as she took up another pair of needles. "You'll make me giddy soon, if you go on turning round

like that." She was now working with fourteen pairs at once, and Alice couldn't help looking at her in great astonishment.

"How *can* she knit with so many?" the puzzled child thought to herself. "She gets more and more like a porcupine every minute!"

"Can you row?" the Sheep asked, handing her a pair of knitting-needles as she spoke.

"Yes, a little—but not on land—and not with needles——" Alice was beginning to say, when suddenly the needles turned into oars in her hands, and she found they were in a little boat, gliding along between banks: so there was nothing for it but to do her best.

"Feather!" cried the Sheep, as she took up another pair of needles.

This didn't sound like a remark that needed any answer: so Alice said nothing, but pulled away. There was something very queer about the water, she thought, as every now and then the oars got fast in it, and would hardly come out again.

"Feather! Feather!" the Sheep cried again, taking more needles. "You'll be catching a crab directly."

"A dear little crab!" thought Alice. "I should like that."

"Didn't you hear me say 'Feather'?" the Sheep cried angrily, taking up quite a bunch of needles.

"Indeed I did," said Alice: "you've said it very often—and very loud. Please where *are* the crabs?"

"In the water, of course!" said the Sheep, sticking some of the needles into her hair, as her hands were full. "Feather, I say!"

"*Why* do you say 'Feather' so often?" Alice asked at last, rather vexed. "I'm not a bird!"

"You are," said the Sheep: "you're a little goose."

This offended Alice a little, so there was no more conversation for a minute or two, while the boat glided gently on, sometimes among beds of weeds (which made the oars stick fast in the water, worse than ever), and sometimes under trees, but always with the same tall river-banks frowning over their heads.

"Oh, please! There are some scented rushes!" Alice cried in a sudden transport of delight. "There really are—and *such* beauties!"

"You needn't say 'please' to *me* about 'em," the Sheep said, without looking up from her knitting: "I didn't put 'em there, and I'm not going to take 'em away."

"No, but I meant—please, may we wait and pick some?" Alice pleaded. "If you don't mind stopping the boat for a minute."

"How am *I* to stop it?" said the Sheep. "If you leave off rowing, it'll stop of itself."

So the boat was left to drift down the stream as it would, till it glided gently in among the waving rushes. And then the little sleeves were carefully rolled up, and the little arms were plunged in elbow-deep, to get hold of the rushes a good long way down before breaking them off— and for a while Alice forgot all about the Sheep and the knitting, as she bent over the side of the boat, with just the ends of her tangled hair dipping into the water—while with bright eager eyes she caught at one bunch after another of the darling scented rushes.

"I only hope the boat won't tipple over!" she said to herself. "Oh, *what* a lovely one! Only I couldn't quite reach it." And it certainly *did* seem a little provoking ("almost as if it happened on purpose," she thought) that, though she managed to pick plenty of beautiful rushes as the boat glided by, there was always a more lovely one that she couldn't reach.

"The prettiest are always further!" she said at last, with a sigh at the obstinacy of the rushes in growing so far off, as, with flushed cheeks and dripping hair and hands, she scrambled back into her place, and began to arrange her new-found treasures.

What mattered it to her just then that the rushes had begun to fade, and to lose all their scent and beauty, from the very moment that she picked them? Even real scented rushes, you know, last only a very little while—and these, being dream-rushes, melted away almost like snow, as they lay in heaps at her feet—but Alice hardly noticed this, there were so many other curious things to think about.

They hadn't gone much farther before the blade of one of the oars got fast in the water and *wouldn't* come out again (so Alice explained it afterwards), and the consequence was that the handle of it caught her under the chin, and, in spite of a series of little shrieks of 'Oh, oh, oh!' from poor Alice, it swept her straight off the seat, and down among the heap of rushes.

However, she wasn't a bit hurt, and was soon up again: the Sheep went on with her knitting all the while, just as if nothing had happened. "That was a nice crab you caught!" she remarked, as Alice got back into her place, very much relieved to find herself still in the boat.

"Was it? I didn't see it," said Alice, peeping cautiously over the side of the boat into the dark water. "I wish it hadn't let go—I should so like a little crab to take home with me!" But the Sheep only laughed scornfully, and went on with her knitting.

"Are there many crabs here?" said Alice.

"Crabs, and all sorts of things," said the Sheep: "plenty of choice, only make up your mind. Now, what *do* you want to buy?"

"To buy!" Alice echoed in a tone that was half astonished and half frightened—for the oars, and the boat, and the river, had vanished all in a moment, and she was back again in the little dark shop.

"I should like to buy an egg, please," she said timidly. "How do you sell them?"

"Fivepence farthing for one—twopence for two," the Sheep replied.

"Then two are cheaper than one?" Alice said in a surprised tone, taking out her purse.

"Only you *must* eat them both, if you buy two," said the Sheep.

"Then I'll have *one*, please," said Alice, as she put the money down on the counter. For she thought to herself, "They mightn't be at all nice, you know."

The Sheep took the money, and put it away in a box: then she said "I never put things into people's hands—that would never do—you must get it for yourself." And so saying, she went off to the other end of the shop, and set the egg upright on a shelf.

"I wonder *why* it wouldn't do?" thought Alice, as she groped her way among the tables and chairs, for the shop was very dark towards the end. "The egg seems to get further away the more I walk towards it. Let me see, is this a chair? Why, it's got branches, I declare! How very odd to find trees growing here! And actually here's a little brook! Well, this is the very queerest shop I ever saw!"

```
      *         *         *         *         *         *
          *         *         *         *         *
      *         *         *         *         *         *
```

So she went on, wondering more and more at every step, as everything turned into a tree the moment she came up to it, and she quite expected the egg to do the same.

CHAPTER VI.

HUMPTY DUMPTY.

HOWEVER, the egg only got larger and larger, and more and more human: when she had come within a few yards of it, she saw that it had eyes and a nose and mouth; and, when she had come close to it, she saw clearly that it was HUMPTY DUMPTY himself. "It ca'n't be anybody else!" she said to herself. "I'm as certain of it, as if his name were written all over his face!"

It might have been written a hundred times, easily, on that enormous face. Humpty Dumpty was sitting, with his legs crossed like a Turk, on the top of a high wall—such a narrow one that Alice quite wondered how he could keep his balance—and, as his eyes were steadily fixed in the opposite direction, and he didn't take the least notice of her, she thought he must be a stuffed figure, after all.

"And how exactly like an egg he is!" she said aloud, standing with her hands ready to catch him, for she was every moment expecting him to fall.

"It's *very* provoking," Humpty Dumpty said after a long silence, looking away from Alice as he spoke, "to be called an egg—*very!*"

"I said you *looked* like an egg, Sir," Alice gently explained. "And some eggs are very pretty, you know," she added, hoping to turn her remark into a sort of compliment.

"Some people," said Humpty Dumpty, looking away from her as usual, "have no more sense than a baby!"

Alice didn't know what to say to this: it wasn't at all like conversation, she thought, as he never said anything to *her;* in fact, his last remark was evidently addressed to a tree—so she stood and softly repeated to herself:—

> *"Humpty Dumpty sat on a wall:*
> *Humpty Dumpty had a great fall.*
> *All the King's horses and all the King's men*
> *Couldn't put Humpty Dumpty in his place again."*

"That last line is much too long for the poetry," she added, almost out loud, forgetting that Humpty Dumpty would hear her.

"Don't stand chattering to yourself like that," Humpty Dumpty said, looking at her for the first time, "but tell me your name and your business."

"My *name* is Alice, but——"

"It's a stupid name enough!" Humpty Dumpty interrupted impatiently. "What does it mean?"

"*Must* a name mean something?" Alice asked doubtfully.

"Of course it must," Humpty Dumpty said with a short laugh: "*my* name means the shape I am—and a good handsome shape it is, too. With a name like yours, you might be any shape, almost."

"Why do you sit out here all alone?" said Alice, not wishing to begin an argument.

"Why, because there's nobody with me!" cried Humpty Dumpty. "Did you think I didn't know the answer to *that?* Ask another."

"Don't you think you'd be safer down on the ground?" Alice went on, not with any idea of making another riddle, but simply in her good-natured anxiety for the queer creature. "That wall is so *very* narrow!"

"What tremendously easy riddles you ask!" Humpty Dumpty growled out. "Of course I don't think so! Why, if ever I *did* fall off—which there's no chance of—but if *I* did——" Here he pursed up his lips, and looked so solemn and grand that Alice could hardly help laughing. "*If I did* fall," he went on, "*the King has promised me*—ah, you may turn pale, if you like! You didn't think I was going to say that, did you? *The King has promised me—with his very own mouth*—to—to——"

"To send all his horses and all his men," Alice interrupted, rather unwisely.

"Now I declare that's too bad!" Humpty Dumpty cried, breaking into

a sudden passion. "You've been listening at doors—and behind trees—and down chimneys—or you couldn't have known it!"

"I haven't, indeed!" Alice said very gently. "It's in a book."

"Ah, well! They may write such things in a *book*," Humpty Dumpty said in a calmer tone. "That's what you call a History of England, that is. Now, take a good look at me! I'm one that has spoken to a King, *I* am: mayhap you'll never see such another: and, to show you I'm not proud, you may shake hands with me!" And he grinned almost from ear to ear, as he leant forwards (and as nearly as possible fell off the wall in doing so) and offered Alice his hand. She watched him a little anxiously as she took it. "If he smiled much more the ends of his mouth might meet behind," she thought: "and then I don't know *what* would happen to his head! I'm afraid it would come off!"

"Yes, all his horses and all his men," Humpty Dumpty went on. "They'd pick me up again in a minute, *they* would! However, this conversation is going on a little too fast: let's go back to the last remark but one."

"I'm afraid I ca'n't quite remember it," Alice said, very politely.

"In that case we start afresh," said Humpty Dumpty, "and it's my turn to choose a subject——" ("He talks about it just as if it was a game!" thought Alice.) "So here's a question for you. How old did you say you were?"

Alice made a short calculation, and said "Seven years and six months."

"Wrong!" Humpty Dumpty exclaimed triumphantly. "You never said a word like it!"

"I thought you meant 'How old *are* you?'" Alice explained.

"If I'd meant that, I'd have said it," said Humpty Dumpty.

Alice didn't want to begin another argument, so she said nothing.

"Seven years and six months!" Humpty Dumpty repeated thoughtfully. "An uncomfortable sort of age. Now if you'd asked *my* advice, I'd have said 'Leave off at seven'——but it's too late now."

"I never ask advice about growing," Alice said indignantly.

"Too proud?" the other enquired.

Alice felt even more indignant at this suggestion. "I mean," she said, "that one ca'n't help growing older."

"*One* ca'n't, perhaps," said Humpty Dumpty; "but *two* can. With proper assistance, you might have left off at seven."

"What a beautiful belt you've got on!" Alice suddenly remarked. (They had had quite enough of the subject of age, she thought: and, if they really were to take turns in choosing subjects, it was *her* turn now.) "At least," she corrected herself on second thoughts, "a beautiful cravat, I should have said—no, a belt, I mean—I beg your pardon!" she added in dismay, for Humpty Dumpty looked thoroughly offended, and she began to wish she hadn't chosen that subject. "If only I knew," she thought to herself, "which was neck and which was waist!"

Evidently Humpty Dumpty was very angry, though he said nothing for a minute or two. When he *did* speak again, it was in a deep growl.

"It is a—*most—provoking*—thing," he said at last, "when a person doesn't know a cravat from a belt!"

"I know it's very ignorant of me," Alice said, in so humble a tone that Humpty Dumpty relented.

"It's a cravat, child, and a beautiful one, as you say. It's a present from the White King and Queen. There now!"

"Is it really?" said Alice, quite pleased to find that she *had* chosen a good subject, after all.

"They gave it me," Humpty Dumpty continued thoughtfully, as he crossed one knee over the other and clasped his hands round it, "they gave it me—for an un-birthday present."

"I beg your pardon?" Alice said with a puzzled air.

"I'm not offended," said Humpty Dumpty.

"I mean, what *is* an un-birthday present?"

"A present given when it isn't your birthday, of course."

Alice considered a little. "I like birthday presents best," she said at last.

"You don't know what you're talking about!" cried Humpty Dumpty. "How many days are there in a year?"

"Three hundred and sixty-five," said Alice.

"And how many birthdays have you?"

"One."

"And if you take one from three hundred and sixty-five, what remains?"

"Three hundred and sixty-four, of course."

Humpty Dumpty looked doubtful. "I'd rather see that done on paper," he said.

Alice couldn't help smiling as she took out her memorandum-book, and worked the sum for him:

$$
\begin{array}{r}
3\,6\,5 \\
1 \\
\hline
3\,6\,4
\end{array}
$$

Humpty Dumpty took the book, and looked at it carefully. "That seems to be done right——" he began.

"You're holding it upside down!" Alice interrupted.

"To be sure I was!" Humpty Dumpty said gaily, as she turned it round for him. "I thought it looked a little queer. As I was saying, that *seems* to be done right—though I haven't time to look it over thoroughly just now—and that shows that there are three hundred and sixty-four days when you might get un-birthday presents——"

"Certainly," said Alice.

"And only *one* for birthday presents, you know. There's glory for you!"

"I don't know what you mean by 'glory,'" Alice said.

Humpty Dumpty smiled contemptuously. "Of course you don't—till I tell you. I meant 'there's a nice knock-down argument for you!'"

"But 'glory' doesn't mean 'a nice knock-down argument,'" Alice objected.

"When *I* use a word," Humpty Dumpty said, in rather a scornful tone, "it means just what I choose it to mean—neither more nor less."

"The question is," said Alice, "whether you *can* make words mean so many different things."

"The question is," said Humpty Dumpty, "which is to be master—— that's all."

Alice was too much puzzled to say anything; so after a minute Humpty Dumpty began again. "They've a temper, some of them—particularly verbs: they're the proudest—adjectives you can do anything with, but not verbs—however, *I* can manage the whole lot of them! Impenetrability! That's what *I* say!"

"Would you tell me, please," said Alice, "what that means?"

"Now you talk like a reasonable child," said Humpty Dumpty, looking very much pleased. "I meant by 'impenetrability' that we've had enough of that subject, and it would be just as well if you'd mention what you mean to do next, as I suppose you don't mean to stop here all the rest of your life."

"That's a great deal to make one word mean," Alice said in a thoughtful tone.

"When I make a word do a lot of work like that," said Humpty Dumpty, "I always pay it extra."

"Oh!" said Alice. She was too much puzzled to make any other remark.

"Ah, you should see 'em come round me of a Saturday night," Humpty Dumpty went on, wagging his head gravely from side to side, "for to get their wages, you know."

(Alice didn't venture to ask what he paid them with; and so you see I ca'n't tell *you*.)

"You seem very clever at explaining words, Sir," said Alice. "Would you kindly tell me the meaning of the poem called 'Jabberwocky'?"

"Let's hear it," said Humpty Dumpty. "I can explain all the poems that ever were invented—and a good many that haven't been invented just yet."

This sounded very hopeful, so Alice repeated the first verse:—

> "'*Twas brillig, and the slithy toves*
> *Did gyre and gimble in the wabe:*
> *All mimsy were the borogoves,*
> *And the mome raths outgrabe.*"

"That's enough to begin with," Humpty Dumpty interrupted: "there are plenty of hard words there. '*Brillig*' means four o'clock in the afternoon—the time when you begin *broiling* things for dinner."

"That'll do very well," said Alice: "and '*slithy*'?"

"Well, '*slithy*' means 'lithe and slimy.' 'Lithe' is the same as 'active.' You see it's like a portmanteau—there are two meanings packed up into one word."

"I see it now," Alice remarked thoughtfully: "and what are '*toves*'?"

"Well, '*toves*' are something like badgers—they're something like lizards—and they're something like corkscrews."

"They must be very curious-looking creatures."

"They are that," said Humpty Dumpty; "also they make their nests under sun-dials—also they live on cheese."

"And what's to '*gyre*' and to '*gimble*'?"

"To '*gyre*' is to go round and round like a gyroscope. To '*gimble*' is to make holes like a gimblet."

"And '*the wabe*' is the grass-plot round a sun-dial, I suppose?" said Alice, surprised at her own ingenuity.

"Of course it is. It's called '*wabe*,' you know, because it goes a long way before it, and a long way behind it——"

"And a long way beyond it on each side," Alice added.

"Exactly so. Well then, '*mimsy*' is 'flimsy and miserable' (there's another portmanteau for you). And a '*borogove*' is a thin shabby-looking bird with its feathers sticking out all round—something like a live mop."

"And then '*mome raths*'?" said Alice. "I'm afraid I'm giving you a great deal of trouble."

"Well, a '*rath*' is a sort of green pig: but '*mome*' I'm not certain about. I think it's short for 'from home'—meaning that they'd lost their way, you know."

"And what does '*outgrabe*' mean?"

"Well, '*outgribing*' is something between bellowing and whistling, with a kind of sneeze in the middle: however, you'll hear it done, maybe—down in the wood yonder—and, when you've once heard it, you'll be *quite* content. Who's been repeating all that hard stuff to you?"

"I read it in a book," said Alice. "But I *had* some poetry repeated to me much easier than that, by—Tweedledee, I think it was."

"As to poetry, you know," said Humpty Dumpty, stretching out one of his great hands, "*I* can repeat poetry as well as other folk, if it comes to that——"

"Oh, it needn't come to that!" Alice hastily said, hoping to keep him from beginning.

"The piece I'm going to repeat," he went on without noticing her remark, "was written entirely for your amusement."

Alice felt that in that case she really *ought* to listen to it; so she sat down, and said "Thank you" rather sadly.

> *In winter, when the fields are white,*
>   *I sing this song for your delight——*

only I don't sing it," he added, as an explanation.

"I see you don't," said Alice.

"If you can *see* whether I'm singing or not, you've sharper eyes than most," Humpty Dumpty remarked severely. Alice was silent.

> *"In spring, when woods are getting green,*
> *I'll try and tell you what I mean:"*

"Thank you very much," said Alice.

> *"In summer, when the days are long,*
> *Perhaps you'll understand the song:*
>
> *In autumn, when the leaves are brown,*
> *Take pen and ink, and write it down."*

"I will, if I can remember it so long," said Alice.

"You needn't go on making remarks like that," Humpty Dumpty said: "they're not sensible, and they put me out."

> *"I sent a message to the fish:*
> *I told them 'This is what I wish.'*
>
> *The little fishes of the sea,*
> *They sent an answer back to me.*
>
> *The little fishes' answer was*
> *'We cannot do it, Sir, because——' "*

"I'm afraid I don't quite understand," said Alice.

"It gets easier further on," Humpty Dumpty replied.

> *"I sent to them again to say*
> *'It will be better to obey.'*
>
> *The fishes answered, with a grin,*
> *'Why, what a temper you are in!'*
>
> *I told them once, I told them twice:*
> *They would not listen to advice.*
>
> *I took a kettle large and new,*
> *Fit for the deed I had to do.*
>
> *My heart went hop, my heart went thump:*
> *I filled the kettle at the pump.*
>
> *Then some one came to me and said*
> *'The little fishes are in bed,'*

I said to him, I said it plain,
'Then you must wake them up again.'

I said it very loud and clear:
I went and shouted in his ear."

Humpty Dumpty raised his voice almost to a scream as he repeated this verse, and Alice thought with a shudder, "I wouldn't have been the messenger for *anything!*"

"But he was very stiff and proud:
He said, 'You needn't shout so loud!'

And he was very proud and stiff:
He said 'I'd go and wake them, if——'

I took a corkscrew from the shelf:
I went to wake them up myself.

And when I found the door was locked,
I pulled and pushed and kicked and knocked.

And when I found the door was shut,
I tried to turn the handle, but——"

There was a long pause.

"Is that all?" Alice timidly asked.

"That's all," said Humpty Dumpty. "Good-bye."

This was rather sudden, Alice thought: but, after such a *very* strong hint that she ought to be going, she felt that it would hardly be civil to stay. So she got up, and held out her hand. "Good-bye, till we meet again!" she said as cheerfully as she could.

"I shouldn't know you again if we *did* meet," Humpty Dumpty replied in a discontented tone, giving her one of his fingers to shake: "you're so exactly like other people."

"The face is what one goes by, generally," Alice remarked in a thoughtful tone.

"That's just what I complain of," said Humpty Dumpty. "Your face is the same as everybody has—the two eyes, so——" (marking their places in the air with his thumb) "nose in the middle, mouth under. It's always the same. Now if you had the two eyes on the same side of the nose, for instance—or the mouth at the top—that would be *some* help."

"It wouldn't look nice," Alice objected. But Humpty Dumpty only shut his eyes, and said "Wait till you've tried."

Alice waited a minute to see if he would speak again, but, as he never opened his eyes or took any further notice of her, she said "Good-bye!" once more, and, getting no answer to this, she quietly walked away: but she couldn't help saying to herself, as she went, "Of all the unsatis-factory——" (she repeated this aloud, as it was a great comfort to have such a long word to say) "of all the unsatisfactory people I *ever* met——" She never finished the sentence, for at this moment a heavy crash shook the forest from end to end.

CHAPTER VII.

THE LION AND THE UNICORN.

THE next moment soldiers came running through the wood, at first in twos and threes, then ten or twenty together, and at last in such crowds that they seemed to fill the whole forest. Alice got behind a tree, for fear of being run over, and watched them go by.

She thought that in all her life she had never seen soldiers so uncertain on their feet: they were always tripping over something or other, and whenever one went down, several more always fell over him, so that the ground was soon covered with little heaps of men.

Then came the horses. Having four feet, these managed rather better than the foot-soldiers; but even *they* stumbled now and then; and it seemed to be a regular rule that, whenever a horse stumbled, the rider fell off instantly. The confusion got worse every moment, and Alice was very glad to get out of the wood into an open place, where she found the White King seated on the ground, busily writing in his memorandum-book.

"I've sent them all!" the King cried in a tone of delight, on seeing Alice. "Did you happen to meet any soldiers, my dear, as you came through the wood?"

"Yes, I did," said Alice: "several thousand, I should think."

"Four thousand two hundred and seven, that's the exact number," the King said, referring to his book. "I couldn't send all the horses, you know, because two of them are wanted in the game. And I haven't sent the two Messengers, either. They're both gone to the town. Just look along the road, and tell me if you can see either of them."

"I see nobody on the road," said Alice.

"I only wish *I* had such eyes," the King remarked in a fretful tone. "To be able to see Nobody! And at that distance too! Why, it's as much as *I* can do to see real people, by this light!"

All this was lost on Alice, who was still looking intently along the road, shading her eyes with one hand. "I see somebody now!" she exclaimed at last. "But he's coming very slowly—and what curious attitudes he goes into!" (For the Messenger kept skipping up and down, and wriggling like an eel, as he came along, with his great hands spread out like fans on each side.)

"Not at all," said the King. "He's an Anglo-Saxon Messenger—and those are Anglo-Saxon attitudes. He only does them when he's happy. His name is Haigha." (He pronounced it so as to rhyme with 'mayor.')

"I love my love with an H," Alice couldn't help beginning, "because he is Happy. I hate him with an H, because he is Hideous. I fed him with—with—with Ham-sandwiches and Hay. His name is Haigha, and he lives——"

"He lives on the Hill," the King remarked simply, without the least idea that he was joining in the game, while Alice was still hesitating for the name of a town beginning with H. "The other Messenger's called Hatta. I must have *two*, you know—to come and go. One to come, and one to go."

"I beg your pardon?" said Alice.

"It isn't respectable to beg," said the King.

"I only meant that I didn't understand," said Alice. "Why one to come and one to go?"

"Don't I tell you?" the King repeated impatiently. "I must have *two*— to fetch and carry. One to fetch, and one to carry."

At this moment the Messenger arrived: he was far too much out of breath to say a word, and could only wave his hands about, and make the most fearful faces at the poor King.

"This young lady loves you with an H," the King said, introducing Alice in the hope of turning off the Messenger's attention from himself— but it was of no use—the Anglo-Saxon attitudes only got more extraordinary every moment, while the great eyes rolled wildly from side to side.

"You alarm me!" said the King. "I feel faint——Give me a ham-sandwich!"

On which the Messenger, to Alice's great amusement, opened a bag that hung round his neck, and handed a sandwich to the King, who devoured it greedily.

"Another sandwich!" said the King.

"There's nothing but hay left now," the Messenger said, peeping into the bag.

"Hay, then," the King murmured in a faint whisper.

Alice was glad to see that it revived him a good deal. "There's nothing like eating hay when you're faint," he remarked to her, as he munched away.

"I should think throwing cold water over you would be better," Alice suggested: "—or some sal-volatile."

"I didn't say there was nothing *better*," the King replied. "I said there was nothing *like* it." Which Alice did not venture to deny.

"Who did you pass on the road?" the King went on, holding out his hand to the Messenger for some hay.

"Nobody," said the Messenger.

"Quite right," said the King: "this young lady saw him too. So of course Nobody walks slower than you."

"I do my best," the Messenger said in a sullen tone. "I'm sure nobody walks much faster than I do!"

"He ca'n't do that," said the King, "or else he'd have been here first. However, now you've got your breath, you may tell us what's happened in the town."

"I'll whisper it," said the Messenger, putting his hands to his mouth in the shape of a trumpet and stooping so as to get close to the King's ear. Alice was sorry for this, as she wanted to hear the news too. However, instead of whispering, he simply shouted, at the top of his voice, "They're at it again!"

"Do you call *that* a whisper?" cried the poor King, jumping up and shaking himself. "If you do such a thing again, I'll have you buttered! It went through and through my head like an earthquake!"

"It would have to be a very tiny earthquake!" thought Alice. "Who are at it again?" she ventured to ask.

"Why, the Lion and the Unicorn, of course," said the King.

"Fighting for the crown?"

"Yes, to be sure," said the King: "and the best of the joke is, that it's *my* crown all the while! Let's run and see them." And they trotted off, Alice repeating to herself, as she ran, the words of the old song:—

"The Lion and the Unicorn were fighting for the crown:
The Lion beat the Unicorn all round the town.
Some gave them white bread, some gave them brown:
Some gave them plum-cake and drummed them out of town."

"Does——the one——that wins——get the crown?" she asked, as well as she could, for the run was putting her quite out of breath.

"Dear me, no!" said the King. "What an idea!"

"Would you—be good enough——" Alice panted out, after running a little further, "to stop a minute—just to get—one's breath again?"

"I'm *good* enough," the King said, "only I'm not *strong* enough. You see, a minute goes by so fearfully quick. You might as well try to stop a Bandersnatch!"

Alice had no more breath for talking; so they trotted on in silence, till they came into sight of a great crowd, in the middle of which the Lion and Unicorn were fighting. They were in such a cloud of dust, that at first Alice could not make out which was which; but she soon managed to distinguish the Unicorn by his horn.

They placed themselves close to where Hatta, the other Messenger, was standing watching the fight, with a cup of tea in one hand and a piece of bread-and-butter in the other.

"He's only just out of prison, and he hadn't finished his tea when he was sent in," Haigha whispered to Alice: "and they only give them oyster-shells in there—so you see he's very hungry and thirsty. How are you, dear child?" he went on, putting his arm affectionately round Hatta's neck.

Hatta looked round and nodded, and went on with his bread-and-butter.

"Were you happy in prison, dear child?" said Haigha.

Hatta looked round once more, and this time a tear or two trickled down his cheek; but not a word would he say.

"Speak, ca'n't you!" Haigha cried impatiently. But Hatta only munched away, and drank some more tea.

"Speak, wo'n't you!" cried the King. "How are they getting on with the fight?"

Hatta made a desperate effort, and swallowed a large piece of bread-and-butter. "They're getting on very well," he said in a choking voice: "each of them has been down about eighty-seven times."

"Then I suppose they'll soon bring the white bread and the brown?" Alice ventured to remark.

"It's waiting for 'em now," said Hatta; "this is a bit of it as I'm eating."

There was a pause in the fight just then, and the Lion and the Unicorn sat down, panting, while the King called out "Ten minutes allowed for refreshments!" Haigha and Hatta set to work at once, carrying round trays of white and brown bread. Alice took a piece to taste, but it was *very* dry.

"I don't think they'll fight any more to-day," the King said to Hatta: "go and order the drums to begin." And Hatta went bounding away like a grasshopper.

For a minute or two Alice stood silent, watching him. Suddenly she brightened up. "Look, look!" she cried, pointing eagerly. "There's the White Queen running across the country! She came flying out of the wood over yonder—— How fast those Queens *can* run!"

"There's some enemy after her, no doubt," the King said, without even looking round. "That wood's full of them."

"But aren't you going to run and help her?" Alice asked, very much surprised at his taking it so quietly.

"No use, no use!" said the King. "She runs so fearfully quick. You might as well try to catch a Bandersnatch! But I'll make a memorandum about her, if you like——She's a dear good creature," he repeated softly to himself, as he opened his memorandum-book. "Do you spell 'creature' with a double 'e'?"

At this moment the Unicorn sauntered by them, with his hands in his pockets. "I had the best of it this time?" he said to the King, just glancing at him as he passed.

"A little—a little," the King replied, rather nervously. "You shouldn't have run him through with your horn, you know."

"It didn't hurt him," the Unicorn said carelessly, and he was going on, when his eye happened to fall upon Alice: he turned round instantly, and stood for some time looking at her with an air of the deepest disgust.

"What—is—this?" he said at last.

"This is a child!" Haigha replied eagerly, coming in front of Alice to introduce her, and spreading out both his hands towards her in an Anglo-Saxon attitude. "We only found it to-day. It's as large as life, and twice as natural!"

"I always thought they were fabulous monsters!" said the Unicorn. "Is it alive?"

"It can talk," said Haigha solemnly.

The Unicorn looked dreamily at Alice, and said "Talk, child."

Alice could not help her lips curling up into a smile as she began: "Do you know, I always thought Unicorns were fabulous monsters, too! I never saw one alive before!"

"Well, now that we *have* seen each other," said the Unicorn, "if you'll believe in me, I'll believe in you. Is that a bargain?"

"Yes, if you like," said Alice.

"Come, fetch out the plum-cake, old man!" the Unicorn went on, turning from her to the King. "None of your brown bread for me!"

"Certainly—certainly!" the King muttered, and beckoned to Haigha. "Open the bag!" he whispered. "Quick! Not that one—that's full of hay!"

Haigha took a large cake out of the bag, and gave it to Alice to hold, while he got out a dish and carving-knife. How they all came out of it Alice couldn't guess. It was just like a conjuring-trick, she thought.

The Lion had joined them while this was going on: he looked very tired and sleepy, and his eyes were half shut. "What's this!" he said, blinking lazily at Alice, and speaking in a deep hollow tone that sounded like the tolling of a great bell.

"Ah, what *is* it, now?" the Unicorn cried eagerly. "You'll never guess! *I* couldn't."

The Lion looked at Alice wearily. "Are you animal—or vegetable—or mineral?" he said, yawning at every other word.

"It's a fabulous monster!" the Unicorn cried out, before Alice could reply.

"Then hand round the plum-cake, Monster," the Lion said, lying down and putting his chin on his paws. "And sit down, both of you," (to the King and the Unicorn): "fair play with the cake, you know!"

The King was evidently very uncomfortable at having to sit down between the two great creatures; but there was no other place for him.

"What a fight we might have for the crown, *now!*" the Unicorn said, looking slyly up at the crown, which the poor King was nearly shaking off his head, he trembled so much.

"I should win easy," said the Lion.

"I'm not so sure of that," said the Unicorn.

"Why, I beat you all round the town, you chicken!" the Lion replied angrily, half getting up as he spoke.

Here the King interrupted, to prevent the quarrel going on: he was very nervous, and his voice quite quivered. "All round the town?" he said. "That's a good long way. Did you go by the old bridge, or the market-place? You get the best view by the old bridge."

"I'm sure I don't know," the Lion growled out as he lay down again. "There was too much dust to see anything. What a time the Monster is, cutting up that cake!"

Alice had seated herself on the bank of a little brook, with the great dish on her knees, and was sawing away diligently with the knife. "It's very provoking!" she said, in reply to the Lion (she was getting quite used to being called 'the Monster'). "I've cut several slices already, but they always join on again!"

"You don't know how to manage Looking-glass cakes," the Unicorn remarked. "Hand it round first, and cut it afterwards."

This sounded nonsense, but Alice very obediently got up, and carried the dish round, and the cake divided itself into three pieces as she did so. "*Now* cut it up," said the Lion, as she returned to her place with the empty dish.

"I say, this isn't fair!" cried the Unicorn, as Alice sat with the knife in her hand, very much puzzled how to begin. "The Monster has given the Lion twice as much as me!"

"She's kept none for herself, anyhow," said the Lion. "Do you like plum-cake, Monster?"

*   *   *   *   *   *

   *   *   *   *   *

*   *   *   *   *   *

But before Alice could answer him, the drums began.

Where the noise came from, she couldn't make out: the air seemed full of it, and it rang through and through her head till she felt quite deafened. She started to her feet and sprang across the little brook in her terror, and had just time to see the Lion and the Unicorn rise to their feet, with angry looks at being interrupted in their feast, before she dropped to her knees, and put her hands over her ears, vainly trying to shut out the dreadful uproar.

"If *that* doesn't 'drum them out of town,'" she thought to herself, "nothing ever will!"

CHAPTER VIII.

"IT'S MY OWN INVENTION."

AFTER a while the noise seemed gradually to die away, till all was dead silence, and Alice lifted up her head in some alarm. There was no one to be seen, and her first thought was that she must have been dreaming about the Lion and the Unicorn and those queer Anglo-Saxon Messengers. However, there was the great dish still lying at her feet, on which she had tried to cut the plum-cake, "So I wasn't dreaming, after all," she said to herself, "unless—unless we're all part of the same dream. Only I do hope it's *my* dream, and not the Red King's! I don't like belonging to another person's dream," she went on in a rather complaining tone: "I've a great mind to go and wake him, and see what happens!"

At this moment her thoughts were interrupted by a loud shouting of "Ahoy! Ahoy! Check!" and a Knight, dressed in crimson armour, came galloping down upon her, brandishing a great club. Just as he reached her, the horse stopped suddenly: "You're my prisoner!" the Knight cried, as he tumbled off his horse.

Startled as she was, Alice was more frightened for him than for herself at the moment, and watched him with some anxiety as he mounted again. As soon as he was comfortably in the saddle, he began once more "You're my——" but here another voice broke in "Ahoy! Ahoy! Check!" and Alice looked round in some surprise for the new enemy.

This time it was a White Knight. He drew up at Alice's side, and tumbled off his horse just as the Red Knight had done: then he got on again, and the two Knights sat and looked at each other for some time without speaking. Alice looked from one to the other in some bewilderment.

"She's *my* prisoner, you know!" the Red Knight said at last.

"Yes, but then *I* came and rescued her!" the White Knight replied.

"Well, we must fight for her, then," said the Red Knight, as he took up his helmet (which hung from the saddle, and was something the shape of a horse's head) and put it on.

"You will observe the Rules of Battle, of course?" the White Knight remarked, putting on his helmet too.

"I always do," said the Red Knight, and they began banging away at each other with such fury that Alice got behind a tree to be out of the way of the blows.

"I wonder, now, what the Rules of Battle are," she said to herself, as she watched the fight, timidly peeping out from her hiding-place. "One Rule seems to be, that if one Knight hits the other, he knocks him off his horse; and, if he misses, he tumbles off himself—and another Rule seems to be that they hold their clubs with their arms, as if they were Punch and Judy——What a noise they make when they tumble! Just like a whole set of fire-irons falling into the fender! And how quiet the horses are! They let them get on and off them just as if they were tables!"

Another Rule of Battle, that Alice had not noticed, seemed to be that they always fell on their heads; and the battle ended with their both falling off in this way, side by side. When they got up again, they shook hands, and then the Red Knight mounted and galloped off.

"It was a glorious victory, wasn't it?" said the White Knight, as he came up panting.

"I don't know," Alice said doubtfully. "I don't want to be anybody's prisoner. I want to be a Queen."

"So you will, when you've crossed the next brook," said the White Knight. "I'll see you safe to the end of the wood—and then I must go back, you know. That's the end of my move."

"Thank you very much," said Alice. "May I help you off with your

helmet?" It was evidently more than he could manage by himself: however, she managed to shake him out of it at last.

"Now one can breathe more easily," said the Knight, putting back his shaggy hair with both hands, and turning his gentle face and large mild eyes to Alice. She thought she had never seen such a strange-looking soldier in all her life.

He was dressed in tin armour, which seemed to fit him very badly, and he had a queer-shaped little deal box fastened across his shoulders, upside-down, and with the lid hanging open. Alice looked at it with great curiosity.

"I see you're admiring my little box," the Knight said in a friendly tone. "It's my own invention—to keep clothes and sandwiches in. You see I carry it upside-down, so that the rain ca'n't get in."

"But the things can get *out*," Alice gently remarked. "Do you know the lid's open?"

"I didn't know it," the Knight said, a shade of vexation passing over his face. "Then all the things must have fallen out! And the box is no use without them." He unfastened it as he spoke, and was just going to throw it into the bushes, when a sudden thought seemed to strike him, and he hung it carefully on a tree. "Can you guess why I did that?" he said to Alice.

Alice shook her head.

"In hopes some bees may make a nest in it—then I should get the honey."

"But you've got a bee-hive—or something like one—fastened to the saddle," said Alice.

"Yes, it's a very good bee-hive," the Knight said in a discontented tone, "one of the best kind. But not a single bee has come near it yet. And the other thing is a mouse-trap. I suppose the mice keep the bees out—or the bees keep the mice out, I don't know which."

"I was wondering what the mouse-trap was for," said Alice. "It isn't very likely there would be any mice on the horse's back."

"Not very likely, perhaps," said the Knight; "but, if they *do* come, I don't choose to have them running all about.

"You see," he went on after a pause, "it's as well to be provided for *everything*. That's the reason the horse has all those anklets round his feet."

"But what are they for?" Alice asked in a tone of great curiosity.

"To guard against the bites of sharks," the Knight replied. "It's an invention of my own. And now help me on. I'll go with you to the end of the wood—What's that dish for?"

"It's meant for plum-cake," said Alice.

"We'd better take it with us," the Knight said. "It'll come in handy if we find any plum-cake. Help me to get it into this bag."

This took a long time to manage, though Alice held the bag open very carefully, because the Knight was so *very* awkward in putting in the dish: the first two or three times that he tried he fell in himself instead. "It's rather a tight fit, you see," he said, as they got it in at last; "there are so many candlesticks in the bag." And he hung it to the saddle, which was already loaded with bunches of carrots, and fire-irons, and many other things.

"I hope you've got your hair well fastened on?" he continued, as they set off.

"Only in the usual way," Alice said, smiling.

"That's hardly enough," he said, anxiously. "You see the wind is so *very* strong here. It's as strong as soup."

"Have you invented a plan for keeping the hair from being blown off?" Alice enquired.

"Not yet," said the Knight. "But I've got a plan for keeping it from *falling* off."

"I should like to hear it, very much."

"First you take an upright stick," said the Knight. "Then you make your hair creep up it, like a fruit-tree. Now the reason hair falls off is because it hangs *down*—things never fall *upwards*, you know. It's a plan of my own invention. You may try it if you like."

It didn't sound a comfortable plan, Alice thought, and for a few minutes she walked on in silence, puzzling over the idea, and every now and then stopping to help the poor Knight, who certainly was *not* a good rider.

Whenever the horse stopped (which it did very often), he fell off in

front; and, whenever it went on again (which it generally did rather suddenly), he fell off behind. Otherwise he kept on pretty well, except that he had a habit of now and then falling off sideways; and, as he generally did this on the side on which Alice was walking, she soon found that it was the best plan not to walk *quite* close to the horse.

"I'm afraid you've not had much practice in riding," she ventured to say, as she was helping him up from his fifth tumble.

The Knight looked very much surprised, and a little offended at the remark. "What makes you say that?" he asked, as he scrambled back into the saddle, keeping hold of Alice's hair with one hand, to save himself from falling over on the other side.

"Because people don't fall off quite so often, when they've had much practice."

"I've had plenty of practice," the Knight said very gravely: "plenty of practice!"

Alice could think of nothing better to say than "Indeed?" but she said it as heartily as she could. They went on a little way in silence after this, the Knight with his eyes shut, muttering to himself, and Alice watching anxiously for the next tumble.

"The great art of riding," the Knight suddenly began in a loud voice, waving his right arm as he spoke, "is to keep——" Here the sentence ended as suddenly as it had begun, as the Knight fell heavily on the top of his head exactly in the path where Alice was walking. She was quite frightened this time, and said in an anxious tone, as she picked him up, "I hope no bones are broken?"

"None to speak of," the Knight said, as if he didn't mind breaking two or three of them. "The great art of riding, as I was saying, is—to keep your balance properly. Like this, you know——"

He let go the bridle, and stretched out both his arms to show Alice what he meant, and this time he fell flat on his back, right under the horse's feet.

"Plenty of practice!" he went on repeating, all the time that Alice was getting him on his feet again. "Plenty of practice!"

"It's too ridiculous!" cried Alice, losing all her patience this time. "You ought to have a wooden horse on wheels, that you ought!"

"Does that kind go smoothly?" the Knight asked in a tone of great interest, clasping his arms round the horse's neck as he spoke, just in time to save himself from tumbling off again.

"Much more smoothly than a live horse," Alice said, with a little scream of laughter, in spite of all she could do to prevent it.

"I'll get one," the Knight said thoughtfully to himself. "One or two— several."

There was a short silence after this, and then the Knight went on again. "I'm a great hand at inventing things. Now, I daresay you noticed, the last time you picked me up, that I was looking rather thoughtful?"

"You *were* a little grave," said Alice.

"Well, just then I was inventing a new way of getting over a gate— would you like to hear it?"

"Very much indeed," Alice said politely.

"I'll tell you how I came to think of it," said the Knight. "You see, I said to myself 'The only difficulty is with the feet: the *head* is high enough already.' Now, first I put my head on the top of the gate—then the head's high enough—then I stand on my head—then the feet are high enough, you see—then I'm over, you see."

"Yes, I suppose you'd be over when that was done," Alice said thoughtfully: "but don't you think it would be rather hard?"

"I haven't tried it yet," the Knight said, gravely; "so I ca'n't tell for certain—but I'm afraid it *would* be a little hard."

He looked so vexed at the idea, that Alice changed the subject hastily. "What a curious helmet you've got!" she said cheerfully. "Is that your invention too?"

The Knight looked down proudly at his helmet, which hung from the saddle. "Yes," he said; "but I've invented a better one than that—like a sugar-loaf. When I used to wear it, if I fell off the horse, it always touched the ground directly. So I had a *very* little way to fall, you see—But there *was* the danger of falling *into* it, to be sure. That happened to me once— and the worst of it was, before I could get out again, the other White Knight came and put it on. He thought it was his own helmet."

The Knight looked so solemn about it that Alice did not dare to laugh. "I'm afraid you must have hurt him," she said in a trembling voice, "being on the top of his head."

"I had to kick him, of course," the Knight said, very seriously. "And then he took the helmet off again—but it took hours and hours to get me out. I was as fast as—as lightning, you know."

"But that's a different kind of fastness," Alice objected.

The Knight shook his head. "It was all kinds of fastness with me, I can assure you!" he said. He raised his hands in some excitement as he said this, and instantly rolled out of the saddle, and fell headlong into a deep ditch.

Alice ran to the side of the ditch to look for him. She was rather startled by the fall, as for some time he had kept on very well, and she was afraid that he really *was* hurt this time. However, though she could see nothing but the soles of his feet, she was much relieved to hear that he was talking on in his usual tone. "All kinds of fastness," he repeated: "but it was careless of him to put another man's helmet on—with the man in it, too."

"How *can* you go on talking so quietly, head downwards?" Alice asked, as she dragged him out by the feet, and laid him in a heap on the bank.

The Knight looked surprised at the question. "What does it matter where my body happens to be?" he said. "My mind goes on working all the same. In fact, the more head-downwards I am, the more I keep inventing new things."

"Now the cleverest thing of the sort that I ever did," he went on after a pause, "was inventing a new pudding during the meat-course."

"In time to have it cooked for the next course?" said Alice. "Well, that *was* quick work, certainly!"

"Well, not the *next* course," the Knight said in a slow thoughtful tone: "no, certainly not the next *course*."

"Then it would have to be the next day. I suppose you wouldn't have two pudding-courses in one dinner?"

"Well, not the *next* day," the Knight repeated as before: "not the next *day*. In fact," he went on, holding his head down, and his voice getting lower and lower, "I don't believe that pudding ever *was* cooked! In fact, I don't believe that pudding ever *will* be cooked! And yet it was a very clever pudding to invent."

"What did you mean it to be made of?" Alice asked, hoping to cheer him up, for the poor Knight seemed quite low-spirited about it.

"It began with blotting-paper," the Knight answered with a groan.

"That wouldn't be very nice, I'm afraid——"

"Not very nice *alone*," he interrupted, quite eagerly: "but you've no idea what a difference it makes, mixing it with other things—such as gunpowder and sealing-wax. And here I must leave you." They had just come to the end of the wood.

Alice could only look puzzled: she was thinking of the pudding.

"You are sad," the Knight said in an anxious tone: "let me sing you a song to comfort you."

"Is it very long?" Alice asked, for she had heard a good deal of poetry that day.

"It's long," said the Knight, "but it's very, *very* beautiful. Everybody that hears me sing it—either it brings the *tears* into their eyes, or else——"

"Or else what?" said Alice, for the Knight had made a sudden pause.

"Or else it doesn't, you know. The name of the song is called 'Haddocks' Eyes.' "

"Oh, that's the name of the song, is it?" Alice said, trying to feel interested.

"No, you don't understand," the Knight said, looking a little vexed. "That's what the name is *called*. The name really is 'The Aged Aged Man.' "

"Then I ought to have said 'That's what the *song* is called'?" Alice corrected herself.

"No, you oughtn't: that's quite another thing! The *song* is called 'Ways and Means': but that's only what it's *called*, you know!"

"Well, what *is* the song, then?" said Alice, who was by this time completely bewildered.

"I was coming to that," the Knight said. "The song really is 'A-sitting On A Gate': and the tune's my own invention."

So saying, he stopped his horse and let the reins fall on its neck: then, slowly beating time with one hand, and with a faint smile lighting up his gentle foolish face, as if he enjoyed the music of his song, he began.

Of all the strange things that Alice saw in her journey Through The Looking-Glass, this was the one that she always remembered most clearly. Years afterwards she could bring the whole scene back again, as if it had been only yesterday—the mild blue eyes and kindly smile of the Knight— the setting sun gleaming through his hair, and shining on his armour in a blaze of light that quite dazzled her—the horse quietly moving about, with the reins hanging loose on his neck, cropping the grass at her feet— and the black shadows of the forest behind—all this she took in like a picture, as, with one hand shading her eyes, she leant against a tree, watching the strange pair, and listening, in a half-dream, to the melancholy music of the song.

"But the tune *isn't* his own invention," she said to herself: "it's '*I give thee all, I can no more.*'" She stood and listened very attentively, but no tears came into her eyes.

> "*I'll tell thee everything I can:*
>   *There's little to relate.*
> *I saw an aged aged man,*
>   *A-sitting on a gate.*
> *'Who are you, aged man?' I said.*
>   *'And how is it you live?'*
> *And his answer trickled through my head,*
>   *Like water through a sieve.*
>
> *He said 'I look for butterflies*
>   *That sleep among the wheat:*
> *I make them into mutton-pies,*
>   *And sell them in the street.*
> *I sell them unto men,' he said,*
>   *'Who sail on stormy seas;*
> *And that's the way I get my bread—*
>   *A trifle, if you please.'*
>
> *But I was thinking of a plan*
>   *To dye one's whiskers green,*
> *And always use so large a fan*
>   *That they could not be seen.*
> *So, having no reply to give*
>   *To what the old man said,*
> *I cried 'Come, tell me how you live!'*
>   *And thumped him on the head.*
>
> *His accents, mild took up the tale:*
>   *He said 'I go my ways,*
> *And when I find a mountain-rill,*
>   *I set it in a blaze;*
> *And thence they make a stuff they call*
>   *Rowland's Macassar-Oil—*
> *Yet twopence-halfpenny is all*
>   *They give me for my toil.'*
>
> *But I was thinking of a way*
>   *To feed oneself on batter,*
> *And so go on from day to day*
>   *Getting a little fatter*
> *I shook him well from side to side,*
>   *Until his face was blue:*
> *'Come, tell me how you live,' I cried,*
>   *'And what it is you do!'*

He said 'I hunt for haddocks' eyes
  Among the heather bright,
And work them into waistcoat-buttons
  In the silent night.
And these I do not sell for gold
  Or coin of silvery shine,
But for a copper halfpenny,
  And that will purchase nine.

'I sometimes dig for buttered rolls,
  Or set limed twigs for crabs:
I sometimes search the grassy knolls
  For wheels of Hansom-cabs.
And that's the way' (he gave a wink)
  'By which I get my wealth—
And very gladly will I drink
  Your Honour's noble health.'

I heard him then, for I had just
  Completed my design
To keep the Menai bridge from rust
  By boiling it in wine.
I thanked him much for telling me
  The way he got his wealth,
But chiefly for his wish that he
  Might drink my noble health.

And now, if e'er by chance I put
    My fingers into glue,
Or madly squeeze a right-hand foot
    Into a left-hand shoe,
Or if I drop upon my toe
    A very heavy weight,
I weep, for it reminds me so
Of that old man I used to know—
Whose look was mild, whose speech was slow,
Whose hair was whiter than the snow,
Whose face was very like a crow,
With eyes, like cinders, all aglow,
Who seemed distracted with his woe,
Who rocked his body to and fro,
And muttered mumblingly and low,
As if his mouth were full of dough,
Who snorted like a buffalo——
That summer evening long ago,
    A-sitting on a gate."

As the Knight sang the last words of the ballad, he gathered up the reins, and turned his horse's head along the road by which they had come. "You've only a few yards to go," he said, "down the hill and over that little brook, and then you'll be a Queen——But you'll stay and see me off first?" he added as Alice turned with an eager look in the direction to which he pointed. "I sha'n't be long. You'll wait and wave your handkerchief when I get to that turn in the road! I think it'll encourage me, you see."

"Of course I'll wait," said Alice: "and thank you very much for coming so far—and for the song—I liked it very much."

"I hope so," the Knight said doubtfully: "but you didn't cry so much as I thought you would."

So they shook hands, and then the Knight rode slowly away into the forest. "It wo'n't take long to see him *off,* I expect," Alice said to herself, as she stood watching him. "There he goes! Right on his head as usual! However, he gets on again pretty easily—that comes of having so many things hung round the horse——" So she went on talking to herself, as she watched the horse walking leisurely along the road, and the Knight tumbling off, first on one side and then on the other. After the fourth or fifth tumble he reached the turn, and then she waved her handkerchief to him, and waited till he was out of sight.

"I hope it encouraged him," she said, as she turned to run down the hill: "and now for the last brook, and to be a Queen! How grand it sounds!" A very few steps brought her to the edge of the brook. "The Eighth Square at last!" she cried as she bounded across,

*   *   *   *   *   *   *
    *   *   *   *   *   *
*   *   *   *   *   *

and threw herself down to rest on a lawn as soft as moss, with little flower-beds dotted about it here and there. "Oh, how glad I am to get here! And what *is* this on my head?" she exclaimed in a tone of dismay, as she put her hands up to something very heavy, that fitted tight all around her head.

"But how *can* it have got there without my knowing it?" she said to herself, as she lifted it off, and set it on her lap to make out what it could possibly be.

It was a golden crown.

CHAPTER IX.

QUEEN ALICE.

"WELL, this *is* grand!" said Alice. "I never expected I should be a Queen so soon—and I'll tell you what it is, your Majesty," she went on, in a severe tone (she was always rather fond of scolding herself), "it'll never do for you to be lolling about on the grass like that! Queens have to be dignified, you know!"

So she got up and walked about—rather stiffly just at first, as she was afraid that the crown might come off: but she comforted herself with the thought that there was nobody to see her, "and if I really am a Queen," she said as she sat down again, "I shall be able to manage it quite well in time."

Everything was happening so oddly that she didn't feel a bit surprised at finding the Red Queen and the White Queen sitting close to her, one on each side: she would have liked very much to ask them how they came there, but she feared it would not be quite civil. However, there would be no harm, she thought, in asking if the game was over. "Please, would you tell me——" she began, looking timidly at the Red Queen.

"Speak when you're spoken to!" the Queen sharply interrupted her.

"But if everybody obeyed that rule," said Alice, who was always ready for a little argument, "and if you only spoke when you were spoken to, and the other person always waited for *you* to begin, you see nobody would ever say anything, so that——"

"Ridiculous!" cried the Queen. "Why, don't you see, child——" here she broke off with a frown, and, after thinking for a minute, suddenly changed the subject of the conversation. "What do you mean by 'If you really are a Queen'? What right have you to call yourself so? You ca'n't be a Queen, you know, till you've passed the proper examination. And the sooner we begin it, the better."

"I only said 'if'!" poor Alice pleaded in a piteous tone.

The two Queens looked at each other, and the Red Queen remarked, with a little shudder, "She *says* she only said 'if'——"

"But she said a great deal more than that!" the White Queen moaned, wringing her hands. "Oh, ever so much more than that!"

"So you did, you know," the Red Queen said to Alice. "Always speak the truth—think before you speak—and write it down afterwards."

"I'm sure I didn't mean——" Alice was beginning, but the Red Queen interrupted her impatiently.

"That's just what I complain of! You *should* have meant! What do you suppose is the use of a child without any meaning? Even a joke should have some meaning—and a child's more important than a joke, I hope. You couldn't deny that, even if you tried with both hands."

"I don't deny things with my *hands*," Alice objected.

"Nobody said you did," said the Red Queen. "I said you couldn't if you tried."

"She's in that state of mind," said the White Queen, "that she wants to deny *something*—only she doesn't know what to deny!"

"A nasty, vicious temper," the Red Queen remarked; and then there was an uncomfortable silence for a minute or two.

The Red Queen broke the silence by saying, to the White Queen, "I invite you to Alice's dinner-party this afternoon."

The White Queen smiled feebly, and said "And I invite *you*."

"I didn't know I was to have a party at all," said Alice; "but, if there is to be one, I think I ought to invite the guests."

"We gave you the opportunity of doing it," the Red Queen remarked: "but I daresay you've not had many lessons in manners yet."

"Manners are not taught in lessons," said Alice. "Lessons teach you to do sums, and things of that sort."

"Can you do Addition?" the White Queen asked. "What's one and one and one and one and one and one and one and one and one and one?"

"I don't know," said Alice. "I lost count."

"She ca'n't do Addition," the Red Queen interrupted. "Can you do Subtraction? Take nine from eight."

"Nine from eight I ca'n't, you know," Alice replied very readily: "but——"

"She ca'n't do Subtraction," said the White Queen. "Can you do Division? Divide a loaf by a knife—what's the answer to *that*?"

"I suppose——" Alice was beginning, but the Red Queen answered for her. "Bread-and-butter, of course. Try another Subtraction sum. Take a bone from a dog: what remains?"

Alice considered. "The bone wouldn't remain, of course, if I took it—and the dog wouldn't remain: it would come to bite me—and I'm sure *I* shouldn't remain!"

"Then you think nothing would remain?" said the Red Queen.

"I think that's the answer."

"Wrong, as usual," said the Red Queen: "the dog's temper would remain."

"But I don't see how——"

"Why, look here!" the Red Queen cried. "The dog would lose its temper, wouldn't it?"

"Perhaps it would," Alice replied cautiously.

"Then if the dog went away, its temper would remain!" the Queen exclaimed triumphantly.

Alice said, as gravely as she could, "They might go different ways." But she couldn't help thinking to herself "What dreadful nonsense we *are* talking!"

"She ca'n't do sums a *bit!*" the Queens said together, with great emphasis.

"Can *you* do sums?" Alice said, turning suddenly on the White Queen, for she didn't like being found fault with so much.

The Queen gasped and shut her eyes. "I can do Addition," she said, "if you give me time—but I ca'n't do Subtraction under *any* circumstances!"

"Of course you know your A B C?" said the Red Queen.

"To be sure I do," said Alice.

"So do I," the White Queen whispered: "we'll often say it over together, dear. And I'll tell you a secret—I can read words of one letter! Isn't *that* grand? However, don't be discouraged. You'll come to it in time."

Here the Red Queen began again. "Can you answer useful questions?" she said. "How is bread made?"

"I know *that!*" Alice cried eagerly. "You take some flour——"

"Where do you pick the flower?" the White Queen asked. "In a garden or in the hedges?"

"Well, it isn't *picked* at all," Alice explained: "it's *ground*——"

"How many acres of ground?" said the White Queen. "You mustn't leave out so many things."

"Fan her head!" the Red Queen anxiously interrupted. "She'll be feverish after so much thinking." So they set to work and fanned her with bunches of leaves, till she had to beg them to leave off, it blew her hair about so.

"She's all right again now," said the Red Queen. "Do you know Languages? What's the French for fiddle-de-dee?"

"Fiddle-de-dee's not English," Alice replied gravely.

"Who ever said it was?" said the Red Queen.

Alice thought she saw a way out of the difficulty, this time. "If you'll tell me what language 'fiddle-de-dee' is, I'll tell you the French for it!" she exclaimed triumphantly.

But the Red Queen drew herself up rather stiffly, and said, "Queens never make bargains."

"I wish Queens never asked questions," Alice thought to herself.

"Don't let us quarrel," the White Queen said in an anxious tone. "What is the cause of lightning?"

"The cause of lightning," Alice said very decidedly, for she felt quite certain about this, "is the thunder—no, no!" she hastily corrected herself. "I meant the other way."

"It's too late to correct it," said the Red Queen: "when you've once said a thing, that fixes it, and you must take the consequences."

"Which reminds me——" the White Queen said, looking down and nervously clasping and unclasping her hands, "we had *such* a thunderstorm last Tuesday—I mean one of the last set of Tuesdays, you know."

Alice was puzzled. "In *our* country," she remarked, "there's only one day at a time."

The Red Queen said "That's a poor thin way of doing things. Now *here*, we mostly have days and nights two or three at a time, and sometimes in the winter we take as many as five nights together—for warmth, you know."

"Are five nights warmer than one night, then?" Alice ventured to ask.

"Five times as warm, of course."

"But they should be five times as *cold*, by the same rule——"

"Just so!" cried the Red Queen. "Five times as warm, *and* five times as cold—just as I'm five times as rich as you are, *and* five times as clever!"

Alice sighed and gave it up. "It's exactly like a riddle with no answer!" she thought.

"Humpty Dumpty saw it too," the White Queen went on in a low voice, more as if she were talking to herself. "He came to the door with a corkscrew in his hand——"

"What did he want?" said the Red Queen.

"He said he *would* come in," the White Queen went on, "because he was looking for a hippopotamus. Now, as it happened, there wasn't such a thing in the house, that morning."

"Is there generally?" Alice asked in an astonished tone.

"Well, only on Thursdays," said the Queen.

"I know what he came for," said Alice: "he wanted to punish the fish, because——"

Here the White Queen began again. "It was *such* a thunderstorm, you ca'n't think!" ("She *never* could, you know," said the Red Queen.) "And part of the roof came off, and ever so much thunder got in—and it went rolling round the room in great lumps—and knocking over the tables and things—till I was so frightened, I couldn't remember my own name!"

Alice thought to herself "I never should *try* to remember my name in the middle of an accident! Where would be the use of it?" but she did not say this aloud, for fear of hurting the poor Queen's feelings.

"Your Majesty must excuse her," the Red Queen said to Alice, taking one of the White Queen's hands in her own, and gently stroking it: "she means well, but she ca'n't help saying foolish things, as a general rule."

The White Queen looked timidly at Alice, who felt she *ought* to say something kind, but really couldn't think of anything at the moment.

"She never was really well brought up," the Red Queen went on: "but it's amazing how good-tempered she is! Pat her on the head, and see how pleased she'll be!" But this was more than Alice had courage to do.

"A little kindness—and putting her hair in papers—would do wonders with her——"

The White Queen gave a deep sigh, and laid her head on Alice's shoulder. "I *am* so sleepy!" she moaned.

"She's tired, poor thing!" said the Red Queen. "Smooth her hair—lend her your nightcap—and sing her a soothing lullaby."

"I haven't got a nightcap with me," said Alice, as she tried to obey the first direction: "and I don't know any soothing lullabies."

"I must do it myself, then," said the Red Queen, and she began:—

> *"Hush-a-by lady, in Alice's lap!*
> *Till the feast's ready, we've time for a nap.*
> *When the feast's over, we'll go to the ball—*
> *Red Queen, and White Queen, and Alice, and all!*

"And now you know the words," she added, as she put her head down on Alice's other shoulder, "just sing it through to *me*. I'm getting sleepy, too." In another moment both Queens were fast asleep, and snoring loud.

"What *am* I to do?" exclaimed Alice, looking about in great perplexity, as first one round head, and then the other, rolled down from her shoulder, and lay like a heavy lump in her lap. "I don't think it *ever* happened before, that any one had to take care of two Queens asleep at once! No, not in all the History of England—it couldn't, you know, because there never was more than one Queen at a time. Do wake up, you heavy things!" she went on in an impatient tone; but there was no answer but a gentle snoring.

The snoring got more distinct every minute, and sounded more like a tune: at last she could even make out words, and she listened so eagerly that, when the two great heads suddenly vanished from her lap, she hardly missed them.

She was standing before an arched doorway, over which were the words "QUEEN ALICE" in large letters, and on each side of the arch there was a bell-handle; one was marked "Visitors' Bell," and the other "Servants' Bell."

"I'll wait till the song's over," thought Alice, "and then I'll ring the—the—*which* bell must I ring?" she went on, very much puzzled by the names. "I'm not a visitor, and I'm not a servant. There *ought* to be one marked 'Queen,' you know——"

Just then the door opened a little way, and a creature with a long beak put its head out for a moment and said "No admittance till the week after next!" and shut the door again with a bang.

Alice knocked and rang in vain for a long time; but at last a very old

Frog, who was sitting under a tree, got up and hobbled slowly towards her: he was dressed in bright yellow, and had enormous boots on.

"What is it, now?" the Frog said in a deep hoarse whisper.

Alice turned round, ready to find fault with anybody. "Where's the servant whose business it is to answer the door?" she began angrily.

"Which door?" said the Frog.

Alice almost stamped with irritation at the slow drawl in which he spoke. "*This* door, of course!"

The Frog looked at the door with his large dull eyes for a minute: then he went nearer and rubbed it with his thumb, as if he were trying whether the paint would come off: then he looked at Alice.

"To answer the door?" he said. "What's it been asking of?" He was so hoarse that Alice could scarcely hear him.

"I don't know what you mean," she said.

"I speaks English, doesn't I?" the Frog went on. "Or are you deaf? What did it ask you?"

"Nothing!" Alice said impatiently. "I've been knocking at it!"

"Shouldn't do that—shouldn't do that——" the Frog muttered. "Wexes it, you know." Then he went up and gave the door a kick with one of his great feet. "You let *it* alone," he panted out, as he hobbled back to his tree, "and it'll let *you* alone, you know."

At this moment the door was flung open, and a shrill voice was heard singing:—

"*To the Looking-Glass world it was Alice that said*
'I've a sceptre in hand, I've a crown on my head.
Let the Looking-Glass creatures, whatever they be,
Come and dine with the Red Queen, the White Queen, and me!'"

And hundreds of voices joined in the chorus:—

"*Then fill up the glasses as quick as you can,*
And sprinkle the table with buttons and bran:
Put cats in the coffee, and mice in the tea—
And welcome Queen Alice with thirty-times-three!"

Then followed a confused noise of cheering, and Alice thought to herself "Thirty times three makes ninety. I wonder if any one's counting?" In a minute there was silence again, and the same shrill voice sang another verse:—

"*'O Looking-Glass creatures,' quoth Alice, 'draw near!*
'Tis an honour to see me, a favour to hear:
'Tis a privilege high to have dinner and tea
Along with the Red Queen, the White Queen, and me!'"

Then came the chorus again:—

"*Then fill up the glasses with treacle and ink,*
Or anything else that is pleasant to drink:
Mix sand with the cider, and wool with the wine—
And welcome Queen Alice with ninety-times-nine!"

"Ninety times nine!" Alice repeated in despair. "Oh, that'll never be done! I'd better go in at once——" and in she went, and there was a dead silence the moment she appeared.

Alice glanced nervously along the table, as she walked up the large hall, and noticed that there were about fifty guests, of all kinds: some were animals, some birds, and there were even a few flowers among them. "I'm glad they've come without waiting to be asked," she thought: "I should never have known who were the right people to invite!"

There were three chairs at the head of the table: the Red and White Queens had already taken two of them, but the middle one was empty. Alice sat down in it, rather uncomfortable at the silence, and longing for some one to speak.

At last the Red Queen began. "You've missed the soup and fish," she said. "Put on the joint!" And the waiters set a leg of mutton before Alice, who looked at it rather anxiously, as she had never had to carve a joint before.

"You look a little shy: let me introduce you to that leg of mutton,"

said the Red Queen. "Alice——Mutton: Mutton——Alice." The leg of
mutton got up in the dish and made a little bow to Alice; and Alice
returned the bow, not knowing whether to be frightened or amused.

"May I give you a slice?" she said, taking up the knife and fork, and
looking from one Queen to the other.

"Certainly not," the Red Queen said, very decidedly: "it isn't etiquette
to cut anyone you've been introduced to. Remove the joint!" And the
waiters carried it off, and brought a large plum-pudding in its place.

"I wo'n't be introduced to the pudding, please," Alice said rather
hastily, "or we shall get no dinner at all. May I give you some?"

But the Red Queen looked sulky, and growled "Pudding——Alice:
Alice——Pudding. Remove the pudding!", and the waiters took it away
so quickly that Alice couldn't return its bow.

However, she didn't see why the Red Queen should be the only one
to give orders; so, as an experiment, she called out "Waiter! Bring back
the pudding!", and there it was again in a moment, like a conjuring-
trick. It was so large that she couldn't help feeling a *little* shy with it, as
she had been with the mutton; however, she conquered her shyness by
a great effort, and cut a slice and handed it to the Red Queen.

"What impertinence!" said the pudding. "I wonder how you'd like it,
if I were to cut a slice out of *you*, you creature!"

It spoke in a thick, suety sort of voice, and Alice hadn't a word to say
in reply: she could only sit and look at it and gasp.

"Make a remark," said the Red Queen: "it's ridiculous to leave all the
conversation to the pudding!"

"Do you know, I've had such a quantity of poetry repeated to me to-day," Alice began, a little frightened at finding that, the moment she opened her lips, there was dead silence, and all eyes were fixed upon her; "and it's a very curious thing, I think—every poem was about fishes in some way. Do you know why they're so fond of fishes, all about here?"

She spoke to the Red Queen, whose answer was a little wide of the mark. "As to fishes," she said, very slowly and solemnly, putting her mouth close to Alice's ear, "her White Majesty knows a lovely riddle—all in poetry—all about fishes. Shall she repeat it?"

"Her Red Majesty's very kind to mention it," the White Queen murmured into Alice's other ear, in a voice like the cooing of a pigeon. "It would be *such* a treat! May I?"

"Please do," Alice said very politely.

The White Queen laughed with delight, and stroked Alice's cheek. Then she began:—

> " *'First, the fish must be caught.'*
> *That is easy: a baby, I think, could have caught it.*
> *'Next, the fish must be bought.'*
> *That is easy: a penny, I think, would have bought it.*
>
> *'Now cook me the fish!'*
> *That is easy, and will not take more than a minute.*
> *'Let it lie in a dish!'*
> *That is easy, because it already is in it.*
>
> *'Bring it here! Let me sup!'*
> *It is easy to set such a dish on the table.*
> *'Take the dish-cover up!'*
> *Ah, that is so hard that I fear I'm unable!*
>
> *For it holds it like glue—*
> *Holds the lid to the dish, while it lies in the middle:*
> *Which is easiest to do,*
> *Un-dish-cover the fish, or dishcover the riddle?"*

"Take a minute to think about it, and then guess," said the Red Queen. "Meanwhile, we'll drink your health—Queen Alice's health!" she screamed at the top of her voice, and all the guests began drinking it directly, and very queerly they managed it: some of them put their glasses upon their heads like extinguishers, and drank all that trickled down their faces—others upset the decanters, and drank the wine as it ran off the edges of the table—and three of them (who looked like kangaroos) scrambled into the dish of roast mutton, and began eagerly lapping up the gravy, "just like pigs in a trough!" thought Alice.

"You ought to return thanks in a neat speech," the Red Queen said, frowning at Alice as she spoke.

"We must support you, you know," the White Queen whispered, as Alice got up to do it, very obediently, but a little frightened.

"Thank you very much," she whispered in reply, "but I can do quite well without."

"That wouldn't be at all the thing," the Red Queen said very decidedly: so Alice tried to submit to it with a good grace.

("And they *did* push so!" she said afterwards, when she was telling her sister the history of the feast. "You would have thought they wanted to squeeze me flat!")

In fact it was rather difficult for her to keep in her place while she made her speech: the two Queens pushed her so, one on each side, that they nearly lifted her up into the air. "I rise to return thanks——" Alice began: and she really *did* rise as she spoke, several inches; but she got hold of the edge of the table, and managed to pull herself down again.

"Take care of yourself!" screamed the White Queen, seizing Alice's hair with both her hands. "Something's going to happen!"

And then (as Alice afterwards described it) all sorts of things happened in a moment. The candles all grew up to the ceiling, looking something like a bed of rushes with fireworks at the top. As to the bottles, they each took a pair of plates, which they hastily fitted on as wings, and so, with forks for legs, went fluttering about in all directions: "and very like birds they look," Alice thought to herself, as well as she could in the dreadful confusion that was beginning.

At this moment she heard a hoarse laugh at her side, and turned to see what was the matter with the White Queen; but, instead of the Queen, there was the leg of mutton sitting in the chair. "Here I am!" cried a voice from the soup-tureen, and Alice turned again, just in time to see the Queen's broad good-natured face grinning at her for a moment over the edge of the tureen, before she disappeared into the soup.

There was not a moment to be lost. Already several of the guests were lying down in the dishes, and the soup-ladle was walking up the table towards Alice's chair, and beckoning to her impatiently to get out of its way.

"I ca'n't stand this any longer!" she cried, as she jumped up and seized the tablecloth with both hands: one good pull, and plates, dishes, guests, and candles came crashing down together in a heap on the floor.

"And as for *you*," she went on, turning fiercely upon the Red Queen, whom she considered as the cause of all the mischief—but the Queen was no longer at her side—she had suddenly dwindled down to the size of a little doll, and was now on the table, merrily running round and round after her own shawl, which was trailing behind her.

At any other time, Alice would have felt surprised at this, but she was far too much excited to be surprised at anything *now*. "As for *you*," she repeated, catching hold of the little creature in the very act of jumping over a bottle which had just lighted upon the table, "I'll shake you into a kitten, that I will!"

CHAPTER X.

SHAKING.

SHE took her off the table as she spoke, and shook her backwards and forwards with all her might.

The Red Queen made no resistance whatever: only her face grew very small, and her eyes got large and green: and still, as Alice went on shaking her, she kept on growing shorter—and fatter—and softer—and rounder—and——

CHAPTER XI.

WAKING.

——and it really *was* a kitten, after all.

CHAPTER XII.

WHICH DREAMED IT?

"Your Red Majesty shouldn't purr so loud," Alice said, rubbing her eyes, and addressing the kitten, respectfully, yet with some severity. "You woke me out of oh! such a nice dream! And you've been along with me, Kitty—all through the Looking-glass world. Did you know it, dear?"

It is a very inconvenient habit of kittens (Alice had once made the remark) that, whatever you say to them, they *always* purr. "If they would only purr for 'yes,' and mew for 'no,' or any rule of that sort," she had said, "so that one could keep up a conversation! But how *can* you talk with a person if they *always* say the same thing?"

On this occasion the kitten only purred: and it was impossible to guess whether it meant 'yes' or 'no.'

So Alice hunted among the chessmen on the table till she had found the Red Queen: then she went down on her knees on the hearth-rug, and put the kitten and the Queen to look at each other. "Now, Kitty!" she cried, clapping her hands triumphantly. "Confess that was what you turned into!"

("But it wouldn't look at it," she said, when she was explaining the thing afterwards to her sister: "it turned away its head, and pretended not to see it: but it looked a *little* ashamed of itself, so I think it *must* have been the Red Queen.")

"Sit up a little more stiffly, dear!" Alice cried with a merry laugh. "And curtsey while you're thinking what to—what to purr. It saves time, remember!" And she caught it up and gave it one little kiss, "just in honour of its having been a Red Queen."

"Snowdrop, my pet!" she went on, looking over her shoulder at the White Kitten, which was still patiently undergoing its toilet, "when *will* Dinah have finished with your White Majesty, I wonder? That must be the reason you were so untidy in my dream.——Dinah! Do you know that you're scrubbing a White Queen? Really, it's most disrespectful of you!"

"And what did *Dinah* turn to, I wonder?" she prattled on, as she settled comfortably down, with one elbow on the rug, and her chin in her hand, to watch the kittens. "Tell me, Dinah, did you turn to Humpty Dumpty? I *think* you did—however, you'd better not mention it to your friends just yet, for I'm not sure.

"By the way, Kitty, if only you'd been really with me in my dream, there was one thing you *would* have enjoyed——I had such a quantity of poetry said to me, all about fishes! To-morrow morning you shall have a real treat. All the time you're eating your breakfast, I'll repeat 'The Walrus and the Carpenter' to you; and then you can make believe it's oysters, dear!

"Now, Kitty, let's consider who it was that dreamed it all. This is a serious question, my dear, and you should *not* go on licking your paw like that—as if Dinah hadn't washed you this morning! You see, Kitty, it *must* have been either me or the Red King. He was part of my dream, of course—but then I was part of his dream, too! *Was* it the Red King, Kitty? You were his wife, my dear, so you ought to know——Oh, Kitty, *do* help to settle it! I'm sure your paw can wait!" But the provoking kitten only began on the other paw, and pretended it hadn't heard the question.

Which do *you* think it was?

A BOAT, beneath a sunny sky
Lingering onward dreamily
In an evening of July—

Children three that nestle near,
Eager eye and willing ear,
Pleased a simple tale to hear—

Long has paled that sunny sky:
Echoes fade and memories die:
Autumn frosts have slain July.

Still she haunts me, phantomwise,
Alice moving under skies
Never seen by waking eyes.

Children yet, the tale to hear,
Eager eye and willing ear,
Lovingly shall nestle near.

In a Wonderland they lie,
Dreaming as the days go by,
Dreaming as the summers die:

Ever drifting down the stream—
Lingering in the golden gleam—
Life, what is it but a dream?

THE END.

THE HUNTING
OF THE SNARK

AN AGONY IN EIGHT FITS

Illustrated by

HENRY HOLIDAY

"SUPPORTING EACH MAN ON THE TOP OF THE TIDE"

INSCRIBED TO A DEAR CHILD:

IN MEMORY OF GOLDEN SUMMER HOURS
AND WHISPERS OF A SUMMER SEA.

Girt with a boyish garb for boyish task,
   Eager she wields her spade: yet loves as well
Rest on a friendly knee, intent to ask
   The tale one loves to tell.

Rude scoffer of the seething outer strife,
   Unmeet to read her pure and simple spright;
Deem, if thou wilt, such hours a waste of life,
   Empty of all delight!

Chat on, sweet Maid, and rescue from annoy
   Hearts that by wiser talk are unbeguiled;
Ah, happy he who owns that tenderest joy,
   The heart-love of a child!

Away, fond thoughts, and vex my soul no more!
   Work claims my wakeful nights, my busy day
Albeit bright memories of that sunlit shore
   Yet haunt my dreaming gaze!

PREFACE.

IF—and the thing is wildly possible—the charge of writing nonsense were ever brought against the author of this brief but instructive poem, it would be based, I feel convinced, on the line (in p. 186)

"Then the bowsprit got mixed with the rudder sometimes:"

In view of this painful possibility, I will not (as I might) appeal indignantly to my other writings as a proof that I am incapable of such a deed: I will not (as I might) point to the strong moral purpose of this poem itself, to the arithmetical principles so cautiously inculcated in it, or to its noble teachings in Natural History—I will take the more prosaic course of simply explaining how it happened.

The Bellman, who was almost morbidly sensitive about appearances, used to have the bowsprit unshipped once or twice a week to be revarnished; and it more than once happened, when the time came for replacing it, that no one on board could remember which end of the ship it belonged to. They knew it was not of the slightest use to appeal to the Bellman about it—he would only refer to his Naval Code, and read out in pathetic tones Admiralty Instructions which none of them had ever been able to understand—so it generally ended in its being fastened on, anyhow, across the rudder. The helmsman* used to stand by with tears in his eyes: *he* knew it was all wrong, but alas! Rule 42 of the Code, *"No one shall speak to the Man at the Helm,"* had been completed by the Bellman himself with the words *"and the Man at the Helm shall speak to no one."* So remonstrance was impossible, and no steering could be done till the next varnishing day. During these bewildering intervals the ship usually sailed backwards.

As this poem is to some extent connected with the lay of the Jabberwock, let me take this opportunity of answering a question that has often been asked me, how to pronounce "slithy toves." The "i" in "slithy" is long, as in "writhe"; and "toves" is pronounced so as to rhyme with "groves." Again, the first "o" in "borogoves" is pronounced like the "o" in "borrow." I have heard people try to give it the sound of the "o" in "worry." Such is Human Perversity.

This also seems a fitting occasion to notice the other hard words in

---

* This office was usually undertaken by the Boots, who found in it a refuge from the Baker's constant complaints about the insufficient blacking of his three pairs of boots.

that poem. Humpty-Dumpty's theory, of two meanings packed into one word like a portmanteau, seems to me the right explanation for all.

For instance, take the two words "fuming" and "furious." Make up your mind that you will say both words, but leave it unsettled which you will say first. Now open your mouth and speak. If your thoughts incline ever so little towards "fuming," you will say "fuming-furious"; if they turn, by even a hair's breadth, towards "furious," you will say "furious-fuming"; but if you have that rarest of gifts, a perfectly balanced mind, you will say "frumious."

Supposing that, when Pistol uttered the well-known words—

"Under which king, Bezonian? Speak or die!"

Justice Shallow had felt certain that it was either William or Richard, but had not been able to settle which, so that he could not possibly say either name before the other, can it be doubted that, rather than die, he would have gasped out "Rilchiam!"

FIT THE FIRST.

THE LANDING.

"JUST the place for a Snark!" the Bellman cried,
    As he landed his crew with care;
Supporting each man on the top of the tide
    By a finger entwined in his hair.

"Just the place for a Snark! I have said it twice:
    That alone should encourage the crew.
Just the place for a Snark! I have said it thrice:
    What I tell you three times is true."

The crew was complete: it included a Boots—
    A maker of Bonnets and Hoods—
A Barrister, brought to arrange their disputes—
    And a Broker, to value their goods.

A Billiard-marker, whose skill was immense,
    Might perhaps have won more than his share—
But a Banker, engaged at enormous expense,
    Had the whole of their cash in his care.

There was also a Beaver, that paced on the deck,
    Or would sit making lace in the bow:
And had often (the Bellman said) saved them from wreck,
    Though none of the sailors knew how.

There was one who was famed for the number of things
    He forgot when he entered the ship:
His umbrella, his watch, all his jewels and rings,
    And the clothes he had bought for the trip.

He had forty-two boxes, all carefully packed,
    With his name painted clearly on each:
But since he omitted to mention the fact,
    They were all left behind on the beach.

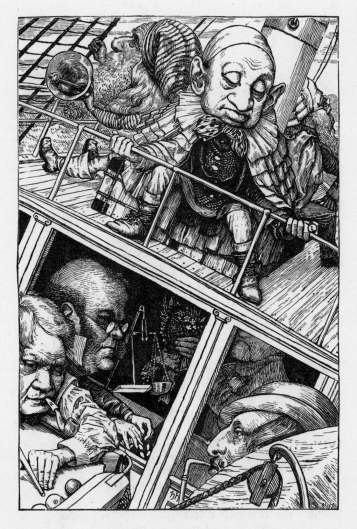

"HE HAD WHOLLY FORGOTTEN HIS NAME"

The loss of his clothes hardly mattered, because
  He had seven coats on when he came,
With three pair of boots—but the worst of it was
  He had wholly forgotten his name.

He would answer to "Hi!" or to any loud cry,
  Such as "Fry me!" or "Fritter my wig!"
To "What-you-may-call-um!" or "What-was-his-name!"
  But especially "Thing-um-a-jig!"

While, for those who preferred a more forcible word,
  He had different names from these:
His intimate friends called him "Candle-ends,"
  And his enemies "Toasted-cheese."

"His form is ungainly—his intellect small—"
  (So the Bellman would often remark)—
"But his courage is perfect! And that, after all,
  Is the thing that one needs with a Snark."

He would joke with hyænas, returning their stare
  With an impudent wag of the head:
And he once went a walk, paw-in-paw, with a bear,
  "Just to keep up its spirits," he said.

He came as a Baker: but owned, when too late—
  And it drove the poor Bellman half-mad—
He could only bake Bride-cake—for which, I may state,
  No materials were to be had.

The last of the crew needs especial remark,
  Though he looked an incredible dunce:
He had just one idea—but, that one being "Snark,"
  The good Bellman engaged him at once.

He came as a Butcher: but gravely declared,
  When the ship had been sailing a week,
He could only kill Beavers. The Bellman looked scared,
  And was almost too frightened to speak:

But at length he explained, in a tremulous tone,
  There was only one Beaver on board;
And that was a tame one he had of his own,
  Whose death would be deeply deplored.

The Beaver, who happened to hear the remark,
  Protested, with tears in its eyes,
That not even the rapture of hunting the Snark
  Could atone for that dismal surprise!

It strongly advised that the Butcher should be
　　Conveyed in a separate ship:
But the Bellman declared that would never agree
　　With the plans he had made for the trip:

Navigation was always a difficult art,
　　Though with only one ship and one bell:
And he feared he must really decline, for his part,
　　Undertaking another as well.

The Beaver's best course was, no doubt, to procure
　　A second-hand dagger-proof coat—
So the Baker advised it—and next, to insure
　　Its life in some Office of note:

This the Baker suggested, and offered for hire
　　(On moderate terms), or for sale,
Two excellent Policies, one Against Fire,
　　And one Against Damage From Hail.

Yet still, ever after that sorrowful day,
　　Whenever the Butcher was by,
The Beaver kept looking the opposite way,
　　And appeared unaccountably shy.

FIT THE SECOND.

THE BELLMAN'S SPEECH.

THE Bellman himself they all praised to the skies—
　　Such a carriage, such ease and such grace!
Such solemnity, too! One could see he was wise,
　　The moment one looked in his face!

He had bought a large map representing the sea,
　　Without the least vestige of land:
And the crew were much pleased when they found it to be
　　A map they could all understand.

"What's the good of Mercator's North Poles and Equators,
  Tropics, Zones, and Meridian Lines?"
So the Bellman would cry: and the crew would reply
  "They are merely conventional signs!

"Other maps are such shapes, with their islands and capes!
  But we've got our brave Captain to thank"
(So the crew would protest) "that he's bought *us* the best—
  A perfect and absolute blank!"

This was charming, no doubt: but they shortly found out
  That the Captain they trusted so well
Had only one notion for crossing the ocean,
  And that was to tingle his bell.

He was thoughtful and grave—but the orders he gave
  Were enough to bewilder a crew.
When he cried "Steer to starboard, but keep her head larboard!"
  What on earth was the helmsman to do?

Then the bowsprit got mixed with the rudder sometimes:
  A thing, as the Bellman remarked,
That frequently happens in tropical climes,
  When a vessel is, so to speak, "snarked."

But the principal failing occurred in the sailing,
  And the Bellman, perplexed and distressed,
Said he *had* hoped, at least, when the wind blew due East,
  That the ship would *not* travel due West!

But the danger was past—they had landed at last,
  With their boxes, portmanteaus, and bags:
Yet at first sight the crew were not pleased with the view
  Which consisted of chasms and crags.

The Bellman perceived that their spirits were low,
  And repeated in musical tone
Some jokes he had kept for a season of woe—
  But the crew would do nothing but groan.

He served out some grog with a liberal hand,
  And bade them sit down on the beach:
And they could not but own that their Captain looked grand,
  As he stood and delivered his speech.

"Friends, Romans, and countrymen, lend me your ears!"
  (They were all of them fond of quotations:
So they drank to his health, and they gave him three cheers,
  While he served out additional rations).

"THE BEAVER KEPT LOOKING THE OPPOSITE WAY"

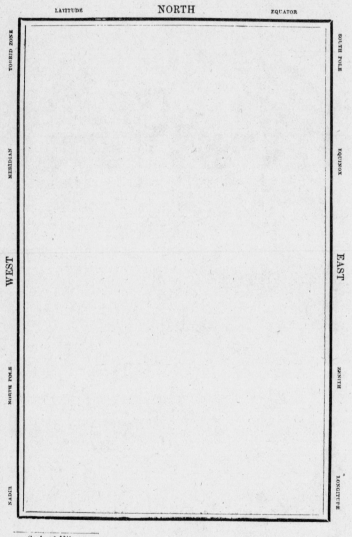

Scale of Miles.

OCEAN-CHART

"We have sailed many months, we have sailed many
weeks,
   (Four weeks to the month you may mark),
But never as yet ('tis your Captain who speaks)
   Have we caught the least glimpse of a Snark!

"We have sailed many weeks, we have sailed many days,
   (Seven days to the week I allow),
But a Snark, on the which we might lovingly gaze,
   We have never beheld till now!

"Come, listen, my men, while I tell you again
   The five unmistakable marks
By which you may know, wheresoever you go,
   The warranted genuine Snarks.

"Let us take them in order. The first is the taste,
   Which is meagre and hollow, but crisp:
Like a coat that is rather too tight in the waist,
   With a flavour of Will-o-the-wisp.

"Its habit of getting up late you'll agree
   That it carries too far, when I say
That it frequently breakfasts at five-o'clock tea,
   And dines on the following day.

"The third is its slowness in taking a jest.
   Should you happen to venture on one,
It will sigh like a thing that is deeply distressed:
   And it always looks grave at a pun.

"The fourth is its fondness for bathing-machines,
   Which it constantly carries about,
And believes that they add to the beauty of scenes—
   A sentiment open to doubt.

"The fifth is ambition. It next will be right
   To describe each particular batch:
Distinguishing those that have feathers, and bite,
   From those that have whiskers, and scratch.

"For, although common Snarks do no manner of harm,
   Yet I feel it my duty to say
Some are Boojums—" The Bellman broke off in alarm,
   For the Baker had fainted away.

FIT THE THIRD.

THE BAKER'S TALE.

THEY roused him with muffins—they roused him with ice—
  They roused him with mustard and cress—
They roused him with jam and judicious advice—
  They set him conundrums to guess.

When at length he sat up and was able to speak,
  His sad story he offered to tell;
And the Bellman cried "Silence! Not even a shriek!"
  And excitedly tingled his bell.

There was silence supreme! Not a shriek, not a scream;
  Scarcely even a howl or a groan,
As the man they called "Ho!" told his story of woe
  In an antediluvian tone.

"My father and mother were honest, though poor—"
  "Skip all that!" cried the Bellman in haste.
"If it once becomes dark, there's no chance of a Snark—
  We have hardly a minute to waste!"

"I skip forty years," said the Baker, in tears,
  "And proceed without further remark
To the day when you took me aboard of your ship
  To help you in hunting the Snark.

"A dear uncle of mine (after whom I was named)
  Remarked, when I bade him farewell—"
"Oh, skip your dear uncle!" the Bellman exclaimed,
  As he angrily tingled his bell.

"He remarked to me then," said that mildest of men,
  " 'If your Snark be a Snark, that is right:
Fetch it home by all means—you may serve it with greens
  And it's handy for striking a light.

" 'You may seek it with thimbles—and seek it with care;
  You may hunt it with forks and hope;
You may threaten its life with a railway-share;
  You may charm it with smiles and soap—' "

("That's exactly the method," the Bellman bold
  In a hasty parenthesis cried,
"That's exactly the way I have always been told
  That the capture of Snarks should be tried!")

" 'But oh, beamish nephew, beware of the day,
  If your Snark be a Boojum! For then
You will softly and suddenly vanish away,
  And never be met with again!'

"It is this, it is this that oppresses my soul,
  When I think of my uncle's last words:
And my heart is like nothing so much as a bowl
  Brimming over with quivering curds!

"It is this, it is this—" "We have had that before!"
  The Bellman indignantly said.
And the Baker replied "Let me say it once more.
  It is this, it is this that I dread!

"I engage with the Snark—every night after dark—
  In a dreamy delirious fight:
I serve it with greens in those shadowy scenes,
  And I use it for striking a light:

"But if ever I meet with a Boojum, that day,
  In a moment (of this I am sure),
I shall softly and suddenly vanish away—
  And the notion I cannot endure!"

FIT THE FOURTH.

THE HUNTING.

THE Bellman looked uffish, and wrinkled his brow.
  "If only you'd spoken before!
It's excessively awkward to mention it now,
  With the Snark, so to speak, at the door!

"BUT OH, BEAMISH NEPHEW, BEWARE OF THE DAY"

"We should all of us grieve, as you well may believe,
  If you never were met with again—
But surely, my man, when the voyage began,
  You might have suggested it then?

"It's excessively awkward to mention it now—
  As I think I've already remarked."
And the man they called "Hi!" replied, with a sigh,
  "I informed you the day we embarked.

"You may charge me with murder—or want of sense—
  (We are all of us weak at times):
But the slightest approach to a false pretence
  Was never among my crimes!

"I said it in Hebrew—I said it in Dutch—
  I said it in German and Greek:
But I wholly forgot (and it vexes me much)
  That English is what you speak!"

"'Tis a pitiful tale," said the Bellman, whose face
  Had grown longer at every word:
"But, now that you've stated the whole of your case,
  More debate would be simply absurd.

"The rest of my speech" (he exclaimed to his men)
  "You shall hear when I've leisure to speak it.
But the Snark is at hand, let me tell you again!
  'Tis your glorious duty to seek it!

"To seek it with thimbles, to seek it with care;
  To pursue it with forks and hope;
To threaten its life with a railway-share;
  To charm it with smiles and soap!

"For the Snark's a peculiar creature, that won't
  Be caught in a commonplace way.
Do all that you know, and try all that you don't:
  Not a chance must be wasted to-day!

"For England expects—I forbear to proceed:
  'Tis a maxim tremendous, but trite:
And you'd best be unpacking the things that you need
  To rig yourselves out for the fight."

Then the Banker endorsed a blank cheque (which he crossed),
  And changed his loose silver for notes:
The Baker with care combed his whiskers and hair,
  And shook the dust out of his coats:

The Boots and the Broker were sharpening a spade—
  Each working the grindstone in turn:
But the Beaver went on making lace, and displayed
  No interest in the concern:

Though the Barrister tried to appeal to its pride,
  And vainly proceeded to cite
A number of cases, in which making laces
  Had been proved an infringement of right.

The maker of Bonnets ferociously planned
  A novel arrangement of bows:
While the Billiard-marker with quivering hand
  Was chalking the tip of his nose.

But the Butcher turned nervous, and dressed himself fine,
  With yellow kid gloves and a ruff—
Said he felt it exactly like going to dine,
  Which the Bellman declared was all "stuff."

"Introduce me, now there's a good fellow," he said,
  "If we happen to meet it together!"
And the Bellman, sagaciously nodding his head,
  Said "That must depend on the weather."

The Beaver went simply galumphing about,
  At seeing the Butcher so shy:
And even the Baker, though stupid and stout,
  Made an effort to wink with one eye.

"Be a man!" cried the Bellman in wrath, as he heard
  The Butcher beginning to sob.
"Should we meet with a Jubjub, that desperate bird,
  We shall need all our strength for the job!"

"TO PURSUE IT WITH FORKS AND HOPE"

FIT THE FIFTH.

THE BEAVER'S LESSON.

THEY sought it with thimbles, they sought it with care
   They pursued it with forks and hope;
They threatened its life with a railway-share;
   They charmed it with smiles and soap.

Then the Butcher contrived an ingenious plan
   For making a separate sally;
And had fixed on a spot unfrequented by man,
   A dismal and desolate valley.

But the very same plan to the Beaver occurred:
   It had chosen the very same place:
Yet neither betrayed, by a sign or a word,
   The disgust that appeared in his face.

Each thought he was thinking of nothing but "Snark"
   And the glorious work of the day;
And each tried to pretend that he did not remark
   That the other was going that way.

But the valley grew narrow and narrower still,
   And the evening got darker and colder,
Till (merely from nervousness, not from good will)
   They marched along shoulder to shoulder.

Then a scream, shrill and high, rent the shuddering sky
   And they knew that some danger was near:
The Beaver turned pale to the tip of its tail,
   And even the Butcher felt queer.

He thought of his childhood, left far far behind—
   That blissful and innocent state—
The sound so exactly recalled to his mind
   A pencil that squeaks on a slate!

"'Tis the voice of the Jubjub!" he suddenly cried.
   (This man, that they used to call "Dunce.")
"As the Bellman would tell you," he added with pride,
   "I have uttered that sentiment once."

"'Tis the note of the Jubjub! Keep count, I entreat;
  You will find I have told it you twice.
'Tis the song of the Jubjub! The proof is complete,
  If only I've stated it thrice."

The Beaver had counted with scrupulous care,
  Attending to every word:
But it fairly lost heart, and outgrabe in despair,
  When the third repetition occurred.

It felt that, in spite of all possible pains,
  It had somehow contrived to lose count,
And the only thing now was to rack its poor brains
  By reckoning up the amount.

"Two added to one—if that could but be done,"
  It said, "with one's fingers and thumbs!"
Recollecting with tears how, in earlier years,
  It had taken no pains with its sums.

"The thing can be done," said the Butcher, "I think.
  The thing must be done, I am sure.
The thing shall be done! Bring me paper and ink,
  The best there is time to procure."

The Beaver brought paper, portfolio, pens,
  And ink in unfailing supplies:
While strange creepy creatures came out of their dens,
  And watched them with wondering eyes.

So engrossed was the Butcher, he heeded them not,
  As he wrote with a pen in each hand,
And explained all the while in a popular style
  Which the Beaver could well understand.

"Taking Three as the subject to reason about—
  A convenient number to state—
We add Seven, and Ten, and then multiply out
  By One Thousand diminished by Eight.

"The result we proceed to divide, as you see,
  By Nine Hundred and Ninety and Two:
Then subtract Seventeen, and the answer must be
  Exactly and perfectly true.

"The method employed I would gladly explain,
  While I have it so clear in my head,
If I had but the time and you had but the brain—
  But much yet remains to be said.

"THE BEAVER BROUGHT PAPER, PORTFOLIO, PENS"

"In one moment I've seen what has hitherto been
    Enveloped in absolute mystery,
And without extra charge I will give you at large
    A Lesson in Natural History."

In his genial way he proceeded to say
    (Forgetting all laws of propriety,
And that giving instruction, without introduction,
    Would have caused quite a thrill in Society),

"As to temper the Jubjub's a desperate bird,
    Since it lives in perpetual passion:
Its taste in costume is entirely absurd—
    It is ages ahead of the fashion:

"But it knows any friend it has met once before:
    It never will look at a bribe:
And in charity-meetings it stands at the door,
    And collects—though it does not subscribe.

"Its flavour when cooked is more exquisite far
    Than mutton, or oysters, or eggs:
(Some think it keeps best in an ivory jar,
    And some, in mahogany kegs:)

"You boil it in sawdust: you salt it in glue:
    You condense it with locusts and tape:
Still keeping one principal object in view—
    To preserve its symmetrical shape."

The Butcher would gladly have talked till next day,
    But he felt that the Lesson must end,
And he wept with delight in attempting to say
    He considered the Beaver his friend:

While the Beaver confessed, with affectionate looks
    More eloquent even than tears,
It had learned in ten minutes far more than all books
    Would have taught it in seventy years.

They returned hand-in-hand, and the Bellman, unmanned
    (For a moment) with noble emotion,
Said "This amply repays all the wearisome days
    We have spent on the billowy ocea!"

Such friends as the Beaver and Butcher became,
    Have seldom if ever been known;
In winter or summer, 'twas always the same—
    You could never meet either alone.

And when quarrels arose—as one frequently finds
    Quarrels will, spite of every endeavour—
The song of the Jubjub recurred to their minds,
    And cemented their friendship for ever!

FIT THE SIXTH.

THE BARRISTER'S DREAM.

They sought it with thimbles, they sought it with care;
    They pursued it with forks and hope;
They threatened its life with a railway-share
    They charmed it with smiles and soap.

But the Barrister, weary of proving in vain
    That the Beaver's lace-making was wrong,
Fell asleep, and in dreams saw the creature quite plain
    That his fancy had dwelt on so long.

He dreamed that he stood in a shadowy Court,
    Where the Snark, with a glass in its eye,
Dressed in gown, bands, and wig, was defending a pig
    On the charge of deserting its sty.

The Witnesses proved, without error or flaw,
    That the sty was deserted when found:
And the Judge kept explaining the state of the law
    In a soft under-current of sound.

The indictment had never been clearly expressed,
    And it seemed that the Snark had begun,
And had spoken three hours, before any one guessed
    What the pig was supposed to have done.

The Jury had each formed a different view
    (Long before the indictment was read),
And they all spoke at once, so that none of them knew
    One word that the others had said.

"'YOU MUST KNOW——' SAID THE JUDGE: BUT THE SNARK EXCLAIMED 'FUDGE!'"

"You must know—" said the Judge: but the Snark exclaimed "Fudge!
   That statute is obsolete quite!
Let me tell you, my friends, the whole question depends
   On an ancient manorial right.

"In the matter of Treason the pig would appear
   To have aided, but scarcely abetted:
While the charge of Insolvency fails, it is clear,
   If you grant the plea 'never indebted.'

"The fact of Desertion I will not dispute:
   But its guilt, as I trust, is removed
(So far as relates to the costs of this suit)
   By the Alibi which has been proved.

"My poor client's fate now depends on your votes."
   Here the speaker sat down in his place,
And directed the Judge to refer to his notes
   And briefly to sum up the case.

But the Judge said he never had summed up before;
   So the Snark undertook it instead,
And summed it so well that it came to far more
   Than the Witnesses ever had said!

When the verdict was called for, the Jury declined,
   As the word was so puzzling to spell;
But they ventured to hope that the Snark wouldn't mind
   Undertaking that duty as well.

So the Snark found the verdict, although, as it owned,
   It was spent with the toils of the day:
When it said the word "GUILTY!" the Jury all groaned
   And some of them fainted away.

Then the Snark pronounced sentence, the Judge being quite
   Too nervous to utter a word:
When it rose to its feet, there was silence like night,
   And the fall of a pin might be heard.

"Transportation for life" was the sentence it gave,
   "And *then* to be fined forty pound."
The Jury all cheered, though the Judge said he feared
   That the phrase was not legally sound.

But their wild exultation was suddenly checked
   When the jailer informed them, with tears,
Such a sentence would have not the slightest effect,
   As the pig had been dead for some years.

The Judge left the Court, looking deeply disgusted:
  But the Snark, though a little aghast,
As the lawyer to whom the defence was intrusted,
  Went bellowing on to the last.

Thus the Barrister dreamed, while the bellowing seemed
  To grow every moment more clear:
Till he woke to the knell of a furious bell,
  Which the Bellman rang close at his ear.

FIT THE SEVENTH.

THE BANKER'S FATE.

THEY sought it with thimbles, they sought it with care;
  They pursued it with forks and hope;
They threatened its life with a railway-share;
  They charmed it with smiles and soap.

And the Banker, inspired with a courage so new
  It was matter for general remark,
Rushed madly ahead and was lost to their view
  In his zeal to discover the Snark.

But while he was seeking with thimbles and care,
  A Bandersnatch swiftly drew nigh
And grabbed at the Banker, who shrieked in despair,
  For he knew it was useless to fly.

He offered large discount—he offered a cheque
  (Drawn "to bearer") for seven-pounds-ten:
But the Bandersnatch merely extended its neck
  And grabbed at the Banker again.

Without rest or pause—while those frumious jaws
  Went savagely snapping around—
He skipped and he hopped, and he floundered and flopped,
  Till fainting he fell to the ground.

The Bandersnatch fled as the others appeared
  Led on by that fear-stricken yell:
And the Bellman remarked "It is just as I feared!"
  And solemnly tolled on his bell.

He was black in the face, and they scarcely could trace
  The least likeness to what he had been:
While so great was his fright that his waistcoat turned white—
  A wonderful thing to be seen!

To the horror of all who were present that day,
  He uprose in full evening dress,
And with senseless grimaces endeavoured to say
  What his tongue could no longer express.

Down he sank in a chair—ran his hands through his hair—
  And chanted in mimsiest tones
Words whose utter inanity proved his insanity,
  While he rattled a couple of bones.

"Leave him here to his fate—it is getting so late!"
  The Bellman exclaimed in a fright.
"We have lost half the day. Any further delay,
  And we sha'n't catch a Snark before night!"

FIT THE EIGHTH.

THE VANISHING.

THEY sought it with thimbles, they sought it with care;
  They pursued it with forks and hope;
They threatened its life with a railway-share;
  They charmed it with smiles and soap.

They shuddered to think that the chase might fail,
  And the Beaver, excited at last,
Went bounding along on the tip of its tail,
  For the daylight was nearly past.

"SO GREAT WAS HIS FRIGHT THAT HIS WAISTCOAT TURNED WHITE"

"There is Thingumbob shouting!" the Bellman said.
    "He is shouting like mad, only hark!
He is waving his hands, he is wagging his head,
    He has certainly found a Snark!"

They gazed in delight, while the Butcher exclaimed
    "He was always a desperate wag!"
They beheld him—their Baker—their hero unnamed—
    On the top of a neighbouring crag,

Erect and sublime, for one moment of time,
    In the next, that wild figure they saw
(As if stung by a spasm) plunge into a chasm,
    While they waited and listened in awe.

"It's a Snark!" was the sound that first came to their ears,
    And seemed almost too good to be true.
Then followed a torrent of laughter and cheers:
    Then the ominous words "It's a Boo—"

Then, silence. Some fancied they heard in the air
    A weary and wandering sigh
That sounded like "—jum!" but the others declare
    It was only a breeze that went by.

They hunted till darkness came on, but they found
    Not a button, or feather, or mark,
By which they could tell that they stood on the ground
    Where the Baker had met with the Snark.

In the midst of the word he was trying to say,
    In the midst of his laughter and glee,
He had softly and suddenly vanished away—
    For the Snark *was* a Boojum, you see.

"THEN, SILENCE"

RHYME?
AND
REASON?

Illustrated by
ARTHUR B. FROST

I have had nor rhyme nor reason

"UPON A BATTLEMENT."

PHANTASMAGORIA.

CANTO I.

The Trystyng.

ONE winter night, at half-past nine,
    Cold, tired, and cross, and muddy,
I had come home, too late to dine,
And supper, with cigars and wine,
    Was waiting in the study.

There was a strangeness in the room,
    And Something white and wavy
Was standing near me in the gloom—
I took it for the carpet-broom
    Left by that careless slavey.

But presently the Thing began
    To shiver and to sneeze:
On which I said "Come, come, my man!
That's a most inconsiderate plan.
    Less noise there, if you please!"

"I've caught a cold," the Thing replies,
    "Out there upon the landing."
I turned to look in some surprise,
And there, before my very eyes,
    A little Ghost was standing!

He trembled when he caught my eye,
    And got behind a chair.
"How came you here," I said, "and why?
I never saw a thing so shy.
    Come out! Don't shiver there!"

He said "I'd gladly tell you how,
    And also tell you why;
But" (here he gave a little bow)
"You're in so bad a temper now,
    You'd think it all a lie.

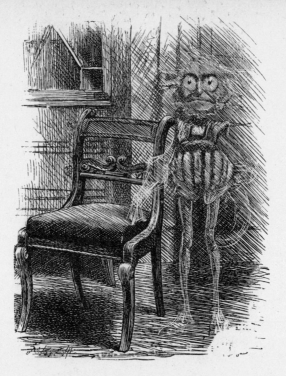

"And as to being in a fright,
    Allow me to remark
That Ghosts have just as good a right,
In every way, to fear the light,
    As Men to fear the dark."

"No plea," said I, "can well excuse
    Such cowardice in you:
For Ghosts can visit when they choose,
Whereas we Humans ca'n't refuse
    To grant the interview."

He said "A flutter of alarm
    Is not unnatural, is it?
I really feared you meant some harm:
But, now I see that you are calm,
    Let me explain my visit.

"Houses are classed, I beg to state,
    According to the number
Of Ghosts that they accommodate:
(The Tenant merely counts as *weight*,
    With Coals and other lumber).

"This is a 'one-ghost' house, and you
    When you arrived last summer,
May have remarked a Spectre who
Was doing all that Ghosts can do
    To welcome the new-comer.

"In Villas this is always done—
    However cheaply rented:
For, though of course there's less of fun
When there is only room for one,
    Ghosts have to be contented.

"That Spectre left you on the Third—
    Since then you've not been haunted:
For, as he never sent us word,
'Twas quite by accident we heard
    That any one was wanted.

"A Spectre has first choice, by right,
    In filling up a vacancy;
Then Phantom, Goblin, Elf, and Sprite—
If all these fail them, they invite
    The nicest Ghoul that they can see.

"The Spectres said the place was low,
    And that you kept bad wine:
So, as a Phantom had to go,
And I was first, of course, you know,
    I couldn't well decline."

"No doubt," said I, "they settled who
    Was fittest to be sent:
Yet still to choose a brat like you,
To haunt a man of forty-two,
    Was no great compliment!"

"I'm not so young, Sir," he replied,
    "As you might think. The fact is,
In caverns by the water-side,
And other places that I've tried,
    I've had a lot of practice:

"But I have never taken yet
    A strict domestic part,
And in my flurry I forget
The Five Good Rules of Etiquette
    We have to know by heart."

"IN CAVERNS BY THE WATER-SIDE"

My sympathies were warming fast
    Towards the little fellow:
He was so utterly aghast
At having found a Man at last,
    And looked so scared and yellow.

"At least," I said, "I'm glad to find
    A Ghost is not a *dumb* thing!
But pray sit down: you'll feel inclined
(If, like myself, you have not dined)
    To take a snack of something:

"Though, certainly, you don't appear
    A thing to offer *food* to!
And then I shall be glad to hear—
If you will say them loud and clear—
    The Rules that you allude to."

"Thanks! You shall hear them by and by
    This *is* a piece of luck!"
"What may I offer you?" said I.
"Well, since you *are* so kind, I'll try
    A little bit of duck.

"*One* slice! And may I ask you for
    Another drop of gravy?"
I sat and looked at him in awe,
For certainly I never saw
    A thing so white and wavy.

And still he seemed to grow more white,
 More vapoury, and wavier—
Seen in the dim and flickering light,
 As he proceeded to recite
His "Maxims of Behaviour."

CANTO II.

Hys Fyve Rules.

"MY First—but don't suppose," he said,
 "I'm setting you a riddle—
s—if your Victim be in bed,
Don't touch the curtains at his head,
 But take them in the middle,

"And wave them slowly in and out,
 While drawing them asunder;
And in a minute's time, no doubt,
He'll raise his head and look about
 With eyes of wrath and wonder.

"And here you must on no pretence
 Make the first observation.
Wait for the Victim to commence:
No Ghost of any common sense
 Begins a conversation.

"If he should say '*How came you here?*'
 (The way that *you* began, Sir,)
In such a case your course is clear—
On the bat's back, my little dear!'
 Is the appropriate answer.

"If after this he says no more,
 You'd best perhaps curtail your
Exertions—go and shake the door,
And then, if he begins to snore,
 You'll know the thing's a failure.

"By day, if he should be alone—
　　At home or on a walk—
You merely give a hollow groan,
To indicate the kind of tone
　　In which you mean to talk.

"But if you find him with his friends,
　　The thing is rather harder.
In such a case success depends
On picking up some candle-ends,
　　Or butter, in the larder.

"With this you make a kind of slide
　　(It answers best with suet),
On which you must contrive to glide,
And swing yourself from side to side—
　　One soon learns how to do it.

"The Second tells us what is right
　　In ceremonious calls:—
'First burn a blue or crimson light'
(A thing I quite forgot to-night),
　　'Then scratch the door or walls.'"

I said "You'll visit *here* no more,
　　If you attempt the Guy.
I'll have no bonfires on *my* floor—
And, as for scratching at the door,
　　I'd like to see you try!"

"AND SWING YOURSELF FROM SIDE TO SIDE"

"The Third was written to protect
    The interests of the Victim,
And tells us, as I recollect,
To treat him with a grave respect,
    And not to contradict him."

"That's plain," said I, "as Tare and Tret,
    To any comprehension:
I only wish *some* Ghosts I've met
Would not so *constantly* forget
    The maxim that you mention!"

"Perhaps," he said, "*you* first transgressed
    The laws of hospitality:
All Ghosts instinctively detest
The Man that fails to treat his guest
    With proper cordiality.

"If you address a Ghost as 'Thing!'
    Or strike him with a hatchet,
He is permitted by the King
To drop all *formal* parleying—
    And then you're *sure* to catch it!

"The Fourth prohibits trespassing
    Where other Ghosts are quartered:
And those convicted of the thing
(Unless when pardoned by the King)
    Must instantly be slaughtered.

"That simply means 'be cut up small':
    Ghosts soon unite anew:
The process scarcely hurts at all—
Not more than when *you're* what you call
    'Cut up' by a Review.

"The Fifth is one you may prefer
    That I should quote entire:—
The King must be addressed as 'Sir.'
This, from a simple courtier,
    Is all the Laws require:

"*But, should you wish to do the thing*
    With out-and-out politeness,
Accost him as 'My Goblin King!'
And always use, in answering,
    The phrase 'Your Royal Whiteness!'

"I'm getting rather hoarse, I fear,
    After so much reciting:
So, if you don't object, my dear,
We'll try a glass of bitter beer—
    I think it looks inviting."

CANTO III.

Scarmoges.

"AND did you really walk," said I,
    "On such a wretched night?
I always fancied Ghosts could fly—
If not exactly in the sky,
    Yet at a fairish height."

"It's very well," said he, "for Kings
    To soar above the earth:
But Phantoms often find that wings—
Like many other pleasant things—
    Cost more than they are worth.

"Spectres of course are rich, and so
    Can buy them from the Elves:
But *we* prefer to keep below—
They're stupid company, you know.
    For any but themselves:

"For, though they claim to be exempt
    From pride, they treat a Phantom
As something quite beneath contempt—
Just as no Turkey ever dreamt
    Of noticing a Bantam."

"They seem too proud," said I, "to go
    To houses such as mine.
Pray, how did they contrive to know
So quickly that 'the place was low,'
    And that I 'kept bad wine'?"

"Inspector Kobold came to you—"
    The little Ghost began.
Here I broke in—"Inspector who?
Inspecting Ghosts is something new!
    Explain yourself my man!"

"His name is Kobold," said my guest:
 "One of the Spectre order:
You'll very often see him dressed
In a yellow gown, a crimson vest,
 And a night-cap with a border.

"He tried the Brocken business first,
 But caught a sort of chill;
So came to England to be nursed,
And here it took the form of *thirst*,
 Which he complains of still.

"Port-wine, he says, when rich and sound,
 Warms his old bones like nectar:
And as the inns, where it is found,
Are his especial hunting-ground,
 We call him the *Inn-Spectre*."

I bore it—bore it like a man—
 This agonizing witticism!
And nothing could be sweeter than
My temper, till the Ghost began
 Some most provoking criticism.

"AND HERE IT TOOK THE FORM OF *THIRST*"

"Cooks need not be indulged in waste;
        Yet still you'd better teach them
Dishes should have *some sort* of taste.
Pray, why are all the cruets placed
        Where nobody can reach them?

"That man of yours will never earn
        His living as a waiter!
Is that queer *thing* supposed to burn?
(It's far too dismal a concern
        To call a Moderator).

"The duck was tender, but the peas
        Were very much too old:
And just remember, if you please,
The *next* time you have toasted cheese,
        Don't let them send it cold.

"You'd find the bread improved, I think,
        By getting better flour:
And have you anything to drink
That looks a *little* less like ink,
        And isn't *quite* so sour?"

Then, peering round with curious eyes,
        He muttered "Goodness gracious!"
And so went on to criticise—
"Your room's an inconvenient size:
        It's neither snug nor spacious.

"That narrow window, I expect,
        Serves but to let the dusk in—"
"But please," said I, "to recollect
'Twas fashioned by an architect
        Who pinned his faith on Ruskin!"

"I don't care who he was, Sir, or
        On whom he pinned his faith!
Constructed by whatever law,
So poor a job I never saw,
        As I'm a living Wraith!

"What a re-markable cigar!
        How much are they a dozen?"
I growled "No matter what they are!
You're getting as familiar
        As if you were my cousin!

"Now that's a thing *I will not stand,*
    And so I tell you flat."
"Aha," said he, "we're getting grand!"
(Taking a bottle in his hand)
    "I'll soon arrange for *that!*"

And here he took a careful aim,
    And gaily cried "Here goes!"
I tried to dodge it as it came,
But somehow caught it, all the same,
    Exactly on my nose.

And I remember nothing more
    That I can clearly fix,
Till I was sitting on the floor,
Repeating "Two and five are four,
    But *five and two* are six."

What really passed I never learned,
    Nor guessed: I only know
That, when at last my sense returned,
The lamp, neglected, dimly burned—
    The fire was getting low—

Through driving mists I seemed to see
    A Thing that smirked and smiled:
And found that he was giving me
A lesson in Biography,
    As if I were a child.

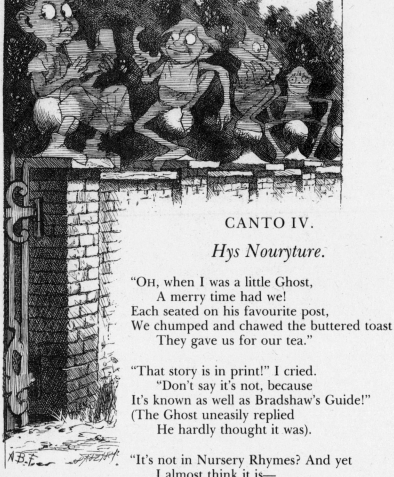

CANTO IV.

Hys Nouryture.

"OH, when I was a little Ghost,
   A merry time had we!
Each seated on his favourite post,
We chumped and chawed the buttered toast
   They gave us for our tea."

"That story is in print!" I cried.
   "Don't say it's not, because
It's known as well as Bradshaw's Guide!"
(The Ghost uneasily replied
   He hardly thought it was).

"It's not in Nursery Rhymes? And yet
   I almost think it is—
'Three little Ghosteses' were set
'On posteses,' you know, and ate
   Their 'buttered toasteses.'

"I have the book; so, if you doubt it—"
   I turned to search the shelf.
"Don't stir!" he cried. "We'll do without it:
I now remember all about it;
   I wrote the thing myself.

"It came out in a 'Monthly,' or
    At least my agent said it did:
Some literary swell, who saw
It, thought it seemed adapted for
    The Magazine he edited.

"My father was a Brownie, Sir;
    My mother was a Fairy.
The notion had occurred to her,
The children would be happier,
    If they were taught to vary.

"The notion soon became a craze;
    And, when it once began, she
Brought us all out in different ways—
One was a Pixy, two were Fays,
    Another was a Banshee;

"The Fetch and Kelpie went to school,
    And gave a lot of trouble;
Next came a Poltergeist and Ghoul,
And then two Trolls (which broke the rule),
    A Goblin, and a Double—

"(If that's a snuff-box on the shelf,"
    He added with a yawn,
"I'll take a pinch)—next came an Elf,
And then a Phantom (that's myself),
    And last, a Leprechaun.

"One day, some Spectres chanced to call,
    Dressed in the usual white:
I stood and watched them in the hall,
And couldn't make them out at all,
    They seemed so strange a sight.

"I wondered what on earth they were,
    That looked all head and sack;
But Mother told me not to stare,
And then she twitched me by the hair,
    And punched me in the back.

"Since then I've often wished that I
    Had been a Spectre born.
But what's the use?" (He heaved a sigh).
"*They* are the ghost-nobility,
    And look on *us* with scorn.

"My phantom-life was soon begun:
    When I was barely six,
I went out with an older one—
And just at first I thought it fun,
    And learned a lot of tricks.

"I've haunted dungeons, castles, towers—
    Wherever I was sent:
I've often sat and howled for hours,
Drenched to the skin with driving showers,
    Upon a battlement.

"It's quite old-fashioned now to groan
    When you begin to speak:
This is the newest thing in tone—"
And here (it chilled me to the bone)
    He gave an *awful* squeak.

"Perhaps," he added, "to *your* ear
    That sounds an easy thing?
Try it yourself, my little dear!
It took *me* something like a year,
    With constant practising.

"And when you've learned to squeak, my man
    And caught the double sob,
You're pretty much where you began:
Just try and gibber if you can!
    That's something *like* a job!

"*I've* tried it, and can only say
    I'm sure you couldn't do it, e-
ven if you practised night and day,
Unless you have a turn that way,
    And natural ingenuity.

"Shakspeare I think it is who treats
    Of Ghosts, in days of old,
Who 'gibbered in the Roman streets,'
Dressed, if you recollect, in sheets—
    They must have found it cold.

"I've often spent ten pounds on stuff,
    In dressing as a Double;
But, though it answers as a puff,
It never has effect enough
    To make it worth the trouble.

"Long bills soon quenched the little thirst
    I had for being funny.
The setting-up is always worst:
Such heaps of things you want at first,
    One must be made of money!

"For instance, take a Haunted Tower,
    With skull, cross-bones, and sheet;
Blue lights to burn (say) two an hour,
Condensing lens of extra power,
    And set of chains complete:

"What with the things you have to hire—
    The fitting on the robe—
And testing all the coloured fire—
The outfit of itself would tire
    The patience of a Job!

"And then they're so fastidious,
    The Haunted-House Committee:
I've often known them make a fuss
Because a Ghost was French, or Russ,
    Or even from the City!

"Some dialects are objected to—
    For one, the *Irish* brogue is:
And then, for all you have to do,
One pound a week they offer you,
    And find yourself in Bogies!"

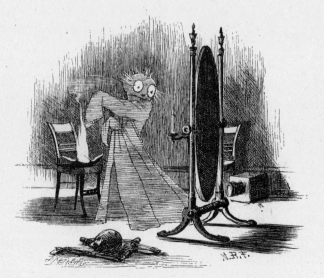

CANTO V.

Byckerment.

"Don't they consult the 'Victims,' though?"
        I said. "They should, by rights,
Give them a chance—because, you know,
The tastes of people differ so,
        Especially in Sprites."

The Phantom shook his head and smiled.
        "Consult them? Not a bit!
'Twould be a job to drive one wild,
To satisfy one single child—
        There'd be no end to it!"

"Of course you can't leave *children* free,"
        Said I, "to pick and choose:
But, in the case of men like me,
I think 'Mine Host' might fairly be
        Allowed to state his views."

He said "It really wouldn't pay—
        Folk are so full of fancies.
We visit for a single day,
And whether then we go, or stay,
        Depends on circumstances.

"And, though we don't consult 'Mine Host'
        Before the thing's arranged,
Still, if he often quits his post,
Or is not a well-mannered Ghost,
        Then you can have him changed.

"But if the host's a man like you—
        I mean a man of sense;
And if the house is not too new—"
"Why, what has *that*," said I, "to do
        With Ghost's convenience?"

"A new house does not suit, you know—
        It's such a job to trim it:
But, after twenty years or so,
The wainscotings begin to go,
        So twenty is the limit."

"To trim" was not a phrase I could
  Remember having heard:
"Perhaps," I said, "you'll be so good
As tell me what is understood
  Exactly by that word?"

"It means the loosening all the doors,"
  The Ghost replied, and laughed:
"It means the drilling holes by scores
In all the skirting-boards and floors,
  To make a thorough draught.

"You'll sometimes find that one or two
  Are all you really need
To let the wind come whistling through—
But *here* there'll be a lot to do!"
  I faintly gasped "Indeed!

"If I'd been rather later, I'll
  Be bound," I added, trying
(Most unsuccessfully) to smile,
"You'd have been busy all this while,
  Trimming and beautifying?"

"Why, no," said he; "perhaps I should
  Have stayed another minute—
But still no Ghost, that's any good,
Without an introduction would
  Have ventured to begin it."

"The proper thing, as you were late,
        Was certainly to go:
But, with the roads in such a state,
I got the Knight-Mayor's leave to wait
        For half an hour or so."

"Who's the Knight-Mayor?" I cried. Instead
        Of answering my question,
"Well! If you don't know *that*," he said,
"Either you never go to bed,
        Or you've a grand digestion!

"He goes about and sits on folk
        That eat too much at night:
His duties are to pinch, and poke,
And squeeze them till they nearly choke."
        (I said "It serves them right!")

"And folk that sup on things like these—
        He muttered, "eggs and bacon—
Lobster—and duck—and toasted cheese—
If they don't get an awful squeeze,
        I'm very much mistaken!

"He is immensely fat, and so
        Well suits the occupation:
In point of fact, if you must know,
We used to call him, years ago,
        The Mayor and Corporation!

"The day he was elected Mayor
        I *know* that every Sprite meant
To vote for *me*, but did not dare—
He was so frantic with despair
        And furious with excitement.

"When it was over, for a whim,
        He ran to tell the King;
And being the reverse of slim,
A two-mile trot was not for him
        A very easy thing.

"So, to reward him for his run
        (As it was baking hot,
And he was over twenty stone),
The King proceeded, half in fun,
        To knight him on the spot."

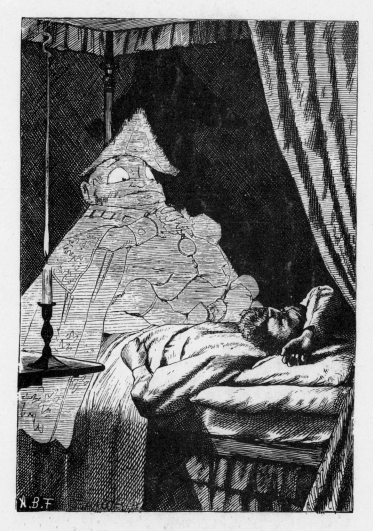

"HE GOES ABOUT AND SITS ON FOLK"

"'Twas a great liberty to take!"
　　(I fired up like a rocket).
"He did it just for punning's sake:
'The man,' says Johnson, 'that would make
　　A pun, would pick a pocket!'"

"A man," said he, "is not a King."
　　I argued for a while,
And did my best to prove the thing—
The Phantom merely listening
　　With a contemptuous smile.

At last, when, breath and patience spent,
　　I had recourse to smoking—
"Your *aim*," he said, "is excellent:
But—when you call it *argument*—
Of course you're only joking?"

Stung by his cold and snaky eye,
　　I roused myself at length
To say "At least I do defy
The veriest sceptic to deny
　　That union is strength!"

"That's true enough," said he, "yet stay—"
　　I listened in all meekness—
"*Union* is strength, I'm bound to say;
In fact, the thing's as clear as day;
　　But *onions*—are a weakness."

CANTO VI.

Dyscomfyture.

As one who strives a hill to climb,
  Who never climbed before:
Who finds it, in a little time,
Grow every moment less sublime,
  And votes the thing a bore:

Yet, having once begun to try,
  Dares not desert his quest,
But, climbing, ever keeps his eye
On one small hut against the sky,
  Wherein he hopes to rest:

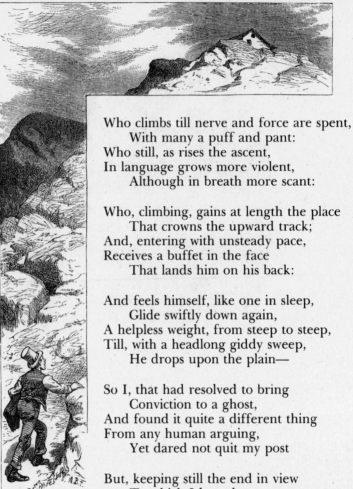

Who climbs till nerve and force are spent,
　　With many a puff and pant:
Who still, as rises the ascent,
In language grows more violent,
　　Although in breath more scant:

Who, climbing, gains at length the place
　　That crowns the upward track;
And, entering with unsteady pace,
Receives a buffet in the face
　　That lands him on his back:

And feels himself, like one in sleep,
　　Glide swiftly down again,
A helpless weight, from steep to steep,
Till, with a headlong giddy sweep,
　　He drops upon the plain—

So I, that had resolved to bring
　　Conviction to a ghost,
And found it quite a different thing
From any human arguing,
　　Yet dared not quit my post

But, keeping still the end in view
　　To which I hoped to come,
I strove to prove the matter true
By putting everything I knew
　　Into an axiom:

Commencing every single phrase
　　With 'therefore' or 'because,'
I blindly reeled, a hundred ways,
About the syllogistic maze,
　　Unconscious where I was.

Quoth he "That's regular clap-trap:
　　Don't bluster any more.

Now *do* be cool and take a nap!
Such a ridiculous old chap
    Was never seen before!

You're like a man I used to meet,
    Who got one day so furious
In arguing, the simple heat
Scorched both his slippers off his feet!"
    I said *"That's very curious!"*

"Well, it *is* curious, I agree,
    And sounds perhaps like fibs:
But still it's true as true can be—
As sure as your name's Tibbs," said he.
    I said "My name's *not* Tibbs."

"*Not* Tibbs!" he cried—his tone became
    A shade or two less hearty—
"Why, no," said I. "My proper name
Is Tibbets—" "Tibbets?" "Aye, the same."
    "Why, then YOU'RE NOT THE PARTY!"

With that he struck the board a blow
    That shivered half the glasses.
"Why couldn't you have told me so
Three quarters of an hour ago,
    You prince of all the asses?

"To walk four miles through mud and rain,
    To spend the night in smoking,
And then to find that it's in vain—
And I've to do it all again—
    It's really *too* provoking!

"Don't talk!" he cried, as I began
    To mutter some excuse.
"Who can have patience with a man
That's got no more discretion than
    An idiotic goose?

"To keep me waiting here, instead
    Of telling me at once
That this was not the house!" he said.
"There, that'll do—be off to bed!
    Don't gape like that, you dunce!"

"SCORCHED BOTH HIS SLIPPERS OFF HIS FEET"

"It's very fine to throw the blame
    On *me* in such a fashion!
Why didn't you enquire my name
The very minute that you came?"
    I answered in a passion.

"Of course it worries you a bit
    To come so far on foot—
But how was *I* to blame for it?"
"Well, well!" said he. "I must admit
    That isn't badly put.

"And certainly you've given me
    The best of wine and victual—
Excuse my violence," said he,
"But accidents like this, you see,
    They put one out a little.

"'Twas *my* fault after all, I find—
    Shake hands, old Turnip-top!"
The name was hardly to my mind,
But, as no doubt he meant it kind,
    I let the matter drop.

"Good-night, old Turnip-top, good-night!
    When I am gone, perhaps
They'll send you some inferior Sprite,
Who'll keep you in a constant fright
    And spoil your soundest naps.

"Tell him you'll stand no sort of trick;
    Then, if he leers and chuckles,
You just be handy with a stick
(Mind that it's pretty hard and thick)
    And rap him on the knuckles!

"Then carelessly remark 'Old coon!
    Perhaps you're not aware
That, if you don't behave, you'll soon
Be chuckling to another tune—
    And so you'd best take care!'

"That's the right way to cure a Sprite
    Of such-like goings-on—
But gacious me! It's getting light!
Good-night, old Turnip-top, good-night!"
    A nod, and he was gone.

CANTO VII.

Sad Souvenaunce.

"What's this?" I pondered. "Have I slept?
    Or can I have been drinking?"
But soon a gentler feeling crept
Upon me, and I sat and wept
    An hour or so, like winking.

"No need for Bones to hurry so!"
    I sobbed. "In fact, I doubt
If it was worth his while to go—
And who is Tibbs, I'd like to know,
    To make such work about?

"If Tibbs is anything like me,
    It's *possible*," I said,
"He won't be over-pleased to be
Dropped in upon at half-past three,
    After he's snug in bed.

"And if Bones plagues him anyhow—
    Squeaking and all the rest of it,
As he was doing here just now—
I prophesy there'll be a row,
    And Tibbs will have the best of it!"

"AND TIBBS WILL HAVE THE BEST OF IT"

Then, as my tears could never bring
    The friendly Phantom back,
It seemed to me the proper thing
To mix another glass, and sing
    The following Coronach.

'And art thou gone, beloved Ghost?
    Best of Familiars!
Nay then, farewell, my duckling roast,
Farewell, farewell, my tea and toast,
    My meerschaum and cigars!

'The hues of life are dull and gray,
    The sweets of life insipid,
When thou, my charmer, art away—
Old Brick, or rather, let me say,
    Old Parallelepiped!'

Instead of singing Verse the Third,
    I ceased—abruptly, rather:
But, after such a splendid word,
I felt that it would be absurd
    To try it any farther.

So with a yawn I went my way
 To seek the welcome downy,
And slept, and dreamed till break of day
Of Poltergeist and Fetch and Fay
 And Leprechaun and Brownie!

For years I've not been visited
 By any kind of Sprite;
Yet still they echo in my head,
Those parting words, so kindly said,
 "Old Turnip-top, good-night!"

ECHOES.

LADY Clara Vere de Vere
Was eight years old, she said:
Every ringlet, lightly shaken, ran itself in golden thread.

She took her little porringer:
Of me she shall not win renown:
For the baseness of its nature shall have strength to
  drag her down.

"Sisters and brothers, little Maid?
There stands the Inspector at thy door:
Like a dog he hunts for boys who know not two and
  two are four."

"Kind words are more than coronets,"
She said, and wondering looked at me:
"It is the dead unhappy night, and I must hurry home
  to tea."

A SEA DIRGE.

THERE are certain things—as, a spider, a ghost,
  The income-tax, gout, an umbrella for three—
That I hate, but the thing that I hate the most
    Is a thing they call the Sea.

Pour some salt water over the floor—
  Ugly I'm sure you'll allow it to be:
Suppose it extended a mile or more,
    That's very like the Sea.

Beat a dog till it howls outright—
  Cruel, but all very well for a spree:
Suppose that he did so day and night,
    That would be like the Sea.

I had a vision of nursery-maids;
  Tens of thousands passed by me—
All leading children with wooden spades,
    And this was by the Sea.

Who invented those spades of wood?
  Who was it cut them out of the tree?
None, I think, but an idiot could—
    Or one that loved the Sea.

"AND THIS WAS BY THE SEA"

It is pleasant and dreamy, no doubt, to float
  With 'thoughts as boundless, and souls as free':
But, suppose you are very unwell in the boat,
    How do you like the Sea?

There is an insect that people avoid
  (Whence is derived the verb 'to flee').
Where have you been by it most annoyed?
    In lodgings by the Sea.

If you like your coffee with sand for dregs,
  A decided hint of salt in your tea,
And a fishy taste in the very eggs—
    By all means choose the Sea.

And if, with these dainties to drink and eat,
  You prefer not a vestige of grass or tree,
And a chronic state of wet in your feet,
    Then—I recommend the Sea.

For *I* have friends who dwell by the coast—
  Pleasant friends they are to me!
It is when I am with them I wonder most
    That any one likes the Sea.

"I HAVE A HORSE"

They take me a walk: though tired and stiff,
  To climb the heights I madly agree;
And, after a tumble or so from the cliff,
  They kindly suggest the Sea.

I try the rocks, and I think it cool
  That they laugh with such an excess of glee,
As I heavily slip into every pool
  That skirts the cold cold Sea.

YE CARPETTE KNYGHTE.

I have a horse—a ryghte goode horse—
  Ne doe Y envye those
Who scoure ye playne yn headye course
  Tyll soddayne on theyre nose
They lyghte wyth unexpected force—
  Yt ys—a horse of clothes.

I have a saddel—"Say'st thou soe?
  Wyth styrruppes, Knyghte, to boote?"
I sayde not that—I answere "Noe"—
  Yt lacketh such, I woote:
Yt ys a mutton-saddel, loe!
  Parte of ye fleecye brute.

I have a bytte—a ryghte good bytte—
  As shall bee seene yn tyme.
Ye jawe of horse yt wyll not fytte;
  Yts use ys more sublyme.
Fayre Syr, how deemest thou of yt?
  Yt ys—thys bytte of rhyme.

HIAWATHA'S PHOTOGRAPHING.

[In an age of imitation, I can claim no special merit for this slight attempt
at doing what is known to be so easy. Any fairly practised writer, with
the slightest ear for rhythm, could compose, for hours together, in the
easy running metre of 'The Song of Hiawatha.' Having, then, distinctly
stated that I challenge no attention in the following little poem to its
merely verbal jingle, I must beg the candid reader to confine his criticism
to its treatment of the subject.]

FROM his shoulder Hiawatha
Took the camera of rosewood,
Made of sliding, folding rosewood;
Neatly put it all together.
In its case it lay compactly,
Folded into nearly nothing;
But he opened out the hinges,
Pushed and pulled the joints and hinges,
Till it looked all squares and oblongs,
Like a complicated figure
In the Second Book of Euclid.
  This he perched upon a tripod—
Crouched beneath its dusky cover—
Stretched his hand, enforcing silence—
Said "Be motionless, I beg you!"

"FIRST THE GOVERNOR, THE FATHER"

Mystic, awful was the process.
  All the family in order
Sat before him for their pictures:
Each in turn, as he was taken,
Volunteered his own suggestions,
His ingenious suggestions.
  First the Governor, the Father:
He suggested velvet curtains
Looped about a massy pillar;
And the corner of a table,
Of a rosewood dining-table.
He would hold a scroll of something,
Hold it firmly in his left-hand;
He would keep his right-hand buried
(Like Napoleon) in his waistcoat;
He would contemplate the distance
With a look of pensive meaning,
As of ducks that die in tempests.
  Grand, heroic was the notion:
Yet the picture failed entirely:
Failed, because he moved a little,
Moved, because he couldn't help it.
  Next, his better half took courage;
She would have her picture taken.
She came dressed beyond description,
Dressed in jewels and in satin
Far too gorgeous for an empress.
Gracefully she sat down sideways,
With a simper scarcely human,
Holding in her hand a bouquet
Rather larger than a cabbage.
All the while that she was sitting,
Still the lady chattered, chattered,
Like a monkey in the forest.
"Am I sitting still?" she asked him.
"Is my face enough in profile?
Shall I hold the bouquet higher?
Will it come into the picture?"
And the picture failed completely.
  Next the Son, the Stunning-Cantab:
He suggested curves of beauty,
Curves pervading all his figure,
Which the eye might follow onward,
Till they centered in the breast-pin,
Centered in the golden breast-pin.
He had learnt it all from Ruskin
(Author of 'The Stones of Venice,'
'Seven Lamps of Architecture,'
'Modern Painters,' and some others);

"NEXT THE SON, THE STUNNING-CANTAB"

And perhaps he had not fully
Understood his author's meaning;
But, whatever was the reason,
All was fruitless, as the picture
Ended in an utter failure.

   Next to him the eldest daughter:
She suggested very little,
Only asked if he would take her
With her look of 'passive beauty.'

   Her idea of passive beauty
Was a squinting of the left-eye,
Was a drooping of the right-eye,
Was a smile that went up sideways
To the corner of the nostrils.

   Hiawatha, when she asked him,
Took no notice of the question,
Looked as if he hadn't heard it;
But, when pointedly appealed to,
Smiled in his peculiar manner,
Coughed and said it 'didn't matter,'
Bit his lip and changed the subject.

   Nor in this was he mistaken,
As the picture failed completely.

   So in turn the other sisters.

   Last, the youngest son was taken:
Very rough and thick his hair was,
Very round and red his face was,
Very dusty was his jacket,
Very fidgety his manner.
And his overbearing sisters
Called him names he disapproved of:
Called him Johnny, 'Daddy's Darling,'
Called him Jacky, 'Scrubby School-boy.'
And, so awful was the picture,
In comparison the others
Seemed, to his bewildered fancy,
To have partially succeeded.

   Finally my Hiawatha
Tumbled all the tribe together,
('Grouped' is not the right expression),
And, as happy chance would have it,
Did at last obtain a picture
Where the faces all succeeded:
Each came out a perfect likeness.

   Then they joined and all abused it,
Unrestrainedly abused it,
As 'the worst and ugliest picture
They could possibly have dreamed of.
Giving one such strange expressions—

"NEXT TO HIM THE ELDEST DAUGHTER"

"LAST, THE YOUNGEST SON WAS TAKEN"

Sullen, stupid, pert expressions.
Really any one would take us
(Any one that did not know us)
For the most unpleasant people!'
(Hiawatha seemed to think so,
Seemed to think it not unlikely).
All together rang their voices,
Angry, loud, discordant voices,
As of dogs that howl in concert,
As of cats that wail in chorus.

But my Hiawatha's patience,
His politeness and his patience,
Unaccountably had vanished,
And he left that happy party.
Neither did he leave them slowly,
With the calm deliberation,
The intense deliberation
Of a photographic artist:
But he left them in a hurry,
Left them in a mighty hurry,
Stating that he would not stand it,
Stating in emphatic language
What he'd be before he'd stand it.

Hurriedly he packed his boxes:
Hurriedly the porter trundled
On a barrow all his boxes:
Hurriedly he took his ticket:

Hurriedly the train received him:
Thus departed Hiawatha.

MELANCHOLETTA.

WITH saddest music all day long
    She soothed her secret sorrow:
At night she sighed "I fear 'twas wrong
    Such cheerful words to borrow.
Dearest, a sweeter, sadder song
    I'll sing to thee to-morrow."

I thanked her, but I could not say
    That I was glad to hear it:
I left the house at break of day,
    And did not venture near it
Till time, I hoped, had worn away
    Her grief, for nought could cheer it!

My dismal sister! Couldst thou know
    The wretched home thou keepest!
Thy brother, drowned in daily woe,
    Is thankful when thou sleepest;
For if I laugh, however low,
    When thou'rt awake, thou weepest!

I took my sister t'other day
    (Excuse the slang expression)
To Sadler's Wells to see the play,
    In hopes the new impression
Might in her thoughts, from grave to gay
    Effect some slight digression.

I asked three gay young dogs from town
    To join us in our folly,
Whose mirth, I thought, might serve to drown
    My sister's melancholy:
The lively Jones, the sportive Brown,
    And Robinson the jolly.

The maid announced the meal in tones
    That I myself had taught her,
Meant to allay my sister's moans
    Like oil on troubled water:
I rushed to Jones, the lively Jones,
    And begged him to escort her.

"AT NIGHT SHE SIGHED"

Vainly he strove, with ready wit,
 To joke about the weather—
To ventilate the last *'on dit'*—
 To quote the price of leather—
She groaned "Here I and Sorrow sit:
 Let us lament together!"

I urged "You're wasting time, you know
 Delay will spoil the venison."
"My heart is wasted with my woe!
 There is no rest—in Venice, on
The Bridge of Sighs!" she quoted low
 From Byron and from Tennyson.

I need not tell of soup and fish
 In solemn silence swallowed,
The sobs that ushered in each dish,
 And its departure followed,
Nor yet my suicidal wish
 To *be* the cheese I hollowed.

Some desperate attempts were made
 To start a conversation;
"Madam," the sportive Brown essayed,
 "Which kind of recreation,
Hunting or fishing, have you made
 Your special occupation?"

Her lips curved downwards instantly,
 As if of india-rubber.
"Hounds *in full cry* I like," said she:
 (Oh how I longed to snub her!)
"Of fish, a whale's the one for me,
 It is so full of blubber!"

The night's performance was "King John."
 "It's dull," she wept, "and so-so!"
A while I let her tears flow on,
 She said they soothed her woe so!
At length the curtain rose upon
 'Bombastes Furioso.'

In vain we roared; in vain we tried
 To rouse her into laughter:
Her pensive glances wandered wide
 From orchestra to rafter—
"*Tier upon tier!*" she said, and sighed;
 And silence followed after.

A VALENTINE.

[Sent to a friend who had complained that I was glad enough to see him when he came, but didn't seem to miss him if he stayed away.]

AND cannot pleasures, while they last,
Be actual unless, when past,
They leave us shuddering and aghast,
    With anguish smarting?
And cannot friends be firm and fast,
    And yet bear parting?

And must I then, at Friendship's call,
Calmly resign the little all
(Trifling, I grant, it is and small)
    I have of gladness,
And lend my being to the thrall
    Of gloom and sadness?

And think you that I should be dumb,
And full *dolorum omnium,*
Excepting when *you* choose to come
    And share my dinner?
At other times be sour and glum
    And daily thinner?

Must he then only live to weep,
Who'd prove his friendship true and deep?
By day a lonely shadow creep,
    At night-time languish,
Oft raising in his broken sleep
    The moan of anguish?

The lover, if for certain days
His fair one be denied his gaze,
Sinks not in grief and wild amaze,
    But, wiser wooer,
He spends the time in writing lays,
    And posts them to her.

And if the verse flow free and fast,
Till even the poet is aghast,
A touching Valentine at last
    The post shall carry,
When thirteen days are gone and past
    Of February.

Farewell, dear friend, and when we meet,
In desert waste or crowded street,
Perhaps before this week shall fleet,
    Perhaps to-morrow,
I trust to find *your* heart the seat
    Of wasting sorrow.

THE THREE VOICES.

The First Voice.

HE trilled a carol fresh and free:
He laughed aloud for very glee:
There came a breeze from off the sea:

It passed athwart the glooming flat—
It fanned his forehead as he sat—
It lightly bore away his hat,

All to the feet of one who stood
Like maid enchanted in a wood,
Frowning as darkly as she could.

With huge umbrella, lank and brown,
Unerringly she pinned it down,
Right through the centre of the crown.

Then, with an aspect cold and grim,
Regardless of its battered rim,
She took it up and gave it him.

A while like one in dreams he stood,
Then faltered forth his gratitude
In words just short of being rude:

For it had lost its shape and shine,
And it had cost him four-and-nine,
And he was going out to dine.

"To dine!" she sneered in acid tone.
"To bend thy being to a bone
Clothed in a radiance not its own!"

The tear-drop trickled to his chin:
There was a meaning in her grin
That made him feel on fire within.

"Term it not 'radiance,'" said he:
"'Tis solid nutriment to me.
Dinner is Dinner: Tea is Tea."

And she "Yea so? Yet wherefore cease?
Let thy scant knowledge find increase.
Say 'Men are Men, and Geese are Geese.'"

He moaned: he knew not what to say.
The thought "That I could get away!"
Strove with the thought "But I must stay."

"To dine!" she shrieked in dragon-wrath.
"To swallow wines all foam and froth!
To simper at a table-cloth!

"UNERRINGLY SHE PINNED IT DOWN"

"Say, can thy noble spirit stoop
To join the gormandising troop
Who find a solace in the soup?

"Canst thou desire or pie or puff?
Thy well-bred manners were enough,
Without such gross material stuff."

"Yet well-bred men," he faintly said,
"Are not unwilling to be fed:
Nor are they well without the bread."

Her visage scorched him ere she spoke:
"There are," she said, "a kind of folk
Who have no horror of a joke.

"Such wretches live: they take their share
Of common earth and common air:
We come across them here and there:

"We grant them—there is no escape—
A sort of semi-human shape
Suggestive of the man-like Ape."

"In all such theories," said he,
"One fixed exception there must be
That is, the Present Company."

Baffled, she gave a wolfish bark:
He, aiming blindly in the dark,
With random shaft had pierced the mark.

She felt that her defeat was plain,
Yet madly strove with might and main
To get the upper hand again.

Fixing her eyes upon the beach,
As though unconscious of his speech,
She said "Each gives to more than each."

He could not answer yea or nay:
He faltered "Gifts may pass away."
Yet knew not what he meant to say.

"If that be so," she straight replied,
"Each heart with each doth coincide.
What boots it? For the world is wide."

"HE FALTERED 'GIFTS MAY PASS AWAY.'"

"The world is but a Thought," said he:
"The vast unfathomable sea
Is but a Notion—unto me,"

And darkly fell her answer dread
Upon his unresisting head,
Like half a hundredweight of lead.

"The Good and Great must ever shun
That reckless and abandoned one
Who stoops to perpetrate a pun.

"The man that smokes—that reads the *Times*—
That goes to Christmas Pantomimes—
Is capable of *any* crimes!"

He felt it was his turn to speak,
And, with a shamed and crimson cheek,
Moaned "This is harder than Bezique!"

But when she asked him "Wherefore so?"
He felt his very whiskers glow,
And frankly owned "I do not know."

While, like broad waves of golden grain,
Or sunlit hues on cloistered pane,
His colour came and went again.

Pitying his obvious distress,
Yet with a tinge of bitterness,
She said "The More exceeds the Less."

"A truth of such undoubted weight,"
He urged, "and so extreme in date,
It were superfluous to state."

Roused into sudden passion, she
In tone of cold malignity:
"To others, yea: but not to thee."

But when she saw him quail and quake,
And when he urged "For pity's sake!"
Once more in gentle tone she spake.

"Thought in the mind doth still abide:
That is by Intellect supplied,
And within that Idea doth hide:

"THIS IS HARDER THAN BEZIQUE!"

"And he, that yearns the truth to know,
Still further inwardly may go,
And find Idea from Notion flow:

"And thus the chain, that sages sought,
Is to a glorious circle wrought,
For Notion hath its source in Thought."

So passed they on with even pace:
Yet gradually one might trace
A shadow growing on his face.

The Second Voice.

THEY walked beside the wave-worn beach
Her tongue was very apt to teach,
And now and then he did beseech

She would abate her dulcet tone,
Because the talk was all her own,
And he was dull as any drone.

She urged "No cheese is made of chalk":
And ceaseless flowed her dreary talk,
Tuned to the footfall of a walk.

Her voice was very full and rich,
And, when at length she asked him "Which?"
It mounted to its highest pitch.

He a bewildered answer gave,
Drowned in the sullen moaning wave,
Lost in the echoes of the cave.

He answered her he knew not what:
Like shaft from bow at random shot,
He spoke, but she regarded not.

She waited not for his reply,
But with a downward leaden eye
Went on as if he were not by:

Sound argument and grave defence,
Strange questions raised on "Why?" and "Whence?"
And wildly tangled evidence.

When he, with racked and whirling brain,
Feebly implored her to explain,
She simply said it all again.

Wrenched with an agony intense,
He spake, neglecting Sound and Sense,
And careless of all consequence:

"Mind—I believe—is Essence—Ent—
Abstract—that is—an Accident—
    Which we—that is to say—I meant—"

When, with quick breath and cheeks all flushed,
At length his speech was somewhat hushed,
She looked at him, and he was crushed.

It needed not her calm reply:
She fixed him with a stony eye,
And he could neither fight nor fly,

While she dissected, word by word,
His speech, half guessed at and half heard,
As might a cat a little bird.

Then, having wholly overthrown
His views, and stripped them to the bone,
Proceeded to unfold her own.

"Shall Man be Man? And shall he miss
Of other thoughts no thought but this,
Harmonious dews of sober bliss?

"What boots it? Shall his fevered eye
Through towering nothingness descry
The grisly phantom hurry by?

"And hear dumb shrieks that fill the air;
See mouths that gape, and eyes that stare
And redden in the dusky glare?

"HE SPAKE, NEGLECTING SOUND AND SENSE."

"SHALL MAN BE MAN?"

"The meadows breathing amber light,
The darkness toppling from the height,
The feathery train of granite Night?

"Shall he, grown gray among his peers,
Through the thick curtain of his tears
Catch glimpses of his earlier years,

"And hear the sounds he knew of yore,
Old shufflings on the sanded floor,
Old knuckles tapping at the door?

"Yet still before him as he flies
One pallid form shall ever rise,
And, bodying forth in glassy eyes

"The vision of a vanished good,
Low peering through the tangled wood,
Shall freeze the current of his blood."

Still from each fact, with skill uncouth
And savage rapture, like a tooth
She wrenched some slow reluctant truth.

Till, like a silent water-mill,
When summer suns have dried the rill,
She reached a full stop, and was still.

Dead calm succeeded to the fuss,
As when the loaded omnibus
Has reached the railway terminus:

When, for the tumult of the street,
Is heard the engine's stifled beat,
The velvet tread of porters' feet.

With glance that ever sought the ground,
She moved her lips without a sound,
And every now and then she frowned.

He gazed upon the sleeping sea,
And joyed in its tranquillity,
And in that silence dead, but she

To muse a little space did seem,
Then, like the echo of a dream,
Harped back upon her threadbare theme.

Still an attentive ear he lent
But could not fathom what she meant:
She was not deep, nor eloquent.

He marked the ripple on the sand:
The even swaying of her hand
Was all that he could understand.

He saw in dreams a drawing-room,
Where thirteen wretches sat in gloom,
Waiting—he thought he knew for whom:

He saw them drooping here and there,
Each feebly huddled on a chair,
In attitudes of blank despair:

Oysters were not more mute than they,
For all their brains were pumped away,
And they had nothing more to say—

Save one, who groaned "Three hours are gone!"
Who shrieked "We'll wait no longer, John!
Tell them to set the dinner on!"

The vision passed: the ghosts were fled:
He saw once more that woman dread:
He heard once more the words she said.

He left her, and he turned aside:
He sat and watched the coming tide
Across the shores so newly dried.

"HE SAT AND WATCHED THE COMING TIDE"

He wondered at the waters clear,
The breeze that whispered in his ear,
The billows heaving far and near,

And why he had so long preferred
To hang upon her every word:
"In truth," he said, "it was absurd."

The Third Voice.

NOT long this transport held its place:
Within a little moment's space
Quick tears were raining down his face.

His heart stood still, aghast with fear;
A wordless voice, nor far nor near,
He seemed to hear and not to hear.

"Tears kindle not the doubtful spark.
If so, why not? Of this remark
The bearings are profoundly dark."

"HE GROANED AGHAST"

"Her speech," he said, "hath caused this pain.
Easier I count it to explain
The jargon of the howling main,

"Or, stretched beside some babbling brook,
To con with inexpressive look,
An unintelligible book."

Low spake the voice within his head,
In words imagined more than said,
Soundless as ghost's intended tread:

"If thou art duller than before,
Why quittedst thou the voice of lore?
Why not endure, expecting more?"

"Rather than that," he groaned aghast,
"I'd writhe in depths of cavern vast,
Some loathly vampire's rich repast."

"'Twere hard," it answered, "themes immense
To coop within the narrow fence
That rings *thy* scant intelligence."

"Not so," he urged, "nor once alone:
But there was something in her tone
That chilled me to the very bone.

"Her style was anything but clear,
And most unpleasantly severe;
Her epithets were very queer.

"And yet, so grand were her replies,
I could not choose but deem her wise;
I did not dare to criticise;

"Nor did I leave her, till she went
So deep in tangled argument
That all my powers of thought were spent."

A little whisper inly slid,
"Yet truth is truth: you know you did."
A little wink beneath the lid.

And, sickened with excess of dread,
Prone to the dust he bent his head,
And lay like one three-quarters dead.

"TORTURED, UNAIDED, AND ALONE"

The whisper left him—like a breeze
Lost in the depths of leafy trees—
Left him by no means at his ease.

Once more he weltered in despair,
With hands, through denser-matted hair,
More tightly clenched than then they were.

When, bathed in Dawn of living red,
Majestic frowned the mountain head,
"Tell me my fault," was all he said.

When, at high Noon, the blazing sky
Scorched in his head each haggard eye,
Then keenest rose his weary cry.

And when at Eve the unpitying sun
Smiled grimly on the solemn fun,
"Alack," he sighed, "what *have* I done?"

But saddest, darkest was the sight,
When the cold grasp of leaden Night
Dashed him to earth, and held him tight.

Tortured, unaided, and alone,
Thunders were silence to his groan,
Bagpipes sweet music to its tone:

"What? Ever thus, in dismal round,
Shall Pain and Mystery profound
Pursue me like a sleepless hound,

"With crimson-dashed and eager jaws,
Me, still in ignorance of the cause,
Unknowing what I broke of laws?"

The whisper to his ear did seem
Like echoed flow of silent stream,
Or shadow of forgotten dream,

The whisper trembling in the wind:
"Her fate with thine was intertwined,"
So spake it in his inner mind:

"Each orbed on each a baleful star:
Each proved the other's blight and bar:
Each unto each were best, most far:

"A SCARED DULLARD, GIBBERING LOW"

"Yea, each to each was worse than foe:
Thou, a scared dullard, gibbering low,
AND SHE, AN AVALANCHE OF WOE!"

TÈMA CON VARIAZIÓNI.

[WHY is it that Poetry has never yet been subjected to that process of
Dilution which has proved so advantageous to her sister-art Music? The
Diluter gives us first a few notes of some well-known Air, then a dozen
bars of his own, then a few more notes of the Air, and so on alternately:
thus saving the listener, if not from all risk of recognising the melody
at all, at least from the too-exciting transports which it might produce
in a more concentrated form. The process is termed "setting" by Com-
posers, and any one, that has ever experienced the emotion of being
unexpectedly set down in a heap of mortar, will recognise the truthfulness
of this happy phrase.

For truly, just as the genuine Epicure lingers lovingly over a morsel
of supreme Venison—whose every fibre seems to murmur "Excelsior!"—
yet swallows, ere returning to the toothsome dainty, great mouthfuls of
oatmeal-porridge and winkles: and just as the perfect Connoisseur in
Claret permits himself but one delicate sip, and then tosses off a pint or
more of boarding-school beer: so also——

I NEVER loved a dear Gazelle—
Nor anything that cost me much:
High prices profit those who sell,
But why should I be fond of such?

To glad me with his soft black eye
My son comes trotting home from school;
He's had a fight, but can't tell why—
He always was a little fool!

But, when he came to know me well,
He kicked me out, her testy Sire:
And when I stained my hair, that Belle,
Might note the change, and thus admire

And love me, it was sure to dye
A muddy green or staring blue:
Whilst one might trace, with half an eye,
The still triumphant carrot through.

A GAME OF FIVES.

FIVE little girls, of Five, Four, Three, Two, One:
Rolling on the hearthrug, full of tricks and fun.

Five rosy girls, in years from Ten to Six:
Sitting down to lessons—no more time for tricks.

Five growing girls, from Fifteen to Eleven:
Music, Drawing, Languages, and food enough for seven!

Five winsome girls, from Twenty to Sixteen:
Each young man that calls, I say "Now tell me which you *mean!*"

Five dashing girls, the youngest Twenty-one:
But, if nobody proposes, what is there to be done?

Five showy girls—but Thirty is an age
When girls may be *engaging,* but they somehow don't *engage.*

Five dressy girls, of Thirty-one or more:
So gracious to the shy young men they snubbed so much before!

    *   *   *   *   *

Five *passé* girls—Their age? Well, never mind!
We jog along together, like the rest of human kind:
But the quondam "careless bachelor" begins to think he knows
The answer to that ancient problem "how the money goes"!

"NOW TELL ME WHICH YOU *MEAN*!"

POETA FIT, NON NASCITUR.

"How shall I be a poet?
  How shall I write in rhyme?
You told me once 'the very wish
  Partook of the sublime.'
Then tell me how! Don't put me off
  With your 'another time'!"

The old man smiled to see him,
  To hear his sudden sally;
He liked the lad to speak his mind
  Enthusiastically;
And thought "There's no hum-drum in him,
  Nor any shilly-shally."

"And would you be a poet
  Before you've been to school?
Ah, well! I hardly thought you
  So absolute a fool.
First learn to be spasmodic—
  A very simple rule.

"For first you write a sentence,
  And then you chop it small;
Then mix the bits, and sort them out
  Just as they chance to fall:
The order of the phrases makes
  No difference at all.

"Then, if you'd be impressive,
  Remember what I say,
That abstract qualities begin
  With capitals alway:
The True, the Good, the Beautiful—
  Those are the things that pay!

"Next, when you are describing
  A shape, or sound, or tint;
Don't state the matter plainly,
  But put it in a hint;
And learn to look at all things
  With a sort of mental squint."

"For instance, if I wished, Sir,
  Of mutton-pies to tell,
Should I say 'dreams of fleecy flocks
  Pent in a wheaten cell'?"
"Why, yes," the old man said: "that phrase
  Would answer very well.

"Then fourthly, there are epithets
  That suit with any word—
As well as Harvey's Reading Sauce
  With fish or flesh, or bird—
Of these 'wild,' 'lonely,' 'weary,' 'strange,'
  Are much to be preferred."

"And will it do, O will it do
  To take them in a lump—
As 'the wild man went his weary way
  To a strange and lonely pump'?"
"Nay, nay! You must not hastily
  To such conclusions jump.

"Such epithets, like pepper,
  Give zest to what you write;
And, if you strew them sparely,
  They whet the appetite:
But if you lay them on too thick,
  You spoil the matter quite!

"THE WILD MAN WENT HIS WEARY WAY"

"Last, as to the arrangement:
　　Your reader, you should show him,
Must take what information he
　　Can get, and look for no im-
mature disclosure of the drift
　　And purpose of your poem.

"Therefore, to test his patience—
　　How much he can endure—
Mention no places, names, or dates,
　　And evermore be sure
Throughout the poem to be found
　　Consistently obscure.

"First fix upon the limit
　　To which it shall extend:
Then fill it up with 'Padding'
　　(Beg some of any friend):
Your great SENSATION-STANZA
　　You place towards the end."

"And what is a Sensation,
　　Grandfather, tell me, pray?
I think I never heard the word
　　So used before to-day:
Be kind enough to mention one
　　'Exempli gratiâ.'"

And the old man, looking sadly
　　Across the garden-lawn,
Where here and there a dew-drop
　　Yet glittered in the dawn,
Said "Go to the Adelphi,
　　And see the 'Colleen Bawn.'

"The word is due to Boucicault—
　　The theory is his,
Where Life becomes a Spasm,
　　And History a Whiz:
If that is not Sensation,
　　I don't know what it is.

"Now try your hand, ere Fancy
　　Have lost its present glow—"
"And then," his grandson added,
　　"We'll publish it, you know:
Green cloth—gold-lettered at the back—
　　In duodecimo!"

Then proudly smiled that old man
  To see the eager lad
Rush madly for his pen and ink
  And for his blotting-pad—
But, when he thought of *publishing,*
  His face grew stern and sad.

SIZE AND TEARS.

WHEN on the sandy shore I sit,
    Beside the salt sea-wave,
And fall into a weeping fit
    Because I dare not shave—
A little whisper at my ear
Enquires the reason of my fear.

I answer "If that ruffian Jones
    Should recognise me here,
He'd bellow out my name in tones
    Offensive to the ear:
He chaffs me so on being stout
(A thing that always puts me out)."

Ah me! I see him on the cliff!
    Farewell, farewell to hope,
If he should look this way, and if
    He's got his telescope!
To whatsoever place I flee,
My odious rival follows me!

For every night, and everywhere,
    I meet him out at dinner;
And when I've found some charming fair,
    And vowed to die or win her,
The wretch (he's thin and I am stout)
Is sure to come and cut me out!

The girls (just like them!) all agree
    To praise J. Jones, Esquire:
I asked them what on earth they see
    About him to admire?
They cry "He is so sleek and slim,
It's quite a treat to look at him!"

They vanish in tobacco smoke,
    Those visionary maids—
I feel a sharp and sudden poke
    Between the shoulder-blades—
"Why, Brown, my boy! You're growing stout!"
(I told you he would find me out!)

"My growth is not *your* business, Sir!"
    "No more it is, my boy!
But if it's *yours*, as I infer,
    Why, Brown, I give you joy!
A man, whose business prospers so,
Is just the sort of man to know!

"HE'S THIN AND I AM STOUT"

"It 's hardly safe, though, talking here—
   I'd best get out of reach:
For such a weight as yours, I fear,
   Must shortly sink the beach!"—
Insult me thus because I'm stout!
I vow I'll go and call him out!

ATALANTA IN CAMDEN-TOWN.

AY, 'twas here, on this spot,
      In that summer of yore,
Atalanta did not
      Vote my presence a bore,
Nor reply to my tenderest talk "She had heard all that
      nonsense before."

She'd the brooch I had bought
      And the necklace and sash on,
And her heart, as I thought,
      Was alive to my passion;
And she'd done up her hair in the style that the
      Empress had brought into fashion.

I had been to the play
    With my pearl of a Peri—
But, for all I could say,
    She declared she was weary,
That "the place was so crowded and hot, and she
    couldn't abide that Dundreary."

Then I thought "'Tis for me
    That she whines and she whimpers!"
And it soothed me to see
    Those sensational simpers,
And I said "This is scrumptious!"—a phrase I had
    learned from the Devonshire shrimpers.

And I vowed "'Twill be said
    I'm a fortunate fellow,
When the breakfast is spread,
    When the topers are mellow,
When the foam of the bride-cake is white, and the
    fierce orange-blossoms are yellow!"

O that languishing yawn!
    O those eloquent eyes!
I was drunk with the dawn
    Of a splendid surmise—
I was stung by a look, I was slain by a tear, by a
    tempest of sighs.

And I whispered "'Tis time!
    Is not Love at its deepest?
Shall we squander Life's prime,
    While thou waitest and weepest?
Let us settle it, License or Banns?—though undoubtedly
    Banns are the cheapest."

"Ah, my Hero," said I,
    "Let me be thy Leander!"
But I lost her reply—
    Something ending with "gander"—
For the omnibus rattled so loud that no mortal could
    quite understand her.

THE LANG COORTIN'.

THE ladye she stood at her lattice high,
    Wi' her doggie at her feet;
Through the lattice she can spy
    The passers in the street.

"There's one that standeth at the door,
    And tirleth at the pin:
Now speak and say, my popinjay,
    If I sall let him in."

Then up and spake the popinjay
    That flew abune her head:
"Gae let him in that tirls the pin:
    He cometh thee to wed."

O when he cam' the parlour in,
    A woeful man was he!
"And dinna ye ken your lover agen,
    Sae well that loveth thee?"

"And how was I ken ye loved me, Sir,
    That have been sae lang away?
And how wad I ken ye loved me, Sir?
    Ye never telled me sae."

Said—"Ladye dear," and the salt, salt tear
    Cam' rinnin' doon his cheek,
"I have sent thee tokens of my love
    This many and many a week.

"O didna ye get the rings, Ladye,
    The rings o' the gowd sae fine?
I wot that I have sent to thee
    Four score, four score and nine."

"They cam' to me," said that fair ladye.
    "Wow, they were flimsie things!"
Said—"that chain o' gowd, my doggie to howd,
    It is made o' thae self-same rings."

"And didna ye get the locks, the locks,
    The locks o' my ain black hair,
Whilk I sent by post, whilk I sent by box,
    Whilk I sent by the carrier?"

"They cam' to me," said that fair ladye;
    "And I prithee send nae mair!"
Said—"that cushion sae red, for my doggie's head,
    It is stuffed wi' thae locks o' hair."

"And didna ye get the letter, Ladye,
    Tied wi' a silken string,
Whilk I sent to thee frae the far countrie,
    A message of love to bring?"

"It cam' to me frae the far countrie
 Wi' its silken string and a' ;
But it wasna prepaid," said that high-born maid,
 "Sae I gar'd them tak' it awa'."

"O ever alack that ye sent it back,
 It was written sae clerkly and well!
Now the message it brought, and the boon that it sought,
 I must even say it mysel'."

Then up and spake the popinjay,
 Sae wisely counselled he.
"Now say it in the proper way:
 Gae doon upon thy knee!"

The lover he turned baith red and pale,
 Went doon upon his knee:
"O Ladye, hear the waesome tale
 That must be told to thee!

"For five lang years, and five lang years,
 I coorted thee by looks;
By nods and winks, by smiles and tears,
 As I had read in books.

"For ten lang years, O weary hours!
 I coorted thee by signs;
By sending game, by sending flowers,
 By sending Valentines.

"For five lang years, and five lang years,
 I have dwelt in the far countrie,
Till that thy mind should be inclined
 Mair tenderly to me.

"Now thirty years are gane and past,
 I am come frae a foreign land:
I am come to tell thee my love at last—
 O Ladye, gie me thy hand!"

The ladye she turned not pale nor red,
 But she smiled a pitiful smile:
"Sic' a coortin' as yours, my man," she said
 "Takes a lang and a weary while!"

"AND OUT AND LAUGHED THE POPINJAY"

"O HUSH THEE, GENTLE POPINJAY!"

And out and laughed the popinjay,
    A laugh of bitter scorn:
"A coortin' done in sic' a way,
    It ought not to be borne!"

Wi' that the doggie barked aloud,
    And up and doon he ran,
And tugged and strained his chain o' gowd,
    All for to bite the man.

"O hush thee, gentle popinjay!
    O hush thee, doggie dear!
There is a word I fain wad say,
    It needeth he should hear!"

Aye louder screamed that ladye fair
    To drown her doggie's bark:
Ever the lover shouted mair
    To make that ladye hark:

Shrill and more shrill the popinjay
    Upraised his angry squall:
I trow the doggie's voice that day
    Was louder than them all!

The serving-men and serving-maids
    Sat by the kitchen fire:
They heard sic' a din the parlour within
    As made them much admire.

Out spake the boy in buttons
    (I ween he wasna thin),
"Now wha will tae the parlour gae,
    And stay this deadlie din?"

And they have taen a kerchief,
    Casted their kevils in,
For wha should tae the parlour gae,
    And stay that deadlie din.

When on that boy the kevil fell
    To stay the fearsome noise,
'Gae in," they cried, "whate'er betide,
    Thou prince of button-boys!"

Syne, he has taen a supple cane
    To swinge that dog sae fat:
The doggie yowled, the doggie howled
    The louder aye for that.

"THE DOGGIE CEASED HIS NOISE"

Syne, he has taen a mutton-bane—
    The doggie ceased his noise,
And followed doon the kitchen stair
    That prince of button-boys!

Then sadly spake that ladye fair,
    Wi' a frown upon her brow:
"O dearer to me is my sma' doggie
    Than a dozen sic' as thou!

"Nae use, nae use for sighs and tears:
    Nae use at all to fret:
Sin' ye've bided sae well for thirty years,
    Ye may bide a wee langer yet!"

Sadly, sadly he crossed the floor
    And tirlëd at the pin:
Sadly went he through the door
    Where sadly he cam' in.

"O gin I had a popinjay
    To fly abune my head,
To tell me what I ought to say,
    I had by this been wed.

"O gin I find anither ladye,"
    He said wi' sighs and tears,
"I wot my coortin' sall not be
    Anither thirty years:

"For gin I find a ladye gay,
  Exactly to my taste,
I'll pop the question, aye or nay,
  In twenty years at maist."

FOUR RIDDLES.

[THESE consist of two Double Acrostics and two Charades.
No. I. was written at the request of some young friends, who had gone to a ball at an Oxford Commemoration—and also as a specimen of what might be done by making the Double Acrostic *a connected poem* instead of what it has hitherto been, a string of disjointed stanzas, on every conceivable subject, and about as interesting to read straight through as a page of a Cyclopædia. The first two stanzas describe the two main words, and each subsequent stanza one of the cross "lights."
No. II. was written after seeing Miss Ellen Terry perform in the play of "Hamlet." In this case the first stanza describes the two main words.
No. III. was written after seeing Miss Marion Terry perform in Mr. Gilbert's play of "Pygmalion and Galatea." The three stanzas respectively describe "My First," "My Second," and "My Whole."]

I.

THERE was an ancient City, stricken down
  With a strange frenzy, and for many a day
They paced from morn to eve the crowded town,
  And danced the night away.

I asked the cause: the aged man grew sad:
  They pointed to a building gray and tall,
And hoarsely answered "Step inside, my lad,
  And then you'll see it all."

———————

Yet what are all such gaieties to me
  Whose thoughts are full of indices and surds?

$$x^2 + 7x + 53$$
$$= 11/3.$$

But something whispered "It will soon be done:
   Bands cannot always play, nor ladies smile:
Endure with patience the distasteful fun
      For just a little while!"

A change came o'er my Vision—it was night:
   We clove a pathway through a frantic throng:
The steeds, wild-plunging, filled us with affright:
      The chariots whirled along.

Within a marble hall a river ran—
   A living tide, half muslin and half cloth:
And here one mourned a broken wreath or fan,
      Yet swallowed down her wrath;

And here one offered to a thirsty fair
   (His words half-drowned amid those thunders tuneful)
Some frozen viand (there were many there),
      A tooth-ache in each spoonful.

There comes a happy pause, for human strength
   Will not endure to dance without cessation;
And every one must reach the point at length
      Of absolute prostration.

At such a moment ladies learn to give,
   To partners who would urge them over-much,
A flat and yet decided negative—
      Photographers love such.

There comes a welcome summons—hope revives,
   And fading eyes grow bright, and pulses quicken:
Incessant pop the corks, and busy knives
      Dispense the tongue and chicken.

Flushed with new life, the crowd flows back again:
   And all is tangled talk and mazy motion—
Much like a waving field of golden grain,
      Or a tempestuous ocean.

And thus they give the time, that Nature meant
   For peaceful sleep and meditative snores,

To ceaseless din and mindless merriment
    And waste of shoes and floors.

And One (we name him not) that flies the flowers,
    That dreads the dances, and that shuns the salads,
They doom to pass in solitude the hours,
    Writing acrostic-ballads.

How late it grows! The hour is surely past
    That should have warned us with its double-knock?
The twilight wanes, and morning comes at last—
    "Oh, Uncle, what's o'clock?"

The Uncle gravely nods, and wisely winks.
    It *may* mean much, but how is one to know?
He opes his mouth—yet out of it, methinks,
    No words of wisdom flow.

II.

EMPRESS of Art, for thee I twine
    This wreath with all too slender skill.
Forgive my Muse each halting line,
    And for the deed accept the will!

O day of tears! Whence comes this spectre grim,
    Parting, like Death's cold river, souls that love?
Is not he bound to thee, as thou to him,
    By vows, unwhispered here, yet heard above?

And still it lives, that keen and heavenward flame,
    Lives in his eye, and trembles in his tone:
And these wild words of fury but proclaim
    A heart that beats for thee, for thee alone!

But all is lost: that mighty mind o'erthrown,
    Like sweet bells jangled, piteous sight to see!
"Doubt that the stars are fire," so runs his moan,
    "Doubt Truth herself, but not my love for thee!"

A sadder vision yet: thine aged sire
    Shaming his hoary locks with treacherous wile!
And dost thou now doubt Truth to be a liar?
    And wilt thou die, that hast forgot to smile?

Nay, get thee hence! Leave all thy winsome ways
  And the faint fragance of thy scattered flowers:
In holy silence wait the appointed days,
  And weep away the leaden-footed hours.

III.

THE air is bright with hues of light
  And rich with laughter and with singing:
Young hearts beat high in ecstasy,
  And banners wave, and bells are ringing:
But silence falls with fading day,
And there's an end to mirth and play.
     Ah, well-a-day!

Rest your old bones, ye wrinkled crones!
  The kettle sings, the firelight dances,
Deep be it quaffed, the magic draught
  That fills the soul with golden fancies!
For Youth and Pleasance will not stay,
And ye are withered, worn, and gray.
     Ah, well-a-day!

O fair cold face! O form of grace,
  For human passion madly yearning!
O weary air of dumb despair,
  From marble won, to marble turning!
"Leave us not thus!" we fondly pray.
"We cannot let thee pass away!"
     Ah, well-a-day!

IV.

My First is singular at best:
    More Plural is my Second:
My Third is far the pluralest—
So plural-plural, I protest
    It scarcely can be reckoned!

My First is followed by a bird:
   My Second by believers
In magic art: my simple Third
Follows, too often, hopes absurd
   And plausible deceivers.

My First to get at wisdom tries—
   A failure melancholy!
My Second men revered as wise:
My Third from heights of wisdom flies
   To depths of frantic folly.

My First is ageing day by day:
   My Second's age is ended:
My Third enjoys an age, they say,
That never seems to fade away,
   Through centuries extended.

My Whole? I need a poet's pen
   To paint her myriad phases:
The monarch, and the slave, of men—
A mountain-summit, and a den
   Of dark and deadly mazes—

A flashing light—a fleeting shade—
   Beginning, end, and middle
Of all that human art hath made
Or wit devised! Go, seek *her* aid,
   If you would read my riddle!

FAME'S PENNY-TRUMPET.

[Affectionately dedicated to all "original researchers" who pant for "endowment."]

BLOW, blow your trumpets till they crack,
   Ye little men of little souls!
And bid them huddle at your back—
   Gold-sucking leeches, shoals on shoals!

Fill all the air with hungry wails—
   "Reward us, ere we think or write!
Without your Gold mere Knowledge fails
   To sate the swinish appetite!"

"GO, THRONG EACH OTHER'S DRAWING-ROOMS"

And, where great Plato paced serene,
  Or Newton paused with wistful eye,
Rush to the chace with hoofs unclean
  And Babel-clamour of the sty!

Be yours the pay: be theirs the praise:
  We will not rob them of their due,
Nor vex the ghosts of other days
  By naming them along with you.

They sought and found undying fame:
  They toiled not for reward nor thanks:
Their cheeks are hot with honest shame
  For you, the modern mountebanks!

Who preach of Justice—plead with tears
  That Love and Mercy should abound—
While marking with complacent ears
  The moaning of some tortured hound:

Who prate of Wisdom—nay, forbear,
  Lest Wisdom turn on you in wrath,
Trampling, with heel that will not spare,
  The vermin that beset her path!

Go, throng each other's drawing-rooms,
  Ye idols of a petty clique:
Strut your brief hour in borrowed plumes,
  And make your penny-trumpets squeak:

Deck your dull talk with pilfered shreds
  Of learning from a nobler time,
And oil each other's little heads
  With mutual Flattery's golden slime:

And when the topmost height ye gain,
  And stand in Glory's ether clear,
And grasp the prize of all your pain—
  So many hundred pounds a year—

Then let Fame's banner be unfurled!
  Sing Pæans for a victory won!
Ye tapers, that would light the world,
  And cast a shadow on the Sun—

Who still shall pour His rays sublime,
  One crystal flood, from East to West,
When *ye* have burned your little time
  And feebly flickered into rest!

THE END.

A
TANGLED
TALE

Illustrated by

ARTHUR B. FROST

"AT A PACE OF SIX MILES IN THE HOUR."

TO MY PUPIL.

Beloved Pupil! Tamed by thee,
    Addish-, Subtrac-, Multiplica-tion,
Division, Fractions, Rule of Three,
    Attest thy deft manipulation!

Then onward! Let the voice of Fame
    From Age to Age repeat thy story,
Till thou hast won thyself a name
    Exceeding even Euclid's glory!

PREFACE

THIS Tale originally appeared as a serial in *The Monthly Packet*, beginning in April, 1880. The writer's intention was to embody in each Knot (like the medicine so dexterously, but ineffectually, concealed in the jam of our early childhood) one or more mathematical questions—in Arithmetic, Algebra, or Geometry, as the case might be—for amusement, and possible edification, of the fair readers of that Magazine.

L. C.

October, 1885.

KNOT I.

EXCELSIOR.

"Goblin, lead them up and down."

THE ruddy glow of sunset was already fading into the sombre shadows of night, when two travellers might have been observed swiftly—at a pace of six miles in the hour—descending the rugged side of a mountain; the younger bounding from crag to crag with the agility of a fawn, while his companion, whose aged limbs seemed ill at ease in the heavy chain armour habitually worn by tourists in that district, toiled on painfully at his side.

As is always the case under such circumstances, the younger knight was the first to break the silence.

"A goodly pace, I trow!" he exclaimed. "We sped not thus in the ascent!"

"Goodly, indeed!" the other echoed with a groan. "We clomb it but at three miles in the hour."

"And on the dead level our pace is—?" the younger suggested; for he was weak in statistics, and left all such details to his aged companion.

"Four miles in the hour," the other wearily replied. "Not an ounce more," he added, with that love of metaphor so common in old age, "and not a farthing less!"

"'Twas three hours past high noon when we left our hostelry," the young man said, musingly. "We shall scarce be back by supper-time. Perchance mine host will roundly deny us all food!"

"He will chide our tardy return," was the grave reply, "and such a rebuke will be meet."

"A brave conceit!" cried the other, with a merry laugh. "And should we bid him bring us yet another course, I trow his answer will be tart!"

"We shall but get our deserts," sighed the elder knight, who had never seen a joke in his life, and was somewhat displeased at his companion's untimely levity. "'Twill be nine of the clock," he added in an undertone, "by the time we regain our hostelry. Full many a mile shall we have plodded this day!"

"How many? How many?" cried the eager youth, ever athirst for knowledge.

The old man was silent.

"Tell me," he answered, after a moment's thought, "what time it was when we stood together on yonder peak. Not exact to the minute!" he added hastily, reading a protest in the young man's face. "An' thy guess be within one poor half-hour of the mark, 'tis all I ask of thy mother's son! Then will I tell thee, true to the last inch, how far we shall have trudged betwixt three and nine of the clock."

A groan was the young man's only reply; while his convulsed features and the deep wrinkles that chased each other across his manly brow, revealed the abyss of arithmetical agony into which one chance question had plunged him.

KNOT II.

ELIGIBLE APARTMENTS.

"Straight down the crooked lane,
And all around the square."

"LET'S ask Balbus about it," said Hugh.

"All right," said Lambert.

"*He* can guess it," said Hugh.

"Rather," said Lambert.

No more words were needed: the two brothers understood each other perfectly.

Balbus was waiting for them at the hotel: the journey down had tired him, he said: so his two pupils had been the round of the place, in search of lodgings, without the old tutor who had been their inseparable companion from their childhood. They had named him after the hero of their Latin exercise-book, which overflowed with anecdotes of that versatile genius—anecdotes whose vagueness in detail was more than compensated by their sensational brilliance. "Balbus has overcome all his enemies" had been marked by their tutor, in the margin of the book, "Successful Bravery." In this way he had tried to extract a moral from every anecdote about Balbus—sometimes one of warning, as in "Balbus had borrowed a healthy dragon," against which he had written "Rashness in Speculation"—sometimes of encouragement, as in the words "Influence of Sympathy in United Action," which stood opposite to the anecdote "Balbus was assisting his mother-in-law to convince the dragon"—and sometimes it dwindled down to a single word, such as "Prudence," which was all he could extract from the touching record that "Balbus, having scorched the tail of the dragon, went away." His pupils liked the short morals best, as it left them more room for marginal illustrations, and in this

"BALBUS WAS ASSISTING HIS MOTHER-IN-LAW TO CONVINCE THE DRAGON."

instance they required all the space they could get to exhibit the rapidity of the hero's departure.

Their report of the state of things was discouraging. That most fashionable of watering-places, Little Mendip, was "chockfull" (as the boys expressed it) from end to end. But in one Square they had seen no less than four cards, in different houses, all announcing in flaming capitals "ELIGIBLE APARTMENTS." "So there's plenty of choice, after all, you see," said spokesman Hugh in conclusion.

"That doesn't follow from the data," said Balbus, as he rose from the easy chair, where he had been dozing over *The Little Mendip Gazette*. "They may be all single rooms. However, we may as well see them. I shall be glad to stretch my legs a bit."

An unprejudiced bystander might have objected that the operation was needless, and that this long, lank creature would have been all the better with even shorter legs: but no such thought occurred to his loving pupils. One on each side, they did their best to keep up with his gigantic strides, while Hugh repeated the sentence in their father's letter, just received from abroad, over which he and Lambert had been puzzling. "He says a friend of his, the Governor of——*what* was that name again, Lambert?" ("Kgovjni," said Lambert.) "Well, yes. The Governor of—— what-you-may-call-it——wants to give a *very* small dinner-party, and he means to ask his father's brother-in-law, his brother's father-in-law, his father-in-law's brother, and his brother-in-law's father: and we're to guess how many guests there will be."

There was an anxious pause. "*How* large did he say the pudding was to be?" Balbus said at last. "Take its cubical contents, divide by the cubical contents of what each man can eat, and the quotient——"

"He didn't say anything about pudding," said Hugh, "—and here's the Square," as they turned a corner and came into sight of the "eligible apartments."

"It *is* a Square!" was Balbus' first cry of delight, as he gazed around him. "Beautiful! Beau-ti-ful! Equilateral! *And* rectangular!"

The boys looked round with less enthusiasm. "Number nine is the first with a card," said prosaic Lambert; but Balbus would not so soon awake from his dream of beauty.

"See, boys!" he cried. "Twenty doors on a side! What symmetry! Each side divided into twenty-one equal parts! It's delicious!"

"Shall I knock, or ring?" said Hugh, looking in some perplexity at a square brass plate which bore the simple inscription "RING ALSO."

"Both," said Balbus. "That's an Ellipsis, my boy. Did you never see an Ellipsis before?"

"I couldn't hardly read it," said Hugh, evasively. "It's no good having an Ellipsis, if they don't keep it clean."

"Which there is *one* room, gentlemen," said the smiling landlady. "And a sweet room too! As snug a little back-room——"

"We will see it," said Balbus gloomily, as they followed her in. "I knew how it would be! One room in each house! No view I suppose?"

"Which indeed there *is*, gentlemen!" the landlady indignantly protested, as she drew up the blind, and indicated the back garden.

"Cabbages, I perceive," said Balbus. "Well, they're green, at any rate."

"Which the greens at the shops," their hostess explained, "are by no means dependable upon. Here you has them on the premises, *and* of the best."

"Does the window open?" was always Balbus' first question in testing a lodging: and "Does the chimney smoke?" his second. Satisfied on all points, he secured the refusal of the room, and they moved on to Number Twenty-five.

This landlady was grave and stern. "I've nobbut one room left," she told them: "and it gives on the back-gyardin."

"But there are cabbages?" Balbus suggested.

The landlady visibly relented. "There is, sir," she said: "and good ones, though I say it as shouldn't. We can't rely on the shops for greens. So we grows them ourselves."

"A singular advantage," said Balbus: and, after the usual questions, they went on to Fifty-two.

"And I'd gladly accommodate you all, if I could," was the greeting that met them. "We are but mortal," ("Irrelevant!" muttered Balbus) "and I've let all my rooms but one."

"Which one is a back-room, I perceive," said Balbus: "and looking out on—on cabbages, I presume?"

"Yes, indeed, sir!" said their hostess. "Whatever *other* folks may do, *we* grows our own. For the shops——"

"An excellent arrangement!" Balbus interrupted. "Then one can really depend on their being good. Does the window open?"

The usual questions were answered satisfactorily; but this time Hugh added one of his own invention—"Does the cat scratch?"

The landlady looked round suspiciously, as if to make sure the cat was not listening, "I will not deceive you, gentlemen," she said. "It *do* scratch, but not without you pulls its whiskers! It'll never do it," she repeated slowly, with a visible effort to recall the exact words of some written agreement between herself and the cat, "without you pulls its whiskers!"

"Much may be excused in a cat so treated," said Balbus, as they left the house and crossed to Number Seventy-three, leaving the landlady curtseying on the doorstep, and still murmuring to herself her parting words, as if they were a form of blessing, "——not without you pulls its whiskers!"

At Number Seventy-three they found only a small shy girl to show the house, who said "yes'm" in answer to all questions.

"The usual room," said Balbus, as they marched in: "the usual back-garden, the usual cabbages. I suppose you can't get them good at the shops?"

"Yes'm," said the girl.

"Well, you may tell your mistress we will take the room, and that her plan of growing her own cabbages is simply *admirable*!"

"Yes'm," said the girl, as she showed them out.

"One day-room and three bed-rooms," said Balbus, as they returned to the hotel. "We will take as our day-room the one that gives us the least walking to do to get to it."

"Must we walk from door to door, and count the steps?" said Lambert.

"No, no! Figure it out, my boys, figure it out!" Balbus gaily exclaimed, as he put pens, ink, and paper before his hapless pupils, and left the room.

"I say! It'll be a job!" said Hugh.

"Rather!" said Lambert.

KNOT III.

MAD MATHESIS.

"I waited for the train."

"WELL, they call me so because I *am* a little mad, I suppose," she said, good-humouredly, in answer to Clara's cautiously-worded question as to how she came by so strange a nick-name. "You see, I never do what sane people are expected to do now-a-days. I never wear long trains, (talking of trains, that's the Charing Cross Metropolitan Station—I've something to tell you about *that*), and I never play lawn-tennis. I can't cook an omelette. I can't even set a broken limb! *There's* an ignoramus for you!"

Clara was her niece, and full twenty years her junior; in fact, she was still attending a High School—an institution of which Mad Mathesis spoke with undisguised aversion. "Let a woman be meek and lowly!" she would say. "None of your High Schools for me!" But it was vacation-time just now, and Clara was her guest, and Mad Mathesis was showing her the sights of that Eighth Wonder of the world—London.

"The Charing Cross Metropolitan Station!" she resumed, waving her hand towards the entrance as if she were introducing her niece to a friend. "The Bayswater and Birmingham Extension is just completed, and the trains now run round and round continuously—skirting the border of Wales, just touching at York, and so round by the east coast back to London. The way the trains run is *most* peculiar. The westerly ones go round in two hours; the easterly ones take three; but they always manage to start two trains from here, opposite ways, punctually every quarter-of-an-hour."

"They part to meet again," said Clara, her eyes filling with tears at the romantic thought.

"No need to cry about it!" her aunt grimly remarked. "They don't meet on the same line of rails, you know. Talking of meeting, an idea strikes me!" she added, changing the subject with her usual abruptness. "Let's go opposite ways round, and see which can meet most trains. No

need for a chaperon—ladies' saloon, you know. You shall go whichever
way you like, and we'll have a bet about it!"

"I never make bets," Clara said very gravely. "Our excellent preceptress
has often warned us——"

"You'd be none the worse if you did!" Mad Mathesis interrupted. "In
fact, you'd be the better, I'm certain!"

"Neither does our excellent preceptress approve of puns," said Clara.
"But we'll have a match, if you like. Let me choose my train," she added
after a brief mental calculation, "and I'll engage to meet exactly half as
many again as you do."

"Not if you count fair," Mad Mathesis bluntly interrupted. "Remember,
we only count the trains we meet *on the way*. You mustn't count the one
that starts as you start, nor the one that arrives as you arrive."

"That will only make the difference of *one* train," said Clara, as they
turned and entered the station. "But I never travelled alone before.
There'll be no one to help me to alight. However, I don't mind. Let's
have a match."

A ragged little boy overheard her remark, and came running after
her. "Buy a box of cigar-lights, Miss!" he pleaded, pulling her shawl to
attract her attention. Clara stopped to explain.

"I never smoke cigars," she said in a meekly apologetic tone, "Our
excellent preceptress——," but Mad Mathesis impatiently hurried her
on, and the little boy was left gazing after her with round eyes of amazement.

The two ladies bought their tickets and moved slowly down the central
platform, Mad Mathesis prattling on as usual—Clara silent, anxiously
reconsidering the calculation on which she rested her hopes of winning
the match.

"Mind where you go, dear!" cried her aunt, checking her just in time.
"One step more, and you'd have been in that pail of cold water!"

"I know, I know," Clara said, dreamily. "The pale, the cold, and the
moony——"

"Take your places on the spring-boards!" shouted a porter.

"What are *they* for!" Clara asked in a terrified whisper.

"Merely to help us into trains." The elder lady spoke with the nonchalance
of one quite used to the process. "Very few people can get into a carriage
without help in less than three seconds, and the trains only stop for one
second." At this moment the whistle was heard, and two trains rushed
into the station. A moment's pause, and they were gone again; but in
that brief interval several hundred passengers had been shot into them,
each flying straight to his place with the accuracy of a Minie bullet—
while an equal number were showered out upon the side-platforms.

Three hours had passed away, and the two friends met again on the
Charing Cross platform, and eagerly compared notes. Then Clara turned
away with a sigh. To young impulsive hearts, like hers, disappointment
is always a bitter pill. Mad Mathesis followed her, full of kindly sympathy.

"Try again, my love!" she said, cheerily. "Let us vary the experiment.
We will start as we did before, but not to begin counting till our trains
meet. When we see each other, we will say 'One!' and so count on till
we come here again."

Clara brightened up. "I shall win *that*," she exclaimed eagerly, "if I may choose my train!"

Another shriek of engine whistles, another upheaving of spring-boards, another living avalanche plunging into two trains as they flashed by: and the travellers were off again.

Each gazed eagerly from her carriage window, holding up her handkerchief as a signal to her friend. A rush and a roar. Two trains shot past each other in a tunnel, and two travellers leaned back in their corners with a sigh—or rather with *two* sighs—of relief. "One!" Clara murmured to herself. "Won! It's a word of good omen. *This* time, at any rate, the victory will be mine!"

But *was* it?

KNOT IV.

THE DEAD RECKONING.

"I did dream of money-bags to-night."

NOONDAY on the open sea within a few degrees of the Equator is apt to be oppressively warm; and our two travellers were now airily clad in suits of dazzling white linen, having laid aside the chain-armour which they had found not only endurable in the cold mountain air they had lately been breathing, but a necessary precaution against the daggers of the banditti who infested the heights. Their holiday-trip was over, and they were now on their way home, in the monthly packet which plied between the two great ports of the island they had been exploring.

Along with their armour, the tourists had laid aside the antiquated speech it had pleased them to affect while in knightly disguise, and had returned to the ordinary style of two country gentlemen of the Twentieth Century.

Stretched on a pile of cushions, under the shade of a huge umbrella, they were lazily watching some native fishermen, who had come on board at the last landing-place, each carrying over his shoulder a small but heavy sack. A large weighing-machine, that had been used for cargo at the last port, stood on the deck; and round this the fishermen had gathered, and, with much unitelligible jabber, seemed to be weighing their sacks.

"More like sparrows in a tree than human talk, isn't it?" the elder tourist remarked to his son, who smiled feebly, but would not exert himself so far as to speak. The old man tried another listener.

"What have they got in those sacks, Captain?" he inquired, as that great being passed them in his never ending parade to and fro on the deck.

The Captain paused in his march, and towered over the travellers—tall, grave, and serenely self-satisfied.

"Fishermen," he explained, "are often passengers in My ship. These five are from Mhruxi—the place we last touched at—and that's the way they carry their money. The money of this island is heavy, gentlemen, but it costs little, as you may guess. We buy it from them by weight—about five shillings a pound. I fancy a ten pound-note would buy all those sacks."

By this time the old man had closed his eyes—in order, no doubt, to concentrate his thoughts on these interesting facts; but the Captain failed to realise his motive, and with a grunt resumed his monotonous march.

Meanwhile the fishermen were getting so noisy over the weighing-machine that one of the sailors took the precaution of carrying off all the weights, leaving them to amuse themselves with such substitutes in the form of winch-handles, belaying-pins, &c., as the could find. This brought their excitement to a speedy end: they carefully hid their sacks in the folds of the jib that lay on the deck near the tourists, and strolled away.

When next the Captain's heavy footfall passed, the younger man roused himself to speak.

"*What* did you call the place those fellows came from, Captain?" he asked.

"Mhruxi, sir."

"And the one we are bound for?"

The Captain took a long breath, plunged into the word, and came out of it nobly. "They call it Kgovjni, sir."

"K—I give it up!" the young man faintly said.

He stretched out his hand for a glass of iced water which the compassionate steward had brought him a minute ago, and had set down, unluckily, just outside the shadow of the umbrella. It was scalding hot, and he decided not to drink it. The effort of making this resolution, coming close on the fatiguing conversation he had just gone through, was too much for him: he sank back among the cushions in silence.

His father courteously tried to make amends for his *nonchalance*.

"Whereabouts are we now, Captain?" said he, "Have you any idea?"

The Captain cast a pitying look on the ignorant landsman. "I could tell you *that*, sir," he said, in a tone of lofty condescension, "to an inch!"

"You don't say so!" the old man remarked, in a tone of languid surprise.

"And mean so," persisted the Captain. "Why, what do you suppose would become of My ship, if I were to lose My Longitude and My Latitude? Could *you* make anything of My Dead Reckoning?"

"Nobody could, I'm sure!" the other heartily rejoined.

But he had overdone it.

"It's *perfectly* intelligible," the Captain said, in an offended tone, "to any one that understands such things." With these words he moved away, and began giving orders to the men, who were preparing to hoist the jib.

Our tourists watched the operation with such interest that neither of them remembered the five money-bags, which in another moment, as the wind filled out the jib, were whirled overboard and fell heavily into the sea.

But the poor fishermen had not so easily forgotten their property. In a moment they had rushed to the spot, and stood uttering cries of fury, and pointing, now to the sea, and now to the sailors who had caused the disaster.

The old man explained it to the Captain.

"Let us make it up among us," he added in conclusion. "Ten pounds will do it, I think you said?"

But the Captain put aside the suggestion with a wave of the hand.

"No, sir!" he said, in his grandest manner. "You will excuse Me, I am sure; but these are My passengers. The accident has happened on board My ship, and under My orders. It is for Me to make compensation." He turned to the angry fishermen. "Come here, my men!" he said, in the Mhruxian dialect. "Tell me the weight of each sack. I saw you weighing them just now."

Then ensued a perfect Babel of noise, as the five natives explained,

all screaming together, how the sailors had carried off the weights, and they had done what they could with whatever came handy.

Two iron belaying-pins, three blocks, six holy-stones, four winch-handles, and a large hammer, were now carefully weighed, the Captain super-intending and noting the results. But the matter did not seem to be settled, even then: an angry discussion followed, in which the sailors and the five natives all joined: and at last the Captain approached our tourists with a disconcerted look, which he tried to conceal under a laugh.

"It's an absurd difficulty," he said. "Perhaps one of you gentlemen can suggest something. It seems they weighed the sacks two at at time!"

"If they didn't have five separate weighings, of course you can't value them separately," the youth hastily decided.

"Let's hear all about it," was the old man's more cautious remark.

"They *did* have five separate weighings," the Captain said, "but— Well, it beats *me* entirely!" he added, in a sudden burst of candour. "Here's the result. First and second sack weighed twelve pounds; second and third, thirteen and a half; third and fourth, eleven and a half; fourth and fifth, eight: and then they say they had only the large hammer left, and it took *three* sacks to weigh it down— that's the first, third and fifth— and *they* weighed sixteen pounds. There, gentlemen! Did you ever hear anything like *that*?"

The old man muttered under his breath "If only my sister were here!" and looked helplessly at his son. His son looked at the five natives. The five natives looked at the Captain. The Captain looked at nobody: his eyes were cast down, and he seemed to be saying softly to himself "Con-template one another, gentlemen, if such be your good pleasure. *I* con-template *Myself*!"

KNOT V.

OUGHTS AND CROSSES.

"Look here, upon this picture, and on this."

"AND what made you choose the first train, Goosey?" said Mad Mathesis, as they got into the cab. "Couldn't you count better than *that*?"

"I took an extreme case," was the tearful reply. "Our excellent preceptress always says 'When in doubt, my dears, take an extreme case.' And I *was* in doubt."

"Does it always succeed?" her aunt enquired.

Clara sighed. "Not *always*," she reluctantly admitted. "And I can't make out why. One day she was telling the little girls—they make such a noise at tea, you know—'The more noise you make, the less jam you will have, and *vice versâ*.' And I thought they wouldn't know what '*vice versâ*' meant: so I explained it to them. I said 'if you make an infinite noise, you'll get no jam: and if you make no noise, you'll get an infinite lot of jam.' But our excellent preceptress said that wasn't a good instance. *Why* wasn't it?" she added plaintively.

Her aunt evaded the question. "One sees certain objections to it," she said. "But how did you work it with the Metropolitan trains? None of them go infinitely fast, I believe."

"I called them hares and tortoises," Clara said—a little timidly, for she dreaded being laughed at. "And I thought there couldn't be so many hares as tortoises on the Line: so I took an extreme case—one hare and an infinite number of tortoises."

"An extreme case, indeed," her aunt remarked with admirable gravity: "and a most dangerous state of things!"

"And I thought, if I went with a tortoise, there would be only *one* hare to meet: but if I went with the hare—you know there were *crowds* of tortoises!"

"It wasn't a bad idea," said the elder lady, as they left the cab, at the entrance of Burlington House. "You shall have another chance to-day. We'll have a match in marking pictures."

Clara brightened up. "I should like to try again, very much," she said. "I'll take more care this time. How are we to play?"

To this question Mad Mathesis made no reply: she was busy drawing lines down the margins of the catalogue. "See," she said after a minute, "I've drawn three columns against the names of the pictures in the long room, and I want you to fill them with oughts and crosses—crosses for good marks and oughts for bad. The first column is for choice of subject, the second for arrangement, the third for colouring. And these are the conditions of the match. You must give three crosses to two or three pictures. You must give two crosses to four or five——"

"Do you mean *only* two crosses?" said Clara. "Or may I count the three-cross pictures among the two-cross pictures?"

"Of course you may," said her aunt. "Any one, that has *three* eyes, may be said to have *two* eyes, I suppose?"

Clara followed her aunt's dreamy gaze across the crowded gallery, half-dreading to find that there was a three-eyed person in sight.

"And you must give one cross to nine or ten."

"And which wins the match?" Clara asked, as she carefully entered these conditions on a blank leaf in her catalogue.

"Whichever marks fewest pictures."

"But suppose we marked the same number?"

"Then whichever uses most marks."

Clara considered. "I don't think it's much of a match," she said. "I shall mark nine pictures, and give three crosses to three of them, two crosses to two more, and one cross each to all the rest."

"Will you, indeed?" said her aunt. "Wait till you've heard all the conditions, my impetuous child. You must give three oughts to one or two pictures, two oughts to three or four, and one ought to eight or nine. I don't want you to be *too* hard on the R.A.'s."

Clara quite gasped as she wrote down all these fresh conditions. "It's a great deal worse than Circulating Decimals!" she said. "But I'm determined to win, all the same!"

Her aunt smiled grimly. "We can begin *here*," she said, as they paused before a gigantic picture, which the catalogue informed them was the "Portrait of Lieutenant Brown, mounted on his favorite elephant."

"He looks awfully conceited!" said Clara. "I don't think he was the elephant's favorite Lieutenant. What a hideous picture it is! And it takes up room enough for twenty!"

"Mind what you say, my dear!" her aunt interposed. "It's by an R.A.!"

But Clara was quite reckless. "I don't care who it's by!" she cried. "And I shall give it three bad marks!"

Aunt and niece soon drifted away from each other in the crowd, and for the next half-hour Clara was hard at work, putting in marks and rubbing them out again, and hunting up and down for suitable pictures. This she found the hardest part of all. "I *can't* find the one I want!" she exclaimed at last, almost crying with vexation.

"What is it you want to find, my dear?" The voice was strange to Clara, but so sweet and gentle that she felt attracted to the owner of it, even before she had seen her; and when she turned, and met the smiling looks of two little old ladies, whose round dimpled faces, exactly alike, seemed never to have known a care, it was as much as she could do—as she confessed to Aunt Mattie afterwards—to keep herself from hugging them both.

"I was looking for a picture," she said, "that has a good subject—and that's well arranged—but badly coloured."

The little old ladies glanced at each other in some alarm. "Calm yourself, my dear," said the one who had spoken first, "and try to remember which it was. What *was* the subject?"

"Was it an elephant, for instance?" the other sister suggested. They were still in sight of Lieutenant Brown.

"I don't know, indeed!" Clara impetuously replied. "You know it doesn't matter a bit what the subject *is*, so long as it's a good one!"

Once more the sisters exchanged looks of alarm, and one of them whispered something to the other, of which Clara caught only the one word "mad."

"They mean Aunt Mattie, of course," she said to herself—fancying, in her innocence, that London was like her native town, where everybody knew everybody else. "If you mean my aunt,"she added aloud, "she's *there*—just three pictures beyond Lieutenant Brown."

"Ah, well! Then you'd better go to her, my dear!" her new friend said, soothingly. "*She'll* find you the picture you want. Good-bye, dear!"

"Good-bye, dear!" echoed the other sister, "Mind you don't lose sight of your aunt!" And the pair trotted off into another room, leaving Clara rather perplexed at their manner.

"They're real darlings!" she soliloquised. "I wonder why they pity me so!" And she wandered on, murmuring to herself "It must have two good marks, and——"

KNOT VI.

HER RADIANCY.

"One piecee thing that my have got,
Maskee* that thing my no can do.
You talkee you no sabey what?
Bamboo."

THEY landed, and were at once conducted to the Palace. About half way they were met by the Governor, who welcomed them in English—a great relief to our travellers, whose guide could speak nothing but Kgovjnian.

"I don't half like the way they grin at us as we go by!" the old man whispered to his son. "And why do they say 'Bamboo!' so often?"

"It alludes to a local custom," replied the Governor, who had overheard the question. "Such persons as happen in any way to displease Her Radiancy are usually beaten with rods."

The old man shuddered. "A most objectional local custom!" he remarked with strong emphasis. "I wish we had never landed! Did you notice that black fellow, Norman, opening his great mouth at us? I verily believe he would like to eat us!"

Norman appealed to the Governor, who was walking at his other side. "Do they often eat distinguished strangers here?" he said, in as indifferent a tone as he could assume.

"Not often—not ever!" was the welcome reply. "They are not good for it. Pigs we eat, for they are fat. This old man is thin."

"And thankful to be so!" muttered the elder traveller. "Beaten we shall be without a doubt. It's a comfort to know it won't be Beaten without the B! My dear boy, just look at the peacocks!"

They were now walking betwen two unbroken lines of those gorgeous birds, each held in check, by means of a golden collar and chain, by a black slave, who stood well behind, so as not to interrupt the view of the glittering tail, with its network of rustling feathers and its hundred eyes.

The Governor smiled proudly. "In your honour," he said, "Her Radiancy has ordered up ten thousand additional peacocks. She will, no doubt, decorate you, before you go, with the usual Star and Feathers."

"It'll be Star without the S!" faltered one of his hearers.

"Come, come! Don't lose heart!" said the other. "All this is full of charm for me."

"You are young, Norman," sighed his father; "young and light-hearted. For me, it is Charm without the C."

"The old one is sad," the Governor remarked with some anxiety. "He has, without doubt, effected some fearful crime?"

---

* *"Maskee,"* in Pigeon-English, means *"without."*

"WHY DO THEY SAY 'BAMBOO!' SO OFTEN?"

"But I haven't!" the poor old gentleman hastily exclaimed. "Tell him I haven't, Norman!"

"He has not, as yet," Norman gently explained. And the Governor repeated, in a satisfied tone, "Not as yet."

"Yours is a wondrous country!" the Governor resumed, after a pause. "Now here is a letter from a friend of mine, a merchant, in London. He and his brother went there a year ago, with a thousand pounds apiece; and on New-Year's-day they had sixty thousand pounds between them!"

"How did they do it?" Norman eagerly exclaimed. Even the elder traveller looked excited.

The Governor handed him the open letter. "Anybody can do it, when once they know how," so ran this oracular document. "We borrowed nought: we stole nought. We began the year with only a thousand pounds apiece: and last New-Year's day we had sixty thousand pounds between us—sixty thousand golden sovereigns!"

Norman looked grave and thoughtful as he handed back the letter. His father hazarded one guess. "Was it by gambling?"

"A Kgovjnian never gambles," said the Governor gravely, as he ushered them through the palace gates. They followed him in silence down a long passage, and soon found themselves in a lofty hall, lined entirely with peacocks' feathers. In the centre was a pile of crimson cushions, which almost concealed the figure of Her Radiancy—a plump little damsel, in a robe of green satin dotted with silver stars, whose pale round face lit up for a moment with a half-smile as the travellers bowed before her, and then relapsed into the exact expression of a wax doll, while she languidly murmured a word or two in Kgovjnian dialect.

The Governor interpreted. "Her Radiancy welcomes you. She notes the Impenetrable Placidity of the old one, and the Imperceptible Acuteness of the youth."

Here the little potentate clapped her hands, and a troop of slaves instantly appeared, carrying trays of coffee and sweetmeats, which they offered to the guests, who had, at a signal from the Governor, seated themselves on the carpet.

"Sugar-plums!" muttered the old man. "One might as well be at a confectioner's! Ask for a penny bun, Norman!"

"Not so loud!" his son whispered. "Say something complimentary!" For the Governor was evidently expecting a speech.

"We thank Her Exalted Potency," the old man timidly began. "We bask in the light of her smile, which——"

"The words of old men are weak!" the Governor interrupted angrily. "Let the youth speak!"

"Tell her," cried Norman, in a wild burst of eloquence, "that, like two grasshoppers in a volcano, we are shrivelled up in the presence of Her Spangled Vehemence!"

"It is well," said the Governor, and translated this into Kgovjnian. "I am now to tell you" he proceeded, "what Her Radiancy requires of you before you go. The yearly competition for the post of Imperial Scarf-maker is just ended; you are the judges. You will take account of the rate of work, the lightness of the scarves, and their warmth. Usually the competitors differ in one point only. Thus, last year, Fifi and Gogo made the same number of scarves in the trial-week, and they were equally light; but Fifi's were twice as warm as Gogo's and she was pronounced twice as good. But this year, woe is me, who can judge it? Three competitors are here, and they differ in all points! While you settle their claims, you shall be lodged, Her Radiancy bids me say, free of expense—in the best dungeon, and abundantly fed on the best bread and water."

The old man groaned. "All is lost!" he wildly exclaimed. But Norman heeded him not: he had taken out his note-book, and was calmly jotting down the particulars.

"Three they be," the Governor proceeded, "Lolo, Mimi, and Zuzu. Lolo makes 5 scarves while Mimi makes 2; but Zuzu makes 4 while Lolo makes 3! Again, so fairylike is Zuzu's handiwork, 5 of her scarves weigh no more than one of Lolo's; yet Mimi's is lighter still—5 of hers will but balance 3 of Zuzu's! And for warmth one of Mimi's is equal to 4 of Zuzu's; yet one of Lolo's is as warm as 3 of Mimi's!"

Here the little lady once more clapped her hands.

"It is our signal of dismissal!" the Governor hastily said. "Pay Her Radiancy your farewell compliments— and walk out backwards."

The walking part was all the elder tourist could manage. Norman simply said "Tell Her Radiancy we are transfixed by the spectacle of Her Serene Brilliance, and bid an agonized farewell to her Condensed Milkiness!"

"Her Radiancy is pleased," the Governor reported, after duly translating this. "She casts on you a glance from Her Imperial Eyes, and is confident that you will catch it!"

"That I warrant we shall!" the elder traveller moaned to himself distractedly.

Once more they bowed low, and then followed the Governor down a winding staircase to the Imperial Dungeon, which they found to be lined with coloured marble, lighted from the roof, and splendidly though not luxuriously furnished with a bench of polished malachite. "I trust you will not delay the calculation," the Governor said, ushering them in with much ceremony. "I have known great inconvenience—great and serious inconvenience—result to those unhappy ones who have delayed to execute the commands of Her Radiancy! And on this occasion she is resolute: she says the thing must and shall be done: and she has ordered up ten thousand additional bamboos!" With these words he left them, and they heard him lock and bar the door on the outside.

"I told you how it would end!" moaned the elder traveller, wringing his hands, and quite forgetting in his anguish that he had himself proposed the expedition, and had never predicted anything of the sort. "Oh that we were well out of this miserable business!"

"Courage!" cried the younger cheerily. "*Hœc olim meminisse juvabit!* The end of all this will be glory!"

"Glory without the L!" was all the poor old man could say, as he rocked himself to and fro on the malachite bench. "Glory without the L!"

KNOT VII.

PETTY CASH.

"Base is the slave that pays."

"AUNT MATTIE!"

"My child?"

"*Would* you mind writing it down at once? I shall be quite *certain* to forget it if you don't!"

"My dear, we really must wait till the cab stops. How can I possibly write anything in the midst of all this jolting?"

"But *really* I shall be forgetting it!"

Clara's voice took the plaintive tone that her aunt never knew how to resist, and with a sigh the old lady drew forth her ivory tablets and prepared to record the amount that Clara had just spent at the Confectioner's shop. Her expenditure was always made out of her aunt's purse, but the poor girl knew, by bitter experience, that sooner or later "Mad Mathesis" would expect an exact account of every penny that had gone, and she waited, with ill-concealed impatience, while the old lady turned the tablets over and over, till she had found the one headed "PETTY CASH."

"Here's the place," she said at last, "and here we have yesterday's luncheon duly entered. *One glass lemonade* (Why can't you drink water, like me?) *three sandwiches* (They never put in half mustard enough. I told the young woman so, to her face; and she tossed her head—like her impudence!) *and seven biscuits. Total one-and-two-pence.* Well, now for to-day's?"

"One glass of lemonade——" Clara was beginning to say, when suddenly the cab drew up, and a courteous railway-porter was handing out the bewildered girl before she had had time to finish her sentence.

Her aunt pocketed the tablets instantly. "Business first," she said: "petty cash—which is a form of pleasure, whatever *you* may think—afterwards." And she proceeded to pay the driver, and to give voluminous orders about the luggage, quite deaf to the entreaties of her unhappy niece that she would enter the rest of the luncheon account.

"My dear, you really must cultivate a more capacious mind!" was all the consolation she vouchsafed to the poor girl. "Are not the tablets of your memory wide enough to contain the record of one single luncheon?"

"Not wide enough! Not half wide enough!" was the passionate reply.

The words came in aptly enough, but the voice was not that of Clara,

A note for American readers: Knot VII. In British currency, a shilling contains twelve pence. The phrase "One and two-pence" (written 1 s. 2 d.) means "one shilling and two-pence."

"I TELL YOU THE CAB-DOOR ISN'T HALF WIDE ENOUGH!"

and both ladies turned in some surprise to see who it was that had so suddenly struck into their conversation. A fat little old lady was standing at the door of a cab, helping the driver to extricate what seemed an exact duplicate of herself: it would have been no easy task to decide which was the fatter, or which looked the more good-humoured of the two sisters.

"I tell you the cab-door isn't half wide enough!" she repeated, as her sister finally emerged, somewhat after the fashion of a pellet from a pop-gun, and she turned to appeal to Clara. "Is it, dear?" she said, trying hard to bring a frown into a face that dimpled all over with smiles.

"Some folks is too wide for 'em," growled the cab-driver.

"Don't provoke me, man!" cried the little old lady, in what she meant for a tempest of fury. "Say another word and I'll put you into the County Court, and sue you for a *Habeas Corpus*!" The cabman touched his hat, and marched off, grinning.

"Nothing like a little Law to cow the ruffians, my dear!" she remarked confidentially to Clara. "You saw how he quailed when I mentioned the *Habeas Corpus*? Not that I've any idea what it means, but it sounds very grand, doesn't it?"

"It's very provoking," Clara replied, a little vaguely.

"Very!" the little old lady eagerly repeated. "And we're very much provoked indeed. Aren't we, sister?"

"I never was so provoked in all my life!" the fatter sister assented, radiantly.

By this time Clara had recognised her picture-gallery acquaintances, and, drawing her aunt aside, she hastily whispered her reminiscences. "I met them first in the Royal Academy—and they were very kind to me—and they were lunching at the next table to us, just now, you know—and they tried to help me to find the picture I wanted—and I'm sure they're dear old things!"

"Friends of yours, are they?" said Mad Mathesis. "Well, I like their looks. You can be civil to them, while I get the tickets. But do try and arrange your ideas a little more chronologically!"

And so it came to pass that the four ladies found themselves seated side by side on the same bench waiting for the train, and chatting as if they had known one another for years.

"Now this I call quite a remarkable coincidence!" exclaimed the smaller and more talkative of the two sisters—the one whose legal knowledge had annihilated the cab-driver. "Not ony that we should be waiting for the same train, and at the same station—*that* would be curious enough—but actually on the same day, and the same hour of the day! That's what strikes *me* so forcibly!" She glanced at the fatter and more silent sister, whose chief function in life seemed to be to support the family opinion, and who meekly responded—

"And me too, sister!"

"Those are not *independent* coincidences——" Mad Mathesis was just beginning, when Clara ventured to interpose.

"There's no jolting here," she pleaded meekly. "*Would* you mind writing it down now?"

Out came the ivory tablets once more. "What was it, then?" said her aunt.

"One glass of lemonade, one sandwich, one biscuit—Oh dear me!" cried poor Clara, the historical tone suddenly changing to a wail of agony.

"Toothache?" said her aunt calmly, as she wrote down the items. The two sisters instantly opened their reticules and produced two different remedies for neuralgia, each marked "unequalled."

"It isn't that!" said poor Clara. "Thank you very much. It's only that I *can't* remember how much I paid!"

"Well, try and make it out, then," said her aunt. "You've got yesterday's luncheon to help you, you know. And here's the luncheon we had the day before—the first day we went to that shop—*one glass lemonade, four sandwiches, ten biscuits. Total, one-and-five pence.*" She handed the tablets to Clara, who gazed at them with eyes so dim with tears that she did not at first notice that she was holding them upside down.

The two sisters had been listening to all this with the deepest interest, and at this juncture the smaller one softly laid her hand on Clara's arm.

"Do you know, my dear," she said coaxingly, "my sister and I are in the very same predicament! Quite identically the very same predicament! Aren't we, sister?"

"Quite identically and absolutely the very——" began the fatter sister, but she was constructing her sentence on too large a scale, and the little one would not wait for her to finish it.

"Yes, my dear," she resumed; "we were lunching at the very same shop as you were—and we had two glasses of lemonade and three sandwiches and five biscuits—and neither of us has the least idea what we paid. Have we, sister?"

"Quite identically and absolutely——" murmured the other, who evidently considered that she was now a whole sentence in arrears, and that she ought to discharge one obligation before contracting any fresh liabilities; but the little lady broke in again, and she retired from the conversation a bankrupt.

"*Would* you make it out for us, my dear?" pleaded the little old lady.

"You can do Arithmetic, I trust?" her aunt said, a little anxiously, as Clara turned from one tablet to another, vainly trying to collect her thoughts. Her mind was a blank, and all human expression was rapidly fading out of her face.

A gloomy silence ensued.

KNOT VIII.

DE OMNIBUS REBUS.

"This little pig went to market:
This little pig staid at home."

"BY Her Radiancy's express command," said the governor, as he conducted the travellers, for the last time, from the Imperial presence, "I shall now have the ecstasy of escorting you as far as the outer gate of the Military Quarter, where the agony of parting—if indeed Nature can survive the shock—must be endured! From that gate grurmstipths start every quarter of an hour, both ways——"

"Would you mind repeating that word?" said Norman. "Grurm—?"

"Grurmstipths," the Governor repeated. "You call them omnibuses in England. They run both ways, and you can travel by one of them all the way down to the harbour."

The old man breathed a sigh of relief; four hours of courtly ceremony had wearied him, and he had been in constant terror lest something should call into use the ten thousand additional bamboos.

In another minute they were crossing a large quadrangle, paved with marble, and tastefully decorated with a pigsty in each corner. Soldiers, carrying pigs, were marching in all directions: and in the middle stood a gigantic officer giving orders in a voice of thunder, which made itself heard above all the uproar of the pigs.

"It is the Commander-in-Chief" the Governor hurriedly whispered to his companions, who at once followed his example in prostrating themselves before the great man. The Commander gravely bowed in return. He was covered with gold lace from head to foot: his face wore an expression of deep misery: and he had a little black pig under each arm. Still the gallant fellow did his best, in the midst of the orders he was every moment issuing to his men, to bid a courteous farewell to the departing guests.

"Farewell, oh old one—carry these three to the South corner—and farewell to thee, thou young one—put this fat one on the top of the others in the Western sty—may your shadows never be less—woe is me, it is wrongly done! Empty out all the sties, and begin again!" And the soldier leant upon his sword, and wiped away a tear.

"He is in distress," the Governor explained as they left the court. "Her Radiancy has commanded him to place twenty-four pigs in those four sties, so that, as she goes round the court, she may always find the number in each sty nearer to ten than the number in the last."

"Does she call ten nearer to ten than nine is?" said Norman.

"Surely," said the Governor. "Her Radiancy would admit that ten is nearer to ten than nine is—and also nearer than eleven is."

"Then I think it can be done," said Norman.

The Governor shook his head. "The Commander has been transferring them in vain for four months," he said. "What hope remains? And Her Radiancy has ordered up ten thousand additional——"

"The pigs don't seem to enjoy being transferred," the old man hastily interrupted. He did not like the subject of bamboos.

"They are only *provisionally* transferred, you know," said the Governor. "In most cases they are immediately carried back again: so they need not mind it. And all is done with the greatest care, under the personal superintendence of the Commander-in-Chief."

"Of course she would only go *once* round?" said Norman.

"Alas, no!" sighed their conductor. "Round and round. Round and round. These are Her Radiancy's own words. But oh, agony! Here is the outer gate, and we must part!" He sobbed as he shook hands with them, and the next moment was briskly walking away.

"He *might* have waited to see us off!" said the old man, piteously.

"And he needn't have begun whistling the very *moment* he left us!" said the young one, severely. "But look sharp—here are two what's-his-names in the act of starting!"

Unluckily, the sea-bound omnibus was full. "Never mind!" said Norman, cheerily. "We'll walk on till the next one overtakes us."

They trudged on in silence, both thinking over the military problem, till they met an omnibus coming from the sea. The elder traveller took out his watch. "Just twelve minutes and a half since we started," he remarked in an absent manner. Suddenly the vacant face brightened; the old man had an idea. "My boy!" he shouted, bringing his hand down upon Norman's shoulder so suddenly as for a moment to transfer his centre of gravity beyond the base of support.

Thus taken off his guard, the young man wildly staggered forwards, and seemed about to plunge into space: but in another moment he had gracefully recovered himself. "Problem in Precession and Nutation," he remarked—in tones where filial respect only just managed to conceal a shade of annoyance. "What is it?" he hastily added, fearing his father might have been taken ill. "Will you have some brandy?"

"When will the next omnibus overtake us? When? When?" the old man cried, growing more excited every moment.

Norman looked gloomy. "Give me time," he said. "I must think it over." And once more the travellers passed on in silence—a silence only broken by the distant squeals of the unfortunate little pigs, who were still being provisionally transferred from sty to sty, under the personal superintendence of the Commander-in-Chief.

KNOT IX.

A SERPENT WITH CORNERS.

"Water, water, every where,
Nor any drop to drink."

"IT'LL just take one more pebble."

"What ever *are* you doing with those buckets?"

The speakers were Hugh and Lambert. Place, the beach of Little Mendip. Time, 1.30, P.M. Hugh was floating a bucket in another a size larger, and trying how many pebbles it would carry without sinking. Lambert was lying on his back, doing nothing.

For the next minute or two Hugh was silent, evidently deep in thought. Suddenly he started.

"I say, look here, Lambert!" he cried.

"If it's alive, and slimy, and with legs, I don't care to," said Lambert.

"Didn't Balbus say this morning that, if a body is immersed in liquid, it displaces as much liquid as is equal to its own bulk?" said Hugh.

"He said things of that sort," Lambert vaguely replied.

"Well, just look here a minute. Here's the little bucket almost quite immersed: so the water displaced ought to be just about the same bulk. And now just look at it!" He took out the little bucket as he spoke, and handed the big one to Lambert. "Why, there's hardly a teacupful! Do you mean to say *that* water is the same bulk as the little bucket?"

"Course it is," said Lambert.

"Well, look here again!" cried Hugh, triumphantly, as he poured the water from the big bucket into the little one. "Why, it doesn't half fill it!"

"That's *its* business," said Lambert. "If Balbus says its the same bulk, why, it *is* the same bulk, you know.,"

"Well, I don't believe it," said Hugh.

"You needn't," said Lambert. "Besides, it's dinner-time. Come along."

They found Balbus waiting dinner for them, and to him Hugh at once propounded his difficulty.

"Let's get you helped first," said Balbus, briskly cutting away at the joint. "You know the old proverb 'Mutton first, mechanics afterwards'?"

The boys did *not* know the proverb, but they accepted it in perfect good faith, as they did every piece of information, however startling, that came from so infallible an authority as their tutor. They ate on steadily in silence, and, when dinner was over, Hugh set out the usual array of pens, ink, and paper, while Balbus repeated to them the problem he had prepared for their afternoon's task.

"A friend of mine has a flower-garden—a very pretty one, though no great size—"

"How big is it?" said Hugh.

"That's what *you* have to find out!" Balbus gaily replied. "All *I* tell you is that it is oblong in shape—just half a yard longer than its width—and that a gravel-walk, one yard wide, begins at one corner and runs all round it."

"Joining into itself?" said Hugh.

"*Not* joining into itself, young man. Just before doing *that*, it turns a corner, and runs round the garden again, alongside of the first portion, and then inside that again, winding in and in, and each lap touching the last one, till it has used up the whole of the area."

"Like a serpent with corners?" said Lambert.

"Exactly so. And if you walk the whole length of it, to the last inch, keeping in the centre the path, it's exactly two miles and half a furlong. Now, while you find out the length and breadth of the garden, I'll see if I can think out that sea-water puzzle."

"You said it was a flower-garden?" Hugh inquired, as Balbus was leaving the room.

"I did," said Balbus.

"Where do the flowers grow?" said Hugh. But Balbus thought it best not to hear the question. He left the boys to their problem, and, in the silence of his own room, set himself to unravel Hugh's mechanical paradox.

"To fix our thoughts," he murmured to himself, as, with hands deep-buried in his pockets, he paced up and down the room, "we will take a cylindrical glass jar, with a scale of inches marked up the side, and fill it with water up to the 10-inch mark: and we will assume that every inch depth of jar contains a pint of water. We will now take a solid cylinder, such that every inch of it is equal in bulk to *half* a pint of water, and plunge 4 inches of it into the water, so that the end of the cylinder comes down to the 6-inch mark. Well, that displaces 2 pints of water. What becomes of them? Why, if there were no more cylinder, they would lie comfortably on the top, and fill the jar up to the 12-inch mark. But unfortunately there *is* more cylinder, occupying half the space between the 10-inch and the 12-inch marks, so that only *one* pint of water can be accommodated there. What becomes of the other pint? Why, if there were no more cylinder, it would lie on the top, and fill the jar up to the 13-inch mark. But unfortunately——Shade of Newton!" he exclaimed, in sudden accents of terror. "When *does* the water stop rising?"

A bright idea struck him. "I'll write a little essay on it," he said.

BALBUS'S ESSAY.

"When a solid is immersed in a liquid, it is well known that it displaces a portion of the liquid equal to itself in bulk, and that the level of the liquid rises just so much as it would rise if a quantity of liquid had been added to it, equal in bulk to the solid. Lardner says, precisely the same process occurs when a solid is *partially* immersed: the quantity of liquid displaced, in this case, equalling the portion of the solid which is immersed, and the rise of the level being in proportion.

"Suppose a solid held above the surface of a liquid and partially immersed: a portion of the liquid is displaced, and the level of the liquid rises. But, by this rise of level, a little bit more of the solid is of course immersed, and so there is a new displacement of a second portion of the liquid, and a consequent rise of level. Again, this second rise of level causes a yet further immersion, and by consequence another displacement of liquid and another rise. It is self-evident that this process must continue till the entire solid is immersed, and that the liquid will then begin to immerse whatever holds the solid, which, being connected with it, must for the time be considered a part of it. If you hold a stick, six feet long, with its end in a tumbler of water, and wait long enough, you must eventually be immersed. The question as to the source from which the water is supplied—which belongs to a high branch of mathematics, and is therefore beyond our present scope—does not apply to the sea. Let us therefore take the familiar instance of a man standing at the edge of the sea, at ebb-tide, with a solid in his hand, which he partially immerses: he remains steadfast and unmoved, and we all know that he must be drowned. The multitudes who daily perish in this manner to attest a philosophical truth, and whose bodies the unreasoning wave casts sullenly upon our thankless shores, have a truer claim to be called the martyrs of science than a Galileo or a Kepler. To use Kossuth's eloquent phrase, they are the unnamed demigods of the nineteenth century."*

"There's a fallacy *somewhere*," he murmured drowsily, as he stretched his long legs upon the sofa. "I must think it over again." He closed his eyes, in order to concentrate his attention more perfectly, and for the next hour or so his slow regular breathing bore witness to the careful deliberation with which he was investigating this new and perplexing view of the subject.

KNOT X.

CHELSEA BUNS.

"Yea, buns, and buns, and buns!"
OLD SONG.

"How very, very sad!" exclaimed Clara; and the eyes of the gentle girl filled with tears as she spoke.

"Sad—but very curious when you come to look at it arithmetically,"

Note by the writer.—For the above Essay I am indebted to a dear friend, now deceased.

"HE REMAINS STEADFAST AND UNMOVED."

was her aunt's less romantic reply. "Some of them have lost an arm in their country's service, some a leg, some an ear, some an eye——"

"And some, perhaps, all!" Clara murmured dreamily, as they passed the long rows of weather-beaten heroes basking in the sun. "Did you notice that very old one, with a red face, who was drawing a map in the dust with his wooden leg, and all the others watching? I *think* it was a plan of battle——"

"The battle of Trafalgar, no doubt," her aunt interrupted, briskly.

"Hardly that, I think," Clara ventured to say. "You see, in that case, he couldn't well be alive——"

"Couldn't well be alive!" the old lady contemptuously repeated. "He's as lively as you and me put together! Why, if drawing a map in the dust—with one's wooden leg—doesn't prove one to be alive, perhaps you'll kindly mention what *does* prove it!"

Clara did not see her way out of it. Logic had never been her *forte*.

"To return to the arithmetic," Mad Mathesis resumed—the eccentric old lady never let slip an opportunity of driving her niece into a calculation—"what percentage do you suppose must have lost all four—a leg, an arm, an eye, and an ear?"

"How *can* I tell?" gasped the terrified girl. She knew well what was coming.

"You can't, of course, without *data*," her aunt replied: "but I'm just going to give you——"

"Give her a Chelsea bun, Miss! That's what most young ladies likes best!" The voice was rich and musical, and the speaker dexterously whipped back the snowy cloth that covered his basket, and disclosed a tempting array of the familiar square buns, joined together in rows, richly egged and browned, and glistening in the sun.

"No, sir! I shall give her nothing so indigestible! Be off!" The old lady waved her parasol threateningly: but nothing seemed to disturb the good-humour of the jolly old man, who marched on, chanting his melodious refrain:—

"Far too indigestible, my love!" said the old lady. "Percentages will agree with you ever so much better!"

Clara sighed, and there was a hungry look in her eyes as she watched the basket lessening in the distance: but she meekly listened to the relentless old lady, who at once proceeded to count off the *data* on her fingers.

"Say that 70 per cent. have lost an eye—75 per cent. an ear—80 per cent. an arm—85 per cent. a leg—that'll do it beautifully. Now, my dear, what percentage, *at least*, must have lost all four?"

No more conversation occurred—unless a smothered exclamation of "Piping hot!" which escaped from Clara's lips as the basket vanished round a corner could be counted as such—until they reached the old Chelsea mansion, where Clara's father was then staying, with his three sons and their old tutor.

Balbus, Lambert, and Hugh had entered the house only a few minutes before them. They had been out walking, and Hugh had been propounding a difficulty which had reduced Lambert to the depths of gloom, and had even puzzled Balbus.

"It changes from Wednesday to Thursday at midnight, doesn't it?" Hugh had begun.

"Sometimes," said Balbus, cautiously.

"Always," said Lambert, decisively.

"*Sometimes*," Balbus gently insisted. "Six midnights out of seven, it changes to some other name."

"I meant, of course," Hugh corrected himself, "when it *does* change from Wednesday to Thursday, it does it at midnight—and *only* at midnight."

"Surely," said Balbus. Lambert was silent.

"Well, now, suppose it's midnight here in Chelsea. Then it's Wednesday *west* of Chelsea (say in Ireland or America) where midnight hasn't arrived yet: and it's Thursday *east* of Chelsea (say in Germany or Russia) where midnight has just passed by?"

"Surely," Balbus said again. Even Lambert nodded this time.

"But it isn't midnight anywhere else; so it can't be changing from one day to another anywhere else. And yet, if Ireland and America and so on call it Wednesday, and Germany and Russia and so on call it Thursday, there *must* be some place—not Chelsea—that has different days on the two sides of it. And the worst of it is, the people *there* get their days in the wrong order: they've got Wednesday *east* of them, and Thursday *west*—just as if their day had changed from Thursday to Wednesday!"

"I've heard that puzzle before!" cried Lambert. "And I'll tell you the explanation. When a ship goes round the world from east to west, we know that it loses a day in its reckoning: so that when it gets home, and calls its day Wednesday, it finds people here calling it Thursday, because we've had one more midnight than the ship has had. And when you go the other way round you gain a day."

"I know all that," said Hugh, in reply to this not very lucid explanation: "but it doesn't help me, because the ship hasn't proper days. One way round, you get more than twenty-four hours to the day, and the other way you get less: so of course the names get wrong: but people that live on in one place always get twenty-four hours to the day."

"I suppose there *is* such a place," Balbus said, meditatively, "though I never heard of it. And the people must find it very queer, as Hugh says, to have the old day *east* of them, and the new one *west:* because, when midnight comes round to them, with the new day in front of it and the old one behind it, one doesn't see exactly what happens. I must think it over."

So they had entered the house in the state I have described—Balbus puzzled, and Lambert buried in gloomy thought.

"Yes, m'm, Master *is* at home, m'm," said the stately old butler. (N.B.— It is only a butler of experience who can manage a series of three M's together, without any interjacent vowels.) "And the *ole* party is a-waiting for you in the libery."

"I don't like his calling your father an *old* party," Mad Mathesis whispered to her niece, as they crossed the hall. And Clara had only just time to whisper in reply "he meant the *whole* party," before they were ushered into the library, and the sight of the five solemn faces there assembled chilled her into silence.

Her father sat at the head of the table, and mutely signed to the ladies to take the two vacant chairs, one on each side of him. His three sons and Balbus completed the party. Writing materials had been arranged round the table, after the fashion of a ghostly banquet: the butler had evidently bestowed much thought on the grim device. Sheets of quarto paper, each flanked by a pen on one side and a pencil on the other, represented the plates—penwipers did duty for rolls of bread—while ink-bottles stood in the places usually occupied by wine-glasses. The *pièce de resistance* was a large green baize bag, which gave forth, as the old man restlessly lifted it from side to side, a charming jingle, as of innumerable golden guineas.

"Sister, daughter, sons—and Balbus—," the old man began, so nervously, that Balbus put in a gentle "Hear, hear!" while Hugh drummed on the table with his fists. This disconcerted the unpractised orator. "Sister—" he began again, then paused a moment, moved the bag to the other side, and went on with a rush, "I mean—this being—a critical occasion— more or less—being the year when one of my sons comes of age—" he paused again in some confusion, having evidently got into the middle of his speech sooner than he intended: but it was too late to go back. "Hear, hear!" cried Balbus. "Quite so," said the old gentleman, recovering his self-possession a little: "when first I began this annual custom—my friend Balbus will correct me if I am wrong—" (Hugh whispered "with a strap!" but nobody heard him except Lambert, who only frowned and shook his head at him) "—this annual custom of giving each of my sons as many guineas as would represent his age—it was a critical time—so Balbus informed me—as the ages of two of you were together equal to that of the third—so on that occasion I made a speech——" He paused so long that Balbus thought it well to come to the rescue with the words "It was a most——" but the old man checked him with a warning look: "yes, made a speech," he repeated. "A few years after that, Balbus pointed out—I say pointed out—" ("Hear, hear"! cried Balbus. "Quite so," said the grateful old man.) "—that it was *another* critical occasion. The ages of two of you were together *double* that of the third. So I made another speech—another speech. And now again it's a critical occasion—so Balbus says—and I am making——" (Here Mad Mathesis pointedly referred to her watch) "all the haste I can!" the old man cried, with wonderful presence of mind. "Indeed, sister, I'm coming to the point now! The number of years that have passed since that first occasion is just two-thirds of the number of guineas I then gave you. Now, my boys, calculate your ages from the *data*, and you shall have the money!"

"But we *know* our ages!" cried Hugh.

"Silence, sir!" thundered the old man, rising to his full height (he was exactly five-foot five) in his indignation. "I say you must use the *data* only! You mustn't even assume *which* it is that comes of age!" He clutched the bag as he spoke, and with tottering steps (it was about as much as he could do to carry it) he left the room.

"And *you* shall have a similar *cadeau*," the old lady whispered to her niece, "when you've calculated that percentage!" And she followed her brother.

Nothing could exceed the solemnity with which the old couple had risen from the table, and yet was it—was it a *grin* with which the father turned away from his unhappy sons? Could it be—could it be a *wink* with which the aunt abandoned her despairing niece? And were those—were those sounds of suppressed *chuckling* which floated into the room, just before Balbus (who had followed them out) closed the door? Surely not: and yet the butler told the cook—but no, that was merely idle gossip, and I will not repeat it.

The shades of evening granted their unuttered petition, and "closed not o'er" them (for the butler brought in the lamp): the same obliging shades left them a "lonely bark" (the wail of a dog, in the back-yard, baying the moon) for "awhile": but neither "morn, alas," (nor any other epoch) seemed likely to "restore" them—to that peace of mind which had once been theirs ere ever these problems had swooped upon them, and crushed them with a load of unfathomable mystery!

"It's hardly fair," muttered Hugh, "to give us such a jumble as this to work out!"

"Fair?" Clara echoed, bitterly. "Well!"

And to all my readers I can but repeat the last words of gentle Clara—

Fare-well!

APPENDIX.

"A knot!" said Alice. "Oh, do let me help to undo it!"

ANSWERS TO KNOT I.

Problem.—"Two travellers spend from 3 o'clock till 9 in walking along a level road, up a hill, and home again: their pace on the level being 4 miles an hour, up hill 3, and down hill 6. Find distance walked: also (within half an hour) time of reaching top of hill."

Answer.—"24 miles: half-past 6."

Solution.—A level mile takes $1/4$ of an hour, up hill $1/3$, down hill $1/6$. Hence to go and return over the same mile, whether on the level or on the hill-side, takes $1/2$ an hour. Hence in 6 hours they went 12 miles out and 12 back. If the 12 miles out had been nearly all level, they would have taken a little over 3 hours; if nearly all up hill, a little under 4. Hence $3 1/2$ hours must be within $1/2$ an hour of the time taken in reaching the peak; thus, as they started at 3, they got there within $1/2$ an hour of $1/2$ past 6.

Twenty-seven answers have come in. Of these, 9 are right, 16 partially right, and 2 wrong. The 16 give the *distance* correctly, but they have failed to grasp the fact that the top of the hill might have been reached at *any* moment between 6 o'clock and 7.

The two wrong answers are from GERTY VERNON and A. NIHILIST. The former makes the distance "23 miles," while her revolutionary companion puts it at "27." GERTY VERNON says "they had to go 4 miles along the plain, and got to the foot of the hill at 4 o'clock." They *might* have done so, I grant; but you have no ground for saying they *did* so. "It was $7 1/2$ miles to the top of the hill, and they reached that at $1/4$ before 7 o'clock." Here you go wrong in your arithmetic, and I must, however reluctantly, bid you farewell. $7 1/2$ miles, at 3 miles an hour, would *not* require $2 3/4$ hours. A. NIHILIST says "Let x denote the whole number of miles; y the number of hours to hill-top; $\therefore 3y$ = number of miles to hill-top, and $x - 3y$ = number of miles on the other side." You bewilder me. The other side of *what*? "Of the hill," you say. But then, how did they get home again? However, to accommodate your views we will build a new hostelry at the foot of the hill on the opposite side, and also assume (what I grant you is *possible*, though it is not *necessarily* true) that there was no level road at all. Even then you go wrong. You say

$$\text{``}y = 6 - \frac{x - 3y}{6}\text{,''} \ldots \ldots \text{(i);}$$

$$\frac{x}{4^{1}/_{2}} = 6 \ldots \ldots \ldots \ldots \text{(ii).''}$$

I grant you (i), but I deny (ii): it rests on the assumption that to go *part* of the time at 3 miles an hour, and the rest at 6 miles an hour, comes to the same result as going the *whole* time at $4^{1}/_{2}$ miles an hour. But this would only be true if the "*part*" were an exact *half*, i.e., if they went up hill for 3 hours, and down hill for the other 3: which they certainly did *not* do.

The sixteen, who are partially right, are AGNES BAILEY, F.K., FIFEE, G.E.B., H.P., KIT, M.E.T., MYSIE, A MOTHER'S SON, NAIRAM, A RE-DRUTHIAN, A SOCIALIST, SPEAR MAIDEN, T.B.C., VIS INERTIÆ, and YAK. Of these, F.K., FIFEE, T.B.C., and VIS INERTIÆ do not attempt the second part at all. F.K. and H.P. give no working. The rest make particular assumptions, such as that there was no level road—that there were 6 miles of level road—and so on, all leading to *particular* times being fixed for reaching the hill-top. The most curious assumption is that of AGNES BAILEY, who says "Let x = number of hours occupied in ascent;

then $\frac{x}{2}$ = hours occupied in descent; and $\frac{4x}{3}$ = hours occupied on the

level." I suppose you were thinking of the relative *rates*, up hill and on the level; which we might express by saying that, if they went x miles up

hill in a certain time, they would go $\frac{4x}{3}$ miles on the level *in the same time*.

You have, in fact, assumed that they took *the same time* on the level that they took in ascending the hill. FIFEE assumes that, when the aged knight said they had gone "four miles in the hour" on the level, he meant that four miles was the *distance* gone, not merely the rate. This would have been—if FIFEE will excuse the slang expression—a "sell," ill-suited to the dignity of the hero.

And now "descend, ye classic Nine!" who have solved the whole problem, and let me sing your praises. Your names are BLITHE, E.W., L.B., A MARLBOROUGH BOY, O.V.L., PUTNEY WALKER, ROSE, SEA BREEZE, SIMPLE SUSAN, and MONEY SPINNER. (These last two I count as one, as they send a joint answer.) ROSE and SIMPLE SUSAN and Co. do not actually state that the hill-top was reached some time between 6 and 7, but, as they have clearly grasped the fact that a mile, ascended and descended, took the same time as two level miles, I mark them as "right." A MARL-BOROUGH BOY and PUTNEY WALKER deserve honourable mention for their algebraical solutions being the only two who have perceived that the question leads to *an indeterminate equation*. E.W. brings a charge of untruthfulness against the aged knight—a serious charge, for he was the very pink of chivalry! She says "According to the data given, the time at the summit affords no clue to the total distance. It does not enable us to state precisely to an inch how much level and how much hill there was on the road." "Fair damsel," the aged knight replies, "— if, as I surmise, thy initials denote Early Womanhood—bethink thee that the word 'enable' is thine, not mine. I did but ask the time of reaching the hill-top as my *condition* for further parley. If *now* thou wilt not grant that I am a truth-loving man, then will I affirm that those same initials denote Envenomed Wickedness!"

CLASS LIST.

I.

A MARLBOROUGH BOY.   PUTNEY WALKER.

II.

BLITHE.   ROSE.
E. W.   SEA BREEZE.
L. B.   SIMPLE SUSAN.
O. V. L.   MONEY-SPINNER.

BLITHE has made so ingenious an addition to the problem, and SIMPLE SUSAN and CO. have solved it in such tuneful verse, that I record both their answers in full. I have altered a word or two in BLITHE'S—which I trust she will excuse; it did not seem quite clear as it stood.

"Yet, stay," said the youth, as a gleam of inspiration lighted up the relaxing muscles of his quiescent features. "Stay. Methinks it matters little *when* we reached that summit, the crown of our toil. For in the space of time wherein we clambered up one mile and bounded down the same on our return, we could have trudged the *twain* on the level. We have plodded, then, four-and-twenty miles in these six mortal hours; for never a moment did we stop for catching of fleeting breath or for gazing on the scene around!"

"Very good," said the old man. "Twelve miles out and twelve miles in. And we reached the top some time between six and seven of the clock. Now mark me! For every five minutes that had fled since six of the clock when we stood on yonder peak, so many miles had we toiled upwards on the dreary mountainside!"

The youth moaned and rushed into the hostel.

BLITHE.

The elder and the younger knight,
   They sallied forth at three;
How far they went on level ground
   It matters not to me;
What time they reached the foot of hill,
   When they began to mount,
Are problems which I hold to be
   Of very small account.

The moment that each waved his hat
   Upon the topmost peak—
To trivial query such as this
   No answer will I seek.
Yet can I tell the distance well
   They must have travelled o'er:
On hill and plain, 'twixt three and nine,
   The miles were twenty-four.

Four miles an hour their steady pace
   Along the level track,
Three when they climbed—but six when they
   Came swiftly striding back
Adown the hill; and little skill
   It needs, methinks, to show,
Up hill and down together told,
   Four miles an hour they go.

For whether long or short the time
   Upon the hill they spent,
Two thirds were passed in going up,
   One third in the descent.
Two thirds at three, one third at six,
   If rightly reckoned o'er,
Will make one whole at four—the tale
   Is tangled now no more.

SIMPLE SUSAN.
MONEY SPINNER.

ANSWERS TO KNOT II.

§ 1. THE DINNER PARTY.

Problem.—"The Governor of Kgovjni wants to give a very small dinner party, and invites his father's brother-in-law, his brother's father-in-law, his father-in-law's brother, and his brother-in-law's father. Find the number of guests."
Answer.—"One."

In this genealogy, males are denoted by capitals, and females by small letters.

The Governor is E and his guest is C.

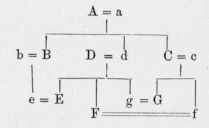

Ten answers have been received. Of these, one is wrong, GALANTHUS NIVALIS MAJOR, who insists on inviting *two* guests, one being the Governor's *wife's brother's father.* If she had taken his *sister's husband's father* instead, she would have found it possible to reduce the guests to *one.*

Of the nine who send right answers, SEA BREEZE is the very faintest breath that ever bore the name! She simply states that the Governor's uncle might fulfill all the conditions "by intermarriages"! "Wind of the western sea," you have had a very narrow escape! Be thankful to appear in the Class-list at all! BOG-OAK and BRADSHAW OF THE FUTURE use genealogies which require 16 people instead of 14, by inviting the Governor's *father's sister's husband* instead of his *father's wife's brother.* I cannot think this so good a solution as one that requires only 14. CAIUS and VALENTINE deserve special mention as the only two who have supplied genealogies.

CLASS LIST.

I.

BEE.	M. M.	OLD CAT.
CAIUS.	MATTHEW MATTICKS.	VALENTINE.

II.

BOG-OAK.　　　　　　BRADSHAW OF THE FUTURE.

III.

SEA-BREEZE.

§ 2. THE LODGINGS.

Problem.—"A Square has 20 doors on each side, which contains 21 equal parts. They are numbered all round, beginning at one corner. From which of the four, Nos. 9, 25, 52, 73, is the sum of the distances, to the other three, least?"
Answer.—"From No. 9."

Let A be No. 9, B No. 25, C
No. 52, and D No. 73.

Then $AB = \sqrt{(12^2 + 5^2)} = \sqrt{169} = 13$;

$AC = 21$;

$AD = \sqrt{(9^2 + 8^2)} = \sqrt{145} = 12 +$;

(N.B. *i.e.* "between 12 and 13.")

$BC = \sqrt{(16^2 + 12^2)} = \sqrt{400} = 20$;

$BD = \sqrt{(3^2 + 21^2)} = \sqrt{450} = 21 +$;

$CD = \sqrt{(9^2 + 13^2)} = \sqrt{250} = 15 +$;

Hence sum of distances from A is between 46 and 47; from B, between 54 and 55; from C, between 56 and 57; from D, between 48 and 51. (Why not "between 48 and 49"? Make this out for yourselves.) Hence the sum is least for A.

Twenty-five solutions have been received. Of these, 15 must be marked "0," 5 are partly right, and 5 right. Of the 15, I may dismiss ALPHABETICAL

PHANTOM, BOG-OAK, DINAH MITE, FIFEE, GALANTHUS NIVALIS MAJOR (I fear the cold spring has blighted our SNOWDROP), GUY, H.M.S. PIN-AFORE, JANET, and VALENTINE with the simple remark that they insist on the unfortunate lodgers *keeping to the pavement*. (I used the words "crossed to Number Seventy-three" for the special purpose of showing that *short cuts* were possible.) SEA BREEZE does the same, and adds that "the result would be the same" even if they crossed the Square, but gives no proof of this. M. M. draws a diagram, and says that No. 9 is the house, "as the diagram shows." I cannot see *how* it does so. OLD CAT assumes that the house *must* be No. 9 or No. 73. She does not explain how she estimates the distances. BEE'S Arithmetic is faulty: she makes $\sqrt{169} + \sqrt{442} + \sqrt{130} = 741$. (I suppose you mean $\sqrt{741}$, which would be a little nearer the truth. But roots cannot be added in this manner. Do you think $\sqrt{9} + \sqrt{16}$ is 25, or even $\sqrt{25}$?) But AYR'S state is more perilous still: she draws illogical conclusions with a frightful calmness. After pointing out (rightly) that AC is less than BD she says, "therefore the nearest house to the other three must be A or C." And again, after pointing out (rightly) that B and D are both within the half-square containing A, she says "therefore" AB + AD must be less than BC + CD. (There is no logical force in either "therefore." For the first, try Nos. 1, 21, 60, 70: this will make your premiss true, and your conclusion false. Similarly, for the second, try Nos. 1, 30, 51, 71.)

Of the five partly-right solutions, RAGS AND TATTERS and MAD HATTER (who send one answer between them) make No. 25 6 units from the corner instead of 5. CHEAM, E. R. D. L., and MEGGY POTTS leave openings at the corners of the Square, which are not in the *data:* moreover CHEAM gives values for the distances without any hint that they are only *approximations*. CROPHI AND MOPHI make the bold and unfounded assumption that there were really 21 houses on each side, instead of 20 as stated by Balbus. "We may assume," they add, "that the doors of Nos. 21, 42, 63, 84, are invisible from the centre of the Square"! What is there, I wonder, that CROPHI AND MOPHI would *not* assume?

Of the five who are wholly right, I think BRADSHAW OF THE FUTURE, CAIUS, CLIFTON C., and MARTREB deserve special paise for their full *analytical* solutions. MATTHEW MATTICKS picks out No. 9, and proves it to be the right house in two ways, very neatly and ingeniously, but *why* he picks it out does not appear. It is an excellent *synthetical* proof, but lacks the analysis which the other four supply.

CLASS LIST.

I.

BRADSHAW OF THE FUTURE.   CLIFTON C.
CAIUS.   MARTREB.

II.

MATTHEW MATTICKS.

III.

CHEAM.	MEGGY POTTS.
CROPHI AND MOPHI.	⎰ RAGS AND TATTERS.
E. R. D. L.	⎱ MAD HATTER.

A remonstrance has reached me from SCRUTATOR on the subject of KNOT I., which he declares was "no problem at all." "Two questions," he says, "are put. To solve one there is no data: the other answers itself." As to the first point, SCRUTATOR is mistaken; there *are* (not "is") data sufficient to answer the question. As to the other, it is interesting to know that the question "answers itself," and I am sure it does the question great credit: still I fear I cannot enter it on the list of winners, as this competition is only open to human beings.

ANSWERS TO KNOT III.

Problem.—(1) "Two travellers, starting at the same time, went opposite ways round a circular railway. Trains start each way every 15 minutes, the easterly ones going round in 3 hours, the westerly in 2. How many trains did each meet on the way, not counting trains met at the terminus itself?" (2) "They went round, as before, each traveller counting as 'one' the train containing the other traveller. How many did each meet?"
Answers.—(1) 19. (2) The easterly traveller met 12; the other 8.

The trains one way took 180 minutes, the other way 120. Let us take the L. C. M., 360, and divide the railway into 360 units. Then one set of trains went at the rate of 2 units a minute and at intervals of 30 units; the other at the rate of 3 units a minute and at intervals of 45 units. An easterly train starting has 45 units between it and the first train it will meet: it does 2–5ths of this while the other does 3–5ths, and thus meets it at the end of 18 units, and so all the way round. A westerly train starting has 30 units between it and the first train it will meet: it does 3–5ths of this while the other does 2–5ths, and thus meets it at the end of 18 units, and so all the way round. Hence if the railway be divided, by 19 posts, into 20 parts, each containing 18 units, trains meet at every post, and, in (1), each traveller passes 19 posts in going round, and so meets 19 trains. But, in (2), the easterly traveller only begins to count after traversing 2–5ths of the journey, *i.e.*, on reaching the 8th post, and so counts 12 posts: similarly the other counts 8. They meet at the end of 2–5ths of 3 hours, or 3–5ths of 2 hours, *i.e.*, 72 minutes.

Forty-five answers have been received. Of these 12 are beyond the reach of discussion, as they give no working. I can but enumerate their names. ARDMORE, E. A., F. A. D., L. D., MATTHEW MATTICKS, M. E. T., POO-POO, and THE RED QUEEN are all wrong. BETA and ROWENA have got (1) right and (2) wrong. CHEEKY BOB and NAIRAM give the right answers, but it may perhaps make the one less cheeky, and induce the other to take a less inverted view of things, to be informed that, if this had been a competition for a prize, they would have got no marks. [N.B.—I have not ventured to put E. A.'s name in full, as she only gave it provisionally, in case her answer should prove right.]

Of the 33 answers for which the working is given, 10 are wrong; 11 half-wrong and half-right; 3 right, except that they cherish the delusion that it was *Clara* who travelled in the easterly train—a point which the data do not enable us to settle; and 9 wholly right.

The 10 wrong answers are from BO-PEEP, FINANCIER, I. W. T., KATE B., M. A. H., Q. Y. Z., SEA-GULL, THISTLEDOWN, TOM-QUAD, and an unsigned one. BO-PEEP rightly says that the easterly traveller met all trains which started during the 3 hours of her trip, as well as all which started during the previous 2 hours, *i.e.*, all which started at the commencements of 20 periods of 15 minutes each; and she is right in striking out the one she met at the moment of starting; but wrong in striking out the *last* train, for she did not meet this at the terminus, but 15 minutes before she got there. She makes the same mistake in (2). FINANCIER thinks that any train, met for the second time, is not to be counted. I. W. T. finds, by a process which is not stated, that the travellers met at the end of 71 minutes and $26\frac{1}{2}$ seconds. KATE B. thinks the trains which are met on starting and on arriving are *never* to be counted, even when met elsewhere. Q. Y. Z. tries a rather complex algebraical solution, and succeeds in finding the time of meeting correctly: all else is wrong. SEA-GULL seems to think that, in (1), the easterly train *stood still* for 3 hours; and says that, in (2), the travellers met at the end of 71 minutes 40 seconds. THISTLEDOWN nobly confesses to having tried no calculation, but merely having drawn a picture of the railway and counted the trains; in (1), she counts wrong; in (2) she makes them meet in 75 minutes. TOM-QUAD omits (1): in (2) he makes Clara count the train she met on her arrival. The unsigned one is also unintelligible; it states that the travellers go "1–24th more than the total distance to be traversed"! The "Clara" theory, already referred to, is adopted by 5 of these, viz., BO-PEEP, FINANCIER, KATE B., TOM-QUAD, and the nameless writer.

The 11 half-right answers are from BOG-OAK, BRIDGET, CASTOR, CHESHIRE CAT, G. E. B., GUY, MARY, M. A. H., OLD MAID, R. W., and VENDREDI. All these adopt the "Clara" theory. CASTOR omits (1). VENDREDI gets (1) right, but in (2) makes the same mistake as BO-PEEP. I notice in your solution a marvellous proportion-sum:—"300 miles: 2 hours: :one mile: 24 seconds." May I venture to advise your acquiring, as soon as possible, an utter disblief in the possibility of a ratio existing between *miles* and *hours*? Do not be disheartened by your two friends' sarcastic remarks on your "roundabout ways." Their short method, of adding 12 and 8, has the slight disadvantage of bringing the answer wrong: even a "roundabout" method is better than *that!* M. A. H., in (2), makes the travellers count "one" *after* they met, not *when* they met. CHESHIRE CAT and OLD MAID get "20" as answer for (1), by forgetting to strike out the train met on arrival. The others all get "18" in various ways. BOG-OAK, GUY, and R. W. divide the trains which the westerly traveller has to meet into 2 sets, viz., those already on the line, which they (rightly) make "11," and those which started during her 2 hours' journey (exclusive of train met on arrival), which they (wrongly) make "7"; and they make a similar mistake with the easterly train. BRIDGET (rightly) says that the westerly traveller met a train every 6 minutes for 2 hours, but (wrongly) makes the number "20"; it should be "21." G. E. B. adopts BO-PEEP'S method, but (wrongly) strikes out (for the easterly traveller) the train which started at the *commencement* of the previous 2 hours. MARY thinks a train, met on arrival, must not be counted, even when met on a *previous* occasion.

The 3, who are wholly right but for the unfortunate "Clara" theory, are F. LEE, G. S. C., and X. A. B.

And now "descend, ye classic Ten!" who have solved the whole problem. Your names are AIX-LES-BAINS, ALGERNON BRAY (thanks for a friendly remark, which comes with a heart-warmth that not even the Atlantic could chill), ARVON, BRADSHAW OF THE FUTURE, FIFEE, H. L. R., J. L. O., OMEGA, S. S. G., and WAITING FOR THE TRAIN. Several of these have put Clara, provisionally, into the easterly train: but they seem to have understood that the data do not decide that point.

CLASS LIST.

I.

AIX-LE-BAINS.	H. L. R.
ALGERNON BRAY.	OMEGA.
BRADSHAW OF THE FUTURE.	S. S. G.
FIFEE.	WAITING FOR THE TRAIN.

II.

ARVON.	J. L. O.

III.

F. LEE.	G. S. C.	X. A. B.

ANSWERS TO KNOT IV.

Problem.—"There are 5 sacks, of which Nos. 1, 2, weigh 12 lbs.; Nos. 2, 3, 13^1/$_2$ lbs.; Nos. 3, 4, 11^1/$_2$ lbs.; nos. 4, 5, 8 lbs.; Nos. 1, 3, 5, 16 lbs. Required the weight of each sack."
Answer.—"5^1/$_2$, 6^1/$_2$, 7, 4^1/$_2$, 3^1/$_2$."

The sum of all the weighings, 61 lbs., includes sack No. 3 *thrice* and each other *twice*. Deducting twice the sum of the 1st and 4th weighings, we get 21 lbs. for *thrice* No. 3, *i.e.*, 7 lbs. for No. 3. Hence, the 2nd and 3rd weighings give 6^1/$_2$ lbs., 4^1/$_2$ lbs for Nos. 2, 4; and hence again, the 1st and 4th weighings give 5^1/$_2$ lbs., 3^1/$_2$ lbs., for Nos. 1, 5.

Ninety-seven answers have been received. Of these, 15 are beyond the reach of discussion, as they give no working. I can but enumerate their names, and I take this opportunity of saying that this is the last time I shall put on record the names of competitors who give no sort of clue to the process by which their answers were obtained. In guessing a conundrum, or in catching a flea, we do not expect the breathless victor to give us afterwards, in cold blood, a history of the mental or muscular efforts by which he achieved success; but a mathematical calculation is another thing. The names of this "mute inglorious" band are COMMON SENSE, D. E. R., DOUGLAS, E. L., ELLEN, I. M. T., J. M. C., JOSEPH, KNOT I, LUCY, MEEK, M. F. C., PYRAMUS, SHAH, VERITAS.

Of the eighty-two answers with which the working, or some approach to it, is supplied, one is wrong: seventeen have given solutions which are (from one cause or another) practically valueless: the remaining sixty-four I shall try to arrange in a Class-list, according to the varying degrees of shortness and neatness to which they seem to have attained.

The solitary wrong answer is from NELL. To be thus "alone in the crowd" is a distinction—a painful one, no doubt, but still a distinction. I am sorry for you, my dear young lady, and I seem to hear your tearful exclamation, when you read these lines, "Ah! This is the knell of all my hopes!" Why, oh why, did you assume that the 4th and 5th bags weighed 4 lbs. each? And why did you not test your answers? However, please try again: and please don't change your *nom-de-plume*: let us have NELL in the First Class next time!

The seventeen whose solutions are practically valueless are ARDMORE, A READY RECKONER, ARTHUR, BOG-LARK, BOG-OAK, BRIDGET, FIRST ATTEMPT, J. L. C., M. E. T., ROSE, ROWENA, SEA-BREEZE, SYLVIA, THISTLEDOWN, THREE-FIFTHS ASLEEP, VENDREDI, and WINIFRED. BOG-LARK tries it by a sort of "rule of false," assuming experimentally that Nos. 1, 2, weigh 6 lbs. each, and having thus produced 17^1/$_2$, instead of 16, as the weight of 1, 3, and 5, she removes "the superfluous pound and a half," but does not explain how she knows from which to take it. THREE-FIFTHS ASLEEP says that (when in that peculiar state) "it seemed perfectly clear" to her that, "3 out of 5 sacks being weighed twice over, $^3/_5$ of $45 = 27$, must be the total weight of the 5 sacks." As to which I can only say, with the Captain, "it beats me entirely!" WINIFRED, on the plea that "one must have a starting-point," assumes (what I fear is a mere guess) that No. 1 weighed $5^1/_2$ lbs. The rest all do it, wholly or partly, by guess-work.

The problem is of course (as any Algebraist sees at once) a case of "simultaneous simple equations." It is, however, easily soluble by Arithmetic only; and, when this is the case, I hold that it is bad workmanship to use the more complex method. I have not, this time, given more credit to arithmetical solutions; but in future problems I shall (other things being equal) give the highest marks to those who use the simplest machinery. I have put into Class I. those whose answers seemed specially short and neat, and into Class III. those that seemed specially long or clumsy. Of this last set, A. C. M., FURZE-BUSH, JAMES, PARTRIDGE, R. W., and WAITING FOR THE TRAIN, have sent long wandering solutions, the substitutions having no definite method, but seeming to have been made to see what would come of it. CHILPOME and DUBLIN BOY omit some of the working. ARVON MARLBOROUGH BOY only finds the weight of *one* sack.

CLASS LIST.

I.

B. E. D.
C. H.
CONSTANCE JOHNSON.
GREYSTEAD.
GUY.
HOOPOE.
J. F. A.
M. A. H.

NUMBER FIVE.
PEDRO.
R. E. X.
SEVEN OLD MEN.
VIS INERTIÆ.
WILLY B.
YAHOO.

II.

AMERICAN SUBSCRIBER.
AN APPRECIATIVE SCHOOLMA'AM.
AYR.
BRADSHAW OF THE FUTURE.
CHEAM.
C. M. G.
DINAH MITE.
DUCKWING.
E. C. M.
E. N. LOWRY.
ERA.
EUROCLYDON.
F. H. W.
FIFEE.
G. E. B.
HARLEQUIN.
HAWTHORN.
HOUGH GREEN.
J. A. B.
JACK TAR.

J. B. B.
KGOVJNI.
LAND LUBBER.
L. D.
MAGPIE.
MARY.
MHRUXI.
MINNIE.
MONEY-SPINNER.
NAIRAM.
OLD CAT.
POLICHINELLE.
SIMPLE SUSAN.
S. S. G.
THISBE.
VERENA.
WAMBA.
WOLFE.
WYKEHAMICUS.
Y. M. A. H.

III.

A. C. M.
ARVON MARLBOROUGH BOY.
CHILPOME.
DUBLIN BOY.
FURZE-BUSH.

JAMES.
PARTRIDGE.
R. W.
WAITING FOR THE TRAIN.

ANSWERS TO KNOT V.

Problem.—To mark pictures, giving 3 ×'s to 2 or 3, 2 to 4 or 5, and 1 to 9 or 10; also giving 3 ○'s to 1 or 2, 2 to 3 or 4 and 1 to 8 or 9; so as to mark the smallest possible number of pictures, and to give them the largest possible number of marks.

Answer.—10 pictures; 29 marks; arranged thus:—

```
×  ×  ×  ×  ×  ×  ×  ×  ×  ○
×  ×  ×  ×  ×     ○  ○  ○  ○
×  ×  ○  ○  ○  ○  ○  ○  ○  ○
```

Solution.—By giving all the ×'s possible, putting into brackets the optional ones, we get 10 pictures marked thus:—

$$× × × × × × × × × (×)$$
$$× × × × (×)$$
$$× × (×)$$

By then assigning ○'s in the same way, beginning at the other end, we get 9 pictures marked thus:—

$$(○) ○$$
$$(○) ○ ○ ○$$
$$(○) ○ ○ ○ ○ ○ ○ ○ ○$$

All we have now to do is to run two wedges as close together as they will go, so as to get the minimum number of pictures——erasing optional marks where by so doing we can run them closer, but otherwise letting them stand. There are 10 necessary marks in the 1st row, and in the 3rd; but only 7 in the 2nd. Hence we erase all optional marks in the 1st and 3rd rows, but let them stand in the 2nd.

———

Twenty-two answers have been received. Of these 11 give no working; so, in accordance with what I announced in my last review of answers, I leave them unnamed, merely mentioning that 5 are right and 6 wrong.

Of the eleven answers with which some working is supplied, 3 are wrong. C. H. begins with the rash assertion that under the given conditions "the sum is impossible. For," he or she adds (these initialed correspondents are dismally vague beings to deal with: perhaps "it" would be a better pronoun), "10 is the least possible number of pictures" (granted): "therefore we must either give 2 ×'s to 6, or 2 ○'s to 5." Why "must," oh alphabetical phantom? It is nowhere ordained that every picture "must" have 3 marks! FIFEE sends a folio page of solution, which deserved a better fate: she offers 3 answers, in each of which 10 pictures are marked, with 30 marks; in one she gives 2 ×'s to 6 pictures; in another to 7; in the 3rd she gives 2 ○'s to 5; thus in every case ignoring the conditions. (I pause to remark that the condition "2 ×'s to 4 or 5 pictures" can only mean "*either* to 4 *or else* to 5": if, as one competitor holds, it might mean *any* number not less than 4, the words "*or 5*" would be superfluous.) I. E. A. (I am happy to say that none of these bloodless phantoms appear this time in the class-list. Is it IDEA with the "D" left out?) gives 2 ×'s to 6 pictures. She then takes me to task for using the word "ought" instead of "nought." No doubt, to one who thus rebels against the rules laid down for her guidance, the word must be distasteful. But does not I. E. A. remember the parallel case of "adder"? That creature was originally "a nadder": then the two words took to bandying the poor "n" backwards and forwards like a shuttlecock, the final state of the game being "an adder." May not "a nought" have similarly become "an ought?" Anyhow, "oughts and crosses" is a very old game. I don't think I ever heard it called "noughts and crosses."

In the following Class-list, I hope the solitary occupant of III. will sheathe her claws when she hears how narrow an escape she has had of not being named at all. Her account of the process by which she got the answer is so meagre that, like the nursery tale of "Jack-a-Minory" (I trust I. E. A. will be merciful to the spelling), it is scarcely to be distinguished from "zero."

CLASS LIST.

I.

GUY.	OLD CAT.	SEA-BREEZE.

II.

AYR.	F. LEE
BRADSHAW OF THE FUTURE.	H. VERNON.

III.

CAT.

ANSWERS TO KNOT VI.

Problem 1.—*A* and *B* began the year with only 1,000*l.* a-piece. They borrowed nought; they stole nought. On the next New-Year's Day they had 60,000*l.* between them. How did they do it?

Solution.—They went that day to the Bank of England. *A* stood in front of it, while *B* went round and stood behind it.

Two answers have been received, both worthy of much honour. AD-DLEPATE makes them borrow "0" and steal "0," and uses both cyphers by putting them at the right-hand end of the 1,000*l.* thus producing 100,000*l.*, which is well over the mark. But (or to express it in Latin) AT SPES INFRACTA has solved it even more ingeniously: with the first cypher she turns the "1" of the 1,000*l.* into a "9," and adds the result to the original sum, thus getting 10,000*l.*: and in this, by means of the other "0," she turns the "1" into a "6," thus hitting the exact 60,000*l.*

CLASS LIST

I.

AT SPES INFRACTA.

II.

ADDLEPATE.

Problem 2.—*L* makes 5 scarves, while *M* makes 2: *Z* makes 4 while *L* makes 3. Five scarves of *Z*'s weigh one of *L*'s; 5 of *M*'s weigh 3 of *Z*'s. One of *M*'s is as warm as 4 of *Z*'s: and one of *L*'s as warm as 3 of *M*'s. Which is best, giving equal weight in the result to rapidity of work, lightness, and warmth?

Answer.—The order is *M, L, Z.*

Solution.—As to rapidity (other things being constant) *L*'s merit is to *M*'s in the ratio of 5 to 2: *Z*'s to *L*'s in the ratio of 4 to 3. In order to get one set of 3 numbers fulfilling these conditions, it is perhaps simplest to take the one that occurs *twice* as unity, and reduce the others to fractions: this gives, for *L, M,* and *Z,* the marks 1, $^2/_5$, $^4/_3$. In estimating for *lightness,* we observe that the greater the weight, the less the merit, so that *Z*'s merit is to *L*'s as 5 to 1. Thus the marks for *lightness* are $^1/_5$, $^5/_3$, 1. And similarly, the marks for warmth are 3, 1, $^1/_4$. To get the total result, we must *multiply L*'s 3 marks together, and do the same for *M* and for *Z.* The final numbers are $1 \times {}^1/_5 \times 3, {}^2/_5 \times {}^5/_3 \times 1, {}^4/_3 \times 1 \times$ $^1/_4$; *i.e* $^3/_5$, $^2/_3$, $^1/_3$; *i.e* multiplying throughout by 15 (which will not alter the proportion), 9, 10, 5; showing the order of merit to be *M, L, Z.*

Twenty-nine answers have been received, of which five are right, and twenty-four wrong. These hapless ones have all (with three exceptions) fallen into the error of *adding* the proportional numbers together, for each candidate, instead of *multiplying.* *Why* the latter is right, rather than the former, is fully proved in textbooks, so I will not occupy space by stating it here: but it can be *illustrated* very easily by the case of length, breadth, and depth. Suppose *A* and *B* are rival diggers of rectangular tanks: the amount of work done is evidently measured by the number of *cubical feet* dug out. Let *A* dig a tank 10 feet long, 10 wide, 2 deep: let *B* dig one 6 feet long, 5 wide, 10 deep. The cubical contents are 200, 300; *i.e. B* is best digger in the ratio of 3 to 2. Now try marking for length, width, and depth, separately; giving a maximum mark of 10 to the best in each contest, and then *adding* the results!

Of the twenty-four malefactors, one gives no working, and so has no real claim to be named; but I break the rule for once, in deference to its success in Problem 1: he, she, or it, is ADDLEPATE. The other twenty-three may be divided into five groups.

First and worst are, I take it, those who put the rightful winner *last;* arranging them as "Lolo, Zuzu, Mimi." The names of these desperate wrong-doers are AYR, BRADSHAW OF THE FUTURE, FURZE-BUSH and POLLUX (who send a joint answer), GREYSTEAD, GUY, OLD HEN, and SIMPLE SUSAN. The latter was *once* best of all; the Old Hen has taken advantage of her simplicity, and beguiled her with the chaff which was the bane of her own chickenhood.

Secondly, I point the finger of scorn at those who have put the worst candidate at the top; arranging them as "Zuzu, Mimi, Lolo." They are GRAECIA, M. M., OLD CAT, and R. E. X. "'Tis Greece, but——."

The third set have avoided both these enormities, and have even succeeded in putting the worst last, their answer being "Lolo, Mimi, Zuzu." Their names are AYR (who also appears among the "quite too too"), CLIFTON C., F. B., FIFEE, GRIG, JANET, and MRS. SAIREY GAMP. F. B. has not fallen into the common error; she *multiplies* together the proportionate numbers she gets, but in getting them she goes wrong, by reckoning warmth as a *de*-merit. Possibly she is "Freshly Burnt," or comes "From Bombay." JANET and MRS. SAIREY GAMP have also avoided this error: the method they have adopted is shrouded in mystery—I scarcely feel competent to criticize it. MRS. GAMP says "if Zuzu makes 4 while Lolo makes 3, Zuzu makes 6 while Lolo makes 5 (bad reasoning), while Mimi makes 2." From this she concludes "therefore Zuzu excels in speed by 1" (*i.e.* when compared with Lolo; but what about Mimi?). She then compares the 3 kinds of excellence, measured on this mystic scale. JANET takes the statement, that "Lolo makes 5 while Mimi makes 2," to prove that "Lolo makes 3 while Mimi makes 1 and Zuzu 4" (worse reasoning than MRS. GAMP'S), and thence concludes that "Zuzu excels in speed by $1/8$!" JANET should have been ADELINE, "mystery of mysteries!"

The fourth set actually put Mimi at the top, arranging them as "Mimi, Zuzu, Lolo." They are MARQUIS AND CO., MARTREB, S. B. B. (first initial scarcely legible: *may* be meant for "J"), and STANZA.

The fifth set consist of AN ANCIENT FISH and CAMEL. These ill-assorted comrades, by dint of foot and fin, have scrambled into the right answer, but, as their method is wrong, of course it counts for nothing. Also AN ANCIENT FISH has very ancient and fishlike ideas as to *how* numbers represent merit: she says "Lolo gains $2^1/_2$ on Mimi." Two and a half *what*? Fish, fish, art thou in thy duty?

Of the five winners I put BALBUS and THE ELDER TRAVELLER slightly below the other three—BALBUS for defective reasoning, the other for scanty working. BALBUS gives two reasons for saying that *addition* of marks is *not* the right method, and then adds "it follows that the decision must be made by *multiplying* the marks together." This is hardly more logical than to say "This is not Spring: *therefore* it must be Autumn."

CLASS LIST.

I.

DINAH MITE.   E. B. D. L.   JORAM.

II.

BALBUS.   THE ELDER TRAVELLER.

———

With regard to Knot V., I beg to express to VIS INERTIÆ and to any others who, like her, understood the condition to be that *every* marked picture must have *three* marks, my sincere regret that the unfortunate phrase "*fill* the columns with oughts and crosses" should have caused them to waste so much time and trouble. I can only repeat that a *literal* interpretation of "fill" would seem to *me* to require that *every* picture in the gallery should be marked. VIS INERTIÆ would have been in the First Class if she had sent in the solution she now offers.

ANSWERS TO KNOT VII.

Problem.—Given that one glass of lemonade, 3 sandwiches, and 7 biscuits, cost 1s. 2d.; and that one glass of lemonade, 4 sandwiches, and 10 biscuits, cost 1s. 5d.: find the cost of (1) a glass of lemonade, a sandwich, and a biscuit; and (2) 2 glasses of lemonade, 3 sandwiches, and 5 biscuits.
Answer.—(1) 8d.; (2) 1s. 7d.

———

Solution.—This is best treated algebraically. Let x = the cost (in pence) of a glass of lemonade, y of a sandwich, and z of a biscuit. Then we have $x + 3y + 7z = 14$, and $x + 4y + 10z = 17$. And we require the values of $x + y + z$, and of $2x + 3y + 5z$. Now, from *two* equations only, we cannot find, *separately*, the values of *three* unknowns: certain *combinations* of them may, however, be found. Also we know that we can, by the help of the given equations, eliminate 2 of the 3 unknowns from the quantity whose value is required, which will then contain one only. If, then, the required value is ascertainable at all, it can only be by the 3rd unknown vanishing of itself: otherwise the problem is impossible.

Let us then eliminate lemonade and sandwiches, and reduce everything to biscuits—a state of things even more depressing than "if all the world were apple-pie"—by subtracting the 1st equation from the 2nd, which eliminates lemonade, and gives $y + 3z = 3$, or $y = 3 - 3z$; and then substituting this value of y in the 1st, which gives $x - 2z = 5$, *i.e.* $x = 5 + 2z$. Now if we substitute these values of x, y, in the quantities whose values are required, the first becomes $(5 + 2z) + (3 - 3z) + z$, *i.e.* 8: and the

A note for American readers: Knot VII. In British currency, a shilling contains twelve pence. The phrase "One and two-pence" (written 1s. 2d.) means "one shilling and two-pence."

second becomes $2(5 + 2z) + 3(3 - 3z) + 5z$, *i.e.* 19. Hence the answers are (1) 8*d*., (2) 1*s*. 7*d*.

The above is a *universal* method: that is, it is absolutely certain either to produce the answer, or to prove that no answer is possible. The question may also be solved by combining the quantities whose values are given, so as to form those whose values are required. This is merely a matter of ingenuity and good luck: and as it *may* fail, even when the thing is possible, and is of no use in proving it *im*possible, I cannot rank this method as equal in value with the other. Even when it succeeds, it may prove a very tedious process. Suppose the 26 competitors, who have sent in what I may call *accidental* solutions, had had a question to deal with where every number contained 8 or 10 digits! I suspect it would have been a case of "silvered is the raven hair" (see "Patience") before any solution would have been hit on by the most ingenious of them.

Forty-five answers have come in, of which 44 give, I am happy to say, some sort of *working*, and therefore deserve to be mentioned by name, and to have their virtues, or vices as the case may be, discussed. Thirteen have made assumptions to which they have no right, and so cannot figure in the Class-list, even though, in 10 of the 12 cases, the answer is right. Of the remaining 28, no less than 26 have sent in *accidental* solutions, and therefore fall short of the highest honours.

I will now discuss individual cases, taking the worst first, as my custom is.

FROGGY gives no working—at least this is all he gives: after stating the given equations, he says "therefore the difference, 1 sandwich + 3 biscuits, = 3*d*.": then follow the amounts of the unknown bills, with no further hint as to how he got them. FROGGY has had a *very* narrow escape of not being named at all!

Of those who are wrong, VIS INERTIÆ has sent in a piece of incorrect working. Peruse the horrid details, and shudder! She takes x (call it "y") as the cost of a sandwich, and concludes (rightly enough) that a biscuit will cost $\dfrac{3 - y}{3}$. She then subtracts the second equation from the first, and deduces $3y + 7 \times \dfrac{3 - y}{3} - 4y + 10 \times \dfrac{3 - y}{3} = 3$. By making two mistakes in this line, she brings out $y = \dfrac{3}{2}$. Try it again, oh VIS INERTIÆ!

Away with INERTIÆ: infuse a little more VIS: and you will bring out the correct (though uninteresting) result, $0 = 0$! This will show you that it is hopeless to try to coax any one of these 3 unknowns to reveal its *separate* value. The other competitor, who is wrong throughout, is either J. M. C. or T. M. C.: but, whether he be a Juvenile Mis-Calculator or a True Mathematician Confused, he makes the answers 7*d*. and 1*s*. 5*d*. He assumes, with Too Much Confidence, that biscuits were $^1\!/_2 d$. each, and that Clara paid for 8, though she only ate 7!

We will now consider the 13 whose working is wrong, though the answer is right: and, not to measure their demerits too exactly, I will take them in alphabetical order. ANITA finds (rightly) that "1 sandwich and 3 biscuits cost 3d.," and proceeds "therefore 1 sandwich = $1^1/2d$., 3 biscuits = $1^1/2d$., 1 lemonade = 6d." DINAH MITE begins like ANITA: and thence proves (rightly) that a biscuit costs less than a 1d.: whence she concludes (wrongly) that it *must* cost $1/2d$. F. C. W. is so beautifully resigned to the certainty of a verdict of "guilty," that I have hardly the heart to utter the word, without adding a "recommended to mercy owing to extenuating circumstances." But really, you know, where *are* the extenuating circumstances? She begins by assuming that lemonade is 4d. a glass, and sandwiches 3d. each, (making with the 2 given equations, *four* conditions to be fulfilled by *three* miserable unknowns!). And, having (naturally) developed this into a contradiction, she then tries 5d. and 2d. with a similar result. (N.B. *This* process might have been carried on through the whole of the Tertiary Period, without gratifying one single Megatherium.) She then, by a "happy thought," tries half-penny biscuits, and so obtains a consistent result. This may be a good solution, viewing the problem as a conundrum: but it is *not* scientific. JANET identifies sandwiches with biscuits! "One sandwich + 3 biscuits" she makes equal to "4." Four *what*? MAYFAIR makes the astounding assertion that the

equation, $s + 3b = 3$, "is evidently only satisfied by $s = \dfrac{3}{2}$, $b = \dfrac{1}{2}$"! OLD

CAT believes that the assumption that a sandwich costs $1^1/2d$. is "the only way to avoid unmanageable fractions." But *why* avoid them? Is there not a certain glow of triumph in taming such a fraction? "Ladies and gentlemen, the fraction now before you is one that for years defied all efforts of a refining nature: it was, in a word, hopelessly vulgar. Treating it as a circulating decimal (the treadmill of fractions) only made matters worse. As a last resource, I reduced it to its lowest terms, and extracted its square root!" Joking apart, let me thank OLD CAT for some very kind words of sympathy, in reference to a correspondent (whose name I am happy to say I have now forgotten) who had found fault with me as a discourteous critic. O. V. L. is beyond my comprehension. He takes the given equations as (1) and (2): thence, by the process [(2)—(1)] deduces (rightly) equation (3) viz. $s + 3b = 3$: and thence again, by the process [× 3] (a hopeless mystery), deduces $3s + 4b = 4$. I have nothing to say about it: I give it up. SEA-BREEZE says "it is immaterial to the answer" (why?) "in what proportion 3d. is divided between the sandwich and the 3 biscuits": so she assumes $s = 1^1/2d$., $b = 1/2d$. STANZA is one of a very irregular metre. At first she (like JANET) identifies sandwiches with biscuits.

She then tries two assumptions ($s = 1$, $b = \dfrac{2}{3}$, and $s = \dfrac{1}{2}$ $b = \dfrac{5}{6}$), and (nat-

urally) ends in contradictions. Then she returns to the first assumption, and finds the 3 unknowns separately: *quod est absurdum*. STILETTO identifies sandwiches and biscuits, as "articles." Is the word ever used by confectioners? I fancied "What is the next article, Ma'am?" was limited to linendrapers. TWO SISTERS first assume that biscuits are 4 a penny, and then that they are 2 a penny, adding that "the answer will of course be the same in both cases." It is a dreamy remark, making one feel something like Macbeth grasping at the spectral dagger. "Is this a statement that I see before me?" If you were to say "we both walked the same way this morning," and *I* were to say "*one* of you walked the same way, but the other didn't," which of the three would be the most hopelessly confused? TURTLE PYATE (what *is* a Turtle Pyate, please?) and OLD CROW, who send a joint answer, and Y. Y., adopt the same method. Y. Y. gets the equation $s + 3b = 3$: and then says "this sum must be apportioned in one of the three following ways." It *may* be, I grant you: but Y. Y. do you say "must?" I fear it is *possible* for Y. Y. to be *two* Y's. The other two conspirators are less positive: they say it "can" be so divided: but they add "either of the three prices being right"! This is bad grammar and bad arithmetic at once, oh mysterious birds!

Of those who win honours, THE SHETLAND SNARK must have the 3rd class all to himself. He has only answered half the question, viz. the amount of Clara's luncheon: the two little old ladies he pitilessly leaves in the midst of their "difficulty." I beg to assure him (with thanks for his friendly remarks) that entrance-fees and subscriptions are things unknown in that most economical of clubs, "The Knot-Untiers."

The authors of the 26 "accidental" solutions differ only in the number of steps they have taken between the *data* and the answers. In order to do them full justice I have arranged the 2nd class in sections, according to the number of steps. The two Kings are fearfully deliberate! I suppose walking quick, or taking short cuts, is inconsistent with kingly dignity: but really, in reading THESEUS' solution, one almost fancied he was "marking time," and making no advance at all! The other King will, I hope, pardon me for having altered "Coal" into "Cole." King Coilus, or Coil, seems to have reigned soon after Arthur's time. Henry of Huntingdon identifies him with the King Coël who first built walls round Colchester, which was named after him. In the Chronicle of Robert of Gloucester we read:—

> "Aftur Kyng Aruirag, of wam we habbeth y told,
> Marius ys sone was kyng, quoynte mon & bold.
> And ys sone was aftur hym, Coil was ys name,
> Bothe it were quoynte men, & of noble fame."

BALBUS lays it down as a general principle that "in order to ascertain the cost of any one luncheon, it must come to the same amount upon two different assumptions." (*Query*. Should not "it" be "we"? Otherwise the *luncheon* is represented as wishing to ascertain its own cost!) He then makes two assumptions—one, that sandwiches cost nothing; the other, that biscuits cost nothing, (either arrangement would lead to the shop being inconveniently crowded!)—and brings out the unknown luncheons as 8*d*. and 19*d*., on each assumption. He then concludes that this agreement of results "shows that the answers are correct." Now I propose to disprove his general law by simply giving *one* instance of its failing. One instance is quite enough. In logical language, in order to disprove a "universal affirmative," it is enough to prove its contradictory, which is a "particular negative." (I must pause for a digression on Logic, and especially on Ladies' Logic. The universal affirmative "everybody says he's a duck" is crushed instantly by proving the particular negative "Peter says he's a goose," which is equivalent to "Peter does *not* say he's a duck." And the universal negative "nobody calls on her" is well met by the particular affirmative "*I* called yesterday." In short, either of two contradictories disproves the other: and the moral is that, since a particular proposition is much more easily proved than a universal one, it is the wisest course, in arguing with a Lady, to limit one's *own* assertions to "particulars," and leave *her* to prove the "universal" contradictory, if she can. You will thus generally secure a *logical* victory: a *practical* victory is not to be hoped for, since she can always fall back upon the crushing remark "*that* has nothing to do with it!"—a move for which Man has not yet discovered any satisfactory answer. Now let us return to BALBUS.) Here is my "particular negative," on which to test his rule. Suppose the two recorded luncheons to have been "2 buns, one queen-cake, 2 sausage-rolls, and a bottle of Zoëdone: total, one-and-ninepence," and "one bun, 2 queen-cakes, a sausage-roll, and a bottle of Zoëdone: total, one-and-fourpence." And suppose Clara's unknown luncheon to have been "3 buns, one queen-cake, one sausage-roll, and 2 bottles of Zoëdone:" while the two little sisters had been indulging in "8 buns, 4 queen-cakes, 2 sausage-rolls, and 6 bottles of Zoëdone." (Poor souls, how thirsty they must have been!) If BALBUS will kindly try this by his principle of "two assumptions," first assuming that a bun is 1*d.* and a queen-cake 2*d.*, and then that a bun is 3*d.* and a queen-cake 3*d.*, he will bring out the other two luncheons, on each assumption, as "one-and-nine-pence" and "four-and-ten-pence" respectively, which harmony of results, he will say, "shows that the answers are correct." And yet, as a matter of fact, the buns were 2*d.* each, the queen-cakes 3*d.*, the sausage-rolls 6*d.*, and the Zoëdone 2*d.* a bottle: so that Clara's third luncheon had cost one-and-sevenpence, and her thirsty friends had spent four-and-fourpence!

Another remark of BALBUS I will quote and discuss: for I think that it also may yield a moral for some of my readers. He says "it is the same thing in substance whether in solving this problem we use words and call it Arithmetic, or use letters and signs and call it Algebra." Now this does not appear to me a correct description of the two methods: the Arithmetical method is that of "synthesis" only; it goes from one known fact to another, till it reaches its goal: whereas the Algebraical method is that of "analysis:" it begins with the goal, symbolically represented, and so goes backwards, dragging its veiled victim with it, till it has reached the full daylight of known facts, in which it can tear off the veil and say "I know you!"

Take an illustration. Your house has been broken into and robbed, and you appeal to the policeman who was on duty that night. "Well, Mum, I did see a chap getting out over your garden-wall: but I was a good bit off, so I didn't chase him, like. I just cut down the short way to the Chequers, and who should I meet but Bill Sykes, coming full split round the corner. So I just ups and says 'My lad, you're wanted.' That's all I says. And he says 'I'll go along quiet, Bobby,' he says, 'without the darbies,' he says." There's your *Arithmetical* policeman. Now try the other method. "I seed somebody a running, but he was well gone or ever *I* got nigh the place. So I just took a look round in the garden. And I noticed the foot-marks, where the chap had come right across your flower-beds. They was good big foot-marks sure-ly. And I noticed as the left foot went down at the heel, ever so much deeper than the other. And I says to myself 'The chap's been a big hulking chap: and he goes lame on his left foot.' And I rubs my hand on the wall where he got over, and there was soot on it, and no mistake. So I says to myself 'Now where can I light on a big man, in the chimbley-sweep line, what's lame of one foot?' And I flashes up permiscuous: and I says 'It's Bill Sykes!' says I." There is your *Algebraical* policeman—a higher intellectual type, to my thinking, than the other.

LITTLE JACK'S solution calls for a word of praise, as he has written out what really is an algebraical proof *in words*, without representing any of his facts as equations. If it is all his own, he will make a good algebraist in the time to come. I beg to thank SIMPLE SUSAN for some kind words of sympathy, to the same effect as those received from OLD CAT.

HECLA and MARTREB are the only two who have used a method *certain* either to produce the answer, or else to prove it impossible: so they must share between them the highest honours.

CLASS LIST.

I.

HECLA. MARTREB.

II.

§ 1 (2 *steps*).
ADELAIDE.
CLIFTON C. . . . .
E. K. C.
GUY.
L'INCONNU.
LITTLE JACK.
NIL DESPERANDUM.
SIMPLE SUSAN.
YELLOW-HAMMER.
WOOLLY ONE.
§ 3 (4 *steps*).
HAWTHORN.
JORAM.
S. S. G.
§ 4 (5 *steps*).
A STEPNEY COACH.

§ 2 (3 *steps*).
A. A.
A CHRISTMAS CAROL.
AFTERNOON TEA.
AN APPRECIATIVE SCHOOLMA'AM.
BABY.
BALBUS.
BOG-OAK.
THE RED QUEEN.
WALL-FLOWER.
§ 5 (6 *steps*).
BAY LAUREL.
BRADSHAW OF THE FUTURE.
§ 6 (9 *steps*).
OLD KING COLE.
§ 7 (14 *steps*).
THESEUS.

ANSWERS TO CORRESPONDENTS.

I HAVE received several letters on the subjects of Knots II. and VI., which lead me to think some further explanation desirable.

In Knot II., I had intended the numbering of the houses to begin at one corner of the Square, and this was assumed by most, if not all, of the competitors. TROJANUS however says "assuming, in default of any information, that the street enters the square in the middle of each side, it may be supposed that the numbering begins at a street." But surely the other is the more natural assumption?

In Knot VI., the first Problem was of course a mere *jeu de mots*, whose presence I thought excusable in a series of Problems whose aim is to entertain rather than to instruct: but it has not escaped the contemptuous criticisms of two of my correspondents, who seem to think that Apollo is in duty bound to keep his bow always on the stretch. Neither of them has guessed it: and this is true human nature. Only the other day—the 31st of September, to be quite exact—I met my old friend Brown, and gave him a riddle I had just heard. With one great effort of his colossal mind, Brown guessed it. "Right!" said I. "Ah," said he, "it's very neat— very neat. And it isn't an answer that would occur to everybody. Very neat indeed." A few yards further on, I fell in with Smith and to him I propounded the same riddle. He frowned over it for a minute, and then gave up. Meekly I faltered out the answer. "A poor thing, sir!" Smith growled, as he turned away. "A very poor thing! I wonder you care to repeat such rubbish!" Yet Smith's mind is, if possible, even more colossal than Brown's.

The second Problem of Knot VI. is an example in ordinary Double Rule of Three, whose essential feature is that the result depends on the variation of several elements, which are so related to it that, if all but one be constant, it varies as that one: hence, if none be constant it varies their product. Thus, for example, the cubical contents of a rectangular tank vary as its length, if breadth and depth be constant, and so on; hence, if none be constant, it varies as the product of the length, breadth, and depth.

When the result is not thus connected with the varying elements, the Problem ceases to be Double Rule of Three and often becomes one of great complexity.

To illustrate this, let us take two candidates for a prize, A and B, who are to compete in French, German, and Italian:

(*a*) Let it be laid down that the result is to depend on their *relative* knowledge of each subject, so that, whether their marks, for French, be "1, 2" or "100, 200," the result will be the same: and let it also be laid down that, if they get equal marks on 2 papers, the final marks are to have the same ratio as those of the 3rd paper. This is a case of ordinary Double Rule of Three. We multiply A's 3 marks together, and do the same for *B*. Note that, if *A* gets a single "0," his final mark is "0," even if he gets full marks for 2 papers while *B* gets only one mark for each paper. This of course would be very unfair on *A*, though a correct solution under the given conditions.

(*b*) The result is to depend, as before, on *relative* knowledge; but French is to have twice as much weight as German or Italian. This is an unusual form of question. I should be inclined to say "the resulting ratio is to be nearer to the French ratio than if we multiplied as in (*a*), and so much nearer that it would be necessary to use the other multipliers *twice* to produce the same result as in (*a*):" *e.g.* if the French Ratio were $9/10$, and the others $4/9$, $1/9$ so that the ultimate ratio, by method (*a*), would be $2/45$, I should multiply instead by $2/3$, $1/3$, giving the result, $1/5$ which is nearer to $9/10$ than if he had used method (*a*).

(*c*) The result is to depend on *actual* amount of knowledge of the 3 subjects collectively. Here we have to ask two questions. (1) What is to be the "unit" (*i.e.* "standard to measure by") in each subject? (2) Are these units to be of equal, or unequal value? The usual "unit" is the knowledge shown by answering the whole paper correctly; calling this "100," all lower amounts are represented by numbers between "0" and "100." Then, if these units are to be of equal value, we simply add *A*'s 3 marks together, and do the same for *B*.

(*d*) The conditions are the same as (*c*), but French is to have double weight. Here we simply double the French marks, and add as before.

(*e*) French is to have such weight, that, if other marks be equal, the ultimate ratio is to be that of the French paper, so that a "0" in this would swamp the candidate: but the other two subjects are only to affect the result collectively, by the amount of knowledge shown, the two being reckoned of equal value. Here I should add *A*'s German and Italian marks together, and multiply by his French mark.

But I need not go on: the problem may evidently be set with many varying conditions, each requiring its own method of solution. The Problem in Knot VI. was meant to belong to variety (*a*), and to make this clear, I inserted the following passage:

"Usually the competitors differ in one point only. Thus, last year, Fifi and Gogo made the same number of scarves in the trial week, and they were equally light; but Fifi's were twice as warm as Gogo's, and she was pronounced twice as good."

What I have said will suffice, I hope, as an answer to BALBUS, who holds that (*a*) and (*c*) are the only possible varieties of the problem, and that to say "We cannot use addition, therefore we must be intended to use multiplication," is "no more illogical than, from knowledge that one was not born in the night, to infer that he was born in the daytime"; and also to FIFEE, who says "I think a little more consideration will show you that our 'error of *adding* the proportional numbers together for each candidate instead of *multiplying*' is no error at all." Why, even if addition *had* been the right method to use, not one of the writers (I speak from memory) showed any consciousness of the necessity of fixing a "unit" for each subject. "No error at all!" They were positively steeped in error!

One correspondent (I do not name him, as the communication is not quite friendly in tone) writes thus:—"I wish to add, very respectfully, that I think it would be in better taste if you were to abstain from the very trenchant expressions which you are accustomed to indulge in when criticising the answer. That such a tone must not be" ("be not?") "agreeable to the persons concerned who have made mistakes may possibly have no great weight with you, but I hope you will feel that it would be as well not to employ it, *unless you are quite certain of being correct yourself.*" The only instances the writer gives of the "trenchant expressions" are "hapless" and "malefactors." I beg to assure him (and any others who may need the assurance: I trust there are none) that all such words have been used in jest, and with no idea that they could possibly annoy any one, and that I sincerely regret any annoyance I may have thus inadvertently given. May I hope that in future they will recognise the distinction between severe language used in sober earnest, and the "words of unmeant bitterness," which Coleridge has alluded to in that lovely passage beginning "A little child, a limber elf"? If the writer will refer to that passage, or to the preface to "Fire, Famine, and Slaughter," he will find the distinction, for which I plead, far better drawn out than I could hope to do in any words of mine.

The writer's insinuation that I care not how much annoyance I give to my readers I think it best to pass over in silence; but to his concluding remark I must entirely demur. I hold that to use language likely to annoy any of my correspondents would not be in the least justified by the plea that I was "quite certain of being correct." I trust that the knot-untiers and I are not on such terms as those!

I beg to thank *G. B.* for the offer of a puzzle—which, however, is too like the old one "Make four 9's into 100."

ANSWERS TO KNOT VIII.

§ 1. THE PIGS.

Problem.—Place twenty-four pigs in four sties so that, as you go round and round, you may always find the number in each sty nearer to ten than the number in the last.

Answer.—Place 8 pigs in the first sty, 10 in the second, nothing in the third, and 6 in the fourth: 10 is nearer ten than 8; nothing is nearer ten than 10; 6 is nearer ten than nothing; and 8 is nearer ten than 6.

This problem is noticed by only two correspondents. BALBUS says "it certainly cannot be solved mathematically, nor do I see how to solve it by any verbal quibble." NOLENS VOLENS makes Her Radiancy change the direction of going round; and even then is obliged to add "the pigs must be carried in front of her!"

§ 2. THE GRURMSTIPTHS.

Problem.—Omnibuses start from a certain point, both ways, every 15 minutes. A traveller, starting on foot along with one of them, meets one in $12^1/_2$ minutes: when will he be overtaken by one?
Answer.—In $6^1/_4$ minutes.

Solution.—Let "a" be the distance an omnibus goes in 15 minutes, and "x" the distance from the starting-point to where the traveller is overtaken. Since the omnibus met is due at the starting-point in $2^1/_2$ minutes, it goes in that time as far as the traveller walks in $12^1/_2$; *i.e.* it goes 5 times as fast. Now the overtaking omnibus is "a" behind the traveller when he starts, and therefore goes "$a + x$" while he goes "x." Hence $a + x = 5x$;

i.e. $4x = a$, and $x = \dfrac{a}{4}$. This distance would be traversed by an omnibus in $\dfrac{15}{4}$ minutes, and therefore by the traveller in $5 \times \dfrac{15}{4}$ Hence he is

overtaken in $18^3/_4$ minutes after starting, *i.e.* in $6^1/_4$ minutes after meeting the omnibus.

Four answers have been received, of which two are wrong. DINAH MITE rightly states that the overtaking omnibus reached the point where they met the other omnibus 5 minutes after they left, but wrongly concludes that, going 5 times as fast, it would overtake them in another minute. The travellers are 5-minutes-walk ahead of the omnibus, and must walk 1-4th of this distance farther before the omnibus overtakes them, which will be 1-5th of the distance traversed by the omnibus in the same time: this will require $1^1/_4$ minutes more. NOLENS VOLENS tries it by a process like "Achilles and the Tortoise." He rightly states that, when the overtaking omnibus leaves the gate, the travellers are 1-5th of "a" ahead, and that it will take the omnibus 3 minutes to traverse this distance; "during which time" the travellers, he tells us, go 1-15th of "a" (this should be 1-25th). The travellers being now 1-15th of "a" ahead, he concludes that the work remaining to be done is for the travellers to go 1-60th of "a," while the omnibus goes 1-12th. The *principle* is correct, and might have been applied earlier.

CLASS LIST.

I.

BALBUS.   DELTA.

ANSWERS TO KNOT IX.

§ 1. THE BUCKETS.

Problem.—Lardner states that a solid, immersed in a fluid, displaces an amount equal to itself in bulk. How can this be true of a small bucket floating in a larger one?

Solution.—Lardner means, by "displaces," "occupies a space which might be filled with water without any change in the surroundings." If the portion of the floating bucket, which is above the water, could be annihilated, and the rest of it transformed into water, the surrounding water would not change its position: which agrees with Lardner's statement.

Five answers have been received, none of which explains the difficulty arising from the well-known fact that a floating body is the same weight as the displaced fluid. HECLA says that "only that portion of the smaller bucket which descends below the original level of the water can be properly said to be immersed, and only an equal bulk of water is displaced." Hence, according to HECLA, a solid, whose weight was equal to that of an equal bulk of water, would not float till the whole of it was below "the original level" of the water: but, as a matter of fact, it would float as soon as it was all under water. MAGPIE says the fallacy is "the assumption that one body can displace another from a place where it isn't," and that Lardner's assertion is incorrect, except when the containing vessel "was originally full to the brim." But the question of floating depends on the present state of things, not on past history. OLD KING COLE takes the same view as HECLA. TYMPANUM and VINDEX assume that "displaced" means "raised above its original level," and merely explain how it comes to pass that the water, so raised, is less in bulk that the immersed portion of bucket, and thus land themselves—or rather set themselves floating— in the same boat as HECLA.

I regret that there is no Class-list to publish for this Problem.

---

§ 2. BALBUS'S ESSAY.

Problem.—Balbus states that if a certain solid be immersed in a certain vessel of water, the water will rise through a series of distances, two inches, one inch, half an inch, &c., which series has no end. He concludes that the water will rise without limit. Is this true?

Solution.—No. This series can never reach 4 inches, since, however many terms we take, we are always short of 4 inches by an amount equal to the last term taken.

Three answers have been received—but only two seem to me worthy of honours.

TYMPANUM says that the statement about the stick "is merely a blind, to which the old answer may well be applied, *solvitur ambulando*, or rather *mergendo*." I trust TYMPANUM will not test this in his own person, by taking the place of the man in Balbus's Essay! He would infallibly be drowned.

OLD KING COLE rightly points out that the series, 2, 1, &c., is a decreasing Geometrical Progression: while VINDEX rightly identifies the fallacy as that of "Achilles and the Tortoise."

CLASS LIST.

I.

OLD KING COLE.   VINDEX.

---

§ 3. THE GARDEN.

Problem.—An oblong garden, half a yard longer than wide, consists entirely of a gravel-walk, spirally arranged, a yard wide and 3,630 yards long. Find the dimensions of the garden.

Answer.—60, 60$^1/_2$.

Solution.—The number of yards and fractions of a yard traversed in walking along a straight piece of walk, is evidently the same as the number of square-yards and fractions of a square-yard, contained in that piece of walk: and the distance, traversed in passing through a square-yard at a corner, is evidently a yard. Hence the area of the garden is 3,630 square-yards: *i.e.* if x be the width, $x(x + \frac{1}{2}) = 3,630$. Solving this Quadratic, we find $x = 60$. Hence the dimensions are 60, $60\frac{1}{2}$.

Twelve answers have been received—seven right and five wrong.

C. G. L., NABOB, OLD CROW, and TYMPANUM assume that the number of yards in the length of the path is equal to the number of square-yards in the garden. This is true, but should have been proved. But each is guilty of darker deeds. C. G. L.'s "working" consists of dividing 3,630 by 60. Whence came this divisor, oh Segiel? Divination? Or was it a dream? I fear this solution is worth nothing. OLD CROW'S is shorter, and so (if possible) worth rather less. He says the answer "is at once seen to be $60 \times 60\frac{1}{2}$!" NABOB'S calculation is short, but "as rich as a Nabob" in error. He says that the square root of 3,630, multiplied by 2, equals the length plus the breadth. That is $60.25 \times 2 = 120\frac{1}{2}$. His first assertion is only true of a *square* garden. His second is irrelevant, since 60.25 is *not* the square-root of 3,630! Nay, Bob, this will *not* do! TYMPANUM says that, by extracting the square-root of 3,630, we get 60 yards with a remainder of $\dfrac{30}{60}$, or half-a-yard, which we add so as to make the oblong $60 \times 60\frac{1}{2}$. This is very terrible: but worse remains behind. TYMPANUM proceeds thus:—"But why should there be the half-yard at all? Because without it there would be no space at all for flowers. By means of it, we find reserved in the very centre a small plot of ground, two yards long by half-a-yard wide, the only space not occupied by walk." But Balbus expressly said that the walk "used up the whole of the area." Oh, TYMPANUM! My tympa is exhausted: my brain is num! I can say no more.

HECLA indulges, again and again, in that most fatal of all habits in computation—the making *two* mistakes which cancel each other. She takes x as the width of the garden, in yards, and $x + \frac{1}{2}$ as its length, and makes her first "coil" the sum of $x - \frac{1}{2}$, $x - \frac{1}{2}$, $x - 1$, $x - 1$, *i.e.* $4x - 3$: but the fourth term should be $x - 1\frac{1}{2}$, so that her first coil is $\frac{1}{2}$ a yard too long. Her second coil is the sum of $x - 2\frac{1}{2}$, $x - 2\frac{1}{2}$, $x - 3$, $x - 3$: here the first term should be $x - 2$ and the last $x - 3\frac{1}{2}$: these two mistakes cancel, and this coil is therefore right. And the same thing is true of every other coil but the last, which needs an extra half-yard to reach the *end* of the path: and this exactly balances the mistake in the first coil. Thus the sum total of the coils comes right though the working is all wrong.

Of the seven who are right, DINAH MITE, JANET, MAGPIE, and TAFFY make the same assumption as C. G. L. and Co. They then solve by a

Quadratic. MAGPIE also tries it by Arithmetical Progression, but fails to notice that the first and last "coils" have special values.

ALUMNUS ETONÆ attempts to prove what C. G. L. assumes by a particular instance, taking a garden 6 by $5\frac{1}{2}$. He ought to have proved it generally: what is true of one number is not always true of others. OLD KING COLE solves it by an Arithmetical Progression. It is right, but too lengthy to be worth as much as a Quadratic.

VINDEX proves it very neatly, by pointing out that a yard of walk measured along the middle represents a square yard of garden, "whether we consider the straight stretches of walk or the square yards at the angles, in which the middle line goes half a yard in one direction and then turns a right angle and goes half a yard in another direction."

CLASS LIST.

I.

VINDEX.

II.

ALUMNUS ETONÆ.   OLD KING COLE.

III.

DINAH MITE.   MAGPIE.
JANET.   TAFFY.

ANSWERS TO KNOT X.

§ 1. THE CHELSEA PENSIONERS.

Problem.—If 70 per cent. have lost an eye, 75 per cent. an ear, 80 per cent. an arm, 85 per cent. a leg: what percentage, *at least*, must have lost all four?

Answer.—Ten.

Solution.—(I adopt that of POLAR STAR, as being better than my own.) Adding the wounds together, we get 70 + 75 + 80 + 85 = 310, among 100 men; which gives 3 to each, and 4 to 10 men. Therefore the least percentage is 10.

Nineteen answers have been received. One is "5," but, as no working is given with it, it must, in accordance with the rule, remain "a deed without a name." JANET makes it "35 and $^7/_{10}$ths." I am sorry she has misunderstood the question, and has supposed that those who had lost an ear were 75 per cent. *of those who had lost an eye;* and so on. Of course, on this supposition, the percentages must all be multiplied together. This she has done correctly, but I can give her no honours, as I do not think the question will fairly bear her interpretation, THREE SCORE AND TEN makes it "19 and $^3/_8$ths." Her solution has given me—I will not say "many anxious days and sleepless nights," for I wish to be strictly truthful, but—some trouble in making any sense at all of it. She makes the number of "pensioners wounded once" to be 310 ("per cent.," I suppose!): dividing by 4, she gets 77 and a half as "average percentage:" again dividing by 4, she gets 19 and $^3/_8$ths as "percentage wounded four times." Does she suppose wounds of different kinds to "absorb" each other, so to speak? Then, no doubt, the *data* are equivalent to 77 pensioners with one wound each, and a half-pensioner with a half-wound. And does she then suppose these concentrated wounds to be *transferable*, so that $^3/_4$ths of these unfortunates can obtain perfect health by handing over their wounds to the remaining $^1/_4$th? Granting these suppositions, her answer is right: or rather, *if* the question had been "A road is covered with one inch of gravel, along 77 and a half per cent. of it. How much of it could be covered 4 inches deep with the same material?" her answer *would* have been right. But alas, that *wasn't* the question! DELTA makes some most amazing assumptions: "let every one who has not lost an eye have lost an ear," "let every one who has not lost both eyes and ears have lost an arm." Her ideas of a battle-field are grim indeed. Fancy a warrior who would continue fighting after losing both eyes, both ears, and both arms! This is a case which she (or "it?") evidently considers *possible.*

Next come eight writers who have made the unwarrantable assumption that, because 70 per cent. have lost an eye, *therefore* 30 per cent. have *not* lost one, so that they have *both* eyes. This is illogical. If you give me a bag containing 100 sovereigns, and if in an hour I come to you (my face *not* beaming with gratitude nearly so much as when I received the bag) to say "I am sorry to tell you that 70 of these sovereigns are bad," do I thereby guarantee the other 30 to be good? Perhaps I have not tested them yet. The sides of this illogical octagon are as follows, in alphabetical order:—ALGERNON BRAY, DINAH MITE, G. S. C., JANE E., J. D. W., MAGPIE (who makes the delightful remark "therefore 90 per cent. have two of something," recalling to one's memory that fortunate monarch, with whom Xerxes was so much pleased that "he gave him ten of everything!"), S. S. G., and TOKIO.

BRADSHAW OF THE FUTURE and T. R. do the question in a piecemeal fashion—on the principle that the 70 per cent. and the 75 per cent., though commenced at opposite ends of the 100, must overlap by *at least* 45 per cent.; and so on. This is quite correct working, but not, I think, quite the best way of doing it.

The other five competitors will, I hope, feel themselves sufficiently glorified by being placed in the first class, without my composing a Triumphal Ode for each!

———————

CLASS LIST.

I.

OLD CAT.   POLAR STAR.
OLD HEN.   SIMPLE SUSAN.
                    WHITE SUGAR.

II.

BRADSHAW OF THE FUTURE.   T. R.

III.

ALGERNON BRAY.   J. D. W.
DINAH MITE.   MAGPIE.
G. S. C.   S. S. G.
JANE E.   TOKIO.

———————

———————

§ 2. CHANGE OF DAY.

I must postpone, *sine die*, the geographical problem—partly because I have not yet received the statistics I am hoping for, and partly because I am myself so entirely puzzled by it; and when an examiner is himself dimly hovering between a second class and a third how is he to decide the position of others?

———————

§ 3. THE SONS' AGES.

Problem.—"At first, two of the ages are together equal to the third. A few years afterwards, two of them are together double of the third. When the number of years since the first occasion is two-thirds of the sum of the ages on that occasion, one age is 21. What are the other two? *Answer.*—"15 and 18."

Solution.—Let the ages at first be x, y, $(x + y)$. Now, if $a + b = 2c$, then $(a - n) + (b - n) = 2(c - n)$, whatever be the value of n. Hence the second relationship, if *ever* true, was *always* true. Hence it was true at first. But it cannot be true that x and y are together double of $(x + y)$. Hence it must be true of $(x + y)$, together with x or y; and it does not matter which we take. We assume, then, $(x + y) + x = 2y$; *i.e.* $y = 2x$. Hence the three ages were, at first, x, $2x$, $3x$; and the number of years, since that time is two-thirds of $6x$, *i.e.* is $4x$. Hence the present ages are $5x$, $6x$, $7x$. The ages are clearly *integers*, since this is only "the year when one of my sons comes of age." Hence $7x = 21$, $x = 3$, and the other ages are 15, 18.

Eighteen answers have been received. One of the writers merely asserts that the first occasion was 12 years ago, that the ages were then 9, 6, and 3; and that on the second occasion they were 14, 11, and 8! As a Roman father, I *ought* to withhold the name of the rash writer; but respect for age makes me break the rule: it is THREE SCORE AND TEN. JANE E. also asserts that the ages at first were 9, 6, 3: then she calculates the present ages, leaving the *second* occasion unnoticed. OLD HEN is nearly as bad; she "tried various numbers till I found one that fitted *all* the conditions"; but merely scratching up the earth, and pecking about, is *not* the way to solve a problem, oh venerable bird! And close after OLD HEN prowls, with hungry eyes, OLD CAT, who calmly assumes, to begin with, that the son who comes of age is the *eldest*. Eat your bird, puss, for you will get nothing from me!

There are yet two zeroes to dispose of. MINERVA assumes that, on *every* occasion, a son comes of age; and that it is only such a son who is "tipped with gold." Is it wise thus to interpret "now, my boys, calculate your ages, and you shall have the money"? BRADSHAW OF THE FUTURE says "let" the ages at first be 9, 6, 3, then assumes that the second occasion was 6 years afterwards, and on these baseless assumptions brings out the right answers. Guide *future* travellers, as thou wilt: thou art no Bradshaw for *this* Age!

Of those who win honours, the merely "honourable" are two. DINAH MITE ascertains (rightly) the relationship between the three ages at first, but then *assumes* one of them to be "6," thus making the rest of her solution tentative. M. F. C. does the algebra all right up to the conclusion that the present ages are $5z$, $6z$, and $7z$; it then assumes, without giving any reason, that $7z = 21$.

Of the more honourable, DELTA attempts a novelty—to discover *which* son comes of age by elimination: it assumes, successively, that it is the middle one, and that it is the youngest; and in each case it *apparently* brings out an absurdity. Still, as the proof contains the following bit of algebra, "$63 = 7x + 4y; \therefore 21 = x + 4$ sevenths of y," I trust it will admit that its proof is not *quite* conclusive. The rest of its work is good. MAGPIE betrays the deplorable tendency of her tribe—to appropriate any stray conclusion she comes across, without having any *strict* logical right to it. Assuming $A, B, C,$ as the ages at first, and D as the number of the years that have elapsed since then, she finds (rightly) the 3 equations, $2A = B,$ $C = B + A, D = 2B.$ She then says "supposing that $A = 1,$ then $B = 2,$ $C = 3,$ and $D = 4.$ Therefore for $A, B, C, D,$ four numbers are wanted which shall be to each other as $1 : 2 : 3 : 4.$" It is in the "therefore" that I detect the unconscientiousness of this bird. The conclusion *is* true, but this is only because the equations are "homogeneous" (*i.e.* having one "unknown" in each term), a fact which I strongly suspect had not been grasped—I beg pardon, clawed—by her. Were I to lay this little pitfall, "$A + 1 = B, B + 1 = C;$ supposing $A = 1,$ then $B = 2,$ and $C = 3.$ *Therefore* for $A, B, C,$ three numbers are wanted which shall be to one another as $1 : 2 : 3,$" would not flutter down into it, oh MAGPIE, as amiably as a Dove? SIMPLE SUSAN is anything but simple to *me*. After ascertaining that the 3 ages at first are as $3 : 2 : 1,$ she says "then, as two-thirds of their sum, added to one of them, $= 21,$ the sum cannot exceed 30, and consequently the highest cannot exceed 15." I suppose her (mental) argument is something like this:—"two-thirds of sum, + one age, $= 21;$ $\therefore$ sum, + 3 halves of one age, $= 31$ and a half. But 3 halves of one age cannot be less than 1 and-a-half (here I perceive that SIMPLE SUSAN would on no account present a guinea to a new-born baby!) hence the sum cannot exceed 30." This is ingenious, but her proof, after that, is (as she candidly admits) "clumsy and roundabout." She finds that there are 5 possible sets of ages, and eliminates four of them. Suppose that, instead of 5, there had been 5 million possible sets? Would SIMPLE SUSAN have courageously ordered in the necessary gallon of ink and ream of paper?

The solution sent in by C. R. is, like that of SIMPLE SUSAN, partly tentative, and so does not rise higher than being Clumsily Right.

Among those who have earned the highest honours, ALGERNON BRAY solves the problem quite correctly, but adds that there is nothing to exclude the supposition that all the ages were *fractional*. This would make the number of answers infinite. Let me meekly protest that I *never* intended my readers to devote the rest of their lives to writing out answers! E. M. RIX points out that, if fractional ages be admissible, any one of the three sons might be the one "come of age"; but she rightly rejects this supposition on the ground that it would make the problem indeterminate. WHITE SUGAR is the only one who has detected an oversight of mine: I had forgotten the possibility (which of course ought to be allowed for) that the son, who came of age that *year*, need not have done so by that *day*, so that he *might* be only 20. This gives a second solution, viz., 20, 24, 28. Well said, pure Crystal! Verily, thy "fair discourse hath been as sugar"!

CLASS LIST.

I.

ALGERNON BRAY.   S. S. G.
AN OLD FOGEY.   TOKIO.
E. M. RIX.   T. R.
G. S. C.   WHITE SUGAR.

II.

C. R.   MAGPIE.
DELTA.   SIMPLE SUSAN.

III.

DINAH MITE.   M. F. C.

I have received more than one remonstrance on my assertion, in the Chelsea Pensioners' problem, that it was illogical to assume, from the *datum* "70 p. c. have lost an eye," that 30 p. c. have *not*. ALGERNON BRAY states, as a parallel case, "suppose Tommy's father gives him 4 apples, and he eats one of them, how many has he left?" and says "I think we are justified in answering, 3." I think so too. There is no "must" here, and the *data* are evidently meant to fix the answer *exactly:* but, if the question were set me "how many *must* he have left?", I should understand the *data* to be that his father gave him 4 *at least*, but *may* have given him more.

I take this opportunity of thanking those who have sent, along with their answers to the Tenth Knot, regrets that there are no more Knots to come, or petitions that I should recall my resolution to bring them to an end. I am most grateful for their kind words; but I think it wisest to end what, at best, was but a lame attempt. "The stretched metre of an antique song" is beyond my compass; and my puppets were neither distinctly *in* my life (like those I now address), nor yet (like Alice and the Mock Turtle) distinctly *out* of it. Yet let me at least fancy, as I lay down the pen, that I carry with me into my silent life, dear reader, a farewell smile from your unseen face, and a kindly farewell pressure from your unfelt hand! And so, good night! Parting is such sweet sorrow, that I shall say "good night!" till it be morrow.

THE END

ALICE'S ADVENTURES UNDER GROUND

Illustrated by
LEWIS CARROLL

"Who will Riddle me the How and the Why?"

So questions one of England's sweetest singers. The "How?" has already been told, after a fashion, in the verses prefixed to "Alice in Wonderland"; and some other memories of that happy summer day are set down, for those who care to see them, in this little book——the germ that was to grow into the published volume. But the "Why?" cannot, and need not, be put into words. Those for whom a child's mind is a sealed book, and who see no divinity in a child's smile, would read such words in vain: while for any one that has ever loved one true child, no words are needed. For he will have known the awe that falls on one in the presence of a spirit fresh from GOD'S hands, on whom no shadow of sin, and but the outermost fringe of the shadow of sorrow, has yet fallen: he will have felt the bitter contrast between the haunting selfishness that spoils his best deeds and the life that is but an overflowing love——for I think a child's *first* attitude to the world is a simple love for all living things: and he will have learned that the best work a man can do is when he works for love's sake only, with no thought of name, or gain, or earthly reward. No deed of ours, I suppose, on this side the grave, is really unselfish: yet if one can put forth all one's powers in a task where nothing of reward is hoped for but a little child's whispered thanks, and the airy touch of a little child's pure lips, one seems to come somewhere near to this.

There was no idea of publication in my mind when I wrote this little book: *that* was wholly an afterthought, pressed on me by the "perhaps too partial friends" who always have to bear the blame when a writer rushes into print: and I can truly say that no praise of theirs has ever given me one hundredth part of the pleasure it has been to think of the sick children in hospitals (where it has been a delight to me to send copies) forgetting, for a few bright hours, their pain and weariness—— perhaps thinking lovingly of the unknown writer of the tale——perhaps even putting up a childish prayer (and oh, how much it needs!) for one who can but dimly hope to stand, some day, not quite out of sight of those pure young faces, before the great white throne. "I am very sure," writes a lady-visitor at a Home for Sick Children, "that there will be many loving earnest prayers for you on Easter morning from the children."

I would like to quote further from her letters, as embodying a suggestion that may perhaps thus come to the notice of some one able and willing to carry it out.

"I want you to send me one of your Easter Greetings for a very dear child who is dying at our Home. She is just fading away, and 'Alice' has brightened some of the weary hours in her illness, and I know that letter would be such a delight to her——especially if you would put 'Minnie' at the top, and she could know you had sent it for her. *She* knows *you*, and would so value it. . . She suffers so much that I long for what I know would so please her." . . . . "Thank you very much for sending me the letter, and for writing Minnie's name. . . . . I am quite sure that all these children will say a loving prayer for the 'Alice-man' on Easter Day: and I am sure the letter will help the little ones to the real Easter joy. How I do wish that you, who have won the hearts and confidence of so many children, would do for them what is so very near my heart, and yet what no one will do, viz. write a book for children about GOD and themselves, which is *not* goody, and which begins at the right end, about religion, to make them see what it really is. I get quite miserable very often over the children I come across: hardly any of them have an idea of *really* knowing that GOD loves them, or of loving and confiding in Him. They will love and trust *me*, and be sure that *I* want them to be happy, and will not let them suffer more than is necessary: but as for going to Him in the same way, they would never think of it. They are dreadfully afraid of Him, if they think of Him at all, which they generally only do when they have been naughty, and they look on all connected with Him as very grave and dull: and, when they are full of fun and thoroughly happy, I am sure they unconsciously hope He is not looking. I am sure I don't wonder they think of Him in this way, for people *never* talk of Him in connection with what makes their little lives the brightest. If they are naughty, people put on solemn faces, and say He is very angry or shocked, or something which frightens them: and, for the rest, He is talked about only in a way that makes them think of church and having to be quiet. As for being taught that all Joy and all Gladness and Brightness is His Joy—that He is wearying for them to be happy, and is not hard and stern, but always doing things to make their days brighter, and caring for them so tenderly, and wanting them to run to Him with *all* their little joys and sorrows, they are not taught that. I do so long to make them trust Him as they trust us, to feel that He will 'take their part' as they do with us in their little woes, and to go to Him in their plays and enjoyments and not only when they say their prayers. I was quite grateful to one little dot, a short time ago, who said to his mother 'when I am in bed, I put out my hand to see if I can feel JESUS and my angel. I thought perhaps *in the dark* they'd touch me, but they never have yet.' I do so want them to *want* to go to Him, and to feel how, if He is there, it *must* be happy."

Let me add—for I feel I have drifted into far too serious a vein for a preface to a fairy-tale—the deliciously naïve remark of a very dear child-friend, whom I asked, after an acquaintance of two or three days, if she had read 'Alice' and the 'Looking-Glass.' "Oh yes," she replied readily, "I've read both of them! And I think" (this more slowly and thoughtfully) "I think 'Through the Looking-Glass' is *more* stupid than 'Alice's Adventures.' Don't *you* think so?" But this was a question I felt it would be hardly discreet for me to enter upon.

Dec. 1886.   LEWIS CARROLL.

POSTSCRIPT.

THE profits, if any, of this book will be given to Children's Hospitals and Convalescent Homes for Sick Children: and the accounts, down to June 30 in each year, will be published in the St. James's Gazette, on the second Tuesday of the following December.

P.P.S.—The thought, so prettily expressed by the little boy, is also to be found in Longfellow's "Hiawatha," where he appeals to those who believe

> "That the feeble hands and helpless,
>   Groping blindly in the darkness,
>   Touch GOD'S right hand in that darkness,
>   And are lifted up and strengthened."

Alice's
Adventures
under
Ground

A Christmas Gift
to
a Dear Child
in Memory
of
a Summer Day.

Chapter I.

Alice was beginning to get very tired of sitting by her sister on the bank, and of having nothing to do: once or twice she had peeped into the book her sister was reading, but it had no pictures or conversations in it, and where is the use of a book, thought Alice, without pictures or conversations? So she was considering in her own mind, (as well as she could, for the hot day made her feel very sleepy and stupid,) whether the pleasure of making a daisy-chain was worth the trouble of getting up and picking the daisies, when a white rabbit with pink eyes ran close by her.

There was nothing very remarkable in that, nor did Alice think it so _very_ much out of the way to hear the rabbit say to itself "dear, dear! I shall be too late!" (when she thought it over afterwards, it occurred to her that she ought to have wondered at this, but at the time it all seemed quite natural); but when the rabbit actually <u>took a watch out of its waistcoat-pocket</u>, looked at it, and then hurried on, Alice started to her feet, for it flashed across her mind that she had never before seen a rabbit with either a waistcoat-pocket or a watch to take out of it, and, full of curiosity, she hurried across the field after it, and was just in time to see it pop down a large rabbit-hole under the hedge. In a moment down went Alice after it, never once considering how in the world she was to get out again.

The rabbit-hole went straight on like a tunnel for some way, and then dipped suddenly down, so suddenly, that Alice had not a moment to think about stopping herself, before she found herself falling down what seemed a deep well. Either the well was very deep, or she fell very slowly, for she had plenty of time as she went down to look about her, and to wonder what would happen next. First, she tried to look down and make out what she was coming to, but it was too dark to see anything: then, she looked at the sides of the well, and noticed that they were filled with cupboards and book-shelves: here and there were maps and pictures hung on pegs. She took a jar down off one of of the shelves as she passed: it was labelled

"Orange Marmalade", but to her great disappoint-
-ment it was empty : she did not like to drop
the jar, for fear of killing somebody underneath,
so managed to put it into one of the cupboards
as she fell past it.

"Well!" thought Alice to herself, "after such
a fall as this, I shall think nothing of tumbling
down stairs! How brave they'll all think me
at home! Why, I wouldn't say anything about
it, even if I fell off the top of the house!" (which
was most likely true.)

Down, down, down. Would the fall never
come to an end? "I wonder how many miles I've
fallen by this time?" said she aloud, "I must
be getting somewhere near the centre of the
earth. Let me see: that would be four thousand
miles down, I think —" (for you see Alice had
learnt several things of this sort in her lessons
in the schoolroom, and though this was not a
very good opportunity of showing off her know-
-ledge, as there was no one to hear her, still
it was good practice to say it over,) "yes, that's
the right distance, but then what Longitude
or Latitude-line shall I be in?" (Alice had no idea

what Longitude was, or Latitude either, but she thought they were nice grand words to say.)

Presently she began again: "I wonder if I shall fall right <u>through</u> the earth! How funny it'll be to come out among the people that walk with their heads downwards! But I shall have to ask them what the name of the country is, you know. Please, Ma'am, is this New Zealand or Australia?" — and she tried to curtsey as she spoke, (fancy <u>curtseying</u> as you're falling through the air! do you think you could manage it?)" and what an ignorant little girl she'll think me for asking! No, it'll never do to ask: perhaps I shall see it written up somewhere."

Down, down, down: there was nothing else to do, so Alice soon began talking again. "Dinah will miss me very much tonight, I should think!" (Dinah was the cat.) "I hope they'll remember her saucer of milk at tea-time! Oh, dear Dinah, I wish I had you here! There are no mice in the air, I'm afraid, but you might catch a bat, and that's very like a mouse, you know, my dear. But do cats eat bats, I wonder?" And here Alice began to get rather sleepy, and kept on saying to herself, in a dreamy sort of way "do cats eat bats? do cats eat bats?" and sometimes, "do bats eat cats?" for, as she couldn't answer either question, it didn't much matter which way she put it. She felt that she was dozing off, and had just begun to dream that she was walking hand in hand with Dinah, and was saying to her very earnestly, "Now, Dinah, my dear, tell me the truth. Did you ever eat a bat?" when suddenly, bump! bump! down she came upon a heap of sticks and shavings, and the fall was over.

Alice was not a bit hurt, and jumped on to her feet directly: she looked up, but it was all dark overhead; before her was another long passage, and the white rabbit was still in sight, hurrying down it. There was not a moment to be lost: away went Alice like the wind, and just heard it say, as it turned a corner, "my ears and whiskers, how late it's getting!" She turned the corner after it, and instantly found herself in a long, low hall, lit up by a row of lamps which hung from the roof.

There were doors all round the hall, but they were all locked, and when Alice had been all round it, and tried them all, she walked sadly down the middle, wondering

how she was ever to get out again: suddenly
she came upon a little three-legged table,
all made of solid glass, there was nothing
lying upon it, but a tiny golden key, and
Alice's first idea was that it might belong
to one of the doors of the hall, but alas! either

the locks were too large,
or the key too small, but
at any rate it would open
none of them However, on
the second time round, she
came to a low curtain,
behind which was a door
about eighteen inches high:
she tried the little key in
the keyhole, and it fitted! Alice opened the door,
and looked down a small passage, not larger
than a rat-hole, into the loveliest garden you
ever saw How she longed to get out of that
dark hall, and wander about among those beds
of bright flowers and those cool fountains, but
she could not even get her head through the
doorway, "and even if my head would go through"
thought poor Alice," it would be very little use
without my shoulders Oh, how I wish I could shut

up like a telescope! I think I could, if I only knew how to begin." For, you see, so many out--of-the-way things had happened lately, that Alice began to think very few things indeed were really impossible.

There was nothing else to do, so she went back to the table, half hoping she might find another key on it, or at any rate a book of rules for shutting up people like telescopes : this time there was a little bottle on it—" which certainly was not there before" said Alice — and tied round the neck of the bottle was a paper label with the words DRINK ME beautifully printed on it in large letters.

It was all very well to say "drink me," "but I'll look first," said the wise little Alice, "and see whether the bottle's marked "poison" or not," for Alice had read several nice little stories about children that got burnt, and eaten up by wild beasts, and other unpleasant things, because they would not remember the simple rules their friends had given them, such as, that, if you get into the fire, it will burn you, and that, if you cut your finger very deeply with a knife, it generally bleeds, and

she had never forgotten that, if you drink a
bottle. marked "poison", it is almost certain
to disagree with you, sooner or later.

However, this bottle was <u>not</u> marked
poison, so Alice tasted it, and finding it very
nice, (it had, in fact, a sort of mixed flavour
of cherry-tart, custard, pine-apple, roast
turkey, toffy, and hot buttered toast,) she very
soon finished it off.

*   *   *   *   *   *

"What a curious feeling!" said Alice,
"I must be shutting up like a telescope!"

It was so indeed : she was now only
ten inches high, and her face brightened up
as it occurred to her that she was now the
right size for going through the little door
into that lovely garden. First, however, she
waited for a few minutes to see whether
she was going to shrink any further : she
felt a little nervous about this, " for it
might end. you know," said Alice to herself,
" in my going out altogether, like a candle,
and what should I be like then, I wonder?"
and she tried to fancy what the flame of a
candle is like after the candle is blown out,

for she could not remember having ever seen one. However, nothing more happened, so she decided on going into the garden at once, but, alas for poor Alice! when she got to the door, she found she had forgotten the little golden key, and when she went back to the table for the key, she found she could not possibly reach it. she could see it plainly enough through the glass, and she tried her best to climb up one of the legs of the table, but it was too slippery, and when she had tired herself out with trying, the poor little thing sat down and cried.

"Come! there's no use in crying!" said Alice to herself rather sharply, "I advise you to leave off this minute!"(she generally gave herself very good advice, and sometimes scolded herself so severely as to bring tears into her eyes, and once she remembered boxing her own ears for having been unkind to herself in a game of croquet she was playing with herself, for this curious child was very fond of pretending to be two people,) "but it's no use now," thought poor Alice, "to pretend to be two people! Why, there's hardly enough of me left to make one respectable person!"

Soon her eyes fell on a little ebony box lying under the table she opened it, and found in it a very small cake, on which was lying a card with the words EAT ME beautifully printed on it in large letters "I'll eat," said Alice, "and if it makes me larger, I can reach the key, and if it makes me smaller, I can creep under the door, so either way I'll get into the garden, and I don't care which happens!"

She eat a little bit, and said anxiously to herself "which way? which way?" and laid her hand on the top of her head to feel which way it was growing, and was quite surprised to find that she remained the same size: to be sure this is what generally happens when one eats cake, but Alice had got into the way of expecting nothing but out-of-the way things to happen, and it seemed quite dull and stupid for things to go on in the common way

So she set to work, and very soon finished off the cake

* * * * *

"Curiouser and curiouser!" cried Alice, (she was so surprised that she quite forgot how to speak good English,) "now I'm opening out like the largest telescope that ever was! Goodbye, feet!" (for when she looked down at her feet, they seemed almost out of sight, they were getting so far off,) "oh, my poor little-feet, I wonder who will put on your shoes and stockings for you now, dears? I'm sure I can't! I shall be a great deal too far off to bother myself about you: you must manage the best way you can— but I must be kind to them", thought Alice, "or perhaps they won't walk the way I want to go! Let me see: I'll give them a new pair of boots every Christmas."

And she went on planning to herself how she would manage it.

"they must go by the carrier," she thought, "and how funny it'll seem, sending presents to one's own feet! And how odd the directions will look! ALICE'S RIGHT FOOT, ESQ.
THE CARPET,
with ALICE'S LOVE.
oh dear! what nonsense I am talking!"

Just at this moment, her head struck against the roof of the hall: in fact, she was now rather more than nine feet high, and she at once took up the little golden key, and hurried off to the garden door.

Poor Alice! it was as much as she could do, lying down on one side, to look through into the garden with one eye, but to get through was more hopeless than ever: she sat down and cried again

"You ought to be ashamed of yourself," said Alice, "a great girl like you," (she might well say this,) "to cry in this way! Stop this instant, I tell you!" But she cried on all the same, shedding gallons of tears, until there was a large pool, about four inches deep, all round her, and reaching half way across the hall After a time, she heard a little pattering of feet in the distance, and

dried her eyes to
see what was coming.
It was the white
rabbit coming back
again, splendidly
dressed, with a
pair of white kid
gloves in one hand,
and a nosegay in
the other. Alice was ready to ask help of any
one, she felt so desperate, and as the rabbit
passed her, she said, in a low, timid voice,
"If you please, Sir ── " the rabbit started
violently, looked up once into the roof of
the hall, from which the voice seemed to come,
and then dropped the nosegay and the white
kid gloves, and skurried away into the dark-
-ness as hard as it could go.

Alice took up the nosegay and gloves,
and found the nosegay so delicious that
she kept smelling at it all the time she
went on talking to herself ── "dear, dear!
how queer everything is today! and yester-
-day everything happened just as usual:
I wonder if I was changed in the night?
Let me think: was I the same when I
got up this morning? I think I remember

feeling rather different But if I'm not the same, who in the world am I? Ah, that's the great puzzle!" And she began thinking over all the children she knew of the same age as herself, to see if she could have been changed for any of them.

"I'm sure I'm not Gertrude," she said, "for her hair goes in such long ringlets, and mine doesn't go in ringlets at all — and I'm sure I can't be Florence, for I know all sorts of things, and she, oh! she knows such a very little! Besides, she's she, and I'm I, and — oh dear! how puzzling it all is! I'll try if I know all the things I used to know. Let me see: four times five is twelve, and four times six is thirteen, and four times seven is fourteen — oh dear! I shall never get to twenty at this rate! But the Multiplication Table don't signify — let's try Geography. London is the capital of France, and Rome is the capital of Yorkshire, and Paris — oh dear! dear! that's all wrong, I'm certain! I must have been changed for Florence! I'll try and say "How doth the little", "and she crossed her hands on her

lap, and began, but her voice sounded
hoarse and strange, and the words did not
sound the same as they used to do:

"How doth the little crocodile
    Improve its shining tail,
And pour the waters of the Nile
    On every golden scale!

How cheerfully it seems to grin!
    How neatly spreads its claws!
And welcomes little fishes in
    With gently-smiling jaws!"

"I'm sure those are not the right
words", said poor Alice, and her eyes filled
with tears as she thought "I must be
Florence after all, and I shall have to go and
live in that poky little house, and have
next to no toys to play with, and oh! ever
so many lessons to learn! No! I've made
up my mind about it: if I'm Florence,
I'll stay down here! It'll be no use their
putting their heads down and saying 'come
up, dear!' I shall only look up and say

who am I, then? answer me that first, and then, if I like being that person, I'll come up: if not I'll stay down here till I'm somebody else —— but oh dear!" cried Alice with a sudden burst of tears, "I do wish they <u>would</u> put their heads down! I am so tired of being all alone here!"

As she said this, she looked down at her hands, and was surprised to find she had put on one of the rabbit's little gloves while she was talking. "How <u>can</u> I have done that?" thought she, "I must be growing small again." She got up and went to the table to measure herself by it, and found that, as nearly as she could guess, she was now about two feet high, and was going on shrinking rapidly: soon she found out that the reason of it was the nosegay she held in her hand: she dropped it hastily, just in time to save herself from shrinking away altogether, and found that she was now only three inches high.

"Now for the garden!" cried Alice,

as she hurried back to the little door, but the little door was locked again, and the little gold key was lying on the glass table as before, and "things are worse than ever!" thought the poor little girl, "for I never was as small as this before, never! And I declare it's too bad, it is!"

At this moment her foot slipped, and splash! she was up to her chin in salt water. Her first idea was that she had fallen into the sea: then she remembered that she was under ground, and she soon made out that it was the pool of tears she had wept when she was nine feet high. "I wish I hadn't cried so much!" said Alice, as she swam about, trying to find her way out, "I shall be punished for it now, I suppose, by being drowned in my own tears! Well! that'll be a queer thing, to be sure! However, every thing is queer today." Very soon she saw something splashing about in the pool near her: at first she thought it must be a walrus or a hippopotamus, but then she remembered how small she was herself, and soon made out that it was only a mouse, that had slipped in like herself.

"Would it be any use, now," thought Alice, "to speak to this mouse? The rabbit is something quite out-of-the-way, no doubt, and so have I been, ever since I came down here, but that is no reason why the mouse should not be able to talk. I think I may as well try."

So she began: "oh Mouse, do you know how to get out of this pool? I am very tired of swimming about here, oh Mouse!" The mouse looked at her rather inquisitively, and seemed to her to wink with one of its little eyes, but it said nothing.

"Perhaps it doesn't understand English," thought Alice; "I daresay it's a French mouse, come over with William the Conqueror!" (for,

with all her knowledge of history, Alice had
no very clear notion how long ago anything
had happened,) so she began again: "où est
"ma chatte?" which was the first sentence
out of her French lesson-book. The mouse
gave a sudden jump in the pool, and seemed
to quiver with fright: "oh, I beg your pardon!"
cried Alice hastily, afraid that she had hurt
the poor animal's feelings, "I quite forgot
"you didn't like cats!"

  "Not like cats!" cried the mouse,
in a shrill, passionate voice, "would _you_
like cats if you were me?"

  "Well, perhaps not," said Alice in
a soothing tone, "don't be angry about it.
"And yet I wish I could show you our
cat Dinah: I think you'd take a fancy to
cats if you could only see her. She is such
a dear quiet thing," said Alice, half to
herself, as she swam lazily about in the
pool," she sits purring so nicely by the fire,
licking her paws and washing her face: and
she is such a nice soft thing to nurse, and
she's such a capital one for catching mice —
oh! I beg your pardon!" cried poor Alice

again, for this time the mouse was bristling all over, and she felt certain that it was really offended, "have I offended you?"

"Offended indeed!" cried the mouse, who seemed to be positively trembling with rage, 'our family always <u>hated</u> cats! Nasty, low, vulgar things! Don't talk to me about them any more!"

"I won't indeed!" said Alice, in a great hurry to change the conversation, "are you — are you — fond of — dogs?" The mouse did not answer, so Alice went on eagerly: "there is such a nice little dog near our house I should like to show you! A little bright-eyed terrier, you know, with oh! such long curly brown hair! And it'll fetch things when you throw them, and it'll sit up and beg for its dinner, and all sorts of things — I can't remember half of them — and it belongs to a farmer, and he says it kills all the rats and — oh dear!" said Alice sadly, "I'm afraid I've offended it again!" for the mouse was swimming away from her as hard as it could go, and making quite a commotion in the pool as it went.

So she called softly after it: "mouse dear! Do come back again, and we won't talk about cats and dogs any more, if you don't like them!" When the mouse heard this, it turned and swam slowly back to her: its face was quite pale, (with passion, Alice thought,) and it said in a trembling low voice "let's get to the shore, and then I'll tell you my history, and you'll understand why it is I hate cats and dogs."

It was high time to go, for the pool was getting quite full of birds and animals that had fallen into it. There was a Duck and a Dodo, a Lory and an Eaglet, and several other curious creatures. Alice led the way, and the whole party swam to the shore.

Chapter 11

They were indeed a curious looking party that assembled on the bank — the birds with draggled feathers, the animals with their fur clinging close to them — all dripping wet, cross, and uncomfortable. The first question of course was, how to get dry: they had a consultation about this, and Alice hardly felt at all surprised at finding her-self talking familiarly with the birds, as if she had known them all her life. Indeed, she had quite a long argument with the Lory, who at last turned sulky, and would only say "I am older than you, and must know best", and this Alice would not admit without knowing how old the Lory was, and as the Lory positively refused to tell its age, there was nothing more to be said

At last the mouse, who seemed to have some authority among them, called out "sit down, all of you, and attend to me! I'll soon make you dry enough!" They all sat down at once, shivering, in a large ring, Alice in the middle, with her eyes anxiously fixed on the mouse, for she felt sure she would catch a bad cold if she did not get dry very soon.

"Ahem!" said the mouse, with a self-important air, "are you all ready? This is the driest thing I know. Silence all round, if you please!

"William the Conqueror, whose cause was favoured by the pope, was soon submitted to by the English, who wanted leaders, and had been of late much accustomed to usurp-ation and conquest. Edwin and Morcar, the earls of Mercia and Northumbria ——"

"Ugh!" said the Lory with a shiver.

"I beg your pardon?" said the mouse, frowning, but very politely, "did you speak?"

"Not I!" said the Lory hastily.

"I thought you did," said the mouse, "I proceed. Edwin and Morcar, the earls of Mercia and Northumbria, declared for him.

and even Stigand, the patriotic archbishop of Canterbury, found it advisable to go with Edgar Atheling to meet William and offer him the crown. William's conduct was at first moderate — how are you getting on now, dear?" said the mouse, turning to Alice as it spoke.

"As wet as ever," said poor Alice," it doesn't seem to dry me at all".

"In that case," said the Dodo solemnly, rising to his feet," I move that the meeting adjourn, for the immediate adoption of more energetic remedies — "

"Speak English!" said the Duck," I don't know the meaning of half those long words, and what's more, I don't believe you do either!" And the Duck quacked a comfortable laugh to itself. Some of the other birds tittered audibly.

"I only meant to say, said the Dodo in a rather offended tone," that I know of a house near here, where we could get the young lady and the rest of the party dried, and then we could listen comfortably to the story which I think you were good enough to promise to tell us," bowing gravely to the mouse.

The mouse made no objection to this, and the whole party moved along the river bank, (for the pool had by this time begun to flow out of the hall, and the edge of it was fringed with rushes and forget-me-nots,) in a slow procession, the Dodo leading the way. After a time the Dodo became impatient, and, leaving the Duck to bring up the rest of the party, moved on at a quicker pace with Alice, the Lory, and the Eaglet, and soon brought them to a little cottage, and there they sat snugly by the fire, wrapped up in blankets, until the rest of the party had arrived, and they were all dry again.

Then they all sat down again in a large ring on the bank, and begged the mouse to begin his story.

"Mine is a long and a sad tale!" said the mouse, turning to Alice, and sighing.

"It _is_ a long tail, certainly," said Alice, looking down with wonder at the mouse's tail, which was coiled nearly all round the party, " but why do you call it sad?" and she went on puzzling about this as the mouse went on speaking, so that her idea of the tale was something like this:

We lived beneath the mat
Warm and snug and fat
But one woe, & that
Was the cat!
To our joys
a clog, In
our eyes a
fog, On our
hearts a log
Was the dog!
When the
cat's away,
Then
the mice
will
play,
But, alas!
one day, (So they say)
Came the dog and
cat, Hunting
for a
rat,
Crushed
the mice
all flat,
Each
one
as
he
sat
Underneath the mat, Warm & snug, & fat — Think of that!

"You are not attending!" said the mouse to Alice severely, "what are you thinking of?"

"I beg your pardon," said Alice very humbly, "you had got to the fifth bend, I think?"

"I had <u>not</u>!" cried the mouse, sharply and very angrily.

"A knot!" said Alice, always ready to make herself useful, and looking anxiously about her, "oh, do let me help to undo it!"

"I shall do nothing of the sort!" said the mouse, getting up and walking away from the party, "you insult me by talking such nonsense!"

"I didn't mean it!" pleaded poor Alice, "but you're so easily offended, you know."

The mouse only growled in reply.

"Please come back and finish your story!" Alice called after it, and the others all joined in chorus "yes, please do!" but the mouse only shook its ears, and walked quickly away, and was soon out of sight.

"What a pity it wouldn't stay!" sighed the Lory, and an old Crab took the oppor-tunity of saying to its daughter "Ah, my dear!

let this be a lesson to you never to lose your temper!" "Hold your tongue, Ma!" said the young Crab, a little snappishly, "you're enough to try the patience of an oyster!"

"I wish I had our Dinah here, I know I do!" said Alice aloud, addressing no one in particular, "she'd soon fetch it back!"

"And who is Dinah, if I might venture to ask the question?" said the Lory.

Alice replied eagerly, for she was always ready to talk about her pet, "Dinah's our cat. And she's such a capital one for catching mice, you can't think! And oh! I wish you could see her after the birds! Why, she'll eat a little bird as soon as look at it!"

This answer caused a remarkable sensation among the party: some of the birds hurried off at once; one old magpie began wrapping itself up very carefully, remarking "I really must be getting home: the night air does not suit my throat," and a canary called out in a trembling voice to its children "come away from her, my dears, she's no fit company for you!" On various pretexts, they all moved off, and Alice was soon left alone.

She sat for some while sorrowful
and silent, but she was not long before
she recovered her spirits, and began talking
to herself again as usual: "I do wish
some of them had stayed a little longer!
and I was getting to be such friends with
them — really the Lory and I were almost
like sisters! and so was that dear little
Eaglet! And then the Duck and the Dodo!
How nicely the Duck sang to us as we came
along through the water: and if the Dodo
hadn't known the way to that nice little
cottage, I don't know when we should have
got dry again —" and there is no knowing
how long she might have prattled on in
this way, if she had not suddenly caught
the sound of pattering feet.

It was the white rabbit, trotting
slowly back again, and looking anxiously
about it as it went, as if it had lost
something, and she heard it muttering
to itself " the Marchioness! the Marchioness!
oh my dear paws! oh my fur and whiskers!
She'll have me executed, as sure as ferrets

are ferrets! Where <u>can</u> I have dropped them,
I wonder?" Alice guessed in a moment that
it was looking for the nosegay and the pair
of white kid gloves, and she began hunting
for them, but they were now nowhere to be
seen — everything seemed to have changed
since her swim in the pool, and her walk
along the river-bank with its fringe of
rushes and forget-me-nots, and the glass
table and the little door had vanished.

Soon the rabbit
noticed Alice, as
she stood looking
curiously about
her, and at once
said in a quick
angry tone, "why,
Mary Ann! what
<u>are</u> you doing out
here? Go home this
moment, and look
on my dressing-table for my gloves and nosegay,
and fetch them here, as quick as you can
run, do you hear?" and Alice was so much
frightened that she ran off at once, without

saying a word, in the direction which the rabbit had pointed out

She soon found herself in front of a neat little house, on the door of which was a bright brass plate with the name W. RABBIT, ESQ. she went in and hurried upstairs, for fear she should meet the real Mary Ann and be turned out of the house before she had found the gloves : she knew that one pair had been lost in the hall, "but of course", thought Alice, "it has plenty more of them in its house How queer it seems to be going messages for a rabbit! I suppose Dinah'll be sending me messages next!" And she began fancying the sort of things that would happen. "Miss Alice! come here directly and get ready for your walk!" "Coming in a minute, nurse! but I've got to watch this mousehole till Dinah comes back, and see that the mouse doesn't get out——" "only I don't think," Alice went on, "that they'd let Dinah stop in the house, if it began ordering people about like that!"

By this time she had found her
way into a tidy little room, with a
table in the window on which was a
looking-glass and, (as Alice had hoped,)
two or three pairs of tiny white kid gloves
she took up a pair of gloves, and was just
going to leave the room, when her eye fell
upon a little bottle that stood near the
looking-glass: there was no label on it
this time with the words "drink me", but
nevertheless she uncorked it and put it

to her lips: "I
know something
interesting is
sure to happen,"
she said to herself,
"whenever I eat
or drink anything
so I'll see what
this bottle does
I do hope it'll
make me grow

larger, for I'm quite tired of being such a
tiny little thing!"

It did so indeed, and much sooner.

than she expected: before she had drunk half the bottle, she found her head pressing against the ceiling, and she stooped to save her neck from being broken, and hastily put down the bottle, saying to herself "that's quite enough— I hope I sha'n't grow any more— I wish I hadn't drunk so much!"

Alas! it was too late: she went on growing and growing, and very soon had to kneel down: in another minute there was not room even for this, and she tried the effect of lying down, with one elbow against the door, and the other arm curled round her head. Still she went on growing, and as a last resource she put one arm out of the window, and one foot up the chimney, and said to herself "now I can do no more — what _will_ become of me?"

Luckily for Alice, the little magic bottle had now had its full effect, and she grew no larger: still it was very uncomfortable, and as there seemed to be no sort of chance of ever getting out of the room again, no wonder she felt unhappy "It was much pleasanter at home," thought poor Alice, "when one wasn't always growing larger and smaller, and being ordered about by mice and rabbits — I almost wish I hadn't gone down that rabbit-hole, and yet, and yet — it's rather curious, you know, this sort of life I do wonder what can have happened to me! When I used to read fairy-tales, I fancied that sort of thing never happened, and now here I am in the middle of one! There ought to be a book written about me, that there ought! and when I grow up I'll write one — but I'm grown up now" said she in a sorrowful tone, "at least there's no room to grow up any more here"

"But then", thought Alice, " shall I never get any older than I am now? That'll be a comfort, one way — never to be an old woman — but then — always to have lessons to learn! Oh, I shouldn't like `that`!"

"Oh, you foolish Alice!" she said again," how can you learn lessons in here? Why, there's hardly room for you, and no room at all for any lesson-books!"

And so she went on, taking first one side, and then the other, and making quite a conversation of it altogether, but. after a few minutes she heard a voice outside, which made her stop to listen.

"Mary Ann! Mary Ann!" said the voice," fetch me my gloves this moment!" Then came a little pattering of feet on the stairs: Alice knew it was the rabbit coming to look for her, and she trembled till she shook the house, quite forgetting that she was now about a thousand times as large as the rabbit, and had no reason to be afraid of it. Presently the rabbit came to the door, and tried to open it, but as it opened inwards, and Alice's elbow was against it, the attempt proved a failure. Alice heard it say to itself "then I'll go round and get in at the window."

"*That* you won't!" thought Alice, and, after waiting till she fancied she heard the rabbit just under the window, she

suddenly spread out her hand, and made a snatch in the air. She did not get hold of anything, but she heard a little shriek and a fall and a crash of breaking glass, from which she concluded that it was just possible it had fallen into a cucumber-frame, or something of the sort.

Next came an angry voice — the rabbit's — "Pat, Pat! where are you?" And then a voice she had never heard before, "shure then I'm here! digging for apples, anyway, yer honour!"

"Digging for apples indeed!" said the rabbit angrily, "here, come and help me out of <u>this</u>!"— Sound of more breaking glass.

"Now, tell me, Pat, what is that coming out of the window?"

"Shure it's an arm, yer honour!"(He pronounced it "arrum".)

"An arm, you goose! Who ever saw an arm that size? Why, it fills the whole window, don't you see?"

"Shure, it does, yer honour, but it's an arm for all that."

"Well, it's no business there: go and take it away!"

There was a long silence after this, and Alice could only hear whispers now and then, such as "shure I don't like it, yer honour, at all at all!" "do as I tell you, you coward!" and at last she spread out her hand again and made another snatch in the air. This time there were <u>two</u> little shrieks, and more breaking glass — "what a number of cucumber-frames there must be!" thought Alice," I wonder what they'll do next! As for pulling me out of the window, I only wish they <u>could</u>! I'm sure <u>I</u> don't want to stop in here any longer!"

She waited for some time without

hearing anything more at last came a rumbling of little cart-wheels, and the sound of a good many voices all talking together: she made out the words "where's the other ladder? — why, I hadn't to bring but one, Bill's got the other — here, put 'em up at this corner — no, tie 'em together first — they don't reach high enough yet — oh, they'll do well enough, don't be particular — here, Bill! catch hold of this rope — will the roof bear? — mind that loose slate — oh, it's coming down! heads below!—" (a loud crash) "now, who did that? — it was Bill, I fancy — who's to go down the chimney? — nay, I shan't! you do it! — that I won't then — Bill's got to go down — here, Bill! the master says you've to go down the chimney!"

"Oh, so Bill's got to come down the chimney, has he?" said Alice to herself, "why, they seem to put everything upon Bill! I wouldn't be in Bill's place for a good deal: the fireplace is a pretty tight one, but I think I can kick a little!"

She drew her foot as far down the chimney as she could, and waited till she

heard a little
animal (she
couldn't guess
what sort it
was) scratching
and scrambling
in the chimney
close above her:
then, saying to
herself "this is
Bill", she gave
one, sharp kick, and waited again to see what
would happen next.

The first thing was a general chorus
of "there goes Bill!" then the rabbit's voice
alone "catch him, you by the hedge!" then
silence, and then another confusion of voices,
"how was it, old fellow? what happened to
you? tell us all about it."

Last came a little feeble squeaking
voice, ("that's Bill" thought Alice,) which said
"well, I hardly know — I'm all of a fluster
myself — something comes at me like a
Jack-in-the-box, and the next minute up I
goes like a rocket!" "And so you did, old
fellow!" said the other voices.

"We must burn the house down!" said the voice of the rabbit, and Alice called out as loud as she could "if you do, I'll set Dinah at you!" This caused silence again, and while Alice was thinking "but how can I get Dinah here?" she found to her great delight that she was getting smaller: very soon she was able to get up out of the uncomfortable position in which she had been lying, and in two or three minutes more she was once more three inches high

She ran out of the house as quick as she could, and found quite a crowd of little animals waiting outside — guinea-pigs, white mice, squirrels, and "Bill" a little green lizard, that was being supported in the arms of one of the guinea-pigs, while another was giving it something out of a bottle. They all made a rush at her the moment she appeared, but Alice ran her hardest, and soon found herself in a thick wood.

Chapter III

"The first thing I've got to do," said Alice to herself, as she wandered about in the wood, "is to grow to my right size, and the second thing is to find my way into that lovely garden I think that will be the best plan"

It sounded an excellent plan, no doubt, and very neatly and simply arranged: the only difficulty was, that she had not the smallest idea how to set about it, and while she was peering anxiously among the trees round her, a little sharp bark just over her head made her look up in a great hurry.

An enormous puppy was looking down at her with large round eyes, and feebly stretching out one paw, trying to reach her. "poor thing!" said Alice in a coaxing tone, and she tried hard to whistle to it, but she was terribly alarmed all the while at the thought that it might be hungry, in which case it would probably devour her in spite of all her coaxing. Hardly knowing what she did, she picked up a little bit of stick, and held it out to the puppy. whereupon the puppy jumped into the air off all its feet at once, and with a yelp of delight rushed at the stick, and made believe to worry it then Alice dodged behind a great thistle to keep herself from being run over, and, the moment she appeared at the other side, the puppy made another dart at the stick, and tumbled head over heels in its hurry to get hold then Alice thinking it was very like having a game of play with a cart-horse, and expecting every moment to be trampled under its feet. ran round the thistle again: then the puppy began a series of short charges at the stick, running a very little way forwards each time and a long way back, and barking hoarsely all the while, till at last it sat down a good way off, panting, with its tongue hanging out of its mouth, and its great eyes half shut.

This seemed to Alice a good opportunity for making her escape : she set off at once, and ran till the puppy's bark sounded quite faint in the distance, and till she was quite tired and out of breath.

"And yet what a dear little puppy it was!" said Alice, as she leant against a buttercup to rest herself, and fanned herself with her hat, "I should have liked teaching it tricks, if — if I'd only been the right size to do it! Oh! I'd nearly forgotten that I've got to grow up again! Let me see: how is it to be managed? I suppose I ought to eat or drink something or other, but the great question is, what?"

The great question certainly was, what? Alice looked all round her. at the flowers and the blades of grass, but could not see anything that looked like the right thing to eat under the circumstances. There is a large mushroom near her, about the same height as herself, and when she had looked under it, and on both sides of it, and behind it, it occurred to her to look and see what was on the top of it.

She stretched herself up on tiptoe, and peeped over the edge of the mushroom, and her eyes immediately met those of a large blue caterpillar, which was sitting with its arms fold- -ed, quietly smoking a long hookah, and taking not the least notice of her or of anything else.

For some time they looked at each other in silence : at last the caterpillar took the hookah out of its mouth, and languidly addressed her.

"Who are you?" said the caterpillar.

This was not an encouraging opening for a conversation : Alice replied rather shyly, "I— I hardly know, sir, just at present— at least I know who I <u>was</u> when I got up this morning, but I think I must have been changed several times since that."

"What do you mean by that?" said the caterpillar, "explain yourself!"

"I ca'nt explain <u>myself</u>, I'm afraid, sir,"

said Alice, 'because I'm not myself, you see.'

"I don't see," said the caterpillar.

"I'm afraid I can't put it more clearly," Alice replied very politely, "for I can't understand it myself, and really to be so many different sizes in one day is very confusing."

"It isn't," said the caterpillar

"Well, perhaps you haven't found it so yet," said Alice, "but when you have to turn into a chrysalis, you know, and then after that into a butterfly, I should think it'll feel a little queer, don't you think so?"

"Not a bit," said the caterpillar.

"All I know is," said Alice, "it would feel queer to me."

"You!" said the caterpillar contemptuously, "who are you?"

Which brought them back again to the beginning of the conversation: Alice felt a little irritated at the caterpillar making such very short remarks, and she drew herself up and said very gravely "I think you ought to tell me who you are, first."

"Why?" said the caterpillar.

Here was another puzzling question:

and as Alice had no reason ready, and the caterpillar seemed to be in a <u>very</u> bad temper, she turned round and walked away.

"Come back!" the caterpillar called after her, "I've something important to say!"

This sounded promising: Alice turned and came back again.

"Keep your temper," said the caterpillar.

"Is that all?" said Alice; swallowing down her anger as well as she could.

"No," said the caterpillar.

Alice thought she might as well wait, as she had nothing else to do, and perhaps after all the caterpillar might tell her something worth hearing For some minutes it puffed away at its hookah without speaking, but at last it unfolded its arms, took the hookah out of its mouth again, and said "so you think you're changed, do you?"

"Yes, sir," said Alice, "I can't remember the things I used to know — I've tried to say "How doth the little busy bee" and it came all different!"

"Try and repeat "You are old, father William"," said the caterpillar.

Alice folded her hands, and began:

1

"You are old, father William," the young man said,
    "And your hair is exceedingly white :
And yet you incessantly stand on your head —
    Do you think, at your age, it is right ?"

2.

"In my youth," father William replied to his son,
    "I feared it might injure the brain :
But now that I'm perfectly sure I have none,
    Why, I do it again and again."

3.

"You are old," said the youth, "as I mentioned before,
  "And have grown most uncommonly fat:
Yet you turned a back-somersault in at the door —
  Pray what is the reason of that?"

4.

"In my youth," said the sage, as he shook his gray locks,
  "I kept all my limbs very supple
By the use of this ointment, five shillings the box —
  Allow me to sell you a couple."

5.

"You are old," said the youth, "and your jaws are too weak

"For anything tougher than suet :

Yet you eat all the goose, with the bones and the beak —

Pray, how did you manage to do it ?"

6.

"In my youth," said the old man, "I took to the law,

And argued each case with my wife,

And the <u>muscular strength</u>, which it gave to my jaw,

Has lasted the rest of my life."

7.

"You are old," said the youth, "one would hardly suppose

"That your eye was as steady as ever:

Yet you balanced an eel on the end of your nose——

What made you so _awfully_ clever ?"

8.

"I have answered three questions, and that is enough,"

Said his father, "don't give yourself airs!

"Do you think I can listen all day to such stuff ?

Be off, or I'll kick you down stairs.!"

"That is not said right," said the caterpillar.

"Not quite right, I'm afraid," said Alice timidly, "some of the words have got altered."

"It is wrong from beginning to end," said the caterpillar decidedly, and there was silence for some minutes: the caterpillar was the first to speak.

"What size do you want to be?" it asked.

"Oh, I'm not particular as to size," Alice hastily replied, "only one doesn't like changing so often, you know."

"Are you content now?" said the caterpillar.

"Well, I should like to be a _little_ larger, sir, if you wouldn't mind," said Alice, "three inches is such a wretched height to be."

"It is a very good height indeed!" said the caterpillar loudly and angrily, rearing itself straight up as it spoke (it was exactly three inches high).

"But I'm not used to it!" pleaded poor Alice in a piteous tone, and she thought to herself "I wish the creatures wouldn't be so easily offended!"

"You'll get used to it in time," said the caterpillar, and it put the hookah into its mouth, and began smoking again.

This time Alice waited quietly until it chose to speak again : in a few minutes the caterpillar took the hookah out of its mouth, and got down off the mushroom, and crawled away into the grass, merely remarking as it went : "the top will make you grow taller, and the stalk will make you grow shorter."

"The top of _what_? the stalk of _what_?" thought Alice.

"Of the mushroom," said the caterpillar, just as if she had asked it aloud, and in another moment it was out of sight.

Alice remained looking thoughtfully at the mushroom for a minute, and then picked it and carefully broke it in two,  taking the stalk in one hand, and the top in the other. "Which does the stalk do?" she said, and nibbled a little bit of it to try: the next mo -ment she felt a violent blow on her chin: it had struck her foot!

She was a good deal frightened by this very sudden change, but as she did not shrink any further, and had not dropped the top of the mushroom, she did not give up hope yet. There was hardly room to open her mouth, with her chin pressing against her foot, but she did it at last, and managed to bite off a little bit of the top of the mushroom

* * * * *

"Come! my head's free at last!" said Alice in a tone of delight, which changed into alarm in another mo-ment, when she found that her shoulders were nowhere to be seen she looked down upon an immense length of neck, which seemed to rise like a stalk out of a sea of green leaves that lay far below her

"What <u>can</u> all that green stuff be?" said Alice, "and where <u>have</u> my shoulders got to? And oh! my poor hands! how is it I can't see you?" She was moving them about as she spoke, but no result seemed to follow, except a little rustling among the leaves. Then she tried to bring her head down to her hands, and was delighted to find that her neck would bend about easily in every direction, like a serpent She had just succeeded in bending it down in a beautiful zig-zag, and was going to dive in among the leaves, which she found to be the tops of the trees of the wood she had been wandering in, when a sharp hiss made her draw back: a large pigeon had flown into her face, and was vio-lently beating her with its wings.

"Serpent!" screamed the pigeon.

"I'm <u>not</u> a serpent!" said Alice indignantly, "let me alone!"

"I've tried every way!" the pigeon said desperately, with a kind of sob: "nothing seems to suit 'em!"

"I haven't the least idea what you mean," said Alice.

"I've tried the roots of trees, and I've tried banks, and I've tried hedges," the pigeon went on without attending to her, "but them serpents! There's no pleasing 'em!"

Alice was more and more puzzled, but she thought there was no use in saying anything till the pigeon had finished.

"As if it wasn't trouble enough hatching the eggs!" said the pigeon, "without being on the look out for serpents, day and night! Why, I haven't had a wink of sleep these three weeks!"

"I'm very sorry you've been annoyed," said Alice, beginning to see its meaning.

"And just as I'd taken the highest tree in the wood," said the pigeon raising its voice to a shriek, "and was just thinking I was free of 'em at last, they must needs come down from the sky! Ugh! Serpent!"

"But I'm not a serpent," said Alice, "I'm a — I'm a —"

"Well! What are you?" said the pigeon, "I see you're trying to invent something."

"I — I'm a little girl," said Alice, rather doubtfully, as she remembered the number of changes she had gone through

"A likely story indeed!" said the pigeon, "I've seen a good many of them in my time, but never <u>one</u> with such a neck as yours! No, you're a serpent, I know <u>that</u> well enough! I suppose you'll tell me next that you never tasted an egg!"

"I <u>have</u> tasted eggs, certainly," said Alice, who was a very truthful child, "but indeed I don't want any of yours. I don't like them raw."

"Well, be off, then!" said the pigeon, and settled down into its nest again. Alice crouched down among the trees, as well as she could, as her neck kept getting entangled among the branches, and several times she had to stop and untwist it Soon she remembered the pieces of mushroom which she still held in her hands, and set to work very carefully, nibbling first at one and then at the other, and growing sometimes taller and sometimes shorter, until she had succeeded in bringing herself down to her usual size.

It was so long since she had been of the right size that it felt quite strange

at first, but she got quite used to it in a
minute or two, and began talking to herself
as usual : "well! there's half my plan done
now! How puzzling all these changes are!
I'm never sure what I'm going to be, from
one minute to another! However, I've got to
my right size again : the next thing is, to
get into that beautiful garden — how is
that to be done, I wonder?"

Just as she said this, she noticed
that one of the trees had a doorway leading
right into it. "That's very curious!" she
thought, " but everything's curious today : I
may as well go in." And in she went.

Once more she found herself in the
long hall, and close to the little glass table:
"now, I'll manage better this time" she said
to herself, and began by taking the little
golden key, and unlocking the door that led
into the garden. Then she set to work eating
the pieces of mushroom till she was about
fifteen inches high : then she walked down
the little passage : and then — she found
herself at last in the beautiful garden, among
the bright flowerbeds and the cool fountains.

Chapter IV

A large rose tree stood near the entrance of the garden. the roses on it were white, but there were three gardeners at it, busily painting them red This Alice thought a very curious thing, and she went near to watch them, and just as she came up she heard one of them say "look out, Five! Don't go splashing paint over me like that!"

"I couldn't help it", said Five in a sulky tone. "Seven jogged my elbow"

On which Seven lifted up his head and said 'that's right, Five! Always lay the blame on others!"

"You'd better not talk!" said Five, "I

heard the Queen say only yesterday she thought of having you beheaded!"

"What for?" said the one who had spoken first.

"That's not your business, Two!" said Seven.

"Yes, it _is_ his business!" said Five, "and I'll tell him: it was for bringing tulip-roots to the cook instead of potatoes."

Seven flung down his brush, and had just begun "well! Of all the unjust things —" when his eye fell upon Alice, and he stopped suddenly. the others looked round, and all of them took off their hats and bowed low.

"Would you tell me, please," said Alice timidly. "why you are painting those roses?"

Five and Seven looked at Two, but said nothing: Two began, in a low voice, "why, Miss the fact is, this ought to have been a red rose tree, and we put a white one in by mistake, and if the Queen was to find it out, we should all have our heads cut off. So. you see, we're doing our best, before she comes, to —" At this moment Five, who had been looking anxiously across the garden called out "the Queen! the Queen!" and

the three gardeners instantly threw them-
-selves flat upon their faces. There was a
sound of many footsteps, and Alice looked
round, eager to see the Queen

First came ten soldiers carrying clubs:
these were all shaped like the three gardeners,
flat and oblong, with their hands and feet at
the corners: next the ten courtiers; these
were all ornamented with diamonds, and
walked two and two, as the soldiers did. After
these came the Royal children: there were ten
of them, and the little dears came jumping
merrily along, hand in hand, in couples: they
were all ornamented with hearts. Next came
the guests, mostly kings and queens, among
whom Alice recognised the white rabbit: it
was talking in a hurried nervous manner,
smiling at everything that was said, and
went by without noticing her. Then followed
the Knave of Hearts, carrying the King's crown
on a cushion, and, last of all this grand pro-
-cession, came THE KING AND QUEEN
OF HEARTS.

When the procession came opposite
to Alice, they all stopped and looked at her, and

the Queen said severely "who is this?" She said it to the Knave of Hearts, who only bowed and smiled in reply.

"Idiot!" said the Queen, turning up her nose, and asked Alice "what's your name?"

"My name is Alice, so please your Majesty," said Alice boldly, for she thought to herself "why, they're only a pack of cards! I needn't be afraid of them!"

"Who are these?" said the Queen, pointing to the three gardeners lying round the rose tree, for, as they were lying on their faces, and the pattern on their backs was the same as the rest of the pack, she could not tell whether they were gardeners, or soldiers, or courtiers, or three of her own children.

"How should I know?" said Alice, surprised at her own courage, "it's no business of mine"

The Queen turned crimson with fury, and, after glaring at her for a minute, began in a voice of thunder "off with her —"

"Nonsense!" said Alice, very loudly and decidedly, and the Queen was silent.

The King laid his hand upon her arm, and said timidly "remember, my dear! She is only a child!"

The Queen turned angrily away from him and said to the Knave "turn them over!"

The Knave did so, very carefully, with one foot.

"Get up!" said the Queen, in a shrill loud voice, and the three gardeners instantly jumped up, and began bowing to the King, the Queen, the Royal children, and everybody else.

"Leave off that!" screamed the Queen, "you make me giddy". And then, turning to the rose tree, she went on "what <u>have</u> you been doing here?"

"May it please your Majesty", said Two very humbly, going down on one knee as he spoke, "we were trying——."

"<u>I</u> see!" said the Queen, who had meantime been examining the roses, "off with their heads!" and the procession moved on, three of the soldiers remaining behind to execute the three unfortunate gardeners, who ran to Alice for protection.

"You shan't be beheaded!" said Alice, and she put them into her pocket: the three soldiers marched once round her, looking for them, and then quietly marched off after the others.

"Are their heads off?" shouted the Queen

"Their heads are gone," the soldiers shouted in reply, "if it please your Majesty."

"That's right!" shouted the Queen, "can you play croquet?"

The soldiers were silent, and looked at Alice, as the question was evidently meant for her.

"Yes!" shouted Alice at the top of her voice.

"Come on then!" roared the Queen, and Alice joined the procession, wondering very much what would happen next.

"It's — it's a very fine day!" said a timid little voice: she was walking by the white rabbit, who was peeping anxiously into her face.

"Very," said Alice, "where's the Marchioness?"

"Hush, hush!" said the rabbit in a low voice, "she'll hear you. The Queen's the Marchioness: didn't you know that?"

"No, I didn't," said Alice, "what of?"

"Queen of Hearts," said the rabbit in a whisper, putting its mouth close to her ear, "and Marchioness of Mock Turtles."

"What are they?" said Alice, but there was no time for the answer, for they had reached the croquet-ground, and the game began instantly.

Alice thought she had never seen such a curious croquet-ground in all her life: it was all in ridges and furrows: the croquet-balls were live hedgehogs, the mallets live ostriches, and the soldiers had to double themselves up, and stand

on their feet and hands, to make the arches.

The chief difficulty which Alice found at first was to manage her ostrich : she got its body tucked away, comfortably enough, under

her arm, with its legs hanging down, but generally, just as she had got its neck straightened out nicely, and was going to give a blow with its head, it would twist itself round, and look up into her face, with such a puzzled expression that she could not help bursting out laughing : and when she had got its head down, and was going to begin again, it was very confusing to find that the hedgehog had unrolled itself, and was in the act of crawling away : besides all this, there was generally a ridge or a furrow in her way, wherever she wanted to send the hedgehog to, and as the doubled-up soldiers were always getting up and walking off to other parts of the ground, Alice soon came to the conclusion that it was a very difficult game indeed.

The players all played at once without waiting for turns, and quarrelled all the while at the tops of their voices, and in a very few minutes the Queen was in a furious passion, and went stamping about and shouting "off with his head!" or "off with her head!" about once in a minute. All those whom she sentenced were taken into custody by the soldiers, who of course had to leave off being arches to do this, so that, by the end of half an hour or so, there were no arches left, and all the players, except the King, the Queen, and Alice, were in custody, and under sentence of execution.

Then the Queen left off, quite out of breath, and said to Alice "have you seen the Mock Turtle?"

"No," said Alice, "I don't even know what a Mock Turtle is."

"Come on then," said the Queen, "and it shall tell you its history."

As they walked off together, Alice heard the King say in a low voice, to the company generally, "you are all pardoned."

"Come, that's a good thing!" thought Alice, who had felt quite grieved at the number of executions which the Queen had ordered.

They very soon came upon a Gryphon, which lay fast asleep in the sun: (if you don't know what a Gryphon is, look at the picture): "up, lazy thing!" said the Queen, "and take this young lady to see the Mock Turtle, and to  hear its history. I must go back and see after some executions I ordered," and she walked off, leaving Alice with the Gryphon. Alice did not quite like the look of the creature, but on the whole she thought it quite as safe to stay as to go after that savage Queen: so she waited.

The Gryphon sat up and rubbed its eyes: then it watched the Queen till she was out of sight: then it chuckled. "What fun!" said the Gryphon, half to itself, half to Alice.

"What _is_ the fun?" said Alice.

"Why, _she_," said the Gryphon; "it's all her fancy, that: they never executes nobody, you know: come on!"

"Everybody says 'come on!' here," thought Alice, as she walked slowly after the Gryphon; "I never was ordered about so before in all my life — never!"

They had not gone far before they saw the Mock Turtle in the distance, sitting sad and lonely on a little ledge of rock, and, as they came nearer, Alice could hear it sighing as if it its heart would break. She pitied it deeply: "what is its sorrow?" she asked the Gryphon, and the Gryphon answered, very nearly in the same words as before, "it's all its fancy, that: it hasn't got no sorrow, you know: come on!"

So they went up to the Mock Turtle, who looked at them with large eyes full of tears, but said nothing.

"This here young lady" said the Gryphon.

"wants for to know your history, she do."

"I'll tell it", said the Mock Turtle, in a deep hollow tone, "sit down, and don't speak till I've finished."

So they sat down, and no one spoke for some minutes: Alice thought to herself "I don't see how it can ever finish, if it doesn't begin" but she waited patiently.

"Once", said the Mock Turtle at last, with a deep sigh, "I was a real Turtle."

These words were followed by a very long silence, broken only by an occasional ex-clamation of "hjckrrh!" from the Gryphon, and the constant heavy sobbing of the Mock Turtle. Alice was very nearly getting up and saying, "thank you, sir, for your interesting story," but she could not help thinking there must be more to come, so she sat still and said nothing.

"When we were little", the Mock Turtle went on, more calmly, though still sobbing a little now and then, "we went to school in the sea The master was an old Turtle—we used to call him Tortoise—"

"Why did you call him Tortoise, if he wasn't one?" asked Alice.

"We called him Tortoise because he taught us," said the Mock Turtle angrily, "really you are very dull!"

"You ought to be ashamed of yourself for asking such a simple question," added the Gryphon, and then they both sat silent and looked at poor Alice, who felt ready to sink into the earth: at last the Gryphon said to the Mock Turtle, "get on, old fellow! Don't be all day!" and the Mock Turtle went on in these words.

"You may not have lived much under the sea—" ("I haven't," said Alice,) "and perhaps you were never even introduced to a lobster—" (Alice began to say "I once tasted—" but hastily checked herself, and said "no, never," instead,) "so you can have no idea what a delightful thing a Lobster Quadrille is!"

"No, indeed," said Alice, "what sort of a thing is it?"

"Why," said the Gryphon, "you form into a line along the sea shore—"

"Two lines!" cried the Mock Turtle, "seals, turtles, salmon, and so on — advance twice—"

"Each with a lobster as partner!" cried the Gryphon.

"Of course," the Mock Turtle said, "advance twice, set to partners —"

"Change lobsters, and retire in same order —" interrupted the Gryphon.

"Then, you know," continued the Mock Turtle, "you throw the —"

"The lobsters!" shouted the Gryphon, with ..a bound into the air.

"As far out to sea as you can —"

"Swim after them!" screamed the Gryphon

"Turn a somersault in the sea!" cried. the Mock Turtle, capering wildly about.

"Change lobsters again!" yelled the Gryphon at the top of its voice, "and then —"

"That's all," said the Mock Turtle, suddenly dropping its voice, and the two creatures, who had been jumping about like mad things all this time, sat down again very sadly and quietly, and looked at Alice

"It must be a very pretty dance," said Alice timidly.

"Would you like to see a little of it?" said the Mock Turtle

"Very much indeed," said Alice.

"Come, let's try the first figure!" said the Mock Turtle to the Gryphon, "we can do it without lobsters, you know. Which shall sing?"

"Oh! you sing!" said the Gryphon,
"I've forgotten the words."

So they began solemnly dancing round
and round Alice,
every now and
then treading on
her toes when they
came too close,
and waxing their
fore-paws to mark
the time, while the
Mock Turtle sang,
slowly and sadly,
these words:

"Beneath the waters of the sea
Are lobsters thick as thick can be—
They love to dance with you and me,
My own, my gentle Salmon!"

The Gryphon joined in singing the chorus,
which was:

"Salmon come up! Salmon go down!
Salmon come twist your tail around!
Of all the fishes of the sea
There's none so good as Salmon!"

"Thank you," said Alice, feeling very glad that the figure was over.

"Shall we try the second figure?" said the Gryphon, "or would you prefer a song?"

"Oh, a song, please!" Alice replied, so eagerly, that the Gryphon said, in a rather offended tone, "hm! no accounting for tastes! Sing her 'Mock Turtle Soup', will you, old fellow!"

The Mock Turtle sighed deeply, and began, in a voice sometimes choked with sobs, to sing this:

"Beautiful Soup, so rich and green,
Waiting in a hot tureen!
Who for such dainties would not stoop?
Soup of the evening, beautiful Soup!
Soup of the evening, beautiful Soup!
    Beau—ootiful Soo—oop!
    Beau—ootiful Soo—oop!
Soo—oop of the e—e—evening,
    Beautiful beautiful Soup!

"Chorus again!" cried the Gryphon, and

the Mock Turtle had just begun to repeat it,
then a cry of "the trial's beginning!" was
heard in the distance.

"Come on!" cried the Gryphon, and,
taking Alice by the hand, he hurried off,
without waiting for the end of the song.

"What trial is it?" panted Alice as
she ran, but the Gryphon only answered "come
on!" and ran the faster, and more and more
faintly came, borne on the breeze that followed
them, the melancholy words

"Soo—oop of the e-e-evening,
Beautiful beautiful Soup!"

The King and Queen were seated on
their throne when they arrived, with a great
crowd assembled around them: the Knave was
in custody: and before the King stood the
white rabbit, with a trumpet in one hand,
and a scroll of parchment in the other.

"Herald! read the accusation!" said
the King.

On this the white rabbit blew three
blasts on the trumpet, and then unrolled the
parchment scroll, and read as follows:

"The Queen of Hearts she made some tarts
All on a summer day:
The Knave of Hearts he stole those tarts,
And took them quite away!"

"Now for the evidence," said the King, "and then the sentence.

"No!" said the Queen, first the sentence, and then the evidence!"

"Nonsense!" cried Alice, so loudly that everybody jumped, "the idea of having the sentence first!

"Hold your tongue!" said the Queen.

"I won't!" said Alice, "you're nothing but a pack of cards! Who cares for you?"

At this the whole pack rose up into the air, and came flying down upon her: she gave a little scream of fright, and tried to beat them off, and found herself lying on the bank, with her head in the lap of her sister, who was gently brushing away some leaves that had fluttered down from the trees on to her face.

"Wake up! Alice dear!" said her sister, "what a nice long sleep you've had!"

"Oh, I've had such a curious dream!" said Alice, and she told her sister all her Adventures Under Ground, as you have read them, and when she had finished, her sister kissed her and said "it _was_ a curious dream, dear, certainly! But now run in to your tea: it's getting late."

So Alice ran off, thinking while she ran (as well she might) what a wonderful dream it had been.

———————————

But her sister sat there some while longer, watching the setting sun, and thinking of little Alice and her Adventures, till she too began dreaming after a fashion, and this was her dream:

She saw an ancient city, and a quiet river winding near it along the plain, and up the stream went slowly gliding a boat with a merry party of children on board — she could hear their voices and laughter like music over the water — and among them was another little Alice, who sat listening with bright eager eyes to a tale that was being told, and she listened for the words of the tale, and lo! it was the dream of her own little sister. So the boat wound slowly along, beneath the bright summer-day, with its merry crew and its music of voices and laughter, till it passed round one of the many turnings of the stream, and she saw it no more.

Then she thought, (in a dream within the dream, as it were,) how this same little Alice would, in the after-time, be herself a grown woman: and how she would keep, through her riper years, the simple and loving heart of her childhood: and how she would gather around her other little children, and make *their* eyes bright and eager with many a wonderful tale, perhaps even with these very adventures of the little Alice of long-age: and how she would feel with all their simple sorrows, and find a pleasure in all their simple joys, remembering her own child-life, and the happy summer days.

THE END.

AN EASTER GREETING

TO

EVERY CHILD WHO LOVES

"Alice."

DEAR CHILD,

Please to fancy, if you can, that you are reading a real letter, from a real friend whom you have seen, and whose voice you can seem to yourself to hear wishing you, as I do now with all my heart, a happy Easter.

Do you know that delicious dreamy feeling when one first wakes on a summer morning, with the twitter of birds in the air, and the fresh breeze coming in at the open window——when, lying lazily with eyes half shut, one sees as in a dream green boughs waving, or waters rippling in a golden light? It is a pleasure very near to sadness, bringing tears to one's eyes like a beautiful picture or poem. And is not that a Mother's gentle hand that undraws your curtains, and a Mother's sweet voice that summons you to rise? To rise and forget, in the bright sunlight, the ugly dreams that frightened you so when all was dark——to rise and enjoy another happy day, first kneeling to thank that unseen Friend, who sends you the beautiful sun?

Are these strange words from a writer of such tales as "Alice"? And is this a strange letter to find in a book of nonsense? It may be so. Some perhaps may blame me for thus mixing together things grave and gay; others may smile and think it odd that any one should speak of solemn things at all, except in church and on a Sunday: but I think——nay, I am sure——that some children will read this gently and lovingly, and in the spirit in which I have written it.

For I do not believe God means us thus to divide life into two halves——to wear a grave face on Sunday, and to think it out-of-place to even so much as mention Him on a week-day. Do you think He cares to see only kneeling figures, and to hear only tones of prayer——and that He does not also love to see the lambs leaping in the sunlight, and to hear the merry voices of the children, as they roll among the hay? Surely their innocent laughter is as sweet in His ears as the grandest anthem that ever rolled up from the "dim religious light" of some solemn cathedral?

And if I have written anything to add to those stores of innocent and healthy amusement that are laid up in books for the children I love so well, it is surely something I may hope to look back upon without shame and sorrow (as how much of life must then be recalled!) when my turn comes to walk through the valley of shadows.

This Easter sun will rise on you, dear child, feeling your "life in every limb," and eager to rush out into the fresh morning air——and many an Easter-day will come and go, before it finds you feeble and gray-headed, creeping wearily out to bask once more in the sunlight——but it is good, even now, to think sometimes of that great morning when the "Sun of Righteousness shall arise with healing in his wings."

Surely your gladness need not be the less for the thought that you will one day see a brighter dawn than this——when lovelier sights will meet your eyes than any waving trees or rippling waters——when angel-hands shall undraw your curtains, and sweeter tones than ever loving Mother breathed shall wake you to a new and glorious day——and when all the sadness, and the sin, that darkened life on this little earth, shall be forgotten like the dreams of a night that is past!

Your affectionate friend,
LEWIS CARROLL.

EASTER, 1876.

CHRISTMAS GREETINGS.

[FROM A FAIRY TO A CHILD.]

LADY dear, if Fairies may
   For a moment lay aside
Cunning tricks and elfish play,
   'Tis at happy Christmas-tide.

We have heard the children say—
   Gentle children, whom we love—
Long ago, on Christmas Day,
   Came a message from above.

Still, as Christmas-tide comes round,
   They remember it again—
Echo still the joyful sound
   "Peace on earth, good-will to men!"

Yet the hearts must childlike be
   Where such heavenly guests abide;
Unto children, in their glee.
   All the year is Christmas-tide!

Thus, forgetting tricks and play
   For a moment, Lady dear,
We would wish you, if we may,
   Merry Christmas, glad New Year!

                LEWIS CARROLL

Christmas, 1867.

SYLVIE AND BRUNO

Illustrated by
HARRY FURNISS

Is all our Life, then, but a dream
Seen faintly in the golden gleam
Athwart Time's dark resistless stream?

Bowed to the earth with bitter woe,
Or laughing at some raree-show,
We flutter idly to and fro.

Man's little Day in haste we spend,
And, from its merry noontide, send
No glance to meet the silent end.

PREFACE.

ONE little picture in this book, the Magic Locket, at p. 530, was drawn by 'Miss Alice Havers.' I did not state this on the title-page, since it seemed only due, to the artist of all these (to my mind) *wonderful* pictures, that his name should stand there alone.

The descriptions, at p. 651, of Sunday as spent by children of the last generation, are quoted *verbatim* from a speech made to me by a child-friend and a letter written to me by a lady-friend.

The Chapters, headed 'Fairy Sylvie' and 'Bruno's Revenge,' are a reprint, with a few alterations, of a little fairy-tale which I wrote in the year 1867, at the request of the late Mrs. Gatty, for 'Aunt Judy's Magazine,' which she was then editing.

It was in 1874, I believe, that the idea first occurred to me of making it the nucleus of a longer story. As the years went on, I jotted down, at odd moments, all sorts of odd ideas, and fragments of dialogue, that occurred to me—who knows how?—with a transitory suddenness that left me no choice but either to record them then and there, or to abandon them to oblivion. Sometimes one could trace to their source these random flashes of thought—as being suggested by the book one was reading, or struck out from the 'flint' of one's own mind by the 'steel' of a friend's chance remark—but they had also a way of their own, of occurring, *à propos* of nothing—specimens of that hopelessly illogical phenomenon, 'an effect without a cause.' Such, for example, was the last line of 'The Hunting of the Snark,' which came into my head (as I have already related in 'The Theatre' for April, 1887) quite suddenly, during a solitary walk: and such, again, have been passages which occurred in *dreams,* and which I cannot trace to any antecedent cause whatever. There are at least *two* instances of such dream-suggestions in this book—one, my Lady's remark, 'it often runs in families, just as a love for pastry does', at p. 535; the other, Eric Lindon's *badinage* about having been in domestic service, at p. 631.

And thus it came to pass that I found myself at last in possession of a huge unwieldy mass of litterature—if the reader will kindly excuse the spelling—which only needed stringing together, upon the thread of a consecutive story, to constitute the book I hoped to write. Only! The task, at first, seemed absolutely hopeless, and gave me a far clearer idea, than I ever had before, of the meaning of the word 'chaos': and I think it must have been ten years, or more, before I had succeeded in classifying these odds-and-ends sufficiently to see what sort of a story they indicated: for the story had to grow out of the incidents, not the incidents out of the story.

I am telling all this, in no spirit of egoism, but because I really believe that some of my readers will be interested in these details of the 'genesis' of a book, which looks so simple and straight-forward a matter, when completed, that they might suppose it to have been written straight off, page by page, as one would write a letter, beginning at the beginning and ending at the end.

It is, no doubt, *possible* to write a story in that way: and, if it be not vanity to say so, I believe that I could, myself,—if I were in the unfortunate position (for I do hold it to be a real misfortune) of being obliged to produce a given amount of fiction in a given time,—that I could 'fulfil my task,' and produce my 'tale of bricks,' as other slaves have done. One thing, at any rate, I could guarantee as to the story so produced—that it should be utterly commonplace, should contain no new ideas whatever, and should be very very weary reading!

This species of literature has received the very appropriate name of 'padding'—which might fitly be defined as 'that which all can write and none can read.' That the present volume contains *no* such writing I dare not avow: sometimes, in order to bring a picture into its proper place, it has been necessary to eke out a page with two or three extra lines: but I can honestly say I have put in no more than I was absolutely compelled to do.

My readers may perhaps like to amuse themselves by trying to detect, in a given passage, the one piece of 'padding' it contains. While arranging the 'slips' into pages, I found that the passage, which now extends from near the top of p. 514 to near the middle of p. 515, was 3 lines too short. I suppplied the deficiency, not by interpolating a word here and a word there, but by writing in 3 consecutive lines. Now can my readers guess *which* they are?

A harder puzzle—if a harder be desired—would be to determine, as to the Gardener's Song, in *which* cases (if any) the stanza was adapted to the surrounding text, and in *which* (if any) the text was adapted to the stanza.

Perhaps the hardest thing in all literature—at least *I* have found it so: by no voluntary effort can I accomplish it: I have to take it as it comes— is to write anything *original*. And perhaps the easiest is, when once an original line has been struck out, to follow it up, and to write any amount more to the same tune. I do not know if 'Alice in Wonderland' was an *original* story—I was, at least, no *conscious* imitator in writing it—but I do know that, since it came out, something like a dozen story-books have appeared, on identically the same pattern. The path I timidly explored—believing myself to be 'the first that ever burst into that silent sea'—is now a beaten high-road: all the way-side flowers have long ago been trampled into the dust: and it would be courting disaster for me to attempt that style again.

Hence it is that, in 'Sylvie and Bruno,' I have striven—with I know not what success—to strike out yet another new path: be it bad or good, it is the best I can do. It is written, not for money, and not for fame, but in the hope of supplying, for the children whom I love, some thoughts that may suit those hours of innocent merriment which are the very life of Childhood; and also in the hope of suggesting, to them and to others, some thoughts that may prove, I would fain hope, not wholly out of harmony with the graver cadences of Life.

If I have not already exhausted the patience of my readers, I would like to seize this opportunity—perhaps the last I shall have of addressing so many friends at once—of putting on record some ideas that have occurred to me, as to books desirable to be written—which I should much like to *attempt,* but may not ever have the time or power to carry through—in the hope that, if *I* should fail (and the years are gliding away *very* fast) to finish the task I have set myself, other hands may take it up.

First, a Child's Bible. The only real *essentials* of this would be, carefully selected passages, suitable for a child's reading, and pictures. One principle of selection, which I would adopt, would be that Religion should be put before a child as a revelation of *love*—no need to pain and puzzle the young mind with the history of crime and punishment. (On such a principle I should, for example, omit the history of the Flood.) The supplying of the pictures would involve no great difficulty: no new ones would be needed: hundreds of excellent pictures already exist, the copyright of which has long ago expired, and which simply need photo-zincography, or some similar process, for their successful reproduction. The book should be handy in size—with a pretty attractive-looking cover—in a clear legible type—and, above all, with abundance of pictures, pictures, pictures!

Secondly, a book of pieces selected from the Bible—not single texts, but passages of from 10 to 20 verses each—to be committed to memory. Such passages would be found useful, to repeat to one's-self and to ponder over, on many occasions when reading is difficult, if not impossible: for instance, when lying awake at night—on a railway-journey—when taking a solitary walk—in old age, when eye-sight is failing or wholly lost—and, best of all, when illness, while incapacitating us for reading or any other occupation, condemns us to lie awake through many weary silent hours: at such a time how keenly one may realise the truth of

David's rapturous cry *'O how sweet are thy words unto my throat: yea, sweeter than honey unto my mouth!'*

I have said 'passages,' rather than single texts, because we have no means of *recalling* single texts: memory needs *links,* and here are none: one may have a hundred texts stored in the memory, and not be able to recall, at will, more than half-a-dozen—and those by mere chance: whereas, once get hold of any portion of a *chapter* that has been committed to memory, and the whole can be recovered: all hangs together.

Thirdly, a collection of passages, both prose and verse, from books other than the Bible. There is not perhaps much, in what is called 'uninspired' literature (a misnomer, I hold: if Shakespeare was not inspired, one may well doubt if any man ever was), that will bear the process of being pondered over, a hundred times: still there *are* such passages— enough, I think, to make a goodly store for the memory.

These two books—of sacred, and secular, passages for memory—will serve other good purposes besides merely occupying vacant hours: they will help to keep at bay many anxious thoughts, worrying thoughts, uncharitable thoughts, unholy thoughts. Let me say this, in better words than my own, by copying a passage from that most interesting book, Robertson's Lectures on the Epistles to the Corinthians, Lecture XLIX. "If a man finds himself haunted by evil desires and unholy images, which will generally be at periodical hours, let him commit to memory passages of Scripture, or passages from the best writers in verse or prose. Let him store his mind with these, as safeguards to repeat when he lies awake in some restless night, or when despairing imaginations, or gloomy, suicidal thoughts, beset him. Let these be to him the sword, turning everywhere to keep the way of the Garden of Life from the intrusion of profaner footsteps."

Fourthly, a "Shakespeare" for girls: that is, an edition in which everything, not suitable for the perusal of girls of (say) from 10 to 17, should be omitted. Few children under 10 would be likely to understand or enjoy the greatest of poets: and those, who have passed out of girlhood, may safely be left to read Shakespeare, in any edition, 'expurgated' or not, that they may prefer: but it seems a pity that so many children, in the intermediate stage, should be debarred from a great pleasure for want of an edition suitable to them. Neither Bowdler's, Chambers's, Brandram's, nor Cundell's 'Boudoir' Shakespeare, seems to me to meet the want: they are not sufficiently 'expurgated.' Bowdler's is the most extraordinary of all: looking through it, I am filled with a deep sense of wonder, considering what he has left in, that he should have cut *anything* out! Besides relentlessly erasing all that is unsuitable on the score of reverence or decency, I should be inclined to omit also all that seems too difficult, or not likely to interest young readers. The resulting book might be slightly fragmentary: but it would be a real treasure to all British maidens who have any taste for poetry.

If it be needful to apologize to any one for the new departure I have taken in this story—by introducing, along with what will, I hope, prove to be acceptable nonsense for children, some of the graver thoughts of human life—it must be to one who has learned the Art of keeping such thoughts wholly at a distance in hours of mirth and careless ease. To him such a mixture will seem, no doubt, ill-judged and repulsive. And that such an Art *exists* I do not dispute: with youth, good health, and sufficient money, it seems quite possible to lead, for years together, a life of unmixed gaiety—with the exception of one solemn fact, with which we are liable to be confronted at *any* moment, even in the midst of the most brilliant company or the most sparkling entertainment. A man may fix his own times for admitting serious thought, for attending public worship, for prayer, for reading the Bible: all such matters he can defer to that 'convenient season', which is so apt never to occur at all: but he cannot defer, for one single moment, the necessity of attending to a message, which may come before he has finished reading this page, '*this night shall thy soul be required of thee.*'

The ever-present sense of this grim possibility has been, in all ages,[1] an incubus that men have striven to shake off. Few more interesting subjects of enquiry could be found, by a student of history, than the various weapons that have been used against this shadowy foe. Saddest of all must have been the thoughts of those who saw indeed an *existence* beyond the grave, but an existence far more terrible than annihilation—an existence as filmy, impalpable, all but invisible spectres, drifting about, through endless ages, in a world of shadows, with nothing to do, nothing to hope for, nothing to love! In the midst of the gay verses of that genial 'bon vivant' Horace, there stands one dreary word whose utter sadness goes to one's heart. It is the word '*exilium*' in the well-known passage

> *Omnes eodem cogimur, omnium*
> *Versatur urnâ serius ocius*
>   *Sors exitura et nos in æternum*
>   *Exilium impositura cymbæ.*[1]

Yes, to him this present life—spite of all its weariness and all its sorrow—was the only life worth having: all else was 'exile'! Does it not seem almost incredible that one, holding such a creed, should ever have smiled?

And many in this day, I fear, even though believing in an existence beyond the grave far more real than Horace ever dreamed of, yet regard it as a sort of 'exile' from all the joys of life, and so adopt Horace's theory, and say 'let us eat and drink, for to-morrow we die.'

We go to entertainments, such as the theatre—I say 'we', for *I* also go to the play, whenever I get a chance of seeing a really good one—and keep at arm's length, if possible, the thought that we may not return alive. Yet how do you know—dear friend, whose patience has carried you through this garrulous preface—that it may not be *your* lot, when mirth is fastest and most furious, to feel the sharp pang, or the deadly

---

[1] At the moment, when I had written these words, there was a knock at the door, and a telegram was brought me, announcing the sudden death of a dear friend.

faintness, which heralds the final crisis—to see, with vague wonder, anxious friends bending over you—to hear their troubled whispers—perhaps yourself to shape the question, with trembling lips, "Is it serious?", and to be told "Yes: the end is near" (and oh, how different all Life will look when those words are said!)—how do you know, I say, that all this may not happen to *you*, this night?

And *dare* you, knowing this, say to yourself "Well, perhaps it *is* an immoral play: perhaps the situations *are* a little too 'risky', the dialogue a little too strong, the 'business' a little too suggestive. I don't say that conscience is *quite* easy: but the piece is so clever, I must see it this once! I'll begin a stricter life to-morrow." *To-morrow, and to-morrow, and to-morrow!*

> "Who sins in hope, who, sinning, says,
>   'Sorrow for sin God's judgement stays!'
> Against God's Spirit he lies; quite stops
> Mercy with insult; dares, and drops,
> Like a scorch'd fly, that spins in vain
>   Upon the axis of its pain,
> Then takes its doom, to limp and crawl,
> Blind and forgot, from fall to fall."

Let me pause for a moment to say that I believe this thought, of the possibility of death—if calmly realised, and steadily faced—would be one of the best possible tests as to our going to any scene of amusement being right or wrong. If the thought of sudden death acquires, for *you*, a special horror when imagined as happening in a *theatre,* then be very sure the theatre is harmful for *you,* however harmless it may be for others; and that *you* are incurring a deadly peril in going. Be sure the safest rule is that we should not dare to *live* in any scene in which we dare not *die.*

But, once realise what the true object *is* in life—that it is *not* pleasure, *not* knowledge, *not* even fame itself, 'that last infirmity of noble minds'— but that it *is* the development of *character,* the rising to a higher, nobler, purer standard, the building-up of the perfect *Man*—and then, so long as we feel that this is going on, and will (we trust) go on for evermore, death has for us no terror; it is not a shadow, but a light; not an end, but a beginning!

One other matter may perhaps seem to call for apology—that I should have treated with such entire want of sympathy the British passion for 'Sport', which no doubt has been in by-gone days, and is still, in some forms of it, an excellent school for hardihood and for coolness in moments of danger. But I am not entirely without sympathy for *genuine* 'Sport': I can heartily admire the courage of the man who, with severe bodily toil, and at the risk of his life, hunts down some 'man-eating' tiger: and I can heartily sympathize with him when he exults in the glorious ex- citement of the chase and the hand-to-hand struggle with the monster brought to bay. But I can but look with deep wonder and sorrow on the hunter who, at his ease and in safety, can find pleasure in what involves, for some defenceless creature, wild terror and a death of agony: deeper, if the hunter be one who has pledged himself to preach to men the Religion of universal Love: deepest of all, if it be one of those *'tender and delicate'* beings, whose very name serves as a symbol of Love—*'thy love to me was wonderful, passing the love of women'*—whose mission here is surely to help and comfort all that are in pain or sorrow!

'Farewell, farewell! but this I tell
To thee, thou Wedding-Guest!
He prayeth well, who loveth well
Both man and bird and beast.

He prayeth best, who loveth best
All things both great and small;
For the dear God who loveth us,
He made and loveth all.'

CHAPTER I.

LESS BREAD! MORE TAXES!

—and then all the people cheered again, and one man, who was more excited than the rest, flung his hat high into the air, and shouted (as well as I could make out) "Who roar for the Sub-Warden?" *Everybody* roared, but whether it was for the Sub-Warden, or not, did not clearly appear: some were shouting "Bread!" and some "Taxes!", but no one seemed to know what it was they really wanted.

All this I saw from the open window of the Warden's breakfast-saloon, looking across the shoulder of the Lord Chancellor, who had sprung to his feet the moment the shouting began, almost as if he had been expecting it, and had rushed to the window which commanded the best view of the market-place.

"What *can* it all mean?" he kept repeating to himself, as, with his hands clasped behind him, and his gown floating in the air, he paced rapidly up and down the room. "I never heard such shouting before—and at this time of the morning, too! And with such unanimity! Doesn't it strike *you* as very remarkable?"

I represented, modestly, that to *my* ears it appeared that they were shouting for different things, but the Chancellor would not listen to my suggestion for a moment. "They all shout the same words, I assure you!" he said: then, leaning well out of the window, he whispered to a man who was standing close underneath, "Keep 'em together, ca'n't you? The Warden will be here directly. Give 'em the signal for the march up!" All this was evidently not meant for *my* ears, but I could scarcely help hearing it, considering that my chin was almost on the Chancellor's shoulder.

The 'march up' was a very curious sight: a straggling procession of men, marching two and two, began from the other side of the market-place, and advanced in an irregular zig-zag fashion towards the Palace, wildly tacking from side to side, like a sailing vessel making way against an unfavourable wind—so that the head of the procession was often

further from us at the end of one tack than it had been at the end of
the previous one.

Yet it was evident that all was being done under orders, for I noticed
that all eyes were fixed on the man who stood just under the window,
and to whom the Chancellor was continually whispering. This man held
his hat in one hand and a little green flag in the other: whenever he
waved the flag the procession advanced a little nearer, when he dipped
it they sidled a little farther off, and whenever he waved his hat they all
raised a hoarse cheer. "Hoo-roah!" they cried, carefully keeping time
with the hat as it bobbed up and down. "Hoo-roah! Noo! Consti! Tooshun!
Less! Bread! More! Taxes!"

"That'll do, that'll do!" the Chancellor whispered. "Let 'em rest a bit
till I give you the word. He's not here yet!" But at this moment the great
folding-doors of the saloon were flung open, and he turned with a guilty
start to receive His High Excellency. However it was only Bruno, and
the Chancellor gave a little gasp of relieved anxiety.

"Morning!" said the little fellow, addressing the remark, in a general
sort of way, to the Chancellor and the waiters. "Doos oo know where
Sylvie is? I's looking for Sylvie!"

"She's with the Warden, I believe, y'reince!" the Chancellor replied with a low bow. There was, no doubt, a certain amount of absurdity in applying this title (which, as of course you see without my telling you, was nothing but 'your Royal Highness' condensed into one syllable) to a small creature whose father was merely the Warden of Outland: still, large excuse must be made for a man who had passed several years at the Court of Fairyland, and had there acquired the almost impossible art of pronouncing five syllables as one.

But the bow was lost upon Bruno, who had run out of the room, even while the great feat of The Unpronounceable Monosyllable was being triumphantly performed.

Just then, a single voice in the distance was understood to shout "A speech from the Chancellor!" "Certainly, my friends!" the Chancellor replied with extraordinary promptitude. "You shall have a speech!" Here one of the waiters, who had been for some minutes busy making a queer-looking mixture of egg and sherry, respectfully presented it on a large silver salver. The Chancellor took it haughtily, drank it off thoughtfully, smiled benevolently on the happy waiter as he set down the empty glass, and began. To the best of my recollection this is what he said.

"Ahem! Ahem! Ahem! Fellow-sufferers, or rather suffering fellows——" ("Don't call 'em names!" muttered the man under the window. "I didn't say *felons!*" the Chancellor explained.) "You may be sure that I always sympa——" ("'Ear, 'ear!" shouted the crowd, so loudly as quite to drown the orator's thin squeaky voice) "——that I always sympa——" he repeated. ("Don't simper quite so much!" said the man under the window. "It makes yer look a hidiot!" And, all this time, "'Ear, 'ear!" went rumbling round the market-place, like a peal of thunder.) "That I always *sympathise!*" yelled the Chancellor, the first moment there was silence. "But your *true* friend is the *Sub-Warden!* Day and night he is brooding on your wrongs—I should say your *rights*—that is to say your *wrongs*—no, I mean your *rights*——" ("Don't talk no more!" growled the man under the window. "You're making a mess of it!") At this moment the Sub-Warden entered the saloon. He was a thin man, with a mean and crafty face, and a greenish-yellow complexion; and he crossed the room very slowly, looking suspiciously about him as if he thought there might be a savage dog hidden somewhere. "Bravo!" he cried, patting the Chancellor on the back. "You did that speech very well indeed. Why, you're a born orator, man!"

"Oh, that's nothing!" the Chancellor replied, modestly, with downcast eyes. "Most orators are *born,* you know."

The Sub-Warden thoughtfully rubbed his chin. "Why, so they are!" he admitted. "I never considered it in that light. Still, you did it very well. A word in your ear!"

The rest of their conversation was all in whispers: so, as I could hear no more, I thought I would go and find Bruno.

I found the little fellow standing in the passage, and being addressed by one of the men in livery, who stood before him, nearly bent double from extreme respectfulness, with his hands hanging in front of him like the fins of a fish. "His High Excellency," this respectful man was saying, "is in his Study, y'reince!" (He didn't pronounce this quite so well as the Chancellor.) Thither Bruno trotted, and I thought it well to follow him.

The Warden, a tall dignified man with a grave but very pleasant face, was seated before a writing-table, which was covered with papers, and holding on his knee one of the sweetest and loveliest little maidens it has ever been my lot to see. She looked four or five years older than Bruno, but she had the same rosy cheeks and sparkling eyes, and the same wealth of curly brown hair. Her eager smiling face was turned upwards towards her father's, and it was a pretty sight to see the mutual love with which the two faces—one in the Spring of Life, the other in its late Autumn—were gazing on each other.

"No, you've never seen him," the old man was saying: "you couldn't, you know, he's been away so long—traveling from land to land, and seeking for health, more years than you've been alive, little Sylvie!"

Here Bruno climbed upon his other knee, and a good deal of kissing, on a rather complicated system, was the result.

"He only came back last night," said the Warden, when the kissing was over: "he's been traveling post-haste, for the last thousand miles or so, in order to be here on Sylvie's birthday. But he's a very early riser, and I dare say he's in the Library already. Come with me and see him. He's always kind to children. You'll be sure to like him."

"Has the Other Professor come too?" Bruno asked in an awe-struck voice.

"Yes, they arrived together. The Other Professor is—well, you won't like him quite so much, perhaps. He's a little more *dreamy*, you know."

"I wiss *Sylvie* was a little more dreamy," said Bruno.

"What *do* you mean, Bruno?" said Sylvie.

Bruno went on addressing his father. "She says she *ca'n't*, oo know. But I thinks it isn't *ca'n't*, it's *wo'n't*."

"Says she *ca'n't* dream!" the puzzled Warden repeated.

"She *do* say it," Bruno persisted. "When I says to her 'Let's stop lessons!', she says 'Oh, I ca'n't *dream* of letting oo stop yet!' "

"He always wants to stop lessons," Sylvie explained, "five minutes after we begin!"

"Five minutes' lessons a day!" said the Warden. "You won't learn much at *that* rate, little man!"

"That's just what Sylvie says," Bruno rejoined. "She says I *wo'n't* learn my lessons. And I tells her, over and over, I *ca'n't* learn 'em. And what doos oo think she says? She says 'It isn't *ca'n't*, it's *wo'n't*!' "

"Let's go and see the Professor," the Warden said, wisely avoiding further discussion. The children got down off his knees, each secured a hand, and the happy trio set off for the Library—followed by me. I had come to the conclusion by this time that none of the party (except, for a few moments, the Lord Chancellor) was in the least able to see me.

"What's the matter with him?" Sylvie asked, walking with a little extra sedateness, by way of example to Bruno at the other side, who never ceased jumping up and down.

"What *was* the matter—but I hope he's all right now—was lumbago, and rheumatism, and that kind of thing. He's been curing *himself*, you know: he's a very learned doctor. Why, he's actually *invented* three new diseases, besides a new way of breaking your collar-bone!"

"Is it a nice way?" said Bruno.

"Well, hum, not *very,*" the Warden said, as we entered the Library. "And here *is* the Professor. Good morning, Professor! Hope you're quite rested after your journey!"

A jolly-looking, fat little man, in a flowery dressing-gown, with a large book under each arm, came trotting in at the other end of the room, and was going straight across without taking any notice of the children. "I'm looking for Vol. Three," he said. "Do you happen to have seen it?"

"You don't see my *children,* Professor!" the Warden exclaimed, taking him by the shoulders and turning him round to face them.

The Professor laughed violently: then he gazed at them through his great spectacles, for a minute or two, without speaking.

At last he addressed Bruno. "I hope you have had a good night, my child?"

Bruno looked puzzled. "I's had the same night *oo've* had," he replied. "There's only been *one* night since yesterday!"

It was the Professor's turn to look puzzled now. He took off his spectacles, and rubbed them with his handkerchief. Then he gazed at them again.

Then he turned to the Warden. "Are they bound?" he enquired.

"No, we aren't," said Bruno, who thought himself quite able to answer *this* question.

The Professor shook his head sadly. "Not even half-bound?"

"Why *would* we be half-bound?" said Bruno. "We're not prisoners!"

But the Professor had forgotten all about them by this time, and was speaking to the Warden again. "You'll be glad to hear," he was saying, "that the Barometer's beginning to move——"

"Well, which way?" said the Warden—adding, to the children, "Not that *I* care, you know. Only *he* thinks it affects the weather. He's a wonderfully clever man, you know. Sometimes he says things that only the Other Professor can understand. Sometimes he says things that *nobody* can understand! Which way is it, Professor? Up or down?"

"Neither!" said the Professor, gently clapping his hands. "It's going sideways—if I may so express myself."

"And what kind of weather does *that* produce?" said the Warden. "Listen, children! Now you'll hear something worth knowing!"

"Horizontal weather," said the Professor, and made straight for the door, very nearly trampling on Bruno, who had only just time to get out of his way.

"*Isn't* he learned?" the Warden said, looking after him with admiring eyes. "Positively he runs over with learning!"

"But he needn't run over *me!*" said Bruno.

The Professor was back in a moment: he had changed his dressing-gown for a frock-coat, and had put on a pair of very strange-looking boots, the tops of which were open umbrellas. "I thought you'd like to see them," he said. "*These* are the boots for horizontal weather!"

"But what's the use of wearing umbrellas round one's knees?"

"In *ordinary* rain," the Professor admitted, "they would *not* be of much use. But if ever it rained *horizontally,* you know, they would be invaluable— simply invaluable!"

"Take the Professor to the breakfast-saloon, children," said the Warden. "And tell them not to wait for me. I had breakfast early, as I've some business to attend to." The children seized the Professor's hands, as familiarly as if they had known him for years, and hurried him away. I followed respectfully behind.

CHAPTER II.

L'AMIE INCONNUE.

As we entered the breakfast-saloon, the Professor was saying "—and he had breakfast by himself, early: so he begged you wouldn't wait for him, my Lady. This way, my Lady," he added, "this way!" And then, with (as it seemed to me) most superfluous politeness, he flung open the door of my compartment, and ushered in "—a young and lovely lady!" I muttered to myself with some bitterness. "And this is, of course, the opening scene of Vol. I. *She* is the Heroine. And *I* am one of those subordinate characters that only turn up when needed for the development of her destiny, and whose final appearance is outside the church, waiting to greet the Happy Pair!"

"Yes, my Lady, change at Fayfield," were the next words I heard (oh that too obsequious Guard!), "next station but one." And the door closed, and the lady settled down into her corner, and the monotonous throb of the engine (making one feel as if the train were some gigantic monster, whose very circulation we could feel) proclaimed that we were once more speeding on our way. "The lady had a perfectly formed nose," I caught myself saying to myself, "hazel eyes, and lips——" and here it occurred to me that to see, for myself, what "the lady" was really like, would be more satisfactory than much speculation.

I looked round cautiously, and—was entirely disappointed of my hope. The veil, which shrouded her whole face, was too thick for me to see more than the glitter of bright eyes and the hazy outline of what *might* be a lovely oval face, but might also, unfortunately, be an equally *unlovely* one. I closed my eyes again, saying to myself "—couldn't have a better chance for an experiment in Telepathy! I'll *think out* her face, and afterwards test the portrait with the original."

At first, no result at all crowned my efforts, though I 'divided my swift mind,' now hither, now thither, in a way that I felt sure would have made: Æneas green with envy: but the dimly-seen oval remained as provokingly blank as ever—a mere Ellipse, as if in some mathematical diagram, without even the Foci that might be made to do duty as a nose and a mouth. Gradually, however, the conviction came upon me that I could, by a certain concentration of thought, *think the veil away,* and so get a glimpse of the mysterious face—as to which the two questions, "is she pretty?" and "is she plain?", still hung suspended, in my mind, in beautiful equipoise.

Success was partial—and fitful—still there *was* a result: ever and anon, the veil seemed to vanish, in a sudden flash of light: but, before I could fully realise the face, all was dark again. In each such glimpse, the face seemed to grow more childish and more innocent: and, when I had at last *thought* the veil entirely away, it was, unmistakeably, the sweet face of little Sylvie!

"So, either I've been dreaming about Sylvie," I said to myself, "and this is the reality. Or else I've really been with Sylvie, and this is a dream! Is Life itself a dream, I wonder?"

To occupy the time, I got out the letter, which had caused me to take this sudden railway-journey from my London home down to a strange fishing-town on the North coast, and read it over again:—

> "DEAR OLD FRIEND,
>
> "I'm sure it will be as great a pleasure to me, as it can possibly be to you, to meet once more after so many years: and of course I shall be ready to give you all the benefit of such medical skill as I have: only, you know, one mustn't violate professional etiquette! And you are already in the hands of a first-rate London doctor, with whom it would be utter affectation for me to pretend to compete. (I make no doubt he is right in saying the heart is affected: all your symptoms point that way.) One thing, at any rate, I have already done in my doctorial capacity—secured you a bedroom on the ground-floor, so that you will not need to ascend the stairs at all.
>
> "I shall expect you by last train on Friday, in accordance with your letter: and, till then, I shall say, in the words of the old song, 'Oh for Friday nicht! Friday's lang a-coming!'
>
> > "Yours always,
> >
> > "ARTHUR FORESTER.
>
> "P.S. Do you believe in Fate?"

This Postscript puzzled me sorely. "He is far too sensible a man," I thought, "to have become a Fatalist. And yet what else can he mean by it?" And, as I folded up the letter and put it away, I inadvertently repeated the words aloud. "Do you believe in Fate?"

The fair 'Incognita' turned her head quickly at the sudden question. "No, I don't!" she said with a smile. "Do you?"

"I—I didn't mean to ask the question!" I stammered, a little taken aback at having begun a conversation in so unconventional a fashion.

The lady's smile became a laugh—not a mocking laugh, but the laugh of a happy child who is perfectly at her ease. "Didn't you?" she said. "Then it was a case of what you Doctors call 'unconscious cerebration'?"

"I am no Doctor," I replied. "Do I look so like one? Or what makes you think it?"

She pointed to the book I had been reading, which was so lying that its title, "Diseases of the Heart," was plainly visible.

"One needn't be a *Doctor,*" I said, "to take an interest in medical books. There's another class of readers, who are yet more deeply interested——"

"You mean the *Patients?*" she interrupted, while a look of tender pity gave new sweetness to her face. "But," with an evident wish to avoid a possibly painful topic, "one needn't be *either,* to take an interest in books of *Science.* Which contain the greatest amount of Science, do you think, the books, or the minds?"

"Rather a profound question for a lady!" I said to myself, holding, with the conceit so natural to Man, that Woman's intellect is essentially shallow. And I considered a minute before replying. "If you mean *living* minds, I don't think it's possible to decide. There is so much *written* Science that no living person has ever *read:* and there is so much *thought-out* Science that hasn't yet been *written.* But, if you mean the whole human race, then I think the *minds* have it: everything, recorded in *books,* must have once been in some *mind,* you know."

"Isn't that rather like one of the Rules in Algebra?" my Lady enquired. ("*Algebra* too!" I thought with increasing wonder.) "I mean, if we consider thoughts as *factors,* may we not say that the Least Common Multiple of all the *minds* contains that of all the *books;* but not the other way?"

"Certainly we may!" I replied, delighted with the illustration. "And what a grand thing it would be," I went on dreamily, thinking aloud rather than talking, "if we could only *apply* that Rule to books! You know, in finding the Least Common Multiple, we strike out a quantity wherever it occurs, except in the term where it is raised to its highest power. So we should have to erase every recorded thought, except in the sentence where it is expressed with the greatest intensity."

My Lady laughed merrily. "*Some* books would be reduced to blank paper, I'm afraid!" she said.

"They would. Most libraries would be terribly diminished in *bulk.* But just think what they would gain in *quality!*"

"When will it be done?" she eagerly asked. "If there's any chance of it in *my* time, I think I'll leave off reading, and wait for it!"

"Well, perhaps in another thousand years or so—"

"Then there's no use waiting!" said my Lady. "Let's sit down. Uggug, my pet, come and sit by me!"

"Anywhere but by *me!*" growled the Sub-Warden. "The little wretch always manages to upset his coffee!"

I guessed at once (as perhaps the reader will also have guessed, if, like myself, he is *very* clever at drawing conclusions) that my Lady was the Sub-Warden's wife, and that Uggug (a hideous fat boy, about the same age as Sylvie, with the expression of a prize-pig) was their son. Sylvie and Bruno, with the Lord Chancellor, made up a party of seven.

"And you actually got a plunge-bath every morning?" said the Sub-

Warden, seemingly in continuation of a conversation with the Professor. "Even at the little roadside-inns?"

"Oh, certainly, certainly!" the Professor replied with a smile on his jolly face. "Allow me to explain. It is, in fact, a very simple problem in Hydrodynamics. (That means a combination of Water and Strength.) If we take a plunge-bath, and a man of great strength (such as myself) about to plunge into it, we have a perfect example of this science. I am bound to admit," the Professor continued, in a lower tone and with downcast eyes, "that we need a man of *remarkable* strength. He must be able to spring from the floor to about twice his own height, gradually turning over as he rises, so as to come down again head first."

"Why, you need a *flea*, not a *man!*" exclaimed the Sub-Warden.

"Pardon me," said the Professor. "This particular kind of bath is *not* adapted for a flea. Let us suppose," he continued, folding his table-napkin into a graceful festoon, "that this represents what is perhaps *the* necessity of this Age—the Active Tourist's Portable Bath. You may describe it briefly, if you like," looking at the Chancellor, "by the letters A. T. P. B."

The Chancellor, much disconcerted at finding everybody looking at him, could only murmur, in a shy whisper, "Precisely so!"

"One great advantage of this plunge-bath," continued the Professor, "is that it requires only half-a-gallon of water——"

"I don't call it a *plunge*-bath," His Sub-Excellency remarked, "unless your Active Tourist goes *right under!*"

"But he *does* go right under," the old man gently replied. "The A. T. hangs up the P. B. on a nail—*thus*. He then empties the water-jug into it—places the empty jug below the bag—leaps into the air—descends head-first into the bag—the water rises round him to the top of the bag—and there you are!" he triumphantly concluded. "The A. T. is as much under water as if he'd gone a mile or two down into the Atlantic!"

"And he's drowned, let us say, in about four minutes——"

"By no means!" the Professor answered with a proud smile. "After about a minute, he quietly turns a tap at the lower end of the P. B.—all the water runs back into the jug—and there you are again!"

"But how in the world is he to get *out* of the bag again?"

"*That*, I take it," said the Professor, "is the most beautiful part of the whole invention. All the way up the P.B., inside, are loops for the thumbs; so it's something like going up-stairs, only perhaps less comfortable; and, by the time the A. T. has risen out of the bag, all but his head, he's sure to topple over, one way or the other—the Law of Gravity secures *that*. And there he is on the floor again!"

"A little bruised, perhaps?"

"Well, yes, a little bruised; but *having had his plunge-bath:* that's the great thing."

"Wonderful! It's almost beyond belief!" murmured the Sub-Warden. The Professor took it as a compliment, and bowed with a gratified smile.

"*Quite* beyond belief!" my Lady added—meaing, no doubt, to be more complimentary still. The Professor bowed, but he didn't smile *this* time.

"I can assure you," he said earnestly, "that, *provided the bath was made,*

I used it every morning. I certainly *ordered* it—*that* I am clear about—
my only doubt is, whether the man ever finished making it. It's difficult
to remember, after so many years——"

At this moment the door, very slowly and creakingly, began to open,
and Sylvie and Bruno jumped up, and ran to meet the well-known
footstep.

CHAPTER III.

BIRTHDAY-PRESENTS.

"It's my brother!" the Sub-Warden exclaimed, in a warning whisper.
"Speak out, and be quick about it!"

The appeal was evidently addressed to the Lord Chancellor, who instantly replied, in a shrill monotone, like a little boy repeating the alphabet,
"As I was remarking, your Sub-Excellency, this portentous movement—"

"You began too soon!" the other interrupted, scarcely able to restrain
himself to a whisper, so great was his excitement. "He couldn't have
heard you. Begin again!"

"As I was remarking," chanted the obedient Lord Chancellor, "this
portentous movement has already assumed the dimensions of a Revolution!"

"And what *are* the dimensions of a Revolution?" The voice was genial
and mellow, and the face of the tall dignified old man, who had just
entered the room, leading Sylvie by the hand, and with Bruno riding
triumphantly on his shoulder, was too noble and gentle to have scared
a less guilty man: but the Lord Chancellor turned pale instantly, and
could hardly articulate the words "The dimensions—your—your High
Excellency? I—I—scarcely comprehend!"

"Well, the length, breadth, and thickness, if you like it better!" And
the old man smiled, half-contemptuously.

The Lord Chancellor recovered himself with a great effort, and pointed
to the open window. "If your High Excellency will listen for a moment
to the shouts of the exasperated populace——" ("of the exasperated
populace!" the Sub-Warden repeated in a louder tone, as the Lord Chancellor, being in a state of abject terror, had dropped almost into a whisper)
"—you will understand what it is they want."

And at that moment there surged into the room a hoarse confused
cry, in which the only clearly audible words were "Less—bread—More—
taxes!" The old man laughed heartily. "What in the world——" he was
beginning: but the Chancellor heard him not. "Some mistake!" he muttered, hurrying to the window, from which he shortly returned with an
air of relief. "*Now* listen!" he exclaimed, holding up his hand impressively.
And now the words came quite distinctly, and with the regularity of the
ticking of a clock "More—bread—Less—taxes!"

"More bread!" the Warden repeated in astonishment. "Why, the new Government Bakery was opened only last week, and I gave orders to sell the bread at cost-price during the present scarcity! What *can* they expect more?"

"The Bakery's closed, y'reince!" the Chancellor said, more loudly and clearly than he had spoken yet. He was emboldened by the consciousness that *here*, at least, he had evidence to produce: and he placed in the Warden's hands a few printed notices, that were lying ready, with some open ledgers, on a side-table.

"Yes, yes, *I* see!" the Warden muttered, glancing carelessly through them. "Order countermanded by my brother, and supposed to be *my* doing! Rather sharp practice! It's all right!" he added in a louder tone. "My name is signed to it: so I take it on myself. But what do they mean by 'Less Taxes'? How *can* they be less? I abolished the last of them a month ago!"

"It's been put on again, y'reince, and by y'reince's own orders!", and other printed notices were submitted for inspection.

The Warden, whilst looking them over, glanced once or twice at the Sub-Warden, who had seated himself before one of the open ledgers, and was quite absorbed in adding it up; but he merely repeated "It's all right. I accept it as my doing."

"And they do say," the Chancellor went on sheepishly—looking much more like a convicted thief than an Officer of State, "that a change of Government, by the abolition of the Sub-Warden—I mean," he hastily added, on seeing the Warden's look of astonishment, "the abolition of the *office* of Sub-Warden, and giving the present holder the right to act as *Vice*-Warden whenever the Warden is absent—would appease all this seedling discontent. I mean," he added, glancing at a paper he held in his hand, "all this *seething* discontent!"

"For fifteen years," put in a deep but very harsh voice, "my husband has been acting as Sub-Warden. It is too long! It is much too long!" My Lady was a vast creature at all times: but, when she frowned and folded her arms, as now, she looked more gigantic than ever, and made one try to fancy what a haystack would look like, if out of temper.

"He would distinguish himself as a Vice!" my Lady proceeded, being far too stupid to see the double meaning of her words. "There has been no such Vice in Outland for many a long year, as he would be!"

"What course would *you* suggest, Sister?" the Warden mildly enquired.

My Lady stamped, which was undignified: and snorted, which was ungraceful. "This is no *jesting* matter!" she bellowed.

"I will consult my brother," said the Warden. "Brother!"

"—and seven makes a hundred and ninety-four, which is sixteen and twopence," the Sub-Warden replied. "Put down two and carry sixteen."

The Chancellor raised his hands and eyebrows, lost in admiration. "*Such* a man of business!" he murmured.

"Brother, could I have a word with you in my Study?" the Warden said in a louder tone. The Sub-Warden rose with alacrity, and the two left the room together.

My Lady turned to the Professor, who had uncovered the urn, and was taking its temperature with his pocket-thermometer. "Professor!" she began, so loudly and suddenly that even Uggug, who had gone to sleep in his chair, left off snoring and opened one eye. The Professor pocketed his thermometer in a moment, clasped his hands, and put his head on one side with a meek smile.

"You were teaching my son before breakfast, I believe?" my Lady loftily remarked. "I hope he strikes you as having talent?"

"Oh, very much so indeed, my Lady!" the Professor hastily replied, unconsciously rubbing his ear, while some painful recollection seemed to cross his mind. "I was very forcibly struck by His Magnificence, I assure you!"

"He is a charming boy!" my Lady exclaimed. "Even his snores are more musical than those of other boys!"

If that *were* so, the Professor seemed to think, the snores of *other* boys must be something too awful to be endured: but he was a cautious man, and he said nothing.

"And he's so clever!" my Lady continued. "No one will enjoy your Lecture more—by the way, have you fixed the time for it yet? You've never given one, you know: and it was promised years ago, before you—"

"Yes, yes, my Lady, *I* know! Perhaps next Tuesday—or Tuesday week——"

"That will do very well," said my Lady, graciously. "Of course you will let the Other Professor lecture as well?"

"I think *not*, my Lady," the Professor said with some hesitation. "You see, he always stands with his back to the audience. It does very well for *reciting;* but for *lecturing*——"

"You are quite right," said my Lady. "And, now I come to think of it, there would hardly be time for more than *one* Lecture. And it will go off all the better, if we begin with a Banquet, and a Fancy-dress Ball——"

"It will indeed!" the Professor cried, with enthusiasm.

"I shall come as a Grass-hopper," my Lady calmly proceeded. "What shall *you* come as, Professor?"

The Professor smiled feebly. "I shall come as—as early as I can, my Lady!"

"You mustn't come in before the doors are opened," said my Lady.

"I ca'n't," said the Professor. "Excuse me a moment. As this is Lady Sylvie's birthday, I would like to——" and he rushed away.

Bruno began feeling in his pockets, looking more and more melancholy as he did so: then he put his thumb in his mouth, and considered for a minute: then he quietly left the room.

He had hardly done so before the Professor was back again, quite out of breath. "Wishing you many happy returns of the day, my dear child!" he went on, addressing the smiling little girl, who had run to meet him. "Allow me to give you a birthday-present. It's a second-hand pincushion, my dear. And it only cost fourpence-halfpenny!"

"Thank you, it's *very* pretty!" And Sylvie rewarded the old man with a hearty kiss.

"And the *pins* they gave me for nothing!" the Professor added in high glee. "Fifteen of 'em, and only *one* bent!"

"I'll make the bent one into a *hook!*" said Sylvie. "To catch Bruno with, when he runs away from his lessons!"

"You ca'n't guess what *my* present is!" said Uggug, who had taken the butter-dish from the table, and was standing behind her, with a wicked leer on his face.

"No, I ca'n't guess," Sylvie said without looking up. She was still examining the Professor's pincushion.

"It's *this!*" cried the bad boy, exultingly, as he emptied the dish over her, and then, with a grin of delight at his own cleverness, looked round for applause.

Sylvie coloured crimson, as she shook off the butter from her frock: but she kept her lips tight shut, and walked away to the window, where she stood looking out and trying to recover her temper.

Uggug's triumph was a very short one: the Sub-Warden had returned, just in time to be a witness of his dear child's playfulness, and in another moment a skilfully-applied box on the ear had changed the grin of delight into a howl of pain.

"My darling!" cried his mother, enfolding him in her fat arms. "Did they box his ears for nothing? A precious pet!"

"It's not for *nothing!*" growled the angry father. "Are you aware, Madam, that *I* pay the house-bills, out of a fixed annual sum? The loss of all that wasted butter falls on *me!* Do you hear, Madam!"

"Hold your tongue, Sir!" My Lady spoke very quietly—almost in a whisper. But there was something in her *look* which silenced him. "Don't you see it was only a *joke?* And a very clever one, too! He only meant that he loved nobody *but* her! And, instead of being pleased with the compliment, the spiteful little thing has gone away in a huff!"

The Sub-Warden was a very good hand at changing a subject. He walked across to the window. "My dear," he said, "is that a *pig* that I see down below, rooting about among your flower-beds?"

"A *pig!*" shrieked my Lady, rushing madly to the window, and almost pushing her husband out, in her anxiety to see for herself. "Whose pig is it? How did it get in? Where's that crazy Gardener gone?"

At this moment Bruno re-entered the room, and passing Uggug (who was blubbering his loudest, in the hope of attracting notice) as if he was quite used to that sort of thing, he ran up to Sylvie and threw his arms round her. "I went to my toy-cupboard," he said with a very sorrowful face, "to see if there were *somefin* fit for a present for oo! And there isn't *nuffin!* They's *all* broken, every one! And I haven't got *no* money left, to buy oo a birthday-present! And I ca'n't give oo nuffin but *this!*" ("*This*" was a very earnest hug and a kiss.)

"Oh, thank you, darling!" cried Sylvie. "I like *your* present best of all!" (But if so, why did she give it back so quickly?)

His Sub-Excellency turned and patted the two children on the head with his long lean hands. "Go away, dears!" he said. "There's business to talk over."

Sylvie and Bruno went away hand in hand: but, on reaching the door,

Sylvie came back again and went up to Uggug timidly. "I don't mind about the butter," she said, "and I—I'm sorry he hurt you!" And she tried to shake hands with the little ruffian: but Uggug only blubbered louder, and wouldn't make friends. Sylvie left the room with a sigh.

The Sub-Warden glared angrily at his weeping son. "Leave the room, Sirrah!" he said, as loud as he dared. His wife was still leaning out of the window, and kept repeating "I *ca'n't* see that pig! Where *is* it?"

"It's moved to the right—now it's gone a little to the left," said the Sub-Warden: but he had his back to the window, and was making signals to the Lord Chancellor, pointing to Uggug and the door, with many a cunning nod and wink.

The Chancellor caught his meaning at last, and, crossing the room, took that interesting child by the ear—the next moment he and Uggug were out of the room, and the door shut behind them: but not before one piercing yell had rung through the room, and reached the ears of the fond mother.

"What *is* that hideous noise?" she fiercely asked, turning upon her startled husband.

"It's some hyæna—or other," replied the Sub-Warden, looking vaguely up to the ceiling, as if that was where they usually were to be found. "Let us to business, my dear. Here comes the Warden." And he picked up from the floor a wandering scrap of manuscript, on which I just caught the words 'after which Election duly holden the said Sibimet and Tabikat his wife may at their pleasure assume Imperial——' before, with a guilty look, he crumpled it up in his hand.

CHAPTER IV.

A CUNNING CONSPIRACY.

THE Warden entered at this moment: and close behind him came the Lord Chancellor, a little flushed and out of breath, and adjusting his wig, which appeared to have been dragged partly off his head.

"But where is my precious child?" my Lady enquired, as the four took their seats at the small side-table devoted to ledgers and bundles and bills.

"He left the room a few minutes ago—with the Lord Chancellor," the Sub-Warden briefly explained.

"Ah!" said my Lady, graciously smiling on that high official. "Your Lordship has a very *taking* way with children! I doubt if any one could *gain the ear* of my darling Uggug so quickly as *you* can!" For an entirely stupid woman, my Lady's remarks were curiously full of meaning, of which she herself was wholly unconscious.

The Chancellor bowed, but with a very uneasy air. "I think the Warden was about to speak," he remarked, evidently anxious to change the subject.

But my Lady would not be checked. "He is a clever boy," she continued with enthusiasm, "but he needs a man like your Lordship to *draw him out!*"

The Chancellor bit his lip, and was silent. He evidently feared that, stupid as she looked, she understood what she said *this* time, and was having a joke at his expense. He might have spared himself all anxiety: whatever accidental meaning her *words* might have, she *herself* never meant anything at all.

"It is all settled!" the Warden announced, wasting no time over preliminaries. "The Sub-Wardenship is abolished, and my brother is appointed to act as Vice-Warden whenever I am absent. So, as I am going abroad for a while, he will enter on his new duties at once."

"And there will really be a Vice after all?" my Lady enquired.

"I hope so!" the Warden smilingly replied.

My Lady looked much pleased, and tried to clap her hands: but you might as well have knocked two feather-beds together, for any noise it made. "When my husband is Vice," she said, "it will be the same as if we had a *hundred* Vices!"

"Hear, hear!" cried the Sub-Warden.

"You seem to think it very remarkable," my Lady remarked with some severity, "that your wife should speak the truth!"

"No, not *remarkable* at all!" her husband anxiously explained. "*Nothing* is remarkable that *you* say, sweet one!"

My Lady smiled approval of the sentiment and went on. "And am I Vice-Wardeness?"

"If you choose to use that title," said the Warden: "but 'Your Excellency'

will be the proper style of address. And I trust that both '*His* Excellency'
and '*Her* Excellency' will observe the Agreement I have drawn up. The
provision I am *most* anxious about is this." He unrolled a large parchment
scroll, and read aloud the words "'*item*, that we will be kind to the poor.'
The Chancellor worded it for me," he added, glancing at that great
Functionary. "I suppose, now, that word '*item*' has some deep legal meaning?"

"Undoubtedly!" replied the Chancellor, as articulately as he could with
a pen between his lips. He was nervously rolling and unrolling several
other scrolls, and making room among them for the one the Warden
had just handed to him. "These are merely the rough copies," he explained:
"and, as soon as I have put in the final corrections—" making a great
commotion among the different parchments, "—a semi-colon or two
that I have accidentally omitted—" here he darted about, pen in hand,
from one part of the scroll to another, spreading sheets of blotting-paper
over his corrections, "all will be ready for signing."

"Should it not be read out, first?" my Lady enquired.

"No need, no need!" the Sub-Warden and the Chancellor exclaimed
at the same moment, with feverish eagerness.

"No need at all," the Warden gently assented. "Your husband and I
have gone through it together. It provides that he shall exercise the full
authority of Warden, and shall have the disposal of the annual revenue
attached to the office, until my return, or, failing that, until Bruno comes
of age: and that he shall then hand over, to myself or to Bruno as the
case may be, the Wardenship, the unspent revenue, and the contents of
the Treasury, which are to be preserved, intact, under his guardianship."

All this time the Sub-Warden was busy, with the Chancellor's help,
shifting the papers from side to side, and pointing out to the Warden
the place where he was to sign. He then signed it himself, and my Lady
and the Chancellor added their names as witnesses.

"Short partings are best," said the Warden. "All is ready for my journey.
My children are waiting below to see me off." He gravely kissed my
Lady, shook hands with his brother and the Chancellor, and left the
room.

The three waited in silence till the sound of wheels announced that
the Warden was out of hearing: then, to my surprise, they broke into
peals of uncontrollable laughter.

"What a game, oh, what a game!" cried the Chancellor. And he and
the Vice-Warden joined hands, and skipped wildly about the room. My
Lady was too dignified to skip, but she laughed like the neighing of a
horse, and waved her handkerchief above her head: it was clear to her
very limited understanding that *something* very clever had been done,
but what it *was* she had yet to learn.

"You said I should hear all about it when the Warden had gone," she
remarked, as soon as she could make herself heard.

"And so you shall, Tabby!" her husband graciously replied, as he
removed the blotting-paper, and showed the two parchments lying side
by side. "This is the one he read but didn't sign: and this is the one he

signed but didn't read! You see it was all covered up, except the place for signing the names——"

"Yes, yes!" my Lady interrupted eagerly, and began comparing the two Agreements. "'*Item,* that he shall exercise the authority of Warden, in the Warden's absence.' Why, that's been changed into 'shall be absolute governor for life, with the title of Emperor, if elected to that office by the people.' What! Are you *Emperor,* darling?"

"Not yet, dear," the Vice-Warden replied. "It won't do to let this paper be seen, just at present. All in good time."

My Lady nodded, and read on. "'*Item,* that we will be kind to the poor.' Why, that's omitted altogether!"

"Course it is!" said her husband. "*We're* not going to bother about the wretches!"

"*Good,*" said my Lady, with emphasis, and read on again. "'*Item,* that the contents of the Treasury be preserved intact.' Why, that's altered into 'shall be at the absolute disposal of the Vice-Warden'! "Well, Sibby, that *was* a clever trick! *All* the Jewels, only think! May I go and put them on directly?"

"Well, not *just* yet, Lovey," her husband uneasily replied. "You see the public mind isn't quite *ripe* for it yet. We must feel our way. Of course we'll have the coach-and-four out, at once. And I'll take the title of Emperor, as soon as we can safely hold an Election. But they'll hardly stand our using the *Jewels,* as long as they know the Warden's alive. We must spread a report of his death. A little Conspiracy——"

"A Conspiracy!" cried the delighted lady, clapping her hands. "Of all things, I *do* like a Conspiracy! It's so interesting!"

The Vice-Warden and the Chancellor interchanged a wink or two. "Let her conspire to her heart's content!" the cunning Chancellor whispered. "It'll do no harm!"

"And when will the Conspiracy——"

"Hist!" her husband hastily interrupted her, as the door opened, and Sylvie and Bruno came in, with their arms twined lovingly round each other—Bruno sobbing convulsively, with his face hidden on his sister's shoulder, and Sylvie more grave and quiet, but with tears streaming down her cheeks.

"Mustn't cry like that!" the Vice-Warden said sharply, but without any effect on the weeping children. "Cheer 'em up a bit!" he hinted to my Lady.

"*Cake!*" my Lady muttered to herself with great decision, crossing the room and opening a cupboard, from which she presently returned with two slices of plum-cake. "Eat, and don't cry!" were her short and simple orders: and the poor children sat down side by side, but seemed in no mood for eating.

For the second time the door opened—or rather was *burst* open, this time, as Uggug rushed violently into the room, shouting "that old Beggar's come again!"

"He's not to have any food——" the Vice-Warden was beginning, but the Chancellor interrupted him. "It's all right," he said, in a low voice: "the servants have their orders."

"He's just under here," said Uggug, who had gone to the window, and was looking down into the court-yard.

"Where, my darling?" said his fond mother, flinging her arms round the neck of the little monster. All of us (except Sylvie and Bruno, who took no notice of what was going on) followed her to the window. The old Beggar looked up at us with hungry eyes. "Only a crust of bread, your Highness!" he pleaded. He was a fine old man, but looked sadly ill and worn. "A crust of bread is what I crave!" he repeated. "A single crust, and a little water!"

"Here's some water, drink this!" Uggug bellowed, emptying a jug of water over his head.

"Well done, my boy!" cried the Vice-Warden. "That's the way to settle such folk!"

"Clever boy!" the Wardeness chimed in. *"Hasn't* he good spirits?"

"Take a stick to him!" shouted the Vice-Warden, as the old Beggar shook the water from his ragged cloak, and again gazed meekly upwards.

"Take a red-hot poker to him!" my Lady again chimed in.

Possibly there was no red-hot poker handy: but some *sticks* were forth-coming in a moment, and threatening faces surrounded the poor old wanderer, who waved them back with quiet dignity. "No need to break my old bones," he said. "I am going. Not even a crust!"

"Poor, *poor* old man!" exclaimed a little voice at my side, half choked with sobs. Bruno was at the window, trying to throw out his slice of plum-cake, but Sylvie held him back.

"He *shall* have my cake!" Bruno cried, passionately struggling out of Sylvie's arms.

"Yes, yes, darling!" Sylvie gently pleaded. "But don't *throw* it out! He's gone away, don't you see? Let's go after him." And she led him out of the room, unnoticed by the rest of the party, who were wholly absorbed in watching the old Beggar.

The Conspirators returned to their seats, and continued their con-versation in an undertone, so as not to be heard by Uggug, who was still standing at the window.

"By the way, there was something about Bruno succeeding to the Wardenship," said my Lady. "How does *that* stand in the new Agreement?"

The Chancellor chuckled. "Just the same, word for word," he said, "with *one* exception, my Lady. Instead of 'Bruno,' I've taken the liberty to put in——" he dropped his voice to a whisper, "—to put in 'Uggug,' you know!"

"Uggug, indeed!" I exclaimed, in a burst of indignation I could no longer control. To bring out even that one word seemed a gigantic effort: but, the cry once uttered, all effort ceased at once: a sudden gust swept away the whole scene, and I found myself sitting up, staring at the young lady in the opposite corner of the carriage, who had now thrown back her veil, and was looking at me with an expression of amused surprise.

CHAPTER V.

A BEGGAR'S PALACE.

THAT I had said *something*, in the act of waking, I felt sure: the hoarse stifled cry was still ringing in my ears, even if the startled look of my fellow-traveler had not been evidence enough: but what could I possibly say by way of apology?

"I hope I didn't frighten you?" I stammered out at last. "I have no idea what I said. I was dreaming."

"You said '*Uggug indeed!*'" the young lady replied, with quivering lips that *would* curve themselves into a smile, in spite of all her efforts to look grave. "At least—you didn't *say* it—you *shouted* it!"

"I'm very sorry," was all I could say, feeling very penitent and helpless. "She *has* Sylvie's eyes!" I thought to myself, half-doubting whether, even now, I were fairly awake. "And that sweet look of innocent wonder is all Sylvie's, too. But Sylvie *hasn't* got that calm resolute mouth—nor that far-away look of dreamy sadness, like one that has had some deep sorrow, very long ago———" And the thick-coming fancies almost prevented my hearing the lady's next words.

"If you had had a 'Shilling Dreadful' in your hand," she proceeded, "something about Ghosts—or Dynamite—or Midnight Murder—one could understand it: those things aren't worth the shilling, unless they give one a Nightmare. But really—with only a *medical treatise*, you know—" and she glanced, with a pretty shrug of contempt, at the book over which I had fallen asleep.

Her friendliness, and utter unreserve, took me aback for a moment; yet there was no touch of forwardness, or boldness, about the child— for child, almost, she seemed to be: I guessed her at scarcely over twenty— all was the innocent frankness of some angelic visitant, new to the ways of earth and the conventionalisms—or, if you will, the barbarisms—of Society. "Even so," I mused, "will *Sylvie* look and speak, in another ten years."

"You don't care for Ghosts, then," I ventured to suggest, "unless they are really terrifying?"

"Quite so," the lady assented. "The regular Railway-Ghosts—I mean the Ghosts of ordinary Railway-literature—are very poor affairs. I feel inclined to say, with Alexander Selkirk, 'Their tameness is shocking to me'! And they never do any Midnight Murders. They couldn't 'welter in gore,' to save their lives!"

"'Weltering in gore' is a very expressive phrase, certainly. Can it be done in *any* fluid, I wonder?"

"I think *not*," the lady readily replied—quite as if she had thought it out, long ago. "It has to be something *thick*. For instance, you might welter in bread-sauce. That, being *white*, would be more suitable for a Ghost, supposing it wished to welter!"

"You have a real good *terrifying* Ghost in that book?" I hinted.

"How *could* you guess?" she exclaimed with the most engaging frankness, and placed the volume in my hands. I opened it eagerly, with a not unpleasant thrill (like what a good ghost-story gives one) at the 'uncanny' coincidence of my having so unexpectedly divined the subject of her studies.

It was a book of Domestic Cookery, open at the article 'Bread Sauce.'

I returned the book, looking, I suppose, a little blank, as the lady laughed merrily at my discomfiture. "It's far more exciting than some

of the modern ghosts, I assure you! Now there was a Ghost last month—
I don't mean a *real* Ghost in—in Supernature—but in a Magazine. It was
a perfectly *flavorless* Ghost. It wouldn't have frightened a mouse! It wasn't
a Ghost that one would even offer a chair to!"

"Three score years and ten, baldness, and spectacles, have their advantages after all!" I said to myself. "Instead of a bashful youth and
maiden, gasping out monosyllables at awful intervals, here we have an
old man and a child, quite at their ease, talking as if they had known
each other for years! Then you think," I continued aloud, "that we ought
sometimes to ask a Ghost to sit down? But have we any authority for it?
In Shakespeare, for instance—there are plenty of ghosts *there*—does
Shakespeare ever give the stage-direction *'hands chair to Ghost'* ? "

The lady looked puzzled and thoughtful for a moment: then she *almost*
clapped her hands. "Yes, yes, he *does!*" she cried. "He makes Hamlet say
'Rest, rest, perturbed Spirit!' "

"And that, I suppose, means an easy-chair?"

"An American rocking-chair, I *think*——"

"Fayfield Junction, my Lady, change for Elveston!" the guard announced, flinging open the door of the carriage: and we soon found
ourselves, with all our portable property around us, on the platform.

The accommodation, provided for passengers waiting at this Junction,
was distinctly inadequate—a single wooden bench, apparently intended
for three sitters only: and even this was already partially occupied by a
very old man, in a smock frock, who sat, with rounded shoulders and
drooping head, and with hands clasped on the top of his stick so as to
make a sort of pillow for that wrinkled face with its look of patient
weariness.

"Come, you be off!" the Station-master roughly accosted the poor old
man. "You be off, and make way for your betters! This way, my Lady!"
he added in a perfectly different tone. "If your Ladyship will take a seat,
the train will be up in a few minutes." The cringing servility of his manner
was due, no doubt, to the address legible on the pile of luggage, which
announced their owner to be "Lady Muriel Orme, passenger to Elveston,
viâ Fayfield Junction."

As I watched the old man slowly rise to his feet, and hobble a few
paces down the platform, the lines came to my lips:—

> *"From sackcloth couch the Monk arose,*
> *With toil his stiffen'd limbs he rear'd;*
> *A hundred years had flung their snows*
> *On his thin locks and floating beard."*

But the lady scarcely noticed the little incident. After one glance at
the 'banished man,' who stood tremulously leaning on his stick, she
turned to me. "This is *not* an American rocking-chair, by any means!
Yet may I say," slightly changing her place, so as to make room for me
beside her, "may I say, in Hamlet's words, 'Rest, rest——' " she broke
off with a silvery laugh.

"——perturbed Spirit!' " I finished the sentence for her. "Yes, that
describes a railway-traveler *exactly!* And here is an instance of it," I added,

as the tiny local train drew up alongside the platform, and the porters bustled about, opening carriage-doors—one of them helping the poor old man to hoist himself into a third-class carriage, while another of them obsequiously conducted the lady and myself into a first-class.

She paused, before following him, to watch the progress of the other passenger. "Poor old man!" she said. "How weak and ill he looks! It was a shame to let him be turned away like that. I'm very sorry——" At this moment it dawned on me that these words were not addressed to *me*, but that she was unconsciously thinking aloud. I moved away a few steps, and waited to follow her into the carriage, where I resumed the conversation.

"Shakespeare *must* have traveled by rail, if only in a dream: 'perturbed Spirit' is such a happy phrase."

"'Perturbed' referring, no doubt," she rejoined, "to the sensational booklets peculiar to the Rail. If Steam has done nothing else, it has at least added a whole new Species to English Literature!"

"No doubt of it," I echoed. "The true origin of all our medical books— and all our cookery-books——"

"No, no!" she broke in merrily. "I didn't mean *our* Literature! *We* are quite abnormal. But the booklets—the little thrilling romances, where the Murder comes at page fifteen, and the Wedding at page forty— surely *they* are due to Steam?"

"And when we travel by Electricity—if I may venture to develop your theory—we shall have leaflets instead of booklets, and the Murder and the Wedding will come on the same page."

"A development worthy of Darwin!" the lady exclaimed enthusiastically. "Only *you* reverse his theory. Instead of developing a mouse into an elephant, you would develop an elephant into a mouse!" But here we plunged into a tunnel, and I leaned back and closed my eyes for a moment, trying to recall a few of the incidents of my recent dream.

"I thought I saw——" I murmured sleepily: and then the phrase insisted on conjugating itself, and ran into "you thought you saw—he thought he saw——" and then it suddenly went off into a song:—

> *"He thought he saw an Elephant,*
> *That practised on a fife:*
> *He looked again, and found it was*
> *A letter from his wife.*
> *'At length I realise,' he said,*
> *'The bitterness of Life!'"*

And what a wild being it was who sang these wild words! A Gardener he seemed to be—yet surely a mad one, by the way he brandished his rake—madder, by the way he broke, ever and anon, into a frantic jig— maddest of all, by the shriek in which he brought out the last words of the stanza!

It was so far a description of himself that he had the *feet* of an Elephant: but the rest of him was skin and bone: and the wisps of loose straw, that bristled all about him, suggested that he had been originally stuffed with it, and that nearly all the stuffing had come out.

Sylvie and Bruno waited patiently till the end of the first verse. Then Sylvie advanced alone (Bruno having suddenly turned shy) and timidly introduced herself with the words "Please, I'm Sylvie!"

"And who's that other thing?" said the Gardener.

"What thing?" said Sylvie, looking round. "Oh, that's Bruno. He's my brother."

"Was he your brother yesterday?" the Gardener anxiously enquired.

"Course I were!" cried Bruno, who had gradually crept nearer, and didn't at all like being talked about without having his share in the conversation.

"Ah, well!" the Gardener said with a kind of groan. "Things change so, here. Whenever I look again, it's sure to be something diferent! Yet I does my duty! I gets up wriggle-early at five——"

"If I was *oo*," said Bruno, "I wouldn't wriggle so early. It's as bad as being a worm!" he added, in an undertone to Sylvie.

"But you shouldn't be lazy in the morning, Bruno," said Sylvie. "Remember, it's the *early* bird that picks up the worm!"

"It may, if it likes!" Bruno said with a slight yawn. "I don't like eating worms, one bit. I always stop in bed till the early bird has picked them up!"

"I wonder you've the face to tell me such fibs!" cried the Gardener.

To which Bruno wisely replied "Oo don't want a *face* to tell fibs wiz— only a *mouf*."

Sylvie discreetly changed the subject. "And did you plant all these flowers?" she said. "What a lovely garden you've made! Do you know, I'd like to live here *always!*"

"In the winter-nights—" the Gardener was beginning.

"But I'd nearly forgotten what we came about!" Sylvie interrupted. "Would you please let us through into the road? There's a poor old beggar just gone out—and he's very hungry—and Bruno wants to give him his cake, you know!"

"It's as much as my place is worth!" the Gardener muttered, taking a key from his pocket, and beginning to unlock a door in the garden-wall.

"How much *are* it wurf?" Bruno innocently enquired.

But the Gardener only grinned. "That's a secret!" he said. "Mind you come back quick!" he called after the children, as they passed out into the road. I had just time to follow them, before he shut the door again.

We hurried down the road, and very soon caught sight of the old Beggar, about a quarter of a mile ahead of us, and the children at once set off running to overtake him. Lightly and swiftly they skimmed over the ground, and I could not in the least understand how it was I kept up with them so easily. But the unsolved problem did not worry me so much as at another time it might have done, there were so many other things to attend to.

The old Beggar must have been very deaf, as he paid no attention whatever to Bruno's eager shouting, but trudged wearily on, never pausing until the child got in front of him and held up the slice of cake. The poor little fellow was quite out of breath, and could only utter the one word "Cake!"—not with the gloomy decision with which Her Excellency had so lately pronounced it, but with a sweet childish timidity, looking up into the old man's face with eyes that loved 'all things both great and small.'

The old man snatched it from him, and devoured it greedily, as some hungry wild beast might have done, but never a word of thanks did he give his little benefactor—only growled "More, more!" and glared at the half-frightened children.

"There *is* no more!" Sylvie said with tears in her eyes. "I'd eaten mine. It was a shame to let you be turned away like that. I'm very sorry——"

I lost the rest of the sentence, for my mind had recurred, with a great shock of surprise, to Lady Muriel Orme, who had so lately uttered these very words of Sylvie's—yes, and in Sylvie's own voice, and with Sylvie's gentle pleading eyes!

"Follow me!" were the next words I heard, as the old man waved his hand, with a dignified grace that ill suited his ragged dress, over a bush, that stood by the road side, which began instantly to sink into the earth. At another time I might have doubted the evidence of my eyes, or at least have felt some astonishment: but, in *this* strange scene, my whole being seemed absorbed in strong curiosity as to what would happen next.

When the bush had sunk quite out of our sight, marble steps were seen, leading downwards into darkness. The old man led the way, and we eagerly followed.

The staircase was so dark, at first, that I could only just see the forms of the children, as, hand-in-hand, they groped their way down after their guide: but it got lighter every moment, with a strange silvery brightness, that seemed to exist in the air, as there were no lamps visible; and, when at last we reached a level floor, the room, in which we found ourselves, was almost as light as day.

It was eight-sided, having in each angle a slender pillar, round which silken draperies were twined. The wall between the pillars was entirely covered, to the height of six or seven feet, with creepers, from which hung quantities of ripe fruit and of brilliant flowers, that almost hid the leaves. In another place, perchance, I might have wondered to see fruit and flowers growing together: here, my chief wonder was that neither fruit nor flowers were such as I had ever seen before. Higher up, each wall contained a circular window of coloured glass; and over all was an arched roof, that seemed to be spangled all over with jewels.

With hardly less wonder, I turned this way and that, trying to make out how in the world we had come in: for there was no door: and all the walls were thickly covered with the lovely creepers.

"We are safe here, my darlings!" said the old man, laying a hand on Sylvie's shoulder, and bending down to kiss her. Sylvie drew back hastily, with an offended air: but in another moment, with a glad cry of "Why, it's *Father!*", she had run into his arms.

"Father! Father!" Bruno repeated: and, while the happy children were being hugged and kissed, I could but rub my eyes and say "Where, then, are the rags gone to?"; for the old man was now dressed in royal robes that glittered with jewels and gold embroidery, and wore a circlet of gold around his head.

CHAPTER VI.

THE MAGIC LOCKET.

"WHERE are we, father?" Sylvie whispered, with her arms twined closely around the old man's neck, and with her rosy cheek lovingly pressed to his.

"In Elfland, darling. It's one of the provinces of Fairyland."

"But I thought Elfland was *ever* so far from Outland: and we've come such a *tiny* little way!"

"You came by the Royal Road, sweet one. Only those of royal blood can travel along it: but *you've* been royal ever since I was made King of Elfland—that's nearly a month ago. They sent *two* ambassadors, to make sure that their invitation to me, to be their new King, should reach me. One was a Prince; so *he* was able to come by the Royal Road, and to come invisibly to all but me: the other was a Baron; so *he* had to come by the common road, and I dare say he hasn't even *arrived* yet."

"Then how far have we come?" Sylvie enquired.

"Just a thousand miles, sweet one, since the Gardener unlocked that door for you."

"A thousand miles!" Bruno repeated. "And may I eat one?"

"Eat a *mile,* little rogue?"

"No," said Bruno. "I mean may I eat one of that fruits?"

"Yes, child," said his father: "and then you'll find out what *Pleasure* is like—the Pleasure we all seek so madly, and enjoy so mournfully!"

Bruno ran eagerly to the wall, and picked a fruit that was *shaped* something like a banana, but had the *colour* of a strawberry.

He ate it with beaming looks, that became gradually more gloomy, and were very blank indeed by the time he had finished.

"It hasn't got no taste at all!" he complained. "I couldn't feel nuffin in my mouf! It's a—what's that hard word, Sylvie?"

"It was a *Phlizz,*" Sylvie gravely replied. "Are they *all* like that, father?"

"They're all like that to *you,* darling, because you don't belong to Elfland—yet. But to *me* they are real."

Bruno looked puzzled. "I'll try anuvver kind of fruits!" he said, and jumped down off the King's knee. "There's some lovely striped ones, just like a rainbow!" And off he ran.

Meanwhile the Fairy-King and Sylvie were talking together, but in such low tones that I could not catch the words: so I followed Bruno, who was picking and eating other kinds of fruit, in the vain hope of finding *some* that had a taste. I tried to pick some myself—but it was like grasping air, and I soon gave up the attempt and returned to Sylvie.

"Look well at it, my darling," the old man was saying, "and tell me how you like it."

"It's just *lovely*," cried Sylvie, delightedly. "Bruno, come and look!" And she held up, so that he might see the light through it, a heart-shaped Locket, apparently cut out of a single jewel, of a rich blue colour, with a slender gold chain attached to it.

"It are welly pretty," Bruno more soberly remarked: and he began spelling out some words inscribed on it. "All—will—love—Sylvie," he made them out at last. "And so they doos!" he cried, clasping his arms round her neck. "*Everybody* loves Sylvie!"

"But *we* love her best, don't we, Bruno?" said the old King, as he took possession of the Locket. "Now, Sylvie, look at *this*." And he showed her, lying on the palm of his hand, a Locket of a deep crimson colour, the same shape as the blue one and, like it, attached to a slender golden chain.

"Lovelier and lovelier!" exclaimed Sylvie, clasping her hands in ecstasy. "Look, Bruno! "

"And there's words on this one, too," said Bruno. "Sylvie—will—love—all."

"Now you see the difference," said the old man: "different colours and different words. Choose one of them, darling. I'll give you whichever you like best."

Sylvie whispered the words, several times over, with a thoughtful smile, and then made her decision. "It's *very* nice to be loved," she said: "but it's nicer to love other people! May I have the red one, Father?"

The old man said nothing: but I could see his eyes fill with tears, as he bent his head and pressed his lips to her forehead in a long loving kiss. Then he undid the chain, and showed her how to fasten it round her neck, and to hide it away under the edge of her frock. "It's for you to *keep*, you know," he said in a low voice, "not for other people to *see*. You'll remember how to use it?"

"Yes, I'll remember," said Sylvie.

"And now, darlings, it's time for you to go back, or they'll be missing you, and then that poor Gardener will get into trouble!"

Once more a feeling of wonder rose in my mind as to how in the world we were to *get* back again—since I took it for granted that, wherever the children went, *I* was to go—but no shadow of doubt seemed to cross *their* minds, as they hugged and kissed him, murmuring, over and over again, "Good-bye, darling Father!" And then, suddenly and swiftly, the darkness of midnight seemed to close in upon us, and through the darkness harshly rang a strange wild song:—

> "He thought he saw a Buffalo
> Upon the chimney-piece:
> He looked again, and found it was
> His Sister's Husband's Niece.
> 'Unless you leave this house,' he said,
> 'I'll send for the Police!'"

"That was *me!*" he added, looking out at us, through the half-opened

door, as we stood waiting in the road. "And that's what I'd have done—as sure as potatoes aren't radishes—if she hadn't have tooken herself off! But I always loves my *pay-rints* like anything."

"Who *are* oor *pay-rints?*" said Bruno.

"Them as pay *rint* for me, a course!" the Gardener replied. "You can come in now, if you like."

He flung the door open as he spoke, and we got out, a little dazzled and stupefied (at least *I* felt so) at the sudden transition from the half-darkness of the railway-carriage to the brilliantly-lighted platform of Elveston Station.

A footman, in a handsome livery, came forwards and respectfully touched his hat. "The carriage is here, my Lady," he said, taking from her the wraps and small articles she was carrying: and Lady Muriel, after shaking hands and bidding me "Good-night!" with a pleasant smile, followed him.

It was with a somewhat blank and lonely feeling that I betook myself to the van from which the luggage was being taken out: and, after giving directions to have my boxes sent after me, I made my way on foot to Arthur's lodgings, and soon lost my lonely feeling in the hearty welcome my old friend gave me, and the cozy warmth and cheerful light of the little sitting-room into which he led me.

"Little, as you see, but quite enough for us two. Now, take the easy-chair, old fellow, and let's have another look at you! Well, you *do* look a bit pulled down!" and he put on a solemn professional air. "I prescribe Ozone, *quant. suff.* Social dissipation, *fiant pilulæ quam plurimæ:* to be taken, feasting, three times a day!"

"But, Doctor!" I remonstrated. "Society doesn't 'receive' three times a day!"

"That's all *you* know about it!" the young Doctor gaily replied. "At home, lawn-tennis, 3 P.M. At home, kettledrum, 5 P.M. At home, music (Elveston doesn't give dinners), 8 P.M. Carriages at 10. There you are!"

It sounded very pleasant, I was obliged to admit. "And I know some of the *lady*-society already," I added. "One of them came in the same carriage with me."

"What was she like? Then perhaps I can identify her."

"The *name* was Lady Muriel Orme. As to what she was *like*—well, *I* thought her very beautiful. Do you know her?"

"Yes—I do know her." And the grave Doctor coloured slightly as he added "Yes, I agree with you. She *is* beautiful."

"*I* quite lost my heart to her!" I went on mischievously. "We talked--"

"Have some supper!" Arthur interrupted with an air of relief, as the maid entered with the tray. And he steadily resisted all my attempts to return to the subject of Lady Muriel until the evening had almost worn itself away. Then, as we sat gazing into the fire, and conversation was lapsing into silence, he made a hurried confession.

"I hadn't meant to tell you anything about her," he said (naming no names, as if there were only one 'she' in the world!) "till you had seen more of her, and formed your own judgment of her: but somehow you surprised it out of me. And I've not breathed a word of it to any one else. But I can trust *you* with a secret, old friend! Yes! It's true of *me*, what I suppose *you* said in jest."

"In the merest jest, believe me!" I said earnestly. "Why, man, I'm three times her age! But if she's *your* choice, then I'm sure she's all that is good and——"

"——and sweet," Arthur went on, "and pure, and self-denying, and true-hearted, and——" he broke off hastily, as if he could not trust himself to say more on a subject so sacred and so precious. Silence followed: and I leaned back drowsily in my easy-chair, filled with bright and beautiful imaginings of Arthur and his lady-love, and of all the peace and happiness in store for them.

I pictured them to myself walking together, lingeringly and lovingly, under arching trees, in a sweet garden of their own, and welcomed back by their faithful gardener, on their return from some brief excursion.

It seemed natural enough that the gardener should be filled with exuberant delight at the return of so gracious a master and mistress—and how strangely childlike they looked! I could have taken them for Sylvie and Bruno—less natural that he should show it by such wild dances, such crazy songs!

> *"He thought he saw a Rattlesnake*
> *That questioned him in Greek:*
> *He looked again, and found it was*
> *The Middle of Next Week.*
> *'The one thing I regret,' he said,*
> *'Is that it cannot speak!'"*

—least natural of all that the Vice-Warden and 'my Lady' should be standing close beside me, discussing an open letter, which had just been handed to him by the Professor, who stood, meekly waiting, a few yards off.

"If it were not for those two brats" I heard him mutter, glancing savagely at Sylvie and Bruno, who were courteously listening to the Gardener's song, "there would be no difficulty whatever."

"Let's hear that bit of the letter again," said my Lady. And the Vice-Warden read aloud:—

"——and we therefore entreat you graciously to accept the Kingship, to which you have been unanimously elected by the Council of Elfland: and that you will allow your son Bruno—of whose goodness, cleverness, and beauty, reports have reached us—to be regarded as Heir-Apparent."

"But what's the difficulty?" said my Lady.

"Why, don't you see? The Ambassador, that brought this, is waiting in the house: and he's sure to see Sylvie and Bruno: and then, when he sees Uggug, and remembers all that about 'goodness, cleverness, and beauty,' why, he's sure to——"

"And *where* will you find a better boy than *Uggug*?" my Lady indignantly interrupted. "Or a wittier, or a lovelier?"

To all of which the Vice-Warden simply replied "Don't you be a great blethering goose! Our only chance is to keep those two brats out of sight. If *you* can manage *that,* you may leave the rest to *me. I'll* make him believe Uggug to be a model of cleverness and all that."

"We must change his name to Bruno, of course?" said my Lady.

The Vice-Warden rubbed his chin. "Humph! No!" he said musingly. "Wouldn't do. The boy's such an utter idiot, he'd never learn to answer to it."

"*Idiot,* indeed!" cried my Lady. "He's no more an idiot than I am!"

"You're right, my dear," the Vice-Warden soothingly replied. "He isn't, indeed!"

My Lady was appeased. "Let's go in and receive the Ambassador," she said, and beckoned to the Professor. "Which room is he waiting in?" she inquired.

"In the Library, Madam."

"And *what* did you say his name was?" said the Vice-Warden.

The Professor referred to a card he held in his hand. "His Adiposity the Baron Doppelgeist."

"Why does he come with such a funny name?" said my Lady.

"He couldn't well change it on the journey," the Professor meekly replied, "because of the luggage."

"*You* go and receive him," my Lady said to the Vice-Warden, "and *I'll* attend to the children."

CHAPTER VII.

THE BARON'S EMBASSY.

I WAS following the Vice-Warden, but, on second thoughts, went after my Lady, being curious to see how she would manage to keep the children out of sight.

I found her holding Sylvie's hand, and with her other hand stroking Bruno's hair in a most tender and motherly fashion: both children were looking bewildered and half-frightened.

"My own darlings," she was saying, "I've been planning a little treat for you! The Professor shall take you a long walk into the woods this beautiful evening: and you shall take a basket of food with you, and have a little picnic down by the river!"

Bruno jumped, and clapped his hands. "That *are* nice!" he cried. "Aren't it, Sylvie?"

Sylvie, who hadn't quite lost her surprised look, put up her mouth for a kiss. "Thank you *very* much," she said earnestly.

My Lady turned her head away to conceal the broad grin of triumph that spread over her vast face, like a ripple on a lake. "Little simpletons!" she muttered to herself, as she marched up to the house. I followed her in.

"Quite so, your Excellency," the Baron was saying as we entered the

Library. "All the infantry were under *my* command." He turned, and was duly presented to my Lady.

"A *military* hero?" said my Lady. The fat little man simpered. "Well, yes," he replied, modestly casting down his eyes. "My ancestors were all famous for military genius."

My Lady smiled graciously. "It often runs in families," she remarked: "just as a love for pastry does."

The Baron looked slightly offended, and the Vice-Warden discreetly changed the subject. "Dinner will soon be ready," he said. "May I have the honour of conducting your Adiposity to the guest-chamber?"

"Certainly, certainly!" the Baron eagerly assented. "It would never do to keep *dinner* waiting!" And he almost trotted out of the room after the Vice-Warden.

He was back again so speedily that the Vice-Warden had barely time to explain to my Lady that her remark about "a love for pastry" was "unfortunate. You might have seen, with half an eye," he added, "that that's *his* line. Military genius, indeed! Pooh!"

"Dinner ready yet?" the Baron enquired, as he hurried into the room.

"Will be in a few minutes," the Vice-Warden replied. "Meanwhile, let's take a turn in the garden. You were telling me," he continued, as the trio left the house, "something about a great battle in which you had the command of the infantry——"

"True," said the Baron. "The enemy, as I was saying, far outnumbered us: but I marched my men right into the middle of——what's that?" the Military Hero exclaimed in agitated tones, drawing back behind the Vice-Warden, as a strange creature rushed wildly upon them, brandishing a spade.

"It's only the Gardener!" the Vice-Warden replied in an encouraging tone. "Quite harmless, I assure you. Hark, he's singing! It's his favorite amusement."

And once more those shrill discordant tones rang out:—

> *"He thought he saw a Banker's Clerk*
> *Descending from the bus:*
> *He looked again, and found it was*
> *A Hippopotamus:*
> *'If this should stay to dine,' he said,*
> *'There won't be much for us!'"*

Throwing away the spade, he broke into a frantic jig, snapping his fingers, and repeating, again and again,

> *"There won't be much for us!*
> *There won't be much for us!"*

Once more the Baron looked slightly offended, but the Vice-Warden hastily explained that the song had no allusion to *him,* and in fact had no meaning at all. "You didn't mean anything by it, now *did* you?" He

appealed to the Gardener, who had finished his song, and stood, balancing himself on one leg, and looking at them, with his mouth open.

"I never means nothing," said the Gardener: and Uggug luckily came up at the moment, and gave the conversation a new turn.

"Allow me to present my son," said the Vice-Warden; adding, in a whisper, "one of the best and cleverest boys that ever lived! I'll contrive for you to see some of his cleverness. He knows everything that other boys *don't* know; and in archery, in fishing, in painting, and in music, his skill is—but you shall judge for yourself. You see that target over there? He shall shoot an arrow at it. Dear boy," he went on aloud, "his Adiposity would like to see you shoot. Bring his Highness' bow and arrows!"

Uggug looked very sulky as he received the bow and arrow, and prepared to shoot. Just as the arrow left the bow, the Vice-Warden trod heavily on the toe of the Baron, who yelled with the pain.

"Ten thousand pardons!" he exclaimed. "I stepped back in my excitement. See! It is a bull's-eye!"

The Baron gazed in astonishment. "He held the bow so awkwardly, it seemed impossible!" he muttered. But there was no room for doubt: there was the arrow, right in the centre of the bull's-eye!

"The lake is close by," continued the Vice-Warden. "Bring his Highness' fishing-rod!" And Uggug most unwillingly held the rod, and dangled the fly over the water.

"A beetle on your arm!" cried my Lady, pinching the poor Baron's arm worse than if ten lobsters had seized it at once. "*That* kind is poisonous," she explained. "But *what* a pity! You missed seeing the fish pulled out!"

An enormous dead cod-fish was lying on the bank, with the hook in its mouth.

"I had always fancied," the Baron faltered, "that cod were *salt*-water fish?"

"Not in *this* country," said the Vice-Warden. "Shall we go in? Ask my son some question on the way—*any* subject you like!" And the sulky boy was violently shoved forwards, to walk at the Baron's side.

"Could your Highness tell me," the Baron cautiously began, "how much seven times nine would come to?"

"Turn to the left!" cried the Vice-Warden, hastily stepping forwards to show the way—so hastily, that he ran against his unfortunate guest, who fell heavily on his face.

"*So* sorry!" my Lady exclaimed, as she and her husband helped him to his feet again. "My son was in the act of saying 'sixty-three' as you fell!"

The Baron said nothing: he was covered with dust, and seemed much hurt, both in body and mind. However, when they had got him into the house, and given him a good brushing, matters looked a little better.

Dinner was served in due course, and every fresh dish seemed to increase the good-humour of the Baron: but all efforts, to get him to express his opinion as to Uggug's cleverness, were in vain, until that interesting youth had left the room, and was seen from the open window, prowling about the lawn with a little basket, which he was filling with frogs.

"So fond of Natural History as he is, dear boy!" said the doting mother. "Now *do* tell us, Baron, what you think of him!"

"To be perfectly candid," said the cautious Baron, "I would like a *little* more evidence. I think you mentioned his skill in——"

"Music?" said the Vice-Warden. "Why, he's simply a prodigy! You shall hear him play the piano." And he walked to the window, "Ug—— I mean my boy! Come in for a minute, *and bring the music-master with you!* To turn over the music for him," he added as an explanation.

Uggug, having filled his basket with frogs, had no objection to obey, and soon appeared in the room, followed by a fierce-looking little man, who asked the Vice-Warden "Vot music vill you haf?"

"The Sonata that His Highness plays so charmingly," said the Vice-Warden.

"His Highness haf not——" the music-master began, but was sharply stopped by the Vice-Warden.

"Silence, Sir! Go and turn over the music for his Highness. My dear," (to the Wardeness) "will you show him what to do? And meanwhile, Baron, I'll just show you a most interesting map we have—of Outland, and Fairyland, and that sort of thing."

By the time my Lady had returned, from explaining things to the music-master, the map had been hung up, and the Baron was already much bewildered by the Vice-Warden's habit of pointing to one place while he shouted out the name of another.

My Lady joining in, pointing out other places, and shouting other names, only made matters worse; and at last the Baron, in despair, took to pointing out places for himself, and feebly asked "Is that great yellow splotch *Fairyland?*"

"Yes, that's Fairyland," said the Vice-Warden: "and you might as well give him a hint," he muttered to my Lady, "about going back to-morrow. He eats like a shark! It would hardly do for *me* to mention it."

His wife caught the idea, and at once began giving hints of the most subtle and delicate kind. "Just see what a short way it is back to Fairyland! Why, if you started to-morrow morning, you'd get there in very little more than a week!"

The Baron looked incredulous. "It took me a full month to *come,*" he said.

"But it's ever so much shorter, going *back,* you know!"

The Baron looked appealingly to the Vice-Warden, who chimed in readily. "You can go back *five* times, in the time it took you to come here *once*—if you start to-morrow morning!"

All this time the Sonata was pealing through the room. The Baron could not help admitting to himself that it was being magnificently played: but he tried in vain to get a glimpse of the youthful performer. Every time he had nearly succeeded in catching sight of him, either the Vice-Warden or his wife was sure to get in the way, pointing out some new place on the map, and deafening him with some new name.

He gave in at last, wished a hasty good-night, and left the room, while his host and hostess interchanged looks of triumph.

"Deftly done!" cried the Vice-Warden. "Craftily contrived! But what means all that tramping on the stairs?" He half-opened the door, looked out, and added in a tone of dismay, "The Baron's boxes are being carried down!"

"And what means all that rumbling of wheels?" cried my Lady. She peeped through the window curtains. "The Baron's carriage has come round!" she groaned.

At this moment the door opened: a fat, furious face looked in: a voice, hoarse with passion, thundered out the words "My room is full of frogs— I leave you!": and the door closed again.

And still the noble Sonata went pealing through the room: but it was *Arthur's* masterly touch that roused the echoes, and thrilled my very soul with the tender music of the immortal 'Sonata Pathetique': and it was not till the last note had died away that the tired but happy traveler could bring himself to utter the words "good-night!" and to seek his much-needed pillow.

CHAPTER VIII.

A RIDE ON A LION.

THE next day glided away, pleasantly enough, partly in settling myself in my new quarters, and partly in strolling round the neighbourhood, under Arthur's guidance, and trying to form a general idea of Elveston and its inhabitants. When five o'clock arrived, Arthur proposed—without any embarrassment this time—to take me with him up to 'the Hall,' in order that I might make acquaintance with the Earl of Ainslie, who had taken it for the season, and renew acquaintance with his daughter Lady Muriel.

My first impressions of the gentle, dignified, and yet genial old man were entirely favourable: and the *real* satisfaction that showed itself on his daughter's face, as she met me with the words "this is indeed an unlooked-for pleasure!", was very soothing for whatever remains of personal vanity the failures and disappointments of many long years, and much buffeting with a rough world, had left in me.

Yet I noted, and was glad to note, evidence of a far deeper feeling than mere friendly regard, in her meeting with Arthur—though this was, as I gathered, an almost daily occurrence—and the conversation between them, in which the Earl and I were only occasional sharers, had an ease and a spontaneity rarely met with except between *very* old friends: and, as I knew that they had not known each other for a longer period than the summer which was now rounding into autumn, I felt certain that 'Love,' and Love alone, could explain the phenomenon.

"How convenient it would be," Lady Muriel laughingly remarked, *à propos* of my having insisted on saving her the trouble of carrying a cup of tea across the room to the Earl, "if cups of tea had no weight at all! Then perhaps ladies would *sometimes* be permitted to carry them for short distances!"

"One can easily imagine a situation," said Arthur, "where things would *necessarily* have no weight, relatively to each other, though each would have its usual weight, looked at by itself."

"Some desperate paradox!" said the Earl. "Tell us how it could be. We shall never guess it."

"Well, suppose this house, just as it is, placed a few billion miles above a planet, and with nothing else near enough to disturb it: of course it falls *to* the planet?"

The Earl nodded. "Of course—though it might take some centuries to do it."

"And is five-o'clock-tea to be going on all the while?" said Lady Muriel.

"That, and other things," said Arthur. "The inhabitants would live their lives, grow up and die, and still the house would be falling, falling, falling! But now as to the relative weight of things. Nothing can be *heavy*, you know, except by *trying* to fall, and being prevented from doing so. You all grant that?"

We all granted that.

"Well, now, if I take this book, and hold it out at arm's length, of course I feel its *weight*. It is trying to fall, and I prevent it. And, if I let go, it falls to the floor. But, if we were all falling together, it couldn't be *trying* to fall any quicker, you know: for, if I let go, what more could it do than fall? And, as my hand would be falling too—at the same rate— it would never leave it, for that would be to get ahead of it in the race. And it could never overtake the falling floor!"

"I see it clearly," said Lady Muriel. "But it makes one dizzy to think of such things! How *can* you make us do it?"

"There is a more curious idea yet," I ventured to say. "Suppose a cord fastened to the house, from below, and pulled down by some one on the planet. Then of course the *house* goes faster than its natural rate of falling: but the furniture—with our noble selves—would go on falling at their old pace, and would therefore be left behind."

"Practically, we should rise to the ceiling," said the Earl. "The inevitable result of which would be concussion of brain."

"To avoid that," said Arthur, "let us have the furniture fixed to the floor, and ourselves tied down to the furniture. Then the five-o'clock-tea could go on in peace."

"With one little drawback!" Lady Muriel gaily interrupted. "We should take the *cups* down with us: but what about the *tea?*"

"I had forgotten the *tea*," Arthur confessed. "*That*, no doubt, would rise to the ceiling—unless you chose to drink it on the way!"

"Which, I think, is *quite* nonsense enough for one while!" said the Earl. "What news does this gentleman bring us from the great world of London?"

This drew *me* into the conversation, which now took a more conventional tone. After a while, Arthur gave the signal for our departure, and in the cool of the evening we strolled down to the beach, enjoying the silence, broken only by the murmur of the sea and the far-away music of some fishermen's song, almost as much as our late pleasant talk.

We sat down among the rocks, by a little pool, so rich in animal, vegetable, and zoöphytic—or whatever is the right word—life, that I became entranced in the study of it, and, when Arthur proposed returning to our lodgings, I begged to be left there for a while, to watch and muse alone.

The fishermen's song grew ever nearer and clearer, as their boat stood in for the beach; and I would have gone down to see them land their cargo of fish, had not the microcosm at my feet stirred my curiosity yet more keenly.

One ancient crab, that was for ever shuffling frantically from side to side of the pool, had particularly fascinated me: there was a vacancy in its stare, and an aimless violence in its behaviour, that irresistibly recalled the Gardener who had befriended Sylvie and Bruno: and, as I gazed, I caught the concluding notes of the tune of his crazy song.

The silence that followed was broken by the sweet voice of Sylvie. "Would you please let us out into the road?"

"What! After that old beggar again?" the Gardener yelled, and began singing:—

> "He thought he saw a Kangaroo
> That worked a coffee-mill:
> He looked again and found it was
> A Vegetable-Pill.
> 'Were I to swallow this' he said,
> 'I should be very ill!'"

"We don't want him to swallow *anything*," Sylvie explained. "He's not hungry. But we want to see him. So will you please——"

"Certainly!" the Gardener promptly replied. "I *always* please. Never displeases nobody. There you are!" And he flung the door open, and let us out upon the dusty high-road.

We soon found our way to the bush, which had so mysteriously sunk into the ground: and here Sylvie drew the Magic Locket from its hiding-place, turned it over with a thoughtful air, and at last appealed to Bruno in a rather helpless way. "What *was* it we had to do with it, Bruno? It's all gone out of my head!"

"Kiss it!" was Bruno's invariable recipe in cases of doubt and difficulty. Sylvie kissed it, but no result followed.

"Rub it the wrong way," was Bruno's next suggestion.

"Which *is* the wrong way?" Sylvie most reasonably enquired. The obvious plan was to try *both* ways.

Rubbing from left to right had no visible effect whatever.

From right to left—"Oh, stop, Sylvie!" Bruno cried in sudden alarm. "Whatever *is* going to happen?"

For a number of trees, on the neighbouring hillside, were moving slowly upwards, in solemn procession: while a mild little brook, that had been rippling at our feet a moment before, began to swell, and foam, and hiss, and bubble, in a truly alarming fashion.

"Rub it some other way!" cried Bruno. "Try up-and-down! Quick!"

It was a happy thought. Up-and-down did it: and the landscape, which had been showing signs of mental aberration in various directions, returned to its normal condition of sobriety—with the exception of a small yellowish-brown mouse, which continued to run wildly up and down the road, lashing its tail like a little lion.

"Let's follow it," said Sylvie: and this also turned out a happy thought. The mouse at once settled down into a business-like jog-trot, with which we could easily keep pace. The only phenomenon, that gave me any uneasiness, was the rapid increase in the *size* of the little creature we were following, which became every moment more and more like a real lion.

Soon the transformation was complete: and a noble lion stood patiently waiting for us to come up with it. No thought of fear seemed to occur to the children, who patted and stroked it as if it had been a Shetland-pony.

"Help me up!" cried Bruno. And in another moment Sylvie had lifted him upon the broad back of the gentle beast, and seated herself behind him, pillion-fashion. Bruno took a good handful of mane in each hand, and made believe to guide this new kind of steed. "Gee-up!" seemed quite sufficient by way of *verbal* direction: the lion at once broke into an easy canter, and we soon found ourselves in the depths of the forest. I say '*we*,' for I am certain that *I* accompanied them—though *how* I managed to keep up with a cantering lion I am wholly unable to explain. But I was certainly one of the party when we came upon an old beggar-man cutting sticks, at whose feet the lion made a profound obeisance, Sylvie and Bruno at the same moment dismounting, and leaping into the arms of their father.

"From bad to worse!" the old man said to himself, dreamily, when the children had finished their rather confused account of the Ambassador's visit, gathered no doubt from general report, as they had not seen him themselves. "From bad to worse! That is their destiny. I see it, but I cannot alter it. The selfishness of a mean and crafty man—the selfishness of an ambitious and silly woman—the selfishness of a spiteful and loveless child—all tend one way, from bad to worse! And you, my darlings, must sufer it awhile, I fear. Yet, when things are at their worst, you can come to me. I can do but little as yet——"

Gathering up a handful of dust and scattering it in the air, he slowly and solemnly pronounced some words that sounded like a charm, the children looking on in awe-struck silence:—

> "*Let craft, ambition, spite,*
> *Be quenched in Reason's night,*
> *Till weakness turn to might,*
> *Till what is dark be light,*

Till what is wrong be right!"

The cloud of dust spread itself out through the air, as if it were alive, forming curious shapes that were for ever changing into others.

"It makes letters! It makes words!" Bruno whispered, as he clung, half-frightened, to Sylvie. "Only I *ca'n't* make them out! Read them, Sylvie!"

"I'll try," Sylvie gravely replied. "Wait a minute—if only I could see that word—"

"I should be very ill!" a discordant voice yelled in our ears.

" 'Were I to swallow this,' he said,
'I should be very ill!' "

CHAPTER IX.

A JESTER AND A BEAR.

YES, we were in the garden once more: and, to escape that horrid discordant voice, we hurried indoors, and found ourselves in the library—Uggug blubbering, the Professor standing by with a bewildered air, and my Lady, with her arms clasped round her son's neck, repeating, over and over again, "and *did* they give him nasty lessons to learn? My own pretty pet!"

"What's all this noise about?" the Vice-Warden angrily enquired, as he strode into the room. "And who put the hat-stand here?" And he hung his hat up on Bruno, who was standing in the middle of the room, too much astonished by the sudden change of scene to make any attempt at removing it, though it came down to his shoulders, making him look something like a small candle with a large extinguisher over it.

The Professor mildly explained that His Highness had been graciously pleased to say he wouldn't do his lessons.

"Do your lessons this instant, you young cub!" thundered the Vice-Warden. "And take *this!*" and a resounding box on the ear made the unfortunate Professor reel across the room.

"Save me!" faltered the poor old man, as he sank, half-fainting, at my Lady's feet.

"Shave you? Of course I will!" my Lady replied, as she lifted him into a chair, and pinned an anti-macassar round his neck. "Where's the razor?"

The Vice-Warden meanwhile had got hold of Uggug, and was belabouring him with his umbrella. "Who left this loose nail in the floor?" he shouted. "Hammer it in, I say! Hammer it in!" Blow after blow fell on the writhing Uggug, till he dropped howling to the floor.

Then his father turned to the 'shaving' scene which was being enacted, and roared with laughter. "Excuse me, dear, I ca'n't help it!" he said as soon as he could speak. "You *are* such an utter donkey! Kiss me, Tabby!"

And he flung his arms round the neck of the terrified Professor, who raised a wild shriek, but whether he received the threatened kiss or not I was unable to see, as Bruno, who had by this time released himself from his extinguisher, rushed headlong out of the room, followed by Sylvie; and I was so fearful of being left alone among all these crazy creatures that I hurried after them.

"We must go to Father!" Sylvie panted, as they ran down the garden. "I'm *sure* things are at their worst! I'll ask the Gardener to let us out again."

"But we ca'n't *walk* all the way!" Bruno whimpered. "How I *wiss* we had a coach-and-four, like Uncle!"

And, shrill and wild, rang through the air the familiar voice:—

> "He thought he saw a Coach-and-Four
> That stood beside his bed:
> He looked again, and found it was
> A Bear without a Head.
> 'Poor thing,' he said, 'poor silly thing!
> It's waiting to be fed!'"

"No, I ca'n't let you out again!" he said, before the children could speak. "The Vice-Warden gave it me, he did, for letting you out last

time! So be off with you!" And, turning away from them, he began
digging frantically in the middle of a gravel-walk, singing, over and over
again,

> " 'Poor thing,' he said, 'poor silly thing!
> It's waiting to be fed!' "

but in a more musical tone than the shrill screech in which he had begun.

The music grew fuller and richer at every moment: other manly voices
joined in the refrain: and soon I heard the heavy thud that told me the
boat had touched the beach, and the harsh grating of the shingle as the
men dragged it up. I roused myself, and, after lending them a hand in
hauling up their boat, I lingered yet awhile to watch them disembark a
goodly assortment of the hard-won 'treasures of the deep.'

When at last I reached our lodgings I was tired and sleepy, and glad
enough to settle down again into the easy-chair, while Arthur hospitably
went to his cupboard, to get me out some cake and wine, without which,
he declared, he could not, as a doctor, permit my going to bed.

And how that cupboard-door *did* creak! It surely could not be *Arthur*,
who was opening and shutting it so often, moving so restlessly about,
and muttering like the soliloquy of a tragedy-queen!

No, it was a *female* voice. Also the figure—half-hidden by the cupboard-
door—was a *female* figure, massive, and in flowing robes. Could it be the
landlady? The door opened, and a strange man entered the room.

"What *is* that donkey doing?" he said to himself, pausing, aghast, on
the threshold.

The lady, thus rudely referred to, was his wife. She had got one of
the cupboards open, and stood with her back to him, smoothing down

a sheet of brown paper on one of the shelves, and whispering to herself "So, so! Deftly done! Craftily contrived!"

Her loving husband stole behind her on tip-toe, and tapped her on the head. "Boh!" he playfully shouted at her ear. "Never tell me again I ca'n't say 'boh' to a goose!"

My Lady wrung her hands. "Discovered!" she groaned. "Yet no—he is one of us! Reveal it not, oh Man! Let it bide its time!"

"Reveal *what* not?" her husband testily replied, dragging out the sheet of brown paper. "What are you hiding here, my Lady? I insist upon knowing!"

My Lady cast down her eyes, and spoke in the littlest of little voices. "Don't make fun of it, Benjamin!" she pleaded. "It's—it's—don't you understand? It's a DAGGER!"

"And what's *that* for?" sneered His Excellency. "We've only got to make people *think* he's dead! We haven't got to *kill* him! And made of tin, too!" he snarled, contemptuously bending the blade round his thumb. "Now, Madam, you'll be good enough to explain. First, what do you call me *Benjamin* for?"

"It's part of the Conspiracy, Love! One *must* have an alias, you know—"

"Oh, an *alias*, is it? Well! And next, what did you get this dagger for? Come, no evasions! You ca'n't deceive *me!*"

"I got it for—for—for——" the detected Conspirator stammered, trying her best to put on the assassin-expression that she had been practising at the looking-glass. "For——"

"For *what,* Madam!"

"Well, for eighteenpence, if you *must* know, dearest! That's what I got it for, on my——"

"Now *don't* say your Word and Honour!" groaned the other Conspirator. "Why, they aren't worth half the money, put together!"

"On my *birthday*," my Lady concluded in a meek whisper. "One *must* have a dagger, you know. It's part of the——"

"Oh, don't talk of Conspiracies!" her husband savagely interrupted, as he tossed the dagger into the cupboard. "You know about as much how to manage a Conspiracy as if you were a chicken. Why, the first thing is to get a disguise. Now, just look at this!"

And with pardonable pride he fitted on the cap and bells, and the rest of the Fool's dress, and winked at her, and put his tongue in his cheek. "Is *that* the sort of thing, now?" he demanded.

My Lady's eyes flashed with all a Conspirator's enthusiasm. "The very thing!" she exclaimed, clapping her hands. "You do look, oh, such a *perfect* Fool!"

The Fool smiled a doubtful smile. He was not quite clear whether it was a compliment or not, to express it so plainly. "You mean a Jester? Yes, that's what I intended. And what do you think *your* disguise is to be?" And he proceeded to unfold the parcel, the lady watching him in rapture.

"Oh, how lovely!" she cried, when at last the dress was unfolded. "What a *splendid* disguise! An Esquimaux peasant-woman!"

"An Esquimaux peasant, indeed!" growled the other. "Here, put it on, and look at yourself in the glass. Why it's a *Bear*, ca'n't you use your eyes?" He checked himself suddenly, as a harsh voice yelled through the room

> *"He looked again, and found it was*
> *A Bear without a Head!"*

But it was only the Gardener, singing under the open window. The Vice-Warden stole on tip-toe to the window, and closed it noiselessly, before he ventured to go on. "Yes, Lovey, a *Bear:* but not without a *head*, I hope! You're the Bear, and me the Keeper. And if any one knows us, they'll have sharp eyes, that's all!"

"I shall have to practise the steps a bit," my Lady said, looking out through the Bear's mouth: "one ca'n't help being rather human just at first, you know. And of course you'll say 'Come up, Bruin!', won't you?"

"Yes, of course," replied the Keeper, laying hold of the chain, that hung from the Bear's collar, with one hand, while with the other he cracked a little whip. "Now go round the room in a sort of a dancing attitude. Very good, my dear, very good. Come up, Bruin! Come up, I say!"

He roared out the last words for the benefit of Uggug, who had just come into the room, and was now standing, with his hands spread out,

and eyes and mouth wide open, the very picture of stupid amazement. "Oh, my!" was all he could gasp out.

The Keeper pretended to be adjusting the bear's collar, which gave him an opportunity of whispering, unheard by Uggug, "*my* fault, I'm afraid! Quite forgot to fasten the door. Plot's ruined if *he* finds it out! Keep it up a minute or two longer. Be savage!" Then, while seeming to pull it back with all his strength, he let it advance upon the scared boy: my Lady, with admirable presence of mind, kept up what she no doubt intended for a savage growl, though it was more like the purring of a cat: and Uggug backed out of the room with such haste that he tripped over the mat, and was heard to fall heavily outside——an accident to which even his doting mother paid no heed, in the excitement of the moment.

The Vice-Warden shut and bolted the door. "Off with the disguises!" he panted. "There's not a moment to lose. He's sure to fetch the Professor, and we couldn't take *him* in, you know!" And in another minute the disguises were stowed away in the cupboard, the door unbolted, and the two Conspirators seated lovingly side-by-side on the sofa, earnestly discussing a book the Vice-Warden had hastily snatched off the table, which proved to be the City-Directory of the capital of Outland.

The door opened, very slowly and cautiously, and the Professor peeped in, Uggug's stupid face being just visible behind him.

"It is a beautiful arrangement!" the Vice-Warden was saying with enthusiasm. "You see, my precious one, that there are fifteen houses in Green Street, *before* you turn into West Street."

"*Fifteen* houses! Is it *possible?*" my Lady replied. "I thought it was fourteen!" And, so intent were they on this interesting question, that neither of them even looked up till the Professor, leading Uggug by the hand, stood close before them.

My Lady was the first to notice their approach. "Why, here's the Professor!" she exclaimed in her blandest tones. "And my precious child too! Are lessons over?"

"A strange thing has happened!" the Professor began in a trembling tone. "His Exalted Fatness" (this was one of Uggug's many titles) "tells me he has just seen, in this very room, a Dancing-Bear and a Court-Jester!"

The Vice-Warden and his wife shook with well-acted merriment.

"Not in *this* room, darling!" said the fond mother. "We've been sitting here this hour or more, reading——," here she referred to the book lying on her lap, "—reading the—the City-Directory."

"Let me feel your pulse, my boy!" said the anxious father. "Now put out your tongue. Ah, I thought so! He's a little feverish, Professor, and has had a bad dream. Put him to bed at once, and give him a cooling draught."

"I ain't been dreaming!" his Exalted Fatness remonstrated, as the Professor led him away.

"Bad grammar, Sir!" his father remarked with some sternness. "Kindly attend to *that* little matter, Professor, as soon as you have corrected the feverishness. And, by the way, Professor!" (The Professor left his distinguished pupil standing at the door, and meekly returned.) "There is a rumour afloat, that the people wish to elect an—in point of fact, an—you understand that I mean an—"

"Not *another Professor!*" the poor old man exclaimed in horror.

"No! Certainly not!" the Vice-Warden eagerly explained. "Merely an *Emperor,* you understand."

"An *Emperor!*" cried the astonished Professor, holding his head between his hands, as if he expected it to come to pieces with the shock. "What will the Warden——"

"Why, the *Warden* will most likely *be* the new Emperor!" my Lady explained. "Where could we find a better? Unless, perhaps——" she glanced at her husband.

"Where indeed!" the Professor fervently responded, quite failing to take the hint.

The Vice-Warden resumed the thread of his discourse. "The reason I mentioned it, Professor, was to ask *you* to be so kind as to preside at the Election. You see it would make the thing *respectable*—no suspicion of anything underhand——"

"I fear I ca'n't, your Excellency!" the old man faltered. "What will the Warden——"

"True, true!" the Vice-Warden interrupted. "Your position, as Court-Professor, makes it awkward, I admit. Well, well! Then the Election shall be held without you."

"Better so, than if it were held *within* me!" the Professor murmured with a bewildered air, as if he hardly knew what he was saying. "Bed, I think your Highness said, and a cooling-draught?" And he wandered dreamily back to where Uggug sulkily awaited him.

I followed them out of the room, and down the passage, the Professor murmuring to himself, all the time, as a kind of aid to his feeble memory, "C, C, C; Couch, Cooling-Draught, Correct-Grammar," till, in turning a corner, he met Sylvie and Bruno, so suddenly that the startled Professor let go of his fat pupil, who instantly took to his heels.

CHAPTER X.

THE OTHER PROFESSOR.

"WE were looking for you!" cried Sylvie, in a tone of great relief. "We *do* want you so much, you ca'n't think!"

"What is it, dear children?" the Professor asked, beaming on them with a very different look from what Uggug ever got from him.

"We want you to speak to the Gardener for us," Sylvie said, as she and Bruno took the old man's hands and led him into the hall.

"He's ever so unkind!" Bruno mournfully added. "They's *all* unkind to us, now that Father's gone. The Lion were *much* nicer!"

"But you must explain to me, please," the Professor said with an anxious look, "*which* is the Lion, and *which* is the Gardener. It's *most* important not to get two such animals confused together. And one's very liable to do it in their case—both having mouths, you know——"

"Doos oo *always* confuses two animals together?" Bruno asked.

"Pretty often, I'm afraid," the Professor candidly confessed. "Now, for instance, there's the rabbit-hutch and the hall-clock." The Professor pointed them out. "One gets a little confused with *them*—both having doors, you know. Now, only yesterday—would you believe it?—I put some lettuces into the clock, and tried to wind up the rabbit!"

"Did the rabbit *go,* after oo wounded it up?" said Bruno.

The Professor clasped his hands on the top of his head, and groaned. "Go? I should think it *did* go! Why, it's *gone!* And where ever it's gone to—that's what I *ca'n't* find out! I've done my best—I've read all the article 'Rabbit' in the great dictionary——Come in!"

"Only the tailor, Sir, with your little bill," said a meek voice outside the door.

"Ah, well, I can soon settle *his* business," the Professor said to the children, "if you'll just wait a minute. How much is it, this year, my man?" The tailor had come in while he was speaking.

"Well, it's been a doubling so many years, you see," the tailor replied, a little gruffly, "and I think I'd like the money now. It's two thousand pound, it is!"

"Oh, that's nothing!" the Professor carelessly remarked, feeling in his pocket, as if he always carried at least *that* amount about with him. "But wouldn't you like to wait just another year, and make it *four* thousand? Just think how rich you'd be! Why, you might be a *King,* if you liked!"

"I don't know as I'd care about being a *King,*" the man said thoughtfully. "But it *dew* sound a powerful sight o' money! Well, I think I'll wait——"

"Of course you will!" said the Professor. "There's good sense in *you,* I see. Good-day to you, my man!"

"Will you ever have to pay him that four thousand pounds?" Sylvie asked as the door closed on the departing creditor.

"*Never,* my child!" the Professor replied emphatically. "He'll go on doubling it, till he dies. You see it's *always* worth while waiting another year, to get twice as much money! And now what would you like to do, my little friends? Shall I take you to see the Other Professor? This would be an excellent opportunity for a visit," he said to himself, glancing at his watch: "he generally takes a short rest—of fourteen minutes and a half—about this time."

Bruno hastily went round to Sylvie, who was standing at the other side of the Professor, and put his hand into hers. "I *thinks* we'd like to go," he said doubtfully: "only please let's go all together. It's best to be on the safe side, oo know!"

"Why, you talk as if you were *Sylvie!*" exclaimed the Professor.

"I know I did," Bruno replied very humbly. "I quite forgotted I wasn't Sylvie. Only I fought he might be rarver fierce!"

The Professor laughed a jolly laugh. "Oh, he's quite tame!" he said. "He never bites. He's only a little——a little *dreamy,* you know." He took hold of Bruno's other hand, and led the children down a long passage I had never noticed before—not that there was anything remarkable in *that:* I was constantly coming on new rooms and passages in that mysterious Palace, and very seldom succeeded in finding the old ones again.

Near the end of the passage the Professor stopped. "This is his room," he said, pointing to the solid wall.

"We ca'n't get in through *there!*" Bruno exclaimed.

Sylvie said nothing, till she had carefully examined whether the wall opened anywhere. Then she laughed merrily. "You're playing us a trick, you dear old thing!" she said. "There's no *door* here!"

"There isn't any door to the room," said the Professor. "We shall have to climb in at the window."

So we went into the garden, and soon found the window of the Other Professor's room. It was a ground-floor window, and stood invitingly open: the Professor first lifted the two children in, and then he and I climbed in after them.

The Other Professor was seated at a table, with a large book open before him, on which his forehead was resting: he had clasped his arms round the book, and was snoring heavily. "He usually reads like that," the Professor remarked, "when the book's very interesting: and then sometimes it's very difficult to get him to attend!"

This seemed to be one of the difficult times: the Professor lifted him up, once or twice, and shook him violently: but he always returned to his book the moment he was let go of, and showed by his heavy breathing that the book was as interesting as ever.

"How dreamy he is!" the Professor exclaimed. "He must have got to a *very* interesting part of the book!" And he rained quite a shower of thumps on the Other Professor's back, shouting "Hoy! Hoy!" all the time. "Isn't it *wonderful* that he should be so dreamy?" he said to Bruno.

"If he's always as *sleepy* as that," Bruno remarked, "a *course* he's dreamy!"

"But what are we to *do?*" said the Professor. "You see he's quite wrapped up in the book!"

"Suppose oo *shuts* the book?" Bruno suggested.

"That's it!" cried the delighted Professor. "Of course that'll do it!" And he shut up the book so quickly that he caught the Other Professor's nose between the leaves, and gave it a severe pinch.

The Other Professor instantly rose to his feet, and carried the book away to the end of the room, where he put it back in its place in the book-case. "I've been reading for eighteen hours and three-quarters," he said, "and now I shall rest for fourteen minutes and a half. Is the Lecture all ready?"

"Very nearly," the Professor humbly replied. "I shall ask you to give me a hint or two—there will be a few little difficulties——"

"And a Banquet, I think you said?"

"Oh yes! The Banquet comes *first*, of course. People never enjoy Abstract Science, you know, when they're ravenous with hunger. And then there's the Fancy-Dress-Ball. Oh, there'll be lots of entertainment!"

"Where will the Ball come in?" said the Other Professor.

"I *think* it had better come at the beginning of the Banquet—it brings people together so nicely, you know."

"Yes, that's the right order. First the Meeting: then the Eating: then the Treating—for I'm sure any Lecture *you* give us will be a treat!" said the Other Professor, who had been standing with his back to us all this time, occupying himself in taking the books out, one by one, and turning them upside-down. An easel, with a black board on it, stood near him: and, every time that he turned a book upside-down, he made a mark on the board with a piece of chalk.

"And as to the 'Pig-Tale'—which *you* have so kindly promised to give us—" the Professor went on, thoughtfully rubbing his chin. "I think that had better come at the *end* of the Banquet: then people can listen to it quietly."

"Shall I *sing* it?" the Other Professor asked, with a smile of delight.

"If you *can*," the Professor replied, cautiously.

"Let me try," said the Other Professor, seating himself at the pianoforte. "For the sake of argument, let us assume that it begins on A flat." And he struck the note in question. "La, la, la! I think that's within an octave of it." He struck the note again, and appealed to Bruno, who was standing at his side. "Did I sing it like *that*, my child?"

"No, oo didn't," Bruno replied with great decision. "It were more like a duck."

"Single notes are apt to have that effect," the Other Professor said with a sigh. "Let me try a whole verse.

> There was a Pig, that sat alone,
>   Beside a ruined Pump.
> By day and night he made his moan:
> It would have stirred a heart of stone
> To see him wring his hoofs and groan,
>   Because he could not jump.

Would you call that a tune, Professor?" he asked, when he had finished.

The Professor considered a little. "Well," he said at last, "some of the notes are the same as others—and some are different—but I should hardly call it a *tune*."

"Let me try it a bit by myself," said the Other Professor. And he began touching the notes here and there, and humming to himself like an angry bluebottle.

"How do you like his singing?" the Professor asked the children in a low voice.

"It isn't very *beautiful*," Sylvie said, hesitatingly.

"It's very extremely *ugly!*" Bruno said, without any hesitation at all.

"All extremes are bad," the Professor said, very gravely. "For instance, Sobriety is a very good thing, when practised *in moderation:* but even Sobriety, when carried to an *extreme*, has its disadvantages."

"What are its disadvantages?" was the question that rose in my mind— and, as usual, Bruno asked it for me. "What *are* its lizard bandages?"

"Well, this is *one* of them," said the Professor. "When a man's tipsy (that's one extreme, you know), he sees one thing as two. But, when he's *extremely* sober (that's the other extreme), he sees two things as one. It's equally inconvenient, whichever happens."

"What does 'illconvenient' mean?" Bruno whispered to Sylvie.

"The difference between 'convenient' and 'inconvenient' is best explained by an example," said the Other Professor, who had overheard the question. "If you'll just think over any Poem that contains the two words—such as——-"

The Professor put his hands over his ears, with a look of dismay. "If you once let him begin a *Poem*," he said to Sylvie, "he'll never leave off again! He never does!"

"Did he ever begin a Poem and not leave off again?" Sylvie enquired.

"Three times," said the Professor.

Bruno raised himself on tiptoe, till his lips were on a level with Sylvie's ear. "What became of them three Poems?" he whispered. "Is he saying them all, now?"

"Hush!" said Sylvie. "The Other Professor is speaking!"

"I'll say it very quick," murmured the Other Professor, with downcast eyes, and melancholy voice, which contrasted oddly with his face, as he had forgotten to leave off smiling. ("At least it wasn't exactly a *smile*," as Sylvie said afterwards: "it looked as if his mouth was made that shape.")

"Go on then," said the Professor. *"What must be must be."*

"Remember that!" Sylvie whispered to Bruno, "It's a very good rule for whenever you hurt yourself."

"And it's a very good rule for whenever I make a noise," said the saucy little fellow. "So *you* remember it too, Miss!"

"Whatever *do* you mean?" said Sylvie, trying to frown, a thing she never managed particularly well.

"Oftens and oftens," said Bruno, "haven't oo told me 'There mustn't be so much noise, Bruno!' when I've tolded oo 'There *must!*' Why, there isn't no rules at all about 'There mustn't'! But oo never believes *me!*"

"As if any one *could* believe *you,* you wicked wicked boy!" said Sylvie. The *words* were severe enough, but I am of opinion that, when you are really *anxious* to impress a criminal with a sense of his guilt, you ought not to pronounce the sentence with your lips *quite* close to his cheek—since a kiss at the end of it, however accidental, weakens the effect terribly.

CHAPTER XI.

PETER AND PAUL.

"As I was saying," the Other Professor resumed, "if you'll just think over any Poem, that contains the words——such as

'Peter is poor,' said noble Paul,
  'And I have always been his friend:
And, though my means to give are small,
  At least I can afford to lend.
How few, in this cold age of greed,
  Do good, except on selfish grounds!
But I can feel for Peter's need,
  And I WILL LEND HIM FIFTY POUNDS!'

How great was Peter's joy to find
  His friend in such a genial vein!
How cheerfully the bond he signed,
  To pay the money back again!
'We ca'n't,' said Paul, 'be too precise:
  'Tis best to fix the very day:
So, by a learned friend's advice,
  I've made it Noon, the Fourth of May.'

'But this is April!' Peter said.
  'The First of April, as I think.
Five little weeks will soon be fled:
  One scarcely will have time to wink!
Give me a year to speculate—
  To buy and sell—to drive a trade—'
Said Paul 'I cannot change the date.
  On May the Fourth it must be paid.'

'Well, well!' said Peter, with a sigh.
  'Hand me the cash, and I will go.
I'll form a Joint-Stock Company,
  And turn an honest pound or so.'
'I'm grieved,' said Paul, 'to seem unkind:
  The money shall of course be lent:
But, for a week or two, I find
  It will not be convenient.'

So, week by week, poor Peter came
  And turned in heaviness away;
For still the answer was the same,
  'I cannot manage it to-day.'
And now the April showers were dry—
  The five short weeks were nearly spent—
Yet still he got the old reply,
  'It is not quite convenient!'

The Fourth arrived, and punctual Paul
  Came, with his legal friend, at noon.
'I thought it best,' said he, 'to call:
  One cannot settle things too soon.'
Poor Peter shuddered in despair:
  His flowing locks he wildly tore:
And very soon his yellow hair
  Was lying all about the floor.

The legal friend was standing by,
  With sudden pity half unmanned:
The tear-drop trembled in his eye,
  The signed agreement in his hand:
But when at length the legal soul
  Resumed its customary force,
'The Law,' he said, 'we ca'n't control:
  Pay, or the Law must take its course!'

Said Paul 'How bitterly I rue
  That fatal morning when I called!
Consider, Peter, what you do!
  You won't be richer when you're bald!

Think you, by rending curls away,
* To make your difficulties less?*
Forbear this violence, I pray:
* You do but add to my distress!'*

'Not willingly would I inflict,'
* Said Peter, 'on that noble heart*
One needless pang. Yet why so strict?
* Is this to act a friendly part?*
However legal it may be
* To pay what never has been lent,*
This style of business seems to me
* Extremely inconvenient!*

'No Nobleness of soul have I,
* Like some that in this Age are found!'*
(Paul blushed in sheer humility,
* And cast his eyes upon the ground.)*

'This debt will simply swallow all,
　And make my life a life of woe!'
'Nay, nay, my Peter!' answered Paul.
　'You must not rail on Fortune so!

'You have enough to eat and drink:
　You are respected in the world:
And at the barber's, as I think,
　You often get your whiskers curled.
Though Nobleness you ca'n't attain—
　To any very great extent—
The path of Honesty is plain,
　However inconvenient!'

' 'Tis true,' said Peter, 'I'm alive:
　I keep my station in the world:
Once in the week I just contrive
　To get my whiskers oiled and curled.
But my assets are very low:
　My little income's overspent:
To trench on capital, you know,
　Is always inconvenient!'

'But pay your debts!' cried honest Paul.
　'My gentle Peter, pay your debts!
What matter if it swallows all
　That you describe as your "assets"?
Already you're an hour behind:
　Yet Generosity is best.
It pinches me—but never mind!
　I WILL NOT CHARGE YOU INTEREST!'

'How good! How great!' poor Peter cried.
　'Yet I must sell my Sunday wig—
The scarf-pin that has been my pride—
　My grand piano—and my pig!'
Full soon his property took wings:
　And daily, as each treasure went,
He sighed to find the state of things
　Grow less and less convenient.

Weeks grew to months, and months to years:
　Peter was worn to skin and bone:
And once he even said, with tears,
　'Remember, Paul, that promised Loan!'
Said Paul 'I'll lend you, when I can,
　All the spare money I have got—
Ah, Peter, you're a happy man!
　Yours is an enviable lot!

'I'm getting stout, as you may see:
    It is but seldom I am well:
I cannot feel my ancient glee
    In listening to the dinner-bell:
But you, you gambol like a boy,
    Your figure is so spare and light:
The dinner-bell's a note of joy
    To such a healthy appetite!'

Said Peter 'I am well aware
    Mine is a state of happiness:
And yet how gladly could I spare
    Some of the comforts I possess!
What you call healthy appetite
    I feel as Hunger's savage tooth:
And, when no dinner is in sight,
    The dinner-bell's a sound of ruth!

'No scare-crow would accept this coat:
   Such boots as these you seldom see.
Ah, Paul, a single five-pound-note
   Would make another man of me!'
Said Paul 'It fills me with surprise
   To hear you talk in such a tone:
I fear you scarcely realise
   The blessings that are all your own!

'You're safe from being overfed:
   You're sweetly picturesque in rags:
You never know the aching head
   That comes along with money-bags:
And you have time to cultivate
   That best of qualities, Content—
For which you'll find your present state
   Remarkably convenient!'

Said Peter 'Though I cannot sound
   The depths of such a man as you,
Yet in your character I've found
   An inconsistency or two.
You seem to have long years to spare
   When there's a promise to fulfil:
And yet how punctual you were
   In calling with that little bill!'

'One can't be too deliberate,'
   Said Paul, 'in parting with one's pelf.
With bills, as you correctly state,
   I'm punctuality itself.
A man may surely claim his dues:
   But, when there's money to be lent,
A man must be allowed to choose
   Such times as are convenient!'

It chanced one day, as Peter sat
   Gnawing a crust—his usual meal—
Paul bustled in to have a chat,
   And grasped his hand with friendly zeal.
'I knew,' said he, 'your frugal ways:
   So, that I might not wound your pride
By bringing strangers in to gaze,
   I've left my legal friend outside!

'You well remember, I am sure,
   When first your wealth began to go,
And people sneered at one so poor,
   I never used my Peter so!

And when you'd lost your little all,
   And found yourself a thing despised,
I need not ask you to recall
   How tenderly I sympathised!

'Then the advice I've poured on you,
   So full of wisdom and of wit:
All given gratis, though 'tis true
   I might have fairly charged for it!
But I refrain from mentioning
   Full many a deed I might relate—
For boasting is a kind of thing
   That I particularly hate.

'How vast the total sum appears
   Of all the kindnesses I've done,
From Childhood's half-forgotten years
   Down to that Loan of April One!
That Fifty Pounds! You little guessed

How deep it drained my slender store:
But there's a heart within this breast,
    And I WILL LEND YOU FIFTY MORE!'

'*Not so,*' *was Peter's mild reply,*
    His cheeks all wet with grateful tears:
'*No man recalls, so well as I,*
    Your services in bygone years:
And this new offer, I admit,
    Is very very kindly meant—
Still, to avail myself of it
    Would not be quite convenient!'

You'll see in a moment what the difference is between 'convenient ' and 'inconvenient.' You quite understand it now, don't you?" he added, looking kindly at Bruno, who was sitting, at Sylvie's side, on the floor.

"Yes," said Bruno, very quietly. Such a short speech was very unusual, for him: but just then he seemed, I fancied, a little exhausted. In fact, he climbed up into Sylvie's lap as he spoke, and rested his head against her shoulder. "What a many verses it was!" he whispered.

CHAPTER XII.

A MUSICAL GARDENER.

THE Other Professor regarded him with some anxiety. "The smaller animal ought to go to bed *at once,*" he said with an air of authority.

"Why *at once?*" said the Professor.

"Because he ca'n't go at twice," said the Other Professor.

The Professor gently clapped his hands. 'Isn't he *wonderful!*" he said to Sylvie. "Nobody else could have thought of the reason, so quick. Why, *of course* he ca'n't go at twice! It would hurt him to be divided."

This remark woke up Bruno, suddenly and completely. "I don't want to be *divided,*" he said decisively.

"It does very well on a *diagram,*" said the Other Professor. "I could show it you in a minute, only the chalk's a little blunt."

"Take care!" Sylvie anxiously exclaimed, as he began, rather clumsily, to point it. "You'll cut your finger off, if you hold the knife so!"

"If oo cuts it off, will oo give it to *me,* please?" Bruno thoughtfully added.

"It's like this," said the Other Professor, hastily drawing a long line upon the black board, and marking the letters 'A,' 'B,' at the two ends, and 'C' in the middle: "let me explain it to you. If AB were to be divided into two parts at C——"

"It would be drownded," Bruno pronounced confidently.

The Other Professor gasped. "*What* would be drownded?"

"Why the bumble-bee, of course!" said Bruno. "And the two bits would sink down in the sea!"

Here the Professor interfered, as the Other Professor was evidently too much puzzled to go on with his diagram.

"When I said it would *hurt* him, I was merely referring to the action of the nerves——"

The Other Professor brightened up in a moment. "The action of the nerves," he began eagerly, "is curiously slow in some people. I had a friend, once, that, if you burnt him with a red-hot poker, it would take years and years before he felt it!"

"And if you only *pinched* him?" queried Sylvie.

"Then it would take ever so much longer, of course. In fact, I doubt if the man *himself* would ever feel it, at all. His grandchildren might."

"I wouldn't like to be the grandchild of a pinched grandfather, would *you*, Mister Sir?" Bruno whispered. "It might come just when you wanted to be happy!"

That would be awkward, I admitted, taking it quite as a matter of course that he had so suddenly caught sight of me. "But don't you *always* want to be happy, Bruno?"

"Not *always*," Bruno said thoughtfully. "Sometimes when I's *too* happy, I wants to be a little miserable. Then I just tell Sylvie about it, oo know, and Sylvie sets me some lessons. Then it's all right."

"I'm sorry you don't like lessons," I said. "You should copy Sylvie. *She's* always as busy as the day is long!"

"Well, so am *I*!" said Bruno.

"No, no!" Sylvie corrected him. "*You're* as busy as the day is *short!*"

"Well, what's the difference?" Bruno asked. "Mister Sir, isn't the day as short as it's long? I mean, isn't it the *same* length?"

Never having considered the question in this light, I suggested that they had better ask the Professor; and they ran off in a moment to appeal to their old friend. The Professor left off polishing his spectacles to consider. "My dears," he said after a minute, "the day is the same length as anything that is the same length as *it*." And he resumed his never-ending task of polishing.

The children returned, slowly and thoughtfully, to report his answer. "*Isn't* he wise?" Sylvie asked in an awestruck whisper. "If *I* was as wise as *that*, I should have a head-ache all day long. I *know* I should!"

"You appear to be talking to somebody—that isn't here," the Professor said, turning round to the children. "Who is it?"

Bruno looked puzzled. "I never talks to nobody when he isn't here!" he replied. "It isn't good manners. Oo should always wait till he comes, before oo talks to him!"

The Professor looked anxiously in my direction, and seemed to look through and through me without seeing me. "Then who are you talking to?" he said. "There isn't anybody here, you know, except the Other Professor—and *he* isn't here!" he added wildly, turning round and round like a teetotum. "Children! Help to look for him! Quick! He's got lost again!"

The children were on their feet in a moment.

"Where shall we look?" said Sylvie.

"Anywhere!" shouted the excited Professor. "Only be quick about it!" And he began trotting round and round the room, lifting up the chairs, and shaking them.

Bruno took a very small book out of the bookcase, opened it, and shook it in imitation of the Professor. "He isn't *here*," he said.

"He *ca'n't* be there, Bruno!" Sylvie said indignantly.

"Course he ca'n't!" said Bruno. "I should have shooked him out, if he'd been in there!"

"Has he ever been lost before?" Sylvie enquired, turning up a corner of the hearth-rug, and peeping under it.

"Once before," said the Professor: "he once lost himself in a wood——"

"And couldn't he find his-self again?" said Bruno. "Why didn't he shout? He'd be sure to hear his-self, 'cause he couldn't be far off, oo know."

"Let's try shouting," said the Professor.

"What shall we shout?" said Sylvie.

"On second thoughts, *don't* shout," the Professor replied. "The Vice-Warden might hear you. He's getting awfully strict!"

This reminded the poor children of all the troubles, about which they had come to their old friend. Bruno sat down on the floor and began crying. "He *is* so cruel!" he sobbed. "And he lets Uggug take away *all* my toys! And such horrid meals!"

"What did you have for dinner to-day?" said the Professor.

"A little piece of a dead crow" was Bruno's mournful reply.

"He means rook-pie," Sylvie explained.

"It *were* a dead crow," Bruno persisted. "And there were a apple-pudding—and Uggug ate it all—and I got nuffin but a crust! And I asked for a orange—and—didn't get it!" And the poor little fellow buried his face in Sylvie's lap, who kept gently stroking his hair, as she went on. "It's all true Professor dear! They *do* treat my darling Bruno very badly! And they're not kind to *me* either," she added in a lower tone, as if *that* were a thing of much less importance.

The Professor got out a large red silk handkerchief, and wiped his eyes. "I wish I could help you, dear children!" he said. "But what *can* I do?"

"We know the way to Fairyland—where Father's gone—quite well," said Sylvie: "if only the Gardener would let us out."

"Won't he open the door for you?" said the Professor.

"Not for *us*," said Sylvie: "but I'm sure he would for *you*. Do come and ask him, Professor dear!"

"I'll come this minute!" said the Professor.

Bruno sat up and dried his eyes. "*Isn't* he kind, Mister Sir?"

"He is *indeed*," said I. But the Professor took no notice of my remark. He had put on a beautiful cap with a long tassel, and was selecting one of the Other Professor's walking-sticks, from a stand in the corner of the room. "A thick stick in one's hand makes people respectful," he was saying to himself. "Come along, dear children!" And we all went out into the garden together.

"I shall address him, first of all," the Professor explained as we went along, "with a few playful remarks on the weather. I shall then question him about the Other Professor. This will have a double advantage. First, it will open the conversation (you can't even drink a bottle of wine without opening it first): and secondly, if he's seen the Other Professor, we shall find him that way: and, if he hasn't, we sha'n't."

On our way, we passed the target, at which Uggug had been made to shoot during the Ambassador's visit.

"See!" said the Professor, pointing out a hole in the middle of the bull's-eye. "His Imperial Fatness had only *one* shot at it; and he went in just *here!*"

Bruno carefully examined the hole. "Couldn't go in *there*," he whispered to me. "He are too *fat!*"

We had no sort of difficulty in *finding* the Gardener. Though he was hidden from us by some trees, that harsh voice of his served to direct us; and, as we drew nearer, the words of his song became more and more plainly audible:

> "He thought he saw an Albatross
> That fluttered round the lamp:
> He looked again, and found it was
> A Penny-Postage-Stamp.
> 'You'd best be getting home,' he said:
> 'The nights are very damp!'"

"Would it be afraid of catching cold?" said Bruno.

"If it got *very* damp," Sylvie suggested, "it might stick to something, you know."

"And *that* somefin would have to go by the post, whatever it was!"

Bruno eagerly exclaimed. "Suppose it was a cow! Wouldn't it be *dreadful* for the other things!"

"And all these things happened to *him*," said the Professor. "That's what makes the song so interesting."

"He must have had a very curious life," said Sylvie.

"You may say that!" the Professor heartily rejoined.

"Of course she may!" cried Bruno.

By this time we had come up to the Gardener, who was standing on one leg, as usual, and busily employed in watering a bed of flowers with an empty watering-can.

"It hasn't got no water in it!" Bruno explained to him, pulling his sleeve to attract his attention.

"It's lighter to hold," said the Gardener. "A lot of water in it makes one's arms ache." And he went on with his work, singing softly to himself

> *"The nights are very damp!"*

"In digging things out of the ground—which you probably do now and then," the Professor began in a loud voice; "in making things into heaps—which no doubt you often do; and in kicking things about with one heel—which you seem never to leave off doing; have you ever happened to notice another Professor, something like me, but different?"

"Never!" shouted the Gardener, so loudly and violently that we all drew back in alarm. "There ain't such a thing!"

"We will try a less exciting topic," the Professor mildly remarked to the children. "You were asking——"

"We asked him to let us through the garden-door," said Sylvie: "but he wouldn't: but perhaps he would for *you!*"

The Professor put the request, very humbly and courteously.

"I wouldn't mind letting *you* out," said the Gardener. "But I mustn't open the door for *children*. D'you think I'd disobey the *Rules?* Not for one-and-sixpence!"

The Professor cautiously produced a couple of shillings.

"That'll do it!" the Gardener shouted, as he hurled the watering-can across the flower-bed, and produced a handful of keys—one large one, and a number of small ones.

"But look here, Professor dear!" whispered Sylvie. "He needn't open the door for *us*, at all. We can go out with *you*."

"True, dear child!" the Professor thankfully replied, as he replaced the coins in his pocket. "That saves two shillings!" And he took the children's hands, that they might all go out together when the door was opened. This, however, did not seem a very likely event, though the Gardener patiently tried all the small keys, over and over again.

At last the Professor ventured on a gentle suggestion. "Why not try the *large* one? I have often observed that a door unlocks *much* more nicely with its *own* key."

The very first trial of the large key proved a success: the Gardener opened the door, and held out his hand for the money.

The Professor shook his head. "You are acting by *Rule*," he explained, "in opening the door for *me*. And now it's open, we are going out by *Rule*—the Rule of *Three*."

The Gardener looked puzzled, and let us go out; but, as he locked the door behind us, we heard him singing thoughtfully to himself

> *"He thought he saw a Garden-Door*
> *That opened with a key:*
> *He looked again, and found it was*
> *A Double Rule of Three:*
> *'And all its mystery,' he said,*
> *'Is clear as day to me!'"*

"I shall now return," said the Professor, when we had walked a few yards: "you see, it's impossible to read *here*, for all my books are in the house."

But the children still kept fast hold of his hands. "*Do* come with us!" Sylvie entreated with tears in her eyes.

"Well, well!" said the good-natured old man. "Perhaps I'll come after you, some day soon. But I *must* go back *now*. You see I left off at a comma, and it's so awkward not knowing how the sentence finishes! Besides, you've got to go through Dogland first, and I'm always a little nervous about dogs. But it'll be quite easy to come, as soon as I've completed my new invention—for carrying one's-*self*, you know. It wants just a *little* more working out."

"Won't that be very tiring, to carry *yourself?*" Sylvie enquired.

"Well, no, my child. You see, whatever fatigue one incurs by *carrying*, one saves by *being carried!* Good-bye, dears! Good-bye, Sir!" he added to my intense surprise, giving my hand an affectionate squeeze.

"Good-bye, Professor!" I replied: but my voice sounded strange and far away, and the children took not the slightest notice of our farewell. Evidently they neither saw me nor heard me, as, with their arms lovingly twined round each other, they marched boldly on.

CHAPTER XIII.

A VISIT TO DOGLAND.

"THERE'S a house, away there to the left," said Sylvie, after we had walked what seemed to me about fifty miles. "Let's go and ask for a night's lodging."

"It looks a very comfable house," Bruno said, as we turned into the road leading up to it. "I doos hope the Dogs will be kind to us, I *is* so tired and hungry!"

A Mastiff, dressed in a scarlet collar, and carrying a musket, was pacing up and down, like a sentinel, in front of the entrance. He started, on catching sight of the children, and came forwards to meet them, keeping his musket pointed straight at Bruno, who stood quite still, though he turned pale and kept tight hold of Sylvie's hand, while the Sentinel walked solemnly round and round them, and looked at them from all points of view.

"Oobooh hooh boohooyah!" He growled at last. "Woobah yahwah oobooh! Bow wahbah woobooyah? Bow wow?" he asked Bruno, severely.

Of course *Bruno* understood all this, easily enough. All Fairies understand Doggee—that is, Dog-language. But, as *you* may find it a little difficult, just at first, I had better put it into English for you. "Humans, I verily believe! A couple of stray Humans! What Dog do you belong to? What do you want?"

"We don't belong to a *Dog!*" Bruno began, in Doggee. ("Peoples *never* belongs to Dogs!" he whispered to Sylvie.)

But Sylvie hastily checked him, for fear of hurting the Mastiff's feelings. "Please, we want a little food, and a night's lodging—if there's room in the house," she added timidly. Sylvie spoke Doggee very prettily: but I think it's almost better, for *you*, to give the conversation in English.

"The *house*, indeed!" growled the Sentinel. "Have you never seen a *Palace* in your life? Come along with me! His Majesty must settle what's to be done with you."

They followed him through the entrance-hall, down a long passage, and into a magnificent Saloon, around which were grouped dogs of all sorts and sizes. Two splendid Blood-hounds were solemnly sitting up, one on each side of the crown-bearer. Two or three Bull-dogs—whom I guessed to be the Body-Guard of the King—were waiting in grim silence: in fact the only voices at all plainly audible were those of two

little dogs, who had mounted a settee, and were holding a lively discussion that looked very like a quarrel.

"Lords and Ladies in Waiting, and various Court Officials," our guide gruffly remarked, as he led us in. Of *me* the Courtiers took no notice whatever: but Sylvie and Bruno were the subject of many inquisitive looks, and many whispered remarks, of which I only distinctly caught *one*—made by a sly-looking Dachshund to his friend—"Bah wooh wahyah hoobah Oobooh, *hah* bah?" ("She's not such a bad-looking Human, *is* she?")

Leaving the new arrivals in the centre of the Saloon, the Sentinel advanced to a door, at the further end of it, which bore an inscription, painted on it in Doggee, "Royal Kennel—Scratch and Yell."

Before doing this, the Sentinel turned to the children, and said "Give me your names."

"We'd rather not!" Bruno exclaimed, pulling Sylvie away from the door. "We want them ourselves. Come back, Sylvie! Come quick!"

"Nonsense!" said Sylvie very decidedly: and gave their names in Doggee.

Then the Sentinel scratched violently at the door, and gave a yell that made Bruno shiver from head to foot.

"Hooyah wah!" said a deep voice inside. (That's Doggee for "Come in!")

"It's the King himself!" the Mastiff whispered in an awestruck tone. "Take off your wigs and lay them humbly at his paws." (What *we* should call "at his *feet*.")

Sylvie was just going to explain, very politely, that really they *couldn't* perform *that* ceremony, because their wigs wouldn't come off, when the door of the Royal Kennel opened, and an enormous Newfoundland Dog put his head out. "Bow wow?" was his first question.

"When His Majesty speaks to you," the Sentinel hastily whispered to Bruno, "you should prick up your ears!"

Bruno looked doubtfully at Sylvie. "I'd rather not, please," he said. "It would hurt."

"It doesn't hurt a bit!" the Sentinel said with some indignation. "Look! It's like this!" And he pricked up his ears like two railway signals.

Sylvie gently explained matters. "I'm afraid we ca'n't manage it," she said in a low voice. "I'm very sorry: but our ears haven't got the right—" she wanted to say "machinery" in Doggee: but she had forgotten the word, and could only think of "steam-engine."

The Sentinel repeated Sylvie's explanation to the King.

"Can't prick up their ears without a steam-engine!" His Majesty exclaimed. "They *must* be curious creatures! I must have a look at them!" And he came out of his Kennel, and walked solemnly up to the children.

What was the amazement—not to say the horror—of the whole assembly, when Sylvie actually *patted his Majesty on the head*, while Bruno seized his long ears and pretended to tie them together under his chin!

The Sentinel groaned aloud: a beautiful Greyhound—who appeared to be one of the Ladies in Waiting—fainted away: and all the other Courtiers hastily drew back, and left plenty of room for the huge New-

foundland to spring upon the audacious strangers, and tear them limb from limb.

Only—he didn't. On the contrary his Majesty actually *smiled*—so far as a Dog *can* smile—and (the other Dogs couldn't believe their eyes, but it was true, all the same) his Majesty *wagged his tail!*

"Yah! Hooh hahwooh!" (that is "Well! I never!") was the universal cry.

His Majesty looked round him severely, and gave a slight growl, which produced instant silence. "Conduct *my friends* to the banqueting-hall!" he said, laying such an emphasis on *"my friends"* that several of the dogs rolled over helplessly on their backs and began to lick Bruno's feet.

A procession was formed, but I only ventured to follow as far as the *door* of the banqueting-hall, so furious was the uproar of barking dogs within. So I sat down by the King, who seemed to have gone to sleep, and waited till the children returned to say good-night, when His Majesty got up and shook himself.

"Time for bed!" he said with a sleepy yawn. "The attendants will show you your room," he added, aside, to Sylvie and Bruno. "Bring lights!" And, with a dignified air, he held out his paw for them to kiss.

But the children were evidently not well practised in Court-manners. Sylvie simply stroked the great paw: Bruno hugged it: the Master of the Ceremonies looked shocked.

All this time Dog-waiters, in splendid livery, were running up with lighted candles: but, as fast as they put them upon the table, other waiters ran away with them, so that there never seemed to be one for *me,* though the Master kept nudging me with his elbow, and repeating "I ca'n't let you sleep *here!* You're not in *bed,* you know!"

I made a great effort, and just succeeded in getting out the words "I know I'm not. I'm in an arm-chair."

"Well, forty winks will do you no harm," the Master said, and left me. I could scarcely hear his words: and no wonder: he was leaning over the side of a ship, that was miles away from the pier on which I stood. The ship passed over the horizon, and I sank back into the arm-chair.

The next thing I remember is that it was morning: breakfast was just over: Sylvie was lifting Bruno down from a high chair, and saying to a Spaniel, who was regarding them with a most benevolent smile, "Yes, thank you, we've had a *very* nice breakfast. Haven't we, Bruno?"

"There was too many bones in the——" Bruno began, but Sylvie frowned at him, and laid her finger on her lips, for, at this moment, the travelers were waited on by a very dignified officer, the Head-Growler, whose duty it was, first to conduct them to the King to bid him farewell, and then to escort them to the boundary of Dogland. The great Newfoundland received them most affably, but, instead of saying "good-bye," he startled the Head-Growler into giving three savage growls, by announcing that he would escort them himself.

"It is a most unusual proceeding, your Majesty!" the Head-Growler exclaimed, almost choking with vexation at being set aside, for he had put on his best Court-suit, made entirely of cat-skins, for the occasion.

"I shall escort them myself," his Majesty repeated, gently but firmly, laying aside the Royal robes, and changing his crown for a small coronet, "and you may stay at home."

"I *are* glad!" Bruno whispered to Sylvie, when they had got well out of hearing. "He were so *welly* cross!" And he not only patted their Royal escort, but even hugged him round the neck in the exuberance of his delight.

His Majesty calmly wagged the Royal tail. "It's quite a relief," he said, "getting away from that Palace now and then! Royal Dogs have a dull life of it, I can tell you! Would you mind" (this to Sylvie, in a low voice, and looking a little shy and embarrassed) "would you mind the trouble of just throwing that stick for me to fetch?"

Sylvie was too much astonished to do anything for a moment: it sounded such a monstrous impossibility that a *King* should wish to run after a stick. But *Bruno* was equal to the occasion, and with a glad shout of "Hi then! Fetch it, good Doggie!" he hurled it over a clump of bushes. The next moment the Monarch of Dogland had bounded over the bushes, and picked up the stick, and came galloping back to the children with it in his mouth. Bruno took it from him with great decision. "Beg for it!" he insisted; and His Majesty begged. "Paw!" commanded Sylvie; and His Majesty gave his paw. In short, the solemn ceremony of escorting the travelers to the boundaries of Dogland became one long uproarious game of play!

"But business is business!" the Dog-King said at last. "And I must go back to mine. I couldn't come any further," he added, consulting a dog-watch, which hung on a chain round his neck, "not even if there were a *Cat* in sight!"

They took an affectionate farewell of His Majesty, and trudged on.

"That *were* a dear dog!" Bruno exclaimed. "Has we to go far, Sylvie? I's tired!"

"Not much further, darling!" Sylvie gently replied. "Do you see that shining, just beyond those trees? I'm almost *sure* it's the gate of Fairyland! I know it's all golden—Father told me so—and so bright, so bright!" she went on dreamily.

"It dazzles!" said Bruno, shading his eyes with one little hand, while the other clung tightly to Sylvie's hand, as if he were half-alarmed at her strange manner.

For the child moved on as if walking in her sleep, her large eyes gazing into the far distance, and her breath coming and going in quick pantings of eager delight. I knew, by some mysterious mental light, that a great change was taking place in my sweet little friend (for such I loved to think her) and that she was passing from the condition of a mere Outland Sprite into the true Fairy-nature.

Upon Bruno the change came later: but it was completed in both before they reached the golden gate, through which I knew it would be impossible for *me* to follow. I could but stand outside, and take a last look at the two sweet children, ere they disappeared within, and the golden gate closed with a bang.

And with *such* a bang! "It never *will* shut like any other cupboard-door," Arthur explained. "There's something wrong with the hinge.

However, here's the cake and wine. And you've had your forty winks. So you really *must* get off to bed, old man! You're fit for nothing else. Witness my hand, Arthur Forester, M.D."

By this time I was wide-awake again. "Not *quite* yet!" I pleaded. "Really I'm not sleepy now. And it isn't midnight yet."

"Well, I did want to say another word to you," Arthur replied in a relenting tone, as he supplied me with the supper he had prescribed. "Only I thought you were too sleepy for it to-night."

We took our midnight meal almost in silence; for an unusual nervousness seemed to have seized on my old friend.

"What kind of a night is it?" he asked, rising and undrawing the window-curtains, apparently to change the subject for a minute. I followed him to the window, and we stood together, looking out, in silence.

"When I first spoke to you about——" Arthur began, after a long and embarrassing silence, "that is, when we first talked about her—for I think it was *you* that introduced the subject—my own position in life forbade me to do more than worship her from a distance: and I was turning over plans for leaving this place finally, and settling somewhere out of all chance of meeting her again. That seemed to be my only chance of usefulness in life."

"Would that have been wise?" I said. "To leave yourself no hope at all?"

"There *was* no hope to leave," Arthur firmly replied, though his eyes glittered with tears as he gazed upwards into the midnight sky, from which one solitary star, the glorious 'Vega,' blazed out in fitful splendour through the driving clouds. "She was like that star to me—bright, beautiful, and pure, but out of reach, out of reach!"

He drew the curtains again, and we returned to our places by the fireside.

"What I wanted to tell you was this," he resumed. "I heard this evening from my solicitor. I ca'n't go into the details of the business, but the upshot is that my worldly wealth is much more than I thought, and I am (or shall soon be) in a position to offer marriage, without imprudence, to any lady, even if she brought nothing. I doubt if there would be anything on *her* side: the Earl is poor, I believe. But I should have enough for both, even if health failed."

"I wish you all happiness in your married life!" I cried. "Shall you speak to the Earl to-morrow?"

"Not yet awhile," said Arthur. "He is very friendly, but I dare not think he means more than that, as yet. And as for—as for Lady Muriel, try as I may, I *cannot* read her feelings towards me. If there *is* love, she is hiding it! No, I must wait, I must wait!"

I did not like to press any further advice on my friend, whose judgment, I felt, was so much more sober and thoughtful than my own; and we parted without more words on the subject that had now absorbed his thoughts, nay, his very life.

The next morning a letter from *my* solicitor arrived, summoning me to town on important business.

CHAPTER XIV.

FAIRY-SYLVIE.

FOR a full month the business, for which I had returned to London, detained me there: and even then it was only the urgent advice of my physician that induced me to leave it unfinished and pay another visit to Elveston.

Arthur had written once or twice during the month; but in none of his letters was there any mention of Lady Muriel. Still, I did not augur ill from his silence: to me it looked like the natural action of a lover, who, even while his heart was singing "She is mine!", would fear to paint his happiness in the cold phrases of a written letter, but would wait to tell it by word of mouth. "Yes," I thought, "I am to hear his song of triumph from his own lips!"

The night I arrived we had much to say on other matters: and, tired with the journey, I went to bed early, leaving the happy secret still untold. Next day, however, as we chatted on over the remains of luncheon, I ventured to put the momentous question. "Well, old friend, you have told me nothing of Lady Muriel—nor when the happy day is to be?"

"The happy day," Arthur said, looking unexpectedly grave, "is yet in the dim future. We need to know—or, rather, *she* needs to know *me* better. I know *her* sweet nature, thoroughly, by this time. But I dare not speak till I am sure that my love is returned."

"Don't wait too long!" I said gaily. "Faint heart never won fair lady!"

"It *is* 'faint heart,' perhaps. But really I *dare* not speak just yet."

"But meanwhile," I pleaded, "you are running a risk that perhaps you have not thought of. Some other man——"

"No," said Arthur firmly. "She is heart-whole: I am sure of that. Yet, if she loves another better than me, so be it! I will not spoil her happiness. The secret shall die with me. But she is my first——and my *only* love!"

"That is all very beautiful *sentiment*," I said, "but it is not *practical*. It is not like *you*.

> He either fears his fate too much,
>   Or his desert is small,
> Who dares not put it to the touch,
>   To win or lose it all."

"I *dare* not ask the question whether there is another!" he said passionately. "It would break my heart to know it!"

"Yet is it wise to leave it unasked? You must not waste your life upon an 'if'!"

"I tell you I *dare* not!"

"May *I* find it out for you?" I asked, with the freedom of an old friend.

"No, no!" he replied with a pained look. "I entreat you to say nothing. Let it wait."

"As you please," I said: and judged it best to say no more just then. "But this evening," I thought, "I will call on the Earl. I may be able to *see* how the land lies, without so much as saying a word!"

It was a very hot afternoon—too hot to go for a walk or do anything— or else it wouldn't have happened, I believe.

In the first place, I want to know—dear Child who reads this! —why Fairies should always be teaching *us* to do our duty, and lecturing *us* when we go wrong, and we should never teach *them* anything? You can't mean to say that Fairies are never greedy, or selfish, or cross, or deceitful, because that would be nonsense, you know. Well then, don't you think they might be all the better for a little lecturing and punishing now and then?

I really don't see why it shouldn't be tried, and I'm almost sure that, if you could only catch a Fairy, and put it in the corner, and give it nothing but bread and water for a day or two, you'd find it quite an improved character—it would take down its conceit a little, at all events.

The next question is, what is the best time for seeing Fairies? I believe I can tell you all about that.

The first rule is, that it must be a *very* hot day—that we may consider as settled: and you must be just a *little* sleepy—but not too sleepy to keep your eyes open, mind. Well, and you ought to feel a little—what one may call "fairyish"—the Scotch call it "eerie," and perhaps that's a prettier word; if you don't know what it means, I'm afraid I can hardly explain it; you must wait till you meet a Fairy, and then you'll know.

And the last rule is, that the crickets should not be chirping. I can't stop to explain that: you must take it on trust for the present.

So, if all these things happen together, you have a good chance of seeing a Fairy—or at least a much better chance than if they didn't.

The first thing I noticed, as I went lazily along through an open place in the wood, was a large Beetle lying struggling on its back, and I went down upon one knee to help the poor thing to its feet again. In some things, you know, you ca'n't be quite sure what an insect would like: for instance, I never could quite settle, supposing I were a moth, whether I would rather be kept out of the candle, or be allowed to fly straight in and get burnt—or again, supposing I were a spider, I'm not sure if I should be *quite* pleased to have my web torn down, and the fly let loose—but I feel quite certain that, if I were a beetle and had rolled over on my back, I should always be glad to be helped up again.

So, as I was saying, I had gone down upon one knee, and was just reaching out a little stick to turn the Beetle over, when I saw a sight that made me draw back hastily and hold my breath, for fear of making any noise and frightening the little creature away.

Not that she looked as if she would be easily frightened: she seemed so good and gentle that I'm sure she would never expect that any one could wish to hurt her. She was only a few inches high, and was dressed in green, so that you really would hardly have noticed her among the long grass; and she was so delicate and graceful that she quite seemed to belong to the place, almost as if she were one of the flowers. I may tell you besides, that she had no wings (I don't believe in Fairies with wings), and that she had quantities of long brown hair and large earnest brown eyes, and then I shall have done all I can to give you an idea of her.

Sylvie (I found out her name afterwards) had knelt down, just as I was doing, to help the Beetle; but it needed more than a little stick for *her* to get it on its legs again; it was as much as she could do, with both arms, to roll the heavy thing over; and all the while she was talking to it, half scolding and half comforting, as a nurse might do with a child that had fallen down.

"There, there! You needn't cry so much about it. You're not killed yet—though if you were, you couldn't cry, you know, and so it's a general rule against crying, my dear! And how did you come to tumble over? But I can see well enough how it was—I needn't ask you that—walking over sand-pits with your chin in the air, as usual. Of course if you go among sand-pits like that, you must expect to tumble. You should look."

The Beetle murmured something that sounded like "I *did* look," and Sylvie went on again.

"But I know you didn't! You never do! You always walk with your chin up—you're so dreadfully conceited. Well, let's see how many legs are broken this time. Why, none of them, I declare! And what's the good of having six legs, my dear, if you can only kick them all about in the air when you tumble? Legs are meant to walk with, you know. Now don't begin putting out your wings yet; I've more to say. Go to the frog that

lives behind that buttercup—give him my compliments—Sylvie's compliments—can you say 'compliments'?"

The Beetle tried and, I suppose, succeeded.

"Yes, that's right. And tell him he's to give you some of that salve I left with him yesterday. And you'd better get him to rub it in for you. He's got rather cold hands, but you mustn't mind that."

I think the Beetle must have shuddered at this idea, for Sylvie went on in a graver tone. "Now you needn't pretend to be so particular as all that, as if you were too grand to be rubbed by a frog. The fact is, you ought to be very much obliged to him. Suppose you could get nobody but a toad to do it, how would you like *that?*"

There was a little pause, and then Sylvie added "Now you may go. Be a good beetle, and don't keep your chin in the air." And then began one of those performances of humming, and whizzing, and restless banging about, such as a beetle indulges in when it has decided on flying, but hasn't quite made up its mind which way to go. At last, in one of its awkward zig-zags, it managed to fly right into my face, and, by the time I had recovered from the shock, the little Fairy was gone.

I looked about in all directions for the little creature, but there was no trace of her—and my 'eerie' feeling was quite gone off, and the crickets were chirping again merrily—so I knew she was really gone.

And now I've got time to tell you the rule about the crickets. They always leave off chirping when a Fairy goes by—because a Fairy's a kind of queen over them, I suppose—at all events it's a much grander thing than a cricket—so whenever you're walking out, and the crickets suddenly leave off chirping, you may be sure that they see a Fairy.

I walked on sadly enough, you may be sure. However, I comforted myself with thinking "It's been a very wonderful afternoon, so far. I'll just go quietly on and look about me, and I shouldn't wonder if I were to come across another Fairy somewhere."

Peering about in this way, I happened to notice a plant with rounded leaves, and with queer little holes cut in the middle of several of them. "Ah, the leafcutter bee!" I carelessly remarked—you know I am very learned in Natural History (for instance, I can always tell kittens from chickens at one glance)—and I was passing on, when a sudden thought made me stoop down and examine the leaves.

Then a little thrill of delight ran through me—for I noticed that the holes were all arranged so as to form letters; there were three leaves side by side, with "B," "R," and "U" marked on them, and after some search I found two more, which contained an "N" and an "O."

And then, all in a moment, a flash of inner light seemed to illumine a part of my life that had all but faded into oblivion—the strange visions I had experienced during my journey to Elveston: and with a thrill of delight I thought "Those visions are destined to be linked with my waking life!"

By this time the 'eerie' feeling had come back again, and I suddenly observed that no crickets were chirping; so I felt quite sure that "Bruno" was somewhere very near.

And so indeed he was—so near that I had very nearly walked over him without seeing him; which would have been dreadful, always supposing that Fairies *can* be walked over—my own belief is that they are something of the nature of Will-o'-the-Wisps: and there's no walking over *them*.

Think of any pretty little boy you know, with rosy cheeks, large dark eyes, and tangled brown hair, and then fancy him made small enough to go comfortably into a coffee-cup, and you'll have a very fair idea of him.

"What's your name, little one?" I began, in as soft a voice as I could manage. And, by the way, why is it we always begin by asking little children their names? Is it because we fancy a name will help to make them a little bigger? You never thought of asking a real large man his name, now, did you? But, however that may be, I felt it quite necessary to know *his* name; so, as he didn't answer my question, I asked it again a little louder. "What's your name, my little man?"

"What's oors?" he said, without looking up.

I told him my name quite gently, for he was much too small to be angry with.

"Duke of Anything?" he asked, just looking at me for a moment, and then going on with his work.

"Not Duke at all," I said, a little ashamed of having to confess it.

"Oo're big enough to be two Dukes," said the little creature. "I suppose oo're Sir Something, then?"

"No," I said, feeling more and more ashamed. "I haven't got any title."

The Fairy seemed to think that in that case I really wasn't worth the trouble of talking to, for he quietly went on digging, and tearing the flowers to pieces.

After a few minutes I tried again. "*Please* tell me what your name is."

"Bruno," the little fellow answered, very readily. "Why didn't oo say 'please' before?"

"That's something like what we used to be taught in the nursery," I thought to myself, looking back through the long years (about a hundred of them, since you ask the question), to the time when I was a little child. And here an idea came into my head, and I asked him "Aren't you one of the Fairies that teach children to be good?"

"Well, we have to do that sometimes," said Bruno, "and a dreadful bother it is." As he said this, he savagely tore a heartsease in two, and trampled on the pieces.

"What *are* you doing there, Bruno?" I said.

"Spoiling Sylvie's garden," was all the answer Bruno would give at first. But, as he went on tearing up the flowers, he muttered to himself "The nasty cross thing—wouldn't let me go and play this morning,— said I must finish my lessons first—lessons, indeed! I'll vex her finely, though!"

"Oh, Bruno, you shouldn't do that!" I cried. "Don't you know that's revenge? And revenge is a wicked, cruel, dangerous thing!"

"River-edge?" said Bruno. "What a funny word! I suppose oo call it cruel and dangerous 'cause, if oo wented too far and tumbleded in, oo'd get drownded."

"No, not river-edge," I explained: "revenge" (saying the word very slowly). But I couldn't help thinking that Bruno's explanation did very well for either word.

"Oh!" said Bruno, opening his eyes very wide, but without trying to repeat the word.

"Come! Try and pronounce it, Bruno!" I said, cheerfully. "Re-venge, re-venge."

But Bruno only tossed his little head, and said he couldn't; that his mouth wasn't the right shape for words of that kind. And the more I laughed, the more sulky the little fellow got about it.

"Well, never mind, my little man!" I said. "Shall I help you with that job?"

"Yes, please," Bruno said, quite pacified. "Only I wiss I could think of somefin to vex her more than this. Oo don't know how hard it is to make her angry!"

"Now listen to me, Bruno, and I'll teach you quite a splendid kind of revenge!"

"Somefin that'll vex her finely?" he asked with gleaming eyes.

"Something that will vex her finely. First, we'll get up all the weeds in her garden. See, there are a good many at this end—quite hiding the flowers."

"But *that* won't vex her!" said Bruno.

"After that," I said, without noticing the remark, "we'll water this highest bed—up here. You see it's getting quite dry and dusty."

Bruno looked at me inquisitively, but he said nothing this time.

"Then after that," I went on, "the walks want sweeping a bit; and I think you might cut down that tall nettle—it's so close to the garden that it's quite in the way——"

"What *is* oo talking about?" Bruno impatiently interrupted me. "All that won't vex her a bit!"

"Won't it?" I said, innocently. "Then, after that, suppose we put in some of these coloured pebbles—just to mark the divisions between the different kinds of flowers, you know. That'll have a very pretty effect."

Bruno turned round and had another good stare at me. At last there came an odd little twinkle into his eyes, and he said, with quite a new meaning in his voice, "That'll do nicely. Let's put 'em in rows—all the red together, and all the blue together."

"That'll do capitally," I said; "and then—what kind of flowers does Sylvie like best?"

Bruno had to put his thumb in his mouth and consider a little before he could answer. "Violets." he said, at last.

"There's a beautiful bed of violets down by the brook——"

"Oh, let's fetch 'em!" cried Bruno, giving a little skip into the air. "Here! Catch hold of my hand, and I'll help oo along. The grass is rather thick down that way."

I couldn't help laughing at his having so entirely forgotten what a big creature he was talking to. "No, not yet, Bruno," I said: "we must consider what's the right thing to do first. You see we've got quite a business before us."

"Yes, let's consider," said Bruno, putting his thumb into his mouth again, and sitting down upon a dead mouse.

"What do you keep that mouse for?" I said. "You should either bury it, or else throw it into the brook."

"Why, it's to measure with!" cried Bruno. "How ever would oo do a garden without one? We make each bed three mouses and a half long, and two mouses wide."

I stopped him, as he was dragging it off by the tail to show me how it was used, for I was half afraid the 'eerie' feeling might go off before we had finished the garden, and in that case I should see no more of him or Sylvie. "I think the best way will be for *you* to weed the beds, while *I* sort out these pebbles, ready to mark the walks with."

"That's it!" cried Bruno. "And I'll tell oo about the caterpillars while we work."

"Ah, let's hear about the caterpillars," I said, as I drew the pebbles together into a heap and began dividing them into colours.

And Bruno went on in a low, rapid tone, more as if he were talking to himself. "Yesterday I saw two little caterpillars, when I was sitting by the brook, just where oo go into the wood. They were quite green, and they had yellow eyes, and they didn't see *me*. And one of them had got a moth's wing to carry—a great brown moth's wing, oo know, all dry, with feathers. So he couldn't want it to eat, I should think—perhaps he meant to make a cloak for the winter?"

"Perhaps," I said, for Bruno had twisted up the last word into a sort of question, and was looking at me for an answer.

One word was quite enough for the little fellow, and he went on merrily. "Well, and so he didn't want the other caterpillar to see the moth's wing, oo know—so what must he do but try to carry it with all his left legs, and he tried to walk on the other set. Of course he toppled over after that."

"After what?" I said, catching at the last word, for, to tell the truth, I hadn't been attending much.

"He toppled over," Bruno repeated, very gravely, "and if *oo* ever saw a caterpillar topple over, oo'd know it's a welly serious thing, and not sit grinning like that—and I sha'n't tell oo no more!"

"Indeed and indeed, Bruno, I didn't mean to grin. See, I'm quite grave again now."

But Bruno only folded his arms, and said "Don't tell *me*. I see a little twinkle in one of oor eyes—just like the moon."

"Why do you think I'm like the moon, Bruno?" I asked.

"Oor face is large and round like the moon," Bruno answered, looking at me thoughtfully. "It doesn't shine quite so bright—but it's more cleaner."

I couldn't help smiling at this. "You know I sometimes wash *my* face, Bruno. The moon never does that."

"Oh, doosn't she though!" cried Bruno; and he leant forwards and added in a solemn whisper, "The moon's face gets dirtier and dirtier every night, till it's black all across. And then, when it's dirty all over—so—" (he passed his hand across his own rosy cheeks as he spoke) "then she washes it."

"Then it's all clean again, isn't it?"

"Not all in a moment," said Bruno. "What a deal of teaching oo wants! She washes it little by little—only she begins at the other edge, oo know."

By this time he was sitting quietly on the dead mouse with his arms folded, and the weeding wasn't getting on a bit: so I had to say "Work first, pleasure afterwards: no more talking till that bed's finished."

CHAPTER XV.

BRUNO'S REVENGE.

AFTER that we had a few minutes of silence, while I sorted out the pebbles, and amused myself with watching Bruno's plan of gardening. It was quite a new plan to me: he always measured each bed before he weeded it, as if he was afraid the weeding would make it shrink; and once, when it came out longer than he wished, he set to work to thump the mouse with his little fist, crying out "There now! It's all gone wrong again! Why don't oo keep oor tail straight when I tell oo!"

"I'll tell you what I'll do," Bruno said in a half-whisper, as we worked. "Oo like Fairies, don't oo?"

"Yes," I said: "of course I do, or I shouldn't have come here. I should have gone to some place where there are no Fairies."

Bruno laughed contemptuously. "Why, oo might as well say oo'd go to some place where there wasn't any air—supposing oo didn't like air!"

This was a rather difficult idea to grasp. I tried a change of subject. "You're nearly the first Fairy I ever saw. Have *you* ever seen any people besides me?"

"Plenty!" said Bruno. "We see 'em when we walk in the road."

"But they ca'n't see *you*. How is it they never tread on you?"

"Ca'n't *tread* on us," said Bruno, looking amused at my ignorance. "Why, suppose oo're walking, here—so—" (making little marks on the ground) "and suppose there's a Fairy—that's me—walking *here*. Very well then, oo put one foot here, and one foot here, so oo doosn't tread on the Fairy."

This was all very well as an explanation, but it didn't convince me. "Why shouldn't I put one foot *on* the Fairy?" I asked.

"I don't know *why,*" the little fellow said in a thoughtful tone. "But I know oo *wouldn't.* Nobody never walked on the top of a Fairy. Now I'll tell oo what I'll do, as oo're so fond of Fairies. I'll get oo an invitation to the Fairy-King's dinner-party. I know one of the head-waiters."

I couldn't help laughing at this idea. "Do the waiters invite the guests?" I asked.

"Oh, not *to sit down!*" Bruno said. "But to wait at table. Oo'd like that, wouldn't oo? To hand about plates, and so on."

"Well, but that's not so nice as sitting at the table, is it?"

"Of course it isn't," Bruno said, in a tone as if he rather pitied my ignorance; "but if oo're not even Sir Anything, oo ca'n't expect to be allowed to sit at the table, oo know."

I said, as meekly as I could, that I didn't expect it, but it was the only way of going to a dinner-party that I really enjoyed. And Bruno tossed his head, and said, in a rather offended tone, that I might do as I pleased—there were many he knew that would give their ears to go.

"Have you ever been yourself, Bruno?"

"They invited me once, last week," Bruno said, very gravely. "It was to wash up the soup-plates—no, the cheese-plates I mean—that was grand enough. And I waited at table. And I didn't hardly make only *one* mistake."

"What was it?" I said. "You needn't mind telling *me*."

"Only bringing scissors to cut the beef with," Bruno said carelessly. "But the grandest thing of all was, *I* fetched the King a glass of cider!"

"That *was* grand!" I said, biting my lip to keep myself from laughing.

"Wasn't it?" said Bruno, very earnestly. "Oo know it isn't every one that's had such an honour as *that!*"

This set me thinking of the various queer things we call "an honour" in this world, but which, after all, haven't a bit more honour in them than what Bruno enjoyed, when he took the King a glass of cider.

I don't know how long I might not have dreamed on in this way, if Bruno hadn't suddenly roused me. "Oh, come here quick!" he cried, in a state of the wildest excitement. "Catch hold of his other horn! I ca'n't hold him more than a minute!"

He was struggling desperately with a great snail, clinging to one of its horns, and nearly breaking his poor little back in his efforts to drag it over a blade of grass.

I saw we should have no more gardening if I let this sort of thing go on, so I quietly took the snail away, and put it on a bank where he couldn't reach it. "We'll hunt it afterwards, Bruno," I said, "if you really want to catch it. But what's the use of it when you've got it?"

"What's the use of a fox when oo've got it?" said Bruno. "I know oo big things hunt foxes."

I tried to think of some good reason why "big things" should hunt foxes, and he should not hunt snails, but none came into my head: so I said at last, "Well, I suppose one's as good as the other. I'll go snail-hunting myself some day."

"I should think oo wouldn't be so silly," said Bruno, "as to go snail-hunting by oorself. Why, oo'd never get the snail along, if oo hadn't somebody to hold on to his other horn!"

"Of course I sha'n't go *alone*," I said, quite gravely. "By the way, is that the best kind to hunt, or do you recommend the ones without shells?"

"Oh, no, we never hunt the ones without shells," Bruno said, with a little shudder at the thought of it. "They're always so cross about it; and then, if oo tumbles over them, they're ever so sticky!"

By this time we had nearly finished the garden. I had fetched some violets, and Bruno was just helping me to put in the last, when he suddenly stopped and said "I'm tired."

"Rest then," I said: "I can go on without you, quite well."

Bruno needed no second invitation: he at once began arranging the dead mouse as a kind of sofa. "And I'll sing oo a little song," he said, as he rolled it about.

"Do," said I: "I like songs very much."

"Which song will oo choose?" Bruno said, as he dragged the mouse into a place where he could get a good view of me. "'Ting, ting, ting' is the nicest."

There was no resisting such a strong hint as this: however, I pretended to think about it for a moment, and then said "Well, I like 'Ting, ting, ting,' best of all."

"That shows oo're a good judge of music," Bruno said, with a pleased look. "How many hare-bells would oo like?" And he put his thumb into his mouth to help me to consider.

As there was only one cluster of hare-bells within easy reach, I said very gravely that I thought one would do *this* time, and I picked it and gave it to him. Bruno ran his hand once or twice up and down the flowers, like a musician trying an instrument, producing a most delicious delicate tinkling as he did so. I had never heard flower-music before— I don't think one can, unless one's in the 'eerie' state—and I don't know quite how to give you an idea of what it was like, except by saying that it sounded like a peal of bells a thousand miles off. When he had satisfied himself that the flowers were in tune, he seated himself on the dead mouse (he never seemed really comfortable anywhere else), and, looking up at me with a merry twinkle in his eyes, he began. By the way, the tune was rather a curious one, and you might like to try it for yourself, so here are the notes.

> "Rise, oh, rise! The daylight dies:
>   The owls are hooting, ting, ting, ting!
> Wake, oh, wake! Beside the lake

The elves are fluting, ting, ting, ting!
Welcoming our Fairy King,
   We sing, sing, sing."

He sang the first four lines briskly and merrily, making the hare-bells chime in time with the music; but the last two he sang quite slowly and gently, and merely waved the flowers backwards and forwards. Then he left off to explain. "The Fairy-King is Oberon, and he lives across the lake—and sometimes he comes in a little boat—and we go and meet him—and then we sing this song, you know."

"And then you go and dine with him?" I said, mischievously.

"Oo shouldn't talk," Bruno hastily said: "it interrupts the song so."

I said I wouldn't do it again.

"I never talk myself when I'm singing," he went on very gravely: "so *oo* shouldn't either." Then he tuned the hare-bells once more, and sang:—

   "Hear, oh, hear! From far and near
     The music stealing, ting, ting, ting!
   Fairy bells adown the dells
     Are merrily pealing, ting, ting, ting!
   Welcoming our Fairy King,
     We ring, ring, ring.

   "See, oh, see! On every tree
     What lamps are shining, ting, ting, ting!
   They are eyes of fiery flies
     To light our dining, ting, ting, ting!
   Welcoming our Fairy King
     They swing, swing, swing.

   "Haste, oh haste, to take and taste
     The dainties waiting, ting, ting, ting!
   Honey-dew is stored——"

"Hush, Bruno!" I interrupted in a warning whisper. "She's coming!"

Bruno checked his song, and, as she slowly made her way through the long grass, he suddenly rushed out headlong at her like a little bull, shouting "Look the other way! Look the other way!"

"Which way?" Sylvie asked, in rather a frightened tone, as she looked round in all directions to see where the danger could be.

"*That* way!" said Bruno, carefully turning her round with her face to the wood. "Now, walk backwards—walk gently—don't be frightened: oo sha'n't trip!"

But Sylvie *did* trip notwithstanding: in fact he led her, in his hurry, across so many little sticks and stones, that it was really a wonder the poor child could keep on her feet at all. But he was far too much excited to think of what he was doing.

I silently pointed out to Bruno the best place to lead her to, so as to get a view of the whole garden at once: it was a little rising ground, about the height of a potato; and, when they had mounted it, I drew back into the shade, that Sylvie mightn't see me.

I heard Bruno cry out triumphantly "*Now* oo may look!" and then followed a clapping of hands, but it was all done by Bruno himself. Sylvie was silent—she only stood and gazed with her hands clasped together, and I was half afraid she didn't like it after all.

Bruno too was watching her anxiously, and when she jumped down off the mound, and began wandering up and down the little walks, he cautiously followed her about, evidently anxious that she should form her own opinion of it all, without any hint from him. And when at last she drew a long breath, and gave her verdict—in a hurried whisper, and without the slightest regard to grammar—"It's the loveliest thing as I never saw in all my life before!" the little fellow looked as well pleased as if it had been given by all the judges and juries in England put together.

"And did you really do it all by yourself, Bruno?" said Sylvie. "And all for me?"

"I was helped a bit," Bruno began, with a merry little laugh at her surprise. "We've been at it all the afternoon—I thought oo'd like—" and here the poor little fellow's lip began to quiver, and all in a moment he burst out crying, and running up to Sylvie he flung his arms passionately round her neck, and hid his face on her shoulder.

There was a little quiver in Sylvie's voice too, as she whispered "Why, what's the matter, darling?" and tried to lift up his head and kiss him.

But Bruno only clung to her, sobbing, and wouldn't be comforted till he had confessed. "I tried—to spoil oor garden—first—but I'll never—never—" and then came another burst of tears, which drowned the rest of the sentence. At last he got out the words "I liked—putting in the flowers—for *oo,* Sylvie—and I never was so happy before." And the rosy little face came up at last to be kissed, all wet with tears as it was.

Sylvie was crying too by this time, and she said nothing but "Bruno, dear!" and "*I* never was so happy before," though why these two children who had never been so happy before should both be crying was a mystery to *me.*

I felt very happy too, but of course I didn't cry: "big things" never do, you know—we leave all that to the Fairies. Only I think it must have been raining a little just then, for I found a drop or two on my cheeks.

After that they went through the whole garden again, flower by flower, as if it were a long sentence they were spelling out, with kisses for commas, and a great hug by way of a full-stop when they got to the end.

"Doos oo know, that was my river-edge, Sylvie?" Bruno solemnly began.

Sylvie laughed merrily. "What *do* you mean?" she said. And she pushed back her heavy brown hair with both hands, and looked at him with dancing eyes in which the big tear-drops were still glittering.

Bruno drew in a long breath, and made up his mouth for a great effort. "I mean re—venge," he said: "now oo under'tand." And he looked so happy and proud at having said the word right at last, that I quite envied him. I rather think Sylvie didn't "under'tand" at all; but she gave him a little kiss on each cheek, which seemed to do just as well.

So they wandered off lovingly together, in among the buttercups, each with an arm twined round the other, whispering and laughing as they went, and never so much as once looked back at poor me. Yes, once, just before I quite lost sight of them, Bruno half turned his head, and nodded me a saucy little good-bye over one shoulder. And that was all the thanks I got for *my* trouble. The very last thing I saw of them was this—Sylvie was stooping down with her arms round Bruno's neck, and saying coaxingly in his ear, "Do you know, Bruno, I've quite forgotten that hard word. Do say it once more. Come! Only this once, dear!"

But Bruno wouldn't try it again.

CHAPTER XVI.

A CHANGED CROCODILE.

THE Marvellous—the Mysterious—had quite passed out of my life for the moment: and the Common-place reigned supreme. I turned in the direction of the Earl's house, as it was now 'the witching hour' of five, and I knew I should find them ready for a cup of tea and a quiet chat.

Lady Muriel and her father gave me a delightfully warm welcome. They were not of the folk we meet in fashionable drawing-rooms—who conceal all such feelings as they may chance to possess beneath the impenetrable mask of a conventional placidity. 'The Man with the Iron Mask' was, no doubt, a rarity and a marvel in his own age: in modern London no one would turn his head to give him a second look! No, these were *real* people. When they *looked* pleased, it meant that they *were* pleased: and when Lady Muriel said, with a bright smile, "I'm *very* glad to see you again!", I knew that it was *true*.

Still I did not venture to disobey the injunctions—crazy as I felt them to be—of the love-sick young Doctor, by so much as alluding to his existence: and it was only after they had given me full details of a projected picnic, to which they invited me, that Lady Muriel exclaimed, almost as an after-thought, "and *do* if you can, bring Doctor Forester with you! I'm sure a day in the country would do him good. I'm afraid he studies too much——"

It was 'on the tip of my tongue' to quote the words "His only books are woman's looks!" but I checked myself just in time—with something of the feeling of one who has crossed a street, and has been all but run over by a passing 'Hansom.'

"—and I think he has too lonely a life," she went on, with a gentle earnestness that left no room whatever to suspect a double meaning. "*Do* get him to come! And don't forget the day, Tuesday week. We can drive you over. It would be a pity to go by rail—there is so much pretty scenery on the road. And our open carriage just holds four."

"Oh, *I'll* persuade him to come!" I said with confidence—thinking "it would take all *my* powers of persuasion to keep him away!"

The picnic was to take place in ten days: and though Arthur readily accepted the invitation I brought him, nothing that I could say would induce him to call—either with me or without me—on the Earl and his daughter in the meanwhile. No: he feared to "wear out his welcome," he said: they had "seen enough of him for one while": and, when at last the day for the expedition arrived, he was so childishly nervous and uneasy that I thought it best so to arrange our plans that we should go separately to the house—my intention being to arrive some time after him, so as to give him time to get over a meeting.

With this object I purposely made a considerable circuit on my way to the Hall (as we called the Earl's house): "and if I could only manage to lose my way a bit," I thought to myself, "that would suit me capitally!"

In this I succeeded better, and sooner, than I had ventured to hope for. The path through the wood had been made familiar to me, by many a solitary stroll, in my former visit to Elveston; and how I could have so suddenly and so entirely lost it—even though I *was* so engrossed in thinking of Arthur and his lady-love that I heeded little else—was a mystery to me. "And this open place," I said to myself, "seems to have some memory about it I cannot distinctly recall—surely it is the very spot where I saw those Fairy-Children! But I hope there are no snakes about!" I mused aloud, taking my seat on a fallen tree. "I certainly do *not* like snakes—and I don't suppose *Bruno* likes them, either!"

"No, he *doesn't* like them!" said a demure little voice at my side. "He's not *afraid* of them, you know. But he doesn't *like* them. He says they're too waggly!"

Words fail me to describe the beauty of the little group—couched on a patch of moss, on the trunk of the fallen tree, that met my eager gaze: Sylvie reclining with her elbow buried in the moss, and her rosy cheek resting in the palm of her hand, and Bruno stretched at her feet with his head in her lap.

"Too waggly?" was all I could say in so sudden an emergency.

"I'm not praticular," Bruno said, carelessly: "but I *do* like straight animals best——"

"But you like a dog when it wags its tail," Sylvie interrupted. "You *know* you do, Bruno!"

"But there's more of a dog, isn't there, Mister Sir?" Bruno appealed to me. "*You* wouldn't like to have a dog if it hadn't got nuffin but a head and a tail?"

I admitted that a dog of that kind would be uninteresting.

"There *isn't* such a dog as that," Sylvie thoughtfully remarked.

"But there *would* be," cried Bruno, "if the Professor shortened it up for us!"

"Shortened it up?" I said. "That's something new. How does he do it?"

"He's got a curious machine—" Sylvie was beginning to explain.

"A *welly* curious machine," Bruno broke in, not at all willing to have the story thus taken out of his mouth, "and if oo puts in—somefinoruvver—at *one* end, oo know—and he turns the handle—and it comes out at the uvver end, oh, ever so short!"

"As short as short!" Sylvie echoed.

"And one day—when we was in Outland, oo know—before we came to Fairyland—me and Sylvie took him a big Crocodile. And he shortened it up for us. And it *did* look so funny! And it kept looking round, and saying 'wherever *is* the rest of me got to?' And then its eyes looked unhappy——"

"Not *both* its eyes," Sylvie interrupted.

"Course not!" said the little fellow. "Only the eye that *couldn't* see wherever the rest of it had got to. But the eye that *could* see wher-ever——"

"How short *was* the crocodile?" I asked, as the story was getting a little complicated.

"Half as short again as when we caught it—*so* long," said Bruno, spreading out his arms to their full stretch.

I tried to calculate what this would come to, but it was too hard for me. Please make it out for me, dear Child who reads this!

"But you didn't leave the poor thing so short as that, did you?"

"Well, no. Sylvie and me took it back again and we got it stretched to—to—how much was it, Sylvie?"

"Two times and a half, and a little bit more," said Sylvie.

"It wouldn't like that better than the other way, I'm afraid?"

"Oh, but it did though!" Bruno put in eagerly. "It *were* proud of its new tail! Oo never saw a Crocodile so proud! Why, it could go round and walk on the top of its tail, and along its back, all the way to its head!"

"Not *quite* all the way," said Sylvie. "It couldn't, you know."

"Ah but it *did,* once!" Bruno cried triumphantly. "Oo weren't looking— but *I* watched it. And it walked on tipplety toe, so as it wouldn't wake itself, 'cause it thought it were asleep. And it got both its paws on its tail. And it walked and it walked all the way along its back. And it walked and it walked on its forehead. And it walked a tiny little way down its nose! There now!"

This was a good deal worse than the last puzzle. Please, dear Child, help again!

"I don't believe no Crocodile never walked along its own forehead!" Sylvie cried, too much excited by the controversy to limit the number of her negatives.

"Oo don't know the *reason* why it did it!" Bruno scornfully retorted. "It had a welly good reason. I *heerd* it say 'Why *shouldn't* I walk on my own forehead?' So a course it *did,* oo know!"

"If *that's* a good reason, Bruno," I said, "why shouldn't *you* get up that tree?"

"*Shall,* in a minute," said Bruno: "soon as we've done talking. Only two peoples *ca'n't* talk comfably togevver, when one's getting up a tree, and the other isn't!"

It appeared to me that a conversation would scarcely be 'comfable' while trees were being climbed, even if *both* the 'peoples' were doing it: but it was evidently dangerous to oppose any theory of Bruno's; so I thought it best to let the question drop, and to ask for an account of the machine that made things *longer.*

This time Bruno was at a loss, and left it to Sylvie. "It's like a mangle," she said: "if things are put in, they get squoze———"

"Squeezeled!" Bruno interrupted.

"Yes." Sylvie accepted the correction, but did not attempt to pronounce the word, which was evidently new to her. "They get—like that—and they come out, oh, ever so long!"

"Once," Bruno began again, "Sylvie and me writed———"

"Wrote!" Sylvie whispered.

"Well, we *wroted* a Nursery-Song, and the Professor mangled it longer for us. It were '*There was a little Man, And he had a little gun, And the bullets—*'"

"I know the rest," I interrupted. "But would you say it *long*—I mean the way that it came *out* of the mangle?"

"We'll get the Professor to *sing* it for you," said Sylvie. "It would spoil it to *say* it."

"I would like to meet the Professor," I said. "And I would like to take you all with me, to see some friends of mine, that live near here. Would you like to come?"

"I don't think the *Professor* would like to come," said Sylvie. "He's *very* shy. But *we'd* like it very much. Only we'd better not come *this* size, you know."

The difficulty had occurred to me already: and I had felt that perhaps there *would* be a slight awkwardness in introducing two such tiny friends into Society. "What size will you be?" I enquired.

"We'd better come as—common *children*," Sylvie thoughtfully replied. "That's the easiest size to manage."

"Could you come to-day?" I said, thinking "then we could have you at the picnic!"

Sylvie considered a little. "Not *to-day,*" she replied. "We haven't got the things ready. We'll come on—Tuesday next, if you like. And now, *really*, Bruno, you must come and do your lessons."

"I *wiss* oo wouldn't say '*really* Bruno!'" the little fellow pleaded, with pouting lips that made him look prettier than ever. "It *always* shows there's something horrid coming! And I won't kiss you, if you're so unkind."

"Ah, but you *have* kissed me!" Sylvie exclaimed in merry triumph.

"Well then, I'll *un*kiss you!" And he threw his arms round her neck for this novel, but apparently not *very* painful, operation.

"It's *very* like *kissing!*" Sylvie remarked, as soon as her lips were again free for speech.

"Oo don't know *nuffin* about it! It were just the *conkery!*" Bruno replied with much severity, as he marched away.

Sylvie turned her laughing face to me. "Shall we come on Tuesday?" she said.

"Very well," I said: "let it be Tuesday next. But where *is* the Professor? Did he come with you to Fairyland?"

"No," said Sylvie. "But he promised he'd come and see us, *some* day. He's getting his Lecture ready. So he has to stay at home."

"At home?" I said dreamily, not feeling quite sure what she had said.

"Yes, Sir. His Lordship and Lady Muriel *are* at home. Please to walk this way."

CHAPTER XVII.

THE THREE BADGERS.

STILL more dreamily I found myself following this imperious voice into a room where the Earl, his daughter, and Arthur, were seated. "So you're come *at last!*" said Lady Muriel, in a tone of playful reproach.

"I was delayed," I stammered. Though *what* it was that had delayed me I should have been puzzled to explain! Luckily no questions were asked.

The carriage was ordered round, the hamper, containing our contribution to the Picnic, was duly stowed away, and we set forth.

There was no need for *me* to maintain the conversation. Lady Muriel and Arthur were evidently on those most delightful of terms, where one has no need to check thought after thought, as it rises to the lips, with the fear '*this* will not be appreciated—*this* will give offence—*this* will sound too serious—this will sound flippant': like very old friends, in fullest sympathy, their talk rippled on.

"Why shouldn't we desert the Picnic and go in some other direction?" she suddenly suggested. "A party of four is surely self-sufficing? And as for *food*, our hamper——"

"Why *shouldn't* we? What a genuine *lady's* argument!" laughed Authur. "A lady never knows on which side the *onus probandi*—the burden of proving—lies!"

"Do *men* always know?" she asked with a pretty assumption of meek docility.

"With *one* exception—the only one I can think of—Dr. Watts, who has asked the senseless question

> '*Why should I deprive my neighbour*
> *Of his goods against his will?*'

Fancy *that* as an argument for Honesty! His position seems to be 'I'm only honest because I see no reason to steal.' And the *thief's* answer is of course complete and crushing. 'I deprive my neighbour of his goods because I want them myself. And I do it against his will because there's no chance of getting him to consent to it!'"

"I can give you one other exception," I said: "an argument I heard only to-day—and *not* by a lady. 'Why shouldn't I walk on my own forehead?'"

"What a curious subject for speculation!" said Lady Muriel, turning to me, with eyes brimming over with laughter. "May we know who propounded the question? And *did* he walk on his own forehead?"

"I ca'n't remember *who* it was that said it!" I faltered. "Nor *where* I heard it!"

"Whoever it was, I hope we shall meet him at the Picnic!" said Lady Muriel. "It's a *far* more interesting question than '*Isn't* this a picturesque ruin?' '*Aren't* those autumn-tints lovely?' I shall have to answer those two questions *ten* times, at least, this afternoon!"

"That's one of the miseries of Society!" said Arthur. "Why ca'n't people let one enjoy the beauties of Nature without having to *say* so every minute? Why should Life be one long Catechism?"

"It's just as bad at a picture-gallery," the Earl remarked. "I went to the R.A. last May, with a conceited young artist: and he *did* torment me! I wouldn't have minded his criticizing the pictures *himself:* but *I* had to agree with him—or else to argue the point, which would have been worse!"

"It was *depreciatory* criticism, of course?" said Arthur.

"I don't see the 'of course' at all."

"Why, did you ever know a conceited man dare to *praise* a picture? The one thing he dreads (next to not being noticed) is *to be proved fallible!* If you once *praise* a picture, your character for *infallibility* hangs by a thread. Suppose it's a figure-picture, and you venture to say 'draws well.' Somebody measures it, and finds one of the proportions an eighth of an inch wrong. *You* are disposed of as a critic! 'Did you say he draws *well?*' your friends enquire sarcastically, while you hang your head and blush. No. The only *safe* course, if any one says 'draws well,' is to shrug your shoulders. '*Draws* well?' you repeat thoughtfully. 'Draws *well?* Humph!' That's the way to become a great critic!"

Thus airily chatting, after a pleasant drive through a few miles of beautiful scenery, we reached the *rendezvous*—a ruined castle—where the rest of the picnic-party were already assembled. We spent an hour or two in sauntering about the ruins: gathering at last, by common consent, into a few random groups, seated on the side of a mound, which commanded a good view of the old castle and its surroundings.

The momentary silence, that ensued, was promptly taken possession of—or, more correctly, taken into custody—by a Voice; a voice so smooth, so monotonous, so sonorous, that one felt, with a shudder, that any other conversation was precluded, and that, unless some desperate remedy were adopted, we were fated to listen to a Lecture, of which no man could foresee the end!

The speaker was a broadly-built man, whose large, flat, pale face was bounded on the North by a fringe of hair, on the East and West by a fringe of whisker, and on the South by a fringe of beard—the whole constituting a uniform halo of stubbly whitey-brown bristles. His features were so entirely destitute of expression that I could not help saying to myself—helplessly, as if in the clutches of a night-mare—"they are only penciled in: no final touches as yet!" And he had a way of ending every sentence with a sudden smile, which spread like a ripple over that vast blank surface, and was gone in a moment, leaving behind it such absolute solemnity that I felt impelled to murmur "it was not *he:* it was somebody else that smiled!"

"Do you observe?" (such was the phrase with which the wretch began each sentence) "Do you observe the way in which that broken arch, at the very top of the ruin, stands out against the clear sky? It is placed *exactly* right: and there is *exactly* enough of it. A little more, or a little less, and all would be utterly spoiled!"

"Oh gifted architect!" murmured Arthur, inaudibly to all but Lady Muriel and myself. "Foreseeing the exact effect his work would have, when in ruins, centuries after his death!"

"And do you observe, where those trees slope down the hill," (indicating them with a sweep of the hand, and with all the patronising air of the man who has himself arranged the landscape), "how the mists rising from the river fill up *exactly* those intervals where we *need* indistinctness, for artistic effect? Here, in the foreground, a few clear touches are not amiss: but a *back*-ground without mist, you know! It is simply barbarous! Yes, we *need* indistinctness!"

The orator looked so pointedly at *me* as he uttered these words, that I felt bound to reply, by murmuring something to the effect that I hardly felt the need *myself*—and that I enjoyed looking at a thing, better, when I could *see* it.

"Quite so!" the great man sharply took me up. "From *your* point of view, that is correctly put. But for any one who has a soul for *Art,* such a view is preposterous. *Nature* is one thing. *Art* is another. *Nature* shows

us the world as it *is*. But *Art*—as a Latin author tells us—*Art,* you know—the words have escaped my memory———"

"*Ars est celare Naturam,*" Arthur interposed with a delightful promptitude.

"Quite so!" the orator replied with an air of relief. "I thank you! *Ars est celare Naturam*—but that isn't it." And, for a few peaceful moments, the orator brooded, frowningly, over the quotation. The welcome opportunity was seized, and *another* voice struck into the silence.

"What a *lovely* old ruin it is!" cried a young lady in spectacles, the very embodiment of the March of Mind, looking at Lady Muriel, as the proper recipient of all really *original* remarks. "And *don't* you admire those autumn-tints on the trees? *I* do, *intensely!*"

Lady Muriel shot a meaning glance at me; but replied with admirable gravity. "Oh yes indeed, indeed! *So* true!"

"And isn't it strange," said the young lady, passing with startling suddenness from Sentiment to Science, "that the mere impact of certain coloured rays upon the Retina should give us such exquisite pleasure?"

"You have studied Physiology, then?" a certain young Doctor courteously enquired.

"Oh *yes!* Isn't it a *sweet* Science?"

Arthur slightly smiled. "It seems a paradox, does it not," he went on, "that the image formed on the Retina should be inverted?"

"It *is* puzzling," she candidly admitted. "Why is it we do not *see* things upside-down?"

"You have never heard the Theory, then, that the *Brain* also is inverted?"

"No *indeed!* What a *beautiful* fact! But how is it *proved?*"

"*Thus,*" replied Arthur, with all the gravity of ten Professors rolled into one. "What we call the *vertex* of the Brain is really its *base:* and what we call its *base* is really its *vertex:* it is simply a question of *nomenclature.*"

This last polysyllable settled the matter. "How truly delightful!" the fair Scientist exclaimed with enthusiasm. "I shall ask our Physiological Lecturer why he never gave us that *exquisite* Theory!"

"I'd give something to be present when the question is asked!" Arthur whispered to me, as, at a signal from Lady Muriel, we moved on to where the hampers had been collected, and devoted ourselves to the more *substantial* business of the day.

We 'waited' on ourselves, as the modern barbarism (combining two good things in such a way as to secure the discomforts of both and the advantages of neither) of having a picnic with servants to wait upon you, had not yet reached this out-of-the-way region—and of course the gentlemen did not even take their places until the ladies had been duly provided with all imaginable creature-comforts. Then I supplied myself with a plate of something solid and a glass of something fluid, and found a place next to Lady Muriel.

It had been left vacant—apparently for Arthur, as a distinguished stranger: but he had turned shy, and had placed himself next to the young lady in spectacles, whose high rasping voice had already cast loose upon Society such ominous phrases as "Man is a bundle of Qualities!", "the Objective is only attainable through the Subjective!". Arthur was bearing it bravely: but several faces wore a look of alarm, and I thought it high time to start some less metaphysical topic.

"In my nursery days," I began, "when the weather didn't suit for an out-of-doors picnic, we were allowed to have a peculiar kind, that we enjoyed hugely. The table cloth was laid *under* the table, instead of upon it: we sat round it on the floor: and I believe we really enjoyed that extremely uncomfortable kind of dinner more than we ever did the orthodox arrangement!"

"I've no doubt of it," Lady Muriel replied. "There's nothing a well-regulated child hates so much as regularity. I believe a really healthy boy would thoroughly enjoy Greek Grammar—if only he might stand on his head to learn it! And your carpet-dinner certainly spared you *one* feature of a picnic, which is to me its chief drawback."

"The chance of a shower?" I suggested.

"No, the chance—or rather the certainty—of *live* things occurring in combination with one's food! *Spiders* are *my* bugbear. Now my father has *no* sympathy with that sentiment—*have* you, dear?" For the Earl had caught the word and turned to listen.

"To each his sufferings, all are men," he replied in the sweet sad tones that seemed natural to him: "each has his pet aversion."

"But you'll never guess *his!*" Lady Muriel said, with that delicate silvery laugh that was music to my ears.

I declined to attempt the impossible.

"He doesn't like *snakes!*" she said, in a stage whisper. "Now, isn't *that* an unreasonable aversion? Fancy not liking such a dear, coaxingly, *clingingly* affectionate creature as a snake!"

"Not like *snakes!*" I exclaimed. "Is such a thing possible?"

"No, he *doesn't* like them," she repeated with a pretty mock-gravity. "He's not *afraid* of them, you know. But he doesn't *like* them. He says they're too waggly!"

I was more startled than I liked to show. There was something so *uncanny* in this echo of the very words I had so lately heard from that little forest-sprite, that it was only by a great effort I succeeded in saying, carelessly, "Let us banish so unpleasant a topic. Won't you sing us something, Lady Muriel? I know you *do* sing without music."

"The only songs I know—without music—are *desperately* sentimental, I'm afraid! Are your tears all ready?"

"Quite ready! Quite ready!" came from all sides, and Lady Muriel—not being one of those lady-singers who think it *de rigueur* to decline to sing till they have been petitioned three or four times, and have pleaded failure of memory, loss of voice, and other conclusive reasons for silence—began at once:—

> *"There be three Badgers on a mossy stone,*
> *Beside a dark and covered way:*
> *Each dreams himself a monarch on his throne,*
> *And so they stay and stay—*
> *Though their old Father languishes alone,*
> *They stay, and stay, and stay.*

"There be three Herrings loitering around,
  Longing to share that mossy seat:
Each Herring tries to sing what she has found
  That makes Life seem so sweet.
Thus, with a grating and uncertain sound,
  They bleat, and bleat, and bleat.

"The Mother-Herring, on the salt sea-wave,
  Sought vainly for her absent ones:
The Father-Badger, writhing in a cave,
  Shrieked out 'Return, my sons!
You shall have buns,' he shrieked, 'if you'll behave!
  Yea, buns, and buns, and buns!'

" 'I fear,' said she, 'your sons have gone astray?
  My daughters left me while I slept.'
'Yes'm,' the Badger said: 'it's as you say.'
  'They should be better kept.'
Thus the poor parents talked the time away,
  And wept, and wept, and wept."

Here Bruno broke off suddenly. "The Herrings' Song wants anuvver tune, Sylvie," he said. "And I ca'n't sing it—not wizout oo plays it for me!"

Instantly Sylvie seated herself upon a tiny mushroom, that happened to grow in front of a daisy, as if it were the most ordinary musical

instrument in the world, and played on the petals as if they were the notes of an organ. And such delicious *tiny* music it was! Such teeny-tiny music!

Bruno held his head on one side, and listened very gravely for a few moments until he had caught the melody. Then the sweet childish voice rang out once more:—

> "Oh, dear beyond our dearest dreams,
> Fairer than all that fairest seems!
> To feast the rosy hours away,
> To revel in a roundelay!
>   How blest would be
>   A life so free—
> Ipwergis-Pudding to consume,
> And drink the subtle Azzigoom!
>
> "And if, in other days and hours,
> Mid other fluffs and other flowers,
> The choice were given me how to dine—
> 'Name what thou wilt: it shall be thine!'
>   Oh, then I see
>   The life for me—
> Ipwergis-Pudding to consume,
> And drink the subtle Azzigoom!"

"Oo may leave off playing *now*, Sylvie. I can do the uvver tune much better wizout a compliment."

"He means 'without *accompaniment*,'" Sylvie whispered, smiling at my puzzled look: and she pretended to shut up the stops of the organ.

> *"The Badgers did not care to talk to Fish:*
>   *They did not dote on Herrings' songs:*
> *They never had experienced the dish*
>   *To which that name belongs:*
> *'And oh, to pinch their tails,' (this was their wish,)*
>   *'With tongs, yea, tongs, and tongs!'"*

I ought to mention that he marked the parenthesis, in the air, with his finger. It seemed to me a very good plan. You know there's no *sound* to represent it—any more than there is for a question.

Suppose you have said to your friend "You are better to-day," and that you want him to understand that you are asking him a *question,* what can be simpler than just to make a "?" in the air with your finger? He would understand you in a moment!

> *"'And are not these the Fish,' the Eldest sighed,*
>   *'Whose Mother dwells beneath the foam?'*
> *'They are the Fish!' the Second one replied.*
>   *'And they have left their home!'*
> *'Oh wicked Fish,' the Youngest Badger cried,*
>   *'To roam, yea, roam, and roam!'*

> *"Gently the Badgers trotted to the shore—*
>   *The sandy shore that fringed the bay:*
> *Each in his mouth a living Herring bore—*
>   *Those aged ones waxed gay:*
> *Clear rang their voices through the ocean's roar,*
>   *'Hooray, hooray, hooray!'"*

"So they all got safe home again," Bruno said, after waiting a minute to see if *I* had anything to say: he evidently felt that *some* remark ought to be made. And I couldn't help wishing there were some such rule in Society, at the conclusion of a song—that the singer *herself* should say the right thing, and not leave it to the audience. Suppose a young lady has just been warbling ('with a grating and uncertain sound') Shelley's exquisite lyric *'I arise from dreams of thee'*: how much nicer it would be, instead of *your* having to say "Oh, *thank* you, *thank* you!" for the young lady herself to remark, as she draws on her gloves, while the impassioned words *'Oh, press it to thine own, or it will break at last!'* are still ringing in your ears, "—but she wouldn't do it, you know. So it *did* break at last."

"And I *knew* it would!" she added quietly, as I started at the sudden crash of broken glass. "You've been holding it sideways for the last minute, and letting all the champagne run out! Were you asleep, I wonder? I'm *so* sorry my singing has such a narcotic effect!"

CHAPTER XVIII.

QUEER STREET, NUMBER FORTY.

LADY MURIEL was the speaker. And, for the moment, that was the only fact I could clearly realise. But how she came to be there—and how *I* came to be there—and how the glass of champagne came to be there—all these were questions which I felt it better to think out in silence, and not commit myself to any statement till I understood things a little more clearly.

'First accumulate a mass of Facts: and *then* construct a Theory.' *That,* I believe, is the true Scientific Method. I sat up, rubbed my eyes, and began to accumulate Facts.

A smooth grassy slope, bounded, at the upper end, by venerable ruins half buried in ivy, at the lower, by a stream seen through arching trees—a dozen gaily-dressed people, seated in little groups here and there—some open hampers—the *débris* of a picnic—such were the *Facts* accumulated by the Scientific Researcher. And now, what deep, far-reaching *Theory* was he to construct from them? The Researcher found himself at fault. Yet stay! One Fact had escaped his notice. While all the rest were grouped in twos and in threes, *Arthur* was alone: while all tongues were talking, *his* was silent: while all faces were gay, *his* was gloomy and despondent. Here was a *Fact* indeed! The Researcher felt that a *Theory* must be constructed without delay.

Lady Muriel had just risen and left the party. Could *that* be the cause of his despondency? The Theory hardly rose to the dignity of a Working Hypothesis. Clearly more Facts were needed.

The Researcher looked round him once more: and now the Facts accumulated in such bewildering profusion, that the Theory was lost among them. For Lady Muriel had gone to meet a strange gentleman, just visible in the distance: and now she was returning with him, both of them talking eagerly and joyfully, like old friends who have been long parted: and now she was moving from group to group, introducing the new hero of the hour: and he, young, tall, and handsome, moved gracefully at her side, with the erect bearing and firm tread of a soldier. Verily, the Theory looked gloomy for Arthur! His eye caught mine, and he crossed to me.

"He is very handsome," I said.

"Abominably handsome!" muttered Arthur: then smiled at his own bitter words. "Lucky no one heard me but you!"

"Doctor Forester," said Lady Muriel, who had just joined us, "let me introduce to you my cousin Eric Lindon—*Captain* Lindon, I should say."

Arthur shook off his ill-temper instantly and completely, as he rose and gave the young soldier his hand. "I have heard of you," he said. "I'm very glad to make the acquaintance of Lady Muriel's cousin."

"Yes, that's all I'm distinguished for, *as yet!*" said Eric (so we soon got to call him) with a winning smile. "And I doubt," glancing at Lady Muriel, "if it even amounts to a good-conduct-badge! But it's something to begin with."

"You must come to my father, Eric," said Lady Muriel. "I think he's wandering among the ruins." And the pair moved on.

The gloomy look returned to Arthur's face: and I could see it was only to distract his thoughts that he took his place at the side of the metaphysical young lady, and resumed their interrupted discussion.

"Talking of Herbert Spencer," he began, "do you really find no *logical* difficulty in regarding Nature as a process of involution, passing from definite coherent homogeneity to indefinite incoherent heterogeneity?"

Amused as I was at the ingenious jumble he had made of Spencer's words, I kept as grave a face as I could.

"No *physical* difficulty," she confidently replied: "but I haven't studied *Logic* much. Would you *state* the difficulty?"

"Well," said Arthur, "do you accept it as self-evident? Is it as obvious, for instance, as that 'things that are greater than the same are greater than one another'?"

"To *my* mind," she modestly replied, "it seems *quite* as obvious. I grasp *both* truths by intuition. But *other* minds may need some logical—I forget the technical terms."

"For a *complete* logical argument," Arthur began with admirable solemnity, "we need two prim Misses——"

"Of course!" she interrupted. "I remember that word now. And they produce——?"

"A Delusion," said Arthur.

"Ye—es?" she said dubiously. "I don't seem to remember that so well. But what is the *whole* argument called?"

"A Sillygism."

"Ah, yes! I remember now. But I don't need a Sillygism, you know, to prove that mathematical axiom you mentioned."

"Nor to prove that 'all angles are equal', I suppose?"

"Why, of course not! One takes such a simple truth as that for granted!"

Here I ventured to interpose, and to offer her a plate of strawberries and cream. I felt really uneasy at the thought that she *might* detect the trick: and I contrived, unperceived by her, to shake my head reprovingly at the pseudo-philosopher. Equally unperceived by her, Arthur slightly raised his shoulders, and spread his hands abroad, as who should say "What else can I say to her?" and moved away, leaving her to discuss her strawberries by 'involution,' or any other way she preferred.

By this time the carriages, that were to convey the revelers to their respective homes, had begun to assemble outside the Castle-grounds: and it became evident—now that Lady Muriel's cousin had joined our party—that the problem, how to convey five people to Elveston, with a carriage that would only hold four, must somehow be solved.

The Honourable Eric Lindon, who was at this moment walking up and down with Lady Muriel, might have solved it at once, no doubt, by announcing his intention of returning on foot. Of *this* solution there did not seem to be the very smallest probability.

The next best solution, it seemed to me, was that *I* should walk home: and this I at once proposed.

"You're sure you don't mind?" said the Earl. "I'm afraid the carriage won't take us all, and I don't like to suggest to Eric to desert his cousin so soon."

"So far from minding it," I said, "I should prefer it. It will give me time to sketch this beautiful old ruin."

"I'll keep you company," Arthur suddenly said. And, in answer to what I suppose was a look of surprise on my face, he said in a low voice, "I *really* would rather. I shall be quite *de trop* in the carriage!"

"I think I'll walk too," said the Earl. "You'll have to be content with *Eric* as your escort," he added, to Lady Muriel, who had joined us while he was speaking.

"You must be as entertaining as Cerberus—'three gentlemen rolled into one'—" Lady Muriel said to her companion. "It will be a grand military exploit!"

"A sort of Forlorn Hope?" the Captain modestly suggested.

"You *do* pay pretty compliments!" laughed his fair cousin. "Good day to you, gentlemen three—or rather deserters three!" And the two young folk entered the carriage and were driven away.

"How long will your sketch take?" said Arthur.

"Well," I said, "I should like an hour for it. Don't you think you had better go without me? I'll return by train. I know there's one in about an hour's time."

"Perhaps that *would* be best," said the Earl. "The Station is quite close."

So I was left to my own devices, and soon found a comfortable seat, at the foot of a tree, from which I had a good view of the ruins.

"It is a very drowsy day," I said to myself, idly turning over the leaves of the sketch-book to find a blank page. "Why, I thought you were a mile off by this time!" For, to my surprise, the two walkers were back again.

"I came back to remind you," Arthur said, "that the trains go every ten minutes——"

"Nonsense!" I said. "It isn't the Metropolitan Railway!"

"It *is* the Metropolitan Railway," the Earl insisted. "This is a part of Kensington."

"Why do you talk with your eyes shut?" said Arthur. "Wake up!"

"I think it's the heat makes me so drowsy," I said, hoping, but not feeling quite sure, that I was talking sense. "Am I awake now?"

"I think *not*," the Earl judicially pronounced. "What do *you* think, Doctor? He's only got one eye open!"

"And he's snoring like anything!" cried Bruno. "Do wake up, you dear old thing!" And he and Sylvie set to work, rolling the heavy head from side to side, as if its connection with the shoulders was a matter of no sort of importance.

And at last the Professor opened his eyes, and sat up, blinking at us with eyes of utter bewilderment. "Would you have the kindness to mention," he said, addressing me with his usual old-fashioned courtesy, "whereabouts we are just now—and *who* we are, beginning with me?"

I thought it best to begin with the children. "This is Sylvie, Sir; and *this* is Bruno."

"Ah, yes! I know *them* well enough!" the old man murmured. "It's *myself* I'm most anxious about. And perhaps you'll be good enough to mention, at the same time, how I got here?"

"A harder problem occurs to *me*," I ventured to say: "and that is, how you're to get back again."

"True, true!" the Professor replied. "That's *the* Problem, no doubt. Viewed *as* a Problem, outside of oneself, it is a *most* interesting one. Viewed as a portion of one's own biography, it is, I must admit, very distressing!" He groaned, but instantly added, with a chuckle, "As to *myself*, I think you mentioned that I am——"

"Oo're the *Professor!*" Bruno shouted in his ear. "Didn't oo know *that*? Oo've come from *Outland!* And it's *ever* so far away from here!"

The Professor leapt to his feet with the agility of a boy. "Then there's no time to lose!" he exclaimed anxiously. "I'll just ask this guileless peasant, with his brace of buckets that contain (apparently) water, if he'll be so kind as to direct us. Guileless peasant!" he proceeded in a louder voice. "Would you tell us the way to Outland?"

The guileless peasant turned with a sheepish grin. "Hey?" was all he said.

"The—way—to—Outland!" the Professor repeated.

The guileless peasant set down his buckets and considered. "Ah dunnot——"

"I ought to mention," the Professor hastily put in, "that whatever you say will be used in evidence against you."

The guileless peasant instantly resumed his buckets. "Then ah says nowt!" he answered briskly, and walked away at a great pace.

The children gazed sadly at the rapidly vanishing figure. "He goes very quick!" the Professor said with a sigh. "But I *know* that was the right thing to say. I've studied your English Laws. However, let's ask this next man that's coming. He is *not* guileless, and he is *not* a peasant—but I don't know that either point is of vital importance."

It was, in fact, the Honourable Eric Lindon, who had apparently fulfilled his task of escorting Lady Muriel home, and was now strolling leisurely up and down the road outside the house, enjoying a solitary cigar.

"Might I trouble you, Sir, to tell us the nearest way to Outland!" Oddity as he was, in outward appearance, the Professor was, in that essential nature which no outward disguise could conceal, a thorough gentleman.

And, as such, Eric Lindon accepted him instantly. He took the cigar from his mouth, and delicately shook off the ash, while he considered. "The name sounds strange to me," he said. "I doubt if I can help you."

"It is not *very* far from *Fairyland*," the Professor suggested.

Eric Lindon's eye-brows were slightly raised at these words, and an amused smile, which he courteously tried to repress, flitted across his handsome face. "A trifle *cracked!*" he muttered to himself. "But what a jolly old patriarch it is!" Then he turned to the children. "And ca'n't *you* help him, little folk?" he said, with a gentleness of tone that seemed to win their hearts at once. "Surely *you* know all about it?

> '*How many miles to Babylon?*
> *Three-score miles and ten.*
> *Can I get there by candlelight?*
> *Yes, and back again!*'"

To my surprise, Bruno ran forwards to him, as if he were some old friend of theirs, seized the disengaged hand and hung on to it with both of his own: and there stood this tall dignified officer in the middle of the road, gravely swinging a little boy to and fro, while Sylvie stood ready to push him, exactly as if a real swing had suddenly been provided for their pastime.

"We don't want to get to *Babylon*, oo know!" Bruno explained as he swung.

"And it isn't *candlelight:* it's *daylight!*" Sylvie added, giving the swing a push of extra vigour, which nearly took the whole machine off its balance.

By this time it was clear to me that Eric Lindon was quite unconscious of my presence. Even the Professor and the children seemed to have lost sight of me: and I stood in the midst of the group, as unconcernedly as a ghost, seeing but unseen.

"How perfectly isochronous!" the Professor exclaimed with enthusiasm. He had his watch in his hand, and was carefully counting Bruno's oscillations. "He measures time quite as accurately as a pendulum!"

"Yet even pendulums" the good-natured young soldier observed, as

he carefully released his hand from Bruno's grasp, "are not a joy *for ever!* Come, that's enough for one bout, little man! Next time we meet, you shall have another. Meanwhile you'd better take this old gentleman to Queer Street, Number——"

"*We'll* find it!" cried Bruno eagerly, as they dragged the Professor away.

"We are much indebted to you!" the Professor said, looking over his shoulder.

"Don't mention it!" replied the officer, raising his hat as a parting salute.

"*What* number did you say!" the Professor called from the distance.

The officer made a trumpet of his two hands. "Forty!" he shouted in stentorian tones. "And not *piano*, by any means!" he added to himself. "It's a mad world, my masters, a mad world!" He lit another cigar, and strolled on towards his hotel.

"What a lovely evening!" I said, joining him as he passed me.

"Lovely indeed," he said. "Where did *you* come from? Dropped from the clouds?"

"I'm strolling your way," I said; and no further explanation seemed necessary.

"Have a cigar?"

"Thanks: I'm not a smoker."

"Is there a Lunatic Asylum near here?"

"Not that I know of."

"Thought there might be. Met a lunatic just now. Queer old fish as ever I saw!"

And so, in friendly chat, we took our homeward ways, and wished each other 'good-night' at the door of his hotel.

Left to myself, I felt the 'eerie' feeling rush over me again, and saw, standing at the door of Number Forty, the three figures I knew so well.

"Then it's the wrong house?" Bruno was saying.

"No, no! It's the right *house,*" the Professor cheerfully replied: "but it's the wrong *street. That's* where we've made our mistake! Our best plan, now, will be to——"

It was over. The street was empty, Commonplace life was around me, and the 'eerie' feeling had fled.

CHAPTER XIX.

HOW TO MAKE A PHLIZZ.

THE week passed without any further communication with the 'Hall,' as Arthur was evidently fearful that we might 'wear out our welcome'; but when, on Sunday morning, we were setting out for church, I gladly agreed to his proposal to go round and enquire after the Earl, who was said to be unwell.

Eric, who was strolling in the garden, gave us a good report of the invalid, who was still in bed, with Lady Muriel in attendance.

"Are you coming with us to church?" I enquired.

"Thanks, no," he courteously replied. "It's not—exactly—in my line, you know. It's an excellent institution—for the *poor*. When I'm with my own folk, I go, just to set them an example. But I'm not known *here:* so I think I'll excuse myself sitting out a sermon. Country-preachers are always so dull!"

Arthur was silent till we were out of hearing. Then he said to himself, almost inaudibly, *"Where two or three are gathered together in my name, there am I in the midst of them."*

"Yes," I assented: "no doubt that *is* the principle on which church-going rests."

"And when he *does* go," he continued (our thoughts ran so much together, that our conversation was often slightly elliptical), "I suppose he repeats the words *'I believe in the Communion of Saints'?"*

But by this time we had reached the little church, into which a goodly stream of worshipers, consisting mainly of fishermen and their families, was flowing.

The service would have been pronounced by any modern æsthetic religionist—or religious æsthete, which is it?—to be crude and cold: to me, coming fresh from the ever-advancing developments of a London church under a *soi-disant* 'Catholic' Rector, it was unspeakably refreshing.

There was no theatrical procession of demure little choristers, trying their best not to simper under the admiring gaze of the congregation: the people's share in the service was taken by the people themselves, unaided, except that a few good voices, judiciously posted here and there among them, kept the singing from going too far astray.

There was no murdering of the noble music, contained in the Bible and the Liturgy, by its recital in a dead monotone, with no more expression than a mechanical talking-doll.

No, the prayers were *prayed,* the lessons were *read,* and—best of all—the sermon was *talked;* and I found myself repeating, as we left the church, the words of Jacob, when he *'awaked out of his sleep.'* "*'Surely the Lord is in this place! This is none other but the house of God, and this is the gate of heaven.'"*

"Yes," said Arthur, apparently in answer to my thoughts, "those 'high' services are fast becoming pure Formalism. More and more the people are beginning to regard them as 'performances,' in which they only 'assist' in the French sense. And it is *specially* bad for the little boys. They'd be much less self-conscious as pantomime-fairies. With all that dressing-up, and stagy-entrances and exits, and being always *en evidence,* no wonder if they're eaten up with vanity, the blatant little coxcombs!"

When we passed the Hall on our return, we found the Earl and Lady Muriel sitting out in the garden. Eric had gone for a stroll.

We joined them, and the conversation soon turned on the sermon we had just heard, the subject of which was 'selfishness.'

"What a change has come over our pulpits," Arthur remarked, "since the time when Paley gave that utterly selfish definition of virtue, *'the doing good to mankind, in obedience to the will of God, and for the sake of everlasting happiness'!"*

Lady Muriel looked at him enquiringly, but she seemed to have learned by intuition, what years of experience had taught *me,* that the way to elicit Arthur's deepest thoughts was neither to assent nor dissent, but simply to *listen.*

"At that time," he went on, "a great tidal wave of selfishness was sweeping over human thought. Right and Wrong had somehow been transformed into Gain and Loss, and Religion had become a sort of commercial transaction. We may be thankful that our preachers are beginning to take a nobler view of life."

"But is it not taught again and again in the *Bible?"* I ventured to ask.

"Not in the Bible as a *whole,"* said Arthur. "In the Old Testament, no doubt, rewards and punishments are constantly appealed to as motives for action. That teaching is best for *children,* and the Israelites seem to have been, mentally, *utter* children. We guide our children thus, at first: but we appeal, as soon as possible, to their innate sense of Right and Wrong: and, when *that* stage is safely past, we appeal to the highest motive of all, the desire for likeness to, and union with, the Supreme Good. I think you will find that to be the teaching of the Bible, *as a whole,* beginning with *'that thy days may be long in the land,'* and ending with *'be ye perfect, even as your Father which is in heaven is perfect.'"*

We were silent for awhile, and then Arthur went off on another tack. "Look at the literature of Hymns, now. How cankered it is, through and through, with selfishness! There are few human compositions more utterly degraded than some modern Hymns!"

I quoted the stanza

> *"Whatever, Lord, we lend to Thee,*
> *Repaid a thousandfold shall be,*
> *Then gladly will we give to Thee,*
> *Giver of all!"*

"Yes," he said grimly: "that is the typical stanza. And the very last charity-sermon I heard was infected with it. After giving many good reasons for charity, the preacher wound up with 'and, for all you give, you will be repaid a thousandfold!' Oh the utter meanness of such a motive, to be put before men who *do* know what self-sacrifice is, who *can* appreciate generosity and heroism! Talk of Original *Sin!"* he went on with increasing bitterness. "Can you have a stronger proof of the Original Goodness there must be in this nation, than the fact that Religion has been preached to us, as a commercial speculation, for a century, and that we still believe in a God?"

"It couldn't have gone on so long," Lady Muriel musingly remarked, "if the Opposition hadn't been practically silenced—put under what the French call *la clôture.* Surely in any lecture-hall, or in private society, such teaching would soon have been hooted down?"

"I trust so," said Arthur: "and, though I don't want to see 'brawling in church' legalised, I must say that our preachers enjoy an *enormous* privilege—which they ill deserve, and which they misuse terribly. We put our man into a pulpit, and we virtually tell him 'Now, you may stand there and talk to us for half-an-hour. We won't interrupt you by so much as a *word!* You shall have it all your own way!' And what does he give us in return? Shallow twaddle, that, if it were addressed to you over a dinner-table, you would think 'Does the man take me for a *fool?'* "

The return of Eric from his walk checked the tide of Arthur's eloquence, and, after a few minutes' talk on more conventional topics, we took our leave. Lady Muriel walked with us to the gate. "You have given me much to think about," she said earnestly, as she gave Arthur her hand. "I'm so glad you came in!" And her words brought a real glow of pleasure into that pale worn face of his.

On the Tuesday, as Arthur did not seem equal to more walking, I took a long stroll by myself, having stipulated that he was not to give the *whole* day to his books, but was to meet me at the Hall at about tea-time. On my way back, I passed the Station just as the afternoon-train came in sight, and sauntered down the stairs to see it come in. But there was little to gratify my idle curiosity: and, when the train was empty, and the platform clear, I found it was about time to be moving on, if I meant to reach the Hall by five.

As I approached the end of the platform, from which a steep irregular wooden staircase conducted to the upper world, I noticed two passengers, who had evidently arrived by the train, but who, oddly enough, had entirely escaped my notice, though the arrivals had been so few. They were a young woman and a little girl: the former, so far as one could judge by appearances, was a nursemaid, or possibly a nursery-governess, in attendance on the child, whose refined face, even more than her dress, distinguished her as of a higher class than her companion.

The child's face was refined, but it was also a worn and sad one, and told a tale (or so I seemed to read it) of much illness and suffering, sweetly and patiently borne. She had a little crutch to help herself along with: and she was now standing, looking wistfully up the long staircase, and apparently waiting till she could muster courage to begin the toilsome ascent.

There are some things one *says* in life—as well as things one *does*—which come automatically, by *reflex action,* as the physiologists say (meaning, no doubt, action *without* reflection, just as *lucus* is said to be derived 'a non lucendo'). Closing one's eyelids, when something seems to be flying into the eye, is one of those actions, and saying "May I carry the little girl up the stairs?" was another. It wasn't that any thought of offering help occurred to me, and that *then* I spoke: the first intimation I had, of being likely to make that offer, was the sound of my own voice, and the discovery that the offer had been made. The servant paused, doubtfully glancing from her charge to me, and then back again to the child. "Would you like it, dear?" she asked her. But no such doubt appeared to cross the child's mind: she lifted her arms eagerly to be taken up. ".Please!" was all she said, while a faint smile flickered on the weary little face. I took her up with scrupulous care, and her little arm was at once clasped trustfully round my neck.

She was a *very* light weight—so light, in fact, that the ridiculous idea crossed my mind that it was rather easier going up, with her in my arms, than it would have been without her: and, when we reached the road above, with its cart-ruts and loose stones—all formidable obstacles for a lame child—I found that I had said "I'd better carry her over this rough place," before I had formed any *mental* connection between its roughness and my gentle little burden. "Indeed it's troubling you too much, Sir!" the maid exclaimed. "She can walk very well on the flat." But the arm, that was twined about my neck, clung just an atom more closely at the suggestion, and decided me to say "She's no weight, really. I'll carry her a little further. I'm going your way."

The nurse raised no further objection: and the next speaker was a ragged little boy, with bare feet, and a broom over his shoulder, who ran across the road, and pretended to sweep the perfectly dry road in front of us. "Give us a 'ap'ny!" the little urchin pleaded, with a broad grin on his dirty face.

"*Don't* give him a 'ap'ny!" said the little lady in my arms. The *words* sounded harsh: but the *tone* was gentleness itself. "He's an *idle* little boy!" And she laughed a laugh of such silvery sweetness as I had never yet heard from any lips but Sylvie's. To my astonishment, the boy actually *joined* in the laugh, as if there were some subtle sympathy between them, as he ran away down the road and vanished through a gap in the hedge.

But he was back in a few moments, having discarded his broom and provided himself, from some mysterious source, with an exquisite bouquet of flowers. "Buy a posy, buy a posy! Only a 'ap'ny!" he chanted, with the melancholy drawl of a professional beggar.

"*Don't* buy it!" was Her Majesty's edict as she looked down, with a lofty

scorn that seemed curiously mixed with tender interest, on the ragged creature at her feet.

But this time I turned rebel, and ignored the royal commands. Such lovely flowers, and of forms so entirely new to me, were not to be abandoned at the bidding of any little maid, however imperious. I bought the bouquet: and the little boy, after popping the halfpenny into his mouth, turned head-over-heels, as if to ascertain whether the human mouth is really adapted to serve as a money-box.

With wonder, that increased every moment, I turned over the flowers, and examined them one by one: there was not a single one among them that I could remember having ever seen before. At last I turned to the nursemaid. "Do these flowers grow wild about here? never saw——" but the speech died away on my lips. The nursemaid had vanished!

"You can put me down, *now*, if you like," Sylvie quietly remarked.

I obeyed in silence, and could only ask myself "Is this a *dream?*", on finding Sylvie and Bruno walking one on either side of me, and clinging to my hands with the ready confidence of childhood.

"You're larger than when I saw you last!" I began. "Really I think we ought to be introduced again! There's so much of you that I never met before, you know."

"Very well!" Sylvie merrily replied. "This is *Bruno*. It doesn't take long. He's only got one name!"

"There's *another* name to me!" Bruno protested, with a reproachful look at the Mistress of the Ceremonies. "And it's—'*Esquire*'!"

"Oh, of course. I forgot," said Sylvie. "Bruno—*Esquire!*"

"And did you come here to meet *me,* my children?" I enquired.

"You know I said we'd come on Tuesday," Sylvie explained. "Are we the proper size for common children?"

"Quite the right size for *children,*" I replied, (adding mentally "though not *common* children, by any means!") "But what became of the nursemaid?"

"It are *gone!*" Bruno solemnly replied.

"Then it wasn't solid, like Sylvie and you?"

"No. Oo couldn't *touch* it, oo know. If oo walked *at* it, oo'd go right froo!"

"I quite expected you'd find it out, once," said Sylvie. "Bruno ran it against a telegraph post, by accident. And it went in two halves. But you were looking the other way."

I felt that I had indeed missed an opportunity: to witness such an event as a nursemaid going 'in two halves' does not occur twice in a lifetime!

"When did oo guess it were Sylvie?" Bruno enquired.

"I didn't guess it, till it *was* Sylvie, I said. "But how did you manage the nursemaid?"

"*Bruno* managed it," said Sylvie. "It's called a Phlizz."

"And how do you make a Phlizz, Bruno?"

"The Professor teached me how," said Bruno. "First oo takes a lot of air——"

"Oh, *Bruno!*" Sylvie interposed. "The Professor said you weren't to tell!"

"But who did her *voice?*" I asked.

"Indeed it's troubling you too much, Sir! She can walk very well on the flat."

Bruno laughed merrily as I turned hastily from side to side, looking in all directions for the speaker. "That were *me!*" he gleefully proclaimed, in his own voice.

"She can indeed walk very well on the flat," I said. "And I think *I* was the Flat."

By this time we were near the Hall. "This is where my friends live," I said. "Will you come in and have some tea with them?"

Bruno gave a little jump of joy: and Sylvie said "Yes, please. You'd like some tea, Bruno, wouldn't you? He hasn't tasted *tea,*" she explained to me, "since we left Outland."

"And *that* weren't *good* tea!" said Bruno. "It were so *welly* weak!"

CHAPTER XX.

LIGHT COME, LIGHT GO.

LADY MURIEL'S smile of welcome could not *quite* conceal the look of surprise with which she regarded my new companions.

I presented them in due form. "This is *Sylvie,* Lady Muriel. And this is *Bruno.*"

"Any surname?" she enquired, her eyes twinkling with fun.

"No," I said gravely. "No surname."

She laughed, evidently thinking I said it in fun; and stooped to kiss the children—a salute to which *Bruno* submitted with reluctance: *Sylvie* returned it with interest.

While she and Arthur (who had arrived before me) supplied the children with tea and cake, I tried to engage the Earl in conversation: but he was restless and *distrait,* and we made little progress. At last, by a sudden question, he betrayed the cause of his disquiet.

"*Would* you let me look at those flowers you have in your hand?"

"Willingly!" I said, handing him the bouquet. Botany was, I knew, a favourite study of his: and these flowers were to me so entirely new and mysterious, that I was really curious to see what a botanist would say of them.

They did *not* diminish his disquiet. On the contrary, he became every moment more excited as he turned them over. "*These* are all from Central India!" he said, laying aside part of the bouquet. "They are rare, even there: and I have never seen them in any other part of the world. *These* two are Mexican—*This* one—" (He rose hastily, and carried it to the window, to examine it in a better light, the flush of excitement mounting to his very forehead) "—is, I am nearly sure—but I have a book of Indian Botany here—" He took a volume from the book-shelves, and turned the leaves with trembling fingers. "Yes! Compare it with this picture! It is the exact duplicate! This is the flower of the Upastree, which usually grows only in the depths of forests; and the flower fades so quickly after being plucked, that it is scarcely possible to keep its form or colour even so far as the outskirts of the forest! Yet this is in full bloom! *Where* did you get these flowers?" he added with breathless eagerness.

I glanced at Sylvie, who, gravely and silently, laid her finger on her lips, then beckoned to Bruno to follow her, and ran out into the garden; and I found myself in the position of a defendant whose two most important witnesses have been suddenly taken away. "Let me give you the flowers!" I stammered out at last, quite 'at my wit's end' as to how to get out of the difficulty. "You know much more about them than I do!"

"I accept them most gratefully! But you have not yet told me—" the

Earl was beginning, when we were interrupted, to my great relief, by the arrival of Eric Lindon.

To *Arthur,* however, the new-comer was, I saw clearly, anything but welcome. His face clouded over: he drew a little back from the circle, and took no further part in the conversation, which was wholly maintained, for some minutes, by Lady Muriel and her lively cousin, who were discussing some new music that had just arrived from London.

"Do just try this one!" he pleaded. "The music looks easy to sing at sight, and the song's quite appropriate to the occasion."

"Then I suppose it's

> *'Five o'clock tea!*
> *Ever to thee*
> *Faithful I'll be,*
> *Five o'clock tea!'* "

laughed Lady Muriel, as she sat down to the piano, and lightly struck a few random chords.

"Not quite: and yet it *is* a kind of 'ever to thee faithful I'll be!' It's a pair of hapless lovers: *he* crosses the briny deep: and *she* is left lamenting."

"That is *indeed* appropriate!" she replied mockingly, as he placed the song before her. "And am *I* to do the lamenting? And who for, if you please?"

She played the air once or twice through, first in quick, and finally in slow, time; and then gave us the whole song with as much graceful ease as if she had been familiar with it all her life:—

> *"He stept so lightly to the land,*
> *All in his manly pride:*
> *He kissed her cheek, he pressed her hand,*
> *Yet still she glanced aside.*
> *'Too gay he seems,' she darkly dreams,*
> *'Too gallant and too gay*
> *To think of me—poor simple me—*
> *When he is far away!'*
>
> *'I bring my Love this goodly pearl*
> *Across the seas,' he said:*
> *'A gem to deck the dearest girl*
> *That ever sailor wed!'*
> *She clasps it tight: her eyes are bright:*
> *Her throbbing heart would say*
> *'He thought of me—he thought of me—*
> *When he was far away!'*
>
> *The ship has sailed into the West:*
> *Her ocean-bird is flown:*
> *A dull dead pain is in her breast,*
> *And she is weak and lone:*

Yet there's a smile upon her face,
  A smile that seems to say
'He'll think of me—he'll think of me—
  When he is far away!

'Though waters wide between us glide,
  Our lives are warm and near:
No distance parts two faithful hearts—
  Two hearts that love so dear:
And I will trust my sailor-lad,
  For ever and a day,
To think of me—to think of me—
  When he is far away!' "

The look of displeasure, which had begun to come over Arthur's face when the young Captain spoke of Love so lightly, faded away as the song proceeded, and he listened with evident delight. But his face darkened again when Eric demurely remarked "Don't you think 'my *soldier*-lad' would have fitted the tune just as well!"

"Why, so it would!" Lady Muriel gaily retorted. "Soldiers, sailors, tinkers, tailors, what a lot of words would fit in! I think 'my *tinker*-lad' sounds best. Don't *you?*"

To spare my friend further pain, I rose to go, just as the Earl was beginning to repeat his particularly embarrassing question about the flowers.

"You have not yet——"

"Yes, I've *had* some tea, thank you!" I hastily interrupted him. "And now we really *must* be going. Good evening, Lady Muriel!" And we made our adieux, and escaped, while the Earl was still absorbed in examining the mysterious bouquet.

Lady Muriel accompanied us to the door. "You *couldn't* have given my father a more acceptable present!" she said, warmly. "He is so passionately fond of Botany. I'm afraid *I* know nothing of the *theory* of it, but I keep his *Hortus Siccus* in order. I must get some sheets of blotting-paper, and dry these new treasures for him before they fade."

"*That* won't be no good at all!" said Bruno, who was waiting for us in the garden.

"Why won't it?" said I. "You know I *had* to give the flowers, to stop questions."

"Yes, it ca'n't be helped," said Sylvie: "but they *will* be sorry when they find them gone!"

"But how will they go?"

"Well, I don't know *how*. But they *will* go. The nosegay was only a *Phlizz*, you know. Bruno made it up."

These last words were in a whisper, as she evidently did not wish Arthur to hear. But of this there seemed to be little risk: he hardly seemed to notice the children, but paced on, silent and abstracted; and when, at the entrance to the wood, they bid us a hasty farewell and ran off, he seemed to wake out of a day-dream.

The bouquet vanished, as Sylvie had predicted; and when, a day or two afterwards, Arthur and I once more visited the Hall, we found the Earl and his daughter, with the old housekeeper, out in the garden, examining the fastenings of the drawing-room window.

"We are holding an Inquest," Lady Muriel said, advancing to meet us: "and we admit you, as Accessories before the Fact, to tell us all you know about those flowers."

"The Accessories before the Fact decline to answer *any* questions," I gravely replied. "And they reserve their defence."

"Well then, turn Queen's Evidence, please! The flowers have disappeared in the night," she went on, turning to Arthur, "and we are *quite* sure no one in the house has meddled with them. Somebody must have entered by the window——"

"But the fastenings have not been tampered with," said the Earl.

"It must have been while you were dining, my Lady," said the housekeeper.

"That was it," said the Earl. "The thief must have seen you bring the flowers," turning to me, "and have noticed that you did *not* take them away. And he must have known their great value—they are simply *priceless!*" he exclaimed, in sudden excitement.

"And you never told us how you got them!" said Lady Muriel.

"Some day," I stammered, "I may be free to tell you. Just now, would you excuse me?"

The Earl looked disappointed, but kindly said "Very well, we will ask no questions."

"But we consider you a *very* bad Queen's Evidence," Lady Muriel added playfully, as we entered the arbour. "We pronounce you to be an accomplice: and we sentence you to solitary confinement, and to be fed on bread and—butter. Do you take sugar?"

"It is disquieting, certainly," she resumed, when all 'creature-comforts' had been duly supplied, "to find that the house has been entered by a thief—in this out-of-the-way place. If only the flowers had been *eatables*, one might have suspected a thief of quite another shape——"

"You mean that universal explanation for all mysterious disappearances, 'the *cat* did it'?" said Arthur.

"Yes," she replied. "What a convenient thing it would be if all thieves had the same shape! It's so confusing to have some of them quadrupeds and others bipeds!"

"It has occurred to me," said Arthur, "as a curious problem in Teleology—the Science of Final Causes," he added, in answer to an enquiring look from Lady Muriel.

"And a Final Cause is——?"

"Well, suppose we say—the last of a series of connected events—each of the series being the cause of the next—for whose sake the first event takes place."

"But the last event is practically an *effect* of the first, isn't it? And yet you call it a *cause* of it!"

Arthur pondered a moment. "The words are rather confusing, I grant

you," he said. "Will this do? The last event is an effect of the first: but the *necessity* for that event is a cause of the *necessity* for the first."

"That seems clear enough," said Lady Muriel. "Now let us have the problem."

"It's merely this. What object can we imagine in the arrangement by which each different size (roughly speaking) of living creatures has its special shape? For instance, the human race has one kind of shape—bipeds. Another set, ranging from the lion to the mouse, are quadrupeds. Go down a step or two further, and you come to insects with six legs—hexapods—a beautiful name, is it not? But beauty, in our sense of the word, seems to diminish as we go down: the creature becomes more—I won't say 'ugly' of any of God's creatures—more uncouth. And, when we take the microscope, and go a few steps lower still, we come upon animalculæ, terribly uncouth, and with a terrible number of legs!"

"The other alternative," said the Earl, "would be a *diminuendo* series of repetitions of the same type. Never mind the monotony of it: let's see how it would work in other ways. Begin with the race of men, and the creatures they require: let us say horses, cattle, sheep, and dogs—we don't exactly require frogs and spiders, do we, Muriel?"

Lady Muriel shuddered perceptibly: it was evidently a painful subject. "We can dispense with *them*," she said gravely.

"Well, then we'll have a second race of men, half-a-yard high——"

"—who would have *one* source of exquisite enjoyment, not possessed by ordinary men!" Arthur interrupted.

"*What* source?" said the Earl.

"Why, the grandeur of scenery! Surely the grandeur of a mountain, to *me*, depends on its *size*, relative to me? Double the height of the mountain, and of course it's twice as grand. Halve *my* height, and you produce the same effect."

"Happy, happy, happy Small!" Lady Muriel murmured rapturously. "None but the Short, none but the Short, none but the Short enjoy the Tall!"

"But let me go on," said the Earl. "We'll have a third race of men, five inches high; a fourth race, an inch high——"

"They couldn't eat common beef and mutton, I'm sure!" Lady Muriel interrupted.

"True, my child, I was forgetting. Each set must have its own cattle and sheep."

"And its own vegetation," I added. "What could a cow, an inch high, do with grass that waved far above its head?"

"That is true. We must have a pasture within a pasture, so to speak. The common grass would serve our inch-high cows as a green forest of palms, while round the root of each tall stem would stretch a tiny carpet of microscopic grass. Yes, I think our scheme will work fairly well. And it would be very interesting, coming into contact with the races below us. What sweet little things the inch-high bull-dogs would be! I doubt if even *Muriel* would run away from one of them!"

"Don't you think we ought to have a *crescendo* series, as well?" said

Lady Muriel. "Only fancy being a hundred yards high! One could use an elephant as a paper-weight, and a crocodile as a pair of scissors!"

"And would you have races of different sizes communicate with one another?" I enquired. "Would they make war on one another, for instance, or enter into treaties?"

"*War* we must exclude, I think. When you could crush a whole nation with one blow of your fist, you couldn't conduct war on equal terms. But anything, involving a collision of *minds* only, would be possible in our ideal world—for of course we must allow *mental* powers to all, irrespective of size. Perhaps the fairest rule would be that, the *smaller* the race, the *greater* should be its intellectual development!"

"Do you mean to say," said Lady Muriel, "that these manikins of an inch high are to *argue* with me?"

"Surely, surely!" said the Earl. "An argument doesn't depend for its logical force on the *size* of the creature that utters it!"

She tossed her head indignantly. "I would *not* argue with any man less than six inches high!" she cried. "I'd make him *work!*"

"What at?" said Arthur, listening to all this nonsense with an amused smile.

"*Embroidery!*" she readily replied. "What *lovely* embroidery they would do!"

"Yet, if they did it wrong," I said, "you couldn't *argue* the question. I don't know *why:* but I agree that it couldn't be done."

"The reason is," said Lady Muriel, "one couldn't sacrifice one's *dignity* so far."

"Of course one couldn't!" echoed Arthur. "Any more than one could argue with a potato. It would be altogether—excuse the ancient pun—*infra dig.!*"

"I doubt it," said I. "Even a pun doesn't *quite* convince me."

"Well, if that is *not* the reason," said Lady Muriel, "what reason would you give?"

I tried hard to understand the meaning of this question: but the persistent humming of the bees confused me, and there was a drowsiness in the air that made every thought stop and go to sleep before it had got well thought out: so all I could say was "That must depend on the *weight* of the potato."

I felt the remark was not so sensible as I should have liked it to be. But Lady Muriel seemed to take it quite as a matter of course. "In that case—" she began, but suddenly started, and turned away to listen. "Don't you hear him?" she said. "He's crying. We must go to him, somehow."

And I said to myself "That's very strange! I quite thought it was *Lady Muriel* talking to me. Why, it's *Sylvie* all the while!" And I made another great effort to say something that should have some meaning in it. "Is it about the potato?"

CHAPTER XXI.

THROUGH THE IVORY DOOR.

"I DON'T know," said Sylvie. "Hush! I must think. I could go to him, by myself, well enough. But I want *you* to come too."

"Let me go with you," I pleaded. "I can walk as fast as *you* can, I'm sure."

Sylvie laughed merrily. "What nonsense!" she cried. "Why, you ca'n't walk a bit! You're lying quite flat on your back! You don't understand these things."

"I can walk as well as *you* can," I repeated. And I tried my best to walk a few steps: but the ground slipped away backwards, quite as fast as I could walk, so that I made no progress at all. Sylvie laughed again.

"There, I told you so! You've no idea how funny you look, moving your feet about in the air, as if you were walking! Wait a bit. I'll ask the Professor what we'd better do." And she knocked at his study-door.

The door opened, and the Professor looked out. "What's that crying I heard just now?" he asked. "Is it a human animal?"

"It's a boy," Sylvie said.

"I'm afraid you've been teasing him?"

"No, *indeed* I haven't!" Sylvie said, very earnestly. "I *never* tease him!"

"Well, I must ask the Other Professor about it." He went back into the study, and we heard him whispering "small human animal—says she hasn't been teasing him—the kind that's called Boy——"

"Ask her *which* Boy," said a new voice. The Professor came out again. "*Which* Boy is it that you haven't been teasing?"

Sylvie looked at me with twinkling eyes. "You dear old thing!" she exclaimed, standing on tiptoe to kiss him, while he gravely stooped to receive the salute. "How you *do* puzzle me! Why, there are *several* boys I haven't been teasing!"

The Professor returned to his friend: and this time the voice said "Tell her to bring them here—*all* of them!"

"I ca'n't, and I wo'n't!" Sylvie exclaimed, the moment he reappeared. "It's *Bruno* that's crying: and he's my brother: and, please, we *both* want to go: he ca'n't walk, you know: he's—he's *dreaming*, you know" (this in a whisper, for fear of hurting my feelings). "*Do* let's go through the Ivory Door!"

"I'll ask him," said the Professor, disappearing again. He returned directly. "He says you may. Follow me, and walk on tip-toe."

The difficulty with me would have been, just then, *not* to walk on tip-toe. It seemed very hard to reach down far enough to just touch the floor, as Sylvie led me through the study.

The Professor went before us to unlock the Ivory Door. I had just time to glance at the Other Professor, who was sitting reading, with his back to us, before the Professor showed us out through the door, and locked it behind us. Bruno was standing with his hands over his face, crying bitterly.

"What's the matter, darling?" said Sylvie, with her arms round his neck.

"Hurted mine self *welly* much!" sobbed the poor little fellow.

"I'm *so* sorry, darling! How ever *did* you manage to hurt yourself so?"

"Course I managed it!" said Bruno, laughing through his tears. "Doos oo think nobody else but *oo* ca'n't manage things?"

Matters were looking distinctly brighter, now Bruno had begun to argue. "Come, let's hear all about it!" I said.

"My foot took it into its head to slip——" Bruno began.

"A foot hasn't got a head!" Sylvie put in, but all in vain.

"I slipted down the bank. And I tripted over a stone. And the stone hurted my foot! And I trod on a Bee. And the Bee stinged my finger!" Poor Bruno sobbed again. The complete list of woes was too much for his feelings. "And it knewed I didn't *mean* to trod on it!" he added, as the climax.

"That Bee should be ashamed of itself!" I said severely, and Sylvie hugged and kissed the wounded hero till all tears were dried.

"My finger's quite unstung now!" said Bruno. "Why doos there be stones? Mister Sir, doos oo know?"

"They're good for *something*," I said: "even if we don't know *what*. What's the good of *dandelions*, now?"

"Dindledums?" said Bruno. "Oh, they're ever so pretty! And stones aren't pretty, one bit. Would oo like some dindledums, Mister Sir?"

"Bruno!" Sylvie murmured reproachfully. "You mustn't say 'Mister' and 'Sir,' both at once! Remember what I told you!"

"You told me I were to say 'Mister' when I spoked *about* him, and I were to say 'Sir' when I spoked *to* him!"

"Well, you're not doing *both*, you know."

"Ah, but I *is* doing bofe, Miss Praticular!" Bruno exclaimed triumphantly. "I wishted to speak *about* the Gemplun—and I wishted to speak *to* the Gemplun. So a course I said 'Mister Sir'!"

"That's all right, Bruno," I said.

"*Course* it's all right!" said Bruno. "Sylvie just knows nuffin at all!"

"There never *was* an impertinenter boy!" said Sylvie, frowning till her bright eyes were nearly invisible.

"And there never was an ignoranter girl!" retorted Bruno. "Come along and pick some dindledums. *That's all she's fit for!*" he added in a very loud whisper to me.

"But why do you say 'Dindledums,' Bruno? *Dandelions* is the right word."

"It's because he jumps about so," Sylvie said, laughing.

"Yes, that's it," Bruno assented. "Sylvie tells me the words, and then, when I jump about, they get shooken up in my head—till they're all froth!"

I expressed myself as perfectly satisfied with this explanation. "But aren't you going to pick me any dindledums, after all?"

"Course we will!" cried Bruno. "Come along, Sylvie!" And the happy children raced away, bounding over the turf with the fleetness and grace of young antelopes.

"Then you didn't find your way back to Outland?" I said to the Professor.

"Oh yes, I did!" he replied, "We never got to Queer Street; but I found another way. I've been backwards and forwards several times since then. I had to be present at the Election, you know, as the author of the new Money-Act. The Emperor was so kind as to wish that *I* should have the credit of it. 'Let come what come may,' (I remember the very words of the Imperial Speech) 'if it *should* turn out that the Warden *is* alive, *you* will bear witness that the change in the coinage is the *Professor's* doing, not *mine!*' I never was so glorified in my life, before!" Tears trickled down his cheeks at the recollection, which apparently was not *wholly* a pleasant one.

"Is the Warden supposed to be *dead?*"

"Well, it's *supposed* so: but, mind you, *I* don't believe it! The evidence is *very* weak—mere hear-say. A wandering Jester, with a Dancing-Bear (they found their way into the Palace, one day) has been telling people he comes from Fairyland, and that the Warden died there. *I* wanted the Vice-Warden to question him, but, most unluckily, he and my Lady were always out walking when the Jester came round. Yes, the Warden's supposed to be dead!" And more tears trickled down the old man's cheeks.

"But what is the new Money-Act?"

The Professor brightened up again. "The Emperor started the thing," he said. "He wanted to make everybody in Outland twice as rich as he was before—just to make the new Government popular. Only there wasn't nearly enough money in the Treasury to do it. So *I* suggested that he might do it by doubling the value of every coin and bank-note in Outland. It's the simplest thing possible. I wonder nobody ever thought of it before! And you never saw such universal joy. The shops are full from morning to night. Everybody's buying everything!"

"And how was the glorifying done?"

A sudden gloom overcast the Professor's jolly face. "They did it as I went home after the Election," he mournfully replied. "It was kindly meant—but I didn't like it! They waved flags all round me till I was nearly blind: and they rang bells till I was nearly deaf: and they strewed the road so thick with flowers that I lost my way!" And the poor old man sighed deeply.

"How far is it to Outland?" I asked, to change the subject.

"About five days' march. But one *must* go back—occasionally. You see, as Court-Professor, I have to be *always* in attendance on Prince Uggug. The Empress would be *very* angry if I left him, even for an hour."

"But surely, every time you come here, you are absent ten days, at least?"

"Oh, more than that!" the Professor exclaimed. "A fortnight, sometimes. But of course I keep a memorandum of the exact time when I started, so that I can put the Court-time back to the very moment!"

"Excuse me," I said. "I don't understand."

Silently the Professor drew from his pocket a square gold watch, with six or eight hands, and held it out for my inspection. "This," he began, "is an Outlandish Watch——"

"So I should have thought."

"—which has the peculiar property that, instead of *its* going with the *time*, the *time* goes with *it*. I trust you understand me now?"

"Hardly," I said.

"Permit me to explain. So long as it is let alone, it takes its own course. Time has *no* effect upon it."

"I have known such watches," I remarked.

"It *goes*, of course, at the usual rate. Only the time has to go *with* it. Hence, if I move the hands, I change the time. To move them *forwards*, in *advance* of the true time, is impossible: but I can move them as much as a month *backwards*—that is the limit. And then you have the events all over again—with any alterations experience may suggest."

"*What* a blessing such a watch would be," I thought, "in real life! To be able to unsay some heedless word—to undo some reckless deed! Might I see the thing done?"

"With pleasure!" said the good natured Professor. "When I move *this* hand back to *here*," pointing out the place, "History goes back fifteen minutes!"

Trembling with excitement, I watched him push the hand round as he described.

"Hurted mine self *welly* much!"

Shrilly and suddenly the words rang in my ears, and, more startled than I cared to show, I turned to look for the speaker.

Yes! There was Bruno, standing with the tears running down his cheeks, just as I had seen him a quarter of an hour ago; and there was Sylvie with her arms round his neck!

I had not the heart to make the dear little fellow go through his troubles a second time, so hastily begged the Professor to push the hands round into their former position. In a moment Sylvie and Bruno were gone again, and I could just see them in the far distance, picking 'dindledums.'

"Wonderful, indeed!" I exclaimed.

"It has another property, yet more wonderful," said the Professor. "You see this little peg? That is called the 'Reversal Peg.' If you push it in, the events of the next hour happen in the reverse order. Do not try it now. I will lend you the Watch for a few days, and you can amuse yourself with experiments."

"Thank you very much!" I said as he gave me the Watch. "I'll take the greatest care of it—why, here are the children again!"

"We could only but find *six* dindledums," said Bruno, putting them into my hands, " 'cause Sylvie said it were time to go back. And here's a big blackberry for *ooself!* We couldn't only find but *two!*"

"Thank you: it's *very* nice," I said. And I suppose *you* ate the other, Bruno?"

"No, I didn't," Bruno said, carelessly."*Aren't* they pretty dindledums, Mister Sir?"

"Yes very: but what makes you limp so, my child?"

"Mine foot's come *hurted* again!" Bruno mournfully replied. And he sat down on the ground, and began nursing it.

The Professor held his head between his hands—an attitude that I knew indicated distraction of mind. "Better rest a minute," he said. "It may be better then—or it may be worse. If only I had some of my medicines here! I'm Court-Physician, you know," he added, aside to me.

"Shall I go and get you some blackberries, darling?" Sylvie whispered, with her arms round his neck; and she kissed away a tear that was trickling down his cheek.

Bruno brightened up in a moment. "That *are* a good plan!" he exclaimed. "I thinks my foot would come *quite* unhurted, if I eated a blackberry— two or three blackberries—six or seven blackberries—"

Sylvie got up hastily. "I'd better go," she said, aside to me, "before he gets into the double figures!"

"Let me come and help you," I said. "I can reach higher up than you can."

"Yes, please," said Sylvie, putting her hand into mine: and we walked off together.

"Bruno *loves* blackberries," she said, as we paced slowly along by a tall hedge, that looked a promising place for them, "and it was so *sweet* of him to make me eat the only one!"

"Oh, it was *you* that ate it, then? Bruno didn't seem to like to tell me about it."

"No; I saw that," said Sylvie. "He's always afraid of being praised. But he *made* me eat it, really! I would much rather he—oh, what's that?" And she clung to my hand, half-frightened, as we came in sight of a hare, lying on its side with legs stretched out, just in the entrance to the wood.

"It's a *hare,* my child. Perhaps it's asleep."

"No, it isn't asleep," Sylvie said, timidly going nearer to look at it: "it's eyes are open. Is it—is it—" her voice dropped to an awestruck whisper, "is it *dead,* do you think?"

"Yes, it's quite dead," I said, after stooping to examine it. "Poor thing! I think it's been hunted to death. I know the harriers were out yesterday. But they haven't touched it. Perhaps they caught sight of another, and left it to die of fright and exhaustion."

"Hunted to *death?*" Sylvie repeated to herself, very slowly and sadly. "I thought hunting was a thing they *played* at—like a game. Bruno and I hunt snails: but we never hurt them when we catch them!"

"Sweet angel!" I thought. "How am I to get the idea of *Sport* into your innocent mind?" And as we stood, hand-in-hand, looking down at the dead hare, I tried to put the thing into such words as she could understand. "You know what fierce wild-beasts lions and tigers are?" Sylvie nodded. "Well, in some countries men *have* to kill them, to save their own lives, you know."

"Yes," said Sylvie: "if one tried to kill *me,* Bruno would kill *it*— if he could."

"Well, and so the men—the hunters—get to enjoy it, you know: the running, and the fighting, and the shouting, and the danger."

"Yes," said Sylvie. "Bruno likes danger."

"Well, but, in *this* country, there aren't any lions and tigers, loose: so they hunt other creatures, you see." I hoped, but in vain, that this would satisfy her, and that she would ask no more questions.

"They hunt *foxes,*" Sylvie said, thoughtfully. "And I think they *kill* them, too. Foxes are very fierce. I daresay men don't love them. Are hares fierce?"

"No," I said. "A hare is a sweet, gentle, timid animal—almost as gentle as a lamb."

"But, if men *love* hares, why—why—" her voice quivered, and her sweet eyes were brimming over with tears.

"I'm afraid they *don't* love them, dear child."

"All *children* love them," Sylvie said. "All *ladies* love them."

"I'm afraid even *ladies* go to hunt them, sometimes."

Sylvie shuddered. "Oh, no, not *ladies!*" she earnestly pleaded. "Not Lady Muriel!"

"No, *she* never does, I'm sure—but this is too sad a sight for *you,* dear. Let's try and find some—"

But Sylvie was not satisfied yet. In a hushed, solemn tone, with bowed head and clasped hands, she put her final question. "Does GOD love hares?"

"Yes!" I said. "I'm *sure* He does! He loves every living thing. Even sinful *men*. How much more the animals, that cannot sin!"

"I don't know what 'sin' means," said Sylvie. And I didn't try to explain it.

"Come, my child," I said, trying to lead her away. "Wish good-bye to the poor hare, and come and look for blackberries."

"Good-bye, poor hare!" Sylvie obediently repeated, looking over her shoulder at it as we turned away. And then, all in a moment, her self-command gave way. Pulling her hand out of mine, she ran back to where the dead hare was lying, and flung herself down at its side in such an agony of grief as I could hardly have believed possible in so young a child.

"Oh, my darling, my darling!" she moaned, over and over again. "And GOD meant your life to be so beautiful!"

Sometimes, but always keeping her face hidden on the ground, she would reach out one little hand, to stroke the poor dead thing, and then once more bury her face in her hands, and sob as if her heart would break.

I was afraid she would really make herself ill: still I thought it best to let her weep away the first sharp agony of grief: and, after a few minutes, the sobbing gradually ceased and Sylvie rose to her feet, and looked calmly at me, though tears were still streaming down her cheeks.

I did not dare to speak again, just yet; but simply held out my hand to her, that we might quit the melancholy spot,

"Yes, I'll come now," she said. Very reverently she kneeled down, and kissed the dead hare; then rose and gave me her hand, and we moved on in silence.

A child's sorrow is violent, but short; and it was almost in her usual voice that she said, after a minute, "Oh stop, stop! Here are some *lovely* blackberries!"

We filled our hands with fruit, and returned in all haste to where the Professor and Bruno were seated on a bank, awaiting our return.

Just before we came within hearing-distance, Sylvie checked me. "Please don't tell *Bruno* about the hare!" she said.

"Very well, my child. But why not?"

Tears again glittered in those sweet eyes, and she turned her head away, so that I could scarcely hear her reply. "He's—he's very *fond* of gentle creatures, you know. And he'd—he'd be so sorry! I don't want him to be made sorry."

"And *your* agony of sorrow is to count for nothing, then, sweet unselfish child!" I thought to myself. But no more was said till we had reached our friends; and Bruno was far too much engrossed, in the feast we had brought him, to take any notice of Sylvie's unusually grave manner.

"I'm afraid it's getting rather late, Professor?" I said.

"Yes, indeed," said the Professor. "I must take you all through the Ivory Door again. You've stayed your full time."

"Mightn't we stay a *little* longer!" pleaded Sylvie.

"Just *one* minute!" added Bruno.

But the Professor was unyielding. "It's a great privilege, coming through at all," he said. "We must go now." And we followed him obediently to the Ivory Door, which he threw open, and signed to me to go through first.

"You're coming too, aren't you?" I said to Sylvie.

"Yes," she said: "but you won't see us after you've gone through."

"But suppose I wait for you outside?" I asked, as I stepped through the doorway.

"In that case," said Sylvie, "I think the potato would be *quite* justified in asking *your* weight. I can quite imagine a really *superior* kidney-potato declining to argue with any one under *fifteen stone!*"

With a great effort I recovered the thread of my thoughts. "We lapse very quickly into nonsense!" I said.

CHAPTER XXII.

CROSSING THE LINE.

"LET us lapse back again," said Lady Muriel. "Take another cup of tea? I hope *that's* sound common sense?"

"And all that strange adventure," I thought, "has occupied the space of a single comma in Lady Muriel's speech! A single comma, for which grammarians tell us to 'count *one*'!" (I felt no doubt that the Professor had kindly put back the time for me, to the exact point at which I had gone to sleep.)

When, a few minutes afterwards, we left the house, Arthur's first remark was certainly a strange one. "We've been there just *twenty minutes*," he said, "and I've done nothing but listen to you and Lady Muriel talking: and yet, somehow, I feel exactly as if *I* had been talking with her for an *hour* at least!"

And so he *had* been, I felt no doubt: only, as the time had been put back to the beginning of the tête-à-tête he referred to, the whole of it had passed into oblivion, if not into nothingness! But I valued my own reputation for sanity too highly to venture on explaining to *him* what had happened.

For some cause, which I could not at the moment divine, Arthur was unusually grave and silent during our walk home. It could not be connected with Eric Lindon, I thought, as he had for some days been away in London: so that, having Lady Muriel almost 'all to himself'—for *I* was only too glad to hear those two conversing, to have any wish to intrude any remarks of my own—he *ought*, theoretically, to have been specially radiant and contented with life. "Can he have heard any bad news?" I said to myself. And, almost as if he had read my thoughts, he spoke.

"He will be here by the last train," he said, in the tone of one who is continuing a conversation rather than beginning one.

"Captain Lindon, do you mean?"

"Yes—Captain Lindon," said Arthur: "I said 'he,' because I fancied we were talking about him. The Earl told me he comes to-night, though *to-morrow* is the day when he will know about the Commission that he's hoping for. I wonder he doesn't stay another day to hear the result, if he's really so anxious about it as the Earl believes he is."

"He can have a telegram sent after him," I said: "but it's not very soldier-like, running away from possible bad news!"

"He's a very good fellow," said Arthur: "but I confess it would be good news for *me*, if he got his Commission, and his Marching Orders, all at once! I wish him all happiness—with *one* exception. Good night!" (We had reached home by this time.) "I'm not good company to-night—better be alone."

It was much the same, next day. Arthur declared he wasn't fit for Society, and I had to set forth alone for an afternoon-stroll. I took the road to the Station, and, at the point where the road from the 'Hall' joined it, I paused, seeing my friends in the distance, seemingly bound for the same goal.

"Will you join us?" the Earl said, after I had exchanged greetings with him, and Lady Muriel, and Captain Lindon. "This restless young man is expecting a telegram, and we are going to the Station to meet it."

"There is also a restless young woman in the case," Lady Muriel added.

"That goes without saying, my child," said her father. "Women are *always* restless!"

"For generous appreciation of all one's *best* qualities," his daughter impressively remarked, "there's nothing to compare with a father, is there, Eric?"

"Cousins are not 'in it,' " said Eric: and then somehow the conversation lapsed into two duologues, the younger folk taking the lead, and the two old men following with less eager steps.

"And when are we to see your little friends again?" said the Earl. "They are singularly attractive children."

"I shall be delighted to bring them, when I can," I said. "But I don't know, myself, when I am likely to see them again."

"I'm not going to question you," said the Earl: "but there's no harm in mentioning that Muriel is simply tormented with curiosity! We know most of the people about here, and she has been vainly trying to guess what house they can possibly be staying at."

"Some day I may be able to enlighten her: but just at present——"

"Thanks. She must bear it as best she can. *I* tell her it's a grand opportunity for practising *patience*. But she hardly sees it from that point of view. Why, there *are* the children!"

So indeed they were: waiting (for *us,* apparently) at a stile, which they could not have climbed over more than a few moments, as Lady Muriel and her cousin had passed it without seeing them. On catching sight of us, Bruno ran to meet us, and to exhibit to us, with much pride, the handle of a clasp-knife—the blade having been broken off—which he had picked up in the road.

"And what shall you use it for, Bruno?" I said.

"Don't know," Bruno carelessly replied: "must think."

"A child's first view of life," the Earl remarked, with that sweet sad smile of his, "is that it is a period to be spent in accumulating portable property. That view gets modified as the years glide away." And he held out his hand to Sylvie, who had placed herself by me, looking a little shy of him.

But the gentle old man was not one with whom any child, human or fairy, could be shy for long; and she had very soon deserted my hand for his—Bruno alone remaining faithful to his first friend. We overtook the other couple just as they reached the Station, and both Lady Muriel and Eric greeted the children as old friends—the latter with the words "So you got to Babylon by candlelight, after all?"

"Yes, and back again!" cried Bruno.

Lady Muriel looked from one to the other in blank astonishment. "What, *you* know them, Eric?" she exclaimed. "This mystery grows deeper every day!"

"Then we must be somewhere in the Third Act," said Eric. "You don't expect the mystery to be cleared up till the Fifth Act, do you?"

"But it's such a *long* drama!" was the plaintive reply. "We *must* have got to the Fifth Act by this time!"

"*Third* Act, I assure you," said the young soldier mercilessly. "Scene, a railway-platform. Lights down. Enter Prince (in disguise, of course) and faithful Attendant. *This* is the Prince—" (taking Bruno's hand) "and here stands his humble Servant! What is your Royal Highness's next command?" And he made a most courtier-like low bow to his puzzled little friend.

"Oo're *not* a Servant!" Bruno scornfully exclaimed. "Oo're a *Gemplun!*"

"*Servant,* I assure your Royal Highness!" Eric respectfully insisted.

"Allow me to mention to your Royal Highness my various situations—past, present, and future."

"What did oo begin wiz?" Bruno asked, beginning to enter into the jest. "Was oo a shoe-black?"

"Lower than that, your Royal Highness! Years ago, I offered myself as a *Slave*—as a *'Confidential* Slave,' I think it's called?" he asked, turning to Lady Muriel.

But Lady Muriel heard him not: something had gone wrong with her glove, which entirely engrossed her attention.

"Did oo get the place?" said Bruno.

"Sad to say, Your Royal Highness, I did *not!* So I had to take a situation as—as *Waiter,* which I have now held for some years—haven't I?" He again glanced at Lady Muriel.

"Sylvie dear, *do* help me to button this glove!" Lady Muriel whispered, hastily stooping down, and failing to hear the question.

"And what will oo be *next?*" said Bruno.

"My next place will, I hope, be that of *Groom.* And after that——"

"Don't puzzle the child so!" Lady Muriel interrupted. "What nonsense you talk!"

"—after that," Eric persisted, "I hope to obtain the situation of *House-keeper,* which—*Fourth Act!*" he proclaimed, with a sudden change of tone. "Lights turned up. Red lights. Green lights. Distant rumble heard. Enter a passenger-train!"

And in another minute the train drew up alongside of the platform, and a stream of passengers began to flow out from the booking office and waiting-rooms.

"Did you ever make *real* life into a drama?" said the Earl. "Now just try. I've often amused myself that way. Consider this platform as our stage. Good entrances and exits on *both* sides, you see. Capital background scene: real engine moving up and down. All this bustle, and people passing to and fro, must have been most carefully rehearsed! How naturally they do it! With never a glance at the audience! And every grouping is quite fresh, you see. No repetition!"

It really was admirable, as soon as I began to enter into it from this point of view. Even a porter passing, with a barrow piled with luggage, seemed so realistic that one was tempted to applaud. He was followed by an angry mother, with hot red face, dragging along two screaming children, and calling, to some one behind, "John! Come on!" Enter John, very meek, very silent, and loaded with parcels. And he was followed, in his turn, by a frightened little nursemaid, carrying a fat baby, also screaming. All the children screamed.

"Capital byplay!" said the old man aside. "Did you notice the nursemaid's look of terror? It was simply *perfect!*"

"You have struck quite a new vein," I said. "To most of us Life and its pleasures seem like a mine that is nearly worked out."

"Worked out!" exclaimed the Earl. "For any one with true dramatic instincts, it is only the Overture that is ended! The real treat has yet to begin. You go to a theatre, and pay your ten shillings for a stall, and what do you get for your money? Perhaps it's a dialogue between a couple of farmers—unnatural in their overdone caricature of farmers' dress—more unnatural in their constrained attitudes and gestures—most unnatural in their attempts at ease and geniality in their talk. Go instead and take a seat in a third-class railway-carriage, and you'll get the same dialogue done *to the life!* Front-seats—no orchestra to block the view—and nothing to pay!"

"Which reminds me," said Eric. "There is nothing to pay on receiving a telegram! Shall we enquire for one?" And he and Lady Muriel strolled off in the direction of the Telegraph-Office.

"I wonder if Shakespeare had that thought in his mind," I said, "when he wrote 'All the world's a stage'?"

The old man sighed. "And so it is," he said, "look at it as you will. Life is indeed a drama; a drama with but few *encores*—and no *bouquets!*" he added dreamily. "We spend one half of it in regretting the things we did in the other half!"

"And the secret of *enjoying* it," he continued, resuming his cheerful tone, "is *intensity!*"

"But not in the modern æsthetic sense, I presume? Like the young lady, in Punch, who begins a conversation with 'Are you *intense?*'"

"By no means!" replied the Earl. "What I mean is intensity of *thought*—a concentrated *attention*. We lose half the pleasure we might have in Life, by not really *attending*. Take any instance you like: it doesn't matter *how* trivial the pleasure may be—the principle is the same. Suppose *A* and *B* are reading the same second-rate circulating-library novel. *A* never troubles himself to master the relationships of the characters, on which perhaps all the interest of the story depends: he 'skips' over all the descriptions of scenery, and every passage that looks rather dull: he doesn't half attend to the passages he does read: he goes on reading—merely from want of resolution to find another occupation—for hours after he ought to have put the book aside: and reaches the 'FINIS' in a state of utter weariness and depression! *B* puts his whole soul *into* the thing—on the principle that 'whatever is worth doing is worth doing *well*': he masters the genealogies: he calls up pictures before his 'mind's eye' as he reads about the scenery: best of all, he resolutely shuts the book at the end of some chapter, while his interest is yet at its keenest, and turns to other subjects; so that, when next he allows himself an hour at it, it is like a hungry man sitting down to dinner: and, when the book is finished, he returns to the work of his daily life like 'a giant refreshed'!"

"But suppose the book were really *rubbish*—nothing to repay attention?"

"Well, suppose it," said the Earl. "My theory meets *that* case, I assure you! *A* never finds out that it *is* rubbish, but maunders on to the end, trying to believe he's enjoying himself. *B* quietly shuts the book, when he's read a dozen pages, walks off to the Library, and changes it for a better! I have yet *another* theory for adding to the enjoyment of Life—that is, if I have not exhausted your patience? I'm afraid you find me a very garrulous old man."

"No indeed!" I exclaimed earnestly. And indeed I felt as if one *could* not easily tire of the sweet sadness of that gentle voice.

"It is, that we should learn to take our pleasures *quickly,* and our pains *slowly.*"

"But why? I should have put it the other way, myself."

"By taking *artificial* pain—which can be as trivial as you please—*slowly,* the result is that, when *real* pain comes, however severe, all you need do is to let it go at its *ordinary* pace, and it's over in a moment!"

"Very true," I said, "but how about the *pleasure?*"

"Why, by taking it quick, you can get so much more into life. It takes *you* three hours and a half to hear and enjoy an opera. Suppose *I* can take it in, and enjoy it, in half-an-hour. Why, I can enjoy *seven* operas, while you are listening to *one!*"

"Always supposing you have an orchestra capable of *playing* them," I said. "And that orchestra has yet to be found!"

The old man smiled. "I have heard an air played," he said, "and by no means a short one—played right through, variations and all, in three seconds!"

"When? And how?" I asked eagerly, with a half-notion that I was dreaming again.

"It was done by a little musical-box," he quietly replied. "After it had been wound up, the regulator, or something, broke, and it ran down, as I said, in about three seconds. But it *must* have played all the notes, you know!"

"Did you *enjoy* it?" I asked, with all the severity of a cross-examining barrister.

"No, I didn't!" he candidly confessed. "But then, you know, I hadn't been trained to that kind of music!"

"I should much like to *try* your plan," I said, and, as Sylvie and Bruno happened to run up to us at the moment, I left them to keep the Earl company, and strolled along the platform, making each person and event play its part in an *extempore* drama for my especial benefit. "What, is the Earl tired of you already?" I said, as the children ran past me.

"No!" Sylvie replied with great emphasis. "He wants the evening-paper. So Bruno's going to be a little news-boy!"

"Mind you charge a good price for it!" I called after them.

Returning up the platform, I came upon Sylvie alone. "Well, child," I said, "where's your little news-boy? Couldn't he get you an evening-paper?"

"He went to get one at the book-stall at the other side," said Sylvie; "and he's coming across the line with it—oh, Bruno, you ought to cross by the bridge!" for the distant thud, thud, of the Express was already audible. Suddenly a look of horror came over her face. "Oh, he's fallen down on the rails!" she cried, and darted past me at a speed that quite defied the hasty effort I made to stop her.

But the wheezy old Station-Master happened to be close behind me: he wasn't good for much, poor old man, but he was good for this; and, before I could turn round, he had the child clasped in his arms, saved from the certain death she was rushing to. So intent was I in watching this scene, that I hardly saw a flying figure in a light grey suit, who shot across from the back of the platform, and was on the line in another second. So far as one could take note of time in such a moment of horror, he had about ten clear seconds, before the Express would be upon him, in which to cross the rails and to pick up Bruno. Whether he did so or not it was quite impossible to guess: the next thing one knew was that the Express had passed, and that, whether for life or death, all was over. When the cloud of dust had cleared away, and the line was once more visible, we saw with thankful hearts that the child and his deliverer were safe.

"All right!" Eric called to us cheerfully, as he recrossed the line. "He's more frightened than hurt!"

He lifted the little fellow up into Lady Muriel's arms, and mounted the platform as gaily as if nothing had happened: but he was as pale as death, and leaned heavily on the arm I hastily offered him, fearing he was about to faint. "I'll just—sit down a moment—" he said dreamily: "—where's Sylvie?"

Sylvie ran to him, and flung her arms round his neck, sobbing as if her heart would break. "Don't do that, my darling!" Eric murmured, with a strange look in his eyes. "Nothing to cry about now, you know. But you very nearly got yourself killed for nothing!"

"For Bruno!" the little maiden sobbed. "And he would have done it for me. Wouldn't you, Bruno?"

"Course I would!" Bruno said, looking round with a bewildered air.

Lady Muriel kissed him in silence as she put him down out of her arms. Then she beckoned Sylvie to come and take his hand, and signed

to the children to go back to where the Earl was seated. "Tell him," she whispered with quivering lips, "tell him——all is well!" Then she turned to the hero of the day. "I thought it was *death*," she said. "Thank God, you are safe! Did you see how near it was?"

"I saw there was just time," Eric said lightly. "A soldier must learn to carry his life in his hand, you know. I'm all right now. Shall we go to the telegraph-office again? I daresay it's come by this time."

I went to join the Earl and the children, and we waited—almost in silence, for no one seemed inclined to talk, and Bruno was half-asleep on Sylvie's lap—till the others joined us. No telegram had come.

"I'll take a stroll with the children," I said, feeling that we were a little *de trop,* "and I'll look in, in the course of the evening."

"We must go back into the wood, now," Sylvie said, as soon as we were out of hearing. "We ca'n't stay this size any longer."

"Then you will be quite tiny Fairies again, next time we meet?"

"Yes," said Sylvie: "but we'll be children again some day—if you'll let us. Bruno's very anxious to see Lady Muriel again."

"She are *welly* nice," said Bruno.

"I shall be very glad to take you to see her again," I said. "Hadn't I better give you back the Professor's Watch? It'll be too large for you to carry when you're Fairies, you know."

Bruno laughed merrily. I was glad to see he had quite recovered from the terrible scene he had gone through. "Oh no, it won't!" he said. "When *we* go small, *it'll* go small!"

"And then it'll go straight to the Professor," Sylvie added, "and you won't be able to use it any more: so you'd better use it all you can, *now.* We *must* go small when the sun sets. Good-bye!"

"Good-bye!" cried Bruno. But their voices sounded very far away, and, when I looked round, both children had disappeared.

"And it wants only two hours to sunset!" I said as I strolled on. "I must make the best of my time!"

CHAPTER XXIII.

AN OUTLANDISH WATCH.

As I entered the little town, I came upon two of the fishermen's wives interchanging that last word "which never was the last": and it occurred to me, as an experiment with the Magic Watch, to wait till the little scene was over, and then to 'encore' it.

"Well, good night t'ye! And ye winna forget to send us word when your Martha writes?"

"Nay, ah winna forget. An' if she isn't suited, she can but coom back. Good night t'ye!"

A casual observer might have thought "and there ends the dialogue!" That casual observer would have been mistaken.

"Ah, she'll like 'em, I war'n' ye! *They'll* not treat her bad, yer may depend. They're varry canny fowk. Good night!"

"Ay, they *are* that! Good night!"

"Good night! And ye'll send us word if she writes?"

"Aye, ah will, yer may depend! Good night t'ye!"

And at last they parted. I waited till they were some twenty yards apart, and then put the Watch a minute back. The instantaneous change was startling: the two figures seemed to flash back into their former places.

"—isn't suited, she can but coom back. Good night t'ye!" one of them was saying: and so the whole dialogue was repeated, and, when they had parted for the second time, I let them go their several ways, and strolled on through the town.

"But the real usefulness of this magic power," I thought, "would be to undo some harm, some painful event, some accident——" I had not long to wait for an opportunity of testing *this* property also of the Magic Watch, for, even as the thought passed through my mind, the accident I was imagining occurred. A light cart was standing at the door of the 'Great Millinery Depôt' of Elveston, laden with card-board packing-cases, which the driver was carrying into the shop, one by one. One of the cases had fallen into the street, but it scarcely seemed worth while to step forward and pick it up, as the man would be back again in a moment. Yet, in that moment, a young man riding a bicycle came sharp round the corner of the street and, in trying to avoid running over the box, upset his machine, and was thrown headlong against the wheel of the spring-cart. The driver ran out to his assistance, and he and I together raised the unfortunate cyclist and carried him into the shop. His head was cut and bleeding; and one knee seemed to be badly injured; and it was speedily settled that he had better be conveyed at once to the only Surgery in the place. I helped them in emptying the cart, and placing in it some pillows for the wounded man to rest on; and it was only when the driver had mounted to his place, and was starting for the Surgery, that I bethought me of the strange power I possessed of undoing all this harm.

"Now is my time!" I said to myself, as I moved back the hand of the Watch, and saw, almost without surprise this time, all things restored to the places they had occupied at the critical moment when I had first noticed the fallen packing-case.

Instantly I stepped out into the street, picked up the box, and replaced it in the cart: in the next moment the bicycle had spun round the corner, passed the cart without let or hindrance, and soon vanished in the distance, in a cloud of dust.

"Delightful power of magic!" I thought. "How much of human suffering I have—not only relieved, but actually annihilated!" And in a glow of conscious virtue, I stood watching the unloading of the cart, still holding the Magic Watch open in my hand, as I was curious to see what would happen when we again reached the exact time at which I had put back the hand.

The result was one that, if only I had considered the thing carefully,

I might have foreseen: as the hand of the Watch touched the mark, the spring-cart—which had driven off, and was by this time half-way down the street, was back again at the door, and in the act of starting, while— oh woe for the golden dream of world-wide benevolence that had dazzled my dreaming fancy!—the wounded youth was once more reclining on the heap of pillows, his pale face set rigidly in the hard lines that told of pain resolutely endured.

"Oh mocking Magic Watch!" I said to myself, as I passed out of the little town, and took the seaward road that led to my lodgings. "The good I fancied I could do is vanished like a dream: the evil of this troublesome world is the only abiding reality!"

And now I must record an experience so strange, that I think it only fair, before beginning to relate it, to release my much-enduring reader from any obligation he may feel to believe this part of my story. *I* would not have believed it, I freely confess, if I had not seen it with my own eyes: then why should I expect it of my reader, who, quite possibly, has never seen anything of the sort?

I was passing a pretty little villa, which stood rather back from the road, in its own grounds, with bright flower-beds in front—creepers wandering over the walls and hanging in festoons about the bow-windows— an easy-chair forgotten on the lawn, with a newspaper lying near it—a small pug-dog "couchant" before it, resolved to guard the treasure even at the sacrifice of life—and a front-door standing invitingly half-open. "Here is my chance," I thought, "for testing the reverse action of the Magic Watch!" I pressed the 'reversal-peg' and walked in. In *another* house, the entrance of a stranger might cause surprise—perhaps anger, even going so far as to expel the said stranger with violence: but *here,* I knew, nothing of the sort could happen. The *ordinary* course of events— first, to think nothing about me; then, hearing my footsteps to look up and see me; and then to wonder what business I had there—would be reversed by the action of my Watch. They would *first* wonder who I was, *then* see me, then look down, and think no more about me. And as to being expelled with violence, *that* event would necessarily come *first* in this case. "So, if I can once get *in,*" I said to myself, "all risk of *expulsion* will be over!"

The pug-dog sat up, as a precautionary measure, as I passed; but, as I took no notice of the treasure he was guarding, he let me go by without even one remonstrant bark. "He that takes my life," he seemed to be saying, wheezily, to himself, "takes trash: But he that takes the *Daily Telegraph*——!" But this awful contingency I did not face.

The party in the drawing-room—I had walked straight in, you un- derstand, without ringing the bell, or giving any notice of my approach— consisted of four laughing rosy children, of ages from about fourteen down to ten, who were, apparently, all coming towards the door (I found they were really walking *backwards*), while their mother, seated by the fire with some needlework on her lap, was saying, just as I entered the room, "Now, girls, you may get your things on for a walk."

To my utter astonishment—for I was not yet accustomed to the action of the Watch—"all smiles ceased" (as Browning says) on the four pretty

faces, and they all got out pieces of needle-work, and sat down. No one noticed *me* in the least, as I quietly took a chair and sat down to watch them.

When the needle-work had been unfolded, and they were all ready to begin, their mother said "Come, *that's* done, at last! You may fold up your work, girls." But the children took no notice whatever of the remark; on the contrary, they set to work at once sewing—if that is the proper word to describe an operation such as *I* had never before witnessed. Each of them threaded her needle with a short end of thread attached to the work, which was instantly pulled by an invisible force through the stuff, dragging the needle after it: the nimble fingers of the little sempstress caught it at the other side, but only to lose it again the next moment. And so the work went on, steadily undoing itself, and the neatly-stitched little dresses, or whatever they were, steadily falling to pieces. Now and then one of the children would pause, as the recovered thread became inconveniently long, wind it on a bobbin, and start again with another short end.

At last all the work was picked to pieces and put away, and the lady led the way into the next room, walking backwards, and making the insane remark "Not yet, dear: we *must* get the sewing done first." After which, I was not surprised to see the children skipping backwards after her, exclaiming "Oh, mother, it *is* such a lovely day for a walk!"

In the dining-room, the table had only dirty plates and empty dishes on it. However the party—with the addition of a gentleman, as good-natured, and as rosy, as the children—seated themselves at it very contentedly.

You have seen people eating cherry-tart, and every now and then cautiously conveying a cherry-stone from their lips to their plates? Well, something like that went on all through this ghastly—or shall we say 'ghostly'?—banquet. An empty fork is raised to the lips: there it receives a neatly-cut piece of mutton, and swiftly conveys it to the plate, where it instantly attaches itself to the mutton already there. Soon one of the plates, furnished with a complete slice of mutton and two potatoes, was handed up to the presiding gentleman, who quietly replaced the slice on the joint, and the potatoes in the dish.

Their conversation was, if possible, more bewildering than their mode of dining. It began by the youngest girl suddenly, and without provocation, addressing her eldest sister. "Oh, you *wicked* story-teller!" she said.

I expected a sharp reply from the sister; but, instead of this, she turned laughingly to her father, and said, in a very loud stage-whisper, "To be a bride!"

The father, in order to do *his* part in a conversation that seemed only fit for lunatics, replied "Whisper it to me, dear."

But she *didn't* whisper (these children never did anything they were told): she said, quite loud, "Of course not! Everybody knows what *Dolly* wants!"

And little Dolly shrugged her shoulders, and said, with a pretty pettishness, "Now, Father, you're not to tease! You know I don't want to be bride's-maid to *anybody!*"

"And Dolly's to be the fourth," was her father's idiotic reply.

Here Number Three put in her oar. "Oh, it *is* settled, Mother dear, really and truly! Mary told us all about it. It's to be next Tuesday four weeks—and three of her cousins are coming to be bride's-maids—and——"

"*She* doesn't forget it, Minnie!" the Mother laughingly replied. "I do wish they'd get it settled! I don't like long engagements."

And Minnie wound up the conversation—if so chaotic a series of remarks deserves the name—with "Only think! We passed the Cedars this morning, just exactly as Mary Davenant was standing at the gate, wishing good-bye to Mister—I forget his name. Of course we looked the other way."

By this time I was so hopelessly confused that I gave up listening, and followed the dinner down into the kitchen.

But to you, O hypercritical reader, resolute to believe no item of this weird adventure, what need to tell how the mutton was placed on the spit, and slowly unroasted—how the potatoes were wrapped in their skins, and handed over to the gardener to be buried—how, when the mutton had at length attained to rawness, the fire, which had gradually changed from red-heat to a mere blaze, died down so suddenly that the cook had only just time to catch its last flicker on the end of a match— or how the maid, having taken the mutton off the spit, carried it (backwards, of course) out of the house, to meet the butcher, who was coming (also backwards) down the road?

The longer I thought over this strange adventure, the more hopelessly tangled the mystery became: and it was a real relief to meet Arthur in the road, and get him to go with me up to the Hall to learn what news the telegraph had brought. I told him, as we went, what had happened at the Station, but as to my further adventures I thought it best, for the present, to say nothing.

The Earl was sitting alone when we entered. "I am glad you are come in to keep me company," he said. "Muriel is gone to bed—the excitement of that terrible scene was too much for her—and Eric has gone to the hotel to pack his things, to start for London by the early train."

"Then the telegram has come?" I said.

"Did you not hear? Oh, I had forgotten: it came in after you left the Station. Yes, it's all right: Eric has got his commission; and, now that he has arranged matters with Muriel, he has business in town that must be seen to at once."

"What arrangement do you mean?" I asked with a sinking heart, as the thought of Arthur's crushed hopes came to my mind. "Do you mean that they are *engaged?*"

"They have been engaged—in a sense—for two years," the old man gently replied: "that is, he has had my promise to consent to it, so soon as he could secure a permanent and settled line in life. I could never be happy with my child married to a man without an object to live for—— without even an object to die for!"

"I hope they will be happy," a strange voice said. The speaker was evidently in the room, but I had not heard the door open, and I looked round in some astonishment. The Earl seemed to share my surprise. "Who spoke?" he exclaimed.

"It was I," said Arthur, looking at us with a worn, haggard face, and eyes from which the light of life seemed suddenly to have faded. "And let me wish *you* joy also, dear friend," he added, looking sadly at the Earl, and speaking in the same hollow tones that had startled us so much.

"Thank you," the old man said, simply and heartily.

A silence followed: then I rose, feeling sure that Arthur would wish to be alone, and bade our gentle host 'Good night': Arthur took his hand, but said nothing: nor did he speak again, as we went home, till we were in the house and had lit our bed-room candles. Then he said, more to himself than to me, *"The heart knoweth its own bitterness.* I never understood those words till now."

The next few days passed wearily enough. I felt no inclination to call again, by myself, at the Hall; still less to propose that Arthur should go with me: it seemed better to wait till Time—that gentle healer of our bitterest sorrows—should have helped him to recover from the first shock of the disappointment that had blighted his life.

Business, however, soon demanded my presence in town; and I had to announce to Arthur that I must leave him for a while. "But I hope to run down again in a month," I added. "I would stay now, if I could. I don't think it's good for you to be alone."

"No, I ca'n't face solitude, *here,* for long," said Arthur. "But don't think about *me.* I have made up my mind to accept a post in India, that has been offered me. Out there, I suppose I shall find something to live for; I ca'n't see *anything* at present. *This life of mine I guard, as God's high gift, from scathe and wrong, Not greatly care to lose!'"*

"Yes," I said: "your name-sake bore as heavy a blow, and lived through it."

"A far heavier one than *mine,"* said Arthur. "The woman *he* loved proved false. There is no such cloud as *that* on my memory of— of——" He left the name unuttered, and went on hurriedly. "But *you* will return, will you not?"

"Yes, I shall come back for a short time."

"Do," said Arthur: "and you shall write and tell me of our friends. I'll send you my address when I'm settled down."

CHAPTER XXIV.

THE FROG'S BIRTHDAY-TREAT.

AND so it came to pass that, just a week after the day when my Fairy-friends first appeared as Children, I found myself taking a farewell-stroll through the wood, in the hope of meeting them once more. I had but to stretch myself on the smooth turf, and the 'eerie' feeling was on me in a moment.

"Put oor ear *welly* low down," said Bruno, "and I'll tell oo a secret! It's the Frogs' Birthday-Treat—and we've lost the Baby!"

"*What* Baby?" I said, quite bewildered by this complicated piece of news.

"The *Queen's* Baby, a course!" said Bruno. "Titania's Baby. And we's *welly* sorry. Sylvie, she's—oh so sorry!"

"*How* sorry is she?" I asked, mischievously.

"Three-quarters of a yard," Bruno replied with perfect solemnity. "And *I'm* a little sorry too," he added, shutting his eyes so as not to see that he was smiling.

"And what are you doing about the Baby?"

"Well, the *soldiers* are all looking for it—up and down—everywhere."

"The *soldiers?*" I exclaimed.

"Yes, a course!" said Bruno. "When there's no fighting to be done, the soldiers doos any little odd jobs, oo know."

I was amused at the idea of its being a 'little odd job' to find the Royal Baby. "But how did you come to lose it?" I asked.

"We put it in a flower," Sylvie, who had just joined us, explained with her eyes full of tears. "Only we ca'n't remember *which!*"

"She says *us* put it in a flower," Bruno interrupted, "'cause she doosn't want *I* to get punished. But it were really *me* what put it there. *Sylvie* were picking Dindledums."

"You shouldn't say '*us* put it in a flower'," Sylvie very gravely remarked.

"Well, *hus,* then," said Bruno. "I never *can* remember those horrid H's!"

"Let me help you to look for it," I said. So Sylvie and I made a 'voyage of discovery' among all the flowers; but there was no Baby to be seen.

"What's become of Bruno?" I said, when we had completed our tour.

"He's down in the ditch there," said Sylvie, "amusing a young Frog."

I went down on my hands and knees to look for him, for I felt very

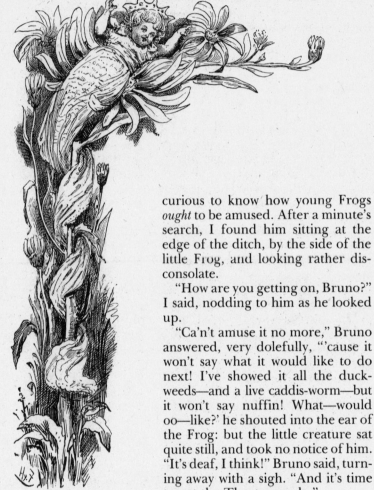

curious to know how young Frogs *ought* to be amused. After a minute's search, I found him sitting at the edge of the ditch, by the side of the little Frog, and looking rather disconsolate.

"How are you getting on, Bruno?" I said, nodding to him as he looked up.

"Ca'n't amuse it no more," Bruno answered, very dolefully, "'cause it won't say what it would like to do next! I've showed it all the duck-weeds—and a live caddis-worm—but it won't say nuffin! What—would oo—like?' he shouted into the ear of the Frog: but the little creature sat quite still, and took no notice of him. "It's deaf, I think!" Bruno said, turning away with a sigh. "And it's time to get the Theatre ready."

"Who are the audience to be?"

"Only but Frogs," said Bruno. "But they haven't comed yet. They wants to be drove up, like sheep."

"Would it save time," I suggested, "if *I* were to walk round with Sylvie, to drive up the Frogs, while *you* get the Theatre ready?"

"That *are* a good plan!" cried Bruno. "But where *are* Sylvie?"

"I'm here!" said Sylvie, peeping over the edge of the bank. "I was just watching two Frogs that were having a race."

"Which won it?" Bruno eagerly inquired.

Sylvie was puzzled. "He *does* ask such hard questions!" she confided to me.

"And what's to happen in the Theatre?" I asked.

"First they have their Birthday-Feast," Sylvie said: "then Bruno does some Bits of Shakespeare; then he tells them a Story."

"I should think the Frogs like the Feast best. Don't they?"

"Well, there's generally very few of them that get any. They *will* keep their mouths shut so tight! And it's just as well they *do*," she added, "because Bruno likes to cook it himself: and he cooks *very* queerly. Now they're all in. Would you just help me to put them with their heads the right way?"

We soon managed this part of the business, though the Frogs kept up a most discontented croaking all the time.

"What *are* they saying?" I asked Sylvie.

"They're saying 'Fork! Fork!' It's very silly of them! You're not going to *have* forks!" she announced with some severity. "Those that want any Feast have just got to open their mouths, and Bruno'll put some of it in!"

At this moment Bruno appeared, wearing a little white apron to show that he was a Cook, and carrying a tureen full of very queer-looking soup. I watched very carefully as he moved about among the Frogs; but I could not see that *any* of them opened their mouths to be fed—except one very young one, and I'm nearly sure it did it accidentally, in yawning. However Bruno instantly put a large spoonful of soup into its mouth, and the poor little thing coughed violently for some time.

So Sylvie and I had to share the soup between us, and to *pretend* to enjoy it, for it certainly was *very* queerly cooked.

I only ventured to take *one* spoonful of it ("Sylvie's Summer-Soup," Bruno said it was), and must candidly confess that it was not *at all* nice; and I could not feel surprised that so many of the guests had kept their mouths shut up tight.

"What's the soup *made* of, Bruno?" said Sylvie, who had put a spoonful of it to her lips, and was making a wry face over it.

And Bruno's answer was anything but encouraging. "Bits of things!"

The entertainment was to conclude with "Bits of Shakespeare," as Sylvie expressed it, which were all to be done by Bruno, Sylvie being fully engaged in making the Frogs keep their heads towards the stage: after which Bruno was to appear in his real character, and tell them a Story of his own invention.

"Will the Story have a Moral to it?" I asked Sylvie, while Bruno was away behind the hedge, dressing for the first 'Bit.'

"I *think* so," Sylvie replied doubtfully. "There generally *is* a Moral, only he puts it in too soon."

"And will he *say* all the Bits of Shakespeare?"

"No, he'll only *act* them," said Sylvie. "He knows hardly any of the words. When I see what he's dressed like, I've to tell the Frogs what character it is. They're always in such a hurry to guess! Don't you hear them all saying 'What? What?'" And so indeed they were: it had only sounded like croaking, till Sylvie explained it, but I could now make out the "Wawt? Wawt?" quite distinctly.

"But why do they try to guess it before they see it?"

"I don't know," Sylvie said: "but they always *do*. Sometimes they begin guessing weeks and weeks before the day!"

(So now, when you hear the Frogs croaking in a particularly melancholy way, you may be sure they're trying to guess Bruno's next Shakespeare 'Bit'. Isn't *that* interesting?)

However, the chorus of guessing was cut short by Bruno, who suddenly rushed on from behind the scenes, and took a flying leap down among the Frogs, to re-arrange them.

For the oldest and fattest Frog—who had never been properly arranged so that he could see the stage, and so had no idea what was going on— was getting restless, and had upset several of the Frogs, and turned others round with their heads the wrong way. And it was no good at all, Bruno said, to do a 'Bit' of Shakespeare when there was nobody to look at it (you see he didn't count *me* as anybody). So he set to work with a stick, stirring them up, very much as you would stir up tea in a cup, till most of them had at least *one* great stupid eye gazing at the stage.

"*Oo* must come and sit among them, Sylvie," he said in despair, "I've put these two side-by-side, with their noses the same way, ever so many times, but they *do* squarrel so!"

So Sylvie took her place as 'Mistress of the Ceremonies,' and Bruno vanished again behind the scenes, to dress for the first 'Bit.'

"Hamlet!" was suddenly proclaimed, in the clear sweet tones I knew so well. The croaking all ceased in a moment, and I turned to the stage, in some curiosity to see what Bruno's ideas were as to the behaviour of Shakespeare's greatest Character.

According to this eminent interpreter of the Drama, Hamlet wore a short black cloak (which he chiefly used for muffling up his face, as if he suffered a good deal from toothache), and turned out his toes very much as he walked. "To be or not to be!" Hamlet remarked in a cheerful tone, and then turned head-over-heels several times, his cloak dropping off in the performance.

I felt a little disappointed: Bruno's conception of the part seemed so wanting in dignity. "Won't he say any more of the speech?" I whispered to Sylvie.

"I *think* not," Sylvie whispered in reply. "He generally turns head-over-heels when he doesn't know any more words."

Bruno had meanwhile settled the question by disappearing from the stage; and the Frogs instantly began inquiring the name of the next Character.

"You'll know directly!" cried Sylvie, as she adjusted two or three young Frogs that had struggled round with their backs to the stage. "Macbeth!" she added, as Bruno re-appeared.

Macbeth had something twisted round him, that went over one shoulder and under the other arm, and was meant, I believe, for a Scotch plaid. He had a thorn in his hand, which he held out at arm's length, as if he were a little afraid of it. "Is this a *dagger?*" Macbeth inquired, in a puzzled sort of tone: and instantly a chorus of "Thorn! Thorn!" arose from the Frogs (I had quite learned to understand their croaking by this time).

"It's a *dagger!*" Sylvie proclaimed in a peremptory tone. "Hold your tongues!" And the croaking ceased at once.

Shakespeare has not told us, so far as I know, that Macbeth had any such eccentric habit as turning head-over-heels in private life: but Bruno evidently considered it quite an essential part of the character, and left the stage in a series of somersaults. However, he was back again in a few moments, having tucked under his chin the end of a tuft of wool (probably left on the thorn by a wandering sheep), which made a magnificent beard, that reached nearly down to his feet.

"Shylock!" Sylvie proclaimed. "No, I beg your pardon!" she hastily corrected herself, "King Lear! I hadn't noticed the crown." (Bruno had very cleverly provided one, which fitted him exactly, by cutting out the centre of a dandelion to make room for his head.)

King Lear folded his arms (to the imminent peril of his beard) and said, in a mild explanatory tone, "Ay, every *inch* a king!" and then paused, as if to consider how this could best be proved. And here, with all possible deference to Bruno as a Shakespearian critic, I *must* express my opinion that the poet did *not* mean his three great tragic heroes to be so strangely alike in their personal habits; nor do I believe that he would have accepted the faculty of turning head-over-heels as any proof at all of royal descent. Yet it appeared that King Lear, after deep meditation, could think of no other argument by which to prove his kingship: and, as this was the last of the 'Bits' of Shakespeare ("We never do more than *three,*" Sylvie explained in a whisper), Bruno gave the audience quite a long series of somersaults before he finally retired, leaving the enraptured Frogs all crying out "More! More!" which I suppose was their way of encoring a performance. But Bruno wouldn't appear again, till the proper time came for telling the Story.

When he appeared at last in his *real* character, I noticed a remarkable change in his behaviour. He tried no more somersaults. It was clearly his opinion that, however suitable the habit of turning head-over-heels might be to such petty individuals as Hamlet and King Lear, it would never do for *Bruno* to sacrifice his dignity to such an extent. But it was equally clear that he did not feel entirely at his ease, standing all alone on the stage, with no costume to disguise him: and though he began, several times, "There were a Mouse—," he kept glancing up and down, and on all sides, as if in search of more comfortable quarters from which to tell the Story. Standing on one side of the stage, and partly overshadowing it, was a tall fox-glove, which seemed, as the evening breeze gently swayed it hither and thither, to offer exactly the sort of accommodation that the orator desired. Having once decided on his quarters, it needed only a second or two for him to run up the stem like a tiny squirrel, and to seat himself astride on the topmost bend, where the fairy-bells clustered most closely, and from whence he could look down on his audience from such a height that all shyness vanished, and he began his Story merrily.

"Once there were a Mouse and a Crocodile and a Man and a Goat and a Lion." I had never heard the 'dramatis personæ' tumbled into a story with such profusion and in such reckless haste; and it fairly took my breath away. Even Sylvie gave a little gasp, and allowed three of the

Frogs, who seemed to be getting tired of the entertainment, to hop away into the ditch, without attempting to stop them.

"And the Mouse found a Shoe, and it thought it were a Mouse-trap. So it got right in, and it stayed in ever so long."

"Wy did it *stay* in?" said Sylvie. Her function seemed to be much the same as that of the Chorus in a Greek Play: she had to encourage the orator, and draw him out, by a series of intelligent questions.

"'Cause it thought it couldn't get out again," Bruno explained. "It were a clever mouse. It knew it couldn't get out of traps!"

"But why did it go in at all?" said Sylvie.

"—and it jamp, and it jamp," Bruno proceeded, ignoring this question, "and at last it got right out again. And it looked at the mark in the Shoe. And the Man's name were in it. So it knew it wasn't its own Shoe."

"Had it thought it *was?*" said Sylvie.

"Why, didn't I tell oo it thought it were a *Mouse-trap?*" the indignant orator replied. "Please, Mister Sir, will oo make Sylvie attend?" Sylvie was silenced, and was all attention: in fact, she and I were most of the audience now, as the Frogs kept hopping away, and there were very few of them left.

"So the Mouse gave the Man his Shoe. And the Man were welly glad, 'cause he hadn't got but one Shoe, and he were hopping to get the other."

Here I ventured on a question. "Do you mean 'hopping,' or 'hoping'?"

"Bofe," said Bruno. "And the Man took the Goat out of the Sack." ("We haven't heard of the *sack* before," I said. "Nor you won't hear of it again," said Bruno). "And he said to the Goat, 'Oo will walk about here till I comes back.' And he went and he tumbled into a deep hole. And the Goat walked round and round. And it walked under the Tree. And it wug its tail. And it looked up in the Tree. And it sang a sad little Song. Oo never heard such a sad little Song!"

"Can you sing it, Bruno?" I asked.

"Iss, I can," Bruno readily replied. "And I sa'n't. It would make Sylvie cry——"

"It wouldn't!" Sylvie interrupted in great indignation. "And I don't believe the Goat sang it at all!"

"It did, though!" said Bruno. "It singed it right froo. I *sawed* it singing with its long beard——"

"It couldn't sing with its *beard*," I said, hoping to puzzle the little fellow: "a beard isn't a *voice*."

"Well then, *oo* couldn't walk with Sylvie!" Bruno cried triumphantly. "Sylvie isn't a *foot!*"

I thought I had better follow Sylvie's example, and be silent for a while. Bruno was too sharp for us.

"And when it had singed all the Song, it ran away—for to get along to look for the Man, oo know. And the Crocodile got along after it— for to bite it, oo know. And the Mouse got along after the Crocodile."

"Wasn't the Crocodile *running?*" Sylvie enquired. She appealed to me. "Crocodiles do run, don't they?"

I suggested "crawling" as the proper word.

"He wasn't running," said Bruno, "and he wasn't crawling. He went struggling along like a portmanteau. And he held his chin ever so high in the air——"

"What did he do *that* for?" said Sylvie.

"'cause he hadn't got a toofache!" said Bruno. "Ca'n't oo make out *nuffin* wizout I 'splain it? Why, if he'd had a toofache, a course he'd have held his head down—like this—and he'd have put a lot of warm blankets round it!"

"If he'd *had* any blankets," Sylvie argued.

"Course he *had* blankets!" retorted her brother. "Doos oo think Crocodiles goes walks wizout blankets? And he frowned with his eyebrows. And the Goat was welly flightened at his eyebrows!"

"I'd never be afraid of *eyebrows!*" exclaimed Sylvie.

"I should think oo *would* though, if they'd got a Crocodile fastened to them, like these had! And so the Man jamp, and he jamp, and at last he got right out of the hole."

Sylvie gave another little gasp: this rapid dodging about among the characters of the Story had taken away her breath.

"And he runned away—for to look for the Goat, oo know. And he heard the Lion grunting——"

"Lions don't grunt," said Sylvie.

"This one did," said Bruno. "And its mouth were like a large cupboard. And it had plenty of room in its mouth. And the Lion runned after the Man—for to eat him, oo know. And the Mouse runned after the Lion."

"But the Mouse was running after the *Crocodile*," I said: "he couldn't run after *both!*"

Bruno sighed over the density of his audience, but explained very patiently. "He *did* runned after *bofe:* 'cause they went the same way! And first he caught the Crocodile, and then he didn't catch the Lion. And when he'd caught the Crocodile, what doos oo think he did—'cause he'd got pincers in his pocket?"

"I ca'n't guess," said Sylvie.

"Nobody couldn't guess it!" Bruno cried in high glee. "Why, he wrenched out that Crocodile's toof!"

"*Which* tooth?" I ventured to ask.

But Bruno was not to be puzzled. "The toof he were going to bite the Goat with, a course!"

"He couldn't be sure about that," I argued, "unless he wrenched out *all* its teeth."

Bruno laughed merrily, and half sang, as he swung himself backwards and forwards, "He did—wrenched—out—*all* its teef!"

"Why did the Crocodile wait to have them wrenched out?" said Sylvie.

"It had to wait," said Bruno.

I ventured on another question. "But what became of the Man who said 'You may wait here till I come back'?"

"He didn't say 'Oo *may*,'" Bruno explained. "He said, 'Oo *will*.' Just like Sylvie says to me 'Oo will do oor lessons till twelve o'clock.' Oh, I *wiss*," he added with a little sigh, "I *wiss* Sylvie would say 'Oo *may* do oor lessons'!"

This was a dangerous subject for discussion, Sylvie seemed to think. She returned to the Story. "But what became of the Man?"

"Well, the Lion springed at him. But it came so slow, it were three weeks in the air——"

"Did the Man wait for it all that time?" I said.

"Course he didn't!" Bruno replied, gliding head-first down the stem of the fox-glove, for the Story was evidently close to its end. "He sold his house, and he packed up his things, while the Lion were coming. And he went and he lived in another town. So the Lion ate the wrong man."

This was evidently the Moral: so Sylvie made her final proclamation to the Frogs. "The Story's finished! And whatever is to be *learned* from it," she added, aside to me, "I'm sure *I* don't know!"

I did not feel *quite* clear about it myself, so made no suggestion: but the Frogs seemed quite content, Moral or no Moral, and merely raised a husky chorus of "Off! Off!" as they hopped away.

CHAPTER XXV.

LOOKING EASTWARD.

"It's just a week," I said, three days later to Arthur, "since we heard of Lady Muriel's engagement. I think *I* ought to call, at any rate, and offer my congratulations. Won't you come with me?"

A pained expression passed over his face. "When must you leave us?" he asked.

"By the first train on Monday."

"Well—yes, I *will* come with you. It would seem strange and unfriendly if I didn't. But this is only Friday. Give me till Sunday afternoon. I shall be stronger then."

Shading his eyes with one hand, as if half-ashamed of the tears that were coursing down his cheeks, he held the other out to me. It trembled as I clasped it.

I tried to frame some words of sympathy; but they seemed poor and cold, and I left them unspoken. "Good night!" was all I said.

"Good night, dear friend!" he replied. There was a manly vigour in his tone that convinced me he was wrestling with, and triumphing over, the great sorrow that had so nearly wrecked his life—and that, on the stepping-stone of his dead self, he would surely rise to higher things!

There was no chance, I was glad to think, as we set out on Sunday afternoon, of meeting *Eric* at the Hall, as he had returned to town the day after his engagement was announced. *His* presence might have disturbed the calm—the almost unnatural calm—with which Arthur met the woman who had won his heart, and murmured the few graceful words of sympathy that the occasion demanded.

Lady Muriel was perfectly radiant with happiness: sadness could not live in the light of such a smile: and even Arthur brightened under it, and, when she remarked "You see I'm watering my flowers, though it *is* the Sabbath-Day," his voice had almost its old ring of cheerfulness as he replied "Even on the Sabbath-Day works of mercy are allowed. But this *isn't* the Sabbath-Day. The Sabbath-Day has ceased to exist."

"I know it's not *Saturday*," Lady Muriel replied: "but isn't Sunday often called 'the Christian Sabbath'?"

"It is so called, I think, in recognition of the *spirit* of the Jewish institution, that one day in seven should be a day of *rest*. But I hold that Christians are freed from the *literal* observance of the Fourth Commandment."

"Then where is our *authority* for Sunday observance?"

"We have, first, the fact that the seventh day was 'sanctified', when God rested from the work of Creation. That is binding on us as *Theists*. Secondly, we have the fact that 'the Lord's Day' is a *Christian* institution. That is binding on us as *Christians*."

"And your practical rules would be——?"

"First, as Theists, to keep it *holy* in some special way, and to make it, so far as is reasonably possible, a day of *rest*. Secondly, as *Christians,* to attend public worship."

"And what of *amusements?*"

"I would say of them, as of all kinds of *work,* whatever is innocent on a week-day, is innocent on Sunday, provided it does not interfere with the duties of the day."

"Then you would allow children to *play* on Sunday?"

"Certainly I should. Why make the day irksome to their restless natures?"

"I have a letter somewhere," said Lady Muriel, "from an old friend, describing the way in which Sunday was kept in her younger days. I will fetch it for you."

"I had a similar description, *vivâ voce,* years ago," Arthur said when she had left us, "from a little girl. It was really touching to hear the melancholy tone in which she said 'On Sunday I mustn't play with my doll! On Sunday I mustn't run on the sands! On Sunday I mustn't dig in the garden!' Poor child! She had indeed abundant cause for hating Sunday!"

"Here is the letter," said Lady Muriel, returning. "Let me read you a piece of it."

> "*When, as a child, I first opened my eyes on a Sunday-morning, a feeling of dismal anticipation, which began at least on the Friday, culminated. I knew what was before me, and my wish, if not my word, was 'Would God it were evening!' It was no day of rest, but a day of texts, of catechisms (Watts'), of tracts about converted swearers, godly charwomen, and edifying deaths of sinners saved.*
>
> "*Up with the lark, hymns and portions of Scripture had to be learned by heart till 8 o'clock, when there were family-prayers, then breakfast, which I was never able to enjoy, partly from the fast already undergone, and partly from the outlook I dreaded.*
>
> "*At 9 came Sunday-School; and it made me indignant to be put into the class with the village-children, as well as alarmed lest, by some mistake of mine, I should be put below them.*
>
> "*The Church-Service was a veritable Wilderness of Zin. I wandered in it, pitching the tabernacle of my thoughts on the lining of the square family-pew, the fidgets of my small brothers, and the horror of knowing that, on the Monday, I should have to write out, from memory, jottings of the rambling disconnected extempore sermon, which might have had any text but its own, and to stand or fall by the result.*
>
> "*This was followed by a cold dinner at 1 (servants to have no work), Sunday-School again from 2 to 4, and Evening-Service at 6. The intervals were perhaps the greatest trial of all, from the efforts I had to make, to be less than usually sinful, by reading books and sermons as barren as the Dead Sea. There was but one rosy spot, in the distance, all that day: and that was 'bed-time,' which never could come too early!*"

"Such teaching was well meant, no doubt," said Arthur; "but it must have driven many of its victims into deserting the Church-Services altogether."

"I'm afraid *I* was a deserter this morning," she gravely said. "I had to write to Eric. Would you—would you mind my telling you something he said about *prayer*? It had never struck me in that light before."

"In what light?" said Arthur.

"Why, that all Nature goes by fixed, regular laws—Science has proved *that*. So that asking God to *do* anything (except of course praying for *spiritual* blessings) is to expect a miracle: and we've no right to do *that*. I've not put it as well as *he* did: but that was the outcome of it, and it has confused me. Please tell me what you can say in answer to it."

"I don't propose to discuss *Captain Lindon's* difficulties," Arthur gravely replied; "specially as he is not present. But, if it is *your* difficulty," (his voice unconsciously took a tenderer tone) "then I will speak."

"It *is* my difficulty," she said anxiously.

"Then I will begin by asking 'Why did you except *spiritual* blessings?' Is not your mind a part of Nature?"

"Yes, but Free-Will comes in there—I can *choose* this or that; and God can influence my choice."

"Then you are not a Fatalist?"

"Oh, no!" she earnestly exclaimed.

"Thank God!" Arthur said to himself, but in so low a whisper that only *I* heard it. "You grant then that I can, by an act of free choice, move this cup," suiting the action to the word, "*this* way or *that* way?"

"Yes, I grant it."

"Well, let us see how far the result is produced by fixed laws. The *cup* moves because certain mechanical forces are impressed on it by my *hand*. My *hand* moves because certain forces—electric, magnetic, or whatever 'nerve-force' may prove to be—are impressed on it by my *brain*. This nerve-force, stored in the brain, would probably be traceable, if Science were complete, to chemical forces supplied to the brain by the blood, and ultimately derived from the food I eat and the air I breathe."

"But would not that be Fatalism? Where would Free-Will come in?"

"In *choice* of nerves," replied Arthur. "The nerve-force in the brain may flow just as naturally down one nerve as down another. We need something more than a fixed Law of Nature to settle *which* nerve shall carry it. That 'something' is Free-Will."

Her eyes sparkled. "I see what you mean!" she exclaimed. "Human Free-Will is an exception to the system of fixed Law. Eric said something like that. And then I think he pointed out that God can only influence Nature by influencing Human Wills. So that we *might* reasonably pray '*give us this day our daily bread*,' because many of the causes that produce bread are under Man's control. But to pray for rain, or fine weather, would be as unreasonable as—" she checked herself, as if fearful of saying something irreverent.

In a hushed, low tone, that trembled with emotion, and with the solemnity of one in the presence of death, Arthur slowly replied "*Shall he that contendeth with the Almighty instruct him?* Shall we, 'the swarm that in the noon-tide beam were born,' feeling in ourselves the power to direct, this way or that, the forces of Nature—of *Nature,* of which we form so trivial a part—shall we, i our boundless arrogance, in our pitiful conceit, *deny* that power to the Ancient of Days? Saying, to our Creator, 'Thus far and no further. Thou madest, but thou canst not rule!'?"

Lady Muriel had covered her face in her hands, and did not look up. She only murmured "Thanks, thanks!" again and again.

We rose to go. Arthur said, with evident effort, "One word more. If you would *know* the power of Prayer—in anything and everything that Man can need—*try* it. *Ask, and it shall be given you.* I—*have* tried it. I *know* that God answers prayer!"

Our walk home was a silent one, till we had nearly reached the lodgings: then Arthur murmured—and it was almost an echo of my own thoughts— *"What knowest thou, O wife, whether thou shalt save thy husband?"*

The subject was not touched on again. We sat on, talking, while hour after hour, of this our last night together, glided away unnoticed. He had much to tell me about India, and the new life he was going to, and the *work* he hoped to do. And his great generous soul seemed so filled with noble ambition as to have no space left for any vain regret or selfish repining.

"Come, it is nearly morning!" Arthur said at last, rising and leading the way upstairs. "The sun will be rising in a few minutes: and, though I *have* basely defrauded you of your last chance of a night's rest here, I'm sure you'll forgive me: for I really *couldn't* bring myself to say 'Good night' sooner. And God knows whether you'll ever see me again, or hear of me!"

"*Hear* of you I am certain I shall!" I warmly responded, and quoted the concluding lines of that strange poem 'Waring':—

> "Oh, never star
> Was lost here, but it rose afar!
> Look East, where whole new thousands are!
> In Vishnu-land what Avatar?"

"Aye, look Eastward!" Arthur eagerly replied, pausing at the staircase window, which commanded a fine view of the sea and the eastward horizon. "The West is the fitting tomb for all the sorrow and the sighing, all the errors and the follies of the Past: for all its withered Hopes and all its buried Loves! From the East comes new strength, new ambition, new Hope, new Life, new Love! Look Eastward! Aye, look Eastward!"

His last words were still ringing in my ears as I entered my room, and undrew the window-curtains, just in time to see the sun burst in glory from his ocean-prison, and clothe the world in the light of a new day.

"So may it be for him, and me, and all of us!" I mused. "All that is evil, and dead, and hopeless, fading with the Night that is past! All that is good, and living, and hopeful, rising with the dawn of Day!

"Fading, with the Night, the chilly mists, and the noxious vapours, and the heavy shadows, and the wailing gusts, and the owl's melancholy hootings: rising, with the Day, the darting shafts of light, and the wholesome morning breeze, and the warmth of a dawning life, and the mad music of the lark! Look Eastward!

"Fading, with the Night, the clouds of ignorance, and the deadly blight of sin, and the silent tears of sorrow: and ever rising, higher, higher, with the Day, the radiant dawn of knowledge, and the sweet breath of purity, and the throb of a world's ecstasy! Look Eastward!

"Fading, with the Night, the memory of a dead love, and the withered leaves of a blighted hope, and the sickly repinings and moody regrets that numb the best energies of the soul: and rising, broadening, rolling upward like a living flood, the manly resolve, and the dauntless will, and the heavenward gaze of faith—*the substance of things hoped for, the evidence of things not seen!*

"Look Eastward! Aye, look Eastward!"

THE END

SYLVIE AND BRUNO CONCLUDED

Illustrated by
HARRY FURNISS

Dreams, that elude the Maker's frenzied grasp—
Hands, stark and still, on a dead Mother's breast,
Which nevermore shall render clasp for clasp,
Or deftly soothe a weeping Child to rest—
In suchlike forms me listeth to portray
My Tale, here ended. Thou delicious Fay—
The guardian of a Sprite that lives to tease thee—
Loving in earnest, chiding but in play
The merry mocking Bruno! Who, that sees thee,
Can fail to love thee, Darling, even as I?—
My sweetest Sylvie, we must say "Good-bye!"

PREFACE.

I MUST begin with the same announcement as in the previous Volume (which I shall henceforward refer to as "Vol. I.," calling the present Volume "Vol. II."), viz. that the Locket, Chapter XXV, was drawn by 'Miss Alice Havers.' And my reason, for not stating this on the title-page—that it seems only due, to the artist of these wonderful pictures, that his name should stand there alone—has, I think, even greater weight in Vol. II. than it had in Vol. I. Let me call especial attention to the three "Little Birds" borders, Chapter XXIII. The way, in which he has managed to introduce the most minute details of the stanzas to be illustrated, seems to me a triumph of artistic ingenuity.

Let me here express my sincere gratitude to the many Reviewers who have noticed, whether favorably or unfavorably, the previous Volume. Their unfavorable remarks were, most probably, well-deserved; the favorable ones less probably so. Both kinds have no doubt served to make the book known, and have helped the reading Public to form their opinions of it. Let me also here assure them that it is not from any want of respect for their criticisms, that I have carefully forborne from reading *any* of them. I am strongly of opinion that an author had far better *not* read any reviews of his books: the unfavorable ones are almost certain to make him cross, and the favorable ones conceited; and *neither* of these results is desirable.

Criticisms have, however, reached me from private sources, to some of which I propose to offer a reply.

One such critic complains that Arthur's strictures, on sermons and on choristers, are too severe, Let me say, in reply, that I do *not* hold myself responsible for *any* of the opinions expressed by the characters in my book. They are simply opinions which, it seemed to me, might probably be held by the persons into whose mouths I put them, and which were worth consideration.

Other critics have objected to certain innovations in spelling, such as "ca'n't," "wo'n't," "traveler." In reply, I can only plead my firm conviction that the popular usage is *wrong*. As to "ca'n't," it will not be disputed that, in all *other* words ending in "n't," these letters are an abbreviation of "not"; and it is surely absurd to suppose that, in this solitary instance, "not" is represented by "'t"! In fact "can't" is the *proper* abbreviation for "can it,"just as "is't" is for "is it." Again, in "wo'n't," the first apostrophe is needed, because the word "would" is here *abridged* into "wo": but I hold it proper to spell "don't" with only *one* apostrophe, because the word "do" is here *complete*. As to such words as "traveler," I hold the correct principle to be, to *double* the consonant when the accent falls on that syllable; otherwise to leave it *single*. This rule is observed in most cases (e.g, we double the "r" in "preferred," but leave it single in "offered"), so that I am only extending, to other cases, an existing rule. I admit, however, that I do not spell "parallel," as the rule would have it; but here we are constrained, by the etymology, to insert the double "l".

In the Preface to Vol. I. were two puzzles, on which my readers might exercise their ingenuity. One was, to detect the 3 lines of "padding," which I found it necessary to supply in the passage in Chapter III. They are the lines that begin "I'll make" and end with "lessons!" The other puzzle was, to determine which (if any) of the 8 stanzas of the Gardener's Song were adapted to the context, and which (if any) had the context adapted to them. The last of them is the only one that was adapted to the context, the "Garden-Door that opened with a key" having been substituted for some creature (a Cormorant, I think) "that nestled in a tree." In the 2nd, 5th, and 7th, the context was adapted to the stanza. In the 4th, neither stanza nor context was altered: the connection between them was simply a piece of good luck.

In the Preface to Vol. I., I gave an account of the making-up of the story of "Sylvie and Bruno." A few more details may perhaps be acceptable to my Readers.

It was in 1873, as I *now* believe, that the idea first occurred to me that a little fairy-tale (written, in 1867, for "Aunt Judy's Magazine," under the title "Bruno's Revenge") might serve as the nucleus of a longer story. This I surmise, from having found the original draft of the last paragraph of Vol. II., dated 1873. So that this paragraph has been waiting 20 years for its chance of emerging into print—more than twice the period so cautiously recommended by Horace for 'repressing' one's literary efforts!

It was in February, 1885, that I entered into negotiations, with Mr. Harry Furniss, for illustrating the book. Most of the substance of *both* Volumes was then in existence in manuscript: and my original intention was to publish the *whole* story at once. In September, 1885, I received from Mr. Furniss the first set of drawings—the four which illustrate "Peter and Paul" (see I., Chapter XI): in November, 1886, I received the second set—the three which illustrate the Professor's song about the "little man" who had "a little gun" (Vol. II, Chapter XVII): and in January, 1887, I received the third set—the four which illustrate the "Pig-Tale."

So we went on, illustrating first one bit of the story, and then another, without any idea of sequence. And it was not till March, 1889, that, having calculated the number of pages the story would occupy, I decided on dividing it into *two* portions, and publishing it half at a time. This necessitated the writing of a *sort* of conclusion for the first Volume: and *most* of my Readers, I fancy, regarded this as the *actual* conclusion, when that Volume appeared in December, 1889. At any rate, among all the letters I received about it, there was only *one* which expressed *any* suspicion that it was not a *final* conclusion. This letter was from a child. She wrote "we were so glad, when we came to the end of the book, to find that there was no ending-up, for that shows us that you are going to write a sequel."

It may interest some of my Readers to know the *theory* on which this story is constructed. It is an attempt to show what might *possibly* happen, supposing that Fairies really existed; and that they were sometimes visible to us, and we to them; and that they were sometimes able to assume human form: and supposing, also, that human beings might sometimes become conscious of what goes on in the Fairy-world—by actual transference of their immaterial essence, such as we meet with in 'Esoteric Buddhism.'

I have supposed a Human being to be capable of various psychical states, with varying degrees of consciousness, as follows:—

(*a*) the ordinary state, with no consciousness of the presence of Fairies;

(*b*) the 'eerie' state, in which, while conscious of actual surroundings, he is *also* conscious of the presence of Fairies;

(*c*) a form of trance, in which, while *un*conscious of actual surroundings, and apparently asleep, he (i.e. his immaterial essence) migrates to other scenes, in the actual world, or in Fairyland, and is conscious of the presence of Fairies.

I have also supposed a Fairy to be capable of migrating from Fairyland into the actual world, and of assuming, at pleasure, a Human form; and also to be capable of various psychical states, viz.

(*a*) the ordinary state, with no consciousness of the presence of Human beings;

(*b*) a sort of 'eerie' state, in which he is conscious, if in the actual world, of the presence of actual Human beings; if in Fairyland, of the presence of the immaterial essences of Human beings. . . .

In the Preface to Vol. I., I gave an account of the *origination* of some of the ideas embodied in the book. A few more such details may perhaps interest my Readers:——

I., Ch. XIV. The very peculiar use, here made of a dead mouse, comes from real life. I once found two very small boys, in a garden, playing a microscopic game of 'Single-Wicket.' The bat was, I think, about the size of a table-spoon; and the utmost distance attained by the ball, in its most daring flights, was some 4 or 5 yards. The *exact* length was of course a matter of *supreme* importance; and it was always carefully measured out (the batsman and the bowler amicably sharing the toil) with a dead mouse!

I., Ch. XVIII. The two quasi-mathematical Axioms, quoted by Arthur ("Things that are greater than the same are greater than one another," and "All angles are equal") were actually enunciated, in all seriousness, by undergraduates at a University situated not 100 miles from Ely.

II., Ch. I. Bruno's remark ("I can, if I like, &c.") was actually made by a little boy.

II., Ch. I. So also was his remark ("I know what it *doesn't* spell.") And his remark ("I just twiddled my eyes, &c.") I heard from the lips of a little girl, who had just solved a puzzle I had set her.

II., Ch. IV. Bruno's soliloquy ("For its father, &c.") was actually spoken by a little girl, looking out of the window of a railway-carriage.

II., Ch. IX. The remark, made by a guest at the dinner-party, when asking for a dish of fruit ("I've been wishing for them, &c.") I heard made by the great Poet-Laureate, whose loss the whole reading-world has so lately had to deplore.

II., Ch. XI. Bruno's speech, on the subject of the age of 'Mein Herr,' embodies the reply of a little girl to the question "Is your grandmother an *old* lady?" "I don't know if she's an *old* lady," said this cautious young person; "she's *eighty-three*."

II., Ch. XIII. The speech about 'Obstruction' is no mere creature of my imagination! It is copied *verbatim* from the columns of the Standard, and was spoken by Sir William Harcourt, who was, at the time, a member of the 'Opposition,' at the 'National Liberal Club,' on July the 16th, 1890.

II., Ch. XXI. The Professor's remark, about a dog's tail, that "it doesn't bite at *that* end," was actually made by a child, when warned of the danger he was incurring by pulling the dog's tail.

II., Ch. XXIII. The dialogue between Sylvie and Bruno about the large slice of cake is a *verbatim* report (merely substituting "cake" for "penny") of a dialogue overheard between two children.

One story in this Volume—'Bruno's Picnic'—I can vouch for as suitable for telling to children, having tested it again and again; and, whether my audience has been a dozen little girls in a village-school, or some thirty or forty in a London drawing-room, or a hundred in a High School, I have always found them earnestly attentive, and keenly appreciative of such fun as the story supplied.

May I take this opportunity of calling attention to what I flatter myself was a successful piece of name-coining, Vol. I., Chapter III. Does not the name 'Sibimet' fairly embody the character of the Sub-Warden? The gentle Reader has no doubt observed what a singularly useless article in a house a brazen trumpet is, if you simply leave it lying about, and never blow it!

Readers of the first Volume, who have amused themselves by trying to solve the two puzzles propounded in the Preface, may perhaps like to exercise their ingenuity in discovering which (if any) of the following parallelisms were intentional, and which (if any) accidental.

"Little Birds."	Events, and Persons.
Stanza 1.	Banquet.
2.	Chancellor.
3.	Empress and Spinach (II., Ch. XX).
4.	Warden's Return.
5.	Professor's Lecture (II., Ch. XXI).
6.	Other Professor's song (I., Ch. X).
7.	Petting of Uggug.
8.	Baron Doppelgeist.
9.	Jester and Bear (I., Ch. IX). Little Foxes.
10.	Bruno's Dinner-Bell; Little Foxes.

I will publish the answer to this puzzle in the Preface to a little book of "Original Games and Puzzles," now in course of preparation.

I have reserved, for the last, one or two rather more serious topics.

I had intended, in this Preface, to discuss more fully, than I had done in the previous Volume, the 'Morality of Sport,' with special reference to letters I have received from lovers of Sport, in which they point out the many great advantages which men get from it, and try to prove that the suffering, which it inflicts on animals, is too trivial to be regarded.

But, when I came to think the subject out, and to arrange the whole of the arguments 'pro' and 'con', I found it much too large for treatment here. Some day, I hope to publish an essay on this subject. At present, I will content myself with stating the net result I have arrived at.

It is, that God has given to Man an absolute right to take the *lives* of other animals, for *any* reasonable cause, such as the supply of food: but that He has *not* given to Man the right to inflict *pain*, unless when *necessary:* that mere pleasure, or advantage, does not constitute such a necessity: and, consequently, that pain, inflicted for the purposes of *Sport*, is cruel, and therefore wrong. But I find it a far more complex question than I had supposed; and that the 'case', on the side of the Sportsman, is a much stronger one than I had supposed. So, for the present, I say no more about it.

Objections have been raised to the severe language I have put into the mouth of 'Arthur', in Chapter XVI, on the subject of 'Sermons,' and in Chapter XIX, on the subjects of Choral Services and 'Choristers.'

I have already protested against the assumption that I am ready to endorse the opinions of characters in my story. But, in these two instances, I admit that I am much in sympathy with 'Arthur.' In my opinion, far too many sermons are expected from our preachers; and, as a consequence, a great many are preached, which are not worth listening to; and, as a consequence of *that*, we are very apt *not* to listen. The reader of this paragraph probably heard a sermon last Sunday morning? Well, let him, if he can, name the text, and state how the preacher treated it!

Then, as to 'Choristers,' and all the other accessories—of music, vestments, processions, &c.,—which have come, along with them, into fashion—while freely admitting that the 'Ritual' movement was sorely needed, and that it has effected a vast improvement in our Church-Services, which had become dead and dry to the last degree, I hold that, like many other desirable movements, it has gone too far in the opposite direction, and has introduced many new dangers.

For the Congregation this new movement involves the danger of learning to think that the Services are done *for* them; and that their bodily *presence* is all they need contribute. And, for Clergy and Congregation alike, it involves the danger of regarding these elaborate Services as *ends in themselves*, and of forgetting that they are simply *means*, and the very hollowest of mockeries, unless they bear fruit in our *lives*.

For the Choristers it seems to involve the danger of self-conceit . . . the danger of regarding those parts of the Service, where their help is not required, as not worth attending to, the danger of coming to regard the Service as a mere outward form—a series of postures to be assumed, and of words to be said or sung, while the *thoughts* are elsewhere—and the danger of 'familiarity' breeding 'contempt' for sacred things.

Let me illustrate these last two forms of danger, from my own experience. Not long ago, I attended a Cathedral-Service, and was placed immediately behind a row of men, members of the Choir; and I could not help noticing that they treated the *Lessons* as a part of the Service to which they needed not to give *any* attention, and as affording them a convenient opportunity for arranging music-books, &c., &c. Also I have frequently seen a row of little choristers, after marching in procession to their places, kneel down, as if about to pray, and rise from their knees after a minute spent in looking about them, it being but too evident that the attitude was a mere mockery. Surely it is very dangerous, for these children, to thus accustom them to *pretend* to pray? As an instance of irreverent treatment of holy things, I will mention a custom, which no doubt many of my readers have noticed in Churches where the Clergy and Choir enter in procession, viz. that, at the end of the private devotions, which are carried on in the vestry, and which are of course inaudible to the Congregation, the final "Amen" is *shouted,* loud enough to be heard all through the Church. This serves as a signal, to the Congregation, to prepare to rise when the procession appears: and it admits of no dispute that it is for this purpose that it is thus shouted. When we remember to Whom that "Amen" is *really* addressed, and consider that it is here *used* for the same purpose as one of the Church-bells, we must surely admit that it is a piece of gross irreverence? To *me* it is much as if I were to see a Bible used as a footstool.

As an instance of the dangers, for the Clergy themselves, introduced by this new movement, let me mention the fact that, according to *my* experience, Clergymen of this school are *specially* apt to retail comic anecdotes, in which the most sacred names and words—sometimes actual texts from the Bible—are used as themes for jesting. Many such things are repeated as having been originally said by *children,* whose utter ignorance of evil must no doubt acquit *them,* in the sight of God, of all blame; but it must be otherwise for those who *consciously* use such innocent utterances as material for their unholy mirth.

Let me add, however, *most* earnestly, that I fully believe that this profanity is, in many cases, *unconscious:* the 'environment' . . . makes all the difference between man and man; and I rejoice to think that many of these profane stories—which *I* find so painful to listen to, and should feel it a sin to repeat—give to *their* ears no pain, and to *their* consciences no shock; and that *they* can utter, not less sincerely than myself, the two prayers, *"Hallowed be Thy Name,"* and *"from hardness of heart, and contempt of Thy Word and Commandment, Good Lord, deliver us!"* To which I would desire to add, for their sake and for my own, Keble's beautiful petition, *"help us, this and every day, To live more nearly as we pray!"* It is, in fact, for its *consequences*—for the grave dangers, both to speaker and to hearer, which it involves—rather than for what it is *in itself* that I mourn over this clerical habit of profanity in social talk. To the *believing* hearer it brings the danger of loss of reverence for holy things, by the mere act of listening to, and enjoying, such jests; and also the temptation to retail them for the amusement of others. To the *unbelieving* hearer it brings a welcome confirmation of his theory that religion is a fable, in the spectacle of its accredited champions thus betraying their trust. And to the speaker himself it must surely bring the danger of *loss of faith*. For surely such jests, if uttered with no consciousness of harm, must necessarily be also uttered with no consciousness, at the moment, of the *reality* of God, as a *living being*, who hears all we say. And he, who allows himself the habit of thus uttering holy words, with no thought of their meaning, is but too likely to find that, for him, God has become a myth, and heaven a poetic fancy—that, for him, the light of life is gone, and that he is at heart an atheist, lost in *"a darkness that may be felt."*

There is, I fear, at the present time, an increasing tendency to irreverent treatment of the name of God and of subjects connected with religion. Some of our theatres are helping this downward movement by the gross caricatures of clergymen which they put upon the stage: some of our clergy are themselves helping it, by showing that they can lay aside the spirit of reverence, along with their surplices, and can treat as jests, when *outside* their churches, names and things to which they pay an almost superstitious veneration when *inside:* the "Salvation Army" has, I fear, with the best intentions, done much to help it, by the coarse familiarity with which they treat holy things: and surely every one, who desires to *live* in the spirit of the prayer *"Hallowed be thy Name,"* ought to do what he can, however little that may be, to check it. So I have gladly taken this unique opportunity, however unfit the topic may seem for the Preface to a book of this kind, to express some thoughts which have weighed on my mind for a long time. I did not expect, when I wrote the Preface to Vol. I, that it would be read to any appreciable extent: but I rejoice to believe, from evidence that has reached me, that it *has* been read by many, and to hope that this Preface will also be so: and I think that, among them, some will be found ready to sympathise with the views I have put forwards, and ready to help, with their prayers and their example, the revival, in Society, of the waning spirit of reverence.

Christmas, 1893.

Editorial Note: This Preface is somewhat abridged; cross references by page number have been deleted.

CHAPTER I.

BRUNO'S LESSONS.

DURING the next month or two my solitary town-life seemed, by contrast, unusually dull and tedious. I missed the pleasant friends I had left behind at Elveston—the genial interchange of thought—the sympathy which gave to one's ideas a new and vivid reality: but, perhaps more than all, I missed the companionship of the two Fairies—or Dream-Children, for I had not yet solved the problem as to who or what they were—whose sweet playfulness had shed a magic radiance over my life.

In office-hours—which I suppose reduce most men to the mental condition of a coffee-mill or a mangle—time sped along much as usual: it was in the pauses of life, the desolate hours when books and newspapers palled on the sated appetite, and when, thrown back upon one's own dreary musings, one strove—all in vain—to people the vacant air with the dear faces of absent friends, that the real bitterness of solitude made itself felt.

One evening, feeling my life a little more wearisome than usual, I strolled down to my Club, not so much with the hope of meeting any friend there, for London was now 'out of town,' as with the feeling that here, at least, I should hear 'sweet words of human speech,' and come into contact with human thought.

However, almost the first face I saw there *was* that of a friend. Eric Lindon was lounging, with rather a 'bored' expression of face, over a newspaper; and we fell into conversation with a mutual satisfaction which neither of us tried to conceal.

After a while I ventured to introduce what was just then the main subject of my thoughts. "And so the Doctor" (a name we had adopted by a tacit agreement, as a convenient compromise between the formality of 'Doctor Forester' and the intimacy—to which Eric Lindon hardly seemed entitled—of 'Arthur') "has gone abroad by this time, I suppose? Can you give me his present address?"

"He is still at Elveston—I believe," was the reply. "But I have not been there since I last met you."

I did not know which part of this intelligence to wonder at most. "And might I ask—if it isn't taking too much of a liberty—when your wedding-bells are to—or perhaps they *have* rung, already?"

"No," said Eric, in a steady voice, which betrayed scarcely a trace of emotion: "*that* engagement is at an end. I am still 'Benedick the *un*married man.'"

After this, the thick-coming fancies—all radiant with new possibilities of happiness for Arthur—were far too bewildering to admit of any further conversation, and I was only too glad to avail myself of the first decent excuse, that offered itself, for retiring into silence.

The next day I wrote to Arthur, with as much of a reprimand for his long silence as I could bring myself to put into words, begging him to tell me how the world went with him.

Needs must that three or four days—possibly more—should elapse before I could receive his reply; and never had I known days drag their slow length along with a more tedious indolence.

To while away the time, I strolled, one afternoon, into Kensington Gardens, and, wandering aimlessly along any path that presented itself, I soon became aware that I had somehow strayed into one that was wholly new to me. Still, my elfish experiences seemed to have so completely faded out of my life that nothing was further from my thoughts than the idea of again meeting my fairy-friends, when I chanced to notice a small creature, moving among the grass that fringed the path, that did not seem to be an insect, or a frog, or any other living thing that I could think of. Cautiously kneeling down, and making an *ex tempore* cage of my two hands, I imprisoned the little wanderer, and felt a sudden thrill of surprise and delight on discovering that my prisoner was no other than *Bruno* himself!

Bruno took the matter *very* coolly, and, when I had replaced him on the ground, where he would be within easy conversational distance, he began talking, just as if it were only a few minutes since last we had met.

"Doos oo know what the *Rule* is," he enquired, "when oo catches a Fairy, withouten its having tolded oo where it was?" (Bruno's notions of English Grammar had certainly *not* improved since our last meeting.)

"No," I said, "I didn't know there was any Rule about it."

"I *think* oo've got a right to *eat* me," said the little fellow, looking up into my face with a winning smile. "But I'm not pruffickly sure, Oo'd better not do it wizout asking."

It did indeed seem reasonable not to take so irrevocable a step as *that*, without due enquiry, "I'll certainly *ask* about it, first," I said. "Besides, I don't know yet whether you would be *worth* eating!"

"I guess I'm *deliciously* good to eat," Bruno remarked in a satisfied tone, as if it were something to be rather proud of.

"And what are you doing here, Bruno?"

"*That's* not my name!" said my cunning little friend. "Don't oo know my name's 'Oh Bruno!'? That's what Sylvie always calls me, when I says mine lessons."

"Well then, what are you doing here, oh Bruno?"

"Doing mine lessons, a-course!" With that roguish twinkle in his eye, that always came when he knew he was talking nonsense.

"Oh, *that's* the way you do your lessons, is it? And do you remember them well?"

"Always can 'member *mine* lessons," said Bruno. "It's *Sylvie's* lessons that's so *dreffully* hard to 'member!" He frowned, as if in agonies of thought, and tapped his forehead with his knuckles. "I *ca'n't* think enough to understand them!" he said despairingly. "It wants *double* thinking, I believe!"

"But where's Sylvie gone?"

"That's just what *I* want to know!" said Bruno disconsolately. "What ever's the good of setting me lessons, when she isn't here to 'splain the hard bits?"

"*I'll* find her for you!" I volunteered; and, getting up, I wandered round the tree under whose shade I had been reclining, looking on all sides for Sylvie. In another minute I *again* noticed some strange thing moving among the grass, and, kneeling down, was immediately confronted with Sylvie's innocent face, lighted up with a joyful surprise at seeing me, and was accosted, in the sweet voice I knew so well, with what seemed to be the *end* of a sentence whose beginning I had failed to catch.

"—and I think he ought to have *finished* them by this time. So I'm going back to him. Will you come too? It's only just round at the other side of this tree."

It was but a few steps for *me;* but it was a great many for Sylvie; and I had to be very careful to walk slowly, in order not to leave the little creature so far behind as to lose sight of her.

To find Bruno's *lessons* was easy enough: they appeared to be neatly written out on large smooth ivy-leaves, which were scattered in some confusion over a little patch of ground where the grass had been worn away; but the pale student, who ought by rights to have been bending over them, was nowhere to be seen: we looked in all directions, for some time, in vain; but at last Sylvie's sharp eyes detected him, swinging on a tendril of ivy, and Sylvie's stern voice commanded his instant return to *terra firma* and to the business of Life.

"Pleasure first and business afterwards" seemed to be the motto of these tiny folk, so many hugs and kisses had to be interchanged before anything else could be done.

"Now, Bruno," Sylvie said reproachfully, "didn't I tell you you were to go on with your lessons, unless you heard to the contrary?"

"But I *did* heard to the contrary!" Bruno insisted, with a mischievous twinkle in his eye.

"*What* did you hear, you wicked boy?"

"It were a sort of noise in the air," said Bruno: "a sort of a scrambling noise. Didn't *oo* hear it, Mister Sir?"

"Well, anyhow, you needn't go to *sleep* over them, you lazy-lazy!" For Bruno had curled himself up, on the largest 'lesson,' and was arranging another as a pillow.

"I *wasn't* asleep!" said Bruno, in a deeply-injured tone. "When I shuts mine eyes, it's to show that I'm *awake!*"

"Well, how much have you learned, then?"

"I've learned a little tiny bit," said Bruno, modestly, being evidently afraid of overstating his achievement. "*Ca'n't* learn no more!"

"Oh Bruno! You know you *can,* if you like."

"Course I can, if I *like*," the pale student replied; "but I ca'n't if I *don't* like!"

Sylvie had a way—which I could not too highly admire—of evading Bruno's logical perplexities by suddenly striking into a new line of thought; and this masterly stratagem she now adopted.

"Well, I must say *one* thing——"

"Did oo know, Mister Sir," Bruno thoughtfully remarked, "that Sylvie ca'n't count? Whenever she says 'I must say *one* thing,' I *know* quite well she'll say *two* things! And she always doos."

"Two heads are better than one, Bruno," I said, but with no very distinct idea as to what I meant by it.

"I shouldn't mind having two *heads*," Bruno said softly to himself: "one head to eat mine dinner, and one head to argue wiz Sylvie—doos oo think oo'd look prettier if oo'd got *two* heads, Mister Sir?"

The case did not, I assured him, admit of a doubt.

"The reason why Sylvie's so cross——" Bruno went on very seriously, almost sadly.

Sylvie's eyes grew large and round with surprise at this new line of enquiry—her rosy face being perfectly radiant with good humour. But she said nothing.

"Wouldn't it be better to tell me after the lessons are over?" I suggested.

"Very well," Bruno said with a resigned air: "only she wo'n't be cross then."

"There's only three lessons to do," said Sylvie. "Spelling, and Geography, and Singing."

"Not *Arithmetic?*" I said.

"No, he hasn't a head for Arithmetic——"

"Course I haven't!" said Bruno. "Mine head's for *hair.* I haven't got a *lot* of heads!"

"—and he ca'n't learn his Multiplication-table——"

"I like *History* ever so much better," Bruno remarked. "Oo has to *repeat* that Muddlecome table——"

"Well, and you have to repeat——"

"No, oo hasn't!" Bruno interrupted. "History repeats itself. The Professor said so!"

Sylvie was arranging some letters on a board—E—V—I—L. "Now, Bruno," she said, "what does *that* spell?"

Bruno looked at it, in solemn silence, for a minute. "I know what it *doosn't* spell!" he said at last.

"That's no good," said Sylvie. "What *does* it spell?"

Bruno took another look at the mysterious letters. "Why, it's 'LIVE,' backwards!" he exclaimed. (I thought it was, indeed.)

"How *did* you manage to see that?" said Sylvie.

"I just twiddled my eyes," said Bruno, "and then I saw it directly. Now may I sing the King-fisher Song?"

"Geography next," said Sylvie. "Don't you know the Rules?"

"I thinks there oughtn't to be such a lot of Rules, Sylvie! I thinks——"

"Yes, there *ought* to be such a lot of Rules, you wicked, wicked boy! And how dare you *think* at all about it? And shut up that mouth directly!"

So, as 'that mouth' didn't seem inclined to shut up of itself, Sylvie shut it for him—with both hands—and sealed it with a kiss, just as you would fasten up a letter.

"Now that Bruno is fastened up from talking," she went on, turning to me, "I'll show you the Map he does his lessons on."

And there it was, a large Map of the World, spread out on the ground. It was so large that Bruno had to crawl about on it, to point out the places named in the 'King-fisher Lesson.'

"When a King-fisher sees a Lady-bird flying away, he says '*Ceylon,* if you *Candia!*' And when he catches it, he says 'Come to *Media!* And if you're *Hungary* or thirsty, I'll give you some *Nubia!*' When he takes it in his claws, he says '*Europe!*' When he puts it into his beak, he says '*India!*' When he's swallowed it, he says '*Eton!*' That's all."

"That's *quite* perfect," said Sylvie. "Now, you may sing the King-fisher Song.'

"Will *oo* sing the chorus?" Bruno said to me.

I was just beginning to say "I'm afraid I don't know the *words*," when Sylvie silently turned the map over, and I found the words were all written on the back. In one respect it was a *very* peculiar song: the chorus to each verse came in the *middle*, instead of at the *end* of it. However, the tune was so easy that I soon picked it up, and managed the chorus as well, perhaps, as it is possible for *one* person to manage such a thing. It was in vain that I signed to Sylvie to help me: she only smiled sweetly and shook her head.

> "*King Fisher courted Lady Bird*—
> **Sing Beans, sing Bones, sing Butterflies!**
> '*Find me my match,*' *he said,*
> '*With such a noble head*—
> *With such a beard, as white as curd*—
> *With such expressive eyes!*'
>
> "'*Yet pins have heads,*' *said Lady Bird*—
> **Sing Prunes, sing Prawns, sing Primrose-Hill!**
> '*And, where you stick them in,*
> *They stay, and thus a pin*
> *Is very much to be preferred*
> *To one that's never still!*'
>
> "'*Oysters have beards,*' *said Lady Bird*—
> **Sing Flies, sing Frogs, sing Fiddle-strings!**
> '*I love them, for I know*
> *They never chatter so:*
> *They would not say one single word*—
> *Not if you crowned them Kings!*'
>
> "'*Needles have eyes,*' *said Lady Bird*—
> **Sing Cats, sing Corks, sing Cowslip-tea!**
> '*And they are sharp—just what*
> *Your Majesty is* not:
> *So get you gone—'tis too absurd*
> *To come a-courting* me!'"

"So he went away," Bruno added as a kind of postscript, when the last note of the song had died away. "Just like he always did."

"Oh, my *dear* Bruno!" Sylvie exclaimed, with her hands over her ears. "You shouldn't say 'like': you should say '*what*.'"

To which Bruno replied, doggedly, "I only says 'what!' when oo doesn't speak loud, so as I can hear oo."

"Where did he go to?" I asked, hoping to prevent an argument.

"He went more far than he'd never been before," said Bruno.

"You should never say 'more far,'" Sylvie corrected him: "you should say '*farther*.'"

"Then *oo* shouldn't say 'more broth,' when we're at dinner," Bruno retorted: "oo should say '*brother*'!"

This time Sylvie evaded an argument by turning away, and beginning to roll up the Map. "Lessons are over!" she proclaimed in her sweetest tones.

"And has there been no *crying* over them?" I enquired. "Little boys *always* cry over their lessons, don't they?"

"I never cries after twelve o'clock," said Bruno: "'cause then it's getting so near to dinner-time."

"Sometimes, in the morning," Sylvie said in a low voice; "when it's Geography-day, and when he's been disobe——"

"*What* a fellow you are to talk, Sylvie!" Bruno hastily interposed. "Doos oo think the world was *made* for oo to talk in?"

"Why, where would you *have* me talk, then?" Sylvie said, evidently quite ready for an argument.

But Bruno answered resolutely. "I'm not going to argue about it, 'cause it's getting late, and there wo'n't be time—but oo's as 'ong as ever oo can be!" And he rubbed the back of his hand across his eyes, in which tears were beginning to glitter.

Sylvie's eyes filled with tears in a moment. "I didn't mean it, Bruno, *darling!*" she whispered; and the rest of the argument was lost 'amid the tangles of Neæra's hair,' while the two disputants hugged and kissed each other.

But this new form of argument was brought to a sudden end by a flash of lightning, which was closely followed by a peal of thunder, and by a torrent of rain-drops, which came hissing and spitting, almost like live creatures, through the leaves of the tree that sheltered us.

"Why, it's raining cats and dogs!" I said.

"And all the *dogs* has come down *first*," said Bruno: "there's nothing but *cats* coming down now!"

In another minute the pattering ceased, as suddenly as it had begun. I stepped out from under the tree, and found that the storm was over; but I looked in vain, on my return, for my tiny companions. They had vanished with the storm, and there was nothing for it but to make the best of my way home.

On the table lay, awaiting my return, an envelope of that peculiar yellow tint which always announces a telegram, and which must be, in the memories of so many of us, inseparably linked with some great and sudden sorrow—something that has cast a shadow, never in this world to be wholly lifted off, on the brightness of Life. No doubt it has *also* heralded—for many of us—some sudden news of joy; but this, I think, is less common: human life seems, on the whole, to contain more of sorrow than of joy. And yet the world goes on. Who knows why?

This time, however, there was no shock of sorrow to be faced: in fact, the few words it contained ("Could not bring myself to write. Come soon. Always welcome. A letter follows this. Arthur.") seemed so like Arthur himself speaking, that it gave me quite a thrill of pleasure, and I at once began the preparations needed for the journey.

CHAPTER II.

LOVE'S CURFEW.

"FAYFIELD Junction! Change for Elveston!"

What subtle memory could there be, linked to these commonplace words, that caused such a flood of happy thoughts to fill my brain? I dismounted from the carriage in a state of joyful excitement for which I could not at first account. True, I had taken this very journey, and at the same hour of the day, six months ago; but many things had happened since then, and an old man's memory has but a slender hold on recent events: I sought 'the missing link' in vain. Suddenly I caught sight of a bench—the only one provided on the cheerless platform—with a lady seated on it, and the whole forgotten scene flashed upon me as vividly as if it were happening over again.

"Yes," I thought. "This bare platform is, for me, rich with the memory

of a dear friend! She was sitting on that very bench, and invited me to
share it, with some quotation from Shakespeare—I forget what. I'll try
the Earl's plan for the Dramatisation of Life, and fancy that figure to
be Lady Muriel; and I won't undeceive myself too soon!"

So I strolled along the platform, resolutely 'making-believe' (as children
say) that the casual passenger, seated on that bench, was the Lady Muriel
I remembered so well. She was facing away from me, which aided the
elaborate cheatery I was practising on myself: but, though I was careful,
in passing the spot, to look the other way, in order to prolong the pleasant
illusion, it was inevitable that, when I turned to walk back again, I should
see who it was. It was Lady Muriel herself!

The whole scene now returned vividly to my memory; and, to make
this repetition of it stranger still, there was the same old man, whom I
remembered seeing so roughly ordered off, by the Station-Master, to
make room for his titled passenger. The same, but 'with a difference':
no longer tottering feebly along the platform, but actually seated at Lady
Muriel's side, and in conversation with her! "Yes, put it in your purse,"
she was saying, "and remember you're to spend it all for *Minnie*. And
mind you bring her something nice, that'll do her real good! And give
her my love!" So intent was she on saying these words, that, although
the sound of my footstep had made her lift her head and look at me,
she did not at first recognise me.

I raised my hat as I approached, and then there flashed across her
face a genuine look of joy, which so exactly recalled the sweet face of
Sylvie, when last we met in Kensington Gardens, that I felt quite bewildered.

Rather than disturb the poor old man at her side, she rose from her
seat, and joined me in my walk up and down the platform, and for a

minute or two our conversation was as utterly trivial and commonplace as if we were merely two casual guests in a London drawing-room. Each of us seemed to shrink, just at first, from touching on the deeper interests which linked our lives together.

The Elveston train had drawn up at the platform, while we talked; and, in obedience to the Station-Master's obsequious hint of "This way, my Lady! Time's up!", we were making the best of our way towards the end which contained the sole first-class carriage, and were just passing the now-empty bench, when Lady Muriel noticed, lying on it, the purse in which her gift had just been so carefully bestowed, the owner of which, all unconscious of his loss, was being helped into a carriage at the other end of the train. She pounced on it instantly. "Poor old man!" she cried. "He mustn't go off, and think he's lost it!"

"Let *me* run with it! I can go quicker than you!" I said. But she was already half-way down the platform, flying ('running' is much too mundane a word for such fairy-like motion) at a pace that left all possible efforts of *mine* hopelessly in the rear.

She was back again before I had well completed my audacious boast of speed in running, and was saying, quite demurely, as we entered our carriage, "and you really think *you* could have done it quicker?"

"No, indeed!" I replied. "I plead 'Guilty' of gross exaggeration, and throw myself on the mercy of the Court!"

"The Court will overlook it—for this once!" Then her manner suddenly changed from playfulness to an anxious gravity.

"You are not looking your best!" she said with an anxious glance. "In fact, I think you look *more* of an invalid than when you left us. I very much doubt if London agrees with you?"

"It *may* be the London air," I said, "or it may be the hard work—or my rather lonely life: anyhow, I've *)not* been feeling very well, lately. But Elveston will soon set me up again. Arthur's prescription—he's my doctor, you know, and I heard from him this morning—is 'plenty of ozone, and new milk, and *pleasant society*'!"

"Pleasant society?" said Lady Muriel, with a pretty make-believe of considering the question. "Well, really I don't know where we can find *that* for you! We have so few neighbours. But new milk we *can* manage. Do get it of my old friend Mrs. Hunter, up there, on the hill-side. You may rely upon the *quality*. And her little Bessie comes to school every day, and passes your lodgings. So it would be very easy to send it."

"I'll follow your advice, with pleasure," I said; "and I'll go and arrange about it to-morrow. I know Arthur will want a walk."

"You'll find it quite an easy walk—under three miles, I think."

"Well, now that we've settled that point, let me retort your own remark upon yourself. I don't think *you're* looking quite your best!"

"I daresay not," she replied in a low voice; and a sudden shadow seemed to overspread her face. "I've had some troubles lately. It's a matter about which I've been long wishing to consult you, but I couldn't easily write about it. I'm *so* glad to have this opportunity!"

"Do you think," she began again, after a minute's silence, and with a visible embarrassment of manner most unusual in her, "that a promise, deliberately and solemnly given, is *always* binding—except, of course, where its fulfilment would involve some actual *sin?*"

"I ca'nt think of any other exception at this moment," I said. "That branch of casuistry is usually, I believe, treated as a question of truth and untruth——"

"Surely that *is* the principle?" she eagerly interrupted. "I always thought the Bible-teaching about it consisted of such texts as '*lie not one to another*'?"

"I have thought about that point," I replied; "and it seems to me that the essence of *lying* is the intention of *deceiving*. If you give a promise, fully *intending* to fulfil it, you are certainly acting truthfully *then;* and, if you afterwards break it, that does not involve any *deception*. I cannot call it *untruthful*."

Another pause of silence ensued. Lady Muriel's face was hard to read: she looked pleased, I thought, but also puzzled; and I felt curious to know whether her question had, as I began to suspect, some bearing on the breaking off of her engagement with Captain (now Major) Lindon.

"You have relieved me from a great fear," she said; "but the thing is of course *wrong*, somehow. What texts would *you* quote, to prove it wrong?"

"Any that enforce the payment of *debts*. If *A* promises something to *B*, *B* has a claim upon *A*. And *A*'s sin, if he breaks his promise, seems to me more analogous to *stealing* than to *lying*."

"It's a new way of looking at it—to me," she said; "but it seems a *true* way, also. However, I won't deal in generalities with an old friend like you! For we *are* old friends, somehow. Do you know, I think we *began* as old friends?" she said with a playfulness of tone that ill accorded with the tears that glistened in her eyes.

"Thank you very much for saying so," I replied. "I like to think of you as an *old* friend," ("—though you don't look it!" would have been the almost necessary sequence, with any other lady; but she and I seemed to have long passed out of the time when compliments, or any such trivialities, were possible.)

Here the train paused at a station, where two or three passengers entered the carriage; so no more was said till we had reached our journey's end.

On our arrival at Elveston, she readily adopted my suggestion that we should walk up together; so, as soon as our luggage had been duly taken charge of—hers by the servant who met her at the station, and mine by one of the porters—we set out together along the familiar lanes, now linked in my memory with so many delightful associations. Lady Muriel at once recommenced the conversation at the point where it had been interrupted.

"You knew of my engagement to my cousin Eric. Did you also hear——"

"Yes," I interrupted, anxious to spare her the pain of giving any details. "I heard it had all come to an end."

"I would like to tell you how it happened," she said; "as that is the very point I want your advice about. I had long realised that we were not in sympathy in religious belief. His ideas of Christianity are very shadowy; and even as to the existence of a God he lives in a sort of dreamland. But it has not affected his life! I feel sure, now, that the most absolute Atheist *may* be leading, though walking blindfold, a pure and noble life. And if you knew half the good deeds——" she broke off suddenly, and turned away her head.

"I entirely agree with you," I said. "And have we not our Saviour's own promise that such a life shall surely lead to the light?"

"Yes, I know it," she said in a broken voice, still keeping her head turned away. "And so I told him. He said he would believe, for *my* sake, if he could. And he wished, for *my* sake, he could see things as I did. But that is all wrong!" she went on passionately. "God *cannot* approve such low motives as that! Still it was not *I* that broke it off. I knew he loved me; and I had *promised;* and——"

"Then it was *he* that broke it off?"

"He released me unconditionally." She faced me again now, having quite recovered her usual calmness of manner.

"Then what difficulty remains?"

"It is *this,* that I don't believe he did it of his own free will. Now, supposing he did it *against* his will, merely to satisfy my scruples, would not his claim on me remain just as strong as ever? And would not my promise be as binding as ever? My father says 'no'; but I ca'n't help fearing he is biased by his love for me. And I've asked no one else. I have many friends—friends for the bright sunny weather; not friends for the clouds and storms of life; not *old* friends like you!"

"Let me think a little," I said: and for some minutes we walked on in silence, while pained to the heart at seeing the bitter trial that had come upon this pure and gentle soul, I strove in vain to see my way through the tangled skein of conflicting motives.

"If she loves him truly," (I seemed at last to grasp the clue to the problem) "is not *that,* for her, the voice of God? May she not hope that she is sent to him, even as Ananias was sent to Saul in his blindness, that he may receive his sight?" Once more I seemed to hear Arthur whispering *"What knowest thou, O wife, whether thou shalt save thy husband?"* and I broke the silence with the words "If you still love him truly——"

"I do *not!*" she hastily interrupted. "At least—not in *that* way. I *believe* I loved him when I promised; but I was very young: it is hard to know. But, whatever the feeling was, it is dead *now.* The motive on *his* side is Love: on *mine* it is—Duty!"

Again there was a long silence. The whole skein of thought was tangled worse than ever. This time *she* broke the silence. "Don't misunderstand me!" she said. "When I said my heart was not *his,* I did not mean it was any one else's! At present I feel bound to *him;* and, till I know I am absolutely free, in the sight of God, to love any other than him, I'll never even *think* of any one else—in *that* way, I mean. I would die sooner!" I had never imagined my gentle friend capable of such passionate utterances.

I ventured on no further remark until we had nearly arrived at the Hall-gate; but, the longer I reflected, the clearer it became to me that no call of Duty demanded the sacrifice—possibly of the happiness of a life—which she seemed ready to make. I tried to make this clear to *her* also, adding some warnings on the dangers that surely awaited a union in which mutual love was wanting. "The only argument for it, worth considering," I said in conclusion, "seems to be his supposed *reluctance* in releasing you from your promise. I have tried to give to that argument its *full* weight, and my conclusion is that it does *not* affect the rights of the case, or invalidate the release he has given you. My belief is that you are *entirely* free to act as *now* seems right."

"I am *very* grateful to you," she said earnestly. "Believe it, please! I ca'n't put it into proper words!" and the subject was dropped by mutual consent: and I only learned, long afterwards, that our discussion had really served to dispel the doubts that had harassed her so long.

We parted at the Hall-gate, and I found Arthur eagerly awaiting my arrival; and, before we parted for the night, I had heard the whole story—how he had put off his journey from day to day, feeling that he *could* not go away from the place till his fate had been irrevocably settled by the wedding taking place: how the preparations for the wedding, and the excitement in the neighbourhood, had suddenly come to an end, and he had learned (from Major Lindon, who called to wish him good-bye) that the engagement had been broken off by mutual consent: how he had instantly abandoned all his plans for going abroad, and had decided to stay on at Elveston, for a year or two at any rate, till his newly-awakened hopes should prove true or false; and how, since that memorable day, he had avoided all meetings with Lady Muriel, fearing to betray his feelings before he had had any sufficient evidence as to how she regarded him. "But it is nearly six weeks since all that happened," he said in conclusion, "and we can meet in the ordinary way, now, with no need for any painful allusions. I would have written to tell you all this: only I kept hoping from day to day that—that there would be *more* to tell!"

"And how should there be *more*, you foolish fellow," I fondly urged, "if you never even go near her? Do you expect the offer to come from *her*?"

Arthur was betrayed into a smile. "No," he said, "I hardly expect *that*. But I'm a desperate coward. There's no doubt about it!"

"And what *reasons* have you heard of for breaking off the engagement?"

"A good many," Arthur replied, and proceeded to count them on his fingers. "First, it was found that she was dying of—something; so *he* broke it off. Then it was found that *he* was dying of—some other thing; so *she* broke it off. Then the Major turned out to be a confirmed gamester; so the *Earl* broke it off. Then the Earl insulted him; so the *Major* broke it off. It got a good deal broken off, all things considered!"

"You have all this on the very best authority, of course?"

"Oh, certainly! And communicated in the strictest confidence! Whatever defects Elveston society suffers from, *want of information* isn't one of them!"

"Nor *reticence*, either, it seems. But, seriously, do you know the real reason?"

"No, I'm quite in the dark."

I did not feel that I had any right to enlighten him; so I changed the subject, to the less engrossing one of "new milk," and we agreed that I should walk over, next day, to Hunter's farm, Arthur undertaking to set me part of the way, after which he had to return to keep a business-engagement.

CHAPTER III.

STREAKS OF DAWN.

NEXT day proved warm and sunny, and we started early, to enjoy the luxury of a good long chat before he would be obliged to leave me.

"This neighbourhood has more than its due proportion of the *very* poor," I remarked, as we passed a group of hovels, too dilapidated to deserve the name of "cottages."

"But the few rich," Arthur replied, "give more than their due proportion of help in charity. So the balance is kept."

"I suppose the *Earl* does a good deal?"

"He *gives* liberally; but he has not the health or strength to do more. Lady Muriel does more in the way of school-teaching and cottage-visiting than she would like me to reveal."

"Then *she,* at least, is not one of the 'idle mouths' one so often meets with among the upper classes. I have sometimes thought they would have a hard time of it, if suddenly called on to give their *raison d'être,* and to show cause why they should be allowed to live any longer!"

"The whole subject," said Arthur, "of what we may call 'idle mouths' (I mean persons who absorb some of the material *wealth* of a community—in the form of food, clothes, and so on—without contributing its equivalent in the form of productive *labour*) is a complicated one, no doubt. I've tried to think it out. And it seemed to me that the simplest form of the problem, to start with, is a community without *money,* who buy and sell by *barter* only; and it makes it yet simpler to suppose the food and other things to be capable of *keeping* for many years without spoiling."

"Yours is an excellent plan," I said. "What is your solution of the problem?"

"The commonest type of 'idle mouths,'" said Arthur, "is no doubt due to money being left by parents to their own children. So I imagined a man—either exceptionally clever, or exceptionally strong and industrious—who had contributed so much valuable labour to the needs of the community that its equivalent, in clothes, &c., was (say) five times as much as he needed for himself. We cannot deny his *absolute* right to give the superfluous wealth as he chooses. So, if he leaves *four* children behind him (say two sons and two daughters), with enough of all the necessaries of life to last them a life-time, I cannot see that the *community* is in any way wronged if they choose to do nothing in life but to 'eat, drink, and be merry.' Most certainly, the community could not fairly say, in reference to *them, 'if a man will not work, neither let him eat.'* Their reply would be crushing. 'The labour has already been *done,* which is a fair equivalent for the food we are eating; and you have had the benefit of it. On what principle of justice can you demand *two* quotas of work for *one* quota of food?' "

"Yet surely," I said, "there is something wrong *somewhere,* if these four people are well able to do useful work, and if that work is actually *needed* by the community, and they elect to sit idle?"

"I think there *is,*" said Arthur: "but it seems to me to arise from a Law of God—that every one shall do as much as he can to help others—and not from any *rights,* on the part of the community, to exact labour as an equivalent for food that has already been fairly earned."

"I suppose the *second* form of the problem is where the 'idle mouths' possess *money* instead of *material* wealth?"

"Yes," replied Arthur: "and I think the simplest case is that of *paper-*money. *Gold* is itself a form of material wealth; but a bank-note is merely a *promise* to hand over so much *material* wealth when called upon to do so. The father of these four 'idle mouths,' had done (let us say) five thousand pounds' worth of useful work for the community. In return for this, the community had given him what amounted to a written promise to hand over, whenever called upon to do so, five thousand pounds' worth of food, &c. Then, if he only uses *one* thousand pounds' worth himself, and leaves the rest of the notes to his children, surely they have a full right to *present* these written promises, and to say 'hand over the food, for which the equivalent labour has been already done.' Now I think *this* case well worth stating, publicly and clearly. I should like to drive it into the heads of those Socialists who are priming our ignorant paupers with such sentiments as 'Look at them bloated haris-tocrats! Doing not a stroke o' work for theirselves, and living on the sweat of *our* brows!' I should like to *force* them to see that the *money,* which those 'haristocrats' are spending, represents so much labour *already done* for the community, and whose equivalent, in *material* wealth, is *due from the community.*"

"Might not the Socialists reply 'Much of this money does not represent *honest* labour *at all.* If you could trace it back, from owner to owner, though you might begin with several legitimate steps, such as gift, or bequeathing by will, or 'value received,' you would soon reach an owner who had no moral right to it but had got it by fraud or other crimes; and of course his successors in the line would have no better right to it than *he* had."

"No doubt, no doubt," Arthur replied. "But surely that involves the logical fallacy of *proving too much?* It is *quite* as applicable to *material* wealth, as it is to *money.* If we once begin to go back beyond the fact that the *present* owner of certain property came by it honestly, and to ask whether any previous owner, in past ages, got it by fraud, would *any* property be secure?"

After a minute's thought, I felt obliged to admit the truth of this.

"My general conclusion," Arthur continued, "from the mere standpoint of human *rights,* man against man, was this—that if some wealthy 'idle mouth,' who has come by his money in a lawful way, even though not one atom of the labour it represents has been his own doing, chooses to spend it on his own needs, without contributing any labour to the community from whom he buys his food and clothes, that community has no *right* to interfere with him. But it's quite another thing, when we come to consider the *divine* law. Measured by *that* standard, such a man is undoubtedly doing wrong, if he fails to use, for the good of those in need, the strength or the skill, that God has given him. That strength and skill do *not* belong to the community, to be paid to *them* as a *debt:* they do *not* belong to the man *himself,* to be used for his *own* enjoyment: they *do* belong to God, to be used according to *His* will; and we are not left in doubt as to what this will is. *'Do good, and lend, hoping for nothing again.'"*

"Anyhow," I said, "an 'idle mouth' very often gives away a great deal in charity."

"In *so-called* 'charity,'" he corrected me. "Excuse me if I seem to speak *un*charitably. I would not dream of *applying* the term to any *individual.* But I would say, *generally,* that a man who gratifies every fancy that occurs to him—denying himself in *nothing*—and merely gives to the poor some part, or even *all,* of his *superfluous* wealth, is only deceiving himself if he calls it *charity.*"

"But, even in giving away *superfluous* wealth, he *may* be denying himself the miser's pleasure in hoarding?"

"I grant you that, gladly," said Arthur. "Given that he *has* that morbid craving, he is doing a good deed in restraining it."

"But, even in spending on *himself,*" I persisted, "our typical rich man often does good, by employing people who would otherwise be out of work: and that is often better than pauperising them by *giving* the money."

"I'm glad you've said that!" said Arthur. "I would not like to quit the subject without exposing the *two* fallacies of that statement—which have gone so long uncontradicted that Society now accepts it as an axiom!"

"What are they?" I said. "I don't even see *one,* myself."

"One is merely the fallacy of *ambiguity*—the assumption that *'doing good'* (that is, benefiting somebody) is necessarily a *good thing to do* (that is, a *right* thing). The other is the assumption that, if one of two specified acts is *better* than another, it is necessarily a *good* act in itself. I should like to call this the fallacy of *comparison*—meaning that it assumes that what is *comparatively* good is therefore *positively* good."

"Then what is *your* test of a good act?"

"That it shall be *our best,*" Arthur confidently replied. "And even *then* *'we are unprofitable servants.'* But let me illustrate the two fallacies. Nothing illustrates a fallacy so well as an extreme case, which fairly comes under it. Suppose I find two children drowning in a pond. I rush in, and save one of the children, and then walk away, leaving the other to drown. Clearly I have *'done good,'* in saving a child's life? But——. Again, supposing I meet an inoffensive stranger, and knock him down, and walk on. Clearly that is *'better'* than if I had proceeded to jump upon him and break his ribs? But——"

"Those 'buts' are quite unanswerable," I said. "But I should like an instance from *real* life."

"Well, let us take one of those abominations of modern Society, a

Charity-Bazaar. It's an interesting question to think out—how much of the money, that reaches the object in view, is *genuine* charity; and whether even *that* is spent in the *best* way. But the subject needs regular classification, and analysis, to understand it properly."

"I should be glad to *have* it analysed," I said: "it has often puzzled me."

"Well, if I am really not boring you. Let us suppose our Charity-Bazaar to have been organised to aid the funds of some Hospital: and that A, B, C *give* their services in making articles to sell, and in acting as salesmen, while X, Y, Z buy the articles, and the money so paid goes to the Hospital.

"There are two distinct species of such Bazaars: one, where the payment exacted is merely the *market-value* of the goods supplied, that is, exactly what you would have to pay at a shop: the other, where *fancy-prices* are asked. We must take these separately.

"First, the 'market-value' case. Here A, B, C are exactly in the same position as ordinary shopkeepers; the only difference being that they give the proceeds to the Hospital. Practically, they are *giving their skilled labour* for the benefit of the Hospital. This seems to me to be genuine charity. And I don't see how they could use it better. But X, Y, Z are exactly in the same position as any ordinary purchasers of goods. To talk of 'charity' in connection with *their* share of the business, is sheer nonsense. Yet they are very likely to do so.

"Secondly, the case of 'fancy-prices.' Here I think the simplest plan is to divide the payment into two parts, the 'market-value' and the excess over that. The 'market-value' part is on the same footing as in the first case: the *excess* is all we have to consider. Well, A, B, C do not *earn* it; so we may put *them* out of the question: it is a gift, from X, Y, Z, to the Hospital. And my opinion is that it is not given in the best way: far better buy what they choose to *buy*, and give what they choose to *give*, as two *separate* transactions: then there is *some* chance that their motive in giving may be real charity, instead of a mixed motive—half charity, half self-pleasing. 'The trail of the serpent is over it all.' And *therefore* it is that I hold all such spurious 'Charities' in *utter* abomination!" He ended with unusual energy, and savagely beheaded, with his stick, a tall thistle at the road-side, behind which I was startled to see Sylvie and Bruno standing. I caught at his arm, but too late to stop him. Whether the stick reached them, or not, I could not feel sure: at any rate they took not the smallest notice of it, but smiled gaily, and nodded to me; and I saw at once that they were only visible to *me:* the 'eerie' influence had not reached to *Arthur*.

"Why did you try to save it?" he said. *"That's* not the wheedling Secretary of a Charity-Bazaar! I only wish it were!" he added grimly.

"Doos oo know, that stick went right froo my head!" said Bruno. (They had run round to me by this time, and each had secured a hand.) "Just under my chin! I *are* glad I aren't a thistle!"

"Well, we've threshed *that* subject out, anyhow!" Arthur resumed. "I'm afraid I've been talking too much, for *your* patience and for my strength. I must be turning soon. This is about the end of my tether."

> *"Take, O boatman, thrice thy fee;*
> *Take, I give it willingly;*
> *For, invisible to thee,*
> *Spirits twain have crossed with me!"*

I quoted, involuntarily.

"For utterly inappropriate and irrelevant quotations," laughed Arthur, "you are 'ekalled by few, and excelled by none'!" And we strolled on.

As we passed the head of the lane that led down to the beach, I noticed a single figure, moving slowly along it, seawards. She was a good way off, and had her back to us: but it was Lady Muriel, unmistakably. Knowing that Arthur had not seen her, as he had been looking, in the other direction, at a gathering rain-cloud, I made no remark, but tried to think of some plausible pretext for sending him back by the sea.

The opportunity instantly presented itself. "I'm getting tired," he said. "I don't think it would be prudent to go further. I had better turn here."

I turned with him, for a few steps, and as we again approached the head of the lane, I said, as carelessly as I could, "Don't go back by the road. It's too hot and dusty. Down this lane, and along the beach, is nearly as short; and you'll get a breeze off the sea."

"Yes, I think I will," Arthur began; but at that moment we came into sight of Lady Muriel, and he checked himself. "No, it's too far round. Yet it certainly *would* be cooler——" He stood, hesitating, looking first one way and then the other—a melancholy picture of utter infirmity of purpose!

How long this humiliating scene would have continued, if *I* had been the only external influence, it is impossible to say; for at this moment Sylvie, with a swift decision worthy of Napoleon himself, took the matter into her own hands. "You go and drive *her,* up this way," she said to Bruno. "I'll get *him* along!" And she took hold of the stick that Arthur was carrying, and gently pulled him down the lane.

He was totally unconscious that any will but his own was acting on the stick, and appeared to think it had taken a horizontal position simply because he was pointing with it. "Are not those *orchises* under the hedge there?" he said. "I think that decides me. I'll gather some as I go along."

Meanwhile Bruno had run on behind Lady Muriel, and, with much jumping about and shouting (shouts audible to no one but Sylvie and myself, much as if he were driving sheep, he managed to turn her round and make her walk, with eyes demurely cast upon the ground, in our direction.

The victory was ours! And, since it was evident that the lovers, thus urged together, *must* meet in another minute, I turned and walked on, hoping that Sylvie and Bruno would follow my example, as I felt sure that the fewer the spectators the better it would be for Arthur and his good angel.

"And what sort of meeting was it?" I wondered, as I paced dreamily on.

CHAPTER IV.

THE DOG-KING.

"THEY shooked hands," said Bruno, who was trotting at my side, in answer to the unspoken question.

"And they looked *ever* so pleased!" Sylvie added from the other side.

"Well, we must get on, now, as quick as we can," I said. "If only I knew the best way to Hunter's farm!"

"They'll be sure to know in this cottage," said Sylvie.

"Yes, I suppose they will. Bruno, would you run in and ask?"

Sylvie stopped him, laughingly, as he ran off. "Wait a minute," she said. "I must make you *visible* first, you know."

"And *audible* too, I suppose?" I said, as she took the jewel, that hung round her neck, and waved it over his head, and touched his eyes and lips with it.

"Yes," said Sylvie: "and *once,* do you know, I made him *audible,* and forgot to make him *visible!* And he went to buy some sweeties in a shop. And the man *was* so frightened! A voice seemed to come out of the air, 'Please, I want two ounces of barley-sugar drops!' And a shilling came *bang* down upon the counter! And the man said 'I ca'n't *see* you!' And Bruno said 'It doosn't sinnify seeing *me,* so long as oo can see the *shilling!*'

But the man said he never sold barley-sugar drops to people he couldn't *see*. So we had to—*Now*, Bruno, you're ready!" And away he trotted.

Sylvie spent the time, while we were waiting for him, in making *herself* visible also. "It's rather awkward, you know," she explained to me, "when we meet people, and they can see *one* of us, and ca'n't see the *other!*"

In a minute or two Bruno returned, looking rather disconsolate. "He'd got friends with him, and he were *cross!*" he said. "He asked me who I were. And I said 'I'm Bruno: who is *these* peoples?' And he said 'One's my half-brother, and t'other's my half-sister: and I don't want no more company! Go along with yer!' And I said 'I ca'n't go along *wizout* mine self!' And I said 'Oo shouldn't have *bits* of peoples lying about like that! It's welly untidy!' And he said 'Oh, don't talk to *me!*' And he pushted me outside! And he shutted the door!"

"And you never asked where Hunter's farm was?" queried Sylvie.

"Hadn't room for any questions," said Bruno. "The room were so crowded."

"Three people *couldn't* crowd a room," said Sylvie.

"They *did*, though," Bruno persisted. "*He* crowded it most. He's such a welly *thick* man—so as oo couldn't knock him down."

I failed to see the drift of Bruno's argument. "Surely *anybody* could be knocked down," I said: "thick or thin wouldn't matter."

"Oo couldn't knock *him* down," said Bruno. "He's more wider than he's high: so, when he's lying down, he's more higher than when he's standing: so a-course oo couldn't knock him *down!*"

"Here's another cottage," I said: "*I'll* ask the way, *this* time."

There was no need to go in, this time, as the woman was standing in the doorway, with a baby in her arms, talking to a respectably dressed man—a farmer, as I guessed—who seemed to be on his way to the town.

"—and when there's *drink* to be had," he was saying, "he's just the worst o' the lot, is your Willie. So they tell me. He gets fairly mad wi' it!"

"I'd have given 'em the lie to their faces, a twelvemonth back!" the woman said in a broken voice. "But a' canna noo! A' canna noo!" She checked herself on catching sight of us, and hastily retreated into the house, shutting the door after her.

"Perhaps you can tell me where Hunter's farm is?" I said to the man, as he turned away from the house.

"I can *that*, Sir!" he replied with a smile. "I'm John Hunter hissel, at your sarvice. It's nobbut half a mile further—the only house in sight, when you get round bend o' the road yonder. You'll find my good woman within, if so be you've business wi' *her*. Or mebbe I'll do as well?"

"Thanks," I said. "I want to order some milk. Perhaps I had better arrange it with your wife?"

"Aye," said the man. "*She* minds all *that*. Good day t'ye, Master—and to your bonnie childer, as well!" And he trudged on.

"He should have said '*child*,' not '*childer*'," said Bruno. "Sylvie's not a *childer!*"

"He meant *both* of us," said Sylvie.

"No, he didn't!" Bruno persisted. "'cause he said 'bonnie', oo know!"

"Well, at any rate he *looked* at us both," Sylvie maintained.

"Well, then he *must* have seen we're not *both* bonnie!" Bruno retorted. "A-*course* I'm much uglier than *oo!* Didn't he mean *Sylvie*, Mister Sir?" he shouted over his shoulder, as he ran off.

But there was no use in replying, as he had already vanished round the bend of the road. When we overtook him he was climbing a gate, and was gazing earnestly into the field, where a horse, a cow, and a kid were browsing amicably together. "For its father, a *Horse*," he murmured to himself. "For its mother, a *Cow*. For their dear little child, a *little* Goat, is the most curiousest thing I ever seen in my world!"

"Bruno's World!" I pondered. "Yes, I suppose every child has a world of his own—and every man, too, for the matter of that. I wonder if *that's* the cause for all the misunderstanding there is in Life?"

"That *must* be Hunter's farm!" said Sylvie, pointing to a house on the brow of the hill, led up to by a cart-road. "There's no other farm in sight, *this* way; and you *said* we must be nearly there by this time."

I had *thought* it, while Bruno was climbing the gate, but I couldn't remember having *said* it. However, Sylvie was evidently in the right. "Get down, Bruno," I said, "and open the gate for us."

"It's a good thing we's with oo, *isn't* it, Mister Sir?" said Bruno, as we entered the field. "That big dog might have bited oo, if oo'd been alone! Oo needn't be *flightened* of it!" he whispered, clinging tight to my hand to encourage me. "It aren't fierce!"

"Fierce!" Sylvie scornfully echoed, as the dog—a magnificent Newfoundland—that had come galloping down the field to meet us, began curveting round us, in gambols full of graceful beauty, and welcoming us with short joyful barks. "Fierce! Why, it's as gentle as a lamb! It's— why, Bruno, don't you know? It's——"

"So it *are!*" cried Bruno, rushing forwards and throwing his arms round its neck. "Oh, you *dear* dog!" And it seemed as if the two children would never have done hugging and stroking it.

"And how *ever* did he get *here?*" said Bruno. "Ask him, Sylvie. I doosn't know how."

And then began an eager talk in Doggee, which of course was lost upon *me;* and I could only *guess,* when the beautiful creature, with a sly glance at me, whispered something in Sylvie's ear, that *I* was now the subject of conversation. Sylvie looked round laughingly.

"He asked me who you are," she explained. "And I said 'He's our *friend.*' And he said 'What's his name?' And I said 'It's *Mister Sir.*' And he said 'Bosh!' "

"What is 'Bosh!' in Doggee?" I enquired.

"It's the same as in English," said Sylvie. "Only, when a *dog* says it, it's a sort of a whisper, that's half a *cough* and half a *bark.* Nero, say '*Bosh!*' "

And Nero, who had now begun gamboling round us again, said "*Bosh!*" several times; and I found that Sylvie's description of the sound was perfectly accurate.

"I wonder what's behind this long wall?" I said, as we walked on.

"It's the *Orchard,*" Sylvie replied, after a consultation with Nero. "See, there's a boy getting down off the wall, at that far corner. And now he's running away across the field. I do believe he's been stealing the apples!"

Bruno set off after him, but returned to us in a few moments, as he had evidently no chance of overtaking the young rascal.

"I couldn't catch him!" he said. "I wiss I'd started a little sooner. His pockets *was* full of apples!"

The Dog-King looked up at Sylvie, and said something in Doggee.

"Why, of *course* you can!" Sylvie exclaimed. "How stupid not to think of it! *Nero*'ll hold him for us, Bruno! But I'd better make him invisible, first." And she hastily got out the Magic Jewel, and began waving it over Nero's head, and down along his back.

"That'll do!" cried Bruno, impatiently. "After him, good Doggie!"

"Oh, Bruno!" Sylvie exclaimed reproachfully. "You shouldn't have sent him off so quick! I hadn't done the tail!"

Meanwhile Nero was coursing like a greyhound down the field: so at least I concluded from all *I* could see of him—the long feathery tail, which floated like a meteor through the air—and in a very few seconds he had come up with the little thief.

"He's got him safe, by one foot!" cried Sylvie, who was eagerly watching the chase. "Now there's no hurry, Bruno!"

So we walked, quite leisurely, down the field, to where the frightened lad stood. A more curious sight I had seldom seen, in all my 'eerie' experiences. Every bit of him was in violent action, except the left foot, which was apparently glued to the ground—there being nothing visibly holding it: while, at some little distance, the long feathery tail was waving gracefully from side to side, showing that Nero, at least, regarded the whole affair as nothing but a magnificent game of play.

"What's the matter with you?" I said, as gravely as I could.

"Got the crahmp in me ahnkle!" the thief groaned in reply. "An' me fut's gone to sleep!" And he began to blubber aloud.

"Now, look here!" Bruno said in a commanding tone, getting in front of him. "Oo've got to give up those apples!"

The lad glanced at me, but didn't seem to reckon *my* interference as worth anything. Then he glanced at Sylvie: *she* clearly didn't count for very much, either. Then he took courage. "It'll take a better man than any of *yer* to get 'em!" he retorted defiantly.

Sylvie stooped and patted the invisible Nero. "A *little* tighter!" she whispered. And a sharp yell from the ragged boy showed how promptly the Dog-King had taken the hint.

"What's the matter *now?*" I said. "Is your ankle worse?"

"And it'll get worse, and worse, and worse," Bruno solemnly assured him, "till oo gives up those apples!"

Apparently the thief was convinced of this at last, and he sulkily began emptying his pockets of the apples. The children watched from a little distance, Bruno dancing with delight at every fresh yell extracted from Nero's terrified prisoner.

"That's all," the boy said at last.

"It *isn't* all!" cried Bruno. "There's three more in that pocket!"

Another hint from Sylvie to the Dog-King—another sharp yell from

the thief, now convicted of lying also—and the remaining three apples were surrendered.

"Let him go, please," Sylvie said in Doggee, and the lad limped away at a great pace, stooping now and then to rub the ailing ankle, in fear, seemingly, that the 'crahmp' might attack it again.

Bruno ran back, with his booty, to the orchard wall, and pitched the apples over it one by one. "I's welly afraid *some* of them's gone under the wrong trees!" he panted, on overtaking us again.

"The *wrong* trees!" laughed Sylvie. "Trees *ca'n't* do wrong! There's no such things as *wrong* trees!"

"Then there's no such things as *right* trees, neither!" cried Bruno. And Sylvie gave up the point.

"Wait a minute, please!" she said to me. "I must make Nero *visible*, you know!"

"No, *please* don't!" cried Bruno, who had by this time mounted on the Royal back, and was twisting the Royal hair into a bridle. "It'll be *such* fun to have him like this!"

"Well, it *does* look funny," Sylvie admitted, and led the way to the farmhouse, where the farmer's wife stood, evidently much perplexed at the weird procession now approaching her. "It's summat gone wrong wi' my spectacles, I doubt!" she murmured, as she took them off, and began diligently rubbing them with a corner of her apron.

Meanwhile Sylvie had hastily pulled Bruno down from his steed, and had just time to make His Majesty wholly visible before the spectacles were resumed.

All was natural, now; but the good woman still looked a little uneasy about it. "My eyesight's getting bad," she said, "but I see you *now*, my darlings! You'll give me a kiss, wo'n't you?"

Bruno got behind me, in a moment: however Sylvie put up *her* face, to be kissed, as representative of *both*, and we all went in together.

CHAPTER V.

MATILDA JANE.

"COME to me, my little gentleman," said our hostess, lifting Bruno into her lap, "and tell me everything."

"I ca'n't," said Bruno. "There wouldn't be time. Besides, I don't *know* everything."

The good woman looked a little puzzled, and turned to Sylvie for help. "Does he like *riding?*" she asked.

"Yes, I *think* so," Sylvie gently replied. "He's just had a ride on *Nero.*"

"Ah, Nero's a grand dog, isn't he? Were you ever outside a *horse*, my little man?"

"*Always!*" Bruno said with great decision. "Never was *inside* one. Was *oo?*"

SWAIN sc

Here I thought it well to interpose, and to mention the business on which we had come, and so relieved her, for a few minutes, from Bruno's perplexing questions.

"And those dear children will like a bit of cake, *I'll* warrant!" said the farmer's hospitable wife, when the business was concluded, as she opened her cupboard, and brought out a cake. "And don't you waste the crust, little gentleman!" she added, as she handed a good slice of it to Bruno. "You know what the poetry-book says about wilful waste?"

"No, I dont," said Bruno. "What doos he say about it?"

"Tell him, Bessie!" And the mother looked down, proudly and lovingly, on a rosy little maiden, who had just crept shyly into the room, and was leaning against her knee. "What's that your poetry-book says about wilful waste?"

"For wilful waste makes woeful want," Bessie recited, in an almost inaudible whisper: *"and you may live to say 'How much I wish I had the crust that then I threw away!'"*

"Now try if *you* can say it, my dear! *For wilful——*"

"For wifful—sumfinoruvver——" Bruno began, readily enough; and then there came a dead pause. "Ca'n't remember no more!"

"Well, what do you *learn* from it, then? You can tell us *that*, at any rate?"

Bruno ate a little more cake, and considered: but the moral did not seem to him to be a very obvious one.

"Always to——" Sylvie prompted him in a whisper.

"Always to——" Bruno softly repeated: and then, with sudden inspiration, "always to look where it goes to!"

"Where *what* goes to, darling?"

"Why the *crust*, a course!" said Bruno. "Then, if I lived to say '*How much I wiss I had the crust*—' (and all that), I'd know where I frew it to!"

This new interpretation quite puzzled the good woman. She returned to the subject of 'Bessie.' "Wouldn't you like to see Bessie's doll, my dears! Bessie, take the little lady and gentleman to see Matilda Jane!"

Bessie's shyness thawed away in a moment. "Matilda Jane has just woke up," she stated, confidentially, to Sylvie. "Wo'n't you help me on with her frock? Them strings *is* such a bother to tie!"

"I can tie *strings*," we heard, in Sylvie's gentle voice, as the two little girls left the room together. Bruno ignored the whole proceeding, and strolled to the window, quite with the air of a fashionable gentleman. Little girls, and dolls, were not at all in his line.

And forthwith the fond mother proceeded to tell me (as what mother is not ready to do?) of all Bessie's virtues (and vices too, for the matter of that) and of the many fearful maladies which, notwithstanding those ruddy cheeks and that plump little figure, had nearly, time and again, swept her from the face of the earth.

When the full stream of loving memories had nearly run itself out, I began to question her about the working men of that neighbourhood, and specially the 'Willie,' whom we had heard of at his cottage. "He was a good fellow once," said my kind hostess: "but it's the drink has ruined him! Not that I'd rob them of the drink—it's good for the most of them—

but there's some as is too weak to stand agin' temptations: it's a thousand pities, for *them*, as they ever built the Golden Lion at the corner there!"

"The Golden Lion?" I repeated.

"It's the new Public," my hostess explained. "And it stands right in the way, and handy for the workmen, as they come back from the brick-fields, as it might be to-day, with their week's wages. A deal of money gets wasted that way. And some of 'em gets drunk."

"If only they could have it in their own houses—" I mused, hardly knowing I had said the words out loud.

"That's it!" she eagerly exclaimed. It was evidently a solution, of the problem, that she had already thought out. "If only you could manage, so's each man to have his own little barrel in his own house—there'd hardly be a drunken man in the length and breadth of the land!"

And then I told her the old story—about a certain cottager who bought himself a little barrel of beer, and installed his wife as bar-keeper: and how, every time he wanted his mug of beer, he regularly paid her over the counter for it: and how she never would let him go on 'tick,' and was a perfectly inflexible bar-keeper in never letting him have more than his proper allowance: and how, every time the barrel needed refilling, she had plenty to do it with, and something over for her money-box: and how, at the end of the year, he not only found himself in first-rate health and spirits, with that undefinable but quite unmistakeable air which always distinguishes the sober man from the one who takes 'a drop too much,' but had quite a box full of money, all saved out of his own pence!

"If only they'd all do like that!" said the good woman, wiping her eyes, which were overflowing with kindly sympathy. "Drink hadn't need to be the curse it is to some——"

"Only a *curse*," I said, "when it is used wrongly. Any of God's gifts may be turned into a curse, unless we use it wisely. But we must be getting home. Would you call the little girls? Matilda Jane has seen enough of company, for *one* day, I'm sure!"

"I'll find 'em in a minute," said my hostess, as she rose to leave the room. "Maybe that young gentleman saw which way they went?"

"Where are they, Bruno?" I said.

"They ain't in the field," was Bruno's rather evasive reply, "'cause there's nothing but *pigs* there, and Sylvie isn't a pig. Now don't interrupt me any more, 'cause I'm telling a story to this fly; and it won't attend!"

"They're among the apples, I'll warrant 'em!" said the Farmer's wife. So we left Bruno to finish his story, and went out into the orchard, where we soon came upon the children, walking sedately side by side, Sylvie carrying the doll, while little Bess carefully shaded its face, with a large cabbage-leaf for a parasol.

As soon as they caught sight of us, little Bess dropped her cabbage-leaf and came running to meet us, Sylvie following more slowly, as her precious charge evidently needed great care and attention.

"I'm its Mamma, and Sylvie's the Head-Nurse," Bessie explained: "and Sylvie's taught me ever such a pretty song, for me to sing to Matilda Jane!"

"Let's hear it once more, Sylvie," I said, delighted at getting the chance I had long wished for of hearing her sing. But Sylvie turned shy and frightened in a moment. "No, *please* not!" she said, in an earnest 'aside' to me. "Bessie knows it quite perfect now. Bessie can sing it!"

"Aye, aye! Let Bessie sing it!" said the proud mother. "Bessie has a bonny voice of her own," (this again was an 'aside' to me) "though I say it as shouldn't!"

Bessie was only too happy to accept the 'encore.' So the plump little Mamma sat down at our feet, with her hideous daughter reclining stiffly across her lap (it was one of a kind that wo'n't sit down, under *any* amount of persuasion), and, with a face simply beaming with delight, began the lullaby, in a shout that *ought* to have frightened the poor baby into fits. The Head-Nurse crouched down behind her, keeping herself respectfully in the back-ground, with her hands on the shoulders of her little mistress, so as to be ready to act as Prompter, if required, and to supply '*each gap in faithless memory void.*'

The shout, with which she began, proved to be only a momentary effort. After a very few notes, Bessie toned down, and sang on in a small but very sweet voice. At first her great black eyes were fixed on her mother, but soon her gaze wandered upwards, among the apples, and she seemed to have quite forgotten that she had any other audience than her Baby, and her Head-Nurse, who once or twice supplied, almost inaudibly, the right note, when the singer was getting a little 'flat.'

> "*Matilda Jane, you never look*
> *At any toy or picure-book:*
> *I show you pretty things in vain—*
> *You must be blind, Matilda Jane!*

"I ask you riddles, tell you tales,
But all *our conversation fails:*
You never *answer me again—*
I fear you're dumb, Matilda Jane!

"Matilda, darling, when I call,
You never seem to hear at all:
I shout with all my might and main—
But you're so *deaf, Matilda Jane!*

"Matilda Jane, you needn't mind:
For, though you're deaf, and dumb, and blind,
There's some one *loves you, its plain—*
And that is me, *Matilda Jane!"*

She sang three of the verses in a rather perfunctory style, but the last stanza evidently excited the little maiden. Her voice rose, ever clearer and louder: she had a rapt look on her face, as if suddenly inspired, and, as she sang the last few words, she clasped to her heart the inattentive Matilda Jane.

"Kiss it now!" prompted the Head-Nurse. And in a moment the simpering meaningless face of the Baby was covered with a shower of passionate kisses.

"What a bonny song!" cried the Farmer's wife. "Who made the words, dearie?"

"I—I think I'll look for Bruno," Sylvie said demurely, and left us hastily. The curious child seemed always afraid of being praised, or even noticed.

"Sylvie planned the words," Bessie informed us, proud of her superior information: "and Bruno planned the music—and *I* sang it!" (this last circumstance, by the way, we did not need to be told).

So we followed Sylvie, and all entered the parlour together. Bruno was still standing at the window, with his elbows on the sill. He had, apparently, finished the story that he was telling to the fly, and had found a new occupation. "Don't imperrupt!" he said as we came in. "I'm counting the Pigs in the field!"

"How many are there?" I enquired.

"About a thousand and four," said Bruno.

"You mean 'about a thousand,'" Sylvie corrected him. "There's no good saying '*and four*': you *ca'n't* be sure about the four!"

"And you're as wrong as ever!" Bruno exclaimed triumphantly. "It's just the *four* I *can* be sure about; 'cause they're here, grubbling under the window! It's the *thousand* I isn't pruffickly sure about!"

"But some of them have gone into the sty," Sylvie said, leaning over him to look out of the window.

"Yes," said Bruno; "but they went so slowly and so fewly, I didn't care to count *them.*"

"We must be going, children," I said. "Wish Bessie good-bye." Sylvie flung her arms round the little maiden's neck, and kissed her: but Bruno stood aloof, looking unusually shy. ("I never kiss *nobody* but Sylvie!" he explained to me afterwards.) The farmer's wife showed us out: and we were soon on our way back to Elveston.

"And that's the new public-house that we were talking about, I suppose?" I said, as we came in sight of a long low building, with the words 'THE GOLDEN LION' over the door.

"Yes, that's it," said Sylvie. "I wonder if *her* Willie's inside? Run in, Bruno, and see if he's there."

I interposed, feeling that Bruno was, in a sort of way, in *my* care. "That's not a place to send a child into." For already the revelers were getting noisy: and a wild discord of singing, shouting, and meaningless laughter came to us through the open windows.

"They wo'n't *see* him, you know," Sylvie explained. "Wait a minute, Bruno!" She clasped the jewel, that always hung round her neck, between the palms of her hands, and muttered a few words to herself. What they were I could not at all make out, but some mysterious change seemed instantly to pass over us. My feet seemed to me no longer to press the ground, and the dream-like feeling came upon me, that I was suddenly endowed with the power of floating in the air. I could still just *see* the children: but their forms were shadowy and unsubstantial, and their voices sounded as if they came from some distant place and time, they were so unreal. However, I offered no further opposition to Bruno's going into the house. He was back again in a few moments. "No, he isn't come yet," he said. "They're talking about him inside, and saying how drunk he was last week."

While he was speaking, one of the men lounged out through the door, a pipe in one hand and a mug of beer in the other, and crossed to where we were standing, so as to get a better view along the road. Two or three others leaned out through the open window, each holding his mug of beer, with red faces and sleepy eyes. "Canst see him, lad?" one of them asked.

"I dunnot know," the man said, taking a step forwards, which brought us nearly face to face. Sylvie hastily pulled me out of his way. "Thanks, child," I said. "I had forgotten he couldn't see us. What would have happened if I had staid in his way?"

"I don't know," Sylvie said gravely. "It wouldn't matter to *us;* but *you* may be different." She said this in her usual voice, but the man took no sort of notice, though she was standing close in front of him, and looking up into his face as she spoke.

"He's coming now!" cried Bruno, pointing down the road.

"He be a-coomin noo!" echoed the man, stretching out his arm exactly over Bruno's head, and pointing with his pipe.

"Then *chorus* agin!" was shouted out by one of the red-faced men in the window: and forthwith a dozen voices yelled, to a harsh discordant melody, the refrain:—

> *"There's him, an' yo,' an' me,*
> *Roarin' laddies!*
> *We loves a bit o' spree,*

>   *Roarin' laddies we,*
>   *Roarin' laddies*
>   *Roarin' laddies!"*

The man lounged back again to the house, joining lustily in the chorus as he went: so that only the children and I were in the road when 'Willie' came up.

CHAPTER VI.

WILLIE'S WIFE.

HE made for the door of the public-house, but the children intercepted him. Sylvie clung to one arm; while Bruno, on the opposite side, was pushing him with all his strength, with many inarticulate cries of "Gee-up! Gee-back! Woah then!" which he had picked up from the waggoners.

'Willie' took not the least notice of them: he was simply conscious that *something* had checked him: and, for want of any other way of accounting for it, he seemed to regard it as his own act.

"I wunnut coom in," he said: "not to-day."

"A mug o'beer wunnut hurt 'ee!" his friends shouted in chorus. "*Two* mugs wunnut hurt 'ee! Nor a dozen mugs!"

"Nay," said Willie. "I'm agoan whoam."

"What, withouten thy drink, Willie man?" shouted the others. But 'Willie man' would have no more discussion, and turned doggedly away, the children keeping one on each side of him, to guard him against any change in his sudden resolution.

For a while he walked on stoutly enough, keeping his hands in his pockets, and softly whistling a tune, in time to his heavy tread: his success, in appearing entirely at his ease, was *almost* complete; but a careful observer would have noted that he had forgotten the second part of the air, and that, when it broke down, he instantly began it again, being too nervous to think of another, and too restless to endure silence.

It was not the old fear that possessed him now—the old fear, that had been his dreary companion every Saturday night he could remember, as he had reeled along, steadying himself against gates and garden-palings, and when the shrill reproaches of his wife had seemed to his dazed brain only the echo of a yet more piercing voice within, the intolerable wail of a hopeless remorse: it was a wholly new fear that had come to him now: life had taken on itself a new set of colours, and was lighted up with a new and dazzling radiance, and he did not see, as yet, how his home-life, and his wife and child, would fit into the new order of things: the very novelty of it all was, to his simple mind, a perplexity and an overwhelming terror.

And now the tune died into sudden silence on the trembling lips, as he turned a sharp corner, and came in sight of his own cottage, where

his wife stood, leaning with folded arms on the wicket-gate, and looking
up the road with a pale face, that had in it no glimmer of the light of
hope—only the heavy shadow of a deep stony despair.

"Fine an' early, lad! Fine an' early!" The words might have been words
of welcoming, but oh, the bitterness of the tone in which she said it!
"What brings thee from thy merry mates, and all the fiddling and the
jigging? Pockets empty, I doubt? Or thou'st come, mebbe, for to see thy
little one die? The bairnie's clemmed, and I've nor bite nor sup to gie
her. But what does *thou* care?" She flung the gate open, and met him
with blazing eyes of fury.

The man said no word. Slowly, and with downcast eyes, he passed
into the house, while she, half terrified at his strange silence, followed
him in without another word; and it was not till he had sunk into a chair,
with his arms crossed on the table and with drooping head, that she
found her voice again.

It seemed entirely natural for us to go in with them: at another time one would have asked leave for this, but I felt, I knew not why, that we were in some mysterious way invisible, and as free to come and to go as disembodied spirits.

The child in the cradle woke up, and raised a piteous cry, which in a moment brought the children to its side: Bruno rocked the cradle, while Sylvie tenderly replaced the little head on the pillow from which it had slipped. But the mother took no heed of the cry, nor yet of the satisfied 'coo' that it set up when Sylvie had made it happy again: she only stood gazing at her husband, and vainly trying, with white quivering lips (I believe she thought he was mad), to speak in the old tones of shrill upbraiding that he knew so well.

"And thou'st spent all thy wages—I'll swear thou hast—on the devil's own drink—and thou'st been and made thysen a beast again—as thou allus dost——"

"Hasna!" the man muttered, his voice hardly rising above a whisper, as he slowly emptied his pockets on the table. "There's th' wage, Missus, every penny on't."

The woman gasped, and put one hand to her heart, as if under some great shock of surprise. "Then *how's* thee gotten th' drink?"

"*Hasna* gotten it," he answered her, in a tone more sad than sullen. "I hanna touched a drop this blessed day. No!" he cried aloud, bringing his clenched fist heavily down upon the table, and looking up at her with gleaming eyes, "nor I'll never touch another drop o' the cursed drink—till I die—so help me God my Maker!" His voice, which had suddenly risen to a hoarse shout, dropped again as suddenly: and once more he bowed his head, and buried his face in his folded arms.

The woman had dropped upon her knees by the cradle, while he was speaking. She neither looked at him nor seemed to hear him. With hands clasped above her head, she rocked herself wildly to and fro. "Oh my God! Oh my God!" was all she said, over and over again.

Sylvie and Bruno gently unclasped her hands and drew them down— till she had an arm round each of them, though she took no notice of them, but knelt on with eyes gazing upwards, and lips that moved as if in silent thanksgiving. The man kept his face hidden, and uttered no sound: but one could *see* the sobs that shook him from head to foot.

After a while he raised his head—his face all wet with tears. "Polly!" he said softly; and then, louder, "Old Poll!"

Then she rose from her knees and came to him, with a dazed look, as if she were walking in her sleep. "Who was it called me old Poll?" she asked: her voice took on it a tender playfulness: her eyes sparkled; and the rosy light of Youth flushed her pale cheeks, till she looked more like a happy girl of seventeen than a worn woman of forty. "Was that my own lad, my Willie, a-waiting for me at the stile?"

His face too was transformed, in the same magic light to the likeness of a bashful boy: and boy and girl they seemed, as he wound an arm about her, and drew her to his side, while with the other hand he thrust from him the heap of money, as though it were something hateful to the touch. "Tak it, lass," he said, "tak it all! An' fetch us summat to eat: but get a sup o' milk, first, for t' bairn."

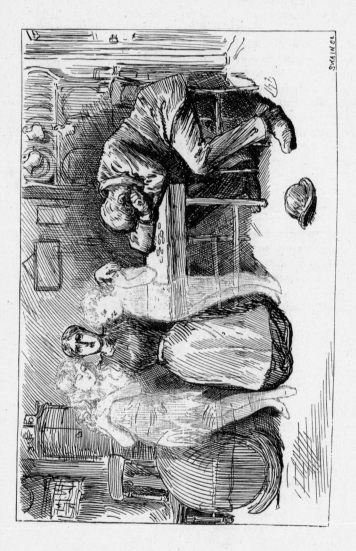

"My *little* bairn!" she murmured as she gathered up the coins. "My own little lassie!" Then she moved to the door, and was passing out, but a sudden thought seemed to arrest her: she hastily returned—first to kneel down and kiss the sleeping child, and then to throw herself into her husband's arms and be strained to his heart. The next moment she was on her way, taking with her a jug that hung on a peg near the door: we followed close behind.

We had not gone far before we came in sight of a swinging sign-board bearing the word 'DAIRY' on it, and here she went in, welcomed by a little curly white dog, who, not being under the 'eerie' influence, saw the children, and received them with the most effusive affection. When I got inside, the dairyman was in the act of taking the money. "Is't for thysen, Missus, or for t' bairn?" he asked, when he had filled the jug, pausing with it in his hand.

"For t' *bairn!*" she said, almost reproachfully. "Think'st tha I'd touch a drop *mysen*, while as *she* hadna got her fill?"

"All right, Missus," the man replied, turning away with the jug in his hand. "Let's just mak sure it's good measure." He went back among his shelves of milk-bowls, carefully keeping his back towards her while he emptied a little measure of cream into the jug, muttering to himself "mebbe it'll hearten her up a bit, the little lassie!"

The woman never noticed the kind deed, but took back the jug with a simple "Good evening, Master," and went her way: but the children had been more observant, and, as we followed her out, Bruno remarked "That were *welly* kind: and I loves that man: and if I was welly rich I'd give him a hundred pounds—and a bun. That little grummeling dog doosn't know its business!" He referred to the dairyman's little dog, who had apparently quite forgotten the affectionate welcome he had given us on our arrival, and was now following at a respectful distance, doing his best to *'speed the parting guest'* with a shower of little shrill barks, that seemed to tread on one another's heels.

"What *is* a dog's business?" laughed Sylvie. "Dogs ca'n't keep shops and give change!"

"Sisters' businesses *isn't* to laugh at their brothers," Bruno replied with perfect gravity. "And dogs' businesses is to *bark*—not like that: it should finish one bark before it begins another: and it should—Oh Sylvie, there's some dindledums!"

And in another moment the happy children were flying across the common, racing for the patch of dandelions.

While I stood watching them, a strange dreamy feeling came upon me: a railway-platform seemed to take the place of the green sward, and, instead of the light figure of Sylvie bounding along, I seemed to see the flying form of Lady Muriel; but whether Bruno had also undergone a transformation, and had become the old man whom she was running to overtake, I was unable to judge, so instantaneously did the feeling come and go.

When I re-entered the little sitting-room which I shared with Arthur, he was standing with his back to me, looking out of the open window, and evidently had not heard me enter. A cup of tea, apparently just tasted and pushed aside, stood on the table, on the opposite side of which was a letter, just begun, with the pen lying across it: an open book lay on the sofa: the London paper occupied the easy chair; and on the little table which stood by it, I noticed an unlighted cigar and an open box of cigar-lights: all things betokened that the Doctor, usually so methodical and so self-contained, had been trying every form of occupation, and could settle to none!

"This is very unlike *you*, Doctor!" I was beginning, but checked myself, as he turned at the sound of my voice, in sheer amazement at the wonderful change that had taken place in his appearance. Never had I seen a face so radiant with happiness, or eyes that sparkled with such unearthly light! "Even thus," I thought, "must the herald-angel have looked, who brought to the shepherds, watching over their flocks by night, that sweet message of *'peace on earth, good-will to men'!*"

"Yes, dear friend!" he said, as if in answer to the question that I suppose he read in my face. "It is true! It is true!"

No need to ask *what* was true. "God bless you both!" I said, as I felt the happy tears brimming to my eyes. "You were made for each other!"

"Yes," he said, simply, "I believe we were. And *what* a change it makes in one's Life! This isn't the same world! That isn't the sky I saw yesterday! Those clouds—I never saw such clouds in all my life before! They look like troops of hovering angels!"

To *me* they looked very ordinary clouds indeed: but then *I* had not fed *'on honeydew, And drunk the milk of Paradise'!*

"She wants to see you—at once," he continued, descending suddenly to the things of earth. "She says *that* is the *one* drop yet wanting in her cup of happiness!"

"I'll go at once," I said, as I turned to leave the room. "Wo'n't you come with me?"

"No, Sir!" said the Doctor, with a sudden effort—which proved an utter failure—to resume his professional manner. "Do I *look* like coming with you? Have you never heard that two is company, and——"

"Yes," I said, "I *have* heard it: and I'm painfully aware that *I* am *Number Three*! But, *when* shall we three meet again?"

"When the hurly-burly's done!" he answered with a happy laugh, such as I had not heard from him for many a year.

CHAPTER VII.

MEIN HERR.

So I went on my lonely way, and, on reaching the Hall, I found Lady Muriel standing at the garden-gate waiting for me.

"No need to *give* you joy, or to *wish* you joy?" I began.

"None *whatever*!" she replied, with the joyous laugh of a child. "We *give* people what they haven't got: we *wish* for something that is yet to come. For *me*, it's all *here!* It's all *mine!* Dear friend," she suddenly broke off, "do you think Heaven ever begins on *Earth*, for any of us?"

"For *some*," I said. "For some, perhaps, who are simple and childlike. You know He said 'of such is the Kingdom of Heaven.'"

Lady Muriel clasped her hands, and gazed up into the cloudless sky, with a look I had often seen in Sylvie's eyes. "I feel as if it had begun for *me*," she almost whispered. "I feel as if *I* were one of the happy children, whom He bid them bring near to Him, though the people would have kept them back. Yes, He has seen me in the throng. He has read the wistful longing in my eyes. He has beckoned me to Him. They have *had* to make way for me. He has taken me up in His arms. He has put His hands upon me and blessed me!" She paused, breathless in her perfect happiness.

"Yes," I said. "I think He has!"

"You must come and speak to my father," she went on, as we stood side by side at the gate, looking down the shady lane. But, even as she said the words, the 'eerie' sensation came over me like a flood: I saw the dear old Professor approaching us, and also saw, what was stranger still, that he was visible to *Lady Muriel!*

What was to be done? Had the fairy-life been merged in the real life? Or was Lady Muriel 'eerie' also, and thus able to enter into the fairy-world along with me? The words were on my lips ("I see an old friend of mine in the lane: if you don't know him, may I introduce him to you?") when the strangest thing of all happened: Lady Muriel spoke.

"I see an old friend of mine in the lane," she said: "if you don't know him, may I introduce him to you?"

I seemed to wake out of a dream: for the 'eerie' feeling was still strong upon me, and the figure outside seemed to be changing at every moment, like one of the shapes in a kaleidoscope: now he was the *Professor*, and now somebody else! By the time he had reached the gate, he certainly was somebody else: and I felt that the proper course was for *Lady Muriel*, not for *me*, to introduce him. She greeted him kindly, and, opening the gate, admitted the venerable old man—a German, obviously—who looked about him with dazed eyes, as if *he*, too, had but just awaked from a dream!

No, it was certainly *not* the Professor! My old friend *could* not have grown that magnificent beard since last we met: moreover, he would have recognised *me*, for I was certain that *I* had not changed much in the time.

As it was, he simply looked at me vaguely, and took off his hat in response to Lady Muriel's words "Let me introduce Mein Herr to you"; while in the words, spoken in a strong German accent, "proud to make your acquaintance, Sir!" I could detect no trace of an idea that we had ever met before.

Lady Muriel led us to the well-known shady nook, where preparations for afternoon-tea had already been made, and, while she went in to look for the Earl, we seated ourselves in two easy-chairs, and 'Mein Herr' took up Lady Muriel's work, and examined it through his large spectacles (one of the adjuncts that made him so provokingly like the Professor).

"Hemming pocket-handkerchiefs?" he said, musingly. "So *that* is what the English miladies occupy themselves with, is it?"

"It is the one accomplishment," I said, "in which Man has never yet rivaled Woman!"

Here Lady Muriel returned with her father; and, after he had exchanged some friendly words with 'Mein Herr,' and we had all been supplied with the needful 'creature-comforts,' the newcomer returned to the suggestive subject of Pocket-handkerchiefs.

"You have heard of Fortunatus's Purse, Miladi? Ah, so! Would you be surprised to hear that, with three of these leetle handkerchiefs, you shall make the Purse of Fortunatus; quite soon, quite easily?"

"Shall I indeed?" Lady Muriel eagerly replied, as she took a heap of them into her lap, and threaded her needle. "*Please* tell me how, Mein Herr! I'll make one before I touch another drop of tea!"

"You shall first," said Mein Herr, possessing himself of two of the handkerchiefs, spreading one upon the other, and holding them up by two corners, "you shall first join together these upper corners, the right to the right, the left to the left; and the opening between them shall be the *mouth* of the Purse."

A very few stitches sufficed to carry out *this* direction. "Now, if I sew the other three edges together," she suggested, "the bag is complete?"

"Not so, Miladi: the *lower* edges shall *first* be joined——ah, not so!" (as she was beginning to sew them together). "Turn one of them over, and join the *right* lower corner of the one to the *left* lower corner of the other, and sew the lower edges together in what you would call *the wrong way*."

"*I* see!" said Lady Muriel, as she deftly executed the order. "And a very twisted, uncomfortable, uncanny-looking bag it makes! But the *moral* is a lovely one. Unlimited wealth can only be attained by doing things *in the wrong way*! And how are we to join up these mysterious— no, I mean *this* mysterious opening?" (twisting the thing round and round with a puzzled air). "Yes, it *is* one opening. I thought it was *two*, at first."

"You have seen the puzzle of the Paper Ring?" Mein Herr said, addressing the Earl. "Where you take a slip of paper, and join its ends together, first twisting one, so as to join the *upper* corner of *one* end to the *lower* corner of the *other?*"

"I saw one made, only yesterday," the Earl replied. "Muriel, my child, were you not making one, to amuse those children you had to tea?"

"Yes, I know that Puzzle," said Lady Muriel. "The Ring has only *one* surface, and only *one* edge. It's very mysterious!"

"The *bag* is just like that, isn't it?" I suggested. "Is not the *outer* surface of one side of it continuous with the *inner* surface of the other side?"

"So it is!" she exclaimed. "Only it *isn't* a bag, just yet. How shall we fill up this opening, Mein Herr?"

"Thus!" said the old man impressively, taking the bag from her, and rising to his feet in the excitement of the explanation. "The edge of the opening consists of *four* handkerchief-edges, and you can trace it continuously, round and round the opening: down the right edge of *one* handkerchief, up the left edge of the *other*, and then down the left edge of the *one*, and up the right edge of the *other!*"

"So you can!" Lady Muriel murmured thoughtfully, leaning her head on her hand, and earnestly watching the old man. "And that *proves* it to be only *one* opening!"

She looked so strangely like a child, puzzling over a difficult lesson, and Mein Herr had become, for the moment, so strangely like the old Professor, that I felt utterly bewildered: the 'eerie' feeling was on me in its full force, and I felt almost *impelled* to say "Do you understand it, Sylvie?" However I checked myself by a great effort, and let the dream (if indeed it *was* a dream) go on to its end.

"Now, this *third* handkerchief," Mein Herr proceeded, "has *also* four edges, which you can trace continuosly round and round: all you need do is to join its four edges to the four edges of the opening. The Purse is then complete, and its outer surface——"

"*I* see!" Lady Muriel eagerly interrupted. "Its *outer* surface will be continuous with its *inner* surface! But it will take time. I'll sew it up after tea." She laid aside the bag, and resumed her cup of tea. "But why do you call it Fortunatus's Purse, Mein Herr?"

The dear old man beamed upon her, with a jolly smile, looking more exactly like the Professor than ever. "Don't you see, my child—I should say Miladi? Whatever is *inside* that Purse, is *outside* it; and whatever is *outside* it, is *inside* it. So you have all the wealth of the world in that leetle Purse!"

His pupil clapped her hands, in unrestrained delight. "I'll certainly sew the third handkerchief in—*some* time," she said: "but I wo'n't take up your time by trying it now. Tell us some more wonderful things, please!" And her face and her voice so *exactly* recalled Sylvie, that I could not help glancing round, half-expecting to see *Bruno* also!

Mein Herr began thoughtfully balancing his spoon on the edge of his

teacup, while he pondered over this request. "Something wonderful—like Fortunatus's Purse? *That* will give you—when it is made—wealth beyond your wildest dreams: but it will not give you *Time!*"

A pause of silence ensued—utilised by Lady Muriel for the very practical purpose of refilling the teacups.

"In *your* country," Mein Herr began with a startling abruptness, "what becomes of all the wasted Time?"

Lady Muriel looked grave. "Who can tell?" she half-whispered to herself. "All one knows is that it is gone—past recall!"

"Well, in *my*—I mean in a country *I* have visited," said the old man, "they store it up: and it comes in *very* useful, years afterwards! For example, suppose you have a long tedious evening before you: nobody to talk to: nothing you care to do: and yet hours too soon to go to bed. How do *you* behave then?"

"I get *very* cross," she frankly admitted: "and I want to throw things about the room!"

"When that happens to—to the people I have visited, they never act *so*. By a short and simple process—which I cannot explain to you—they store up the useless hours: and, on some *other* occasion, when they happen to *need* extra time, they get them out again."

The Earl was listening with a slightly incredulous smile. "Why cannot you *explain* the process?" he enquired.

Mein Herr was ready with a quite unanswerable reason. "Because you have no *words*, in *your* language, to convey the ideas which are needed. I could explain it in—in—but you would not understand it!"

"No indeed!" said Lady Muriel, graciously dispensing with the *name* of the unknown language. "I never learnt it—at least, not to speak it *fluently*, you know. *Please* tell us some more wonderful things!"

"They run their railway-trains without any engines——nothing is needed but machinery to *stop* them with. Is *that* wonderful enough, Miladi?"

"But where does the *force* come from?" I ventured to ask.

Mein Herr turned quickly round, to look at the new speaker. Then he took off his spectacles, and polished them, and looked at me again, in evident bewilderment. I could see he was thinking—as indeed *I* was also—that we *must* have met before.

"They use the force of *gravity*," he said. "It is a force known also in *your* country, I believe?"

"But that would need a railway going *down-hill*," the Earl remarked. "You ca'n't have *all* your railways going down-hill?"

"They *all* do," said Mein Herr.

"Not from *both* ends?"

"From *both* ends."

"Then I give it up!" said the Earl.

"Can you explain the process?" said Lady Muriel. "Without using that language, that I ca'n't speak fluently?"

"Easily," said Mein Herr. "Each railway is in a long tunnel, perfectly straight: so of course the *middle* of it is nearer the centre of the globe than the two ends: so every train runs half-way *down*-hill, and that gives it force enough to run the *other* half *up*-hill."

"Thank you. I understand that perfectly," said Lady Muriel. "But the velocity, in the *middle* of the tunnel, must be something *fearful!*"

'Mein Herr' was evidently much gratified at the intelligent interest Lady Muriel took in his remarks. At every moment the old man seemed to grow more chatty and more fluent. "You would like to know our methods of *driving?*" he smilingly enquired. "To us, a run-away horse is of no import at all!"

Lady Muriel slightly shuddered. "To *us* it is a very real danger," she said.

"That is because your carriage is wholly *behind* your horse. Your horse runs. Your carriage follows. Perhaps your horse has the bit in his teeth. Who shall stop him? You fly, ever faster and faster! Finally comes the inevitable upset!"

"But suppose *your* horse manages to get the bit in his teeth?"

"No matter! We would not concern ourselves. Our horse is harnessed in the very centre of our carriage. Two wheels are in front of him, and two behind. To the roof is attached one end of a broad belt. This goes under the horse's body, and the other end is attached to a leetle—what you call a 'windlass,' I think. The horse takes the bit in his teeth. He runs away. We are flying at ten miles an hour! We turn our little windlass, five turns, six turns, seven turns, and——poof! Our horse is off the ground! *Now* let him gallop in the air as much as he pleases: our *carriage* stands still. We sit round him, and watch him till he is tired. Then we let him down. Our horse is glad, very much glad, when his feet once more touch the ground!"

"Capital!" said the Earl, who had been listening attentively. "Are there any other peculiarities in your carriages?"

"In the *wheels*, sometimes, my Lord. For your health, *you* go to sea: to be pitched, to be rolled, occasionally to be drowned. *We* do all that on land: we are pitched, as you: we are rolled, as you; but *drowned*, no! There is no water!"

"What are the wheels like, then?"

"They are *oval*, my Lord. Therefore the carriages rise and fall."

"Yes, and pitch the carriage backwards and forwards: but how do they make it *roll?*"

"They do not match, my Lord. The *end* of one wheel answers to the *side* of the opposite wheel. So first one side of the carriage rises, then the other. And it pitches all the while. Ah, you must be a good sailor, to drive in our boat-carriages!"

"I can easily believe it," said the Earl.

Mein Herr rose to his feet. "I must leave you now, Miladi," he said, consulting his watch. "I have another engagement."

"I only wish we had stored up some extra time!" Lady Muriel said, as she shook hands with him. "Then we could have kept you a little longer!"

"In *that* case I would gladly stay," replied Mein Herr. "As it is——I fear I must say good-bye!"

"Where did you first meet him?" I asked Lady Muriel, when Mein Herr had left us. "And where does he live? And what is his real name?"

"We first—met—him——" she musingly replied, "really, I ca'n't remember *where!* And I've no idea where he lives! And I never heard any other name! It's very curious. It never occurred to me before to consider what a mystery he is!"

"I hope we shall meet again," I said: "he interests me very much."

"He will be at our farewell-party, this day fortnight," said the Earl. "Of course you will come? Muriel is anxious to gather all our friends around us once more, before we leave the place."

And then he explained to me—as Lady Muriel had left us together— that he was so anxious to get his daughter away from a place full of so many painful memories connected with the now-canceled engagement with Major Lindon, that they had arranged to have the wedding in a month's time, after which Arthur and his wife were to go on a foreign tour.

"Don't forget Tuesday week!" he said as we shook hands at parting. "I only wish you could bring with you those charming children, that you introduced to us in the summer. Talk of the mystery of Mein Herr! That's *nothing* to the mystery that seems to attend *them!* I shall never forget those marvellous flowers!"

"I will bring them if I possible can," I said. But how to *fulfil* such a promise, I mused to myself on my way back to our lodgings, was a problem entirely beyond my skill!

CHAPTER VIII.

IN A SHADY PLACE.

THE ten days glided swiftly away: and, the day before the great party was to take place, Arthur proposed that we should stroll down to the Hall, in time for afternoon-tea.

"Hadn't you better go *alone?*" I suggested. "Surely *I* shall be very much *de trop?*"

"Well, it'll be a kind of *experiment,*" he said. *"Fiat experimentum in corpore vili!"* he added, with a graceful bow of mock politeness towards the unfortunate victim. "You see I shall have to bear the sight, to-morrow night, of my lady-love making herself agreable to everybody *except* the right person, and I shall bear the agony all the better if we have a dress-rehearsal beforehand!"

"My part in the play being, apparently, that of the sample *wrong* person?"

"Well, no," Arthur said musingly, as we set forth: "there's no such part in a regular company. 'Heavy Father'? *That* won't do: that's filled already. 'Singing Chambermaid'? Well, the 'First Lady' doubles *that* part. 'Comic Old Man'? You're not comic enough. After all, I'm afraid there's no part for you but the 'Well-dressed Villain': only," with a critical side-glance, "I'm a *leetle* uncertain about the dress!"

We found Lady Muriel alone, the Earl having gone out to make a call, and at once resumed old terms of intimacy, in the shady arbour where the tea-things seemed to be always waiting. The only novelty in the arrangements (one which Lady Muriel seemed to regard as *entirely* a mattter of course), was that two of the chairs were placed *quite* close together, side by side. Strange to say, *I* was not invited to occupy *either* of them!

"We have been arranging, as we came along, about letter-writing," Arthur began. "He will want to know how we're enjoying our Swiss tour: and of course we must pretend we *are?*"

"Of course," she meekly assented.

"And the skeleton-in-the-cupboard———" I suggested.

"—is always a difficulty," she quickly put in, "when you're traveling about, and when there are no cupboards in the hotels. However, *ours* is a *very* portable one; and will be neatly packed, in a nice leather case—"

"But please don't think about *writing,*" I said, "when you've anything more attractive on hand. I delight in *reading* letters, but I know well how tiring it is to *write* them."

"It *is,* sometimes," Arthur assented. "For instance, when you're very shy of the person you have to write to."

"Does that show itself in the *letter?*" Lady Muriel enquired. "Of course, when I hear any one *talking—you,* for instance—I can see how *desperately* shy he is! But can you see that in a *letter?*"

"Well, of course, when you hear any one talk *fluently—you,* for instance— you can see how desperately *un*-shy she is—not to say saucy! But the shyest and most intermittent talker must *seem* fluent in letter-writing. He may have taken half-an-hour to *compose* his second sentence; but there it is, close after the first!"

"Then letters don't express all that they *might* express?"

"That's merely becaue our system of letter-writing is incomplete. A shy writer *ought* to be able to show that he is so. Why shouldn't he make *pauses* in writing, just as he would do in speaking? He might leave blank spaces—say half a page at a time. And a *very* shy girl—if there *is* such a thing—might write a sentence on the *first* sheet of her letter—then put in a couple of *blank* sheets—then a sentence on the *fourth* sheet: and so on."

"I quite foresee that *we*—I mean this clever little boy and myself—" Lady Muriel said to me, evidently with the kind wish to bring me into the conversation, "—are going to become famous—of course all our inventions are common property now—for a new Code of Rules for Letter-writing! Please invent some more, little boy!"

"Well, another thing *greatly* needed, little girl, is some way of expressing that we *don't* mean anything."

"Explain yourself, little boy! Surely *you* can find no difficulty in expressing a *total* absence of meaning?"

"I mean that you should be able, when you *don't* mean a thing to be taken seriously, to express that wish. For human nature is so constituted that whatever you write seriously is taken as a joke, and whatever you mean as a joke is taken seriously! At any rate, it is so in writing to a *lady!*"

"Ah! you're not used to writing to ladies!" Lady Muriel remarked, leaning back in her chair, and gazing thoughtfully into the sky. "You should try."

"Very good," said Arthur. "How many ladies may I begin writing to? As many as I can count on the fingers of both hands?"

"As many as you can count on the *thumbs* of *one* hand!" his lady-love replied with much severity. "What a *very* naughty little boy he is! *Isn't* he?" (with an appealing glance at me).

"He's a little fractious," I said. "Perhaps he's cutting a tooth." While to myself I said "How *exactly* like Sylvie talking to Bruno!"

"He wants his tea." (The naughty little boy volunteered the information.) "He's getting very tired, at the mere *prospect* of the great party to-morrow!"

"Then he shall have a good rest beforehand!" she soothingly replied. "The tea isn't made yet. Come, little boy, lean well back in your chair, and think about nothing—or about *me*, whichever you prefer!"

"All the same, all the same!" Arthur sleepily murmured, watching her with loving eyes, as she moved her chair away to the tea-table, and began to make the tea. "Then he'll wait for his tea, like a good, patient little boy!"

"Shall I bring you the London Papers?" said Lady Muriel. "I saw them lying on the table as I came out, but my father said there was nothing in them, except that horrid murder-trial." (Society was just then enjoying its daily thrill of excitement in studying the details of a specially sensational murder in a thieves' den in the East of London.)

"I have no appetite for horrors," Arthur replied. "But I hope we have learned the lesson they should teach us—though we are very apt to read it backwards!"

"You speak in riddles," said Lady Muriel. "Please explain yourself. See now," suiting the action to the word, "I am sitting at your feet, just

as if you were a second Gamaliel! Thanks, no." (This was to me, who had risen to bring her chair back to its former place.) "Pray don't disturb yourself. This tree and the grass make a very nice easy-chair. *What* is the lesson that one always reads wrong?"

Arthur was silent for a minute. "I would like to be clear what it *is* I mean," he said, slowly and thoughtfully, "before I say anything to *you*— because you *think* about it."

Anything approaching to a compliment was so unusual an utterance for Arthur, that it brought a flush of pleasure to her cheek, as she replied "It is *you,* that give me the ideas to think about."

"One's first thought," Arthur proceeded, "in reading of anything specially vile or barbarous, as done by a fellow-creature, is apt to be that we see a new depth of Sin revealed *beneath* us: and we seem to gaze down into that abyss from some higher ground, far apart from it."

"I think I understand you now. You mean that one ought to think— not 'God, I thank Thee that I am not as other men are'—but 'God, be merciful to me also, who might be, but for Thy grace, a sinner as vile as he!'"

"No," said Arthur. "I meant a great deal more than that."

She looked up quickly, but checked herself, and waited in silence.

"One must begin further back, I think. Think of some other man, the same age as this poor wretch. Look back to the time when they both began life—before they had sense enough to know Right from Wrong. *Then,* at any rate, they were equal in God's sight?"

She nodded assent.

"We have, then, two distinct epochs at which we may contemplate the two men whose lives we are comparing. At the first epoch they are, so far as moral responsibility is concerned, on precisely the same footing: they are alike incapable of doing right or wrong. At the second epoch the one man—I am taking an extreme case, for contrast—has won the esteem and love of all around him: his character is stainless, and his name will be held in honour hereafter: the other man's history is one unvaried record of crime, and his life is at last forfeited to the outraged laws of his country. Now what have been the causes, in each case, of each man's condition being what it is at the second epoch? They are of two kinds—one acting from within, the other from without. These two kinds need to be discussed separately—that is, if I have not already tired you with my prosing?"

"On the contrary," said Lady Muriel, "it is a special delight to me to have a question discussed in this way—analysed and arranged, so that one can understand it. Some books, that profess to argue out a question, are to me intolerably wearisome, simply because the ideas are all arranged hap-hazard—a sort of 'first come, first served.'"

"You are very encouraging," Arthur replied, with a pleased look. "The causes, acting from *within,* which make a man's character what it is at any given moment, are his successive acts of volition—that is, his acts of choosing whether he will do this or that."

"We are to assume the existence of Free-Will?" I said, in order to have that point made quite clear.

"If not," was the quiet reply, "*cadit quaestio:* and I have no more to say."

"We *will* assume it!" the rest of the audience—the majority, I may say, looking at it from Arthur's point of view—imperiously proclaimed. The orator proceeded.

"The causes, acting from *without,* are his surroundings—what Mr. Herbert Spencer calls his 'environment.' Now the point I want to make clear is this, that a man is responsible for his acts of choosing, but *not* responsible for his environment. Hence, if these two men make, on some given occasion, when they are exposed to equal temptation, equal efforts to resist and to choose the right, their condition, in the sight of God, must be the same. If He is pleased in the one case, so will He be in the other; if displeased in the one case, so also in the other."

"That is so, no doubt: I see it quite clearly," Lady Muriel put in.

"And yet, owing to their different environments, the one may win a great victory over the temptation, while the other falls into some black abyss of crime."

"But surely you would not say those men were equally guilty in the sight of God?"

"Either that," said Arthur, "or else I must give up my belief in God's perfect justice. But let me put one more case, which will show my meaning even more forcibly. Let the one man be in a high social position—the other, say, a common thief. Let the one be tempted to some trivial act of unfair dealing—something which he can do with the absolute certainty that it will never be discovered—something which he can with perfect ease forbear from doing—and which he distinctly knows to be a sin. Let the other be tempted to some terrible crime—as men would consider it—but under an almost overwhelming pressure of motives—of course not *quite* overwhelming, as that would destroy all responsibility. Now, in this case, let the second man make a *greater* effort at resistance than the first. Also suppose *both* to fall under the temptation—I say that the second man is, in God's sight, *less* guilty than the other."

Lady Muriel drew a long breath. "It upsets all one's ideas of Right and Wrong—just at first! Why, in that dreadful murder-trial, you would say, I suppose, that it was possible that the least guilty man in the Court was the murderer, and that possibly the judge who tried him, by yielding to the temptation of making one unfair remark, had committed a crime outweighing the criminal's whole career!"

"Certainly I should," Arthur firmly replied. "It sounds like a paradox, I admit. But just think what a grievous sin it must be, in God's sight, to yield to some very slight temptation, which we could have resisted with perfect ease, and to do it deliberately, and in the full light of God's Law. What penance can atone for a sin like *that?*"

"I ca'n't reject your theory," I said. "But how it seems to widen the possible area of Sin in the world!"

"Is that so?" Lady Muriel anxiously enquired.

"Oh, not so, not so!" was the eager reply. "To me it seems to clear away much of the cloud that hangs over the world's history. When this view first made itself clear to me, I remember walking out into the fields, repeating to myself that line of Tennyson *'There seemed no room for sense of wrong!'* The thought, that perhaps the real guilt of the human race was infinitely less than I fancied it—that the millions, whom I had thought of as sunk in hopeless depths of sin, were perhaps, in God's sight, scarcely sinning at all—was more sweet than words can tell! Life seemed more bright and beautiful, when once that thought had come! *'A livelier emerald twinkles in the grass, A purer sapphire melts into the sea!'* " His voice trembled as he concluded, and the tears stood in his eyes.

Lady Muriel shaded her face with her hand, and was silent for a minute. "It is a beautiful thought," she said, looking up at last. "Thank you—Arthur, for putting it into my head!"

The Earl returned in time to join us at tea, and to give us the very unwelcome tidings that a fever had broken out in the little harbour-town that lay below us—a fever of so malignant a type that, though it had only appeared a day or two ago, there were already more than a dozen down in it, two or three of whom were reported to be in imminent danger.

In answer to the eager questions of Arthur—who of course took a deep scientific interest in the matter—he could give very few *technical* details, though he had met the local doctor. It appeared, however, that it was an almost *new* disease—at least in *this* century, though it *might* prove to be identical with the 'Plague' recorded in History—*very* infectious, and frightfully rapid in its action. "It will not, however, prevent our party to-morrow," he said in conclusion. "None of the guests belong to the infected district, which is, as you know, exclusively peopled by fish-ermen: so you may come without any fear."

Arthur was very silent, all the way back, and, on reaching our lodgings, immediately plunged into medical studies, connected with the alarming malady of whose arrival we had just heard.

CHAPTER IX.

THE FAREWELL-PARTY.

ON the following day, Arthur and I reached the Hall in good time, as only a few of the guests—it was to be a party of eighteen—had as yet arrived; and these were talking with the Earl, leaving us the opportunity of a few words apart with our hostess.

"Who is that *very* learned-looking man with the large spectacles?" Arthur enquired. "I haven't met him here before, have I?"

"No, he's a new friend of ours," said Lady Muriel: "a German, I believe. He *is* such a dear old thing! And quite the most learned man I ever met—with *one* exception, of course!" she added humbly, as Arthur drew himself up with an air of offended dignity.

"And the young lady in blue, just beyond him, talking to that foreign-looking man. Is *she* learned, too?"

"I don't know," said Lady Muriel. "But I'm told she's a wonderful piano-forte-player. I hope you'll hear her to-night. I asked that foreigner to take her in, because *he's* very musical, too. He's a French Count, I believe; and he sings *splendidly!*"

"Science—music—singing—you have indeed got a complete party!" said Arthur. "I feel quite a privileged person, meeting all these stars. I *do* love music!"

"But the party isn't *quite* complete!" said Lady Muriel. "You haven't brought us those two beautiful children," she went on, turning to me. "He brought them here to tea, you know, one day last summer," again addressing Arthur: "and they *are* such darlings!"

"They are, *indeed*," I assented.

"But why haven't you brought them with you? You promised my father you *would*."

"I'm very sorry," I said; "but really it was impossible to bring them with me." Here I most certainly *meant* to conclude the sentence: and it was with a feeling of utter amazement, which I cannot adequately describe, that I heard myself *going on speaking*. "—but they are to join me here in the course of the evening" were the words, uttered in *my* voice, and seeming to come from *my* lips.

"I'm *so* glad!" Lady Muriel joyfully replied. "I *shall* enjoy introducing them to some of my friends here! When do you expect them?"

I took refuge in silence. The only *honest* reply would have been "That was not *my* remark. *I* didn't say it, and *it isn't true!*" But I had not the moral courage to make such a confession. The character of a 'lunatic' is not, I believe, very difficult to *acquire:* but it is amazingly difficult to *get rid of:* and it seemed quite certain that any such speech as *that* would quite justify the issue of a writ *'de lunatico inquirendo.'*

Lady Muriel evidently thought I had failed to hear her question, and turned to Arthur with a remark on some other subject; and I had time to recover from my shock of surprise—or to awake out of my momentary 'eerie' condition, whichever it was.

When things around me seemed once more to be real, Arthur was saying "I'm afraid there's no help for it: they *must* be finite in number."

"I should be sorry to have to believe it," said Lady Muriel. "Yet, when one comes to think of it, there *are* no new melodies, now-a-days. What people talk of as 'the last new song' always recalls to *me* some tune I've known as a child!"

"The day must come—if the world lasts long enough——" said Arthur, "when every possible tune will have been composed—every possible pun perpetrated——" (Lady Muriel wrung her hands, like a tragedy-queen) "and, worse than that, every possible *book* written! For the number of *words* is finite."

"It'll make very little difference to the *authors*," I suggested. "Instead of saying '*what* book shall I write?' an author will ask himself '*which* book shall I write?' A mere verbal distinction!"

Lady Muriel gave me an approving smile. "But *lunatics* would always write new books, surely?" she went on. "They *couldn't* write the same books over again!"

"True," said Arthur. "But *their* books would come to an end, also. The number of lunatic *books* is as finite as the number of lunatics."

"And *that* number is becoming greater every year," said a pompous man, whom I recognised as the self-appointed showman on the day of the picnic.

"So they say," replied Arthur. "And, when ninety per cent of us are lunatics," (he seemed to be in a wildly nonsensical mood) "the asylums will be put to their proper use."

"And that is——?" the pompous man gravely enquired.

"*To shelter the sane!*" said Arthur. "*We* shall bar ourselves in. The lunatics will have it all their own way, *outside*. They'll do it a little queerly, no doubt. Railway-collisions will be always happening: steamers always blowing up: most of the towns will be burnt down: most of the ships sunk——"

"And most of the men *killed!*" murmured the pompous man, who was evidently hopelessly bewildered.

"Certainly," Arthur assented. "Till at last there will be *fewer* lunatics than sane men. Then *we* come out: *they* go in: and things return to their normal condition!"

The pompous man frowned darkly, and bit his lip, and folded his arms, vainly trying to think it out. "He is *jesting!*" he muttered to himself at last, in a tone of withering contempt, as he stalked away.

By this time the other guests had arrived; and dinner was announced. Arthur of course took down Lady Muriel: and *I* was pleased to find myself seated at her other side, with a severe-looking old lady (whom I had not met before, and whose name I had, as is usual in introductions, entirely failed to catch, merely gathering that it sounded like a compound-name) as my partner for the banquet.

She appeared, however, to be acquainted with Arthur, and confided to me in a low voice her opinion that he was "a very argumentative young man." Arthur, for his part, seemed well inclined to show himself worthy of the character she had given him, and, hearing her say "I never take wine with my soup!" (this was *not* a confidence to me, but was launched upon Society, as a matter of general interest), he at once challenged a combat by asking her "*when* would you say that property *commence* in a plate of soup?"

"This is *my* soup," she sternly replied: "and what is before you is *yours.*"

"No doubt," said Arthur: "but *when* did I begin to own it? Up to the moment of its being put into the plate, it was the property of our host: while being offered round the table, it was, let us say, held in trust by the waiter: did it become mine when I accepted it? Or when it was placed before me? Or when I took the first spoonful?"

"He is a *very* argumentative young man!" was all the old lady would say: but she said it audibly, this time, feeling that Society had a right to know it.

Arthur smiled mischievously. "I shouldn't mind betting you a shilling," he said, "that the Eminent Barrister next you" (It certainly *is* possible to say words so as to make them begin with capitals!) "ca'n't answer me!"

"I *never* bet," she sternly replied.

"Not even sixpenny points at *whist?*"

"Never!" she repeated. *"Whist* is innocent enough: but whist played for *money!"* She shuddered.

Arthur became serious again. "I'm afraid I ca'n't take that view," he said. "I consider that the introduction of small stakes for card-playing was one of the most *moral* acts Society ever did, *as* Society."

"How was it so?" said Lady Muriel.

"Because it took Cards, once for all, out of the category of games at which *cheating* is possible. Look at the way Croquet is demoralising Society. Ladies are beginning to cheat at it, terribly: and, if they're found out, they only laugh, and call it fun. But when there's *money* at stake, that is out of the question. The swindler is *not* accepted as a wit. When a man sits down to cards, and cheats his friends out of their money, he doesn't get much *fun* out of it—unless he thinks it fun to be kicked down stairs!"

"If all gentlemen thought as badly of ladies as *you* do," my neighbour remarked with some bitterness, "there would be very few—very few——." She seemed doubtful how to end her sentence, but at last took "honeymoons" as a safe word.

"On the contrary," said Arthur, the mischievous smile returning to his face, "if only people would adopt *my* theory, the number of honeymoons—quite of a new kind—would be greatly increased!"

"May we hear about this new kind of honeymoon?" said Lady Muriel.

"Let *X* be the gentleman," Arthur began, in a slightly raised voice, as he now found himself with an audience of *six,* including 'Mein Herr,' who was seated at the other side of my polynomial partner. "Let *X* be the gentleman, and *Y* the lady to whom he thinks of proposing. He applies for an Experimental Honeymoon. It is granted. Forthwith the young couple—accompanied by the great-aunt of *Y,* to act as chaperone— start for a month's tour, during which they have many a moonlight-walk, and many a *tête-à-tête* conversation, and each can form a more correct estimate of the other's character, in four *weeks,* than would have been possible in as many *years,* when meeting under the ordinary restrictions of Society. And it is only after their *return* that *X* finally decides whether he will, or will not, put the momentous question to *Y!"*

"In nine cases out of ten," the pompous man proclaimed, "he would decide to break it off!"

"Then, in nine cases out of ten," Arthur rejoined, "an unsuitable match would be prevented, and *both* parties saved from misery!"

"The only really *unsuitable* matches," the old lady remarked, "are those made without sufficient *Money. Love* may come *afterwards.* Money is needed *to begin with!"*

This remark was cast loose upon Society, as a sort of general challenge; and, as such, it was at once accepted by several of those within hearing: *Money* became the key-note of the conversation for some time; and a fitful echo of it was again heard, when the dessert had been placed upon the table, the servants had left the room, and the Earl had started the wine in its welcome progress round the table.

"I'm very glad to see you keep up the old customs," I said to Lady Muriel as I filled her glass. "It's really delightful to experience, once more, the peaceful feeling that comes over one when the waiters have left the room—when one can converse without the feeling of being overheard, and without having dishes constantly thrust over one's shoulder. How much more sociable it is to be able to pour out the wine for the ladies, and to hand the dishes to those who wish for them!"

"In that case, kindly send those peaches down here," said a fat red-faced man, who was seated beyond our pompous friend. "I've been wishing for them—diagonally—for some time!"

"Yes, it *is* a ghastly innovation," Lady Muriel replied, "letting the waiters carry round the wine at dessert. For one thing, they *always* take it the wrong way round—which of course brings bad luck to *everybody* present!"

"Better go the *wrong* way than not go *at all!*" said our host. "Would you kindly help yourself?" (This was to the fat red-faced man.) "You are not a teetotaler, I think?"

"Indeed but I *am!*" he replied, as he pushed on the bottles. "Nearly twice as much money is spent in England on *Drink,* as on any other article of food. Read this card." (What faddist ever goes about without a pocketful of the appropriate literature?) "The stripes of different colours represent the amounts spent of various articles of food. Look at the highest three. Money spent on butter and on cheese, thirty-five millions: on bread, seventy millions: on *intoxicating liquors,* one hundred and thirty-six millions! If I had my way, I would close every public-house in the land! Look at that card, and read the motto. *That's where all the money goes to!*"

"Have you seen the *Anti-Teetotal Card?*" Arthur innocently enquired.

"No, Sir, I have not!" the orator savagely replied. "What is it like?"

"Almost exactly like this one. The coloured stripes are the same. Only, instead of the words 'Money spent on,' it has 'Incomes derived from sale of'; and, instead of 'That's where all the money goes to,' its motto is *'That's where all the money comes from!'* "

The red-faced man scowled, but evidently considered Arthur beneath his notice. So Lady Muriel took up the cudgels. "Do you hold the theory," she enquired, "that people can preach teetotalism more effectually by being teetotalers themselves?"

"Certainly I do!" replied the red-faced man. "Now, here is a case in point," unfolding a newspaper-cutting: "let me read you this letter from a teetotaler. *To the Editor. Sir, I was once a moderate drinker, and knew a man who drank to excess. I went to him. 'Give up this drink,' I said. 'It will ruin your health!' 'You drink,' he said: 'why shouldn't I?' 'Yes,' I said, 'but I know when to leave off.' He turned away from me. 'You drink in your way,' he said: 'let me drink in mine. Be off!' Then I saw that, to do any good with him, I must forswear drink. From that hour I haven't touched a drop!*"

"There! What do you say to *that?*" He looked round triumphantly, while the cutting was handed round for inspection.

"How very curious!" exclaimed Arthur, when it had reached him. "Did you happen to see a letter, last week, about early rising? It was strangely like this one."

The red-faced man's curiosity was roused. "Where did it appear?" he asked.

"Let me read it to you," said Arthur. He took some papers from his pocket, opened one of them, and read as follows. *To the Editor. Sir, I was once a moderate sleeper, and knew a man who slept to excess. I pleaded with him. 'Give up this lying in bed,' I said. 'It will ruin your health!' 'You go to bed,' he said: 'why shouldn't I?' 'Yes,' I said, 'but I know when to get up in the morning.' He turned away from me. 'You sleep in your way,' he said: 'let me sleep in mine. Be off!' Then I saw that to do any good with him, I must forswear sleep. From that hour I haven't been to bed!"*

Arthur folded and pocketed his paper, and passed on the newspaper-cutting. None of us dared to laugh, the red-faced man was evidently so angry. "Your parallel doesn't run on all fours!" he snarled.

"*Moderate* drinkers never do so!" Arthur quietly replied. Even the stern old lady laughed at this.

"But it needs many other things to make a *perfect* dinner!" said Lady Muriel, evidently anxious to change the subject. "Mein Herr! What is *your* idea of a perfect dinner-party?"

The old man looked round smilingly, and his gigantic spectacles seemed more gigantic than ever. "A *perfect* dinner-party?" he repeated. "First, it must be presided over by our present hostess!"

"That, of *course!*" she gaily interposed. "But what *else,* Mein Herr?"

"I can but tell you what I have seen," said Mein Herr, "in mine own— in the country I have traveled in."

He paused for a full minute, and gazed steadily at the ceiling—with so dreamy an expression on his face, that I feared he was going off into a reverie, which seemed to be his normal state. However, after a minute, he suddenly began again.

"That which chiefly causes the failure of a dinner-party, is the running-short—not of meat, nor yet of drink, but of *conversation.*"

"In an *English* dinner-party," I remarked, "I have never known *small-talk* run short!"

"Pardon me," Mein Herr respectfully replied, "I did not say 'small-talk.' I said 'conversation.' All such topics as the weather, or politics, or local gossip, are unknown among us. They are either vapid or controversial. What we need for *conversation* is a topic of *interest* and of *novelty.* To secure these things we have tried various plans—Moving-Pictures, Wild-Creatures, Moving-Guests, and a Revolving-Humorist. But this last is only adapted to *small* parties."

"Let us have it in four separate Chapters, please!" said Lady Muriel, who was evidently deeply interested—as, indeed, most of the party were, by this time: and, all down the table, talk had ceased, and heads were leaning forwards, eager to catch fragments of Mein Herr's oration.

"Chapter One! Moving-Pictures!" was proclaimed in the silvery voice of our hostess.

"The dining-table is shaped like a circular ring," Mein Herr began, in low dreamy tones, which, however, were perfectly audible in the silence. "The guests are seated at the inner side as well as the outer, having ascended to their places by a winding-staircase, from the room below. Along the middle of the table runs a little railway; and there is an endless train of trucks, worked round by machinery; and on each truck there are two pictures, leaning back to back. The train makes two circuits during dinner; and, when it has been *once* round, the waiters turn the pictures round in each truck, making them face the other way. Thus *every* guest sees *every* picture!"

He paused, and the silence seemed deader than ever. Lady Muriel looked aghast. "Really, if this goes on," she exclaimed, "I shall have to drop a pin! Oh, it's *my* fault, is it?" (In answer to an appealing look from Mein Herr.) "I was forgetting my duty. Chapter Two! Wild-Creatures!"

"We found the Moving-Pictures a *little* monotonous," said Mein Herr. "People didn't care to talk Art through a whole dinner; so we tried Wild-Creatures. Among the flowers, which we laid (just as *you* do) about the table, were to be seen, here a mouse, there a beetle; here a spider," (Lady Muriel shuddered) "there a wasp; here a toad, there a snake;" ("Father!" said Lady Muriel, plaintively. "Did you hear *that?*") "so we had plenty to talk about!"

"And when you got stung——" the old lady began.

"They were all chained-up, dear Madam!"

And the old lady gave a satisfied nod.

There was no silence to follow, *this* time. "Third Chapter!" Lady Muriel proclaimed at once. "Moving-Guests!"

"Even the Wild-Creatures proved monotonous," the orator proceeded. "So we left the guests to choose their own subjects; and, to avoid monotony, we changed *them*. We made the table of *two* rings; and the inner ring moved slowly round, all the time, along with the floor in the middle and the inner row of guests. Thus *every* inner guest was brought face-to-face with *every* outer guest. It was a little confusing, sometimes, to have to *begin* a story to one friend and *finish* it to another; but *every* plan has its faults, you know."

"Fourth Chapter!" Lady Muriel hastened to announce. "The Revolving-Humorist!"

"For a *small* party we found it an excellent plan to have a round table, with a hole cut in the middle large enough to hold *one* guest. Here we placed our *best* talker. He revolved slowly, facing every other guest in turn: and he told lively anecdotes the whole time!"

"I shouldn't like it!" murmured the pompous man. "It would make me giddy, revolving like that! I should decline to——" here it appeared to dawn upon him that perhaps the assumption he was making was not warranted by the circumstances: he took a hasty gulp of wine, and choked himself.

But Mein Herr had relapsed into reverie, and made no further remark. Lady Muriel gave the signal, and the ladies left the room.

CHAPTER X.

JABBERING AND JAM.

WHEN the last lady had disappeared, and the Earl, taking his place at the head of the table, had issued the military order "Gentlemen! Close up the ranks, if you please!", and when, in obedience to his command, we had gathered ourselves compactly round him, the pompous man gave a deep sigh of relief, filled his glass to the brim, pushed on the wine, and began one of his favorite orations. "They are charming, no doubt! Charming, but very frivolous. They drag us down, so to speak, to a lower level. They——"

"Do not all pronouns require antecedent *nouns?*" the Earl gently enquired.

"Pardon me," said the pompous man, with lofty condescension. "I had overlooked the noun. The ladies. We regret their absence. Yet we console ourselves. *Thought is free.* With them, we are limited to *trivial* topics— Art, Literature, Politics, and so forth. One can bear to discuss *such* paltry matters with a lady. But no man, in his senses—" (he looked sternly round the table, as if defying contradiction) "—ever yet discussed *WINE* with a lady!" He sipped his glass of port, leaned back in his chair, and slowly raised it up to his eye, so as to look through it at the lamp. "The vintage, my Lord?" he enquired, glancing at his host.

The Earl named the date.

"So I had supposed. But one likes to be certain. The *tint* is, perhaps, slightly pale. But the *body* is unquestionable. And as for the *bouquet*—"

Ah, that magic Bouquet! How vividly that single word recalled the scene! The little beggar-boy turning his somersault in the road—the sweet little crippled maiden in my arms—the mysterious evanescent nursemaid—all rushed tumultuously into my mind, like the creatures of a dream: and through this mental haze there still boomed on, like the tolling of a bell, the solemn voice of the great connoisseur of *WINE!*

Even *his* utterances had taken on themselves a strange and dream-like form. "No," he resumed—and *why* is it, I pause to ask, that, in taking up the broken thread of a dialogue, one *always* begins with this cheerless monosyllable? After much anxious thought, I have come to the conclusion that the object in view is the same as that of the schoolboy, when the sum he is working has got into a hopeless muddle, and when in despair he takes the sponge, washes it all out, and begins again. Just in the same way the bewildered orator, by the simple process of denying *everything* that has been hitherto asserted, makes a clean sweep of the whole discussion, and can 'start fair' with a fresh theory. "No," he resumed: "there's nothing like cherry-jam, after all. That's what *I* say!"

"Not for *all* qualities!" an eager little man shrilly interposed. "For *richness* of general tone I don't say that it *has* a rival, But for *delicacy* of modulation—for what one may call the '*harmonics*' of flavour—give *me* good old *raspberry*-jam!"

"Allow me one word!" The fat red-faced man, quite hoarse with excitement, broke into the dialogue. "It's too important a question to be settled by Amateurs! I can give you the views of a *Professional*—perhaps the most experienced jam-taster now living. Why, I've known him fix the age of strawberry-jam, to a *day*—and we all know what a difficult jam it is to give a date to—on a single tasting! Well, I put to him the *very* question you are discussing. His words were '*cherry*-jam is best, for mere *chiaroscuro* of flavour: *raspberry*-jam lends itself best to those resolved discords that linger so lovingly on the tongue: but, for rapturous *utterness* of saccharine perfection, it's *apricot-jam first and the rest nowhere!'* That was well put, *wasn't* it?"

"Consummately put!" shrieked the eager little man.

"I know your friend well," said the pompous man. "As a jam-taster, he has no rival! Yet I scarcely think——"

But here the discussion became general: and his words were lost in a confused medley of names, every guest sounding the praises of his own favorite jam. At length, through the din, our host's voice made itself heard. "Let us join the ladies!" These words seemed to recall me to waking life; and I felt sure that, for the last few minutes, I had relapsed into the 'eerie' state.

"A strange dream!" I said to myself as we trooped upstairs. "Grown men discussing, as seriously as if they were matters of life and death, the hopelessly trivial details or mere *delicacies,* that appeal to no higher human function than the nerves of the tongue and palate! What a humiliating spectacle such a discussion would be in waking life!"

When, on our way to the drawing-room, I received from the housekeeper my little friends, clad in the daintiest of evening costumes, and looking, in the flush of expectant delight, more radiantly beautiful than I had ever seen them before, I felt no shock of surprise, but accepted the fact with the same unreasoning apathy with which one meets the events of a dream, and was merely conscious of a vague anxiety as to how they would acquit themselves in so novel a scene—forgetting that Court-life in Outland was as good training as they could need for Society in the more substantial world.

It would be best, I thought, to introduce them as soon as possible to some good-natured lady-guest, and I selected the young lady whose piano-forte-playing had been so much talked of. "I am sure you like children," I said. "May I introduce two little friends of mine? This is Sylvie—and this is Bruno."

The young lady kissed Sylvie very graciously. She would have done the same for *Bruno,* but he hastily drew back out of reach. "Their faces are new to me," she said. "Where do you come from, my dear?"

I had not anticipated so inconvenient a question; and, fearing that it might embarrass Sylvie, I answered for her. "They come from some distance. They are only here just for this one evening."

"How far have you come, dear?" the young lady persisted.

Sylvie looked puzzled. "A mile or two, I *think,*" she said doubtfully.

"A mile or *three,*" said Bruno.

"You shouldn't say 'a mile or *three,*'" Sylvie corrected him.

The young lady nodded approval. "Sylvie's quite right. It isn't usual to say 'a mile or *three.*'"

"It would be usual—if we said it often enough," said Bruno.

It was the young lady's turn to look puzzled now. "He's very quick, for his age!" she murmured. "You're not more than seven, are you, dear?" she added aloud.

"I'm not so many as *that,*" said Bruno. "I'm *one.* Sylvie's *one.* Sylvie and me is *two. Sylvie* taught me to count."

"Oh, I wasn't *counting* you, you know!" the young lady laughingly replied.

"Hasn't oo *learnt* to count?" said Bruno.

The young lady bit her lip. "Dear! What embarrassing questions he *does* ask!" she said in a half-audible 'aside.'

"Bruno, you shouldn't!" Sylvie said reprovingly.

"Shouldn't *what?*" said Bruno.

"You shouldn't ask—that sort of questions."

"*What* sort of questions?" Bruno mischievously persisted.

"What *she* told you not," Sylvie replied, with a shy glance at the young lady, and losing all sense of grammar in her confusion.

"Oo ca'n't pronounce it!" Bruno triumphantly cried. And he turned to the young lady, for sympathy in his victory. "I *knewed* she couldn't pronounce 'umbrella-sting'!"

The young lady thought it best to return to the arithmetical problem. "When I asked if you were *seven,* you know, I didn't mean 'how many *children?*' I meant 'how many *years*——'"

"Only got *two* ears," said Bruno. "Nobody's got *seven* ears.

"And you belong to this little girl?" the young lady continued, skilfully evading the anatomical problem.

"No I doosn't belong to *her!*" said Bruno. "Sylvie belongs to *me!*" And he clasped his arms round her as he added "She are my very mine!"

"And, do you know," said the young lady, "I've a little sister at home, exactly like *vour* sister? I'm sure they'd love each other."

"They'd be very extremely useful to each other," Bruno said, thoughtfully. "And they wouldn't want no looking-glasses to brush their hair wiz."

"Why not, my child?"

"Why, each one would do for the other one's looking-glass, a-course!" cried Bruno.

But here Lady Muriel, who had been standing by, listening to this bewildering dialogue, interrupted it to ask if the young lady would favour us with some music; and the children followed their new friend to the piano.

Arthur came and sat down by me. "If rumour speaks truly," he whispered, "we are to have a real treat!" And then, amid a breathless silence, the performance began.

She was one of those players whom Society talks of as 'brilliant,' and she dashed into the loveliest of Haydn's Symphonies in a style that was clearly the outcome of years of patient study under the best masters. At first it seemed to be the perfection of piano-forte-playing; but in a few minutes I began to ask myself, wearily, "*What* is it that is wanting? *Why* does one get no pleasure from it?"

Then I set myself to listen intently to every note; and the mystery explained itself. There *was* an almost-perfect mechanical *correctness*— and there was nothing else! False notes, of course, did not occur: she knew the piece too well for *that;* but there was just enough irregularity of *time* to betray that the player had no real 'ear' for music—just enough inarticulateness in the more elaborate passages to show that she did not think her audience worth taking real pains for—just enough mechanical monotony of accent to take all *soul* out of the heavenly modulations she was profaning—in short, it was simply irritating; and, when she had rattled off the finale and had struck the final chord as if, the instrument being now done with, it didn't matter how many wires she broke, I could not even *affect* to join in the stereotyped "Oh, *thank* you!" which was chorused around me.

Lady Muriel joined us for a moment. "Isn't it *beautiful?*" she whispered, to Arthur, with a mischievous smile.

"No, it isn't!" said Arthur. But the gentle sweetness of his face quite neutralised the apparent rudeness of the reply.

"Such execution, you know!" she persisted.

"That's what she *deserves*," Arthur doggedly replied: "but people are so prejudiced against capital——"

"Now you're beginning to talk nonsense!" Lady Muriel cried. "But you *do* like Music, don't you? You said so just now."

"Do I like *Music?*" the Doctor repeated softly to himself. "My dear Lady Muriel, there is Music and Music. Your question is painfully vague. You might as well ask 'Do you like *People?*'"

Lady Muriel bit her lip, frowned, and stamped with one tiny foot. As a dramatic representation of ill-temper, it was distinctly *not* a success. However, it took in *one* of her audience, and Bruno hastened to interpose, as peacemaker in a rising quarrel, with the remark "*I* likes Peoples!"

Arthur laid a loving hand on the little curly head. "What? *All* Peoples?" he enquired.

"Not *all* Peoples," Bruno explained. "Only but Sylvie—and Lady Muriel—and him—" (pointing to the Earl) "and oo—and oo!"

"You shouldn't point at people," said Sylvie. "It's very rude."

"In Bruno's World," I said, "there are only *four* People—worth mentioning!"

"In Bruno's World!" Lady Muriel repeated thoughtfully. "A bright and flowery world. Where the grass is always green, where the breezes always blow softly, and the rain-clouds never gather; where there are no wild beasts, and no deserts——"

"There *must* be deserts," Arthur decisively remarked. "At least if it was *my* ideal world."

"But what possible use is there in a *desert?*" said Lady Muriel. "*Surely* you would have no wilderness in your ideal world?"

Arthur smiled. "But indeed I *would!*" he said. "A wilderness would be more necessary than a railway; and *far* more conducive to general happiness than church-bells!"

"But what would you use it for?"

"*To practise music in*," he replied. "All the young ladies, that have no ear for music, but insist on learning it, should be conveyed, every morning, two or three miles into the wilderness. There each would find a comfortable room provided for her, and also a cheap second-hand piano-forte, on which she might play for hours, without adding one needless pang to the sum of human misery!"

Lady Muriel glanced round in alarm, lest these barbarous sentiments should be overheard. But the fair musician was at a safe distance. "At any rate you must allow that she's a sweet girl?" she resumed.

"Oh, certainly. As sweet as *eau sucrée*, if you choose—and nearly as interesting!"

"You are incorrigible!" said Lady Muriel, and turned to me. "I hope you found Mrs. Mills an interesting companion?"

"Oh, *that's* her name, is it?" I said. "I fancied there was *more* of it."

"So there is: and it will be 'at your proper peril' (whatever that may mean) if you ever presume to address her as 'Mrs. Mills.' She is 'Mrs. Ernest—Atkinson—Mills'!"

"She is one of those would-be grandees," said Arthur, "who think that, by tacking on to their surname all their spare Christian-names, with hyphens between, they can give it an aristocratic flavour. As if it wasn't trouble enough to remember *one* surname!"

By this time the room was getting crowded, as the guests, invited for the evening-party, were beginning to arrive, and Lady Muriel had to devote herself to the task of welcoming them, which she did with the sweetest grace imaginable. Sylvie and Bruno stood by her, deeply interested in the process.

"I hope you like my friends?" she said to them. "Specially my dear old friend, Mein Herr (What's become of him, I wonder? Oh, there he is!), that old gentleman in spectacles, with a long beard?"

"He's a grand old gentleman!" Sylvie said, gazing admiringly at 'Mein Herr,' who had settled down in a corner, from which his mild eyes beamed on us through a gigantic pair of spectacles. "And what a lovely beard!"

"What does he call his-self?" Bruno whispered.

"He calls himself 'Mein Herr,'" Sylvie whispered in reply.

Bruno shook his head impatiently. "That's what he calls his *hair*, not his *self* oo silly!" He appealed to me. "What doos he call his *self*, Mister Sir?"

"That's the only name *I* know of," I said. "But he looks very lonely. Don't you pity his grey hairs?"

"I pities his *self*," said Bruno, still harping on the misnomer; "but I doosn't pity his *hair*, one bit. His *hair* ca'n't feel!"

"We met him this afternoon," said Sylvie. "We'd been to see Nero and we'd had *such* fun with him, making him invisible again! And we saw that nice old gentleman as we came back."

"Well, let's go and talk to him, and cheer him up a little," I said: "and perhaps we shall find out what he calls himself."

CHAPTER XI.

THE MAN IN THE MOON.

THE children came willingly. With one of them on each side of me, I approached the corner occupied by 'Mein Herr.' "You don't object to *children*, I hope?" I began.

"*Crabbed age and youth cannot live together!*" the old man cheerfully replied, with a most genial smile. "Now take a good look at me, my children! You would guess me to be an *old* man, wouldn't you?"

At first sight, though his face had reminded me so mysteriously of "the Professor," he had seemed to be decidedly a *younger* man: but, when I came to look into the wonderful depth of those large dreamy eyes, I felt, with a strange sense of awe, that he was incalculably *older:* he seemed to gaze at us out of some by-gone age, centuries away.

"I don't know if oo're an *old* man," Bruno answered, as the children, won over by the gentle voice, crept a little closer to him. "I thinks oo're *eighty-three.*"

"He is very exact!" said Mein Herr.

"Is he anything like right?" I said.

"There are reasons," Mein Herr gently replied, "reasons which I am not at liberty to explain, for not mentioning *definitely* any Persons, Places, or Dates. One remark only I will permit myself to make—that the period of life, between the ages of a hundred-and-sixty-five and a hundred-and-seventy-five, is a specially *safe* one."

"How do you make that out?" I said.

"Thus. You would consider swimming to be a very safe amusement, if you scarcely ever heard of any one dying of it. Am I not right in thinking that you never heard of any one dying between those two ages?"

"I see what you mean," I said: "but I'm afraid you ca'n't prove *swimming* to be safe, on the same principle. It is no uncommon thing to hear of some one being *drowned.*"

"In *my* country," said Mein Herr. "no one is *ever* drowned."

"Is there no water deep enough?"

"Plenty! But we ca'n't *sink*. We are all *lighter than water*. Let me explain," he added, seeing my look of surprise. "Suppose you desire a race of *pigeons* of a particular shape or colour, do you not select, from year to year, those that are nearest to the shape or colour you want, and keep those, and part with the others?"

"We do," I replied. "We call it 'Artificial Selection.'"

"Exactly so," said Mein Herr. "Well, *we* have practised that for some centuries—constantly selecting the *lightest* people: so that, now, *everybody* is lighter than water."

"Then you never can be drowned at *sea?*"

"Never! It is only on the *land*—for instance, when attending a play in a theatre—that we are in such a danger."

"How can that happen at a *theatre?*"

"Our theatres are all *underground*. Large tanks of water are placed above. If a fire breaks out, the taps are turned, and in one minute the theatre is flooded, up to the very roof! Thus the fire is extinguished."

"*And* the audience, I presume?"

"That is a minor matter," Mein Herr carelessly replied. "But they have the comfort of knowing that, whether drowned or not, they are all *lighter than water*. We have not yet reached the standard of making people lighter than *air* but we are *aiming* at it; and, in another thousand years or so——"

"What doos oo do wiz the peoples that's too heavy?" Bruno solemnly enquired.

"We have applied the same process," Mein Herr continued, not noticing Bruno's question, "to many other purposes. We have gone on selecting *walking-sticks*— always keeping those that walked *best*—till we have obtained some, that can walk by themselves! We have gone on selecting *cotton-wool*, till we have got some lighter than air! You've no idea what a useful material it is! We call it 'Imponderal.'"

"What do you use it for?"

"Well, chiefly for *packing* articles, to go by Parcel-Post. It makes them weigh *less than nothing*, you know."

"And how do the Post-Office people know what you have to pay?"

"That's the beauty of the new system!" Mein Herr cried exultingly. "They pay *us:* we don't pay *them!* I've often got as much as five shillings for sending a parcel."

"But doesn't your Government object?"

"Well, they *do* object, a little. They say it comes so expensive, in the long run. But the thing's as clear as daylight, by their own rules. If I send a parcel, that weighs a pound *more* than nothing, I *pay* three-pence: so, of course, if it weighs a pound *less* than nothing, I ought to *receive* three-pence."

"It is *indeed* a useful article!" I said.

"Yet even 'Imponderal' has its disadvantages," he resumed. "I bought some, a few days ago, and put it into my *hat*, to carry it home, and the hat simply floated away!"

"Had oo some of that funny stuff in oor hat *to-day?*" Bruno enquired. "Sylvie and me saw oo in the road, and oor hat were ever so high up! Weren't it, Sylvie?"

"No, that was quite another thing," said Mein Herr. "There was a drop or two of rain falling: so I put my hat on the top of my stick—as an umbrella, you know. As I came along the road," he continued, turning to me, "I was overtaken by——"

"——a shower of rain?" said Bruno.

"Well, it *looked* more like the tail of a dog," Mein Herr replied. "It was the most curious thing! Something rubbed affectionately against my knee. And I looked down. And I could see *nothing!* Only, about a yard off, there was a dog's tail, wagging, all by itself!"

"Oh, *Sylvie!*" Bruno murmured reproachfully. "Oo didn't finish making him visible!"

"I'm *so* sorry!" Sylvie said, looking very penitent. "I meant to rub it along his back, but we were in such a hurry. We'll go and finish him tomorrow. Poor thing! Perhaps he'll get no supper tonight!"

"*Course* he won't!" said Bruno. "Nobody never gives bones to a dog's tail!"

Mein Herr looked from one to the other in blank astonishment. "I do not understand you," he said. "I had lost my way, and I was consulting a pocket-map, and somehow I had dropped one of my gloves, and this invisible *Something,* that had rubbed against my knee, actually brought it back to me!"

"Course he did!" said Bruno. "He's *welly* fond of fetching things."

Mein Herr looked so thoroughly bewildered that I thought it best to change the subject. "What a useful thing a pocket-map is!" I remarked.

"That's another thing we've learned from *your* Nation," said Mein Herr, "map-making. But we've carried it much further than *you.* What do you consider the *largest* map that would be really useful?"

"About six inches to the mile."

"Only *six inches!*" exclaimed Mein Herr. "We very soon got to six *yards* to the mile. Then we tried a *hundred* yards to the mile. And then came the grandest idea of all! We actually made a map of the country, on the scale of a *mile to the mile!*"

"Have you used it much?" I enquired.

"It has never been spread out, yet," said Mein Herr: "the farmers objected: they said it would cover the whole country, and shut out the sunlight! So we now use the country itself, as its own map, and I assure you it does nearly as well. Now let me ask you *another* question. What is the smallest *world* you would care to inhabit?"

"*I* know!" cried Bruno, who was listening intently. "I'd like a little teeny-tiny world, just big enough for Sylvie and me!"

"Then you would have to stand on opposite sides of it," said Mein Herr. "And so you would never see your sister *at all!*"

"And I'd have no *lessons,*" said Bruno.

"You don't mean to say you've been trying experiments in *that* direction!" I said.

"Well, not *experiments* exactly. We do not profess to *construct* planets.

But a scientific friend of mine, who has made several balloon-voyages, assures me he has visited a planet so small that he could walk right round it in twenty minutes! There had been a great battle, just before his visit, which had ended rather oddly: the vanquished army ran away at full speed, and in a very few minutes found themselves face-to-face with the victorious army, who were marching home again, and who were so frightened at finding themselves between *two* armies, that they surrendered at once! Of course that lost them the battle, though, as a matter of fact, they had killed *all* the soldiers on the other side."

"Killed soldiers *ca'n't* run away," Bruno thoughtfully remarked.

" 'Killed' is a technical word," replied Mein Herr. "In the little planet I speak of, the bullets were made of soft black stuff, which marked everything it touched. So, after a battle, all you had to do was to count how many soldiers on each side were 'killed'—that means 'marked on the *back*,' for marks in *front* didn't count."

"Then you couldn't 'kill' any, unless they ran away?" I said.

"My scientific friend found out a better plan than *that*. He pointed out that, if only the bullets were sent *the other way round the world*, they would hit the enemy in the *back*. After that, the *worst* marksmen were considered the *best* soldiers; and *the very worst of all* always got First Prize."

"And how did you decide which was *the very worst of all?*"

"Easily. The *best* possible shooting is, you know, to hit what is exactly in *front* of you: so of course the *worst* possible is to hit what is exactly *behind* you."

"They were strange people in that little planet!" I said.

"They were indeed! Perhaps their method of *government* was the strangest of all. In *this* planet, I am told, a Nation consists of a number of Subjects, and one King: but, in the little planet I speak of, it consisted of a number of *Kings,* and one *Subject!*"

"You say you are 'told' what happens in *this* planet," I said. "May I venture to guess that you yourself are a visitor from some *other* planet?"

Bruno clapped his hands in his excitement. "Is oo the Man-in-the-Moon?" he cried.

Mein Herr looked uneasy. "I am *not* in the Moon, my child," he said evasively. "To return to what I was saying. I think *that* method of government ought to answer *well*. You see, the Kings would be sure to make Laws contradicting each other: so the Subject could never be punished, because, *whatever* he did, he'd be obeying *some* Law."

"And, whatever he did, he'd be disobeying *some* Law!" cried Bruno. "So he'd *always* be punished!"

Lady Muriel was passing at the moment; and caught the last word. "Nobody's going to be punished *here!*" she said, taking Bruno in her arms. "This is Liberty-Hall! Would you lend me the children for a minute?"

"The children desert us, you see," I said to Mein Herr, as she carried them off: "so we old folk must keep each other company!"

The old man sighed. "Ah, well! We're old folk *now;* and yet I was a child myself, once—at least I fancy so."

It *did* seem a rather unlikely fancy, I could not help owning to myself—

looking at the shaggy white hair, and the long beard—that he could *ever* have been a child. "You are fond of young people?" I said.

"Young *men*," he replied. "Not of *children* exactly. I used to teach young men—many a year ago—in my dear old University!"

"I didn't quite catch its *name?*" I hinted.

"I did not name it," the old man replied mildly. "Nor would you know the name if I did. Strange tales I could tell you of all the changes I have witnessed there! But it would weary you, I fear."

"No, *indeed!*" I said. "Pray go on. What kind of changes?"

But the old man seemed to be more in a humour for questions than for answers. "Tell me," he said, laying his hand impressively on my arm, "tell me something. For I am a stranger in your land, and I know little of *your* modes of education: yet something tells me *we* are further on than *you* in the eternal cycle of change—and that many a theory *we* have tried and found to fail, *you* also will try, with a wilder enthusiasm: you also will find to fail, with a bitterer despair!"

It was strange to see how, as he talked, and his words flowed more and more freely, with a certain rhythmic eloquence, his features seemed to glow with an inner light, and the whole man seemed to be transformed, as if he had grown fifty years younger in a moment of time.

CHAPTER XII.

FAIRY-MUSIC.

THE silence that ensued was broken by the voice of the musical young lady, who had seated herself near us, and was conversing with one of the newly-arrived guests. "Well!" she said in a tone of scornful surprise. "We *are* to have something new in the way of music, it appears!"

I looked round for an explanation, and was nearly as much astonished as the speaker herself: it was *Sylvie* whom Lady Muriel was leading to the piano!

"Do try it, my darling!" she was saying. "I'm sure you can play very nicely!"

Sylvie looked round at me, with tears in her eyes. I tried to give her an encouraging smile, but it was evidently a great strain on the nerves of a child so wholly unused to be made an exhibition of, and she was frightened and unhappy. Yet here came out the perfect sweetness of her disposition: I could see that she was resolved to forget herself, and do her best to give pleasure to Lady Muriel and her friends. She seated herself at the instrument, and began instantly. Time and expression, so far as one could judge, were perfect: but her touch was one of such extraordinary lightness that it was at first scarcely possible, through the hum of conversation which still continued, to catch a note of what she was playing.

But in a minute the hum had died away into absolute silence, and we all sat, entranced and breathless, to listen to such heavenly music as none then present could ever forget.

Hardly touching the notes at first, she played a sort of introduction in a minor key—like an embodied twilight; one felt as though the lights were growing dim, and a mist were creeping through the room. Then there flashed through the gathering gloom the first few notes of a melody so lovely, so delicate, that one held one's breath, fearful to lose a single note of it. Ever and again the music dropped into the pathetic minor key with which it had begun, and, each time that the melody forced its way, so to speak, through the enshrouding gloom into the light of day, it was more entrancing, more magically sweet. Under the airy touch of the child, the instrument actually seemed to *warble*, like a bird. *"Rise up, my love, my fair one,"* it seemed to sing, *"and come away! For lo, the winter is past, the rain is over and gone; the flowers appear on the earth; the time of the singing of birds is come!"* One could fancy one heard the tinkle of the last few drops, shaken from the trees by a passing gust—that one saw the first glittering rays of the sun, breaking through the clouds.

The Count hurried across the room in great excitement. "I *cannot* remember myself," he exclaimed, "of the name of this so charming an air! It is of an opera, most surely. Yet not even will the *opera* remind his name to me! What you call him, dear child?"

Sylvie looked round at him with a rapt expression of face. She had ceased playing, but her fingers still wandered fitfully over the keys. All

fear and shyness had quite passed away now, and nothing remained but the pure joy of the music that had thrilled our hearts.

"The title of it!" the Count repeated impatiently. "How call you the opera?"

"I don't know what an opera *is*," Sylvie half-whispered.

"How, then, call you the *air*?"

"I don't know any name for it," Sylvie replied, as she rose from the instrument.

"But this is marvellous!" exclaimed the Count, following the child, and addressing himself to me, as if I were the proprietor of this musical prodigy, and so *must* know the origin of her music. "You have heard her play this, sooner—I would say 'before this occasion'? How call you the air?"

I shook my head; but was saved from more questions by Lady Muriel, who came up to petition the Count for a song.

The Count spread out his hands apologetically, and ducked his head. "But, Milady, I have already respected—I would say prospected—all your songs; and there shall be none fitted to my voice! They are not for basso voices!"

"Wo'n't you look at them again?" Lady Muriel implored.

"Let's help him!" Bruno whispered to Sylvie. "Let's get him—*you* know!"

Sylvie nodded. "Shall *we* look for a song for you?" she said sweetly to the Count.

"Mais *oui!*" the little man exclaimed.

"Of course we may!" said Bruno, while, each taking a hand of the delighted Count, they led him to the music-stand.

"There is still hope!" said Lady Muriel over her shoulder, as she followed them.

I turned to 'Mein Herr,' hoping to resume our interrupted conversation. "You were remarking——" I began: but at this moment Sylvie came to call Bruno, who had returned to my side, looking unusually serious. "*Do* come, Bruno!" she entreated. "You know we've nearly found it!" Then, in a whisper, "The locket's in my *hand*, now. I couldn't get it out while they were looking!"

But Bruno drew back. "The man called me names," he said with dignity.

"What names?" I enquired with some curiosity.

"I asked him," said Bruno, "which sort of song he liked. And he said 'A song of *a* man, not of *a* lady.' And I said 'Shall Sylvie and me find you the song of Mister Tottles?' And he said 'Wait, eel!' And I'm *not* an eel, oo know!"

"I'm *sure* he didn't mean it!" Sylvie said earnestly. "It's something French—you know he ca'n't talk English so well as——"

Bruno relented visibly. "Course he knows no better, if he's Flench! Flenchmen *never* can speak English so goodly as *us!*" And Sylvie led him away, a willing captive.

"Nice children!" said the old man, taking off his spectacles and rubbing them carefully. Then he put them on again, and watched with an approving smile, while the children tossed over the heap of music, and we just caught Sylvie's reproving words, "We're *not* making hay, Bruno!"

"This has been a long interruption to our conversation," I said. "Pray let us go on!"

"Willingly!" replied the gentle old man. "I was much interested in what you——" He paused a moment, and passed his hand uneasily across his brow. "One forgets," he murmured. "What was I saying? Oh! Something you were to tell me. Yes. Which of your teachers do you value the most highly, those whose words are easily understood, or those who puzzle you at every turn?"

I felt obliged to admit that we generally admired most the teachers we couldn't quite understand.

"Just so," said Mein Herr. "That's the way it begins. Well, *we* were at that stage some eighty years ago—or was it ninety? Our favourite teacher got more obscure every year; and every year we admired him more— just as *your* Art-fanciers call *mist* the fairest feature in a landscape, and admire a view with frantic delight when they can see nothing! Now I'll tell you how it ended. It was Moral Philosophy that our idol lectured on. Well, his pupils couldn't make head or tail of it, but they got it all by heart; and, when Examination-time came, they wrote it down; and the Examiners said 'Beautiful! What depth!' "

"But what good was it to the young men *afterwards?*"

"Why, don't you see?" replied Mein Herr. "*They* became teachers in their turn, and *they* said all these things over again; and *their* pupils wrote it all down; and the Examiners accepted it; and nobody had the ghost of an idea what it all meant!"

"And how did it end?"

"It ended this way. We woke up one fine day, and found there was no one in the place that knew *anything* about Moral Philosophy. So we abolished it, teachers, classes, examiners, and all. And if any one wanted to learn anything about it, he had to make it out for himself; and after another twenty years or so there were several men that really knew something about it! Now tell me another thing. How long do you teach a youth before you examine him, in your Universities?"

I told him, three or four years.

"Just so, just what *we* did!" he exclaimed. "We taught 'em a bit, and, just as they were beginning to take it in, we took it all out again! We pumped our wells dry before they were a quarter full—we stripped our orchards while the apples were still in blossom—we applied the severe logic of arithmetic to our chickens, while peacefully slumbering in their shells! Doubtless it's the early bird that picks up the worm—but if the bird gets up so outrageously early that the worm is still deep underground, what *then* is its chance of a breakfast?"

Not much, I admitted.

"Now see how that works!" he went on eagerly. "If you want to pump your wells so soon—and I suppose you tell me that is what you *must* do?"

"We must," I said. "In an over-crowded country like this, nothing but Competitive Examinations——"

Mein Herr threw up his hands wildly. "What, *again?*" he cried. "I thought it was dead, fifty years ago! Oh this Upas-tree of Competitive Examinations! Beneath whose deadly shade all the original genius, all the exhaustive research, all the untiring life-long diligence by which our fore-fathers have so advanced human knowledge, must slowly but surely wither away, and give place to a system of Cookery, in which the human mind is a sausage, and all we ask is, how much indigestible stuff can be crammed into it!"

Always, after these bursts of eloquence, he seemed to forget himself for a moment, and only to hold on to the thread of thought by some single word. "Yes, *crammed*," he repeated. "We went through all that stage of the disease—had it bad, I warrant you! Of course, as the Examination was all in all, we tried to put in just what was wanted—and the *great* thing to aim at was, that the Candidate should know absolutely *nothing* beyond the needs of the Examination! I don't say it was ever *quite* achieved: but one of my own pupils (pardon an old man's egotism) came very near it. After the Examination, he mentioned to me the few facts which he knew but had *not* been able to bring in, and I can assure you they were trivial, Sir, absolutely trivial!"

I feebly expressed my surprise and delight.

The old man bowed, with a gratified smile, and proceeded. "At that time, no one had hit on the much more rational plan of watching for the individual scintillations of genius, and rewarding them as they occurred. As it was, we made our unfortunate pupil into a Leyden-jar, charged him up to the eyelids—then applied the knob of a Competitive Examination, and drew off one magnificent spark, which very often cracked the jar! What mattered *that*? He labeled it 'First Class Spark,' and put it away on the shelf."

"But the more rational system——?" I suggested.

"Ah, yes! *that* came next. Instead of giving the whole reward of learning in one lump, we used to pay for every good answer as it occurred. How well I remember lecturing in those days, with a heap of small coins at my elbow! It was 'A *very* good answer, Mr. Jones!' (that meant a shilling, mostly). 'Bravo, Mr. Robinson!' (that meant half-a-crown). Now I'll tell you how *that* worked. Not one single fact would any of them take in, without a fee! And when a clever boy came up from school, he got paid more for learning than we got paid for teaching him! Then came the wildest craze of all."

"What, *another* craze?" I said.

"It's the last one," said the old man. "I must have tired you out with my long story. Each College wanted to get the clever boys: so we adopted a system which we had heard was very popular in England: the Colleges competed against each other, and the boys let themselves out to the highest bidder! What geese we were! Why, they were bound to come to the University *somehow*. We needn't have paid 'em! And all our money went in getting clever boys to come to one College rather than another! The competition was so keen, that at last mere money-payments were not enough. Any College, that wished to secure some specially clever young man, had to waylay him at the station, and hunt him through the streets. The first who touched him was allowed to have him."

"That hunting-down of the scholars, as they arrived, must have been a curious business," I said. "Could you give me some idea of what it was like?"

"Willingly!" said the old man. "I will describe to you the very last Hunt that took place, before that form of Sport (for it was actually reckoned among the *Sports* of the day: we called it 'Cub-Hunting') was finally abandoned. I witnessed it myself, as I happened to be passing by at the moment, and was what we called 'in at the death.' I can see it now!" he went on in an excited tone, gazing into vacancy with those large dreamy eyes of his. "It seems like yesterday; and yet it happened——" He checked himself hastily, and the remaining words died away into a whisper.

"*How* many years ago did you say?" I asked, much interested in the prospect of at last learning *some* definite fact in his history.

"*Many* years ago," he replied. "The scene at the Railway-Station had been (so they told me) one of wild excitement. Eight or nine Heads of Colleges had assembled at the gates (no one was allowed inside), and the Station-Master had drawn a line on the pavement, and insisted on their all standing behind it. The gates were flung open! The young man darted through them, and fled like lightning down the street, while the Heads of Colleges actually *yelled* with excitement on catching sight of him! The Proctor gave the word, in the old statutory form, '*Semel! Bis! Ter! Currite!*,' and the Hunt began! Oh, it was a fine sight, believe me! At the first corner he dropped his Greek Lexicon: further on, his railway-rug: then various small articles: then his umbrella: lastly, what I suppose he prized most, his hand-bag; but the game was up: the spherical principal of—of——"

"Of *which* College?" I said.

"—of *one* of the Colleges," he resumed, "had put into operation the Theory—his own discovery—of Accelerated Velocity, and captured him just opposite to where I stood. I shall never forget that wild breathless

struggle! But it was soon over. Once in those great bony hands, escape was impossible!"

"May I ask why you speak of him as the '*spherical*' Principal?" I said.

"The epithet referred to his *shape,* which was a perfect *sphere.* You are aware that a bullet, another instance of a perfect sphere, when falling in a perfectly straight line, moves with Accelerated Velocity?"

I bowed assent.

"Well, my spherical friend (as I am proud to call him) set himself to investigate the *causes* of this. He found them to be *three.* One; that it is a perfect *sphere.* Two; that it moves in a *straight line.* Three; that its direction is *not upwards.* When these three conditions are fulfilled, you get Accelerated Velocity."

"Hardly," I said: "if you will excuse my differing from you. Suppose we apply the theory to *horizontal* motion. If a bullet is fired *horizontally,* it——"

"—it does *not* move in a *straight line,*" he quietly finished my sentence for me.

"I yield the point," I said. "What did your friend do next?"

"The next thing was to apply the theory, as you rightly suggest, to *horizontal* motion. But the moving body, ever tending to *fall,* needs *constant support,* if it is to move in a true horizontal line. 'What, then,' he asked himself, 'will give *constant support to a moving body?* And his answer was '*Human legs!*' *That* was the discovery that immortalised his name!"

"His name being——?" I suggested.

"I had not mentioned it," was the gentle reply of my most unsatisfactory informant. "His next step was an obvious one. He took to a diet of suet-dumplings, until his body had become a perfect sphere. *Then* he went out for his first experimental run—which nearly cost him his life!"

"How was *that?*"

"Well, you see, he had no idea of the *tremendous* new Force in Nature that he was calling into play. He began too fast. In a very few minutes he found himself moving at a hundred miles an hour! And, if he had not had the presence of mind to charge into the middle of a haystack (which he scattered to the four winds) there can be no doubt that he would have left the Planet he belonged to, and gone right away into Space!"

"And how came that to be the *last* of the Cub-Hunts?" I enquired.

"Well, you see, it led to a rather scandalous dispute between two of the Colleges. *Another* Principal had laid his hand on the young man, so nearly at the same moment as the *spherical* one, that there was no knowing which had touched him first. The dispute got into print, and did us no credit, and, in short, Cub-Hunts came to an end. Now I'll tell you what cured us of that wild craze of ours, the bidding against each other, for the clever scholars, just as if they were articles to be sold by auction! Just when the craze had reached its highest point, and when one of the Colleges had actually advertised a Scholarship of one thousand pounds *per annum,* one of our tourists brought us the manuscript of an old African legend—I happen to have a copy of it in my pocket. Shall I translate it for you?"

"Pray go on," I said, though I felt I was getting *very* sleepy.

CHAPTER XIII.

WHAT TOTTLES MEANT.

MEIN Herr unrolled the manuscript, but, to my great surprise, instead of *reading* it, he began to *sing* it, in a rich mellow voice that seemed to ring through the room.

> *"One thousand pounds per annum*
> *Is not so bad a figure, come!"*
> *Cried Tottles. "And I tell you, flat,*
> *A man may marry well on that!*
> *To say 'the Husband needs the Wife'*
> *Is* not *the way to represent it.*
> *The crowning joy of Woman's life*
> *Is* Man!" *said Tottles (and he meant it).*

> *The blissful Honey-moon is past:*
> *The Pair have settled down at last:*

Mamma-in-law their home will share,
And make their happiness her care.
"Your income is an ample one:
Go it, my children!" (And they went it).
"I rayther *think this kind of fun*
Won't last!" said Tottles (and he meant it).

They took a little country-box—
A box at Covent Garden also:
They lived a life of double-knocks,
Acquaintances began to call so:
Their London house was much the same
(It took three hundred, clear, to rent it):
"Life is a very jolly game!"
Cried happy Tottles (and he meant it).

'Contented with a frugal lot'
(He always used that phrase at Gunter's),
He bought a handy little yacht—
A dozen serviceable hunters—
The fishing of a Highland Loch—
A sailing-boat to circumvent it—
"The sounding of that Gaelic 'och'
Beats me!" *said Tottles (and he meant it)."*

Here, with one of those convulsive starts that wake one up in the very act of dropping off to sleep, I became conscious that the deep musical tones that thrilled me did *not* belong to Mein Herr, but to the French Count. The old man was still conning the manuscript.

"I *beg* your pardon for keeping you waiting!" he said. "I was just making sure that I knew the English for all the words. I am quite ready now." And he read me the following Legend:—

"In a city that stands in the very centre of Africa, and is rarely visited by the casual tourist, the people had always bought eggs—a daily necessary in a climate where egg-flip was the usual diet—from a Merchant who came to their gates once a week. And the people always bid wildly against each other: so there was quite a lively auction every time the Merchant came, and the last egg in his basket used to fetch the value of two or three camels, or thereabouts. And eggs got dearer every week. And still they drank their egg-flip, and wondered where all their money went to.

"And there came a day when they put their heads together. And they understood what donkeys they had been.

"And next day, when the Merchant came, only *one* Man went forth. And he said 'Oh, thou of the hook-nose and the goggle-eyes, thou of the measureless beard, how much for that lot of eggs?'

"And the Merchant answered him 'I *could* let thee have that lot at ten thousand piastres the dozen.'

"And the Man chuckled inwardly, and said '*Ten* piastres the dozen I offer thee, and no more, oh descendant of a distinguished grandfather!'

"And the Merchant stroked his beard, and said 'Hum! I will await the coming of thy friends.' So he waited. And the Man waited with him. And they waited both together."

"The manuscript breaks off here," said Mein Herr, as he rolled it up again; "but it was enough to open our eyes. We saw what simpletons we had been—buying our Scholars much as those ignorant savages bought their eggs—and the ruinous system was abandoned. If only we could have abandoned, along with it, all the *other* fashions we had borrowed from you, instead of carrying them to their logical results! But it was not to be. What ruined my country, and drove me from my home, was the introduction—into the *Army*, of all places—of your theory of Political Dichotomy!"

"Shall I trouble you too much," I said, "if I ask you to explain what you mean by 'the Theory of Political Dichotomy'?"

"No trouble at all!" was Mein Herr's most courteous reply. "I quite enjoy talking, when I get so good a listener. What started the thing, with us, was the report brought to us, by one of our most eminent statesmen, who had stayed some time in England, of the way affairs were managed there. It was a political necessity (so he assured us, and we believed him, though we had never discovered it till that moment) that there should be *two* Parties, in every affair and on every subject. In *Politics*, the two parties, which you had found it necessary to institute, were called, he told us, 'Whigs' and 'Tories'."

"That must have been some time ago?" I remarked.

"It *was* some time ago," he admitted. "And this was the way the affairs of the British Nation were managed. (You will correct me if I misrepresent it. I do but repeat what our traveler told us.) These two Parties—which were in chronic hostility to each other—took turns in conducting the Government; and the Party, that happened *not* to be in power, was called the 'Opposition', I believe?"

"That is the right name," I said. "There have always been, so long as we have had a Parliament at all, *two* Parties, one 'in', and one 'out'."

"Well, the function of the 'Ins' (if I may so call them) was to do the best they could for the national welfare—in such things as making war or peace, commercial treaties, and so forth?"

"Undoubtedly," I said.

"And the function of the 'Outs' was (so our traveler assured us, though we were very incredulous at first) to *prevent* the 'Ins' from succeeding in any of these things?"

"To *criticize* and to *amend* their proceedings," I corrected him. "It would be *unpatriotic* to *hinder* the Government in doing what was for the good of the Nation! We have always held a *Patriot* to be the greatest of heroes, and an *unpatriotic* spirit to be one of the worst of human ills!"

"Excuse me for a moment," the old gentleman courteously replied, taking out his pocket-book. "I have a few memoranda here, of a correspondence I had with our tourist, and, if you will allow me, I'll just refresh my memory—although I quite agree with you—it is, as you say, one of the worst of human ills——" And, here Mein Herr began singing again:—

> But oh, the worst of human ills
> (Poor Tottles found) are 'little bills'!
> And, with no balance in the Bank,
> What wonder that his spirits sank?
> Still, as the money flowed away,
> He wondered how on earth she spent it.
> "You cost me twenty pounds a day,
> At least!" cried Tottles (and he meant it).
>
> She sighed. "Those Drawing Rooms, you know!
> I really never thought about it:
> Mamma declared we ought to go—
> We should be Nobodies without it.
> That diamond-circlet for my brow—
> I quite believed that she had sent it,
> Until the Bill came in just now——"
> "Viper!" cried Tottles (and he meant it).
>
> Poor Mrs. T. could bear no more,
> But fainted flat upon the floor.

Mamma-in-law, with anguish wild,
Seeks, all in vain, to rouse her child.
"Quick! Take this box of smelling-salts!
Don't scold her, James, or you'll repent it,
She's a dear *girl, with all her faults——"*
"She is!" groaned Tottles *(and he meant it).*

"I was a donkey," Tottles cried,
"To choose your daughter for my bride!
'Twas you *that bid us cut a dash!*
'Tis you *have brought us to this smash!*
You don't suggest one single thing
That can in any way prevent it——
Then what's the use of arguing?
Shut up!" *cried Tottles (and he meant it).*

Once more I started into wakefulness, and realised that Mein Herr was not the singer. He was still consulting his memoranda.

"It is exactly what my friend told me," he resumed, after conning over various papers. " '*Unpatriotic*' is the very word I had used, in writing to him, and '*hinder*'is the very word he used in his reply! Allow me to read you a portion of his letter:—

> " '*I can assure you,*' he writes, '*that, unpatriotic as you may think it, the recognised function of the 'Opposition' is to hinder, in every manner not forbidden by the Law, the action of the Government. This process is called 'Legitimate Obstruction': and the greatest triumph the 'Opposition' can ever enjoy, is when they are able to point out that, owing to their 'Obstruction', the Government have failed in everything they have tried to do for the good of the Nation!*' "

"Your friend has not put it *quite* correctly," I said. "The Opposition would no doubt be glad to point out that the Government had failed *through their own fault;* but *not* that they had failed on account of *Obstruction!*"

"You think so?" he gently replied. "Allow me now to read to you this newspaper-cutting, which my friend enclosed in his letter. It is part of the report of a public speech, made by a Statesman who was at the time a member of the 'Opposition':—

> " '*At the close of the Session, he thought they had no reason to be discontented with the fortunes of the campaign. They had routed the enemy at every point. But the pursuit must be continued. They had only to follow up a disordered and dispirited foe.*' "

"Now to what portion of your national history would you guess that the speaker was referring?"

"Really, the number of *successful* wars we have waged during the last century," I replied, with a glow of British pride, "is *far* too great for me to guess, with any chance of success, *which* it was we were then engaged in. However. I will name *'India'* as the most probable. The Mutiny was no doubt, all but crushed, at the time that speech was made. What a fine, manly, *patriotic* speech it must have been!" I exclaimed in an outburst of enthusiasm.

"You think so?" he replied, in a tone of gentle pity. "Yet my friend tells me that the *'disordered and dispirited foe'* simply meant the Statesmen who happened to be in power at the moment; that the *'pursuit'* simply meant 'Obstruction'; and that the words *'they had routed the enemy'* simply meant that the 'Opposition' had succeeded in hindering the Government from doing any of the work which the Nation had empowered them to do!"

I thought it best to say nothing.

"It seemed queer to *us,* just at first," he resumed, after courteously waiting a minute for me to speak: "but, when once we had mastered the idea, our respect for your Nation was so great that we carried it into every department of life! It was *'the beginning of the end'* with us. My country never held up its head again!" And the poor old gentleman sighed deeply.

"Let us change the subject," I said. "Do not distress yourself, I beg!"

"No, no!" he said, with an effort to recover himself. "I had rather finish my story! The next step (after reducing our Government to impotence, and putting a stop to all useful legislation, which did not take us long to do) was to introduce what we called 'the glorious British Principle of Dichotomy' into *Agriculture.* We persuaded many of the well-to-do farmers to divide their staff of labourers into two Parties, and to set them one against the other. They were called, like our political Parties, the 'Ins' and the 'Outs': the business of the 'Ins' was to do as much of ploughing, sowing, or whatever might be needed, as they could manage in a day, and at night they were paid according to the amount they had *done:* the business of the 'Outs' was to hinder them, and *they* were paid for the amount they had *hindered.* The farmers found they had to pay only *half* as much wages as they did before, and they didn't observe that the amount of work done was only a *quarter* as much as was done before: so they took it up quite enthusiastically, *at first.*"

"And *afterwards*——?" I enquired.

"Well, *afterwards* they didn't like it quite so well. In a very short time, things settled down into a regular routine. No work *at all* was done. So the 'Ins' got no wages, and the 'Outs' got full pay. And the farmers never discovered, till most of them were ruined, that the rascals had agreed to manage it so, and had shared the pay between them! While the thing lasted, there were funny sights to be seen! Why, I've often watched a ploughman, with two horses harnessed to the plough, doing his best to get it *forwards;* while the opposition-ploughman, with three donkeys harnessed at the *other* end, was doing his best to get it *backwards!* And the plough never moving an inch, *either* way!"

"But *we* never did anything like *that!*" I exclaimed.

"Simply because you were less *logical* than we were," replied Mein

Herr. "There is *sometimes* an advantage in being a donk—Excuse me! No *personal* allusion intended. All this happened *long ago,* you know!"

"Did the Dichotomy-Principle succeed in *any* direction?" I enquired.

"In *none,*" Mein Herr candidly confessed. "It had a *very* short trial in *Commerce.* The shop-keepers *wouldn't* take it up, after once trying the plan of having half the attendants busy in folding up and carrying away the goods which the other half were trying to spread out upon the counters. They said the Public didn't like it!"

"I don't wonder at it," I remarked.

"Well, we tried 'the British Principle' for some years. And the end of it all was—" His voice suddenly dropped, almost to a whisper; and large tears began to roll down his cheeks. "—the end was that we got involved in a war; and there was a great battle, in which we far out-numbered the enemy. But what could one expect, when only *half* of our soldiers were fighting, and the other half pulling them back? It ended in a crushing defeat—an utter rout. This caused a Revolution; and most of the Government were banished. I myself was accused of Treason, for having so strongly advocated 'the British Principle.' My property was all forfeited, and—and—I was driven into exile! 'Now the mischief's done,' they said, 'perhaps you'll kindly leave the country?' It nearly broke my heart, but I had to go!"

The melancholy tone became a wail: the wail became a chant: the chant became a song—though whether it was *Mein Herr* that was singing, this time, or somebody else, I could not feel certain.

> *"And, now the mischief's done, perhaps*
> *You'll kindly go and pack your traps?*
> *Since* two *(your daughter and your son)*
> *Are Company, but* three *are none.*
> *A course of saving we'll begin:*
> *When change is needed,* I'll *invent it:*
> *Don't think to put* your *finger in*
> *This* pie!" *cried Tottles (and he meant it).*

The music seemed to die away. Mein Herr was again speaking in his ordinary voice. "Now tell me one thing more," he said. "Am I right in thinking that in *your* Universities, though a man may reside some thirty or forty years, you examine him, once for all, at the end of the first three or four?"

"That is so, undoubtedly," I admitted.

"Practically, then, you examine a man at the *beginning* of his career!" the old man said to himself rather than to me. "And what guarantee have you that he *retains* the knowledge for which you have rewarded him—beforehand, as *we* should say?"

"None," I admitted, feeling a little puzzled at the drift of his remarks. "How do *you* secure that object?"

"By examining him at the *end* of his thirty or forty years—not at the beginning," he gently replied. "On an average, the knowledge then found is about one-fifth of what it was at first—the process of forgetting going on at a very steady uniform rate—and he, who forgets *least,* gets *most* honour, and most rewards."

"Then you give him the money when he needs it no longer? And you make him live most of his life on *nothing!*"

"Hardly that. He gives his orders to the tradesmen: they supply him, for forty, sometimes fifty, years, at their own risk: then he gets his Fellowship—which pays him in *one* year as much as *your* Fellowships pay in fifty—and then he can easily pay all his bills, with interest."

"But suppose he fails to get his Fellowship? That must occasionally happen."

"That occasionally happens." It was Mein Herr's turn, now, to make admissions.

"And what becomes of the tradesmen?"

"They calculate accordingly. When a man appears to be getting alarmingly ignorant, or stupid, they will sometimes refuse to supply him any longer. You have no idea with what enthusiasm a man will begin to rub up his forgotten sciences or languages, when his butcher has cut off the supply of beef and mutton!"

"And who are the Examiners?"

"The young men who have just come, brimming over with knowledge. You would think it a curious sight," he went on, "to see mere boys examining such old men. I have known a man set to examine his own grandfather. It was a little painful for both of them, no doubt. The old gentleman was as bald as a coot——"

"How bald would that be?" I've no idea why I asked this question. I felt I was getting foolish.

CHAPTER XIV.

BRUNO'S PICNIC.

"As bald as bald," was the bewildering reply. "Now, Bruno, I'll tell you a story."

"And I'll tell *oo* a story," said Bruno, beginning in a great hurry for fear of Sylvie getting the start of him: "once there were a Mouse—a little tiny Mouse—such a tiny little Mouse! Oo never saw such a tiny Mouse——"

"Did nothing ever happen to it, Bruno?" I asked. "Haven't you anything more to tell us, besides its being so tiny?"

"Nothing never happened to it," Bruno solemnly replied.

"Why did nothing never happen to it?" said Sylvie, who was sitting, with her head on Bruno's shoulder, patiently waiting for a chance of beginning *her* story.

"It were too tiny," Bruno explained.

"*That's* no reason!" I said. "However tiny it was, things might happen to it."

Bruno looked pityingly at me, as if he thought me very stupid. "It were too tiny," he repeated. "If anything happened to it, it would die—it were so *very* tiny!"

"Really that's enough about its being tiny!" Sylvie put in. "Haven't you invented any more about it?"

"Haven't invented no more yet."

"Well then, you shouldn't begin a story till you've invented more! Now be quiet, there's a good boy, and listen to *my* story."

And Bruno, having quite exhausted all his inventive faculty, by beginning in too great a hurry, quietly resigned himself to listening. "Tell about the other Bruno, please," he said coaxingly.

Sylvie put her arms round his neck, and began:—

"The wind was whispering among the trees," ("That wasn't good manners!" Bruno interrupted. "Never mind about manners," said Sylvie) "and it was evening—a nice moony evening, and the Owls were hooting——"

"Pretend they weren't Owls!" Bruno pleaded, stroking her cheek with his fat little hand. "I don't like Owls. Owls have such great big eyes. Pretend they were Chickens!"

"Are you afraid of their great big eyes, Bruno?" I said.

"Aren't *'fraid* of nothing," Bruno answered in as careless a tone as he could manage: "they're ugly with their great big eyes. I think if they cried, the tears would be as big—oh, as big as the moon!" And he laughed merrily. "Doos Owls cry ever, Mister Sir?"

"Owls cry never," I said gravely, trying to copy Bruno's way of speaking: "they've got nothing to be sorry for, you know."

"Oh, but they have!" Bruno exclaimed. "They're ever so sorry, 'cause they killed the poor little Mouses!"

"But they're not sorry when they're *hungry,* I suppose?"

"Oo don't know nothing about Owls!" Bruno scornfully remarked. "When they're hungry, they're very, *very* sorry they killed the little Mouses, 'cause if they *hadn't* killed them there'd be sumfin for supper, oo know!"

Bruno was evidently getting into a dangerously inventive state of mind, so Sylvie broke in with "Now I'm going on with the story. So the Owls—the Chickens, I mean—were looking to see if they could find a nice fat Mouse for their supper——"

"Pretend it was a nice 'abbit!" said Bruno.

"But it *wasn't* a nice habit, to kill Mouses," Sylvie argued. "I can't pretend *that!*"

"I didn't say 'habit,' oo silly fellow!" Bruno replied with a merry twinkle in his eye. " *'abbits*—that runs about in the fields!"

"Rabbit? Well it can be a Rabbit, if you like. But you mustn't alter my story so much, Bruno. A Chicken *couldn't* eat a Rabbit!"

"But it might have wished to see if it could try to eat it."

"Well, it wished to see if it could try—oh, really, Bruno, that's nonsense! I shall go back to the Owls."

"Well, then, pretend they hadn't great eyes!"

"And they saw a little Boy," Sylvie went on, disdaining to make any further corrections. "And he asked them to tell him a story. And the

Owls hooted and flew away——" ("Oo shouldn't say 'flewed;' oo should
say 'flied,'" Bruno whispered. But Sylvie wouldn't hear.) "And he met a
Lion. And he asked the Lion to tell him a story. And the Lion said 'yes,'
it would. And, while the Lion was telling him the story, it nibbled some
of his head off——"

"Don't say 'nibbled'!" Bruno entreated. "Only little things nibble—
little thin sharp things, with edges——"

"Well, then, it 'nubbled,'" said Sylvie. "And when it had nubbled all
his head off, he went away, and he never said 'thank you'!"

"That were very rude," said Bruno. "If he couldn't speak, he might
have nodded—no, he couldn't nod. Well, he might have shaked hands
with the Lion!"

"Oh, I'd forgotten that part!" said Sylvie. "He did shake hands with
it. He came back again, you know, and he thanked the Lion very much,
for telling him the story."

"Then his head had growed up again?" said Bruno.

"Oh yes, it grew up in a minute. And the Lion begged pardon, and
said it wouldn't nubble off little boys' heads—not never no more!"

Bruno looked much pleased at this change of events. "Now that are
a really nice story!" he said. "Aren't it a nice story, Mister Sir?"

"Very," I said. "I would like to hear another story about that Boy."

"So would I," said Bruno, stroking Sylvie's cheek again. "Please tell
about Bruno's picnic; and don't talk about nubbly Lions!"

"I won't, if it frightens you," said Sylvie.

"Flightens me!" Bruno exclaimed indignantly. "It isn't that! It's 'cause
'nubbly''s such a grumbly word to say—when one person's got her head
on another person's shoulder. When she talks like that," he exclaimed
to me, "the talking goes down bofe sides of my face—all the way to my
chin—and it doos tickle so! It's enough to make a beard grow, that it is!"

He said this with great severity, but it was evidently meant for a joke:
so Sylvie laughed—a delicious musical little laugh, and laid her soft cheek
on the top of her brother's curly head, as if it were a pillow, while she
went on with the story. "So this Boy——"

"But it wasn't me, oo know!" Bruno interrupted. "And oo needn't try
to look as if it was, Mister Sir!"

I represented, respectfully, that I was trying to look as if it wasn't.

"—he was a middling good Boy——"

"He were a welly good Boy!" Bruno corrected her. "And he never did
nothing he wasn't told to do——"

"That doesn't make a good Boy!" Sylvie said contemptuously.

"That do make a good Boy!" Bruno insisted.

Sylvie gave up the point. "Well, he was a very good Boy, and he always
kept his promises, and he had a big cupboard——"

"—for to keep all his promises in!" cried Bruno.

"If he kept all his promises," Sylvie said, with a mischievous look in
her eyes, "he wasn't like some Boys I know of!"

"He had to put salt with them, a-course," Bruno said gravely: "oo ca'n't
keep promises when there isn't any salt. And he kept his birthday on
the second shelf."

"How long did he keep his birthday?" I asked. "I never can keep *mine* more than twenty-four hours."

"Why, a birthday *stays* that long by itself!" cried Bruno. "Oo doosn't know how to keep birthdays! This Boy kept *his* a whole year!"

"And then the next birthday would begin," said Sylvie. "So it would be his birthday *always*."

"So it were," said Bruno. "Doos *oo* have treats on *oor* birthday, Mister Sir?"

"Sometimes," I said.

"When oo're *good*, I suppose?"

"Why, it *is* a sort of treat, being good, isn't it?" I said.

"A sort of *treat!*" Bruno repeated. "It's a sort of *punishment*, I think!"

"Oh, Bruno!" Sylvie interrupted, almost sadly. "How *can* you?"

"Well, but it *is*," Bruno persisted. "Why, look here, Mister Sir! *This* is being good!" And he sat bolt upright, and put on an absurdly solemn face. "First oo must sit up as straight as pokers——"

"—as *a* poker," Sylvie corrected him.

"—as straight as *pokers*," Bruno firmly repeated. "Then oo must clasp oor hands—*so*. Then—'Why hasn't oo brushed oor hair? Go and brush it *toreckly!*' Then—'Oh, Bruno, oo mustn't dog's-ear the daisies!' Did oo learn *oor* spelling wiz daisies, Mister Sir?"

"I want to hear about that Boy's *Birthday*," I said.

Bruno returned to the story instantly. "Well, so this Boy said 'Now it's my Birthday!' And so—I'm tired!" he suddenly broke off, laying his head in Sylvie's lap. "Sylvie knows it best. Sylvie's grown-upper than me. Go on, Sylvie!"

Sylvie patiently took up the thread of the story again. "So he said 'Now it's my Birthday. Whatever shall I do to keep my Birthday?' All *good* little Boys——" (Sylvie turned away from Bruno, and made a great pretence of whispering to *me*) "—all *good* little Boys—Boys that learn their lessons quite perfect—they always keep their birthdays, you know. So of course *this* little Boy kept *his* Birthday."

"Oo may call him Bruno, if oo like," the little fellow carelessly remarked. "It weren't *me*, but it makes it more interesting."

"So Bruno said to himself 'The properest thing to do is to have a Picnic, all by myself, on the top of the hill. And I'll take some Milk, and some Bread, and some Apples: and first and foremost, I want some *Milk!*' So, first and foremost, Bruno took a milk-pail——"

"And he went and milkted the Cow!" Bruno put in.

"Yes," said Sylvie, meekly accepting the new verb. "And the Cow said 'Moo! What are you going to do with all that Milk?' And Bruno said 'Please'm, I want it for my Picnic.' And the Cow said 'Moo! But I hope you wo'n't *boil* any of it?' And Bruno said 'No, *indeed* I won't! New Milk's so nice and so warm, it wants no boiling!'"

"It doesn't want no boiling," Bruno offered as an amended version.

"So Bruno put the Milk in a bottle. And then Bruno said 'Now I want some Bread!' So he went to the Oven, and he took out a delicious new Loaf. And the Oven——"

"—ever so light and so puffy!" Bruno impatiently corrected her. "Oo shouldn't leave out so many words!"

Sylvie humbly apologised. "—a delicious new Loaf, ever so light and so puffy. And the Oven said——" Here Sylvie made a long pause. "Really I don't know *what* an Oven begins with, when it wants to speak!"

Both children looked appealingly at me; but I could only say, helplessly, "I haven't the least idea! *I* never heard an Oven speak!"

For a minute or two we all sat silent; and then Bruno said, very softly, "Oven begins wiz 'O'."

"Good little boy!" Sylvie exclaimed. "He does his spelling *very* nicely. *He's cleverer than he knows!"* she added, aside, to *me.* "So the Oven said 'O! What are you going to do with all that Bread?' And Bruno said 'Please——' Is an Oven 'Sir' or ''m,' would you say?" She looked to me for a reply.

"Both, I think," seemed to me the safest thing to say.

Sylvie adopted the suggestion instantly. "So Bruno said 'Please, Sirm, I want it for my picnic.' And the Oven said 'O! But I hope you wo'n't *toast* any of it?' And Bruno said, 'No, *indeed* I wo'n't! New Bread's so light and so puffy, it wants no toasting!'"

"It never doesn't want no toasting," said Bruno. "I *wiss* oo wouldn't say it so short!"

"So Bruno put the Bread in the hamper. Then Bruno said 'Now I want some Apples!' So he took the hamper, and he went to the Apple-Tree, and he picked some lovely ripe Apples. And the Apple-Tree said"—— Here followed another long pause.

Bruno adopted his favourite expedient of tapping his forehead; while Sylvie gazed earnestly upwards, as if she hoped for some suggestion from the birds, who were singing merrily among the branches overhead. But no result followed.

"What *does* an Apple-Tree begin with, when it wants to speak?" Sylvie murmured despairingly, to the irresponsive birds.

At last, taking a leaf out of Bruno's book, I ventured on a remark. "Doesn't 'Apple-tree' always begin with 'Eh!'?"

"Why, of *course* it does! How *clever* of you!" Sylvie cried delightedly. Bruno jumped up, and patted me on the head. I tried not to feel conceited.

"So the Apple-Tree said 'Eh! What are you going to do with all those Apples?' And Bruno said 'Please, Sir, I want them for my Picnic.' And the Apple-Tree said 'Eh! But I hope you wo'n't *bake* any of them?' And Bruno said 'No, *indeed* I wo'n't! Ripe Apples are so nice and so sweet, they want no baking!'"

"They never doesn't——" Bruno was beginning, but Sylvie corrected herself before he could get the words out.

" 'They never doesn't nohow want no baking.' So Bruno put the Apples in the hamper, along with the Bread, and the bottle of Milk. And he set off to have a Picnic, on the top of the hill, all by himself——"

"He wasn't greedy, oo know, to have it all by himself," Bruno said, patting me on the cheek to call my attention; "'cause he hadn't got no brothers and sisters."

"It was very sad to have no *sisters,* wasn't it?" I said.

"Well, I don't know," Bruno said thoughtfully; "'cause he hadn't no lessons to do. So he didn't mind."

Sylvie went on. "So, as he was walking along the road, he heard behind him such a curious sort of noise—a sort of a Thump! Thump! Thump! 'Whatever *is* that?' said Bruno. 'Oh, I know!' said Bruno. 'Why, it's only my Watch a-ticking!' "

"*Were* it his Watch a-ticking?" Bruno asked me, with eyes that fairly sparkled with mischievous delight.

"No doubt of it!" I replied. And Bruno laughed exultingly.

"Then Bruno thought a little harder. And he said 'No! It *ca'n't* be my Watch a-ticking; because I haven't *got* a Watch!' "

Bruno peered up anxiously into my face, to see how I took it. I hung my head, and put a thumb into my mouth, to the evident delight of the little fellow.

"So Bruno went a little further along the road. And then he heard it again, that queer noise—Thump! Thump! Thump! 'What ever *is* that?' said Bruno. 'Oh, I know!' said Bruno. 'Why, it's only the Carpenter a-mending my Wheelbarrow!' "

"*Were* it the Carterpenter a-mending his Wheelbarrow?" Bruno asked me.

I brightened up, and said "It *must* have been!" in a tone of absolute conviction.

Bruno threw his arms round Sylvie's neck. "Sylvie!" he said, in a perfectly audible whisper. "He says it *must* have been!"

"Then Bruno thought a little harder. And he said 'No! It *ca'n't* be the Carpenter a-mending my Wheelbarrow, because I haven't *got* a Wheelbarrow!' "

This time I hid my face in my hands, quite unable to meet Bruno's look of triumph.

"So Bruno went a little further along the road. And then he heard that queer noise again—Thump! Thump! Thump! So he thought he'd look round, *this* time, just to *see* what it was. And what should it be but a great Lion!"

"A great big Lion," Bruno corrected her.

"A great big Lion. And Bruno was ever so frightened, and he ran——"

"No, he wasn't *flightened* a bit!" Bruno interrupted. (He was evidently anxious for the reputation of his namesake.) "He runned away to get a good look at the Lion; 'cause he wanted to see if it were the same Lion what used to nubble little Boys' heads off; and he wanted to know how big it was!"

"Well, he ran away, to get a good look at the Lion. And the Lion trotted slowly after him. And the Lion called after him, in a very gentle voice, 'Little Boy, little Boy! You needn't be afraid of *me!* I'm a very *gentle* old Lion now. I *never* nubble little Boys' heads off, as I used to do.' And so Bruno said 'Don't you *really,* Sir? Then what do you live on?' And the Lion——"

"Oo *see* he weren't a bit flightened!" Bruno said to me, patting my cheek again. "'cause he remembered to call it 'Sir,' oo know."

I said that no doubt that was the *real* test whether a person was frightened or not.

"And the Lion said 'Oh, I live on bread-and-butter, and cherries, and marmalade, and plum-cake——' "

"——and *apples!*" Bruno put in.

"Yes, 'and apples.' And Bruno said 'Won't you come with me to my Picnic?' And the Lion said 'Oh, I should like it *very much indeed!*' And Bruno and the Lion went away together." Sylvie stopped suddenly.

"Is that *all?*" I asked, despondingly.

"Not *quite* all," Sylvie slily replied. "There's a sentence or two more. Isn't there, Bruno?"

"Yes," with a carelessness that was evidently put on: "just a sentence or two more."

"And, as they were walking along, they looked over a hedge, and who should they see but a little black Lamb! And the Lamb was ever so frightened. And it ran——"

"It were *really* flightened!" Bruno put in.

"It ran away. And Bruno ran after it. And he called 'Little Lamb! You needn't be afraid of *this* Lion! It *never* kills things! It lives on cherries, and marmalade——' "

"——and *apples!*" said Bruno. "Oo *always* forgets the apples!"

"And Bruno said 'Wo'n't you come with us to my Picnic?' And the Lamb said 'Oh, I should like it *very much indeed,* if my Ma will let me!' And Bruno said 'Let's go and ask your Ma!' And they went to the old Sheep. And Bruno said 'Please, may your little Lamb come to my Picnic?' And the Sheep said 'Yes, if it's learnt all its lessons.' And the Lamb said 'Oh yes, Ma! I've learnt *all* my lessons!' "

"Pretend it hadn't any lessons!" Bruno earnestly pleaded.

"Oh, that would never do!" said Sylvie. "I ca'n't leave out all about the lessons! And the old Sheep said 'Do you know your A B C yet? Have you learnt A?' And the Lamb said 'Oh yes, Ma! I went to the A-field, and I helped them to make A!' 'Very good, my child! And have you learnt B?' 'Oh yes, Ma! I went to the B-hive, and the B gave me some honey!' 'Very good, my child! And have you learnt C?' 'Oh yes, Ma! I went to the C-side, and I saw the ships sailing on the C!' 'Very good, my child! You may go to Bruno's Picnic.'

"So they set off. And Bruno walked in the middle, so that the Lamb mightn't see the Lion——"

"It were *flightened,*" Bruno explained.

"Yes, and it trembled so; and it got paler and paler; and, before they'd got to the top of the hill, it was a *white* little Lamb—as white as snow!"

"But *Bruno* weren't flightened!" said the owner of that name. "So *he* staid black!"

"No, he *didn't* stay black! He staid *pink!*" laughed Sylvie. "I shouldn't kiss you like this, you know, if you were *black!*"

"Oo'd *have* to!" Bruno said with great decision. "Besides, Bruno wasn't

Bruno, oo know—I mean, Bruno wasn't *me*—I mean—don't talk nonsense, Sylvie!"

"I won't do it again!" Sylvie said very humbly. "And so, as they went along, the Lion said 'Oh, I'll tell you what I used to do when I was a young Lion. I used to hide behind trees, to watch for little Boys.'" (Bruno cuddled a little closer to her.) "'And, if a little thin scraggy Boy came by, why, I used to let him go. But, if a little fat juicy——'"

Bruno could bear no more. "Pretend he wasn't juicy!" he pleaded, half-sobbing.

"Nonsense, Bruno!" Sylvie briskly replied. "It'll be done in a moment! '—if a little fat juicy Boy came by, why, I used to spring out and gobble him up! Oh, you've no *idea* what a delicious thing it is—a little juicy Boy!' And Bruno said 'Oh, if you please, Sir, *don't* talk about eating little boys! It makes me so *shivery!*'"

The real Bruno shivered, in sympathy with the hero.

"And the Lion said 'Oh, well, we won't talk about it, then! I'll tell you what happened on my wedding-day——'"

"I like *this* part better," said Bruno, patting my cheek to keep me awake.

"'There was, oh, such a lovely wedding-breakfast! At *one* end of the table there was a large plum-pudding. And at the other end there was a nice roasted *Lamb!* Oh, you've no *idea* what a delicious thing it is—a nice roasted Lamb!' And the Lamb said 'Oh, if you please, Sir, *don't* talk about eating Lambs! It makes me so *shivery!*' And the Lion said 'Oh, well, we won't talk about it, then!' "

CHAPTER XV.

THE LITTLE FOXES.

"So, when they got to the top of the hill, Bruno opened the hamper: and he took out the Bread, and the Apples, and the Milk: and they ate, and they drank. And when they'd finished the Milk, and eaten half the Bread and half the Apples, the Lamb said 'Oh, my paws is so sticky! I want to wash my paws!' And the Lion said 'Well, go down the hill, and wash them in the brook, yonder. We'll wait for you!' "

"It never comed back!" Bruno solemnly whispered to me.

But Sylvie overheard him. "You're not to whisper, Bruno! It spoils the story! And when the Lamb had been gone a long time, the Lion said to Bruno 'Do go and see after that silly little Lamb! It must have lost its way.' And Bruno went down the hill. And when he got to the brook, he saw the Lamb sitting on the bank: and who should be sitting by it but an old Fox!"

"Don't know who *should* be sitting by it," Bruno said thoughtfully to himself. "A old Fox *were* sitting by it."

"And the old Fox were saying," Sylvie went on, for once conceding the grammatical point, " 'Yes, my dear, you'll be ever so happy with us, if you'll only come and see us! I've got three little Foxes there, and we do love little Lambs so dearly!' And the Lamb said 'But you never *eat* them, do you, Sir?' And the Fox said 'Oh, no! What, *eat* a Lamb? We never *dream* of doing such a thing!' So the Lamb said 'Then I'll come with you.' And off they went, hand in hand."

"That Fox were welly extremely wicked, *weren't* it?" said Bruno.

"No, no!" said Sylvie, rather shocked at such violent language. "It wasn't quite so bad as that!"

"Well, I mean, it wasn't nice," the little fellow corrected himself.

"And so Bruno went back to the Lion. 'Oh, come quick!' he said. 'The Fox has taken the Lamb to his house with him! I'm *sure* he means to eat it!' And the Lion said 'I'll come as quick as ever I can!' And they trotted down the hill."

"Do oo think he caught the Fox, Mister Sir?" said Bruno. I shook my head, not liking to speak: and Sylvie went on.

"And when they got to the house, Bruno looked in at the window. And there he saw the three little Foxes sitting round the table, with their clean pinafores on, and spoons in their hands——"

"Spoons in their hands!" Bruno repeated in an ecstasy of delight.

"And the Fox had got a great big knife—all ready to kill the poor little Lamb——" ("Oo needn't be flightened, Mister Sir!" Bruno put in, in a hasty whisper.)

"And just as he was going to do it, Bruno heard a great ROAR——" (The real Bruno put his hand into mine, and held tight), "and the Lion came *bang* through the door, and the next moment it had bitten off the old Fox's head! And Bruno jumped in at the window, and went leaping round the room, and crying out 'Hooray! Hooray! The old Fox is dead! The old Fox is dead!'"

Bruno got up in some excitement. "May I do it now?" he enquired.

Sylvie was quite decided on this point. "Wait till afterwards," she said. "The speeches come next, don't you know? You always love the speeches, *don't* you?"

"Yes, I doos," said Bruno: and sat down again.

"The Lion's speech. 'Now, you silly little Lamb, go home to your mother, and never listen to old Foxes again. And be very good and obedient.'

"The Lamb's speech. 'Oh, indeed, Sir, I will, Sir!' and the Lamb went away." ("But *oo* needn't go away!" Bruno explained. "It's quite the nicest part—what's coming now!" Sylvie smiled. She liked having an appreciative audience.)

"The Lion's speech to Bruno. 'Now, Bruno, take those little Foxes home with you, and teach them to be good obedient little Foxes! Not like that wicked old thing there, that's got no head!'" ("That hasn't got no head," Bruno repeated.)

"Bruno's speech to the Lion. 'Oh, indeed, Sir, I will, Sir!' And the Lion went away." ("It gets betterer and betterer, now," Bruno whispered to me, "right away to the end!")

"Bruno's speech to the little Foxes. 'Now, little Foxes, you're going to have your first lesson in being good. I'm going to put you into the hamper, along with the Apples and the Bread: and you're not to eat the Apples: and you're not to eat the Bread: and you're not to eat *anything*— till we get to my house: and then you'll have your supper.'

"The little Foxes' speech to Bruno. The little Foxes said nothing.

"So Bruno put the Apples into the hamper—and the little Foxes— and the Bread—" ("They had picnicked all the Milk," Bruno explained in a whisper) "—and he set off to go to his house." ("We're getting near the end now," said Bruno.)

"And, when he had got a little way, he thought he would look into the hamper, and see how the little Foxes were getting on."

"So he opened the door——" said Bruno.

"Oh, Bruno!" Sylvie exclaimed, *"you're* not telling the story! So he opened the door, and behold, there were no Apples! So Bruno said 'Eldest little Fox, have *you* been eating the Apples?' And the eldest little Fox said 'No no no!'" (It is impossible to give the tone in which Sylvie repeated this rapid little 'No no no!' The nearest I can come to it is to say that it was much as if a young and excited duck had tried to quack the words. It was too quick for a quack, and yet too harsh to be anything else.) "Then he said 'Second little Fox, have *you* been eating the Apples?' And the

second little Fox said 'No no no!' Then he said 'Youngest little Fox, have *you* been eating the Apples?' And the youngest little Fox *tried* to say 'No no no!' but its mouth was so full, it couldn't, and it only said 'Wauch! Wauch! Wauch!' And Bruno looked into its mouth. And its mouth was full of Apples! And Bruno shook his head, and he said 'Oh dear, oh dear! What bad creatures these Foxes are!'"

Bruno was listening intently: and, when Sylvie paused to take breath, he could only just gasp out the words "About the Bread?"

"Yes," said Sylvie, "the Bread comes next. So he shut the door again; and he went a little further; and then he thought he'd just peep in once more. And behold, there was no Bread!" ("What do 'behold' *mean?*" said Bruno. "Hush!" said Sylvie.) "And he said 'Eldest little Fox, have *you* been eating the Bread?' And the eldest little Fox said 'No no no!' 'Second little Fox, have *you* been eating the Bread?' And the second little Fox only said 'Wauch! Wauch! Wauch!' And Bruno looked into its mouth, and its mouth was full of Bread!" ("It might have chokeded it," said Bruno.) "So he said 'Oh dear, oh dear! What *shall* I do with these Foxes?' And he went a little further." ("Now comes the most interesting part," Bruno whispered.)

"And when Bruno opened the hamper again, what do you think he saw?" ("Only *two* Foxes!" Bruno cried in a great hurry.) "You shouldn't tell it so quick. However, he *did* see only *two* Foxes. And he said 'Eldest little Fox, have you been eating the youngest little Fox?' And the eldest little Fox said 'No no no!' 'Second little Fox, have *you* been eating the youngest little Fox?' And the second little Fox did its very best to say 'No no no!' but it could only say 'Weuchk! Weuchk! Weuchk!' And when Bruno looked into its mouth, it was half full of Bread, and half full of Fox!" (Bruno said nothing in the pause this time. He was beginning to pant a little, as he knew the crisis was coming.)

"And when he'd got nearly home, he looked once more into the hamper, and he saw——"

"Only——" Bruno began, but a generous thought struck him, and he looked at me. "*Oo* may say it, this time, Mister Sir!" he whispered. It was a noble offer, but I wouldn't rob him of the treat. "Go on, Bruno," I said, "you say it much the best." "Only—but—*one*—Fox!" Bruno said with great solemnity.

"'Eldest little Fox,'" Sylvie said, dropping the narrative-form in her eagerness, "'you've been *so* good that I can hardly believe *you've* been disobedient: but I'm *afraid* you've been eating your little sister?' And the eldest little Fox said 'Whihuauch! Whihuauch!' and then it choked. And Bruno looked into its mouth, and it *was* full!" (Sylvie paused to take breath, and Bruno lay back among the daisies, and looked at me triumphantly. "Isn't it *grand*, Mister Sir?" said he. I tried hard to assume a critical tone. "It's grand," I said: "but it frightens one so!" "Oo may sit a little closer to *me*, if oo like," said Bruno.)

"And so Bruno went home: and took the hamper into the kitchen, and opened it. And he saw——" Sylvie looked at *me*, this time, as if she

thought I had been rather neglected and ought to be allowed *one* guess, at any rate.

"He ca'n't guess!" Bruno cried eagerly. "I 'fraid I *must* tell him! There weren't——*nuffin* in the hamper!" I shivered in terror, and Bruno clapped his hands with delight. "He *is* flightened, Sylvie! Tell the rest!"

"So Bruno said 'Eldest little Fox, have you been eating *yourself*, you wicked little Fox?' And the eldest little Fox said 'Whihuauch!' And then Bruno saw there was only its *mouth* in the hamper! So he took the mouth, and he opened it, and shook, and shook! And at last he shook the little Fox out of its own mouth! And then he said 'Open your mouth again, you wicked little thing!' And he shook, and shook! And he shook out the second little Fox! And he said 'Now open *your* mouth!' And he shook, and shook! And he shook out the youngest little Fox, and all the Apples, and all the Bread!

"And then Bruno stood the little Foxes up against the wall: and he made them a little speech. 'Now, little Foxes, you've begun very wickedly— and you'll have to be punished. First you'll go up to the nursery, and wash your faces, and put on clean pinafores. Then you'll hear the bell ring for supper. Then you'll come down: and *you won't have any supper:* but you'll have a good *whipping!* Then you'll go to bed. Then in the morning you'll hear the bell ring for breakfast. *But you won't have any breakfast!* You'll have a good *whipping!* Then you'll have your lessons. And, perhaps, if you're *very* good, when dinner-time comes, you'll have a little dinner, and no more whipping!' " ("How *very* kind he was!" I whispered to Bruno. *"Middling* kind," Bruno corrected me gravely.)

"So the little Foxes ran up to the nursery. And soon Bruno went into the hall, and rang the big bell. 'Tingle, tingle, tingle! Supper, supper, supper!' Down came the little Foxes, in such a hurry for their supper! Clean pinafores! Spoons in their hands! And, when they got into the dining-room, there was ever such a white table-cloth on the table! But there was nothing on it but a big whip. And they had *such* a whipping!" (I put my handkerchief to my eyes, and Bruno hastily climbed upon my knee and stroked my face. "Only *one* more whipping, Mister Sir!" he whispered. "Don't cry more than oo ca'n't help!")

"And the next morning early, Bruno rang the big bell again. 'Tingle, tingle, tingle! Breakfast, breakfast, breakfast!' Down came the little Foxes! Clean pinafores! Spoons in their hands! No breakfast! Only the big whip! Then came lessons," Sylvie hurried on, for I still had my handkerchief to my eyes. "And the little Foxes were ever so good! And they learned their lessons backwards, and forwards, and upside-down. And at last Bruno rang the big bell again. 'Tingle, tingle, tingle! Dinner, dinner, dinner!' And when the little Foxes came down——" ("Had they clean pinafores on?" Bruno enquired. "Of course!" said Sylvie. "And spoons?" "Why, you *know* they had!" "Couldn't be *certain,*" said Bruno.) "—they came as slow as slow! And they said 'Oh! There'll be no dinner! There'll only be the big whip!' But, when they got into the room, they saw the most *lovely* dinner!" ("Buns?" cried Bruno, clapping his hands.) "Buns, and cake, and—" ("—and jam?" said Bruno.) "Yes, jam—and soup—and—" ("—and *sugar plums!*" Bruno put in once more; and Sylvie seemed satisfied.)

"And ever after that, they *were* such good little Foxes! They did their lessons as good as gold—and they never did what Bruno told them not to—and they never ate each other any more—and *they never ate themselves!*"

The story came to an end so suddenly, it almost took my breath away; however I did my best to make a pretty speech of thanks. "I'm sure it's very—very—very much so, I'm sure!" I seemed to hear myself say.

CHAPTER XVI.

BEYOND THESE VOICES.

"I DIDN'T quite catch what you said!" were the next words that reached my ear, but certainly *not* in the voice either of Sylvie or of Bruno, whom I could just see, through the crowd of guests, standing by the piano, and listening to the Count's song. Mein Herr was the speaker. "I didn't quite catch what you said!" he repeated. "But I've no doubt you take *my* view of it. Thank you *very* much for your kind attention. There is only but *one* verse left to be sung!" These last words were not in the gentle voice of Mein Herr, but in the deep bass of the French Count. And, in the silence that followed, the final stanza of 'Tottles' rang through the room.

> *See now this couple settled down*
> *In quiet lodgings, out of town:*
> *Submissively the tearful wife*
> *Accepts a plain and humble life:*
> *Yet begs one boon on bended knee:*
> *'My ducky-darling, don't resent it!*
> *Mamma might come for two or three——'*
> *'NEVER!' yelled Tottles. And he meant it.*

The conclusion of the song was followed by quite a chorus of thanks and compliments from all parts of the room, which the gratified singer responded to by bowing low in all directions. "It is to me a great privilege," he said to Lady Muriel, "to have met with this so marvellous a song. The accompaniment to him is so strange, so mysterious: it is as if a new music were to be invented! I will play him once again so as that to show you what I mean." He returned to the piano, but the song had vanished.

The bewildered singer searched through the heap of music lying on an adjoining table, but it was not there, either. Lady Muriel helped in the search: others soon joined: the excitement grew. "What *can* have become of it?" exclaimed Lady Muriel. Nobody knew: one thing only was certain, that no one had been near the piano since the Count had sung the last verse of the song.

"Nevare mind him!" he said, most good-naturedly. "I shall give it you with memory alone!" He sat down, and began vaguely fingering the notes; but nothing resembling the tune came out. Then he, too, grew excited. "But what oddness! How much of singularity! That I might lose, not the words alone, but the tune also—that is quite curious, I suppose?"

We all supposed it, heartily.

"It was that sweet little boy, who found it for me," the Count suggested. "Quite perhaps *he* is the thief?"

"Of course he is!" cried Lady Muriel. "Bruno! Where are you, my darling?"

But no Bruno replied: it seemed that the two children had vanished as suddenly, and as mysteriously, as the song.

"They are playing us a trick!" Lady Muriel gaily exclaimed. "This is only an *ex tempore* game of Hide-and-Seek! That little Bruno is an embodied Mischief!"

The suggestion was a welcome one to most of us, for some of the guests were beginning to look decidedly uneasy. A general search was set on foot with much enthusiasm: curtains were thrown back and shaken, cupboards opened, and ottomans turned over; but the number of possible hiding-places proved to be strictly limited; and the search came to an end almost as soon as it had begun.

"They must have run out, while we were wrapped up in the song," Lady Muriel said, addressing herself to the Count, who seemed more agitated than the others; "and no doubt they've found their way back to the housekeeper's room."

"Not by *this* door!" was the earnest protest of a knot of two or three gentlemen, who had been grouped round the door (one of them actually leaning against it) for the last half-hour, as they declared. "*This* door has not been opened since the song began!"

An uncomfortable silence followed this announcement. Lady Muriel ventured no further conjectures, but quietly examined the fastenings of the windows, which opened as doors. They all proved to be well fastened, *inside*.

Not yet at the end of her resources, Lady Muriel rang the bell. "Ask the housekeeper to step here," she said, "and to bring the children's walking-things with her."

"I've brought them, my Lady," said the obsequious housekeeper, entering after another minute of silence. "I thought the young lady would have come to my room to put on her boots. Here's your boots, my love!" she added cheerfully, looking in all directions for the children. There was no answer, and she turned to Lady Muriel with a puzzled smile. "Have the little darlings hid themselves?"

"I don't see them, just now," Lady Muriel replied, rather evasively. "You can leave their things here, Wilson. *I'll* dress them, when they're ready to go."

The two little hats, and Sylvie's walking-jacket, were handed round among the ladies, with many exclamations of delight. There certainly was a sort of witchery of beauty about them. Even the little boots did not miss their share of favorable criticism. "Such natty little things!" the musical young lady exclaimed, almost fondling them as she spoke. "And what tiny tiny feet they must have!"

Finally, the things were piled together on the centre-ottoman, and the guests, despairing of seeing the children again, began to wish good-night and leave the house.

There were only some eight or nine left—to whom the Count was explaining, for the twentieth time, how he had had his eye on the children during the last verse of the song; how he had then glanced round the room, to see what effect "de great chest-note" had had upon his audience; and how, when he looked back again, they had both disappeared—when exclamations of dismay began to be heard on all sides, the Count hastily bringing his story to an end to join in the outcry.

The walking-things had all disappeared!

After the utter failure of the search for the *children*, there was a very half-hearted search made for their *apparel*. The remaining guests seemed only too glad to get away, leaving only the Count and our four selves.

The Count sank into an easy-chair, and panted a little.

"Who then *are* these dear children, I pray you?" he said. "Why come they, why go they, in this so little ordinary a fashion? That the music should make itself vanish—that the hats, the boots, should make themselves to vanish—how is it, I pray you?"

"I've no idea where they are!" was all I could say, on finding myself appealed to, by general consent, for an explanation.

The Count seemed about to ask further questions, but checked himself.

"The hour makes himself to become late," he said. "I wish to you a very good night, my Lady. I betake myself to my bed—to dream—if that indeed I be not dreaming now!" And he hastily left the room.

"Stay awhile, stay awhile!" said the Earl, as I was about to follow the Count. *"You* are not a guest, you know! Arthur's friend is at *home* here!"

"Thanks!" I said, as, with true English instincts, we drew our chairs together round the fire-place, though no fire was burning—Lady Muriel having taken the heap of music on her knee, to have one more search for the strangely-vanished song.

"Don't you sometimes feel a wild longing," she said, addressing herself to me, "to have something more to do with your hands, while you talk, than just holding a cigar, and now and then knocking off the ash? Oh, I know all that you're going to say!" (This was to Arthur, who appeared about to interrupt her.) "The Majesty of Thought supersedes the work of the fingers. A Man's severe thinking, *plus* the shaking-off a cigar-ash, comes to the same total as a Woman's trivial fancies, *plus* the most elaborate embroidery. *That's* your sentiment, isn't it, only better expressed?"

Arthur looked into the radiant, mischievous face, with a grave and very tender smile. "Yes," he said resignedly: "that is my sentiment, exactly."

"Rest of body, and activity of mind," I put in. "Some writer tells us *that* is the acme of human happiness."

"Plenty of *bodily* rest, at any rate!" Lady Muriel replied, glancing at the three recumbent figures around her. "But what you call activity of *mind*——"

"—is the privilege of young Physicians *only*," said the Earl. "We old men have no claim to be active! *What can an old man do but die?*"

"A good many other things, I should *hope*," Arthur said earnestly.

"Well, maybe. Still you have the advantage of me in many ways, dear boy! Not only that *your* day is dawning while *mine* is setting, but your *interest* in Life—somehow I ca'n't help envying you *that*. It will be many a year before you lose your hold of *that*."

"Yet surely many human interests *survive* human Life?" I said.

"Many do, no doubt. And *some* forms of Science; but only *some*, I think. Mathematics, for instance: *that* seems to possess an endless interest: one ca'n't imagine *any* form of Life, or *any* race of intelligent beings, where Mathematical truth would lose its meaning. But I fear *Medicine* stands on a different footing. Suppose you discover a remedy for some disease hitherto supposed to be incurable. Well, it is delightful for the moment, no doubt—full of interest—perhaps it brings you fame and fortune. But what then? Look on, a few years, into a life where disease has no existence. What is your discovery worth, *then*? Milton makes Jove promise too much. *'Of so much fame in heaven expect thy meed.'* Poor comfort, when one's 'fame' concerns matters that will have ceased to have a meaning!"

"At any rate, one wouldn't care to make any *fresh* medical discoveries," said Arthur. "I see no help for *that*—though I shall be sorry to give up my favorite studies. Still, medicine, disease, pain, sorrow, sin—I fear they're all linked together. Banish sin, and you banish them all!"

"*Military* science is a yet stronger instance," said the Earl. "Without sin, *war* would surely be impossible. Still any mind, that has had in this life any keen interest, not in *itself* sinful, will surely find itself *some* congenial line of work hereafter. Wellington may have no more *battles* to fight— and yet—

> 'We doubt not that, for one so true,
> There must be other, nobler work to do,
> Than when he fought at Waterloo,
>   And Victor he must ever be!' "

He lingered over the beautiful words, as if he loved them: and his voice, like distant music, died away into silence.

After a minute or two he began again. "If I'm not wearying you, I would like to tell you an idea of the future Life which has haunted me for years, like a sort of waking nightmare—I ca'n't reason myself out of it."

"Pray do," Arthur and I replied, almost in a breath. Lady Muriel put aside the heap of music, and folded her hands together.

"The one idea," the Earl resumed, "that has seemed to me to overshadow all the rest, is that of *Eternity*—involving, as it seems to do, the necessary *exhaustion* of all subjects of human interest. Take Pure Mathematics, for instance—a Science independent of our present surroundings. I have studied it, myself, a little. Take the subject of circles and ellipses—what we call 'curves of the second degree.' In a future Life, it would only be a question of so many years (or *hundreds* of years, if you like), for a man to work out *all* their properties. Then he *might* go to curves of the third degree. Say *that* took ten times as long (you see we have *unlimited* time to deal with). I can hardly imagine his *interest* in the subject holding out even for those; and, though there is no limit to the *degree* of the curves he might study, yet surely the time, needed to exhaust *all* the novelty and interest of the subject, would be absolutely *finite?* And so of all other branches of Science. And, when I transport myself, in thought, through some thousands or millions of years, and fancy myself possessed of as much Science as one created reason can carry, I ask myself 'What then? With nothing more to learn, can one rest content on *knowledge,* for the eternity yet to be lived through?' It has been a very wearying thought to me. I have sometimes fancied one *might,* in that event, say 'It is better *not* to be,' and pray for personal *annihilation*—the Nirvana of the Buddhists."

"But that is only half the picture," I said. "Besides working for *oneself,* may there not be the helping of *others?*"

"Surely, surely!" Lady Muriel exclaimed in a tone of relief, looking at her father with sparkling eyes.

"Yes," said the Earl, "so long as there *were* any others needing help. But, given ages and ages more, surely all created reasons would at length reach the same dead level of *satiety.* And *then* what is there to look forward to?"

"I know that weary feeling," said the young Doctor. "I have gone through it all, more than once. Now let me tell you how I have put it to myself. I have imagined a little child, playing with toys on his nursery-floor, and yet able to *reason,* and to look on, thirty years ahead. Might he not say to himself 'By that time I shall have had enough of bricks and ninepins. How weary Life will be!' Yet, if we look forward through those thirty years, we find him a great statesman, full of interests and joys far more intense than his baby-life could give—joys wholly inconceivable to his baby-mind—joys such as no baby-language could in the faintest degree describe. Now, may not our life, a million years hence, have the same relation, to our life now, that the man's life has to the child's? And, just as one might try, all in vain, to express to that child, in the language of bricks and ninepins, the meaning of 'politics,' so perhaps all those descriptions of Heaven, with its music, and its feasts, and its streets of gold, may be only attempts to describe, in *our* words, things for which we *really* have no words at all. Don't you think that, in *your* picture of another life, you are in fact transplanting that child into political life, without making any allowance for his growing up?"

"I think I understand you," said the Earl. "The music of Heaven *may* be something beyond our powers of thought. Yet the music of Earth is sweet! Muriel, my child, sing us something before we go to bed!"

"Do," said Arthur, as he rose and lit the candles on the cottage-piano, lately banished from the drawing-room to make room for a 'semi-grand.' "There is a song here, that I have never heard you sing.

> *"Hail to thee, blithe spirit!*
> *Bird thou never wert,*

That from Heaven, or near it,
Pourest thy full heart!' "

he read from the page he had spread open before her.

"And our little life here," the Earl went on, "is, to that grand time, like a child's summer-day! One gets tired as night draws on," he added, with a touch of sadness in his voice, "and one gets to long for bed! For those welcome words 'Come, child, 'tis bed-time!' "

CHAPTER XVII.

TO THE RESCUE!

"IT *isn't* bed-time!" said a sleepy little voice. "The owls hasn't gone to bed, and I s'a'n't go to seep wizout oo sings to me!"

"Oh, Bruno!" cried Sylvie. "Don't you know the owls have only just got up? But the *frogs* have gone to bed, ages ago."

"Well, *I* aren't a frog," said Bruno.

"What shall I sing?" said Sylvie, skilfully avoiding the argument.

"Ask Mister Sir," Bruno lazily replied, clasping his hands behind his curly head, and lying back on his fern-leaf, till it almost bent over with his weight. "This aren't a comfable leaf, Sylvie. Find me a comfabler— please!" he added, as an after-thought, in obedience to a warning finger held up by Sylvie. "I doosn't like being feet-upwards!"

It was a pretty sight to see—the motherly way in which the fairy-child gathered up her little brother in her arms, and laid him on a stronger leaf. She gave it just a touch to set it rocking, and it went on vigorously by itself, as if it contained some hidden machinery. It certainly wasn't the wind, for the evening-breeze had quite died away again, and not a leaf was stirring over our heads.

"Why does that one leaf rock so, without the others?" I asked Sylvie. She only smiled sweetly and shook her head. "I don't know *why*," she said. "It always does, if it's got a fairy-child on it. It *has* to, you know."

"And can people see the leaf rock, who ca'n't see the Fairy on it?"

"Why, of course!" cried Sylvie. "A leaf's a leaf, and everybody can see it; but Bruno's Bruno, and they ca'n't see *him*, unless they're eerie, like you."

Then I understood how it was that one sometimes sees—going through the woods in a still evening—one fern-leaf rocking steadily on, all by itself. Haven't you ever seen that? Try if you can see the fairy-sleeper on it, next time; but don't *pick* the leaf, whatever you do; let the little one sleep on!

But all this time Bruno was getting sleepier and sleepier. "Sing, sing!" he murmured fretfully. Sylvie looked to me for instructions. "What shall it be?" she said.

"Could you sing him the nursery-song you once told me of?" I suggested.

"The one that had been put through the mind-mangle, you know. '*The little man that had a little gun,*' I think it was."

"Why, that are one of the *Professor's* songs!" cried Bruno. "I likes the little man; and I likes the way they spinned him—like a teetle-totle-tum." And he turned a loving look on the gentle old man who was sitting at the other side of his leaf-bed, and who instantly began to sing, accompanying himself on his Outlandish guitar, while the snail, on which he sat, waved its horns in time to the music.

> *In stature the Manlet was dwarfish—*
> *No burly big Blunderbore he:*
> *And he wearily gazed on the crawfish*
> *His Wifelet had dressed for his tea.*
> *"Now reach me, sweet Atom, my gunlet,*
> *And hurl the old shoelet for luck:*
> *Let me hie to the bank of the runlet,*
> *And shoot thee a Duck!"*
>
> *She has reached him his minikin gunlet:*
> *She has hurled the old shoelet for luck:*
> *She is busily baking a bunlet,*
> *To welcome him home with his Duck.*
> *On he speeds, never wasting a wordlet,*
> *Though thoughtlets cling, closely as wax,*
> *To the spot where the beautiful birdlet*
> *So quietly quacks.*
>
> *Where the Lobsterlet lurks, and the Crablet*
> *So slowly and sleepily crawls:*

Where the Dolphin's at home, and the Dablet
   Pays long ceremonious calls:
Where the Grublet is sought by the Froglet:
   Where the Frog is pursued by the Duck:
Where the Ducklet is chased by the Doglet—
      So runs the world's luck!

He has loaded with bullet and powder:
   His footfall is noiseless as air:

But the Voices grow louder and louder,
  And bellow and bluster, and blare.
They bristle before him and after,
  They flutter above and below,
Shrill shriekings of lubberly laughter,
          Weird wailings of woe!

They echo without him, within him:
  They thrill through his whiskers and beard:
Like a teetotum seeming to spin him,
  With sneers never hitherto sneered.
"Avengement," they cry, "on our Foelet!
  Let the Manikin weep for our wrongs!
Let us drench him, from toplet to toelet,
          With Nursery-Songs!

"He shall muse upon 'Hey! Diddle! Diddle!'
  On the Cow that surmounted the Moon:
He shall rave of the Cat and the Fiddle,
  And the Dish that eloped with the Spoon:
And his soul shall be sad for the Spider,
  When Miss Muffet was sipping her whey,
That so tenderly sat down beside her,
          And scared her away!

"The music of Midsummer-madness
  Shall sting him with many a bite,
Till, in rapture of rollicking sadness,
  He shall groan with a gloomy delight:

He shall swathe him, like mists of the morning,
*   In platitudes luscious and limp,*
Such as deck, with a deathless adorning,
*   The Song of the Shrimp!*

"When the Ducklet's dark doom is decided,
*   We will trundle him home in a trice:*
And the banquet, so plainly provided,
*   Shall round into rose-buds and rice:*
In a blaze of pragmatic invention
*   He shall wrestle with Fate, and shall reign:*
But he has not a friend fit to mention,
*   So hit him again!"*

He has shot it, the delicate darling!
*   And the Voices have ceased from their strife:*
Not a whisper of sneering or snarling,
*   As he carries it home to his wife:*
Then, cheerily champing the bunlet
*   His spouse was so skilful to bake,*
He hies him once more to the runlet,
*   To fetch her the Drake!*

"He's sound asleep now," said Sylvie, carefully tucking in the edge of a violet-leaf, which she had been spreading over him as a sort of blanket: "good night!"

"Good night!" I echoed.

"You may well say 'good night'!" laughed Lady Muriel, rising and shutting up the piano as she spoke. "When you've been nid—nid—nodding all the time I've been singing for your benefit! What was it all about, now?" she demanded imperiously.

"Something about a duck?" I hazarded. "Well, a bird of some kind?" I corrected myself, perceiving at once that *that* guess was wrong, at any rate.

"*Something about a bird of some kind!*" Lady Muriel repeated, with as much withering scorn as her sweet face was capable of conveying. "And that's the way he speaks of Shelley's Sky-Lark, is it? When the Poet particularly says '*Hail to thee, blithe spirit!* Bird *thou never wert!*'"

She led the way to the smoking-room, where, ignoring all the usages of Society and all the instincts of Chivalry, the three Lords of the Creation reposed at their ease in low rocking-chairs, and permitted the one lady who was present to glide gracefully about among us, supplying our wants in the form of cooling drinks, cigarettes, and lights. Nay, it was only *one* of the three who had the chivalry to go beyond the common-place "thank you," and to quote the Poet's exquisite description of how Geraint, when waited on by Enid, was moved

"To stoop and kiss the tender little thumb
That crossed the platter as she laid it down,"

and to suit the action to the word—an audacious liberty for which, I feel
bound to report, he was *not* duly reprimanded.

As no topic of conversation seemed to occur to any one, and as we
were, all four, on those delightful terms with one another (the only terms,
I think, on which any friendship, that deserves the name of *intimacy*, can
be maintained) which involve no sort of necessity for *speaking* for mere
speaking's sake, we sat in silence for some minutes.

At length I broke the silence by asking "Is there any fresh news from
the harbour about the Fever?"

"None since this morning," the Earl said, looking very grave. "But
that was alarming enough. The Fever is spreading fast: the London
doctor has taken fright and left the place, and the only one now available
isn't a regular doctor at all: he is apothecary, and doctor, and dentist,
and I don't know what other trades, all in one. It's a bad outlook for
those poor fishermen—and a worse one for all the women and children."

"How many are there of them altogether?" Arthur asked.

"There were nearly one hundred, a week ago," said the Earl: "but
there have been twenty or thirty deaths since then."

"And what religious ministrations are there to be had?"

"There are three brave men down there," the Earl replied, his voice trembling with emotion, "gallant heroes as ever won the Victoria Cross! I am certain that no one of the three will ever leave the place merely to save his own life. There's the Curate: his wife is with him: they have no children. Then there's the Roman Catholic Priest. And there's the Wesleyan Minister. They go amongst their own flocks, mostly; but I'm told that those who are dying like to have *any* of the three with them. How slight the barriers seem to be that part Christian from Christian, when one has to deal with the great facts of Life and the reality of Death!"

"So it must be, and so it should be——" Arthur was beginning, when the front-door bell rang, suddenly and violently.

We heard the front-door hastily opened, and voices outside: then a knock at the door of the smoking-room, and the old house-keeper appeared, looking a little scared.

"Two persons, my Lord, to speak with Dr. Forester."

Arthur stepped outside at once, and we heard his cheery "Well, my men?" but the answer was less audible, the only words I could distinctly catch being "ten since morning, and two more just——"

"But there *is* a doctor there?" we heard Arthur say: and a deep voice, that we had not heard before, replied "Dead, Sir. Died three hours ago."

Lady Muriel shuddered, and hid her face in her hands: but at this moment the front-door was quietly closed, and we heard no more.

For a few minutes we sat quite silent: then the Earl left the room, and soon returned to tell us that Arthur had gone away with the two fishermen, leaving word that he would be back in about an hour. And, true enough, at the end of that interval—during which very little was said, none of us seeming to have the heart to talk—the front-door once more creaked on its rusty hinges, and a step was heard in the passage, hardly to be recognised as Arthur's, so slow and uncertain was it, like a blind man feeling his way.

He came in, and stood before Lady Muriel, resting one hand heavily on the table, and with a strange look in his eyes, as if he were walking in his sleep.

"Muriel—my love—" he paused, and his lips quivered: but after a minute he went on more steadily. "Muriel—my darling—they—*want* me—down in the harbour."

"*Must* you go?" she pleaded, rising and laying her hands on his shoulders, and looking up into his face with her great eyes brimming over with tears. "Must *you* go, Arthur? It may mean—death!"

He met her gaze without flinching. "It *does* mean death," he said, in a husky whisper: "but—darling—I am *called*. And even my life it-self——" His voice failed him, and he said no more.

For a minute she stood quite silent, looking upwards with a helpless gaze, as if even prayer were now useless, while her features worked and quivered with the great agony she was enduring. Then a sudden inspiration seemed to come upon her and light up her face with a strange sweet smile. "*Your* life?" she repeated. "It is not *yours* to give!"

Arthur had recovered himself by this time, and could reply quite firmly, "That is true," he said. "It is not *mine* to give. It is *yours*, now, my—wife that is to be! And you—do *you* forbid me to go? Will you not spare me, my own beloved one?"

Still clinging to him, she laid her head softly on his breast. She had never done such a thing in my presence before, and I knew how deeply she must be moved. "I *will* spare you," she said, calmly and quietly, "to God."

"And to God's poor," he whispered.

"And to God's poor," she added. "When must it be, sweet love?"

"To-morrow morning," he replied. "And I have much to do before then."

And then he told us how he had spent his hour of absence. He had been to the Vicarage, and had arranged for the wedding to take place at eight the next morning (there was no legal obstacle, as he had, some time before this, obtained a Special License) in the little church we knew so well. "My old friend here," indicating me, "will act as 'Best Man,' I know: your father will be there to give you away: and—and—you will dispense with bride's-maids, my darling?"

She nodded: no words came.

"And then I can go with a willing heart—to do God's work—knowing

that we are *one*—and that we are together in *spirit,* though not in bodily presence—and are most of all together when we pray! Our *prayers* will go up together——"

"Yes, yes!" sobbed Lady Muriel. "But you must not stay longer now, my darling! Go home and take some rest. You will need all your strength to-morrow——"

"Well, I will go," said Arthur. "We will be here in good time to-morrow. Good night, my own own darling!"

I followed his example, and we two left the house together. As we walked back to our lodgings, Arthur sighed deeply once or twice, and seemed about to speak—but no words came, till we had entered the house, and had lit our candles, and were at our bedroom-doors. Then Arthur said "Good night, old fellow! God bless you!"

"God bless you!" I echoed from the very depths of my heart.

We were back again at the Hall by eight in the morning, and found Lady Muriel and the Earl, and the old Vicar, waiting for us. It was a strangely sad and silent party that walked up to the little church and back; and I could not help feeling that it was much more like a funeral than a wedding: to Lady Muriel it *was* in fact, a funeral rather than a wedding, so heavily did the presentiment weigh upon her (as she told us afterwards) that her newly-won husband was going forth to his death.

Then we had breakfast; and, all too soon, the vehicle was at the door, which was to convey Arthur, first to his lodgings, to pick up the things he was taking with him, and then as far towards the death-stricken hamlet as it was considered safe to go. One or two of the fishermen were to meet him on the road, to carry his things the rest of the way.

"And are you quite sure you are taking all that you will need?" Lady Muriel asked.

"All that I shall need as a *doctor,* certainly. And my own personal needs are few: I shall not even take any of my own wardrobe—there is a fisherman's suit, ready-made, that is waiting for me at my lodgings. I shall only take my watch, and a few books, and—stay—there *is* one book I should like to add, a pocket-Testament—to use at the bedsides of the sick and dying——"

"Take mine!" said Lady Muriel: and she ran upstairs to fetch it. "It has nothing written in it but 'Muriel,'" she said as she returned with it: "shall I inscribe——"

"No, my own one," said Arthur, taking it from her. "What *could* you inscribe better than that? Could any human name mark it more clearly as my own individual property? Are *you* not mine? Are you not," (with all the old playfulness of manner) "as Bruno would say, 'my *very mine*'?"

He bade a long and loving adieu to the Earl and to me, and left the room, accompanied only by his wife, who was bearing up bravely, and was—*outwardly,* at least—less overcome than her old father. We waited in the room a minute or two, till the sounds of wheels had told us that Arthur had driven away; and even then we waited still, for the step of Lady Muriel, going upstairs to her room, to die away in the distance. Her step, usually so light and joyous, now sounded slow and weary, like one who plods on under a load of hopeless misery; and I felt almost as hopeless, and almost as wretched, as she. "Are we four destined *ever* to meet again, on this side the grave?" I asked myself, as I walked to my home. And the tolling of a distant bell seemed to answer me, "No! No! No!"

CHAPTER XVIII.

A NEWSPAPER-CUTTING.

EXTRACT FROM THE "FAYFIELD CHRONICLE."

Our readers will have followed with painful interest, the accounts we have from time to time published of the terrible epidemic which has, during the last two months, carried off most of the inhabitants of the little fishing-harbour adjoining the village of Elveston. The last survivors, numbering twenty-three only, out of a population which, three short months ago, exceeded on hundred and twenty, were removed on Wednesday last, under the authority of the Local Board, and safely lodged in the County Hospital: and the place is now veritably 'a city of the dead,' without a single human voice to break its silence.

The rescuing party consisted of six sturdy fellows—fishermen from the neighbourhood—directed by the resident Physician of the Hospital, who came over for that purpose, heading a train of hospital-ambulances. The six men had been selected—from a much larger number who had volunteered for this peaceful 'forlorn hope'—for their strength and robust health, as the expedition was considered to be, even now, when the malady has expended its chief force, not unattended with danger.

Every precaution that science could suggest, against the risk of infection, was adopted: and the sufferers were tenderly carried on litters, one by one, up the steep hill, and placed in the ambulances which, each provided with a hospital nurse, were waiting on the level road. The fifteen miles, to the Hospital, were done at a walking-pace, as some of the patients were in too prostrate a condition to bear jolting, and the journey occupied the whole afternoon.

The twenty-three patients consist of nine men, six women, and eight children. It has not been found possible to identify them all, as some of the children—left with no surviving relatives—are infants; and two men and one woman are not yet able to make rational replies, the brain-powers being entirely in abeyance. Among a more well-to-do-race, there would no doubt have been names marked on the clothes; but here no such evidence is forthcoming.

Besides the poor fishermen and their families, there were but five persons to be accounted for: and it was ascertained, beyond a doubt, that all five are numbered with the dead. It is a melancholy pleasure to place on record the names of these genuine martyrs—than whom none, surely, are more worthy to be entered on the glory-roll of England's heroes! They are as follows:—

The Rev. James Burgess, M.A., and Emma his wife. He was the Curate at the Harbour, not thirty years old, and had been married only two years. A written record was found in their house, of the dates of their deaths.

Next to theirs we will place the honoured name of Dr. Arthur Forester, who, on the death of the local physician, nobly faced the imminent peril of death, rather than leave these poor folk uncared for in their last extremity. No record of his name, or of the date of his death, was found: but the corpse was easily identified, although dressed in the ordinary fisherman's suit (which he was known to have adopted when he went down there), by a copy of the New Testament, the gift of his wife, which was found, placed next his heart, with his hands crossed over it. It was not thought prudent to remove the body, for burial elsewhere: and accordingly it was at once committed to the ground, along with four others found in different houses, with all due reverence. His wife, whose maiden name was Lady Muriel Orme, had been married to him on the very morning on which he undertook his self-sacrificing mission.

Next we record the Rev. Walter Saunders, Wesleyan Minister. His death is believed to have taken place two or three weeks ago, as the words 'Died October 5' were found written on the wall of the room which he is known to have occupied— the house being shut up, and apparently not having been entered for some time.

Last—though not a whit behind the other four in glorious self-denial and devotion to duty—let us record the name of Father Francis, a young Jesuit Priest who had been only a few months in the place. He had not been dead many hours when the exploring party came upon the body, which was identified, beyond the possibility of doubt, by the dress, and by the crucifix which was, like the young Doctor's Testament, clasped closely to his heart.

Since reaching the hospital, two of the men and one of the children have died. Hope is entertained for all the others: though there are two or three cases where the vital powers seem to be so entirely exhausted that it is but 'hoping against hope' to regard ultimate recovery as even possible.

CHAPTER XIX.

A FAIRY-DUET.

THE year—what an eventful year it had been for me!—was drawing to a close, and the brief wintry day hardly gave light enough to recognise the old familiar objects, bound up with so many happy memories, as the train glided round the last bend into the station, amid the hoarse cry of "Elveston! Elveston!" resounded along the platform.

It was sad to return to the place, and to feel that I should never again see the glad smile of welcome, that had awaited me here so few months ago. "And yet, if I were to find him here," I muttered, as in solitary state I followed the porter, who was wheeling my luggage on a barrow, "and if he *were* to *'strike a sudden hand in mine, And ask a thousand things of home,'* I should not—no, *'I should not feel it to be strange'!*"

Having given directions to have my luggage taken to my old lodgings, I strolled off alone, to pay a visit, before settling down in my own quarters, to my dear old friends—for such I indeed felt them to be, though it was barely half a year since first we met—the Earl and his widowed daughter.

The shortest way, as I well remembered, was to cross through the churchyard. I pushed open the little wicket-gate and slowly took my way among the solemn memorials of the quiet dead, thinking of the many who had, during the past year, disappeared from the place, and had gone to 'join the majority.' A very few steps brought me in sight of the object of my search. Lady Muriel, dressed in the deepest mourning, her face hidden by a long crape veil, was kneeling before a little marble cross, round which she was fastening a wreath of flowers.

The cross stood on a piece of level turf, unbroken by any mound, and I knew that it was simply a memorial-cross, for one whose dust reposed elsewhere, even before reading the simple inscription:—

In loving Memory of
ARTHUR FORESTER, M.D.
whose mortal remains lie buried by the sea:
whose spirit has returned to God who gave it.

"Greater love hath no man than this, that
a man lay down his life for his friends."

She threw back her veil on seeing me approach, and came forwards to meet me, with a quiet smile, and far more self-possessed than I could have expected.

"It is quite like old times, seeing *you* here again!" she said, in tones of genuine pleasure. "Have you been to see my father?"

"No," I said: "I was on my way there, and came through here as the shortest way. I hope he is well, and you also?"

"Thanks, we are both quite well. And you? Are you any better yet?"

"Not much better, I fear: but no worse, I am thankful to say."

"Let us sit here awhile, and have a quiet chat," she said. The calmness—almost indifference—of her manner quite took me by surprise. I little guessed what a fierce restraint she was putting upon herself.

"One can be so quiet here," she resumed. "I come here every—every day."

"It is very peaceful," I said.

"You got my letter?"

"Yes, but I delayed writing. It is so hard to say—on *paper*——"

"I know. It was kind of you. You were with us when we saw the last of——" She paused a moment, and went on more hurriedly. "I went down to the harbour several times, but no one knows which of those vast graves it is. However, they showed me the house he died in: that was some comfort. I stood in the very room where—where——." She struggled in vain to go on. The flood-gates had given way at last, and the outburst of grief was the most terrible I had ever witnessed. Totally regardless of my presence, she flung herself down on the turf, burying her face in the grass, and with her hands clasped round the little marble cross, "Oh, my darling, my darling!" she sobbed. "And God meant your life to be so beautiful!"

I was startled to hear, thus repeated by Lady Muriel, the very words of the darling child whom I had seen weeping so bitterly over the dead hare. Had some mysterious influence passed, from that sweet fairy-spirit, ere she went back to Fairyland, into the human spirit that loved her so dearly? The idea seemed too wild for belief. And yet, are there not '*more things in heaven and earth than are dreamt of in our philosophy*'?

"God *meant* it to be beautiful," I whispered, "and surely it *was* beautiful? God's purpose never fails!" I dared say no more, but rose and left her. At the entrance-gate to the Earl's house I waited, leaning on the gate and watching the sun set, revolving many memories—some happy, some sorrowful—until Lady Muriel joined me.

She was quite calm again now. "Do come in," she said. "My father will be so pleased to see you!"

The old man rose from his chair, with a smile, to welcome me; but his self-command was far less than his daughter's, and the tears coursed down his face as he grasped both my hands in his, and pressed them warmly.

My heart was too full to speak; and we all sat silent for a minute or two. Then Lady Muriel rang the bell for tea. "You *do* take five o'clock tea, I know!" she said to me, with the sweet playfulness of manner I remembered so well, "even though you *ca'n't* work your wicked will on the Law of Gravity, and make the teacups descend into Infinite Space, a little faster than the tea!"

This remark gave the tone to our conversation. By a tacit mutual consent, we avoided, during this our first meeting after her great sorrow, the painful topics that filled our thoughts, and talked like light-hearted children who had never known a care.

"Did you ever ask yourself the question," Lady Muriel began, *à propos* of nothing, "what is the *chief* advantage of being a Man instead of a Dog?"

"No, indeed," I said: "but I think there are advantages on the *Dog's* side of the question, as well."

"No doubt," she replied, with that pretty mock-gravity that became her so well: "but, on *Man's* side, the chief advantage seems to me to consist in *having pockets!* It was borne in upon me—upon *us*, I should say; for my father and I were returning from a walk—only yesterday. We met a dog carrying home a bone. What it wanted it for, I've no idea: certainly there was no *meat* on it——"

A strange sensation came over me, that I had heard all this, or something exactly like it, before: and I almost expected her next words to be "perhaps he meant to make a cloak for the winter?" However what she really said was "and my father tried to account for it by some wretched joke about *pro bono publico*. Well, the dog laid down the bone—*not* in disgust with the pun, which would have shown it to be a dog of taste—but simply to rest its jaws, poor thing! I *did* pity it so! Won't you join my *Charitable Association for supplying dogs with pockets?* How would *you* like to have to carry your walking-stick in your mouth?"

Ignoring the difficult question as to the *raison d'être* of a walking-stick, supposing one had no *hands*, I mentioned a curious instance, I had once witnessed, of reasoning by a dog. A gentleman, with a lady, and child, and a large dog, were down at the end of a pier on which I was walking. To amuse his child, I suppose, the gentleman put down on the ground his umbrella and the lady's parasol, and then led the way to the other end of the pier, from which he sent the dog back for the deserted articles. I was watching with some curiosity. The dog came racing back to where I stood, but found an unexpected difficulty in picking up the things it had come for. With the umbrella in its mouth, its jaws were so far apart that it could get no firm grip on the parasol. After two or three failures, it paused and considered the matter.

Then it put down the umbrella and began with the parasol. Of course that didn't open its jaws nearly so wide, and it was able to get a good hold of the umbrella, and galloped off in triumph. One couldn't doubt that it had gone through a real train of logical thought.

"I entirely agree with you," said Lady Muriel: "but don't orthodox writers condemn that view, as putting Man on the level of the lower animals? Don't they draw a sharp boundary-line between Reason and Instinct?"

"That certainly *was* the orthodox view, a generation ago," said the Earl. "The truth of Religion seemed ready to stand or fall with the assertion that Man was the only reasoning animal. But that is at an end now. Man can still claim *certain* monopolies—for instance, such a use of *language* as enables us to utilise the work of many, by 'division of labour.' But the belief, that we have a monopoly of *Reason,* has long been swept away. Yet no catastrophe has followed. As some old poet says, '*God is where he was.*'"

"Most religious believers would *now* agree with Bishop Butler," said I, "and not reject a line of argument, even if it led straight to the conclusion that animals have some kind of *soul,* which survives their bodily death."

"I *would* like to know *that* to be true!" Lady Muriel exclaimed. "If only for the sake of the poor horses. Sometimes I've thought that, if anything *could* make me cease to believe in a God of perfect justice, it would be the sufferings of horses—without guilt to deserve it, and without any compensation!"

"It is only part of the great Riddle," said the Earl, "why innocent beings *ever* suffer. It *is* a great strain on Faith—but not a *breaking* strain, I think."

"The sufferings of *horses,*" I said, "are chiefly caused by *Man's* cruelty. So *that* is merely one of the many instances of Sin causing suffering to others than the Sinner himself. But don't you find a greater difficulty in sufferings inflicted by animals upon each other? For instance, a cat playing with a mouse. Assuming it to have no *moral* responsibility, isn't that a greater mystery than a man over-driving a horse?"

"I think it *is,*" said Lady Muriel, looking a mute appeal to her father.

"What right have we to make that assumption?" said the Earl. "*Many* of our religious difficulties are merely deductions from unwarranted assumptions. The wisest answer to most of them, is, I think, '*behold, we know not anything.*'"

"You mentioned 'division of labour,' just now," I said. "Surely it is carried to a wonderful perfection in a hive of bees?"

"So wonderful—so entirely super-human—" said the Earl, "and so entirely inconsistent with the intelligence they show in other ways—that I feel no doubt at all that it is *pure* Instinct, and *not,* as some hold, a very high order of Reason. Look at the utter stupidity of a bee, trying to find its way out of an open window! It *doesn't* try, in any reasonable sense of the word: it simply bangs itself about! We should call a puppy *imbecile,* that behaved so. And yet we are asked to believe that its intellectual level is above Sir Isaac Newton!"

"Then you hold that *pure* Instinct contains no *Reason* at all?"

"On the contrary," said the Earl, "I hold that the work of a bee-hive involves Reason of the *highest* order. But none of it is done by the *Bee. God* has reasoned it all out, and has put into the mind of the Bee the *conclusions,* only, of the reasoning process."

"But how do their minds come to work *together?"* I asked.

"What right have we to assume that they *have* minds?"

"Special pleading, special pleading!" Lady Muriel cried, in a most unfilial tone of triumph. "Why, you yourself said, just now, 'the mind of the Bee'!"

"But I did *not* say '*minds,*' my child," the Earl gently replied. "It has occurred to me, as the most probable solution of the 'Bee'-mystery, that a swarm of Bees *have only one mind among them.* We often see one mind animating a most complex collection of limbs and organs, *when joined together.* How do we know that any material connection is necessary? May not mere neighbourhood be enough? If so, a swarm of bees is simply a single animal whose many limbs are not quite close together!"

"It is a bewildering thought," I said, "and needs a night's rest to grasp it properly. Reason and Instinct *both* tell me I ought to go home. So, good-night!"

"I'll 'set' you part of the way," said Lady Muriel. "I've had no walk to-day. It will do me good, and I have more to say to you. Shall we go through the wood? It will be pleasanter than over the common, even though it *is* getting a little dark."

We turned aside into the shade of interlacing boughs, which formed an architecture of almost perfect symmetry, grouped into lovely groined arches, or running out, far as the eye could follow, into endless aisles, and chancels, and naves, like some ghostly cathedral, fashioned out of the dream of a moon-struck poet.

"Always, in this wood," she began after a pause (silence seemed natural in this dim solitude), "I begin thinking of Fairies! May I ask you a question?" she added hesitatingly. "Do you believe in Fairies?"

The momentary impulse was so strong to tell her of my experiences in this very wood, that I had to make a real effort to keep back the words that rushed to my lips. "If you mean, by 'believe,' 'believe in their *possible* existence,' I say 'Yes.' For their *actual existence,* of course, one would need *evidence.*"

"You were saying, the other day," she went on, "that you would accept *anything,* on good evidence, that was not *à priori* impossible. And I think you named *Ghosts* as an instance of a *provable* phenomenon. Would *Fairies* be another instance?"

"Yes, I think so." And again it was hard to check the wish to say more: but I was not yet sure of a sympathetic listener.

"And have you any theory as to what sort of place they would occupy in Creation? Do tell me what you think about them! Would they, for instance (supposing such beings to exist), would they have any moral responsibility? I mean" (and the light bantering tone suddenly changed to one of deep seriousness) "would they be capable of *sin?*"

"They can reason—on a lower level, perhaps, than men and women—never rising, I think, above the faculties of a child; and they have a moral sense, most surely. Such a being, without *free will*, would be an absurdity. So I am driven to the conclusion that they *are* capable of sin."

"You believe in them?" she cried delightedly, with a sudden motion as if about to clap her hands. "Now tell me, have you any reason for it?"

And still I strove to keep back the revelation I felt sure was coming. "I believe that there is *life* everywhere—not *material* only, not merely what is palpable to our senses—but immaterial and invisible as well. We believe in our own immaterial essence—call it 'soul,' or 'spirit,' or what you will. Why should not other similar essences exist around us, *not* linked on to a visible and *material* body? Did not God make this swarm of happy insects, to dance in this sunbeam for one hour of bliss, for no other object, that we can imagine, than to swell the sum of conscious happiness? And where shall we dare to draw the line, and say 'He has made all these and no more'?"

"Yes, yes!" she assented, watching me with sparkling eyes. "But these are only reasons for not *denying*. You have more reasons than this, have you not?"

"Well, yes," I said, feeling I might safely tell all now. "And I could not find a fitter time or place to say it. I have *seen* them—and in this very wood!"

Lady Muriel asked no more questions. Silently she paced at my side, with head bowed down and hands clasped tightly together. Only, as my tale went on, she drew a little short quick breath now and then, like a child panting with delight. And I told her what I had never yet breathed to any other listener, of my double life, and, more than that (for *mine* might have been but a noonday-dream), of the double life of those two dear children.

And when I told her of Bruno's wild gambols, she laughed merrily; and when I spoke of Sylvie's sweetness and her utter unselfishness and trustful love, she drew a deep breath, like one who hears at last some precious tidings for which the heart has ached for a long while; and the happy tears chased one another down her cheeks.

"I have often longed to meet an angel," she whispered, so low that I could hardly catch the words. "I'm *so* glad I've seen Sylvie! My heart went out to the child the first moment that I saw her—— Listen!" she broke off suddenly. "That's Sylvie singing! I'm sure of it! Don't you know her voice?"

"I have heard *Bruno* sing, more than once," I said: "but I never heard Sylvie."

"I have only heard her *once*," said Lady Muriel. "It was that day when you brought us those mysterious flowers. The children had run out into the garden; and I saw Eric coming in that way, and went to the window to meet him: and Sylvie was singing, under the trees, a song I had never heard before. The words were something like 'I think it is Love, I feel it is Love.' Her voice sounded far away, like a dream, but it was beautiful beyond all words—as sweet as an infant's first smile, or the first gleam of the white cliffs when one is coming *home* after weary years—a voice that seemed to fill one's whole being with peace and heavenly thoughts— Listen!" she cried, breaking off again in her excitement. "That *is* her voice, and that's the very song!"

I could distinguish no words, but there was a dreamy sense of music in the air that seemed to grow ever louder and louder, as if coming nearer to us. We stood quite silent, and in another minute the two children appeared, coming straight towards us through an arched opening among the trees. Each had an arm round the other, and the setting sun shed a golden halo round their heads, like what one sees in pictures of saints. They were looking in our direction, but evidently did not see us, and I soon made out that Lady Muriel had for once passed into a condition familiar to *me,* that we were both of us 'eerie', and that, though we could see the children so plainly, we were quite invisible to *them.*

The song ceased just as they came into sight: but, to my delight, Bruno instantly said "Let's sing it all again, Sylvie! It *did* sound so pretty!" And Sylvie replied "Very well. It's *you* to begin, you know."

So Bruno began, in the sweet childish treble I knew so well:—

> *Say, what is the spell, when her fledgelings are cheeping,*
> *That lures the bird home to her nest?*
> *Or wakes the tired mother, whose infant is weeping,*
> *To cuddle and croon it to rest?*
> *What's the magic that charms the glad babe in her arms,*
> *Till it cooes with the voice of the dove?"*

And now ensued quite the strangest of all the strange experiences that marked the wonderful year whose history I am writing—the experience of *first* hearing Sylvie's voice in song. Her part was a very short one— only a few words—and she sang it timidly, and very low indeed, scarcely audibly, but the *sweetness* of her voice was simply indescribable; I have never heard any earthly music like it.

> *"'Tis a secret, and so let us whisper it low—*
> *And the name of the secret is Love!"*

On me the first effect of her voice was a sudden sharp pang that seemed to pierce through one's very heart. (I had felt such a pang only once before in my life, and it had been from *seeing* what, at the moment, realised one's idea of perfect beauty—it was in a London exhibition, where, in making my way through a crowd, I suddenly met, face to face, a child of quite unearthly beauty.) Then came a rush of burning tears to the eyes, as though one could weep one's soul away for pure delight.

And lastly there fell on me a sense of awe that was almost terror—some such feeling as Moses must have had when he heard the words *"Put off thy shoes from off thy feet, for the place whereon thou standest is holy ground."* The figures of the children became vague and shadowy, like glimmering meteors: while their voices rang together in exquisite harmony as they sang:—

> *"For I think it is Love,*
> *For I feel it is Love,*
> *For I'm sure it is nothing but Love!"*

By this time I could see them clearly once more. Bruno again sang by himself:—

> *"Say, whence is the voice that, when anger is burning,*
> *Bids the whirl of the tempest to cease?*
> *That stirs the vexed soul with an aching—a yearning*
> *For the brotherly hand-grip of peace?*
> *Whence the music that fills all our being—that thrills*
> *Around us, beneath, and above?"*

Sylvie sang more courageously, this time: the words seemed to carry her away, out of herself:—

> *"'Tis a secret: none knows how it comes, how it goes:*
> *But the name of the secret is Love!"*

And clear and strong the chorus rang out:—

> *"For I think it is Love,*
> *For I feel it is Love,*
> *For I'm sure it is nothing but Love!"*

Once more we heard Bruno's delicate little voice alone:—

> *"Say whose is the skill that paints valley and hill,*
> *Like a picture so fair to the sight?*
> *That flecks the green meadow with sunshine and shadow,*
> *Till the little lambs leap with delight?"*

And again uprose that silvery voice, whose angelic sweetness I could hardly bear:—

> *"'Tis a secret untold to hearts cruel and cold,*
> *Though 'tis sung, by the angels above,*
> *In notes that ring clear for the ears that can hear—*
> *And the name of the secret is Love!"*

And then Bruno joined in again with

"For I think it is Love,
For I feel it is Love,
For I'm sure it is nothing but Love!"

"That *are* pretty!" the little fellow exclaimed, as the children passed us—so closely that we drew back a little to make room for them, and it seemed we had only to reach out a hand to touch them: but this we did not attempt.

"No use to try and stop them!" I said, as they passed away into the shadows. "Why, they could not even see us!"

"No use at all," Lady Muriel echoed with a sigh. "One would *like* to meet them again, in living form! But I feel, somehow, *that* can never be. They have passed out of *our* lives!" She sighed again; and no more was said, till we came out into the main road, at a point near my lodgings.

"Well, I will leave you here," she said. "I want to get back before dark: and I have a cottage-friend to visit, first. Good night, dear friend! Let us see you soon—and often!" she added, with an affectionate warmth that went to my very heart. *"For those are few we hold as dear!"*

"Good night!" I answered. "Tennyson said that of a worthier friend than me."

"Tennyson didn't know what he was talking about!" she saucily rejoined, with a touch of her old childish gaiety, and we parted.

CHAPTER XX.

GAMMON AND SPINACH.

My landlady's welcome had an extra heartiness about it: and though, with a rare delicacy of feeling, she made no direct allusion to the friend whose companionship had done so much to brighten life for me, I felt sure that it was a kindly sympathy with my solitary state that made her so specially anxious to do all she could think of to ensure my comfort, and make me feel at home.

The lonely evening seemed long and tedious: yet I lingered on, watching the dying fire, and letting Fancy mould the red embers into the forms and faces belonging to bygone scenes. Now it seemed to be Bruno's roguish smile that sparkled for a moment, and died away: now it was Sylvie's rosy cheek: and now the Professor's jolly round face, beaming with delight. "You're welcome, my little ones!" he seemed to say. And then the red coal, which for the moment embodied the dear old Professor, began to wax dim, and with its dying lustre the words seemed to die away into silence. I seized the poker, and with an artful touch or two revived the waning glow, while Fancy—no coy minstrel she—sang me once again the magic strain I loved to hear.

"You're welcome, little ones!" the cheery voice repeated. "I told them you were coming. Your rooms are all ready for you. And the Emperor and the Empress—well, I think they're rather pleased than otherwise! In fact, Her Highness said 'I hope they'll be in time for the Banquet!' Those were her very words, I assure you!"

"Will Uggug be at the Banquet?" Bruno asked. And both children looked uneasy at the dismal suggestion.

"Why, of course he will!" chuckled the Professor. "Why, it's his *birthday,* don't you know? And his health will be drunk, and all that sort of thing. What would the Banquet be without *him?*"

"Ever so much nicer," said Bruno. But he said it in a *very* low voice, and nobody but Sylvie heard him.

The Professor chuckled again. "It'll be a jolly Banquet, now *you've* come, my little man! I *am* so glad to see you again!"

"I 'fraid we've been very long in coming," Bruno politely remarked.

"Well, yes," the Professor assented. "However, you're very short now you're come: that's *some* comfort." And he went on to enumerate the plans for the day. "The Lecture comes first," he said. *"That* the Empress *insists* on. She says people will eat so much at the Banquet, they'll be too sleepy to attend to the Lecture afterwards—and perhaps she's right. There'll just be a little *refreshment,* when the people first arrive—as a kind of surprise for the Empress, you know. Ever since she's been—well, not *quite* so clever as she once was—we've found it desirable to concoct little surprises for her. *Then* comes the Lecture——"

"What? The Lecture you were getting ready—ever so long ago?" Sylvie enquired.

"Yes—that's the one," the Professor rather reluctantly admitted. "It *has* taken a goodish time to prepare. I've got so many other things to attend to. For instance, I'm Court-Physician. I have to keep all the Royal Servants in good health—and that reminds me!" he cried, ringing the bell in a great hurry. "This is Medicine-Day! We only give Medicine once a week. If we were to begin giving it every day, the bottles would *soon* be empty!"

"But if they were ill on the *other* days?" Sylvie suggested.

"What, ill on the wrong *day!*" exclaimed the Professor. "Oh, that would never do! A Servant would be dismissed *at once,* who was ill on the wrong day! This is the Medicine for *today,*" he went on, taking down a large jug from a shelf. "I mixed it, myself, first thing this morning. Taste it!" he said, holding out the jug to Bruno. "Dip in your finger, and taste it!"

Bruno did so, and made such an excruciatingly wry face that Sylvie exclaimed, in alarm, "Oh, Bruno, you mustn't!"

"It's welly extremely nasty!" Bruno said, as his face resumed its natural shape.

"Nasty?" said the Professor. "Why, of *course* it is! What would Medicine be, if it wasn't *nasty?*"

"Nice," said Bruno.

"I was going to say—" the Professor faltered, rather taken aback by the promptness of Bruno's reply, "—that *that* would never do! Medicine *has* to be nasty, you know. Be good enough to take this jug, down into the Servants' Hall," he said to the footman who answered the bell: "and tell them it's their Medicine for *today*."

"Which of them is to drink it?" the footman asked, as he carried off the jug.

"Oh, I've not settled *that* yet!" the Professor briskly replied. "I'll come and settle that, soon. Tell them not to begin, on any account, till I come! It's really *wonderful*" he said, turning to the children, "the success I've had in curing Diseases! Here are some of my memoranda." He took down from the shelf a heap of little bits of paper, pinned together in twos and threes. "Just look at *this* set, now. *'Under-Cook Number Thirteen recovered from Common Fever—Febris Communis.'* And now see what's pinned to it. *'Gave Under-Cook Number Thirteen a Double Dose of Medicine.'* That's something to be proud of, isn't it?"

"But which happened *first?*" said Sylvie, looking very much puzzled.

The Professor examined the papers carefully. "They are not *dated,* I find," he said with a slightly dejected air: "so I fear I ca'n't tell you. But they *both* happened: there's no doubt of *that.* The *Medicine's* the great thing, you know. The *Diseases* are much less important. You can keep a *Medicine,* for years and years: but nobody ever wants to keep a *Disease!* By the way, come and look at the platform. The Gardener asked me to come and see if it would do. We may as well go before it gets dark."

"We'd like to, very much!" Sylvie replied. "Come, Bruno, put on your hat. Don't keep the dear Professor waiting!"

"Ca'n't find my hat!" the little fellow sadly replied. "I were rolling it about. And it's rolled itself away!"

"Maybe it's rolled in *there*," Sylvie suggested, pointing to a dark recess, the door of which stood half open: and Bruno ran in to look. After a minute he came slowly out again, looking very grave, and carefully shut the cupboard-door after him.

"It aren't in there," he said, with such unusual solemnity, that Sylvie's curiosity was roused.

"What *is* in there, Bruno?"

"There's cobwebs—and two spiders—" Bruno thoughtfully replied, checking off the catalogue on his fingers, "—and the cover of a picture-book—and a tortoise—and a dish of nuts—and an old man."

"An old man!" cried the Professor, trotting across the room in great excitement. "Why, it must be the Other Professor, that's been lost for ever so long!"

He opened the door of the cupboard wide: and there he was, the Other Professor, sitting in a chair, with a book on his knee, and in the act of helping himself to a nut from a dish, which he had taken down off a shelf just within his reach. He looked round at us, but said nothing till he had cracked and eaten the nut. Then he asked the old question. "Is the Lecture all ready?"

"It'll begin in an hour," the Professor said, evading the question. "First, we must have something to surprise the Empress. And then comes the Banquet——"

"The Banquet!" cried the Other Professor, springing up, and filling

the room with a cloud of dust. "Then I'd better go and—and brush myself a little. What a state I'm in!"

"He *does* want brushing!" the Professor said, with a critical air. "Here's your hat, little man! I had put it on by mistake. I'd quite forgotten I had *one* on, already. Let's go and look at the pl atform."

"And there's that nice old Gardener singing still!" Bruno exclaimed in delight, as we went out into the garden. "I do believe he's been singing that very song ever since we went away!"

"Why, of course he has!" replied the Professor. "It wouldn't be the thing to leave off, you know."

"Wouldn't be *what* thing?" said Bruno: but the Professor thought it best not to hear the question. "What are you doing with that hedgehog?" he shouted at the Gardener, whom they found standing upon one foot, singing softly to himself, and rolling a hedgehog up and down with the other foot.

"Well, I wanted fur to know what hedgehogs lives on: so I be a-keeping this here hedgehog—fur to see if it eats potatoes——"

"Much better keep a potato," said the Professor; "and see if hedgehogs eat it!"

"That be the roight way, sure-ly!" the delighted Gardener exclaimed. "Be you come to see the platform?"

"Aye, aye!" the Professor cheerily replied. "And the children have come back, you see!"

The Gardener looked round at them with a grin. Then he led the way to the Pavilion; and as he went he sang:—

> "He looked again, and found it was
> A Double Rule of Three:
> 'And all its Mystery,' he said,
> 'Is clear as day to me!'"

"You've been *months* over that song," said the Professor. "Isn't it finished yet?"

"There be only one verse more," the Gardener sadly replied. And, with tears streaming down his cheeks, he sang the last verse:—

> "He thought he saw an Argument
> That proved he was the Pope:
> He looked again, and found it was
> A Bar of Mottled Soap.
> 'A fact so dread,' he faintly said,
> 'Extinguishes all hope!'"

Choking with sobs, the Gardener hastily stepped on a few yards ahead of the party, to conceal his emotion.

"Did *he* see the Bar of Mottled Soap?" Sylvie enquired, as we followed.

"Oh, certainly!" said the Professor. "That song is his own history, you know."

Tears of an ever-ready sympathy glittered in Bruno's eyes. "I's *welly* sorry he isn't the Pope!" he said. "Aren't *you* sorry, Sylvie?"

"Well—I hardly know," Sylvie replied in the vaguest manner. "Would it make him any happier?" she asked the Professor.

"It wouldn't make the *Pope* any happier," said the Professor. "Isn't the platform *lovely?*" he asked, as we entered the Pavilion.

"I've put an extra beam under it!" said the Gardener, patting it affectionately as he spoke. "And now it's that strong, as—as a mad elephant might dance upon it!"

"Thank you *very* much!" the Professor heartily rejoined. "I don't know that we shall exactly require-but it's convenient to know." And he led the children upon the platform, to explain the arrangements to them. "Here are three seats, you see, for the Emperor and the Empress and Prince Uggug. But there must be two more chairs here!" he said, looking down at the Gardener. "One for Lady Sylvie, and one for the smaller animal!"

"And may I help in the Lecture?" said Bruno. "I can do some conjuring-tricks."

"Well, it's not exactly a *conjuring* lecture," the Professor said, as he arranged some curious-looking machines on the table. "However, what can you do? Did you ever go through a table, for instance?"

"Often!" said Bruno. *"Haven't* I, Sylvie?"

The Professor was evidently surprised, though he tried not to show it. "This must be looked into," he muttered to himself, taking out a note-book. "And first—what kind of table?"

"Tell him!" Bruno whispered to Sylvie, putting his arms round her neck.

"Tell him yourself," said Sylvie.

"Ca'n't," said Bruno. "It's a *bony* word."

"Nonsense!" laughed Sylvie. "You can say it well enough, if you only try. Come!"

"Muddle—" said Bruno. "That's a bit of it."

"What does he say?" cried the bewildered Professor.

"He means the multiplication-table," Sylvie explained.

The Professor looked annoyed, and shut up his note-book again. "Oh, that's *quite* another thing," he said.

"It are ever so many other things," said Bruno. *"Aren't* it, Sylvie?"

A loud blast of trumpets interrupted this conversation. "Why, the entertainment has *begun!"* the Professor exclaimed, as he hurried the children into the Reception-Saloon. "I had no idea it was so late!"

A small table, containing cake and wine, stood in a corner of the Saloon; and here we found the Emperor and Empress waiting for us. The rest of the Saloon had been cleared of furniture, to make room for the guests. I was much struck by the great change a few months had made in the faces of the Imperial Pair. A vacant stare was now the *Emperor's* usual expression; while over the face of the *Empress* there flitted, ever and anon, a meaningless smile.

"So you're come at last!" the Emperor sulkily remarked, as the Professor and the children took their places. It was evident that he was *very* much out of temper: and we were not long in learning the cause of this. He did not consider the preparations, made for the Imperial party, to be such as suited their rank. "A common mahogany table!" he growled, pointing to it contemptuously with his thumb. "Why wasn't it made of gold, I should like to know?"

"It would have taken a very long——" the Professor began, but the Emperor cut the sentence short.

"Then the cake! Ordinary plum! Why wasn't it made of—of——" He broke off again. "Then the wine! Merely old Madeira! Why wasn't it——Then this chair! That's worst of all. Why wasn't it a throne? One *might* excuse the other omissions, but I *ca'n't* get over the chair!"

"What *I* ca'n't get over," said the Empress, in eager sympathy with her angry husband, "is the *table!"*

"Pooh!" said the Emperor.

"It is much to be regretted!" the Professor mildlly replied, as soon as he had a chance of speaking. After a moment's thought he strengthened the remark. *"Everything,"* he said, addressing Society in general, "is *very much* to be regretted!"

A murmur of "Hear, hear!" rose from the crowded Saloon.

There was a rather awkward pause: the Professor evidently didn't

know how to begin. The Empress leant forwards, and whispered to him. "A few jokes, you know, Professor—just to put people at their ease!"

"True, true, Madam!" the Professor meekly replied. "This little boy——"

"Please don't make any jokes about *me!"* Bruno exclaimed, his eyes filling with tears.

"I won't if you'd rather I didn't," said the kind-hearted Professor. "It was only something about a Ship's Buoy: a harmless pun—but it doesn't matter." Here he turned to the crowd and addressed them in a loud voice. "Learn your A's!" he shouted. "Your B's! Your C's! And your D's! *Then* you'll be at your ease!"

There was a roar of laughter from all the assembly, and then a great deal of confused whispering. *"What* was it he said? Something about bees, I fancy——"

The Empress smiled in her meaningless way, and fanned herself. The poor Professor looked at her timidly: he was clearly at his wits' end again, and hoping for another hint. The Empress whispered again.

"Some spinach, you know, Professor, as a surprise."

The Professor beckoned to the Head-Cook, and said something to him in a low voice. Then the Head-Cook left the room, followed by all the other cooks.

"It's difficult to get things started," the Professor remarked to Bruno. "When once we get started, it'll go on all right, you'll see."

"If oo want to startle people," said Bruno, "oo should put live frogs on their backs."

Here the cooks all came in again, in a procession, the Head-Cook coming last and carrying something, which the others tried to hide by waving flags all round it. "Nothing but flags, Your Imperial Highness! Nothing but flags!" he kept repeating, as he set it before her. Then all the flags were dropped in a moment, as the Head-Cook raised the cover from an enormous dish.

"What is it?" the Empress said faintly, as she put her spy-glass to her eye. "Why, it's *Spinach,* I declare!"

"Her Imperial Highness is surprised," the Professor explained to the attendants: and some of them clapped their hands. The Head-Cook made a low bow, and in doing so dropped a spoon on the table, as if by accident, just within reach of the Empress, who looked the other way and pretended not to see it.

"I *am* surprised!" the Empress said to Bruno. "Aren't you?"

"Not a bit," said Bruno. "I heard—" but Sylvie put her hand over his mouth, and spoke for him. "He's rather tired, I think. He wants the Lecture to begin."

"I want the *supper* to begin," Bruno corrected her.

The Empress took up the spoon in an absent manner, and tried to balance it across the back of her hand, and in doing this she dropped it into the dish: and, when she took it out again, it was full of spinach. "How curious!" she said, and put it into her mouth. "It tastes just like *real* spinach! I thought it was an imitation—but I do believe it's real!" And she took another spoonful.

"It wo'n't be real much longer," said Bruno.

But the Empress had had enough spinach by this time, and somehow—I failed to notice the exact process—we all found ourselves in the Pavilion, and the Professor in the act of beginning the long-expected Lecture.

CHAPTER XXI.

THE PROFESSOR'S LECTURE.

"IN Science—in fact, in most things—it is usually best *to begin at the beginning*. In *some* things, of course, it's better to begin at the *other* end. For instance, if you wanted to paint a dog green, it *might* be best to begin with the *tail*, as it doesn't bite at *that* end. And so——"

"May *I* help oo?" Bruno interrupted.

"Help me to do *what?*" said the puzzled Professor, looking up for a moment, but keeping his finger on the book he was reading from, so as not to lose his place.

"To paint a dog green!" cried Bruno. *"Oo* can begin wiz its *mouf,* and I'll——"

"No, no!" said the Professor. "We haven't got to the *Experiments* yet. And so," returning to his note-book, "I'll give you the Axioms of Science. After that I shall exhibit some Specimens. Then I shall explain a Process or two. And I shall conclude with a few Experiments. An *Axiom,* you know, is a thing that you accept without contradiction. For instance, if I were to say 'Here we are!', that would be accepted without any contradiction, and it's a nice sort of remark to *begin* a conversation with. So it would be an *Axiom.* Or again, supposing I were to say, 'Here we are not!,' *that* would be——"

"—a fib!" cried Bruno.

"Oh, *Bruno!*" said Sylvie in a warning whisper. "Of course it would be an *Axiom,* if the Professor said it!"

"—that would be accepted, if people were civil," continued the Professor; "so it would be *another* Axiom."

"It *might* be an Axledum," Bruno said: "but it wouldn't be *true!*"

"Ignorance of Axioms," the Lecturer continued, "is a great drawback in life. It wastes so much time to have to say them over and over again. For instance, take the Axiom '*Nothing is greater than itself*'; that is, '*Nothing can contain itself.*' How often you hear people say 'He was so excited, he was quite unable to contain himself.' Why, *of course* he was unable! The *excitement* had nothing to do with it!"

"I say, look here, you know!" said the Emperor, who was getting a little restless. "How many Axioms are you going to give us? At *this* rate, we sha'n't get to the *Experiments* till to-morrow-week!"

"Oh, sooner than *that,* I assure you!" the Professor replied, looking up in alarm. "There are only," (he referred to his notes again) "only *two* more, that are really *necessary.*"

"Read 'em out, and get on to the *Specimens*," grumbled the Emperor.

"The *First* Axiom," the Professor read out in a great hurry, "consists of these words, *'Whatever is, is.'* And the Second consists of *these* words, *'Whatever isn't, isn't.'* We will now go on to the *Specimens*. The first tray contains Crystals and other Things." He drew it towards him, and again referred to his note-book. "Some of the labels—owing to insufficient adhesion——" Here he stopped again, and carefully examined the page with his eyeglass. "I ca'n't read the rest of the sentence," he said at last, "but it *means* that the labels have come loose, and the Things have got mixed——"

"Let *me* stick 'em on again!" cried Bruno eagerly, and began licking them, like postage-stamps, and dabbing them down upon the *Crystals* and the other Things. But the Professor hastily moved the tray out of his reach. "They *might* get fixed to the *wrong* Specimens, you know!" he said.

"Oo shouldn't have any *wrong* peppermints in the tray!" Bruno boldly replied. *"Should* he, Sylvie?"

But Sylvie only shook her head.

The Professor heard him not. He had taken up one of the bottles, and was carefully reading the label through his eye-glass. "Our first Specimen——" he announced, as he placed the bottle in front of the other Things, "is—that is, it is called——" here he took it up, and examined the label again, as if he thought it might have changed since he last saw it, "is called Aqua Pura—common water—the fluid that cheers——"

"Hip! Hip! Hip!" the Head-Cook began enthusiastically.

"—but *not* inebriates!" the Professor went on quickly, but only just in time to check the "Hooroar!" which was beginning.

"Our second Specimen," he went on, carefully opening a small jar, "is——" here he removed the lid, and a large beetle instantly darted out, and with an angry buzz went straight out of the Pavilion, "—is—or rather, I should say," looking sadly into the empty jar, "it *was*—a curious kind of Blue Beetle. Did any one happen to remark—as it went past—three blue spots under each wing?"

Nobody had remarked them.

"Ah, well!" the Professor said with a sigh. "It's a pity. Unless you remark that kind of thing *at the moment,* it's very apt to get overlooked! The *next* Specimen, at any rate, will not fly away! It is—in short, or perhaps, more correctly, at *length*— an *Elephant.* You will observe——" Here he beckoned to the Gardener to come up on the platform, and with his help began putting together what looked like an enormous dog-kennel, with short tubes projecting out of it on both sides.

"But we've seen *Elephants* before," the Emperor grumbled.

"Yes, but not through a *Megaloscope!*" the Professor eagerly replied. "You know you can't see a *Flea*, properly, without a *magnifying*-glass— what we call a *Microscope*. Well, just in the same way, you can't see an *Elephant,* properly, without a *minimifying*-glass. There's one in each of these little tubes. And *this* is a *Megaloscope!* The Gardener will now bring in the next Specimen. Please open *both* curtains, down at the end there, and make way for the Elephant!"

There was a general rush to the sides of the Pavilion, and all eyes were turned to the open end, watching for the return of the Gardener, who had gone away singing *"He thought he saw an Elephant That practised on a Fife!"* There was silence for a minute: and then his harsh voice was heard again in the distance. *"He looked again—come up then! He looked again, and found it was—woa back! and found it was A letter from his—make way there! He's a-coming!"*

And in marched, or waddled—it is hard to say which is the right word—an Elephant, on its hind-legs, and playing on an enormous fife which it held with its fore-feet.

The Professor hastily threw open a large door at the end of the Megaloscope, and the huge animal, at a signal from the Gardener, dropped the fife, and obediently trotted into the machine, the door of which was at once shut by the Professor. "The Specimen is now ready for observation!" he proclaimed. "It is exactly the size of the common Mouse—*Mus Communis!*"

There was a general rush to the tubes, and the spectators watched with delight the minikin creature, as it playfully coiled its trunk round the Professor's extended finger, finally taking its stand upon the palm of his hand, while he carefully lifted it out, and carried it off to exhibit to the Imperial party.

"Isn't it a *darling?*" cried Bruno. "May I stroke it, please? I'll touch it *welly* gently!"

The Empress inspected it solemnly with her eye-glass. "It is very small," she said in a deep voice. "Smaller than elephants usually are, I believe?"

The Professor gave a start of delighted surprise. "Why, that's *true!*"

he murmured to himself. Then louder, turning to the audience, "Her Imperial Highness has made a remark which is perfectly sensible!" And a wild cheer arose from that vast multitude.

"The next Specimen," the Professor proclaimed, after carefully placing the little Elephant in the tray, among the Crystals and other Things, "is a *Flea*, which we will enlarge for the purposes of observation." Taking a small pill-box from the tray, he advanced to the Megaloscope, and reversed all the tubes. "The Specimen is ready!" he cried, with his eye at one of the tubes, while he carefully emptied the pill-box through a little hole at the side. "It is now the size of the Common Horse—*Equus Communis!*"

There was another general rush, to look through the tubes, and the Pavilion rang with shouts of delight, through which the Professor's anxious tones could scarcely be heard. "Keep the door of the Microscope *shut!*" he cried. "If the creature were to escape, *this size*, it would——" But the mischief was done. The door had swung open, and in another moment the Monster had got out, and was trampling down the terrified, shrieking spectators.

But the Professor's presence of mind did not desert him. "Undraw those curtains!" he shouted. It was done. The Monster gathered its legs together, and in one tremendous bound vanished into the sky.

"Where *is* it?" said the Emperor, rubbing his eyes.

"In the next Province, I fancy," the Professor replied. "That jump would take it at *least* five miles! The next thing is to explain a Process or two. But I find there is hardly room enough to operate—the smaller animal is rather in my way——"

"Who does he mean?" Bruno whispered to Sylvie.

"He means *you!*" Sylvie whispered back. "Hush!"

"Be kind enough to move—angularly—to *this* corner," the Professor said, addressing himself to Bruno.

Bruno hastily moved his chair in the direction indicated. "Did I move angrily enough?" he inquired. But the Professor was once more absorbed in his Lecture, which he was reading from his note-book.

"I will now explain the Process of—the name is blotted, I'm sorry to say. It will be illustrated by a number of—of——" here he examined the page for some time, and at last said "It seems to be either 'Experiments' or 'Specimens'——"

"Let it be *Experiments*," said the Emperor. "We've seen plenty of *Specimens*."

"Certainly, certainly!" the Professor assented. "We will have some Experiments."

"May *I* do them?" Bruno eagerly asked.

"Oh dear no!" The Professor looked dismayed. "I really don't know what would happen if *you* did them!"

"Nor nobody doosn't know what'll happen if *oo* doos them!" Bruno retorted.

"Our First Experiment requires a Machine. It has two knobs—only *two*—you can count them, if you like."

The Head-Cook stepped forwards, counted them, and retired satisfied.

"Now you *might* press those two knobs together—but that's not the way to do it. Or you *might* turn the Machine upside-down—but *that's* not the way to do it!"

"What *are* the way to do it?" said Bruno, who was listening very attentively.

The Professor smiled benignantly. "Ah, yes!" he said, in a voice like the heading of a chapter. "The Way To Do It! Permit me!" and in a moment he had whisked Bruno upon the table. "I divide my subject," he began, "into three parts——"

"I think I'll get down!" Bruno whispered to Sylvie. "It aren't nice to be divided!"

"He hasn't got a knife, silly boy!" Sylvie whispered in reply. "Stand still! You'll break all the bottles!"

"The first part is to take hold of the knobs," putting them into Bruno's hands. "The second part is——" Here he turned the handle, and, with a loud "Oh!", Bruno dropped both the knobs, and began rubbing his elbows.

The Professor chuckled in delight. "It had a sensible effect. *Hadn't* it?" he enquired.

"No, it hadn't a *sensible* effect!" Bruno said indignantly. "It were very silly indeed. It jingled my elbows, and it banged my back, and it crinkled my hair, and it buzzed among my bones!"

"I'm sure it *didn't!*" said Sylvie. "You're only inventing!"

"Oo doesn't know nuffin about it!" Bruno replied. "Oo wasn't there to see. Nobody ca'n't go among my bones. There isn't room!"

"Our Second Experiment," the Professor announced, as Bruno returned to his place, still thoughtfully rubbing his elbows, "is the production of that seldom-seen-but-greatly-to-be-admired phenomenon, Black Light! You have seen White Light, Red Light, Green Light, and so on: but never, till this wonderful day, have any eyes but mine seen *Black Light!* This box," carefully lifting it upon the table, and covering it with a heap of blankets, "is quite full of it. The way I made it was this—I took a lighted candle into a dark cupboard and shut the door. Of course the cupboard was then full of *Yellow* Light. Then I took a bottle of Black ink, and poured it over the candle: and, to my delight, every atom of the Yellow Light turned *Black!* That was indeed the proudest moment of my life! Then I filled a box with it. And now—would anyone like to get under the blankets and see it?"

Dead silence followed this appeal: but at last Bruno said "*I'll* get under, if it won't jingle my elbows."

Satisfied on this point, Bruno crawled under the blankets, and, after a minute or two, crawled out again, very hot and dusty, and with his hair in the wildest confusion.

"What did you see in the box?" Sylvie eagerly enquired.

"I saw *nuffin!*" Bruno sadly replied. "It were too dark!"

"He has described the appearance of the thing exactly!" the Professor exclaimed with enthusiasm. "Black Light, and Nothing, look so extremely alike, at first sight, that I don't wonder he failed to distinguish them! We will now proceed to the Third Experiment."

The Professor came down, and led the way to where a post had been driven firmly into the ground. To one side of the post was fastened a chain, with an iron weight hooked on to the end of it, and from the other side projected a piece of whalebone, with a ring at the end of it. "This is a *most* interesting Experiment!" the Professor announced. "It will need *time*, I'm afraid: but that is a trifling disadvantage. Now observe. If I were to unhook this weight, and let go, it would fall to the ground. You do not deny *that?*"

Nobody denied it.

"And in the same way, if I were to bend this piece of whalebone round the post—thus—and put the ring over this hook—thus—it stays bent: but, if I unhook it, it straightens itself again. You do not deny *that?*"

Again, nobody denied it.

"Well, now, suppose we left things just as they are, for a long time. The force of the *whalebone* would get exhausted, you know, and it would stay bent, even when you unhooked it. Now, *why* shouldn't the same thing happen with the *weight?* The *whalebone* gets so used to being bent, that it ca'n't *straighten* itself any more. Why shouldn't the *weight* get so used to being held up, that it ca'n't *fall* any more? That's what *I* want to know!"

"That's what *we* want to know!" echoed the crowd.

"How long must we wait?" grumbled the Emperor.

The Professor looked at his watch. "Well, I *think* a thousand years will do to *begin* with," he said. "Then we will cautiously unhook the weight:

and, if it *still* shows (as perhaps it will) a *slight* tendency to fall, we will hook it on to the chain again, and leave it for *another* thousand years."

Here the Empress experienced one of those flashes of Common Sense which were the surprise of all around her. "Meanwhile there'll be time for another Experiment," she said.

"There will *indeed!*" cried the delighted Professor. "Let us return to the platform, and proceed to the *Fourth* Experiment!"

"For this concluding Experiment, I will take a certain Alkali, or Acid— I forget which. Now you'll see what will happen when I mix it with Some——" here he took up a bottle, and looked at it doubtfully, "— when I mix it with—with Something——"

Here the Emperor interrupted. "What's the *name* of the stuff?" he asked.

"I don't remember the *name*," said the Professor: "and the label has come off." He emptied it quickly into the other bottle, and, with a tremendous bang, both bottles flew to pieces, upsetting all the machines, and filling the Pavilion with thick black smoke. I sprang to my feet in terror, and—and found myself standing before my solitary hearth, where the poker, dropping at last from the hand of the sleeper, had knocked over the tongs and the shovel, and had upset the kett e, filling the air with clouds of steam. With a weary sigh, I betook myself to bed.

CHAPTER XXII.

THE BANQUET.

"Heaviness may endure for a night: but joy cometh in the morning." The next day found me quite another being. Even the memories of my lost friend and companion were sunny as the genial weather that smiled around me. I did not venture to trouble Lady Muriel, or her father, with another call so soon: but took a walk into the country, and only turned homewards when the low sunbeams warned me that day would soon be over.

On my way home, I passed the cottage where the old man lived, whose face always recalled to me the day when I first met Lady Muriel; and I glanced in as I passed, half-curious to see if he were still living there.

Yes: the old man was still alive. He was sitting out in the porch, looking just as he did when I first saw him at Fayfield Junction—it seemed only a few days ago!

"Good evening!" I said, pausing.

"Good evening, Maister!" he cheerfully responded. "Wo'n't ee step in?"

I stepped in, and took a seat on the bench in the porch. "I'm glad to see you looking so hearty," I began. "Last time, I remember, I chanced to pass just as Lady Muriel was coming away from the house. Does she still come to see you?"

"Ees," he answered slowly. "She has na forgotten me. I don't lose her bonny face for many days together. Well I mind the very first time she come, after we'd met at Railway Station. She told me as she come to mak' amends. Dear child! Only think o' that! To mak' amends!"

"To make amends for what?" I enquired. "What could *she* have done to need it?"

"Well, it were loike this, you see? We were both on us a-waiting fur t' train at t' Junction. And I had setten mysen down upat t' bench. And Station-Maister, *he* comes and he orders me off—fur t' mak' room for her Ladyship, you understand?"

"I remember it all," I said. "I was there myself, that day."

"*Was* you, now? Well, an' she axes my pardon fur 't. Think o' that, now! *My* pardon! An owd ne'er-do-weel like me! Ah! She's been here many a time, sin' then. Why, she were in here only yestere'en, as it were, a-sittin', as it might be, where you're a-sitting now, an' lookin' sweeter and kinder nor an angel! An' she says 'You've not got your Minnie, now,' she says, 'to fettle for ye.' Minnie was my grand-daughter, Sir, as lived wi' me. She died, a matter of two months ago—or it may be three. She was a bonny lass—and a good lass, too. Eh, but life has been rare an' lonely without her!"

He covered his face in his hands: and I waited a minute or two, in silence, for him to recover himself.

"So she says, 'Just tak' *me* fur your Minnie!' she says. 'Didna Minnie mak' your tea fur you?' says she. 'Ay,' says I. An' she mak's the tea. 'An' didna Minnie light your pipe?' says she. 'Ay,' says I. An' she lights the pipe for me. 'An' didna Minnie set out your tea in t' porch?' An' I says 'My dear,' I says, 'I'm thinking you're Minnie hersen!' An' she cries a bit. We both on us cries a bit——"

Again I kept silence for a while.

"An' while I smokes my pipe, she sits an' talks to me—as loving an' as pleasant! I'll be bound I thowt it were Minnie come again! An' when she gets up to go, I says 'Winnot ye shak' hands wi' me?' says I. An' she says 'Na,' she says: 'a cannot *shak' hands* wi' thee!' she says."

"I'm sorry she said *that*," I put in, thinking it was the only instance I had ever known of pride of rank showing itself in Lady Muriel.

"Bless you, it werena *pride!*" said the old man, reading my thoughts. "She says '*Your* Minnie never *shook hands* wi' you!' she says. 'An' *I'm* your Minnie now,' she says. An' she just puts her dear arms about my neck—and she kisses me on t' cheek—an' may God in Heaven bless her!" And here the poor old man broke down entirely, and could say no more.

"God bless her!" I echoed. "And good night to you!" I pressed his hand, and left him. "Lady Muriel," I said softly to myself as I went homewards, "truly you know how to 'mak' amends'!"

Seated once more by my lonely fireside, I tried to recall the strange vision of the night before, and to conjure up the face of the dear old Professor among the blazing coals. "That black one—with just a touch of red—would suit him well," I thought. "After such a catastrophe, it would be sure to be covered with black stains—and he would say:—

"The result of *that* combination—you may have noticed?—was an *Ex-plosion!* Shall I repeat the Experiment?"

"No, no! Don't trouble yourself!" was the general cry. And we all trooped off, in hot haste, to the Banqueting-Hall, where the feast had already begun.

No time was lost in helping the dishes, and very speedily every guest found his plate filled with good things.

"I have always maintained the principle," the Professor began, "that it is a good rule to take some food—occasionally. The great advantage of dinner—parties—" he broke off suddenly. "Why, actually here's the Other Professor!" he cried. "And there's no place left for him!"

The Other Professor came in reading a large book, which he held close to his eyes. One result of his not looking where he was going was that he tripped up, as he crossed the Saloon, flew up into the air, and fell heavily on his face in the middle of the table.

"*What* a pity!" cried the kind-hearted Professor, as he helped him up.

"It wouldn't be *me,* if I didn't trip," said the Other Professor.

The Professor looked much shocked. "Almost *anything* would be better than *that!*" he exclaimed. "It never does," he added, aside to Bruno, "to be anybody else, does it?"

To which Bruno gravely replied "I's got nuffin on my plate."

The Professor hastily put on his spectacles, to make sure that the *facts* were all right, to begin with: then he turned his jolly round face upon the unfortunate owner of the empty plate. "And what would you like next, my little man?"

"Well," Bruno said, a little doubtfully, "I think I'll take some plum-pudding, please—while I think of it."

"Oh, Bruno!" (This was a whisper from Sylvie.) "It isn't good manners to ask for a dish before it comes!"

And Bruno whispered back "But I might forget to ask for some, when it comes, oo know—I *do* forget things, sometimes," he added, seeing Sylvie about to whisper more.

And *this* assertion Sylvie did not venture to contradict.

Meanwhile a chair had been placed for the Other Professor, between the Empress and Sylvie. Sylvie found him a rather uninteresting neighbour: in fact, she couldn't afterwards remember that he had made more than *one* remark to her during the whole banquet, and that was "What a comfort a Dictionary is!" (She told Bruno, afterwards, that she had been too much afraid of him to say more than "Yes, Sir," in reply; and that had been the end of their conversation. On which Bruno expressed a very decided opinion that *that* wasn't worth calling a "conversation" at all. "Oo should have asked him a riddle!" he added triumphantly "Why, *I* asked the Professor *three* riddles! One was that one that you asked me in the morning, 'How many pennies are there in two shillings?' And another was——" "Oh, Bruno!" Sylvie interrupted. "*That* wasn't a riddle!" "It *were!*" Bruno fiercely replied.)

By this time a waiter had supplied Bruno with a plateful of *something,* which drove the plum-pudding out of his head.

"Another advantage of dinner-parties," the Professor cheerfully explained, for the benefit of any one that would listen, "is that it helps you

to *see* your friends. If you want to *see* a man, offer him something to eat. It's the same rule with a mouse."

"This Cat's very kind to the Mouses," Bruno said, stooping to stroke a remarkably fat specimen of the race, that had just waddled into the room, and was rubbing itself affectionately against the leg of his chair. "Please, Sylvie, pour some milk in your saucer. Pussie's ever so thirsty!"

"Why do you want *my* saucer?" said Sylvie. "You've got one yourself!"

"Yes, I know," said Bruno: "but I wanted *mine* for to give it some *more* milk in."

Sylvie looked unconvinced: however it seemed quite impossible for her *ever* to refuse what her brother asked: so she quietly filled her saucer with milk, and handed it to Bruno, who got down off his chair to administer it to the cat.

"The room's very hot, with all this crowd," the Professor said to Sylvie. "I wonder why they don't put some lumps of ice in the grate? You fill it with lumps of coal in the winter, you know, and you sit round it and enjoy the warmth. How jolly it would be to fill it now with lumps of ice, and sit round it and enjoy the coolth!"

Hot as it was, Sylvie shivered a little at the idea. "It's very cold *outside*," she said. "My feet got almost frozen to-day."

"That's the *shoemaker's* fault!" the Professor cheerfully replied. "How often I've explained to him that he *ought* to make boots with little iron frames under the soles, to hold lamps! But he never *thinks*. No one would suffer from cold, if only they would *think* of those little things. I always use hot ink, myself, in the winter. Very few people ever think of *that!* Yet how simple it is!"

"Yes, it's very simple," Sylvie said politely. "Has the cat had enough?" This was to Bruno, who had brought back the saucer only half-emptied.

But Bruno did not hear the question. "There's somebody scratching at the door and wanting to come in," he said. And he scrambled down off his chair, and went and cautiously peeped out through the door-way.

"Who was it wanted to come in?" Sylvie asked, as he returned to his place.

"It were a Mouse," said Bruno. "And it peepted in. And it saw the Cat. And it said 'I'll come in another day.' And I said 'Oo needn't be flightened. The Cat's *welly* kind to Mouses.' And it said 'But I's got some imporkant business, what I *must* attend to.' And it said 'I'll call again to-morrow.' And it said 'Give my love to the Cat.'"

"What a fat cat it is!" said the Lord Chancellor, leaning across the Professor to address his small neighbour, "It's quite a wonder!"

"It was awfully fat when it camed in," said Bruno: "so it would be more wonderfuller if it got thin all in a minute."

"And that was the reason, I suppose," the Lord Chancellor suggested, "why you didn't give it the rest of the milk?"

"No," said Bruno. "It were a betterer reason. I tooked the saucer up 'cause it were so discontented!"

"It doesn't look so to *me*," said the Lord Chancellor. "What made you think it was discontented?"

"'cause it grumbled in its throat."

"Oh, Bruno!" cried Sylvie. "Why, that's the way cats show they're *pleased!*"

Bruno looked doubtful. "It's not a good way," he objected. "Oo wouldn't say *I* were pleased, if I made that noise in my throat!"

"What a singular boy!" the Lord Chancellor whispered to himself: but Bruno had caught the words.

"What do it mean to say 'a *singular* boy'?" he whispered to Sylvie.

"It means *one* boy," Sylvie whispered in return. "And *plural* means two or three."

"Then I's welly glad I *is* a singular boy!" Bruno said with great emphasis. "It would be *horrid* to be two or three boys! P'raps they wouldn't play with me!"

"Why *should* they?" said the Other Professor, suddenly waking up out of a deep reverie. "They might be asleep, you know."

"Couldn't, if *I* was awake," Bruno said cunningly.

"Oh, but they might indeed!" the Other Professor protested. "Boys don't all go to sleep at once, you know. So these boys—but who are you talking about?"

"He *never* remembers to ask that first!" the Professor whispered to the children.

"Why, the rest of *me*, a-course!" Bruno exclaimed triumphantly. "Supposing I was two or three boys!"

The Other Professor sighed, and seemed to be sinking back into his reverie; but suddenly brightened up again, and addressed the Professor. "There's nothing more to be done *now*, is there?"

"Well, there's the dinner to finish," the Professor said with a bewildered smile: "and the heat to bear. I hope you'll enjoy the dinner—such as it is; and that you won't mind the heat—such as it isn't."

The sentence *sounded* well, but somehow I couldn't quite understand it; and the Other Professor seemed to be no better off. "Such as it isn't *what*?" he peevishly enquired.

"It isn't as hot as it might be," the Professor replied, catching at the first idea that came to hand.

"Ah, I see what you mean *now!*" the Other Professor graciously remarked. "It's very badly expressed, but I quite see it *now!* Thirteen minutes and a half ago," he went on, looking first at Bruno and then at his watch as he spoke, "you said 'this Cat's very kind to the Mouses.' It must be a singular animal!"

"So it *are*," said Bruno, after carefully examining the Cat, to make sure how many there were of it.

"But how do you know it's kind to the Mouses—or, more correctly speaking, the *Mice*?"

"'cause it *plays* with the Mouses," said Bruno; "for to amuse them, oo know."

"But that is just what I *don't* know," the Other Professor rejoined. "My belief is, it plays with them to *kill* them!"

"Oh, that's quite a *accident!*" Bruno began, so eagerly, that it was evident he had already propounded this very difficulty to the Cat. "It 'splained all that to me, while it were drinking the milk. It said 'I teaches the Mouses new games: the Mouses likes it ever so much.' It said 'Sometimes little accidents happens: sometimes the Mouses kills theirselves.' It said 'I's always *welly* sorry, when the Mouses kills theirselves.' It said——"

"If it was so *very* sorry," Sylvie said, rather disdainfully, "it wouldn't *eat* the Mouses after they'd killed themselves!"

But this difficulty, also, had evidently not been lost sight of in the exhaustive ethical discussion just concluded. "It said——" (the orator constantly omitted, as superfluous, his own share in the dialogue, and merely gave us the replies of the Cat) "It said 'Dead Mouses *never* objecks to be eaten.' It said 'There's no use wasting good Mouses.' It said 'Wifful—' sumfinoruvver. It said 'And oo may live to say "How much I wiss I had the Mouse that then I frew away!'" It said——."

"It hadn't *time* to say such a lot of things!" Sylvie interrupted indignantly.

"Oo doesn't know how Cats speaks!" Bruno rejoined contemptuously. "Cats speaks *welly* quick!"

CHAPTER XXIII.

THE PIG-TALE.

By this time the appetites of the guests seemed to be nearly satisfied, and even *Bruno* had the resolution to say, when the Professor offered him a fourth slice of plum-pudding, "I thinks three helpings is enough!"

Suddenly the Professor started as if he had been electrified. "Why, I had nearly forgotten the most important part of the entertainment! The Other Professor is to recite a Tale of a Pig—I mean a Pig-Tale," he corrected himself. "It has Introductory Verses at the beginning, and at the end."

"It ca'n't have Introductory Verses at the *end*, can it?" said Sylvie.

"Wait till you hear it," said the Professor: "then you'll see. I'm not sure it hasn't some in the *middle*, as well." Here he rose to his feet, and there was an instant silence through the Banqueting-Hall: they evidently expected a speech.

"Ladies, and gentlemen," the Professor began, "the Other Professor is so kind as to recite a Poem. The title of it is 'The Pig-Tale.' He never recited it before!" (General cheering among the guests.) "He will never recite it again!" (Frantic excitement, and wild cheering all down the hall, the Professor himself mounting the table in hot haste, to lead the cheering, and waving his spectacles in one hand and a spoon in the other.)

Then the Other Professor got up, and began:—

Little Birds are dining
  Warily and well,
    Hid in mossy cell:
Hid, I say, by waiters
Gorgeous in their gaiters—
    I've a Tale to tell.

Little Birds are feeding
  Justices with jam,
    Rich in frizzled ham:
Rich, I say, in oysters
Haunting shady cloisters—
    That is what I am.

Little Birds are teaching
  Tigresses to smile,
    Innocent of guile:
Smile, I say, not smirkle—
Mouth a semicircle,
    That's the proper style!

Little Birds are sleeping
  All among the pins,
    Where the loser wins:
Where, I say, he sneezes
When and how he pleases—
    So the Tale begins.

There was a Pig that sat alone
  Beside a ruined Pump:
By day and night he made his moan—

It would have stirred a heart of stone
To see him wring his hoofs and groan,
  Because he could not jump.

A certain Camel hear him shout—
  A Camel with a hump.
"Oh, is it Grief, or is it Gout?
What is this bellowing about?"
That Pig replied, with quivering snout,
  "Because I cannot jump!"

That Camel scanned him, dreamy-eyed.
  "Methinks you are too plump.
I never knew a Pig so wide—
That wobbled so from side to side—
Who could, however much he tried,
  Do such a thing as jump!

"Yet mark those trees, two miles away,
  All clustered in a clump:
If you could trot there twice a day,
Nor ever pause for rest or play,
In the far future—Who can Say?—
  You may be fit to jump."

That Camel passed, and left him there
  Beside the ruined Pump.
Oh, horrid was that Pig's despair!
His shrieks of anguish filled the air.
He wrung his hoofs, he rent his hair,
  Because he could not jump.

There was a Frog that wandered by—
  A sleek and shining lump:
Inspected him with fishy eye,
And said "O Pig, what makes you cry?"
And bitter was that Pig's reply,
  "Because I cannot jump!"

That Frog he grinned a grin of glee,
  And hit his chest a thump.
"O Pig," he said, "be ruled by me,
And you shall see what you shall see.
This minute, for a trifling fee,
  I'll teach you how to jump!

"You may be faint from many a fall,
  And bruised by many a bump:
But, if you persevere through all,
And practise first on something small,
Concluding with a ten-foot wall,
  You'll find that you can jump!"

That Pig looked up with joyful start:
  "Oh Frog, you are a trump!
Your words have healed my inward smart—
Come, name your fee and do your part:
Bring comfort to a broken heart,
  By teaching me to jump!"

"My fee shall be a mutton-chop,
  My goal this ruined Pump.
Observe with what an airy flop
I plant myself upon the top!
Now bend your knees and take a hop,
  For that's the way to jump!"

Uprose that Pig, and rushed, full whack,
  Against the ruined Pump:
Rolled over like an empty sack,
And settled down upon his back,
While all his bones at once went 'Crack!'
  It was a fatal jump.

When the Other Professor had recited this Verse, he went across to
the fire-place, and put his head up the chimney. In doing this, he lost
his balance, and fell head-first into the empty grate, and got so firmly
fixed there that it was some time before he could be dragged out again.

Bruno had had time to say "I thought he wanted to see how many
peoples was up the chimbley."

And Sylvie had said *"Chimney*—not chimbley."

And Bruno had said "Don't talk 'ubbish!"

All this, while the Other Professor was being extracted.

"You must have blacked your face!" the Empress said anxiously. "Let
me send for some soap?"

"Thanks, no," said the Other Professor, keeping his face turned away.
"Black's quite a respectable colour. Besides, soap would be no use without
water."

Keeping his back well turned away from the audience, he went on
with the Introductory Verses:—

Little Birds are writing
    Interesting books,
    To be read by cooks:
Read, I say, not roasted—
Letterpress, when toasted,
Loses its good looks.

    Little Birds are playing
    Bagpipes on the shore,
    Where the tourists snore:
'Thanks!' they cry. "'Tis thrilling!
Take, oh take this shilling!
    Let us have no more!"

Little Birds are bathing
    Crocodiles in cream,
    Like a happy dream!
Like, but not so lasting—
Crocodiles, when fasting,
    Are not all they seem!

That Camel passed, as Day grew dim
    Around the ruined Pump.
"O broken heart! O broken limb!
It needs," that Camel said to him,
"Something more fairy-like and slim,
    To execute a jump!"

That Pig lay still as any stone,
    And could not stir a stump:
Nor ever, if the truth were known,

Was he again observed to moan,
Nor ever wring his hoofs and groan,
Because he could not jump.

That Frog made no remark, for he
Was dismal as a dump:

> *He knew the consequence must be*
> *That he would never get his fee—*
> *And still he sits, in miserie,*
> *Upon that ruined Pump!*

"It's a miserable story!" said Bruno. "It begins miserably, and it ends miserablier. I think I shall cry. Sylvie, please lend me your handkerchief."

"I haven't got it with me," Sylvie whispered.

"Then I won't cry," said Bruno manfully.

"There are more Introductory Verses to come," said the Other Professor, "but I'm hungry." He sat down, cut a large slice of cake, put it on Bruno's plate, and gazed at his own empty plate in astonishment.

"Where did you get that cake?" Sylvie whispered to Bruno.

"He gived it me," said Bruno.

"But you shouldn't ask for things! You *know* you shouldn't!"

"I *didn't* ask," said Bruno, taking a fresh mouthful: "he *gived* it me."

Sylvie considered this for a moment: then she saw her way out of it. "Well, then, ask him to give *me* some!"

"You seem to enjoy that cake?" the Professor remarked.

"Doos that mean 'munch'?" Bruno whispered to Sylvie.

Sylvie nodded. "It means 'to munch' and 'to *like* to munch.'"

Bruno smiled at the Professor. "I *doos* enjoy it," he said.

The Other Professor caught the word. "And I hope you're enjoying *yourself*, little Man?" he enquired.

Bruno's look of horror quite startled him. "No, *indeed* I aren't!" he said.

The Other Professor looked thoroughly puzzled. "Well, well!" he said. "Try some cowslip wine!" And he filled a glass and handed it to Bruno. "Drink this, my dear, and you'll be quite another man!"

"Who shall I be?" said Bruno, pausing in the act of putting it to his lips.

"Don't ask so many questions!" Sylvie interposed, anxious to save the poor old man from further bewilderment. "Suppose we get the Professor to tell us a story."

Bruno adopted the idea with enthusiasm. "*Please* do!" he cried eagerly. "Sumfin about tigers—and bumble-bees—and robin-redbreasts, oo knows!"

"Why should you always have *live* things in stories?" said the Professor. "Why don't you have events, or circumstances?"

"Oh, *please* invent a story like that!" cried Bruno.

The Professor began fluently enough. "Once a coincidence was taking a walk with a little accident, and they met an explanation—a *very* old explanation—so old that it was quite doubled up, and looked more like a conundrum——" he broke off suddenly.

"*Please* go on!" both children exclaimed.

The Professor made a candid confession. "It's a very difficult sort to invent, I find. Suppose Bruno tells one, first."

Bruno was only too happy to adopt the suggestion.

"Once there were a Pig, and a Accordion, and two Jars of Orange-marmalade——"

"The *dramatis personæ*," murmured the Professor. "Well, what then?"

"So, when the Pig played on the Accordion," Bruno went on, "one of the Jars of Orange-marmalade didn't like the tune, and the other Jar of Orange-marmalade did like the tune—I *know* I shall get confused among those Jars of Orange-marmalade, Sylvie!" he whispered anxiously.

"I will now recite the other Introductory Verses," said the Other Professor.

Little Birds are choking
    Baronets with bun,
    Taught to fire a gun:
Taught, I say, to splinter
Salmon in the winter—
    Merely for the fun.

Little Birds are hiding
    Crimes in carpet-bags,
    Blessed by happy stags:
Blessed, I say, though beaten—
Since our friends are eaten
    When the memory flags.

Little Birds are tasting
    Gratitude and gold,
    Pale with sudden cold:
Pale, I say, and wrinkled—
When the bells have tinkled,
    And the Tale is told.

"The next thing to be done," the Professor cheerfully remarked to the Lord Chancellor, as soon as the applause, caused by the recital of the Pig-Tale, had come to an end, "is to drink the Emperor's health, is it not?"

"Undoubtedly!" the Lord Chancellor replied with much solemnity, as he rose to his feet to give the necessary directions for the ceremony. "Fill your glasses!" he thundered. All did so, instantly. "Drink the Emperor's health!" A general gurgling resounded all through the Hall. "Three cheers for the Emperor!" The faintest possible sound followed *this* announcement: and the Chancellor, with admirable presence of mind, instantly proclaimed "A speech from the Emperor!"

The Emperor had begun his speech almost before the words were uttered. "However unwilling to be Emperor—since you all wish me to be Emperor—you know how badly the late Warden managed things—with such enthusiasm as you have shown—he persecuted you—he taxed you too heavily—you know who is fittest man to be Emperor—my brother had no sense——."

How long this curious speech might have lasted it is impossible to say, for just at this moment a hurricane shook the palace to its foundations, bursting open the windows, extinguishing some of the lamps, and filling the air with clouds of dust, which took strange shapes in the air, and seemed to form words.

But the storm subsided as suddenly as it had risen—the casements swung into their places again: the dust vanished: all was as it had been a minute ago—with the exception of the Emperor and Empress, over whom had come a wondrous change. The vacant stare, the meaningless smile, had passed away: all could see that these two strange beings had returned to their senses.

The Emperor continued his speech as if there had been no interruption. "And we have behaved—my wife and I—like two arrant Knaves. We deserve no better name. When my brother went away, you lost the best Warden you ever had. And I've been doing my best, wretched hypocrite that I am, to cheat you into making me an Emperor. Me! One that has hardly got the wits to be a shoe-black!"

The Lord Chancellor wrung his hands in despair. "He is mad, good people!" he was beginning. But both speeches stopped suddenly—and, in the dead silence that followed, a knocking was heard at the outer door.

"What is it?" was the general cry. People began running in and out. The excitement increased every moment. The Lord Chancellor, forgetting all the rules of Court-ceremony, ran full speed down the hall, and in a minute returned, pale and gasping for breath.

CHAPTER XXIV.

THE BEGGAR'S RETURN.

"YOUR Imperial Highnesses!" he began. "It's the old Beggar again! Shall we set the dogs at him?"

"Bring him here!" said the Emperor.

The Chancellor could scarcely believe his ears. *"Here,* your Imperial Highness? Did I rightly understand——"

"Bring him here!" the Emperor thundered once more. The Chancellor tottered down the hall—and in another minute the crowd divided, and the poor old Beggar was seen entering the Banqueting-Hall.

He was indeed a pitiable object: the rags, that hung about him, were all splashed with mud: his white hair and his long beard were tossed about in wild disorder. Yet he walked upright, with a stately tread, as if used to command: and—strangest sight of all—Sylvie and Bruno came with him, clinging to his hands, and gazing at him with looks of silent love.

Men looked eagerly to see how the Emperor would receive the bold intruder. Would he hurl him from the steps of the daïs? But no. To their utter astonishment, the Emperor knelt as the beggar approached, and with bowed head murmured "Forgive us!"

"Forgive us!" the Empress, kneeling at her husband's side, meekly repeated.

The Outcast smiled. "Rise up!" he said. "I forgive you!" And men saw with wonder that a change had passed over the old beggar, even as he spoke. What had seemed, but now, to be vile rags and splashes of mud,

were seen to be in truth kingly trappings, broidered with gold, and sparkling with gems. All knew him now, and bent low before the Elder Brother, the true Warden.

"Brother mine, and Sister mine!" the Warden began, in a clear voice that was heard all through that vast hall. "I come not to disturb you. Rule on, as Emperor, and rule wisely. For I am chosen King of Elfland. To-morrow I return there, taking nought from hence, save only—save only——" his voice trembled, and with a look of ineffable tenderness, he laid his hands in silence on the heads of the two little ones who clung around him.

But he recovered himself in a moment, and beckoned to the Emperor to resume his place at the table. The company seated themselves again— room being found for the Elfin-King between his two children—and the Lord Chancellor rose once more, to propose the next toast.

"The next toast—the hero of the day—why, he isn't here!" he broke off in wild confusion.

Good gracious! Everybody had forgotten Prince Uggug!

"He was told of the Banquet, of course?" said the Emperor.

"Undoubtedly!" replied the Chancellor. "*That* would be the duty of the Gold Stick in Waiting."

"Let the Gold Stick come forwards!" the Emperor gravely said.

The Gold Stick came forwards. "I attended on His Imperial Fatness," was the statement made by the trembling official. "I told him of the Lecture and the Banquet——."

"What followed?" said the Emperor: for the unhappy man seemed almost too frightened to go on.

"His Imperial Fatness was graciously pleased to be sulky. His Imperial Fatness was graciously pleased to box my ears. His Imperial Fatness was graciously pleased to say 'I don't care!'"

"'Don't-care' came to a bad end," Sylvie whispered to Bruno. "I'm not sure, but I *believe* he was hanged."

The Professor overheard her. "*That* result," he blandly remarked, "was merely a case of mistaken identity."

Both children looked puzzled.

"Permit me to explain. 'Don't-care' and 'Care' were twin-brothers. 'Care,' you know, killed the Cat. And they caught 'Don't-care' by mistake, and hanged him instead. And so 'Care' is alive still. But he's very unhappy without his brother. That's why they say 'Begone, dull Care!'"

"Thank you!" Sylvie said, heartily. "It's very extremely interesting. Why, it seems to explain *everything!*"

"Well, not quite *everything,*" the Professor modestly rejoined. "There are two or three scientific difficulties——"

"What was your general impression as to His Imperial Fatness?" the Emperor asked the Gold Stick.

"My impression was that His Imperial Fatness was getting more——"

"More *what?*"

All listened breathlessly for the next word.

"More PRICKLY!"

"He must be sent for *at once!*" the Emperor exclaimed. And the Gold Stick went off like a shot. The Elfin-King sadly shook his head. "No use, no use!" he murmured to himself. "Loveless, loveless!"

Pale, trembling, speechless, the Gold Stick came slowly back again.

"Well?" said the Emperor. "Why does not the Prince appear?"

"One can easily guess," said the Professor. "His Imperial Fatness is, without doubt, a little preoccupied."

Bruno turned a look of solemn enquiry on his old friend. "What do that word mean?"

But the Professor took no notice of the question. He was eagerly listening to the Gold Stick's reply.

"Please your Highness! His Imperial Fatness is——" Not a word more could he utter.

The Empress rose in an agony of alarm. "Let us go to him!" she cried. And there was a general rush for the door.

Bruno slipped off his chair in a moment. "May we go too?" he eagerly asked. But the King did not hear the question, as the Professor was speaking to him. *"Preoccupied,* your Majesty!" he was saying. "That is what he is, no doubt!"

"May we go and see him?" Bruno repeated. The King nodded assent, and the children ran off. In a minute or two they returned, slowly and gravely. "Well?" said the King. "What's the matter with the Prince?"

"He's—what *you* said," Bruno replied, looking at the Professor. "That hard word." And he looked to Sylvie for assistance.

"Porcupine," said Sylvie.

"No, no!" the Professor corrected her. " '*Pre-occupied,*' you mean."

"No, it's *porcupine,*" persisted Sylvie. "Not that other word at all. And please will you come? The house is all in an uproar." ("And oo'd better bring an uproar-glass wiz oo!" added Bruno.)

We got up in great haste, and followed the children upstairs. No one took the least notice of *me,* but I wasn't at all surprised at this, as I had long realised that I was quite invisible to them all—even to Sylvie and Bruno.

All along the gallery, that led to the Prince's apartment, an excited crowd was surging to and fro, and the Babel of voices was deafening: against the door of the room three strong men were leaning, vainly trying to shut it—for some great animal inside was constantly bursting it half open, and we had a glimpse, before the men could push it back again, of the head of a furious wild beast, with great fiery eyes and gnashing teeth. Its voice was a sort of mixture—there was the roaring of a lion, and the bellowing of a bull, and now and then a scream like a gigantic parrot. "There is no judging by the voice!" the Professor cried in great excitement. "What is it?" he shouted to the men at the door. And a general chorus of voices answered him "Porcupine! Prince Uggug has turned into a Porcupine!"

"A new Specimen!" exclaimed the delighted Professor. "Pray let me go in. It should be labeled at once!"

But the strong men only pushed him back. "Label it, indeed! Do you want to be eaten up?" they cried.

"Never mind about Specimens, Professor!" said the Emperor, pushing his way through the crowd. "Tell us how to keep him safe!"

"A large cage!" the Professor promptly replied. "Bring a large cage," he said to the people generally, "with strong bars of steel, and a portcullis made to go up and down like a mouse-trap! Does anyone happen to have such a thing about him?"

It didn't sound a likely sort of thing for anyone to have about him; however, they brought him one directly: curiously enough, there happened to be one standing in the gallery.

"Put it facing the opening of the door, and draw up the portcullis!" This was done in a moment.

"Blankets now!" cried the Professor. "This is a most interesting Experiment!"

There happened to be a pile of blankets close by: and the Professor had hardly said the word, when they were all unfolded and held up like curtains all around. The Professor rapidly arranged them in two rows, so as to make a dark passage, leading straight from the door to the mouth of the cage.

"Now fling the door open!" This did not need to be done: the three men had only to leap out of the way, and the fearful monster flung the door open for itself, and, with a yell like the whistle of a steam-engine, rushed into the cage.

"Down with the portcullis!" No sooner said than done: and all breathed freely once more, on seeing the Porcupine safely caged.

The Professor rubbed his hands in childish delight. "The Experiment has succeeded!" he proclaimed. "All that is needed now is to feed it three times a day, on chopped carrots and——"

"Never mind about its food, just now!" the Emperor interrupted. "Let us return to the Banquet. Brother, will you lead the way?" And the old man, attended by his children, headed the procession down stairs. "See the fate of a loveless life!" he said to Bruno, as they returned to their places. To which Bruno made reply, "I always loved Sylvie, so I'll never get prickly like that!"

"He *is* prickly, certainly," said the Professor, who had caught the last words, "but we must remember that, however porcupiny, he is royal still! After this feast is over, I'm going to take a little present to Prince Uggug—just to soothe him, you know: it isn't pleasant living in a cage."

"What'll you give him for a birthday-present?" Bruno enquired.

"A small saucer of chopped carrots," replied the Professor. "In giving birthday-presents, *my* motto is—cheapness! I should think I save forty pounds a year by giving—oh, *what* a twinge of pain!"

"What is it?" said Sylvie anxiously.

"My old enemy!" groaned the Professor. "Lumbago—rheumatism— that sort of thing. I think I'll go and lie down a bit." And he hobbled out of the Saloon, watched by the pitying eyes of the two children.

"He'll be better soon!" the Elfin-King said cheerily. "Brother!" turning to the Emperor, "I have some business to arrange with you to-night. The Empress will take care of the children." And the two Brothers went away together, arm-in-arm.

The Empress found the children rather sad company. They could talk of nothing but "the dear Professor," and "what a pity he's so ill!", till at last she made the welcome proposal "Let's go and see him!"

The children eagerly grasped the hands she offered them: and we went off to the Professor's study, and found him lying on the sofa, covered up with blankets, and reading a little manuscript-book. "Notes on Vol. Three!" he murmured, looking up at us. And there, on a table near him, lay the book he was seeking when first I saw him.

"And how are you now, Professor?" the Empress asked, bending over the invalid.

The Professor looked up, and smiled feebly. "As devoted to your Imperial Highness as ever!" he said in a weak voice. "All of me, that is not Lumbago, is Loyalty!"

"A sweet sentiment!" the Empress exclaimed with tears in her eyes. "You seldom hear anything so beautiful as that—even in a Valentine!"

"We must take you to stay at the seaside," Sylvie said, tenderly. "It'll do you ever so much good! And the Sea's so grand!"

"But a Mountain's grander!" said Bruno.

"What is there grand about the Sea?" said the Professor. "Why, you could put it all into a teacup!"

"*Some* of it," Sylvie corrected him.

"Well, you'd only want a certain number of teacups to hold it *all*. And *then* where's the grandeur? Then as to a Mountain—why, you could carry it all away in a wheel-barrow, in a certain number of years!"

"It wouldn't look grand—the bits of it in the wheel-barrow," Sylvie candidly admitted.

"But when oo put it together again—" Bruno began.

"When you're older," said the Professor, "you'll know that you *ca'n't* put Mountains together again so easily! One lives and one learns, you know!"

"But it needn't be the *same* one, need it?" said Bruno. "Wo'n't it do, if *I* live, and if *Sylvie* learns?"

"I *ca'n't* learn without living!" said Sylvie.

"But I *can* live without learning!" Bruno retorted. "Oo just try me!"

"What I meant, was—" the Professor began, looking much puzzled, "—was—that you don't know *everything*, you know."

"But I *do* know everything I know!" persisted the little fellow. "I know ever so many things! Everything, 'cept the things I *don't* know. And Sylvie knows all the rest."

The Professor sighed, and gave it up. "Do you know what a Boojum is?"

"*I* know!" cried Bruno. "It's the thing what wrenches people out of their boots!"

"He means 'bootjack,'" Sylvie explained in a whisper.

"You ca'n't wrench people out of *boots*," the Professor mildly observed.

Bruno laughed saucily. "Oo *can*, though! Unless they're *welly* tight in."

"Once upon a time there was a Boojum—" the Professor began, but stopped suddenly. "I forget the rest of the Fable," he said. "And there was a lesson to be learned from it. I'm afraid I forget *that* too."

"*I'll* tell oo a Fable!" Bruno began in a great hurry. "Once there were a Locust, and a Magpie, and a Engine-driver. And the Lesson is, to learn to get up early——"

"It isn't a bit interesting!" Sylvie said contemptuously. "You shouldn't put the Lesson so soon."

"When did you invent that Fable?" said the Professor. "Last week?"

"No!" said Bruno. "A deal shorter ago than that. Guess again!"

"I ca'n't guess," said the Professor. "How long ago?"

"Why, it isn't invented yet!" Bruno exclaimed triumphantly. "But I *have* invented a lovely one! Shall I say it?"

"If you've *finished* inventing it," said Sylvie. "And let the Lesson be 'to try again'!"

"No," said Bruno with great decision. "The Lesson are '*not* to try again'!" "Once there were a lovely china man, what stood on the chimbley-piece. And he stood, and he stood. And one day he tumbleded off, and he didn't hurt his self one bit. Only he *would* try again. And the next time he tumbleded off, he hurted his self welly much, and breaked off ever so much varnish."

"But how did he come back on the chimney-piece after his first tumble?" said the Empress. (It was the first sensible question she had asked in all her life.)

"*I* put him there!" cried Bruno.

"Then I'm afraid you know something about his tumbling," said the Professor. "Perhaps you pushed him?"

To which Bruno replied, very seriously, "Didn't pushed him *much*— he were a *lovely* china man," he added hastily, evidently very anxious to change the subject.

"Come, my children!" said the Elfin-King, who had just entered the room. "We must have a little chat together, before you go to bed." And he was leading them away, but at the door they let go his hands, and ran back again to wish the Professor good night.

"Good night, Professor, good night!" And Bruno solemnly shook hands with the old man, who gazed at him with a loving smile, while Sylvie bent down to press her sweet lips upon his forehead.

"Good night, little ones!" said the Professor. "You may leave me now— to ruminate. I'm as jolly as the day is long, except when it's necessary to ruminate on some very difficult subject. All of me," he murmured sleepily as we left the room, "all of me, that isn't *Bonhommie*, is Rumination!"

"*What* did he say, Bruno?" Sylvie enquired, as soon as we were safely out of hearing.

"I *think* he said 'All of me that isn't Bone-disease is Rheumatism.' Whatever *are* that knocking, Sylvie?"

Sylvie stopped, and listened anxiously. It sounded like some one kicking at a door. "I *hope* it isn't that Porcupine breaking loose!" she exclaimed.

"Let's go on!" Bruno said hastily. "There's nuffin to wait for, oo know!"

CHAPTER XXV.

LIFE OUT OF DEATH.

THE sound of kicking, or knocking, grew louder every moment: and at last a door opened somewhere near us. "Did you say 'come in!' Sir?" my landlady asked timidly.

"Oh yes, come in!" I replied. "What's the matter?"

"A note has just been left for you, Sir, by the baker's boy. He said he was passing the Hall and they asked him to come round and leave it here."

The note contained five words only. "Please come at once. Muriel."

A sudden terror seemed to chill my very heart. "The Earl is ill!" I said to myself. "Dying, perhaps!" And I hastily prepared to leave the house.

"No bad news, Sir, I hope?" my landlady said, as she saw me out. "The boy said as some one had arrived unexpectedly——"

"I hope that is it!" I said. But my feelings were those of fear rather than of hope: though, on entering the house, I was somewhat reassured by finding luggage lying in the entrance, bearing the initials "E. L."

"It's only Eric Lindon after all!" I thought, half relieved and half annoyed. "Surely she need not have sent for me for *that!*"

Lady Muriel met me in the passage. Her eyes were gleaming—but it was the excitement of joy, rather than of grief. "I have a surprise for you!" she whispered.

"You mean that Eric Lindon is here?" I said, vainly trying to disguise the involuntary bitterness of my tone. *"'The funeral baked meats did coldly furnish forth the marriage-tables,'"* I could not help repeating to myself. How cruelly I was misjudging her!

"No, no!" she eagerly replied. "At least—Eric *is* here. But——," her voice quivered, "but there is *another!"*

No need for further question. I eagerly followed her in. There on the bed, he lay—pale and worn—the mere shadow of his old self—my old friend come back again from the dead!

"Arthur!" I exclaimed. I could not say another word.

"Yes, back again, old boy!" he murmured, smiling as I grasped his hand. *"He,"* indicating Eric, who stood near, "saved my life—*He* brought me back. Next to God, we must thank *him,* Muriel, my wife!"

Silently I shook hands with Eric and with the Earl: and with one consent we moved into the shaded side of the room, where we could talk without disturbing the invalid, who lay, silent and happy, holding his wife's hand in his, and watching her with eyes that shone with the deep steady light of Love.

"He has been delirious till to-day," Eric explained in a low voice: "and even to-day he has been wandering more than once. But the sight of *her* has been new life to him." And then he went on to tell us, in would-be careless tones—I knew how he hated any display of feeling—how he had insisted on going back to the plague-stricken town, to bring away a man whom the doctor had abandoned as dying, but who *might,* he fancied, recover if brought to the hospital: how he had seen nothing in the wasted features to remind him of Arthur, and only recognised him when he visited the hospital a month after: how the doctor had forbidden him to announce the discovery, saying that any shock to the over-taxed brain might kill him at once: how he had staid on at the hospital, and nursed the sick man by night and day—all this with the studied indifference of one who is relating the commonplace acts of some chance acquaintance!

"And this was his *rival!"* I thought. "The man who had won from him the heart of the woman he loved!"

"The sun is setting," said Lady Muriel, rising and leading the way to the open window. "Just look at the western sky! What lovely crimson tints! We shall have a glorious day to-morrow——" We had followed her across the room, and were standing in a little group, talking in low tones in the gathering gloom, when we were startled by the voice of the sick man, murmuring words too indistinct for the ear to catch.

"He is wandering again," Lady Muriel whispered, and returned to the bedside. We drew a little nearer also: but no, this had none of the incoherence of delirium. *"What reward shall I give unto the Lord,"* the tremulous lips were saying, *"for all the benefits that He hath done unto me? I will receive the cup of salvation, and call——and call——"* but here the poor weakened memory failed, and the feeble voice died into silence.

His wife knelt down at the bedside, raised one of his arms, and drew

it across her own, fondly kissing the thin white hand that lay so listlessly in her loving grasp. It seemed to me a good opportunity for stealing away without making her go through any form of parting: so, nodding to the Earl and Eric, I silently left the room. Eric followed me down the stairs, and out into the night.

"Is it Life or Death?" I asked him, as soon as we were far enough from the house for me to speak in ordinary tones.

"It is *Life!*" he replied with eager emphasis. "The doctors are quite agreed as to *that*. All he needs now, they say, is rest, and perfect quiet, and good nursing. He's quite sure to get rest and quiet, here: and, as for the nursing, why, I think it's just *possible*——" (he tried hard to make his trembling voice assume a playful tone) "he may even get fairly well nursed, in his present quarters!"

"I'm sure of it!" I said. "Thank you so much for coming out to tell me!" And, thinking he had now said all he had come to say, I held out my hand to bid him good night. He grasped it warmly, and added, turning his face away as he spoke, "By the way, there is one other thing I wanted to say. I thought you'd like to know that—that I'm not—not in the mind I was in when last we met. It isn't—that I can accept Christian belief—at least, not yet. But all this came about so strangely. And she had prayed, you know. And I had prayed. And—and——" his voice broke, and I could only just catch the concluding words, *"there is a God that answers prayer!* I know it for certain now." He wrung my hand once more, and left me suddenly. Never before had I seen him so deeply moved.

So, in the gathering twilight, I paced slowly homewards, in a tumultuous whirl of happy thoughts: my heart seemed full, and running over, with joy and thankfulness: all that I had so fervently longed for, and prayed for, seemed now to have come to pass. And, though I reproached myself, bitterly, for the unworthy suspicion I had for one moment harboured against the true-hearted Lady Muriel, I took comfort in knowing it had been but a passing thought.

Not Bruno himself could have mounted the stairs with so buoyant a step, as I felt my way up in the dark, not pausing to strike a light in the entry, as I knew I had left the lamp burning in my sitting-room.

But it was no common *lamplight* into which I now stepped, with a strange, new, dreamy sensation of some subtle witchery that had come over the place. Light, richer and more golden than any lamp could give, flooded the room, streaming in from a window I had somehow never noticed before, and lighting up a group of three shadowy figures, that grew momently more distinct—a grave old man in royal robes, leaning back in an easy chair, and two children, a girl and a boy, standing at his side.

"Have you the Jewel still, my child?" the old man was saying.

"Oh, *yes!*" Sylvie exclaimed with unusual eagerness. "Do you think I'd *ever* lose it or forget it?" She undid the ribbon round her neck, as she spoke, and laid the Jewel in her father's hand.

Bruno looked at it admiringly. "What a lovely brightness!" he said. "It's just like a little red star! May I take it in my hand?"

Sylvie nodded: and Bruno carried it off to the window, and held it aloft against the sky, whose deepening blue was already spangled with stars. Soon he came running back in some excitement. "Sylvie! Look here!" he cried. "I can see right through it when I hold it up to the sky. And it isn't red a bit: it's, oh such a lovely blue! And the words are all different! Do look at it!"

Sylvie was quite excited, too, by this time; and the two children eagerly held up the Jewel to the light, and spelled out the legend between them, "ALL WILL LOVE SYLVIE."

"Why, this is the *other* Jewel!" cried Bruno. "Don't you remember, Sylvie? The one you *didn't* choose!"

Sylvie took it from him, with a puzzled look, and held it, now up to the light, now down. "It's blue *one* way," she said softly to herself, "and it's red the *other* way! Why, I thought there were *two* of them—Father!" she suddenly exclaimed, laying the Jewel once more in his hand, "I do believe it was the *same* Jewel all the time!"

"Then you choosed it from *itself*," Bruno thoughtfully remarked. "Father, *could* Sylvie choose a thing from itself?"

"Yes, my own one," the old man replied to Sylvie, not noticing Bruno's embarrassing question, "it *was* the same Jewel—but you chose quite right." And he fastened the ribbon round her neck again.

"SYLVIE WILL LOVE ALL—ALL WILL LOVE SYLVIE," Bruno murmured, raising himself on tiptoe to kiss the 'little red star.' "And, when you look *at* it, it's red and fierce like the sun—and, when you look *through* it, it's gentle and blue like the sky!"

"God's own sky," Sylvie said, dreamily.

"God's own sky," the little fellow repeated, as they stood, lovingly clinging together, and looking out into the night. "But oh, Sylvie, what makes the sky such a *darling* blue?"

Sylvie's sweet lips shaped themselves to reply, but her voice sounded faint and very far away. The vision was fast slipping from my eager gaze: but it seemed to me, in that last bewildering moment, that not Sylvie but an angel was looking out through those trustful brown eyes, and that not Sylvie's but an angel's voice was whispering

"It is Love."

THE END.

THREE SUNSETS
AND
OTHER POEMS

Illustrated by
E. GERTRUDE THOMSON

PREFACE

NEARLY the whole of this volume is a reprint of the serious portion of *Phantasmagoria and other Poems*, which was first published in 1869 and has long been out of print. "The Path of Roses" was written soon after the Crimean War, when the name of Florence Nightingale had already become a household-word. "Only a Woman's Hair" was suggested by a circumstance mentioned in *The Life of Dean Swift*, viz., that, after his death, a small packet was found among his papers containing a single lock of hair and inscribed with those words. "After Three Days" was written after seeing Holman Hunt's picture, *The Finding of Christ in the Temple*.

The two poems, "Far Away" and "A Song of Love," are reprinted from *Sylvie and Bruno* and *Sylvie and Bruno Concluded*, books whose high price (made necessary by the great cost of production) has, I fear, put them out of the reach of most of my readers.* "A Lesson in Latin" is reprinted from *The Jabberwock*, a Magazine got up among the Members of "The Girls' Latin School, Boston, U.S.A." The only poems, here printed for the first time, are put together under the title of "Puck Lost and Found," having been inscribed in two books—*Fairies*, a poem by Allingham, illustrated by Miss E. Gertrude Thomson, and *Merry Elves*, a story-book, by whom written I do not know, illustrated by C. O. Murray—which were presented to a little girl and boy, as a sort of memento of a visit paid by them to the author one day, on which occasion he taught them the pastime—dear to the hearts of children—of folding paper-"pistols," which can be made to imitate, fairly well, the noise of a real one.

Jan., 1898.

* *Editorial Note*: These two poems have not been reprinted in the present edition, as they appear elsewhere in this volume: "Far Away" in *Sylvie and Bruno*, Chapter XX; "A Song of Love" in *Sylvie and Bruno Concluded*, Chapter XIX.

THREE SUNSETS.

HE saw her once, and in the glance,
  A moment's glance of meeting eyes,
His heart stood still in sudden trance:
  He trembled with a sweet surprise—
All in the waning light she stood,
The star of perfect womanhood.

That summer-eve his heart was light:
  With lighter step he trod the ground:
And life was fairer in his sight,
  And music was in every sound:
He blessed the world where there could be
So beautiful a thing as she.

There once again, as evening fell
  And stars were peering overhead,
Two lovers met to bid farewell:
  The western sun gleamed faint and red,
Lost in a drift of purple cloud
That wrapped him like a funeral-shroud.

Long time the memory of that night—
  The hand that clasped, the lips that kissed,
The form that faded from his sight
  Slow sinking through the tearful mist—
In dreamy music seemed to roll
Through the dark chambers of his soul.

So after many years he came
  A wanderer from a distant shore:
The street, the house, were still the same,
  But those he sought were there no more:
His burning words, his hopes and fears,
Unheeded fell on alien ears.

Only the children from their play
  Would pause the mournful tale to hear,
Shrinking in half-alarm away,
  Or, step by step, would venture near
To touch with timid curious hands
That strange wild man from other lands.

He sat beside the busy street,
　　There, where he last had seen her face;
And thronging memories, bitter-sweet,
　　Seemed yet to haunt the ancient place:
Her footfall ever floated near:
Her voice was ever in his ear.

He sometimes, as the daylight waned
　　And evening mists began to roll,
In half-soliloquy complained
　　Of that black shadow on his soul,
And blindly fanned, with cruel care,
The ashes of a vain despair.

The summer fled: the lonely man
　　Still lingered out the lessening days;
Still, as the night drew on, would scan
　　Each passing face with closer gaze—
Till, sick at heart, he turned away,
And sighed "she will not come to-day."

So by degrees his spirit bent
　　To mock its own despairing cry,
In stern self-torture to invent
　　New luxuries of agony,
And people all the vacant space
With visions of her perfect face.

Then for a moment she was nigh,
　　He heard no step, but she was there;
As if an angel suddenly
　　Were bodied from the viewless air,
And all her fine ethereal frame
Should fade as swiftly as it came.

So, half in fancy's sunny trance,
　　And half in misery's aching void
With set and stony countenance
　　His bitter being he enjoyed,
And thrust for ever from his mind
The happiness he could not find.

As when the wretch, in lonely room,
　　To selfish death is madly hurled,
The glamour of that fatal fume
　　Shuts out the wholesome living world—
So all his manhood's strength and pride
One sickly dream had swept aside.

Yea, brother, and we passed him there,
　But yesterday, in merry mood,
And marveled at the lordly air
　That shamed his beggar's attitude,
Nor heeded that ourselves might be
Wretches as desperate as he;

Who let the thought of bliss denied
　Make havoc of our life and powers,
And pine, in solitary pride,
　For peace that never shall be ours,
Because we will not work and wait
In trustful patience for our fate.

And so it chanced once more that she
　Came by the old familiar spot:
The face he would have died to see
　Bent o'er him, and he knew it not;
Too rapt in selfish grief to hear,
Even when happiness was near.

And pity filled her gentle breast
　For him that would not stir nor speak
The dying crimson of the west,
　That faintly tinged his haggard cheek,
Fell on her as she stood, and shed
A glory round the patient head.

Ah, let him wake! The moments fly:
　This awful tryst may be the last.
And see, the tear, that dimmed her eye,
　Had fallen on him ere she passed—
She passed: the crimson paled to gray:
And hope departed with the day.

The heavy hours of night went by,
　And silence quickened into sound,
And light slid up the eastern sky,
　And life began its daily round—
But light and life for him were fled:
His name was numbered with the dead.

Nov., 1861.

THE PATH OF ROSES.

IN the dark silence of an ancient room,

Whose one tall window fronted to the West,
Where, through laced tendrils of a hanging vine,
The sunset-glow was fading into night,
Sat a pale Lady, resting weary hands
Upon a great clasped volume, and her face
Within her hands. Not as in rest she bowed,
But large hot tears were coursing down her cheek,
And her low-panted sobs broke awefully
Upon the sleeping echoes of the night.
  Soon she unclasp'd the volume once again,
And read the words in tone of agony,
As in self-torture, weeping as she read:—

> "He crowns the glory of his race:
>   He prayeth but in some fit place
>   To meet his foeman face to face:
>
> "And, battling for the True, the Right,

From ruddy dawn to purple night,
To perish in the midmost fight:

"Where hearts are fierce and hands are strong,
Where peals the bugle loud and long,
Where blood is dropping in the throng:

"Still, with a dim and glazing eye,
To watch the tide of victory,
To hear in death the battle-cry:

"Then, gathered grandly to his grave,
To rest among the true and brave,
In holy ground, where yew-trees wave:

"Where, from church-windows sculptured fair,
Float out upon the evening air
The note of praise, the voice of prayer:

"Where no vain marble mockery
Insults with loud and boastful lie
The simple soldier's memory:

"Where sometimes little children go,
And read, in whisper'd accent slow,
The name of him who sleeps below."

Her voice died out: like one in dreams she sat.
"Alas!" she sighed. "For what can Woman do?
Her life is aimless, and her death unknown:
Hemmed in by social forms she pines in vain.
Man has his work, but what can Woman do?"
　　And answer came there from the creeping gloom,
The creeping gloom that settled into night:
"Peace! For thy lot is other than a man's:
His is a path of thorns: he beats them down:
He faces death: he wrestles with despair
Thine is of roses, to adorn and cheer
His lonely life, and hide the thorns in flowers."
　　She spake again: in bitter tone she spake:
"Aye, as a toy, the puppet of an hour,
Or a fair posy, newly plucked at morn,
But flung aside and withered ere the night."
　　And answer came there from the creeping gloom,
The creeping gloom that blackened into night:
"So shalt thou be the lamp to light his path,
What time the shades of sorrow close around."
　　And, so it seemed to her, an awful light
Pierced slowly through the darkness, orbed, and grew,

Until all passed away—the ancient room—
The sunlight dying through the trellised vine—
The one tall window—all had passed away,
And she was standing on the mighty hills.
 Beneath, around, and far as eye could see,
Squadron on squadron, stretched opposing hosts,
Ranked as for battle, mute and motionless.
Anon a distant thunder shook the ground,
The tramp of horses, and a troop shot by—
Plunged headlong in that living sea of men—
Plunged to their death: back from that fatal field
A scattered handful, fighting hard for life,
Broke through the serried lines; but, as she gazed,
They shrank and melted, and their forms grew thin—
Grew pale as ghosts when the first morning ray
Dawns from the East—the trumpet's brazen blare
Died into silence—and the vision passed—
Passed to a room where sick and dying lay
In long, sad line—there brooded Fear and Pain—
Darkness was there, the shade of Azrael's wing.
But there was one that ever, to and fro,
Moved with light footfall: purely calm her face,
And those deep steadfast eyes that starred the gloom:
Still, as she went, she ministered to each
Comfort and counsel; cooled the fevered brow
With softest touch, and in the listening ear
Of the pale sufferer whispered words of peace.
The dying warrior, gazing as she passed,
Clasped his thin hands and blessed her. Bless her too,
Thou, who didst bless the merciful of old!
 So prayed the Lady, watching tearfully
Her gentle moving onward, till the night
Had veiled her wholly, and the vision passed.
 Then once again the solemn whisper came:
"So in the darkest path of man's despair,
Where War and Terror shake the troubled earth,
Lies woman's mission; with unblenching brow
To pass through scenes of horror and affright
Where men grow sick and tremble: unto her
All things are sanctified, for all are good.
Nothing so mean, but shall deserve her care:
Nothing so great, but she may bear her part.
No life is vain: each hath his place assigned:
Do thou thy task, and leave the rest to God."
And there was silence, but the Lady made
No answer, save one deeply-breathed "Amen."
 And she arose, and in that darkening room
Stood lonely as a spirit of the night—
Stood calm and fearless in the gathered night—

And raised her eyes to heaven. There were tears
Upon her face, but in her heart was peace,
Peace that the world nor gives nor takes away!

April 10, 1856.

THE VALLEY OF THE SHADOW
OF DEATH.

HARK, *said the dying man, and sighed*,
  To that complaining tone—
Like sprite condemned, each eventide,
  To walk the world alone.
At sunset, when the air is still,
I hear it creep from yonder hill:
It breathes upon me, dead and chill,
  A moment, and is gone.

My son, it minds me of a day
  Left half a life behind,

That I have prayed to put away
   For ever from my mind.
But bitter memory will not die:
It haunts my soul when none is nigh:
I hear its whisper in the sigh
   Of that complaining wind.

And now in death my soul is fain
   To tell the tale of fear
That hidden in my breast hath lain
   Through many a weary year:
Yet time would fail to utter all—
The evil spells that held me thrall,
And thrust my life from fall to fall,
   Thou needest not to hear.

The spells that bound me with a chain,
   Sin's stern behests to do,
Till Pleasure's self, invoked in vain,
   A heavy burden grew—
Till from my spirit's fevered eye,
A hunted thing, I seemed to fly
Through the dark woods that underlie
   Yon mountain-range of blue.

Deep in those woods I found a vale
   No sunlight visiteth,
Nor star, nor wandering moonbeam pale;
   Where never comes the breath
Of summer-breeze—there in mine ear,
Even as I lingered half in fear,
I heard a whisper, cold and clear,
   "This is the gate of Death.

"O bitter is it to abide
   In weariness alway:
At dawn to sigh for eventide,
   At eventide for day.
Thy noon hath fled: thy sun hath shone.
The brightness of thy day is gone:
What need to lag and linger on
   Till life be cold and gray?

"O well," it said, "beneath yon pool,
   In some still cavern deep,
The fevered brain might slumber cool,
   The eyes forget to weep:
Within that goblet's mystic rim
Are draughts of healing, stored for him

Whose heart is sick, whose sight is dim,
  Who prayeth but to sleep!"

The evening-breeze went moaning by,
  Like mourner for the dead,
And stirred, with shrill complaining sigh,
  The tree-tops overhead:
My guardian-angel seemed to stand
And mutely wave a warning hand—
With sudden terror all unmanned,
  I turned myself and fled!

A cottage-gate stood open wide:
  Soft fell the dying ray
On two fair children, side by side,
  That rested from their play—
Together bent the earnest head,
As ever and anon they read
From one dear Book: the words they said
  Come back to me to-day.

Like twin cascades on mountain-stair
  Together wandered down
The ripples of the golden hair,
  The ripples of the brown:
While, through the tangled silken haze,
Blue eyes looked forth in eager gaze,
More starlike than the gems that blaze
  About a monarch's crown.

My son, there comes to each an hour
  When sinks the spirit's pride—
When weary hands forget their power
  The strokes of death to guide:
In such a moment, warriors say,
A word the panic-rout may stay,
A sudden charge redeem the day
  And turn the living tide.

I could not see, for blinding tears,
  The glories of the west:
A heavenly music filled mine ears,
  A heavenly peace my breast.
"Come unto Me, come unto Me—
All ye that labour, unto Me—
Ye heavy-laden, come to Me—
  And I will give you rest."

The night drew onward: thin and blue

The evening mists arise
To bathe the thirsty land in dew,
   As erst in Paradise—
While, over silent field and town,
The deep blue vault of heaven looked down;
Not, as of old, in angry frown,
   But bright with angels' eyes.

Blest day! Then first I heard the voice
   That since hath oft beguiled
These eyes from tears, and bid rejoice
   This heart with anguish wild—
Thy mother, boy, thou hast not known;
So soon she left me here to moan—
Left me to weep and watch, alone,
   Our one beloved child.

Though, parted from my aching sight,
   Like homeward-speeding dove,
She passed into the perfect light
   That floods the world above;
Yet our twin spirits, well I know—
Though one abide in pain below—
Love, as in summers long ago,
   And evermore shall love.

So with a glad and patient heart
   I move toward mine end:
The streams, that flow awhile apart,
   Shall both in ocean blend.
I dare not weep: I can but bless
The Love that pitied my distress,
And lent me, in Life's wilderness,
   So sweet and true a friend.

But if there be—O if there be
   A truth in what they say,
That angel-forms we cannot see
   Go with us on our way;
Then surely she is with me here,
I dimly feel her spirit near—
The morning-mists grow thin and clear,
   And Death brings in the Day.

April, 1868.

SOLITUDE.

I LOVE the stillness of the wood:

I love the music of the rill:
I love to couch in pensive mood
    Upon some silent hill.

Scarce heard, beneath yon arching trees,
    The silver-crested ripples pass;
And, like a mimic brook, the breeze
    Whispers among the grass.

Here from the world I win release,
    Nor scorn of men, nor footstep rude,
Break in to mar the holy peace
    Of this great solitude.

Here may the silent tears I weep
    Lull the vexed spirit into rest,
As infants sob themselves to sleep
    Upon a mother's breast.

But when the bitter hour is gone,
  And the keen throbbing pangs are still,
Oh sweetest then to couch alone
    Upon some silent hill!

To live in joys that once have been,
  To put the cold world out of sight,
And deck life's drear and barren scene
    With hues of rainbow-light.

For what to man the gift of breath,
  If sorrow be his lot below;
If all the day that ends in death
    Be dark with clouds of woe?

Shall the poor transport of an hour
    Repay long years of sore distress—
The fragrance of a lonely flower
    Make glad the wilderness?

Ye golden hours of Life's young spring,
  Of innocence, of love and truth!
Bright, beyond all imagining,
    Thou fairy-dream of youth!

I'd give all wealth that years have piled,
  The slow result of Life's decay,
To be once more a little child
    For one bright summer-day.
           March 16, 1853.

BEATRICE.

IN her eyes is the living light
  Of a wanderer to earth
From a far celestial height:
    Summers five are all the span—
    Summers five since Time began
To veil in mists of human night
  A shining angel-birth.

Does an angel look from her eyes?
  Will she suddenly spring away,
And soar to her home in the skies?
    Beatrice! Blessing and blessed to be!
    Beatrice! Still, as I gaze on thee,
Visions of two sweet maids arise,
  Whose life was of yesterday:

Of a Beatrice pale and stern,
    With the lips of a dumb despair,
With the innocent eyes that yearn—
        Yearn for the young sweet hours of life,
        Far from sorrow and far from strife,
For the happy summers, that never return,
    When the world seemed good and fair:

Of a Beatrice glorious, bright—
    Of a sainted, ethereal maid,
Whose blue eyes are deep fountains of light,
        Cheering the poet that broodeth apart,
        Filling with gladness his desolate heart,

Like the moon when she shines thro' a cloudless night
  On a world of silence and shade.

And the visions waver and faint,
  And the visions vanish away
That my fancy delighted to paint—
    She is here at my side, a living child,
    With the glowing cheek and the tresses wild,
Nor death-pale martyr, nor radiant saint,
  Yet stainless and bright as they.

For I think, if a grim wild beast
  Were to come from his charnel-cave,
From his jungle-home in the East—
    Stealthily creeping with bated breath,
    Stealthily creeping with eyes of death—
He would all forget his dream of the feast,
  And crouch at her feet a slave.

She would twine her hand in his mane:
  She would prattle in silvery tone,
Like the tinkle of summer-rain—
    Questioning him with her laughing eyes,
    Questioning him with a glad surprise,
Till she caught from those fierce eyes again
  The love that lit her own.

And be sure, if a savage heart,
  In a mask of human guise,
Were to come on her here apart—
    Bound for a dark and a deadly deed,
    Hurrying past with pitiless speed—
He would suddenly falter and guiltily start
  At the glance of her pure blue eyes.

Nay, be sure, if an angel fair,
  A bright seraph undefiled,
Were to stoop from the trackless air,
    Fain would she linger in glad amaze—
    Lovingly linger to ponder and gaze,
With a sister's love and a sister's care,
  On the happy, innocent child.

                    Dec. 4, 1862.

STOLEN WATERS.

THE light was faint, and soft the air
  That breathed around the place;
And she was lithe, and tall, and fair,

And with a wayward grace
Her queenly head she bare.

With glowing cheek, with gleaming eye,
   She met me on the way:
My spirit owned the witchery
   Within her smile that lay:
I followed her, I know not why.

The trees were thick with many a fruit,
   The grass with many a flower:
My soul was dead, my tongue was mute,
   In that accursèd hour.

And, in my dream, with silvery voice,
   She said, or seemed to say,
"Youth is the season to rejoice—"
   I could not choose but stay:
   I could not say her nay.

She plucked a branch above her head,
   With rarest fruitage laden:

"Drink of the juice, Sir Knight," she said:
  "'Tis good for knight and maiden."

Oh, blind mine eye that would not trace—
  Oh, deaf mine ear that would not heed—
The mocking smile upon her face,
  The mocking voice of greed!

I drank the juice; and straightway felt
  A fire within my brain:
My soul within me seemed to melt
  In sweet delirious pain.

"Sweet is the stolen draught," she said:
  "Hath sweetness stint or measure?
Pleasant the secret hoard of bread:
  What bars us from our pleasure?"

"Yea, take we pleasure while we may,"
  I heard myself replying.
In the red sunset, far away,
  My happier life was dying:
My heart was sad, my voice was gay.

And unawares, I knew not how,
  I kissed her dainty finger-tips,
I kissed her on the lily brow,
  I kissed her on the false, false lips—
That burning kiss, I feel it now!

"True love gives true love of the best:
  Then take," I cried, "my heart to thee!"
The very heart from out my breast
  I plucked, I gave it willingly:
  Her very heart she gave to me—
Then died the glory from the west.

In the gray light I saw her face,
  And it was withered, old, and gray;
The flowers were fading in their place,
  Were fading with the fading day.

Forth from her, like a hunted deer,
  Through all that ghastly night I fled,
And still behind me seemed to hear
  Her fierce unflagging tread;
And scarce drew breath for fear.

Yet marked I well how strangely seemed

The heart within my breast to sleep:
Silent it lay, or so I dreamed,
   With never a throb or leap.

For hers was now my heart, she said,
   The heart that once had been mine own:
And in my breast I bore instead
   A cold, cold heart of stone.
So grew the morning overhead.

The sun shot downward through the trees
   His old familiar flame:
All ancient sounds upon the breeze
   From copse and meadow came—
   But I was not the same.

They call me mad: I smile, I weep,
   Uncaring how or why:
Yea, when one's heart is laid asleep,
   What better than to die?
So that the grave be dark and deep.

To die! To die? And yet, methinks,
   I drink of life, to-day,
Deep as the thirsty traveler drinks
   Of fountain by the way:
My voice is sad, my heart is gay.

When yestereve was on the wane,
   I heard a clear voice singing
So sweetly that, like summer-rain,
   My happy tears came springing:
My human heart returned again.

   "A rosy child,
Sitting and singing, in a garden fair,
   The joy of hearing, seeing,
   The simple joy of being—
Or twining rosebuds in the golden hair
   That ripples free and wild.

   "A sweet pale child—
Wearily looking to the purple West—
   Waiting the great For-ever
   That suddenly shall sever
The cruel chains that hold her from her rest—
   By earth-joys unbeguiled.

   "An angel-child—

Gazing with living eyes on a dead face:
The mortal form forsaken,
That none may now awaken,
That lieth painless, moveless in her place,
As though in death she smiled!

"Be as a child—
So shalt thou sing for very joy of breath—
So shalt thou wait thy dying,
In holy transport lying—
So pass rejoicing through the gate of death,
In garment undefiled."

Then call me what they will, I know
    That now my soul is glad:
If this be madness, better so,
    Far better to be mad,
Weeping or smiling as I go.

For if I weep, it is that now
    I see how deep a loss is mine,
And feel how brightly round my brow
    The coronal might shine,
Had I but kept mine early vow:

And if I smile, it is that now
    I see the promise of the years—
The garland waiting for my brow,
    That must be won with tears,
With pain—with death—I care not how.

                May 9, 1862.

THE WILLOW-TREE.

THE morn was bright, the steeds were light,
    The wedding guests were gay:
Young Ellen stood within the wood
    And watched them pass away.
She scarcely saw the gallant train:
    The tear-drop dimmed her ee:
Unheard the maiden did complain
    Beneath the Willow-Tree.

"Oh, Robin, thou didst love me well,
    Till, on a bitter day,
She came, the Lady Isabel,
    And stole thy heart away.

My tears are vain: I live again
  In days that used to be,
When I could meet thy welcome feet
  Beneath the Willow-Tree.

"Oh Willow gray, I may not stay
  Till Spring renew thy leaf;
But I will hide myself away,
  And nurse a lonely grief.
It shall not dim Life's joy for him:
  My tears he shall not see:
While he is by, I'll come not nigh
  My weeping Willow-Tree.

"But when I die, oh let me lie
  Beneath thy loving shade,
That he may loiter careless by,
  Where I am lowly laid.
And let the white white marble tell,
  If he should stoop to see,
'Here lies a maid that loved thee well,
  Beneath the Willow-Tree.'"

1859.

ONLY A WOMAN'S HAIR.

'ONLY a woman's hair'! Fling it aside!
  A bubble on Life's mighty stream:
Heed it not, man, but watch the broadening tide
    Bright with the western beam.

Nay! In those words there rings from other years
    The echo of a long low cry,
Where a proud spirit wrestles with its tears
    In loneliest agony.

And, as I touch that lock, strange visions throng
    Upon my soul with dreamy grace—
Of woman's hair, the theme of poet's song
    In every time and place.

A child's bright tresses, by the breezes kissed
    To sweet disorder as she flies,
Veiling, beneath a cloud of golden mist,
    Flushed cheek and laughing eyes—

Or fringing, like a shadow, raven-black,
    The glory of a queen-like face—
Or from a gipsy's sunny brow tossed back
    In wild and wanton grace—

Or crown-like on the hoary head of Age,
    Whose tale of life is well-nigh told—
Or, last, in dreams I make my pilgrimage
    To Bethany of old.

I see the feast—the purple and the gold—
    The gathering crowd of Pharisees,
Whose scornful eyes are centred to behold
    Yon woman on her knees.

The stifled sob rings strangely on mine ears,
    Wrung from the depth of sin's despair:
And still she bathes the sacred feet with tears,
    And wipes them with her hair.

He scorned not then the simple loving deed
    Of her, the lowest and the last;
Then scorn not thou, but use with earnest heed
    This relic of the past.

The eyes that loved it once no longer wake:
   So lay it by with reverent care—
Touching it tenderly for sorrow's sake—
   It is a woman's hair.

Feb. 17, 1862.

THE SAILOR'S WIFE.

SEE! There are tears upon her face—
   Tears newly shed, and scarcely dried:
Close, in an agonised embrace,
   She clasps the infant at her side.

Peace dwells in those soft-lidded eyes,
   Those parted lips that faintly smile—
Peace, the foretaste of Paradise,
   In heart too young for care or guile.

No peace that mother's features wear;
   But quivering lip, and knotted brow,
And broken mutterings, all declare
   The fearful dream that haunts her now.

The storm-wind, rushing through the sky,
   Wails from the depths of cloudy space;
Shrill, piercing as the seaman's cry
   When death and he are face to face.

Familiar tones are in the gale:
   They ring upon her startled ear:
And quick and low she pants the tale
   That tells of agony and fear:

"Still that phantom-ship is nigh—
   With a vexed and life-like motion,
All beneath an angry sky,
   Rocking on an angry ocean.

"Round the straining mast and shrouds
   Throng the spirits of the storm:
Darkly seen through driving clouds,
   Bends each gaunt and ghastly form.

"See! The good ship yields at last!
   Dumbly yields, and fights no more;
Driving, in the frantic blast,
   Headlong on the fatal shore.

"Hark! I hear her battered side,
   With a low and sullen shock,
Dashed, amid the foaming tide,
   Full upon a sunken rock.

"His face shines out against the sky,
   Like a ghost, so cold and white;
With a dead despairing eye
   Gazing through the gathered night.

"Is he watching, through the dark

Where a mocking ghostly hand
Points a faint and feeble spark
　　Glimmering from the distant land?

"Sees he, in this hour of dread,
　　Hearth and home and wife and child?
Loved ones who, in summers fled,
　　Clung to him and wept and smiled?

"Reeling sinks the fated bark
　　To her tomb beneath the wave:
Must he perish in the dark—
　　Not a hand stretched out to save?

"See the spirits, how they crowd!
　　Watching death with eyes that burn!
Waves rush in——" she shrieks aloud,
　　Ere her waking sense return.

The storm is gone: the skies are clear:
　　Hush'd is that bitter cry of pain:
The only sound, that meets her ear,
　　The heaving of the sullen main.

Though heaviness endure the night,
　　Yet joy shall come with break of day:
She shudders with a strange delight—
　　The fearful dream is pass'd away.

She wakes: the grey dawn streaks the dark:
　　With early song the copses ring:
Far off she hears the watch-dog bark
　　A joyful bark of welcoming!
　　　　　　　　　　　　Feb. 23, 1857.

AFTER THREE DAYS.

I STOOD within the gate
Of a great temple, 'mid the living stream
Of worshipers that thronged its regal state
　　Fair-pictured in my dream.

Jewels and gold were there;
And floors of marble lent a crystal sheen
To body forth, as in a lower air,
　　The wonders of the scene.

Such wild and lavish grace
Had whispers in it of a coming doom;

As richest flowers lie strown about the face
  Of her that waits the tomb.

  The wisest of the land
Had gathered there, three solemn trysting-days,
For high debate: men stood on either hand
  To listen and to gaze.

  The aged brows were bent,
Bent to a frown, half thought, and half annoy,
That all their stores of subtlest argument
  Were baffled by a boy.

  In each averted face
I marked but scorn and loathing, till mine eyes
Fell upon one that stirred not in his place,
  Tranced in a dumb surprise.

  Surely within his mind
Strange thoughts are born, until he doubts the lore
Of those old men, blind leaders of the blind,
  Whose kingdom is no more.

Surely he sees afar
A day of death the stormy future brings;
The crimson setting of the herald-star
 That led the Eastern kings.

Thus, as a sunless deep
Mirrors the shining heights that crown the bay,
So did my soul create anew in sleep
 The picture seen by day.

Gazers came and went—
A restless hum of voices marked the spot—
In varying shades of critic discontent
 Prating they knew not what.

"Where is the comely limb,
The form attuned in every perfect part,
The beauty that we should desire in him?"
 Ah! Fools and slow of heart!

Look into those deep eyes,
Deep as the grave, and strong with love divine;
Those tender, pure, and fathomless mysteries,
 That seem to pierce through thine.

Look into those deep eyes,
Stirred to unrest by breath of coming strife,
Until a longing in thy soul arise
 That this indeed were life:

That thou couldst find Him there,
Bend at His sacred feet thy willing knee,
And from thy heart pour out the passionate prayer,
 "Lord, let me follow Thee!"

But see the crowd divide:
Mother and sire have found their lost one now:
The gentle voice, that fain would seem to chide
 Whispers "Son, why hast thou"—

In tone of sad amaze—
"Thus dealt with us, that art our dearest thing?
Behold, thy sire and I, three weary days,
 Have sought thee sorrowing."

And I had stayed to hear
The loving words, "How is it that ye sought?"—
But that the sudden lark, with matins clear,
 Severed the links of thought.

Then over all there fell
Shadow and silence; and my dream was fled,
As fade the phantoms of a wizard's cell
   When the dark charm is said.

  Yet, in the gathering light,
I lay with half-shut eyes that would not wake,
Lovingly clinging to the skirts of night
   For that sweet vision's sake.

Feb. 16, 1861.

FACES IN THE FIRE.

THE night creeps onward, sad and slow:
In these red embers' dying glow
The forms of Fancy come and go.

An island-farm—broad seas of corn
Stirred by the wandering breath of morn—
The happy spot where I was born.

The picture fadeth in its place:
Amid the glow I seem to trace
The shifting semblance of a face.

'Tis now a little childish form—
Red lips for kisses pouted warm—
And elf-locks tangled in the storm.

'Tis now a grave and gentle maid,
At her own beauty half afraid,
Shrinking, and willing to be stayed.

Oh, Time was young, and Life was warm,
When first I saw that fairy-form,
Her dark hair tossing in the storm.

And fast and free these pulses played,
When last I met that gentle maid—
When last her hand in mine was laid.

Those locks of jet are turned to gray,
And she is strange and far away
That might have been mine own to-day—

That might have been mine own, my dear,
Through many and many a happy year—
That might have sat beside me here.

Ay, changeless through the changing scene,
The ghostly whisper rings between,
The dark refrain of 'might have been.'

The race is o'er I might have run:
The deeds are past I might have done;
And sere the wreath I might have won.

Sunk is the last faint flickering blaze:
The vision of departed days
Is vanished even as I gaze.

The pictures, with their ruddy light,
Are changed to dust and ashes white,
And I am left alone with night.

Jan., 1860.

A LESSON IN LATIN.

OUR Latin books, in motley row,
Invite us to our task—

Gay Horace, stately Cicero:
Yet there's one verb, when once we know,
  No higher skill we ask:
This ranks all other lore above—
We've learned "'*Amare*' means '*to love*'!"

So, hour by hour, from flower to flower,
  We sip the sweets of Life:
Till, all too soon, the clouds arise,
And flaming cheeks and flashing eyes
  Proclaim the dawn of strife:
With half a smile and half a sigh,
"*Amare! Bitter One!*" we cry.

Last night we owned, with looks forlorn,
  "Too well the scholar knows
There is no rose without a thorn"—
But peace is made! We sing, this morn,
  "No thorn without a rose!"
Our Latin lesson is complete:
We've learned that Love is Bitter-Sweet!

May, 1888.

PUCK LOST AND FOUND.

PUCK has fled the haunts of men:
  Ridicule has made him wary:
In the woods, and down the glen,
  No one meets a Fairy!

"Cream!" the greedy Goblin cries—
  Empties the deserted dairy—
Steals the spoons, and off he flies.
  Still we seek our Fairy!

Ah! What form is entering?
  Lovelit eyes and laughter airy!
Is not this a better thing,

Child, whose visit thus I sing,
   Even than a Fairy?

Nov. 22, 1891.

———————

PUCK has ventured back agen:
   Ridicule no more affrights him:
In the very haunts of men
   Newer sport delights him.

Capering lightly to and fro,
   Ever frolicking and funning—
"Crack!" the mimic pistols go!
   Hark! The noise is stunning!

All too soon will Childhood gay
   Realise Life's sober sadness.
Let's be merry while we may,
Innocent and happy Fay!
   Elves were made for gladness!

Nov. 25, 1891.

———————

THE END.

LEWIS CARROLL:

A BIOGRAPHICAL CHRONOLOGY

1832   Charles Lutwidge Dodgson born (January 27) at Daresbury Parsonage, Cheshire, the third of eleven children and the eldest son of the Reverend Charles Dodgson and Frances Jane Lutwidge Dodgson.

1843   Dodgson family moves to Croft Rectory, Yorkshire, when father becomes Rector.

1844–5   The young Charles attends the nearby Richmond Grammar School (from August 1) to prepare to enter a public school. Up until that time, he had been educated at home. At the Richmond School he earns high marks and receives good reports.

1845   Contributing poems and drawings, he produces the first of several family magazines, *Useful and Instructive Poetry;* he follows this with *The Rectory Magazine,* which he edits for his family (revising repeatedly until 1850) and to which he contributes stories, poems, and drawings.

1846–9   Attends Rugby School (from January 27), the celebrated public school. He does well but retains unhappy memories of the period. Continues to write creatively for his family, including a series of parodies, and also organizes marionette shows.

1850   Matriculates at Christ Church, Oxford (May 23). He continues his preparation for Oxford at home and contributes verse, drawings, and prose to another family magazine, *The Rectory Umbrella.*

1851   Takes up residence at Christ Church (January 24 until his death). His mother dies (January 26).

1852   Passes the first part of his examinations, doing exceptionally well in mathematics. He becomes a life member of Christ Church when he is made a Student (Fellow), a teacher attached to the college who is elected and paid by the college.

1854   Obtains his B.A. with First Class Honors in Mathematics and Second Class Honors in Classics. He begins to publish his humorous writing, contributing to the *Oxonian Advertiser* and the *Whitby Gazette*.

1855   Begins teaching duties at Christ Church as a Mathematical Lecturer (until 1881) and becomes Sub-Librarian, Christ Church (until 1857). He publishes some parodies in the *Comic Times* and composes the first stanza of "Jabberwocky," which he preserves in his scrapbook *Mischmasch*. His uncle Skeffington Lutwidge arouses his interest in photography; he composes "Photography Extraordinary." He also begins his lifelong practice of regularly attending the London theatre.

1856   "Lewis Carroll" appears in print for the first time; Edmund Yates, editor of *The Train*, selects the name from a list of potential pseudonyms submitted by Dodgson; several parodies by Carroll appear in the comic paper. He meets Alice Pleasance Liddell, the child of the Dean of Christ Church (April 24). He purchases a complete set of photographic equipment and takes his first successful photographs.

1857   Obtains M.A. degree. Meets Holman Hunt, John Ruskin, and William Makepeace Thackeray. Visits and photographs Tennyson and his family at Coniston, in the Lake District. He actively pursues his hobby of photography and writes "Hiawatha's Photographing."

1858   Exhibits four of his photographs in the fifth annual exhibition of the Photographic Society of London.

1860   Publishes "A Photographer's Day Out" in *South Shields Amateur Magazine, Rules for Court Circular,* and *A Syllabus of Plane Algebraical Geometry.*

1861   Ordained Deacon (December 22). Contributes to *College Rhymes*.

1862   Tells the story of Alice's adventures for the first time on an afternoon boating trip up the river Isis to Godstow in the company of Alice, Lorina, and Edith Liddell, and Robinson Duckworth (July 4). Begins to revise and write down *Alice's Adventures Under Ground* for Alice Liddell.

1863   Completes *Alice's Adventures Under Ground* and his friends, George MacDonald and his family, urge him to publish it. Meets and photographs Dante Gabriel and Christina Rossetti.

1864   John Tenniel agrees to illustrate, and Macmillan to publish, the expanded and retitled manuscript, *Alice's Adventures in Wonderland*. Presents Alice Liddell with the manuscript of *Alice's Adventures Under Ground*. Meets John Everett Millais and Arthur Hughes.

1865   Publishes *Alice's Adventures in Wonderland* (July), but withdraws it due to poor printing; the faulty sheets are shipped to America. Sends a presentation copy to Alice Liddell (July 4). A new edition of *Alice's Adventures in Wonderland* is published (November, but dated 1866). Publishes the satirical pamphlet *The Dynamics of a Parti-cle*.

1866   Publishes *Condensation of Determinants*. Meets Charlotte M. Yonge.

1867   Travels on the Continent to Russia with H. P. Liddon (July 13–September 14). Contributes "Bruno's Revenge," which contains the kernel of the *Sylvie and Bruno* books, to *Aunt Judy's Magazine*. Begins writing *Through the Looking-Glass and What Alice Found There*. Publishes *An Elementary Treatise on Determinants*.

1868   Father dies (June 21). As "head of the family" Dodgson acquires "The Chestnuts," Guildford, Surrey, for his sisters and moves the family. He himself moves to new rooms in Tom Quad, Christ Church, which he occupies until his death.

1869   Publishes *Phantasmagoria and Other Poems*.

1871   Completes *Through the Looking-Glass and What Alice Found There*, which John Tenniel reluctantly illustrates. The volume is published in December in time for Christmas (although dated 1872).

1872   Becomes involved in a university controversy over Dean Liddell's architectural plans and anonymously publishes a strong attack on Liddell's position in the first of his political pamphlets, *The New Belfry of Christ Church, Oxford*. Has a glass house built on top of Tom Quad to facilitate taking photographs.

1873   Publishes another Oxford political pamphlet, *Vision of the Three T's*. Develops *Sylvie and Bruno*, telling stories to Maud and Gwendolen Cecil at Hatfield House.

1874   Begins *The Hunting of the Snark* when the last line "For the Snark *was* a Boojum, you see" suddenly came into his head during a walk on a hillside near Guildford. Publishes several mathematical works under his real name and *Notes by an Oxford Chiel*, a collection of six pamphlets (five previously published), anonymously.

1875   Works on and completes the *Snark* during the summer at Sandown, Isle of Wight, where he meets a new child-friend, Gertrude Chataway, to whom he dedicates the poem. Publishes "Some Popular Fallacies about Vivisection" in the *Fortnightly Review*.

1876   Publishes *The Hunting of the Snark* (March), illustrated by Henry Holiday.

1877   Takes up summer lodgings (July 31) for the first time at the shore in Eastbourne, where he spends subsequent Augusts until his death.

1879   Publishes *Euclid and his Modern Rivals* under his own name.

1880   Gives up his hobby of photography without explanation.

1881   Resigns Mathematical Lectureship (but retains Studentship) in order to devote more time to writing.

1882   Elected Curator of the Senior Common Room, Christ Church (December 8, 1882 to February 21, 1892).

1883   Publishes a collection of verses, mostly old ones, as *Rhyme? and Reason?*, with new illustrations by A. B. Frost.

1884   Begins publishing a series of pamphlets on proportional representation.

1885   Publishes *A Tangled Tale*, which originally appeared in the *Monthly Packet*, in book form with illustrations by Arthur B. Frost.

1886   Publishes a facsimile edition of *Alice's Adventures Under Ground*. A stage version of *Alice in Wonderland* by Savile Clarke appears at the Prince of Wales Theatre, London (December 23). Lectures at one of the women's colleges at Oxford, Lady Margaret Hall.

1887   Publishes *The Game of Logic* (February); an edition printed the previous December was withdrawn due to poor printing and shipped to America. Publishes "Alice on the Stage" in *The Theatre*. Teaches logic in a girls' senior high school in Oxford.

1888   Publishes, under his own name, *Curiosa Mathematica, Part I,* a new theory of parallels and an analysis and attempt to improve Euclid's axiom about two lines unequally inclined to a transversal.

1889   Publishes *Sylvie and Bruno* with a dedicatory acrostic to his child-friend Isa Bowman, who played Alice in the 1888 revival of Savile Clarke's stage version of *Alice in Wonderland*.

1890   Publishes *The Nursery "Alice"* for very young children. Invents "The Wonderland Postage-Stamp Case."

1892   Resigns Curatorship of Senior Common Room, Christ Church.

1893   Publishes *Sylvie and Bruno Concluded* and *Curiosa Mathematica, Part II (Pillow Problems)*, and *Syzgyies and Lanrick: A Word-Puzzle and a Game for Two Players*.

1894   Publishes in *Mind* "A Logical Paradox" and "What the Tortoise Said to Achilles," problems (largely in the form of dialogues) involving hypothetical propositions.

1896   Publishes *Symbolic Logic, Part I: Elementary* (February 21). (A reconstructed *Part II: Advanced* was published for the first time in 1976.)

1898   Develops bronchitis and dies (January 14) at Guildford, where he is buried. *Three Sunsets and Other Poems*, a collection of previously published poems, which were at the printer at the time of his death, is published posthumously.

SELECTED BIBLIOGRAPHY OF BOOKS

Works, Diaries, and Letters

The Complete Works of Lewis Carroll. New York: Random House; London: Nonesuch Press, 1939; New York: Vintage (paperback), 1976. The Nonesuch/Modern Library edition, despite its title, is far from complete; still, a most useful anthology.

Alice in Wonderland: Authoritative Texts of Alice's Adventures in Wonderland, Through the Looking-Glass, The Hunting of the Snark / Backgrounds / Essays in Criticism. Ed., Donald Gray. A Norton Critical Edition. New York: Norton, 1971.

The Annotated Alice: Alice's Adventures in Wonderland and Through the Looking-Glass. Ed., Martin Gardner. New York: Clarkson N. Potter, 1960.

The Annotated Snark: The Full Text of Lewis Carroll's Great Nonsense Epic "The Hunting of the Snark" and the Original Illustrations by Henry Holiday. Ed., Martin Gardner. 1962; revised edition included in *The Hunting of the Snark*. Los Altos, California: William Kaufmann, Inc., 1981.

The Wasp in a Wig: A "Suppressed" Episode of Through the Looking-Glass and what Alice found there. Ed., Martin Gardner. New York: Lewis Carroll Society of North America; London: Macmillan; New York: Clarkson N. Potter, 1977.

The Rectory Umbrella and Mischmasch. 1932; rpt. New York: Dover, 1971. Two of Dodgson's juvenile family magazines.

Useful and Instructive Poetry. London: Geoffrey Bles, 1954. Dodgson's early (1845) poetry.

The Rectory Magazine. Austin: Univ. of Texas Press, 1975. One of Dodgson's juvenile family magazines.

Lewis Carroll's Symbolic Logic. Pt. 1: *Elementary,* 1896. 5th ed. Pt. 2: *Advanced, Never Previously Published.* Ed., William Warren Bartley, III. New York: Clarkson N. Potter, 1977.

The Diaries of Lewis Carroll. Ed., Roger Lancelyn Green. 2 vols. London: Cassell, 1953; New York: Oxford Univ. Press, 1954.

The Russian Journal and Other Selections from the Works of Lewis Carroll. Ed., John Francis McDermott. 1935; rpt. New York: Dover, 1977. Contains Dodgson's journal of his trip to Russia in 1867.

The Letters of Lewis Carroll. Ed., Morton N. Cohen with the assistance of Roger Lancelyn Green. 2 vols. London: Macmillan; New York: Oxford Univ. Press, 1979.

Lewis Carroll and the Kitchins: Containing Twenty-five Letters Not Previously Published and Nineteen of His Photographs. Ed., Morton N. Cohen. New York: Argosy Bookstore; also The Lewis Carroll Society of North America, 1980.

BIBLIOGRAPHY AND REFERENCE

Guiliano, Edward. *Lewis Carroll: An Annotated International Bibliography.* Charlottesville: Univ. Press of Virginia; Brighton, England: Harvester Press, 1980.

Ovenden, Graham, ed. *The Illustrators of Alice in Wonderland.* Introduction by John Davis. London: Academy; New York: St. Martin's, 1979.

Stern, Jeffrey, ed. *Lewis Carroll's Library.* Carroll Studies No. 5. New York: Lewis Carroll Society of North America, distributed by the Univ. Press of Virginia, 1981.

Weaver, Warren. *Alice in Many Tongues: The Translations of Alice in Wonderland.* Madison: Univ. of Wisconsin Press, 1964.

Williams, Sidney Herbert, Falconer Madan, Roger Green, and Denis Crutch. *The Lewis Carroll Handbook.* Revised edition. Folkestone, England: Dawson; Hamden, Conn.: Archon Books, 1979.

BIOGRAPHY

Bowman, Isa. *Lewis Carroll as I Knew Him.* Introduction by Morton N. Cohen. New York: Dover, 1972. Reprint, with new introduction, of the 1899 *The Story of Lewis Carroll Told for Young People by the Real Alice in Wonderland.* Isa Bowman was a child-friend of Dodgson who played Alice in the Savile Clarke theatrical adaption of the *Alice* books.

Clark, Ann. *Lewis Carroll: A Biography.* London: Dent; New York: Schocken Books, 1979. The first full biography written with access to Dodgson's ms. diaries and to a transcript of the *Letters of Lewis Carroll.*

Collingwood, Stuart Dodgson. *The Life and Letters of Lewis Carroll*. 1899; rpt. Detroit: Gale, 1967. The family biography, written by Dodgson's nephew; still valuable.

Gattégno, Jean. *Lewis Carroll: Fragments of a Looking-Glass*. New York: Crowell, 1976. A collection of biographical essays organized by theme. Translation of a biography which first appeared in French in 1974.

Greenacre, Phyllis. *Swift and Carroll: A Psychoanalytic Study of Two Lives*. New York: International Universities Press, 1955.

Hudson, Derek. *Lewis Carroll: An Illustrated Biography*. London: Constable, 1976; New York: Clarkson N. Potter, 1977. Update of 1954 edition and still considered the best biography available.

Lennon, Florence Becker. *The Life of Lewis Carroll: Victoria Through the Looking-Glass*. Revised edition. New York: Dover; London: Constable, 1972. First published in 1945.

Pudney, John. *Lewis Carroll and His World*. London: Thames & Hudson; New York: Charles Scribner's Sons, 1976. Pictorial biography.

Reed, Langford. *The Life of Lewis Carroll*. London: W. & G. Foyle, 1932.

Wood, James Playstead. *The Snark was a Boojum: A Life of Lewis Carroll*. New York: Pantheon, 1966. Intended for adolescents; contains drawings by David Levine.

PHOTOGRAPHY

Cohen, Morton N. *Lewis Carroll's Photographs of Nude Children*. Philadelphia: The Philip H. & A.S.W. Rosenbach Foundation, 1978; New York; Clarkson N. Potter, 1979.

Gernsheim, Helmut. *Lewis Carroll: Photographer*. 1949; rpt. New York: Dover; London: Peter Smith, 1969.

Lewis Carroll at Christ Church. Introduction by Morton N. Cohen. London: The National Portrait Gallery, 1974.

COMMENTARIES

Blake, Kathleen. *Play, Games, and Sport: The Literary Works of Lewis Carroll*. London and Ithaca, New York: Cornell Univ. Press, 1974.

Gattégno, Jean. *Lewis Carroll*. Paris: José Corti, 1970. In French.

Guiliano, Edward, ed. *Lewis Carroll: A Celebration*. New York: Clarkson N. Potter, 1982. A collection of fifteen new essays by various authors on diverse aspects of Carroll's life and art. Contains photographs and illustrations.

Guiliano, Edward, ed. *Lewis Carroll Observed*. New York: Clarkson N. Potter, 1976. Another anthology of fifteen new essays. Illustrations.

Guiliano, Edward, and James R. Kincaid, eds. *Soaring with the Dodo: Essays on Lewis Carroll's Life and Art*. Charlottesville: LCSNA and Univ. Press of Virginia, 1982. Contains photographs and illustrations.

Heath, Peter, ed. *The Philosopher's Alice: Alice's Adventures in Wonderland & Through the Looking-Glass*. An annotated edition of the *Alice* books from a philosophical perspective.

Kelly, Richard. *Lewis Carroll*. Boston: Twayne, 1977.

Parisot, Henri, ed. *Lewis Carroll*. Cahiers de l'Herne 17. Paris: Edition de l'Herne, 1971. Collection of diverse essays in French.

Phillips, Robert, ed. *Aspects of Alice: Lewis Carroll's Dreamchild as seen through the Critic's Looking-Glass, 1865–1971*. New York: Vanguard, 1971; London: Gollancz, 1972; Harmondsworth, England: Penguin (paperback), 1974; New York: Vintage (paperback), 1977. Valuable anthology of criticism of the *Alice*s.

Reichert, Klaus. *Lewis Carroll—Studien zum literarischen Unsinn*. Munich: Carl Hanser, 1974. Philosophical, psychoanalytical, and linguistic analysis of Carroll's nonsense; in German.

Sewell, Elizabeth. *The Field of Nonsense*. London: Chatto and Windus, 1952.

Sutherland, Robert D. *Language and Lewis Carroll*. The Hague: Mouton, 1970.

Taylor, Alexander L. *The White Knight: A Study of C. L. Dodgson (Lewis Carroll)*. Edinburgh: Oliver & Boyd, 1952.

JORGE LUIS BORGES

JORGE LUIS BORGES

A Literary Biography

Emir Rodriguez Monegal

E.P. DUTTON • NEW YORK

*This book is dedicated
to all the sisters of
Clementina Villar and Beatriz Viterbo,
and especially to
the one who is
"dark, despotic, and beautiful."*

Contents

Eight pages of photographs follow page 278

Part One

1.
The Family Museum

Borges once said that for years he believed he had been brought up on the outskirts of Buenos Aires in "a suburb of adventurous streets and visible sunsets." But, he added, "the truth is that I grew up in a garden, behind a speared railing, and in a library of unlimited English books" (*Carriego,* 1955, p. 9).* Years later he simplified the account of his life further by stating: "If I were asked to name the chief event in my life, I should say my father's library. In fact, sometimes I think I have never strayed outside that library" ("Essay," 1970, p. 209).

Borges' imaginary life finds its roots in this library, and, up to a point, it would be possible to write his literary biography without leaving that magic space of "unlimited English books." But the truth is more complex: Borges lived, simultaneously, inside and outside of his father's library; he was an inhabitant of an imaginary world created by books in English and of a real world, a Buenos Aires district with an Italian name, Palermo, where, in a house with a garden, he actually spent his childhood.

Borges was born in 1899 in a house at 840 Tucumán Street, close to the downtown area. It was a "small unassuming" house: "Like most of the houses of that day, it had a flat roof; a long, arched entranceway, called a *zaguán;* a cistern where we got our water; and two patios" (ibid., p. 203). This house, which years later his sister, Norah, depicted in her drawings and paintings, belonged to his mother's parents. Borges' mother had been born there in 1876.

Both maternal grandparents were still alive at the turn of the century, when Georgie—as he was called at home—was born. In his

*See the Bibliography for full data.

3

younger years the grandfather, Isidoro de Acevedo Laprida, had fought in the civil war against Rosas, the "tyrant" who ruled Argentina from 1835 to 1852. Later Don Isidoro retired to a long, secluded life at home. Borges knew very little of him. In his poem "Isidoro Acevedo," he admits he has only a few dates and place names to remember his grandfather by: "Frauds and failings of the words." But what he knew was enough. He knew that in dying, in 1905, his grandfather had relived his distant days and met the death of a hero.

> While a lung ailment ate away at him
> and hallucinatory fevers distorted the face of the day,
> he assembled the burning documents of his memory
> for the forging of his dream.
> . . . .
> In the visionary defense of his country that his faith
>   hungered for (and not that his fever imposed)
> he plundered his days
> and rounded up an army of Buenos Aires ghosts
> so as to get himself killed in the fighting.
>
> That was how, in a bedroom that looked onto the garden,
> he died out of devotion for his city.
>   (*Poems,* 1972, translated by
>   Norman Thomas di Giovanni, pp. 53–55)

The poem also documents Georgie's incredulity at the news of his grandfather's death, the first he had experienced.

> It was in the metaphor of a journey that I was told
>   of his death, and I did not believe it.
> I was a boy, who knew nothing of dying; I was immortal,
> and afterward for days I searched the sunless rooms for him.
>   (Ibid., p. 55)

Many years later Borges based one of his stories, "The Other Death," on his grandfather's last dream. Since it was customary then for young couples to live with their relatives during the first years of marriage, Jorge Guillermo and Leonor were staying at her parents' home when their first child was born. Some six years before his grandfather's death, in the winter of 1899—August 24 to be precise—Jorge Luis had been born, prematurely, in the eighth month of his mother's pregnancy. As blindness was endemic in the Borges family, Borges' father, who had very poor eyesight, made sure to examine his son's eyes. He discovered that the baby had blue eyes, like his wife. "He is saved," he told her. "He has your eyes." When Borges' mother told me this anecdote in 1971, she apparently was not aware that all babies have blue eyes. His father was also wrong in his hopeful prediction: Georgie would be affected, like him, with near blindness for the better part of his life; he is the sixth generation of the Borgeses to be so afflicted.

For a while the family had no worries. A second child, a daughter, Norah, was born in 1901. In photographs of the time both parents look splendid, thriving and fashionable.

Georgie never addressed his parents as Mummy and Daddy. He always used the formal Mother and Father, a traditional form that suggests the Victorian household. Both parents came from old families, established in South America since the time of the Spanish conquest. On her paternal side, Mother was related to Francisco Narciso de Laprida, who presided in 1816 over the Congress of Tucumán, which declared Argentine independence. He died in 1829, in an early civil war. More than a century later Borges dedicated to him his "Conjectural Poem," in which he presents Laprida evoking his own death at the hands of the rebellious gauchos and contrasts his own destiny with Laprida's savage end:

> I who longed to be someone else, to weigh
> judgments, to read books, to hand down the law,
> will lie in the open out in these swamps;
> but a secret joy somehow swells my breast.
> I see at last that I am face to face
> with my South American destiny.
> I was carried to this ruinous hour
> by the intricate labyrinth of steps
> woven by my days from a day that goes
> back to my birth. At last I've discovered
> the mysterious key to all my years,
> the fate of Francisco de Laprida,
> the missing letter, the perfect pattern
> that was known to God from the beginning.
> In this night's mirror I can comprehend
> my unsuspected true face. The circle's
> about to close. I wait to let it come.
>
> My feet tread the shadows of the lances
> that spar for the kill. The taunts of my death,
> the horses, the horsemen, the horses' manes,
> tighten the ring around me . . . Now for the first
> blow, the lance's hard steel ripping my chest,
> and across my throat the intimate knife.
> (*Poems,* 1972, translated by
> Norman Thomas di Giovanni, pp. 83–85)

Mother's maternal grandfather, Colonel Isidoro Suárez, had also fought in the war of independence and went into exile in Uruguay at the time of the Rosas dictatorship. He married into a Uruguayan family, the Haedos, which had been very active in political and artistic life. Borges later dedicated a poem to him. Titled "A Page to Commemorate Colonel Suárez, Victor at Junín," the poem refers, like others devoted to the family pantheon of heroes, to a single instant: the heroic deed at Junín that the old man continuously reenacts. But there is a difference. At the very end of the poem the distant past is suddenly made present, and Borges' ancestor's fight is made one with the fight against another unnamed dictator ruling Argentina in 1953:

> His great-grandson is writing these lines,
> and a silent voice comes to him out of the past,
> out of the blood:
>
> "What does my battle at Junín matter if it is only
> a glorious memory, or a date learned by rote
> for an examination, or a place in the atlas?
> The battle is everlasting and can do without
> the pomp of actual armies and of trumpets.
> Junín is two civilians cursing a tyrant
> on a street corner
> or an unknown man somewhere, dying in prison."
> (Ibid., translated by Alastair Reid, p. 91)

Borges' family piety reflects his mother's attitude toward her ancestors. Georgie was born and brought up in a house that was, up to a point, a family museum, presided over by the almost ghostly presence of grandfather Acevedo. The place of honor went to the swords that had liberated South America at Junín and Cepeda; the uniforms were carefully preserved against injury from moths; the daguerreotypes framed in black velvet memorialized a parade of dark, sad gentlemen or reserved ladies, many of them prematurely widowed. Georgie was surrounded by the sacred objects of family history and the ritual repetition of the deeds of his heroic ancestors. These stories of courage and silent dignity in defeat, of poverty and pride, were a permanent part of his heritage. Many years later he was to acknowledge: "On both sides of my family, I have military forebears; this may account for my yearning after that epic destiny which my gods denied me, no doubt wisely" ("Essay," 1970, p. 208).

Father belonged to an even older family. One of his ancestors, Jerónimo Luis de Córdoba, was the founder of Córdoba, the most traditional and Catholic of Argentine cities, the one most like Boston in the history of the United States. For the traditional Cordobeses, Buenos Aires will always be, like New York for Bostonians, the immigrant's city. It is populated mainly by poor foreigners, illiterate Spaniards and Italians not worthy of representing European culture. But Father himself had not been born in Córdoba. In the nineteenth century the family had moved closer to the Buenos Aires area. His own father had been born in Paraná, Entre Ríos, and at the time Father was born Grandfather Borges was a colonel in the Santa Fe garrison, in the pampas. Both provinces belonged to a more primitive and simple world: the frontier between the Argentine settlers and the still unruly Indians. From Entre Ríos came the caudillo (chieftain) Justo José de Urquiza, the man who in 1852 finally defeated Rosas at Pavón.

Father was not so devoted to the memory of his heroic ancestors as Mother was. But he maintained interest in the political struggle in Paraná; and in 1921, when he was retired and living in Spain, he wrote a curiously anachronistic novel, *El caudillo* (The Chieftain), which recaptures the romantic climate of violence, intrigue, and passion that surrounded so many Borges males during the civil wars.

On his mother's side, Father had a completely different tradition. Frances Haslam had been born in 1845 in Staffordshire, England, of Northumbrian stock. Borges has described her arrival in Argentina:

> A rather unlikely set of circumstances brought her to South America. Fanny Haslam's elder sister married an Italian-Jewish engineer named Jorge Suárez, who brought the first horse-drawn tramcars to Argentina, where he and his wife settled and sent for Fanny. I remember an anecdote concerning this venture. Suárez was a guest at General Urquiza's "palace" in Entre Ríos, and very improvidently won his first game of cards with the General, who was the stern dictator of that province and not above throat-cutting. When the game was over, Suárez was told by alarmed fellow guests that if he wanted the license to run his tramcars in the province, it was expected of him to lose a certain amount of gold coins each night. Urquiza was such a poor player that Suárez had a great deal of trouble losing the appointed sums.
>
> It was in Paraná, the capital city of Entre Ríos, that Fanny Haslam met Colonel Francisco Borges. This was in 1870 or 1871, during the siege of the city by the *montoneros,* or gaucho militia of Ricardo López Jordán. Borges, riding at the head of his regiment, commanded the troops defending the city. Fanny Haslam saw him from the flat roof of her house; that very night a ball was given to celebrate the arrival of the government relief forces. Fanny and the Colonel met, danced, fell in love, and eventually married. ("Essay," 1970, pp. 204–205)

Colonel Francisco Borges was twelve years older than his wife. Very little is known about the marriage except that they seemed happy and had two sons. Father was the younger. In 1874 Colonel Borges was killed by a Remington rifle in one of the civil wars. He was barely forty-one. His grandson discovered an irony in his death:

> In the complicated circumstances surrounding his defeat at La Verde, he rode out slowly on horseback, wearing a white poncho and followed by ten or twelve of his men, toward the enemy lines, where he was struck by two Remington bullets. This was the first time Remington rifles were used in the Argentine, and it tickles my fancy to think that the firm that shaves me every morning bears the same name as the one that killed my grandfather. (Ibid., pp. 205–206)

The stories his grandmother told him about living on the frontier resurfaced many years later in "The Story of the Warrior and the Captive." The first half summarizes and expands on a story taken from different European sources (Croce, Gibbon, Dante); the second half is based on one of Fanny Haslam's frontier tales. An English girl, taken by the Indians in one of their raids, is forced to marry a warrior and is converted to barbarism. Grandmother had met her briefly at the army post her husband commanded and had tried to persuade her to return to civilization. She failed, and the girl went back to her man and two children. In the conclusion of the story Borges explores one of the meanings of this symbolic confrontation between the two English exiles: "Perhaps the two women felt for an instant as sisters; they were far from their beloved island and in an incredible country; . . . perhaps then my grandmother was able to perceive in this other woman, also held captive and transformed by the implacable continent, a monstrous mirror of her own destiny" (*Labyrinths*, 1964; p. 130). In a sense, the story is right: Fanny Haslam was also a captive. Although she had married a colonel and a gentleman, and she had been able to preserve her native tongue and even to transmit it to her sons and grandchildren, she still was a captive in a primitive and violent land, imprisoned forever in a world dominated by an alien tongue.

Her husband's death left Fanny Haslam very much on her own. She had two sons to care for and bring up. Undaunted, she opened her home to paying guests, young American women who came to Argentina to teach under an educational program conceived by President Sarmiento when he visited the United States. Borges does not tell this part of his grandmother's story in his "Autobiographical Essay"; nor has he ever mentioned it in his interviews. He prefers to emphasize the less prosaic details of her life, the frontier adventures. But although not picturesque, Fanny Haslam's solid Victorian upbringing saved the day. She managed to keep the family within the bounds of middle-class respectability and saw to it that both her sons had a position in life. The elder followed in his father's footsteps and became a naval officer; Father became a lawyer. Perhaps the fact that Father inherited the Borges blindness explains the choice of a civil career. The consequence of this decision was that he was to remain very much under his mother's influence; that is, under the British influence. This was decisive for his son's fate.

Although Father was proud of his English ancestry and especially of English culture, he was not a fanatic. Borges has pointed out that "he used to joke about it, saying with feigned perplexity, 'After all, what are the English? Just a pack of German agriculture laborers' " ("Essay," 1970, p. 206). Borges writes:

> My father, Jorge Guillermo Borges, worked as a lawyer. He was a philosophical anarchist—a disciple of Spencer's—and also a teacher of psychology at the Normal School for Modern Languages, where he gave his course in English, using as his text William James' shorter book of psychology. . . .
>
> My father was very intelligent and, like all intelligent men, very kind. Once, he told me that I should take a good look at soldiers, uniforms, barracks, flags, churches, priests, and butcher shops, since all these things were about to disappear, and I could tell my children that I had actually seen them. The prophecy has not yet come true, unfortunately. My father was such a modest man that he would have liked being invisible. . . . His idols were Shelley, Keats, and Swinburne. As a reader, he had two interests. First, books on metaphysics and psychology (Berkeley, Hume, Royce, and William James). Second, literature and books about the East (Lane, Burton, and Payne). It was he who revealed the power of poetry to me—the fact that words are not only a means of communication but also magic symbols and music. . . . He also, without my being aware of it, gave me my first lessons in philosophy. When I was still quite young, he showed me, with the aid of a chessboard, the paradoxes of Zeno—Achilles and the tortoise, the unmoving flight of the arrow, the impossibility of motion. Later, without mentioning Berkeley's name, he did his best to teach me the rudiments of idealism. (Ibid., pp. 204–207)

By his ancestors, by his double cultural origins, Father at once confirmed and modified Mother's familial museum. He added more colonial prototypes and more army brass to the pantheon, more vivid memories of heroic deeds. He also incorporated an element that was totally absent in Mother's piety: irony, a mind gifted with the most elegant skepticism. Georgie inherited this gift.

2.
The Personal
Myth

From his father's side, the family museum, this private *pietas,* was seen through very ironic glasses. In a book-length interview with Jean de Milleret, Borges has explained his peculiar interpretation of the family tradition. While he readily admits that the Borgeses can be traced back to the Spanish conquerors, his own pantheon does not go back that far: "I am so much an Argentine that I can't really be interested in my distant ancestors, those who came before 1810. You know that I never talk about them . . . I am also very ignorant of their lives. Besides, they were people with very little intelligence, Spanish professional soldiers, and from Old Spain" (De Milleret, 1967, p. 203). In contrast to Mother's attitude of family worship—the carefully preserved genealogical tree, the daguerreotypes, the sacred swords and uniforms—Borges' dismissal of the family's colonial inheritance reflects Father's sense of irony and subtle understatement. The difference was rooted in the conflict between Spanish and English values, a conflict that culminated in the wars between England and Spain but did not end there: in Latin America it is alive today.

For the boy, that conflict must have been muted by affection, buried in the deepest and darkest layers of subconscious feeling. In the everyday experience of life at home, as in a childish charade, Georgie was confronted by the cultural abyss that separated his father's side of the family from his mother's. Some sixty years later, in the same long interview, Borges gives his view of his mother's family: "The Acevedos are incredibly ignorant. For instance, for them, descendants of the old Spanish settlers, to be a Protestant is synonymous with being a Jew, that is, an atheist, or a freethinker, or a heretic; in short, they put everything in the same bag. There is no real difference between these words

10

for them" (ibid., p. 39). It is obvious that Borges is here simplifying and exaggerating the Acevedos' prejudices, which mirrored those of many ignorant Argentine Catholics. But it is the irreverent tone that is particularly significant. It makes explicit Georgie's subconscious reaction to the two sides of his family.

Borges later defined the traditional character of the Acevedos by stating: "When I was growing up, religion belonged to women and children; most men in Buenos Aires were freethinkers—though, had they been asked, they might have called themselves Catholic" ("Essay," 1970, p. 207). Although irony is absent here, it is evident that Borges is subtly antagonistic to his mother's religious stand. In the same essay, Borges praises what he calls his mother's "hospitable mind." To illustrate that hospitality, he writes: "From the time she learned English, through my father, she has done most of her reading in that language" (ibid., p. 207). English is once more presented as a certificate of culture, of an open and hospitable mind, to be opposed implicitly to the narrow, ignorant, Catholic mind of the Acevedos. But Borges also remarks on the limitations of the cult of Englishness: "My fondness for such a Northern past has been resented by some of my countrymen, who dub me an Englishman, but I hardly need point out that many things English are utterly alien to me: tea, the Royal Family, 'manly' sports, the worship of every line written by the uncaring Shakespeare" (ibid., p. 252). Thus, in recollection at least, Borges seems equally distant to both the Spanish and the English sides of his family.

Borges' memory in the "Autobiographical Essay" is selective. He makes no mention of his Portuguese origins. His surname is undoubtedly Portuguese: Borges means a citizen of the *burgos,* or cities, a bourgeois. In a late poem called "The Borges" he refers to these unknown ancestors:

> My Portuguese forebears. They were a ghostly race,
> Who still play in my body their mysterious
> Disciplines, habits, and anxieties.
> Indecipherably they form a part
> Of time, of earth, and of oblivion.
> $\qquad$ (*Poems,* 1972, translated by Alastair Reid, p. 137)

In a 1970 interview for the Brazilian weekly *Veja* Borges dwells on these shadowy Portuguese ancestors and on the possibility that through them he may be connected with the wandering tribes of Israel. He asks rhetorically:

I, Borges Ramalho, descendant of a Portuguese sailor and, on top of that, having a mother called Acevedo: might I not be a Jew? . . . When I visited

11

Lisbon many years ago, I tried to do some research on my origins. I looked into the phone book and got the scare of my life: all the people there were my relatives, because those who were not Borges were Ramalho or Acevedo! I didn't know I had such a family and just in Lisbon! . . . Whatever the case, I would be very proud to belong to one of the civilized races in the world, to a branch of humanity that had already invented Job's story and *The Song of Songs* while other countries were still submerged in the original barbarism. (Ribeiro, 1970, pp. 4–5)

The question of Borges' Jewish origins, lightly and humorously touched on here, was a very sensitive one in Argentina, especially in the 1930s and 1940s, when the army was aping the Italians and Germans and the Church and the upper classes were solidly anti-Semitic. In those days a nationalistic magazine called *Crisol* (The Crucible) accused Borges of being a Jew. He thereupon wrote a piece for the journal *Megáfono* entitled "I, a Jew," which is a masterpiece of teasing. He begins by stating that he has played more than once with the idea that he had some Jewish ancestors; he admits that Acevedo is generally included in a list of surnames of Jewish origin compiled by an Argentine historian who was trying to prove that practically all the families in Rosas' time had a "Jewish-Portuguese" ancestry. On the other hand, research done by a member of his family had proved that the Acevedos came not from Portugal but from Spain—and, to be more precise, from Catalonia. He concludes then that it is a hopeless task to try to prove his Jewish ancestry. Apart from the ironic value of this "search," it is obvious that Borges did not take the question seriously. Not a word is said about the obvious Portuguese origin of his surname, which could have helped to establish the missing Jewish link. But in ambiguously denying his ancestors (which he recognizes in 1970), Borges aimed to destroy the basis of the accusation. The end of the article presents a new argument:

Statistically speaking, the Jews were very few. What would we think of some-one in the year 4000 who discovers everywhere descendants of the inhabi-tants of the San Juan province [one of the least populated in Argentina]? Our inquisitors are seeking Hebrews, never Phoenicians, Numidians, Scyth-ians, Babylonians, Huns, Vandals, Ostrogoths, Ethiopians, Illyrians, Paph-lagonians, Sarmatians, Medes, Ottomans, Berbers, Britons, Lybians, Cy-clops, and Lapiths. The nights of Alexandria, Babylon, Carthage, Memphis have never succeeded in engendering one single grandfather: only the tribes of the bituminous Black Sea had that power. (*Megáfono*, April 1934, p. 10)

In poking fun at the Fascist obsession with Jewish ancestors as proof of some obscure blemish or original sin, Borges even includes the mythological Cyclops and Lapiths among the old tribes who failed to engender one grandfather. His jokes advance the main object of the article: to demythify the subject once and for all. If to be a Jew means that somewhere in the past a Jewish ancestor looms, then who can be sure, in Spain and Portugal, in Latin America, of not having at least one great-grandfather of that origin? From that point of view, to be a Jew has no meaning. An irony revealed by Borges' "research" must not be overlooked. It is the very Catholic and traditional branch of the Acevedos that seems the most likely carrier of the Jewish blood into Borges' ancestry—they who shared, with the nationalist and the Fascist in Argentina, the cult of the universal religion of Rome and who believed that any freethinker, any Protestant, any mason, was a Jew. Such ignorance turned Borges from his mother's side of the family.

It is obvious that this aspect of the family conflict was not self-evident to Georgie, at least in his childhood. Although his father was an agnostic and his paternal grandmother a Protestant, he was probably brought up as a Catholic in a Catholic household. Religious instruction, if any, was in his mother's hands, and his father probably accepted it. But if the conflict was not evident at that stage, it was nevertheless part of the personal myth Georgie was already developing. If English was the language of culture, Spanish was to become the language associated with the deeds of arms and the gods of war. In constantly being reminded of the family past, in hearing once and again the tales of brave feats accomplished especially by the Suárezes and the Acevedos, Georgie was initiated into another religion: the worship of the family gods and of manly courage. In this religion the differences between Father's and Mother's side were erased: all ancestors were united in the family cult. In his "Autobiographical Essay" Borges indicates explicitly how Georgie reacted to this heroic ancestry: "I was always very nearsighted and wore glasses, and I was rather frail. As most of my people had been soldiers . . . and I knew I would never be, I felt ashamed, quite early, to be a bookish kind of person and not a man of action" ("Essay," 1970, p. 208).

The two sides of the Borges household represent, as in an allegorical tableau, the famous contrast between arms and letters, a topic to which Don Quixote had something to add. Although on both sides of the family Georgie had professional soldiers, it was the Acevedo branch that at the time of his birth offered vivid examples. The only grandfather still living was Isidoro de Acevedo Laprida, who had fought so bravely and died in a dream of battles long ago. On his father's side what prevailed was not the image of Colonel Francisco Borges (who died twenty-five years before Georgie was born) but that of Fanny Haslam, the English grandmother who held the key to the world of En-

13

glish and of English books, the world of culture. Father himself was a lawyer and a man of books, the owner of that infinite library.

The personal myth of Borges begins here: it is, at the same time, a myth of despair at not having been a man of arms and a myth of compensation. The reader and the writer found in books, in the desire and guilt aroused by books, what was lacking in his "real" life. Because Father had preceded him in this path—he too was a descendant of warriors who chose books and the law—Borges would have to find, many years later, a solution to the latent Oedipal conflict. In his case, parricide would assume a most unexpected disguise: total submission to his father's will.

3.
The Act of
Reading

Borges learned to read English before he could read Spanish. He first read *Don Quixote* in English translation. From the very beginning the English language was inseparably related to the act of reading. For Georgie, it was the code that gave him access to the world of books. That world, limited only by the imagination, came to be more fabulous than the real world. Here lies the origin of his personal myth and of his well-known predilection for British—and, by extension, North American—letters. At the same time, something more important also originated here: the dual emotions of desire and guilt that haunted the child and later the writer.

Borges' familiarity with English and English letters did not make him an English writer. He never felt that English really belonged to him. Turning to the subject in his "Autobiographical Essay," with a humility that sometimes seems excessive but that is undoubtedly authentic, he mentions his conflict with a language "I am unworthy to handle, a language I often wish had been my birthright" ("Essay," 1970, p. 258). On the other side was his exasperation, and attitude of resignation, regarding the Spanish language, which did belong to him as his birthright.

The fact that he learned to read English before he could read Spanish, which now seems so strange and even artificial (he seemed to be the victim of a baroque experiment, like Prince Segismundo in *Life Is a Dream*), was not at all artificial to Georgie as a conscious experience. Linguistic duality was a basic fact of his home life. Living with his parents was his paternal grandmother, Frances Haslam, who had been born in England. Though she had come to Argentina as a young woman and had married an Argentine gentleman, Fanny continued to inhabit an English-speaking world. Like so many of her compatriots, she carried the imperial language with her. She taught English not only to her son but to her grandson as well. Even her daughter-in-law would eventually be colonized. The peculiar conditions that gave rise to the bilingualism of the Borges household explain why speaking and reading, and later even writing, in a language which was not that of his native country was not unusual to Georgie. In his home (a closed, autarchical world) English was, equally, a natural language. Not until he went to school did Georgie discover that this language belonged to him a little less than Spanish did.

Since both English and Spanish were spoken at home, Georgie was unaware for some time that they were two different languages. Years later he told one of his interviewers, Rita Guibert: "When I was talking to my paternal grandmother I had to speak in a manner that I afterward discovered was called English, and when I was talking to my mother or her parents I had to talk a language that afterward turned out to be Spanish" (Guibert, 1973, p. 81). It is obvious that in Georgie's experience, rather than being two different languages, English and Spanish more nearly resembled two systems of address, like calling someone by his surname instead of his Christian name.

The conflict approached the critical stage when Georgie started reading in English, for it was his paternal grandmother who took charge of this part of his education. Alicia Jurado, one of his biographers, who was undoubtedly relying on information confided to her by Borges or his mother, evokes this scene: "Before he learned the alphabet, Fanny Haslam used to sit him on her lap and read to him from some children's magazines in English, bound in a very heavy volume he called the 'lectionary,' a word that united the idea of both a dictionary and a lecture" (Jurado, 1964, p. 26). Perhaps this bound volume contained a collection of the popular Victorian magazine *The Boy's Own Journal* or the no less famous *Tit-Bits,* though the latter might have been too melodramatic for Fanny Haslam. The fact that the volume was bound suggests that the grandmother had used it for the father's education as well.

After a time the child passed from the stage of being read to and started reading himself. His instruction was placed in the hands of an English governess, Miss Tink, who also looked after his sister, Norah, two years younger. The reason the family gave for not sending the children to school, where instruction was naturally in Spanish, was its dread of contagious childhood diseases. That is at least what Alicia Jurado reports (ibid., p. 28). But Borges is perhaps more candid in his "Autobiographical Essay": "I did not start school until I was nine. This was because my father, as an anarchist, distrusted all enterprises run by the State" ("Essay," 1970, pp. 211–212). One must remember that when Borges says that his father was an anarchist he means it in a purely philosophical sense, since his father counted himself among the followers of Spencer, not Bakunin.

Perhaps there were religious motives as well to avoid the state schools. As religious instruction was regularly given in those schools, his father probably did not wish to have the children exposed at such an early age to dogmatic instruction. Besides, the English grandmother was a Protestant. At any rate, the immediate consequence of not attending school and of having instead an English governess was that Georgie continued to develop his knowledge of English as the language of culture. Spanish was relegated to strictly domestic concerns. On the other hand, even if Georgie had gone to the state schools at a very young age, his attitude toward the Spanish language as a literary code would probably not have been much different. English was too deeply rooted in him. Looking back, Borges has spoken of his bilingualism in these bilingual terms: "I'm used to thinking in English, and I also believe some English words are untranslatable, so I occasionally use them *for the sake of precision. I'm not showing off.* Since *I've done most of my reading in English,* it's natural that the first word that comes to mind is often an English one" (Guibert, 1973, p. 100; the italicized words are in English in the Spanish original of this interview: Guibert, 1968, p. 55).

The Borgeses' attitude toward the state schools was not unusual in Argentina at the turn of the century. The Argentine upper classes were ambivalent toward everything Hispanic, which in a subtle way also affected the language. Many cultivated Argentines preferred to call Spanish the *idioma nacional* (national tongue) so as to avoid peninsular connotations. There was also a question of status, which Borges reveals:

> In Buenos Aires, Spaniards always held menial jobs—as domestic servants, waiters, and laborers—or were small tradesmen, and we Argentines never thought of ourselves as Spanish. We had, in fact, left off being Spaniards in 1816, when we declared our independence from Spain. When, as a boy, I read Prescott's *Conquest of Peru,* it amazed me to find that he portrayed the conquistadors in a romantic way. To me, descended from certain of these officials, they were an uninteresting lot. ("Essay," 1970, pp. 218–219).

Where Georgie's father did not hold with the tradition of the Argentine upper classes was in the choice of cultural model. In Argentina, as in almost all of Latin America, that model was the French one. Well-to-do people sent their children to French schools. Many writers (especially women) preferred that language as their mode of expression. One of the most remarkable cases was that of Victoria Ocampo, who was later to be so influential in Borges' literary career. She was schooled by a French governess, was given diction lessons with Marguerite Moréno—an outstanding actress from the Comédie Française and the wife of the writer Marcel Schwob—and wrote her first books in French. Even though her native language was Spanish, French was her literary language. In time Victoria Ocampo learned to write in Spanish as well. But her case, while perhaps extreme, was not exceptional.

Argentina at that time (like the United States in the nineteenth century) was a land of immigrants still clinging to Old World traditions and languages. Of the immigrants who came to Argentina, those most firmly attached to their native language were the English (a category that in Argentina included Scots, Welsh, and even Irish). As if it were their only heritage of value, the English preserved their language against all possible contamination. The oldest among them got along with an almost total ignorance of Spanish or with the barest vocabulary. The second generation (of which Borges' father was a good example) was perforce bilingual but did not abandon its attachment to the original language; rather, it changed English into an instrument of culture, a tool of the spirit. No effort seemed excessive to them when it came to defending that umbilical cord that tied them to the center of the British empire. They lived in Argentina as their compatriots did in India. It is not surprising, then, that Borges felt such admiration for the work of Rudyard Kipling.

Though the Borgeses were not wealthy, they had a British governess to protect their children from all forms of contagion, not just from childhood diseases. In addition to these solid family reasons, there was then rampant in Argentina a sort of pro-British snobbery that would dominate Buenos Aires society as the century advanced. French fashions were gradually giving way to English ones. This change had an economic base. Even though Argentina had been within a French-influenced cultural sphere since the beginning of the nineteenth century, from an economic standpoint the independence of the River Plate area was achieved under the aegis of British diplomacy and commerce. Until World War II, Argentina belonged to the pound sterling international trading zone and was virtually part of the Commonwealth. When Perón seized power, at the end of the war, English imperialism remained one of his main targets. Sometime later, in 1955, England openly supported the military revolt that overthrew him. Owing to these circumstances, it was not unusual for Argentine families without any English members whatsoever to send their children to local British schools or, in the case of wealthy families, to have British governesses. What today seems very unusual was, at the time, merely a consequence of the colonial status of the economy and of Argentine culture. In Borges' case, that cultural colonialism was even more justified because the unwitting colonizer was already permanently set up at home.

That paradoxical situation, normal in appearance to the child though in reality profoundly anomalous, would not provoke a crisis until much later. Even though Georgie was "naturally" bilingual, his bilingualism contained the seeds of a fateful distinction between the two languages. The act of reading in English when he had still not learned to do it in Spanish established a radical and decisive difference between the two codes. English became the key to reading and writing. Imagination, dreams, and longings that were aroused or intensified by books would become known to Georgie in English. In English and only in English would they exist for him. In that language he would subsequently find a key to decipher invisible words. Spanish, by contrast, was not only the language of his mother's side of the family (less valid from a cultural point of view because the child could not read it) but the language of servants, those anonymous Galicians and Basques who kept coming to the River Plate area in search of an elusive El Dorado. Thus, until the child was well along in years, Spanish was not a language of culture and, still less, a literary code.

As Georgie grew and became even more aware of the world outside his home, the strangeness of his fate began to dawn on him. Like the Minotaur in Borges' story "The House of Asterion," Georgie had no idea of his uniqueness. But away from the confines of his home he found that things happened in a different way; people spoke a single language, and their values were different. Inside, the restricted and bilingual world of English and Spanish (in that order of cultural and even social importance) alternated smoothly. Outside the garden gate began the exclusive domain of Spanish, a powerful but undeniably common language. No wonder that for Georgie Spanish was associated with a more primitive or elemental form of life, while English gave him access to a higher level of life, to a dream and desire tantalizingly controlled by words and books. Of the two linguistic codes that the boy learned in his childhood, his mother's would be the culturally inferior one.

To this linguistic crisis which pervaded his experience he would attempt to give a paradoxical solution in works that, while written in that inferior language, Spanish, are syntactically closer to the English tongue. On the literary as well as the biographical level, Georgie would become Borges. The child who had an early access to the English code of reading and writing and who theoretically could have become an English writer (George Borges) was to transform himself into an Hispanic writer (Jorge Luis Borges), reverting to the code originally taught by his mother. But though Borges might develop an awesome mastery of Spanish and become the language's foremost writer, he would always feel that in this accomplishment he had sacrificed total mastery of the other code.

The future struggle between English and Spanish on the level of writing and literary production appeared in an already defined form (though visible only at the unconscious level) in the basic act of reading. On the conscious level the child accepted and learned the two languages, went from one to the other with complete ease, and handled all the rules without apparent effort. But on the unconscious level the linguistic conflict was implanted in the core of his experience and caused an inner split in Georgie before doing likewise to Borges. As soon as Georgie reached total awareness, through the basic act of reading, of those two languages that were his without his knowing it, a sense of dualism took root in him. The two codes appeared facing each other, as in a mirror. On learning to read, the child had had no choice but to accept his bilingualism. Now he realized that the garden gate separated something more than home and the city. It was the dividing line between two linguistic systems. It was Alice's mirror. Gradually Georgie would learn to cross at will from one side to the other. The unconscious daily experience of bilingualism would become the conscious experience, accepted without argument and accomplished without the effort of crossing "through the looking glass." It would be, in the end, trivial. But dualism, once consciously discovered, would never be abandoned.

4.
The Two Mothers:
The Two Codes

There is obviously much more in Borges' relationship with his parents than has been indicated here. Some of his autobiographical texts talk freely about Mother, but they reveal little that is relevant to his childhood years. He mentions the help he received from her after his father's death and after his own blindness made it very difficult for him to read and write. About his father, on the contrary, he is always explicit and precise. Even when he is confronted with an interviewer, like Jean de Milleret, who is determined to subject him to a bit of simplified Freudianism, Borges is adamant. Again and again he dodges a question about his mother's supposedly dominant personality and attributes everything to his father's strong will. When he is asked, rather directly, if he thinks that his was "an oppressive mother," he answers that it was his father who was a decisive influence on his life because it was through him that he learned English and had access to a vast library. When pressed again to admit that Mother was a sort of tyrannical Genitrix, he refuses to accept such a characterization and wonders aloud who could have thought of that. He denies any mother fixation and predictably concludes: "It was my father who had an influence on her and not the reverse. My mother was a young woman of a good Argentine family and my father was a liberal and cultivated man: his mother was English and a Protestant; he had a good library at home. I must say that he lived, intellectually speaking, in a more complex world than my mother" (De Milleret, 1967, p. 213). It is obvious that Borges is here denying any attempt to "psychoanalyze" him or his relationship with his parents.

Borges' resistance to any type of analysis (not only to the instant one attempted by De Milleret) is well known. In another interview he even makes a joke about it: "I've rather forgotten the time I spent in my mother's womb—although, according to the Freudians, it must have been very important to me" (*Triunfo*, November 15, 1969, p. 36). More straightforward is an exchange recorded by Richard Burgin:

BURGIN: I take it you don't think much of Freud, either.

BORGES: No, I always disliked him. But I've always been a great reader of Jung. I read Jung in the same way as, let's say, I might read Pliny or Frazer's *Golden Bough;* I read it as a kind of mythology, or as a kind of museum or encyclopedia of curious lores.

BURGIN: When you say that you dislike Freud, what do you mean?

BORGES: I think of him as a kind of madman, no? A man laboring over a sexual obsession. Well, perhaps he didn't take it to heart. Perhaps he was just doing it as a kind of game. I tried to read him, and I thought of him either as a charlatan or as a madman, in a sense. After all, the world is far too complex to be boiled down to that all-too-simple scheme. But in Jung, well, of course, Jung I have read far more widely than Freud, but in Jung you feel a wide and hospitable mind. In the case of Freud, it all boils down to a few rather unpleasant facts. But, of course, that's merely my ignorance or my bias. (Burgin, 1969, p. 109)

Borges' resistance to Freud is revealing and, in a sense, as curious as that shown by Nabokov. They even use similar words. While Nabokov calls Freud a "crank," Borges suggests he is either a "charlatan" or a "madman." Borges is obviously overreacting, and it is this overreaction that attracts attention. At the root of his bilingualism is an unconscious conflict whose symptoms and origins are clear. The fact that he was taught Spanish by his mother and English by his grandmother established from the beginning a conflict between the two codes. The immediate manifestations of this conflict are well known. He had some difficulty in learning to talk. According to Mother, "when he was very small, he had the most extraordinary way of talking: Perhaps he didn't hear well? He disfigured completely many words" (Mother, 1964, p. 10). Later on he developed a slight stammer that became more evident when he was in the company of strangers or when he had to talk in public. Not until he was forty-five did he seriously attempt to overcome his stammer. The fact that it was his English grandmother who taught him the English code and who introduced him to the world of books added some confusion to the already confusing double language he learned to use while a child. Georgie had two "mothers" instead of one, as he had two languages. At the level of the personal myth, the fact that the second mother was his father's mother only increased Father's sphere of influence. Father became duplicated: he was represented by a virile figure who ran everything at home and by a maternal version who was (implicitly) Mother's rival in teaching the boy how to speak. In view of the complexity of that original configuration, it is easy to understand Borges' resistance to De Milleret's "Freudian" line of questioning.

At the conscious level, he always saw Mother under the influence of Father, and there was no doubt about that. It is possible to go one step further and assume that for Georgie Mother had a secondary role in her own household: she was also under Fanny Haslam's influence because Grandmother was the owner of the most powerful linguistic code—English. Mother was like the beautiful concubine in some of the tales of the *One Thousand and One Nights* that Father (and later Georgie) loved to read in Richard Burton's unexpurgated translation. She was a sort of slave who was tolerated as the Heir's mother, but the real Queen, the only legitimate wife, was Father's mother. This configuration explains the part Mother plays in Borges' personal myth: she is always there, she is always courteously referred to, but she is always kept (in a very subtle way) in a subordinate position.

A purely psychoanalytical reading of this situation is impossible here. It has been attempted more than once with various results. The best analysis so far is one done by Didier Anzieu in 1971. Although the French psychoanalyst lacked all the necessary biographical information and had less than complete bibliographical data, he was able to develop many original insights. Instead of following the traditional Freudian line, he relied both on Melanie Klein's theories about the relationship between the body and the unconscious (Klein, 1975) and also on Jacques Lacan's subtle reading and rewriting of Freud (Lacan, 1966). According to these views, the child continues to be one with the mother long after the umbilical cord has been severed and the child is being breast-fed; the unity of his and his mother's body survives even the weaning, because the mother never ceases to talk to him; that is, to teach him the linguistic code. The teaching of that code creates a link that substitutes for the umbilical cord. One may call the new bond the vocal cord. Because it is the mother who teaches the child the first sounds, and later the first words and phrases, her teachings become for him deeply associated with the other functions she performs. Feeding him, nursing him, talking to him: all become one. From this point of view, the mouth of the mother is another breast.

In Georgie's case, there was another mother who did not breast-feed him but who also took care of him and (after the weaning) helped to feed him. This second mother, being an Englishwoman, had a different linguistic code; she taught Georgie this second code. If the sharing of the linguistic code is nothing but a symbolization of the unity of the body of the mother and that of the child, to adopt a second

Perhaps those who use it in this imperial way (as distinct from those who know him) are themselves partho-types.

No doubt!

!

23

*Erikson
a more
appro-
priate
inter-
preter.*

linguistic code implies that the original unity is threatened and the body is split. Georgie accepted the double code but at the cost of becoming permanently injured. His body rebelled. It is known that he had difficulty in speaking and "disfigured completely many words." At the conscious level, the splitting of the original unity into two different codes (two mothers, two bodies) was accepted. At the unconscious level, the seeds of a tragic conflict were sown.

*Incoher-
ent.*

The rebellion of Georgie's unconscious was quenched after a while. He stopped making mistakes; he learned to speak properly and to separate the two languages. But deep inside him, at the level where the poems he was to write and the stories he was to tell were already being formed, at the truly archaic level, prior to any discovery of the differences between the sexes and the Oedipus complex, something irreversible had happened. It would take almost four decades of unconscious work for the conflict to come out into the open. In the stories Borges wrote after his father's death in 1938 the conflict at last emerges in beautiful and mysterious formulations.

Two of these stories have been singled out by Anzieu to prove his views. "The God's Script," originally included in *The Aleph* (1949), presents a Mayan priest who has been thrown into a cell by Alvarado, the Spanish conquistador. In the next cell is a beautiful jaguar. The priest spends endless nights attempting to understand the meaning of the defeat of his god. He finally decides that his god has left, somewhere, a secret message to his followers:

> The god, foreseeing that at the end of time there would be devastation and ruin, wrote on the first day of Creation a magical sentence with the power to ward off those evils. He wrote it in such a way that it would reach the most distant generations and not be subject to chance. No one knows where it was written nor with what characters, but it is certain that it exists, secretly, and that a chosen one will read it. I considered that we were now, as always, at the end of time and that my destiny as the last priest of the god would give me access to the privilege of intuiting the script. (*Labyrinths,* 1962, p. 170)

Slowly, painfully, the priest comes to the conclusion that the message is inscribed in the jaguar's skin. After more long sessions of dreaming and thinking and suffering, he has a mystical vision and is made one with the god. He is now ready to decipher the inscription.

> It is a formula of fourteen random words (they appear random) and to utter it in a loud voice would suffice to make me all-powerful. To say it would suffice to abolish this stone prison, to have daylight break into my night, to be young, to be immortal, to have the tiger's jaws crush Alvarado, to sink the

This is the road we all must travel, [handwritten left margin]

to die before our death, and to resurrect ourselves. [handwritten right margin]

sacred knife into the breasts of Spaniards, to reconstruct the pyramid, to reconstruct the empire. Forty syllables, fourteen words, and I, Tzinacán, would rule the lands Moctezuma ruled. But I know I shall never say those words, because I no longer remember Tzinacán.

May the mystery lettered on the tigers die with me. Whoever has seen the universe, whoever has beheld the fiery designs of the universe, cannot think in terms of one man, of that man's trivial fortunes or misfortunes, though he be that very man. That man *has been he* and now matters no more to him. What is the life of that other to him, the nation of that other to him, if he, now, is no one? This is why I do not pronounce the formula, why, lying here in the darkness, I let the days obliterate me. (Ibid., p. 173)

Nonsense. [handwritten]   In mastering his god's code, Tzinacán has reached his goal: the mystical union with the divine. Now that he has the secret of the divine script, he doesn't need to use it. Interpreting the story, Anzieu points out that the mystical union through language symbolizes the fusion with the mother: Tzinacán is happy in the depths of his prison because he is now one with his god; in the same way, the child is happy outside his mother's body because the possession of the linguistic code makes the two bodies one (Anzieu, 1971, pp. 185–186). One could add that even the fact that Tzinacán keeps the secret formula to himself stresses the character of a private and unique relationship that the child has with his mother. *Now we know why some are critics.* [handwritten]

The other story, "The Library of Babel," is according to Anzieu Borges' best. It came out originally in *The Garden of Forking Paths* (1941) and was later included in *Ficciones* (1944). To Anzieu, the infinite library is a symbol of the unconscious: "It has all the characteristics of the unconscious, not only according to Freud, but also according to Lacan; it is universal, eternal and, also, it is structured like a language" (ibid., p. 196). There is another link between the library of Babel and the unconscious: both are susceptible to infinite combinations. "To the point where the body articulates itself with the code, where the child talks then writes for his mother, whose mouth speaks and later writes for him, the unconscious proposes to the discourse many possibilities of fantastic combinations, because of their number, their form, and their content." Thus, according to Anzieu, "the mystical journey of the narrator through the library of Babel is a symbolical exploration of the mother's body—a feeding breast which is also a mouth that speaks, a mouth that teaches the entranced child the phonological code" (ibid., p. 198). *"The Book of Sand"* [handwritten]

This story also contains traces of the trauma caused by the double linguistic code. The collection of books in the library is infinite and at the same time monstrous. In his report on the library the anonymous narrator recalls some axioms, the second of which is:

25

The orthographical symbols are twenty-five in number.[1] This finding made it possible, three hundred years ago, to formulate a general theory of the Library and solve satisfactorily the problem which no conjecture had deciphered: the formless and chaotic nature of almost all the books. One which my father saw in a hexagon on circuit fifteen ninety-four was made up of the letters MCV, perversely repeated from the first line to the last. Another (very much consulted in this area) is a mere labyrinth of letters, but the next-to-last page says *Oh time thy pyramids.* This much is already known: for every sensible line of straightforward statement, there are leagues of senseless cacophonies, verbal jumbles and incoherences.

[1] The original manuscript does not contain digits or capital letters. The punctuation has been limited to the comma and the period. These two signs, the space and the twenty-two letters of the alphabet are the twenty-five symbols considered sufficient by this unknown author. *Editor's note.* (*Labyrinths,* 1962, p. 53)

The body of the library that contains such books has been destroyed by chaos, quartered and made absurd by the application of an insane code. The dream of order has turned into a nightmare. In the same way, for Georgie, the institution of a second code (based more on a conscious than on an unconscious logic) will destroy the unity of Mother's body. Thus, the role of the second mother, of Grandmother Haslam, would, at the unconscious level, be that of the disruptive element of chaos. But the conflict will remain hidden in Georgie's unconscious until he first learns to read, in English and not in Spanish. Then, by a strange permutation, Grandmother's code becomes the first, and Father, who had so far remained in the background, becomes the most important person in the household. As a carrier of English (the privileged code), Father drastically displaces both Mother and Grandmother Haslam and assumes the role of teacher, the master of the new code of reading. At the conscious level, Georgie accepts the change. But at the unconscious level (at the level where all his fantastic tales had already started to be produced), he never accepts it. And only in Mother's discarded and despised code—Spanish—will he later succeed in symbolizing all that archaic repressed material: the stuff bodies (and poetry) are made of.

I think it sensible to speak of a primordial identity, but babbling to speak of its trauma. Traumas are a dyslogistic term for experience, which is also primordial

5.
The Playmate

For the better part of his childhood Georgie had an accomplice. ?
It was his sister, Norah, two years his junior. Although in the "Autobiographical Essay" very little space is devoted to Norah—she is mentioned only four or five times—in Georgie's emotional experience
Norah was very important. For some fifteen years they shared everything: every evening they had to leave the adult world and go upstairs
to sleep in their separate bedrooms; they were taught English by the
same governess; they spent their holidays together, playing endless
games invented by Georgie in which Norah had the leading roles, as
guide and protector. They shared love, dreams, terrors. If Georgie was
older, Norah had a more determined character. She did not inherit the
Borges blindness. On the contrary, her eyes were enormous, as if
slightly bewildered by the world's profusion of shapes and colors. In
the extant photographs of their childhood Norah's eyes are strong and
inquisitive, a petulant smile on her lips, while Georgie's eyes are dream-
ier, more evasive. Norah was destined to become a painter and a
draftswoman, and in her works she leaves testimony of the familial
world she shared with her brother. Her paintings and drawings offer
an almost infantile, naïve vision of that world, as if her eyes could ✔
remember the garden only before the Fall.

In her reminiscences to a French interviewer Mother commented on their close relationship: "He was shy, extremely reserved.
He adored his sister, and they both invented an infinite number of extraordinary games. They never quarreled and they were always
together before Georgie found in Switzerland some schoolmates"
(Mother, 1964, p. 9). In a more neutral tone, Borges evokes the same
period of his childhood: "I have already said that I spent a great deal of

my boyhood indoors. Having no childhood friends, my sister and I invented two imaginary companions, named, for some reason or other, Quilos and the Windmill. (When they finally bored us, we told our mother that they had died.)" ("Essay," 1970, p. 208).

This short reference is tantalizing because of its reticent evocation of a period that was so important in his life. It is also revealing for the hints it gives of Georgie's precocious gift for language. The names of the imaginary characters are significant. Quilos suggests immediately the phonetic transcription of the Spanish plural *kilos* (kilograms); but it may come from another, more scholarly, source that Georgie could have picked up in a dictionary. In Spanish the digestive juices are called *quilos* (from the Greek *khylós*, according to Corominas, 1967, p. 487); this opens up the possibility of a pun. The other character's name, the Windmill, is easier to place. The garden of the Borgeses' house on the outskirts of Buenos Aires had a windmill. During a storm, the windmill's whining and screeching used to scare Georgie. In a poem he wrote when he was thirty, "Natural Fluency of Memory" (included in *San Martín Copybook*, 1929), which evokes his childhood home and neighborhood, he singles out the windmill. It was red and had a laborious wheel; it was "the honor of our home" because the neighbors did not have windmills and had to get their water from carriers who came from the river with their wooden wagons. He vividly recalls the windmill's circular basement, "its jail of subtle water" (*Poemas*, 1943, pp. 126–127).

The poem also recalls the garden and the neighborhood. In attempting to capture the magic and beauty of those days, Borges cannot help adding a few sinister touches. He remembers the beautiful tree in which a magpie had settled to devour her offspring despite the protests of the other birds. The horror of the occasion is concentrated in a single word: depredation. Addressing the garden, Borges says:

> The sleep of your trees and mine
> still blend in darkness
> and the depredation of the magpie
> left an old fear in my blood.
>
> (Ibid., p. 127)

Mother remembered that Georgie loved to play in the garden near the palm tree that is mentioned in the poem:

> Palm tree, the highest of that heaven
> and little bird's tenement
>
> (Ibid., p. 126)

"Under that palm tree," Mother recalled, "he invented with his sister games, dreams, projects; they created characters with whom they played; it was their island (Mother, 1964, p. 10).

Norah has also confided her memories of those days. In Alicia Jurado's book it is her version that prevails. She recalls the games and the terrors, the windmill and the magpie. But she adds other images to their childhood iconography. According to that source, Norah could see Georgie

> in her memory, always reading, lying on his stomach on the ground dressed in a light brown wrapper. He didn't like any manual work or any game of skill, except the diavolo [a game played with a wooden hoop], but he liked to reenact with her scenes taken from books: he was a prince and she the queen, his mother; standing on a staircase, they leaned over to hear the acclamations of an imaginary multitude; or they traveled to the moon in a missile built by folding a red silk Chinese screen, embroidered with golden birds and flowers, into which they tumbled after sliding down the banister of the staircase. Sometimes, they traveled dangerously on the flat roofs, searching for a room where they'd never been, a mysterious place that ought perforce to exist. (Jurado, 1964, p. 29)

They used to spend their summers in Uruguay, visiting Mother's relatives in a villa on the outskirts of Montevideo or on a ranch up the Uruguay River, near Fray Bentos. There they had a playmate, a cousin, Esther Haedo, who also had been educated by an English governess. According to Norah's reminiscences, at Esther's place

> there was a lookout tower, with a spiral staircase and colored windows, from which came undoubtedly the red and green lozenges of Triste-le-Roy [a villa in Borges' story "Death and the Compass"]. In that lonely place, the children founded the Society of the Three Crosses, created to defend the boy from an imaginary enemy who wanted to kill him. General headquarters was a gazebo of painted wood with a gallery whose only access was through a little bridge. They wrote messages in a code invented by the supposed victim, and they roamed around the villa with cloth masks. (Ibid., pp. 29–30)

As a child, Georgie had been fascinated and repelled by masks. At carnival time he used to peer out from the safety of the garden into the street, where the masked revelers filled the air with their drums and riotous water play. In the poem quoted above he mentions the "coarse carnival." Perhaps he had had a bad experience with masks: Mother confided to Alicia Jurado that as a child Georgie only once "consented to put on a disguise, and then he insisted—perhaps significantly—on a devil's costume" (ibid., p. 26). This childhood fear of masks prevailed in later years. One of his closest friends, Silvina

Ocampo, described Borges' astonishing reaction once "when some masked and costumed friends crashed in during carnival time" (ibid., p. 26).

In his fiction Borges has always associated masks and disguises with evil or murder. In *A Universal History of Infamy,* one of the most revealing stories is "The Masked Dyer, Hakim of Merv," about a false prophet who hides his leprosy under a mask of gold. In one episode of "Death and the Compass" (a story later included in *Ficciones*), the criminal uses masks to lure the detective into a plot that endangers his life. Masks are terrifying not only because they hide one's real features but because on them the expression of character is forever fixed. They are absolutes in a world of contingency and change. Masks are also a symbol of the duality of man: the two that fight inside each person. Perhaps Georgie was not consciously aware of the meaning of masks, but he felt that they were disgusting and rejected them, or wore them only when he wanted to play a sinister role: the devil (in Mother's reminiscences) or the persecuted victim (in Norah's recollections).

His games of pursuit with Norah and Esther came to a climax one day: "A whole summer they lived in terror of the fabrications of their own imagination, which came to be so vivid that once, at siesta time, the three saw the murderer reflected in one of the terrible mirrors of the wardrobe. It was, Norah tells, blurred and green-colored" (Jurado, 1964, pp. 29–30). The haunting, sleepless mirror is one of the recurrent images in Borges' work. But before becoming a literary image, it had been an obsession. According to Alicia Jurado:

> Norah still remembers the nights of terror [when] they were left alone upstairs in their bedrooms. Georgie was afraid even of the vague reflection of his face in the polished mahogany of his bed. Many years later, we will recognize that mood in a poem in which he talks about the
>
> > masked
> > mahogany mirror which in the mist
> > of red twilight erases
> > that face which looks and is looked upon.
> > (Ibid., pp. 25–26)

This poem, "The Mirror," continues revealingly:

> Glasses spy on us. If between the four
> walls of my bedroom there is a mirror,
> I am no longer alone. There is another one.
> There is the reflection
> which creates a silent theater at dawn.
> (*Obra,* 1964, pp. 183–85)

Georgie's fear and even horror of mirrors seems to go against everything that is known about children's reactions to them. According to Jacques Lacan's theory about the importance of the mirror stage in the evolution of the subconscious, the child discovers in the mirror an image of himself as a unified body, a totality; before that experience, he has only a partial image of himself. This discovery brings joy to him because he thus anticipates in his imagination his future control over his own body (Lacan, 1966, pp. 93–100). In Georgie's case, this joy did not seem to have existed. To him—as Didier Anzieu has suggested in his psychoanalytical study (Anzieu, 1971, p. 200)—the specular reflection only confirms the fact that his body has been torn apart from the body of his mother. Instead of reassuring Georgie, the discovery ratifies the pain, the intolerable awareness of being another. What he sees in the mirror is the other; that is, himself. To put it in a different way, he sees himself not as he wants to be (one with his mother) but as he is (the other). That could be the origin of an obsession that his bilingualism could only have strengthened.

A different reading of the same obsession, to which Anzieu only alludes in his study (ibid., pp. 199 and 202), could be attempted. On several occasions, but chiefly in his clinical study of the Wolf-Man, Sigmund Freud identified another, related trauma that sometimes involves mirrors: the primal scene. Often the parents' sexual activities are discovered accidentally by children through the reflection in a mirror. The fact that George was haunted by a mirror in his own bedroom, and that he was even afraid of seeing his image in the polished mahogany of his bed, seems to suggest the possibility of that reading.

There are other hints that point to the same connection in several of Borges' stories. On many occasions he establishes an unexpected link between mirrors and copulation. The first time he does it is in "The Masked Dyer, Hakim of Merv," a story mentioned earlier for its use of masks. In a section of that story called The Abominable Mirrors, Borges summarizes the protagonist's cosmogony: "The world we live in is a mistake, a clumsy parody. Mirrors and fatherhood, because they multiply and confirm the parody, are abominations. Revulsion is the cardinal virtue" (*Infamy*, 1972, p. 84). Although Borges quotes at the end of *A Universal History of Infamy* a list of historical sources for the stories in the book, it has been proved satisfactorily that no source exists for that particular "cosmogony." In a second story, "Tlön, Uqbar, Orbis Tertius," Borges attributes a similar concept to an even more exotic source. It is presented as the opinion of a heresiarch from Uqbar. According to the story, Borges was having dinner with a friend, Adolfo Bioy Casares, and at a certain point in their conversation Bioy recalled that one of the heresiarchs of Uqbar had declared that "mirrors and copulation are abominable, because they increase the number of men" (*Labyrinths,* 1964, p. 3).

This is the starting point for a long and eventually successful quest for the exact source of that quotation, which Borges calls "a memorable observation." When Bioy Casares produces the volume of the Anglo-American Encyclopedia that contains the article on Uqbar, the heresiarch's doctrine is quoted again: "The heresiarch's name was not forthcoming, but there was a note on his doctrine, formulated in words almost identical to those he [Bioy] had repeated, though perhaps literarily inferior. He had recalled: *Copulation and mirrors are abominable.* The text of the encyclopedia said: *For one of those gnostics, the visible universe was an illusion or (more precisely) a sophism. Mirrors and fatherhood are abominable because they multiply and disseminate that universe*" (ibid., p. 4).

Perhaps it would be useful to point out that in the Spanish text both Bioy Casares' rendering of the heresiarch's statement and the heresiarch's slightly different wording are given in English and then translated into Spanish, to increase perhaps the verisimilitude of the passage. But what is even more important is the confrontation of the three basic texts: the one in "The Masked Dyer" and the two in "Tlön." They seem to state the same thing, but their contexts differ considerably. In Hakim of Merv's cosmogony "mirrors and fatherhood" are compared, as they are in the heresiarch's version in "Tlön," while Bioy Casares' version makes a more explicit and general reference to "copulation and mirrors."

There are other differences between the three texts. In "The Masked Dyer" the comparison between mirrors and fatherhood is based on the fact that they both "multiply and confirm" the world we live in, which is (for Hakim) a "parody." In the first quotation from "Tlön" Bioy Casares refers explicitly to the fact that they "increase the number of men." In the heresiarch's text there is a return to Hakim's notion: there is one universe, real, and another one, reflected, multiplied, and disseminated by mirrors and fatherhood. Again, the similarity between Hakim's and the heresiarch's versions suggests a common doctrine. It is easy to recognize in them an allusion to the gnostic belief that the world was created not by God but by subaltern gods (or demons) who actually parodied God's creation.

In spite of this similarity, there are important differences between the first and the last text. Both state that mirrors and fatherhood "multiply" the universe. But they differ in the second verb: the first text talks about confirming the world; the second, about disseminating it. The change is significant and is even clearer in the Spanish original. There Borges does not use the verb *diseminar* (disseminate) but the verb *divulgar* (divulge), which etymologically implies to spread among the *vulgo,* the common people. In James E. Irby's translation the word "disseminate" carries another weight: it contains the concept of semen or seminal, which is obviously implied in Borges' text. The translation thus makes even more explicit the underlying sexual meaning of the "memorable observation."

This kind of reading of "Tlön" not only seems legitimate but is suggested by the text itself. Very significantly, the whole story evolves from a discussion in which "Borges" and "Bioy" are concerned about "the composition of a novel in the first person, whose narrator would omit or disfigure the facts and indulge in various contradictions which would permit a few readers—very few readers—to perceive an atrocious or banal reality" (*Labyrinths,* 1962, p. 3). If the word "story" is substituted for "novel," as some critics have suggested, the text would contain a reference to "Tlön" itself because the story describes an imaginary world that is actually the earth—"Orbis Tertius," as it was called in Renaissance cosmography. Behind the elaborate mask of Uqbar, an atrocious or banal reality is hidden: the reality of a world that is a parody, created by inferior gods, and that perpetuates itself through mirrors and fatherhood.

How much of this revulsion for the act of fatherhood (or copulation, as Bioy Casares remembered it) has to do with the discovery of the primal scene through the complicity of a mirror? The only evidence that exists is the one buried in Borges' texts. In another part of the poem "The Mirror" the tantalizing link is again established:

> Infinite I see them, elementary
> executors of an old pact,
> to multiply the world as the generative
> act, sleepless and fatal.
>
> (*Obra,* 1964, p. 184)

The gnostics did not know genetics. Nothing is more wonderful than the world itself.

In his writings the impact of that primal scene proliferates in tantalizing allusions and, sometimes, in very explicit statements. There is another story, "The Sect of the Phoenix," originally published in *Sur* (Buenos Aires, September–October 1952) and later included in the 1956 edition of *Ficciones.* It is disguised as a historical reconstruction of an obscure pagan sect. Camouflaged under many observations that are not always false, Borges talks about the "Secret" which assures immortality to the worshippers of the Phoenix.

> This Secret . . . is transmitted from generation to generation, but good usage prefers that mothers should not teach it to their children, nor that priests should; initiation into the mystery is the task of the lowest individuals. A slave, a leper, and a beggar serve as mystagogues. Also one child may

indoctrinate another. The act in itself is trivial, momentary, and requires no description. The materials are cork, wax, or gum arabic. (In the liturgy, mud is mentioned; this is often used as well.) There are no temples especially dedicated to the celebration of this cult, but certain ruins, a cellar, or an entrance hall are considered propitious places. The Secret is sacred but is always somewhat ridiculous; its performance is furtive and even clandestine and the adept do not speak of it. There are no decent words to name it, but it is understood that all words name it or, rather, inevitably allude to it and thus, in a conversation, I say something or other and the adept smile or become uncomfortable, for they realize I have touched upon the Secret. . . . A kind of sacred horror prevents some faithful believers from performing this very simple rite; the others despise them, but they despise themselves even more.

. . . I have attained in three continents the friendship of many devotees of the Phoenix; I know that the Secret, at first, seemed to them banal, embarrassing, vulgar, and (what is even stranger) incredible. They could not bring themselves to admit their parents had stooped to such manipulations. What is odd is that the Secret was not lost long ago; in spite of the vicissitudes of the Universe, in spite of wars and exoduses, it reaches, awesomely, all the faithful. Someone has not hesitated to affirm that it is now instinctive. (*Labyrinths*, 1962, pp. 102–104)

The Secret, which Borges wishes to reveal to the reader gradually, is none other than copulation, which insures the reproduction of the species and therefore grants "eternity to a lineage óf its members, generation after generation, would perform the rite" (ibid., p. 102). But not all readers decipher the Secret. At least one, Ronald Christ, dared to ask Borges about it. As he tells the story, he approached the writer in New York in 1968. Borges' reaction was to keep him guessing for another day; when they met again at a reception the following evening, he "leaned over and whispered into my ear so that no one else could hear: 'Well, the act is what Whitman says "the divine husband knows, from the work of fatherhood." When I first heard about this act, when I was a boy, I was shocked, shocked to think that my mother, my father had performed it. It is an amazing discovery, no? But then too it is an act of immortality, a rite of immortality, isn't it?' " (Christ, 1969, p. 190).

In the story itself Borges notes the astonishment of some believers when told of the act: "They could not bring themselves to admit that their parents had stooped to such manipulations." The same reaction occurs in an earlier story by Borges, one of the few that touches on a sexual subject, "Emma Zunz," first published in *Sur* (September 1948) and later included in *The Aleph* (1949). It is about a young woman whose father is forced by a business partner to commit suicide. To avenge his death, she plans to accuse the partner of having raped her and then to kill him. But one fact threatens to undermine her story: she is still a virgin. In order to lose her virginity, she sells herself to an unknown sailor. (The plot, the weakest aspect of the story, was given to Borges by a woman friend.) Borges describes Emma's reaction during coitus:

> During that time outside of time, in that perplexing disorder of disconnected and atrocious sensations, did Emma Zunz think *once* about the dead man who motivated the sacrifice? It is my belief that she did think once, and in that moment she endangered her desperate undertaking. She thought (she was unable not to think) that her father had done to her mother the hideous thing that was being done to her now. She thought of it with weak amazement and took refuge, quickly, in vertigo. (*Labyrinths,* 1962, p. 135)

The roots of Borges' evasiveness, reticence, and even self-censorship when dealing with sexual subjects—as has been illustrated by the above quotations—can be found in Georgie's discovery of the mystery of sex. It is impossible to know how much of this knowledge he shared with Norah. The differences in their adult lives indicate a radical difference in the impact these childhood games and discoveries in the secluded garden or in the mirrored bedrooms had for each of them. In her late twenties Norah married the Spanish critic and poet Guillermo de Torre; George remained a bachelor until his late sixties, and the marriage lasted only three years. While Norah had two sons, Georgie never fathered a child.

In that Palermo garden Norah and Georgie were closer than ever. She was his protector, a mother surrogate and a good alter ego, not the one that haunted mirrors. She and Esther Haedo, the Uruguayan cousin, defended Georgie from an imaginary enemy. In their eagerness to protect him, they even shared his hallucinations, and one day (Norah is our witness) they both saw the murderer's hideous image reflected in a mirror. Contagious magic, as Frazer would say? Probably, because both girls were totally submissive to Georgie's imagination and will. But they also shared his taste for dreams and art. Regarding his own visual style and Norah's, Borges has commented:

BURGIN: You love painting and architecture, don't you? I mean your stories seem to me very vivid visually.
BORGES: Are they really visual, or does the visibility come from Chesterton?
BURGIN: You seem to have that ability to make a purely imagined world, such as the city of the immortals, come to life.
BORGES: I wonder if they really come to life.
BURGIN: For me they do. I can only speak for myself.

BORGES: Yes, of course. Now my sister paints. She's a fine painter.

BURGIN: What style does she paint in?

BORGES: She's always painting, well, large gardens and old-fashioned pink houses or if not those, angels, but angels who are musicians. She's a very unobtrusive painter. For example, well, she studied perspective drawing and so on. But people who know little or nothing about painting think of her paintings as being just scrawls done by a child. (Burgin, 1969, p. 99)

Borges' subtle irony is at his best here; moving around Burgin's naïve questions, he plays a gentler Johnson to a twentieth-century Boswell. The reference to Chesterton as a source for his "visual" style is one of his critical leitmotifs. But what really matters most is his observation about how people are fooled by Norah's lack of visible skills and her apparent naïveté. That is the precise quality that helped her to maintain a child's vision in works done with the utmost sophistication. Her paintings and drawings preserve the world she shared with Georgie, but in a completely different tonality from that used by her brother. With simple lines and pastel colors, she re-creates the houses and patios, the little squares and monuments, the men and women and children (all with big, round, black eyes) of their childhood. Her work is the positive of the negative inscribed by Georgie. She shows the light of her brother's world of darkness: a world in which an enemy is always hidden in the dark reflection of mirrors. Her private mythology is not the opposite but the complement of her brother's.

One more observation about their childhood games—it is significant that, in playing Kings and Queens, Norah (who was two years younger) became the Queen Mother and not the Princess, as might have been expected at that healthy incestuous stage of their lives. The powerful repression of the Oedipal conflict seems to be at work already. In changing his sister (his equal) into his "mother" (a superior; thus an unreachable being), Georgie was exorcising a potential incestuous relationship that would have been normal at their age. The garden at Palermo was to be Eden; no serpent was allowed to weave its way into that secluded space.

6.
The Inhabitant of the Labyrinth

The garden at Palermo was a privileged place from which Georgie could watch the outside world. It was a holy place. But it was also the door that gave access to another reality: the reality of people who lived next to him in houses of only one story, people who had no water of their own and didn't know the security of possessing their own gardens. Very seldom did Georgie and Norah leave their haven. Apart from visits to relatives, especially to the two grandmothers, the only place they went to regularly was the Buenos Aires zoo, which was located not very far from home. In her recollections Mother evoked some of Georgie's reactions to these excursions: "He was passionate about animals, especially wild beasts. When we visited the zoo, it was difficult to make him leave. And I, who was small, I was afraid of him, so big and strong. I was afraid that he'd get into a rage and beat me. . . . However, he was very kind. When he did not want to give in, I took his books away. That was decisive" (Mother, 1964, p. 10).

Mother's image of a raging, bullying Georgie is unsettling. Even more disturbing are her feelings of being weak and small in front of him: a giant of a boy although generally kind. To overcome her feelings of inferiority, she had to resort to drastic measures. By taking away his books (or perhaps only threatening to do so), she regained her authority. Her method was effective, but it must have been damaging to her relationship with Georgie. From the moment he learned to read in English before he could read in Spanish, the balance tipped toward the first language. Now the punishment of taking his books away when he misbehaved came from the parent who was associated with Spanish. Mother's method might have been effective, but it only confirmed the child's prejudices.

Taking away books was not the only punishment Mother used. She confided to Alicia Jurado that one day Georgie had to be shut in his room "after a horrid tantrum he threw because he had been taken from the zoo at a time he thought was too soon. He was offered a reprieve if he would say tht he didn't mean to react in the way he did." He refused and continued to shout, " 'I did mean it,' until the punishment was over" (Jurado, 1964, p. 25). There is an untranslatable pun in Georgie's words. In Spanish "I didn't mean it" is "Lo hice *sin* querer" (literally: I did it *without* willing it). But Georgie revises the idiomatic phrase and shouts "Lo hice *con* querer" (literally: I did it *with* willing it). The episode seems significant not only in what it shows of Georgie's mettle and determination but especially in what it proves of the child's linguistic imagination. He was already coining his own phrases.

It is obvious that he took language seriously, almost as seriously as going to the zoo. Of all the animals he saw there, his favorite was the √tiger. His maternal grandmother, Leonor Suárez de Acevedo, used to chide him for the preference and tried unsuccessfully to persuade him that lambs were prettier. But he insisted on "the ferocious tiger," as he used to say in English, according to Mother's reminiscences as transmitted by Alicia Jurado (ibid., p. 26). In an interview in the French publication *L'Herne,* Mother completed the picture:

> When he was very young, he would draw animals. Lying down on his stomach on the floor, he would always begin at the end, drawing the feet first. He would draw tigers, which were his favorite animals. Later, from tigers and other savage beasts, he moved to prehistoric animals, about which for two years he read all he could get hold of. Then he became enthusiastic about Egyptian things, and he read about them—read with no end in sight—until he threw himself into Chinese literature; he has a lot of books on the subject. In short, he loves everything that is mysterious. (Mother, 1964, p. 11)

When Georgie was very young his paternal grandmother, Fanny Haslam, probably read him Blake's poem "The Tiger," which develops the comparison between that beast and fire and contains the biblical opposition with the lamb that Grandmother Acevedo had presented as an alternative. But in adoring the tiger, Georgie was not only being true to these literary or religious prototypes. He was being true to one side of his family: to those ancestors who fought first for Spain during the conquest and later for Argentina during the wars of independence; men who died on the battlefield, covered with wounds, or less heroically but not less truly in their own beds, dreaming of a violence that had been finally denied them. In Borges' future work the tiger comes to symbolize many things but always of the same kind. It is darkness and fire, primeval innocence and evil, the sexual instinct and the blind violence that obliterate everything. In text after text the tiger emerges as a symbol of time, which devours men (as in the lyrical conclusion to his essay "A New Refutation of Time," collected in *Inquisitions,* 1964) or as a "string of labored tropes" the poet is trying vainly to capture in the seclusion of a library (as in the poem "The Other Tiger," written when Borges was almost sixty; *Poems,* 1972, pp. 129–131). But for Georgie there was only one tiger: the real one he used to watch at the Palermo zoo. To that tiger (and to the memories and dreams it engendered) Borges devoted one of his most eloquent pieces. It was written in the 1930s and published for the first time in the literary section of the Argentine newspaper *Crítica* (September 15, 1934), under the pseudonym of Francisco Bustos. Not until 1960 was it collected in a volume of Borges' writing, *El hacedor* (*Dreamtigers,* 1964). The title of the piece, "Dreamtigers," is in English in the Spanish original:

> In my childhood I was a fervent worshipper of the tiger: not the jaguar, the spotted "tiger" of the Amazonian tangles and the isles of vegetation that float down the Paraná, but that striped, Asiatic, royal tiger, that can be faced only by a man of war, on a castle atop an elephant. I used to linger endlessly before one of the cages at the zoo; I judged vast encyclopedias and books of natural history by the splendor of their tigers. (I still remember those illustrations: I who cannot rightly recall the brow or smile of a woman.) Childhood passed away, and the tigers and my passion for them grew old, but still they are in my dreams. At that submerged or chaotic level they keep prevailing. And so, as I sleep, some dream beguiles me, and suddenly I know I am dreaming. Then I think: This is a dream, a pure diversion of my will; and now that I have unlimited power, I am going to cause a tiger.
>
> Oh, incompetence: Never can my dreams engender the wild beast I long for. The tiger indeed appears, but stuffed or flimsy, or with impure variations of shape, or of an implausible size, or all too fleeting, or with a touch of the dog or the bird. (*Dreamtigers,* 1964, p. 24)

The tiger Borges was trying to dream was similar to the ones Georgie used to draw, which are preserved in his childhood notebooks. It is shapeless, ambiguous, wrong. But it is, nevertheless, a symbol of what was lacking in the child's life: adventure, passion, violence. The tiger was also, unconsciously, associated in Georgie's mythology with other incomprehensible forces. In a poem written when he was in his seventies Borges summarizes what the tiger was to him in the different periods of his long life. It is called "El oro de los tigres" (The Gold of the Tigers) and is the last poem in the book of the same name (1973). He begins by recalling the many times he saw (as a child) the powerful Bengal tiger

> toing and froing on its paced-out path
> behind the labyrinthine iron bars,
> never suspecting them to be a prison.

Later, he would meet other tigers: Blake's blazing tiger, "the amorous gold shower disguising Zeus," the ring from the *Edda Minor* that every ninth night

> gives light to nine rings more, and these, nine more,
> and there is never an end.
>
> (*Gold,* 1977, p. 47)

The poem concludes on a very personal note. His blindness has obliterated all colors but yellow: the gold of the tigers, the primeval gold, and the even more precious gold of his loved one's hair.

Moving from the first image of the tiger in the Palermo zoo to the gold of the woman he longs for, Borges establishes the link between the wild beast and the sexual appetite that engenders and perpetuates life. The allusion to a passage in the *Edda Minor* (which is elucidated in a note to the poem) makes the image of the tiger as a progenitor very clear. The insistence on the nine nights that engender the nine rings contains an allusion to the nine months of gestation and stresses the same obsession with fatherhood that he had dealt with in "The Sect of the Phoenix." Another clue is contained in a reference to one of Zeus' metamorphoses. The tiger thus becomes the symbol of terrifying parenthood. The primal scene finds its primeval symbol.

Tigers were not the only beasts in Georgie's imaginary zoo. In Mother's recollections she mentions prehistoric animals. According to Alicia Jurado, "Norah and he had a toy collection made of such animals" (Jurado, 1964, p. 27). But that was to be a passing fancy. Of all the other beasts he discovered as a child, only the Minotaur became as central to his personal myth as the tiger. Although Borges dedicated one of his most tantalizing stories to the Minotaur, and the Minoan labyrinth, the symbol that is perhaps the most obviously Borgesian of all, critics have not discussed it at length. Borges himself provides some clues in an interview with Herbert Simon, an American computer scientist. They met in Buenos Aires in 1971, and their conversation was recorded and published by the Argentine weekly *Primera Plana* (January 5, 1971, pp. 42–45). Borges confides to Simon that he remembers "having seen an engraving of the labyrinth in a French book" when he was a boy. The book must have been Lemprière's Greek mythology, to which he makes a passing reference in his autobiographical sketch ("Essay," 1970, p. 211). The conversation with Simon continues on a rather ironic note: that illustration showed the labyrinth as "a circular building without doors but with many windows."

BORGES: I used to look at the engraving and I thought that if I used a magnifying glass I would be able to see the Minotaur.
SIMON: Did you find it?
BORGES: As a matter of fact my eyesight was never very good. Later I discovered a bit about life's complexity, as if it were a game. I'm talking about chess now. (Simon, 1971, p. 43)

To illustrate his thoughts, he quotes a poem about being too old to love but not so old as not to see the immense night that surrounds us; not so old not to be still amazed by something hidden in love and passion. Once again, Borges uses a quotation to mask his thoughts; once again, he moves from the subject of the labyrinth and the Minotaur to the subject of passionate love. They are, in fact, closely related: the Minotaur was conceived by Pasiphae out of her bestial passion for a white bull; the labyrinth was the house built by Daedalus to hide (mask) the monster offspring of that union. Love is still amazing. That is, literally, love throws you into a maze. For Borges, as he tells Simon: "Such is the form in which I perceive life. A continuous amazement. A continuous bifurcation of the labyrinth" (ibid., p. 43). Further on in the same conversation he explains that he was less attracted to the idea of the Minotaur than "by another name attributed to that mythological being. I found the name, *Asterion,* in a dictionary. It had connotations of an asteroid or a star. It is an image which I always thought could please the readers" (ibid., p. 43). For Borges, the Minotaur is not just a symbol or a mythological character; it is a name, a word he has found in a dictionary. Images, words: those are the stuff Borges' (and obviously Georgie's) dreams were made on.

In using the myth of the Minotaur and the labyrinth, Borges is aware of its tradition. In a piece he wrote for *The Book of Imaginary Beings* he points out that the invention of the labyrinth is even more strange than that of its inhabitant: "The idea of a house built so that people could become lost in it is perhaps more unusual than that of a man with a bull's head; both ideas go well together and the image of the labyrinth fits with the image of the Minotaur. It is equally fitting that in the corner of a monstrous house there be a monstrous inhabitant" (*Imaginary,* 1969, p. 158).

But the labyrinth was not only built to confuse and mislead people. It was built both to protect the Minotaur and to imprison him. If it is difficult to find a way into the labyrinth, it is equally difficult to find the way out. A paradoxical place, the labyrinth fixes forever the symbolical movement from the exterior into the interior, from the form to the contemplation, from time to the absence of time. It also represents the opposite movement, from inside out, according to a well-known progression. In the center of the labyrinth there is a being, a monster or a god (because monstrosity is sometimes a divine attribute). God or monster, at the center of the labyrinth there is a mystery.

Labyrinths thus become, according to tradition, the representation of ordered chaos, a chaos submitted to human intelligence, a deliberate disorder that contains its own code. They also represent nature in its least human aspects—an immense river is a labyrinth of water; a jungle is a labyrinth of trees—and some of the proudest human achievements—a library is a labyrinth of processed trees; a city is a labyrinth of streets. The same symbol can also be used to invoke the invisible reality of human fate, of God's will, the mystery of artistic creation.

All these allusions can be found in Borges' work. Some of his favorite authors (Joyce and Kafka, for instance) have been attracted by the same image. In spite of that, the explicit symbol of the labyrinth appears very rarely in his work until 1938, when he began to write some of his strangest fiction. The symbol is even less frequent in his verse. The first mention occurs in the poem "Of Heaven and Hell," written in 1942. From then on it is almost constantly present. "Conjectural Poem" (1943), which dramatizes the fate of one of his ancestors, is really a poem on man's labyrinthine fate.

Borges tries to unravel the mystery of the labyrinth in a story called "The House of Asterion," collected for the first time in *The Aleph* (1949). A quotation from Apollodorus (*The Library,* III, 1) which briefly states that the Queen gave birth to a son called Asterion, opens the story, which is divided into two parts. The first part consists of Asterion's monologue. He says that he lives alone in an unfurnished palace whose plan (the reader slowly realizes) is that of a labyrinth. Some observations make perfectly clear that Asterion is a vain young man, very ignorant of the uses of this world. It is also clear that every nine years he kills nine men and that he is waiting with hope for his redeemer to come. The brief second part (some five lines) identifies the redeemer as Theseus and indicates obliquely the death of the Minotaur. As in stories such as "Streetcorner Man" and "The Shape of the Sword," the first-person narrative helps Borges to omit part of the tale and hide its real meaning until the very last lines of the text. In this particular case, he is trying to hide from the reader the real identity of Asterion. By avoiding the words "Minotaur" and "labyrinth," he manages to keep the mystery and enhance the suspense, as in any good detective story. Unfortunately, Di Giovanni's translation (in spite of its merit) makes a crucial error in substituting for Borges' ambiguous rendering of Apollodorus' words the more scholarly translation: "And she gave birth to Asterius, who was called the Minotaur" (*Review*, 1973, p. 63).

Borges is also concerned with defining, in an oblique manner, the true nature of the Minotaur. Only indirectly, by allusion, is its monstrous nature indicated. In order to prove that he is free to move around and even to go out in the streets, Asterion says:

> As a matter of fact, one evening I did step out into the street; if I came back before nightfall I did so out of the horror that the faces of the common people stirred in me—colorless, flattened faces like an open palm. The sun had already set, but the helpless wail of a child and the crude supplications of the mob showed that they knew me. Men uttered prayers, fled, fell before me on their knees. Some clambered up the steps of the Temple of the Axes, others gathered stones. One or two, I believe, sought refuge beneath the waves. Not for nothing was my mother a queen; I cannot mingle with the crowd, even if my modesty were to allow it. (Ibid., p. 63)

In this indirect way Borges provides the reader with important information: Asterion lives in a house next to the Temple of the Axes, which alludes to one of the possible etymologies for labyrinth (from the Greek *labrys,* the two-headed ax); his mother was a queen, that is, Pasiphae, wife of Minos, the king of Crete; even more important, his face is neither colorless nor flat. Asterion's reaction to the human face is strong—he feels horror—but the crowd's reaction to him is no less strong. People are also horrified, although Asterion is vain enough not to notice it. Later, in describing his innocent pastimes, he adds another significant detail: "Like a butting ram, I rush down these stone passages until I fall to the ground in a daze." He also describes a game he plays with his double, an imaginary Asterion who comes to visit him and to whom he shows the house: "Bowing low, I say to him: 'Now we are back at the same crossway,' or 'Now we find our way into a new courtyard,' or 'I knew you'd like this water trough,' or 'Now you're about to see a cistern that has filled with sand,' or 'Now you'll see how the cellar branches right and left.' Sometimes I make a mistake and the two of us have a good laugh" (ibid., p. 63).

In the last paragraph of the monologue, when Asterion describes how he greets the nine men whom he has "to deliver from all evil," as he euphemistically puts it, there also are some hints about his monstrous nature: "I hear their footsteps or their voices along the stone passages and, full of joy, I rush to find them. The ceremony lasts only minutes. One after the other they go down, and my hands are unsullied. Where they fall they remain; these corpses help me to tell apart one passageway from another" (ibid., pp. 63–64). The fact that he kills them without using his hands suggests that he does it with his horns; the charging of the bull is also alluded to in the words "I rush to find them." In the last phrases of the monologue, when he is pondering the coming of a redeemer prophesied by one of his victims, he asks himself: "What will my redeemer be like? I ask myself. Will he be a bull or a man? Can he possibly be a bull with a man's face? Or will he be like me?" (ibid., p. 64). In a later text, which is included in *The Book of Imaginary Beings,* Borges explains the problems raised by the representation of a monster, half bull, half man. "Ovid in a line that is meant to be clever speaks of the *semibovemque vitum, semivirumque bovem* ('the man half bull, the bull half man'). Dante, who was familiar with the writings of the ancients but not with their coins or monuments, imagined the Minotaur with a man's head and bull's body (*Inferno,* XII, 1–30)" (*Imaginary,* 1969, p. 158). In the same text Borges summarizes the legend:

> The Minotaur . . . was born of the furious passion of Pasiphae, Queen of Crete, for a white bull that Neptune brought out of the sea. Daedalus, who invented the artifice that carried the Queen's unnatural desires to gratification, built the labyrinth destined to confine and keep hidden her monstrous son. The Minotaur fed on human flesh and for its nourishment the King of Crete imposed on the City of Athens a yearly tribute of seven young men and seven maidens. Theseus resolved to deliver his country from this burden when it fell to his lot to be sacrificed to the Minotaur's hunger. Ariadne, the King's daughter, gave him a thread so that he could trace his way out of the windings of the labyrinth's corridors: the hero killed the Minotaur and was able to escape from the maze. (Ibid., p. 158)

There are very important differences between Borges' rendering of the myth and Asterion's version. Some facts are omitted in the latter's monologue. There is no indication that he feeds on the body of his victim, although this could be taken as an oversight on his part. But there are more significant differences. His monologue indicates another cycle for the tribute to be paid: nine years instead of every year; nine men instead of seven young men and seven maidens. Asterion (in Borges' story) is not concerned at all with women. The change in the figure (nine instead of seven) could be attributed to the fact, already indicated in the story, that Asterion cannot read or write, and that he does not know how to count. Also, by prolonging the period of tribute, Borges avoids the cannibalistic implication of the sacrifice and by changing it to nine reinforces the allusion to the months of gestation.

There is an interesting difference between the Spanish text of the piece on the Minotaur in *The Book of Imaginary Beings* and the English version done by Di Giovanni in collaboration with the author. The principal change concerns the words used to describe Pasiphae's attachment to the bull. In Spanish Borges twice uses the same euphemistic word, *amores,* which means "loves." In the English translation he is more explicit but still reticent: "furious passion" the first time; "unnatural desires" the second. But the main point is that the three expressions avoid using the exact word: lust. And that is what the myth is all about. At the end of the article on the Minotaur Borges writes: "The worship of the bull and of the two-headed ax . . . was typical of pre-Hellenic religions, which held sacred bullfights. Human forms with bull-heads figured, to judge by wall paintings, in the demonology of Crete. Most likely the Greek fable of the Minotaur is a late and clumsy version of far older myths, the shadow of other dreams still more full of horror" (ibid., p. 159). On this tantalizing note, the piece ends. One can only conjecture about these far older myths and dreams. But Borges gives another hint in the epilogue to the Spanish edition of *The Aleph,* where he indicates some of the sources of the story: "To a painting by Watts, done in 1896, I owe 'The House of Asterion' and the character of its sad protagonist" (*El Aleph,* 1949, p. 171). The painting shows Asterion in profile and from the back, leaning on one of the palace's parapets and looking rather longingly to the world outside. It is this feeling of sadness and loneliness which Borges has taken from Watts and subtly introduced in the story.

In a text quoted by Di Giovanni in his introduction to the English version of the story, Borges recognizes this. "It is a sad story—a story of loneliness and stupidity. . . . It stands for feeling lonesome, for feeling useless" (*Review,* 1973, p. 62). The story was originally published in the magazine *Los Anales de Buenos Aires,* which Borges edited between 1946 and 1948. According to Di Giovanni, Borges wrote it in two days in 1947. He was closing an issue of the magazine and discovered he had two pages to fill. "He commissioned a half-page drawing of the Minotaur on the spot and then sat down and wrote his tale to measure." Knowing Borges' extremely slow process of composition, especially at the time he was writing those stories, it seems hard to believe that he wrote "The House of Asterion" just like that. He probably had some notes, a sketch or a first draft somewhere, and the pressure to fill those two pages must have acted as a spur. But if he actually did complete the story in two days, it might have been because the theme of the labyrinth and its monstrous inhabitant cut very deeply into his own being. Somehow the story began to be written while Georgie was poring over Lemprière's book with the engraving of the labyrinth, believing that if he looked hard enough and with a magnifying glass, he might be able to see poor, sad Asterion.

In identifying himself with the Minotaur, Georgie was paving the way for Borges' future mythology. At the time, he probably felt, somewhat obscurely, that he was a bit like Asterion. He didn't live alone in a palace built like a labyrinth; but his garden was a labyrinth, and from its gates he could watch strange people moving around in the streets, busy with their mysterious errands, different, alien. Inside the garden life was simpler. Only at night, when the garden was closed and it was time to go to bed, did the horrors of everyday life take over. From mirrors came terror. The other self was waiting there, shapeless and green-colored. These were the really old myths, "the shadow of other dreams still more full of horror" that Borges talks about in his piece on the Minotaur in *The Book of Imaginary Beings*.

Georgie even had with him (like the imaginary double with which Asterion played) a carnal double, his sister, Norah, always ready to participate in his games and to share his dreams and obsessions. But her more important function—that of protecting him against a ruthless and invisible enemy—is also presented, in symbolic form, in the myth of the Minotaur. At the end of "The House of Asterion" Borges quietly incorporates this new element. The last paragraph of the story says:

> The morning sun glinted off the bronze sword.
> It no longer showed even a trace of blood.
> "Would you believe it, Ariadne?" said Theseus.
> "The Minotaur barely put up a fight."
> (*Review*, 1973, p. 64)

The Minotaur's reaction can be explained by the fact that he believed Theseus to be his redeemer. And up to a point he was right, because Theseus' function was to free him from his monstrosity. Death was a liberation. In shifting the narrative focus from Asterion's monologue to an impersonal narrator who follows very closely Theseus' actions and words, Borges also shifts his allegiances and those of his reader. The protagonist of the story is no longer Asterion but Theseus. And from this new point of view, Asterion is reduced to a monster that had to be slain. But that is not the real meaning of the shift. What Borges insinuates is that Asterion and Theseus are doubles: two sides of the same personality. Asterion's sacrifice or redemption is really a metamorphosis: out of the labyrinth comes Theseus, the new Asterion.

A new character is introduced obliquely at the end of the story: Ariadne, the invisible and silent presence to whom Theseus' words are addressed. She is the daughter of Minos and Pasiphae, and in giving Theseus the thread to get safely out of the labyrinth, she goes against her father's authority. She is also an ambiguous, or double, character. In helping Theseus to kill the Minotaur, she seems to be against her half-brother. But as Theseus is also the redeemer, her action is finally beneficial to the Minotaur. In her duplicity, Ariadne stands for Norah: both were linked to their brothers by blood; their function was to protect the best part of them. Both succeeded in bringing them alive out of the labyrinth.

As happens in dreams, each section of the story shifts points of view and changes the identity of the characters. The stories told by dreams play on permutation and metamorphoses. In the dreams written by authors, the same happens. Out of those dreams, and the daydreamings of childhood, tales are written. Thus in 1947 Borges could compose in two days a story Georgie probably never told anybody but endlessly and symbolically rehearsed with the help of Norah, his playmate, his Ariadne, his guide in the labyrinth of his inner self.

7.
The Italian Quarter

Before Norah was born, the Borgeses moved to Palermo, a poor neighborhood on the outskirts of Buenos Aires. Georgie was only two. In a poem written in 1929 and explicitly dedicated to "The Mythological Foundation of Buenos Aires" (he changed the adjective later to "Mythical"), Borges tells how he discovered his native city: first, in the history books he read at school; later, through his own experience. The identification of the poet with his city is made explicit in the fourth stanza, where he disputes the history books' claim that Buenos Aires was founded in the Riachuelo district:

> but that is a story dreamed up in the Boca.
> It was really a city block in my district—Palermo.

> A whole square block, but set down in open country,
> attended by dawns and rains and hard southeasters.
> identical to that block which still stands in my neighborhood:
> Guatemala—Serrano—Paraguay—Gurruchaga.
> (*Poems,* 1972, translated by Alastair Reid, pp. 48–49)

The city block he mentions is where his home stood—at 2135 Serrano Street. In a 1964 conversation with Napoleon Murat he gives these recollections of Palermo:

When I was a boy, the town ended there, fifty yards from our home. There was a rather dirty stream which was called Maldonado, then some empty lots, and the town began again at Belgrano. What was in between the Pacific bridge and Belgrano was not the countryside, that word would be too beautiful, but empty lots, and villas. The neighborhood was very poor. At Serrano Street there were only three two-story houses with patios. One had the feeling of being at the edge of town. When I wrote the biography of Carriego, I looked for old folks and they told me a lot of stories of those days, stories that had to do with the tango, etc. However, and this is rather strange, I do not have personal memories of those things. . . . (Murat, 1964, p. 373)

In his 1930 biography of Carriego, a popular neighborhood poet, Borges also included a description of Palermo as it might have been in the late nineteenth century. In his description there is perhaps an echo of how the place looked to Georgie some years later. Using and perhaps abusing the rhetorical device called hypallage—in which a quality of one object is displaced to another object—Borges writes:

> Toward the boundary with Balvanera in the east, there were sprawling houses with strings of patios, the sprawling yellow or ocher houses with an arched door—an arch which was mirrored by another arch in the inner door of the house, delicately cast in iron. When the impatient nights of October took chairs and people out to the sidewalks and the profound houses opened up for inspection their backyards, and there was a yellow light in the patios, the street was cozy and light and the empty houses were like lanterns in a row. (*Carriego,* 1930, p. 20)

But perhaps those recollections were purely literary, carefully made up of words drawn from Carriego's verses or writings about his life. Writing much later, when he was seventy, Borges included in his "Autobiographical Essay" memories that confirm, or elaborate on, what he had already said to Napoleon Murat:

> I cannot tell whether my first memories go back to the eastern or to the western bank of the muddy, slow-moving Río de la Plata—to Montevideo, where we spent long, lazy holidays in the villa of my uncle Francisco Haedo, or to Buenos Aires. I was born there, in the very heart of that city, in 1899, on Tucumán Street, between Suipacha and Esmeralda, in a small, unassuming house belonging to my maternal grandparents. . . . We must have moved out to the suburb of Palermo quite soon, because there I have my first memories of another house with two patios, a garden with a tall windmill pump, and on the other side of the garden an empty lot. Palermo at that time—the Palermo where we lived, Serrano and Guatemala—was on the shabby northern outskirts of town, and many people, ashamed of saying they lived there, spoke in a dim way of living on the Northside. We lived in one of the few two-story homes on our street; the rest of the neighborhood was made up of low houses and vacant lots. I have often spoken of this area as a slum, but I do not quite mean that in the American sense of the word. In Palermo lived shabby, genteel people as well as more undesirable sorts. There was also a Palermo of hoodlums, called *compadritos,* famed for their

knife fights, but this Palermo was only later to capture my imagination, since we did our best—our successful best—to ignore it. Unlike our neighbor Evaristo Carriego, however, who was the first Argentine poet to explore the literary possibilities that lay there at hand. As for myself, I was hardly aware of the existence of *compadritos,* since I lived essentially indoors. ("Essay," 1970, pp. 203–204)

Although Georgie's knowledge of Palermo was limited, some of the neighborhood's most colorful aspects caught the boy's attention. In the poem dedicated to his home garden, Borges gives tantalizing glimpses of what could be seen from the garden or from the second floor of their house. He talks about the horse carriages and the carnival, the sound of popular music and the hoodlums who hung around the general store: a world teeming with strange, almost exotic life. The Borgeses were doubly alienated from Palermo: they were half English and came from old Argentine stock. Palermo, on the contrary, was a town where immigrants settled, a kind of no-man's land where the "poor but respectable" working class lived next door to petty criminals whose energies were devoted to pimping, whoring, and random violence.

As its name indicates, Palermo had Italian origins. According to one source quoted by Borges in his biography of Carriego, the neighborhood took its name from an Italian called Domenico who changed his name into the more Spanish Domínguez and added the name of his native town, Palermo, as homage. This happened in the early seventeenth century. Two centuries later, the Italian immigrants who came to Argentina chose that neighborhood, perhaps because of its name, perhaps because it was cheap and not too far from the downtown area. In his reminiscences Borges never mentions the Italians or the Italian origin of the word "Palermo," possibly because he was writing for an Argentine audience that already had that information. The only proof that he was aware of the Italians in the Palermo of his childhood is one specific mention of the Calabrese in his reminiscences with Napoleon Murat, already quoted. But why the Calabrese and not the Neapolitans or the Genovese? In his book on Carriego there is a short explanation; in describing the Maldonado, a small and dirty stream close to his home, Borges writes: "Toward the Maldonado, native hoodlums were scarce, their places taken by the Calabrese, people with whom nobody wanted to get involved because of the dangerously long time they bore grudges or the long-lasting scars of their knifings" (*Carriego,* 1930, p. 22).

To understand Borges' prejudice against the Italians it is necessary to point out that in the years before Borges was born, Argentina had a predominantly Spanish population. Borges' ancestors on both sides had their roots in the colonial period: warriors who had conquered the land, settlers who had tamed it, heroes who had fought to free it from Spain and from local tyrants. They were the icons of Borges' family museum. But these pious traditions clashed brutally with Argentine reality at the turn of the century. Some eight million Italians had come to the River Plate area in the last decades of the nineteenth century. They were peasants from the poorest parts of Italy, illiterate and hungry, and they viewed Argentina as the new El Dorado. The Argentine government had opened up the country to them because it needed them to populate the vast spaces of the pampas, to till the fields, to work in the new factories. President Sarmiento had initiated this policy, which he took (with so many other things) from the United States. As happened also in the United States, the Italian immigrants began to influence the national character. By the time Borges was born and his parents had decided to move to Palermo, Buenos Aires was beginning to look like an Italian city. But Georgie knew little of this. He continued to live in his garden, protected from the world outside by his imagination and the stories his English grandmother read to him.

The house where he had been born, close to the downtown area, was still part of the traditional Buenos Aires of people of Spanish stock. But Palermo was already another country. His father's decision to move there must have been prompted by financial considerations. He probably could not afford a two-story house with a garden in any other part of Buenos Aires. Borges recalled many years later that many "shabby, genteel people" lived there. What he does not say in his "Essay" is that many of these people were Italians.

Today it is hard to understand his omission. The Italian component of Argentine culture is so strong that it seems impossible not to acknowledge it. But in a symbolic sense Georgie never left Father's library of English books or Mother's secluded Hispanic garden. Although he later learned Italian well enough to read and reread Dante, Ariosto, and Croce, he has always maintained that he cannot understand spoken Italian; he has claimed he seldom goes to see an Italian movie because he cannot follow the dialogue. (Subtitles have always been too small for him to read.) His prejudice is as strong as the one he holds against Spaniards. The roots are similar. In Borges' household the language of culture and refinement was English. Spanish was only second best, because it was the language of servants and illiterate people. Italian was not even considered. It was the language of peasants who could not speak it properly and had little to do with the great Italian poets and novelists. Georgie refused to even acknowledge its existence. He might have heard a few words of Italian slang in the conversations between servants and delivery boys, but he fails to acknowledge even this, possibly because the Italians corrupted not only their own language (the tongue of Dante and Petrarch) but also Argentine Spanish.

The slang spoken in the slums of Buenos Aires was called *lunfardo* (from *lunfa,* a petty thief). Experts agree that it was not a language but an argot: words and idioms used to hide more than reveal what the speakers were saying. It had the same origin as the famous language of Germania, spoken by Spanish soldiers who came home from the German wars of the sixteenth century and widely used in picaresque novels, even in *Don Quixote. Lunfardo* was metaphorical, vivid, and colorful, and it spread to all classes of Argentine society mainly through tango lyrics and the short fiction and popular theater of the day. In a 1927 lecture called "El idioma de los argentinos" (The Language of the Argentines), later collected in a book of the same title, Borges has this to say:

> There is no general dialect of our popular classes: the language spoken in the slums is not it. The old native Argentines do not use it, women seldom speak it, even the local hoodlums only parade it to look tougher. The vocabulary is extremely poor: it is formed by some twenty concepts, and a sick proliferation of synonyms complicates it. So narrow is it that the popular playwrights have to invent words and have even resorted to the very telling ingenuity of inverting the common ones. That destitution is not normal, because the language of the slums is nothing but a decantation or divulgation of *lunfardo,* which is a jargon invented to conceal what thieves had to say. *Lunfardo* is a trade vocabulary, as with so many others; it is the technology of the *furca* (half-Nelson or lock) and the skeleton key. (*Idioma,* 1928, pp. 166–167)

Once more, Borges avoids mentioning the linguistic components of *lunfardo.* It was based on Spanish but with a strong Italian influence, plus some specific words from the argot used by French pimps and whores. Those were the days when a French prostitute was highly prized and a profitable traffic was established between Marseilles and Buenos Aires. That part of *lunfardo* was as technical (to use Borges' expression) as one could desire. But if Borges omits mention of Italian or French, it is only because he is more interested in other things. In the book on Carriego written in 1930 he says very little about *lunfardo.* Carriego, who was born in the provinces, used it sparingly. Only a few of his writings are cited in José Gobello's excellent *Lunfardia* (1953). More probably exist, but for the most part Carriego used the common speech of Buenos Aires and not a limited patois. And that is what Borges was interested in proving.

In reissuing the book some twenty-five years later, Borges added a few new pieces. The most important is "History of the Tango," in which he rewrites and updates an article published in 1927 under the title "Progeny of the Tango." As the most popular music produced in the River Plate area, the tango has come to symbolize Argentina. Borges deplored this identification, primarily because the most widely known tango form is not the one he likes best (or dislikes least, to be more precise). The popular tango is either the choreographed version Valentino illustrated in the Paris sequence of *The Four Horsemen of the Apocalypse* (Metro, 1920) or the sentimental ballad forever associated with the name of Carlos Gardel, the Sinatra of that era. Borges considered the Paris version a fake. The tango was born in the brothels of Montevideo and Buenos Aires and for decades was considered too obscene to be danced in public. Only the hoodlums dared to dance it in the streets, and then both dancers were always men. For Borges, the Valentino version was despicable. His opinion of Gardel was no less critical. He believed that the sentimentality of the lyrics the singer had made so popular and his affected delivery of them ruined a music which could easily do without lyrics. Against the most popular topics of tango lyrics (unmanly lament for a lost love or a betrayal), Borges stresses in his writings that the tango originated in the rivalry among hoodlums, confronting each other in a game of power, violence, and deadly skills. The fact that the tango began in brothels had served to emphasize its heterosexual connotations. But men do not go to brothels just to meet women; they also go to meet, and compete, with other men. The men who danced the tango in the streets were engaged in a show of physical skill with sexual undertones.

In "History of the Tango" Borges reports that "as a boy I could see in Palermo, and years later in Chacarita and Boedo, that it was danced on the streetcorners by couples of men, because working-class women didn't want to have anything to do with a tramp's dance" (*Carriego*, 1955, p. 145).

This brief glimpse of Georgie, at the garden gate or in the street, watching a couple of hoodlums going through the elaborate motions of the tango is tantalizing. The boy couldn't have had a precise idea of what he was seeing, except that it was a very reprehensible activity because not even working-class women would stoop to it. At the time Georgie was living in Palermo, the tango had not yet become fashionable in Europe, and upper-class Buenos Aires society, as well as the respectable poor, rejected it completely. Both the upper and the lower classes were right to do so, because in aiming at respectability they rejected physical violence. But the hoodlums could survive only through violence. And sexual violence as it was practiced in the brothel was not too far from the violence men did to each other in their fights for supremacy. The tango, according to Borges, expressed both sides of the coin:

> The sexual character of the tango was noticed by many, but not its quarrel-some nature. It is true that both are modes or manifestations of the same impulse, and thus the word *man,* in all the languages I know, has a connota-tion both of sexual capacity and fighting capacity, and the word *virtus,* which in Latin means courage, comes from *vir,* which is man. Similarly, in one of *Kim*'s pages, an Afghan states: "When I was fifteen, I had shot my man and begot my man," as if the two acts were essentially the same. (Ibid., pp. 146–147)

In this interpretation the tango is not only an elaborate ritual to conceal and reveal the mating urge; it is also a test of manliness, a close fight (body against body) with a rival as skillful and powerful as oneself. The latent homosexual component of that fight, on which Borges does not comment, is thus made visible.

In criticizing the tango, Borges has some good words to say about one of the tango's ancestors, the milonga. Although it never at-tained the tango's international fame, the milonga is considered supe-rior by some aficionados. Its rhythm is quicker; it avoids elaborate footwork and requires a certain agility. And its lyrics are generally free of sentimentality. In his later years Borges composed lyrics for some milongas, celebrating the courage and skill of the infamous hoodlums.

In "History of the Tango" Borges rectifies his earlier view of Italian immigrants:

> I recall that around 1926 I was fond of attributing to the Italians . . . the decline of the tango. In that myth, or fantasy, of a "native" tango ruined by the "wops," I see now a clear symptom of some nationalistic heresies which later ravaged the world—promoted by the "wops," of course. It was not the accordion, which I once called cowardly, nor the dutiful composers of the waterfront which made the tango what it is, but the whole nation. Besides, the old native folk who engendered the tango were called Bevilacqua, Greco, or de Bassi. (Ibid., p. 162)

Besides an occasional glimpse of two hoodlums dancing an elaborate dance on a streetcorner, Georgie had few contacts with the tango and its world. One of these may have been John Tink, an au-thentic hoodlum who was a cousin of Miss Tink, Georgie's English governess. Like so many of Borges' heroes and heroines, John Tink was a soul divided between two loyalties: to a European tradition of culture represented by his cousin, and to a native, more barbarous experience. As with the English captive in Borges' tale "The Story of the Warrior and the Captive," John Tink was ensnared by the environment and became "Juan Tink, el inglés," one of the hoodlums who hung around streetcorners (De Milleret, 1967, p. 23). It is not known how much Georgie knew about him, nor with what Victorian sternness Miss Tink reacted to her cousin's fate. What is known is that the only hoodlum Georgie saw at close quarters was an Englishman. Not until years later, upon writing his biography of Carriego, would Borges come across the real native product.

Georgie met one other representative of the tango and its strange world. One of his paternal cousins, Alvaro Melián Lafinur, was a minor writer and a bit of a bohemian. He had relatives in Uruguay and apparently had a wide experience of brothels on both sides of the River Plate. Alvaro, like Prince Danilo in Strauss' *Merry Widow,* burned his candle at both ends. In his escapades he did not confine himself to prostitutes; maidens, married women, and widows were also fair game. From Alvaro, Georgie gained some tantalizing glimpses of a life he would experience briefly during his residence in Spain. Alvaro was also very fond of tangos and, accompanied by his own guitar, used to sing them on the Sundays he came to visit the Borgeses.

Thus a whiff of the forbidden world outside the garden reached Georgie every once in a while.

8.
The Other Bank of the River

Borges had few memories of the Palermo quarter where he lived as a child, but among his most vivid recollections were the holidays spent with his family in Uruguay, on the other bank of the River Plate. Every February, when Father was on vacation, the Borgeses crossed the muddy, wide river to spend a whole month at the villa of Mother's cousin Francisco Haedo. The villa was located on the outskirts of Montevideo in Paso Molino (literally: the pass to the mill). Once a rural village, Paso Molino, by the beginning of the twentieth century, was a small town that had been swallowed by Montevideo. In those days South Americans were just beginning to discover the beauty of a suntan and the stimulation of sea air. Beaches and all the amenities of the coastline had until then been left to fishermen and beachcombers. Since respectable grown-ups did not spend much time on the coast, the children had to amuse themselves in the garden surrounding the villa, one considerably larger than the garden at Palermo. Francisco's daughter, Esther, became a valued and trusted participant in Georgie and Norah's games. She was always willing to help Norah to come to the boy's defense against unseen but ever present enemies.

Summer days (which in that part of the world correspond exactly to winter in the Northern hemisphere) were long and lazy, made tolerable only by the children's imagination. When the heat was unbearable—and it can be unbearable in the months of January and February in the low-lying, humid River Plate basin, where the big tropical rivers of the south come finally to the sea—the children were taken to the river banks and neighboring Capurro beach. In those days Capurro still had some pretensions to gentility. There were villas and a promenade overlooking the River Plate, which at that point is so wide that it is impossible to see the Argentine bank. Nearby, as a backdrop to the beach, the volcanolike structure of Montevideo's small Cerro could be seen. This modest, conical hill, topped by a Spanish fortress, probably gave the town its name. (One of the etymologies of Montevideo is *monte vide eu,* which perhaps meant "I have seen a mountain," a statement attributed to one of Magellan's Portuguese sailors, who discovered it in 1519.) The children were probably taken to see the fortress, a sturdy building constructed by the Spaniards in 1724 to contain and control the already worrisome Portuguese expansion southward from Brazil.

Today Capurro is a slum. The whole Cerro area has become part of a working-class town, with meat-packing factories and tenements, big oil tanks, and an active traffic of small vessels. There is a busy crowd now where ladies and gentlemen of the Belle Epoque once strolled with their children, their dogs, and their servants. A French engineer, visiting Montevideo in the first decade of the twentieth century, made a quick inspection of the shoreline and recommended to President Batlle (the man who shaped modern Uruguay) that the city be developed not toward the west or the north but toward the east. There, a string of beaches with the softest white sand and invigorating breezes coming from the Atlantic Ocean made the summer bearable. President Batlle took the advice to heart, and in implementing it he created one of the sources of Uruguayan prosperity for decades to come. Summer resorts eventually extended along the entire northern bank of the River Plate toward the Atlantic and the Brazilian frontier.

But when the Borgeses went summering in Paso Molino, all this belonged to the future. Instead of the wavy coastline of Punta del Este and La Paloma, they met only the sweet and mildly polluted waters of Capurro. Many years later Borges celebrated the river with a famous line in his poem "The Mythological Founding of Buenos Aires," calling it "that torpid, muddy river" (*Poems,* 1972, p. 49). In the Spanish text the river is described not as "torpid" but as "sleepy." The River Plate must have seemed sleepy and muddy to Georgie every summer. The usual way of crossing the river in those days was on a large ferryboat with paddles which took no less than twelve hours to reach Montevideo. It had elegant drawing rooms and a good restaurant, with comfortable first-class cabins. It left Buenos Aires in the evening and reached Montevideo in the early hours of the next morning. Adults used to stay awake all night—to see dawn, they claimed, but probably to get drunk and/or do some explorations of their own in the darkest corners of the boat. But children, after having exhausted the possibilities of adventure on the many staircases and corridors, were sent to bed.

The Haedos came from the northwest and had a ranch near

Fray Bentos, on the Uruguay River. (Uruguay gets its name from that river, which separates it from Argentina and runs almost directly northward into the River Plate.) The Borgeses used to go to the ranch in the summer. Many years later, in a short story called "Funes, the Memorious," Borges evoked some memories of the San Francisco ranch and the Haedos, although placing the anecdote in a time, 1884, when he had not yet been born. Georgie learned to swim on the waters of the Uruguay River. They were swift, live waters, and only a strong swimmer could withstand the currents. Georgie became a very good swimmer. Fifteen years later, when swimming in the Rhone in Geneva or, even later, in the Mediterranean, he boasted of his early training in the swift waters of the Uruguay. (He also boasts about his swimming skills in his "Autobiographical Essay," p. 219.)

Georgie did some swimming too in a small stream close to the Paso Molino villa. The water there was not so swift and thus was less challenging, but the children welcomed the chance to escape from the heat of the summer. Either on the Uruguay or in the small stream in Paso Molino, Georgie spent part of each summer practicing the only sport he really liked. Only when forced by his poor eyesight, following an accident in which the retina of one of his eyes was separated, did he give up swimming for good. Borges' poem "Poema del cuarto elemento" ("Poem to the Fourth Element") echoes these childhood experiences:

> Water, I beg you. For this sleepy
> Chain of numbered words I am telling you,
> Remember Borges, your swimmer, your friend,
> Do not make yourself scarce at the very last moment.
> (*Obra,* 1964, p. 151)

On the Uruguayan bank life seemed easier. Georgie always considered Uruguay, and especially Montevideo, more traditional than Buenos Aires, more authentically rooted in the River Plate's history and old ways. Years later, in a poem originally published in 1924 and later collected in *Moon Across the Way* (1925), Borges expressed his feelings for the town that belonged to him through his Acevedo and Haedo ancestors:

> You are the Buenos Aires we had, the one that quietly went away,
> You are backwatery and clear in the afternoon as the memories of a
>   smooth friendship.
> Fondness grows in your stones as a humble grass.
> You belong to us, you're like a party, as the star that the waters reflect.
> False exits to time, your streets look at the lightest past.

Light from your morning comes to us, over the sweet muddiness of waters.
Before lighting up my shades your low sun brings happiness to your villas.
City that sounds like a verse.
Streets with patio light.

(Poemas, 1943, pp. 91–92)

"Montevideo" summarizes Borges' feelings for his mother's native country and the hospitality the Haedos always gave him. In the fourth line the Spanish text is even more explicit. It literally says "You are ours and holidaylike"; in the sixth verse there is a description of the slow River Plate waters he had to cross every summer.

Three years after writing that poem, Borges stated in a prologue to Ildefonso Pereda Valdés' *Anthology of Modern Uruguayan Poetry* his rights to be and feel like an Uruguayan:

What is my justification for being at the entrance-door [of this book]? None except that river of Uruguayan blood that goes through my chest; none except for the Uruguayan days there are in my days and whose memories I know I deserve. Those stories—the Montevidean grandfather who left to join the Grand Army in 1851 and lived twenty years of war; the grandmother from Mercedes who united in the same tone of rejection Oribe and Rosas—allow me to participate, in a mysterious but constant way, in Uruguay. Then, there are my memories, also. Many of them ancient, I found, belong to Montevideo; some—a siesta, the smell of wet earth, a different light—I could not tell from which river bank they come. That fusion or confusion, that community, can be beautiful. (Valdés, 1927, pp. 219–220)

The prologue ends by comparing the differing attitude of Argentines and Uruguayans toward their respective countries:

We Argentines live in the lazy conviction of belonging to a great country, a country whose excessive extension makes us visible enough because of the multiplicity of its bulls and the fertility of its plains. If the providential rain and the providential Italian immigrant do not fail us, we will become the Chicago of this side of the planet and even its bakery. But the Uruguayans do not behave like that. Thus, their heroic disposition to differentiate themselves [from us], their persistence in being themselves, their searching and early-rising soul. If on many occasions, they not only search but find, it will be mean to envy them for it. The sun, in the mornings, passes by San Felipe of Montevideo before it comes here. (Ibid., p. 221)

The last words of the prologue (which, by the way, was printed as an epilogue) repeat the image already used in the seventh verse of "Montevideo." But if Borges was then trying to stress both the differences and similarities between the two banks of the River Plate, in another piece written only three years later he erased the distinctions to show what they had in common: the tradition of their origins and development, which both countries share so intimately and which is expressed in Borges' own ancestors. The piece was published as an introduction to a book on the Uruguayan painter Pedro Figari, who lived a very important part of his life in Buenos Aires and painted subjects that belong to both countries: "Figari paints the Argentine memoir. I say *Argentine* and in using that word I am not practicing an absent-minded annexation of Uruguay, but I am making an irreproachable reference to the River Plate, which, unlike the metaphorical one of death, has two banks: the one as Argentine as the other, both selected by my hope" (*Figari,* 1930).

The feeling of these references to Uruguay and his own Montevidean experiences is also reflected in some of his more recent interviews. Here and there, a small detail surfaces from the depths of the past. In talking to Jean de Milleret about the house in which he was born, Borges evokes one of his most peculiar childhood memories: that of a cistern where the rainwater was collected.

> At the bottom of the cistern there was a tortoise, to purify the water, people believed. Mother and I have drunk for years that tortoise water without ever thinking about it even though the water was rather "unpurified" by the tortoise. But that was the custom and nobody paid any attention. Nevertheless, when you rented a house you always asked if there was a tortoise in the cistern. . . . But in Montevideo things were different. Estela Canto once told me that they had toads there and not tortoises. Thus, when you were renting a house and asked the question, they answered, "Don't you worry, Madam, there is a toad," and then you drank the rain water purified by that live filter, without any qualms whatsoever. (De Milleret, 1967, pp. 18–19)

In a later interview, with Cesar Fernández Moreno, he refers to the same anecdote and concludes:

> The first memories I have are the memories of a garden, a railing, a rainbow, but I don't known on which side of the river they were located. It could be in Palermo, it could be a villa in Adrogué, or it could be the villa of an uncle of mine, Francisco Haedo, in Paso Molino, Montevideo. Yes, they are like that, very vague, and I don't know on which bank of the River Plate to place them: on the east or the west bank. (Fernández Moreno, 1967, p. 8)

To the Uruguayan side of his family Georgie owes another discovery of his childhood: the pampas. Visiting the ranch of one of his Acevedo uncles, he came across a place which had till then loomed larger in his reading than in actual experience. According to the "Autobiographical Essay," he was almost ten when he went to a place near San Nicolás, northwest of Buenos Aires. His recollections are limited but precise: "I remember that the nearest house was a kind of blur on the horizon. This endless distance, I found out, was called the pampa" ("Essay," 1970, pp. 212–213). When he learned that the farmhands were gauchos, Georgie was moved: he had already met them in books, and that fact "gave them a certain glamour." Borges can recall only a few details of the gaucho life Georgie saw:

> Once, I was allowed to accompany them on horseback, taking cattle to the river early one morning. The men were small and darkish and wore *bombachas,* a kind of wide, baggy trouser. When I asked them if they knew how to swim, they replied, "Water is meant for cattle." My mother gave a doll, in a large cardboard box, to the foreman's daughter. The next year, we went back and asked after the little girl. "What a delight the doll has been to her!" they told us. And we were shown it, still in its box, nailed to the wall like an image. Of course, the girl was allowed only to look at it, not to touch it, for it might have been soiled or broken. There it was, high up, put out of harm's way, worshipped from afar. (Ibid., p. 213)

In telling these anecdotes, Borges seems intent on depriving the gauchos of the mythological trappings that a century and a half of regionalist literature had given them. To the poetic image of the gaucho and his habitat, he opposes the commonsense attitude of the real farmhands, who had very limited notions about the country they lived in (swimming doesn't come to their minds) or about the joys of life (a toy becomes an icon). But in stressing only this aspect of gaucho life and reducing the pampas to a vast emptiness, Borges deliberately omits everything that justifies the mythology. Perhaps Georgie was unable to see it at the time, and Borges is now trying to recapture his original perspective. Not until his return from Europe in 1921 could Georgie truly discover his native city and, a few years later, the entire country. The pampas and the gauchos, and all the writers who had written about them, would then be the object of several of his essays. But for Georgie in 1909, the excursion to one of the places where the River Plate nations originated was rather disappointing. He was still very much under the influence of a family who had long memories of fighting the gauchos and the gauchos' hated chieftains: Rosas, López, Jordán, Urquiza. As Borges told Leo Gilson Ribeiro, in one of his most interesting interviews, his mother never spared the gauchos. When she called somebody "a gaucho," it was not as praise: she meant he was "rough, coarse, and illiterate" (Ribeiro, 1970, p. 4).

Little by little, at the garden in Palermo or in the zoo, on the summer excursions to the other bank of the river, and even in the discovery of the pampas, Georgie was collecting the feelings and experiences that would later be essential to Borges. The roots of his rather unexpected regionalism can be found in these modest beginnings.

9.
The House of the Body

The Borgeses spent some of their summer holidays in Argentina. To avoid humid and hot Buenos Aires, they rented a house in Adrogué, a small town some ten or fifteen miles to the south of the capital. Borges recalls that

> during all these years, we usually spent our summers out in Adrogué . . .
> where we had a place of our own—a large, one-story house with grounds,
> two summer houses, a windmill, and a shaggy brown sheepdog. Adrogué
> then was a lost and undisturbed maze of summer houses surrounded by
> iron fences with masonry planters on the gate posts, of parks, of streets that
> radiated out of the many plazas, and of the ubiquitous smell of eucalyptus
> trees. We continued to visit Adrogué for decades. ("Essay," 1970, p. 212)

The house was located in front of a square. It had a red-tiled roof and a veranda to protect the rooms from excessive heat. In his "Essay" Borges fails to mention the fact that they did not keep the house for long. Although they continued spending their summer holidays in Adrogué, they went instead to the Hotel Las Delicias (The Pleasures), whose long corridors with mirrors and "effusive honeysuckles" are mentioned in "Tlön, Uqbar, Orbis Tertius" as part of the setting for the presentation of Herbert Ashe, a fictitious Englishman modeled on Borges' father.

The real hotel was a sort of neoclassical building, done in the Belle Epoque style, which was probably modeled with due modesty on some half-forgotten Riviera prototype. An engraving done later by Norah, and reproduced in *Borgès par lui même* (Rodríguez Monegal, 1970, pp. 78–79), shows the portico with columns and the niches with half-dressed, or half-undressed nymphs, opening on a patio with black and white diamond-shaped tiles. Alicia Jurado recalls a visit with Borges to the hotel: "I went with him to say good-by to the Adrogué Hotel before it was demolished; we walked in darkness through ravaged floors, glimpsing patios and windows which brought memories to him, sitting on the broken bench of a ruined garden he loved and in a square full of trees and covered with fallen leaves from which he pointed out to me the house they had had for many a summer" (Jurado, 1964, p. 20). This melancholy excursion may have occurred during the 1950s. But long before that Borges had transformed his memories of the hotel into the villa owned by General Berkeley in "The Shape of the Sword": "The house was less than a century old, but it was decayed and shadowy and flourished in puzzling corridors and in pointless antechambers" (*Labyrinths*, 1964, p. 69).

Those few words condense more than the memories of the story's protagonist. Georgie's own astonishment in walking along the seemingly endless and mazelike corridors and antechambers of the Adrogué Hotel is preserved there as well. In another story, "Death and the Compass," Borges creates a nightmarish vision of the hotel to which he probably added a few touches from the Haedo villa at Paso Molino. In the first paragraph of the story he warns the reader that the "intermittent stories of murders which constitute the plot will come to a culmination amid the incessant odor of eucalyptus trees at the villa Triste-le-Roy" (*The Aleph*, 1970, p. 65). In a note to the story he wrote for the American edition he acknowledges that

> Triste-le-Roy, a beautiful name invented by Amanda Molina Vedia, stands for the now demolished Hotel Las Delicias in Adrogué. (Amanda had painted a map of an imaginary island on the wall of her bedroom; on her map I discovered the name Triste-le-Roy.)
>
> . . . I have embedded many memories of Buenos Aires and its southern outskirts in this wild story. Triste-le-Roy itself is a heightened and distorted version of the roomy and pleasant Hotel Las Delicias, which still survives in so many memories. (Ibid., pp. 268–269)

Perhaps Borges was struck by the name not only because it was beautiful but also because, in its association with the Adrogué Hotel and his childhood games, he could invest it with the terrors of his early years, when he was a prince who had to be protected from some powerful unseen enemy by his sister (the queen mother) and his cousin Esther. In the story's last episode the protagonist, Eric Lönnrot, finally reaches the villa where the fourth murder is going to be committed and discovers that he has fallen into the trap of his archenemy, Red Scharlach; that he is the last victim. Critics have pointed out that Lönnrot and Scharlach are really doubles, a sort of Dr. Jekyll and Mr. Hyde: the detective and the criminal share the same symbolic color, red, which is evident in Scharlach's nickname and barely hidden in Lönnrot's. (*Rot* means red in German and Scandinavian.) Borges relies on his memories of the Adrogué Hotel to describe the villa:

Night was falling when he saw the rectangular mirador of the villa Triste-le-Roy, almost as tall as the surrounding black eucalyptus trees. . . .

A rusted iron fence bounded the villa's irregular perimeter. The main gate was shut. Lönnrot, without much hope of getting in, walked completely around the place. Before the barred gate once again, he stuck a hand through the palings—almost mechanically—and found the bolt. The squeal of rusted iron surprised him. With clumsy obedience, the whole gate swung open.

Lönnrot moved forward among the eucalyptus trees, stepping on the layered generations of fallen leaves. Seen from up close, the house was a clutter of meaningless symmetries and almost insane repetitions: one icy Diana in a gloomy niche matched another Diana in a second niche; one balcony appeared to reflect another; double outer staircases crossed at each landing. A two-faced Hermes cast a monstrous shadow. Lönnrot made his way around the house as he had made his way around the grounds. He went over every detail; below the level of the terrace he noticed a narrow shutter.

He pushed it open. A few marble steps went down into a cellar. Lönnrot, who by now anticipated the architect's whims, guessed that in the opposite wall he would find a similar set of steps. He did. Climbing them, he lifted his hands and raised a trapdoor.

A strain of light led him to a window. He opened it. A round yellow moon outlined two clogged fountains in the unkempt garden. Lönnrot explored the house. Through serving pantries and along corridors he came to identical courtyards and several times to the same courtyard. He climbed dusty stairways to circular anterooms, where he was multiplied to infinity in facing mirrors. He grew weary of opening or peeping through windows that revealed, outside, the same desolate garden seen from various heights and various angles; and indoors he grew weary of the rooms of furniture, each draped in yellowing slipcovers, and the crystal chandeliers wrapped in tarlatan. A bedroom caught his attention—in it, a single flower in a porcelain vase. At a touch, the ancient petals crumbled to dust. On the third floor, the last floor, the house seemed endless and growing. The house is not so large, he thought. This dim light, the sameness, the mirrors, the many years, my unfamiliarity, the loneliness are what make it large.

By a winding staircase he reached the mirador. That evening's moon streamed in through the diamond-shaped panes; they were red, green, and yellow. He was stopped by an awesome, dizzying recollection. (Ibid., pp. 73–75)

The recollection is of the diamond-shaped objects that had been used as emblems in previous murders. Too late, Lönnrot realizes he has fallen into a trap. The rather banal and summery reality of the Adrogué Hotel and (perhaps) the Paso Molino villa has been transformed by Borges' nightmarish imagination into these decayed corridors, these haunted mirrors, these sinister staircases and menacing windowpanes. Perhaps the transformation did not happen in 1942, when Borges published "Death and the Compass" in *Sur*, but much earlier when Georgie was roaming the endless corridors, the symmetrical staircases, the labyrinthine construction that the sedate Adrogué Hotel became in his childhood imagination.

Borges never stopped writing variations on the labyrinthine corridors of the Adrogué Hotel. In two other stories it is possible to see how that playground of his childhood is metamorphosed by the dreams of the adult. In describing the hideous and ruined City of the Immortals in the story "The Immortals," Borges manages to produce a space that is the perversion of all architecture. Before reaching the city, the narrator has a nightmarish experience among some very primitive tribes. He longs to get into the city he can see from afar: "At the foot of the mountain, an impure stream spread noiselessly, clogged with débris and sand; on the opposite bank (beneath the last sun or beneath the first) shone the evident City of the Immortals. I saw walls, arches, façades and fora: the base was a stone plateau" (*Labyrinths*, 1964, p. 108). But soon the protagonist discovers the difficulties of reaching the city.

I had to skirt several irregular ravines which seemed to me like quarries; obfuscated by the City's grandeur, I had thought it nearby. Toward midnight, I set foot upon the black shadow of its walls, bristling out in idolatrous forms on the yellow sand. I was halted by a kind of sacred horror. Novelty and the desert are so abhorred by man that I was glad one of the troglodytes had followed me to the last. I closed my eyes and awaited (without sleeping) the light of day.

I have said that the City was founded on a stone plateau. This plateau, comparable to a high cliff, was no less arduous than the walls. In vain I fatigued myself: the black base did not disclose a single door. The force of the sun obliged me to seek refuge in a cave; in the rear was a pit, in the pit a stairway which sank down abysmally into the darkness below. I went down; through a chaos of sordid galleries I reached a vast circular chamber, scarcely visible. There were nine doors in this cellar; eight led to a labyrinth that treacherously returned to the same chamber; the ninth (though another labyrinth) led to a second circular chamber equal to the first. I do not know the total number of these chambers; my misfortune and anxiety multiplied them. The silence was hostile and almost perfect; there was no sound in this deep stone network save that of a subterranean wind, whose cause I did not discover; noiselessly, tiny streams of rusty water disappeared between the crevices. Horribly, I became habituated to this doubtful world; I found it incredible that there could be anything but cellars with nine doors and long branched-out cellars; I do not know how long I must have walked beneath the ground; I know that I once confused, in the same nostalgia, the atrocious village of the barbarians and my native city, amid the clusters.

In the depths of a corridor, an unforeseen wall halted me; a remote light fell from above. I raised my confused eyes; in the vertiginous, extreme heights I saw a circle of sky so blue that it seemed purple. Some metal rungs scaled the wall. I was limp with fatigue, but I climbed up, stopping only at times to sob clumsily with joy. I began to glimpse capitals and astragals, triangular pediments and vaults, confused pageants of granite and marble. Thus I was afforded this ascension from the blind region of dark interwoven labyrinths into the resplendent city.

I emerged into a kind of little square or, rather, a kind of courtyard. It was surrounded by a single building of irregular form and variable height; to this heterogenous building belonged the different cupolas and columns. Rather than by any other trait of this incredible monument, I was held by the extreme age of its fabrication. I felt that it was older than mankind, than the earth. This manifest antiquity (though in some way terrible to the eyes) seemed to me in keeping with the work of immortal builders. At first cautiously, later indifferently, at last desperately, I wandered up the stairs and along the pavements of the inextricable palace. (Afterwards I learned that the width and height of the steps were not constant, a fact which made me understand the singular fatigue they produced.) "This palace is a fabrication of the gods," I thought at the beginning. I explored the uninhabited interiors and corrected myself: "The gods who built it were mad!" I said it, I know, with an incomprehensible reprobation which was almost remorse, with more intellectual horror than palpable fear. To the impression of enormous antiquity others were added: that of the interminable, that of the atrocious, that of the complexly senseless. I had crossed a labyrinth, but the nitid City of the Immortals filled me with fright and repugnance. A labyrinth is a structure compounded to confuse men; its architecture, rich in symmetries, is subordinated to that end. In the palace I imperfectly explored, the architecture lacked any such finality. It abounded in dead-end corridors, high unattainable windows, portentous doors which led to a cell or a pit, incredible inverted stairways whose steps and balustrades hung downward. Other stairways, clinging airily to the side of a monumental wall, would die without leading anywhere, after making two or three turns in the lofty darkness of the cupolas. I do not know if all the examples I have enumerated are literal; I know that for many years they infested my nightmares; I am no longer able to know if such and such a detail is a transcription of reality or of the forms which unhinged my nights. "This City" (I thought) "is so horrible that its mere existence and perdurance, though in the midst of a secret desert, contaminates the past and the future and in some ways even jeopardizes the stars. As long as it lasts, no one in the world can be strong or happy." I do not want to describe it; a chaos of heterogenous words, the body of a tiger or a bull in which teeth, organs, and heads monstrously pullulate in mutual conjunction and hatred can (per-haps) be approximate images.

I do not remember the stages of my return, amid the dusty and damp hypoges. I only know I was not abandoned by the fear that, when I left the last labyrinth, I would again be surrounded by the nefarious City of the Im-mortals. I can remember nothing else. This oblivion, now insuperable, was perhaps voluntary; perhaps the circumstances of my escape were so un-pleasant that, on some day no less forgotten as well, I swore to forget them. (Ibid., pp. 109–111)

The literary sources of this story are so obvious—Poe's "The Pit and the Pendulum" as well as Richard Burton's books of his journeys in the Near East and Franz Kafka's *The Castle*—that the reader may over-look how much of the story is based on Borges' insomnia, which he suf-fered from for years. It is the "atrocious lucidity of insomnia" (as he once called it) that the story tries to capture on its surface. But under-neath that experience is Borges' nightmarish view of reality. The City of the Immortals is another version of the haunted, abandoned villa he calls Triste-le-Roy in "Death and the Compass," as well as the house where Asterion lives in the story of that name. That is, it is a labyrinth, a hideous place. These stories have at their root a recurring nightmare: the house that protects is also a prison.

Many centuries before Borges was born, an Italian artist en-graved a series of nightmarish palaces very much in the style of the City of the Immortals. In calling them *carceri* (prisons), Gianbattista Piranesi revealed their hidden meaning. These monumental ruins of nonexistent palaces, this horrid fabric of brick and stone and stucco, could have been built only in the dreams and terrors of man. Borges has always been very fond of Piranesi and obviously conceived his City of the Immortals along the lines of the etchings. But he was also follow-ing another model, one that (for him) was even older: Georgie's uncon-scious obsessions.

Both "Death and the Compass" and, in a more revealing way, "The Immortals" allude to the experience of being trapped in a laby-rinth. In both stories the search for a center becomes the search for a solution. In "Death and the Compass" the answer, when found, is death. In "The Immortals" it is the reverse, immortality, but at the price of total forgetfulness; that is, at the price of the death of memory. Coming out of the labyrinth into the "real" world, the solution is sim-pler, as "The House of Asterion" shows: there is no way out but through death, and the fact that the story is told from the naïve (and thus comic) point of view of the Minotaur only helps to disguise its hor-ror. Death or forgetfulness is the only way out of the labyrinth. Why? Anzieu has pointed out in his psychoanalytical study that the house is the mother's body, the womb where the child finds his first abode. In Borges' "The Immortals" (as in Poe's "The Pit and the Pendulum") some details of the journey inside the labyrinth have very revealing connotations. When talking about the vast circular chamber through which he would eventually find access to the City of the Immortals, the narrator indicates that it had "nine doors" that led to nine labyrinths, only one of which, "the ninth," did not return to the same chamber. The choice of the number nine and the emphasis put on the ninth indicate the importance of that figure, which corresponds to the nine months of gestation, of life inside the labyrinth of the mother's womb, from which the child is bound to emerge in the ninth month. The other connotations of that secret chamber are also indicative. It is silent except for the sound of wind and water; the way out, when found, is through a remote hole in the ceiling through which the blue, almost purple sky can be seen.

Even the rejection that the City of the Immortals inspires in the narrator corresponds to the rejection of the brutality and violence of the external world that is so common in infants. The loss of memory that follows the experience of discovering the City of the Immortals (that is, of getting into the world) is equally characteristic of the birth trauma. Even in the sinisterly comic version of the same myth in "The House of Asterion" Borges could not refrain from including an allusion to the nine months of gestation. The subconscious identity between the space of these stories, the space of Georgie's and Borges' nightmares, and the mother's womb is clear.

10.
The Infinite Library

"I have always been a greater reader than a writer," Borges once told Richard Burgin, and he has never tired of recalling the adventure of reading, the inexhaustible source of pleasure and horror books represented to him (Burgin, 1969, p. 4). It all began at home. Father was not only an avid reader but also an aspiring author. He had collected a large library of English books that Georgie's imagination would make as limitless as the universe. Without setting a foot outside, Georgie had the world of fable and romance at hand. He spent the better part of his childhood in the library, and in retrospect, as he grew old, the memories of that library assumed epic proportions. He remembered having spent more time reading Father's books than playing with his sister in the garden or exploring the neighborhood. The library became his habitat.

One of the first occasions on which Borges talks publicly about this library is in the prologue to the second edition of his biography of Evaristo Carriego; there he contrasts the world of books with the real world he had so much trouble in mastering.

For years I believed I had grown up in one of the suburbs of Buenos Aires, a suburb of adventurous streets and visible sunsets. The truth is that I grew up in a garden, behind a speared railing, and in a library of unlimited English books. In every corner of Palermo (I have been told) knives and guitars were teeming, but those who filled my mornings and gave a horrid pleasure to my nights were Stevenson's blind buccaneer, dying under the horses' hoofs, and the traitor who abandoned his friend on the moon, and the time traveler who brought from the future a faded flower, and the spirit incarcerated for centuries in Solomon's jar, and the veiled prophet of Khorassan who hid behind precious stones and silk, his face ravaged by leprosy. (*Carriego,* 1955, p. 9)

This list of his readings does not attempt to be complete. Borges alludes not to the central subjects of the books but to episodes that caught his childhood fancy. Thus Stevenson's *Treasure Island* is identified not by any reference to the protagonist, Jim Hawkins, or his even more famous antagonist, Long John Silver, but through a minor character, the sinister, blind Pew, whose brutal death must have haunted Georgie's nightmares. In Wells' science-fiction masterpiece *The First Men on the Moon* Borges' memory selects not the success of the space journey but the betrayal and fearful destiny of the man left behind; again, in Wells' *The Time Machine,* it is not the conception of a flight through time that he recalls but the inexplicable flower of the future that the time traveler brings back to earth. In an article published in 1945 and later included in *Other Inquisitions* (1952) Borges develops the haunting notion of a flower made of time. It is called "The Flower of Coleridge" and links Wells' invention to James' *The Sense of the Past* and to Coleridge's note on the same subject. The image had sunk deep into Georgie's mind.

The other two books mentioned are older and reflect a different type of literature. To the *One Thousand and One Nights* belongs the story of the genie imprisoned in the bottle; to Thomas Moore's *Lalla Rookh, an Eastern Romance* belongs the story of the veiled prophet of Khorassan. Georgie must have read the first in Father's copy of the unexpurgated Richard Burton translation. Many years later Borges wrote an article, "The Translators of the *One Thousand and One Nights,*" collected in *History of Eternity* (1936), which discusses the merits of the different translations of that book. Moore's silly romance became one of the sources of "The Masked Dyer, Hakim of Merv," a tale written by Borges in 1933 and later included in *A Universal History of Infamy* (1935). Again, what matters is not the sources but what Borges' (and Georgie's) memory selected from them. In the vast, sprawling, and occasionally obscene *One Thousand and One Nights* his memory selected the imprisoned spirit; in *Lalla Rookh* (a book teeming with cloying sentimentality and tepid eroticism), the horrifying face of the leper behind the bejeweled and silky mask. Those were Georgie's images, the ones that haunted him as a child and were more real than the house, the garden, and the slightly dilapidated suburb of Buenos Aires in which he lived.

In recalling those same childhood years for his "Autobiographical Essay," Borges emphasizes the importance of that first contact with English books:

If I were asked to name the chief event in my life, I should say my father's library. In fact, I sometimes think I have never strayed outside that library. I can still picture it. It was in a room of its own, with glass-fronted shelves, and must have contained several thousand volumes. Being so nearsighted, I have forgotten most of the faces of that time (perhaps even when I think of my grandfather Acevedo I am thinking of his photograph), and yet I vividly remember so many of the steel engravings in *Chambers' Encyclopaedia* and in the *Britannica*. ("Essay," 1970, p. 209)

A private library of several thousand volumes was not unusual then in the River Plate countries. Public libraries were generally poor and out of date, and carried very few books in languages other than Spanish or French. English was then too exotic, and only a small segment of the population—generally, wealthy people—read it. So readers of English used to collect their own books. A few bookstores catered to them; the most famous was Mitchell's, in the downtown area. Father had a very good excuse to become a book collector. The fact that he acquired the Burton translation of the *Arabian Nights* (a very expensive edition limited to subscribers) proves that for him books were not only to be read. The actual title of that famous translation is *The Book of the Thousand Nights and a Night*, and it was published in seventeen volumes in London around 1885. The volumes contain suggestive illustrations and long, explicit notes about the sexual mores of the Arab world, which explains why its sale was limited to wealthy subscribers. Pornography (or what Mrs. Grundy believed to be pornography) was tolerated in Victorian England only if it was expensive.

In his "Autobiographical Essay" Borges recalls: "The Burton, filled with what was then considered obscenity, was forbidden, and I had to read it hiding up on the roof. But at the time, I was so carried away with the magic that I took no notice whatever of the objectionable parts, reading the tales unaware of any other significance" (ibid., p. 209).

Borges' selective memory omits any mention of the illustrations, which stressed the erotic significance of the book. These illustrations, in a coy academic style, would be considered rather mild today; nevertheless, they were there, opening up a tantalizing perspective for the young child. Nor does he mention Burton's explicit notes, which never tired of discussing some of the most fashionable perversions of the Near East. Mrs. Burton, as is well known, was not amused. Nor, apparently, was Father, because the Burton translation was out of bounds for Georgie. That did not prevent the child from finding a time and place to enjoy the magical erotic tales in private.

There is nothing in the "Autobiographical Essay" about *Lalla Rookh*, which played such an important part in the second prologue to *Evaristo Carriego* and is mentioned by Borges in a note to *A Universal*

History of Infamy. In talking about the sources of "The Masked Dyer, Hakim of Merv," he says: "The Prophet's fame in the West is owed to a long-winded poem by Thomas Moore, laden with all the sentimentality of an Irish patriot" (*Infamy,* 1972, p. 79).

The story of the veiled prophet is only one of the four tales told by Moore in *Lalla Rookh;* instead of concentrating his narrative on the prophet, Moore prefers the point of view of one of his captives, Zelica, who had to face a destiny worse than death at the hands of the prophet. Forty lines are devoted to the seduction of poor Zelica by the sadistic fiend. After a short introduction in which he stresses the links that tie Zelica to him and makes mockery of their wedding—

> Yes, my sworn bride, let others seek in bow'rs
> Their bridal place—the charnel vault was ours!

—before taking her to the harem, he unveils his face:

> And now thou seest my *soul*'s angelic hue,
> 'Tis time these *features* were uncurtain'd too—
> This brow, whose light—o rare celestial light!
> Hath been reserv'd to bless thy favour'd sight;
> These dazzling eyes, before whose shrouded might
> Thou'st seen immortal Man kneel down and quake—
> Would that they *were* heaven's lightnings for his sake!
> But turn and look—then wonder, if thou wilt,
> That I should hate, should take revenge, by guilt,
> Upon the hand, whose mischief or whose mirth
> Sent me thus maim'd and monstrous upon earth;
> And on that race who, though more vile they be
> Than mowing apes, are demigods to me!
> Here—judge if hell, with all its power to damn,
> Can add one curse to the foul thing I am!—
> He rais'd his veil—the Maid turn'd slowly round,
> Look'd round at him—shriek'd—and sank upon the ground!
>   (Moore, 1929, pp. 359–360)

The image of the lepered prophet remained in Georgie's imagination long enough to become the source of a tale written some twenty-five years later; but instead of developing the sado-masochistic destiny of the prophet along the romantic lines indicated by Moore, Borges develops the almost metaphysical problem of appearance and reality expressed by the gold mask over the leprous face. Again, what attracts him is the monster that lurks inside, like the Minotaur in his labyrinth. In Borges' story, "The Masked Dyer Hakim of Merv," only a few references to the prophet's excesses of the flesh remain. One has already been discussed here: his belief that mirrors and fatherhood are abominable. The other is equally terse but more ironic: "The petty tasks of government were delegated to six or seven devotees. Ever mindful of serenity and meditation, the Prophet kept a harem of a hundred and fourteen blind women, who did their best to satisfy the needs of his divine body" (*Infamy,* 1972, p. 83).

Another book may have added to Georgie's horror of masks and mirrors. In talking to Jean de Milleret, he recalls:

> There was a book which also made me afraid, especially its illustrations. I believe its title is *The Viscount of Bragelonne,* in which there is the Iron Mask. There was an engraving which represented a nobleman with the Iron Mask who was promenading very sadly on a terrace over the sea, I believe; and all that frightened me. That got mixed up with a Moore poem on the veiled prophet of Khorassan, who was a leper. Those two images—the idea of the Persian veiled prophet and the idea of the Iron Mask—all that went together and frightened me. (De Milleret, 1967, pp. 24–25)

Although this is the only time Borges has ever mentioned reading Alexandre Dumas' crowded novel, it is singular that he chose that particular episode. *Le vicomte de Bragelonne* is the third and last book in the Musketeers saga. It is an episodic novel, full of incidents. One of the episodes concerns the Iron Mask, a famous political prisoner during Louis XIV's time who was condemned to wear a mask over his face to avoid identification. For reasons of his own, and against historical evidence, Dumas made him into the king's twin brother. But what Borges remembers is not the plot but the vivid image of the Iron Mask's loneliness, an image that can be linked to Watts' painting of the Minotaur, which spawned "The House of Asterion." A masked Persian prophet, the Iron Mask, the Minotaur: Georgie's heroes have two traits in common—monstrosity and loneliness.

In the "Autobiographical Essay" Borges gives a list of childhood reading: "The first novel I ever read through was *Huckleberry Finn.* Next came *Roughing It* and *Flush Days in California.* I also read books by Captain Marryat, Wells' *First Men on the Moon,* Poe, a one-volume edition of Longfellow, *Treasure Island,* Dickens, *Don Quixote, Tom Brown's School Days,* Grimm's *Fairy Tales,* Lewis Carroll, *The Adventures of Mr. Verdant Green* (a now forgotten book), Burton's *A Thousand Nights and a Night*" ("Essay," 1970, p. 209). The list is singular not only for the books not mentioned in previous listings but also for the ones it omits. In the *Evaristo Carriego* prologue he alludes to only five books, all English, even if one (the Burton) is only a translation. Sixteen years later, in mentioning his childhood readings, he omits two of the books alluded to in 1955: Wells' *The Time Machine* and Moore's *Lalla Rookh*. If these omissions are puzzling, no less intriguing is the inclusion of a title such as *The Adventures of Mr. Verdant Green, an Oxford Freshman,* written by Edward Bradley and originally published in 1853–1857. It is the only mention in the vast Borgesian corpus of such a forgotten novel. Other titles are more predictable: Grimm's *Fairy Tales* and Captain Marryat's works were the usual fare for children of those days, along with Dickens' novels, *Tom Brown's School Days,* Lewis Carroll's Alice books, and the already mentioned Wells' *Time Machine* and Stevenson's *Treasure Island.*

What is really new in the 1970 list is the place taken by North American authors. In an interview with Rita Guibert, Borges stresses the importance of his North American readings: "From those days of my childhood in which I read Mark Twain, Bret Harte, Hawthorne, Jack London, Edgar Allan Poe, I have been very fond of the United States and I am still fond of it" (Guibert, 1973, p. 49).

In both lists the first author mentioned is Mark Twain. In an earlier interview with Ronald Christ, Borges says:

> Look here, I'm talking to an American: there's a book I *must* speak about—nothing unexpected about it—that book is *Huckleberry Finn*. I thoroughly dislike *Tom Sawyer*. I think that Tom Sawyer spoils the last chapters of *Huckleberry Finn*. All those silly jokes. They are all pointless jokes; but I suppose Mark Twain thought it was his duty to be funny, even when he wasn't in the mood. The jokes had to be worked in somehow. According to what George Moore said, the English always thought: "Better a bad joke than no joke." I think that Mark Twain was one of the really great writers but I think he was rather unaware of the fact. But perhaps in order to write a really great book, you *must* be rather unaware of the fact. (Christ, 1967, p. 132)

The same year, in a manual written with the help of Esther Zemborain de Torres, Borges dedicated a few lines to *Huckleberry Finn:* "From this great book, which abounds in admirable evocations of mornings and evenings and of the dismal banks of the river, there have arisen in time two others whose outline is the same—*Kim* (1901) by Kipling and *Don Segundo Sombra* (1926) by Ricardo Güiraldes" (*American Literature,* 1971, p. 37).

Georgie obviously found much to his liking in *Huckleberry Finn.* His experience of both banks of the wide River Plate, the lazy summers spent at Paso Molino or at Fray Bentos, on the banks of the Uruguay River, must have provided the necessary elements for an identification. And the fact that Borges would comment on his hatred for the good Tom Sawyer and would reject Mark Twain's feeble attempts at developing a plot at the end of the book indicates very clearly that what

Georgie loved was the free flow of the narrative, its dreamy pastoral quality.

Of the other North American authors mentioned, Borges singles out Bret Harte. As evidence of his interest, he wrote a preface to a Spanish version of Harte's California tales. In it he defends Harte against DeVoto's accusation that he was "a literary charlatan." He argues that the critic was trying to debunk Harte to exalt Mark Twain. At the end of his preface Borges stresses a faculty that Bret Harte shared with Chesterton and Stevenson: "the invention (and the bold design) of memorable visual traits. Perhaps the most strange is one that I read when I was twelve and that will follow me, I know, to the end of the road: the white and black card nailed by a firm blade to the trunk of the monumental tree, over the body of John Oakhurst, gambler" (*Prólogos*, 1975, p. 83).

But the best proof of how much Harte and Mark Twain impressed Georgie can be found in one of the tales included in *A Universal History of Infamy*, "The Dread Redeemer Lazarus Morell." Although he was probably much older when he read the two books listed as sources at the end of the volume—Mark Twain's *Life on the Mississippi* and Bernard DeVoto's *Mark Twain's America*—the melodramatic, almost Gothic vision and the terse, epigrammatic imagery of Borges' story are rooted in Georgie's readings of Harte and Twain. The other two North American authors he mentions—Hawthorne and Jack London—left different traces. About the first he wrote one of his most elaborate essays, published in *Other Inquisitions* (1952); to the second he devoted exactly one page of his *Introduction to American Literature,* filled with biographical data but also containing a very personal selection of works:

> He died at forty, leaving behind some fifty volumes. Of these we shall mention *The People of the Abyss,* for which he personally explored the low quarters of London; *The Sea Wolf,* whose leading character is a sea captain who preaches and practices violence; and *Before Adam,* a novel on a prehistoric theme, whose narrator recovers in fragmentary dreams the troubled days through which he had lived during a previous incarnation. Jack London also wrote admirable adventure stories and some fantastic tales, among which is "The Shadow and the Flash," which tells of the rivalry and the final duel of two invisible men. His style is realistic, but he re-creates and exalts a reality of his own. The vitality which permeated his life also permeates his work, which will continue to attract young readers. (*American Literature,* 1971, pp. 38–39)

It is possible that Borges' selection did not coincide with Georgie's, to whom *White Fang* and *The Call of the Wild* may have been more appealing. In his reevaluation of London's works, he devotes half the space he gives Mark Twain but twice what he dedicates to Bret Harte.

The inclusion of Longfellow's poetry in the "Autobiographical Essay" list may have more to do with Father's love for his poetry than with Georgie's own taste. Longfellow rates only half a page in the *Introduction to American Literature*. One sentence summarizes Borges' opinion: "Many of the compositions of his book *Voices of the Night* [1839] won him the affection and admiration of his contemporaries, and they still endure in the anthologies. Reread now, they leave us the impression that all they lack is a final touch (ibid., p. 29).

Perhaps the place of honor given by Borges to North American writers in his "Autobiographical Essay" owes something to the fact that the piece was written especially for the North American edition of *The Aleph* (1970). In an interview with Ronald Christ, Borges explicitly indicates how aware he always is of the background of the person to whom he is talking. In spite of that, it is obvious that for Georgie North American and British authors were not basically different: they all shared the language which had become for the child *the* code of reading, the key to the world of desire and imagination. In his daydreaming he may have moved with ease from Stevenson's blind buccaneer to Poe's haunted protagonists, from Huckleberry Finn's madcap adventures to Oliver Twist's more Gothic ones. Myths and nightmares, dreams and romance, all came to him in the language that was Father's and Grandmother's and that, as a reader, he would possess forever.

The only book in the 1970 list that does not belong to the Anglo-Saxon tradition (which could also include Grimm's *Fairy Tales*) was *Don Quixote*, but even that book reached Georgie in an English version. Apparently Father's library lacked the Spanish text:

> When later I read *Don Quixote* in the original, it sounded like a bad translation to me. I still remember those red volumes with the gold lettering of the Garnier edition. At some point, my father's library was broken up, and when I read the *Quixote* in another edition I had the feeling that it wasn't the real *Quixote*. Later, a friend got me the Garnier, with the same steel engravings, the same footnotes, and also the same errata. All those things form part of the book for me; this I consider the real *Quixote*. ("Essay," 1970, pp. 209–210)

It would be easy to dismiss this statement as an exercise in paradox. It is better to recognize in it one of the basic tenets of Borges' poetics: that the reading (not the writing) creates the work. This concept is developed in a famous story written in 1939, "Pierre Menard, Author of the *Quixote*," later included in *Ficciones* (1944). In imagining a French author who attempts to rewrite Cervantes' masterpiece in its literal entirety, Borges is not only poking fun at the notion of originality but also proving how much to write is to rewrite (that is, to write once more what has already been written) and to what extent to rewrite is simply to read. But for the child, *Don Quixote* was the source of adventure and dreams. One of his earliest attempts at writing preempted Menard's quest. He confides in his "Autobiographical Essay": "My first story was a rather nonsensical piece after the manner of Cervantes, an old-fashioned romance called 'La visera fatal'—The Fatal Helmet" (ibid., p. 211). Many years later, while living in Spain, Borges returned to *Don Quixote* and read it in the original. The book eventually became one of the most influential in developing his concept of narrative.

How much of these readings were under the guidance of Father, or done with his approval? Some books were obviously out of bounds, but it seems reasonable to assume that the majority were suggested by Father and that some books were bought especially for him. Georgie was encouraged to read by Father's example. In *Les mots* (his partial autobiography) Jean-Paul Sartre dwells on the notion that one becomes a writer by sheer imitation. It is even truer that one becomes a reader for the same reason. Georgie had a formidable model at home. But to be the kind of reader he became, more than the impulse to imitate is needed. Because Georgie became an addict. Reading was so much his passion that Mother soon discovered that for punishment when he misbehaved she had only to take away his books. Reading was for him what Valery Larbaud once called "ce vice impuni" (that unpunished vice). But Mother knew best and used books as other parents used candies.

The addiction was made even more dangerous by the fact that the child had weak eyesight. He had inherited the Borges blindness and eventually became the sixth generation to be totally blind. While he was beginning his fantastic explorations in the library of unlimited English books, he could see his own father growing blind. He himself would soon have to resort to glasses. Reading (the unpunished vice) carries its own punishment. To read is to race against blindness; that is, against time. In his ever weakening eyes, Georgie could measure his own time.

11.
The Son

When he was six, Georgie told Father he wanted to be a writer. This statement—reported by Mother (De Milleret, 1967, p. 24)—places exactly the time the child discovered his vocation. It was not unexpected: Georgie had been brought up in a library and spent most of his childhood reading. Borges later told De Milleret that when reading as a child "I tended to identify with the author, or one of his characters; for instance, when I was eleven, I was Lesage or Cervantes" (ibid., p. 21). This precocious identification, not just with the characters (which is rather common) but with the author, reveals his vocation and anticipates those poetic dramatizations in which Borges assumes the persona of Milton or Averroes, Shakespeare or Spinoza. But if the anecdote is eloquent, it tends to simplify a process which, in a sense, was even more dramatic.

Any child models himself on the person he adores. The person Georgie adored was Father, and Father was always a literary man, with a frustrated poetic vocation. Literature was in Father's blood. In his "Autobiographical Essay" Borges recalls:

A tradition of literature ran through my father's family. His great-uncle Juan Crisóstomo Lafinur was one of the first Argentine poets, and he wrote an ode on the death of his friend General Manuel Belgrano, in 1820. One of my father's cousins, Alvaro Melián Lafinur, whom I knew from childhood, was a leading minor poet and later found his way into the Argentine Academy of Letters. My father's maternal grandfather, Edward Young Haslam, edited one of the first English papers in Argentina, the *Southern Cross,* and was a Doctor of Philosophy or Letters, I'm not sure which, of the University of Heidelberg. Haslam could not afford Oxford or Cambridge, so he made his way to Germany, where he got his degree, going through the whole course in Latin. Eventually, he died in Paraná. ("Essay," 1970, p. 210)

Father himself had tried his hand at several genres. According to Borges, he published "some fine sonnets" after the style of the Argentine poet Enrique Banchs, who was a postsymbolist. He also published a historical novel, *El caudillo* (The Chieftain), while he was living in Majorca in 1921. But the major part of his work remained unpublished and was eventually destroyed by its author; it included a book of essays, a book of Oriental stories ("in the manner of the *Arabian Nights,"* according to Borges), and a drama, *Hacia la nada* (Toward Nothingness), "about a man's disappointment in his son" (ibid., p. 211).

Father never considered himself a professional writer. To find time to write, he had to fight against many odds. He was practically an orphan. His own father, Colonel Borges, had been killed in action the same year he was born; his mother, Fanny Haslam, was left with two small children in a foreign country still ravaged by civil war. In reaching adolescence, Father had to choose a more lucrative profession than writing. He read law and eventually devoted himself to this profession. He also taught psychology in the English department of a school of modern languages. But he never really gave up his literary ambitions.

He had another handicap: he belonged to the fifth recorded generation of Borgeses to have very poor eyesight. In the "Autobiographical Essay" his son observes that "blindness ran in my family; a description of the operation performed on the eyes of my great-grandfather, Edward Young Haslam, appeared in the pages of the London medical journal, the *Lancet*" (ibid., p. 250). Grandmother Haslam also became totally blind before dying. Father, in turn, became partially blind in his late thirties. At forty he was forced to retire; and in spite of several operations, he was completely blind for the remaining years of his life. The little he wrote was done in his spare time or dictated when blindness had overcome him. Borges explains the link between Father's frustrated literary ambitions and his: "From the time I was a boy, when blindness came to him, it was tacitly understood that I had to fulfill the literary destiny that circumstances had denied my father. This was something that was taken for granted (and such things are far more important than things that are merely said). I was expected to be a writer" (ibid., p. 211).

This version subtly contradicts what Mother reported to Jean de Milleret, not only because it lacks drama (the child at six declaring to Father he wanted to be a writer) but especially because it changes the accent. In the "Autobiographical Essay" it is not Georgie's decision that matters any longer but Father's. The position of both characters has changed radically: now Father occupies center stage while Georgie becomes his echo. The dramatic situation is different: instead of Siegfried, going out to kill dragons, one has Hamlet, burdened by the task of fulfilling another man's destiny.

Which of the two versions is closer to reality? It is difficult to know. Perhaps one day, when he was six, Georgie stated solemnly to Father: "I want to be a writer." This statement (transformed by Mother's recollection into an "anecedote") does not exclude the other version: a flat statement about what Father took for granted about Georgie's future. The emphasis is on his duty: fate as something inherited. By accepting the destiny of writer as a kind of paternal bequest, Georgie accepts the fact that he is a son. It will be seen later in what a curious and even paradoxical way he fulfills his mandate.

It is difficult to know if Father was *really* a writer or only a man who wanted to be a writer. He may have used circumstances to justify the lack of true literary ambitions; he may have been the kind of person who has the aptitude for a certain esthetic activity but lacks the talent and drive to produce anything valuable. In her reminiscences Mother states bluntly that he "was a very intelligent man, as intelligent as Georgie, but he lacked the genius his son has" (De Milleret, 1967, p. 67).

In a more indirect way Borges also comes to a negative conclusion about Father's work. His conversations with Richard Burgin begin with that subject:

BURGIN: Was there ever a time when you didn't love literature?
BORGES: No, I always knew, I always thought of myself as a writer, even before I wrote a book. Let me say that even when I had written nothing, I knew that I would. I do not think of myself as a good writer but I knew that my destiny or my fate was a literary one, no? I never thought of myself as being anything else.
BURGIN: You never thought about taking up any career? I mean, your father was a lawyer.
BORGES: Yes. But, after all, he had tried to be a literary man and failed. He wrote some very nice sonnets. But he thought that I should fulfill that destiny, no? (Burgin, 1969, p. 1)

Although Borges' attempts to soften the harsh judgment (Father had failed as a writer) by remembering his "nice" sonnets, it is obvious that on that matter he shares Mother's opinion. It is also obvious that his own literary destiny was molded by that failure. Somehow, he had to fulfill Father's project; he had to vindicate him. That was his main task in life.

It is difficult to assess the quality of Father's work. With a single exception—(the novel *El caudillo*)—his writings are inaccessible or have been destroyed. The novel was written around 1919, at the time the family was living in Majorca, and it was published there at his own expense in 1921. Borges recalls that Father "had some five hundred copies of the book printed and brought them back to Buenos Aires, where he gave them away to friends" ("Essay," 1970, p. 219).

Today the novel is a bibliographical rarity, even harder to get than some of Borges' early books. Father must have been forty-six when he wrote it. But it is obvious that it had been planned long before. It has all the defects of a first novel, and one written probably very quickly. Although it is amateurish, it does not lack interest. It centers on an imaginary episode during the civil war of the 1860s in Entre Ríos, Father's native province. The protagonist is Carlos DuBois, son of a landowner who emigrated to Argentina after the French revolution of 1848. Because his father is sick and has to live in Buenos Aires, Carlos goes back to the ranch, after getting a law degree. There he plans to develop a meat-packing plant. His principal neighbor is Andrés Tavares, the local caudillo, a violent and despotic man, who in the forthcoming civil war would throw his weight in favor of the province's strongman, López Jordán. Tavares has a daughter, María Isabel, also strong-willed and determined to seduce Carlos in spite of the young man's decision to be faithful to the word given to the fiancée he left in Buenos Aires. Carlos' final resistance is overcome when a flood forces Marisabel (as she is called at home) to spend the night at his ranch. The caudillo believes Carlos has deliberately abducted his daughter and sends a henchman to kill him under the pretext that the young man doesn't want to join the López Jordán forces. The ending is truly tragic. After Carlos' death, the caudillo comes to his ranch and walks by his daughter without making a sign of recognition. She is also dead to him.

The novel is perhaps better than the above résumé suggests. It begins with an Indian legend in which a young warrior attempts to hunt and destroy a big crocodile, the representative of the god of the tribe, to gain the favors of his fiancée. Although he succeeds, the god's revenge is terrible: a flood destroys the whole tribe. The legend functions as both introduction and symbolic statement. The Indian couple defy and violate the religious principles of their community as much as the novel's protagonists defy and violate those of their community. The terrifying reptile is the equivalent of the caudillo. In both stories, the flood is a symbol of God's wrath; in both, it is the woman who behaves as seductress and leads to damnation.

The novel has many clumsily told episodes; the chronology is erratic, the romantic couple too conventional. The only character who is really alive is the caudillo. From a purely literary point of view, the novel is an anachronism. Although it was written in the late 1910s, its models belong to nineteenth-century literature. A mixture of romance and the realistic novel, *El caudillo* mishandles both. The conflict between Carlos and Marisabel is trite; more fascinating is the one that opposes Carlos to the caudillo, and even more interesting is the one (revealed only at the end) between Marisabel and her father. But the author does not explore these conflicts thoroughly enough.

To what extent did Father's novel anticipate some of Borges' own stories? The central subject of *El caudillo* (a strong man who destroys a younger rival) can be seen in one of Borges' best gaucho stories, "The Dead Man," originally published in 1946 and later included in *The Aleph*. The caudillo Otálora is really a more sinister version of Tavares, with some sado-masochistic elements added. He pretends to be overwhelmed by the young man and even humiliated by him, because from the very beginning he has planned a deadly revenge. Like Tavares, he is deaf to compassion. Another theme anticipated by Father's novel and recurrent in Borges' fiction is that of the man brought up in the city who has to face a rural destiny. In "The South" (originally published in 1953), the protagonist—a clerk in a municipal library—ends up fighting a knife duel in the pampas, a fate anticipated by Carlos' final confrontation with the caudillo's henchman. It is true that Carlos does not accept the challenge and prefers to be murdered, whereas Borges' Juan Dahlmann meekly accepts his fate. But that difference does not alter the basic similarity of both situations.

More than a coincidence of subjects and themes is implicit here. There is in both writers a preoccupation, almost an obsession, with a certain kind of confrontation: between powerful, primitive men and weak, educated men. Father was (like his son) an intellectual who learned to make his living through the practice of law and the teaching of psychology. But his own father had been a colonel, a man of action. In Father's situation one can already recognize the conflict between arms and letters that Georgie would have to face later. It is easy to recognize in the protagonist of *El caudillo,* in that half-European Carlos, an alter ego of the author. In many respects, they were similar. But what is really important is that in trying to portray his own predicament Father was also concerned with understanding the caudillo's psychology. In confronting Carlos with the caudillo, Father was exploring one of his private obsessions: the feeling of inadequacy he felt in contrasting his fate with that of his own father. One of the works he had projected and apparently even wrote, according to Borges, was the drama *Toward Nothingness,* "about a man's disappointment in his son" ("Essay," 1970, p. 211). In the plot of that drama it is possible to read a recognition of his shortcomings as a man, when measured against the heroic proportions of his father, Colonel Borges. The feeling was inherited by Georgie.

In spite of its literary clumsiness, *El caudillo* deserves serious reading. Borges even believes that it ought to be reissued—in a new version, of course. He mentions in his "Autobiographical Essay" that he had in mind revising "and perhaps rewriting my father's novel *El caudillo*, as he asked me to years ago. We had gone as far as discussing many of the problems; I like to think of the undertaking as a continued dialogue and a very real collaboration" (ibid., p. 259). So far, he doesn't seem to have attempted it.

The most ambitious poetical work produced by Father was a Spanish version of Edward FitzGerald's English translation of Omar Khayyam's *Rubaiyat*. It was done in the same meter as the original and was first published in a little magazine, *Proa* (Prow), edited by Borges and some friends in the mid-1920s. In an introductory note Georgie not only talks about the translation's author and praises his work but also finds words of praise for *El caudillo*. (The note was later included in *Inquisiciones*, 1925, pp. 127–130.) In spite of the explicit introduction, the translation was later attributed to Borges in a learned bibliography published in Buenos Aires (Lucio and Revello, 1961, p. 75). Bibliographers, it is a well-known fact, do not read the items they record.

Many years later Borges wrote an essay on the English translation of Omar Khayyam; it is called "The Enigma of Edward FitzGerald" and is included in *Other Inquisitions* (1952). It starts with short, parallel biographies of the Persian poet and his Victorian translator and comes to the conclusion that, since Omar Khayyam believed in the doctrine of the transmigration of souls, his soul must have migrated into FitzGerald's. But immediately Borges suggests that the same effect could have been caused by "a beneficent change":

> Sometimes clouds form the shapes of mountains or lions; Edward FitzGerald's unhappiness and a manuscript of yellow paper with purple letters, forgotten on a shelf of the Bodleian at Oxford, formed the poem for our benefit. All collaboration is mysterious. That by the Englishman and the Persian was more mysterious than any because the two were very different and perhaps in life they would not have become friends; death and vicissitudes and time caused one to know of the other and made them into a single poet. (*Inquisitions*, 1964, p. 78)

There is not one word in the article about the fact that Father had translated FitzGerald's English translation into Spanish. But it is obvious that the critic's theory could be extended to include him too, as a third reincarnation of the Persian poet: a reincarnation that is closer to the Victorian prototype than to the remote original. One passage in the article may well be taken as a disguised portrait of Father. According to Borges, FitzGerald

> is less intellectual than Omar, but perhaps more sensitive and more sad. FitzGerald knows that his true destiny is literature, and he practices it with indolence and tenacity. He reads and rereads the *Quixote,* which seems to him almost the best of all books (but he does not wish to be unjust with Shakespeare and with "dear old Virgil"), and his love extends to the dictionary in which he seeks words. He knows that every man who has any music in his soul can write verses ten or twelve times in the natural course of his life, if the stars are propitious, but he does not propose to abuse that modest privilege. He is a friend of famous persons (Tennyson, Carlyle, Dickens, Thackeray), to whom he does not feel inferior in spite of the fact that he is both modest and courteous. (Ibid., pp. 76–77)

With a few alterations of names and dates, those words could have been written about Father. Borges has told us how much he loved poetry, and if one substitutes Swinburne, Shelley, or Keats for Shakespeare, Cervantes, or Virgil, one would have Father's roll of poets. By changing FitzGerald's friends into Macedonio Fernández, Marcelo del Mazo, Evaristo Carriego, and Enrique Larreta, the same function would be performed. Father had never felt inferior to his more successful friends. Other details of FitzGerald's biography seem applicable to Father. In spite of having a home, a wife, and children, Father was essentially a solitary man, sensitive and sad. He was, after all, a Victorian gentleman, with some music in his soul: a man destined to literature but indolent in spite of his lucidity. Like FitzGerald, he even took advantage of some propitious stars to versify ten or twelve times in his life.

The article also presents a kind of paradigm of the man of letters. Many of the comments can be applied to Borges himself. It is not by chance that Borges quotes FitzGerald's concept of poetry as an occasional activity for any man who had some music in his soul, in an epigraph to his *San Martín Copybook* (*Poemas,* 1943, p. 119). But if he shared some of FitzGerald's traits, Borges obviously was not a Victorian gentleman. On the contrary, he had always taken literature seriously and was closer to Samuel Johnson than to FitzGerald in his professionalism.

There is another aspect of Borges' article that is worth underlining. In writing about the metamorphoses of Omar Khayyam's poems into FitzGerald's, he suggests a concept of literature as palimpsest: for him, a literary text is always based on another text, which in turn is based on a previous text, and so on and so forth. But Borges goes even further: poets are also palimpsests. The poet who was Omar

Khayyam can be seen through the mask of the poet who was Edward FitzGerald in the same way FitzGerald can be seen through the mask that was Father. When Georgie came to his father at six to state that he wanted to be a writer, was he consciously assuming for the first time a mask that had been inherited, or bequeathed to him?

12.
The Act of Writing

Georgie inherited Father's literary vocation. He also inherited his literary habits. Because Father loved to read English poetry aloud, Georgie continued that custom, carrying his imitation to the point of perfection. In his "Autobiographical Essay" Borges observes: "When I recite poetry in English now, my mother tells me I take on his very voice" ("Essay," 1970, p. 207). On many occasions I have heard Borges recite English poems. His voice has a deeper, warmer, almost a longing tone. The accent seems older than the one he normally uses when speaking English. A sort of rough North Country sound is superimposed on the clipped precision of the Oxonian prototype learned by Borges as a child. More than once I have thought, "He sounds like a nineteenth-century gentleman." Not until I read that passage from his autobiography did I discover why: the voice that endlessly quotes from the treasures of English poetry is Father's. Perhaps in that voice there are also echoes of the grandmother who was born in Staffordshire, of Northumbrian stock.

Another of Father's literary habits inherited by Georgie was the fruitful consultation of dictionaries and encyclopedias. It is not an Argentine or Hispanic habit. As a distinguished Spanish philologist once put it: "Spaniards consult the dictionary to see if it is right." But Georgie soon learned to trust the dictionary and always look in it first. In her interview with *L'Herne* Mother stressed the importance of Father's example in shaping Georgie's mind: "As his father did, every time a word or a theme attracts his attention . . . he searches for information in a dictionary" (Mother, 1964, p. 9). In recalling his first readings, Borges never forgets to mention the two reference works he consulted most: the *Encylopaedia Britannica* and *Chambers' Encyclopaedia*.

Those books not only contain the key to knowledge; they also give access to other books. They are really a library condensed into a few volumes.

That seed (like the seed of reading) was planted by Fanny Haslam. She used to sit Georgie on her lap and read from the bound copies of an English magazine for children. Alicia Jurado mentions that Georgie called the volume a "leccionario"—a portmanteau word that combines the concepts of "diccionario" (dictionary) and "lección" (lesson) (Jurado, 1964, p. 26). From the English "leccionario" Grandmother Haslam read to him, Georgie moved to the "diccionario." There he learned the meaning of words, their origins, their curious, fascinating life; he also learned to decipher the world of objects these words refer to.

Soon the encyclopedias became Georgie's chief source of information, and a model of prose writing. Consulting encyclopedias and dictionaries became a habit of Georgie's literary life. Some anecdotes preserved by his family and retold by his biographers show how deeply embedded that habit was. When Georgie was nineteen, he asked for a German encyclopedia as a birthday present. The family was then living in Lugano, Switzerland. Georgie had just completed his secondary schooling in Geneva. The German encyclopedia became his third important instrument in the search for knowledge. A few years later, when the Borgeses returned to Argentina to settle for good, Georgie visited the National Library regularly to consult the *Encyclopaedia Britannica*. By then Father's library had been dismantled. Many years later, after Borges had been appointed director of the National Library, he answered a query from Ronald Christ about his predilection for encyclopedias:

BORGES: Ah, yes, I'm very fond of that, I remember a time when I used to come here to read. I was a very young man, and I was far too timid to ask for a book. Then, I was rather, I won't say poor, but I wasn't too wealthy in those days—so I used to come every night here and pick out a volume of the *Encyclopaedia Britannica*, the old edition.

CHRIST: The eleventh?

BORGES: The eleventh or twelfth because those editions are far above the new ones. They were meant to be *read*. Now they are merely reference books. While in the eleventh or twelfth edition of the *Encyclopaedia Britannica*, you had long articles by Macaulay, by Coleridge; no, not by Coleridge, by—

CHRIST: By De Quincey?

BORGES: Yes, by De Quincey and so on. So that I used to take any volume from the shelves—there was no need to ask for them; they were reference books—and then I opened the book till I found an article that interested me, for example about the Mormons or about any particular writer. I sat down and read it because those articles were really monographs, really books or short books. The same goes for the German encyclopedias—Brockhaus or Meyers. (Christ, 1967, p. 154)

Eventually, Georgie owned a set of the *Encyclopaedia Britannica.* When awarded the second prize in the 1929 Municipal Literary Competition, he spent the money on a secondhand *Britannica.* The eleventh edition, of course. Because of his taste for encyclopedias and dictionaries, he has been accused of faulty scholarship. In his conversations with Jean de Milleret, Borges freely admits his debt to the *Britannica.* His only regret is not having been able to read more of it:

If I had read it entirely, I believe I would know a lot. Really, I believe that no one in the world knows as much as any encyclopedia. The majority of the contributors do not know what the others have written; thus, as a whole, encyclopedias know more than anybody. And I am sure about their worth because to begin the study of any subject, it is necessary to read the corresponding article in a good encyclopedia. That would permit you to sketch an idea, to trace a plan of work; in short, to trim the question. (De Milleret, 1967, pp. 197–198)

Borges is the reverse of a scholar: a man whose intellectual landscape is narrowed to a precise field and whose scope is voluntarily limited. Borges is a generalist: a man who approaches books and culture with an immense appetite but without any illusions about the possibility of mastering them. Because he admits his limitations, he can move freely in the world of culture. And because he does not have any pretense to specialization, he can (very humbly) start his quest by consulting an encyclopedia. He knows, of course, that the all-embracing view given by such a tool is incomplete. He knows it is the result of a convention: a game of scholarship. In two of his most celebrated stories he offers a hallucinatory image of encyclopedias and libraries. In "Tlön, Uqbar, Orbis Tertius," written in 1940 and collected in *Ficciones* (1944), he tells of the search for a missing article in a somewhat dubious if not totally piratical encyclopedia; in "The Library of Babel" (of the same book), he satirizes the concept of a total library. More recently, in *The Book of Sand* (1975), he conceives a book of infinite pages that contains all books: the total library concentrated in a single, monstrous object.

Even more interesting than the use Borges makes of encyclopedias as a literary subject, or motif, is the fact that encyclopedias, as literary structures and as prototypes of a certain style of writing, serve as models not only for Borges' essays but for many of his most celebrated stories. Thus he generally begins an article or a story by

89

summarizing the subject; he then moves to an analysis of the chief theme; finally, he offers conclusions that usually contradict (totally or partially) the starting point. The technique is like a reduction, by way of his skill at minimal art, of the structure of articles in the *Encyclopaedia Britannica*. Even the technique of including at the end a note with a basic bibliography corresponds to the model. The only difference (*the* difference) is that Borges' texts are not just a reduction of the model but also a parody. In parading his scholarship, Borges undermines it by introducing not only false leads but false sources, apocryphal books, misquoted texts. Long before the concept of "misreading" became a useful if popular tool in critical analysis, Borges had exhausted its parodic possibilities.

Another habit of Father's that Borges inherited was the now forgotten art of conversation. Father was not a great talker or an indiscriminate conversationalist. But he had a few friends with whom it was worth breaking the code of silence. One of his most intimate was his cousin Alvaro Melián Lafinur. Born in 1889, he was some fifteen years younger than Father. Although he had literary ambitions, his life was primarily spent in teaching and journalism. Nevertheless, he became a member of Argentina's Academy of Letters in 1936. He used to visit the Borgeses in the evenings. According to one of Borges' biographers, he always came with his guitar and used to make Georgie cry by singing "The Pirate's Song" (Jurado, 1964, p. 31).

Alvaro had an important role in Georgie's education. Being Father's young cousin and only ten years older than Georgie, he was less an uncle than an older brother, a model for a different kind of life than the one the child had at home. Apparently, Alvaro was familiar with the low life of brothels, easy women, and the tango. Once Borges told an interviewer that he learned from him how much prostitutes charged in those days. In an interview with Rita Guibert he alludes to Alvaro while discussing the origins of the tango. It began in brothels around 1880, according to what "was told to me by an uncle who was a bit of a rogue. I believe that the proof can be found in the fact that if the tango had been popular, the basic instrument would have been the guitar, as it was in the case of the milonga. Instead, the tango was always played on piano, flute, and violin, all instruments which belong to a higher economic level" (Guibert, 1968, p. 53). In Georgie's imagination, Alvaro, with his guitar and his aura of being a ladies' man, must have been a tantalizing figure. To the child who lived in a house with a garden from which evil was excluded, Alvaro's visits introduced a bit of the sounds and shapes of the sinful outside world.

Another visitor was to leave a deeper mark on Georgie's imagination. Evaristo Carriego, a popular poet and a friend of Father, came from Father's province of Entre Ríos and had been living for some time in the same Palermo neighborhood. Born in 1883, Carriego was nine years younger than Father but shared with him similar political experiences. Their families had fought against the local caudillo, Urquiza, and had finally emigrated to Buenos Aires. He also shared Father's love of poetry. But while the latter wrote only occasionally, and generally preferred to read and reread his favorite authors, Carriego was a professional poet, and a very successful one. He wrote about the lives and sentimental experiences of the poor: their joys and disappointments, their miseries and celebrations. His muse was humble and bathetic. Many of his poems were easily transformed into tango lyrics.

There was another difference: Carriego lived in the Palermo of the poor people; Father lived in the only two-storied house in sight. He was Carriego; Father was Dr. Borges. But they were friends, and Carriego used to call every Sunday upon returning from the horse races. In a literary biography of Carriego published in 1930 Borges evokes some of these visits. For him, Carriego's image is inseparable from Palermo: this poet and the neighborhood are one. In discussing one of Carriego's poems, "The Neighborhood Dogs," he interpolates his own memories of those mongrels who actually owned Palermo's streets and were perpetually rounded up by the police in a contraption called *la perrera* (the dog warden). To Borges, the wagon is a symbol of dark forces. Quoting some of Carriego's lines, he writes:

> I want to repeat this verse
>   when they drink moon-water in the pools
> and the other one about
>   howling exorcisms against the dog wagon,
> which brings back one of my stronger memories: the
> absurd visit of that little hell, anticipated by
> painful barks, and preceded—very closely—by a
> cloud of dust made of poor children who, shouting
> and throwing stones, scared another cloud of dust
> made of dogs, to save them from the noose.
>   (*Carriego*, 1930, p. 63)

There is little more about Carriego's contacts with the Borgeses in that book. But in his "Autobiographical Essay," written some forty years later, Borges tells us that Carriego's career

followed the same evolution as the tango—rollicking, daring, courageous at first, then turning sentimental. In 1912, at the age of twenty-nine, he died of tuberculosis, leaving behind a single volume of his work. I remember that a copy of it, inscribed to my father, was one of several Argentine books we had taken to Geneva and that I read and reread there. Around 1909, Carriego had dedicated a poem to my mother. Actually, he had written it in her album. In it, he spoke of me: "And may your son . . . go forth, led by the trusting wing of inspiration, to carry out the vintage of a new annunciation, which from lofty grapes will yield the wine of Song." ("Essay," 1970, pp. 233–234)

The lines do not seem memorable except for one thing: they bear witness that as early as 1909, when Georgie was ten, it was obvious at home that he was destined to be a poet, so obvious that the most popular Argentine poet of his time was ready to assume the prophetic mode to celebrate his verses to come.

How much of Carriego's conversation with Father was available to Georgie? In his biography Borges mentions many occasions on which Carriego talked about the books he liked, the poets he admired or hated, the people he despised (Italians and Spanish immigrants, in that order). But it is hard to say if these opinions were based on actual recollections or on Father's later reminiscences of Carriego. Because it can be assumed that talking about Carriego's visits was a normal occupation at the Borgeses'. Georgie's early reaction to Carriego may be found in Mother's reminiscences. Talking to a French interviewer, she once said: "At the beginning, Georgie did not like the visits of my husband's friends; later, he got used to it. And then, when for instance Carriego called on us, he loved to remain downstairs with the grownups, listening to the poet read his own poems, or Almafuerte's 'The Missionary'; then, he used to stay there, with his eyes wide open" (Mother, 1964, p. 10).

These two contrasted images of Georgie are worth considering. Proust has already described in minute detail the exquisite tortures of childhood when one was forced to go upstairs to sleep when a brilliant visitor was entertaining the grown-ups. Osbert Sitwell has devoted a whole volume of his five-part autobiography to the feelings of being excluded from real life when in the evening laughter pours in from the next room. But a moment came for Georgie when he was allowed to stay downstairs and hear Carriego read from his own poetry, or from the poets he admired. Then Georgie not only shared the excitement of the evening but probably got more out of it than the adults. His eyes wide open, he had the chance to see and hear a prodigy: a man who not only wrote occasional poems (as Father did) but actually devoted his entire life to writing. Carriego was to become Georgie's first literary prototype. That single volume of verses which the poet had dedicated to Father was to become Georgie's favorite reading in his long Geneva exile.

There is a third Argentine writer Father knew. Although he is now out of fashion, at the beginning of this century he was *the* most famous Latin American novelist. Born in 1873, only one year before Father, Enrique Rodríguez Larreta read law at Buenos Aires University with Macedonio Fernández and Father. They all graduated in 1898 and probably attended the same banquets to celebrate their newly minted degrees. But there is no record of any friendship after that date. Ten years later, after dropping the name Rodríguez as being too common (it is the equivalent of a name such as Smith in English), Enrique Larreta published his most successful book, *The Glory of Don Ramiro,* a historical novel of the age of Philip II, when the sun never set on the Spanish empire. A cold, precise, decorative reconstruction, the novel was written in a pastiche of Spanish Golden Age prose and became immensely popular—as popular as *One Hundred Years of Solitude* is now. Today it is hardly read; its pastry-shop style is no longer accepted. Father probably didn't think much of Dr. Larreta. In a 1945 interview Borges recalls a conversation with Father in which Dr. Larreta's name was mentioned. They were discussing one of the most famous utterances of General San Martín, Argentina's national hero: "You will be what you have to be, or you will be nothing." According to Father, it meant that "you will be a gentleman, a Catholic, an Argentine, a member of the Jockey Club, an admirer of Uriburu [the general who in 1930 deposed President Irigoyen], an admirer of Quirós' vast rustic characters—*or you will be nothing*—you will be a Jew, an anarchist, a bum, a lowly clerk; the National Commission of Culture will ignore your books and Dr. Rodríguez Larreta will not send you copies of his, enhanced by his autograph" (*Latitud,* February 1945, p. 4).

Calling the successful Larreta by his full surname and with the addition of "Dr." is one of the oldest tricks in the art of abuse, about which Borges wrote a devastatingly comic article in 1932. But there is more than abuse in the text just quoted. A whole view of Argentine life in this century is condensed here. To Father, Argentine society was deeply rooted in privilege, in social inequality, in racism and snobbery. To be somebody there one had to assume the mask of the Catholic gentleman, a supporter of army intervention in the affairs of state and an admirer of native subjects in painting. To be somebody meant to get prizes in the official literary competitions and autographed copies of Larreta's books. In short, to be somebody was to belong to the establishment. And Father was very determined not to belong to it, in spite of the fact that he came from an old family, was a lawyer, and had married a woman who belonged to an old Catholic family.

Compared with Macedonio Fernández or Evaristo Carriego, Father was part of the establishment. But compared with Dr. Rodríguez Larreta, he did not pass the test. There was too much in him of the anarchist, the freethinker, and the foreigner. The fact that he had chosen to live in Palermo, a rundown neighborhood, did not attend the Jockey Club (except for the annual banquets of the class of 1898), and had not supported Uriburu or ever admired Quirós helped to alienate him from the establishment. Furthermore (and this is the most important point) he was never graced with an autographed copy of Larreta's novels. In talking to Georgie about San Martín's dictum and in expanding and decoding it, Father was pursuing his main task of indoctrination. He wanted Georgie to become a poet and fulfill his frustrated literary vocation, but he wanted him to be different: a philosophical anarchist; not a tamed writer but a truly independent one. Father taught Georgie to shun prizes and despise honors. With his example and the corrosive wit of his conversation, he offered the best example of a man who chose to be marginal in a society in which every poet attempted to reach the center of the ring.

Georgie learned the lesson of marginality so well that he ended up making his peripheral activities the center of another (but purely literary) establishment. Many years later, when answering one of his interviewer's questions, Borges recalled an anecdote of his childhood days. Once he had told Father that he wanted to be a *raté;* that is, a failure (Arias, 1971, pp. 2–3). The French expression was rather commonly used in Argentina in those days; there was even a popular play by Henri Lenormand (*Les ratés*) on the subject. Georgie probably had heard the expression and, not knowing French well, mistook it for something desirable. But if he was wrong about the exact meaning of the word, he was right about its symbolic meaning. For the Argentine establishment of those days, what Father and Georgie really wanted to be was exactly that: *ratés,* and not the success that Dr. Rodríguez Larreta so ponderously represented.

On several occasions Borges has evoked his literary beginnings under the invisible but firm hand of Father. The versions differ only in detail. This is what he has to say in the "Autobiographical Essay":

> I first started writing when I was six or seven. I tried to imitate classic writers of Spanish—Miguel de Cervantes, for example. I had set down in quite bad English a kind of handbook on Greek mythology, no doubt cribbed from Lemprière. This may have been my first literary venture. My first story was a rather nonsensical piece after the manner of Cervantes, an old-fashioned romance called "La visera fatal" (The Fatal Helmet). I very neatly wrote these things into copybooks. My father never interfered. He wanted me to commit all my own mistakes, and once said, "Children educate their parents, not the other way around." When I was nine or so, I translated Oscar Wilde's "The Happy Prince" into Spanish, and it was published in one of the Buenos Aires dailies, *El País*. Since it was signed merely "Jorge Borges,"

people naturally assumed the translation was my father's. ("Essay," 1970, p. 211)

In talking to Richard Burgin he stresses other details:

BORGES: I began [writing] when I was a little boy. I wrote an English handbook ten pages long on Greek mythology, in very clumsy English. That was the first thing I ever wrote.

BURGIN: You mean "original mythology" or a translation?

BORGES: No, no, no, no. It was just saying, for example, well, "Hercules attempted twelve labors" or "Hercules killed the Nemean Lion."

BURGIN: So you must have been reading those books when you were very young.

BORGES: Yes, of course, I'm very fond of mythology. Well, it was nothing, it was just a, it must have been fifteen pages long . . . with the story of the Golden Fleece and the Labyrinth and Hercules, he was my favorite, and then something about the loves of the gods, and the tale of Troy. That was the first thing I ever wrote. I remember it was written in a very short and crabbed handwriting because I was very short-sighted. That's all I can tell you about it. In fact, I think my mother kept a copy for some time, but as we've travelled all over the world, the copy got lost, which is as it should be, of course, because we thought nothing whatever about it, except for the fact that it was written by a small boy. (Burgin, 1969, pp. 2–3)

The choice of a handbook on Greek mythology for a first attempt at literary composition may seem odd in any six-year-old writer, but not in Georgie. Georgie was anticipating some of Borges' most famous works (*The Book of Imaginary Beings,* for instance), and he was already creating a literary space of his own: the space of myth. But not all the Greek myths would survive childhood. Hercules never made the grade. Or perhaps only degraded versions of Hercules did, versions in which the hero is fatally flawed and weak. But the labyrinth, on the contrary, became one of Borges' most personal symbols: the very image of life's absurdity and man's puzzling predicament. In evoking many years later, in *The Book of Imaginary Beings,* the image of the monster who sits at the center of the labyrinth, Borges writes: "Most likely the Greek fable of the Minotaur is a late and clumsy version of older myths, the shadow of other dreams still more full of horror" (*Imaginary,* 1969, p. 159). It is obvious that for Borges (and perhaps for Georgie) what was really attractive in Greek mythology in general and in the myth of the Minotaur in particular was its deep roots in the unconscious, where nightmares are produced.

In his conversation with Burgin, Borges returns to the subject of his first piece of fiction, the old-fashioned romance "La visera fatal."

He recalls that after reading a chapter or two of *Don Quixote,* he tried to write archaic Spanish: "And that saved me from trying to do the same thing some fifteen years afterward, no? Because I had already attempted that game and failed at it" (Burgin, 1969, p. 3). According to Mother, this first fictional attempt was a short tale, in "old Spanish," some "four or five pages long" (Mother, 1964, p. 10). Quoting Mother as a source, Victoria Ocampo reports that it was a story written "in a style similar to *The Glory of Don Ramiro*" and adds: "In that story, people did not die; they departed" (Ocampo, 1964, p. 21).

If Victoria Ocampo's recollections are correct, the story must have been written when Georgie was older, because *The Glory of Don Ramiro* did not come out until 1908, when the boy was nine. The point is a minor one, but what is ironic about a possible connection between Georgie's first fiction and Larreta's novel is the fact that its author was to become for him the epitome of the literary fake. More significant still is the fact that in starting his literary career Georgie had chosen as a model the exact book one of his characters would attempt to rewrite so earnestly in the 1939 short story called "Pierre Menard, Author of the *Quixote.*"

There is a little anecote attached to Georgie's literary beginnings. When his translation of Wilde's "The Happy Prince" was published, a friend of Father's, Ricardo Blemey Lafont, a teacher at the Institute of Living Languages, where Father taught psychology, not only congratulated Father for the translation but adopted it as a text in one of his classes (Jurado, 1964, p. 31). The mistake is significant. Georgie's first published work would be attributed to Father. Many years later, in one of the first full-length bibliographies of his work, included among Borges' translations was Father's version of Omar Khayyam (Lucio and Revello, 1961, p. 75). The circle of false attribution was by then completed: Georgie, who became Father's specular image, had finally reached the stage in his career where Father would become his specular image.

Another of his childhood productions of which very little is known is a gaucho poem mentioned in the "Autobiographical Essay": "I think I began writing a poem about gauchos, probably under the influence of the poet Ascasubi, before I went to Geneva. I recall trying to work in as many gaucho words as I could, but the technical difficulties were beyond me. I never got past a few stanzas" ("Essay," 1970, p. 213). Borges never attempted such a task again. It was already hopelessly anachronistic by the time he tried his hand at it. Ascasubi, one of the most prolific of the gaucho poets, had died in 1875, exactly one year after Father's birth. The tradition of gaucho poetry was practically dead in Argentina, and only a few such poets remained in

Uruguay (Elías Regules, "El Viejo Pancho," Fernán Silva Valdés) to practice a genre that used to be the most popular in the River Plate area. In discussing why Uruguay kept the gaucho tradition longer than Argentina, Borges has pointed out that it is a more primitive country, a country in which gauchos still participated actively in national life. In Argentina, the fast industrialization which took place in the second half of the nineteenth century made the gaucho, and gaucho poetry, obsolete.

Not much is known about Georgie's early works, but in them we can find a key to his interests and even his obsessions. The fact that we have only titles or short descriptions to go on should not be a great obstacle. Borges has already shown how to deal with writers (Pierre Menard, Herbert Quain, Jaromir Hládik, Ts'ui Pên, Nils Runenberg, Carlos Argentino Daneri, Joseph Cartaphilus, Julio Platero Haedo, Suárez Miranda, Gasper Camerarius) of whose works there remain only a title, a fragment, an incomplete quotation, a plot summary. That much has been saved so far of Georgie Borges' works. Perhaps in the near future some devoted scholar will unearth the "lost" notebooks and will publish them with all the critical paraphernalia these crumbs will undoubtedly merit. Then it will be forever impossible to continue to speculate about Georgie's lost works.

13.
The Eton Boy

The only formal schooling Georgie had before he was nine was given him by his English grandmother or by an English governess, Miss Tink, who took care of him and his sister, Norah. Father was always there, but his teachings were of a different kind.

In 1908, when Georgie was almost nine, a momentous decision was made: to send him to the state school. As he had already learned many odd things, including English, he was placed directly in fourth grade.

The school was a day school for boys. Georgie had been used to learning in the quiet of his home, helped by people who loved him and who shared his cultural code: English. At the state school English was worse than useless; it was positively exotic and, as he soon learned, dangerous. For the first time in his life he found himself in a totally hostile world. Not until 1937, when he began working at a municipal library, would he experience similar alienation and terror. In the descriptions of his early schooldays in the "Autobiographical Essay" Borges' generally ironical narrative takes on a slightly sinister tone: "I take no pleasure whatever in recalling my early schooldays. . . . As I wore spectacles and dressed in an Eton collar and tie, I was jeered at and bullied by most of my schoolmates, who were amateur hooligans. I cannot remember the name of the school but recall that it was on Thames Street" ("Essay," 1970, p. 212).

The decision to send Georgie to a state school, disguised as an Eton boy, proved how alien the Borgeses were to the world around them. Georgie's dress, his nearsightedness, his stammering, made him the favorite target of the bullies. The thought that in an English public school he would have probably received even more brutal treatment

98

could not have provided much consolation. Another mention of his schooldays can be found in his conversations with Richard Burgin; to a question about childhood fights, Borges replies:

Well, my eyesight was bad; it was very weak and I was generally defeated. But it had to be done. Because there was a code and, in fact, when I was a boy, there was even a code of dueling. But I think dueling is a very stupid custom, no? After all, it's quite irrelevant. If you quarrel with me and I quarrel with you, what has our swordsmanship or our marksmanship to do with it? Nothing—unless you have the mystical idea that God will punish the wrong. I don't think anybody has that kind of idea, no? Well, suppose we get back to more . . . because, I don't know why, I seem to be rambling on. (Burgin, 1969, p. 29)

What is striking in this testimony about his schooldays is Borges' emotional tone of voice. It is possible to detect even in the written transcript the revulsion that such a "code of honor" still arouses in him. The violence and terror of those early fights were never erased.

There is an irony here. The same Georgie who suffered the humiliation of being made a scapegoat will become (much later and as a writer) a champion of physical courage, of the old skills of gun and knife play and the mythology of violence. The conflict between his military forebears and his literary vocation, between the sword and the library, here takes on a more squalid form. It comes as no surprise that Borges calls his schoolmates "amateur hooligans," but the code of honor so deeply imbedded in the Borgeses forced Georgie to conquer his revulsion and face the hooligans, participating in fights he knew he could never win.

There is an interesting lapse in Borges' school recollections: he has forgotten the name of the school, although he remembers that it was located, of all places, on Thames Street. Mother had a better memory. In a conversation with me in 1971 she remembered one of Georgie's classmates, Roberto Godel, from French stock, who used to see Georgie after school. According to her, they continued to be friends. They probably went together to the National School for their secondary studies. He is the only name that survives from those schooldays.

In discussing oblivion with Burgin, Borges observes that it is "the highest form of revenge" and adds: "If I were insulted by a stranger in the street, I don't think I would give the matter a second thought. I would just pretend I hadn't heard him and go on, because, after all, I don't exist for him, so why should he exist for me?" (Burgin, 1969, p. 28). Years later, in one of his most famous short stories, "The South," Borges dramatizes this observation. When the protagonist,

Juan Dahlmann (of mixed Scandinavian and Argentine stock), is challenged by some drunks in a tavern set in the middle of nowhere, he decides not to pay any attention to them until he is recognized by the owner and called by his name. Then he has to fight. There is an echo here of that old chivalric code which forces one to accept the challenge of another knight but never the challenge of a villain. In the same way, Georgie at school accepted his classmates' challenge and fought hopeless fights. Sixty years later, in recalling those days for Richard Burgin, his voice betrayed him: he still was fighting those nightmarish duels.

The scars that his days at school left on Georgie are still visible in the writing of Borges. One of the scars was left by his schoolmates' coarse descriptions of the mysteries of sex. In some of the stories Borges later wrote—"The Sect of the Phoenix" and "Emma Zunz" are the most revealing—it is still possible to see how shocked Georgie was.

Little is known about what Georgie actually learned at school. According to Mother, he was a good student but had some trouble with mathematics. He preferred history and ("naturally") literature, as well as grammar and philosophy (Mother, 1964, p. 11). Borges recalls that his father

> used to say that Argentine history had taken the place of the catechism, so we were expected to worship all things Argentine. We were taught Argentine history, for example, before we were allowed any knowledge of the many lands and many centuries that went into its making. As far as Spanish composition goes, I was taught to write in a flowery way: *Aquellos que lucharon por una patria libre, independiente, gloriosa* . . . (Those who struggled for a free, independent, and glorious nation . . .). Later on, in Geneva, I was to be told that such writing was meaningless and that I must see things through my own eyes. ("Essay," 1970, p. 212)

Georgie's experience helped to confirm everything that Father had been saying about the low level of the state schools. It was a further proof (if any were needed) of the backwardness and general inferiority of Argentine culture. The gap that Georgie's bilingualism had already created at home began to widen at school. Nothing that he could have learned there would erase the prejudices against everything Hispanic that he inherited from Father's side. A long residence in Spain, which led to the discovery of the poetical possibilities of Spanish and later the rediscovery of his native Buenos Aires, was needed to alter Georgie's prejudices.

But if the level of teaching and learning at the state school was rather low, Georgie continued to have the best of mentors at home. Father began to guide him firmly into the labyrinths of philosophy. According to Mother, "he read a lot and he talked to his father. . . . They began to talk about philosophy when Georgie was ten" (Mother, 1964, p. 11). In his "Autobiographical Essay" Borges mentions how Father taught him Zeno's paradoxes with the aid of a chessboard; and in Father's only novel, *El caudillo,* the protagonist, Carlos DuBois, uses a similar method to teach one of the foreman's sons the rudiments of the alphabet. Talking to Burgin, Borges indicates the importance of such a training:

BURGIN: Of course most people live and die without ever, it seems, really thinking about the problems of time or space or infinity.

BORGES: Well, because they take the universe for granted. They take things for granted. They take themselves for granted. That's true. They never wonder at anything, no? They don't think it's strange that they should be living. I remember the first time I felt that was when my father said to me, "What a queer thing," he said, "that I should be living, as they say, behind my eyes, inside my head. I wonder if that makes sense?" And then, it was the first time I felt that, and then instantly I pounced upon that because I knew what he was saying. But many people can hardly understand that. And they say, "Well, but where else could you live?" (Burgin, 1969, p. 6)

A few pages later, after a digression on women, Borges returns to the subject:

BURGIN: So you think that remark of your father's heralded the beginning of your own metaphysics?

BORGES: Yes, it did.

BURGIN: How old were you then?

BORGES: I don't know. I must have been a very young child. Because I remember he said to me, "Now, look here; this is something that may amuse you," and then, he was very fond of chess, he was a very good chess player, and then he took me to the chessboard, and he explained to me the paradoxes of Zeno, Achilles and the Tortoise, you remember, the arrows, the fact that movement was impossible because there was always a point in between, and so on. And I remember him speaking of these things to me and I was very puzzled by them. And he explained them with the help of a chessboard. (Ibid., p. 9)

Many years later Borges would make the game that Father played with Georgie into his own literary game, a game he plays endlessly in poems, short stories, and essays. In talking to Herbert Simon, Borges adds a few anecdotes about his early training:

BORGES: I inherited from Father the taste for this type of reasoning. He used to take me apart to talk or to ask me questions about my beliefs. Once he took an orange and asked me: According to you, the taste is in the orange? I told

101

him it was. Then he asked me: Well, then you think that the orange is constantly tasting itself?

SIMON: It can be assumed that the solution to this type of questioning would take one deeply into the field of solipsism.

BORGES: Actually, Father did not lead me to the philosophical sources. He only asked concrete problems. Only after quite a long time he showed me a history of philosophy in which I found the origin of all these questions. In the same way he taught me to play chess. Although I have always been a poor player and he was very good. (Simon, 1971, p. 43)

After discussing some basic ideas about combinatory analysis, the infinite, and the labyrinth, Borges predictably concludes: "I got many of my ideas from books on logic and mathematics which I have read, but to be honest, every time I have attempted reading these books, they have defeated me; I haven't been able to interpret them thoroughly. Now, the majority of these ideas I got from Father's observations" (ibid., p. 45).

As a teacher of psychology and a follower of William James, Father also used his experiences in the classroom to introduce Georgie gradually to the complexities of thinking. In his conversations with Burgin, Borges recalls one lesson:

BORGES: I remember my father said to me something about memory, a very saddening thing. He said, "I thought I could recall my childhood when we first came to Buenos Aires, but now I know that I can't." I said, "Why?" He said, "Because I think that memory"—I don't know if this was his own theory; I was so impressed by it that I didn't ask him whether he found it or whether he evolved it—but he said, "I think that if I recall something, for example, if today I look back on this morning, then I get an image of what I saw this morning. But if tonight, I'm thinking back on this morning, then what I'm really recalling is not the first image in morning. So that every time I recall something, I'm not recalling it really. I'm recalling the last time I recalled it, I'm recalling my last memory of it. So that really," he said, "I have no memories whatever, I have no images whatever, about my childhood, about my youth." And then he illustrated that, with a pile of coins. He piled one coin on top of the other and said, "Well, now this first coin, the bottom coin, this would be the first image, for example, of the house of my childhood. Now this second would be a memory I had of that house when I went to Buenos Aires. Then the third one another memory and so on. And as in every memory there's a slight distortion, I don't suppose that my memory of today ties in with the first image I had. So that," he said, "I try not to think of things in the past because if I do I'll be thinking back on those memories and not on the actual images themselves." And then that saddened me. To think maybe we have no true memories of youth.

BURGIN: That the past was invented, fictitious.

BORGES: That it can be distorted by successive repetition. Because if in every repetition you get a slight distortion, then in the end you will be a long way off from the issue. It's a saddening thought. I wonder if it's true, I wonder what other psychologists would have to say about that. (Burgin, 1969, pp. 10–11)

The strangest thing about this anecdote is not what it says about Father's theory of memory. It is the fact that Borges did not realize that it was another version of Zeno's second paradox about the impossibility of Achilles ever reaching the tortoise. By parceling space, Zeno proved the race could never be won by the fastest Greek warrior. In Father's theory the imaginary space of memory is equally divided into infinite segments, until memory (that is, the actual and new recollection of something that once happened to us) becomes impossible. After this exercise, Father and Georgie are left with only a sad feeling. Memory also becomes part of the fictional world Father's idealist philosophy had created for Georgie to live in. The mentor had reached a point at which he could rest. The pupil is forever programmed to believe reality and fiction are one and the same.

Part Two

1.
Trapped in Switzerland

Perhaps the most momentous decision ever made by Father was his sudden determination to visit Europe in the summer of 1914. As he was becoming totally blind, he felt he could no longer pursue his career as a lawyer. He was approaching forty at the time and decided on early retirement. In his "Autobiographical Essay" Borges has this to say:

> In 1914, we moved to Europe. My father's eyesight had begun to fail and I remember him saying, "How on earth can I sign my name to legal papers when I am unable to read them?" Forced into early retirement, he planned our trip in exactly ten days. The world was unsuspicious then; there were no passports or other red tape. . . . The idea of the trip was for my sister and me to go to school in Geneva; we were to live with my maternal grandmother, who traveled with us and eventually died there, while my parents toured the Continent. At the same time, my father was to be treated by a famous Genevan eye doctor. ("Essay," 1970, pp. 213–214)

Implicit in Borges' account is the fact that the journey was to be long enough to justify the children's going to school in Geneva and to allow the parents to do some sightseeing. The trip to Europe was then, as it still is, considered essential in the education of an Argentine gentleman. It was the equivalent of the Grand Tour that eighteenth-century English gentlemen used to take after they had graduated from Oxford or Cambridge: a chance to gain a firsthand acquaintance with Western culture. Purely for economic reasons, Father had postponed the trip since his own graduation. But now he hesitated no longer. In ten days he had everybody packed, and they sailed for the Old World.

107

The moment seemed auspicious. The Pax Victoriana, prolonged by the Entente Cordiale between England and France, seemed eternal. Europe had not had a major upheaval since the Franco-Prussian war of 1870. Wars (civil or international) seemed cozily confined to the marginal areas of Asia, Africa, and Latin America. The Borgeses sailed off to meet a war that was to be called *The* World War before it became World War I. Borges underscores the irony of the situation in a 1967 interview with César Fernández Moreno: "When my father had to retire because of his blindness, the family decided to travel in Europe. We were so ignorant about universal history, and especially about the immediate future, that we traveled in 1914 and got stuck in Switzerland" (Fernández Moreno, 1967, pp. 8–9).

The decision to move to Europe for a few months to live under the care of their maternal grandmother, Leonor Suárez Acevedo probably did not appeal to Georgie and Norah. To understand their strong feelings of abandonment, one has to remember how closely united the family had been till then, how inbred their affective life was, how little the children had seen of the outside world. They must have been miserable.

From Father's point of view, the plan was simple and feasible. His pension was small, but in those days the Argentine peso was strong. Those were the years when landowners in Argentina, made rich by the meat and dairy products of their ranches, used to spend a great part of their fortune in Europe; when European elegance was carefully copied on both banks of the River Plate; and when the wealthy journeyed to Europe with their servants and sometimes even with their favorite cows. Apparently they did not trust the quality of the European product. Vicente Blasco Ibáñez described them in his best-seller *The Four Horsemen of the Apocalypse,* later immortalized in a 1920 movie directed by Fred Niblo. In that film Rudolph Valentino epitomized the Argentine male of those years: a suave, beautiful, vaselinized Latin lover, teaching the French ladies hcw to tango in and out of bed.

The Borgeses had little to do with those people. Father's pension was not large and he was no Latin lover, although he had a fondness for easy young women. (Borges once told me that his father was "a bit of a rogue" in these matters.) If Father failed to conform to the tango prototype, he represented very effectively another less publicized Argentine prototype: the cultivated gentleman for whom Europe is a string of museum cities. The family's itinerary seems to support this view. Skipping Spain for the time being, they went directly to England, where Georgie had a glimpse of London's "red labyrinth" and of Cambridge; then they crossed the Channel to Paris. In his "Autobiographical Essay" Borges is not kind to the great city: "We first spent some weeks in Paris, a city that neither then nor since has particularly charmed me, as it does every other good Argentine. Perhaps, without knowing it, I was always a bit of a Britisher; in fact, I always think of Waterloo as a victory" ("Essay," 1970, p. 213). From Paris the Borgeses went to Geneva. With the children safely tucked away at school, Father and Mother continued their tour alone. They were in Germany when war broke out and had some difficulty in returning to Switzerland. But as Latin Americans they were luckier than many other stranded tourists. In due time they managed to reach Geneva, where they remained until the end of the war.

In Switzerland the Borgeses re-created the family cell they had formed while living in Palermo. The family found shelter in the beautiful and melancholy city by the lake. There Georgie invented another secluded, holy space in which to continue his reading, his daydreaming with Norah, his permanent conversation with Father.

Father and Mother were still young and extremely handsome; the children had dark, sensitive features. In two studio photographs, taken in Geneva, in 1914 and 1915, they look well and prosperous, although their faces are sad.

Georgie was unhappy in Switzerland. In a short autobiographical piece he wrote for a 1927 anthology of Argentine poetry, he summarizes his experience there: "I spent the war years in Geneva; [it was] a no-exit time, tight, made of drizzle, which I'll always remember with some hatred" (Vignale, 1927, p. 93). For a boy used to the bright sun and the hot summers of Buenos Aires, Geneva's misty, damp, and cold weather must have been painful enough. What justified the hatred was probably the feeling of being trapped there. But his attitude changed with time. In a 1967 interview with Fernández Moreno, Borges recalls only the brighter of those days in Geneva:

BORGES: I came to know Switzerland very thoroughly, and to love it very much.
FERNÁNDEZ MORENO: You had remembered those days as "gray, and tight with drizzle," in a 1927 statement.
BORGES: Yes, but that was then; not now. Now, when I returned to Switzerland after forty years, I was greatly moved and had the feeling of returning home also. Because the experiences of adolescence, all that, happened there. . . . Geneva is a city I know better than Buenos Aires. Besides, Geneva can be learned because it is a normal-size city, shall we say, while Buenos Aires is such an outrageous city that nobody can ever learn it. (Fernández Moreno, 1967, p. 9)

He returns to the subject in his "Autobiographical Essay," describing the everyday routine of his life in Geneva: "We lived in a flat on the southern, or old, side of town. I still know Geneva far better than I know Buenos Aires, which is easily explained by the fact that in Geneva no two streetcorners are alike and one quickly learns the differences. Every day, I walked along that green and icy river, the Rhone, which runs through the very heart of the city, spanned by seven quite different-looking bridges" ("Essay," 1970, p. 215).

The apartment house where the Borgeses lived is still there, in the old quarter, not too far from the Collège Calvin, which Georgie attended for four years. It belongs to a whole block of nineteenth-century townhouses in the style that Baron Haussmann's reforms made so popular in Paris: solid, dignified, a bit dull. The only change brought about by this century is in the name of the street, then called Rue Malagnou and now called Rue Ferdinand Hodler to celebrate the twentieth-century Swiss painter. The whole quarter, built on a hill, still has winding roads and a few medieval landmarks. In a 1975 story called "The Other" there is a fleeting evocation of those cold days by the river in an imaginary encounter between two Borgeses (the 1914 one, the 1969 one) on a bench on the banks of the Charles River in Cambridge, Massachusetts, which is also a bench on the Rhone in Geneva.

Although the Grand Tour plans had to be shelved because of the war, the Borgeses still wanted to see Europe. From Geneva, the safest summer tour seemed to be to the south, crossing the slopes to visit northern Italy. In his "Autobiographical Essay" Borges recalls: "I have vivid memories of Verona and Venice. In the vast and empty amphitheater of Verona I recited, loud and bold, several gaucho verses from Ascasubi" (ibid., p. 214). The selection of Ascasubi may seem less a homage to one of the masters of Argentine gaucho verse than a sort of challenge to the Old World. To have quoted Shakespeare in Verona would have seemed trite to Georgie. Ascasubi had the advantage of being untainted by sophistication. He provided a way for Georgie to espress his longing for his native land and speech. Borges gives no further details of his "vivid" memories of Venice.

The other important family event of those European years was the arrival in Switzerland of Fanny Haslam, the English grandmother. She may have decided to join the Borgeses because, with their prolonged absence, she was lonely in Buenos Aires. The "Autobiographical Essay" makes only a short reference to her visit: "As a result of the war—apart from the Italian trip and journeys inside Switzerland—we did no traveling. Later on, braving German submarines and in the company of only four or five passengers, my English grandmother joined us" (ibid., p. 215).

Fanny Haslam's courage is a subject that Borges loves to discuss. She had proved it in her early years in Argentina when she shared frontier life with her husband, Colonel Borges. Now, in facing the German submarines, Grandmother showed her truly British spirit. With her arrival in Geneva, the original Borges clan was restored. Life in Geneva began to take on features of life in Palermo.

Before his grandmother's arrival, Georgie had sent her post-cards which revealed his homesickness.

DE MILLERET: It's true, some of the postcards you sent your grandmother at the time show regrets which are not specifically addressed to her.

BORGES: It was a lack of tact on my part, no? When one is twelve or thirteen one is not a man of the world. (De Milleret, 1967, p. 20)

Borges uses irony here to disguise his feelings. He had attached to Buenos Aires the longing he felt for the close-knit world of Palermo. Too proud to tell his grandmother he missed her, he talked of his native city. There is another revelation in these reminiscences. By slightly reducing his real age (he was nearly fifteen when he went to Europe), Borges tries to make more acceptable the fact that he was still so attached to his grandmother's apron strings.

Grandmother was not the only relative to visit the Borgeses in Switzerland. Around 1916 some of Mother's Uruguayan cousins came to Europe. They belonged to the Haedo branch of the family. To celebrate the visit, Father took some photographs which show at least three generations of Haedo women surrounding Doñã Leonor, the maternal grandmother. Among these women (eight in all), Georgie cuts a strange figure. Even with his closest relatives he seems the odd man out, the stranger. The difference is visible in the expression of the face, the sadness of the eyes behind the thick glasses, and the terribly unhappy mouth. It is also evident in the way he sits or stands, always so clumsily, as if his body, growing too quickly and with a will of its own, bothered him too much.

In those difficult days Georgie could not forget he had a body. Infrequent but tantalizing references in his poems or short stories make quite clear that Georgie did not weather the sexual problems of adolescence easily. In the story called "The Other," in which he describes a meeting between himself as an old man and as a very young man in Geneva, to convince the young Georgie that he really is his future self, Borges adduces some evidence only he could have:

> I can prove I'm not lying. . . . I'm going to tell you things a stranger couldn't possibly know. At home [in Geneva] we have a silver maté cup with a base in the form of entwined serpents. Our great-grandfather brought it from Peru. There's also a silver washbasin that hung from his saddle. In the wardrobe of your room are two rows of books: the three volumes of Lane's *One Thousand and One Nights,* with steel engravings and with notes in small

type at the end of each chapter; Quicherat's Latin dictionary; Tacitus' *Germania* in Latin and also in Grodon's English translation; a *Don Quixote* published by Garnier; Rivera Indarte's *Tablas de sangre,* inscribed by the author; Carlyle's *Sartor Resartus;* a biography of Amiel; and, hidden behind the other volumes, a book in paper covers about sexual customs in the Balkans. Nor have I forgotten one evening on a certain second floor of the Place Dubourg."

"Dufour," he corrected.

"Very well—Dufour." (*Sand,* 1977, pp. 11–12)

The context in which that mysterious evening on the second floor of Dufour Square is mentioned may seem purely literary. But some of the books mentioned—Lane's translation, Amiel's biography, and the hidden volume on Balkan erotic habits—are specifically associated with a forbidden subject: sex. Lane's version of the *One Thousand and One Nights* (published in 1839) bowdlerized the famous original. In an article devoted to different European translations of the book Borges discusses at some length the virtues and omissions of that version. Lane lived in Cairo for five years and learned the language and mores thoroughly, but he never relinquished (according to Borges) "his British sense of decorum." Instead of having the elegant reticence of Antoine Galland, the French translator who omitted all controversial references, Lane did not "pact with silence." He did not translate the more pornographic passages but he mentioned each omission. In his article Borges quotes expressions such as "I overlooked a most reprehensible episode," "I eliminate a disgusting explanation," "Here a line too gross to translate," "Here the story of Bujait, the slave, totally inadequate to be translated." What Borges criticizes is Lane's tendency to evade some of the original's specifics. He quotes an example: "In night 217 there is a king who slept with two women, one night with one, the following night with the other, and in that way they were all happy. Lane explains the monarch's venture by saying he treated his women 'with impartiality.' " Borges concludes that "one of the reasons [for such an evasion] is that Lane had oriented his work to the 'parlor table,' the center of alarmless reading and reticent conversation" (*Eternidad,* 1936, pp. 76–77).

In calling Lane's version of the *Arabian Nights* "a mere encyclopedia of evasion" (ibid., p. 76), Borges offers a clue to his own reticence. Like Lane, he generally avoids saying things explicitly, but at the same time, very conscientiously, he leaves tantalizing clues here and there. In a subtler way he points obliquely to the places where something has been left unsaid. In the fragment from "The Other" quoted above, the signs are clear. Not only Lane's version but also the brief reference to a biography of Amiel work as indexes: they point to what is missing. Amiel, a well-known Swiss essayist whose *Diary* was widely read, had a troubled sexual life. In not identifying which biography of Amiel Georgie possessed, Borges is playing again with the reader. But is is fair to assume that Amiel's sexual problems were not omitted in that biography. Less reticent is the reference to a book on Balkan sexual mores. The fact that the book was hidden from a casual viewer's eyes is very telling. It might have been one of those books which, according to Rousseau's famous mot, are read with one hand only. If Georgie used it for that purpose, he would have been doing only what any normal adolescent would do. But even now, writing a story that evokes that younger self, he cannot bring himself to abandon his reticence. And then there is the tantalizing reference to Dufour Square.

Only gossip is available to elucidate the reference, but it is gossip that has been around long enough to acquire a certain respectability. According to Borges' confidences to several friends, he was once taken by Father to one of those complaisant Geneva girls who catered to foreigners, loners, and young men in distress. He performed his task so quickly that he was overcome by the power of orgasm. The "little death," as the French call it, was too close to real death for him. From then on Georgie viewed sex with fear. There is another side to the story which may have more complex implications. In being initiated into sex through the offices of his father, Georgie may have assumed that the girl had performed the same services for Father; having to share the same woman with Father disturbed deep-seated taboos.

It will never be known exactly what happened at Dufour Square, if that was the place. What is known is that Borges cared enough about the episode to repeat it to friends in confidence and to include a tantalizing reference to it in one of his stories.

In his conversation with Fernández Moreno, quoted above, Borges mentions that he was greatly moved upon returning to Switzerland after forty years: he "had the feeling of returning home also. Because the experiences of adolescence, all that, happened there." Again, reticence; but if one connects this statement with the allusion in the story, things begin to fall into place. Geneva was where adolescence came to Georgie.

2.
The French Circulating Library

To be admitted to the Collège Calvin, Georgie had first to learn French. He began by taking lessons with a private teacher, then spent some time at an academy. He finally passed the admission test, although his French was still shaky. It was the third linguistic code he had had to master, but at fifteen the situation was less traumatic than when, as a child, he had had to learn Spanish and English almost simultaneously. The fact that French was a totally alien language to him, even though most educated Argentines of that era had some rudiments of French, emphasizes the paradoxical nature of his cultural upbringing. But if Georgie had to learn French the hard way, he also had to learn it thoroughly—something few of his countrymen bother to do.

Although Georgie had a rough time with the new language, his sister, Norah, mastered it very quickly. In his "Autobiographical Essay" he notes that her "French soon became so good she even dreamed in it. I remember my mother's coming home one day and finding Norah hidden behind a red plush curtain, crying out in fear, *'Une mouche, une mouche!'* It seems she had adopted the French notion that flies are dangerous. 'You come out of there,' my mother told her, somewhat unpatriotically. 'You were born and bred among flies!' " ("Essay," 1970, p. 215).

Borges also recalls some of the difficulties he had in adjusting to the Collège Calvin: "That first fall—1914—I started school at the College of Geneva, founded by John Calvin. It was a day school. In my class there were some forty of us; a good half were foreigners. The chief subject was Latin, and I soon found out that one could let other studies slide a bit as long as one's Latin was good" (ibid., p. 214).

Latin became his fourth code. Although it was never to be one

114

of his major languages (later, in Majorca he improved his mastery of it), it gave Georgie a firm syntactic structure and an awareness of etymology that were later reflected in Borges' prose style. Combined with French, Latin erased the rhetorical vagueness inherent in Spanish and the untidiness of nineteenth-century English. Learning Latin and French simultaneously gave Georgie the linguistic discipline Borges later put to such good use.

In spite of hard work, Georgie had trouble keeping pace. Besides studying French as a separate language, he had to study all his other courses—"algebra, chemistry, physics, mineralogy, botany, zoology," he recalls (ibid., p. 214)—in that language. At the end of the year he passed all his exams except French. His schoolmates were so aware of his efforts that they decided to speak on his behalf:

> Without a word to me, my fellow schoolmates sent a petition around to the headmaster, which they had all signed. They pointed out that I had to study all of the different subjects in French, a language I also had to learn. They asked the headmaster to take this into account, and he very kindly did so. At first, I had not even understood when a teacher was calling on me, because my name was pronounced in the French manner, in a single syllable (rhyming roughly with "forge"), while we pronounce it with two syllables, the "g" sounding like a strong Scottish "h." Every time I had to answer, my schoolmates would nudge me. (Ibid., pp. 214–215)

Georgie must have responded to the warmth and concern of his schoolmates, especially in contrast to his experiences at school in Buenos Aires. Here in Geneva his singularity, even his foreignness, was not so strange. Many of the students in his class were also foreigners. To be "different" here was normal. Very soon Georgie had found among his schoolmates two of his closest friends, both two years younger. "My two friends were of Polish-Jewish origin—Simon Jichlinski and Maurice Abramowicz. One became a lawyer and the other a physician. I taught them to play *truco,* and they learned so well and fast that at the end of our first game they left me without a cent" ("Essay," p. 215).

I had the chance to visit Geneva in May 1975 and called on Dr. Jichlinski and Maître Abramowicz. They are both prosperous. Dr. Jichlinski had seen Borges again in the mid-1960s and had had the chance to refresh his memories. He told me that Borges exaggerated their ease in learning to play *truco.* He believed that Borges' account was part of his tendency to put himself in an ironic situation. Dr. Jichlinski recalled long conversations about literature while walking along the streets of the old quarter, bouts of drinking in the evening, endless meetings to discuss everything and nothing.

If Dr. Jichlinski shared more of Georgie's everyday life, it was Maître Abramowicz who shared more of his literary life. A lawyer by profession but a writer and a poet by avocation, he seemed to have total recall in talking about Georgie, whom he met at Geneva's municipal library, and read to me some of the letters Georgie wrote him from Spain in the late 1910s and early 1920s, checking on dates, names, figures.

More than once Borges has included Maître Abramowicz in a short list of his lifelong friends or has mentioned some of the writers Abramowicz taught him to love. In his conversations with Jean de Milleret, Borges acknowledges his debt to Abramowicz:

> Yes, he initiated me in the reading of Rimbaud. I remember one evening we were by the Rhone and he kept repeating:
>
> > J'ai vu des archipels sidéraux! et des îles
> > Dont les ciels délirants sont ouverts au voyageur:
> > —Est-ce en ces nuits sans fonds que tu dors et t'exiles,
> > Million d'oiseaux d'or, ô future Vigueur?
> > J'ai rêvé la nuit verte aux neiges éblouies,
> > Baisers montant aux yeux des mers avec lenteurs,
> > La circulation des sèves inouïes,
> > Et l'éveil jaune et bleu des phosphores chanteurs!
> > Mais, vrai, j'ai trop pleuré! les Aubes sont navrantes,
> > Toute lune est atroce et tout soleil amer.
>
> > (De Milleret, 1967, p. 25)

In quoting Rimbaud's *Le bateau ivre* (strophes 10, 20, 23), Borges makes a few mistakes which De Milleret corrects in a footnote. The mistakes are not important if one remembers that Borges was quoting in 1966 verses he must have learned some fifty years earlier. But what really matters is that he learned them not from a book but from Abramowicz's memory.

In a theological fantasy called "Three Versions of Judas," included in *Ficciones* (1944), Borges pays an oblique homage to their friendship. In a footnote he quotes a disparaging comment on Nils Runeberg, the protagonist of the story, and attributes that comment to none other than Maurice Abramowicz. It is doubtful that Abramowicz himself ever discussed the imaginary works of Nils Runeberg, but Borges loves to insert the names of his friends in his stories, as a form of private homage and public mystification. He did it with Bioy Casares and other literary friends in "Tlön, Uqbar, Orbis Tertius"; he included Patricio Gannon and myself in the story "The Other Death" (collected in *The Aleph,* 1949). To have Maurice Abramowicz discuss Runeberg's heresies is part of a private joke.

One of the things Georgie did as soon as he was settled in Geneva was to subscribe to a French circulating library. Thus he got the key to a literature he hardly knew. Soon French literature became the second most important of his youth. Critics have followed Borges' lead in underplaying the importance of French literature in shaping his writings; but the truth is that in spite of his preference for England and English letters, and without ever publicly admitting it, Borges was influenced by the concept of logical discourse and the subtle reasoning of French essayists. He also learned from France's poets and short-story writers.

In his conversations with Jean de Milleret, Borges recalls the names of some French writers he read while in Geneva. It is a rambling list which mentions, in the same breath, Daudet's comic masterpiece *Tartarin de Tarascon* and Gyp's rather naughty high-society novels. To justify his mentioning Gyp (who was considered extremely conservative and even anti-Semitic), Borges notes in another interview that Nietzsche also admired Gyp (*L'Herne,* 1964, p. 373). But Georgie's response to Gyp was hardly literary. Upon reaching the passage in her novel *The Passionate Woman* in which the baroness commits suicide because her lover deserts her, Georgie cried. To justify his youthful reaction, Borges ironically comments: "When one is a child, one is very snobbish, and then Gyp (the Comtesse de Martel) introduces you to a world of barons, marquises, dukes, eh!" (De Milleret, 1967, p. 26).

Gyp and Daudet were only two of his discoveries. He also read Zola very thoroughly (the whole of the Rougon-Macquart novels), many of Maupassant's books, and Victor Hugo's *Les misérables.* In reviewing with De Milleret those early readings, Borges comments: "Some ten years ago I tried to reread *L'assommoir* [The Drunkard]; I couldn't do it. In the same way, I've tried to read *Les misérables* and failed. While I can always read Hugo's poetry, that novel is so terribly emphatic" (ibid., p. 26). There is an invisible thread that links all the books mentioned by Borges: they all embody more or less the realist and naturalist style of narrative developed in the second half of the nineteenth century. This style had an enormous influence in Europe and the United States, but especially in Latin America. Even today (after the Borgesian revolution in writing) one can still find novelists and critics who praise the virtues of that long-forgotten school or attempt to refloat it under some fashionable new name. The fact that Borges, the man most responsible for having undermined its acceptance among younger writers, was exposed in his youth to the French classics of realism and naturalism is seldom mentioned by the critics. But such reading made Georgie aware of the conventions of story-telling (narrative continuity, character description, landscape) in a way that would prove useful to the future writer of *Ficciones*.

Another important aspect of reading the French realist and naturalist writers lies in their handling of the relationship between the sexes. Zola, Maupassant, and even Gyp displayed a candor (or brutal-ity) that was new in nineteenth-century literature. In the case of Zola, well known for his socialist views, this preoccupation with a subject the romantics treated only from the point of view of feeling was reinforced by an acute perception of class conflict and an active interest in the coming struggle for power between the workers and the bourgeoisie. Because Father had been (and still was) a philosophical anarchist, Georgie accepted the view of political and social forces that Zola ex-posed in his novels. They paved the way for his later spontaneous, even joyful embrace of the 1917 Russian revolution.

A writer he first read then, and continued to read throughout his life, was Flaubert. In his mature years Borges devoted two essays to him (both published originally in 1954): the first, to discuss and defend *Bouvard and Pécuchet;* the second, to underline Flaubert's creation of a poetic persona, a literary mask that took the place of the writer's own personality and even obliterated it. It is obvious that Georgie could not have read Flaubert that way. He probably perused *Madame Bovary* and the celebrated *Three Stories.* (Gertrude Stein had already published her own rewriting of one of those stories in *Three Lives* in 1909.) His view of Flaubert as a sort of precursor of Valéry, or perhaps of Pierre Men-ard, came to fruition later.

Another French writer he read while in Geneva was the now al-most forgotten but then extremely popular Henri Barbusse. During the war years Barbusse became one of the most influential French writers. His novel *The Fire* (1916) described the horrors of war in the trenches, the endless carnage that the stalemate between Germany and the Allied forces had created. Later, the German writer Erich Maria Remarque wrote *All Quiet on the Western Front* (1929), a novel that achieved even greater popularity. According to Borges in a 1937 ar-ticle, Barbusse's novel was superior. But the Barbusse novel he pre-ferred was an earlier one, *Hell* (1908), in which a man lives in a hotel and through a hole in the wall spies on his next-door neighbors. Borges has this to say about the book:

In the mixed pages of *Hell,* Barbusse attempted the writing of a classic, a timeless work. He wanted to fix the essential activities of man, free from the

varied colors of space and time. He wanted to reveal the general book that
lies beneath all books. Neither the plot—the poetical prose dialogues and the
salacious or lethal episodes which a hole in the wall affords the narrator—
nor the style, more or less derived from Hugo, allowed a good execution of
that Platonic concept, which is totally inaccessible in any case. Since 1919 I
had no chance to reread that book; I still remember the deep passion of its
prose. Also, its more or less adequate statement about man's central loneliness. (*El Hogar*, March 19, 1937, p. 28)

In stressing the novel's basic preoccupations with man's loneliness (or alienation, as it would be called later), Borges calls attention to
its major subject, one prominent in French fiction of the twentieth century, as Céline's *Voyage au bout de la nuit* (1932), Sartre's *La nausée*
(1938), Camus' *L'étranger* (1942), and Alain Robbe-Grillet's *Le voyeur*
(1950) bear witness. In spite of the differences in style and writing, all
these novels share a preoccupation with the central loneliness in their
main characters' view of life: a loneliness that makes them desperate
witnesses to other people's lives. Barbusse's protagonist is a voyeur; that
is, a true child of this century.

The reading of *Hell* must have had a great influence on
Georgie's view of the adult world. With the exception of the book on
Balkan sex life, *Hell* was probably the first book he came across that
dealt explicitly with sex. He had already read Burton's and Lane's
translations of the *One Thousand and One Nights*. Lane's explicit omissions and Burton's detailed footnotes on sexual mores and perversions
in the Islamic world must have alerted Georgie. But the Arabian stories
lacked prurience in their handling of sex. They were explicit and even
salacious but never titillating. In Zola or Maupassant, Georgie may have
found a more complex and even suggestive treatment of sex, although
both writers had to conform to a nineteenth-century concept of decorum that was absent in the Oriental classic. But in *Hell* Georgie found
something else: a vivid description of the sexual encounter as seen
from the passive (and perhaps also active) point of view of the voyeur:
sex is something that happens to you while you are watching what is
happening to others. The voyeur is like a reader of novels; he is participating through his imagination more than through his senses in a vi-
carious experience.

Another popular French book that Georgie read was *Jean Christophe,* the ten-volume novel by Romain Rolland about the life and loves
of a German composer. Rolland was a musicologist who in 1903 had
published a celebrated biography of Beethoven. The long novel was, in
a sense, an outcome of his interests both in Beethoven and in the
mystique of the artist's life. Like Barbusse, Rolland was also famous for
his socialist views. A firm believer in peace, he preferred exile in Swit-

zerland to participation in the nationalistic hysteria that the war brought about. Georgie must have read *Jean Christophe* around 1917. In a short piece on Rolland written twenty years later, he points out that the protagonist is a "fusion of Beethoven and Rolland," and that even more admirable than the work is its success: "I remember that around 1917 people still repeated '*Jean Christophe* is the password of the new generation' " (*El Hogar,* July 25, 1937, p. 30). Borges' words are colored with irony. In the same article, to indicate the scope and quality of Rolland's followers, he adds: "Rolland's glory seems very firm. In Argentina, he is admired by the admirers of Joaquin V. González; in the Caribbean Sea, by those of Martí; in the United States, by those of Hendrik Willem van Loon. In the French-speaking world, he would never lack the support of Belgium and Switzerland. His virtues, by the way, are less literary than moral, less syntactic than 'panhumanist,' to use a word that makes him happy" (ibid., p. 30).

In poking fun at Rolland's admirers, Borges also pokes fun at Georgie. The irony with which he describes the kinds of admirers Rolland has (readers of best-sellers like those written by van Loon, of sentimental poets like González and Martí) or the places where he is celebrated (marginal to Paris), or even the reason for his fame (his "panhumanism") indicates very clearly the bitterness with which Borges has turned against what he once probably loved. On the other hand, it gives a glimpse of what he thought in 1937 about Switzerland in 1917: it was a place where Rolland had followers.

But in those days Georgie probably read *Jean Christophe* with passion; he must have discussed it with Maurice Abramowicz and Simon Jichlinski and discovered in it the password for his generation. In describing the book's appeal, Borges uses three adjectives: "intimate, silent, and heartfelt." While the war was still going on and people had no time to reflect on their feelings, Rolland's "panhumanism" may have seemed uplifting to all those provincial souls. The Russian revolution of 1917 and the 1918 Wilsonian peace first kindled, then drastically dissipated, the aura of that "panhumanism."

Rimbaud was not the only French poet Georgie favored. In his conversations with De Milleret, he quotes a whole list: "It was especially Rimbaud whom I loved to recite, and a forgotten poet, Ephraim Michael. I read them all in a yellow-covered book published by the *Mercure de France,* an anthology of French modern poetry where you could find Stuart Merrill, obviously Mallarmé, Rimbaud, Verlaine of course, and several minor poets of the symbolist movement. I read, I reread all that. . . . I knew many poems by heart" (De Milleret, 1967, pp. 20–21).

There is very little trace in Borges' work of those readings of his adolescence. But the few references here and there prove his famil-

iarity with those books. In a short piece written in 1937 to review two
new books on Rimbaud (one by a Catholic writer, the other by two
Marxists), he not only praises Rimbaud highly but defends French literature against the accusation that instead of producing geniuses it has
the talent only to "organize and polish foreign importations"; Borges
also quotes a long passage from Rimbaud's *Season in Hell*. The quotation is truncated and the words are out of order; but that only proves
again that Borges was quoting by heart.

A poet he forgets to mention in his conversations with De Milleret is Baudelaire, although he was naturally included in the *Mercure
de France* anthology and is mentioned by Borges in Murat's interview,
where he acknowledges that there "was a time I knew *Les fleurs du mal*
by heart. But now I find myself far from Baudelaire. I believe that if I
had to name one French poet, it would be Verlaine" (Murat, 1964, p.
383).

His resistance to Baudelaire comes across rather strongly in
another piece written in 1937. In telling an anecdote about the Indian
poet Rabindranath Tagore (who had recently visited Buenos Aires),
Borges introduces a reference to Baudelaire:

> Three years ago I had the slightly terrible honor of talking with the ven-
> erated and honey-tongued Rabindranath Tagore. We talked about Baude-
> laire's poetry and somebody repeated "La mort des amants," that sonnet so
> cluttered with beds, divans, flowers, fireplaces, shelves, mirrors, and angels.
> Tagore listened to it attentively but said at the end: "I don't like your furni-
> ture poet!" I deeply sympathized with him. Now, rereading his works, I sus-
> pect that he was moved less by any horror of romantic bric-à-brac than by
> his invincible love of vagueness. (*El Hogar,* June 11, 1937, p. 30)

Once more, Borges' memory is playing a trick on him. There is
no mention of actual fireplaces or mirrors in Baudelaire's poems. The
fires and mirrors are metaphors for the lovers' hearts, burning with the
ardor that is reflected in their souls:

> Nos deux cœurs seront deux vastes flambeaux,
> Qui réflechiront leurs doubles lumières
> Dans nos deux esprits, ces miroirs jumeaux.
> (Baudelaire, 1951, p. 193)

But the beauty of Borges' recollection of how Tagore reacted to Baudelaire's poem is that it allows him to disparage both poets simultaneously.

What is missing in Borges' recollections of the French poets
Georgie read is a more detailed account of his reactions to Mallarmé.

In later years Borges quoted Mallarmé occasionally and always in an important context. His persona (the poet who is totally dedicated to writing and to whom the world makes sense only in a book) influenced Borges' own concept of literature and of the literary mind. Traces of Mallarmé can be detected in the invention of Pierre Menard. But if Borges has been reticent in making explicit his adolescent reaction to Mallarmé, he has been more forthright in talking about Rémy de Gourmont, another important French symbolist writer he read in Geneva. He readily admits that he read "a lot of De Gourmont in those days" (De Milleret, 1967, p. 382). De Gourmont (who died in 1915) was a dedicated critic and one of the founders, in 1889, of the *Mercure de France,* the same journal that published the symbolist anthology Georgie learned by heart. De Gourmont was then vastly read: he was quoted with respect by Eliot, had an enormous following among the Latin American poets of the turn of the century, and in a sense played the part Jean Paulhan would play in the period between the two world wars.

De Gourmont was also a novelist of a refined and slightly perverse turn of mind, and the author of a celebrated erotic treatise, *La physique de l'amour* (1903), written in the spirit of the Greek materialists Epicure and Democritus and their famous disciple, Lucretius. How much of these works Georgie read is not known. But there is one aspect of De Gourmont that he probably knew very well: his appetite for philosophical discussion, the encyclopedic criticism that knew how to balance contrary theories or find the right word to deflect them. One of his critics once pointed out that De Gourmont "is always ready to untie what he had just tied, he proclaims that the 'death of some truth is of a great benefit to men' because it has become nothing but a commonplace . . . worn-out, outdated, and bothersome" (Clouard, 1947, p. 392).

It was probably this cultivated and paradoxical side of De Gourmont that most attracted Georgie. In his essays (collected under the titles of *Promenades littéraires* and *Promenades philosophiques*), Georgie may have found the model for a certain type of writing he later developed and perfected. There are other more obvious links between De Gourmont and the future writer. De Gourmont had translated into French Enrique Larreta's *The Glory of Don Ramiro,* a book that Georgie knew from childhood. In an essay De Gourmont collected in the fourth series of his *Literary Walks* (1912), he explains his method: "I have translated his book as literally as was compatible with the elegance our language demands; one can be sure that there is nothing of the Spanish redundance. It is a clear and logical spirit" (De Gourmont, 1912, p. 121). Georgie probably laughed at De Gourmont's French prejudice against Spanish when he came across this book; he probably shared his laugh with Father.

There is another article in the same series that Georgie may have read. It is dedicated to "Louis Ménard, a Mystical Pagan." Ménard was an inventor (he discovered collodium, so useful in photography), a painter of the Barbizon school, and a poet. His more lasting work was in the domain of parody. In his youth he attempted to rewrite some of the lost plays of the Greek tragic poets and even attempted a version of Aeschylus' lost *Prometheus Unbound* which for the convenience of his readers he wrote in French, in spite of having preferred (according to De Gourmont) to write it in Aeschylus' own Greek (ibid., p. 163). His second major parody was a piece called "The Devil at the Café," which he attributed to Diderot and almost managed to smuggle into a collection of that writer's work then in progress. (Unfortunately, Anatole France exposed the hoax in time.) According to De Gourmont, Ménard liked to practice a sort of anachronistic reading of the classics: "When he read Homer, he thought about Shakespeare, placed Helen under the absent-minded eyes of Hamlet, and imagined the plaintive Desdemona at Achilles' feet" (ibid., p. 163).

Louis Ménard's literary habits (the rewriting of lost or nonexistent works, his anachronistic reading of literature) anticipate those of his namesake Pierre Menard (without any accent on the *e*), the strange postsymbolist French poet Borges invented in 1939 to poke fun at the conventions of literary criticism.

How much of what one reads into De Gourmont's article on Louis Ménard is determined by one's previous reading of Borges' short story? Is this a case of that anachronistic influence that he talks about in "Kafka and His Precursors," where the reading of a contemporary writer influences the reading of the classics? It is difficult to say. Georgie probably read De Gourmont's article on Ménard, and somewhere in his vast memory a trace was left. Twenty years later his own Menard would come into being, transforming a delightful little piece about an odd character into one of the comic masterpieces of this century. De Gourmont's Ménard was probably the small seed which, with the help of many other writers (Mallarmé, Valéry, Unamuno, perhaps Larreta, and of course Carlyle and De Quincey), finally became Borges' Menard.

A footnote to Louis Ménard. In De Gourmont's article, in talking about the invention of collodium, the author indicates that an American inventor "rediscovered" collodium and took the precaution of taking out an international patent under his own name, which was (confusion compounded) Maynard: a name that in French sounds almost the same as Ménard. The whole story is already too Borgesian.

Although Borges in years to come tried to forget how much he owed to French culture, at a time when his mind and memory were impressionable he spent the better part of five years reading Zola and Maupassant, Barbusse and Romain Rolland, Hugo and Rimbaud, Verlaine and Rémy de Gourmont. In Geneva he learned to understand and love a culture that left its traces, ineffaceable as a watermark, on his writing.

3.
The Ambassadors

Georgie's discovery of French literature in Geneva did not dull his appetite for English literature. On the contrary, he was able to continue his readings in that field thanks to a German publisher who had reprinted some of the best English and American writers in cheap, paperback editions. All books published by Bernhard Tauchnitz in Leipzig carried this sentence on the cover: "Not to be introduced into the British empire." They thus preserved the original British or American copyrights and were meant only for circulation among foreign students of Anglo-American literature or English-speaking tourists who strayed onto the Continent. They were also sold in the colonies and, naturally, in South America. In Buenos Aires Georgie was probably already familiar with their plain covers and their small, neat print.

Three of the English authors he discovered while living in Geneva had a lasting influence. These were Thomas De Quincey, Thomas Carlyle, and Gilbert Keith Chesterton. Of the three, De Quincey is the most widely read today; both Carlyle and Chesterton have gone out of fashion, although Chesterton's Father Brown mystery stories are still popular.

Borges has singled out De Quincey as the most important influence. In writing about the *Biathanatos,* the long, obscure text on suicide by John Donne, he says that his own debt to De Quincey "is so vast that to specify a part of it seems to repudiate or to silence the rest" (*Inquisitions,* 1964, p. 89). Yet it would be useless to search among Borges' essays for one explicitly dedicated to De Quincey. The omission (deliberate, of course) makes it more difficult to document his readings. Fortunately, some specifics are mentioned in a 1962 interview with James E. Irby:

I read De Quincey when I was sixteen; since then I have read and reread him innumerable times. He is a very suggestive writer, with an almost inexhaustible curiosity and erudition. As an explorer of dream life, he is unique in literature. His style is excellent, except when he attempts to be humoristic. I remember a long essay . . . which is one of his best, "The Last Days of Immanuel Kant," the description of how a powerful intelligence is put out: something intense, very sad. (Irby, 1962, p. 10)

When Borges says that De Quincey's style is excellent (with the proviso that he fails when attempting to be comic), he is stressing something that separates his model's writings from his own: where Borges is short and precise, De Quincey (in the best tradition of romantic prose) is digressive, prolix, highly emotional. In the vast collection of De Quincey's *Writings* (Borges generally quotes from the 1897 David Masson edition) Georgie discovered a model of discourse. By a process that can be compared to the miniaturization achieved in electronic circuits, Borges learned to pack into his short, fragmentary pieces the substance of De Quincey's sprawling articles. The model's digressiveness is condensed into one parenthesis; the tension of one of De Quincey's emotional paragraphs is reduced to one unexpected adjective; the serpentine footnotes of the original, which wind their way from page to page, are replaced by spare notes at the end of a piece or by pointed, reticent prologues. Where De Quincey expands, Borges contracts; where De Quincey lets passion flow, Borges becomes reticent or argumentative; where De Quincey muses, Borges is painfully lucid. But in spite of all the differences in their writings, the effect of their texts is similar.

The rather chaotic erudition of De Quincey (a journalist, after all) is equally chaotic in Borges, in spite of the latter's more professional system of quotes. Passion runs as deeply under Borges' writing as it runs on the sentimental surface of De Quincey's. Although Borges' digressions are cleverly disguised by the French method of composition he learned so well in Geneva, they are no less capricious than those of his model. If one reads De Quincey after having read Borges (the kind of reverse operation "Pierre Menard" suggests), it is impossible not to recognize the kinship.

Other forms of kinship are perhaps more obvious. Both De Quincey and Borges had well-developed memories and the rare ability to perceive analogical relationships. In his *Confessions of an English Opium Eater,* De Quincey boasts about both gifts: "Having the advantage of a prodigious memory, and the far greater advantage of a logical instinct for feeling in a moment the secret analogies or parallelisms that connected things else apparently remote, I enjoyed these two peculiar gifts for conversation" (De Quincey, 1897, p. 332). Borges could have subscribed to these words.

Another characteristic that unites them is insomnia. For many long years Borges suffered from it to the point that he even attempts to recapture in "Funes, the Memorious" what he calls its "atrocious lucidity." De Quincey, on the other hand, attributed to insomnia his craving for opium.

They also share an interest in certain subjects: strange heresies, secret societies, philosophical or religious problems (suicide is one of the most noticeable), odd linguistic theories, murder and violent death. But it is De Quincey's literary persona that chiefly influenced Borges. In him, Georgie found his prototype of the literary man, not under the guise of the successful and rather terrifying Dr. Johnson, but in the strange, slightly marginal, but intensely attractive one of De Quincey. Georgie must have been highly impressed by a writer who, from the etymological study of a word, could move quickly to a philosophical doctrine and even to a coherent view of the world. His conversations with Father, and the reading of Herbert Spencer and William James, had prepared Georgie for De Quincey's hospitable and penetrating mind, one of whose tasks would be to facilitate Georgie's entry into German philosophy. From that point of view, his piece on "The Last Days of Immanuel Kant" had a lasting impact.

In that article Georgie probably discovered another very important aspect of De Quincey's method of writing. In telling of Kant's last days, the English writer created a single text out of different narratives written by several witnesses (Wasianski, Jachman, Rink, and Borowski, among others); but instead of indicating the source in each case, he preferred to present this collage of texts as a single narrative attributed to Wasianski for the sake of unity. Borges followed De Quincey's method in composing his biographies of infamous men for *A Universal History of Infamy*. Here again, the unity of the text masks the subtle collage of sources, which are partially indicated in a note at the end of the biographical section of that book.

Another aspect of De Quincey's works which Borges underlines in his conversations with Irby is his value as an "explorer of dream life." Besides the two versions of *Confessions of an English Opium Eater* (1821, 1856) and the *Suspiria de Profundis* (1845), in which De Quincey develops his hallucinations and explores his dreams of opium, there are other, less well-known pieces—such as the description of one of Piranesi's engravings which he never saw but which (he claims) Coleridge once described to him—in which De Quincey reveals a visionary quality that must have impressed Georgie deeply. In all these essays, visions are presented not as opposed to reality but as part of it: hallucinations are not fictions but a natural dimension of the real.

On many occasions De Quincey achieves an almost surreal dimension. One of his most famous passages is the description of his life in London when, as a teenager, he was totally lost in that "red labyrinth." There he met a fifteen-year-old prostitute who befriended him and for several months was his constant companion. In the 1821 version of the *Confessions* De Quincey manages to convey the almost hallucinatory experiences of those two children in a style that preserves their innocence. Isolated from the rest of his writings as it is generally read now, this episode seems merely an anticipation of what years later both Dickens and Wilkie Collins would attempt to capture in their more robust melodramas. But if the episode is inserted in the autobiographical sequence provided by other De Quincey texts, it is easy to see its real significance. What is known of his life (mainly through his *Autobiographical Sketches*) confirms his deep affection for young girls. De Quincey's father had died when he was only seven, and his mother had always been absent, taking care of the family's business. He had been brought up in a house dominated by his older sisters and by female servants. He even congratulates himself for having spent most of his childhood under "the gentlest of sisters." In the same memoirs he remembers among the most intense experiences of his life the deaths of two of his sisters: one died at three when he was only one year and a half; the other died at nine when he was just six. Visiting the room where she was being mourned, the child had a vision in which death was contrasted with the beauty of the summer day.

When De Quincey reaches London at age sixteen, it is not as a boy who has just lost his mother, but as someone who has lost his whole family of little mothers: his sisters. In finding the fifteen-year-old prostitute and an even younger girl who shared his empty lodgings, he succeeds somehow in rebuilding, in the middle of corrupted Soho, the paradise of his childhood.

It is possible to recognize in De Quincey's emotional attachment to his real and surrogate sisters the same kind of affection that linked Georgie to his only sister, Norah. Like De Quincey, he grew up under his sister's active devotion. Although she was two years younger, she had a more outgoing personality, and in their childhood games she always played the part of the mother, protecting him from invisible and hideous enemies. In Switzerland, where he was isolated from his familiar surroundings, Norah must have continued to be his Electra, in the sense De Quincey used the word in describing the woman he eventually married and the daughter who cared for him in his last invalid years.

The parallel must not be pursued further. There is nothing in Georgie's family setup equal to the hardships that beset De Quincey. Mother was not absent. Father was very much present and cast a powerful shadow over the boy. Another decisive element was missing: the necrophiliac feelings that the death of his two older sisters aroused in De Quincey. But in spite of obvious differences, at the level of a dream (a fiction half lived, half imagined), Georgie must have found in De Quincey's autobiographical writings a key to some of the most obscure experiences of his adolescence.

Borges' debt to Carlyle is of a very different sort. At the time Georgie discovered his work, he came to think that Carlyle summarized literature. To quote from the concluding statement of one of his most important articles, "The Flower of Coleridge": "Those who carefully copy a writer do it impersonally, do it because they confuse that writer with literature, do it because they suspect that to leave him at any point is to deviate from reason and orthodoxy. For many years I thought that the almost infinite world of literature was in one man. That man was Carlyle, he was Johannes Becher, he was Walt Whitman, he was Rafael Cansinos-Asséns, he was De Quincey" (*Inquisitions,* 1964, p. 13).

As Borges generally lists writers in chronological order (that is, in the order of their birthdates), the disorder of the above list can only mean that he is citing them in the order he read them. Carlyle thus comes first not only in the text but in Borges' experience as a reader. He must have been the one to open up for Georgie a new literary perspective. The list shows something else that is relevant. If Carlyle once represented literature, he was soon displaced by other writers, and rather quickly too: Becher, Whitman, and Cansinos-Asséns were all discovered by Georgie before he was twenty-one.

Carlyle's ascent and sudden dismissal can be attributed to an inner resistance Borges later experienced to the views Carlyle commonly expressed. If at the time he discovered his works Georgie paid little attention to Carlyle's ideology, fifty years later Borges chose to discuss that aspect of his work almost exclusively. In an interview with Ronald Christ he says rather bluntly: "I rather dislike him: I think he invented Nazism and so on—one of the fathers or forefathers of such things" (Christ, 1967, p. 130). The same year, he discussed Carlyle's politics with De Milleret. Concentrating his objections on the subject of slavery, Borges accused Carlyle of being a racist and believing the fate of the blacks was to be slaves. Similar views of Carlyle have been advanced in other Borges works.

In a 1956 prologue Borges wrote for a Spanish translation of Carlyle's *On Heroes and Hero Worship,* he discusses Herbert Spencer's criticism of Carlyle's religion and summarizes the latter's political theory in one word: Nazism. The authors he quotes to substantiate his arguments are Bertrand Russell (*The Ancestry of Fascism,* 1935) and

G. K. Chesterton (*The End of the Armistice,* 1940). Using both critics and quoting Carlyle's own writings, Borges proves his relationship with totalitarianism.

This political view of Caryle was not current in Geneva. It is obvious that it was formed later, in the period between the two world wars, as the dates of Russell's and Chesterton's books indicate. The war with Germany put Carlyle's authoritarian texts in a purely political perspective. In spite of that, Borges is able to recognize other aspects of his literary personality. In the same prologue Borges adds:

> Such affirmations do not invalidate Carlyle's sincerity. Nobody has felt like him that this world is unreal (unreal like a nightmare, and atrocious). Of this general ghostliness, he saves one thing only, work: not its outcome, let's make clear, which is mere vanity, mere image, but its performance. He writes (*Reminiscences: James Carlyle*): "All human work is transitory, small, in itself contemptible; only the worker, and the spirit that dwells in him, is significant." (Prólogos, 1975, pp. 36–37)

This was probably the Carlyle Georgie read so avidly: the stoic, undefeatable, slightly mad Carlyle, not the apologist of slavery and totalitarianism. From his book on heroes and from his historical essays and biographies, Georgie must have taken the impulse to see life as a dream, a nightmare, made real only by an effort of the will. From this point of view, Carlyle must have served for Georgie as an ambassador to more complex writers: Schopenhauer and Nietzsche, whom he avidly read while in Geneva.

Among Carlyle's writings is a fictional biography that contains long excerpts from an apocryphal book. *Sartor Resartus* was, at the time it was published in three volumes (1831), merely an oddity, an elaborate joke on the same art of biography that Carlyle had practiced with some persistence (his life of Frederick the Great takes up seven volumes in the collected edition of his works; his Cromwell, three). The book can be read as a tedious parody of German romantic philosophy, very much in fashion then. But there is more in *Sartor Resartus* than meets the eye. In pretending to review and summarize a nonexistent book, Carlyle developed a format that Borges would take to its most delicate consequences: the fake review of an imaginary work by a nonexistent writer. As early as 1936 Borges included in one of his books of essays, *History of Eternity,* under the general title of "Two Notes," the "review" of a detective story called "The Approach to al-Mu'tasim," supposedly written by Mir Bahadur Ali. Although Borges even quotes some previous reviews of the book, the article is a hoax: everything, from the name of the author and the title of the novel to the English quotations in the review, was invented by Borges. Five years later, collecting "The Approach to al-Mu'tasim" in a book of short stories (*The Garden of Forking Paths*, 1941), Borges acknowledged the hoax and even justified it in a prologue:

> The composition of vast books is a laborious and impoverishing extravagance. To go on for five hundred pages developing an idea whose perfect oral exposition is possible in a few minutes! A better course of procedure is to pretend that these books already exist, and then to offer a résumé, a commentary. Thus proceeded Carlyle in *Sartor Resartus*. Thus Butler in *The Fair Haven*. These are works which suffer the imperfection of being themselves books, and of being no less tautological than the others. (*Ficciones*, 1962, p. 15)

To avoid tautology, Borges preferred to write "notes upon imaginary books." Those "notes" are "Tlön, Uqbar, Orbis Tertius," "An Examination of the Work of Herbert Quain," and "The Approach to al-Mu'tasim": all texts collected in *The Garden*.

If Borges' 1941 criticism of Carlyle reflects the viewpoint of the mature writer he had by then become, Georgie's view in 1916 must have been different. He probably was fascinated as much by Carlyle's paradoxical mind as by his flamboyant and even turgid style. At that time, he was about to enter a phase of his reading that would lead to his first published writings: a series of poems written in a rather passionate and exalted style. In this, as in his anticipation of Schopenhauer and Nietzsche, Carlyle also functioned as an ambassador.

The third English writer Georgie discovered in Geneva was one of Carlyle's most active opponents. In his prologue to the Argentine edition of *On Heroes* Borges quotes from one of Chesterton's outbursts against Carlyle. It can be found in *The End of the Armistice* and was written when Chesterton was sixty-six: "A man who has reveled in Carlyle as a boy, reacted against him as a man, re-reacted with saner appreciation as an older man, and ended, he will hope, by seeing Carlyle more or less where he really stands, can only be amazed at this sudden reappearance of all that was bad and barbarous and stupid and ignorant in Carlyle, without a touch of what was really quaint and humorous in him" (Chesterton, 1940, p. 66).

But it was not this pamphleteering side of Chesterton that Georgie discovered in Geneva; it was the master of the short story. Borges told James E. Irby that Chesterton belonged with Stevenson and Kipling to a trilogy of writers whose stories he had read so much that "I can almost re-create them in their entirety in my memory" (Irby, 1962, p. 10). In the prologue to his first collection of stories, *A Universal History of Infamy*, Borges publicly acknowledges his debt to Chesterton and Stevenson. Two years before, in one of his most important essays, "Narrative Art and Magic" (included in *Discusión,* 1932), Borges used some of Chesterton's stories to illustrate some points of his argument. According to him, magical narratives have a tightly knit structure:

> Every episode in a painstaking piece of fiction prefigures something still to come. Thus, in one of Chesterton's phantasmagorias ["The Honest Quack," from *Four Faultless Felons,* 1930], a man suddenly shoves a stranger out of the road to save him from an oncoming motorcar, and this necessary but alarming violence foreshadows the first man's later act of declaring the other man insane so that he may not be hanged for a murder. In another Chesterton story ["The Loyal Traitor," from the same collection], a vast and dangerous conspiracy consisting of a single man (aided by false beards, masks, and aliases) is darkly heralded by the lines:
>
> > As all stars shrivel in the single sun,
> > The words are many, but the Word is one.
>
> This comes to be unraveled at the end through a shift of capital letters:
>
> > The words are many, but the word is One.
>
> In a third story ["The Arrow of Heaven," from *The Incredulity of Father Brown,* 1926], the initial prototype—the passing mention of an Indian who throws his knife at another man and kills him—is the complete reverse of the plot: a man stabbed to death by his friend with an arrow beside the open window of a tower. A knife turned into an arrow, an arrow turned into a knife. Between the two there is a long repercussion. (*Prose,* 1972, pp. 214–215)

Borges remembered these Chestertonian inventions at the time he began to write his own stories. Unexplained behavior, the use of masks and disguises, emblematic situations that anticipate (in reverse) the solution of the mystery: all these tricks can be found in his stories as well as in Chesterton's.

In a note about one of his most successful stories, "The Dead Man," Borges acknowledges Chesterton's influence on the delineation of the protagonist: "Azevedo Bandeira, in that story, is a man from Rivera or Cerro Largo [two provinces in the north of Uruguay] and he is also a rough god, a mulatto, an uncouth version of Chesterton's incomparable Sunday" (*El Aleph,* 1949, p. 145). In the American edition of the book this note is replaced by one in which Borges omits all allusion to *The Man Who Was Thursday* (1908) and comments on the real sources of the story. But at the time the story was first published in book form, Chesterton was foremost in his thoughts. From the very beginning of his discovery of Chesterton, Georgie fell under his spell. He not only read and reread his stories; he came to know them by heart. And from the storehouse of concrete details he found in his narratives, Borges would continue to pick up words, sentences, tricks. His conversations with Richard Burgin include the following exchange:

BURGIN: You love painting and architecture, don't you? I mean, your stories seem to me very vivid visually.
BORGES: Are they really visual, or does the visibility come from Chesterton? (Burgin, 1969, p. 99)

His debt to Chesterton goes even further. In his concept of the detective story, as well as in his sense of evil, Borges later borrowed heavily from Chesterton. He dedicated several essays and a warm article to him on his death. Although in a 1968 interview with Rita Guibert he has admitted that many of Chesterton's surprises and tricks do not stand the wear and tear of time, while his old rival Shaw has the chance of a longer posthumous life, Borges feels that it would be a pity if Chesterton's "flavor" were ever lost.

4.
The Philosopher's Code

If the Borgeses were ignorant of the imminent outbreak of World War I when they decided to travel to Europe, they were also unwise about predicting its end. The war seemed to have reached a stalemate in the trenches of France; neither side was strong enough to make the last, decisive push. But two events of 1917 ought to have alerted the Borgeses. The entrance of the United States into the war and the October revolution in Russia were portents of the conflict's end, and also of the end of Europe as it had been viewed in the last four hundred years. At that precise moment two marginal countries were making decisions that would affect the destiny of all Europeans.

The Borgeses did not possess that kind of vision. Very few people in Europe did. Therefore, Georgie continued his studies and completed his fourth year at the Collège Calvin, avidly reading anything that was available in the French circulating library, in Tauchnitz's convenient reprints, or in the libraries of Geneva. He also continued to develop his friendship with Abramowicz and Jichlinski.

His stay in Geneva came to an abrupt end in 1918, when his maternal grandmother died. The family decided to leave Geneva and move farther up Lake Leman to Lugano. They settled at the Hotel du Lac. Georgie spent long hours there, endlessly reading, or rowing in the lake with Norah. The move to Lugano brought him close to his sister once again. Isolated from his Geneva friends and classmates, Georgie went back to her. While rowing, he used to recite to her poems from Baudelaire and the symbolists. Verlaine was probably one of his favorites, as was Rimbaud's *Le bateau ivre,* so appropriate to the occasion. He probably knew by heart Baudelaire's "Invitation au voyage," which echoes *The Song of Songs* in the way the lover addresses his mistress:

134

> Mon enfant, ma sœur,
> Songe à la douceur
> D'aller là-bas vivre ensemble!

Perhaps Georgie and Norah found in the poet's longing for a paradise in the tropics a metaphor for their own longings to return to the lost paradise of the garden in Palermo. In his own recollections in the "Autobiographical Essay," Borges omits all reference to those days spent on the lake with Norah and concentrates almost exclusively on his linguistic and poetic pursuits:

> We remained in Switzerland until 1919. After three or four years in Geneva, we spent a year in Lugano. I had my bachelor's degree by then, and it was now understood that I should devote myself to writing. I wanted to show my manuscripts to my father, but he told me he didn't believe in advice and that I must work my way all by myself through trial and error. I had been writing sonnets in English and in French. The English sonnets were poor imitations of Wordsworth, and the French, in their own watery way, were imitative of symbolist poetry. I still recall one line of my French experiments: *"Petite boîte noire pour le violon cassé."* The whole piece was titled "Poème pour être récité avec un accent russe." As I knew I wrote a foreigner's French, I thought a Russian accent better than an Argentine one. In my English experiments, I affected some eighteenth-century mannerisms, such as "o'er" instead of "over" and, for the sake of metrical ease, "doth sing" instead of "sings." I knew, however, that Spanish would be my unavoidable destiny. ("Essay," 1970, p. 218)

The year spent at Lugano was a hard one. Although Switzerland had been spared the horrors of war, it suffered, like the rest of Europe, from an acute shortage of food. Recalling those days in an interview with Gloria Alcorta, Borges says: "I had never experienced hunger except in the last year of World War I. . . . I remember that we thought [then] that the only thing we wanted was a little more bread, or one extra grain of rice" (Alcorta, 1964, p. 412). Not far from Lugano, in Prague, Kafka was experiencing hunger, and his body was being further undermined by it. But in 1918 Georgie hadn't yet heard of Kafka. He kept hunger away by reading the symbolists and by writing his first poems. Soon he was to discover a new linguistic world. German was the third language he acquired while in Switzerland. He did it on his own, with the help of a German-English dictionary. Borges recalls that it was Carlyle's *Sartor Resartus* which sent him on "this adventure":

> [The book] dazzled and also bewildered me. The hero, Diogenes Devil's-dung, is a German professor of idealism. In German literature, I was look-

ing for something Germanic, akin to Tacitus, but I was only later to find this in Old English and Old Norse. German literature turned out to be romantic and sickly. At first, I tried Kant's *Critique of Pure Reason* but was defeated by it, as most people—including most Germans—are. Then I thought verse would be easier, because of its brevity. So I got hold of a copy of Heine's early poems the *Lyrisches Intermezzo*, and a German-English dictionary. Little by little, owing to Heine's simple vocabulary, I found I could do without the dictionary. Soon I had worked my way into the loveliness of the language. ("Essay," 1970, p. 216).

On two previous occasions Borges had told his interviewers how he learned German. In 1967 he said to Ronald Christ that it took him "two or three months" to get "fairly good" at reading Heine's poetry "without the aid of a dictionary" (Christ, 1967, p. 130). To De Milleret he confided his feeling that it was better to read Kant's *Critique of Pure Reason* in any language but German: "Mauthner says that in that book Kant writes with a dazzling dryness, but I found more of the dryness than of the dazzlingness; the phrases are too long" (De Milleret, 1967, p. 27).

If Spanish and English had come to Georgie naturally, and Latin and French had to be taken as part of the Collège Calvin curriculum, German was the first language he chose to learn. By that time, with four languages at his command, Georgie must have realized that he was, as he put it in an ironic autobiographical piece, "a polyglot" (Vignale, 1927). But Georgie was always selective: he chose languages for their value as keys to segments of the literary world he wanted to possess. German was for him, mainly, the language of the philosophers. He was attracted to it by Carlyle's outrageous parody of German idealism; but the fact that he attempted to begin with Kant's *Critique* shows how deadly serious he was. His defeat, and the shortcut that reading Heine's *Lyrical Intermezzo* implied, did not change his plan. He would master the language first by reading poets and novelists in order to be able to return to the philosophers.

The first book in German he managed to read in its entirety was a novel by the Viennese writer Gustav Meyrink. *The Golem* (1915) is loosely based on a cabalistic legend about a Prague rabbi who creates a creature out of mud and makes him his servant. The legend is a vehicle for Meyrink to indulge in his love for the occult and the vague Indian philosophy of redemption and even for Madame Blavatsky's theosophy, as has been pointed out by his critics. Only one paragraph in the "Autobiographical Essay" refers to this book, which influenced Borges in a very curious way: "I also managed to read Meyrink's novel *Der Golem*. (In 1969, when I was in Israel, I talked over the Bohemian legend of the Golem with Gershom Scholem, a leading scholar of Jewish mysticism, whose name I had twice used as the only possible rhyming word in a poem of my own on the Golem.)" ("Essay," 1970, p. 216).

The mention cannot be more oblique. Instead of discussing the Meyrink book, he recalls a conversation he had years later with Gershom Scholem. Even the Scholem book he alludes to—*Major Trends in Jewish Mysticism* (1941)—devotes only half a page to the legend and doesn't even mention Meyrink's novel. Probably Borges had also read another Scholem book, *On the Cabala and Its Symbolism* (1960), which devotes two pages to Meyrink in the last chapter, "The Idea of the Golem." If Borges ever read this last text, he must have been surprised at the disdain with which Scholem treats the novel.

Borges discusses *The Golem* in another piece, written in 1936. In reviewing Meyrink's *Der Engel von westlich Fenster,* he says: "This novel, more or less theosophic—*The Angel of the Western Window*—is less beautiful than its title. Its author, Gustav Meyrink, was made famous by the fantastic novel *The Golem,* an extraordinarily visual book which graciously put together mythology, eroticism, tourism, Prague's local color, premonitory dreams, dreams of alien or previous lives, and even reality. That happy book was followed by other less agreeable ones" (*El Hogar,* October 16, 1936).

In this short evaluation it is possible to get closer to what Georgie must have discovered in the rambling, atmospheric, and suggestive novel. More than likely, it was not only the Golem legend that attracted his interest but also the fact that Meyrink proved that the legend was another version of the theme of the double. In his novel the protagonist and the Golem are, in a sense, doubles. At the end, in a swift change of point of view, the narrator of the story and the protagonist (who had seemed up to that point to be the same) are revealed to be two distinct characters. The narrator had, in a trance, become the protagonist.

Twenty-five years later Borges wrote a story about an Indian mystic who worships fire and creates a disciple to propagate his faith. "The Circular Ruins," collected in *Ficciones* (1944), can be seen as an anticipation of the poem on the Golem that Borges mentions in his "Autobiographical Essay." In the story an abyssal perspective is opened when the reader realizes that the mystic has also been created by another, the god Fire, while in the poem the rabbi who has created the Golem is shown to be the creation of his god. Both the story and the poem suggest that all these characters are creations of the writer, the real god of his creatures. That perspective was already implicit in Meyrink's novel.

One reason for Borges' silence in his "Autobiographical Essay" on these aspects of Meyrink's novel may be the fact that the novel is written in a highly emotional style and lacks a coherent structure. In the 1930s Georgie reacted against this aspect of fantastic writing and successfully began to develop his own brand of short, concise narratives, in which baroque rhetoric is tightly controlled by a corrosive irony. The stories, collected in *A Universal History of Infamy* (1935), have very little kinship with Meyrink's style, but in more than one sense they belong to the same world of nightmarish reality.

Georgie soon discovered two other German writers. One was the romantic Jean-Paul Richter. Borges recalls that around 1917 he tried to get interested in him "for Carlyle's and De Quincey's sake . . . but I soon discovered that I was very bored by the reading. Richter, in spite of his two English champions, seemed to me very long-winded and perhaps a passionless writer" ("Essay," 1970, p. 216). More successful was his experience with Fritz Mauthner. He does not mention him in the "Autobiographical Essay," but in his interview with Irby he talks extensively about him:

> He was a Jew, of Czech origin, who lived at the end of the last century. He published some very bad novels, but his philosophical papers are excellent. He is a wonderful writer, very ironic, whose style recalls that of the eighteenth century. He believed language only serves either to hide reality or for esthetic expression. His dictionary of philosophy, one of the books I have consulted with great pleasure, is really a collection of essays on different subjects, such as the soul, the world, the spirit, the conscience, etc. The historical part is also good; Mauthner was a scholar. He wanted his dictionary to be read in a skeptical mood. He makes some very good jokes. He talks, for instance, of the German verb *stehen* (*to stand,* in English), which has no equivalent in French or Spanish, where you have to say *être debout* or *estar de pie,* which is not the same thing. But he observes that in both French and Spanish they had to know the concept of *stehen;* otherwise they would fall to the ground. (Irby, 1962, p. 9)

Some forty years after his first encounter with Mauthner's book, Borges was still able to recall a scholarly joke he once had found amusing. More significantly, in many of his essays on philosophical subjects he takes advantage of Mauthner's scholarship and wit to help him to present a problem or find a new argument or an illustration. In discussing Korzybski's theories in a 1928 article, he quotes Mauthner to prove that the theories presented by the former in his *Manhood of Humanity* are not really new; in 1934 he uses Mauthner to discuss Nietzsche's theory of the eternal return; in 1942 Mauthner is one of the sources for his discussion of John Wilkins' analytical language. Time and again, Borges is indebted to Georgie's discovery of Mauthner.

Another German writer he read in Switzerland was the now almost forgotten Max Stirner. A sort of precursor of Nietzsche, Stirner died in 1856, but his main work, *The Ego and His Own,* had a short revival at the turn of the century. Borges has never devoted an article to Stirner or really acknowledged his influence. But there is an independent source for his knowledge of Stirner. In a brief description of how Georgie looked at the time of his first visit to Spain in 1919, Guillermo de Torre presents him in this colorful language: "He arrived [from Switzerland] drunk with Whitman, equipped by Stirner, following Romain Rolland" (De Torre, 1925, p. 62). Both Whitman and Rolland have been duly acknowledged by Borges, but the silence about Stirner is total. That makes it more tantalizing. Probably it was only a phase; soon Georgie was to discover two German philosophers whose work was to be decisive for his intellectual development: Arthur Schopenhauer and Friedrich Nietzsche. Borges does not mention the latter in his "Autobiographical Essay," but he singles out the former for an extraordinary tribute: "At some point while in Switzerland, I began reading Schopenhauer. Today, were I to choose a single philosopher, I would choose him. If the riddle of the universe can be stated in words, I think these words would be in his writings. I have read him many times over, both in German and, with my father and his close friend Macedonio Fernández, in translation" ("Essay," 1970, pp. 216–217).

From Schopenhauer, Georgie got the philosophical guidance he had looked for in vain in his attempt to decode Kant's *Critique of Pure Reason.* Implicit in that earlier failure was more than a question of language or philosophical training. While Kant wrote in the most impenetrable manner, Schopenhauer was elegant and witty. But *The World as Will and Representation* was more than an entertaining piece of writing. It was conceived by Schopenhauer to carry Kant's theories to their radical ends. If Kant had shown that the world is a product of our mind, and that the supernatural is unreachable, Schopenhauer went one step further to prove that even what we call nature is only a disguise assumed by the will, and that to escape from insanity it is necessary to elevate and transfigure the will into representation. In Kant's *Critique of Judgment* the artist is presented as free to create according to his intentions a totally arbitrary work. From the point of view of art, to attempt to be faithful to nature, to have a moral purpose, to stick to empirical truth or to a religion is totally irrelevant. Art is an end in itself. Kant also revealed the gulf between logical discourse and artistic discourse, between art and empirical experience. As some critics have pointed out, Kant completed Rousseau, while Schopenhauer completed (from this point of view) Kant. In Schopenhauer, Georgie may have found the notion that art is the only way to meaning, that art (as much as science) creates a meaningful natural cosmos out of the crumbling social order. It is possible to conjecture that Schopenhauer's paradoxical combination of idealism and nihilism (or pessimism) was extremely attractive to Georgie, who was then passing through the normal crisis of adolescence.

But Georgie may have been attracted to another side of Schopenhauer's philosophy: its denial of the existence of time and its erosion of the concepts of external reality and individual personality. Georgie had been trained by Father to understand Berkeleyan solipsism, and in reading Schopenhauer at Geneva he must have availed himself of the opportunity to discuss with Father the German philosopher's theories about reality. As he indicates in his "Autobiographical Essay," he continued to discuss Schopenhauer with his father and his father's friend Macedonio Fernández upon his return to Buenos Aires in 1921. In his first attempts at philosophical speculation—two articles printed in his first collection of essays, *Inquisiciones* (1925)— Schopenhauer is invariably quoted to forward the argument. In the more important of the two, "The Nothingness of Personality," after stressing some contradictions he finds in the German philosopher's theories, Borges quotes a dazzling sentence in which Schopenhauer maintains that "everyone who said I during all that time before I was born, was truly I." From that Borges concludes that the ego is not "individual" but a "mere logical urgency" (*Inquisiciones,* 1925, p. 95). To put it in more contemporary terms, the "I" is a *shifter:* everyone who uses it is "I" and nobody is exclusively "I." Borges was already looking in Schopenhauer for arguments to build his theory of the nonexistence of time and space, and consequently of the individual personality. In his most ambitious "metaphysical" piece, "A New Refutation of Time" (1947), he returns to Schopenhauer for arguments.

Georgie was probably very impressed (and perhaps even influenced) by Schopenhauer's pessimism. The latter's essays against women and marriage were extremely popular then, both in Spain and in Latin America. Cheap collections of some of his essays, generally translated from inexpensive French versions, flooded the market. They were generally printed in atrocious editions, on a brownish paper, and were plagued by misprints. It was probably that misogynistic side of Schopenhauer which attracted the attention of Georgie and his schoolmates.

Soon he moved on to an even more radical philosopher, Friedrich Nietzsche. If he fails to mention him in his "Autobiographical Essay," he has the following to say to Richard Burgin about his thinking:

BURGIN: Well, speaking about the will, I have the feeling that you aren't too fond of Nietzsche as a thinker.

BORGES: No. Well, I think that I am unfair to Nietzsche, because though I have read and reread many of his books, well, I think that if you omit *Thus Spoke Zarathustra,* if you omit that book—a kind of sham Bible, no?—I mean, a sham biblical style—but if you omit that book you get very interesting books.

BURGIN: *Beyond Good and Evil?*

BORGES: Yes, I've read them in German. And I greatly enjoyed them. But yet, somehow, I have never felt any sympathy for him as a man, no? I mean, I feel a great sympathy for Schopenhauer, or for ever so many writers, but in the case of Nietzsche I feel there is something hard and I won't say priggish—I mean, as a person he has no modesty about him. The same thing happens to me with Blake. I don't like writers who are making sweeping statements all the time. Of course, you might argue that what I'm saying is a sweeping statement also, no? Well, one has to say things with a certain emphasis.

BURGIN: Don't you feel, though, in the case of Nietzsche, he might be somewhat akin to Whitman? In that the personae of their works are quite different from the actual men behind them?

BORGES: Yes, but in the case of Whitman he gives you a very attractive persona. In the case of Nietzsche he gives you a very disagreeable one; at least to me. I feel I can sympathize with Whitman, but I can hardly sympathize with Nietzsche. In fact, I don't suppose he wanted people to sympathize with him. (Burgin, 1969, pp. 102–103)

It is obvious that this view of the German philosopher is not the one Georgie had in Geneva. The fact that Borges admits having read and reread him is proof enough of his early interest. Nietzsche's name and theories are generally present in Borges' philosophical essays, especially in those dedicated to refuting the existence of time. One of his most important pieces, "The Doctrine of the Cycles," written in 1934 and collected in *History of Eternity* (1936), discusses Nietzsche's theory of the eternal return. It is true that he quotes Nietzsche to disagree with him, but the essay shows a great familiarity with his work and advances a subtle interpretation of the basic conflict between Nietzsche's personality and his philosophy. Borges points out that although Nietzsche knew that the theory of the eternal return was not his, he preferred to ignore this fact and maintain with pride: "Immortal the instant in which I engendered the eternal return. For that instant I can stand the return" (*Unschuld des Werdens,* II, 1308). According to Borges, that instant is one of Nietzsche's honors. His explanation (as he indicates) is "grammatical, I almost say, syntactical":

Nietzsche knew that the eternal return is one of the fables or fears or entertainments which return eternally, but he also knew that the most effective of the grammatical persons is the first. For a prophet, it is possible to say that it is the only one. To derive his revelation from a treatise, or from the *Historia*

Philosophiae Greco-Romans written by the Assistant Professors Ritter and Preller, was impossible for Zarathustra, for reasons of voice and anachronism—when not for typographical reasons. The prophetic style does not allow quotes or the scholarly presentation of books and authors. . . .

   If my human flesh assimilates brutal flesh of mutton, who will prevent the human mind from assimilating human mental states? Because he thought about it and he suffered it so much, the eternal return of things now belongs to Nietzsche and not to somebody who is dead and is just a Greek name. (*Eternidad,* 1936, pp. 63–64)

In the rest of the essay Borges quotes from other Nietzschean texts (especially the *Nachlass,* his private notebooks) and comments on his physical sufferings and the curse of insomnia, which the German philosopher tried to alleviate with chloral. The end of the second part of the essay includes a memorable paragraph:

Nietzsche wanted to be Walt Whitman, he wanted to fall thoroughly in love with his destiny. He followed a heroic method: he unearthed the intolerable Greek hypothesis of the eternal repetition and tried to educe from this mental nightmare an occasion for joy. He searched for the most horrible idea in the world and he proposed it to men's delectation. Weak optimists try to imagine they are Nietzschean; Nietzsche faces them with the circles of his eternal return and thus he spits them out of his mouth. (Ibid., pp. 64–65)

   A doomed Nietzsche, a desperate Nietzsche, caught in the atrocious lucidity of insomnia as in one of Dante's circles: that is the Nietzsche which Borges reveals here. This tortured Nietzsche had very little to do with the one Borges would soon denounce as one of the precursors of Nazism, the Nietzsche he dislikes so intensely and unfairly in his conversations with Richard Burgin. The change in perspective can be attributed to the politics that led to World War II. Today we know that Nietzsche's sister not only edited his unpublished manuscripts but altered them to suit her Nazi husband's beliefs.

   Borges' real readings of Nietzsche are to be found in his adolescent admiration for *Zarathustra* and in the brilliant 1934 essay. The Nietzsche Georgie read was the follower of Schopenhauer who dared to carry some of his teacher's lessons perhaps too far. If Schopenhauer was too "bourgeois" to deplore the blind destructiveness of the will, Nietzsche was wild enough to rejoice in it and even foresee the possibility of an ecstatic union with the will. Nietzsche also carried forward Schopenhauer's view of the artist as one who gives meaning to the world, to the extreme of maintaining the artist's right to be amoral and become a law unto himself. Georgie and his schoolmates must have been very impressed by this Dionysian vitalism and these dreams of a

Superman. The old Borges may now reject *Zarathustra* because of its "sham biblical style" and forget how much Georgie was carried away by it. But at the time Georgie read Nietzsche, it was not only himself and the small group of alienated young poets of the Collège Calvin who were spellbound by his apocalyptic texts; a whole generation of young poets and playwrights, painters, and musicians was seduced by his spirit. Georgie was a child of his times. In reading Nietzsche as well as Schopenhauer, he learned not only the philosopher's code but a code for the poetry that was being written in Europe at the time, the poetry he himself would be writing very soon.

The summer of 1918 marks the moment when Georgie's involvement with German literature and philosophy began. On his nineteenth birthday (August 24) he asked for and got as a present a German encyclopedia. Now he possessed a key to a whole new cultural world.

5.
A Brotherhood
of Poets

Heine was not the only German poet Georgie knew by heart. While in Switzerland, he discovered the works of Rilke and the expressionists. Borges speaks of Rilke only in passing references. In his article "Apollinaire's Paradox," written in 1946, he compares him favorably with the French poet and concludes that Rilke is "closer to us" (*Los Anales,* August 1946, p. 49). Some twenty years later he returns to the subject in an interview but no longer seems to appreciate Rilke's closeness: "I have the feeling he's been greatly overrated. I think of him as a very pleasant poet. I know some of his pieces by heart, or at least I did. But I could never be very interested in him" (Marx and Simon, 1968, p. 109).

Yet it is obvious that Georgie was extremely susceptible to German poetry. In his readings he had come across a group of young poets who wrote violently about love and war, about despair and hope, about a world brotherhood. They were called "expressionists" and were related to the avant-garde poets, called cubists or futurists, dadaists or imagists, who since the beginning of the century had one thing in common: the need to radically change the literary and artistic establishment's concept of art and of the world. The expressionists were the first truly modern poets Georgie read, the ones who introduced him to the new poetics. They achieved what neither Father with his nineteenth-century taste nor his closest Swiss friends with their fondness for symbolism could do: they made him truly conversant with what was revolutionary in contemporary letters.

In evoking those days of his adolescence in his "Autobiographical Essay," Borges states firmly that expressionism was "beyond other contemporary schools, such as imagism, cubism, futurism, surrealism, and so on" ("Essay," 1970, p. 216). In his interview with Irby he

144

summarizes in more detailed terms the impact expressionism had on modern letters and on his own reading. Although at the time Georgie was living in Geneva he did not participate in the scholarly and literary life of the city and knew nothing about the quiet revolution in linguistics that Ferdinand de Saussure's posthumous *Course in General Linguistics* (1916) was producing, he did make good use of the French circulating library and also availed himself of the city's municipal libraries. Furthermore, he was in constant communication with aspiring young poets, such as Maurice Abramowicz. At Lugano he was more isolated. He resorted to German to fill the emptiness of his literary life. The discovery of expressionism made a lasting impact on him. As he told Irby, expressionism already contained "everything which is essential in later literature. I like it better than surrealism or dadaism, which seem frivolous to me. Expressionism is more serious and reflects a whole series of deep preoccupations: magic, dreams, Eastern religions and philosophies, the aspiration toward a world brotherhood. . . . Besides, German, with its almost infinite verbal possibilities, lends itself more easily to strange metaphors" (Irby, 1962, p. 6).

Some of the first critical pieces Georgie wrote a few years later, while in Spain, reflect the first impact of that movement on his literary imagination. For Georgie, it was to be associated with the impact produced by the seemingly endless war. Although he was a foreigner and was living in a neutral country, the war only made more evident his double exile: from faraway Argentina, its language, its people, and from the continent on which he was then living. A foreigner to Switzerland, he was also a foreigner to the war that was decimating the generation to which he belonged. In an article published in Spain in 1921—a review of *Die Aktion-Lyrik, 1914–1916,* an anthology of expressionist poetry—he points out that the majority of these self-conscious, hard, painful poems were written in the trenches of Poland, Russia, and France, where the young poets had been stationed to defend the fatherland. In another article on the same subject, written in Buenos Aires in 1923 and later collected in his first book of essays, *Inquisiciones* (1925), he comments on the note of discord expressionism brought to German literature. Expressionism aimed at intensity and the "effectiveness of details: the unusual assurance of adjectives, the brusque thrusting of verbs" (*Inquisiciones,* 1925, p. 147). Borges attributes this intensity to the experience of war. By placing everything in danger, war made the poets realize the value of life and taught them to question established notions about the world and the arts:

If for the mind, the war had been insignificant, because it only intensified Europe's diminished status, there is no doubt that for participants in the tragic farce, it was a very intense experience. How many hard visions crowded their views! To have known in the soldier's immediate experience the lands of Russia and Austria and France and Poland; to have participated in the first victories, as terrible as defeats, when the infantry in pursuit of skies and armies crossed dull fields where death looked satiated and the injury caused by arms was universal, is a desirable but certain suffering. Add to this succession of witches' Sabbaths the innermost feeling that life, your own warm and swift life, is contingent and not certain. It is no wonder that many [poets] in that perfection of pain had resorted to immortal words to make pain recede. . . . Thus, in trenches, in hospitals, in desperate and reasonable hate, expressionism grew. War did not make it but it justified it. (Ibid., pp. 147–148)

Borges readily admits that the expressionists did not achieve "perfect works." On the other hand, he points out that three of the poets who preceded them—Karl Gustav Moeller, Rainer Maria Rilke, and Hugo von Hofmannsthal—did. But the expressionists excelled in something different: the intensity of their feelings and of the poetry through which they communicate those feelings. "Vehemence in the attitudes, and in the depth of their poetry, abundance of images and the postulation of universal brotherhood: that was expressionism" (ibid., p. 148). It was this intensity that Georgie tried to capture in his first poetical attempts.

In both articles, as well in others published during the same period in Spain, Georgie includes translations of expressionist poets. They all belong to the group closely associated with war. Of the dozen chosen by him, only four are still considered important: Johannes Beecher, Wilhelm Klemm, Ernst Stadler, and August Stramm. The first is probably the most widely known today because of his postexpressionist career, which included an activist phase as a communist poet in Hitler's Germany, a long exile in the Soviet Union, and a triumphal return as the head of cultural activities for the German Democratic Republic. Georgie was particularly interested in his poetry and believed him to be the best German poet of the time (*Cervantes*, October 1920, p. 103). In those early days Becher believed in assaulting the reader's sensitivity with aggressive and erotic metaphors. Aggressive also was the poetry of Wilhelm Klemm. (He is included in all four of the selections of expressionist poetry made by Georgie.) Klemm's violence and humanitarianism later found an outlet in Nazism: a path as alien to Borges as the one Becher took. Georgie admired him for having declared that his heart was "as wide as Germany and France reunited" and was being pierced "by the bullets of the whole world" (*Inquisiciones*, 1925, p. 152).

The other poets, Ernst Stadler and August Stramm, shared a

146

common fate. Both were killed on the battlefield: the first on the Western front; the second on the Russian front. But they were very different. Stadler was an Alsatian who never fully became an expressionist. He had a Whitmanesque love for mankind that owed something also to one of Whitman's French followers, the Belgian Emile Verhaeren. Stramm, on the other hand, was one of the leaders of a loosely connected group of poets who began publishing their verses in *Sturm* magazine before the war and quickly attracted attention. In his use of the possibilities of German for coining words, Stramm was second to none and has often been compared with Joyce. After his death on the Eastern front, a volume of his war poems was published in 1919. He also left a volume, *Liebesgedichte* (Love Poetry) (1919), which inspired Georgie's own erotic poems.

The other expressionist poets to whom Georgie called attention in his articles and translations were less impressive, but at the time he read them their cruel, erotic, dazzling images represented the new poetry. There was more in their poetry than challenging images or the feeling that war was hell. They all expressed, in different ways and according to different ideologies and credos, a belief in a brotherhood of man. The experience of war had made them pacifists. They had come to realize that war was always fought by those who did not start it; that its price was always paid by the sons and not the fathers. Patricide, as the Oedipus myth reveals, is only the second most evident stage of a conflict that usually begins with a filicide. It was Laius who first attempted to take his son's life. The expressionist poets had to fight a war that was one of the most tragic filicides in human history. Suddenly, under the very eyes of a society that was considered civilized, a whole generation was butchered.

Georgie had been protected from the carnage because he was an Argentine who lived in a neutral country. Nevertheless, he could not help feeling the impact of those poems that violently attacked war and proclaimed the need for all men to unite in a universal brotherhood. He discovered another link with the expressionist poets: they also had been taught by Schopenhauer and Nietzsche to believe that will, and will only, gave meaning to a chaotic world; they had discovered in *Zarathustra* the vitalism they needed to face the horrors of war and destruction. They sided with Nietzsche in preferring "the Dionysian *afflatus* over Apollonian intellectual balance," as one art critic has put it (Zigrosser, 1957, p. 11). In those days Georgie was obviously closer to Dionysius than to Apollo.

But the greatest debt Georgie incurred to the expressionists was that they led him to a poet who was to become for him *the* poet.

One day, reading an expressionist annual, he found a translation of some of Walt Whitman's verses. He tells the story in his "Autobiographical Essay":

> I first met Walt Whitman through a German translation by Johannes Schlaf (*"Als ich in Alabama meinen Morgengang machte"*—"As I have walk'd in Alabama my morning walk"). Of course, I was struck by the absurdity of reading an American poet in German, so I ordered a copy of *Leaves of Grass* from London. I remember it still—bound in green. For a time, I thought of Whitman not only as a great poet but as the *only* poet. In fact, I thought all poets the world over had been merely leading up to Whitman until 1855, and that not to imitate him was a proof of ignorance. This feeling had already come over me with Carlyle's prose, which is now unbearable to me, and with the poetry of Swinburne. These were phases I went through. ("Essay," 1970, p. 217)

Later Georgie learned to overcome his infatuation with Carlyle's prose and Swinburne's poetry, but he never really got over Whitman. Remembering those Geneva days, he told Irby in 1962 that for many years he used Whitman as a canon to judge all poetry; he then believed Whitman *was* poetry. In some of the first critical articles he wrote (later collected in *Inquisiciones*) Whitman's name is mentioned not only with reverence but with insight. In "The Nothingness of Personality," an elaborate essay which attempts to deny the existence of the individual "I," Borges discusses Whitman; he sees him as the first to express in his verses not only his own personality but the entire world's soul. As Borges puts it:

> To attempt to express yourself and to want to express life in its totality is one and the same thing. . . . Whitman was the first Atlante to attempt to perform this fierce task and put the world on his shoulders. He believed that it was enough to enumerate things to immediately taste how unique and astonishing they are. Thus, in his poems, next to many beautiful [products of] rhetoric, can be found a string of gaudy words, sometimes copied from geography or history textbooks, burning with admiration marks which imitate lofty enthusiasm. (*Inquisiciones,* 1925, p. 91)

It is possible to detect here a certain detachment that becomes even more noticeable in another piece in which Borges compares Whitman with a very fine Spanish writer, Ramón Gómez de la Serna. He stresses that both had the same appetite for things. For Ramón (as he is usually called), "things are not corridors that lead to God."

> He loves them, he pets them and caresses them, but the satisfaction he gets from them is unbinding and without any taint of oneness. In that indepen-

dence of his love we find the essential distinction which separates him from Walt Whitman. We can also see in Whitman the whole business of living; in Whitman also breathes the miraculous gratitude for the concrete and tactile and many-colored ways things are. But Walt's gratitude was satisfied with the enumeration of objects whose accumulation is the world, while the Spaniard has written comic and passionate commentaries on the individuality of each object. (Ibid., p. 125)

In spite of these reservations, Georgie continued to admire Whitman and to follow him in his discoveries of a universal brotherhood and the secrets of poetry. His reading of Whitman completed the task the expressionists had begun. Now he was ready to begin writing a new kind of poetry. The lessons of the symbolists were forgotten; Whitman and the expressionists were to dominate his imagery and feelings. One of the first poems of the new cycle he wrote is dedicated to the war. It is called "Trenches":

> Anguish.
> At the highest point a mountain walks
> Earth-colored men drown in the lowest crevice
> Fate yokes the souls of those
> who bathed their little hope in the pools of night.
> The bayonets dream of the nuptial mess.
> The world has been lost and the eyes of the dead
> look for it
> Silence howls in the sunken horizons.
> (Videla, 1963, pp. 100–101)

Living in the seclusion of Geneva or Lugano, protected by the love of his family, and doubly exiled from the war, Georgie turned to Whitmanesque verse and to the expressionists' obsession with war to find the proper outlet for his feelings. The phallic allusion in the sixth line puts the whole poem in perspective. Lost in the violent experiences of his adolescence, fighting against the anguish of a world that was being torn to pieces while he remained intact, in anguished impotence, Georgie finds in the imaginary experience of war, in the naked, brutal butchery of war, a metaphor for his own desperate feelings.

6.
Back to the
Old Country

The Borgeses' European experience did not end with the close of the war. They were in no special rush to return home, since Georgie's poor eyesight exempted him from military service. Thus, before returning to Argentina, they decided to spend a year or so vacationing in Spain. As Borges tells the story in his "Autobiographical Essay," the idea seemed very reasonable:

> Spain at that time was slowly being discovered by Argentines. Until then, even eminent writers like Leopoldo Lugones and Ricardo Güiraldes deliberately left Spain out of their European travels. This was no whim. In Buenos Aires, Spaniards always held menial jobs—as domestic servants, waiters, and laborers—or were small tradesmen, and we Argentines never thought of ourselves as Spanish. . . . Through French eyes, however, Latin Americans saw the Spaniards as picturesque, thinking of them in terms of the stock in trade of García Lorca—gypsies, bullfights, and Moorish architecture. But though Spanish was our language and we came mostly of Spanish and Portuguese blood, my own family never thought of our trip in terms of going back to Spain after an absence of some three centuries. ("Essay," 1970, pp. 218–219)

Borges' reaction reflects his anti-Spanish bias, but it is also based on fact. There was very little admiration for the grandeur of the Spanish conquest in the River Plate area. Historically, it was the last outpost of the Spanish empire and was not competely settled and organized under Spanish rule until the eighteenth century. Therefore, it was spared the worst abuses of a corrupt Spanish administration and was in effect left free to follow its own path. The descendents of the conquistadors soon developed an appetite for freedom. The notion of a federation of South American states, closely based on the North American model, began to be formed. While the Argentine San Martín succeeded in making his dreams of freedom true and went as far as Peru in his liberation campaign, the Uruguayan José Artigas failed in implementing the ideal of federation and had to leave Montevideo to seek refuge in Paraguay.

The independence achieved by Argentina and Uruguay was only independence from Spanish authority, which was quickly replaced by North American and French authority as cultural models. Latin America throughout the nineteenth century was solidly anti-Spain, and when in the second half of that century the Spaniards returned to the newly independent republics they came as poor immigrants, much as the Irish came to the United States. They were generally illiterate, and the Spanish they spoke was not elegant. They settled at the lower levels of society. Argentines and Uruguayans never thought of them as the master race.

Thus the Borgeses' trip to Spain did not imply a return to the old country in search of valid roots, although Georgie had in fact descended from the conquistadors. His genealogical tree goes back, on both sides of the family, to people who came to America at the beginning of the sixteenth century. On the Borges side there is Don Alonso de la Puente, who participated in the conquest of Peru in 1532, and Don Gonzalo Martel de la Puente, who also came to Peru at that time. There was Juan de Sanabria, one of the first settlers of Argentina, and among his ancestors were two important historical figures: Don Juan de Garay, the founder of Buenos Aires in 1591, and Don Hernando Arias de Saavedra (better known as Hernandarias), who was instrumental in settling the River Plate area and who introduced cattle with the success later centuries would prove. No less important were Don Gerónimo Luis de Cabrera y Toledo, founder of Córdoba del Tucumán in 1571, and Don Jerónimo Luis de Cabrera y Garay, who was governor of the province of the River Plate in 1641. On his mother's side Borges' ancestors lacked such resplendent titles, but they were distinguished enough.

Although once Georgie corrected a Spaniard who was boasting about the exploits of his ancestors in America with a curt "We are the descendants of the conquistadors; you descend only from the cousins who stayed at home," he never took his genealogical tree too seriously. He was chiefly attracted to the ancestors who fought the Spaniards in 1810 and freed the River Plate area. Besides, the influence of a British and Swiss education had made him less susceptible to the grandeur of Spain. In cultural matters, Spain and Spanish did not rank too high.

Not all Argentines shared the Borgeses' prejudices against

Spain. In spite of what Borges says in his "Autobiographical Essay," the River Plate area had a contingent of educated people who loved and respected the Spanish culture. Some writers, such as Enrique Larreta (who had been Father's classmate at law school) and the Uruguayan Carlos Reyles, not only lived in Spain for long periods but produced some of their most important work on Spanish subjects. At the turn of the century the Spanish-American war turned the emotional tide in favor of Spain. Now that the old country was defeated by a new empire, it was time to bury the independence hatchets and revise the purely negative attitude toward all things Spanish. In doing so, both Larreta and Reyles (and many others with them) rediscovered a culture that was a decisive part of Latin America's heritage. Before them, and in a momentous 1900 essay, *Ariel,* the Uruguayan José Enrique Rodó had pointed the way to recovery of a lost or mislaid tradition.

Georgie was not at all interested in that recovery. He was living a most contemporary life. Having discovered Whitman and the expressionists, he was concerned only with being modern, and that emphatically did not include Spain. Although it was his fate to discover in that neglected if not despised Spain a first hint of his literary gifts, in retelling the story in his "Autobiographical Essay," Borges prefers to return to the ironical view he probably had in 1919.

The Borgeses traveled by train to Barcelona and from there by boat to Majorca, in the Balearic Islands. They first settled in Palma, at the Hotel Continental, facing St. Michael's Church. In the "Autobiographical Essay" (which does not have a word to say about Barcelona) Borges writes:

> We went to Majorca because it was cheap, beautiful, and had hardly any tourists but ourselves. We lived there nearly a whole year, in Palma and Valldemosa, a village high up in the hills. I went on studying Latin, this time under the tutelage of a priest, who told me that since the innate was sufficient to his needs, he had never attempted reading a novel. We went over Virgil, of whom I still think highly. I remember I astonished the natives by my fine swimming, for I had learned in different swift rivers, such as the Uruguay and the Rhone, while Majorcans were used only to a quiet, tideless sea. ("Essay," 1970, p. 219)

The study of Latin, under the Valldemosa vicar, was the major literary event Borges now remembers of those Majorcan days. It completed and perfected the possession of a linguistic code that was to be decisive for his writings. Borges' extraordinary command of syntax, his almost uncanny feeling for words (especially for their etymological meaning), and his awareness of the infinite possibilities of the Spanish language were all enhanced by his study of Latin and of French.

The only personal note about his life in Majorca is his proud remark about his abilities as a swimmer. By the time he went to Spain he was probably as good as he claimed to be. Swimming was not yet as popular in Europe as it later came to be. People used to go to the beaches more for the sun and the fresh air than for the sea. They entered the water covered by an excess of clothes, caps, and rubber shoes. The most they attempted was a few hysterical strokes, never losing a foothold on firm ground. Children jumped and frolicked on the shoreline. A swimmer such as Georgie must have caused quite a sensation in the Majorca of those days.

The island is especially remembered in the "Autobiographical Essay" as the place where Father finally came to grips with his literary avocation and produced his first and only novel, *The Chieftain*.

> My father was writing his novel, which harked back to old times during the civil war of the 1870s in his native Entre Ríos. I recall giving him some quite bad metaphors, borrowed from the German expressionists, which he accepted out of resignation. He had some five hundred copies of the book printed, and brought them back to Buenos Aires, where he gave them away to friends. Every time the word "Paraná"—his home town—had come up in the manuscript, the printers changed it to "Panamá," thinking they were correcting a mistake. Not to give them trouble, and also seeing it was funnier that way, my father let this pass. (Ibid., p. 219)

Borges' memory plays a trick on him here. Only once in the book (which was published in 1921) does the word "Paraná" appear altered. On page 126 it is spelled "Paramá," which is a sort of Joycean hybrid of "Paraná" and "Panamá." Borges' faulty recollection makes the story sound better. But if his memory fails him, he is right about the intrusion of some expressionist images in a rather old-fashioned text.

Not all the bad images in the book come from the expressionists. Many are taken straight from nineteenth-century romantic and postromantic literature; some reflect more recent readings: the decadents and the Spanish modernists, for instance. Father was an avid reader who had very little literary training; so he borrowed right and left. But a close reading of the novel permits the identification of some of those expressionist (or para-expressionist) images that Borges talks about in his "Autobiographical Essay." Thus, on page 7, the text describes a bridge which "scars the brook"; on page 86 the same bridge crosses the brook "from side to side with the easiness of a tense muscle." The inundation, which is the protagonist's moment of truth, is described as follows on page 141: "Water in the ravine's groove jumped to the conquest of space the way a god in the fullness of hate could do it." After the storm, the sky, "terse and resplendent, was a majolica bowl with metallic reflections." In describing a pastoral scene on page 24, the text says: "The very clear sky kept a watch over its blues."

In recalling his interference with Father's prose, Borges adds in the "Autobiographical Essay": "Now I repent of my youthful intrusions into his book. Seventeen years later, before he died, he told me that he would very much like me to rewrite the novel in a straightforward way, with all the fine writing and purple patches left out" (ibid., pp. 219–220).

If Father had misgivings about the expressionist images, why did he accept them? Borges' explanation in his "Autobiographical Essay"—that he did it "out of resignation"—does not seem good enough. It was probably Father's diffidence and skepticism about all human endeavors that let him accept Georgie's corrections. Besides, he always believed that sons educated their fathers and not the other way around. And in accepting Georgie's expressionist images he was following his own convictions.

While Father was writing his novel, Georgie was busy with his own projects. In the "Autobiographical Essay" he mentions one: "I myself in those days wrote a story about a werewolf and sent it to a popular magazine in Madrid, *La Esfera,* whose editors very wisely turned it down" (ibid., p. 220). This is all he has to say about that first story, but he gives more details about its origins in an interview with Jean de Milleret. It was obviously based on a River Plate version of the lycanthrope myth. Borges begins by pointing out that there are two local names for the werewolf in that area: (1) *lobisón* (from *lobo,* wolf), used both in Uruguay, where some of Mother's relatives came from, and in Entre Ríos, Father's native province; and (2) *capiango,* a name of African origin, used in the province of Córdoba, where there was a great slave market and where the Spanish ancestors of the Borgeses came from. According to the legend, as he recalls it, "it is on Saturday evenings that in some quarters of town men change into pigs or dogs; while in Córdoba they change into *tigers*" (De Milleret, 1967, p. 29). He adds that the famous gaucho chieftain Facundo Quiroga spread the notion that "he had a regiment of *capiangos,* men who at the time of fighting became tigers; well . . . jaguars" (ibid., p. 30). In describing the legend to a foreigner, Borges makes the necessary linguistic clarifications, but he forgets to mention one important aspect of the legend, at least as it is commonly told in Uruguay: that the *lobisón* is the seventh male son in a family and that he turns into a werewolf not every Saturday evening (which would make him look more like a weekend reveler) but on nights when the moon is full. The story Georgie wrote seems lost, or at least that was what Borges wanted to suggest to De Milleret, who chided him: "You have destroyed it. You are an iconoclast" (ibid., p. 29).

In mentioning his first serious attempts at publication, Borges fails to record in his "Autobiographical Essay" an article he succeeded in having published at the time. It was a book review he wrote in French and sent to Maurice Abramowicz in Geneva. After correcting the text, Abramowicz submitted it to *La Feuille,* which published it on August 20, 1919. Titled "Chronique des lettres espagnoles" and more modestly subtitled "Trois nouveaux livres," the article was devoted mainly to reviewing two new books of essays by leading Spanish writers: Pío Baroja, best known as a prolific novelist, and Azorín, one of the most influential essayists of the time. The writing foreshadows the kind of irony which Borges later made famous. It begins with the observation that Spanish writers, when they are sincere, are always either skeptical or sad. In defining Baroja, Borges underlines his achievements as the author of "a long and remarkable series of realistic novels" and calls him "a biting, skeptical, and vigorous writer." Baroja's pessimism is not unique. According to Georgie, "all the intelligent Spaniards will tell you that their country is not worth anything now." That feeling was in part a consequence of the defeat suffered by Spain in the Spanish-American war: the Disaster, as it was called. Both Baroja and Azorín belonged to what was then baptized the Generation of 1898, to mark forever the date of the defeat. That generation had helped to eliminate the decaying traditions of the empire and had updated Spanish culture. Among his contemporaries, Baroja was considered the wildest. He was an anarchist and, as such, a loner and a permanent cause of scandal. Although the Nobel Prize was never his, when Hemingway received it he went to see Baroja to tell him that he considered himself his disciple. Being a Basque, Baroja was also an oddity in not conforming to the clericalism of his countrymen. Georgie sums up his portrait of the rebel with these words: "He is perhaps the most hated man among his [literary] confrères and especially among the clericals on whom he makes furious war."

In analyzing Baroja's latest book, *Momentum catastrophicum* (the title is in mock Latin), Georgie underlines the irony and vigor of its pages but finds it difficult to summarize its arguments. Among other targets, Baroja turns his fire on the Spanish traditionalists and praises Woodrow Wilson ambiguously for his peace crusade; he calls him a "Marcus Aurelius of the great republic of trusts and sewing machines, the one and only, the apostle and arbiter of international affairs, the flower of the arrivistes." In his commentary Georgie adds that he "had welcomed with joy the allusion to Wilson." Although Baroja's praise was not sung without some irony, Georgie favored him as long as the

Basque supported the peace movement. Those were the days when, inspired by Whitman's panhumanism and the expressionists' credo of a universal brotherhood, Georgie truly believed in mankind. In selecting Baroja's book for review, he was obviously using it to make a political statement. The same applies to Azorín's book. Titled *Between Spain and France,* it is described by Georgie as "the calmest book to have been inspired by the war." Azorín's dialectic, according to Georgie, consists in attempting to make his points by quoting extensively from the classics and being gentle with everybody. It is obvious that Georgie prefers Baroja's quick temper to Azorín's politeness.

A third book is briefly mentioned in the article: *An Apology for Christianity,* written by the Jesuit Ruiz Amado. Georgie dismisses it in a few ironic paragraphs. The author seems to believe that the first chapter of Genesis is in perfect accord with the most recent scientific discoveries; he praises the benefits of the Inquisition and fiercely attacks Voltaire (whom Georgie identifies by his real name, Arouet). The reviewer concludes: "It is curious that in a country where only scholars know the *Philosophical Dictionary* poor Arouet continues to be the scarecrow, the bête noire of the pious."

The importance of this article, a minor piece in itself, is in what it reveals about Georgie's state of mind at the time he was living in Majorca. Like many of his contemporaries, he was an aspiring poet who sided with the antitraditionalists and seriously believed in a universal brotherhood of man. Father's philosophical anarchism had helped him to develop a deep sympathy for any system or credo that attacked the establishment and offered a utopian vision of society. On the eve of his entrance into literary life, Georgie appeared to be a bonafide member of the avant-garde.

7.
A New Master

In 1919, when winter came, the Borgeses moved to the Continent. They settled for a while in Seville, the most lively of the three principal Andalusian cities. While Córdoba and Granada continued to live off the splendors of the Moorish and imperial past, Seville aimed to be modern. It had an intense literary life. Its poets and novelists were always launching little magazines, holding noisy gatherings to read their own verse or endlessly criticize their rivals; they loved to produce manifestos and in general call attention to their existence.

Seville was the center of the tourist trade, especially during Holy Week, with its carnivallike atmosphere and its numerous processions of different, rival images of the Virgin Mary, to whom the Sevillans never failed to address reverent and sometimes obscene songs. But Seville was also a city large enough to have a life of its own the rest of the year, and at the same time to preserve, in the old quarter, the feel and immediacy of a medieval town. Today the Santa Cruz (Holy Cross) neighborhood is still a labyrinth of winding streets that lead to small squares that lead to winding streets. Several imposing monuments break the monotony of its small, beautiful houses with their enclosed gardens permanently perfumed by flowers. Some of these streets—such as the one named after a famous inn, The Moor's—were favored by the young poets in their endless walks under Seville's bright, starry, overwhelming sky. In that ideal setting, which winter could not totally dull, Georgie found for the first time in his life a group of poets to whom he immediately felt close. To James E. Irby he confided: "I didn't discover anything special [in Spain] except a generous style of oral life; that atmosphere, so lively and genuine, of literary gatherings and cafés, in which literature was alive in a very striking way: an atmosphere which . . . had never existed in Argentina. In Geneva . . .

157

there was no literary life, although I had there many literary friends of different nationalities, and there were excellent bookstores where one could find the best of the current literature" (Irby, 1962, p. 6).

Seville was at the time deeply affected by the discovery of the avant-garde. The cultural establishment was still very powerful and totally committed to maintaining the tourist's image of the city, living off its glorious past as the commercial and administrative center of the New World during the Spanish conquest. But the youth of Seville cared little about that tradition. Through a local master, Rafael Cansinos-Asséns—who had already moved to Madrid—they discovered the modern movement that in only two decades had profoundly changed European literature. In little magazines published in Madrid and Seville they had come across some of the key names of the period: Mallarmé and Apollinaire, Marinetti and Tzara, Cendrars and Max Jacob. They knew little French and no English or German. Georgie was shocked by the carelessness with which they tossed around names and works they had barely read.

Recalling Seville's literary scene in his "Autobiographical Essay," he does not spare them:

> In Seville, I fell in with the literary group formed around *Grecia*. This group, who called themselves ultraists, had set out to renew literature, a branch of the arts of which they knew nothing whatever. One of them once told me his whole reading had been the Bible, Cervantes, Darío, and one or two of the books of the Master, Rafael Cansinos-Asséns. It baffled my Argentine mind to learn that they had no French and no inkling at all that such a thing as English literature existed. I was even introduced to a local worthy popularly known as "the Humanist" and was not long in discovering that his Latin was far smaller than mine. As for *Grecia* itself, the editor, Isaac del Vando Villar, had the whole corpus of his poetry written for him by one or another of his assistants. I remember one of them telling me one day, "I'm very busy—Isaac is writing a poem." ("Essay," 1970, pp. 220–221)

Borges' memory has reduced to a few ironies and a couple of anecdotes what was for Georgie a decisive if brief experience. It is true that compared with the other avant-garde movements, which Georgie already knew through books and magazines, the Seville branch must have seemed hopelessly provincial. But it was Georgie's first real contact with literary life. In the second-rate and misled poets of Seville, Georgie found his first fellow writers.

As limited as Seville was, it afforded Georgie the possibility of somehow controlling his shyness and learning to participate in literary life. Seville also was the place of another first: one of his poems was printed in *Grecia* on December 31, 1919. The magazine had been founded a little more than a year earlier (on October 12, 1918, the anniversary of Columbus' arrival in America), by a group of poets led by Isaac del Vando Villar.

At the beginning, as its name implied, *Grecia* was still under the influence of the modernists, who were the Hispanic equivalents of the French symbolists. But on April 30, 1919, Cansinos-Asséns' name appears on its editorial board. From then on, the magazine became open to the young. According to Borges, the poem he published there, "Hymn to the Sea," was very derivative.

> In the poem, I tried my hardest to be Walt Whitman:
>
>> O sea! O myth! O wide resting place!
>> I know why I love you. I know that we are both very old,
>> that we have known each other for centuries . . .
>> O Protean, I have been born of you—
>> both of us chained and wandering,
>> both of us hungering for stars,
>> both of us with hopes and disappointments . . .
>
> Today, I hardly think of the sea, or even of myself, as hungering for stars. Years after, when I came across Arnold Bennett's phrase "the third-rate grandiose," I understood at once what he meant. And yet when I arrived in Madrid a few months later, as this was the only poem I had ever printed, people there thought of me as a singer of the sea. (Ibid., p. 220)

If Seville was (at least retrospectively) somewhat disappointing, Madrid brought a personal revelation. There Georgie met the wise polyglot Rafael Cansinos-Asséns. Born in Seville in 1883, Cansinos (as he was generally called) had led a curious if not eccentric life. He did not conform at all to the conventional image of the Spanish man of letters. In the first place, instead of underlining his *casticismo*, or native origins, as all did, he stressed his Jewish background. According to Borges, he studied for the priesthood in Seville "but, having found the name Cansinos in the archives of the Inquisition, he decided he was a Jew. This led him to the study of Hebrew, and later on he even had himself circumcised" (ibid., p. 221). At the time, this insistence on his real or imaginary Jewish roots was extremely unwelcome in Spain. Years later a distinguished essayist and historian, Américo Castro, began to openly explore in depth the Jewish influence on Spanish culture. But for his time Cansinos was unique. He was also unique in having an inexhaustible appetite for languages: eventually he mastered eleven. A third aspect of his personality was equally extraordinary: he was extremely tolerant of other writers' failings, and instead of praising only the powerful and influential he loved to devote long articles and

159

reviews to unknown and even second-rate young writers. The combination of these qualities made him an ideal master for young poets.

Cansinos had an enormous impact on Georgie. Borges calls his meeting him "the great event" of his life in Madrid.

> I still like to think of myself as his disciple. Literary friends from Andalusia took me to meet him. I timidly congratulated him on a poem *he* had written about the sea. "Yes," he said, "and how I'd like to see it before I die." He was a tall man with the Andalusian contempt for all things Castilian. The most remarkable fact about Cansinos was that he lived completely for literature, without regard for money or fame. He was a fine poet and wrote a book of psalms—chiefly erotic—called *El candelabro de los siete brazos* [The Menorah, or The Seven-branched Candelabrum], which was published in 1915. He also wrote novels, stories, and essays, and, when I knew him, presided over a literary circle.
>
> Every Saturday, I would go to the Café Colonial, where we met at midnight, and the conversation lasted until daybreak. Sometimes there were as many as twenty or thirty of us. The group despised all Spanish local color—*cante jondo* [gypsy folk songs] and bullfights. They admired American jazz, and were more interested in being Europeans than Spaniards. Cansinos would propose a subject—The Metaphor, Free Verse, The Traditional Forms of Poetry, Narrative Poetry, The Adjective, The Verb. In his own quiet way, he was a dictator, allowing no unfriendly allusions to contemporary writers and trying to keep the talk on a high plane. (Ibid., pp. 221–222)

What Borges forgets to mention here is that the level of discussion was not always very high. To De Milleret he confides that one evening at the Café Colonial they had argued about the most memorable verse in all literature. They had come to the conclusion that it was one of Apollinaire's which Borges could not recall very well but in Spanish was something like "Tu lengua pez rojo en el acuario de tu voz." ("Your tongue red fish in the aquarium of your voice.") "I believe it was the worst verse Apollinaire ever wrote. . . . And that was quoted as a flower of literature. That astonished me" (De Milleret, 1967, p. 33).

In criticizing the Spanish admirers of Apollinarie, Borges nevertheless attempts to excuse the poet. "He has written very good poems, for instance his war poems," he tells De Milleret, and to prove it he quotes by heart some lines from two of Apollinaire's most famous pieces: "Désir" and "Tristesse d'une étoile." In the first poem Borges makes a couple of minor mistakes, but it is obvious that he had at one time read Apollinaire carefully.

In the "Autobiographical Essay" Borges completes his portrait of Cansinos by discussing his vast reading and his translations (De

160

Quincey's *Opium Eater,* the *Meditations of Marcus Aurelius,* Barbusse's novels, the complete works of Goethe and Dostoevski, the *Arabian Nights,* among others) and by describing a visit to his home: "Once, I went to see him and he took me into his library. Or, rather, I should say his whole house was a library. It was like making your way through a wood. He was too poor to have shelves, and the books were piled one on top of the other from floor to ceiling, forcing you to thread your way among the vertical columns" ("Essay," 1970, p. 222).

In praising Cansinos, he is not blind to his shortcomings:

> But he had a perversity that made him fail to get on with his leading contemporaries. It lay in writing books that lavishly praised second- or third-rate writers. At the time, Ortega y Gasset was at the height of his fame, but Cansinos thought of him as a bad philosopher and a bad writer. What I got from him, chiefly, was the pleasure of literary conversation. Also, I was stimulated by him to far-flung reading. In writing, I began aping him. He wrote long and flowing sentences with an un-Spanish and strongly Hebrew flavor to them. (Ibid., p. 222)

For the first time in his life Georgie had met a well-rounded man of letters. The impact was so great that he not only began to imitate Cansinos but acknowledged him as his master—a view that now seems hard to share.

There is a small error in Borges' reminiscences of Cansinos in the "Autobiographical Essay." He attributes to him the invention of the term "ultraism," the name of the movement led by the group of poets Georgie had first met in Seville. It is still a matter of controversy whether Cansinos really coined the word. The matter would be of secondary importance if the name were not (according to Ortega y Gasset's tart remark) the only good thing about the movement. But if Cansinos did not invent it, he helped to promote it and even contributed to the movement with some "short, laconic ultraist pieces" under the pen name of Juan Las. (The adjectives are from Borges' "Essay.") In private, Cansinos probably voiced some misgivings about the general quality of what was then being written by the young. Or at least that is the impression that Borges conveys in his "Essay": "The whole thing—I see now—was done in a spirit of mockery. But we youngsters took it very seriously" (ibid., p. 222).

Borges also fails to mention that ultraism did not originate in Spain. Before Cansinos had dreamed of supporting any avant-garde movement there, two Hispanic writers had gone to France and had returned to Spain with the new gospel. Borges mentions only one in his "Essay," and in a slightly derogatory context:

In Madrid at this time, there was another group gathered around [Ramón] Gómez de la Serna. I went there once and didn't like the way they behaved. They had a buffoon who wore a bracelet with a rattle attached. He would be made to shake hands with people and the rattle would rattle and Gómez de la Serna would invariably say, "Where's the snake?" That was supposed to be funny. Once, he turned to me proudly and remarked, "You've never seen this kind of thing in Buenos Aires, have you?" I owned, thank God, that I hadn't. (Ibid., p. 223)

Georgie's memories of Ramón Gómez de la Serna are kinder. He devoted at least two articles to him in his first book of essays, *Inquisiciones* (1925). In one he chronicles the two rival groups that dominated the literary scene: Cansinos' and Ramón's. Although Georgie openly admits he preferred the first, he has some good words for the second. In describing the differences between the two masters, he points out that whereas Ramón, a Castilian from Madrid, is thick, dense, and fleshy, Cansinos, an Andalusian, is tall like a flame and clumsy like a tree. He also opposes the first's appetite for reality to the second's sad and slow delivery, in which an old sorrow can be detected. Ramón presided over the Saturday gathering of his followers in the tight, almost jaillike bar of Pombo; Cansinos preferred the mirrored expanses of the Café Colonial for his Saturday meetings. In reviewing their rivalry, Georgie admits that Ramón finally won the day. In spite of his bias for Cansinos, he recognizes in Ramón not only the successful clown but also the tragic spirit that lies beneath layers of frivolity.

Ramón was instrumental in introducing the avant-garde to Spain. He was eight years younger than Cansinos-Asséns. In 1909 he had begun to write about futurism in *Prometeo,* a Madrid magazine he edited, and had translated for the same journal the founding manifesto published by Marinetti in *Le Figaro* (Paris, February 20, 1909). One year later *Prometeo* included a futurist proclamation to the Spaniards, written by Marinetti and translated by Ramón. In his own work Ramón had proclaimed similar ideas and had even invented a new epigrammatic form, the *greguería,* which was based on a mathematical formula: "humor + metaphor = *greguería*." His aim was (as he once said) to "fumigate nature with new images" (Videla, 1963, p. 129). There was a lot of mystification in his attitude, and because of that many young poets did not take him too seriously. Perhaps it was this characteristic that put off Georgie. He obviously preferred Cansinos' subtle irony to the robust and slightly coarse Castilian humor of Ramón.

Cansinos himself, in an article written in 1919, praised Ramón for having introduced futurism to Spain. Cansinos also called attention in 1919 to a second champion of the new poetry, the Chilean Vicente Huidobro. Huidobro had spent two decisive years in Paris, working in close contact with Apollinaire, Max Jacob, and Pierre Reverdy and having his portrait done by Picasso, Juan Gris, and Hans Arp. He had written some graphic poems in French and had achieved a certain notoriety as a cubist and dadaist poet. His stay in Madrid in the summer of 1919 was instrumental in introducing the avant-garde into Spanish literature. After he left for Chile, ultraism was founded.

Georgie probably never met Huidobro personally, but through Cansinos he may have become acquainted with his poetry and theories. A mocking reference in one of his essays to a metaphor coined by Huidobro (*Inquisiciones*, 1925, p. 29) makes clear that he was not greatly amused by the kind of innocent playfulness found in the Chilean's poetry.

The greatest omission in Borges' chronicle of ultraist days in Spain is the part he himself played in the movement. Georgie not only sat at the feet of Cansinos, briefly visited Ramón's literary group at Pombo, and published three or four poems in little magazines, as the "Essay" indicates; he also contributed decisively to the organization and diffusion of the movement. It was his task to bring to it an original critical mind, a firsthand knowledge of contemporary literature, and a daring poetic imagination. His contribution went beyond participating in some of the movement's noisier events, such as the one that took place in Madrid on the evening of January 28, 1921. According to a colorful chronicle (Videla, 1963, p. 230), the ultraists attempted to shock the audience with tactics that had been perfected by the futurists. Georgie is included among those who then read their "beautiful poems, which had the incomparable virtue of arousing the morons"—to quote the chronicle's exalted style.

Georgie also struck up a friendship with one of the young leaders of the movement. In the "Autobiographical Essay" Borges devotes three terse lines to him: "Another of the earnest followers was Guillermo de Torre, whom I met in Madrid that spring [1920] and who married my sister Norah nine years later" ("Essay," 1970, pp. 222–223). De Torre was one year younger than Georgie, and when they met he had already been converted to the avant-garde. He had one of the largest collections of little magazines, pamphlets, and manifestos in Europe, traveled regularly to Paris, and corresponded actively with every promising young writer. He eventually chronicled the movement in a polemical book, *Avant-Garde European Literature* (1925; reissued in 1965 in a longer, more sedate and scholarly version as *History of the Avant-Garde Literatures*). What marred De Torre's efforts was his egocentrism: he was not a very good poet, and as a leader he lacked charisma. He knew more and worked harder than his colleagues, but he never commanded the attention Huidobro, Cansinos, or Ramón did. In spite of his devotion to literature, he lacked true critical insight. To stress in his book the importance of ultraism, he inverted chronology, relegating futurism to the last chapter, and started by studying the newer movement. (In 1965 he restored the normal order of things.)

De Torre seemed to have liked Georgie. In his 1925 book he quotes from him extensively and with unlimited praise. In his enthusiasm he even reproduces some of Georgie's worst poems. Norah must have been another link between the two. She used to contribute some of her graphic art to the ultraists' little magazines. Although Georgie seems to have returned the friendship, he showed an amused detachment toward De Torre's naïve promotion of ultraism, especially toward a "vertical" manifesto published as a poster by De Torre with some woodcuts by Norah. According to Enrique Díez-Canedo, a sober chronicler of ultraism, Borges, "who has talent, laughs at the cuteness of 'vertical'" (Videla, 1963, p. 58). In spite of his detachment, he continued to be friends with De Torre, and from Buenos Aires he eventually sent an ultraist manifesto of his own making to be signed and published by the vertical poet.

Georgie's main contribution to the movement at this stage of his career was the constant flow of articles and poems he published in little magazines. He dedicated no less than three articles to discussing and translating the German expressionist poets. He also wrote an article called "On the Margins of Modern Lyrics" (*Grecia,* January 31, 1920) which stressed the importance in ultraist poetry of a new spirit, a new point of view, and linked it with a "dynamic conception of the world." For him, "the fertile premise which considers words not as bridges to ideas but as ends in themselves finds in ultraism its culmination" (Videla, 1963, pp. 201–204). He also wrote an important piece, "Anatomy of My Ultra," which was published in *Grecia* on May 20, 1921. In defining his poetical intentions, he affirms his interest in the *sensation in itself* and not in the description of the spatial or temporal premises that constitute its setting; he longs for an art that can translate the naked emotion, free from the additional data which surround it; an art that avoids the superficial, the metaphysical, the egocentric, and the ironic. To achieve it, he stresses the importance of rhythm and metaphor, or as he puts it, "the acoustic element and the luminous element. Rhythm: not imprisoned in the metrical pentagrams, but in winding, loose, liberated, suddenly truncated Metaphor: that verbal curve which generally traces between two—spiritual—points the shortest way" (Fernández, 1967, p. 493).

In spite of the arch language and heavy imagery of its prose, the piece shows how clearly Georgie viewed what was essential in the new poetry. In insisting on rhythm and metaphor—he wrote another article on metaphor for *Cosmópolis* (Madrid, November 1921, pp. 395–402)—he was preaching what his new poems were practicing. No less than eleven have been identified in several little magazines of the time. In the "Autobiographical Essay," Borges admits that "three or four" found "their way into magazines." What he has to say there about his ultraist writing in Spain is pitifully brief. He mentions two books he wrote while there—one of essays and one of some twenty poems—then adds that he destroyed both books: the latter in Spain, "on the eve of departure"; the former in Buenos Aires because he failed to find a publisher for it ("Essay," 1970, p. 223).

Perhaps Borges is right in dismissing his early work, but he shows an excess of pleasure in talking about the destruction of both manuscripts. What he remembers about the book of essays does not seem too promising: "[The book] was called, I now wonder why, *Los naipes del tahur* (The Sharper's Cards). They were literary and political essays (I was still an anarchist and a freethinker and in favor of pacifism), written under the influence of Pío Baroja. Their aim was to be bitter and relentless, but they were, as a matter of fact, quite tame. I went in for using such words as 'fools,' 'harlots,' 'liars' " (ibid., p. 223). The article on Baroja, Azorín, and the Jesuit priest in *La Feuille* could probably be viewed as an example of the kind of essay Georgie had included in the first book. He may have also included other pieces on Spanish brothels, ultraist poetry, and German expressionism. The second book is easier to evaluate. According to Borges, it "was titled either *The Red Psalms* or *The Red Rhythms*. It was a collection of poems— perhaps some twenty in all—in free verse and in praise of the Russian revolution, the brotherhood of man, and pacifism." He then quotes the titles of three: "Bolshevik Epic," "Trenches," and "Russia" (ibid., p. 223).

The poems that have survived in magazines, or in scholarly works about the period, do not seem memorable. They are interesting for what they reveal about Georgie's apprenticeship. He was obsessed with a war he had seen from a distance ("Trenches"), with a revolution that for a while filled the youth of Europe with hope for social and political justice ("Bolshevik Epic," "Russia"). But in the majority of the verses he was chiefly concerned with expressing his view of reality through rare metaphors and striking similes. He had learned his poetics from Whitman and the German expressionists; he favored free verse and long-lined poems that he called (following Cansinos' example) psalms. What is still memorable today is the violence of many of his images. Thus in "Morning," published in *Ultra* (Madrid, January 1921), the sun, with its spears, claws the mirrors; in "Russia" the bayonets "carry the morning on their tips"; and in "Bolshevik Epic" the Red army is seen as a fresh forest of masts made of bayonet spouts, a candelabrum of one thousand and one phalluses (all these quotes are from De Torre, 1965, pp. 556–558).

That Georgie was obviously passing through an erotic phase is confirmed by one of the articles, "Maison Elena (Toward an Esthetic of the Whorehouses in Spain)," also published in *Ultra* (October 1921). In praising the "easy curves of a girl," Georgie cannot avoid a literary simile: he finds them "sculpted like a phrase by Quevedo" (Fernández Moreno, 1967, p. 141). Perhaps for Georgie (who had been so innocent of what was going on in Palermo's brothels until his cousin Alvaro Melián Lafinur gave him some information), literary life in Madrid was not limited to meetings to discuss poetry, manifestos, and poems. It is well known that an important part of the night life in Spain is traditionally spent in whorehouses, which are a mixture of brothel, social club, and even political caucus.

The reference to Quevedo above stresses another great discovery of Georgie's Spanish sojourn. For the first time in his life he became truly acquainted with the classics of his native language. At the same time that they were getting acquainted with the avant-garde, young Spanish poets disinterred a neglected period of Spanish letters, the baroque. They came to recognize, in Góngora's experiments with a Latinate syntax and elaborate imagery, in Quevedo's play with conceit, and in Cervantes' labyrinthine use of fiction within fiction, preoccupations similar to their own. Some of the older masters (Baroja, Unamuno, Jiménez, the Machado brothers, Valle Inclán) had also been preoccupied with these poetic problems. Georgie read them all and chose a few among them—Quevedo and Cervantes, Unamuno and Baroja—to be his guides for a while. In later essays, written and published in Buenos Aires, he discussed them, imitated them, and (finally) overcame them. If there is very little in the "Autobiographical Essay" about his reading or about all the writing he did in Spain at that time, the fault is in Borges' memory. For Georgie, the ultraist experience was decisive. Only after reaching Buenos Aires in 1921 would he be in a position to evaluate its importance.

8.
The Mythological Foundation of Buenos Aires

Georgie was barely fifteen when he left Buenos Aires, or rather Palermo, the only neighborhood of his native city he really knew. Until that time the child had seldom ventured outside the two-story house and the garden. He was familiar only with certain places: when visiting relatives, he would have a glimpse of the city; during the summer he would go to Adrogué, a small town some fifteen miles to the south of Buenos Aires, or would cross the River Plate to swim on the Uruguayan side or go north to bathe in the swift waters of the Uruguay River. Monotonous, reassuring, foreseeable, his life in Buenos Aires before 1914 made Georgie into an introverted, quiet adolescent. When he returned home in 1921, almost seven years had passed. He was a young man and had lived in Switzerland and Spain; had learned Latin, French, and German; had participated vicariously in some avant-garde movements and become an active member of a new group, the ultraists; had published reviews, articles, and a few poems; had even written two books. At twenty-one he was still shy but he was no longer unseasoned.

Buenos Aires was different too. In his "Autobiographical Essay" Borges concentrates his narrative mainly on the changes he noticed in his native city:

We returned to Buenos Aires on the *Reina Victoria Eugenia* toward the end of March 1921. It came to me as a surprise, after living in so many European cities—after so many memories of Geneva, Zurich, Nîmes, Córdoba, and Lisbon—to find that my native town had grown, and that it was now a very large, sprawling, and almost endless city of low buildings with flat roofs, stretching west toward what geographers and literary hands call the pampas.

It was more than a homecoming; it was a rediscovery. I was able to see Buenos Aires keenly and eagerly because I had been away from it for a long time. Had I never gone abroad, I wonder whether I would ever have seen it with the peculiar shock and glow that it now gave me. The city—not the whole city, of course, but a few places in it that became emotionally significant to me—inspired the poems of my first published book, *Fervor de Buenos Aires*. ("Essay," 1970, pp. 223–224)

The Borgeses had settled in a house on Bulnes Street, not far from their old Palermo neighborhood, and lived there for the next two years. Georgie there began a habit that he kept well into his fifties: walking endlessly along Buenos Aires streets, covering enormous distances, alone or with friends, musing and perhaps sketching poems or articles in his mind, talking about anything that took his fancy. Thus he *learned* Buenos Aires, or at least *his* Buenos Aires; it was an inch-by-inch, repetitive covering of a territory that his writings would cover just as closely. Buenos Aires had existed before Georgie discovered it, but very few of its writers had taken the trouble of reinventing it so thoroughly and with such success. From 1921 onward Buenos Aires became his as much as Manhattan was Whitman's.

In recalling those days in his "Autobiographical Essay," Borges subtly downplays his literary activities. He prefers to stress the first impact of the city on his poetic imagination. The only thing he has to say about his literary life is, "I am still known to literary historians as the 'father of Argentine ultraism' " (ibid., p. 225), but he fails to explain why he has earned such a title. The truth is that as soon as he settled in Buenos Aires he became the leader of a group of young poets—among them his cousin Guillermo Juan Borges, Eduardo González Lanuza, Norah Lange, and Francisco Piñero—who were also interested in avant-garde literature and with whom he published a literary magazine, *Prisma* (Prism). Only two issues came out: December 1921 and March 1922. Borges recalls the more picturesque aspects of the enterprise: "Our small ultraist group was eager to have a magazine of its own, but a real magazine was beyond our means. I had noticed billboard ads, and the thought came to me that we might similarly print a 'mural magazine' and paste it up ourselves on the walls of the buildings in different parts of town" (ibid., p. 234). The idea of having a mural magazine was very much in line with all that the European avant-garde had been practicing since the cubist painters started to paste bits and pieces of journals on their canvases, Apollinaire began drawing his *Calligrammes,* and Marinetti used posters to advance the cause of futurism. Perhaps Norah also had something to do with the idea. She had contributed her woodcuts to several ultraist publications in Spain, and now in Argentina she became one of Georgie's most constant collaborators. A cursory examination of the little magazines of the 1920s in Argentina shows how much she was also part of the movement.

In his "Essay" Borges gives a few more picturesque details about *Prisma:* "Each issue was a large single sheet and contained a manifesto and some six or eight short, laconic poems, printed with plenty of white space around them, and a woodcut by my sister. We sallied forth at night—González Lanuza, Piñero, my cousin, and I— armed with pastepots and brushes provided by my mother, and, walking miles on end, slapped them up along Santa Fe, Callao, Entre Ríos, and Mexico streets" (ibid., p. 234). This itinerary required Georgie and his friends to work their way down Santa Fe to the downtown section; there, crossing Rivadavia Street (which divides Buenos Aires in two), they entered the Southside, where the National Library is located on Mexico Street. The journey must have taken most of the night.

The first ultraist manifesto ever signed by Georgie came out in the December issue of *Prisma.* In exalted language it begins by criticizing traditional poets who continued to use the worn-out approaches of symbolism or indulged in autobiography. It also concentrates its fire on the waste of time and energy long novels or prolix poems represent. The manifesto complains that to achieve one good, valid verse the traditionalists write a whole sonnet or take two hundred pages to say what could be said in two lines. In a parenthesis it prophesies that the psychological novel is doomed. Against all these errors, the ultraists proclaim the need to free art from its decrepit state. Poetry must concentrate on its basic element: metaphor. "Each verse of one of our poems has an individual life and represents a new vision" (Videla, 1963, pp. 199–210). The manifesto ends by stating that the task of *Prisma* is to make the new poetry available to all.

As Georgie's signature is the first on the manifesto, we can assume he was chiefly responsible for its wording. A few of its ideas (the rejection of autobiography, the attack on the novel) were very much in line with his poetical and philosophical convictions, and in spite of a radical change in his style of writing, Borges still subscribes to them.

In his recollections Borges does not mention the manifesto or the fact that *Prisma* had some impact in Madrid. On the contrary, he takes a rather dim view of the mural magazine's effect on Buenos Aires citizens: "Most of our handiwork was torn down by baffled readers, almost at once, but luckily for us Alfredo Bianchi, of *Nosotros,* saw one of them and invited us to publish an ultraist anthology among the pages of his solid magazine" ("Essay," 1970, pp. 234–235). Once more, Borges fails to mention that Bianchi did more than just ask the group to contribute its poems; he also asked Georgie to write an article explaining to the sedate readers of *Nosotros* what ultraism was about.

Georgie accepted, and his contribution (the first of many to that magazine) was published in the December 1921 issue. Because he was writing for a middle-aged audience and in a magazine that was part of the establishment (it was already in its thirty-ninth year of publication), he made an effort to write in a less baroque style, so that while the article presents the same views aired in the *Prisma* manifesto, the style is more subdued and the arguments tighter. After dismissing the symbolists and the autobiographers, he offers ultraism as "one of the answers" to the crisis of modern poetry. The most important part of the article is a four-point résumé of ultraist principles:

1. Reduction of lyric poetry to its basic element: metaphor.
2. Elimination of links, connecting phrases, and superfluous adjectives.
3. Abolition of ornamental implements, confessionalism, circumstantial evidence, preaching, and deliberate vagueness.
4. Synthesis of two or more images in one, which thus enlarges its capacity for suggestion. (Fernández Moreno, 1967, p. 495)

The article includes quotations from ultraist poetry, written by Spanish and Argentine poets. From that point of view, it was a preface to the anthology that Borges mentions in his "Autobiographical Essay" and that came out in *Nosotros* in September 1922. It includes poems by Georgie ("Saturdays," later collected in his first book of poems) and by the other *Prisma* poets. The selection is, to say the least, eclectic.

The article Georgie wrote for *Nosotros* also mentions a long list of established writers who contributed to ultraism, including Ramón, Ortega y Gasset, Jiménez, Valle Inclán, and the Chilean Vicente Huidobro. Obviously, he was trying to impress the *Nosotros* reader with this list of prominent personalities and thus find a way to legitimize the movement. In his conclusion he repeats one of his chief psychological observations: the mistake of believing in the existence of an individual ego. "Every new state which can be added to those already existing becomes an essential part of the ego and expresses it: this is true not only of that which was already part of *each individual* but also of what was *alien* to it. Any event, any perception, any idea, expresses us with identical efficacy; that is, it can be added to our *us*." For Georgie, the concept of the impersonality of the ego found its best expression in ultraist poetry, whose aim was "the transmutation of the world's concrete reality into an inner emotional reality" (ibid., p. 495).

Perhaps these metaphysical views were not shared by all Argentine ultraist poets; perhaps they represent only Georgie's views, for they appear time and again in Georgie's poems and articles. They are the result of endless discussions with Father on the subject of philosophical idealism and on Georgie's own readings of Hume, Berkeley, and Schopenhauer. Also, on his return to Buenos Aires, he had become friends with one of Father's schoolmates, Macedonio Fernández, who was also a lawyer and had a truly philosophical turn of mind. In his "Autobiographical Essay" Borges writes: "Perhaps the major event of my return was Macedonio Fernández. Of all the people I have met in my life—and I have met some quite remarkable men—no one has ever made so deep and so lasting an impression on me as Macedonio. A tiny figure in a black bowler hat, he was waiting for us on the Dársena Norte when we landed, and I came to inherit his friendship with my father" ("Essay," 1970, p. 227).

Soon Georgie began to meet Macedonio every Saturday at the Perla Café, in the busy Plaza del Once. The new ritual took the place of Cansinos' Saturdays in Spain.

> As in Madrid Cansinos had stood for all learning, Macedonio now stood for pure thinking. At the time, I was a great reader and went out very seldom (almost every night after dinner, I used to go to bed and read), but my whole week was lit up with the expectation that on Saturday I'd be seeing and hearing Macedonio. He lived quite near us and I could have seen him whenever I wanted, but I somehow felt that I had no right to that privilege and that in order to give Macedonio's Saturday its full value I had to forgo him throughout the week. (Ibid., p. 227)

Macedonio was not a great talker like Cansinos. On the contrary, on those Saturdays he would speak "perhaps only three or four times, risking only a few quiet observations," which he generally pretended had been drawn from something his listeners had said or thought. He had a great fondness for philosophical speculation and once had even exchanged some letters with William James. But if he had a mind of his own, he was no inventor of systems:

> Readers of Hume and Schopenhauer may find little that is new in Macedonio, but the remarkable thing about him is that he arrived at his conclusions by himself. Later on, he actually read Hume, Schopenhauer, Berkeley, and William James, but I suspect he had not done much other reading, and he always quoted the same authors. . . . I think of Macedonio as reading a page or so and then being spurred into thought. He not only argued that we are such stuff as dreams are made on, but he really believed that we are all living in a dream world. (Ibid., p. 229)

The impact Macedonio had on Georgie was immense. This is how Borges describes it:

> Before Macedonio, I had always been a credulous reader. His chief gift to me was to make me read skeptically. At the outset, I plagiarized him de-

171

votedly, picking up certain stylistic mannerisms of his that later I came to regret. I look back on him now, however, as an Adam bewildered by the Garden of Eden. His genius survives in but a few of his pages; his influence was of a Socratic nature. I truly loved the man, on this side idolatry, as much as any. (Ibid., p. 230)

If Macedonio was Socrates, Georgie would eventually become Plato. Unknown to anyone but his most intimate friends, Macedonio had been writing (and sometimes quietly publishing) since 1896. He lacked, nevertheless, the necessary impulse to complete some of his most ambitious projects—a book of metaphysical essays, a novel—and continued to accumulate manuscripts that were stuck in boxes and drawers and sometimes even got lost in one of Macedonio's constant changes of boardinghouses. Georgie was instrumental in helping him save and organize some of his works. He even persuaded Macedonio to join him and a few friends in the launching of a new magazine, *Proa* (Prow), which published three issues between August 1922 and July 1923. Each issue had only six pages; it was actually "a single sheet printed on both sides and folded twice," according to Borges' description (ibid., p. 235). On the editorial board Georgie and Macedonio were joined by other young poets. Norah again contributed her woodcuts. A note to the reader in the first issue warned that "Ultraism is not a sect designed as a prison." On the contrary, it can be seen as an open field, "an insatiable longing for faraway lands," or as an "exaltation of the metaphor." Of these two views ("intuitive the first and intellectual the second"), the reader may choose whichever he prefers.

Macedonio contributed at least three pieces to the magazine, while Georgie carried the main responsibility for its editing. In the meantime, he continued to contribute to other publications such as *Nosotros*—an article on Berkeley's metaphysics, another on Unamuno as a poet—and to *Inicial* (Initial), an avant-garde little magazine for which he wrote an article on German expressionist poets and published a few derogatory remarks on a new book by Argentina's leading poet, Leopoldo Lugones. Georgie had discovered in Seville and Madrid the pleasures of literary life; now in Buenos Aires he discovered the exhilaration of having a tribune to air his ideas. His career as editor and reviewer had begun.

Very little of his frantic activity in this period is registered in the "Autobiographical Essay." The whole period is soberly described as follows:

When I talked things over at the time with fellow poets Eduardo González Lanuza, Norah Lange, Francisco Piñero, my cousin Guillermo Juan (Borges), and Roberto Ortelli, we came to the conclusion that Spanish ultraism was overburdened—after the manner of futurism—with modernity and gadgets. We were unimpressed by railway trains, by propellers, by airplanes, and by electric fans. While in our manifestos we still upheld the primacy of the metaphor and the elimination of transitions and decorative adjectives, what we wanted to write was essential poetry—poems beyond the here and now, free of local color and contemporary circumstances. (Ibid., pp. 225–226)

The ironic summary is basically right. In articles published at the time, and later collected in *Inquisiciones,* Georgie offers a similar perspective but in a less ironic mode. Reviewing *Prisma,* a book of poems by González Lanuza, he stresses the differences between Spanish and Argentine ultraism:

Ultraism in Seville and Madrid was a desire for renewal; it was a desire to define a new cycle in the arts; it was a poetry written as if with big red letters on the leaves of a calendar and whose proudest emblems—airplanes, antennae, and propellers—plainly state a chronological nowness. Ultraism in Buenos Aires was the ambition to obtain an absolute art which did not depend on the uncertain prestige of words and which lasted in the eternity of language as a conviction of beauty. Under the powerful brightness of the lamps, the names of Huidobro and Apollinaire were usually mentioned in the Spanish gatherings. We, in the meantime, tested lines from Garcilaso [a Renaissance poet], wandering ponderously under the stars on the outskirts of town, asking for an art which was as atemporal as the eternal stars. We abhorred the blurred shades of rubenism [the Spanish American brand of symbolism] and were inflamed by metaphors because of the precision they have, because of their algebraical quality of relating remote things. (*Inquisiciones,* 1925, pp. 96–97)

In analyzing his friend's book, Georgie verifies a fact which astonishes him: without meaning to, the ultraist "had fallen into another type of rhetoric, as linked as the old ones to verbal deception. . . . I have seen that our poetry, whose flight we considered free and careless, has been drawing a geometrical figure in the air of time. What a beautiful and sad surprise to discover that our gesture, so spontaneous and easy then, was nothing but the clumsy beginning of a rite" (ibid., pp. 97–98).

In a similar vein, Georgie recalls the origins of Argentine ultraism in a prologue to a book of poems by another friend, Norah Lange. He again stresses the differences between the Spanish and the local brand:

Its desire for renewal, which was prankish and bouncing in Seville, sounded loyally and passionately among us. . . . For us, contemporary poetry was as

useless as worn-out incantations, and we felt an urgency to make a new poetry. We were fed up with the insolence of words and the musical vagueness
the turn-of-the-century poets loved, and we asked for a unique and effective
art in which beauty would be undeniable. . . . . We practiced the image, the
sentence, and the epithet, swiftly compendious. (Ibid., pp. 76–77)

A third article, "After the Images," recalls the ultraists' infatuation with images, metaphors, tropes—all the rhetorical paraphernalia
that had also seduced English and North American imagists. Georgie
evokes the time when they discovered in metaphors the power to undermine the rigidity of the world: "For the believer, things are the ac-
tualization of the word of God—first the light was named and then it
shined over the world; for the positivist, they are necessities in an in-
terlocking system. Metaphor, by relating separate objects, breaks this
double rigidity" (ibid., p. 27).

With the perspective afforded by three years, Georgie is ready
to admit that "now" anyone can and does indulge in metaphors. In
praising the power the image has to transform the world ("it is witch-
craft," he writes), he also raises a voice of warning:

It is not enough to say, as all poets do, that mirrors are like water. Nor is it
enough to take this hypothesis as absolute and pretend, like any Huidobro,
that coolness comes out of mirrors or that thirsty birds drink out of them
and the frame becomes empty. We have to move beyond these games. We
have to express this whim made into a reality of one mind: we have to show
a man who gets into the glass and who persists in his imaginary country
(where there are figures and colors but they are ruled by still silence) and
who feels the shame of being nothing but a simulacrum which nights obliterate and which the twilight admits. (Ibid., p. 29)

Apart from documenting Georgie's attitude toward the use and abuse
of metaphors in ultraist poetry, the last sentence anticipates a subject
that Borges later develops in one of his most famous short stories, "The
Circular Ruins," collected in *Ficciones* (1944).

Although Borges never admitted it, the best poetry produced
by Argentine ultraism (and perhaps by Hispanic ultraism as a whole)
can be found in his own *Fervor de Buenos Aires*—a title that may be
translated as "Adoration of Buenos Aires." It is the first of three volumes in which Georgie collected his early poetry. In his "Autobiographical Essay" Borges tells the story of the book in a rather colorful
way:

I wrote these poems in 1921 and 1922, and the volume came out early in
1923. . . . I had bargained for sixty-four pages, but the manuscript ran too
long and at the last minute five poems had to be left out—mercifully. I can't

remember a single thing about them. The book was produced in a some-what boyish spirit. No proofreading was done, no table of contents was provided, and the pages were unnumbered. My sister made a woodcut for the cover, and three hundred copies were printed. ("Essay," 1970, p. 224)

Today the book is one of the most sought-after of his early works. It is a nicely printed, unassuming little white volume, with a woodcut in which Norah offered her own version of Georgie's Buenos Aires: the one-storied, balconied, palm-treed town the poems described in words. Borges' own evaluation in his "Autobiographical Essay" is predictably understated: "The book was essentially romantic, though it was written in a rather lean style and abounded in laconic metaphors. It celebrated sunsets, solitary places, and unfamiliar corners; it ventured into Berkeleyan metaphysics and family history; it recorded early loves" (ibid., p. 225). The style was, according to him, a mimicry of the Spanish baroque poets with some touches of Sir Thomas Browne's rhetoric. (It had a quotation from *Religio Medici* in the preface.) This is Borges' final summation: "I'm afraid the book was a plum pudding—there was just too much in it. And yet, looking back on it now, I think I have never strayed beyond that book. I feel that all my subsequent writing has only developed themes first taken up there; I feel that all during my lifetime I have been rewriting that one book" (ibid., p. 225).

In the "Essay" Borges wonders if the poems in *Fervor de Buenos Aires* are truly "ultraist poetry." After reviewing the origins of ultraism in Argentina and the role he played in that movement, and quoting one of its most representative poems, he comes to the conclusion that the poems are "a far cry from the timid extravagances of my earlier Spanish ultraist exercises, when I saw a trolley car as a man shouldering a gun, the sunrise as a shout, or the setting sun as being crucified in the west. A sane friend to whom I later recited such absurdities remarked, 'Ah, I see you held the view that poetry's chief aim is to startle.' " He also recalls that another friend, his French translator Néstor Ibarra, once said that he "left off being an ultraist poet with the first ultraist poem he wrote." Borges' conclusion is mockingly humble: "I can now only regret my early ultraist excesses. After nearly a half-century, I find myself still striving to live down that awkward period of my life" (ibid., pp. 226–227).

Memory deserts Borges once more. Some of the images he credits to the (discarded) Spanish period of his poetry found their way into *Fervor*. In "Prismas," a poem originally published in *Ultra* (Madrid, March 1, 1921), one line—"The new moon is a small voice up there in heaven"—is later used in a poem of the same period, "Montaña" (Mountain), published in *Tableros* (Madrid, no. 2, 1921), and also in

"Campos atardecidos" (Fields in the Evening), one of the last poems in *Fervor*. In other poems, when describing the sunsets of Buenos Aires, Georgie tends to lapse into expressionist rhetoric: hyperbole takes over, simile suggests the Apocalypse, and a Christian imagery pervades every line. In "Villa Urquiza" he talks about "the Final Judgment of every evening" (*Poemas*, 1943, p. 27); in "Arrabal" (Slums) he sees a Via Crucis in the quiet, suffering streets on the outskirts of Buenos Aires (p. 34); in "La noche de San Juan" sunset is presented as cutting distances with the edge of its sword (p. 61); in "Atardeceres" (Sunsets) a poor sunset mutilates the evening (p. 70). In "Campos atardecidos" Georgie uses this expressionist image:

> Sunset standing like an Archangel
> tyrannized the path.
> (Ibid., p. 71)

In spite of these purple passages, the general tone of the book is less violent than the expressionist exercises Georgie had published in Spain. The dominant mood conveyed is his rediscovery of Buenos Aires. In the very first poem "Calles" (Streets) Georgie explains which part of his native city he prefers:

> The streets of Buenos Aires
> are already the entrails of my soul.
> Not the lively streets
> bothered with haste and agitation,
> but the sweet streets of the outskirts
> softened by trees and sunsets
> (Ibid., p. 11)

The young poet prefers roaming around at sunset, when the bustling modern city begins to be more human. In poem after poem he talks about the square and the trees, the houses and the patios, the fields to which the last streets open up. He wanders and meditates, he feels and dreams, he is overcome by longings and hallucinations. A constant metaphysical quest runs under his wanderings. He finds refuge only in the stillness of cemeteries or in the house where his fiancée lives. Because he is in love. The joys and pains of love pervade the book. The discovery of her beauty, the longing for her, the realization that he is bound to return to Europe for another year: these permeate the book and make it a sort of diary of a young poet in love. It is a moving book, still awkward but already showing promise of the poet Georgie was to become in time.

A few of the poems in the collection deal with metaphysical

speculation. One of them, "El truco" (pp. 21–22), is fully achieved. In describing the popular card game he taught to his Geneva schoolmates, Georgie avoids the pitfalls of local color and concentrates on what makes the game eternal. The permutations of the cards, although innumerable in limited human experience, are not infinite: given enough time, they will come back again and again. Thus the cardplayers not only are repeating hands that have already come up in the past. In a sense, they are repeating the former players as well; they are the former players. In a note Borges added to the 1943 collected edition of his poems (ibid., p. 173), he explains that the intention behind the poem was to apply the Leibnitzian principle of the indiscernible to the problems of individuality and time. He also quotes from a footnote to a 1940 story, "Tlön, Uqbar, Orbis Tertius," in which he postulates that all men who perform the same basic activity (coitus, reciting a line from Shakespeare) *are* the same man. The identity of the activity assures the identity of the performers.

Another group of poems is devoted to family piety. In "Recoleta" Georgie again visits the cemetery where his ancestors are buried and where he will eventually be buried too (*Poemas,* 1943, p. 13); in "Sepulchral Inscription" he evokes the shadow of Isidoro Suárez, one of Argentina's founding fathers, who fought for independence at Junín and died in bitter exile (*Poems,* 1972, p. 5), and in "Rosas," he describes the most famous of all Argentina's dictators and a personal enemy of his family (ibid., p. 11). Georgie had already discovered the elegiac mode, which he would return to in many later pieces.

A few poems seem misplaced in this basically Argentine collection. One is dedicated to Benares, an Indian city that Georgie never visited but that haunted him from early readings of Kipling (*Poemas,* 1943, p. 51). Another, redolent of the expressionist poets, is called "Judería," a title changed to "Judengasse" in 1943 to underline the German connotations of the poem (ibid., p. 53). Although they are out of place in this collection, they anticipate the poems Borges wrote in his maturity: poems about places or men he never knew who still occupy his imagination.

The original edition of *Fervor de Buenos Aires* is a collector's item. In reissuing the book, Borges took enormous liberties with its contents. The first time he reprinted it, as part of the 1943 collection of his verses, he eliminated eight pieces and considerably altered many of the remaining poems, deleting lines, changing words, and altering some of the most explicit references to his fiancée—including her name, Concepción Guerrero, which was reduced to the initials "C.G." in the poem "Sábados" (Saturdays, ibid., p. 62). In the most recent reprint of the book, made in 1969, he eliminated another seven poems but to compensate included three new ones. He also added a preface in which he compared the poet of 1923 with the poet of the present. In stressing the similarities—"We are the same; the two of us do not believe in failure or success, in literary schools and their dogmas; the two of us are devoted to Schopenhauer, Stevenson, and Whitman"—he nevertheless comes to the conclusion that they had different tastes: "In those days, I was after sunsets, outskirts, and unhappiness; now, mornings, downtown, and serenity" (*Fervor,* 1969, p. 9).

9.
A Small Poetic
Reputation

Father's eyesight was getting worse, so he decided in 1923 to return to Geneva to consult his doctor. The moment was not well chosen from Georgie's point of view. He was deeply in love with a young woman whose beautiful hair had inspired some of his verses, and his first book of poems, *Fervor de Buenos Aires,* was just off the press. But as he depended entirely on Father for his living, and was determined not to compromise his poetic pursuits by getting a job, he accepted Father's decision. He wrote a sad poem to his fiancée and did his best to speed the distribution of *Fervor* among the happy few. To this end, he devised an original method:

Having noticed that many people who went to the offices of *Nosotros* . . . left their overcoats hanging in the cloak room, I brought fifty or a hundred copies to Alfredo Bianchi, one of the editors. Bianchi stared at me in amazement and said, "Do you expect me to sell these books for you?" "No," I answered. "Although I've written them, I'm not altogether a lunatic. I thought I might ask you to slip some of these books into the pockets of those coats hanging out there." He generously did so. ("Essay," 1970, pp. 224–225)

Upon his return to Argentina, Georgie found that some of the people had read the book and had even written about it.

The new journey to Europe may, in fact, have appealed to him as providing an opportunity to return to Spain with a small poetic reputation, or so it seems in retrospect. After visiting London and Paris, and consulting Father's doctor in Geneva, the Borgeses finally reached Madrid. They remained in Spain for almost a year, visiting Andalusia and Majorca to renew their impressions and memories, and also ex-

179

ploring neighboring Portugal. The Spanish literary scene was rapidly changing. By 1924 the ultraist movement had disintegrated. All the little magazines had died, and the more sedate journals accepted only what was safer in ultraism. The sense of adventure was already gone. The avant-garde was no longer necessary because Spain had finally updated its culture. Perhaps the surest sign of the change was the launching, in July 1923, of a new journal, *Revista de Occidente* (The Western Review), which was published until the outbreak of the civil war. Its founder was José Ortega y Gasset, then the leading intellectual figure of Spain. Born in 1883 and educated in Germany, Ortega was slightly younger than the men (Baroja, Unamuno, Azorín, the Machados, Jiménez) who represented the generation of 1898—the one that had had to face Spain's defeat in Cuba that same year. He was also more conversant with the latest philosophical theories in Germany and the new avant-garde writing in France. The journal launched became *the* cultural organ of the new Spain—as decisive as T. S. Eliot's *Criterion* in London or the *Nouvelle Revue Française* in Paris. Ortega also started a publishing house under the journal's imprint that was devoted mainly to the translation of important new German books.

The name of the journal had obvious links to Oswald Spengler's monumental *Decline of the West*, which was published in Germany between 1918 and 1922. Ortega had, in fact, recommended the translation of that book to one of the publishing houses he had helped to found and even wrote a prologue for it. But in the Spanish context "Western" had a different meaning. It meant that the journal's purpose was to go against the grain of all that was traditional and thus strictly peninsular in Spanish culture: the excessive nationalism, the endless exaltation of regionalism and local color, the indifference to what was happening on the other side of the Pyrenees. The 1898 Spanish-American war and the isolationism created by World War I, in which Spain fiercely kept its neutrality, had strengthened both nationalism and provincialism. Against them Ortega raised his *Revista de Occidente*.

Georgie's poems found a welcome in the journal. None other than Ramón Gómez de la Serna was to review *Fervor de Buenos Aires*. His article in the April 24 issue begins by recalling Georgie's visits to his Saturday meetings at Pombo and contrasts his presence in Madrid with the half-imagined, half-real vision of a younger Georgie, a "pale boy of great sensitivity" hidden among the thick curtains of a traditional household. The article also makes affectionate references to Norah. "Jorge Luis always seems to me close to Norah, the disturbing girl with the same pale skin of her brother's and, like him, lost among the curtains." Ramón recalls a conversation in which Norah described their home in Buenos Aires, where the "very united and patriarchal Borges family" kept themselves tightly indoors. While Norah talked, Georgie remained silent. Ramón calls him "unsociable, remote, unruly"—which for him means he is destined to become a poet. In commenting on his book, Ramón makes some perceptive observations. He discovers in Georgie's affectionate poem about the streets of Buenos Aires an echo of the equally "silent and moving" streets of Granada. He defines him as "a Góngora more conversant in things than in rhetoric" and quotes several of the poem's more striking images. Ramón's article was not only the first really important piece of criticism devoted to Georgie; it was decisive to his reputation because of the magazine in which it appeared. A second important review came out in the leading newspaper, *España;* it was signed by Enrique Díez-Canedo, one of the most perceptive critics of the new literature. All in all, Georgie's return to Spain was a success. His reputation as a young poet was certainly not small, as Borges unfairly suggests in the "Autobiographical Essay."

Georgie himself contributed two important pieces to Spanish periodicals. The first was a two-part article on metaphor published in *Alfar* (May and June–July 1924), a magazine sponsored by the Casa América de Galicia, an institute created in the north of Spain to better the relations between Latin America and the mother country. *Alfar* was at the time edited by a Uruguayan poet, Julio J. Casal, who doubled as consul of his native country. Georgie must have believed the article was worthy, because he reprinted it in his first book of essays, *Inquisiciones* (1925). It contains an elaborate defense of the role of metaphor in poetry, very much in line with ultraist theories; but what distinguishes it from others he wrote then is its approach. He begins by quoting the Spanish Luis de Granada and the French Bernard Lamy (now very much in fashion among structuralist critics) to argue that metaphors were invented to compensate for the limitations of normal language. He then proceeds to show that metaphors are scarce if nonexistent in popular poetry. Finally, he gives a general classification of metaphors. The quotations range from popular lyrics to the most unexpected learned sources (Virgil and Browning are placed next to Johannes Becher and Guillermo de Torre). Georgie's impressive range of reading and his talent for extracting the most quotable lines from a text are already evident. In future articles he repeats his basic ideas about metaphor but never again attempts such an ambitious classification.

The most important article he published in Spain at the time was one on "Quevedo's Grandeur and Defamation" in *Revista de Occidente* (October–December 1924). The great baroque poet was perhaps the most important discovery he had made during his previous visit to Spain. Other baroque writers (Cervantes, Gracián, Góngora, Villarroel) also attracted his attention, but Quevedo was the one he singled out to represent his concept of literature. In this article he is interested mainly in viewing Quevedo's work as a whole, in its excellences and limitations, as the title of the article rather elaborately indicates. Georgie stresses Quevedo's eroticism, his "fierce intellectualism," the perfection of his metaphors, antitheses, and adjectives. For Georgie, Quevedo's main virtue is to be able to "feel" the world, to be not just a part of reality but an "extra reality." The article compares Góngora's and Quevedo's schools of poetry and favors the latter: "Gongorism was an attempt urged by grammarians to alter the Castilian phrase according to the disorder of Latin; an attempt made without realizing that in Latin such a disorder is only apparent while in Spanish it would be real because of the lack of declensions. Quevedoism is psychological; it aims at restoring to all ideas the risky and abrupt character which made them astonishing the first time they came to mind."

In 1924 Georgie saw Góngora and Góngora's followers as poets exclusively interested in the formal aspect of verse; he saw Quevedo and his disciples as writers more concerned with intelligence and ideas. For him, Quevedo was chiefly interested in language as a tool of thought. Years later Borges admitted that he was wrong in believing Góngora was inferior to Quevedo (*Carriego,* 1955, p. 55). But at the time that Georgie was determined to be a poet, he saw in Quevedo a model for the kind of verse he wanted to write: a verse in which the act of thinking is itself part of the poetic subject matter. In the same article he makes an allusion that links Góngora's formal quest to the symbolists, who had greatly influenced Spanish and Spanish American poetry. In putting these two movements into the same category, Georgie also establishes a parallel link between Quevedo and the kind of ultraist poetry he was interested in.

Georgie's reading of Góngora was not popular in Spain at the time. In 1924 there were already signs of a renewal of interest in Góngora's poetry. The third centenary of his death would be celebrated in 1927 by new studies and a scholarly edition of his *Soledades,* done by a young poet, Dámaso Alonso, who was also interested in avant-garde poetry and had translated Joyce's *Portrait of the Artist as a Young Man* into Spanish.

Georgie's article on Quevedo was his first and only original contribution to *Revista de Occidente.* Perhaps he was too busy participating in Buenos Aires' hectic literary life to have time to send articles or poems to the journal. There may be another explanation. If we remember Cansinos-Asséns' rather lukewarm attitude toward Ortega and Georgie's allegiance to the Andalusian master, it is not too difficult to conjecture why he was not keen on contributing to *Revista.* Besides, he probably did not care much for Ortega's ideas about the avant-garde. In 1925 the Spanish essayist had already published his celebrated *The Dehumanization of Art,* which contained some "Ideas on the Novel" that Borges later demolished in a 1940 prologue to Adolfo Bioy Casares' *The Invention of Morel.* Perhaps already in 1924 Georgie was not terribly impressed with Ortega, and not being impressed with the Spanish master was the worst possible way to insure a permanent flow of contributions to the journal. Like any autocratic editor, Ortega was not only brilliant; he was also vain. Years later, when the Spanish essayist moved to Argentina for the duration of the Spanish civil war, Georgie avoided meeting him, although they had many friends in common.

It was during his visit to Spain in 1923–1924 that Georgie discovered Oswald Spengler's *Decline of the West.* He began to read it in the Spanish translation Ortega had sponsored, of which only two volumes had been published; eager to read it through, Georgie got the German original. Spengler's obvious debt to Nietzsche must have eased Georgie's acceptance of his apocalyptic ideas. In 1962 Borges told James E. Irby:

> Now [Spengler] is condemned for being too pessimistic, for having become a Nazi in his last years. He is being forgotten in favor of Toynbee. This may be right but I prefer Spengler. Look here: it is all right to read books for the truth they hold, but is also nice to read them for the marvelous things they contain. . . . In this way, I read Freud or Jung, for instance. Spengler was very German but he was not confined to his own country; his point of view embraced all cultures. And he was an admirable stylist, which Toynbee is not. You have to notice the poetry of German language. Observe the title of Spengler's work: *Der Untergang des Abendlandes,* which is generally translated as *The Decline of the West.* But literally it means *the going down of the evening land.* How beautiful, no? Perhaps a German-speaking person would not notice it, but those metaphors are there, in the words. (Irby, 1962, pp. 9–10)

Borges' recollection tends to minimize the impact Spengler's ideas probably had on Georgie.

By mid-1924 the Borgeses were back in Buenos Aires. For a while they stayed at the Garden Hotel. Later they moved to a two-story house closer to the downtown area than the one they had rented in 1921. It was located at 222 Avenida Quintana and had a small garden, decorated with a fountain and a nymph. A charming woodcut by Norah (reproduced in Jurado, 1964, p. 89) preserves a view of the house, which no longer exists. (It was torn down to make way for an apartment building.) The fiancée to whom Georgie had written so many sad and charming poems had suffered a metamorphosis during his absence. Her celebrated tresses had been cut, and when Georgie met her again he realized he had lost interest in her. At least that is what Mother told Alicia Jurado (ibid., p. 37). But Mother had always taken a skeptical view of Georgie's endless fiancées. In spite of his reputation as an intellectual and a bookworm, Georgie was terribly susceptible to beautiful young women. He was constantly though briefly falling madly in love.

Borges' own view of passion is ambiguous. In a 1964 interview a very old friend, Gloria Alcorta, tried to get him to speak of it:

ALCORTA: Tell me, why in your work is there so little, or nothing, about love? (*Borges stiffens, turns his face away, astonished by the question and apparently not ready to answer it.*)

BORGES: Perhaps (*he answered after a few seconds of reflection*) I was too concerned about love in my private life to talk about it in my books. Or perhaps because what really moves me in literature is the epic. For instance, I have never cried at the movies except at pirate or gangster movies, never at a sentimental one. . . .

ALCORTA: I have seen you surrounded by women.

BORGES: Then if I do not write about that subject it is out of modesty. . . . I have experienced passion like everybody else.

ALCORTA: Not like everybody. There are people incapable of passion.

BORGES: [They must be] very egotistic people, or very vain . . . or very reasonable. . . . (Alcorta, 1964, p. 404)

To another interviewer, Carlos Peralta, Borges confided that same year: "With a certain sadness, I have discovered that I've spent all my life thinking about one woman or another. I thought I was seeing countries, cities, but always there was a woman as a screen between the object and myself. Perhaps it's possible to be in love and not behave like that. I would have preferred to be able to devote myself entirely to the enjoyment of metaphysics, or linguistics, or other subjects" (Peralta, 1964, p. 410). Two years later, when María Angélica Correa asked him to comment on the fact that there were so few love poems in his works, he observed that if she looked carefully she would see that he had written many. He is right, but the poems he alludes to are not explicitly erotic, and some are cleverly disguised as translations. The best example is a two-line poem attributed in *Dreamtigers* to a certain Gasper Camerarius:

> I, who have been so many men, have never been
> The one in whose embrace Matilde Urbach swooned.
> (*Dreamtigers,* 1964, p. 92)

By placing this poem at the end of the book and, at the same time, attributing it to a nonexistent poet, Borges both affirms and denies (or tries to deny) the importance of these lines, in which the longings of carnal love are so subtly put into words. In the same interview with María Angélica Correa, he indicates that his reticence in talking openly about love is due to the fact that he is afraid of being sentimental, that he prefers to hide his emotions because he is shy. Two years later Borges was confronted again with the same question, this time worded more bluntly. The interviewers were North American journalists:

Mr. Borges, one subject very rarely, if at all, shows up in your work, and that is sex. What would you say was the reason for that?

BORGES: I suppose the reason is that I think too much about it. When I write, I try to get away from personal feelings. I suppose that's the reason. But there has to be another reason. The other reason may be that it's been worked to death, and I know that I can't say anything new or very interesting about it. Of course, you may say that the other subjects I treat have also been worked to death. For example, loneliness, identity. And yet somehow I feel that I can do more with the problems of time and identity than with what was treated by Blake when he spoke of "weaving through dreams a sexual strife, and weeping o'er the web of life." Well, I wonder if I have woven through dreams the sexual strife. I don't think so. But after all, my business is to weave dreams. I suppose I may be allowed to choose the material. (Marx and Simon, 1968, pp. 109–110)

Borges sidesteps the subject, and once more he fails to correct the statement that the subject of sex "very rarely, if at all, shows up in your work." At the time the interview was held, Borges had already published not only many erotic poems but a few stories ("The Sect of the Phoenix," "The Intruder," "Emma Zunz," "The Dead Man," "Streetcorner Man," "The Masked Dyer, Hakim of Merv," to mention only the most important) in which sex plays a decisive role. With Adolfo Bioy Casares he had written in 1946 a parody of the detective novel, "A Model for Death," in which explicit sexual slang is used. But Borges, in answering his interviewers, preserved their ignorance and preferred to discuss his own view of the subject. As usual, it involves a paradox: one writes not to describe what one thinks of obsessively but to get away from personal feelings. Borges' answer coincides almost literally with Marcel Proust's opinion on the same subject. In *Against Sainte-Beuve* Proust objected to the French critic's biographical method of analyzing a literary work, arguing that such a work does not reflect life literally. The second part of Borges' answer is less evasive and contains a clue missed by his interviewers. In quoting Blake, Borges is suggesting an answer to the riddle: sex is not explicitly presented in most of his work because it is presented in a different manner: "weaving through dreams a sexual strife." Once again, as in his conversation with Ronald Christ about "The Sect of the Phoenix," Borges approaches the repressed subject through the web of a quotation: Whitman then, now Blake. This attitude reveals the method of his writing. Just as sex is woven in the texture of his dreams, so it is woven in the texture of the quotations he uses to mask his private voice.

But if he was shy or reticent in his writings, in his private life Georgie did not hide his feelings. Two or three years after his return to Argentina he met a woman who was destined to have, forty years later, a decisive influence on him. Around 1927 Georgie regularly visited Professor Pedro Henríquez Ureña, who taught at the University of La Plata, a small town located some sixty miles to the south of Buenos Aires. Henríquez Ureña had been born in Santo Domingo but was forced into exile because dictator Trujillo was too fond of his beautiful wife. He was the most distinguished Spanish American critic and scholar of his time and a very good friend of Georgie. Among the young women who visited Henríquez Ureña's house was a seventeen-year-old girl, Elsa Astete Millán, to whom Georgie took a fancy. Apparently she did not encourage him at all and eventually married another man. But Georgie never forgot her. When she was a widow, and he a sixty-seven-year-old bachelor, they met again and married.

10.
The Battle of the Magazines

While ultraism was almost dead (if not already buried) in Spain, the avant-garde movements were just beginning to gather strength in the River Plate area. In February 1924 the first issue of *Martín Fierro* came out in Buenos Aires. This journal was to become the most popular of the little magazines. Five years earlier a periodical called *Martín Fierro* had been founded and died. The new one, in spite of using the same name and pretending to continue its approach, was a completely different publication. The first was a political review; thus it amply justified using the name of Hernández's epic hero as its title. The second *Martín Fierro* could be called political only in the first four issues, which attacked the Pope and the Argentine Catholics, the czarist Russian ambassador (still active in Argentina in spite of the October revolution), the Liga Patriótica (equivalent to the American Legion), the mayor of Buenos Aires, the Spanish immigrants from Galicia, and a few of the most famous poets of the old generation. These attacks were generally brutal and sometimes almost obscene. There was no coherent ideology behind them except for total rejection of the establishment, the Church, the army, and cultural traditions. The tone was more dadaist than ultraist, and the editors seemed interested more in destroying than in defending a new way of thinking and writing. The editor-in-chief, Evar Méndez, was a rather mild and generous provincial poet who belonged to an older group; but the real intellectual force behind the magazine was Oliverio Girondo, a young futurist poet with a wit that later verged on the macabre. After the fifth issue (May 15–June 15, 1924), the magazine concerned itself almost exclusively with cultural matters.

As soon as he had finished unpacking, Georgie began to participate in Buenos Aires' literary life. He contributed to *Martín Fierro* one of his best poems, "Montevideo" (August–September 1924), and two articles, one on Cansinos-Asséns (October–November 1924) and a second on Ramón (January 24, 1925). The poem was later included in his second book of poems; the articles were collected in *Inquisiciones*. But by August Georgie had launched his own journal, a new *Proa*. The first had been published with the help of some young poets, under the intellectual patronage of Macedonio Fernández. For the second, Georgie had the help of Ricardo Güiraldes, the most contemporary writer of the previous generation. He was thirty-eight when he met Georgie. A postsymbolist poet and short-story writer, Güiraldes had been attracted early to the avant-garde movements he had learned of on his regular visits to France. He was a wealthy man, son of a ranchowner, and knew how to combine his enthusiasm for contemporary French and German literature with an authentic if slightly exalted love for his native country. At the time he met Georgie he was known only to a few, but he was already planning the book that was to make him the most famous Argentine novelist of the first half of the century.

In his "Autobiographical Essay" Borges tells how the second *Proa* was founded:

> One afternoon, Brandán Caraffa, a young poet from Córdoba, came to see me at the Garden Hotel. He told me that Ricardo Güiraldes and Pablo Rojas Paz had decided to found a magazine that would represent the new literary generation, and that everyone had said that if that were its goal I could not possibly be left out. Naturally, I was flattered. That night, I went around to the Phoenix Hotel, where Güiraldes was staying. He greeted me with these words: "Brandán told me that the night before last all of you got together to found a magazine of young writers, and everyone said I couldn't be left out." At that moment, Rojas Paz came in and told us excitedly, "I'm quite flattered." I broke in and said, "The night before last, the three of us got together and decided that in a magazine of new writers you couldn't be left out." Thanks to this innocent stratagem, *Proa* was born. Each of us put in fifty pesos, which paid for an edition of three to five hundred copies with no misprints and on fine paper. But a year and a half and fifteen issues later, for lack of subscriptions and ads, we had to give it up. ("Essay," 1970, p. 235)

In spite of Brandán Caraffa's innocent mystification, the group worked together nicely, and *Proa* became the best little magazine of the period. Although it did not have the impact of *Martín Fierro* (its distribution was almost clandestine), from the point of view of literary coherence and quality it was superior. In a sense, there was a lot of collaboration between the two magazines. Not only did the writers who contributed to *Proa* also contribute to *Martín Fierro*, but the latter's editor-in-chief became a member of the board of directors of a new publishing house under the *Proa* imprint, founded by Güiraldes and his group. If *Martín Fierro* was too eclectic and lacked a firm purpose, *Proa* had its goals perfectly set. In his "Autobiographical Essay," discussing the friends with whom he launched all these enterprises, Borges recalls: "Behind our work was a sincerity; we felt we were renewing both prose and poetry. Of course, like all young men, I tried to be as unhappy as I could—a kind of Hamlet and Raskolnikov rolled into one. What we achieved was quite bad, but our comradeships endured" (ibid., pp. 235–236).

Among the new friends, the one who immediately gained an important place in Georgie's affection was Ricardo Güiraldes. Borges recalls his literary generosity: "I would give him a quite clumsy poem and he would read between the lines and divine what I had been trying to say but what my literary incapacity had prevented me from saying. He would then speak of the poem to other people, who were baffled not to find these things in the text" (ibid., p. 236). In spite of Borges' ironic attempt to laugh at the poetry he was then writing, his recollection shows how kind and considerate Güiraldes really was.

In his conversations with De Milleret Borges recalls other instances of Güiraldes' generosity. According to Borges, he had a very peculiar view of contemporary French literature; Güiraldes sincerely believed Valery Larbaud and Léon-Paul Fargue to be outstanding, and once he stated that "the only Valéry I knew is Valery Larbaud." Borges, obviously, did not share his opinion and believed both Fargue and Larbaud to be writers of secondary importance. But he attributed Güiraldes' devotion to them to the fact that they were his friends. Borges also recalls that Güiraldes was very loyal to the gauchos and resented Macedonio Fernández's usual jokes about them. In the same conversation with De Milleret, Borges recalls one occasion when he told Güiraldes what one of his Uruguayan relatives, Luis Melián Lafinur, had once said about the gauchos: "Our peasants lack any remarkable traits except, of course, incest." Güiraldes' reaction was patriotic: "Perhaps that was true on the Uruguayan bank but here the gaucho was a hero." Borges, of course, refused to see any heroic difference between Argentine and Uruguayan gauchos (De Milleret, 1967, pp. 43–45).

In spite of Güiraldes' naïveté, Borges respected and loved him. In his conversations with Rita Guibert he says: "I must say I have an excellent memory of Güiraldes, of his generous friendship, of his singular fate." Then he comments on the paradoxical nature of his destiny: "Güiraldes had written many books which had been taken as gentlemen's entertainments, and then, suddenly, when he published *Don Segundo Sombra,* people saw in him a great writer. . . . Thus fame, perhaps glory, came late to Güiraldes. He published *Don Segundo Sombra* in 1926 and he enjoyed the light that was projected then on him. Later he began to feel the first symptoms of illness, went to Paris, and in 1927 died of cancer" (Guibert, 1968, p. 60). Borges once told me that the first time they met, Güiraldes admitted to him that he did not know English and added: "How lucky you are that you can read *Kim* in the original." Rudyard Kipling's novel and *Huckleberry Finn* were the two models Güiraldes used for his tale of a boy who grew up to be a gaucho under the affectionate care of an older man.

A completely different version of Borges' attitude toward Güiraldes can be seen in an interview with Estela Canto published in 1949. According to her, Borges maintained toward Güiraldes

> what could be called "gentle animosity." That is, although he respects Güiraldes—everything makes us believe that he respects him in an almost objective way—he doesn't admire *Don Segundo Sombra*.
> *Don Segundo Sombra* is a good book but undoubtedly inferior to *El paisano Aguilar*. With this observation, Borges means to say that Amorim knows much more, has been much more in contact with rural life than Güiraldes. Güiraldes had a distorted view of Don Segundo. The view not of the real gaucho but of the ranchowner. The view of one who is able to see all the tragedy and the courage of being a cattle driver. Not of one who, because he is a cattle driver, sees that heroism is something natural; somebody for whom landscape exists only as something menacing or benign, not for its esthetic value. (Canto, 1949, p. 5)

Estela Canto understood why Borges took exception to the general wave of admiration that greeted Güiraldes' *Don Segundo Sombra* in Argentina and why he found Enrique Amorim's *El paisano Aguilar* a better and more accurate description of gaucho life. She also detected the subtle mixture of attraction and rejection that was at the heart of their friendship.

Being seriously ill and too absorbed in writing his novel, Güiraldes could not devote his time to *Proa;* but as he was a wealthy man, he continued to help the magazine financially and partially supported the publishing house that had the same imprint. (It was that house which later published *Don Segundo Sombra* in book form.) In August 1925 he sent a letter to his younger friends announcing his departure. The ultraist poet Francisco Luis Bernárdez (another contributor to *Martín Fierro*) replaced him after the twelfth issue. The magazine's last issue was its fifteenth (January 1926). In it, an ironical letter signed by Georgie announced its death. The letter was later included in his second book of essays, *El tamaño de mi esperanza* (The Dimension of My Hope, 1926). The best part of the letter is its description of an editorial meeting. According to Georgie, Güiraldes played the guitar while Brandán Caraffa (who was very small) made a paper airplane out of one of his long verses and let it fly and Macedonio Fernández hid behind a cigarette his power of inventing and destroying a whole world in the time it takes to sip through two matés. Georgie also recalled other fellow poets: Pablo Rojas Paz, Francisco Luis Bernárdez, and Leopoldo Marechal, among the Argentine ultraists; Pedro Leandro Ipuche, among the Uruguayans. In spite of the affectionate tone, the letter ends on a chilly note of defiant acceptance of defeat. Georgie, admitting that each one of them would probably go his own way, says that "one hundred streets on the outskirts are waiting for me, with their moon, their loneliness, and some strong liquor." The last words are addressed to Güiraldes' wife, Adelina del Carril: Georgie asks for the hat and the cane he is sure she will deliver with her usual grace.

If at the beginning *Proa* had been the work of many, in the last issues it was mainly the work of Georgie. It was proper then that he sign the magazine's "certificate of death." For a while rumors of the revival of *Proa* under Georgie's sole editorship appeared in Buenos Aires' literary magazines. But it never happened. By the time the second *Proa* had come to an end, Georgie was too involved in his own work.

To the second *Proa* Georgie contributed three sets of poems, three reviews, and seventeen articles. The majority of these items were later collected in his second volume of poetry, *Luna de enfrente* (Moon Across the Way, 1925), and his first two volumes of essays, *Inquisiciones* (1925) and *El tamaño de mi esperanza* (1926). The range of the articles is wide: Georgie comments on his fellow ultraists' poetry, on the new gaucho verses being written in Uruguay, on some neglected baroque writers (Torres Villarroel, a disciple of Quevedo, and Sir Thomas Browne, a writer totally unknown in Latin America); he reviews some new works such as James Joyce's *Ulysses,* whose last page he translates for the magazine. In all he wrote then, a preoccupation with the new and an original reading of the old are blended. Georgie was already more concerned with discovering what was still alive in Argentine tradition than with being totally up to date. Both in his poetry and in his more important articles he attempted to capture the essence of a certain Argentine tone of voice, a form of the national identity that had been ignored by those who wanted the country to be progressive and modern. On the contrary, he found the real Argentina in gaucho poetry and in the humble outskirts of Buenos Aires. But he also rejected the folklorists' reactionary attempt to re-create a dead past. His recovery of the past was done by intuition and feeling, by an imaginative projection into an extra dimension of time.

If in his "Autobiographical Essay" Borges recalls his comrades with affection, he does not display the same warmth in remembering the group that edited *Martín Fierro:* "I disliked what *Martín Fierro* stood for, which was the French idea that literature is being continually renewed—that Adam is reborn every morning—and also for the idea that, since Paris had literary cliques that wallowed in publicity and bickering, we should be up to date and do the same. One result of this was that a sham literary feud was cooked up in Buenos Aires—that between Florida and Boedo" ("Essay," 1970, p. 236). Florida is still today a busy commercial street in downtown Buenos Aires, next to the theater and movie district, filled with cafés and bars, foreign bookshops, and art galleries. To find an equivalent of what Florida represented in the 1920s it would be necessary to imagine a street that combined Fifth Avenue with Broadway and 42nd Street (minus the porno shops). Boedo, on the other hand, was in a working-class neighborhood and stood for a kind of proletarian literature. In the same recollections Borges readily admits:

> I'd have preferred to be in the Boedo group, since I was writing about the old Northside and slums, sadness, and sunsets. But I was informed by one of the two conspirators—they were Ernesto Palacio, of Florida, and Roberto Mariani, of Boedo—that I was already one of the Florida warriors and that it was too late for me to change. The whole thing was just a put-up job. Some writers belonged to both groups—Roberto Arlt and Nicolás Olivari, for example. This sham is now taken into serious consideration by "credulous universities." But it was partly publicity, partly a boyish prank. (Ibid., p. 236)

There was more than a sophomoric prank in the artificial division of young Argentine writers into two rival groups. The publicity stunt was part of a determined effort by some writers more or less connected with the emerging Argentine Communist Party to gain control of or destroy the avant-grade movement. By dividing the new literature along party lines, Roberto Mariani, a novelist and short-story writer, was trying to call attention to his own brand of proletarian realism. In open letters sent to *Martín Fierro* and in their promotion of the mock rivalry, Mariani and his friends encouraged confrontation.

Borges, who preferred a simple, elemental view of Argentine reality, felt closer to the so-called proletarian writers of Boedo. But they rejected him for his patrician origins, for his European sophistication, and for his concept of literature as nonpolitical. On the other hand, the Boedo group attempted to enroll the novelist and playwright Roberto Arlt because of his proletarian origins and in spite of the fact that he had been Güiraldes' secretary and contributed regularly to the establishment's literary pages. The lines were thus drawn by Mariani and the Boedo group not according to literary affiliation but according to a purely political evaluation of a writer's class origins.

At the time, in a famous 1928 manifesto, the Russian formalists Jurii Tynianov and Roman Jakobsen had criticized this view; but Argentine leftists were not at all interested in a serious discussion of the problem such as was then taking place in the Soviet Union between the formalists on one side and Stalin's commissars on the other. They also ignored the polemics that currently divided the French surrealists. Their only concern was to stir up a bogus feud between Florida and Boedo. The dispute was unimportant and even ridiculous from a purely literary point of view, but its effect on Argentine literary history has been lasting. Even today the dispute is presented as an authentic confrontation between equal champions and not as a purely strategical gambit invented by leftist writers to gain notoriety and take control of the avant-garde.

Although *Martín Fierro* sidestepped the political side of the feud, it could not ignore some of the leftists' attacks and retaliated with vigor and humor against the old-fashioned realism the Boedo group was hailing as future proletarian literature. Another dispute that occupied the *Martín Fierro* contributors was even more grotesque. *La Gaceta Literaria,* a new magazine launched in Spain in 1927 with Guillermo de Torre, the champion of ultraism, as assistant editor, published an article which claimed that the "literary meridian" of Spanish America passed through Madrid. The metaphor and the article belonged to De Torre. *Martín Fierro*'s contributors reacted swiftly (June 10–July 10, 1927, pp. 6–7). Unanimously they claimed that from the Argentine point of view Paris and London were then more important than Madrid, and that as early as the turn of the century Spanish American poetry had begun to influence Spanish poetry, not the other way around. They could have also claimed that it was through the offices of Huidobro and Borges, as much as through Ramón Gómez de la Serna and Cansinos-Asséns, that avant-garde literature was finally being accepted in Spain. The discussion continued through articles in *La Gaceta* and *Martín Fierro*. De Torre apologized for his mistake. The only reasonable voice came from Miguel de Unamuno, who observed in a private letter—published in *Carátula* (Mask, October 1, 1927) and immediately reproduced in *Martín Fierro* (November 15, 1927, p. 10)—that the dispute was based on a mistake: if De Torre had said that the "publishing" meridian of Spanish America passed through Madrid, nobody would have objected because it was a fact that Spanish publishers dominated the book market. But to talk about a "literary" meridian smacked of imperialism. Georgie's contribution to the polemics was a short but barbed article in *Martín Fierro* (June 10–July 10, 1927,

p. 9) in which he enumerates chaotically and with comic effect the many instances that prove how badly Madrid understands Spanish America: the Castilians cannot play a tango without first removing its soul; they are unable to distinguish a Mexican from a Uruguayan accent; they believe that the adjective "invidious" can be used as a word of praise. After a parting shot about the Spanish obsession with "gallicisms" (words taken from the French, which Spanish academicians abhor), Georgie stresses his decision to keep intact his good memories of Madrid, although the time is not for sweet words but for truths.

Borges tends today to dismiss the *Martín Fierro* group and to emphasize his dislike for their concept of literature, fashioned on Paris and its literary coteries. But Georgie contributed actively and generously to the magazine. At least twenty-two pieces have been recorded by bibliographers. They include poems (three), articles (twelve), and reviews (seven). In addition, he participated anonymously in a popular section called the "Satirical Parnassus," in which the editors aired their prejudices in comic and sometimes outrageous epitaphs in verse. He also contributed to a translation by "B.M." of a Rudyard Kipling poem dedicated to Argentina (March 28, 1927, p. 4). It was a hoax perpetrated by Georgie and a friend (Leopoldo Marechal or Evar Méndez) to poke fun at Argentine nationalism. Kipling's well-known jingoism was the basis of the parody.

Like all avant-garde groups, the contributors to *Martín Fierro* loved to attract attention by organizing literary gatherings and banquets to celebrate the launching of a book or the arrival of some transatlantic guest. No less than eight banquets are registered in the pages of *Martín Fierro:* there were banquets in honor of the Uruguayan painter Pedro Figari, who used a distinctly fauvist technique (August–September, 1924); Jules Supervielle, the Franco-Uruguayan poet (January 24, 1925); *Martín Fierro*'s own editor, Evar Méndez (May 5, 1925); the futurist poet Oliverio Girondo (May 17, 1925); F. T. Marinetti, the futurist leader who was visiting Argentina (July 8, 1926); Ernest Ansermet, the Swiss composer and conductor (October 5, 1926); and Alfonso Reyes, the Mexican humanist who had been appointed ambassador to Buenos Aires (August 31–November 15, 1927). There was even a banquet to celebrate simultaneously the launching of Georgie's second book of poems, *Luna de enfrente,* and Sergio Piñero's book of travel chronicles, *El puñal de Orión* (Orion's Knife). On this last occasion Georgie contributed a comic poem called "The Aura with Lunch and Other Misprints," which he has mercifully left out of his collections of poems.

In these celebrations, dutifully recorded by chronicles and photographs in *Martín Fierro*'s pages, the dark, round, and rather sad face of Georgie almost always appears. At the banquet for Evar Méndez he is seen seated in the first row while the supposedly Boedo novelist Roberto Arlt is among those standing in the back; at the Girondo banquet Georgie shares the same back row with Roberto Mariani, the inventor of the Florida–Boedo feud and one of the so-called proletarian novelists.

If *Martín Fierro* was successful as propaganda, from a purely literary point of view it was too eclectic to have a lasting influence. Georgie generally selected his most ephemeral or journalistic pieces for the magazine, keeping the more thoughtful or poetic ones for publication in his own *Proa* or in other journals. By the mid-1920s he had developed into a full-fledged professional writer. Apart from the magazines already mentioned, he contributed regularly to the literary pages of *La Prensa,* one of the largest Latin American newspapers, and to a new journal, *Síntesis* (Synthesis), which was launched in June 1927 by a group of writers of diverse tendencies. Georgie's name was included last on the masthead. To it he contributed mainly literary articles and reviews. But the initial avant-garde enthusiasm was beginning to wane. The so-called revolution of 1930, in which the army took over the Argentine government, put an end to *Síntesis* and also to the period. Ultraism was dead, and the sordid realities of Argentina's political life were becoming too obvious to be ignored. The partying was over.

11.
The Return of the Native

"For many years," Borges told Rita Guibert, "I was the most secret writer in Buenos Aires" (Guibert, 1968, p. 55). But on his return from Europe in 1924 he became the acknowledged leader of the young and one of the most public writers in Argentina's literary history. As a founder of magazines (the two *Proas*) and as a frequent contributor to some of the most important little reviews (*Martín Fierro, Inicial, Valoraciones*) as well as to established periodicals (*Nosotros, La Prensa, Criterio*), Georgie became the most ubiquitous writer of that time and place.

That was only one part of his incredible activity. Before the decade was over he had published two more volumes of poetry (*Luna de enfrente*, 1925; *Cuaderno San Martín* [San Martín Copybook], 1929), three volumes of essays (*Inquisiciones*, 1925; *El tamaño de mi esperanza*, 1926; *El idioma de los argentinos* [The Language of the Argentines], 1928) and had already begun writing a literary biography of Evaristo Carriego, which he published in 1930. His poems were included in three anthologies of the period: Julio Noé's academic *Antología de la poesía argentina moderna: 1900–1925,* published by the conservative magazine *Nosotros* (1926); the avant-garde but chaotic *Indice de la nueva poesía americana,* edited by the Peruvian Alberto Hidalgo (1926), and the youthful *Exposición de la actual poesía argentina: 1922–1927,* compiled by Pedro-Juan Vignale and César Tiempo (1927).

In all three anthologies Georgie's poems have an important place. The least conspicuous is, of course, the one assigned to him in Noé's compilation. The book was aimed at reinforcing the establishment's view of contemporary Argentine poetry. The place of honor was given to Leopoldo Lugones, a major Latin American symbolist who was still active in the 1920s. He favored standard metrical patterns and rhyme, used a vast, bookish vocabulary, and in spite of having very little Greek had "translated" Homer and written about the classics. The young poets attacked him without mercy and, generally, without taste. He replied with disdain or with poetical decrees.

At the time, Georgie sided with his young friends, although he used to take his books to Lugones, who always thanked him and never said a word about them. Lugones also sent his books to Georgie. But there was no dialogue. In his 1967 interview with César Fernández Moreno, Borges recalls some of the occasions on which he met Lugones. He was

> a solitary and dogmatic man, a man who did not open up easily. . . . Conversation was difficult with him because he used to bring everything to a close with a phrase which was literally a period. . . . Then you had to begin again, to find another subject. . . . And that subject was also dissolved with a period. . . . His kind of conversation was brilliant but tiresome. And many times his assertions had nothing to do with what he really believed; he just had to say something extraordinary. . . . What he wanted was to control the conversation. Everything he said was final. And . . . we had a great respect for him. (Fernández Moreno, 1967, pp. 10–11)

In a photograph (reproduced in Jurado, 1964, p. 97) of a meeting of the Sociedad Argentina de Escritores (Argentine Society of Writers), which was chaired by Lugones, Georgie can be seen standing respectfully in the rear and looking down. Was he ashamed of participating in the activities of the literary establishment? Perhaps. But he was not always so respectful. Barely one year after that photograph was taken Georgie contributed to a parody on one of Lugones' celebrated "Romances"; it was published in *Martín Fierro* (July 8, 1926) under the pseudonym Mar-Bor-Vall-Men, which barely hid the names of *Mare*-chal, *Bor*ges, *Vall*ejo, and *Mén*dez. Today, the parody seems sophomoric. The quartet plays with Lugones' name and produces a ridiculous variant, "Leogoldo Lupones," with the stress on "goldo" (a childish pronunciation of *gordo*, fat) and "lupones" (*lupo*, wolf). Lugones was not fat or particularly wolfish.

Lugones also became the recipient of another type of attack. In 1925 in a speech in Lima he had stated bluntly his mistrust of politicians and his preference for military regimes. He had coined the phrase "It is the hour of the sword," which became a rallying cry for all the rightest elements in Argentina. Although the ultraists abstained from attacking him on political grounds, his reactionary ideology further alienated him from a group that was more sympathetic to anarchism than to authoritarianism. But the real disagreement with Lugones was based on a different conception of what poetry ought to be. From that point of view, Georgie must have hated Noé's anthology. In spite of having used some of his best poems, the editor was obviously an established man and devoted sixty-six pages to Lugones, while thirty young poets were packed into 121 pages (Georgie got six and a half).

The Hidalgo anthology, on the contrary, excluded all established poets. It meant to be an index of new Spanish American poetry and at the outset featured three polemical prologues. The first was signed by the editor and attacked "Hispano-Americanism" as a foolish political notion; Hidalgo paraded his anarchism and in general made a fool of himself. In the second prologue the Chilean Vicente Huidobro used aphorisms to defend the new poetry and the need to be constantly creative. The third prologue was written by Georgie and summarized his views of ultraism, the metaphor, and the new kind of Spanish written in Argentina. He made a rather unkind reference to Lugones, describing him as a foreigner with a tendency to make everything Greek, fond of vague landscapes built exclusively out of rhymes. Georgie's poems were allotted the same space as in Noé's anthology, but nobody else got much more. Today the Hidalgo anthology is a bibliographical rarity and also a curiosity. For the first time the important young poets of Spanish America were gathered under one roof: the Chileans Huidobro, Pablo de Rokha, and Neruda; the Peruvians César Vallejo and Juan Parra del Riego; the Mexican Salvador Novo; the Uruguayan Fernán Silva Valdés; the Argentines Borges and Ricardo Molinari. A few older poets were also included—the Mexican José Juan Tablada and the Argentines Macedonio Fernández and Ricardo Güiraldes—but they were closer to the young than to the writers of their own generation.

The third anthology was almost exclusively a young poets' book; in it Georgie had six pages. The short autobiographical note that introduces his poems is written with humor and contains at least two inaccuracies: he claimed to have been born in 1900 and to have visited Spain for the first time in 1918. He had said the same in Noé's anthology. Probably Georgie was trying to use round figures. It is hard to believe that at twenty-eight he was trying to pass for twenty-seven. But the small mystification is typical of his disdain for precision. At the back of the book a list of the poets' professions and addresses informs the reader: "Jorge Luis Borges, Polyglot. Av. Quintana 222, B.A."

By the late 1920s it was obvious in Buenos Aires that Georgie was the most important young poet there and a leader of the avant-garde writers. He was respected by the establishment, loved by the ultraists, attacked by the Boedo group. *Martín Fierro*'s "Satirical Parnassus" includes some comic epitaphs about him. The best is the one that, in alluding to the two magazines he edited under the same name, *Proa* (Prow), calls him "the man with two *Prows*" (September–October 1924, p. 12). Georgie's reputation for being finicky in matters of grammar is reflected in another epitaph which claims that he was killed by the Inquisition because he omitted one comma (August 5, 1925, p. 8). Still another epitaph (September 25, 1925, p. 8) pokes fun at his peculiar spelling, especially his tendency to omit the final *d* in any word. (It is seldom pronounced in Andalusia and the River Plate area, although it is dutifully used in writing.) The epitaph is signed "D." Sometimes Georgie's friends were less than kind; in a section called "Tall Tales" there is a line that begins "Borges saw . . .," in which his near blindness is unmercifully stressed. The final issue of *Martín Fierro* carried on its last page a parting epitaph by Leopoldo Marechal that alludes to Georgie's interest in baroque poetry (Argote is Góngora's second surname):

> Here lies, professor of dreams,
> Jorge Luis Quevedo y Argote.
> Rhetoric lost her master.
> To galvanize him is a vain task:
> He died for the lack of a mustache.
> (*Martin Fierro*,
> August 31–November 15, 1927, p. 14)

The Boedo group was less sprightly. In a magazine ponderously called *Los Pensadores* (The Thinkers) they celebrated the termination of the second *Proa:*

> The contributors to that magazine—if one can give that name to a catalogue of jokes—belong to a fortunately small number of Sarrasani-type writers [Sarrasani was the owner of a famous circus of the time]. They all try to make you laugh, and those who are serious really succeed. Superior to that magazine was the one published by the sane inmates of the state insane asylum. At least there was nobody there who claimed to have discovered the hole in the maté gourd, as did the popular troubador J. L. Borges, because that is what that type wants to prove by writing "espaciosidá" ["espaciosidad"] and "falsiada" ["falseada"] to sound native; and, who knows, with all that jingle and all that silliness, perhaps he doesn't even know how to ride a horse. (*Los Pensadores,* February 1926)

Georgie's discovery of his native town was beginning to annoy a group that pretended to be the sole arbiter of what was and was not truly national. Georgie did not bother to reply.

At the time, he was seriously interested in recovering some lost elements of the Argentine past. He went about this in a rather excessive way perhaps, but there is no doubt about his sincerity. In a sense, what he was trying to do was to integrate his personality, to claim the other side of his inheritance, which had been neglected by his English education and his French and Latin studies in Geneva, his knowledge of several languages, and his avid reading of foreign literature. Returning to Argentina, he felt like a prodigal son. He plunged into the space of Buenos Aires and into the past of those River Plate provinces with the enthusiasm of a convert. He began to spend evenings in pursuit of the remnants of an old Buenos Aires he could find only in the southern district or on the old Northside. He cultivated acquaintanceship with some hoodlums who talked, nostalgically, about the days when everybody admitted to at least one death. He learned to dance the tango and to drink the hard local liquor known as *caña*. Perhaps there was a touch of snobbery in all of it: slumming was then, as now, an activity practiced by the middle and upper classes as part of the exacting business of killing time. But it was more than that for Georgie. It was also a way out of the confined and sweetly repressive atmosphere at home. Father and Mother corresponded too closely to the prototypes of bourgeois respectability, and Georgie, in his late twenties, was experiencing a sort of delayed adolescent rebellion. Father was less strict, of course, and the episode with the young prostitute in Geneva may have established a tacit masculine complicity between the two of them. But if visiting prostitutes or even having an affair was tolerated in polite society, as long as it was done with tact and no visible consequences, to go regularly to the slums and write enthusiastically about them was not admissible. The times were still very hypocritical, and bourgeois morality wanted things done in a certain discreet way.

How far did Georgie go in his explorations of the slums? Although he has given many hints in his writings of the period, he is as usual reticent about the details. To find out more it is necessary to refer to a *roman à clef* written by a friend of the ultraist period, the poet Leopoldo Marechal, who produced in his novel *Adán Buenosayres* (1948) a portrait of the times. Marechal had been Georgie's accomplice in some of the most dadaist happenings sponsored by *Martín Fierro*. Once, to celebrate the bearded Ernest Ansermet, they and a group of friends wore false beards for the occasion (October 5, 1926, pp. 7 and 12). Marechal also wrote some of the best epitaphs for Georgie's *Inquisiciones* and reviewed *Luna de enfrente* (December 29, 1925, p. 4) in the most flattering terms. He claimed that the book was "the best argument against the old-fashioned theories of Lugones" and praised "the virile affirmation of its verses." Ten issues later (December 12, 1926, p. 8) Georgie, in turn, praised Marechal's *Días como flechas* (Days Like Arrows) and maintained that such a book "adds days and nights to reality." They also contributed to two merciless parodies: the one of Lugones already mentioned, and one of Enrique Larreta, the author of *La gloria de Don Ramiro,* who had published a new novel, *Zogoibi,* about an unhappy gaucho.

When Marechal began writing his novel in the late 1920s, his aim was to recapture in a vast book, loosely inspired by *Ulysses,* the flavor of those days. He was then living in Paris, and the self-imposed exile stimulated his recollections. But the book was put aside on his return to Argentina and was not completed until twenty years later. By then the ultraist movement had been forgotten, Georgie was Borges, and Marechal had developed into an important figure in both the Catholic and Peronist establishment. The novel suffered from the delay. Instead of a celebration of friendship, of adventure, of a collective madness, it became a subconscious retaliation against a time and a place Marechal believed he had loved but had in truth hated. Under thinly disguised names and features, the ultraists are pictured as incompetent, crass, and stupid loafers whose only merit is to provide a chorus for the protagonist, a romantic projection of Marechal as a Young Catholic Artist of unrecognized genius. Georgie is reduced to a caricature under the name of "Luis Pereda." The character is introduced as one of a small group of revelers, young poets obsessed with folklore and especially with the tango. He is described as rather stout and walking like a blind wild boar, searching rather ineffectively through a stack of records for one on which the authentic nasal voice of a primitive tango singer could be heard (Marechal, 1948, pp. 152–153). His friends are not too impressed with his act. One of them, Frank Admundsen (perhaps Francisco Luis Bernárdez in real life), makes an unkind remark: "They've sent him to Oxford to read Greek, to the Sorbonne to read literature, to Zurich to read philosophy, and he comes back to Buenos Aires to get up to his ears in a sort of phonographic nativism! Psh! The guy's crazy!" (ibid., p. 154). (Marechal knew, of course, that Georgie had never studied at Oxford, the Sorbonne, or Zurich, but he was trying to disguise the facts a bit.) Later Frank insists: "A pitiful madman! . . . If he is not a terminal case of intellectual masturbation, I'll eat my hat!" The presentation is unkind, although it does not bother "Pereda," who continues to listen to the scratchy record and laugh. Throughout the 741-page novel "Luis Pereda" is presented in the same sophomoric vein. His protuberant mouth is described as a "nobly aggressive mug" (p. 155). His walks through the poorer quarters of the city, whistling some old tango while meditating on the future avatars of Buenos Aires hoodlums, are recalled (p. 193). He is seen reciting some mildly erotic country song (pp. 203–204), attending a wake with his friends (pp. 266–286), or getting drunk with them and visiting a brothel from which they are expelled before they can perform any practical function except to talk their heads off (pp. 326–348). The only descriptions of "Luis Pereda" are scornful: "philosopher of nativism" (p. 291); "grammarian" (p. 291); "pocket agnostic," spoiled by his Calvinist education in Geneva (p. 306). (This time Marechal forgot he had "Pereda" studying philosophy at Zurich.) The culmination of the novel is a long dream sequence in which the protagonist visits an allegorical version of Buenos Aires. It is a hell divided (like Dante's) into circles according to the seven deadly sins. In the seventh, which is devoted to those who have been ravaged by wrath, and among the "pseudogogs" or false teachers, "Luis Pereda" is accused by the False Euterpe (the muse of music and lyrical poetry) of acting like a hoodlum: walking the slums of Buenos Aires with a killer's slanted stare, spitting out of the corner of his mouth, and mumbling with clenched teeth the imperfectly learned lyrics of a tango (p. 665). The False Euterpe adds that "Pereda" attempted to bring to literature "his mystico-slummy effusions, to the point of inventing a false mythology in which Buenos Aires hoodlums reach not only heroic proportions but even vague metaphysical outlines" (p. 665).

Perhaps Marechal was only trying to evoke the sophomoric atmosphere of *Martín Fierro* and the "Satirical Parnassus"—as he has pleaded in his article "Keys to *Adán Buenosayres*" (Marechal, 1966, p. 133)—but the jokes had become stale. Besides, in 1948 the circumstances were different. In 1924–1927 everybody was young and more or less shared the same ideas. When *Adán Buenosayres* was published some twenty years later, both Borges and Marechal were closer to fifty than to twenty-five and were radically opposed politically. As a Catholic and a Peronist, Marechal had been on the side of the Fascists and the Nazis during World War II, while Borges had defended the Allied cause and attacked Hitler and Mussolini long before 1939. The fact that Marechal was part of the establishment and Borges had been abruptly dismissed in 1946 by the Peronists from his modest position in a municipal library only helped to stress the differences. Marechal's cold jokes had a sinister meaning in the Buenos Aires of 1948; they smack of the jokes benevolent executioners tend to make. At least that was the way they were read then. The image of "Luis Pereda" as a fake regionalist, a bad poet, and a sissy was precisely the image of Borges that the Boedo group and its descendants, the Peronist literati, were promoting. But the real Georgie was far more complex and elusive than the inane "Luis Pereda" Marechal had sketched. His regionalism had other roots. The native had returned, but not just to the Argentina of the 1920s.

12.
A Theory of Regionalism

Looking back on this period of his literary life in his "Autobiographical Essay," Borges asserts that it

> was one of great activity, but much of it was perhaps reckless and even pointless. . . . This productivity now amazes me as much as the fact that I feel only the remotest kinship with the work of these years. Three of the four essay collections—whose names are best forgotten—I have never allowed to be reprinted. In fact, when in 1953 my present publisher—Emecé—proposed to bring out my "complete writings," the only reason I accepted was that it would allow me to keep those preposterous volumes suppressed. ("Essay," 1970, p. 230)

About one of those collections, *El tamaño de mi esperanza* (The Dimension of My Hope, 1926), he has this to say: "I tried to be as Argentine as I could. I got hold of Segovia's dictionary of Argentinisms and worked in so many local words that many of my countrymen could hardly understand it. Since I have mislaid the dictionary, I'm not sure I would any longer understand the book myself, and so have given it up as utterly hopeless" (ibid., p. 231). In spite of his warnings, we must turn to these books to find out what his regionalism was about.

The first collection contains many pieces on ultraism, expressionism, and metaphor, and on the young and old masters of the avant-garde. The title Georgie chose for it, *Inquisiciones* (Inquisitions), plays on the etymological sense of the word, which is even more evident in another word of the same family: inquiry. But the title also reveals one of Georgie's interests at the time: the search for the Latin roots of Spanish words. In the "Autobiographical Essay" he condemns the book by stating:

203

When I wrote these pieces [on Sir Thomas Browne, the metaphor, the nonexistence of the ego], I was trying to play the sedulous age to two Spanish baroque seventeenth-century writers, Quevedo and Saavedra Fajardo, who stood in their own stiff, arid, Spanish way for the same kind of writing as Sir Thomas Browne in "Urne-Buriall." I was doing my best to write Latin in Spanish, and the book collapses under the sheer weight of its involutions and sententious judgments. (Ibid., p. 231)

Borges is right about the style, but he is too negative in his evaluation of *Inquisiciones*. There is more in it than what he recalls. In the first place, a note at the end of the volume suggests that Georgie was already convinced that current rhetoric was not adequate to discuss modern literature, and that a new rhetoric was necessary: "What has always been the aim of my writing is a rhetoric that would have its point of departure not in adjusting today's literature to forms already fixed by classical doctrine but in the direct examination of it, and that would categorize the *greguería* [Ramón's own brand of dadaist aphorisms], the confessional novel, and the contemporary use of traditional figures. 'Examination of Metaphors' is a chapter of that possible rhetoric" (*Inquisiciones*, 1925, p. 160). Today Borges may ridicule that article, recalling that it "set out to classify metaphors as though other poetic elements, such as rhythm and music, could be safely ignored" ("Essay," 1970, p. 231). Lugones raised the same objections at the time. But what Borges misses is the other aspect of that article: the attempt to create a new rhetoric. From that point of view, the article is the forerunner of pieces written by Borges in the 1930s and 1940s to categorize the new type of fiction he was already writing. In attempting to explore new rhetorical paths, Georgie was doing exactly what Pound and Eliot had done in the previous decade: developing a critical theory to suit his poetical experiments.

There is another article in *Inquisiciones* which Borges now passes over in silence but which at the time had some relevance. It is devoted to Joyce's *Ulysses*, a book then known to Hispanic readers largely by reputation. (The Spanish translation did not appear until 1948.) Georgie claims to be the "first Hispanic traveler to have reached Joyce's book," which he presents under the metaphor of "a tangled and uncouth country." At the same time, he has no qualms about admitting he has not read the entire book. To justify himself he says: "I confess not having cleared away the seven hundred pages which constitute it, I confess having experienced it only in bits; nevertheless, I know what it is, with the adventurous and legitimate certitude that one has when stating one's knowledge of a city without pretending to know intimately all its streets" (*Inquisiciones*, 1925, pp. 20–21). He then gives a short biographical sketch of Joyce and a brief evaluation of the book, whose perfect amalgam of dream and reality he seems to admire; he also praises the lack of distinction between what is important and what is ephemeral in everyday life. He quotes Kant and Schopenhauer and concludes that "Minerva's olive tree projects a longer shadow on its pages than [Apollo's] laurel," which is an elaborate way of saying that it is more an intellectual than a poetic book. For Georgie, total reality is alive in *Ulysses:* both the reality of the flesh and the reality of the soul. He praises Joyce for his success in achieving the concrete presence of things and can find a parallel only in Ramón's own concrete books. He singles out Chapter 15 (the brothel scene) for its hallucinating felicity and comments enthusiastically on the wealth of words and styles the book possesses. To conclude his review, he quotes Lope de Vega's comment about Góngora as a way of indicating the baroque affiliation of *Ulysses.* (In summarizing Joyce's biography, Georgie points out that Joyce had been taught by Jesuits, masters of the baroque style.)

Among the pieces collected in *Inquisiciones* are four that reveal Georgie's early preoccupation with native reality. The first is devoted to one of the most prolific of nineteenth-century Argentine poets, Hilario Ascasubi, who fought against Rosas' dictatorship and wrote a long, rambling poem, *Santos Vega,* about a gaucho troubador. One essay is dedicated to Pedro Leandro Ipuche and one to Fernán Silva Valdés, both of whom have continued and updated the tradition of gaucho poetry in Uruguay. The last piece attempts to define a native Argentine. What Georgie praises in Ascasubi and finds still very much alive in Ipuche and Silva Valdés is a certain leisurely attitude toward life and literature, a striving not for perfection or intensity but for the reader's friendship. Ascasubi (who wrote the better part of his work in his old age while living in Paris) seems to Georgie to be an old gentleman who, in talking, takes care to pronounce every syllable distinctly and likes to evoke the past with a few grave, scornful undertones. His fate was to inspire some of the best pages of his disciple, Estanislao del Campo, and of the real master of gaucho poetry, José Hernández, the author of *Martín Fierro.* But in his imperfect verses Georgie detects a tone of voice he likes and a true, deep knowledge of the countryside and the gauchos. In the last page of his article on Ipuche, Georgie acknowledges his own limitations: "I have felt the shame of my blurred condition as inhabitant of a city" (ibid., p. 60). He also confirms what his poems state: his sadness on hearing a guitar, his love for the deep patios of old houses.

In these limitations and that nostalgia for a past that belongs to his forefathers can be found the roots of Georgie's regionalism. The last article on the subject makes it explicit. In the same way he had rejected in his poems the bustling, modern Buenos Aires of the downtown area in favor of the humble outskirts or the proletarian districts, he now rejects the conventional image of the native Argentine (a noisy patriot with an aggressive concept of progress) in favor of the real image. According to Georgie, the native Argentine prefers silence to verbal excess, is reticent and ironic. That attitude springs from a certain determinism which encourages a lack of illusion. The same traits can be recognized in Argentina's native poetry. The Spaniard's original vehemence seems there subdued; the language is softer, the images more austere. As in the best tradition of Spanish literature (*Don Quixote* is proof), failure is exalted, and suffering and nostalgia become the permanent themes of Argentine popular poetry. In quoting examples of the kind of verses he prefers, Georgie goes back to Estanislao del Campo and José Hernández, and even praises one aspect of Lugones: his reticence. He also includes William Henry Hudson (who wrote in English but was very Argentine) in his list of favorite writers. At the time Georgie wrote these essays, nativism did not imply the necessity to accept a showy nationalism. Also, it had not been contaminated by the excesses of the folklorists. What he saw in the old Argentina were the values and virtues of his own forefathers, the men who had fought for independence and were too proud and gentlemanly to boast about it. Georgie's nativism really implied a return to his own family roots. Even in praising some minor Uruguayan poets he was reclaiming one part of his heritage, the part Mother had brought to the family.

In the second book of essays Georgie further defines his nativism. The first article, "The Dimension of My Hope," gives its title to the whole volume and constitutes a sort of manifesto. In examining what is really native in Argentina, Georgie addresses himself to those readers who believe they are going to live and die in that land, not to "those who believe that the sun and the moon are in Europe" (*Tamaño,* 1926, p. 5). A summary of what the Argentines had achieved historically and literally follows. Once more he mentions Estanislao del Campo and José Hernández, and he now adds Sarmiento, Lucio V. Mansilla, and Eduardo Wilde to the honors list. The tango gets special mention because it summarizes that whole world of hoodlums and easy women, Saturday nights in the slums, and a certain way of walking that is almost dancing. In this century he finds only Evaristo Carriego, Macedonio Fernández, and Ricardo Güiraldes worth praising. He believes rather modestly that Argentina is poor in creativity: "Not one single mystic or metaphysician . . . has been engendered in this land! Our greatest man is still Juan Manuel [de Rosas]: a great example of the individual's strength, with a great confidence in his own capacity for life, but unable to build anything spiritual, and dominated by his own tyrannical power and his bureaucratic instincts" (ibid., pp. 7–8). He goes on to emphasize the difference between the greatness of true Argentine life and the barrenness of its intellectual reality. After quoting Emerson (an 1844 speech on the literary future of America), he comes to the conclusion that "Buenos Aires is already more than a city; it is a country and it is necessary to find the poetry and the music and the painting and the religion and the metaphysics which are suited to its greatness. That is the dimension of my hope, which invites every one of us to become like gods and to work to make possible its reality" (ibid., p. 9). In a last paragraph he rejects the usual Argentine view of progress (an attempt to be "almost" North American or European; that is, to be somebody else) and the usual concept of nativism, or regionalism, which to him is a concept similar to that used to define the reaction of men on horseback to those who do not know how to ride. Now it expresses only nostalgia for a pastoral life that is no longer possible. Georgie feels the need to enlarge the concept to make nativism a return not just to a lost golden age but to a reality that includes the whole external world and the ego, God, and death.

The book itself illustrates this program. Although it includes some pieces on subjects that have little to do with regionalism—"A History of the Angels," a review of a novel by Cansinos-Asséns, a review of Shaw's *Saint Joan,* an essay on Wilde's "The Ballad of Reading Gaol," a discussion of one line by Apollinaire, a commentary on Milton's condemnation of rhyme, an examination of a sonnet by Góngora, a discussion of the infinitude of language and the function of adjectives—the majority of its twenty-three pieces are devoted to nativism. There is an enthusiastic rereading of Estanislao del Campo's poem *Fausto,* in which a gaucho attends a performance of Gounod's opera and later tells a friend what he has made of it. Georgie believes that poem to be "the best thing said by our America" (ibid., p. 13). In another article he maintains that "the pampas and the slums are gods" and lists those writers who dealt with both myths, including his own name—"as long as I live there will be someone to praise me" (ibid., p. 22)—and also the name of Roberto Arlt. The favorable mention of Arlt (one of the writers promoted by the Boedo group) proves once more how false the dispute between Florida and Boedo was.

A third article is devoted to Evaristo Carriego and is a sort of dry run for the book he wrote on the same subject in 1930. He calls Carriego a "great scorpion," meaning he had a tongue that stung like the scorpion's tail; he also recalls that Carriego used to visit Father on Sundays. A fourth article is devoted to *The Purple Land,* a novel about the Uruguayan civil wars written in English by William Henry Hudson (a friend of Joseph Conrad), who was born in Argentina of North American parents. That novel is for Georgie one of the masterpieces of

Argentine regional literature; he hopes that one day it will be returned to the Spanish language, in which it was originally conceived. There is a fifth article on the Uruguayan poets' reverence for trees which repeats the now familiar notion that the poetry is (for Georgie at least) more rooted in native reality than in contemporary Argentine literature. A long article on popular Argentine songs, whose origins can be traced back to Spain, allows him to demonstrate that the real nativism is a certain humor and a certain capacity for skepticism. A section of book reviews gives him the chance to update some of his opinions on Silva Valdés' nativism (he seems to like it less and less in spite of some praise), to hail his fellow poet Oliverio Girondo's *Calcomanías* (Decals), and to criticize rather severely Leopoldo Lugones' new book of poems, *Romancero,* a collection of ballads that follow the old medieval lyric form but are loaded with sentimental contemporary subjects.

There is a last article on *lunfardo,* the pseudo-slang of the slums. While the real slang of hoodlums is purely functional (its aim is to avoid being understood by anybody outside the group), the slang of those who go slumming is only an imitation of the real thing: "Bullies who want to pretend they are outlaws and toughs, and whose bad deeds are limited to getting drunk with friends in a dive" imitate the vocabulary of jails and brothels. In its place, Georgie praises the "decent native language of our forebears" (ibid., pp. 136–137). He finds that some writers know how to use slang; but the majority do not: they only point up the limitations of a dialect that is poor in words and even poorer in meanings. The only way out of this dilemma is to find a poet who will write not the epic of the gaucho (as Hernández attempted in *Martín Fierro*) but the epic of the slums, or at least a novel of the slums. The article ends on a note of caution: it would be very difficult to write such a novel entirely in the native language. There is an emotional barrier to cross: when really moved, Argentines speak a language that goes back to their Castilian roots. Even Martín Fierro's nostalgia is expressed not in the gaucho dialect but in the purest Castilian.

Throughout the book (which contains many autobiographical allusions and includes personal anecdotes) an almost inaudible note can be heard. Georgie talks explicitly about his hopes for a new form of regionalism, for a language that will truly express the soul and the essence of his native land, its humor, and its sense of destiny; he also tacitly expresses his ambition to be the poet or the novelist who will capture that soul and that essence. He probably was then planning to write a book that would convey his feelings for the slums, a prose epic on the real hoodlums and their mythology. Georgie also offers a "Profession of Literary Faith." Near the end, he comments on the fact that each word has to be lived by the writer before it is used. He warns his colleagues: "Let nobody dare to write *slums* without having first walked endlessly along their high pavements; without having longed and suffered for them as one does for a girl; without having felt the high adobe walls, empty lots, the moon shining over humble stores, as a gift" (ibid., p. 153).

In two short pieces he includes in his next book of essays, *El idioma de los argentinos* (The Language of the Argentines), he attempts to capture the soul and essence of the slums. They can be read as fragments of the long prose poem, or novel, Georgie had outlined in his second book of essays. The shorter of the two pieces is called "Men Fought" and had previously been published in *Martín Fierro* (February 26, 1927) under the title "Police Legend." It is a narrative about the knife duel between two famous hoodlums: El Chileno (The Chilean), who came from the Southside, on the banks of the river; and El Mentao (The Famous One), whose turf was the Northside, in Palermo. Some six years later Georgie developed the same situation in a longer and more famous version, "Streetcorner Man." But in 1927 it was only a sketch.

More important is the second piece, which Georgie later included in his "A New Refutation of Time" in *Other Inquisitions* (1952). It is called "Feeling in Death" and has German metaphysical undertones. It describes an experience Georgie had one evening while walking the streets of Buenos Aires in the late 1920s. He had been roaming along the outskirts of Palermo, the neighborhood of his childhood. He arrived at an unfamiliar part of Barracas, a district that he knew more through words than in reality and that was "familiar and mythological at the same time." Suddenly he found himself on a streetcorner.

On the muddy and chaotic ground a rose-colored adobe wall seemed not to harbor moonglow but to shed a light of its own. I suspect that there can be no better way of denoting tenderness than by means of that rose color. I stood there looking at that simplicity. I thought, no doubt aloud, "This is the same as it was thirty years ago." I guessed at the date: a recent time in other countries, but already remote in this changing part of the world. Perhaps a bird was singing and I felt for him a small, bird-sized affection. What stands out most clearly: in the already vertiginous silence the only noise was the intemporal sound of the crickets. The easy thought, "I am in the eighteen hundreds," ceased to be a few careless words and deepened into reality. I felt dead—that I was an abstract perceiver of the world; I felt an undefined fear imbued with knowledge, the supreme clarity of metaphysics. No, I did not believe I had traveled across the presumptive waters of Time; rather I suspected I was the possessor of the reticent or absent meaning of the inconceivable word *eternity*. Only later was I able to define that imagining.

And now I shall write it like this: that pure representation of homogeneous facts—clear night, limpid wall, rural scent of honeysuckle, elemental clay—is not merely identical to the scene on that corner so many years ago; it is, without similarities or repetitions, the same. If we can perceive that identity, time is a delusion; the indifference and inseparability of one moment of time's apparent yesterday and another of its apparent today are enough to disintegrate it. (*Inquisitions*, 1964, pp. 179–180)

One of the literary sources of this passage is another night in another suburb, more than one hundred years before, when a romantic poet heard a nightingale sing in Hampstead. In interpretating this incident, which Borges does in a later article, "The Nightingale of Keats," also collected in *Other Inquisitions,* he suggests that the English poet discovered that the bird which was singing for him was the same bird which had sung for kings and buffoons, and for Ruth

> when, sick for home,
> She stood in tears amid the alien corn.

Each nightingale is every nightingale; its immortality and the immortality of its song are guaranteed by the immortality of the species.

In Georgie's piece the allusion to the famous ode is found in a single phrase, "Perhaps a bird was singing," a phrase that immediately leads to an observation, both prosaic and ironic: "What stands out most clearly: in the already vertiginous silence the only noise was the intemporal sound of the crickets." (Georgie knew that there are no nightingales in Argentina, but there *are* crickets.) If Keats discovers his own mortality by listening to the song of the immortal bird, Georgie, on the contrary, feels annihilated in the face of mortal time; he feels transformed into an "abstract perceiver of the world" and finds, not the personal identity that the romantic poet seeks and that Proust manages to escape only through art, but the impersonal identity of the perceiver and the object perceived: "that pure representation of homogeneous facts—clear night, limpid wall, rural scent of honeysuckle, elemental clay." Time is thus abolished, not because he feels eternal or because his art is capable of preserving him forever in the eternity of his work, but because he isn't anybody. <u>Or, better said, he *is* nobody</u>.

At this level of reading, Georgie's regionalism has very little to do with what the Boedo group, or even some of his fellow poets of the *Martín Fierro* crusade, had in mind. Georgie was really attempting to find a tone of voice and viewpoint that would capture not just the colorful images of the slums and the hoodlums but the essence and the soul of a part of Argentine reality which, for him, was closely linked with his family roots. He did not achieve all he wanted, but he was on the right path. The next decade would be spent exploring, in a dif-

This is a universal insight interrumated by systems to gain spurious authenticity.

ferent genre, the possibilities of a nativism that was determined not to renounce the hidden essences of reality.

Looking back on those attempts in his "Autobiographical Essay," Borges singles out the short narrative "Men Fought" for commentary:

> I was creeping out of the second book's style and slowly going back to sanity, to writing with some attempt at logic and at making things easy for the reader rather than dazzling him with purple passages. One such experiment, of dubious value, was "Hombres pelearon" (Men Fought), my first venture into the mythology of the old Northside of Buenos Aires. In it, I was trying to tell a purely Argentine story in an Argentine way. This story is one I have been retelling, with small variations, ever since. It is the tale of the motiveless, or disinterested, duel—of courage for its own sake. I insisted when I wrote it that in our sense of the language we Argentines were different from the Spaniards. Now, instead, I think we should try to stress our linguistic affinities. I was still writing, but in a milder way, so that Spaniards would not understand me—writing, it might be said, to be un-understood. ("Essay," 1970, pp. 231–232)

The most important piece in his third volume of essays, and the one that gives it its title, is a lecture called "The Language of the Argentines," which a friend read for Georgie at the Popular Institute of Lectures in Buenos Aires in 1927. In it, Georgie claims not that there is an "Argentine language" but that the Argentines use the Spanish language with a different intonation and a different feeling. What matters to him are precisely those differences: "We have not changed the intrinsic meaning of words but their connotations. That difference, unnoticeable in argumentative or didactic speech, is enormous in the matter of feeling. Our arguments may be Spanish but our poetry and our humor are already from this side of the Atlantic" (*Idioma,* 1928, p. 179). To reinforce his arguments, he quotes a few examples: the word "subject," which was normally used in monarchical Spain, has negative connotations in democratic South America; the expression "worthy of envy" implies praise in Spain, while in Argentina it seems base; two words that express two important realities—"slums" and "pampas"— have no emotional content for a Spaniard. In short, what Georgie wanted was a language that reflected a certain unique reality, the reality of his native country.

The other seventeen pieces in *The Language of the Argentines* are an assortment of articles, notes, and book reviews similar to those in Georgie's first two collections. The short prologue to the book insists on its origin in laziness. The book was made by the accumulation of prologues, that is (etymologically), "of inaugurations and commencements." Commenting on both the encyclopedic and chaotic aspects of the book, Georgie indicates the three basic preoccupations that give it its bearings: language, eternity, and Buenos Aires. To the first belongs an article on how a sentence is understood, illustrated by a word-by-word analysis of the famous beginning of *Don Quixote:* "In a certain village of La Mancha, whose name I do not wish to recall. . . ." The examination leads Georgie to the conclusion that <u>one does not *understand* separately each articulation of the phrase but rather grasps the phrase as a totality.</u> Then, with the help of quotations from Croce and Spiller, among others, he proceeds to analyze the mechanisms of understanding. The article is a forerunner of his more original and witty writings on the subject. To the same group of articles on rhetorical subjects belongs a new note on metaphor along with discussions of a school of Spanish baroque poetry called culteranism and of a Quevedo sonnet; of Góngora's images and Góngora's critics (he pokes fun *en passant* at some literal readings of Dámaso Alonso); of Cervantes' narrative habits; of Jorge Manrique's elegiac couplets; of the pleasure derived from poetry. The last article contains an anticipation of some of Borges' key critical concepts. Georgie discusses the metaphor "Fire, with ferocious jaws, devours the fields," without revealing its true source, as if it had been written in a different period of literary history.

Let us suppose that in a café on Corrientes or the Avenida de Mayo a writer presents the metaphor as his own. I would think: Making metaphors is now a very common task; to substitute "devour" for "burn" is not a very profitable exchange; the mention of "jaws" perhaps will astonish someone, but it shows the poet's weakness, a mere sequel to the expression "devouring fire," an automatism; in short, nothing. . . . Let us suppose now that it is presented to me as the work of a Chinese or Siamese poet. I would think: Everything becomes a dragon to the Chinese and I'll imagine a fire, lighted like a party and serpentine-shaped, and I'll like it. Let us suppose that it is used by the witness to a fire or, even better, by someone who was menaced by the flames. I would think: The concept of a fire with jaws comes really from a nightmare, from horror, and adds a human odious malignity to an unconscious fact. That phrase is almost mythological and powerful. Let us suppose that somebody tells me that the father of the image is Aeschylus and that it <u>was in Prometheus' tongue (which is true) and that the arrested Titan, bound to a rock cliff by Force and Violence, two very severe ministers, told it to the Ocean, an aging gentleman who came to visit his calamity in a winged chariot.</u> Then the sentence will seem appropriate and even perfect to me, considering the extravagant nature of the characters and the (already poetical) distance of its origin. I'll do what the reader did: suspend judgment until I can be sure to whom the phrase belongs. (Ibid., pp. 105–106)

The essay drifts, later, to other related subjects, but Georgie has already made his point: all judgment is relative; criticism is an activity as imaginary as that of fiction or poetry. It is possible to recognize here the critical seed of the story "Pierre Menard, Author of the *Quixote*." The conclusion that Georgie implicitly reaches is very different from the lessons Dr. I. A. Richards derives, for example, from similar exercises in *Practical Criticism* (1929). Both start from the same experience: the discussion of a text whose author is unknown to the reader and which, therefore, can only be deciphered by itself. Yet, contrary to Dr. Richards, Georgie postulates the utter impossibility of scientific criticism. To put it differently, for him every critic (every reader) places himself, willingly or not, in a conditioned perspective; before judging, every reader prejudges. Criticism, or reading, creates the text anew.   *Hirsch.*

The book also includes essays on Argentine writers (the apocalyptic poet Almafuerte, the ultraist Ricardo E. Molinari, the ironic turn-of-the-century narrator Eduardo Wilde) and on some Argentine subjects (the origins of the tango, the three lives of the milonga, the *truco*) that by now constitute permanent features of any book by Georgie. There is also an affectionate review of one of Alfonso Reyes' books, *Reloj de Sol* (Sun Dial), to which Georgie reserves the highest word of praise: it is a spoken book. The article is an anticipation of his later comments on the Mexican humanist, whom he considers his master in matters of style. Subtly, ironically, through his example, Reyes would lead Georgie away from the baroque and teach him how to write the best Spanish prose of the century.

13.
The Gift of
Friendship

In the late 1920s the Borgeses moved to a sixth-floor apartment in a new and imposing building on the corner of Las Heras and Pueyrredón; it had seven balconies overlooking a busy midtown district, with the Recoleta cemetery in the background. The building is still there, and the neighborhood has changed very little. For eleven years that was the Borgeses' residence. In spite of its monotony, which he liked to stress, Georgie's life was being subtly modified by age and literary success. In fact, the whole family was experiencing change. Father was becoming totally blind and Mother's role had turned into nurse and reader. Her English had always been very poor, but now she felt compelled to improve it, to become, as she later put it, her husband's eyes. Her education and outlook broadened. Speaking about her in his "Autobiographical Essay," Borges comments on the change: "My mother has always had a hospitable mind. From the time she learned English, through my father, she has done most of her reading in that language" ("Essay," 1970, p. 207). Unaware of it, she was preparing for the role she would assume some twenty years later: being her son's eyes. Georgie's eyesight was getting worse. In 1927 he had to be operated on for cataracts by Dr. Amadeo Natale. Mother told me in 1971 that while the operation went on, she stood next to him, holding his hand as if he were a baby. The operation was successful, and for the time being Georgie was allowed to continue reading and writing. That was the first of eight eye operations he had to go through before near blindness set in for good.

Those were the years in which Georgie formed lasting friendships. He thought he had inherited the gift of friendship from Mother (ibid., p. 207), but it is an old Argentine trait. In the desolate vastness of the pampas a friend is the most important person in the world.

In the "Autobiographical Essay" Borges recalls the 1920s as quite happy years because "they stood for many friendships" (ibid., p. 235). Among those friends, he mentions Father, Father's classmate Macedonio Fernández, and some young poets with whom he launched ultraism in Argentina: Norah Lange and Francisco Piñero. The first was a beautiful blonde, of Norwegian stock, five years younger than Georgie. He wrote a generous prologue to her first book of poems, *La calle de la tarde* (The Afternoon Street, 1925). In her short autobiographical sketch for the *Exposición de la actual poesía argentina* (1927) she calls him her "sole teacher" and remembers their Saturday meetings at her family's villa on Tronador Street, where they shared friends and some favorite tangos. She also published in *Martín Fierro* (April 28, 1927, p. 6) a short commentary on Georgie's poems in which she praises him highly with only one reservation: in his books Buenos Aires looks too quiet and Sundaylike. A few years later, Norah married a member of the ultraist movement, the poet Oliverio Girondo. In the 1930s she stopped writing poetry and devoted herself entirely to prose. Francisco Piñero was a young lawyer who had helped Georgie to launch his first literary magazine, *Prisma,* and the first *Proa.* He also contributed regularly to *Martín Fierro* and shared with Georgie the banquet held by the magazine (December 29, 1925, p. 7) to celebrate the simultaneous publication of his own book of travels, *El puñal de Orión,* and Georgie's *Luna de enfrente.* In the thirty-fifth issue of *Martín Fierro* (November 5, 1926) a short note informs its readers that Piñero had left the magazine because he was too busy to continue contributing regularly to it. And when Georgie founded the second *Proa,* Piñero was no longer on its masthead.

Borges mentions other friends in the same section of his "Autobiographical Essay": Ricardo Güiraldes, one of the editors of the second *Proa,* who died in 1927; Silvina and Victoria Ocampo, with whom Georgie collaborated in the 1930s and 1940s; the poet Carlos Mastronardi and the novelist Eduardo Mallea, both of whom Borges continues to see regularly even now; and especially Alejandro Schultz, whom he calls by his pseudonym, Xul-Solar:

> In a rough and ready way, it may be said that Xul, who was a mystic, a poet, and a painter, is our William Blake. I remember asking him on one particularly sultry afternoon about what he had done that stifling day. His answer was "Nothing whatever, except for founding twelve religions after lunch." Xul was also a philologist and the inventor of two languages. One was a philosophical language after the manner of John Wilkins and the other a reformation of Spanish with many English, German, and Greek words. He came of Baltic and Italian stock. Xul was his version of Schultz and Solar of Solari. ("Essay," 1970, p. 237)

Xul-Solar was slightly older than his ultraist friends. He was born in 1887, and while in his middle twenties he had started on a journey in a cargo boat to the Far East that was cut short at a Mediterranean port. For ten years he lived in Europe (France, England, Germany, and Italy). World War I caught him in Paris. In 1920 he shared the first exhibit of his paintings with the Italian sculptor Martini. In July 1924 he returned to Argentina and became one of the *Martín Fierro* group. Although they were both in Europe at the same time, Xul and Georgie did not meet then. *Martín Fierro* brought them together. Norah was also a link: both in 1926 and in 1940 she showed her paintings alongside those of Xul in a collective exhibition. The first show was honored by a lecture on avant-garde art given by Marinetti, who was then visiting Argentina. *Martín Fierro* duly chronicled the event (July 8, 1926, p. 1). Reproductions of Xul's strange paintings are on the front page and page 3 of that issue; in a review of the show, the architect and critic Alberto Presbich singled out Xul's "mysterious and symbolical art." Xul's paintings at that time could be easily related to Paul Klee's and (in a way) to Kafka's drawings. They have the same angularity, the phallic agressiveness, the slightly sinister humor. That fall *Martín Fierro* published a few satirical rhymes written by Georgie with the help of his cousin Guillermo Juan. One plays with the *x* in their friend's name:

> With Xul, on the street called Mexico
> We did reform the lexicon.
> (*Martín Fierro*, September 3, 1926, p. 12)

Three of Georgie's books are illustrated by Xul. The first two belong to the 1920s. Five drawings are reproduced as endpapers in *El tamaño de mi esperanza* (1926); six in *El idioma de los argentinos* (1928). They all concern the subject of war and suggest primitive warriors engaged in blurred melees or advancing behind colorful shields while flying the Argentine banner. A commentary on Georgie's nativism, a subtle parody of patriotism, an anticipation of the army's future intervention in Argentina's political affairs? Who knows. Those drawings still haunt the pages of Georgie's early books. The third and last book illustrated by Xul-Solar is the pseudonymous *Un modelo para la muerte* (A Model for Death), a parody of the detective novel, signed "B. Suárez Lynch" and actually written by Borges and Adolfo Bioy Casares. To the first, private 1946 edition of that book Xul-Solar contributed seven unsigned vignettes that look Chinese. On page 27 a four-winged, headless pig is shown. On page 83 a fat man is being carried, very erect and alive, on a stick by two porters; the stick holding him goes through a hole in his chest.

The influence of Xul-Solar on Borges' work has never been studied, although it is considerable. Up to a point, some of the strangest aspects of the literary career of "Pierre Menard" can be traced to Xul. At least five of the nineteen items in Menard's bibliography are related to some of Xul's preoccupations with language (items *b* and *c*), with the game of chess (items *e* and *g*) and with the occult (item *f*). In one of Borges' most intricate stories, "Tlön, Uqbar, Orbis Tertius," some aspects of the invented language of Tlön are similar to one of the two languages invented by Xul, the "neocriollo," or "new native." In the story Borges explains that in that language there are no words corresponding to the noun "moon," but that there is a verb, "to moon" or "to moondle." He gives the following example: *The moon rose over the sea* could be written *hlör u fang axaxaxas mlö,* or, to put it in order: *upward beyond the constant flow there was moondling.* (Xul-Solar translates it succinctly: *upward beyond the onstreaming it mooned.*) (*Ficciones,* 1962, p. 23).

Xul-Solar's unique personality is the model for one of Adán Buenosayres' friends in Marechal's novel of that name. He is thinly disguised as the astrologer and some examples of his "new nativism" are quoted in the book. But by the time the novel was published in 1948, Xul-Solar had parted company with Borges. He had become attracted to Peronism. Borges still admired him to the point of calling him, in a piece written then, "one of the most singular things that had happened in our time." In describing Xul, he also said: "A man familiar with all fields of study, curious about all mysteries, father of languages, of utopias, of mythologies, author of the 'universal chess' ['panchess' in his language], an astrologer, perfect in his indulgent irony and in his generous friendship" (quoted in Xul-Solar's obituary, *La Nación,* Buenos Aires, April 11, 1963, p. 4). In mentioning Xul in his "Autobiographical Essay," Borges chooses to remember the friendship and forget the political disagreement.

He also recalls with affection the Mexican humanist Alfonso Reyes, who was appointed ambassador to Argentina in 1927. Reyes used to invite Georgie to dinner every Sunday at the embassy. A long-lasting friendship began there. Reyes had been very precocious. His first book of essays, *Problems of Esthetics,* was published in 1911, when he was barely twenty-two. After a long sojourn in Spain, where he worked at the Center for Historical Studies and produced the first authoritative edition of Góngora's *Polifemo,* he entered the diplomatic service. He had been a close friend of Pedro Henríquez Ureña while the latter was living in Mexico. Through Don Pedro, Georgie heard of Reyes. A chronicle written by Ricardo Molinari and published in *Martín Fierro* (April 28, 1927, p. 5) refers to an occasion, "during one of our usual

217

visits to La Plata last fall," when Henríquez Ureña read some new poems by Reyes to Molinari, Georgie, and other friends. Even before his arrival in Buenos Aires, the *Martín Fierro* group had begun to direct the attention of its readers to the Mexican humanist's work. In the issue of September 3, 1926, a note on page 8 announces his appointment as ambassador and the banquet that was being organized by Georgie and Don Pedro. Reyes' arrival was delayed and the celebration did not take place until the fall of 1927. A photograph of the banquet is reproduced in *Martín Fierro* (August 31–November 15, 1927, p. 8). A note makes reference to a "dadaist speech" read by Georgie and Marechal; unfortunately, the speech is not printed. On many occasions Borges has mentioned his friendship with Alfonso Reyes and his admiration for his prose style. In the "Autobiographical Essay" he says of him: "I think of Reyes as the finest Spanish prose stylist of this century, and in my writing I learned a great deal about simplicity and directness from him" ("Essay," 1970, p. 237).

Reyes had mastered the art of being succinct and direct without being thin or prosaic. At the time Georgie met him, Reyes already had perfected a subtle, poetic, and extremely condensed prose. Georgie was still very much under the influence of Cansinos-Asséns, who tended to be long-winded and elliptical, and Macedonio Fernández, whose stylistic mannerisms Georgie followed very closely. In the "Autobiographical Essay," while praising Macedonio and proclaiming his devotion to him, he admits that he was a bad influence on his writing (ibid., p. 230). Reyes, on the contrary, was a liberating influence. He anticipated the new writing Georgie developed so brilliantly in the 1930s.

In listing the friends of that period, Borges omits his sister, Norah. She had been very active both in *Prisma* and the two *Proas*, had illustrated Georgie's first two books of poetry, and had attended the meetings at Norah Lange's villa and other literary and artistic gatherings. Her drawings and paintings were regularly featured in *Martín Fierro*. Throughout this period, Norah's career had moved parallel to Georgie's. But if they continued to be associated in their artistic pursuits, in their private lives they were beginning to part. Georgie was more absorbed every day in his explorations of the slums, a world totally inaccessible to Norah, while she had become more and more emotionally involved with Guillermo de Torre, the Spanish poet and critic whom they had met in Spain. In his book on the avant-garde, *Literaturas europeas de vanguardia* (1925), Guillermo comments on the importance of Norah's woodcuts and in a very exalted style describes her as having a "delicate temperament, extraradial[*sic*], unique." To explain what he means, he adds: "The fibers of her marvelous sensitivity are chisels that mark the diagram of her sensitive and intellectual undulations" (De Torre, 1925, p. 55). He also compares her with more famous women artists: the French painters Marie Laurencin and Maria Blanchard.

In the same book he devotes three and a half pages to Georgie's poetry. He notes his importance as a theoretician of the ultraist movement and quotes him extensively, generally with warm approval. But he has reservations about certain characteristics of Georgie's poetry after his return to Buenos Aires: the metaphysical concepts and the baroque style. His appraisal concludes on a very positive note. Georgie, on the other hand, reviewing Guillermo's book for *Martín Fierro* (August 5, 1925, p. 4), adopts a slightly patronizing tone. Although he praises it, he calls it a "rebellious directory of literature" and points out that Guillermo is a man of the world who knows things that are out of Georgie's reach: for instance, how to choose a tie or play tennis. In a more serious vein, he warns Guillermo that in wanting to be so up to date he runs the risk of being old-fashioned. After all, progress was invented not by Spengler but by Spencer. Then, after pointing out the North American influence on European literature (he mentions Poe, Emerson, and Whitman but not Pound and Eliot), he accurately predicts that the Spanish Americans' turn is coming.

From Spain, Guillermo had contributed regularly to Argentina's little magazines. He also wrote on Spanish and Spanish American authors for *Martín Fierro*. But in 1927 he made the fateful mistake of publishing an article in Madrid's *La Gaceta Literaria* in which he maintained that Spanish America's "literary meridian" passed through Madrid. I have already told of the cries of outrage that greeted this statement. Guillermo was visiting Argentina at the time and was probably making plans to marry Norah. He was quick to apologize for his faux pas and his apologies were accepted. But his lack of tact did not endear him to Georgie, who had always been slightly scornful of Guillermo's enthusiasm for the avant-garde and his zeal as a crusader for ultraism. Now Guillermo was plainly making a fool of himself. On a still deeper level, Norah's understanding with Guillermo must have alienated both of them from Georgie's affections. He probably thought his sister had made the wrong choice. In 1928 Norah and Guillermo married and went to live in Spain. Perhaps Georgie unconsciously felt that his Ariadne had deserted the family labyrinth to join forces with an unworthy carrier of the sword. From that moment on, Norah was no longer a part of his daydreaming life. Her role as mother surrogate had come to an end.

In "Singladura" (The Day's Run), a poem he included in his second book of verses, *Luna de enfrente,* there is a revealing reference to Norah. The poem, which may have been written on board a ship when the Borgeses crossed the Atlantic, describes the sea at night with lofty ultraist images; Georgie sees it as a "numerous sword," a "plenitude of poverty," "alone like a blindman," and "impenetrable as carved stone." From the contemplation of the sea, his eyes are raised to the sky to watch the moon "twisted around one of the masts." The poem ends with this long line:

> On deck, quietly, I share the evening with my sister, as if it were a
> piece of bread.
>
> (*Poemas,* 1943, p. 100)

Part Three

1.
The End of a Mythology

More than a dissatisfaction and impatience with ultraism can be detected in the articles written by Georgie in the late 1920s. In questioning the movement, he was also questioning his own attempts to create something different. He still practiced nativism but was already beginning to realize that his poetic powers of invention were not unlimited. He felt a bit stale. His youthful ambition to be a Walt Whitman or a Johannes Becher—that is, an all-embracing, cosmic poet—seemed more and more unattainable. On the first page of his *San Martín Copybook* (1929) he includes a quotation from Edward FitzGerald that indicates his vanishing hope: "As to an occasional copy of verses, there are few men who have leisure to read and are possessed of any music in their souls, who are not capable of versifying on some ten or twelve occasions during their natural lives: at a proper conjunction of the stars. There is no harm in taking advantage of such occasions" (*Poemas,* 1943, p. 121). Those words are perhaps more suited to Father's practice of poetry than to a young poet who had published three books of poems in seven years.

In retrospect, Borges is even more negative about the poems of that period. In the "Autobiographical Essay" he laments not having completely suppressed *Luna de enfrente* (1925) and calls it

a riot of sham local color. Among its tomfooleries were the spelling of my first name in the nineteenth-century Chilean fashion as "Jorje" (it was a half-hearted attempt at phonetic spelling); the spelling of the Spanish for "and" as *i* instead of *y* (our greatest writer, Sarmiento, had done the same, trying to be as un-Spanish as he could); and the omission of the final *d* in words like *autoridá* and *ciudá.* In later editions, I dropped the worst poems, pruned the eccentricities, and successively—through several reprintings—revised and toned down the verses. ("Essay," 1970, p. 232)

As a matter of fact, Borges eliminated eight poems in the first collective reprint (1943) and to compensate added two. In spite of his strictures, there are some good poems in that book. One of the most famous is "General Quiroga Rides to His Death in a Carriage," in which he brilliantly relates the brutal murder of one of the most notorious caudillos of Argentina. Georgie based his dramatic reduction of that episode on Sarmiento's masterful biography of Facundo Quiroga, but what makes the poem unique is the vigor of its images. The last quatrain is an epic evocation of Quiroga entering hell:

> Now dead, now on his feet, now immortal, now a ghost,
> he reported to the Hell marked out for him by God,
> and under his command there marched, broken and bloodless,
> the souls in purgatory of his soldiers and his horses.
> (*Poems,* 1972, translated by Alastair Reid, p. 35)

Another poem is dedicated to the pampas. Its Latin title, "Dulcia Linquimus Arua," comes from Virgil's first *Eclogue,* line 3—*nos patriae finis et dulcia linquimus arua*—which has been rendered by Dudley Fitts as "We depart from our own country, from the sweet fields [of home]," according to information provided by the editor (ibid., p. 293). Contrasting his own urban destiny with that of his ancestors, who made the pampas their home, Georgie says:

> As a town dweller I no longer know these things.
> I come from a city, a neighborhood, a street:
> distant streetcars enforce my nostalgia
> with the wail they let loose in the night.
> (Ibid., translated by Norman Thomas di Giovanni, p. 39)

San Martín Copybook fares slightly better in Borges' "Autobiographical Essay." After explaining that the title has nothing to do with Argentina's national hero General José de San Martín, and that it is "merely the brand name of the out-of-fashion copybook into which I wrote the poems," he admits that it contains some "quite legitimate pieces." He mentions "La noche que en el Sur lo velaron," whose title (according to him) has been "strikingly translated" by Robert Fitzgerald as "Deathwatch on the Southside," and "Muertes de Buenos Aires" (Deaths of Buenos Aires), a poem "about the two chief graveyards of the Argentine capital." But in spite of the more favorable evaluation, he cannot refrain from adding: "One poem in the book (no favorite of mine) has somehow become a minor Argentine classic: 'The Mythical Founding of Buenos Aires.' This book too has been improved, or purified, by cuts and revisions down through the years" ("Essay," 1970, p. 233). Actually, it lost one poem in the collected edition of 1943, and a second in the 1969 reprint.

"The Mythical Founding of Buenos Aires," which was incorrectly called "The Mythological Founding" in the first edition, is colorful and showy; at the same time, it beautifully expresses Georgie's discovery of his native city upon his return from Europe. The last two lines condense his feelings:

> Hard to believe Buenos Aires had any beginning.
> I feel it to be as eternal as air and water.
> (*Poems*, 1972, translated by Alastair Reid, p. 51)

The main tone of the book is of mourning. The section on "Deaths of Buenos Aires" shows Georgie's liking for the imagery of graveyards and tombs. Nevertheless, there was very little in him of the romantic agony. His elegiac poetry goes further back, to Latin models through the hard verses of Quevedo, the great Spanish baroque poet. In recalling the ancestors who fought and died bravely, such as his maternal grandfather, Isidoro Acevedo, or the sudden death of a poet friend, Francisco López Merino, who took his own life at twenty-four, Georgie was exploring a new territory.

Although these two books were not badly received, Georgie practically stopped writing poetry after the second was published. In the next decade he wrote exactly six poems, only four of which were published. In his 1966 conversations with De Milleret, Borges could find no reason to justify that silence except to speculate that he was not too happy with his poetry (De Milleret, 1967, p. 48). In spite of that, in 1929 *San Martín Copybook* won second prize at the annual literary competition held by the city of Buenos Aires. The prize money was three thousand pesos (one thousand dollars approximately), "which in those days was a lordly sum of money," according to Borges' recollections ("Essay," 1970, p. 233). Georgie's first decision was to spend part of the money on a secondhand set of the *Encyclopaedia Britannica,* eleventh edition. But the more important consequence of the prize was that it somehow legitimized his dedication to literature. Although Father had always supported (if not thoroughly invented) his vocation and had regularly answered inquiries from his friends about his son's occupation with a now famous phrase, "He is very busy: he is writing," Georgie probably felt that he was taking advantage of his father. The prize money freed him temporarily from that feeling and allowed him to attempt a major literary enterprise. He had always wanted to write a "longish book on a wholly Argentine subject." In the "Essay" he recalls a conversation with his parents on this topic: "My mother wanted me to write about any of three worthwhile poets—Ascasubi, Almafuerte, or Lugones. I now wish I had. Instead, I chose to write about a nearly invisible popular poet, Evaristo Carriego. My mother and father pointed out that his poems were not good. 'But he was a friend and a neighbor of ours,' I said. 'Well, if you think that qualifies him as the subject for a book, go ahead,' they said" (ibid., p. 233).

His choice was not so capricious after all. As Borges himself points out:

> Carriego was the man who discovered the literary possibilities of the run-down and ragged outskirts of the city—the Palermo of my boyhood. His career followed the same evolution as the tango—rollicking, daring, courageous at first, then turning sentimental. In 1912, at the age of twenty-nine, he died of tuberculosis, leaving behind a single volume of his work. I remember that a copy of it, inscribed to my father, was one of several Argentine books we had taken to Geneva and that I read and reread there. (Ibid., pp. 233–234)

In a sense, writing about Carriego was a roundabout way of writing about himself and his old neighborhood. But there was more to it, although Borges seems not to remember. Choosing Carriego as a fit subject for a major work, Georgie was quietly stressing his rebellion against family values. To discard major Argentine poets such as those he mentions in the "Essay" in favor of this truly minor one indicated a decision to challenge established literary values. It was another way of confirming to his parents his perverse preference for the slums, the tango, and the hoodlums: all the images that Georgie was then trying so hard to metamorphose into a new poetic mythology of Buenos Aires.

In preparing Carriego's biography, Georgie researched the scarce printed matter thoroughly, but his best sources were his family's memories of the poet, some close friends' recollections, and his own exploration of the slums. He interviewed Marcelo del Mazo, a classmate of Father and the person who was probably Carriego's closest friend. But perhaps the person who helped Georgie most to imagine what life was like in the slums at the time Carriego was alive was a famous hoodlum, Don Nicolás Paredes. He was the boss of Palermo when the poet was only fourteen and needed someone to admire. In those days hoodlums were instrumental in deciding elections: they were responsible for controlling the ballots and used to terrorize those who protested against the authority of the local caudillo. In his portrait of Paredes (more colorful and attractive than Carriego's), Georgie stresses the man's native dignity, "the entire possession of his part of reality," and describes him as he might have been on that evening in 1897 when the adolescent Carriego sought his friendship: "the chest bulging with virility, the authoritarian presence, the insolent black mane of hair, the flaming mustache, the usually grave voice which becomes effeminate and crawls with mockery when he is challenging someone, the ponderous walk, the handling of some possibly historical anecdote, of some slangy expression, of the skillful card game, of a knife and a guitar, the infinite certainty" (*Carriego,* 1930, p. 41). In Georgie's portrait, the Paredes of 1897 and the man Georgie visited thirty years later are subtly combined to project a larger-than-life character. In evoking him, Georgie also conveys the aura of a man who really didn't have to use his knife to impose discipline among his followers: the short gaucho whip he always carried, or the hard palm of his hand, was enough. Nearly forty years after Georgie's first meeting with Paredes, Borges told me a few more anecdotes about him. In 1927 Paredes was already retired and lived very frugally in a small room in the slums. He was always neat and courteous. Once he challenged Georgie to a game of *truco,* the native poker. They played for very modest stakes. Georgie won the first round, but then his "luck" turned, and in no time he lost quite a bit to his more skillful rival. When they stopped playing, Paredes refused to take his money and told him that they had been playing for fun. To perfect that object lesson, he gave Georgie an orange for the road, because (he said) he did not want anyone to leave his house empty-handed.

Georgie never forgot the man. Another anecdote about Paredes comes up in his interview with Ronald Christ, although this time he does not mention his name:

> I remember I once saw a man challenging another to fight and the other caved in. But he caved in, I think, because of a trick. One was an old hand, he was seventy, and the other was a young and vigorous man, he must have been between twenty-five and thirty. Then the old man came back with two daggers, and one was a span longer than the other. He said: "Here, choose your weapon." So he gave the other the chance of choosing the longer weapon and having an advantage over him; but that also meant that he felt so sure of himself that he could afford that handicap. The other apologized and caved in, of course. I remember that when I was a young man in the slums, a brave man was always supposed to carry a short dagger, and it was worn here. Like this (*pointing to his armpit*), so it could be taken out at a moment's notice. And the slum word for the knife, or one of the slum words— well, and that has been quite lost; it's a pity—was el *vaivén,* the "come-and-go." In the word *come-and-go* (*making a gesture*) you see the flash of the knife, the sudden flash. (Christ, 1967, p. 140)

Borges had a change of heart while writing *Evaristo Carriego:*

When I began writing my book the same thing happened to me that happened to Carlyle as he wrote his *Frederick the Great.* The more I wrote, the less I cared about my hero. I had started out to do a straight biography, but on the way I became more and more interested in oldtime Buenos Aires. Readers, of course, were not slow in finding out that the book hardly lived up to its title, *Evaristo Carriego,* and so it fell flat. When the second edition appeared twenty-five years later, in 1955, . . . I enlarged the book with several new chapters, one a "History of the Tango." As a consequence of these additions, I feel *Evaristo Carriego* has been rounded out for the better. ("Essay," 1970, p. 234)

In more than one sense, Georgie's book on Carriego was a failure. It was not a good biography of the man, and as criticism of his verses it was too ironical to be of much use. But if it failed as a well-rounded literary study, it contained some fascinating glimpses of Palermo and the atmosphere that made the tango possible. It was also important as Georgie's first attempt to come to terms with the narrative problems of presenting a man's destiny. The portrait of Carriego was the first of a series of character studies Georgie created in the next decade.

Evaristo Carriego was printed on September 30, 1930, exactly twenty-four days after the army coup that deposed President Hipólito Irigoyen. That episode ended a fourteen-year period of democratic rule in Argentina, during which universal suffrage had been established, elections had been untainted by vote tampering or by terrorizing the voters, and the country's economy had been put on a solid basis by increasing its main exports (meat, wool, wheat) and by partially nationalizing oil. The army takeover began a ten-year period that Argentine historians later baptized the "infamous decade." President Irigoyen belonged to one of the established families, but he had always had a populist vision of a new Argentina: a country in which the capital and the provinces, the descendants of the old settlers and the new immigrants, the bourgeois and the workers, could find social justice and happiness. He was also a Latin Americanist in the sense that he understood perfectly that political freedom without economic independence was an illusion. He fought hard to free Argentina from the rule of local landowners and businessmen, but he fought even harder against the powerful British and North American oil and meat-packing interests. He had already served one term as president in 1916–1922. The man who followed him, Marcelo T. Alvear, had been hand-picked by him. Although Alvear proved to be easy prey to the conservative forces,

Irigoyen pretty much ran the show from behind the scenes. He engineered a triumphant comeback in 1928, when he was overwhelmingly elected to a second presidency.

Irigoyen was a strange sort of man for a politician. Instead of parading his power and seducing the masses with his eloquence, he preferred solitude and silence. He was nicknamed "El Peludo," not because he was hairy but because, like the mole, he loved to hide in his hole. In spite of his modern ideology, he was a born caudillo, a leader; he understood the masses intuitively. There was something in him of the witchdoctor, and that made him even more irresistible to the people. In his first presidency he had built an immense following which remained emotionally faithful to him until the last day of his second presidency.

For Georgie, Irigoyen's downfall was an ominous sign. He had always admired the Mole, and in one of the first essays in which he attempted to define the essence of Argentine nativism he had compared him with Juan Manuel de Rosas, the infamous nineteenth-century dictator:

> Silence combined with fatalism is effectively embodied in the major caudillos who have captured Buenos Aires' soul: Rosas and Irigoyen. Don Juan Manuel, in spite of his misdeeds and all the blood he uselessly spilled, was much loved by the people. Irigoyen, in spite of the official masquerades, governs us still. What the people loved in Rosas, understood in Roca, and now admire in Irigoyen is the scorn of theatricals, or the fact that if they use some, they do it with a comic sense. (*Inquisiciones*, 1925, p. 132)

Georgie published this article in 1925, after Irigoyen's first term was over, but he knew perfectly well that the Mole continued to pull the strings. The comparison with Rosas was meant to be favorable. It may seem paradoxical that Georgie, who came from people who had been Don Juan Manuel's mortal enemies and had fought bravely against him, could express such feelings. But he was then passing through a quiet but rebellious phase, and his return to Argentina meant (among other things) a total revision of the family museum. In Irigoyen he saw another Don Juan Manuel, a charismatic leader who in spite of his failings knew what was good for the country in a way the more articulate and perhaps more cautious leaders did not. At the time, many of Irigoyen's enemies also compared him with Rosas, stressing their arbitrariness, authoritarianism, and lack of respect for political niceties. They called them cruel tyrants and dictators. To Georgie, the parallel only stressed the favorable traits they had in common.

When Irigoyen began his campaign for a second presidency, Georgie was prominent among his supporters. A now forgotten chronicle written in 1944 by one member of that group, Ulyses Petit de Murat, offers an unexpected view of him as a political activist. Probably under the influence of a mutual friend, the young poet Francisco López Merino, Georgie and Ulyses decided to join Irigoyen's forces. According to Ulyses, they believed that the Mole had no chance of being reelected, that his enemies were going to tamper with the votes; and because his seemed a lost cause, they devoted all their enthusiasm to it. They came up with the idea of forming a Committee of Young Intellectuals, and soon Francisco Luis Bernárdez, Leopoldo Marechal, Enrique and Raúl González Tuñon, and Sixto Pondal Ríos joined them. The day they went to visit Buenos Aires' Central Committee they were received by the chairman, whose speeches bored them to tears. Suddenly, using a hoodlum's accent, Georgie turned to Ulyses and said: "Eh . . . when are they going to hand out the meat pies wrapped up in commissions?" (Petit de Murat, 1944, p. 6). Georgie's reaction was typical. Those committees were crude offices of patronage, and to attract voters they used to offer, along with the traditional wine and meat pies, the irresistible promise of an official job.

Not all the young intellectuals were attracted to Irigoyen as a lost cause. Many abstained from politics altogether. *Martín Fierro* published an editorial (August 31–November 15, 1927, p. 6) disclaiming any connection with the Committee of Young Intellectuals, many of whose members were regular contributors to the magazine. Georgie and Ulyses did not like the disclaimer and from then on ceased to participate in *Martín Fierro*'s activities. A different type of reaction came from the Boedo group. In their journal *Claridad* (April 1928) they published a poem, supposedly written by members of the committee, that included the following prayer to Irigoyen:

> Destroyer of old and obsolete regimes,
> When at last you cross the much desired threshold
> of the great presidential room,
> listen to our prayers, understand our gestures
> and give us consulates, university chairs and other commissions,
> Unequalled and extraordinary man!
>
> (Alén, 1975, p. 245)

Once more, the Boedo group and the ultraist poets were in confrontation, but this time there was an apparent change in their respective positions. While the supposedly bourgeois and even alienated intellectuals of Florida were in favor of the caudillo, the Boedo group opposed him for the same reasons the Communists would later oppose another charismatic leader, Perón: out of political alienation. The fact that Georgie was not seeking any commission (Father was his patron), and that he himself had laughed at the patronage dispensed by the chairman of the Buenos Aires Central Committee, must have been completely lost on the Boedo group. They continued to weave their neat abstractions while Argentine politics pursued its own course.

It is obvious that Georgie's enthusiasm for Irigoyen as a lost cause did not survive the Mole's triumphant return as president. Instead of claiming the meat pies and the commission, he became highly critical of the new government. And he had some justification. When the Mole was elected for a second term, he was already seventy-seven and was too tired and confused to be able to run the country efficiently. In his first presidency he had Argentina's economic prosperity, enhanced by the World War I boom in its meat and wool exports, to back his reformist political and financial measures. At that time, he not only changed the institutions but consolidated his country's wealth. Six years later, in his second term, he inherited a weaker economy, undermined by his successor's complacency with big business and the international trusts. No sooner was he in power than he had to face the 1929 crash, which damaged the national economy. His enemies accused him of mismanagement and even of stealing. Irigoyen was no longer strong enough to face them, but he did not know it. His own party was divided and he had to fight a rebellious and corrupted Congress. Surrounded by a mediocre staff, he trusted no one. His ingrained tendency to silence and secrecy became worse with age; he took too long to make decisions and, at the same time, insisted on his authority in every single piece of official business. In the last days of his regime he had alienated the best of his friends and was ruling ineffectively through people who awaited his sudden departure in the hope of sharing in the spoils. A severe flu gave them the opportunity to force his temporary resignation. Immediately the army took over. Georgie's reaction to the coup can be seen in some letters he wrote to Alfonso Reyes, who had been transferred to Rio de Janeiro. At the time that Reyes had been Mexican ambassador to Argentina, he had been an admirer of Irigoyen. To his anxious questions about what had happened to the president, Georgie made a measured if subjective reply. He called Irigoyen "el *Doctor,*" which was a way of distancing him ironically:

About the suppression of the *Doctor,* I can assure you that, in spite of the fact that it was needed, it was necessary, it was just, it has created a very disagreeable atmosphere. The revolution (or army coup supported by the people) is a victory of common sense against incompetence, against the usual dishonesty and the arbitrariness, but all these bad things corresponded to a mythology, to a tenderness, to a happiness, to the extravagant image of the *Doctor* conspiring from the presidential palace itself. Buenos Aires had to repudiate his domestic mythology and build very quickly some enthusiasm for

231

acts of heroism in which nobody really believes, on the basis (insignificant for the spirit) that these soldiers are not thieves. To sacrifice Myth to Lucidity, what do you think? Bernard Shaw, undoubtedly, would approve. I don't know if I make myself clear: before (I repeat) we had stupidity but with it the noisy opposition newspapers, the "Long Live" and "Death To" which flourished on the walls, in tangos and milongas; now we have *Independence Under Martial Law,* a fawning press, . . . and the established myth that the former regime was cruel and tyrannical. (*L'Herne,* 1964, p. 56)

In closing, Georgie includes a few vignettes of the "revolution"—a nonlethal shooting in the Plaza del Once; a machine gun positioned at Junín Street, two steps from home; two gunsmith shops sacked in Rivadavia Street by a gang not too sure of itself—and also promises to send the *Carriego* "in ten days." The letter shows that Georgie had finally come to believe all that a corrupted press had said about Irigoyen and his friends. But Georgie was right about the Irigoyen myth, and that was what really mattered.

Less than one year after the publication of the book, in an article Georgie wrote for a new literary review, *Sur* (South), he has a few disillusioned and ironical words to say about the government. In stressing one of Argentina's most negative traits, resentment, he gives as an example "the incomparable spectacle of a conservative government that is pushing the whole Republic to become socialist, only to annoy and sadden a middle-of-the-road party" (*Discusión,* 1932, p. 17). Georgie's political skepticism had reached its lowest point.

2.
The Invention of an Audience

At the beginning of the "infamous decade" Borges could look around him and see that he had been left with very little. Gone was the enthusiasm that made him the apostle of ultraism, the untiring founder of small magazines, the brightest new poet in Argentina. *Evaristo Carriego,* published in the wake of the army coup against Irigoyen, went practically unnoticed. Borges was quickly dissatisfied with it. He had gambled on a popular poet, and his small, sophisticated audience had not responded well. "The happy few" were ready to listen to his poetry or to his brief, ironic essays, but a rather long book on a facile and sentimental poet did not interest them. Borges himself was a bit unsure about what to do next. He had come to realize that poetry would never be his chief concern or his lasting claim to fame. He still was interested in exploring the dimensions of Argentina's reality but didn't know exactly how to go about it. By then he must have realized that to succeed in inventing a new writing, he had to invent a new kind of reader. At that precise point in his literary career he began contributing to *Sur,* the journal founded by Victoria Ocampo; it was to become for the next three decades the most influential literary publication in Latin America.

Borges had already met Victoria (as everybody has always called her) in 1925, at the time he was editing *Proa* with Ricardo Güiraldes. Ricardo and his wife, Adelina, had taken Victoria to meet the Borgeses. Borges was twenty-five at the time, and Victoria, nine years older, found him to be "a young man . . . with a certain shyness apparent in the way he walked, in his voice, in his handshake and his eyes of 'voyant' (seer) or medium, similar to those of his ravishingly beautiful sister Norah" (Ocampo, 1964, pp. 21–22). In an earlier mention, written when Borges received the 1961 Formentor Prize, Victoria gives more details:

233

Adelina and Ricardo used to sing praises of Georgie: "You're going to see how charming the Borgeses are!" Soon I had the chance to verify it. I went into that house, which was presided over by the smiling Leonor, and where her two *enfants terribles* were growing (no longer materially but spiritually)— they were magically terrible because of their uniqueness, let's make it clear. They both, in their different ways, seemed to walk a few inches above the earth we all tread on. . . .

One of the first times I spoke to that child with the angelic face who was called Norah, she asked me: "What do you like better, a rose or a lemon?" Immediately I saw the rose of the rose and the yellow of the lemon because Norah herself was probably seeing them. . . . Everything was happening in the world of the invisible, only visible for moments, and visible in a way that even today man hasn't been able to capture or science to name. In the same way that Norah transmitted to me (with questions which may seem childish because they are exactly the contrary of a cliché) the rose and yellow colors . . . , her brother too transmitted to me . . . everything that his words touched. Everything that belongs to us and that is supposed to be ours and that I, like he, feel as ours, as the most ours of all. (Ocampo, 1961, p. 76)

Many years later, in a 1975 conversation with me, Victoria summarized her final impression of the family group: "They were all so beautiful and gifted."

That encounter marked the beginning of a long friendship, but it was to be a friendship characterized by shyness on both sides, by reticence and reserve, by curiously comic misunderstandings that persist until today. From the very beginning, Victoria's imposing physical presence (she was one of the most handsome and regal of Argentine women), her fastidious and expensive taste in clothing, and her dominant character marked even more deeply than her seniority in age the tone of their friendship. She had a way of ordering people around— terribly well-bred but inarguable—that Borges once described to me as follows: "When Victoria invited you to visit her at San Isidro, she didn't ask you; she summoned you." Like her British namesake, Victoria had something despotic about her.

At the time they met, Victoria had already published three volumes of essays at the influential *Revista de Occidente* press. She was a friend of Ortega y Gasset, who owned the journal and the publishing house that published her first book. It came out in 1924, with an epilogue by Ortega that was half as long as her text. The book was a study of Dante's treatment of the medieval theme of sacred and profane love and started Victoria in her career as a feminist. Ortega's epilogue was respectful, warm, and patronizing: in those days even intelligent men were slightly surprised (as Dr. Johnson once suggested) that women could write at all. In Argentina, Victoria was generally viewed as an amateur, a society lady who enjoyed writing and lecturing with her beautiful, grave, educated voice. Everybody knew that she belonged to one of the oldest families, and that she was wealthy and fiercely independent. Although married very young to a distinguished member of the upper class, she lived on her own and was (at a time women in Argentina hardly ventured outside without a chaperone) what was then called, in the wake of a famous Norma Shearer movie, a free soul. Her writings were idiosyncratic and totally personal.

In fact, she didn't even write in Spanish. Educated by a French governess, she found literary French easier to cope with and had her books translated into Spanish before publication in her native language. In a sense, Victoria looked much like the caricature of the bluestocking ladies Molière and Sheridan had poked fun at. But she was closer to George Eliot and George Sand in her single-minded devotion to writing and her intellectual toughness. Only Argentina's literary machismo prevented the literary world from understanding exactly what she wanted. The sophisticated readers of the time found her style too private, her wealth and tendency to sit at the feet of great writers (Ortega, Tagore, Huxley, Valéry, Virginia Woolf) too snobbish, her feminism too militant. They were used to intelligent women who kept their places or wrote (if they ever wrote) like subdued men. Victoria's attitude was to upset and challenge these assumptions. Without breaking the rules of the upper class in which she was born and brought up, she started to change them, as quietly and effectively as she had done with the marriage conventions. The founding of *Sur* was her first step in leaving a lasting mark on Argentine culture.

The journal that began in 1931 was the result of the joint efforts at persuasion of a young Argentine novelist, Eduardo Mallea (who was Victoria's protégé), and Waldo Frank, an American novelist and essayist who was then visiting South America for the first time. They pleaded and pestered her until she agreed to launch and finance *Sur*. The title was provided by Ortega, who was hastily consulted over the phone. (The call itself has become a legend; in those days only Victoria could afford a long-distance call of that sort.) *Sur*'s logo (an arrow pointing south) made explicit the intentions of the journal. In Victoria's mind it was to serve both as a showplace for Argentine, and eventually Latin American, culture—a permanent exhibition of what it had to offer the West—and as a place where distinguished representatives of European and North American culture could mingle with local talents. In a sense, Victoria was as deeply interested in revealing the new native writing to the Argentines as in introducing the latest fashions in letters into Argentina. As one of the voices in Marcos Victoria's *Colloquium on Victoria Ocampo* (1934) said, she paid as much attention to choosing her

235

gloves or her hats as she did to choosing "the British novelist to be worn this spring or the German philosopher to be worn next winter." The mere fact that in 1934 a pamphlet was published to discuss Victoria shows the impact she had already made.

In her recollections of Borges, Victoria stresses his role in launching *Sur.* Along with Frank and Mallea, she "counted on Borges as the chief contributor to the journal and adviser to the whole enterprise" (Ocampo, 1964, p. 22). Borges had more experience than her Argentine colleagues in editing a literary magazine. In the 1920s he had founded and edited three little reviews and had contributed to a score of others, writing regularly for several of them. Although he had not yet started to make a living from literary journalism, he was a professional in a sense that neither Victoria nor Mallea would ever be. And his contributions to *Sur* would be an asset to that journal. It was a labor of love.

Because Victoria had to finance the journal out of her own pocket, for the first ten years she could not afford to pay its contributors. At the beginning it was an elegant quarterly that came out in a rather square format, with wide, white margins and large typography, obviously inspired by Paul Valéry's *Commerce.* In the first issue Victoria insisted on including some photographs that documented the range of Argentina's topography: the pampas, the Iguazú waterfalls, the Andes, and Patagonia. Many years later Borges told Napoleon Murat that he was amazed when he saw the illustrations, and that he assumed Victoria had published the photographs to show her friends in Europe what Argentina looked like. For him it was "a real geography manual . . . but a bit funny in Buenos Aires" (Murat, 1964, p. 377). In a quick rebuttal Victoria observed that her purpose had been to show Argentina to the Argentines, who were then rather ignorant about their native land and more interested in Europe (Ocampo, 1964b, p. 41).

The disagreement over those illustrations was symptomatic of a larger one between Victoria and Borges. In spite of their friendship, they had vastly different views about literature and life, about culture, and mainly about what a journal should look like. These differences never prevented Borges from being one of *Sur*'s most faithful contributors or prevented Victoria from thinking very highly of this brilliant but unorthodox young man. In his conversations with De Milleret, Borges recalls his misgivings about some aspects of *Sur:*

> The magazine was run in a strange way. At the beginning it was a bit exclusive, had a small circulation; it was a quarterly, and after three months the previous issue was as good as forgotten. Besides, Victoria had strange ideas about what a literary journal was: she wanted to publish only pieces by famous writers and didn't want notes on plays, films, concerts, books . . . all

that is the life of a journal, no? That is, what the reader wants: if he finds a forty-page article signed Homer and a fifty-page one signed Victor Hugo, that bores him and he doesn't think that it is a journal. . . . Besides, I think that the only way to have a journal is to have a group of people who have the same convictions, the same hatreds; a collection of pieces by famous authors does not make a journal . . . in spite of that, *Sur* has been and still is a decisive element in Argentine culture and that is, essentially, Victoria Ocampo's value. (De Milleret, 1967, pp. 60–61)

There are some photographs which document the launching of *Sur*. They were taken at Victoria's Bauhaus-style house in San Isidro. Apart from her, Mallea, and Borges, the group included Pedro Henríquez Ureña, then the foremost Latin American literary historian; Francisco Romero, a leading historian of philosophy; two former ultraist poets, Oliverio Girondo and Guillermo de Torre; Eduardo Bullrich, an architect and art critic who had contributed regularly to *Martín Fierro;* Ernest Ansermet, the French composer and music critic; and Ramón Gómez de la Serna, the dadaist Spanish writer who had finally made good his often announced and regularly postponed visit to Argentina. Not present at the time the photographs were taken were two of *Sur*'s guardian angels: Ortega y Gasset and Alfonso Reyes. Reyes' son was to be the first managing editor of the journal. The cast was very impressive and showed Victoria's success in attracting the stars of the Hispanic world. Photographs taken at the launching of *Sur* also reveal the unobtrusive presence of Raimundo Lida, an unassuming philologist who for a while held the position of managing editor before leaving Argentina for a more scholarly career as editor of the *New Review of Hispanic Philology* at El Colegio de México and later as professor of Spanish literature at Harvard.

But in spite of the credentials of all those writers, thinkers, and critics, the three people who were to make a lasting impact on *Sur* were Victoria, Mallea, and Borges. *Sur* would become Victoria's tribune, the place where she could influence and change Argentine culture. By introducing new subjects or authors, by reassessing old ones, she waged a persistent and effective campaign to update Argentine (and Latin American) culture. Bitterly discussed, even mocked and vilified, she published *Sur* well into the 1960s, changing the staff, discovering bright young talents, always busy with her cultural enterprises. Today *Sur* is no longer a journal, but it continues to publish under its imprint books and volumes of essays generally organized around a common subject.

If Victoria's task was usually challenged by those who could not accept a beautiful, wealthy woman as their cultural leader, the work produced by both Mallea and Borges had a different reception. They would dominate Argentina's literary life for the next thirty years. Mallea was four years younger than Borges. Although he started his career as a short-story writer—his first book had the fanciful title *Cuentos para una inglesa desesperada* (Stories for a Desperate Englishwoman, 1928)—he very shortly began to publish novels and book-length essays. The most important of his early works was *Historia de una pasión argentina* (History of an Argentine Passion, 1937), which was a "confession" of his hopes and anguish as a true Argentine. His theory of the "invisible Argentines" who would eventually come to the fore to redirect their country toward lofty moral goals was in a sense an answer to the depressing mediocrity of the army-ruled government. But it was too optimistic and vague about the recuperative powers of a nation already seriously damaged. In spite of its weaknesses, *Sur*'s readers were led to believe, by several reviewers, that the answer to all of Argentina's problems could be found in those elegant, uplifting pages. The appointment of Mallea as literary editor of the powerful Sunday supplement of *La Nación* consolidated his fame and influence.

Because Borges wrote only very short essays, and later short stories, it was taken for granted that Mallea, who published rather bulky novels, was the more important of the two. Readers then (as now) believed that the thickness of a book guaranteed the writer's soundness. Besides, Borges' pieces always seemed frivolous or ironic. Mallea's novels, on the other hand, were determined to prove that hard thinking and solemn, unsmiling prose were what was needed in South America. His books appealed mainly to the kind of audience that liked its Pascal and Kierkegaard in quotable doses and that was also fond of the Catholic novels of François Mauriac and Graham Greene (not the latter's entertainments, of course, which were more in Borges' province). Mallea was soon translated into English, French, and Italian, hailed by specialists in Latin American literature, and included in the required reading lists of Latin American seminars.

The fare Borges offered to *Sur*'s readers was totally different. Instead of ponderous essays on Argentine life and culture, he published short, oblique pieces on isolated, sometimes banal aspects of his country's reality: one article on a forgotten, second-rate gaucho poet; another on the funny inscription horse wagons then had; a series of very short reviews of current European and American movies. Borges' irony and wit were too dazzling, his deliberate selection of minor subjects too pointed. The majority of the readers (and probably Victoria herself) were not terribly amused. But slowly and firmly he began to form a group of followers, an almost secret society whose members looked like those secret provincial young men Valéry once told Mallarmé were ready to die for him.

One of the first, if not *the* first, of those faithful young men was

Néstor Ibarra. Born in France of an Argentine father who was the son of a French Basque émigré, Néstor Ibarra went to the University of Buenos Aires around 1925 to complete his graduate education. While attending the Faculty of Philosophy and Letters he discovered Borges' poems and fell under their spell. He attempted to persuade his teachers to let him write a thesis on Borges' ultraist poetry. As the poet was not yet thirty, his teachers rejected Ibarra's plan and told him to choose a safer subject. (He eventually wrote a thesis on the late Spanish baroque writer Villarroel, whom Borges had rediscovered in the early 1920s.) The failure to convince the academic world that Borges was worth a thesis did not deter Ibarra. In 1930 he published a book called *La nueva poesía argentina: ensayo crítico sobre el ultraísmo, 1921–1929* (The New Argentine Poetry: A Critical Essay on Ultraism).

Ibarra was barely twenty when he met Borges in 1928 or 1929. For fifteen years he lived in Buenos Aires, becoming so closely acquainted with the man and his writings that Borges once paid him the tribute of acknowledging: "Ibarra knows me more intimately than anybody else" (De Milleret, 1967, p. 132). By reading and rereading Borges, by talking and arguing endlessly with him (Ibarra is no sycophant), the young Basque managed to know Borges from the *inside,* as it were. That is, he was able to decode all the shades of irony, the elaborate system of deceptions and false confessions that form the fabric of Borges' texts. Ibarra's mature view of Borges can be found in his study *Borges et Borges,* which came out in 1969. It is an elaboration of a long piece he had previously published in *L'Herne*'s special issue on Borges (1964).

Many of his memories of Borges go back to those days in the late 1920s and early 1930s when he followed the slightly older master around Buenos Aires, walking endlessly until the small hours of the morning, stopping only to rest for a while in a café or to carefully watch some rose-colored streetcorner. They had first met at one of those literary dinners so common in Argentina's banquet years. According to Ibarra's recollections: "Chance had placed us next to each other in some dinner I cannot now recall; we walked out together and he made me do fifteen kilometers in two hours. A similar adventure happened to Paul Morand later, but he did not pass the test. *After the third block, the globetrotter gave up,* Borges told me" (Ibarra, 1969, p. 16). Morand was then famous for his slightly erotic travel books, but he was a lazy traveler, fond of big hotels, slow transatlantic steamships, and luxury trains. Borges was a born walker, and allied to Johnson in his passion for roaming around the streets of his city.

Soon conversations between Borges and Ibarra took the form of a ritual. They invented a new language, coined out of the etymological meaning of words, with some surrealist (or ultraist) touches added. Ibarra recalls:

> We had a small, warm slang (in the elaboration of which I had a very secondary place) . . . but totally decodable. . . . *Hypogeous* [in Latin: subterranean] meant the subway; *aquarium,* the bathroom. *Phanerogamic* was meant to designate male and female swimmers who were a shade too naked. A *seminar* was something you bought at the drugstore. [*Seminar* comes from *semen;* hence a prophylactic.] Sometimes we suddenly crossed the street to avoid being approached by an *anthropomorphous* Italian [an Italian in the form of a man]. (Ibid., pp. 16–17)

Ibarra also recalls Borges' dislike of Italians and quotes a saying by Carriego he liked to repeat: "Others are happy to hate the Italians. I hate to defame them." He also recalls Borges' dislike of Spaniards, which was almost equally irrational. Ibarra describes the Borges he then knew:

> He is big enough, comfortably wide. . . . His hard and prominent eyebrows give his eyes sometimes a withdrawn expression, even a melancholic one. But as soon as his eyes look at you, you realize your mistake. Lastly, everything is alive and clear in him. In all the meanings of the word. Clear, smooth, subtle. The skin is very white. . . . The hair is very dark. Pushed back, always a bit too long. From indifference, of course, not to look like an artist. He combs it with two fingers when it tickles his temples. (Ibarra, 1964, p. 420)

Of their endless conversations Ibarra recalls mostly the joy, the intelligence, the freshness, the healthiness, and especially the inexhaustible sense of humor: "I believe that he is literally the best-humored man I ever met" (ibid., p. 21). Some of the anecdotes of those days—Borges' refusal to answer negatively a self-serving inquiry made by a hat manufacturer because he was afraid of "being accused of being at the service of the manufacturers of nonhats"; his invention of a new French school, identism, in which objects were always compared to themselves; or the suggestion that an avant-garde review should be called *Papers for the Suppression of Reality*—give some of the flavor of the iconoclastic, untiring joker Borges then was. That he was more than that is proved by Ibarra's unceasing devotion. The faithful young man Valéry talked to Mallarmé about had found a witty reincarnation in Ibarra.

3.
Discussing the Discussant

Néstor Ibarra may have been Borges' first secret young man (in the sense Valéry used the expression), but Adolfo Bioy Casares became his first, very public disciple. Born in 1914, he was barely seventeen when he met Borges, but he had already authored two books.

The exact date of their meeting is hard to pinpoint. In his recollections Borges states flatly: "We met in 1930 or 1931, when he was about seventeen and I was just thirty" ("Essay," 1970, p. 245). In a recent chronology of his life Bioy seems to prefer 1932 (Bioy, 1975, p. 36). If the exact date is irretrievable, the place and the occasion are well known: they met at Victoria Ocampo's house in San Isidro. When the visit was over, Bioy took Borges back to Buenos Aires in his car, and they had the first of their many conversations. Bioy recalls that first meeting:

> Borges was then one of our best-known young writers and I was a young man with a book published privately and another under a pseudonym. When he asked me about my favorite authors, I took the floor and, braving my shyness, which prevented me from keeping the syntax straight for a whole sentence, I launched into praise of the dull prose of a poetaster who edited the literary section of a Buenos Aires newspaper. Perhaps to clear the air, Borges widened the question.
>
> "Of course," he admitted, "but apart from So-and-So, whom else do you admire, in this or any other century?"
>
> "Gabriel Miró, Azorín, James Joyce," I answered.
>
> What do you do with such an answer? I couldn't explain what I found in Miró's vast biblical or even ecclesiastical frescoes, in Azorín's small rural pictures, or in Joyce's garrulous and half-understood cascades from which rose, like rainbowed vapor, all the prestige of what was hermetic, strange, and

241

modern. Borges said something to the effect that only in writers devoted to the charm of words can young men find literature in quantities enough to satisfy them. Then, talking about my admiration for Joyce: "Of course. It is an intention, an act of faith, a promise. The promise that they"—he was talking about young men—"are going to like him when they read him." (Bioy, 1968, pp. 139–140)

Borges' polite irony can be seen here at its deadliest. But Bioy didn't mind. On the contrary, he sensed that he had finally found the mentor he was looking for. In her reminiscences of Borges, Victoria Ocampo acknowledges the part she played in bringing them together:

When Adolfo Bioy Casares was only Adolfito, his mother came to see me one day and talked at length about her unique and admired son's adolescent literary inclinations. She was concerned and proud. She asked me who would be able to guide the object of her worries, which Argentine writer could take him under his wing. Without any vacillation, I said Borges. "Are you sure?" she asked me. "Absolutely," I answered. And I was not mistaken. Between the two, and in spite of the difference in age, a great friendship was about to begin. I anticipated it but could not imagine it was going to be so strong . . . . (Ocampo, 1964, p. 23)

Borges and Bioy began to see each other regularly. In a few years' time (around 1936) they began to collaborate on some very unorthodox literary ventures. Victoria was right about Borges being the mentor Adolfito needed, but she was even shrewder in foreseeing Borges' future influence on Argentine literature. By 1932, with the publication of *Discusión* (his fifth book of prose and fourth of assorted essays), Borges became finally visible.

The fifteen pieces collected in that book were written in the late 1920s and early 1930s and reveal a few basic preoccupations. Some show Borges still very much concerned with the "essence" and "true nature" of Argentina, a subject that had occupied his writings during the 1920s. In two articles devoted to the study of two gaucho poets—Ascasubi and José Hernández, the author of *Martín Fierro*—Borges uses their texts to attempt to define a certain tone of voice, a style of conversation typical of the old "criollos." In selecting their most characteristic verses, he proves to have an ear subtly attuned to the native speech. It seems obvious that he thinks highly of both men, although he points out their limitations and defects and is very harsh with the critics who have attempted to canonize one of them (*Martín Fierro* is a sort of Argentine national epic) or to prove that Ascasubi was nothing but a "precursor" of Hernández. On the contrary, Borges rejects the concept of "precursor" and believes very strongly that Ascasubi is at his best when he doesn't sound at all like Hernández; he also believes that *Martín Fierro*'s most solid claim to fame is the fact that it is *not* an epic poem but a novel in verse. In reading both authors from a new critical perspective, Borges is performing a necessary task: going back to the canonical texts of Argentine culture to discover what they still have to say. In the same critical spirit, he wrote a piece called "Nuestras imposibilidades" (the literal translation "Our Inadequacies" misses the pun in the title), in which he heaps scorn on the average citizen of Buenos Aires: the "porteño." Written in a sort of direct, colloquial Argentine, it is a strong example of the kind of satire generally associated with Juvenal.

Borges is terribly upset about the habits of the porteño. Using the well-known device of "chaotic enumeration," he quickly sketches a portrait of that "mysterious everyday specimen" who venerates the low professions of public auctioneer and meat packer, who travels in buses but believes them to be lethal, who despises the United States and is happy that Buenos Aires can almost compete with Chicago in its number of murders, who rejects the possibility of an uncircumcized and beardless Jew, who intuits a secret relation between perverse or nonexistent virility and American cigarettes (true porteños prefer the Gauloise type of dark tobacco), who in nights of joyous celebration ingests pieces of the digestive, evacuative, or genital tracts of cows, who is proud of his Latin idealism but cherishes his native trickery and naïvely believes only in trickery.

The portrait brings out the worst aspects of the type: the contradictions between what the porteño believes and what he practices show how stupid, how gross, he is. The rest of the article is devoted to commenting on his most characteristic traits. The first is a lack of imagination. Everything that is unusual is, for the porteño, monstrous. To be a foreigner is to be inexcusable, wrong, slightly unreal. Borges does not spare the upper classes and pokes fun at those illustrated magazines devoted entirely to recording the elegance of such summer resorts as Mar del Plata. (The fact that he himself occasionally visited Mar del Plata to see Victoria Ocampo or Adolfito Bioy does not stop him from being nasty.) The second trait he wants to stress is the pleasure the porteño gets out of seeing somebody fail. It is the humiliation of the defeated that he is interested in watching. In the porteño's vocabulary, "to bear up" does not mean to endure with dignity; it is an exhortation addressed to the victim in order not to spoil the pleasure of watching pain. In the same way, if an Argentine woman wants to extol the pleasures of her summer holiday, she will say to her listener, "Take that," meaning "I had all this while you had nothing."

To properly enjoy what they have, the porteños need to be sure that others are deprived of it. Further, it is always a consolation to be able to hurt somebody. Borges closes that part of his article with a reference to the tolerance with which active sodomites are regarded, while the passives are viewed only with scorn. A parting shot is addressed to the military regime that had recently deposed President Irigoyen only to prove itself unable to run the country. According to Borges, in trying to ruin the moderates, whom Irigoyen represented, the army succeeded in leading people to socialism as the only alternative. Borges believes that the army's mistake was based on a grudge against Irigoyen. The article ends with these sad words: "I have been an Argentine for several generations; it is without any joy that I formulate these complaints" (*Discusión*, 1932, p. 17).

The article was originally published in *Sur* (no. 4, 1931) and reflects Borges' immediate disenchantment with the new Argentina that the army was trying to build. It also reflects a more general uneasiness with its culture, its lack of discrimination, its chaotic integration of different ethnic traits, its cult of trickery, and its primitive machismo. Borges' concern with the double standard in matters of sodomy shows how aware he already was of one of the most appalling contradictions of Argentine machismo. While pretending to abhor sodomy in all its forms and proclaiming openly his normal heterosexual appetites, the Argentine reveals in his conversation an obsession with anal intercourse that is slightly embarrassing. Borges avoids tackling that specific situation, but in pointing out the double standard he anticipates a correct reading of native sexual mores.

Borges' article was abrasive, and by placing it at the very beginning of *Discusión* he obviously wanted the reader not to miss the point made by the title. The rest of the book can be easily divided into two groups of articles: those that reveal his permanent preoccupation with philosophical matters and those that discuss rhetorical points. To the first belong "The Penultimate Version of Reality," in which he discusses Korzybski's theories as they had been condensed in an article by Francisco Luis Bernárdez; "A Vindication of the Cabala," which summarizes his knowledge of that esoteric doctrine; "A Vindication of the False Basilides," in which he develops an interpretation of gnosticism; "The Duration of Hell," in which he attempts to cope with the problems of eternity and evil; and "The Perpetual Race Between Achilles and the Tortoise," in which he discusses Zeno's paradox about the impossibility of movement.

In all these articles unexpected erudition, wit, and arbitrariness abound. Borges does not pretend to know everything about a given subject, and he repeatedly stresses the limitations of his scholarship. The fact that he did not take the trouble to read Korzybski directly is telling. What matters is not his scholarship but what the articles reveal about his main metaphysical preoccupations. The negation of space (seen as an attribute of time), the questioning of the reality of time, the doubts about our capacity to perceive reality—these are the real subjects that underlie the topics he discusses. At a very early age he was trained by Father to discuss them. In his first book of essays, *Inquisiciones* (1925) he had a go at them. Now he returns to the attack, this time with a more sophisticated technique, a better, more varied bibliography, and a subtler sense of humor. But he is still far from his goal. Not until 1947 would he be able to communicate coherently his preoccupations with the nonexistence of time and space.

More substantial are the articles that discuss rhetorical questions. If the Borges who seems so preoccupied with metaphysics can be compared to De Quincey (and the comparison has already been made), the Borges who is so concerned with rhetoric is closer to T. S. Eliot. In a sense, he is doing exactly what Eliot did in the articles he put together in his *Collected Essays,* published that same year: 1932. In reevaluating Shakespeare and the Jacobean dramatists, Dante and Baudelaire, and the English metaphysical poets, Eliot was paving the way for his experiments in writing dramatic verse and philosophical poems. Both *Murder in the Cathedral* and *The Four Quartets* are implicit in the *Collected Essays.* In the same way, Borges, in his discussions of Zeno and Korzybski, Bergson and Bertrand Russell, Nietzsche and Mauthner, was developing (very quietly) a new vision that would enable him to write his metaphysical poems and stories; and in his analyses of important aspects of the rhetoric of narrative, he anticipated his own experiments in short-story writing. He had always been a critic, but not of the disinterested sort. His criticism belongs to the category Eliot had named criticism of the practicants; that is, the criticism practiced by those who are paving the way for their own creative writing. From that point of view, the essays on rhetorical matters collected in *Discusión* are of extreme importance.

Two essays, "The Other Walt Whitman" and "Paul Groussac," appear to avoid large rhetorical questions, but even these are primarily concerned with placing a particular writer in a context of ideas; they do not confine their observations to the writer's work or personality. Whitman is seen not only in his texts (Borges translates three of his poems elegantly) but as a model of a certain type of writer. In a footnote Borges appends to the article, as if it were an afterthought, he points out that in discussing Whitman's work critics tend to fall prey to two different types of errors: first, they identify the writer with the larger-than-life poetic character about whom *Leaves of Grass* has so much to say; second, they write about Whitman aping his own extraordinary style and vocabulary. The footnote is not so casual as it seems. It helps to clarify the title of the article: the "other" Whitman Borges is talking about is the writer himself, not the poetic character. The distinction is essential for Borges' theory of literature. Avoiding the biographical trap, he points directly to what really matters in criticism: the study of the texts as texts, not as expressions of a certain writer's life or dreams or as documents of a given society. His attitude is antiholistic. The article does not develop this theory any further. In 1947 Borges returned to the subject in another article, "Note on Walt Whitman," later collected in *Other Inquisitions* (1952).

The article on Paul Groussac seems even less promising. In the prologue Borges calls it "dispensable." It is a harsh sentence, not only because the article contains a witty evaluation of a man who had a decisive influence on Argentine culture (he was a French émigré who became director of the National Library and the foremost literary critic of his time) but also because it places Groussac very firmly among the writers who had a major influence on Borges' style. He begins the article by admitting that he is a hedonistic reader: "I've never let a sense of duty interfere with so personal a habit as buying books; nor have I given a second chance to an unruly author." Thus he finds very significant that in his select library he has no fewer than ten books by Paul Groussac. He concludes that Groussac's readableness (a word Borges uses in English in his text) is due to the easiness of his style. "In Spanish it is a very rare virtue: all conscientious style communicates to the reader part of the trouble that went into producing it. Apart from Groussac, I have found only in Alfonso Reyes a similar concealment or invisibility of effort" (*Discusión,* 1932, p. 125).

The statement may seem merely witty but it is more than that. It is a recognition of the two masters who taught Borges how to overcome the excesses of both baroque and ultraist prose. Borges learned from Groussac and Reyes how to avoid parading the kind of style he was going to become famous for. In the last paragraph of the article he admits that if Groussac had lived and worked in Europe or the United States he would perhaps have been only a second-rate writer. But in this "forsaken republic" he is undoubtedly a master. In writing about Groussac, Borges is not only trying to give him his due. He is also using him as a symbol and prototype of the kind of writer he prefers.

Of the three articles that deal exclusively with rhetorical questions, the clearest is "La supersticiosa ética del lector" (The Superstitious Ethics of the Reader), a piece that can be seen as a complement of the one on Groussac. Borges attacks the Argentine reader's habit of paying more attention to the details of style than to the conviction or emotion the text conveys. For him, Argentines "pay attention not to the effectiveness of the mechanism [of style] but to the way the parts are distributed. They subordinate emotion to ethics, or better, to an unchallenged etiquette" (ibid., p. 44). The rest of the article debunks the notion of a "perfect" style and defends colloquial speech. In attacking the concept of perfection, Borges is also paving the way for the view of reality—as transitory, changing, unreliable—he would present in his forthcoming fiction. The article attacked some ingrained notions Argentines had about literature and was very popular.

Less popular but more important are the other two articles: "La postulación de la realidad" (The Postulation of Reality) and "El arte narrativo y la magia" (Narrative Art and Magic). They are closely connected. The first is devoted primarily to discussing the problem of verisimilitude; that is, the problem of how to present reality in literature and make it believable. To explain his point of view, Borges uses Croce's identification between the esthetic and the expressive. More than a hint of that theory can be recognized in the previous article on style: in censuring the reading habits of the Argentines, Borges was actually complaining that they were not able to recognize the need for expressiveness in style. In this new article, Borges uses Croce's theory to point out the difference between the classicists, who seem to shun expression, and the romantics, who emphasize expression. Borges empties these categories of any historical sense; they represent for him two different ways of handling literature. The classical writer has no need to express reality; he is content with mentioning it. To put it differently, he attempts to present reality not in its immediacy but only in its final elaboration as concepts. Thus the classical writer does not try to reproduce every state of mind, every feeling, every thought of his characters; he accepts the fact that literature (like real life) is not always precise and believes that vagueness is more tolerable or believable in literature than the romantic pretension of transcribing reality in all its peculiarities. It is obvious that for Borges (although he does not put it that way) realism is, from this point of view, also "romantic."

A paradox can be detected here. Because classical writers shun a total expression of reality, they get closer to it than the romantics (or realists), who by including all the unnecessary details tend to destroy reality. In selecting his examples, Borges does not pay too much attention to conventional literary periods. Cervantes and Gibbon are presented as classicists, although from the point of view of literary history one is really a baroque writer and the other a neoclassicist. But, for Borges, both have one trait in common: they do not attempt to portray reality in its entirety; they do not make precision their goal. In the same way, the Victorian William Morris and the Argentine modernist Enrique Larreta are quoted, along with H. G. Wells, Daniel Defoe, and the films of Josef von Sternberg, to illustrate a point about the invention of circumstantial details. Borges is not really trying to do away with the usual literary labels. He is more concerned with defining a certain concept of verisimilitude. For him, verisimilitude is not what conforms to the real, or what a certain literary period or a certain genre claims to be the real. It is what gives more feeling or expresses more reality in a certain text. Verisimilitude has less to do with reality than with the conventions of a certain culture about how to portray reality.

Unfortunately, the article is not at all clear, and to be properly understood it not only needs a very careful reading but must be read along with Borges' complementary piece on narrative art and magic. Here Borges expands his point of view and defines it with greater accuracy. In attempting to study narrative techniques, he begins by admitting that the subject is relatively new and that the study of narrative has not yet reached the sophisticated stage of the study of poetry or of the art of speechmaking. With these provisos, he attempts to define a certain type of narrative: one that follows the procedures of magic. Opposing the realistic type of narrative to that one, Borges contends that writers who deal in extraordinary subjects always attempt to present the extraordinary as normal. He cites two rather unexpected examples: *The Life and Death of Jason,* a novel in verse by William Morris, and Edgar Allan Poe's only novel, *The Narrative of A. Gordon Pym.* He underlines how carefully Morris introduces centaurs and mermaids in his narrative; how cleverly Poe avoids any reference to white in describing an imaginary tribe's horror of whiteness. From his analysis he concludes that there are two types of narratives: the realistic type, which pretends to present chaotic reality in all its details and follows the arbitrary (that is, conventional) descriptions of science; and the magical type, which follows magic in its lucid and beautifully organized way of presenting reality. He concludes that because magic is more rigorous than science and does not leave anything to chance, magic works within a very formal framework. In magical narratives everything is relevant; there are no loose ends. A perfect structure forces every part to correspond to the whole. From the point of view of narrative, it means that texts are built according to a rigorous plot. All episodes have an ulterior consequence. Borges' view of narrative is based on causality. At the end of his article, he postulates a teleology of narrative, illustrating his thesis with examples from Chesterton's short fictions, Joyce's *Ulysses,* and the films of von Sternberg.

Read in connection with the previous article, "Narrative Art and Magic" becomes clearer. But with a perversity that his readers know very well, Borges separates the two articles by a series of short pieces on film. This little trick, and the fact that many early readers found it extremely difficult to follow his arguments, has perpetuated the separation between the two pieces. Even today, when criticism of Borges' texts has reached a high level of accuracy, critics tend to ignore the first article or to overlook the fact that both are based on a similar concept of verisimilitude. Today it is obvious that in those articles Borges laid the foundation for a theory of fantastic literature that he would later develop in important articles and, especially, in his fiction.

The short pieces on film show another aspect of Borges' versatile criticism. In commenting on some films by Fedor Ozep (*The Brothers Karamazov*), Charles Chaplin (*City Lights*), Josef von Sternberg (*Morocco*) and King Vidor (Elmer Rice's *Street Scene*), Borges demonstrates his familiarity with the main cinematographic trends of the 1920s and early 1930s. He also reveals a marked preference for the American cinema, especially for von Sternberg, whose visual images and use of discontinuous montage would have a great influence on his own narrative style. In "Narrative Art and Magic" and in the prologue to his first book of short stories (*A Universal History of Infamy*, 1935), he does in fact pay tribute to von Sternberg's style. Film criticism was an intermittent occupation for him. On and off, he followed the development of cinematic art, from Chaplin's *The Gold Rush* (which he reviewed in the newspaper *La Nación*) to Orson Welles' *Citizen Kane* (reviewed in *Sur*). Even today, when he is no longer able to see a movie, he loves to go to the cinema to listen to the dialogue, while an occasional companion gives him some hint of what is happening on screen.

Borges' previous books of essays had been read only by his closest friends and were, in a sense, almost underground books. With *Evaristo Carriego*, he began to find a larger audience for his prose, but it was *Discusión* that made him truly visible. The book was published as the first volume in a collection of new Argentine writers. It immediately caught the attention of the critics. In 1933 the magazine *Megáfono* devoted the second half of its August issue to a "Discussion on Jorge Luis Borges." It was the first of many attempts to evaluate his work. In its efforts to be polemical, it used a device that could be called the one-way writers' roundtable. The first writer passed his text to the next, who could refute or complement it; the second writer passed the two texts to a third; and so on. The contributors were mainly aspiring young writers. Some were enthusiastic about Borges, some tepid, some totally hostile and even rude. The result, from an intellectual point of view, was rather thin. The best pieces were written by slightly older men—the French writer Pierre Drieu la Rochelle, the Spanish linguist and critic Amado Alonso—who had a broader perspective. Drieu, a very influential novelist and essayist, had met Borges while visiting Argentina as a guest of Victoria Ocampo. In a short piece written on his way back to France, he coined a phrase that is still remembered:

"Borges vaut le voyage"—"Borges is worth the trip" (*Megáfono,* August 1933, p. 14). He was one of the first to recognize not only the extraordinary intelligence but also the sense of humor and the passion with which Borges grasped reality. For Amado Alonso, Borges was maturing into a writer totally responsible for the meaning of words. He praises him for having changed from a baroque writer whose effort to achieve an effect was too visible into a stylist whose writing seems almost effortless. He concurs with Borges' own evaluation of style in the piece, already quoted, about Paul Groussac.

The younger contributors either praised Borges too much or failed to recognize any value in his poems or essays. While Alonso had applauded his literary behavior, which he summarized in the words "responsibility, sincerity, and [a desire for] precision" (ibid., p. 19), several contributors deplored the lack of coherence in his arguments—Ignacio B. Anzoátegui claimed that the article on hell was "unworthy of a chicken's brain" (ibid., p. 17)—or lamented the fragmentary nature of his pieces. Even a faithful admirer such as Enrique Mallea (brother of Eduardo) insisted that his fragmentary approach was a negative quality, without realizing that it was a form of composition and not a defect. In a similar fashion he could have lamented that sonnets are short. Some attacked Borges for not being aware of Argentina's social and political reality. Among these, Enrique Anderson Imbert cut a striking figure: he seemed to be emphatically committed to the socialist cause and claimed to be "living a profound social enthusiasm," an attitude that was quickly satirized by another participant. Anderson Imbert was then only twenty-three; today, after living and teaching in the United States for the last thirty years, his social enthusiasm has not waned, but his judgment about Borges' place in Argentine literature has obviously changed.

If the critical level of the discussion on *Discusión* was not totally satisfactory, the importance of that special issue of *Megáfono,* as an indicator of how Borges was then evaluated, cannot be overlooked. For the first time, a member of the new generation of Argentine writers was taken seriously enough by his colleagues to be the object of a collective evaluation. The fact that the discussion even took place is what really matters. It confirmed Borges' status as the most important young writer in Argentina. Those secret young men who had been gathering around him, and of whom both Néstor Ibarra and Adolfo Bioy Casares were already so representative, were no longer the only ones to be attracted to his writings. A larger audience was slowly being formed. Borges was on the verge of an important breakthrough in his literary career.

4.
The Yellow Literary Press

The month of August 1933, when *Megáfono* published its "Discussion on Jorge Luis Borges," saw a new literary magazine in Buenos Aires. It was called *Revista Multicolor de los Sábados* (Saturday Multicolored Review) and was distributed free to the buyers of *Crítica,* the most popular Argentine newspaper of the time. *Crítica* was the best of many publications that appealed to a mass audience. It was a good example of how to produce a sensational and, at the same time, literate paper. The editor, Natalio Botana, had introduced the style and method of United States' tabloids into Argentina. If the news wasn't striking or scandalous enough, *Crítica* invented it. Once the paper went so far as to report an imaginary uprising among the Chaco Indians in northern Argentina which culminated, when the news value of the hoax was exhausted, with a bold headline: CRÍTICA MAKES PEACE AT CHACO.

Botana had always wanted to have a cultural magazine attached to *Crítica.* After several trials, he launched the *Saturday Multicolored Review.* It was designed to compete with the long-established and high-brow Sunday literary supplement published by *La Nación,* which had been edited by Eduardo Mallea since 1931. Botana decided to hire Borges as literary editor of the *Saturday Multicolored Review.* Thus, for a while, two of Victoria Ocampo's brightest young men were able to shape the taste of the Argentine audience.

Borges had more experience in literary journalism than Mallea. His contributions to *Martín Fierro* and to *Síntesis* in the late 1920s had shown his skill at writing short pieces on books and authors. Writing for *Sur* and other literary publications did not consume all his time. Thus, when Botana came up with the offer to edit the *Saturday Multicolored Review,* Borges was ready to accept. The pay was small, Botana

very demanding, and the pace killing. But he took to the job with enthusiasm. Ulyses Petit de Murat, one of his friends from the *Martín
Fierro* days, was there to help him; he was an ultraist poet, eight years
younger. He and Borges had been active in the committee of young
writers who supported Irigoyen's second term. Petit de Murat worked
as film critic for *Crítica,* and it was perhaps through him that Botana
approached Borges.

Apart from contributing at least twenty-nine original pieces to
the magazine, Borges also selected and translated pieces from his favorite authors for *Crítica.* Chesterton, Kipling, Wells, and the German-
Czech author Gustav Meyrink shared with Swift, Novalis, and James
Frazer the gaudy pages of the supplement. He also introduced some of
his closest friends' works. Articles by Néstor Ibarra (on Ernst Lubitsch),
Xul-Solar, his cousin Guillermo Juan Borges, and the Uruguayan nov-
elist Enrique Amorim all found in Borges a generous promoter. His
own contributions were varied and, in some cases, extraordinary.
There were a few reviews of new books by Argentine, Uruguayan, and
Brazilian writers, the best of which is a short evaluation of Ezequiel
Martínez Estrada's *Radiografía de la pampa,* published in the issue of
September 16, 1933. The book (translated into English as *X-Ray of the
Pampas*) was a metaphysical and lyrical attempt to reveal the mystery of
Argentina's vast emptiness. In his short review Borges begins by linking
Martínez Estrada with a lineage of intense German writers. According
to him, they

> have invented a new literary genre: the pathetic interpretation of the pa-
> thetic history of history and even of geography. Oswald Spengler is the most
> distinguished practitioner of that way of writing history, which excludes the
> novelesque charm of biography and anecdotes, but also the skully digres-
> sions of Lombroso, the sordid shopkeeper's arguments of the economic
> school, and the intermittent heroes, always indignant and moral, which Car-
> lyle prefers. The circumstantial does not interest the new interpreters of his-
> tory, nor individual destinies, in a mutual play of activities and passions. Its
> theme is not succession but the eternity of each man or each type of man:
> the peculiar style of intuiting death, time, the I, the others, the circum-
> stances, and the world. (Rivera, 1976, p. 23)

In pointing out Martínez Estrada's models, Borges does not fail
to mention Keyserling and Waldo Frank. Both writers had visited
South America recently and had described vividly their impressions of
Argentina. Borges finds Martínez Estrada not inferior to his models,
and he praises his prose without reservation. In commenting on his
strictures against Argentina, he has this to say: "He is a writer of splendid bitterness. I'll say more: of the most burning and difficult bitter-

ness, that goes well with passion and even with love" (Rivera, 1976, p. 23). Borges' appraisal of Martínez Estrada's book was prophetic. At the time, very few people in Argentina recognized the author's distinction. Borges never doubted it. In his criticism he anticipated the judgment of the next thirty years.

The other reviews were of less interest and in a sense were an example of the kind of supportive criticism the French call *critique de soutien*. Old friends and accomplices from the *Martín Fierro* days— Norah Lange, Ricardo Güiraldes, the Uruguayan poet Ildefonso Pereda Valdés—predominate. But if the reviews are disappointing in general, some pieces Borges wrote under the pseudonym of F[rancisco] Bustos (a family surname) were outstanding. Three of them, when collected in 1960 in *El hacedor* (called *Dreamtigers* in the English translation), show how far Borges had already gone in developing his own style. The best-known piece is "Dreamtigers," a sort of Kafkaesque parable about the tigers that he was so fond of as a child and that continued to visit his adult dreams. A second piece, "The Draped Mirrors," reveals another well-known obsession. With the utmost economy, he tells the story of a woman friend haunted by Borges' image: when looking at herself in a mirror, she sees him. The third, an even shorter piece called "Toenails," celebrates the blind obstinacy of those parts of his body that would continue to grow long after he was dead.

The major piece that Borges published under a pseudonym was a short story called "Hombre de la esquina rosada" ("Streetcorner Man" in Di Giovanni's translation). It is an expansion of an anecdote told in "Hombres pelearon" (Men Fought), which was collected in *El idioma de los argentinos* (1928). But what had been there just the bare outline of a knife duel between two hoodlums is now an elaborate narrative, written in the first person and purporting to be the oral report given to Borges by a witness to the encounter. The fight has some dramatic qualities: the challenger, Francisco Real, arrives from the north deliberately to engage Rosendo Juárez, one of Nicolás Paredes' hoodlums. Juárez does not react to the challenge and instead flees, leaving Francisco Real not only victorious but also in possession of Juárez's woman, La Lujanera (The Woman from Luján). The narrator, a young man who belongs to Juárez's gang, tells of his humiliation at his boss's cowardice, his longing for revenge, and the sudden and brutal ending: Francisco Real (after having taken La Lujanera outside with him for a quickie) comes back to the party to die from wounds inflicted in a duel. Who killed him? Juárez, the woman, somebody else? The narrator does not say. But there are two clues which hint that the narrator himself did it, to avenge the gang's honor.

The story was Borges' first, but he didn't dare acknowledge his paternity. The pseudonym helped him to face the challenge of a new genre. In a sense, the fact that the story is also about a man who hides behind the name of a narrator to avoid boasting is very relevant.

"Streetcorner Man" became one of Borges' more popular stories, but he soon grew tired of it. In recalling the period of his contributions to *Crítica,* he attempts to dismiss it:

> It took me six years, from 1927 to 1933, to go from that all too self-conscious sketch "Hombres pelearon" to my first outright short story, "Hombre de la esquina rosada" (Streetcorner Man). A friend of mine, Don Nicolás Paredes, a former political boss and professional gambler of the Northside, had died, and I wanted to record something of his voice, his anecdotes, and his particular way of telling them. I slaved over my every page, sounding out each sentence and striving to phrase it in his exact tones. . . . Originally titled "Hombres de las orillas" (Men from the Edge of Town), the story appeared in the Saturday supplement, which I was editing, of a yellow-press daily called *Crítica.* But out of shyness, and perhaps a feeling that the story was a bit beneath me, I signed it with a pen name—the name of one of my great-great-grandfathers, Francisco Bustos. Although the story became popular to the point of embarrassment (today I only find it stagy and mannered and the characters bogus), I never regarded it as a starting point. It simply stands there as a kind of freak. ("Essay," 1970, p. 238)

Borges is too severe with the story. Although it is a bit stagy and mannered and the characters are probably bogus, it reveals an extraordinary sense of narrative for someone who had, so far, written only poems and essays. He has followed some obvious models: Agatha Christie's *The Murder of Roger Ackroyd* (1926), for the surprise ending (in that novel, it is again the killer who tells the story without describing the murder itself); Chesterton and Kipling for the invention of circumstantial details and vivid visual images; and von Sternberg's movies for the cutting and editing, which is sharp, lean, taut.

There is more to Borges' use of a pseudonym than shyness and a fear of criticism. In the "Autobiographical Essay," after telling how he tried to reproduce Nicolás Paredes' exact tone of voice, he adds: "We were living out in Adrogué at the time and, because I knew my mother would heartily disapprove of the subject matter, I composed it in secret over a period of several months" (ibid., p. 238). The information is revealing. In 1930 Borges had already had trouble convincing Father and Mother that the popular poet Evaristo Carriego was a suitable subject for a biography. Although they were friends of the man, they did not think highly of his poetry or of the subject he handled in his works: the slums of Buenos Aires. Borges' friendship with Nicolás Paredes (who helped him in his search for authenticity while writing the Carriego book) must have also seemed wrong to them. In this context, it is not surprising that Borges used a pseudonym. But always contradictory, by choosing the name of one of Father's ancestors, he was flaunting the pseudonym. The selection of the pen name was the kind of subtle practical joke Mother's snobbery deserved.

The most important contributions Borges made to *Crítica* were six stories he later collected (with "Streetcorner Man" and some other pieces) in his next book, *A Universal History of Infamy* (1935). In the preface to the second Spanish edition of that book (1954) he explains, rather apologetically, that the pieces "are the irresponsible game of a shy young man who dared not write stories and so amused himself by falsifying and distorting (without any esthetic justification whatsoever) the tales of others" (*Infamy*, 1972, pp. 11–12). In his "Autobiographical Essay" Borges returns to the subject to add a few more details. After discussing "Streetcorner Man," he says:

> The real beginning of my career as a story writer starts with the series of sketches entitled *Historia universal de la infamia* (A Universal History of Infamy), which I contributed to the columns of *Crítica* in 1933 and 1934. The irony of it is that "Streetcorner Man" really was a story, but these sketches and several of the fictional pieces which followed them, and which very slowly led me to legitimate stories, were in the nature of hoaxes and pseudo-essays. In my *Universal History*, I did not want to repeat what Marcel Schwob had done in his *Imaginary Lives*. He had invented biographies of real men about whom little or nothing is recorded. I, instead, read up on the lives of known persons and then deliberately varied and distorted them according to my own whims. For example, after reading Herbert Ashbury's *The Gangs of New York*, I set down my free version of Monk Eastman, the Jewish gunman, in flagrant contradiction of my chosen authority. I did the same for Billy the Kid, for John Murrel (whom I rechristened Lazarus Morell), for the Veiled Prophet of Khorassan, for the Tichborne Claimant, and for several others. I never thought of book publication. The pieces were meant for popular consumption in *Crítica* and were pointedly picturesque. I suppose now the secret value of those sketches—apart from the sheer pleasure the writing gave me—lay in the fact that they were narrative exercises. Since the general plots or circumstances were all given me, I had only to embroider sets of vivid variations. ("Essay," 1970, pp. 238–239)

Once more, in recalling the past and summarizing his intentions, Borges telescopes too much. A careful comparison between the stories and the sources reveals that he did more than "vivid variations." In some cases ("The Dread Redeemer Lazarus Morell" and "Tom Castro, the Implausible Impostor") he radically changed the axis of the story; in at least one case, "The Masked Dyer, Hakim of Merv," he added so many new things (including a whole fictional cosmogony) that

255

the original sources were totally forgotten. Besides, many of the sources he acknowledges in the list at the end of the volume were also invented—as was the case with *Die Vernichtung der Rose* (*The Annhilation of the Rose*), Leipzig, 1927, attributed to an unknown Alexander Schulz, a name that thinly disguises Xul-Solar's real name. Borges was using the list of sources as an extra mask.

Even in the case of a story that had its roots in a real, identifiable source—such as "Tom Castro, the Implausible Impostor," based on an article by Thomas Secombe in the *Encyclopaedia Britannica* (eleventh ed.; XXVI, 932–933)—Borges altered the story substantially. The original anecdote is rather simple. A man called Arthur Orton attempts to pass himself off as Roger Charles Tichborne, the heir of one of England's wealthiest Catholic families, who had disappeared in a shipwreck off the coast of Brazil fourteen years ago. In the *Britannica* Orton is the one who conceives the impersonation scheme. He secures the help of Bogle, a black servant (who worked for the Tichbornes), only to get some information about the family. In Borges' version Bogle is the mastermind. He not only coaches Orton but guides and supports him throughout the dangerous enterprise, stage-manages the climactic encounter with Lady Tichborne, and finally defends him until his very last gasp. The *Britannica* is silent about Bogle's prominence and devotes exactly one sentence to him. In developing this incidental character into the most decisive one from the point of view of plot, Borges changes what was a rather banal narrative about a failed case of swindling into a drama. Orton and Bogle are presented as parodies of Faust and Mephistopheles. The fact that the intellectual leader is black and the protagonist is white makes it more telling.

A detailed study of the source and Borges' version reveals not only changes in emphasis but also important alterations in the actual circumstances of the story. The first encounter between Orton and Lady Tichborne is managed by Bogle with the brilliance of a stage director. In the *Britannica* the encounter, which takes place on a dark January afternoon in a Paris hotel, proves Orton's cowardice: he hides in bed, his face turned to the wall, to avoid as much as possible Lady Tichborne's questioning eyes. In Borges' version Bogle accompanies Orton to Paris and, instead of hiding him, takes him to Lady Tichborne's hotel. The January afternoon is (in the story) sunny. Upon entering, Bogle goes to the window and throws open the blinds: "The light created a mask, and the mother, recognizing her prodigal son, drew him into her eager embrace" (*Infamy*, 1972, p. 35). The dramatic boldness of Bogle's action is characteristic of Borges' boldness with his sources.

One of the general sources Borges never mentioned in print

prior to writing the "Autobiographical Essay" is Marcel Schwob's *Imaginary Lives*. Although he did not use any of the French symbolist's stories, it is obvious to any reader of both writers that the model for the Borges stories could be found in Schwob's book, especially in the best story, "MM. Burke and Hare, Murderers." According to Suzanne Jill Levine, Borges once remarked that the "concept" of *Imaginary Lives* "was superior to the book itself, and added that the last story, 'Burke and Hare,' was the best and the only one in which Schwob achieved his concept" (Levine, 1972, p. 25). "The key to this emphatic style is precisely the selection of relevant details," comments Levine. In the preface to the first edition of *A Universal History of Infamy* Borges had already acknowledged the style without identifying the general source:

> The exercises in narrative prose that make up this book were written in 1933 and 1934. They stem, I believe, from my rereadings of Stevenson and Chesterton, and also from Sternberg's early films, and perhaps from a certain biography of Evaristo Carriego. They overly exploit certain tricks: random enumerations, sudden shifts of continuity, and the paring down of a man's whole life to two or three scenes. . . . They are not, they do not try to be, psychological. (*Infamy*, 1972, p. 13)

In spite of not mentioning Schwob in the preface to that book, Borges had acknowledged at the time his interest in Schwob. One story from *Imaginary Lives* was included among the pieces he had recommended for publication in *Crítica*. "Burke and Hare" was the one he chose.

5.
The Irresponsible Games

Although Borges had written poems about the pampas and essays on the gaucho poets, his actual knowledge of gaucho life was limited. His first real experience of that region of Argentina came around 1909, when he was ten, and produced the memory of an empty space in which the "nearest house was a kind of blur on the horizon" ("Essay," 1970, p. 212). It was not until he was thirty-five that he had the chance to visit an area where gaucho life was still commonplace. In the summer of 1934 he went to visit the Amorims, wealthy relatives who lived in Salto Oriental, overlooking the Uruguay River. Enrique Amorim was a Uruguayan novelist, a year younger than Borges, and had married Esther Haedo, Borges' cousin and companion in his childhood games. Enrique had studied in Buenos Aires and used to live part of each year in Argentina and part in his native town of Salto, in Uruguay's northwest. The Amorims had land and cattle. Although the business side was left to one of his brothers, Enrique loved to visit the countryside and even wrote some fine novels about the present-day gauchos.

Enrique's home was a beautiful, white Bauhaus-style house he himself had designed. It was called "Las Nubes" (The Clouds), because it was built on a hill which dominated the old town, closer to the sky than to the active river port. Enrique was a convivial host and loved to take home movies of his guests. Borges' visit was duly recorded in a sequence that has extremely funny moments. Like so many vacationers, Borges had let his mustache and beard grow, had completely forgotten to comb his hair, and sported a rather uncouth look. On his visit he was accompanied by his sister, Norah, and his brother-in-law, Guillermo de Torre. Borges constantly poked fun at Guillermo's truly Spanish ignorance of native things. In one of the shots Borges is seen poking Guillermo with a long pole that cattlemen use to prod cattle. The scene was symbolic in more than one sense. In assuming the gaucho side, Borges was underlining not only his hostility to Spaniards but also his undisguised lack of sympathy for Guillermo. Some other photographic documents of the visit show Borges, freshly shaved and conventionally dressed in a dark suit, at the helm of the ferry that took them up the Uruguay River.

At least five of the stories Borges wrote in the next fifteen years were influenced by that rather short visit. During his stay Borges came face to face with a type of violence he had found so far only in books and films. In those days the frontier between Uruguay and Brazil was still very rough country. Except in two places where a wide river marked the boundary (the Cuareim in the west, the Yaguarón in the east), the line that divided the two countries existed only on maps. At one point, where the Uruguayan city of Rivera met the Brazilian city of Santa Anna do Livramento, the frontier was a long, open boulevard with no customhouse whatsoever. Landowners had ranches on both sides of the frontier, an arrangement highly conducive to smuggling cattle. It was the River Plate equivalent of the Far West. Life was cheap there, and the ranchowners' hired hands were as careless with their own and other people's blood as the legendary gauchos. It was in Santa Anna do Livramento that Borges was witness to a casual killing.

In some notes he dictated for the American translation of *The Aleph and Other Stories* (1970), Borges summarizes the episode:

A ten days' stay on the Uruguay-Brazil border seems to have impressed me far more than all the kingdoms of the world and the glory of them, since in my imagination I keep going back to that one not very notable experience. (At the time, I thought of it as boring, though on one of those days I did see a man shot down before my very eyes.) A likely explanation for this is that everything I then witnessed—the stone fences, the longhorn cattle, the horses' silver trappings, the bearded gauchos, the hitching posts, the ostriches—was so primitive, and even barbarous, as to make it more a journey into the past than a journey through space. (*The Aleph,* 1970, p. 271)

In 1964 he reconstructed the episode in more vivid terms for one of his interviewers, Carlos Peralta. Talking about his limited knowledge of Latin America at the time, Borges indicated that he spent a few days in Santa Anna do Livramento,

where I had the chance to see a man killed. We were in a bar with Amorim, and at the next table sat the bodyguard of a very important person, a *capanga*. A drunkard came too close to him and the *capanga* shot him twice.

Next morning, the said *capanga* was in the same bar, having a drink. All that had happened at the table next to us, but I'm telling you what I was told later, and that memory is clearer than reality. I only saw a man who stopped, and the noise of the shots. (Peralta, 1964, p. 413)

With that very limited material, which somehow kept coming back to him, Borges built a few dramatic episodes that he distributed among several stories to lend them verisimilitude. One of the first uses of the visit was a sequence in "Tlön, Uqbar, Orbis Tertius," a story he originally published in 1940. In the second part of the story, when the narrator is trying to solve the riddle of that mysterious land, interpolated into reality by an apocryphal volume of a second-rate encyclopedia, he introduces a new character, Herbert Ashe, a British engineer from the Argentine Southern Railway. Recalling a conversation with Ashe about the sexagesimal system of numbering (in which 60 is written as 10), he points out that the engineer made a reference to Río Grande do Sul. "We talked of country life, of the *capanga,* of the Brazilian etymology of the word *gaucho* (which some old Uruguayans still pronounce *gaúcho*) and nothing more was said—may God forgive me—of duodecimal functions" (*Labyrinths,* 1962, p. 6).

Later, in the same story, Borges puts his experiences on the frontier to even better use. Displacing the time of the episode to suit the fantastic chronology of the story, he dates in 1942 (in a story published in 1940) the visit to the north of Uruguay. The place he now evokes is a country store owned by a Brazilian in Cuchilla Negra, on the Uruguayan side of the frontier. "Amorim and I were returning from Sant'Anna. The river Tacuarembó had flooded and we were obliged to sample (and endure) the proprietor's rudimentary hospitality. He provided us with some creaking cots in a large room cluttered with barrels and hides" (ibid., p. 16). The rest of the episode belongs to Borges' fantasy.

The same frontier setting is used in another story, "The Shape of the Sword," which he included in his second book of "legitimate" short stories, *Ficciones* (1944). The protagonist accidentally meets a man called by his neighbors the "Englishman from La Colorada" (from the name of the ranch he rented); the action takes place in Tacuarembó.

The Englishman came from the border, from Rio Grande del Sur; there are many who say that in Brazil he had been a smuggler. The fields were overgrown with grass, the waterholes brackish; the Englishman, in order to correct those deficiencies, worked fully as hard as his laborers. . . . The last time I passed through the northern provinces, a sudden overflowing of the Caraguatá stream compelled me to spend the night at La Colorada. . . . After dinner we went outside to look at the sky. It had cleared up, but beyond the low hills the southern sky, streaked and gashed by lightning, was conceiving another storm. (Ibid., pp. 67–68)

A comparison between the two episodes reveals a common element: the sudden overflowing of a stream in a desolate country, which forces the narrator to seek refuge among strangers. But in "Tlön" the place is the river Tacuarembó; in "The Shape of the Sword" it is the Caraguatá stream. Borges was obviously displacing an actual incident, which happened somewhere among the wilds of Tacuarembó, to suit the needs of each story.

Two more stories he wrote in the next few years are also located in Uruguay. One is called "The Dead Man" and was included by Borges in his third collection of stories, *El Aleph* (1949). Although the main setting is basically the same (Tacuarembó), the story has been set in the 1890s, a displacement that allows Borges to include tales told perhaps by members of his family who had a Uruguayan background. At only one point in the story does the experience of the author coincide with that of the main character (an Argentine hoodlum who becomes the *capanga* of a Uruguayan chieftain of smugglers): when the young thug visits the north for the first time.

> For Otálora a new kind of life opens up, a life of far-flung sunrises and long days in the saddle, reeking of horses. It is an untried and at times unbearable life, but it's already in his blood, for just as the men of certain countries worship and feel the call of the sea, we Argentines in turn (including the man who weaves these symbols) yearn for the boundless plains that ring under a horse's hooves. (*The Aleph,* 1970, p. 95)

By using Otálora as a mask, Borges is able to convey something of his experience in the wilds of Uruguay's north. There is a subtle hint that in weaving the symbols of that story he was trying to leave some indication of his personal involvement. The names of the two main characters are family names. In a note he dictated for the American edition of *The Aleph,* Borges elucidates the allusion: "Otálora is an old family name of mine; so is Azevedo, but with a Spanish *c* instead of the Portuguese *z*. Bandeira was the name of Enrique Amorim's head gardener, and the word *bandera* (flag) also suggests the Portuguese *bandeirantes,* or conquistadors" (ibid., p. 272). What Borges fails to say is that both names come from Mother's side of the family, and that the real Otálora was a slave trader in eighteenth-century Argentina. Even such a small detail as the name of the ranch where the story's plot unravels, "El Suspiro" (The Sigh), is taken from that visit to the north. "During that 1934 trip, we actually spent one night at a ranch called El Suspiro," Borges says in his note to the story (ibid., p. 272).

In the second story, called "The Other Death," the displacement is both chronological and spatial. The story basically takes place in the years 1904 and 1946, which do not coincide at all with Borges' visit to Tacuarembó, and the main Uruguayan setting is Cerro Largo, Tacuarembó's eastern neighbor. The setting is a part of Uruguay Borges never visited. It is the birthplace of the last of the great gaucho chieftains, Aparicio Saravia. In choosing that particular place, Borges was trying to recapture not just the past (as the plot of the story suggests) but a style of life, the style he discovered in his 1934 trip. One sentence in the story alludes to Uruguay's national hero, a chieftain who had also been, like Azevedo Bandeira, a smuggler. The story itself is based on the "assumption (perhaps undeniable) that Uruguay is more primitive than Argentina and therefore physically braver" (ibid., p. 106). An echo of Georgie's conflicts with the heroic traditions of his family, and his own experience while attending the state school in Buenos Aires, can be detected here. All his life Borges had lamented not having been a man of action; all his life he had felt that to be a writer was to be a coward. Now, in writing about these primitive men and about the land of Mother's ancestors, he is still trying to exorcise these feelings.

In another story, "The South," which is set exclusively in Argentina, the conflict is brought into the open. It is one of Borges' most famous stories, and was included in the second edition of *Ficciones* (1956). Under the mask of Juan Dahlmann, Borges dramatizes the conflict of a man who has both Argentine and European ancestors. In the last scene of the story, when Dahlmann is challenged to a knife duel in the pampas, there are some echoes of the day in 1934 when Borges saw a man killed. The setting is again a general store, badly lighted, with a pervasive "odor and sound of the earth" that "penetrated the iron bars of the window." Dahlmann is served a typical meal: canned sardines, some roast meat, and red wine. He relishes "the tart savor of the wine" and lets his gaze wander over the shop, noticing the kerosene lamps that hang from a beam and a group of noisy drunkards, farm workers with mestizo-type features (*Ficciones*, 1962, p. 172). The challenge made by one of these drunkards is probably based on memories of the episode of the *capanga* and the drunkard, except that in the story, for dramatic reasons, everything seems to happen in slow motion and the duel is fought with knives. But it is not the plot (a dream or nightmare Borges once had that now is Dahlmann's) but the general atmosphere which is rooted in the 1934 experience.

But perhaps it was rooted more in Borges' memory of the experience than in its actuality. In the notes to "The Dead Man" he indicates his puzzlement at the persistence in his memory of the things he then saw. The fact that he was able to use them in no less than five stories is significant. Nevertheless, he realized at the time that the experience in itself was commonplace. According to what Amorim once told me, Borges was more than ready to see wonders on that trip. On one occasion, he pointed out a group of men to his guide and with a childish relish said: "Look at those gauchos." Amorim, who was very familiar with the land and its inhabitants, corrected him with a laugh: "They are only farmhands." But in spite of his gentle warning, in Borges' imagination those farmhands were to become epic heroes, brothers to the gauchos whom he had read about in Ascasubi and Del Campo and Hernández and whom he had finally met (or believed he met) in primitive Uruguay.

That ten-day visit did not produce immediate results. Borges went back to Buenos Aires and resumed his task as literary editor of *Crítica*'s *Saturday Multicolored Review*. In 1935 he collected in *A Universal History of Infamy* the six imaginary biographies published between 1933 and 1934 in the magazine, plus "Streetcorner Man" and a few pieces (translations, adaptations, imitations) he had first published there. He added a seventh biography, that of "The Disinterested Killer Bill Harrigan," a name under which he disguised the notorious Billy the Kid. A prologue indicates some of the models for the stories and has this to say about the pieces that were appended to the book in a section called "Etcetera":

> As for the examples of magic that close the volume, I have no other rights to them than those of translator and reader. Sometimes I suspect that good readers are even blacker and rarer swans than good writers. Will anyone deny that the pieces attributed by Valéry to his pluperfect Edmond Teste are, on the whole, less admirable than those of Teste's wife and friends? Reading, obviously, is an activity which comes after that of writing; it is more modest, more unobtrusive, more intellectual. (*Infamy*, 1972, p. 13)

A few years later Borges would develop in his short story "Pierre Menard, Author of the *Quixote*" a whole poetics of reading as opposed to the poetics of writing. Here he is only trying to put into some perspective the "examples of magic" he had anticipated in *Crítica*. The perspective is that of a translator and reader. But he was more than a translator of some. As Norman Thomas di Giovanni has proved with Borges' amused collaboration, at least one of the five pieces was not a translation. It is called "The Mirror of Ink," and was then wrongly attributed to Richard Burton's *The Lake Regions of Central Equatorial Africa,* a volume Borges "has never laid eyes on," according to Di Giovanni (ibid., p. 11). The real source is another text: Edward William

Lane's *Manners and Customs of the Modern Egyptians,* "one of Borges' favorite books." The false attributions and the distortion of the sources
are typical of his method of using sources as masks. Burton, like Lane,
had translated the *Arabian Nights;* thus Borges attributes to him a story
he picked up in Lane. That helps to confuse the traces and allows him
more freedom. Because the story was included in the last section of *A
Universal History* it has never been considered a legitimate Borges story.
It is worth studying because it contains not only the seed of many
stories to come—a man haunted by his own destiny as seen in a mirror
of ink—but because the mirror itself is an Aleph, as Di Giovanni points
out: a place that contains all places and all times. In "El Aleph," the title
story of his third book of fictions (1949) Borges perfects the vision that
makes it a symbol of his own world of writing. But already in the
masked story the link between the vision and the act of writing is established. The mirror is, after all, made of ink.

The stories in *A Universal History of Infamy* were designed and
written for a popular audience. In collecting them, Borges attempted
to preserve their nature by keeping the melodramatic title under which
they were printed in *Crítica's Saturday Multicolored Review.* Furthermore,
the book came out as one volume in a series of paperbacks edited by
the magazine *Megáfono* (which had organized the 1933 colloquium on
Discusión) and published by a mass publisher, Editorial Tor. But
Borges, being Borges, could not avoid giving the volume some very
sophisticated touches. The original 1935 prologue calls the stories "exercises in narrative prose," and in indicating some of its models Borges
goes so far as to point out their limitations; he also disclaims any rights
over the "examples of magic" that close the book. After these less than
encouraging words, a dedication *in English* confronts the untutored
Spanish reader: "I inscribe this book to I.J.: English, innumerable, and
an Angel. Also: I offer her that kernel of myself that I have saved,
somehow—the central heart that deals not in words, traffics not with
dreams, and is untouched by time, by joy, by adversity" (*Infamia,* 1935,
p. 7).

The dedication is memorable because it is the first published
example of Borges' English prose. But for the mass reader the English
dedication was probably as forbidding as the "Index of Sources" at the
end of the book. With all these handicaps, *A Universal History of Infamy*
did not attract a large audience. Borges had to return to his core of
faithful readers, those secret young men in the provinces and some not
so secret in the capital.

The same year the book came out, Borges was already practicing another form of deception. He had written a story that was to be
published as a book review in a book of essays. In his "Autobiographical Essay" he tells the story behind the story:

My next story, "The Approach to al-Mu'tasim," written in 1935, is both a hoax *and* a pseudo-essay. It purported to be a review of a book published originally in Bombay three years earlier. I endowed its fake second edition with a real publisher, Victor Gollancz, and a preface by a real writer, Dorothy L. Sayers. But the author and the book are entirely my own invention. I gave the plot and details of some chapters—borrowing from Kipling and working in the twelfth-century Persian mystic Farid ud-Din Attar—and then carefully pointed out its shortcomings. The story appeared the next year in a volume of my essays, *Historia de la eternidad* (A History of Eternity), buried at the back of the book together with an article on the "Art of Insult." Those who read "The Approach to al-Mu'tasim" took it at face value, and one of my friends even ordered a copy from London. It was not until 1942 that I openly published it as a short story in my first story collection, *El jardín de senderos que se bifurcan* (The Garden of Forking Paths). Perhaps I have been unfair to this story; it now seems to me to foreshadow and even to set the pattern for those tales that were somehow awaiting me, and upon which my reputation as a storyteller was to be based. ("Essay," 1970, pp. 239–240)

The Garden of Forking Paths came out in 1941, not in 1942. But that is not the relevant point. In recalling the episode, Borges finally admits the importance of a hoax that was so successful that it fooled even Adolfo Bioy Casares, the anonymous friend who ordered the book from Gollancz. He was not the only one: I also believed in the existence of that novel and dutifully made an entry in my notebooks under the name of the imagined author.

More important than the success of the hoax is the fact that Borges had finally discovered a format for his future fiction which was unmistakably original. It was a combination of fiction and essay—two literary genres that convention had generally kept apart but that in Borges' peculiar view of reality were bound to mesh. By pretending that a story has already been told in a published book, Borges could offer, instead of a retelling of the story, a critique of it. The narrative discourse was submerged, masked under the critical discourse. Fiction became truth because what was invented was not the fact that the story may have happened (a commonplace task in discussing fiction) but that the story preexisted its telling. By pretending that the story had already been invented, Borges again claimed the rights of a reader, not of an author.

In including "The Approach to al-Mu'tasim" in the 1941 volume of short stories—later reissued as the first part of *Ficciones* (1944)—Borges had to finally acknowledge his paternity. In a prologue he defends his method of composition, which is "to pretend that these books already exist, and then to offer a résumé, a commentary. Thus proceeded Carlyle in *Sartor Resartus*. Thus Butler in *The Fair Haven*.

These are works which suffer the imperfection of being themselves books, and of being no less tautological than the others. More reasonable, more inept, more indolent, I have preferred to write notes upon imaginary books" (*Ficciones,* 1962, pp. 15–16). He goes on to identify the three stories based on that method: "Tlön, Uqbar, Orbis Tertius," "An Examination of the Work of Herbert Quain," and "The Approach to al-Mu'tasim." He omits the most dazzling of all his fictions, "Pierre Menard, Author of the *Quixote,*" in which he invents not only a book but the entire production of an imaginary writer.

The next book Borges published was a collection of essays called *Historia de la eternidad* (History of Eternity). It came out in 1936 under the imprint of Viau y Zona, a bookseller that specialized in bibliophile editions and occasionally published some books. Apart from the hoax played on the reader by the inclusion of "The Approach to al-Mu'tasim" as a book review, *History of Eternity* is a totally legitimate collection of essays. Its five pieces can easily be divided into two large categories: metaphysical and rhetorical. To the first belong two essays, the one that gives the volume its title and a companion piece called "La doctrina de los ciclos" (The Doctrine of Cycles). In attempting to define eternity, Borges had to go back first to the metaphysical problem of time, which had haunted him since his childhood, when Father taught him, as part of the games they shared, Zeno's paradox and the principles of Berkeleyan idealism. From those games, through some pieces already collected in *Inquisiciones* and *El idioma de los argentinos,* to the present text, Borges had traveled far and wide. In denying the notion of eternity and playing with the concept of infinity, he was paving the way for the total negation he would attempt in his most important piece on the matter, "A New Refutation of Time" (1947).

The essay on eternity is attractive but not terribly convincing. In a 1953 essay Maurice Blanchot discusses Borges' notion of infinity and proves it can be linked to what Hegel called "the bad infinite," a notion that is strictly literary. Blanchot does not criticize Borges for being a writer rather than a philosopher. On the contrary, he praises his honesty in dealing with these problems at the only level he is entitled to. Borges himself would agree with that reading of his essays. His interest in metaphysics is permeated by esthetics. In the essay on eternity, for instance, he rejects the concept of the Trinity not only for its logical difficulties (who was first, etc.) but also because it is ugly: "Conceived as a whole, the conception of a father, a son, and a ghost, articulated into a single organism, seems a case of intellectual teratology, a deformation which only the horror of a nightmare could have brought forth" (*Eternidad,* 1936, p. 20). In discussing Albertus Magnus' concept of the *universalia ante res,* he observes that scholasticism does not even suspect that God's categories may not be those of the Latin language that the theologians generally used. The other sign that Borges is not really terribly interested in discovering truth is that in indicating the bibliographical sources he has used, he points out that he has been relying too much on his own small library. The admission amounts to an exhibition of his unscholarly and hedonistic methods. In the title of the essay there is a contradiction in terms: to write the "history" of eternity implies using a method (historical discourse) for a subject that precisely denies the substance (time) on which the method is based. In the final notes Borges calls the essay a "biography" of eternity, reducing even more the scope of his attempt.

The second piece in the collection is no less personal. In reviewing the story of the concept of cyclical time, Borges actually composes a dramatic essay on Nietzsche's discovery of the concept. The core of the essay evokes that day in August 1881, in the woods near Silvaplana, when the German philosopher had the revelation of the eternal return. For his presentation of the dramatic episode, Borges uses the posthumously published *Die Unschuld des Werdens* (The Innocence of the Future, 1931) and also some passages from the *Nachlass* (Personal Notebooks). He wants to show that Nietzsche had chosen to forget that he was acquainted with the Greek philosophers who had already anticipated the concept, in order to believe that the revelation of cyclical time had come to him out of the blue. Thus dramatized, Nietzsche becomes Zarathustra; that is (in Borges' view), a sort of Walt Whitman. By bringing together these two prophets, Borges underlines the poetic vision of his own essay. In the second edition of *History of Eternity* (1953) he adds another essay on the same subject, "El tiempo circular" (Circular Time), less dramatic and more concerned with summarizing the different doctrines. The essay was originally written in 1943; by that time, it was obvious that Borges had taken the trouble to consult books other than those in his library.

An underlying rhetorical preoccupation can also be detected in his metaphysical essays. It is no wonder, then, that the three other pieces collected in the first edition of *History of Eternity* continue his rhetorical quest. One, "Las Kenningar," is a study of the system of metaphors used by the old Icelandic poets. Originally published in *Sur* in 1932, it was reprinted in pamphlet form in 1933 to correct a mistake Borges had made in translating the title into Spanish (he had originally written "Los Kenningar," making the metaphors masculine). In the corrected version the essay is basically a compilation of and a commentary on those very elaborate rhetorical figures and their code. Quoting extensively from the Eddas, Borges relates that long-forgotten poetry to the efforts made in the baroque age by Spanish poets such as Quevedo,

Góngora, and Gracián, and to the experiments of the ultraists. As a matter of fact, the essay ends with these lines: "The dead ultraist, whose ghost still inhabits me, enjoys these games. I dedicate them to a luminous companion of those heroic days, to Norah Lange, whose blood may by chance recognize them" (*Eternidad,* 1936, p. 56). There is an allusion there to Norah's Norwegian origin. In the second edition Borges added a less rambling and more important piece called "La metáfora" (The Metaphor), written in 1952, in which he quotes extensively from all kinds of literature to conclude that the basic number of analogies poets can unveil is not infinite, although the ways of indicating these basic analogies is unlimited.

The longest piece in the volume is a three-part essay, "The Translators of the *One Thousand and One Nights.*" If one remembers that in Greek the word "metaphor" meant translation, it is easy to see that Borges is still on safe rhetorical ground. To write about translations is to write about one of writing's most conscious operations: the one that perhaps lays open the function of writing as a manipulation of words and not of realities. In translating (as in parodying), the referent is not some elusive external or internal reality but the reality of words already fixed in a literary form. In this long essay Borges follows his usual method of commenting on selected texts, bringing in, at the same time, other texts to clarify or illustrate a point. It is a method of criticism that is closer to the English tradition than to the French. Only once in the essay does he attempt to indulge in a bit of theorizing. In discussing Richard Burton's translation and its relationship to Galland's and Lane's, Borges refers briefly to the famous dispute between Cardinal Newman and Matthew Arnold in 1861–1862. While Newman defended the literal approach, "the maintaining of all the verbal singularities," Arnold proposed the elimination of all the details that distract or stop the reading. Borges ironically comments: "To translate the spirit is such an enormous and ghostly intention that it may be taken as harmless; to translate the letter, such an extravagant precision that there is no risk anybody would attempt it" (ibid., p. 78).

The last piece in the book is a short exercise called the "Art of Insult." Apart from quoting some brilliant examples, Borges puts together some reflections and observations on the rhetorical aspects of insult that complete his work on metaphor, translation, and narrative techniques in this and the previous volume of essays.

The importance of *History of Eternity* in Borges' work became evident when Borges decided to have his books collected in a multivolume edition incorrectly called *Obras completas* (The Complete Works). They are far from complete and, in a sense, they are closer to being the official or canonical edition; that is, the edition by which

Borges wants to be judged. For the first volume of that collection he chose *History of Eternity*. It was a wise selection, because the book shows his maturity as an essayist at the same time that it points toward his future work. The rhetorical and metaphysical problems it raises are developed later in his best book of essays, *Other Inquisitions* (1952); the experiments in narrative anticipated in "The Approach to al-Mu'tasim" are enlarged in *Ficciones*. All things considered, *History of Eternity* is a seminal book, the first to offer in one volume all aspects of the mature writer Borges would soon become. It is a pity that the book came out under the imprint of a bookseller too small and exclusive to give it proper distribution. From that point of view, the book was a failure.

In his 1966 interview with Ronald Christ, Borges attempts to dismiss the whole enterprise as a joke:

> I remember I published a book . . . and at the end of the year I found out that no less than thirty-seven copies had been sold! . . . At first I wanted to find every single one of the buyers to apologize because of the book and also to thank them for what they had done. There is an explanation for that. If you think of thirty-seven people—those people are real, I mean, every one of them has a face of his own, a family, he lives in his own particular street. Why, if you sell, say two thousand copies, it is the same thing as if you sold nothing at all, because two thousand is too vast—I mean, for the imagination to grasp. While thirty-seven people—perhaps thirty-seven are too many, perhaps seventeen would have been better or even seven—but still thirty-seven are still within the scope of one's imagination. (Christ, 1967, p. 126)

Masking his disappointment in self-mockery is another way of avoiding coming to terms with it. In a sense, to have accepted the publication of the book under such conditions amounted to keeping it unpublished. It meant continuing to play the game of masks, deceptions, and hoaxes, this time not with the reader but with himself. Borges' shyness did more than just prevent him from acknowledging his short stories as such; it went so far as to prevent the production and distribution of the books themselves.

6.
The Dread Lucidity of Insomnia

The same year Borges visited Enrique Amorim and observed the last remaining gaucho frontier in the River Plate area, he met a young poetess who was to become one of his best and most durable friends. Silvina Ocampo was Victoria's younger sister and a close friend of Norah Borges, with whom she shared a passion for painting. It was amazing that Silvina and Borges hadn't met earlier, but the fact that she was seven years younger and extremely shy may account for it. Her interest in Borges' work preceded their friendship. In 1927 *Martín Fierro* had published a few of her sketches based on Borges' poems (see the June 10–July 10 issue). They were naïve drawings that featured a patio lighted by the moon and a rose-colored streetcorner. The drawings, which probably reached him through Norah, were published in the magazine with Borges' approval.

It took Silvina seven years to get to know him personally. In a portrait of Borges she wrote in 1964 for *L'Herne,* she remarks that she doesn't seem to remember where and when she first met Borges: "It seems to me that I have always known him, as it happens with everything one loves. He had a mustache and big, astonished eyes." That observation helps to date their meeting, because the first and last time Borges sported a mustache was after his return from visiting the Amorims. "I have detested him sometimes," Silvina adds with her usual frankness. "I have detested him because of a dog, and he has detested me, I suppose, because of a masked costume" (Silvina Ocampo, 1964, p. 26). She then describes the episode of the dog with all the minute details only a dog lover could appreciate. Apparently, once Borges had been visiting the Ocampos at the summer resort of Mar del Plata and Silvina's dog got lost. She searched the neighborhood, knocking at every door and giving a very precise description of her dog. Borges was amazed at her thoroughness:

> "Are you sure you will be able to recognize your dog?" he asked, perhaps to console me.
>
> I was angry with him, thinking he lacked compassion.
>
> To hate Borges is very difficult because he doesn't realize it. I hated him; I thought: "He is mean, he is stupid, he annoys me; my dog is more intelligent than he, because he knows every person is different, while Borges thinks every dog is the same."
>
> Borges could not understand my pain. However, it was I who did not understand a thing, I found out later. Borges believes animals are gods or great magicians; he also thinks, whimsically, that any member of the species represents all of it. When he [now] opens the door to his office at the National Library, I know he asks the cat who belongs to that institution, "May I go in?" Perplexed, he thinks: "But the neighbor's cat I will meet on leaving is perhaps the same cat I met when I got here!" If he finds the cat sitting on his chair, he sits in another chair, not to upset him. He loves animals in his fashion. (Ibid., pp. 26–27)

The other anecdote has to do with Borges' fear of disguises. It was at carnival time. One evening after dinner Silvina and a girl friend, already disguised for a party, were walking in the garden when they met Borges. They did not pretend to hide their identity:

> Without changing our voices, we talked to him, but he didn't answer.
>
> "It's me, Borges. Don't you recognize me?"
>
> Only after I had taken off my disguise and my mask did he answer. He leaned against a leafy tree whose branches scratched his face and muttered: "Is this one also wearing a costume?" (Ibid., p. 27)

Borges' fear of masks was as old as his memory. As a child, he had been frightened by the masks he saw through the garden rails at Palermo, and he had once written a poem about the "coarse carnival." Many years later, in a detective story called "Death and the Compass," he used carnival time as the occasion for one of the story's most elaborate murders.

In her portrait, Silvina also mentions Borges' well-known susceptibility to women:

> Borges has an artichoke heart. He loves beautiful women. Especially if they are ugly, because then he can invent their faces more freely. He falls in love with them. One woman who was jealous of another woman he admired, once told him:
>
> "I do not find her so beautiful. She's totally bald. She has to wear a wig

271

even in bed when she is sleeping, because she's afraid of finding people she loves, or even a mirror, in dreams."

"Nobody would dare to be so bald," he observed with admiration. "Of course, she doesn't need a wig because she is beautiful all the same." And he added with a sincere curiosity: "Has she become bald naturally? Is it really natural?"

To my mind the lady in question became beautiful two or three years ago, when the wig fashion started. (Ibid., p. 27)

At the time Silvina met Borges she also met Adolfo Bioy Casares, whom she married six years later. She joined the two men on many summer trips and endless walks in the most destitute districts of Buenos Aires, as well as in unusual literary projects and a few original anthologies. In Silvina, Borges found a companion who was too independent to be his disciple but congenial enough to be a long-lasting friend.

Those were years when friends counted a lot, because at the core of his artichoke heart Borges was very lonely and unhappy. The unhappiness can be detected in his writings, especially in two poems he wrote then. They were written in English to help him conceal, under the mask of a langage that he knew well but did not normally use for poetry, how deeply miserable he was. They were addressed to a certain "I.J.," to whom he also dedicated *A Universal History of Infamy.* Her identity is less important now than the function she is assigned in the poems. She is the unreachable object of desire, the muse and the Beatrice of this lonely poet. In the first poem Borges is seen at dawn, after a night described with an ultraist metaphor as a "proud wave":

> The surge, the night, left me the customary shreds and odds and ends:
> some hated friends to chat with, music for dreams, and the smoking of
> bitter ashes. The things my hungry heart has no use for.
> The big wave brought you.
> Words, any words, your laughter; and you so lazily and incessantly
> beautiful. We talked and you have forgotten the words.

Dawn, the "useless dawn," finds him standing alone in a deserted street, with only the "toys" she has left behind:

> Your profile turned away, the sounds that go to make your name, the
> lilt of your laughter
> . . . .
> Your dark rich life.

Those toys are not enough. The poet really wants to get at her, "somehow."

272

> I want your hidden look, your real smile—that lonely
> mocking smile your cool mirrors know.
>
> *(Poemas,* 1943, pp. 157–158)

This is precisely what is denied to him. Like Dante, he would be able to have only those "toys."

The second poem is even more desperate. It begins with the eternal question:"What can I hold you with?" In summarizing the catalogue of things that make him what he is—lean streets, desperate sunsets, the moon of the ragged suburbs, the bitterness of a lonely man, his heroic ancestors, the personal insights, what "my books may hold," the manliness or humor of his life, the loyalty of an unloyal man, his central heart "that deals not in words, traffics not with dreams, and is untouched by time, by joy, by adversities"—he is terribly aware of the unworthiness of all these "toys." The last three phrases are humorous and pathetic at the same time:

> I offer you the memory of a yellow rose seen at sunset, years before
> you were born.
> I offer you explanations of yourself, theories about yourself,
> authentic and surprising news of yourself.
> I can give you my loneliness, my darkness, the hunger of my heart; I am
> trying to bribe you with uncertainty, with danger, with defeat.
>
> (Ibid., p. 160)

Part of the second poem he later used for the dedication to *A Universal History of Infamy* (1935), adding to the book's literary hoaxes the fact that it is inscribed in English to a rather tantalizingly unidentified woman. But this is only the beginning of a series of hoaxes Borges would play with her identity. In the second Spanish edition of the book, published in 1953, the initials are changed to "S.D." (*Infamía,* 1953, p. 13); and in the second edition of his collected verses, published one year later, he further identifies the recipient of the first poem (but not of the second) as Beatriz Bibiloni Webster de Bullrich (*Poemas,* 1954, p. 143). If both poems had been inscribed first to "I.J." and then to "S.D.," how on earth can only one be later inscribed to a third lady? Or is there any lady? It is well known that Alexander Pope, in publishing letters he had written, used to change not only the text but the addressee. What mattered for him was the addresser. Borges, who sincerely believed all cats and dogs were the same, must have also believed all Beatrices were one. The initials, or the complete name, really mattered little. What counted was that he had been torn by desire, that he had been lonely and miserable.

The pangs of desire were also visible in the allusions and even the topics of the literary essays collected in *Historia de la eternidad*. He may have had a literary interest in the *One Thousand and One Nights* to the point of carefully comparing several translations of it to English, French, and German. But his interest was not exclusively poetic. The book, and some of its translators and annotators, proved to be an inexhaustible mine of sexual folklore. In an article Borges repeatedly points out the different attitudes toward the book's eroticism one finds in Galland or Mardrus, Burton or Lane. In discussing Burton's translation (the most explicit about sexual matters), he comments on the translator's original contribution to the subject, which takes the form of notes to the text. Of the ones Borges singles out in his article, some are very telling: one is devoted to discussing the hairs on Queen Belkis' legs; another to the secret Night of Power or Night of Nights, which deals explicitly with one of man's oldest obsessions: the size and vigor of the penis; a third to the precise area covered by the pudenda in males and females; a fourth to the project of breeding monkeys with women to obtain a suitable race of workers. Borges' comments on Burton's comments show him at his ironical best: "At fifty, any man has accumulated tenderness, ironies, obscenities, and many anecdotes; Burton unloaded them in his notes" (*Eternidad,* 1936, p. 87). Borges, at thirty-five, was already unloading his.

The article on the translators of the *One Thousand and One Nights* was not unique in that respect. In the article that gives the volume its title, and while discussing very seriously the concept of eternity, he quotes Lucretius' elegant and precise lines about the fallacy of desire and the impossibility of attaining satisfaction in sexual embrace (ibid., p. 28). In another essay, while discussing some metaphors of the ancient Icelandic poets, he appends a note about the fights among breeding horses for the possession of "urgent mares," adding: "Of a captain who fought bravely in front of his lady, the historian observes how that stallion would not fight if he were watched by the mare" (ibid., p. 53n). In the same article, when commenting on the roots of the concept of eternity, he says epigrammatically: "The style of desire is eternity" (ibid., p. 30). Having reached the threshold of maturity, this still young man knew too well how tantalizing desire was. He also knew how destructive it was.

At the time, and for a number of years, Borges had been the victim of insomnia. In one of his articles he talks about its "atrocious lucidity." The Latinate word "atrocious" does not convey in English the colloquial undertone of the Spanish *atroz*. Perhaps it ought to be translated "fiendlike," because insomnia is generally experienced as a sort of possession by another's will—except that in this case the master and the slave are one and the same. In a poem he wrote around 1936 Borges comes to terms with it. Entitled "Insomnia," it was published for the first time in *Sur* (December 1936, pp. 71–72) and was later included in the 1943 edition of *Poemas*. Borges sees himself as the "hateful watcher" of Buenos Aires nights, unable to obliterate from memory all the things he has seen, felt, and done, all the places he has visited, his friends and enemies, his own body, the circulation of his blood and the advance of dental cavities, the inescapable universal history. Written in Adrogué while Borges was on a summer vacation, the poem has some striking lines:

> The universe of this night has the vastness
> of forgetfulness and the precision of fever.
>
> In vain I want to divert my attention from my body
> and from the wakefulness of an incessant mirror
> which multiplies and haunts it
> and from the house which repeats its patios
> and from the world which goes on as far as the broken outskirts
> of paths of clumsy mud where the wind grows tired.
>
> In vain I wait
> for the distintegration and symbols which precede sleep.
> (*Poemas*, 1943, p. 162)

It ends with a sort of desperate metaphysical consolation. The poet has come to believe in a "terrible immortality," that of "horrid wakefulness." Dawn, crapulous dawn ("Coarse, lye-colored clouds would dishonor the sky"), will find him still awake, with his eyelids tightly closed.

Many years later, after insomnia had somehow abated, Borges wrote a short story about a man who had a fantastic memory, "Funes, the Memorious." Originally published in *La Nación* (June 7, 1942), it was later included in *Ficciones* (1944). The protagonist, a young man from the eastern side of Uruguay, "had been thrown by a wild horse" and is "hopelessly crippled." Funes does not move from his cot and spends his days with his eyes madly "fixed on the backyard fig tree, or on a cobweb." The narrator goes to visit him and finds out what the fall had done to him.

> He told me that previous to the rainy afternoon when the blue-tinted horse threw him, he had been—like any man—blind, deaf-mute, somnambulistic, memoryless. . . . For nineteen years, he said, he had lived like a person in a dream: he looked without seeing, heard without hearing, forgot everything—almost everything. On falling from the horse, he lost consciousness; when he recovered it, the present was almost intolerable [because] it was so rich and bright; the same was true of the most ancient and most trivial memories. A little later he realized he was crippled. This fact scarcely interested

275

him. He reasoned (or felt) that immobility was a minimum price to pay. And now, his perception and his memory were infallible. (*Ficciones,* 1962, p. 112)

As a character in a story, Funes belongs to the race of Bartleby and Joseph K., characters afflicted, like him, with some mysterious psychological disease more than with any specific monstrosity. What is really fantastic in them is their behavior: the way Bartleby refuses to budge, or Joseph to react to his fate, or Funes to be astonished by his own pathological memory. But as a mask or persona, Funes is closer to the unhappy Borges of the 1930s. In attempting to explain how his memory worked, Funes comes to these conclusions: *"I have more memories in myself alone than all men have had since the world was a world.* And again: *My dreams are like your vigils.* And again, toward dawn: *My memory, sir, is like a garbage disposal"* (ibid., p. 112).

Haunted by his own memory, unable to forget, Funes spends his days and nights reconstructing his days and his dreams. "Two or three times he had reconstructed an entire day." To illustrate some of Funes' memory exploits, Borges uses images similar to the ones he had already used in his poem "Insomnia": "Swift writes that the emperor of Lilliput could discern the movement of the minute hand; Funes could continuously make out the tranquil advance of corruption, of caries, of fatigue. He noted the progress of death, of moisture. He was the solitary and lucid spectator of a multiform world which was instantaneously and almost intolerably exact" (ibid., p. 114). It is almost impossible for Funes to go to sleep because to sleep "is to be abstracted from the world; Funes, on his back in his cot, in the shadows, imagined every crevice and every molding of the various houses which surrounded him." In order to sleep, he had to turn his face toward the part of town that he hadn't visited and that for him was only "black, compact, made of a single obscurity" (ibid., p. 115).

In a note to the second part of *Ficciones* Borges indicates that the story is "a long metaphor of insomnia," because not being able to sleep amounts to not being able to forget. The daily rite of forgetfulness we call sleep is what the insomniac Borges (as his fictional counterpart, Funes) could hardly perform. His nights, like those of Funes, were spent in the obsessive rehearsing of everything he once did or saw or read. Funes' total recall was a metaphor of insomnia's total lucidity. On that painful and endless torture were grounded the scholarly essays and the masked stories Borges was then writing. Both "The Approach to al-Mu'tasim" and "The Translators of the *One Thousand and One Nights"* sprang from that experience: those days and nights in which Borges (as Funes) believed himself to be "the solitary and lucid spectator of a multiform world." And if Funes was crippled after the accident, Borges had also been symbolically crippled by insomnia: riveted to his bed by a pitiless disease of the mind.

At thirty-five, Borges had achieved a unique position in Argentine letters. He was considered one of the most original poets and essayists of his time. But he was really known only to a small minority of readers made up of young writers, many even younger than himself. In spite of his contributions to the most exclusive as well as the most popular literary magazines, his books were generally overlooked. *History of Eternity* had sold only thirty-seven copies in one year—a figure that is difficult to take. The paradox is that, at the same time, Borges was almost secretly engaged in fictional and critical experiments that not only would change the main course of Argentine and Latin American literature but deeply influence contemporary culture (the movies included) in France and England, Spain and Italy, the United States and Germany. Although Borges at thirty-five continued to be the exclusive object of an underground cult of young writers, he was on the verge of producing the kind of literature that would be truly revolutionary.

He was undoubtedly aware of the paradox of his position, and in some of his essays, under the mask of irony, he faced the problem. As early as the article on Paul Groussac, written in 1929, one can find his view of what it was to be a distinguished writer in Argentina. The case of Groussac was, of course, extreme. Born in France in 1848, he arrived in Buenos Aires at eighteen without any knowledge of Spanish. After a few years of hard work, he became one of the major Argentine writers of the second half of the nineteenth century, the head of the National Library, a respected and even dreaded critic, a master of style. But Groussac always felt and once even wrote that to be a master of Argentine prose was to be a nobody. In discussing Groussac, Borges points out that to see him as a mere traveling salesman of French culture among the mulattoes ("a missionary of Voltaire") was to devalue Argentine culture and Groussac's role in it. He was, Borges concluded, the Dr. Johnson of Argentina. At the same time, Borges observes that Groussac's immortality is "merely South American" (*Discusión*, 1932, p. 128); but he claims, or pretends to claim, that that immortality is enough. Nevertheless, the use of the adverb "merely" is significant. It returns with some obsessive regularity in several texts of the period. In discussing Enno Littmann's German version of the *One Thousand and One Nights,* and after comparing it with those of Burton, Lane, Galland, Mardrus, and others, Borges disagrees with the *Encyclopaedia Britannica*'s opinion that Littmann's is the best: "I hear that the Arabists agree; it is of no importance that a mere writer—and of the merely

Argentine Republic—prefers to dissent" (*Eternidad,* 1936, p. 101). The defensive attitude, the self-criticism, the paradoxical irony: those are the masks Borges had to wear to disguise his hypersensitive realization that he was engaged in a hopeless cultural enterprise.

A mere South American writer, a readership of (exactly) thirty-seven buyers: on these shaky premises Borges was to base the revolutionary work of his maturity. But to produce that incredible breakthrough (he was to be the first Latin American writer to influence Western culture), he had to go through the most elaborate and deadly ritual of initiation: the death and rebirth of the hero.

ABOVE, LEFT: *Colonel Isidoro Suárez (1799 –1846), Borges' maternal great-grandfather.*
ABOVE, RIGHT: *Colonel Francisco Borges (1833 –1874), Borges' paternal grandfather.*
BELOW: *Fanny Haslam de Borges, the English grandmother, in Paris, 1869.*

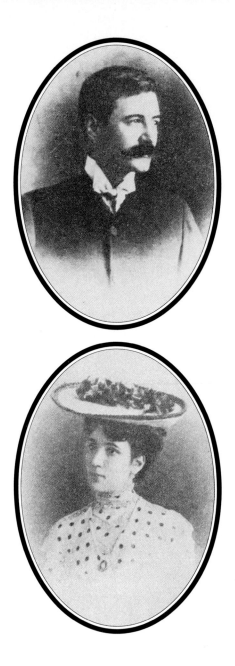

ABOVE: *Jorge Borges and Leonor Acevedo de Borges, his parents.*

OPPOSITE, ABOVE: *Norah Borges, ca. 1918.*

OPPOSITE, BELOW: *His sister Norah (left, rear) with Borges (right, front) in Geneva, 1916.*

LEFT: *Borges in his teens.*
BELOW: *Borges as a young man.*

Norah Borges

LEFT: *A drawing of her brother by Norah,*
ca. *1926.*

BELOW: *Silvina Ocampo and Borges.*

BOTTOM: *Bioy Cesares and Borges.*

ABOVE: *Borges with C. M. Moreno and E. R. Monegal in Montevideo, ca. 1948.*

BELOW: *Borges being interviewed for the BBC, London, 1963.*

OPPOSITE, ABOVE: *Borges with his mother in London, 1963.*

OPPOSITE, BELOW: *Borges at Harvard, 1967. (Charles Phillips, © Time Inc.)*

Borges at the University of Wisconsin, 1976. (Penny A. Wallace)

7.
A Guide to His Literary Mind

In spite of Borges' pessimistic attitude toward Argentine culture, Buenos Aires was then a busy literary center and attracted writers from all parts of the world. Two of the most famous young poets of the Hispanic world visited Buenos Aires in 1934. Federico García Lorca (already thirty-five and at the peak of his fame as a poet and playwright) spent several months in South America, mainly in Buenos Aires, where he gave lectures and recitals and attended the premières of several of his plays. Pablo Neruda (only thirty and still largely unknown outside his native Chile) was for a short time the Chilean consul in Buenos Aires. Neruda and Lorca met at the house of an Argentine friend and immediately struck up a friendship that became as intimate as the common pursuit of poetry and pleasure could make it. They recited verses together, made poems and drawings together, spoke publicly together to celebrate Rubén Darío, the great modernist poet. Once they disguised themselves as bearded sailors for a party, got gloriously drunk, and let their double masked images be recorded for posterity. The only thing they did not have together was sex. Federico was a homosexual, while Pablo was notoriously heterosexual. Federico and Pablo were feted by the Argentine intellectuals and got to know practically everybody, Borges included.

In his conversations with Richard Burgin, Borges could not bring himself to agree with his interviewer on the excellence of Lorca's plays:

BORGES: I don't like them. I never could enjoy Lorca.
BURGIN: Or his poetry either?
BORGES: No. I saw *Yerma* and found it so silly that I walked away. I couldn't stand it. Yet I suppose that's a blind spot because . . .

279

BURGIN: Lorca, for some reason, is idealized in this country.

BORGES: I suppose he had the good luck to be executed, no? I had an hour's chat with him in Buenos Aires. He struck me as a kind of play actor, no? Living up to a certain role. I mean being a professional Andalusian.

BURGIN: The way Cocteau was supposed to be, as I understand it.

BORGES: Yes, I suppose he was. But in the case of Lorca, it was very strange because I lived in Andalusia and the Andalusians aren't a bit like that. His were stage Andalusians. Maybe he thought that in Buenos Aires he had to live up to that character, but in Andalusia, people are not like that. In fact, if you are in Andalusia, if you are talking to a man of letters and you speak to him about bullfights, he'll say, "Oh, well, that sort of thing pleases people, I suppose, but really the *torero* works in no danger whatsoever." Because they are bored by those things, because every writer is bored by the local color in his own country, no? Well, when I met Lorca he was being a professional Andalusian. (Burgin, 1969, pp. 93–94)

Borges' reaction is typical of the intellectual who is fed up with local color, in Spain or in Argentina. Like another great Andalusian poet, Juan Ramón Jiménez, he preferred to pursue less trivial subjects and aimed at some sort of essential poetry. In doing this, he was bound to miss some of what makes Lorca unique, especially his sense of the theatrical, which he (like Cocteau or Noel Coward) carried into everyday life.

BORGES: . . . Lorca wanted to astonish us. He said to me that he was very much troubled about a very important character in the contemporary world—a character in whom you could see all the tragedy of American life. And then he went on in this way until I asked him who the character was, and it turned out the character was Mickey Mouse. I suppose he was trying to be clever. And I thought, that's the kind of thing you might say when you are very young and you want to astonish somebody. But after all, he was a grown man, he had no need, he could have talked in a different way. But when he started about Mickey Mouse being a symbol of America, there was a friend of mine there and he looked at me and I looked at him and we both walked away because we were both too old for that kind of game, no? Even at the time. . . . Even then we felt that that was what you call sophomoric. (Ibid., p. 94)

Faced with Lorca's mischievous sense of humor and of comic impersonation, Borges reacts with disdain. To Burgin's comment that Lorca was perhaps not a thinker but had a "gift for words," he replies:

BORGES: But I think there is very little behind the words.

BURGIN: He had a gift for hearing words.

BORGES: Well, a gift for gab. For example, he makes striking metaphors, but I wonder if he makes striking metaphors for *him*, because I think that his world was mostly verbal. I think that he was fond of playing words against each other, the contrast of words, but I wonder if he knew what he was doing. (Ibid., p. 95)

At the time they met, Borges had left ultraism behind and no longer believed in the power of striking metaphors; he was moving toward a greater simplicity, toward classicism, as he once said. Lorca, on the contrary, had been seduced by surrealism and had become famous for his unexpected, brilliant metaphors. Dialogue between these two poets was impossible.

With Neruda, things went better. Borges probably met him for the first time in 1927, when Neruda visited Buenos Aires briefly. In his conversations with Burgin he is not very specific about the exact occasion:

BORGES: I met him once. And we were both quite young at the time. And then we fell to speaking of the Spanish language. And we came to the conclusion that nothing could be done with it, because it was such a clumsy language, and I said that was the reason that nothing whatever had ever been done with it, and he said, "Well, of course, there's no Spanish literature, no?" and I said, "Well, of course not." And then we went on in that way. The whole thing was a kind of joke. (Ibid., p. 95)

To Burgin's direct question about whether he admired Neruda's poetry, he answers:

BORGES: I think of him as a very fine poet, a very fine poet. I don't admire him as a man. I think of him as a very mean man.
BURGIN: Why do you say that?
BORGES: Well, he wrote a book—well, maybe here I'm being political—he wrote a book about the tyrants of South America, and then he had several stanzas against the United States. Now he knows that that's rubbish. And he had not a word against Perón. Because he had a lawsuit in Buenos Aires, that was explained to me afterward, and he didn't care to risk anything. And so, when he was supposed to be writing at the top of his voice, full of noble indignation, he had not a word to say against Perón. And he was married to an Argentine lady; he knew that many of his friends had been sent to jail. He knew all about the state of our country, but not a word against him [Perón]. At the same time, he was speaking against the United States, knowing that the whole thing was a lie, no? But, of course, that doesn't mean anything against his poetry. Neruda is a very fine poet, a great poet in fact. And when that man [Miguel Angel Asturias] got the Nobel Prize I said that it should have been given to Neruda. (Ibid., pp. 95–96)

Although it is doubtful that Neruda spared Perón just because he had a lawsuit pending in Buenos Aires, it is true that Neruda in his

Canto general blames the United States for all the evils of imperialism but has nothing to say against Perón. It was not his decision to spare Perón. The Argentine Communists, in spite of being regularly tortured and even sent to jail in freezing Patagonia, had and still have an ambivalent attitude toward Peronism. Because Perón was a populist and had helped the working class to get some overdue privileges, the Communists were afraid of alienating the workers if they opposed him too openly. They preferred to fight underground and to keep the door open for a reconciliation. Neruda, being a loyal party member, did not want to disturb that policy.

There is no record about a possible meeting between Borges and Neruda at the time he and Lorca met in Buenos Aires. Lorca went back to Spain, and to his tragic death in Granada, without ever realizing that he had briefly met the man who was to make his style of writing obsolete, both in the Hispanic and in the Western world. But Neruda left a record of his first reactions to Borges. After his brief visit to Buenos Aires in 1927, he went on a long journey which took him first to Europe and Japan and then to Burma, Ceylon, and Indonesia. From Ceylon, he wrote to Héctor Eandi, one of his Argentine friends; in a letter (dated April 24, 1929) he had this to say about Borges:

> He seems to me more worried about problems of culture and society, which do not seduce me at all, which are not at all human. I like good wines, love, suffering, and books as consolation for the inevitable solitude. I even have a certain disdain for culture; as an interpretation of things, a type of knowledge without antecedents, a physical absorption of the world, seems to me better, in spite of and against ourselves. History, the problems "of knowledge," as they call them, seems to be lacking some dimension. How many of them would fill up the vacuum? Every day I see fewer and fewer ideas around and more and more bodies, sun, and sweat. I am tired. (Neruda, 1974, p. 12)

Neruda's letter has to be placed in the context of his traumatic experiences in the Far East. The journey to that faraway land, which he had probably expected to be one of continuous discovery of the marvelous, had actually been a descent into a private inferno, out of which he derived the burning poems of his *Residence on Earth.*

Some years later, in a 1970 interview with Rita Guibert, Neruda answered some questions about Borges:

> He's a great writer and thank heavens for that! All Spanish-speaking races are very proud that Borges exists. And Latin Americans in particular, because before Borges we had very few writers to compare with European authors. We have had great writers, but a universal one, such as Borges, is a

rarity in our countries. He was one of the first. I can't say that he is the *greatest,* and I only hope there may be a hundred others to surpass him, but at all events he made the breakthrough and attracted the attention and intellectual curiosity of Europe toward our countries. That's all I can say. But to quarrel with Borges, just because everyone wants to make me quarrel with Borges—that I'll never do. If he thinks like a dinosaur, that has nothing to do with my thinking. He doesn't understand a thing about what's happening in the modern world, and he thinks that I don't either. Therefore, we are in agreement. (Guibert, 1973, p. 30)

In his conversations with Burgin, Borges tells an anecdote which shows how these two so-called enemies had come to terms with each other late in life. After attacking the winner of the 1967 Nobel Prize, the Guatemalan novelist Miguel Angel Asturias, Borges tells his interviewer what Neruda did at the time Borges visited Chile.

He went on a holiday during the three or four days I was there, so there was no occasion for our meeting. But I think he was acting politely, no? Because he knew that people would be playing him up against me, no? I mean I was an Argentine poet, he a Chilean poet; he's on the side of the Communists, I'm against them. So I felt that he was behaving very wisely in avoiding a meeting that would be quite uncomfortable for both of us. (Burgin, 1969, p. 96)

But that politeness was a late development. At the time they first met, Borges and Neruda had no political quarrel: Borges was then an intellectual anarchist. Neruda tended to sympathize with the political anarchists; he did not become a Communist until the outbreak of the Spanish civil war, in 1936. But their different attitudes toward life and letters were already settled.

In 1935 Borges met a writer who would be his friend for life. His name was José Bianco and he was ten years younger. In an article written for *L'Herne*'s special issue on Borges, Bianco evokes their first meeting. It took place near the end of April at a literary party at Victoria Ocampo's home in Buenos Aires. Borges was then engaged in translating Virginia Woolf's *Orlando* for Victoria's publishing house, and he was very busy teasing Angélica Ocampo by comparing her with one of the supposed portraits of the protagonist included in that book. Angélica was, like her sister Victoria, tall and majestic. Both loved to defy Argentina's conventions by standing, like gentlemen, erect against the fireplace with cigarettes in their hands. Bianco was then only twenty-five and was duly impressed by Victoria's prestige as well as by Angélica's striking features. But he was even more impressed by Borges. Neither Adolfo Bioy Casares nor Silvina Ocampo were present that evening; thus Borges, left to himself, "moved from group to group, introducing chaos." He was discussing *Sur,* which had already reached its tenth issue, and was pleading with Victoria to make it less "anthological," which for Bianco meant, perhaps, to make it less boring. Borges also insisted on the need to have "a punctual, devoted, modest, and intelligent contributor," who for obvious reasons had to be an imaginary being, like the sickly Mr. Banbury in *The Importance of Being Earnest.* The best way to produce such a virtuous character was by collective action. "In the forthcoming issues, and under a common pseudonym, everybody ought to write without any reservations what they really thought. [Borges] advanced several pseudonyms; and each name invented by him, a composite one, very Argentine, absurd, strangely believable, made us laugh and lightened the meeting's atmosphere" (Bianco, 1964, p. 13). Unfortunately, *Sur* was too serious-minded to perpetrate that kind of hoax.

The idea of creating a totally fictitious *homme de lettres* was not new. Pope, Swift, and some friends had attempted to introduce into eighteenth-century English literature the works of a certain Martin Scribblerus. The project didn't get very far, although it produced one masterpiece, Swift's *Gulliver's Travels.* Borges had to wait until 1946, when he became editor of a literary magazine, to practice a similar innocent deception on the Argentine public.

Bianco has this to say about Borges' style of conversation:

. . . He enunciates rather shyly, doubtfully, not his ideas but his opinions, as if he were hoping somebody would contradict him with an interesting opinion which he was ready to acknowledge and to reconcile with his own in the most logical and, generally, in the most unpredictable way. Those who now attend his lectures and classes cannot help but admit the superiority of this distant and enigmatic man who has the gift to associate everything with everything. . . . Nevertheless, it is different to hear him talk behind a desk than privately with you or with a few friends. Another of Borges' characteristics is that he never raises his voice. Once he wrote, in a review of an Américo Castro book which caused a lot of angry reactions: "I have never observed that Spaniards spoke better than we (they speak louder, it is true, with the confidence of those who ignore doubt)." Let us add that he is interested in other people. He has also written, in a page on Bernard Shaw: "In any dialogue, one of the speakers is not the sum or average of what he says: he may be quiet and show he is intelligent, he may say intelligent things and suggest stupidity." However, as Borges is so intelligent, when talking to him, he gives us the feeling we are also intelligent. (Bianco, 1964, p. 13)

In recalling the first evening he met Borges, Bianco admits that he was too impressed to talk to him:

I just observed that young man, already famous among those of us who were much younger than he, unkempt, cheerful, aware of the world around him and at the same time distant from it, free of all solemnity and totally unconcerned about the impression he was making on others. Although courteous, Borges resembled Professor Higgins in *Pygmalion* in believing that "the great secret is not having bad manners or good manners or any particular sort of manners, but having the same manners for all human souls: in short, behaving as if you were in heaven, where there are no third-class carriages, and one soul is as good as another." Trained in the stimulating exercise of paradox, he tended to deliberately demolish tedious conversations with a joke. . . . He hasn't lost this good habit. (Ibid., p. 14)

Bianco also describes another meeting, in the summer of either 1935 or 1936, when he first went to visit the Borgeses at the Hotel Las Delicias in Adrogué. When introducing Mother, Borges asked very proudly: "How old do you think Mother is?" Bianco recalls: "Women then used very heavy makeup. . . . Mrs. Borges didn't even condescend to paint her lips. She didn't seem to be her son's eldest sister but his sister merely. Borges added, proud of his mother's youth: 'She's going to be sixty' " (ibid., p. 15).

For Bianco, Borges' mother was like the rope that keeps the kite firmly moored to the ground. Without her, "this man, so alien to life's realities," would have been lost in the clouds. Bianco also offers a snapshot of Father, "a good-looking man, reticent, with black, extinguished eyes." Bianco returned to the hotel more than once to have dinner with the Borgeses. He recalls that Father hardly ever said a word, except to bother about their guest: "Perhaps Bianco would like to have wine. Why don't you offer Bianco more of this dessert, which seems not too bad?" (ibid., p. 15). Years later, when reading Borges' story "Tlön, Uqbar, Orbis Tertius," Bianco recognized in the faded English engineer Herbert Ashe a portrait of Father.

Father's silence, his reticence, was more than justified at the time. He had never been an optimist, and now his health was declining rapidly. Totally blind and suffering from a heart condition, Father was attended with the utmost care by Mother. His will to live had been further undermined by his own mother's recent death. Fanny Haslam had lived with the Borgeses since 1901. Georgie had been very close to her; it was through her influence that an English governess was hired to teach him to read English before he learned to read Spanish. In his "Autobiographical Essay" Borges evokes his grandmother in her eighties:

Fanny Haslam was a great reader. When she was over eighty, people used to say, in order to be nice to her, that nowadays there were no writers who could vie with Dickens and Thackeray. My grandmother would answer, "On the whole, I rather prefer Arnold Bennett, Galsworthy, and Wells." When she died at the age of ninety, in 1935, she called us to her side and said, in English (her Spanish was fluent but poor), in her thin voice, "I am only an old woman dying very, very slowly. There is nothing remarkable or interesting about this." She could see no reason whatever why the whole household should be upset, and she apologized for taking so long to die. ("Essay," 1970, p. 206)

With Father declining rapidly, Borges felt the need to secure a permanent income of his own. Although he contributed regularly to *Sur* and other magazines, he earned very little. Through friends he got a commission to write for *El Hogar* (The Home), an illustrated magazine that was tailored to the interests of Argentina's upper and middle classes and that also had some literary and cultural aspirations. Some of the more established Argentine and Spanish writers contributed regularly to it. The magazine had two sections which alternated every week. One was devoted to "Books and Authors of the Spanish Language"; the other, to "Foreign Books and Authors." It was this latter page that was offered to Borges. He was also asked to write occasional critical articles for the magazine. The format of the book page had already been established when Borges began editing it on October 16, 1936. At one side, or at the top, a section called "Biografías sintéticas" (Short Biographies) summarized the life and career of an important modern writer. The rest of the page was devoted to book reviews of current titles (one long, several short) and news of the "literary life." In the last issue done by Anne Keen, Borges' predecessor, there was a biography of François Mauriac, one long review of Dos Passos' *The Big Money,* and short reviews of books by Grazia Deledda, Compton Mackenzie, and Joseph Kessel, plus some assorted news about Phillip Guedalla, Jacques Maritain, and Sigrid Undset.

Although Borges accepted the magazine's layout and format, he soon introduced some changes. In the first place, he chose less obvious writers, both for the biographies and for the reviews. Instead of writing about best-sellers or Nobel prizewinners, Borges in the first three months discussed Carl Sandburg, Virginia Woolf, Lion Feuchtwanger, T. E. Lawrence, Benedetto Croce, Victoria Sackville-West, Edgar Lee Masters, Louis Golding, and Oswald Spengler. He also gave samples, in his own translations, of the writers reviewed—a poem by Sandburg or a fragment of Mrs. Woolf's *Orlando.* And he shunned the impersonality of criticism, always writing in the first person, making statements that were very idiosyncratic. As a matter of fact, the section so thoroughly reflects his own likes and dislikes that it offers perhaps the best introduction to his critical mind. It is a hospitable and curious mind but it is also a mind that knows, and even parades, its limitations. Borges is very frank about his habits as a reader, admitting that he hadn't succeeded in getting to the last page of some very famous books (Dostoevski's *The Brothers Karamazov* and Flaubert's *Madame Bovary* are prominent among the unreadable ones) and that he has a weakness for second-rate books with interesting plots (detective novels, science-fiction stories). Sometimes he even indicates the exact amount of time he spent reading a certain book: two successive nights, from nine o'clock on; or a whole afternoon and an evening. But what makes his handling of the section so peculiar is his inexhaustible and perfect timing. Even the less promising subjects (a biography of Joan of Arc, Spengler's biography) are made irresistible by his irony and gift for paradox.

The scope of the section was truly encyclopedic; as sources, Borges used some biographical dictionaries, the *Columbia Encyclopedia* of 1935 (edited by Clarke F. Ansley), some reputable journals (the *Nouvelle Revue Française,* the *Times Literary Supplement*), and press releases from American and European publishers. He also had a passion for book browsing, which can be detected in allusions to the best English bookstore in Buenos Aires at the time (Mitchell's). Under Borges, the section lived up to its subtitle, "A Guide to Reading." The question that probably arose in many literary circles then was: How many of *El Hogar's* readers could avail themselves of such a cicerone, one who guided them unflinchingly through French, English, Italian, and German books, one who would not hesitate to recommend a philosophical interpretation of history (Spengler's) on the same page that he praised a murder story (Golding's *The Pursuer*) or a biography of an imaginary poet (Mrs. Woolf's *Orlando*)? Borges wrote as if every reader of *El Hogar* was as polyglot as he was. It was a large assumption. The fact that the section survived for almost three years, until mid-1939, proves that if few of the readers of *El Hogar* read, or even attempted to peruse, the books Borges mentioned or reviewed, at least they loved to read about them and probably used his witty remarks as suitable (not attributed) quotations at the cocktail parties they attended.

It was at that time that I first came across Borges' name. I was reading *El Hogar* (October 30, 1936) and found in the "Foreign Books and Authors" section a short biography of Virginia Woolf which included a page from *Orlando,* some odd reviews—a book of songs from the Mississippi, an Ellery Queen detective novel, a novel by Henry de Montherlant, a reissue of a study of neurotic writers by Arvede Barine—and a note headed "Literary Life" that was devoted to Joyce and included an anecdote of his meeting with Yeats. (Joyce was quoted as saying to Yeats that it was a pity they hadn't met before because "now you are said to be influenced by me.") I was barely fifteen then and was promptly seduced by Borges' wit and impeccable style and the vast range of his reading. From *El Hogar* I graduated to *Sur* and in no time began to comb Montevideo's bookshops for Borges' own books. I found one of the many unsold copies of *A Universal History of Infamy* (1935) and a secondhand copy of *Inquisiciones* (1925). In 1936 or 1937 those books were not the collector's items they are today.

If I was unaware at the time of the momentous decision I was making in allowing myself to become a Borges addict, I was totally conscious of the unique value of Borges' criticism and of the rare quality of his style. My case was not so singular as it seems, and that is why I mention it. For many young readers, Borges was already beginning to perform the task of mentor: the wittiest, the most irreverent mentor that ever was. In a sense, the page he published every two weeks in *El Hogar* was, and still is, the best possible introduction to his mind and work.

8.
The Start of a Lifelong Collaboration

Although Borges had several literary outlets—the fortnightly book page in *El Hogar,* his almost monthly contributions to *Sur,* some occasional articles for *La Prensa*'s literary supplement—in 1936 he helped Bioy Casares to start a new literary magazine, *Destiempo* (Untime). The journal was as odd as its title. It consisted of exactly six pages in tabloid format, published monthly. Only three issues came out, of which the third seems irretrievably lost. Both Bioy Casares and Borges claim to have mislaid their copies, and in Sergio Provenzano's noted collection of Argentine literary magazines only the first two issues (October and November 1936) survive. Another oddity: neither Bioy Casares' nor Borges' name is on the masthead, which carries only the name of Ernesto Pissavini as "secretario," or editor. Recently Bioy Casares admitted that Pissavini was the janitor of his apartment house, on 174 Avenida Quintana.

The two extant issues show that the magazine was a rather private affair. All the well-known contributors (the Mexican writer Alfonso Reyes, the critic Pedro Henríquez Ureña, the Argentine poet Fernández Moreno, the local metaphysician Macedonio Fernández) were mentors or friends of Borges. Among the not so well known—the poet Carlos Mastronardi, the linguist and painter Xul-Solar, the short-story writer Manuel Peyrou—Borges' friends predominated. Even the translations—one of a story by Kafka, a second from Erskine Caldwell—indicate his preferences at the time. Another Borgesian contribution was the section called "Museum," which featured fragments of curious and unknown works. Some of these fragments were perhaps invented. Borges' signed contributions were few: a collection of four short pieces, under the general title of "Inscriptions," three of which

289

had already been published in *Crítica* (September 15, 1934). The only one that was new was, characteristically, a "Dialogue About a Dialogue," in which A and Z discuss a conversation A had once with Macedonio Fernández about suicide, in which they had come to the conclusion that they ought to try it. Z's only contribution to the dialogue is this observation:

> z (teasingly): But I suspect you decided against it.
> A (lost in a mystical trance): Frankly, I do not remember if we tried it that evening. (*Destiempo*, October 1936, p. 3)

Bioy Casares' contributions were less polished. He was then only twenty-two and was still trying to tame an undisciplined surrealist imagination.

Silvina Ocampo also contributed regularly to *Destiempo*. The journal was underwritten by Bioy Casares' family. They owned a large dairy ranch plus some 130 milk bars in Buenos Aires alone; the chain was called "La Martona" in honor of Bioy's mother, Marta Casares. If the advertisement for the Bioys' dairy products published in *Destiempo*'s first issue was rather sober, the one in the second was less so; it began:

> Yoghurt "La Martona"
> Disintoxicating food recommended
> to those who lead a sedentary life
> (*Destiempo*, November 1936, p. 6)

It is possible to detect Borges' voice in that sound piece of advice.

About this time Bioy and Borges spent a week on the family ranch in Pardo in order to write a "commercial pamphlet, apparently scientific, about the merits of some more or less Bulgarian food," as Bioy recalls. The unnamed "Bulgarian food" is, of course, yoghurt. "It was cold, the house was in ruins, we didn't leave the dining room, where some eucalyptus logs crackled in the fireplace. That pamphlet was a valuable lesson to me; after writing it, I was a different writer, more experienced and skillful. Any collaboration with Borges is the equivalent of years of work" (Bioy Casares, 1968, p. 140).

Bioy also recalls some of the other things they did that week. They attempted to write an enumerative sonnet, of which one line read: "The mills, the angels, the *l*'s" (ibid., p. 141). They discussed a detective story, based on Borges' ideas, about a Dr. Pretorius, a "vast and smooth" German headmaster who, using games and pleasant music, tortured children to death. This story, never written, was the germ of their collaboration much later under the pseudonyms of Bustos Domecq and Suárez Lynch. In his recollections Bioy also mentions *Destiempo:*

> The title indicated our desire to escape the superstitions of the time. We objected especially to the tendency of some critics to overlook the intrinsic qualities of some works and to waste time on their folkloric, telluric aspects, or on those that had to do with literary history or the statistical and sociological disciplines. We believed that the notable antecedents of a literary school were sometimes as worthy of oblivion as the inevitable trilogies on the gauchos, middle-class seamstresses, etc. (Ibid., p. 143)

About the publication of the first issue of *Destiempo,* he offers this anecdote: "On the September morning we came out of the Colombo print shop with the journal's first issue, Borges suggested, half jokingly, half seriously, that we ought to have a picture taken for posterity. We did it at a modest neighborhood photographer. The photograph got lost so quickly that I can't even remember it" (ibid., p. 143).

For Bioy, *Destiempo* must have been a valuable first experience as editor. For Borges, it meant a diversion from more important literary projects. In those years his contributions to *El Hogar* and *Sur* took up most of his time. His output was extraordinary, both in quantity and quality. Apart from writing his twice-a-month section for *El Hogar,* he contributed to the magazine page-long articles on assorted literary subjects. In 1936 he commented on Eugene O'Neill's Nobel Prize (November 13) and celebrated the twenty-five years of poetic silence of one of Argentina's leading poets, Enrique Banchs (December 25), a writer who had influenced, with his meticulous, reticent sonnets, both Father and Borges. In 1937 he published seven special articles on subjects as diverse as the Huxleys' intellectual dynasty (January 15); the death of Unamuno (January 29); Buenos Aires as a city hospitable to provincial Argentine writers (February 26); Kipling's autobiography (March 26); a reevaluation of Jorge Isaacs' *María,* the most famous of Latin America's romantic novels (May 7); and a commentary on Raymond Lull's thinking machine (October 15). Some of these articles could be seen as an extension of his "Foreign Books and Authors" section, but the rest were on Hispanic subjects and showed how much *El Hogar* had taken to Borges. The article on Lugones (February 26, 1937)—in which he recanted his ultraist past and praised the old poet—was the object of a rejoinder from a former ultraist poet and colleague, Eduardo González Lanuza (March 12). Borges did not reply to Lanuza's well-reasoned arguments; he had already made up his mind about the subject, and nothing was going to change it.

During that same period, he also contributed regularly to *Sur.* In the magazine's first seven years (1931–1937) his name appears in eleven of its thirty-nine issues, and in some issues he had collaborations (see especially Summer 1932, September 1936, and December 1936). He wrote articles on philosophical, literary, and social subjects, book and film reviews; and, after years of poetical silence, he published a poem, "Insomnia" (December 1936). Some of the work he did for *Sur* overlapped with his writing for *El Hogar.* A note about Chesterton in *Sur* (July 1936) preceded two reviews of his books in *El Hogar* (*The Paradoxes of Mr. Pond,* May 14, 1936; *Autobiography,* October 1, 1937). An article on T. E. Lawrence's translation of the *Odyssey* in *Sur* (October 1936) anticipated by a month a review of a new biography of Lawrence of Arabia in *El Hogar* (November 13). Reviews of two novels by H. G. Wells in *El Hogar* (*Star Begotten,* July 25, 1937; *Brynhild,* October 29, 1937) followed a long review of William Cameron Menzies' movie version of Wells' *Things to Come* in *Sur* (November 1936). On the occasion of Unamuno's death, he wrote two quite different articles with subtly different titles: "Unamuno's Immortality" for *Sur* (January 1937) and "Miguel de Unamuno's Presence" for *El Hogar* (January 29, 1937). In a sense, his book reviewing in *Sur* can be seen as an extension of the work he was doing for *El Hogar.*

What was new in his contributions to *Sur* in that period was his film criticism. Borges had been a film buff since his childhood, but not until the late 1920s did he start writing regularly about movies. An article in *La Prensa,* "El cinematógrafo, el biógrafo" (April 28, 1929), played in its title with the two terms most generally used in the River Plate area to designate the "seventh art." While the upper middle classes preferred "cinematógrafo" as a more fashionable word, the lower middle classes and the workers used the old-fashioned "biógrafo," a relic from the heyday of the Biograph Company. But Borges did more than just play with words in that article; he also wrote perceptively about Chaplin's *The Gold Rush.* He started to review films in *Sur* by the third issue (Winter 1931). It took some effort to persuade Victoria Ocampo that the journal ought to include regular reviews. In his conversations with Jean de Milleret, Borges mentions Victoria's reluctance to include in her journal (which she saw as an anthology of the best possible writing) such ephemeral items as reviews of plays, movies, concerts, and books. Borges, on the other hand, believed them to be "the life of the magazine . . . all that the reader wants to find" (De Milleret, 1967, p. 60).

The first article Borges wrote, under the modest title "Films," comments on Fedor Ozep's *Der Mörder Dimitri Karamasov* (a 1931 German adaptation of Dostoevski's novel), Chaplin's *City Lights,* and von Sternberg's *Morocco.* While informing the reader about his opinions, Borges sketches briefly but firmly the basic differences between the

German, French, and North American cinemas of the time. Short, tantalizing references to other movies, and even to Garbo's "zenithal shoulders," indicate his familiarity with the medium. That article was the first of eleven that appeared up to the end of 1937. In them, he reviewed films by King Vidor, John Ford, von Sternberg, William Cameron Menzies, Alfred Hitchcock, and James Whale, as well as lesser-known directors. He also reviewed two Argentine films: Luis Saslavsky's *La fuga* (Escape), which he praised with some qualifications, and Manuel Romero's *Los muchachos de antes no usaban gomina* (The Boys of Yesteryear Did Not Use Hair Tonic), an apologia for old-fashioned machismo which Borges killed with one joke: "It is one of the best Argentine movies I've seen; that is, one of the world's worst" (Cozarinsky, 1974, p. 52).

If Victoria needed persuasion to let Borges review films in *Sur,* she was determined to have him translate some of her favorite authors. She commissioned three translations: André Gide's *Persephone* (first published in *Sur* and later issued in pamphlet form by the same magazine, 1936); Virginia Woolf's *A Room of One's Own* (in pamphlet form, 1937) and *Orlando* (1937). Borges had already attracted *El Hogar's* readers to the last in a capsule biography of Virginia Woolf which he illustrated with a fragment from *Orlando* (October 30, 1936). In judging the novel, he stressed its originality: "undoubtedly Virginia Woolf's most intense and one of the most singular and hopeless books of our time." He added: "Magic, bitterness, and joy collaborate in this book. It is, also, a musical book, not only in the euphonic virtues of its prose but in the structure of its composition, made of a limited number of themes which return and intertwine." The translation was soon to become a model. Borges had succeeded in keeping in Spanish the musical quality of Mrs. Woolf's prose.

Borges later attempted to disclaim responsibility for the translation. Writing about Mother's translations from the English, he claims in the "Autobiographical Essay" that she was the real author of those that had been attributed to him, and he mentions specifically the translations of Melville, Virginia Woolf, and William Faulkner ("Essay," 1970, p. 207). But in talking about his work of the period, he says explicitly: "On holidays, I translated Faulkner and Virginia Woolf" (ibid., p. 242). A lapse of memory, a friendly hoax, a filial accolade? It is hard to say. Probably Mother helped him with those translations. She may have even done the first draft. But the Spanish style is so unmistakably Borgesian that it would have taken Mother years of hard labor to be able to imitate it. The most one can safely assume is that, in helping him, she became another of his already distinguished corps of collaborators.

The same year, 1937, another collaboration came to light. It was the *Classical Anthology of Argentine Literature,* which Borges edited with Pedro Henríquez Ureña. Borges' friendship with the Dominican critic and scholar dated from the 1920s. He had always admired Ureña's vast knowledge and his reticent style. In a review of Ureña's collection of essays, *Seis ensayos en busca de nuestra expresión* (Six Essays in Search of Our Expression), in *La Palabra* (September 30, 1928, p. 11), Borges praised both the style and the careful research each of the six pieces reveals. In joining forces with Henríquez Ureña for this anthology, Borges accepted a secondary role. Henríquez Ureña was fifteen years his senior, and his knowledge of Latin American literature was vaster and more balanced than Borges'. As usual, Borges disclaimed any responsibility for the book. He once told me that it was done entirely by Henríquez Ureña. Perhaps, but it is possible that Borges suggested at least some less obvious authors such as William Henry Hudson, who was born in Argentina and wrote in English about River Plate subjects. In the anthology Hudson is rightfully considered one of Argentina's classic authors. Borges had already written about one of his masterpieces, *The Purple Land,* in the second *Proa* (November 1925). Some years later he wrote a definitive piece on that same book for an anthology of Hudson's prose, published in Buenos Aires in 1947. Later he included the piece in *Other Inquisitions* (1952), thus certifying his constant interest in a novel that for him was "perhaps unexcelled by any work of gaucho literature" (*Inquisitions,* 1964, p. 142). There is no record that Henríquez Ureña had ever praised Hudson so much.

9.
The Pen and the Sword

World War II was approaching. In Europe, Mussolini started his imperial expansion by attacking Abyssinia in 1935 and challenging British naval supremacy in the Mediterranean. After occupying the Rhineland, Hitler was putting pressure on Austria in the second stage of his plan to recover the lost pieces of the mystical Fatherland. In the Soviet Union, Stalin had successfully crushed the last remnants of an alternative socialism (Trotsky had found temporary refuge in Mexico) and was getting ready for the inevitable confrontation with Germany. In the Far East, Japan was methodically carving an empire out of a divided and weak China. England and France were major powers, but they were overwhelmed by national unrest, economic crises, and social demands. The United States was coming out of the Depression with a president who was both an aristocrat and a populist. In that scheme of things, Latin America had no say. It was a formerly colonized continent that was still economically dependent on the major European powers.

The example of fascism in two of the most important European countries helped to promote it in Latin America. In Brazil, Getulio Vargas designed his own version of the corporate state, while Plinio Salgado paraded his Green Shirts to match Mussolini's Black and Hitler's Brown Shirts. In Chile, General Ibáñez was a harsh ruler. Even in democratic and small Uruguay, a mild coup d'état secured President Terra's power for a long while.

Argentina was ruled by General Justo with the complicity of the army and all the trappings of democracy. Economically and financially, Argentina still belonged to the sterling area: its meat and wheat were marketed chiefly in England. But politically it was closer to the fascism of Mussolini and, by association, to Hitler's Nazism. Some of the leading army officers were of Italian descent and went back to the mother country to study the regime and pay homage to Il Duce. One of the brightest was Juan Domingo Perón, who was ready to believe that the Italian model could be easily imported into Argentina to prevent economic chaos and fight creeping communism. He was not the only one with this belief.

When, following the outbreak of the Spanish civil war in July 1936, Franco asked for and got help from Italy and Germany, the Argentines found another powerful motive to sympathize with fascism. Many were of Spanish extraction and saw Franco as the savior of Spain's tradition and culture. For the upper and middle classes of Argentina, it was fashionable to be very Catholic and fascist. The government shared both ideologies. On the other hand, the liberal tradition of French culture and the appeal of the British style of life were powerful among the smaller journals like *Sur* and colored the selection of topics and authors in the larger journals *La Nación* and *La Prensa*. Even in *El Hogar* that tradition was accepted, although the magazine catered to the conservative taste of a middle-class, Catholic, feminine audience. Another group, the left-wing intelligentsia, gathered together—under an uneasy alliance—Socialists, Communists, and even anarchists.

As if to show how few political differences existed between these groups, the reaction of both *Sur* and the left-wing intellectuals toward the Spanish civil war was similar. They shared a liberal attitude in spite of so-called ideological differences. It was the time of the popular fronts in France and Spain, the time of ironing out differences in the face of fascism, the common enemy; and although *Sur* did not participate in this movement under its banner, many of its contributors did. In the opposite camp, the Catholic and fascist establishment closed ranks around Franco and his allies. If the inane dispute between "Florida" and "Boedo" had divided the *Martín Fierro* contributors into opposite bands, now the fight for Spain, and the coming fight for Europe, would divide the Argentine intelligentsia even more drastically—although along different lines. Writers such as Leopoldo Marechal and Francisco Luis Bernárdez were to come to the defense of the Catholic establishment, while Victoria Ocampo, Eduardo Mallea, and Borges would be in the opposite camp. It was in that context that the Fourteenth International Congress of the PEN Club met in Buenos Aires on September 5–15, 1936.

The proceedings of the meeting—published in Buenos Aires in 1937—do not make for amusing reading. Some of the stars of the international PEN Club were unable to be present. André Gide was off visiting the USSR, a fateful journey that was to mark the end of his short affair with Stalinism. H. G. Wells, the PEN Club's president, was too busy with his own work to attend and sent, like Gide, a warm message. Most of the members who came to Buenos Aires either were unknown then (one, Halldor Laxness, from Iceland, eventually won a Nobel Prize in 1955) or would never show any other title to fame but their membership in the club. Still, enough truly important writers arrived to make the occasion an elaborate production. The Spanish philosopher José Ortega y Gasset and the Mexican humanist Alfonso Reyes were among the guests of honor; but if they attended the sessions, they did not participate in any of the debates. The Colombian Baldomero Sanin Cano's only function was to preside over one session. The Argentine delegation included Carlos Ibarguren, who was also the president of the congress; Victoria Ocampo, who served as vice-president; Manuel Gálvez, a naturalist novelist of large popular appeal; and Eduardo Mallea, Victoria's protégé and one of the most distinguished young writers of the time.

The fact that both the president of the congress and Gálvez were notoriously sympathetic to fascism gave a certain Alice in Wonderland flavor to the proceedings. The PEN Club had been created in the 1920s to defend culture and literature from every variety of censorship and oppression. As Wells had put it in his message: "Our club . . . is . . . small but it carries an immense and splendid banner: that of free thinking and open discussion" (PEN, 1936, p. 33). At the time the PEN Club was meeting in Buenos Aires, that freedom had already been destroyed in Italy and Germany, had been severely limited in the Soviet Union by the official association of writers, and was being attacked successfully in Spain. But not only were the citizens of these countries persecuted for their ideas. A whole group of intellectuals, among the most important in the Western world, were being deprived of physical freedom and even of their lives for belonging to the Jewish community. Racism in Germany had openly killed or exiled some of the most distinguished writers in the German language. Among the guests of the PEN Club congress were two representatives of that group: the Austrian Stefan Zweig and the German Emil Ludwig.

Also among the guests were two prominent Fascists: the one-time futurist Filippo Tommaso Marinetti and the poet Giuseppe Ungaretti. There was an almost epic clash between Marinetti and some of the liberal participants, particularly two members of the French delegation, the novelist Jules Romains (who was then completing his monumental saga *Les hommes de bonne volonté*) and Benjamin Crémieux, of Jewish extraction and a specialist in Italian literature. The exchange

gave the PEN Club debates—generally bland to the point of being
soporific—an unusual tone. Emil Ludwig contributed an acerbic speech
in which he denounced the Hitler regime. Members of the audience
came vocally to the defense of intellectual freedom; they were not reticent in demonstrating their disgust for Marinetti's histrionics and fascist rhetoric. In the end, concord prevailed, especially because the
avowed policy of the PEN Club was to bring writers together in a peace
movement that would help to avoid war.

The paradox was that the regime that hosted the congress and
even the president of the congress were more sympathetic to Franco
and Mussolini than to the democratic regimes to which they paid lip
service. If the general tone of the debates was political, the papers read
at the conference oscillated between the obvious and the tedious. With
a few exceptions—the Belgian poet Henri Michaux, the Franco-
Uruguayan Jules Supervielle, the Catholic philosopher Jacques Maritain (who was a Jew)—the participants were neither original nor brilliant. Comic relief was provided by Marinetti's gross misinterpretation
of a reference made in a speech by Victoria Ocampo. Attempting to
define her literary position as that of a "common reader" and acknowledging her debt to both Virginia Woolf and Samuel Johnson for that
expression, Victoria had to suffer the humiliation of having Marinetti
distort her words. He seemed to take them as a defense of the common
man and as a not too subtle exhortation to write for the lowest possible
readership. Victoria attempted lamely to explain that her "common
reader" was a cultivated and almost specialized type. Marinetti's ignorance of both Dr. Johnson and Mrs. Woolf made him unresponsive.
Victoria had to ask for extra time to restore her words to their original
meaning.

As usual in this type of meeting, many words were produced,
many egos were exhibited, and very little was accomplished. The importance of the congress resided exclusively in its place and time.
Argentina in 1936 was hardly the locale where a liberal organization
such as the PEN Club could speak its mind—but then how many places
were still left in the world? The fact that the Fascist delegation succeeded in having Italy appointed as the meeting place for the next
congress, with Japan chosen as host for 1940, indicates very clearly that
the PEN Club was hopelessly confused about the future.

Although Victoria Ocampo and Eduardo Mallea participated
rather actively in the congress, Borges seems not to have attended. He
was not listed among the guests of honor or participants, although he
was already better known, nationally and internationally, than both
Victoria and Mallea. There was a very good reason. At the time, Borges
hated to speak in public. Even in small gatherings, he was uncomfort-

able and quickly developed an audible stammer. He had always refused to lecture, and on the rare occasions when he accepted, he had his paper read by a friend while he sat in the back mouthing every word of a text he knew by heart. But he probably had other motives in avoiding the PEN Club congress. He did not suffer fools easily, and literary congresses are generally the province of fools. But he was well informed about what was going on in the congress. In *El Hogar* (September 17, 1937, p. 24), reviewing Jules Romains' long poem *L'homme blanc,* Borges identifies Romains as the one who "demolished" Marinetti at the PEN Club congress. That is the only allusion to the congress in his writings, but it is not the only political dig against Marinetti that Borges made during those years.

In another short notice written for *El Hogar* (March 4, 1938, p. 24) he laughed at one of Marinetti's new "inventions." According to a telegram from Rome, he had recommended that Italian women add to the red of their lips and nails a "light touch of the green of the Lombard plains and the white of the Alpine snows." In Borges' witty retort, those "attractive tricolor lips will utter perfect words of love and kindle the desire for a kiss in those rude soldiers who return undefeated from the wars." He also ridiculed another of Marinetti's "inventions": the substitution of sound native words for all foreign expressions which are contaminating the Italian language. Instead of the French "chic," Italians ought to use "elettrizzante" (electrifying); instead of "bar," they ought to indicate "qui si beve" (here one drinks). After pointing out that each Italian expression is longer than the foreign one, Borges stresses the similarity between Marinetti's puritanism and the preoccupations of conservative bodies such as the Spanish Royal Academy of Language. The conclusion to the short piece is that the one-time futurist impresario is not up to this kind of joke. Even more damaging is the beginning of the article: "F. T. Marinetti is perhaps the most famous example of the kind of writer who lives by his inventions and who hardly ever invents anything."

People who have come lately to Borges' work, with little knowledge of his intellectual and ideological development, tend to think that he was and is totally apolitical. The truth is that Borges always had political opinions, but as he was brought up by Father to be an intellectual anarchist (not a political one), his opinions depended less on the ephemeral strategy of newspaper headlines or the compulsion to get a place in the sun than on the deep conviction that the less government of any kind the better. He thus favored, in general, democracy, because it allowed a sort of balance of power and rejected all one-party regimes because they made dissent almost impossible. True, while a teenager in Geneva, Georgie had admired bloody revolutions and had even sung to

the Red Dawn of Moscow. But soon he came to the conclusion that revolutions only change the staff while perpetuating the bureaucracy of
power. In Argentine politics he only once made a feeble attempt to
participate in political life, at the time of Irigoyen's second bid for the
presidency. After Irigoyen proved to be inept and was deposed by the
army, Borges' political skepticism grew and hardened. He stopped having anything to do with local politics; only World War II would make
him react strongly.

In the meantime, he took advantage of *El Hogar* to load his
"Guide to Reading" with political digs and plainly stated ideological
arguments. A few references to the Spanish civil war can be gleaned
here and there. One is a review (March 18, 1938, p. 14) of H. G. Wells'
novel *The Brothers,* which was set in Spain at the time of the civil war.
Borges stressed the rather obvious parable about the twins who command the two sides of the war, and the pedagogical solution put forth
by Wells: men had to be better educated to avoid wars. About the war,
which was coming to a tragic conclusion with the victory of the Fascists,
Borges said nothing, but it is obvious which side he was on, by the mere
fact that he liked the novel and liked the author even more. Several of
Wells' new books were reviewed in *El Hogar* over a two-year period:
The Croquet Player (February 3, 1937, p. 36); *Star Begotten* (July 23,
1937, p. 30); *Brynhild* (October 29, 1937, p. 28); *A Propos of Dolores*
(December 2, 1938, p. 89), which he reviewed a second time, in *Sur*
(November 1938); and *The Holy Terror* (March 24, 1939, p. 89). Borges'
interest in Wells was not exclusively political, of course. He had been
reading his works since he was a child and discovered *The First Men on
the Moon* and *The Invisible Man.* But the writer Georgie had once read
was no longer the writer Borges reviewed. Now the preoccupation with
the future of mankind had taken over. Of the six novels reviewed in *El
Hogar,* only two (*Brynhild, A Propos of Dolores*) were concerned more with
the individual than with the species, and with private problems rather
than public destinies.

Not all the reviews Borges wrote of Wells' novels were favorable. On more than one occasion he pointed out obvious faults and observed that although Wells' books were never boring they were not
always good. In his review of *The Holy Terror* he observes that it is easy
to prove a priori that the novel is unreadable because it is badly shaped.
But he also observes that such a course is useless. To convince his
reader, he declares: "I—who had been unable to read *Madame Bovary,*
or *The Brothers Karamazov,* or *Marius, the Epicurean,* or *Vanity Fair*—have
read in a day and a night this formless novel. The fact is telling." It is,
of course, in more than one sense. It tells about Borges' impatience
with some "classics of the novel"; it also reveals his interest in the litera-

ture that was then being written. The Wells of that period had for Borges the prestige of being a modern writer.

In reviewing *The Brothers,* Borges singles out one sentence: "Marx stinks of Herbert Spencer and Herbert Spencer stinks of Marx." He does not expand on Wells' utterance, but it is obvious that he was pleased with the link thus established between the holy text of socialism and the representative of old-fashioned positivism. In Wells, Borges found ammunition to fight the pomposities and fallacies of the totalitarians.

Discussing Kipling in an article published in *El Hogar* (March 26, 1937, p. 9), Borges observes that while Kipling's works are more complex than the ideas they are supposed to illustrate, the reverse is true about Marxist art: "The thesis is complex, because it comes out of Hegel, but the art that illustrates it is rudimentary." On another occasion, while discussing Isaac Babel's life, he comments ironically on the fact that Babel had to fight the czarist bureaucracy only to have to face the Soviet bureaucracy. At the time Borges wrote that article for *El Hogar* (February 4, 1938), he obviously did not know that Babel was already in disgrace and that he would become one of the most prominent victims of Stalinism.

In another article (December 2, 1938) he discusses the Marxist point of view in literature. The pretext is a manifesto called "For an Independent Revolutionary Art," signed by André Breton and the Mexican painter Diego Rivera. In the title of his article, "Copious Manifesto by Breton," Borges calls his reader's attention to the French poet's authorship. In a short introductory paragraph Borges laughs at the avant-garde mania for manifestos and ironically stresses the fact that they generally serve to attack the basis of the art they are talking about. If signed by writers, they attack rhyme and metaphor; if by painters, they vindicate (or insult) the basic colors; if by musicians, they praise cacophony; if by architects, they prefer a gas station to Milan's "excessive cathedral." Borges quickly reaches the conclusion that every one of these silly pamphlets has been surpassed by the one "emitted" by Breton and Rivera. After quoting the pamphlet's full title (a subtitle also claims to be in favor of the "final liberation of art"), Borges observes that the text is even more emotional and stuttering than the title:

> It consisted of some three thousand words that say exactly two things (that are incompatible). The first is . . . that art should be free and it isn't in Russia. Rivera-Breton observe: "Under the influence of the USSR's totalitarian regime, a deep dusk has fallen over the entire world, hostile to all kinds of spiritual values. A dusk of mud and blood in which, disguised as intellectuals and artists, men who have made a resource of servilism, a game of the denial of their principles, a habit of venal false testimony, and a pleasure of the

apology of crime, practice their deceptions. The official art of the Stalinist era reflects their ridiculous efforts to cheat and disguise their mercenary role. . . . To those who urge us, be it today or tomorrow, to admit that art can be submitted to a discipline we consider radically incompatible with its means, we oppose a refusal without any appellation, and our deliberate decision to stick to the formula "All sorts of license in art."

What conclusion can we draw from those words? I believe this, and only this: Marxism (like Lutheranism, the moon, a horse, a line from Shakespeare) may be an incitement to art, but it is absurd to postulate that it is the only one. It is absurd to believe that art is a department of politics. However, that is what this incredible manifesto claims. As soon as Breton has printed the formula "All sorts of license in art," he repents his daring and dedicates two furtive pages to denying that reckless statement. He rejects "political indifference," attacks pure art, "which generally serves the most impure aims of reaction," and proclaims "that the supreme task of contemporary art is to participate consciously and actively in the preparation of revolution." Immediately he proposes "the organization of modest local and international congresses." Urged to exhaust the excesses of rhymed prose, he announces that "in the next stage [of the plan] there will be world congresses which officially will celebrate the foundation of the International Federation of Independent Revolutionary Art (IFIRA)."

Poor independent art they are concocting, subordinated to pedantic committees and five capital letters! (*El Hogar,* December 2, 1938, p. 89)

In attacking Breton, Borges once more stood at a distance to judge the avant-garde. In the same way he had already rejected ultraism and futurism, he was now implicitly rejecting surrealism, which he mistakenly took to be a mere offshoot of dadaism and, especially, of German expressionism.

He had other points of disagreement. Borges' rejection of Freud and his theories could also explain his distaste for a movement that relied so much on Freud.

The article appeared at a time when surrealism was fighting to avoid being engulfed by Stalinism. But Borges was unaware of that dramatic situation. He cared little about French, or Latin American, literary strategy. He was also unaware of the fact—revealed only much later—that the real co-author of the pamphlet was not Rivera but Trotsky. The manifesto was written as a consequence of a visit to Mexico made by Breton in 1938.

If Borges was disdainful of Marinetti and futurism, attacked fascism and Stalinism, and laughed at Breton's attempts to find a way out of "revolutionary" art, he reserved his harsher political criticism for Nazism. The most damaging references contained in the articles he published in *El Hogar* are addressed to Nazism's destruction of German culture, to anti-Semitism and the cult of war. In a short review of a

German school primer on racism, *Trau keinem Jud bei seinem Eid* (literally: *Trust No Jew by His Oath*), Borges describes without any comments some of the book's illustrations:

> The first . . . is based on the thesis that the "Devil is the Jew's father."
> The second represents a Jewish creditor who confiscates the pigs and the cow of his debtor.
> The third [shows] the perplexity of a German miss, overwhelmed by a lecherous Jew who offers her a necklace.
> The fourth [shows] a Jewish millionaire (with a cigar and a Turkish cap) driving out two beggars of the Nordic race.
> The fifth [is] a Jewish butcher who tramples on meat.
> The sixth celebrates the decision of a German girl who refuses to buy a puppet at a Jewish toy shop.
> The seventh accuses Jewish lawyers; the eighth, doctors.
> The ninth comments on Jesus' words "The Jew is an assassin."
> The tenth, unexpectedly Zionist, shows a pitiful line of expelled Jews, set for Jerusalem.
> There are twelve more, no less ingenious and indisputable. Of the text itself, it would be enough to translate these verses: "The German Führer is loved by German children; God in heaven is loved by them; the Jew is despised." And then: "Germans walk, Jews crawl." (*El Hogar,* May 20, 1937, p. 26)

Two more references to the anti-Semitic campaign that was then at its shrillest in Germany can be found in *El Hogar.* One is a review (June 11, 1937) of a catalogue produced by Insel-Verlag, one of Germany's biggest publishing houses. In going over it, Borges stresses the fact that it contains only twenty-four new titles and observes that that is a very small number for such a house. Examining the books more closely, he discovers that the protagonist of one of six novels devoted to "proclaiming the merits of fishermen, woodsmen, and peasants is an unforgettable blond giant." Another book praises the founders of the British empire; a third admires the military ethic of the samurai. There is also an illustrated volume of anecdotes on the life of Frederick the Great. Another volume, *Form and Soul,* contains sixty-four reproductions of Leo von Köning's paintings, which "reflect mankind today in its most unmistakable representatives: the soldier (Hindenburg), the politician (Goebbels), the sportsman (von Cramm)." Borges also mentions *Goethe and the Olympic Idea,* a book that naturally won a prize given by the Committee on Olympic Games in Germany and that pretended to demonstrate "the importance of gymnastics in Goethe's life and thought." After this cursory examination, he reaches a terse conclusion: "Germany, literarily, is poor."

A very short item in *El Hogar* (September 3, 1937) informs the reader: "Ludendorff's magazine, *From the Sacred Source of German Strength,* continues from Munich its inexorable and fortnightly campaign against Jews, the Pope, the Buddhists, the masons, the theosophists, the Society of Jesus, communism, Dr. Martin Luther, England, and Goethe's memory." Ludendorff was one of the heroes of World War I. In another article Borges reviews a new edition of one of his most popular works, *Der Totale Krieg* (Total War). In rejecting Ludendorff's prophecies, Borges observes:

> In fifteenth-century Italy, war reached a perfection many people would call ridiculous. When two armies came face to face, generals compared the number, courage, and readiness of the opposing force and thus decided which one had to accept defeat. Chance had been eliminated, and the spilling of blood. That way of making war would not merit perhaps the lovable expression "totalitarian," but I found it wiser and more lucid than the vast sacrifice of millions of men which Ludendorff prophesies. (*El Hogar,* January 21, 1938, p. 26)

Borges' irony is at its best here. The trouble is that the joke is on him. Ludendorff was right in his prophecies. In less than two years' time Germany would begin to move its catastrophic war machine. But if Borges was wrong about the nearness of war, or about its "totalitarian" character, he knew perfectly well what war was about. While in Europe, he had shared the horror of the young for the World War I holocaust. In reviewing *The Men I Killed,* a book by the British general F. P. Crozier, Borges points out the irony in the title: the general is alluding less to the enemies he has ordered killed than to his own soldiers— cowardly men who are killed by their own officers or comrades to prevent panic in battles. They die for their country, but not in the way they are expected to. With a candor unusual in a man of his rank, Crozier admits that he always had in his battalion a man ready to execute the fainthearted ones. And he concludes: "People do not suspect these things: people imagine that battles are won with courage and not with murder" (*El Hogar,* February 18, 1938, p. 28). Borges observes that the book is dedicated both to those soldiers who "stuck it to the end" in the battlefield and to those pacifists who did it in jail. It is because he knows that war, any war, is genocide that he can find words of praise for this very unusual general.

El Hogar's women readers were probably not quite ready for these articles. Perhaps for them, Stalinism and anti-Semitism, the Nazis and the Fascists, surrealists and Trotskyites, were too remote. It is to Borges' honor that he never once asked himself if it was wise or profitable to voice such opinions in the Argentina of the time. He went on writing and commenting on books, unaffected by questions of opportunity or convenience, leaving in the pages of the magazine a sort of ironic journal of his reactions to the coming war.

10.
Life in the
Library

In spite of being quite famous in Buenos Aires, Borges was nearing forty without having established his position in Argentine society. The many literary activities in which he was engaged—his regular contributions to *El Hogar, Sur,* and other journals—failed to assure him a regular income. He was still dependent on Father's limited pension, further eroded by inflation, and was in the awkward position of being a mature man living with his parents as if he were still an adolescent. Since Father's health was declining rapidly, Borges realized that he had to secure a permanent job. In 1937, through friends, he found a job at the Miguel Cané municipal library, named after the author of one of the most popular nineteenth-century Argentine books, *Juvenilia,* a humorous account of life in a high school. The library was located on Avenida La Plata and Carlos Calvo, and its director was the poet Francisco Luis Bernárdez, one of Borges' colleagues from the ultraist days.

Reminiscing about his work at the library in the "Autobiographical Essay," Borges begins by summarizing the "small editing tasks" which had up till then been his sole remunerative occupation: the *Crítica* supplement, the book section at *El Hogar,* and some even more obscure work his biographers have failed to identify precisely: "I had also written newsreel texts and had been editor of a pseudo-scientific magazine called *Urbe,* which was really a promotional organ of a privately owned Buenos Aires subway system" ("Essay," 1970, p. 240). Although it seems unfair to lump together his creative contributions to *Crítica* and *El Hogar* with the hack work he also did, the general conclusion he reaches is correct: "These had all been small-paying jobs, and I was long past the age when I should have begun contributing to our household upkeep." He took his first regular full-time job as a first as-

306

sistant in the Miguel Cané library, which was located, according to him, in "a drab and dreary part of town to the southwest." His position on the library's staff was low: "While there were Second and Third Assistants below me, there were also a Director and First, Second, and Third Officials above me. I was paid two hundred and ten pesos a month and later went up to two hundred and forty. These were sums roughly equivalent to seventy or eighty American dollars" (*ibid.,* pp. 240–241).

The position was also dreary. There was very little work to do, and even that had to be evenly divided among some fifty people. Borges does not conceal his sarcasm in describing his reponsibilities at that patronage-ridden institution:

> At the library, we did very little work. There were some fifty of us producing what fifteen could easily have done. My particular job, shared with fifteen or twenty colleagues, was classifying and cataloguing the library's holdings, which until that time were uncatalogued. The collection, however, was so small that we knew where to find the books without the system, so the system, though laboriously carried out, was never needed or used. The first day, I worked honestly. On the next, some of my fellows took me aside to say that I couldn't do this sort of thing because it showed them up. "Besides," they argued, "as this cataloguing has been planned to give us some semblance of work, you'll put us out of our jobs." I told them I had classified four hundred titles instead of their one hundred. "Well, if you keep that up," they said, "the boss will be angry and won't know what to do with us." For the sake of realism, I was told that from then on I should do eighty-three books one day, ninety another, and one hundred and four the third. (Ibid., p. 241)

In a 1962 interview with James E. Irby, Borges gives a minute description of life at the library. In a sense, that oral report is less reticent and even more personal than the one included in the "Autobiographical Essay." In talking, Borges generally reveals more and even lets his feelings come to the surface more easily. He admits to Irby, for instance, that it was through the influence of some friends that he got a small raise in his salary, under the condition that the friends wouldn't press for another raise for him in the future.

Borges recommended a small collection of English books to improve the library's holdings (Irby, 1962, p. 8). But reading, and the accessibility of books, did not blunt the pain of having to work in such a low position. In the "Essay" Borges is not at all reticent about it: "I stuck to the library for about nine years. They were nine years of solid unhappiness. At work, the other men were interested in nothing but horse racing, soccer matches, and smutty stories. Once, a woman, one of the readers, was raped on her way to the ladies' room. Everybody said such things were bound to happen, since the men's and ladies' rooms were adjoining" ("Essay," 1970, p. 241).

To Irby, Borges confides another anecdote about the hoodlums he had for colleagues: "One day, in the men's room, one of my colleagues took off his shirt to show me the scars he had on his chest, from knife fights he had had." Understandably, Borges concludes: "That whole atmosphere depressed me" (Irby, 1962, p. 8). The irony of the situation is that for many years Georgie had roamed the outskirts of Buenos Aires, slumming for hours, getting acquainted with hoodlums, prostitutes, and pimps and talking endlessly about knife fights, courage, and sex. A great part of Georgie's writings in the late 1920s and early 1930s showed his preoccupation with violence, brutality, and death. But faced with the chance to be on almost intimate terms with such violence, he recoiled with disgust.

The paradox of his predicament was emphasized by the fact that outside of the library Borges' fame continued to grow. If Eliot had been depressed by a clerical job at a bank in London, Borges found his ordeal at the library even more sordid, in violent contrast to the kind of experiences he had outside the library. In the "Autobiographical Essay" he tells a comic anecdote about the difference between these two worlds: "One day, two rather posh and well-meaning friends—society ladies—came to see me at work. They phoned me a day or two later to say, 'You may think it amusing to work in a place like that, but promise us you will find at least a nine-hundred-peso job before the month is out.' I gave them my word that I would" ("Essay," 1970, pp. 241–242). There is a double irony in the situation. The ladies didn't seem to realize that Borges had no way of landing a better job, and he was too proud to tell them the truth. They probably wouldn't have believed it; they thought perhaps that Borges' love for slumming and his rather perverse sense of humor accounted for his choosing such a sordid place to spend his working hours.

If his position was difficult to explain to his friends, it was even more difficult to explain to his colleagues at the library. Borges recalls the humor of the situation: "Ironically, at the time I was a quite well-known writer—except at the library. I remember a fellow employee's once noting in an encyclopedia the name of a certain Jorge Luis Borges—a fact that set him wondering at the coincidence of our identical names and birthdates" (ibid., p. 242). To Irby, he tells a similar anecdote. Some of his colleagues were young lower-middle-class women who always treated him with indifference until one day they found out that he had those posh friends. They were terribly impressed the day Elvira de Alvear, one of the most dazzling of these ladies, phoned Borges to have him for tea. From that day on, the women began to pay attention to him and to ask questions about his friends, whom they tried to emulate. The questions, instead of soothing Borges' pain, must have added to his feeling of being ridiculous. While their male counterparts cared only about races or rape, those young women cared only about what was fashionable to wear that year at Palermo's horse race course.

For Borges, the situation must have been impossible. Although he was at ease with his society friends, he never shared their snobbery or their taste for expensive things. There was nothing in him of the Scott Fitzgeralds of this world. On the contrary, as a member of an old, traditional family with no money or power left, he despised worldly possessions and always had an authentic disinterest in clothes, furniture, houses, cars, and all the other material things that encumber life. If he was a friend of Elvira de Alvear, it was because he was in love with her—hopelessly in love, of course, because Elvira did not love him. But what Borges loved was her eccentricity, not her surname or her fortune. Glimpses of Elvira de Alvear can be seen (conveniently altered to suit the literary needs of the story) in some aspects of Beatriz Viterbo in his story "The Aleph." But it is not a flattering portrait.

And now Borges had the added humiliation of being respected at the library not because he was Borges—that is, one of the best Argentine writers of the time—but because he was Elvira de Alvear's friend. In his interview with Irby he summarizes his predicament: "I found myself in a very awkward position. Many people believed I was a good writer. I contributed to *Sur* and other journals, foreign writers came to Buenos Aires to see me as if I were a famous person. But my everyday life did not agree with that assumed fame: it was a curiously anonymous, annoying life" (Irby, 1962, p. 11). In the "Autobiographical Essay" he adds a few touches that communicate the grimness and pain of his position: "Now and then during these years, we municipal workers were rewarded with gifts of a two-pound package of maté to take home. Sometimes in the evening, as I walked the ten blocks to the tramline, my eyes would be filled with tears. These small gifts from above always underlined my menial and dismal existence" ("Essay," 1970, p. 242). For Borges, and Borges' family, to become a proletarian was the last stage in the journey back to the Haslams' humble rural origins.

If his personal experiences at the Miguel Cané library were humiliating, Borges succeeded, as all good writers do, in transforming them into the most unexpected literary material. He recalls the way he managed to survive the depressing atmosphere of that library: "Though my colleagues thought of me as a traitor for not sharing their boisterous fun, I went on with work of my own in the basement, or, when the weather was warm, up on the flat roof" (ibid., p. 243). Borges is obviously referring to the articles and reviews he wrote for several journals, particularly for *El Hogar* and *Sur*. But he is also alluding to other writing more specifically related to his personal experiences at the library. The most famous of these is his short story "The Library of Babel," which

> was meant as a nightmare version or magnification of that municipal library, and certain details in the text have no particular meaning. The number of books and shelves that I recorded in the story were literally what I had at my elbow. Clever critics have worried over those ciphers, and generously endowed them with mystic significance. "The Lottery in Babylon," "Death and the Compass," and "The Circular Ruins" were written, in whole or part, while I played truant. (Ibid., pp. 243–244)

Originally published in *The Garden of Forking Paths* (1941), "The Library of Babel" seemed so remote from Argentine reality that very few of his readers could have recognized then the subtle hints Borges gives of an "atrocious but commonplace reality," as he once said in another context. The story is full of allusions to the number or shape of the real shelves; there are less obvious references to the small closets where one can sleep standing up or satisfy "fecal necessities" and to the rather mysterious letters that the books have on their spines. They "do not indicate or prefigure what the pages will say," observes Borges in a disguised reference to the signs which indicate the classification of each volume. But what perhaps reflects more poignantly the atmosphere of the Miguel Cané library is the general feeling of despair, of boredom and horror, that the story conveys so effectively. In describing the insane and infinite library, Borges is describing what he felt at the time. He was stuck in an inferior, degrading activity, surrounded by hoodlums or by people who were totally indifferent to the meaning of the function they were supposed to be performing. The library of Babel was infinite and stultifying because Borges was then experiencing the horror of an absurd, pointless job.

A sort of essay version of the same experience was published in *Sur* in August 1939. Called "The Total Library," it was explicitly dedicated to discussing the origin of the concept of a library that included all books. Very formally, Borges traces the utopia of the total library back to Aristotle and Cicero; the latter coined the idea of arbitrarily juggling all the letters of the alphabet to eventually produce, or reproduce, a poetic masterpiece. In the nineteenth century Huxley perfected (or mechanized) the notion by suggesting that half a dozen monkeys, armed with typewriters, could produce, with the help of eternity, all the books contained in the British Museum library. In a note Borges observes that a single immortal monkey would do. Other writers (Lewis

Carroll, Kurd Lasswitz) added interesting details. But what really matters for Borges is not the concept of the infinite that a total library implies but its emotional consequences. In describing the infinite library he produces a chaotic enumeration that includes not only some lost masterpieces (Aeschylus' *The Egyptians*) and Novalis' conjectural encyclopedia, the never written chapters of *Edwin Drood* or Berkeley's unpublished paradoxes on time, but even some very private personal experiences ("my dreams and half-dreams on the morning of August the 14th, 1934"). The final experience conveyed by reading the essay is of chaos, absurdity, and horror. The library's shelves (which were modeled on the Miguel Cané's shelves) create vertigo; they "obliterate the day and in them chaos resides." The conviction that even the horror is "subaltern" (that is, mediocre) adds a touch of commonplace evil to the essay. Before Hannah Arendt, Borges had discovered in his own experience "the banality of evil."

In those years Borges had begun reading Franz Kafka, and it is obvious that both the essay and the story on the total library were under his influence. There are some articles on Kafka in the book page he wrote regularly for *El Hogar*. On August 6, 1937, he reviewed the English translation of *The Trial*, done by Edwin and Willa Muir. Although the review is more informative than critical (Kafka was then totally unknown in Argentina), Borges shows a familiarity with his works, quotes several of his stories, and discusses some of the critical reactions his works had already produced: they are nightmares, they are intense, they can be interpreted from a theological point of view. Borges objects to the last of these interpretations because "they are not inadequate—we know that Kafka was devoted to Pascal and Kierkegaard—but they are not necessary." He also mentions an observation, advanced by "a friend," on the connections between Kafka's fiction and Zeno's paradoxes. The friend might have been Bioy Casares, but perhaps it was only Borges' modest way of masking his own ideas. Many years later he developed this point of view in a now famous essay, "Kafka and His Precursors" (collected in *Other Inquisitions*, 1952).

In a capsule biography of Kafka published in *El Hogar* (October 29, 1937) Borges repeats the observation about Zeno's paradoxes, without quoting any friend. Among the pieces he singles out for praise are several short stories and parables. Many of these he later translated for the first collection of Kafka's stories ever published in Spanish: *La metamorfosis* (The Metamorphosis, Buenos Aires, 1938). It was not his first attempt at translating Kafka. He translated the story "Ante la ley" (Before the Law) for *El Hogar* on May 27, 1938. It comes from an early collection of stories, *A Country Doctor* (Leipzig, 1919) and was later used by Kafka as a parable in *The Trial,* a fact which Borges seems to have overlooked. He did not include it in his collection of Kafka stories.

In the preface to *La metamorfosis* Borges expands and deepens his view of Kafka's life and work. About Kafka's relationship with his father Borges writes, in parentheses: "From that conflict and his stubborn meditations on the strange mercies and unlimited demands of paternal power, he himself has declared, comes his entire work." There is a personal note here. Although Kafka felt, correctly, that he was despised by his father while Borges knew Father loved and even doted on him, there is a curious similarity between the two fathers and the two sons. The expressions Borges uses to define that similarity—"strange mercies" and "unlimited demands"—were applicable in both cases. Borges may have believed that a kind father could be more tyrannical than a harsh one. Talking about World War I and what it meant to Kafka, he observes: "The war's depression is in those works: that oppression whose most atrocious trait is the pretense of happiness and of courageous enthusiasm which forces people into. . . ." Obviously he had come a long way from his youthful enthusiasm for the war poetry of the expressionists.

In evaluating Kafka's work, Borges stresses two ideas, or obsessions, which shape it—subordination and the infinite—and comments briefly on passages in Kafka's novels and tales that illustrate both. He points out that Kafka's critics generally lament that his novels are unfinished, then argues (repeating arguments already advanced in *El Hogar*) that they are "unfinished" deliberately because Kafka wanted to emphasize the infinite number of obstacles their protagonists had to face. Their vicissitudes are as unending as those in hell. He again warns against a theological interpretation of Kafka's work, concluding: "The full enjoyment of Kafka's work . . . may precede any interpretation and does not depend on it." In the last paragraph of the preface he underlines Kafka's most unquestionable virtue: his ability to invent intolerable situations, and observes that Kafka's development of the situation is less admirable than its invention. There is only one character: the *homo domesticus,* so Jewish and German, who only wants a place, no matter how humble, in the order of things, "any Order: the universe, a ministry, an insane asylum, a prison." Plot and atmosphere are, according to Borges, essential in Kafka, "not the evolution of the fable or psychological insight." Thus he believes that his stories are superior to his novels and that a collection of them offers "in its totality the range of this singular writer" (*La metamorfosis,* 1938, p. 11).

The preface takes up only five pages of the small volume, but it contains a complete view of Kafka, and also of Borges. The importance of this volume—which preceded by some months the writing of Borges' first revolutionary story, "Pierre Menard, Author of the *Quixote*," and by three years the publication of his first volume of fantastic stories, *The Garden of Forking Paths*—lies in the fact that it was translated and published at the time Borges was getting ready to take the plunge and devote himself completely to writing fiction. The reading and translating of Kafka helped him to make this decision. In the same way that Eliot began reading and commenting on the English metaphysical poets or the Greek and Elizabethan playwrights at the time he was experimenting with a new form of verse play, Borges studied and discussed Kafka when he was about to begin a new career as a storyteller.

Perhaps his unhappiness at the Miguel Cané library also influenced that decision, for it obviously helped him to understand Kafka's predicament. The library was his ghetto, his penal colony; it was the bureaucratic hell (both horrifying and commonplace) that Kafka presented so well. Out of his misery Borges derived the strength to present not just an ironic, urbane view of the world but a view that showed its real nature. But he had still to go through an experience of symbolical death and rebirth before being able to create his own brand of hell. In the meantime, his daily life replayed the Cinderella myth: hard, unpleasant, degrading conditions of work at the library during the afternoons, and the return to a warm, friendly, affluent world in the evenings. To survive, Borges read incessantly. In his "Autobiographical Essay" he tells about the reading of that period:

> A couple of hours each day, riding back and forth on the tram, I made my way though the *Divine Comedy,* helped as far as "Purgatory" by John Aitken Carlyle's prose translation and then ascending the rest of the way on my own. I would do all my library work in the first hour and then steal away to the basement and pass the other five hours in reading or writing. I remember in this way rereading the six volumes of Gibbon's *Decline and Fall* and the many volumes of Vicente Fidel López's *History of the Argentine Republic.* I read Léon Bloy, Claudel, Groussac, and Bernard Shaw. . . . At some point, I was moved up to the dizzying heights of Third Official. ("Essay," 1970, p. 242)

The irony of the last sentence cannot hide the pain of his situation. But reading, writing, and translating helped him. He put to good use his careful rereading of Gibbon. At least one tale ("The Story of the Warrior and the Captive," collected in *The Aleph,* 1949) and the background for another ("The Theologians") he owed to Gibbon. From López's *History* he undoubtedly took many details of his Argentine poems and tales. The debt to Bloy, Groussac, and Shaw is more diffuse: book reviews or essays show its mark. About the influence of Claudel on his writing nothing has yet been done. It is not at all appar-

313

ent, and if Borges hadn't mentioned his name, it is doubtful that any critic would have thought of it. What is apparent is that three of the writers in that list are important if not great Catholic writers: Dante, Bloy, and Claudel. The fact that Bernárdez, the director of the Miguel Cané library, was a Catholic poet—then much in favor in Catholic Argentina—helps to explain the presence of those writers in the library. In 1962 Borges told James Irby that it seemed a bit incongruous to find such works in a library set in such a proletarian neighborhood, and attributed their presence to Bernárdez's beliefs. What he did not explain is why he, being an agnostic, felt tempted to read Bloy's works, "which I liked a lot," and Claudel's, "which I didn't like that much" (Irby, 1962, p. 8). Perhaps he sought some sort of consolation. But he found more. What he invariably quotes from Bloy is a sentence about self-knowledge: "No one knows who he is," which he extracted and condensed from a longer one in *L'âme de Napoléon* (1912). He has also written of the links between one of Bloy's stories and Kafka's use of infinite postponement. But only one of his many articles is entirely devoted to Bloy. "The Mirror of the Enigmas" shows Borges' familiarity with the French writer. What he likes in him is what clearly makes him a precursor of Borges: his view of the world as a language whose code we have lost or can hardly decipher. In summarizing Bloy, he stresses his own skepticism, but at the same time he praises his invention:

> It is doubtful that the world has a meaning: it is more doubtful still, the incredulous will observe, that it has a double and triple meaning. I agree; but I believed that the hieroglyphic world postulated by Bloy best befits the dignity of the intellectual God of the theologians. "No one knows who he is," said Léon Bloy. Who could have illustrated that intimate knowledge better than he? He believed himself to be a strict Catholic and he was a continuer of the cabalists, a secret brother of Swedenborg and Blake: heresiarchs. (*Inquisitions,* 1964, p. 128)

Borges' Bloy is, like Borges' Kafka, an enigmatic mirror.

His reading of Dante was to have an even more lasting influence on his work. He wrote several articles on the *Divine Comedy,* one of which ("The Meeting in a Dream") was included in *Other Inquisitions,* and in 1949 he wrote a long study, to date not included in his collected works, for an Argentine edition of the *Commedia.* Both the articles and the essay show how deeply Dante's poem had affected him. Its influence is clear in one of his strangest and most complex stories, "The Aleph."

Another writer he read while traveling in the tramcar that took him to and from the Miguel Cané library was Ariosto. The *Orlando Furioso* is not mentioned in the "Autobiographical Essay," but it is included in Alicia Jurado's biography (Jurado, 1964, p. 42). Ariosto's imagination—his power of escaping through poetic dreams from his native Ferrara into the colorful medieval world or to the moon, his gifts of showing "in the disorder of a kaleidoscope" the passions and marvels of a whole era—is celebrated by Borges in a beautiful poem, "Ariosto y los árabes" (Ariosto and the Arabs). There he stresses the supreme irony of the poet's fate: to have dominated the European imagination for two centuries and to have influenced both Cervantes and Milton, among others, only to be reduced in the eighteenth century to being the author of "a dream nobody dreams any longer." (When the tales of the *Arabian Nights* were first translated into French, they changed the shape of Western imagination so drastically that the *Orlando Furioso* was practically forgotten.) Borges observes:

> reduced to
> Mere scholarship, mere history
> [the poem] is alone, dreaming itself. (Glory
> Is one of the forms of oblivion.)
> *(Obra,* 1964, p. 212)

If readers had abandoned *Orlando* by the eighteenth century, Borges rediscovered it in the late 1930s. The poem became, next to the *Arabian Nights,* a challenge to his own capacity to invent dreams and to charm readers. Why, then, does he omit any reference to Ariosto in the pertinent passage of the "Autobiographical Essay"? The omission may be accidental, a lapse in recalling around 1969 what he had been reading thirty years before. But it may also be another sign of Borges' conscious resistance to acknowledging anything but his English and American sources. He invariably reports on the most obscure English-speaking writers he ever perused, but he rarely makes specific reference to Spanish and Spanish American writers or to Italian and even French books (in spite of Borges' schooling in Geneva). This is not because he is trying to hide his sources, as other writers often do. It is because his influences must be made to conform to the persona, the mask, he chose long ago: an eccentric Englishman lost in the cultural emptiness of the Spanish-speaking world. The persona is effective but, obviously, false.

Bloy, Ariosto, Dante: those were some of the writers who helped to make Borges' life at the library less miserable. They provided, in different ways, an escape into the world of imagination and dreams: dreams of carnal love and adventure; dreams of transcendence and metaphysical excursions.

Perhaps Borges needed that brutal sojourn in the library to finally emerge from his overprotected existence. If the library was, to begin with, a daily excursion into hell, it soon became a season in purgatory. Borges had still to pass through a last trial to discover the Paradiso of writing his own fiction.

11.
A Death in the Family

By the beginning of 1937 Father was too ill to leave any doubts about the coming end. He was only sixty-four, but he had been plagued all his life with weak eyesight and had been forced into retirement when he was barely forty. He was now totally blind and had developed a heart condition which forced him to rely more and more on Mother's care.

She had already become his eyes. As soon as it grew obvious that he was going blind, she made an effort to perfect her rather rudimentary English, so that by the time he could no longer read she knew the language well enough to help him.

Father was always a shy man. He was, in Borges' words, "such a modest man that he would have liked to be invisible" ("Essay," 1970, p. 206). Short of achieving that elusive goal, he used to keep quiet for hours on end. Even when there were visitors at home, he would hardly utter a word. His silence was extremely polite. On the rare occasions when he said something, it was generally to inquire about the visitor's comfort. In one of Borges' stories, "Tlön, Uqbar, Orbis Tertius," there is a minor character, Herbert Ashe, who was obviously modeled on Father:

In life, he suffered from a sense of unreality, as so many Englishmen do; dead, he is not even the ghostly creature he was then. . . . . I remember him in the corridor of the hotel, a mathematics textbook in his hand, gazing now and again at the passing colors of the sky. One afternoon, we discussed the duodecimal numerical system (in which twelve is written 10). . . . In September, 1937, . . . Herbert Ashe died of an aneurysmal rupture. (*Ficciones*, 1962, p. 21)

If one remembers that it was Father who taught Georgie both the general principles of mathematics and the fundamentals of metaphysical idealism, the reference to the character's "sense of unreality" is very telling. The image of Ashe, sitting quietly and looking at the sky, was also inspired by the many occasions in which Georgie had seen Father gazing and musing thus at the same hotel. Even the cause of Herbert Ashe's death duplicated Father's. It was his heart that finally failed him.

In one of the most reticent passages of his "Autobiographical Essay" Borges describes the event: "One morning, my mother rang me up [at the Miguel Cané library] and I asked for leave to go home, arriving just in time to see my father die. He had undergone a long agony and was very impatient for his death" ("Essay," 1970 p. 242). He died—as his mother, Fanny Haslam, had died two years before; as his own widow, Leonor Acevedo, would die almost forty years later—welcoming death as a relief, a way out from the pain of living. Borges, as usual, does not give the exact date. It was February 24, 1938. From that moment on, he became the head of the household. He was thirty-eight and had only recently begun to contribute regularly to the family budget.

On the surface, very little was changed with Father's death. Except for the relief of not having to witness his long agony, things went on as usual at home. Borges' literary and bureaucratic life continued unaltered. He went every day to the Miguel Cané library, wrote regularly for *El Hogar,* and continued to see Adolfo Bioy Casares and Silvina Ocampo in his spare time. The only external change was a subtle one. For five months he stopped contributing to *Sur.* He could not afford to stop working for *El Hogar,* which at least paid him something, but he was in no mood to write the more demanding reviews and articles *Sur* needed. His regular contributions to the journal resumed in the August 1938 issue with a review of *La amortajada* (The Shrouded Woman), a novel, by the Chilean writer María Luisa Bombal, about the dreams and hallucinations of a dead woman. The author was a friend of his, and Borges wanted to help to promote a book that had been published by *Sur.* The novel was important for him because it was the type of fantastic fiction he himself was exploring quietly at the time.

His last contribution to *Sur* had been, coincidentally, a note about Leopoldo Lugones' suicide. Lugones had been one of the major forces in shaping Georgie's poetry. At the time the young man began to publish his own poems, in the early 1920s, Lugones was undoubtedly the most important Argentine writer: a man whose work cast a long shadow over the ultraist generation. In an article written for *El Hogar* on February 26, 1937, exactly one year before Lugones' suicide, Borges discusses his influence on young poets. Entitled "The New Literary

Generations," the article attacks the then current notion that the young had stormed and conquered the Bastille of literary prejudices and forwarded the cause of new esthetic ideas. Borges laughs discreetly at the pomposity of that view and claims that it was based on a misconception or perhaps a lie. He affirms that the main preoccupation of the ultraists was the metaphor, which for them represented the whole of poetry. In discarding rhyme, the young believed they surpassed Lugones, who still believed in it. According to Borges, their independence was a delusion; they were "unwilling and fatal disciples" of Lugones' pioneering book, *Lunario sentimental* (Sentimental Moon Calendar). The book had been published in 1909; ten or twelve years later the young poets were still developing what was already contained in it. "We were," Borges concludes, "the tardy heirs of only one of Lugones' profiles."

One of Borges' companions in the ultraist crusade, Eduardo González Lanuza, wrote a rejoinder that was also published in *El Hogar* (March 12, 1937). The tone was friendly but the rebuttal firm. Borges did not reply; he was convinced that his was the right view and did not want to spend any more time arguing. But once Lugones died, he forgot his old arguments. In the article he wrote for *Sur* and later enlarged for a special issue on Lugones published by *Nosotros* in 1938, he summarizes his importance:

> To say that the first Argentine writer has died, to say that the first Spanish-speaking writer has died, is to say the mere truth and is to say very little. After Groussac's death, he is entitled to the first honor; after the death of Unamuno, to the second; but both proceed from a comparison and elimination; the two talk about Lugones and other people, not about the private Lugones; the two leave him very much alone. The two, finally (although not difficult to prove), are vague as any superlative. (*Lugones,* 1955, p. 81)

The ranking is Borges' way of beginning the discussion of Lugones' importance for Hispanic letters. The article does not attempt to hide Lugones' controversial attitudes. In registering his change from atheism to Catholicism, Borges observes curtly: "Only politicians do not change. For them, political fraud and democratic preaching are not incompatible." He also points out that Lugones' ideas were less attractive than his rhetoric and that his arguments rarely were convincing, although the words he used were. In mentioning some of his best pages, Borges also admits that Lugones had bad taste, but he finds an excuse in the fact that it is not so uncommon: for instance, Ortega y Gasset's style is also terrible. Borges points out: "In life, Lugones was judged by the most recent occasional article which his indifference had tolerated. Dead, he has the posthumous right to be judged for his best work" (ibid., p. 84).

The last paragraph of his article contains a subtle allusion to Lugones' suicide: "About the rest, about what we know . . . in the third of his *Hellenic Studies* one can find these words: 'Master of his own life, he is also of his death.' (The context deserves to be remembered. Ulysses refuses the immortality Calypso had offered him; Lugones argues that to refuse immortality is the equivalent of committing suicide, in the long run.)" (ibid., p. 84). Borges believes Lugones had the right to commit suicide and, very discreetly, approves it. In the context of the Argentine society of the time, such a statement was daring. The Catholic Lugones had committed a sin that would condemn his soul to eternal damnation. But Borges does not agree with that view. He prefers to place Lugones in a context the poet would have liked: that of a culture which respected the dignity of suicide. The suicide of Lugones, followed so closely by Father's death, must have affected Borges deeply. In a sense, Lugones was a father figure to him, but a figure he was not bound to respect. Remote, solitary, aloof, Lugones had represented a model against which Georgie could measure himself, a model which he could openly discuss and even defy—complementary, in more than one sense, to the model Father was.

If the surface of Borges' life was altered very little by Father's death, the full impact of his absence was enormous. An accident that Borges had on Christmas Eve 1938 reveals how deeply he had been affected. The episode has been described at least twice by him. In his "Autobiographical Essay" he has this to say:

It was on Christmas Eve of 1938—the same year my father died—that I had a severe accident. I was running up a stairway and suddenly felt something brush my scalp. I had grazed a freshly painted open casement window. In spite of first-aid treatment, the wound became poisoned, and for a period of a week or so I lay sleepless every night and had hallucinations and high fever. One evening, I lost the power of speech and had to be rushed to the hospital for an immediate operation. Septicemia had set in, and for a month I hovered, all unknowingly, between life and death. (Much later, I was to write about this in my story "The South.") ("Essay," 1970, pp. 242–243)

In "The South," after introducing the protagonist, Juan Dahlmann, in the first paragraph of the story, Borges describes what happened to Juan during "the last days of February 1939." There is a change of dates, perhaps to avoid Christmas' religious connotations and to mark (secretly) the exact time of Borges' own recuperation.

Dahlmann had succeeded in acquiring, on that very afternoon, an imperfect copy of Weil's edition of *The Thousand and One Nights*. Avid to examine this find, he did not wait for the elevator but hurried up the stairs. In the obscurity, something brushed by his forehead: a bat, a bird? On the face of the woman who opened the door to him he saw horror engraved, and the hand he wiped across his face came away red with blood. The edge of a recently painted window which someone had forgotten to close had caused his wound. (*Ficciones*, 1962, pp. 167–168)

If one compares this version with the one in the "Autobiographical Essay," it is possible to conclude that Borges invented some narrative details to make the story more concrete and believable: the finding of a copy of an obscure German translation of the *One Thousand and One Nights* (a translation he had reviewed in *History of Eternity*, 1936); the joy and greed that find brings to Dahlmann; his discovery of being wounded by the expression on the face of the woman who opens the door to him and the blood on his own hands. (These last two details are very cinematographic and show Borges' familiarity with both Hitchcock's and von Sternberg's imaginative style of editing.) But if one looks at another testimony of the real accident, it is easy to see that the fictional version presented in "The South" is perhaps closer to reality than the autobiographical summary. It comes from Mother:

He had another horrible accident. . . . He was for a time between life and death. It was Christmas Eve, and Georgie had gone to pick up a girl who was coming to lunch with us. But Georgie didn't come back! I was in anguish till we had a call from the police. . . . It seemed that, the elevator being out of service, he had climbed the stairs very quickly and did not see an open window; pieces of glass had gotten into his head. The scars are still visible. Because the wound had not been properly disinfected before it was sutured, he had a fever of 105 degrees the next day. The fever went on and it was finally necessary to operate, in the middle of the night. (Mother, 1964, p. 11)

By giving more details about the context of the real accident, Mother adds one significant element missing from Borges' accounts. The young woman he had gone to pick up is reduced to a horrified anonymous face in "The South" and is not mentioned at all in the "Essay." The anticipation of the Christmas Eve lunch is transferred in the story (very adequately, Freud would have said) to Dahlmann's greed upon discovering a copy of Weil's rare translation of the *One Thousand and One Nights*. Knowing Borges' reticence in romantic matters, it is understandable that he suppresses all reference to the girl in the "Essay" and alludes to her only briefly in the story.

The young woman has been identified by Borges' biographers as a Chilean friend. She was pretty and Borges apparently was fond of her, but he was fond of practically all pretty young women. She is important to the accident because in Borges' texts she is the repressed element that gives a clue to the story and to the real source of it.

What one has to bear in mind is that Borges had gone to the girl's house to pick her up and take her to lunch with Mother. Being in a hurry, he made a fatal decision that led to the accident. The rush to get upstairs, and the emotionally charged context of the occasion, is what makes the accident revealing. Borges' reticence about the young woman makes it impossible to determine if the occasion had another meaning for him. Was he introducing the young woman to Mother for the first time? Was an engagement contemplated?

If he was really taking the young woman to see Mother for the first time, the whole accident takes on a different meaning. It can be seen as a way of escaping the responsibility of that type of situation, which symbolically implied taking another step toward maturity. Borges was not only the head of the household but was taking a young woman to meet Mother. The fact that, because of the accident, the meeting failed and, because of the accident, Borges temporarily became (like Father) an invalid totally dependent on Mother gives the whole episode another coloration. The accident can then be seen as a way of perpetuating his dependency, a refusal to enter fully into maturity.

But we do not know the exact circumstances of that frustrated lunch. And it would be wise not to speculate too much. What we know is that the accident made Borges more dependent than before on Mother's help. It also had another consequence: it freed him symbolically from Father's tutelage forever. To understand this we must look at the accident from a completely different point of view.

12.
Reading as
Writing

One of the immediate consequences of his accident on Christmas Eve 1938 was Borges' fear that he had lost his capacity to read and write. In his "Autobiographical Essay" he reports:

When I began to recover, I feared for my mental integrity. I remember that my mother wanted to read to me from a book I had just ordered, C. S. Lewis' *Out of the Silent Planet,* but for two or three nights I kept putting her off. At last, she prevailed, and after hearing a page or two I fell to crying. My mother asked me why the tears. "I'm crying because I understand," I said. A bit later, I wondered whether I could ever write again. I had previously written quite a few poems and dozens of short reviews. I thought that if I tried to write a review now and failed I'd be all through intellectually, but that if I tried something I had never really done before and failed at that it wouldn't be so bad and might even prepare me for the final revelation. I decided I would try to write a story. The result was "Pierre Menard, Author of the *Quixote.*" ("Essay," 1970, p. 243)

As usual, Borges summarizes a longer and more complex process. In Mother's account of the accident there are added details:

For two weeks, he was between life and death, with [a fever of] 105 or 106 degrees; at the end of the first week, the fever began to abate and he told me: "Read me a book, read me a page." He had had hallucinations, he had seen animals creeping in through the door, etc. I read him a page, and then he told me: "That's all right." —"What do you mean?" —"Yes, now I know I'm not going to be insane, I've understood everything." He began to write fantastic stories afterward, a thing that had never happened to him before. . . . As soon as he was back home again, he began to write a fantastic story, his first one. . . . And afterward, he wrote only fantastic stories, which scare

323

me a little because I don't understand them very well. I asked him once: "Why don't you write again the same things you used to write?" He answered: "Do not insist, do not insist." And he was right. (Mother, 1964, p. 11)

The difference between the two accounts is not only in the details but in the point of view. While Borges makes it very plain that it was Mother who insisted on reading him Lewis' book, she says that it was he who did it. Eyewitness accounts are bound to differ but not so drastically. Perhaps the difference corresponds only to the shifting of the narrative "I." In his version of the accident Borges is more concerned with communicating to the reader his fears for his "mental integrity," while Mother seems more interested in communicating both her concern for her son's health and her devotion to him. In her reminiscences she always presents herself as being totally at his service, while Borges generally underlines her independence and strength of character. This discrepancy is inevitable: mothers tend to believe they are slaves to their children while children know how dominant and insistent doting mothers can be.

The other major difference is one of tone. Mother is dramatic where Borges is detached and, apparently, devoid of any emotion. Even when he talks about how moved he was and admits to crying, he is distant. The emotional quality of his reaction when he discovered he was able to understand C. S. Lewis' book can be found in "The God's Script," collected in *The Aleph* (1949). Near the end, when the protagonist, an imprisoned Mayan priest, has a mystical vision of the Wheel (which is the universe, which is his god), he exclaims: "O bliss of understanding, greater than the bliss of imagining or feeling" (*Labyrinths,* 1962, p. 172). From that zone between life and death in which he had lingered, Borges (like the Mayan priest) slowly returned to the bliss of understanding.

His account of how he became a fiction writer is also foreshortened and contains a glaring anachronism. Borges had been writing fiction at least since 1933, when he published, in the multicolored pages of *Crítica*'s Saturday supplement, a story called "Streetcorner Man," later collected in *A Universal History of Infamy* (1935). Many of the short biographies of that book were partly fictitious as well. And in his last book of essays, *History of Eternity* (1936), he had already planted a short story, under the guise of a book review of an imaginary detective novel published in Bombay. "The Approach to al-Mu'tasim" was actually the model of what was to be "Pierre Menard, Author of the *Quixote.*" The links between that story and the new one are obvious: both are presented as literary essays that discuss the work of a writer who doesn't exist and give all kinds of bogus information (date and place of publication, name of publisher or journal, quotations from other critics) to make the hoax more believable. Both deal with a certain concept of what fiction is. Both use the trick of introducing a literary reality that is false.

There is, of course, a great difference between the two texts. The first story reviews a book that might have been written and published in Bombay (there is nothing fantastic in that kind of fiction); because of that, it was successful as a hoax. The second story gives the game away because it is based not only on an imaginary writer but on a writer who attempts an impossible task: to rewrite (not copy) *Don Quixote* literally. The fantastic is in Pierre Menard's behavior. It is difficult to see what this has to do with C. S. Lewis' novel. On the other hand, the links with Kafka seem obvious. In many of his novels and tales one finds examples of such "fantastic" conduct. But not in Lewis.

Borges deliberately misguides readers of his "Autobiographical Essay," leading them to believe that he came out of the accident transformed into a fiction writer directly influenced by C. S. Lewis' novel. Still, there is a grain of truth in what he says. If he is wrong in the chronology of events (he had already started his career as a fiction writer) and in the connection he establishes between "Pierre Menard" and *Out of the Silent Planet,* he is right in stressing the influence of Lewis' novel on his new fiction. (The story he ought to have mentioned is "Tlön, Uqbar, Orbis Tertius," in which an imaginary planet is superimposed on our planet.) He is also right about the importance of the accident in radically changing his writing. The accident did bring about a transformation: not as the original cause but as the end product of a complex metamorphosis Borges had undergone since Father's death.

In retelling the story of the accident, Borges makes an incidental remark: "It was on Christmas Eve of 1938—the same year my father died . . ." ("Essay," 1970, p. 242). Father's death had freed Borges, at thirty-eight, from a tutelage that had lasted too long. Since he was a child, and as long as he could remember, Father had led him to fulfill a literary destiny that his own lack of ambition and (perhaps) his rather modest resources had prevented him from accomplishing. Georgie was bound to become a writer because that was what Father had in mind for him. From that point of view, like many parents, Father had wanted Georgie to succeed where he had failed, to be his other self and even a better self than the one he had been. Father's failures as a poet, dramatist, and storyteller would be compensated for by Georgie's successes. This decision, which the child never questioned and the young man accepted and implemented, had placed an enormous responsibility on his shoulders. It is no wonder that Georgie had always been obsessed with the theme of the double and had found in Gustav

Meyrink's novel *The Golem* an adequate symbol for his own feelings of having been "made" by another. He was Father's Golem.

But there was another side to this situation. Father had been a reticent poet and a psychological novelist, while Georgie had attempted to fulfill his ambitions without following too closely the models Father respected. He had written poems, but his source was the cosmic Whitman, not the self-effacing Enrique Banchs; he had avoided psychological narrative and had worked hard at creating (almost surreptitiously) a different type of fiction: critical and even fantastic. With Father's death, the responsibility of fulfilling his destiny continued, but Borges was free to pursue the kind of writing he really liked.

The accident dramatized Borges' guilt over Father's death and his deep, totally unconscious need to be set free at last from Father's tutelage. From a symbolical point of view, the accident represented both a death (by suicide) and a rebirth. After the accident Borges emerged as a different writer, a writer this time engendered by himself. And that precisely is what he is trying to suggest when he says in the "Essay" that after the accident (and Father's death) he "tried something [he] had never really done before" (ibid., p. 243). That is, he tried to write openly a fantastic short story that was meant to be taken as a fantastic short story. He had, literarily, come out of the closet.

This new Borges would go further than Father had ever planned or even dreamed about. In attempting symbolically to kill himself, Borges was actually killing the self that was only Father's reflection. He assumed a new identity through the mythical experience of death and rebirth.

Borges did not dismiss the old self completely. The fantastic story he wrote after recuperating from blood poisoning was presented under the guise of a critical essay and was published in *Sur* (May 1939) with no indication that it was a piece of fiction. The new Borges did not mind being seen as the old one—"The other, the same," as the title of one of his volumes of poems puts it. The metamorphosis was not yet visible but it was final. "Pierre Menard, Author of the *Quixote*" was the first text written by the new Borges.

As soon as Borges was well enough, he resumed his contributions to *El Hogar*. There had been a lapse of more than a month between the last article he published before the accident (December 2, 1938, with the attack on Breton's manifesto) and the reappearance of the section "Foreign Books and Authors" on January 6, 1939. Although two of the pieces in that issue are unmistakably his (a review of Thomas Mann's book on Schopenhauer, another of a book of short stories), the rest of the section may have been put together by the staff of the magazine, using copy left over from previous issues. But the next issue, dated January 27, was obviously written by somebody else. It reveals some mistakes in translation Borges would never make ("El libro *es* terminado," instead of "El libro termina") and shows a Spanish, not Argentine, use of verbs ("no me dejar*íais* decir," instead of the simpler "no me dejar*ían* decir"). It also proliferates in clichés that reveal the hand of a wearied journalist. At the time the issue was put to bed, Borges was in the hospital and *El Hogar* probably had to rely on members of its staff. But by February 10 Borges was back in business. And the longest review of that issue was dedicated precisely to C. S. Lewis' *Out of the Silent Planet.*

The title of the review sets the tone: "A First Memorable Book." It begins by making a pointed reference to the fact that Wells now prefers "political or sociological divagation to the rigorous invention of imaginary events. . . . Luckily, two witty followers compensate for his abstractions." The first is Olaf Stapledon, a writer often reviewed in those pages. The other is C. S. Lewis. After summarizing the book, Borges observes: "It is a psychological book; the three strange 'mankinds' [that the visitor to the silent planet finds] and the vertiginous geography of Mars are less important to the reader than the reaction of the hero who begins by finding them atrocious and almost intolerable, and ends up by identifying with them." His enthusiasm for the novel does not blind Borges. He admits that "Lewis' imagination is limited. . . . What is admirable is the infinite honesty of that imagination, the coherent and thorough truth of that fantastic world."

From the review alone there is little to indicate that Lewis' novel had such an impact on Borges' work. To understand that impact it is necessary to place the novel and the review in the context of Borges' friendship and collaboration with Adolfo Bioy Casares and Silvina Ocampo. That is the context out of which "Pierre Menard" and "Tlön, Uqbar, Orbis Tertius" came to be written. The three friends used to meet at Victoria Ocampo's place in San Isidro to discuss literature and to plan works in collaboration. Some of these works were later published; others never reached that stage and remained fragments of vast enterprises. Among the planned works, Bioy Casares says in an article, "was a story about a young French provincial writer who is attracted to the work of an obscure master, deceased, whose fame has been limited to the select few. With patience and devotion, he collects the works of the master—a speech to praise the sword used by French academicians, written in an extremely correct style and full of clichés; a short pamphlet on the fragments of Varro's *Treatise of the Latin Language;* a collection of sonnets, as cold in their form as in their subject. Unable to reconcile the reputation of the master with these rather disappointing samples, the young man searches for and finally finds his unpublished manuscripts: they consist of rough drafts, "brilliant, hopelessly incomplete" (Bioy Casares, 1968, p. 145). Among the papers left by the master was a list of things a writer ought not to do, a list which Bioy transcribes. It is too long to be quoted here, but its substance is that the best thing is to avoid doing anything. One of the negative recommendations is to shun praise or censure in literary criticism. This wise precept is attributed to a certain Menard (ibid., p. 148).

Although the story was never written, Borges later decided to use it as the starting point for his "Pierre Menard, Author of the *Quixote.*" According to Bioy, the same day that they were jotting down the long list of prohibitions, Borges told them about his new story (ibid., p. 149). The real source of "Pierre Menard" is there. But Borges' imagination transformed an exercise in literary satire (modeled more or less on the artists' and writers' stories written by Henry James) into a truly fantastic story. In his version the original idea—the disillusionment of a young provincial writer upon realizing how frail fame is—is metamorphosed into the story of a writer who attempts the impossible: to rewrite in every detail, and without copying it, a famous text. By changing the focus from the young writer to the master and making the latter a sort of martyr to creative writing, Borges introduces the fantastic element that was lacking in the original plan. Now Menard's mad pursuit becomes the center of the story. Like Melville's Bartleby or Kafka's Hunger Artist, Menard sets himself an impossible task.

The actual story uses enough of the planned satire to be seen as a realization of it. In a sense, the never written work serves as a framework for the story. But instead of showing the young man's disappointing quest for the unpublished work of the master, Borges makes the young man the narrator of the tale and changes his point of view. Instead of being disillusioned by the actual work of Menard, he is enthusiastic. The story is presented as a parody of the kind of article written in defense of a misunderstood genius by one of his followers. By changing the perspective, Borges heightens the satirical aspects of the tale. It becomes a brilliant parody of French literary life, with its touches of bigotry, anti-Semitism, and adulation of the upper classes.

The first part of the story is dedicated to the petty disputes over Menard's work in which several characters are engaged: the anonymous narrator; Madame Henri Bachelier, a society lady too busy to write her own poems; and the Countess of Bagnoregio, another literary lady friend of Menard, married to an American philanthropist. The catalogue of Menard's work offered at the beginning of the story is a takeoff on Mallarmé's pursuit of the trivial and on Valéry's Monsieur Teste. The second part of the story is devoted to commenting on Menard's efforts to rewrite, literally, *Don Quixote*. Here Borges satirizes some of the Cervantists and Cervantophiles who are the plague of Spanish literature. The attempt to rewrite *Don Quixote* is not new. As early as 1614, one year before Cervantes' second part came out, a pseudonymous writer, Alonso Fernández de Avellaneda, published his own second part. Later Juan Montalvo of Ecuador and the Spaniards Miguel de Unamuno and Azorín wrote their own versions of the book and its characters. But none attempted to reproduce the work literally. It is that ambition which separates Menard's mad project from the rest.

As is well known, Menard succeeds in writing a few chapters. In comparing them, the narrator finds that they are literally the same but have a completely different meaning:

> Cervantes' text and Menard's are verbally identical, but the second is almost infinitely richer. (More ambiguous, his detractors will say, but ambiguity is richness.) It is a revelation to compare Menard's *Don Quixote* with Cervantes'. The latter, for example, wrote (part one, chapter nine):
>
> > . . . truth, whose mother is history, rival of time, depository of deeds, witness of the past, exemplar and adviser to the present, and the future's counselor.
>
> Written in the seventeenth century, written by the "lay genius" Cervantes, this enumeration is a mere rhetorical praise of History. Menard, on the other hand, writes:
>
> > . . . truth, whose mother is history, rival of time, depository of deeds, witness of the past, exemplar and adviser to the present, and the future's counselor.
>
> History, the *mother* of truth: the idea is astounding. Menard, a contemporary of William James, does not define history as an inquiry into reality but as its origin. Historical truth, for him, is not what had happened; it is what we judged to have happened. The final phrases—*exemplar and adviser to the present and the future's counselor*—are brazenly pragmatic. The contrast in style is also vivid. The archaic style of Menard—quite foreign, after all—suffers from a certain affectation. Not so that of his forerunner, who handles with ease the current Spanish of his time. (*Labyrinths*, 1962, pp. 42–43)

There is a joke within the joke: the phrase which Borges selected belongs to a passage in which Cervantes, introducing the "Arab historian" Cide Hamete Benengeli as the real author of *Don Quixote*, is laughing at the pretensions of the chivalric romances to tell the truth and nothing but the truth. The text that the narrator of "Pierre Menard" takes so literally was already satirical and contained a parody of the literary model Cervantes was attempting to discredit. But Borges does not mention this. His own joke points to a different goal. More unexpected than his dazzling exercise in critical jugglery over a fixed text is the story's conclusion:

Menard (perhaps without wanting it) has enriched, by means of a new technique, the halting and rudimentary art of reading: this technique is that of the deliberate anachronism and the erroneous attribution. This technique, whose applications are infinite, prompts us to go through the *Odyssey* as if it were posterior to the *Aeneid* and the book *Le jardin du Centaure* of Madame Henri Bachelier as if it were by Madame Henri Bachelier. This technique fills the most placed works with adventure. To attribute the *Imitatio Christi* to Louis Ferdinand Céline or to James Joyce, is this not a sufficient renovation of its tenuous spiritual indications? (ibid., p. 44)

Another of Borges' whims? That is what some readers believed, and the fact that "Pierre Menard" was first included in a collection of stories, *The Garden of Forking Paths* (1941), and reappeared in the more comprehensive collection *Ficciones* (1944), helped to heighten the impression of game playing and irresponsible invention that many readers had when they discovered the story in *Sur*. Nevertheless, some readers probably detected ideas that Borges had expressed in earlier essays. One of these, "La fruición literaria" (Literary Fruition), was originally published in *La Nación* (January 23, 1927) before it was included in *El idioma de los argentinos* (1928). Here Borges examines a metaphor about fire without revealing until the very end the name of the author. By discussing the metaphor as if it were coined by a contemporary poet, an ancient Chinese or Siamese poet, a witness to a fire, or the poet Aeschylus, Borges shows that we judge the metaphor differently according to its literary context. It is the context that fixes the reading and thus changes the text. In another article, "Elementos de preceptiva" (Elements of the Preceptive), published in *Sur* (April 1933), he comes to the conclusion that it is impossible to judge any work of some merit as a whole by simply "a marvelous emission of terrified praise, and without analyzing a single line." This essay, written only six years before "Pierre Menard," agrees on "the final impossibility of an esthetics."

Instead of taking the views of those skeptical articles literally, or merely laughing at the conclusion of "Pierre Menard," we can see in them the foundation of a new poetics, based not on the actual writing of a work but on its reading. This approach to Borges' texts has been favored by French critics since Gérard Genette's 1964 article "La littérature selon Borges." Taking as his starting point the final lines of "Pierre Menard," Genette stresses the importance of the Borgesian intuition that the most delicate and important operation of all those which contribute to the writing of a book is reading it. He concludes his analysis with these words:

> The genesis of a work in historic time and in the life of an author is the most contingent and most insignificant moment of its duration. . . . The time of a book is not the limited time of its writing, but the limitless time of reading and memory. The meaning of books is in front of them and not behind them; it is in us: a book is not a ready-made meaning, a revelation we have to suffer; it is a reserve of forms that are waiting to have some meaning; it is the "imminence of a revelation that is not yet produced" and that every one of us has to produce for himself. (Genette, 1964, p. 132)

Genette's last lines contain a reference to a key passage in Borges' essay "The Wall and the Books," first published in *La Nación* (October 22, 1950) and later collected in *Other Inquisitions* (1952): "That imminence of a revelation that is not yet produced is, perhaps, the esthetic reality" (*Inquisitions*, 1964, p. 5).

If "Pierre Menard" was meant to be a satire on French literary circles (which were, of course, the model for similar circles in Argentina), Borges soon changed the original project and took advantage of the occasion to create not only a fantastic story but also a critical essay on the poetics of reading. From that point of view, "Pierre Menard" is both a culmination of the many hoaxes he had played in two decades of writing and, above all, the beginning of his fully mature work. With his next story, "Tlön, Uqbar, Orbis Tertius," Borges would move even further.

13.
A Distorted Mirror to Reality

In May 1940, one year exactly after the publication of "Pierre Menard, Author of the *Quixote*" in *Sur,* the same journal published "Tlön, Uqbar, Orbis Tertius." This time, the story did not pretend to be an essay, although it had all the external characteristics of one. It began by reporting a conversation between Bioy Casares and the author about a puzzling quotation the first had found in an odd volume of a pirate encyclopedia; it told of the efforts made by both to locate that volume, which they finally did; it offered a summary of the article on "Uqbar," the unknown land which was the subject of the original conversation; it added more information about Uqbar that the author had gathered later under the most unusual circumstances; it revealed the existence of a whole encyclopedia devoted to describing Tlön, the planet to which Uqbar belonged; finally, it explained, calmly, that the whole affair was a hoax perpetrated by a group of eighteenth-century philosophers and carried to its completion in this century through the patronage of an American millionaire. In a postscript, which appears to put the hoax theory in question, the reader is informed, again calmly, that objects made in Uqbar have begun to be introduced on earth.

The postscript gives the game away because it is dated 1947 and reads: "I reproduce the preceding article just as it appeared in number 68 of *Sur*—jade green covers, May 1940." The fact that the reader of *Sur* had in his hands that jade green issue and that he was unmistakably reading it in May 1940 and not in 1947, created a curious perspective—a "mise en abîme," as André Gide used to say and the French critics now repeat. In the same way that the label of a tin of biscuits shows a picture of a tin of biscuits and so on, creating an infinite retrogression, Borges' text was *originally* published in the sixty-eighth issue of *Sur* as a *reproduction* of a text already published in the sixty-eighth issue of *Sur*.

By dating the postscript 1947, Borges defined the "article" unmistakably as a piece of science fiction. From that point of view, it would be easy to establish the links between "Tlön, Uqbar, Orbis Tertius" and C. S. Lewis' novel *Out of the Silent Planet*. Both belong basically to the same genre: utopian science fiction. In both there is a great concern with imaginary languages: while Lewis describes in detail the efforts of the protagonist, a Cambridge linguist named Ransom, to learn the language of one of the three tribes of people in Malacandra, the narrator of "Tlön" describes in detail the language of that planet. There are even minor coincidences in the phonological value of words in both languages. They favor an almost Scandinavian grouping of consonants: one of the tribes' names in Lewis is "Hross," while in Borges some imaginary objects produced in Tlön are called "hrönir."

But what chiefly brings the two works together is their allegorical point of view. In describing Malacandra (which happens to be Mars, the red planet), Lewis is placing a mirror up to earth. In the best tradition of Thomas More and Swift, he describes an imaginary visit to that planet and the society he finds there, to best describe our world, the silent planet of the title. Borges, in a more oblique way, does the same: his Tlön is described as an inverted version of earth. It is a world in which matter is denied and imaginary objects become real. That is, it is a world made according to the theories about reality of the eighteenth-century British philosopher George Berkeley. The fact that the encyclopedic hoax was originated in the eighteenth century and that the American millionaire's surname is Buckley—which sounds almost like the British pronunciation of Berkeley—corroborates the identification proposed by James E. Irby (Irby, 1971, p. 420). Both Lewis and Borges are using one of the oldest methods of describing reality: through the distorted mirror of utopia.

Even the political allusions contained in Lewis' novel and Borges' tale function in a similar context (utopias, from Plato onward, were always political). While Lewis shows that red Mars is really a planet of peace (implying that silent earth is the planet of war), Borges shows that Tlön, being a rational version of earth, is a totalitarian world: the excess of reason leads to totalitarianism. And in the end, when objects made in Tlön begin to appear on this planet, Borges says:

> The dissemination of objects from Tlön over different countries would complement this plan. . . . The fact is that the international press infinitely proclaimed the "find." Manuals, anthologies, summaries, literal versions, authorized re-editions and pirated editions of the Greatest Works of Man

flooded and still flood the earth. Almost immediately, reality yielded on more than one account. The truth is that it longed to yield. Ten years ago any symmetry with a semblance of order—dialectical materialism, anti-Semitism, Nazism—was sufficient to entrance the minds of men. How could one do other than submit to Tlön, to the minute and vast evidence of an orderly planet? (*Labyrinths*, 1962, p. 17)

The reference to totalitarian regimes and ideologies is clear. One must remember that both *Out of the Silent Planet* and "Tlön, Uqbar, Orbis Tertius" were conceived and written at the time of the Spanish civil war, the time of the Munich and the Nazi-Soviet pacts, when Hitler had already begun to prepare his armies for the conquest of Europe. They are both works that belong to the prologue to World War II.

But it would be wrong to overstress the links between the two texts. The differences between them are more relevant. While Lewis writes in the tradition of utopian science fiction, concentrating on the protagonist's adventure in the No-place land, Borges changes the focus: instead of writing about the adventure of the discovery of utopia, he concentrates on the adventure of the discovery of texts about utopia. Lewis' Ransom "actually" travels to Malacandra, while Borges' narrator only reads about Tlön. At the end, by a switch that is typically Borgesian, the reality of Tlön is interpolated into the narrator's (the reader's) reality. To explain this switch it is necessary to study the other sources of the story.

There is no denying the impact that the reading of *Out of the Silent Planet* had on Borges while he lay in the hospital slowly recovering from the accident of Christmas Eve 1938. That reading was decisive because it happened at the right time. But Borges may already have found what he needed in the fictions of H. G. Wells and the other utopians. As a matter of fact, in a review written two years before, Borges advanced many of the points of view he later developed in "Tlön, Uqbar, Orbis Tertius." The review is of Adolfo Bioy Casares' collection of short stories, *La estatua casera* (The Domestic Statue), and was published in *Sur* in March 1936. The opening paragraph gives Borges' notion of utopian science fiction:

I suspect that a general scrutiny of fantastic literature would reveal that it is not very fantastic. I have visited many utopias—from the eponymous one of More to *Brave New World*—and I have not yet found a single one that exceeds the cozy limits of satire or sermon and describes in detail an imaginary country, with its geography, its history, its religion, its language, its literature, its music, its government, its metaphysical and theological controversy . . . its encyclopaedia in short; all of it organically coherent, of course, and (I know I'm very demanding) with no reference whatsoever to the horrible injustices suffered by the artillery captain Alfred Dreyfus. Of Wells' (and even Swift's) imaginary theories, we know that there is in each of them only one fantastic element; of the *One Thousand and One Nights,* that a good part of its marvel is involuntary because thirteenth-century Egyptians believed in talismans and in exorcisms. In short: I wouldn't be surprised if the Universal Library of Fantastic Literature did not contain more than a volume by Lewis Carroll, a couple of Disney films, a poem by Coleridge, and (because of the absent-mindedness of its author) Manuel Galvez's *Opera omnia. (Sur,* March 1936, pp. 85–86)

Borges is being facetious. The last phrase contains a dig at one of Argentina's most successful realistic narrators. His ironical reference implies that "realism" is a branch of fantastic literature. But what is really important in his statement is the notion that utopian literature is generally not very specific in describing the aspects that matter most in an imaginary world. His criticism is relevant not only as a general observation about utopias but, especially, because it already contains the germ of "Tlön, Uqbar, Orbis Tertius." When he presents that imaginary planet, Borges does not omit either its geography or its history, its religion or its poetry, its metaphysics or its music. A blueprint of the story can be seen here, as Irby has correctly pointed out. He also has indicated another source: one of Macedonio Fernández's most curious fantasies, that of becoming the president of Argentina by "very subtly insinuating his name among the populace." Macedonio began by inspiring a collective novel, *El hombre que será presidente* (The Man Who Will Become President), for which Borges and other friends served simultaneously as authors and characters. Only the first two chapters were completed. The novel had a secondary plot which concerned the attempt by a group of "neurotic and perhaps insane millionaires" to further the same campaign by undermining people's resistance through the gradual dissemination of "disturbing inventions." According to Irby's summary, these "were usually contradictory artifacts whose effects ran counter to their apparent form or function, including certain very small and disconcertingly heavy objects (like the cone found by Borges and Amorim toward the end of 'Tlön, Uqbar, Orbis Tertius'), scrambled passages in detective novels (somewhat like the interpolated entry on Uqbar, and dadaist creations like the 'transparent tigers' and 'towers of blood' in Tlön)." Irby concludes that "the novel's techniques and language were meant to enact as well as relate this whole process by introducing more and more such objects in a less and less casual way and by slowly gravitating toward a baroque style of utter delirium" (Irby, 1971, p. 417).

Another important piece in the puzzle that led to the writing of "Tlön, Uqbar, Orbis Tertius" is a literary discussion that Borges had with Adolfo Bioy Casares and Silvina Ocampo in the 1930s. The story itself begins by calling attention to it:

> I owe the discovery of Uqbar to the conjunction of a mirror and an encyclopaedia. The mirror troubled the depths of a corridor in a country house on Gaona Street in Ramos Mejía; the encyclopaedia is fallaciously called *The Anglo-American Cyclopaedia* (New York, 1917) and is a literal but delinquent reprint of the *Encyclopaedia Britannica* of 1902. The event took place some five years ago. Bioy Casares had had dinner with me that evening and we became lengthily engaged in a vast polemics concerning the composition of a novel in the first person, whose narrator would omit or disfigure the facts and indulge in various contradictions which would permit a few readers—very few readers—to perceive an atrocious or banal reality. (*Labyrinths*, 1962, p. 3)

The novel, as such, was never written, but both friends separately attempted versions of it: Bioy in 1945 with the novel *A Plan for Escape,* which presents just such a distorted reality; Borges in 1940 with "Tlön, Uqbar, Orbis Tertius," which ends by revealing a banal reality— Tlön is the real world. The conversation with Bioy is the seed of Borges' story in the same way that Borges' review of *La estatua casera* is the seed of Bioy's novel. The comic reference Borges makes in that review to the destiny of the artillery captain Alfred Dreyfus is taken literally, and parodied, by Bioy in *A Plan for Escape,* which is set on Devil's Island. One of the chief characters is a convict called Dreyfus whose real name is Bordenave.

There is still another text which sheds unexpected light on the writing of "Tlön, Uqbar, Orbis Tertius." It is an article Borges published in *El Hogar* on June 2, 1939, and it is titled "When Fiction Lives Inside Fiction." Its subject is the presence of a work of art inside another work of art. Borges makes explicit reference to well-known examples such as Velázquez's *Las meninas,* which he saw at the Museo del Prado, and Cervantes' *Don Quixote,* which includes a short novel of adultery in Part I. To this and other rather literal attempts to introduce fiction inside fiction, Borges opposes more elaborate versions, such as the Night 602 of the *One Thousand and One Nights,* when Scheherazade begins to tell the king his own story and thus almost creates a totally circular book. In Shakespeare's *Hamlet* the players in Act III present a fragment of a play which has some telling relation to the main story. Borges quotes De Quincey's opinion that the style of that fragmentary play makes Shakespeare's style more realistic; Borges argues that its essential purpose is to make the "reality" of the play more unreal. He gives other examples: Corneille's *L'illusion comique,* in which a magician shows the protagonist his son's life in a vision to reveal finally that what he has seen is not real—the son is a comedian, and his adventures are plays; and Gustav Meyrink's *The Golem,* which tells the story of a dream that contains dreams. But the most complex of these verbal labyrinths is the one Borges leaves for the end: a novel just published by Flann O'Brien, *At Swim Two Birds,* in which a Dublin student writes a novel about a Dublin innkeeper who writes a novel about his clients, one of whom is the student. After indicating the influence of Joyce on O'Brien, Borges concludes: "Arthur Schopenhauer wrote once that dreams and vigil were leaves of the same book and that to read them in order was to live, and to leaf through them was to dream. Paintings inside paintings, books that split into books, help us to intuit that identity" (*El Hogar,* June 2, 1939, p. 6).

The mention of Schopenhauer makes more explicit the general trend of the article. Borges is interested less in the poetic effect of including a work of art inside another work of art than in the metaphysical effect produced by works which erase the distinction between reality and dreams. If we apply this notion to the reading of "Tlön, Uqbar, Orbis Tertius," it is easy to see how Borges reaches the same conclusion. He begins by creating, inside the text of the story, the search for another text. When that text is found, it is described, analyzed, and finally declared a hoax. But precisely at that point, Tlön itself begins to proliferate: it creates objects which are introduced into the reality of Borges' text; it ends up by disseminating itself into that fictional reality, superimposing itself over it and probably obliterating it. At the end of the story, the narrator realizes that Tlön is taking over:

> The contact and habit of Tlön have disintegrated this world. Enchanted by its rigor, humanity forgets over and again that it is a rigor of chess masters, not of angels. . . . A scattered dynasty of solitary men has changed the face of the world. Their task continues. If our forecasts are not in error, a hundred years from now someone will discover the hundred volumes of the Second Encyclopaedia of Tlön. Then English and French and mere Spanish will disappear from the globe. The world will be Tlön. I pay no attention to all this and go on revising, in the still days at the Adrogué Hotel, an uncertain Quevedian translation (which I do not intend to publish) of Browne's *Urn Burial.* (*Labyrinths,* 1962, p. 18)

The search for an article in an encyclopedia has ended with the discovery that the world is being taken over by the encyclopedia. The limits between fiction and reality have been erased. In reaction, the narrator resigns himself to a remote corner of a remote country, devoting himself entirely to a useless occupation: the translation of a book, written by an Engish baroque writer, about funeral inscriptions. By relentless artifice, Borges has created in "Tlön, Uqbar, Orbis Tertius" more than a mirror to reality: he has created a mirror to the writing of fiction as well. The story finally reflects only itself.

The first seeds of "Tlön" were planted (as Irby has shown) in the early 1920s in conversations and literary projects Borges shared with Macedonio Fernández. They were brought to life again in the 1930s in conversations and literary projects Borges shared with Bioy Casares and Silvina Ocampo and in his own articles of the period. They came to fruition after the accident of Christmas Eve 1938 and the timely reading of Lewis' *Out of the Silent Planet*. With "Tlön, Uqbar, Orbis Tertius" Borges had become a new writer.

Part Four

1.
The Shape of Things to Come

At the time of the accident on Christmas Eve 1938, Norah and Guillermo de Torre had been living for a while with the Borgeses. They had been forced to leave Spain and return to Argentina that same year because it was obvious that the civil war was taking a turn for the worse. After the accident, the family decided to move to a house at 1972 Anchorena Street. It was a two-story building in the Andalusian style, with a garden. They lived there until 1943, when the De Torres moved elsewhere and the Borgeses rented an apartment on Quintana Avenue.

In his conversations with De Milleret, Borges stresses the change that Father's death brought to the household: Mother was forced to become a career woman at sixty-three.

> I must say that when my father died, she didn't even know how to draw a check; she was unfamiliar with what one does in a bank; she didn't know how to place her money, and now she is very good at it. And all that she learned after my father's death, in the same way she learned English correctly, because at the beginning she spoke a simple kind of English, an oral English to talk to my grandmother. Now she can even read and scan English verses. . . . And all this is very remarkable because in her family they had a cult of ignorance. (De Milleret, 1969, pp. 214–215)

Another less dramatic change brought about by 1939 was the format and location of Borges' literary section in *El Hogar*. The magazine's editors had already given signs that they were not totally satisfied with the section, which normally had appeared in the first part of the magazine, generally on page 28 or 29. Suddenly, on September 16,

1938, the section appeared on page 88. In the following issue (September 30) there was a change of a different nature: the capsule biography, one of its most important features, was excluded. It reappeared on February 10, 1939, but was again discontinued on March 24, this time for good. Other, more decisive alterations took place later. On May 5 the section was reduced to half a page of book reviews and continued to be published as such, squeezed among advertisements for Lux Soap, Ovaltine, Suchard chocolates, and other products an Argentine woman could not do without. The last time the section appeared was on July 7.

I once asked Borges, rather naïvely, why he had stopped contributing to *El Hogar*. In his usual self-mocking style, he told me that, probably because he had noticed that the magazine editors did not seem too enthusiastic, he had once forgotten to send in his copy. Realizing that nobody had called to ask for it, he came to the conclusion that they were relieved by his oversight. Probably *El Hogar*'s editors had discovered at last that Borges' section was not entirely suited to the kind of woman whose chief objective in life was the purchase of luxury consumer items.

From Borges' point of view, the almost four years of work at *El Hogar* had been a formative experience, not only because it was his first important job in literary journalism but also because, by subtly enlarging and upgrading the rather anonymous section he had inherited from Anne Keen, he had practically created a new form: the book review page, which is a sort of literary microcosm, a magazine inside a magazine. Besides, the task of preparing the fortnightly section kept Borges busy reading new books and catalogues, wittily commenting on events of literary life, and led him into condensing and updating his views on many subjects. Some of the topics that appear constantly in the section—the detective novel, fantastic and science-fiction stories, the problems of narrative technique, the increasing possibility of a European war—are the themes and subjects of his most important writing in the next decade. In a sense, the section was a sort of open workshop, a place where Borges could present, once every two weeks, his views on literary matters and rehearse his many inventions. It was also a public performance that, somehow, taught him to write for a larger audience. Unfortunately, the experience had to stop precisely at a time when Borges had added responsibilities as the head of a household and needed to make more money.

By degrees, Borges had become involved in the actual editing of *Sur*. Victoria Ocampo had never had the patience or the editorial talent required to run a journal. She had the inspiration and the enthusiasm but was more than willing to let somebody do the dreary, boring, everyday work. Thus *Sur* had had a series of young promising writers as managing editors. The first was the son of Mexican humanist Alfonso Reyes; the second, the scholarly Raimundo Lida. But they did not last long in the job. Although careless about the actual details of editing, Victoria had very clear ideas about what she wanted and how the journal ought to look. The managing editor had to be somebody who was efficient and respectful of her views at the same time. Besides, she traveled a lot, spending practically every winter in Europe, so the managing editor for much of the year had to produce the journal almost on his own. Although Borges was not suited to the position, he was very helpful. And when finally Victoria persuaded José Bianco to become managing editor, Borges came to his rescue. He was always available to help with the correct wording of a quotation, the title of a book, or the spelling of a little-known author's name. He was a living encyclopedia.

During the twenty-three years Bianco was in charge of *Sur*, Borges paid regular visits to the journal's office in downtown Buenos Aires. In his reminiscences of Borges, Bianco describes these visits: " 'When do you expect the proofs to be ready?' Borges used to ask me while delivering his copy. And as soon as I told him that they were ready, he immediately came by. After publication, he never complained about a misprint. 'Bettered by misprints' was a phrase that he loved to repeat" (Bianco, 1964, p. 17). Bianco also contrasts the quality and wit of Borges' contributions to *Sur* with the other writers' contributions. For him, his copy "justified the publication, raised its content, and on some occasions made it uneven, producing in some issues frightful bottomless pits, such was the distance between Borges' metaphysical and esthetic preoccupations, the swiftness and daring of his style," and the rest of the journal's content (ibid., p. 18). The paradox was, according to Bianco, that because Borges was exceptional he could afford to be modest, while the other contributors were always more concerned about their own inflated egos than about the quality of their copy. Borges, on the contrary, was simplicity itself.

Bianco recalls meetings with Borges, Silvina Ocampo, and Bioy Casares in which they discussed literary matters and poked fun at everything and everybody. They all had excellent memories and loved to quote from unexpected sources. According to Bianco, they created "an atmosphere in which the real and the unreal got confused. Literature was, for the three, the most intoxicating of drugs: they were exalted by it, moved, became thoughtful. It also made them laugh" (ibid., p. 15). When Silvina and Bioy married in the summer of 1940, in Las Flores, a small suburban community, Borges was the best man. To inform Bianco of the event, which had been decided on rather suddenly, they sent him a telegram written in a language they invented, comprised of English, Italian, and Spanish words. It had been inspired by a certain article by De Quincey about a man named Pinkerton. The telegram, written in pure "Pinkertonio," said literally: "Mucho registro civil, mucha iglesia, dont tell anybodini whateverano." Roughly translated it would be: "Lots of civil marriage, lots of church, don't tell anybody [with an Italian ending] whatsoever [and also: what a summer]." The telegram showed the kind of humor Joyce had made famous in *Finnegans Wake*. It consisted of coining new words by unexpectedly combining two or more already existing ones. Borges had already discussed Joyce's last book in *El Hogar* (June 16, 1939) and in a *Sur* article, "Joyce and Neologisms," published in November 1939. Although his verdict was not totally favorable, he devoted some time in both pieces to discussing the portmanteau words. His contribution to "Pinkertonio" showed that he was not immune to that type of verbal wit.

By the summer of 1940 the European war (which later would be called World War II) was already some months old. In two weeks of September 1939, Hitler with some help from the Soviet Union had destroyed the Polish army and occupied the country. But the hostilities on the Western front, with the two armies separated by the Maginot line and the Siegfried line, had reached a sort of impasse. That period was to be called the "phony war" and would produce some satires, such as Evelyn Waugh's *Put Out More Flags*, which Hitler's subsequent destruction of Holland, Belgium, and France made obsolete. But still, in the summer of 1940, the war seemed at a stalemate, as if no country really wanted to fight seriously. In the River Plate area the war had been brought home unexpectedly by the naval battle fought late in 1939 between the German pocket battleship the *Graf Spee* and three British cruisers in the waters of the river near the Uruguayan resort of Punta del Este. The three cruisers were too light to sink the German ship, but in spite of heavy losses they forced her to seek refuge in Montevideo harbor. At the time, the Uruguayan government supported the Allies and did its best to send the battleship back into the open seas, where a British fleet was gathering. The Germans preferred to sink the ship themselves outside Montevideo and cross the river to seek asylum in Argentina, where the government was pro-Nazi. That was the only moment in which the European war came near the River Plate area.

Borges was clearly and outspokenly in favor of England. There was a small but very vocal contingent of British supporters in Argentina at the time, especially among the upper and upper middle classes, many of whom had British ancestors. Many young Argentines went to England to fight for the empire. Borges was, of course, too old and too nearsighted to contemplate such a move, but he took advantage of the occasion to write some articles on the war. Instead of defending England, he chose to attack Germany, especially the favor Germany enjoyed among Argentine nationalists. One of his best articles on the subject was published on the front page of *El Hogar* on December 13, 1940, at the time Hitler's armies had pushed England out of the Continent at Dunkirk, the Luftwaffe was mercilessly bombarding London, and Germany had occupied France. The article is entitled "Definition of the Germanophile." It begins with an apparent digression on the mysteries of etymology:

> The implacable enemies of etymology argue that the origin of words does not teach what they now mean; the defenders may argue that it always teaches what they do not mean now. It teaches, for instance, that pontifices are not bridge builders; that miniatures are not painted with minium; that the matter of crystal is not ice; that the leopard is not a hybrid of panther and lion; that a candidate may not have been whitened; that sarcophagi are not the contrary of vegetarians; that rubrics are not as red as blushing; that the discoverer of America was not Amerigo Vespucci; and that the Germanophiles are not devoted to Germany. (*El Hogar*, December 13, 1940, p. 1)

The surprise ending of that paragraph is typically Borgesian. It introduces the subject in the most unexpected manner. The point Borges is trying to make is that Germanophiles are not really interested in Germany. To prove it, he argues that on the many occasions he has had a chance to talk to Argentine Germanophiles, he has discovered that they are not conversant with the names of Holderlin, Schopenhauer, and Leibnitz, and that their interest in Germany is only a sign of their hostility to England, actually based on the fact that England ruled the Falkland Islands, which the Argentines call Malvinas and claim to this day as their legitimate possession.

Another characteristic of the Germanophiles, according to Borges, is that they are saddened by the fact that British stockholders own the Argentine railways and that the British had finally won the 1902 war against the Boers in South Africa; they also are anti-Semitic and want to expel from Argentina "a Slavo-Germanic community in which German surnames predominate (Rosenblatt, Gruenberg, Nierestein, Lilenthal) and which speaks a German dialect: Yiddish or Juedisch." All these signs indicate that the Germanophiles are really Anglophobes. "They perfectly ignore Germany but resign themselves to being enthusiastic about a country that fights against England."

To illustrate his point, Borges sketches a typical conversation with a Germanophile. It begins with a discussion of the 1919 peace treaty at Versailles, which was so unfair to Germany. When Borges agrees with his speaker and observes that even then, the treaty was strongly condemned by Wells and Bernard Shaw, the speaker assents and maintains that a victorious country has to set aside oppression and revenge. But where Borges and the Germanophile part is in the conclusion the latter draws from this discussion: he sincerely believes that Germany has the right, now that it is victorious, "to destroy not only England and France (why not Italy?) but also Denmark, Holland, Norway: free of all guilt in that injustice. In 1919, Germany was badly treated by its enemies: this powerful reason allows it to burn, raze, and conquer all the nations of Europe and perhaps of the world. . . . The argument is monstrous, as you can see."

Very timidly, Borges points out this monstrosity, but the speaker laughs at his old-fashioned scruples and argues that ends justify means, and so on and so forth. "There is no other law than the will of the most powerful: the Reich is strong, the Reich's planes have destroyed Coventry, etc." Borges murmurs that if this is true, we cannot be sorry for what happened to Germany in 1919. But the speaker does not listen to the argument and starts a speech in praise of Hitler in which Borges finally discovers an irony: his opponent loves Hitler not in spite of his bombs and the blitzkrieg but because of them. "He is exhilarated by the evil, the atrocious in him. German victory matters less to him than the humiliation of England, the satisfactory burning of London." Borges comes to the conclusion that the Hitlerite is invariably "a spiteful person, a secret and sometimes public admirer of . . . cruelty." The article ends with these words: "It is not impossible that Adolf Hitler may have some justification; I know that the Germanophiles have none."

The fact that *El Hogar* printed the article on the first page showed that Borges' point of view had some backing in the magazine. Unfortunately, it was not equally popular in the rest of Argentina. In coming out openly not only against Nazi Germany but, especially, against the nationalists who in their hatred of England adored Germany and praised its destruction of Europe, Borges was taking a very unpopular stand. It was a stand that would become more and more unpopular with the development of the war and the increased leaning toward fascism of the Argentine army.

2.
A Theory of Fantastic Literature

Now that Silvina and Adolfito were married, a sort of routine was established. Borges visited them regularly and over dinner discussed literary projects or chatted endlessly. On Friday afternoons the Bioys held open house for their literary friends. Many were old acquaintances of Borges and even collaborators from the ultraist days, such as the painter and neolinguist Xul-Solar and the Dominican critic Pedro Henríquez Ureña. But the majority were younger writers who had come together under the *Sur* banner; among them were Eduardo Mallea, Ernesto Sábato (who was then beginning to publish very short, ironic essays in Borges' manner), Adolfo de Obieta (Macedonio Fernández's son), the Chilean novelist María Luisa Bombal, and the poet Ezequiel Martínez Estrada. In her biography Alicia Jurado observes that Borges was never too sociable on those occasions and that "Silvina remembers that . . . he always talked to one person at a time, as if the others were not there, as if his shyness would prevent him from ever giving up his privacy" (Jurado, 1964, p. 52).

But in the security of person-to-person talk Borges opened up a bit, and with some people he even became friendly. Among the visitors to the Bioys' apartment on Friday afternoons were a few who to this day are among Borges' most loyal friends. The poet Carlos Mastronardi was one; also the Dabove brothers, Santiago and César, and Manuel Peyrou, a journalist who worked for *La Prensa* and whose slightly fantastic detective stories Borges praised untiringly. They often met in the evenings in a downtown café, the favored place being the Florida's Richmond, not far from the offices of *La Prensa* and *La Nación*. There, echoes of English coffeehouses and American cocktail bars were discreetly blended with the Latin tastes of the customers. From

347

the Richmond, Borges and his friends could command the busiest part of downtown Buenos Aires. The café was near both Corrientes Street, a main thoroughfare with large movie houses and legitimate theaters, cabarets, and restaurants, and Lavalle Street, where the twenty-odd smaller cinemas were packed with moviegoers all day long. Not too far away was the Southside, where Borges loved to roam and where old-style cafés with tango orchestras and billiard tables were not uncommon. Borges' evenings were thus taken up with the male ritual of going out after dinner to meet friends, to converse until the small hours about everything and nothing, or occasionally to even catch a late movie. Although he loved to maintain this ritual, his shyness prevented him from settling down in one particular café and having a regular *peña:* the sort of literary club he had attended while in Spain. He was not expected to pontificate the way Ramón Gómez de la Serna had done in the Pombo bar in the early 1920s or to subtly keep the conversation going, mastering it unobtrusively, the way Rafael Cansinos-Asséns had done in the Café Colonial during the same period. He despised the role of literary master and always preferred to carry on his endless questioning and probing in a smaller group. His notion of a literary café was more that of a place to meet informally and to use as a starting point for exploring the solitary and quiet streets of Buenos Aires' poorest suburbs.

In spite of the many excellent friends he had then, Borges led a terribly solitary life. He had always been haunted by the idea of suicide, and in writing about Lugones in 1938 he came as close as he would ever come to defending it. Since Father's death and the accident of Christmas Eve, suicide had become an obsession. In a piece he wrote in 1940, which he did not allow to be published until 1973, he described in the third person his own "suicide" at the Adrogué Hotel. An attached poem attempts to give some clue to it. As the poem was never finished, it is not easy to see from the published text how the different parts would have been finally connected. What is clear is that Borges was examining the paradox of attempting to use the same hand trained to write for putting a bullet in his head. To move from the pen to the revolver; from his life as an obscure municipal clerk to a rival of his heroic ancestors; from metaphysical speculation about death to the actual test of that speculation—in short, to move from inaction to action—that is what suicide promised him.

More striking than the argument itself are some details of the poem:

> Am I the municipal employee who brings home the kilo of
> yerba given to him at the office, and one who knows the
> habit of a key and a bus, the obese and epicene (terrible)

```
        lurks
face that        in (mirrors and windows + metals
        floats
and glass)?
```
(Yates, 1973, p. 322)

In another stanza the poem also makes an explicit reference to two decisive episodes in his life:

Or perhaps I have died
two years ago on a murky stairway on Ayacucho Street,
twenty years ago in a venal bedroom in the heart of Europe.
(Ibid., p. 323)

The first reference is to the 1938 accident; the second to the day he was initiated into sex by a prostitute in Geneva—an episode he craftily introduces in the story "The Other," collected in *El libro de arena* (The Book of Sand, 1975). Suicide, then, is not just the result of a metaphysical temptation or a deep *tedium vitae* (which he himself relates to Seneca's stoic writings). It is deeply connected with experiences that had shamed him: the symbolical suicide of 1938, after Father's death; the overwhelming realization that orgasm was too close to real death for him. His hatred of mirrors—which cruelly reflected his "obese" and "epicene" face and multiplied men, as copulation did—can now be seen in the context of an unconscious horror of his own body and of the activities it blindly, obsessively performs. In another, much earlier piece which Borges wrote between 1924 and 1926 he describes in moving, awkward words his disgust with his own naked flesh. "Boletín de una noche" (Report on a Night) is the original title; one of its passsges describes his return home very late at night and his undressing in darkness: "I am a palpable man (I tell myself) but with black skin, black skeleton, black gums, black blood that flows through intimate black flesh. . . . I undress, I am (an instant) that shameful, furtive beast, now inhuman and somehow estranged from itself that is a naked being" (ibid., p. 319). That naked being was carefully kept in the dark by Borges. None of his close friends ever saw it.

By 1940 Borges' literary life was beginning to settle into a pattern that would not be significantly altered until 1956, when encroaching blindness forced him to limit his outings. In this routine the visits to the Bioys' comfortable apartment were the main event. They produced not only the most stimulating conversation but some revolutionary projects. At the time, Argentina's literary life had been deeply changed by the outcome of the Spanish civil war. Even before its tragic ending, some of the most important Spanish publishing houses had moved their quarters to Argentina. It was in Buenos Aires that Espasa Calpe

349

launched its very popular Colección Austral, paperback editions of the classics and books of current interest. Soon thereafter one of the editors of that collection, Gonzalo Losada, founded a publishing house under his own name. He was a publisher with a sure literary instinct and a close friend of his authors, two of whom would later receive the Nobel Prize: the Guatemalan novelist Miguel Angel Asturias (1967) and the Chilean poet Pablo Neruda (1971). Don Gonzalo, as everybody called him, created a series of collections, edited by some of the leading Spanish and Spanish American intellectuals, that were to place Argentina in the forefront of the Hispanic publishing business. Borges' brother-in-law, Guillermo de Torre, became the principal literary editor. In 1938 Borges translated a collection of Kafka's stories for Losada's series of unusual contemporary works, La Pajarita de Papel (Paper Birds).

Following Espasa Calpe's and Losada's lead, other Spanish émigrés founded new publishing houses in Buenos Aires. One of the most important was Editorial Sudamericana, which made an agreement with *Sur* to use its imprint in one of its collections and which borrowed from the journal's vast reservoir of talent. Sudamericana published two anthologies, edited by Borges and the Bioys, that were instrumental in shaping the writers who were to become the avant-garde of the resurgence of Latin American literature. The first anthology, published on December 24, 1940, was entitled *Antología de la literatura fantástica* (Anthology of Fantastic Literature). To this day it is one of the most curious and unorthodox compilations on the subject. It includes texts from the East (Tsao Hsue-kin, the *One Thousand and One Nights,* Chuang Tzu) next to classics of Western literature (Petronius, Don Juan Manuel, Rabelais, Carlyle, Poe, Carroll, Maupassant, Kipling); famous modern masters (Wells, Chesterton, Kafka, Joyce) shared billing with local talent (María Luisa Bombal, Borges, Santiago Dabove, Macedonio Fernández, Arturo Cancela, Pilar de Luzarreta). The anthology was highly personal and (in the best sense of the word) arbitrary. The prologue, written and signed by Bioy, summarizes the trio's ideas about fantastic literature. It is divided into three parts. In the first, devoted to the history of the genre, Bioy observes that "old as fear, fantastic fictions are older than literature" (Bioy Casares, 1940, p. 7). He quotes stories with ghosts from the Zend-Avesta to the Chinese classics, mentioning in passing the Bible, Homer, and the *One Thousand and One Nights*. But as a genre, more or less defined, fantastic literature really belongs to the English literature of the nineteenth century. Bioy does not forget the precursors, and he quotes Don Juan Manuel, Rabelais, Quevedo, Defoe, Horace Walpole, and Hoffmann in nineteenth-century German literature.

In the second part, which discusses the technique of the fantastic story, Bioy observes that "literature is constantly changing its readers and, as a consequence, they demand a continuous changing in literature" (ibid., p. 8). Although he would like to accept a rigid set of rules, he is forced to admit that there is not one type of fantastic story but several; he believes that each writer has to follow the general rules while at the same time discovering his own. Then he makes some general observations on topics such as "atmosphere," "surprises," "the yellow peril," and "the yellow room." The last item contains a comic allusion to a well-known detective novel, *The Mystery of the Yellow Room,* by Maurice Leblanc, which discusses a murderous attack committed in a tightly closed room. By linking it with the famous scare slogan about the danger China represents to Western civilization ("the yellow peril"), Bioy pokes fun at both topics. He correctly observes that the earliest fantastic stories depended primarily on a certain type of atmosphere; later, writers discovered that it was more effective to introduce a single fantastic element into a rather banal reality. Wells is the master of what can be called the realistic tendency in fantastic literature. Writing about surprise, Bioy distinguishes between stylistic and thematic surprise. He does not seem to put too much value on that device but observes that it is almost inevitable in the genre. The last topic he discusses is somewhat frivolous. It applies a joke made by Chesterton about the detective story (the yellow peril is the danger of introducing too many suspicious characters) to fantastic literature. He praises Wells for having restrained himself in inventing a single invisible man and not a legion of invisible men.

In the same section Bioy lists the fantastic plots that writers seemed to prefer: they are based on the use of ghosts, travel in time, the realization of three wishes, travels into hell, dreams, metamorphoses, parallel actions which work analogically, immortality. In a closing paragraph Bioy describes very accurately the type of metaphysical story Borges was then inventing: it is "a new literary genre which is both essay and fiction; they are exercises of unceasing intelligence and fortunate imagination, they lack all languor, all *human elements,* pathetic or sentimental," and are aimed at "intellectual readers, interested in philosophy, and almost specialists in literature" (ibid., p. 13). Before ending his classification, Bioy includes two more items: Kafkaesque stories and stories that deal with vampires and castles. Although he likes the former, he finds the latter not very interesting and pointedly indicates that they have been excluded from the anthology. As an afterthought, he notes that fantastic stories can also be classified by their dénouements and establishes three categories: (1) those which need a supernatural explanation; (2) those which have a fantastic but not super-

natural explanation; and (3) those which can be explained both super-
naturally and naturally.

The last section is devoted to explaining the origin of the
present anthology: "One evening in 1937 when we were talking about
fantastic literature, we discussed the stories we preferred; one of us
suggested that if we put them together and added fragments of the
same nature we had collected in our notebooks, we would have a good
book. We have done that book" (ibid., p. 13).

Bioy's prologue was, to say the least, disorganized. But if it was
weak in theory and logic, it was effective in revealing the trio's literary
intentions. The anthology appeared at a time when nineteenth-century
realism was still the prevalent mode in Latin American letters. In calling attention to an alternate tradition in literature, the anthology
helped both writers and readers to discover a new dimension for Latin
American literature.

On November 14, 1940, a few weeks before publication of the
anthology, Bioy Casares' novel *La invención de Morel* (The Invention of
Morel) had been published by Losada. It carried a prologue by Jorge
Luis Borges which amounted to a manifesto for literature of the fantastic. The prologue begins by discussing the ideas (then widely accepted
in the Hispanic world) of José Ortega y Gasset about the contemporary
novel. In 1925 Ortega had published a short essay called "The Dehumanization of Art" in which he claimed that modern readers were too
sophisticated to be interested in adventure stories, that the invention of
interesting plots was no longer possible, that the novel of the future
was to be "psychological." Borges strongly disagrees, attacking the psychological novel on several counts. The first is poetic: "The typical psychological novel is formless. The Russians and their disciples have dem-
onstrated, tediously, that nobody is impossible. A person may kill
himself because he is so happy, for example, or commit murder as an
act of benevolence. And one man can inform on another out of fervor
or humility. In the end, such complete freedom is tantamount to
chaos" (*Morel,* 1964, p. 6). But the psychological novel also pretended
to be realistic; that is, "to have us forget that it is a verbal artifice, for it
uses each vain precision (or each languid obscurity) as a new proof of
verisimilitude." Disagreeing with Ortega, Borges finds Proust boring
and claims there are pages (and even chapters) in his novels that are
unacceptable as inventions. "We unwittingly resign ourselves to them as
we resign ourselves to the insipidity and the emptiness of each day."

The adventure story, on the other hand, does not attempt to be
"a transcription of reality." According to Borges, "it must have a rigid
plot if it is not to succumb to the mere sequential variety of *The Golden
Ass,* the *Seven Voyages of Sinbad,* or the *Quixote.*" This criticism of the

linear adventure story did not imply an absolute dismissal of the *Quixote;* if he objected to this aspect of the book, he admired the whole concept. He had already written extensively on Cervantes' craft as a novelist, and in 1949, in one of his most important articles, he would explain the "Partial Enchantments of the *Quixote.*" The essay was published in *La Nación* (November 6) and was later included in *Other Inquisitions* (1952). But in the prologue to *The Invention of Morel* he is chiefly concerned with criticizing Ortega's theories.

In the second paragraph he attempts to prove that Ortega was wrong in believing this century "lacks the ability to devise interesting plots." Borges compares Stevenson's inventions with Chesterton's, De Quincey's with Kafka's: all writers he admires. In both cases he finds the twentieth-century author superior, as a creator of plots, to his nineteenth-century counterpart. The sentence ending the paragraph is strong: "I believe I am free from every superstition of modernity, or any illusion that yesterday differs intimately from today or will differ from tomorrow; but I maintain that during no other era have there been novels with such admirable plots as *The Turn of the Screw, Der Prozess, Le voyageur sur la terre,* and the one you are about to read, which was written in Buenos Aires by Adolfo Bioy Casares" (ibid., p. 6).

In the next paragraph Borges takes still another shot at Ortega. He points out that "another popular genre in this so-called plotless century is the detective story, which tells of mysterious events that are later explained and justified by a reasonable occurrence." Then he observes that in his novel Bioy "easily solves a problem perhaps more difficult. The odyssey of marvels he unfolds seems to have no possible explanation other than hallucination or symbolism, and he uses a single fantastic but not supernatural postulate to decipher it" (ibid., p. 7).

What Borges does not explain in his prologue is that Bioy's novel belongs to the science-fiction variety of the adventure story and is modeled after Wells' famous *Island of Dr. Moreau,* published in 1896. In his novel Bioy has the protagonist shipwrecked on a deserted island. To his (and the reader's) surprise, he finds that at some hours of the day the island is the meeting place for a very elegant group of people; among them is a woman, Faustine, with whom he falls in love. The solution to the mystery of the deserted but populated island involves a movie machine which projects three-dimensional images and the protagonist's decision to become part of the film, at the risk of his own life, in order to share the same "reality" with Faustine.

In his prologue to Bioy's novel Borges, besides attempting to discredit Ortega's theories, is revising and expanding his own views on magic or fantastic literature. These views had been previously sketched in his article "Narrative Art and Magic" (*Discusión,* 1932) and would

Fantastic literature is not "the psychological novel" but is instead intellectual & metaphysical. It does not attempt a realistic depiction of obscure motives; instead, it questions the assumptions about the real.

My own work is similar, realistic stories based on dreams and juxtaposing (tacitly) parallel, compatible but hermetic, assumptions about what is going on... all seen from outside by a limited narr.

later be repeated in essays and lectures given during the 1940s as well as in stories written at the time and collected first in *The Garden of Forking Paths* (1941), later included in *Ficciones* (1944), and completed in the new stories collected in *The Aleph* (1949). Against mimetic realism, against the psychological novel, Borges defends a fiction that follows the order and the logic of magic, not of the chaotic "real" world of science and nature.

Although Borges never makes any explicit reference to surrealism, it is obvious that in his rejection of realistic and mimetic literature he is closer to Breton's approach as stated in the first *Manifesto of Surrealism* (1924) than to the Spanish American theoreticians of the time. Borges and Breton coincide in criticizing, although for different motives, both Dostoevski and Proust. A connection could be established between Borges' concept of the "magical" and the "fantastic" and Breton's own attempt to reach a "surrealité" through fiction. Their major point of disagreement lies in the question of plot. Breton seems not to be interested in plot at all, preferring what he calls "le hasard"—the chance meeting of his characters, illustrated in his 1928 novel *Nadja*—and rejecting any excessively rigorous concatenation of events. Borges, on the other hand, shows an almost Aristotelian concern with plot, both as a structural device in narrative and as a teleological key to the world. The fact that Borges developed his theories without any explicit reference to surrealism does not alter the importance of the connections between what he was then saying and what Breton had advanced in his *Manifesto.* At the critical level, Borges and Breton are linked not because Borges owed any allegiance to the surrealist movement but because both he and Breton believed that the chief concern of fiction was the creation of purely verbal objects.

Such a view was not popular in Latin America at the time. The literary establishment was still interested in realism of the nineteenth-century variety, while some of the new novelists were trying to apply social realism to the presentation of Latin America's grim realities. Borges' concept of fiction clashed with both those who had accepted Ortega's ideas about the psychological novel and the practitioners of social realism. In addition, by expressing admiration for popular genres such as the adventure story, the detective novel, and science fiction, Borges offended both groups. The social realists considered those genres escapist because they presented reality in a distorted way; the establishment rejected them as frivolous.

Bioy's novel as well as Borges' prologue found few supporters. The former remained largely unread, and the latter was ignored by many of Borges' critics. But the effect of the novel and the prologue would be lasting. They were carefully read by a small group of writers who would come to dominate Latin American fiction and criticism in the next two decades—people such as Octavio Paz, Juan José Arreola, Julio Cortázar, and Alejo Carpentier. In less than fifteen years those few readers would become a large audience.

Writers can create audiences . . . over time . . . by suggesting altvs. in perspective.

3.
A New Type of Fiction

One year exactly after the *Anthology of Fantastic Literature* came out, the same publisher launched the *Antología poética argentina* (Anthology of Argentine Poetry). The scope of the anthology was clearly defined by the jacket: it covered the 1900–1941 period in Argentine poetry and was "objective," not reflecting "a school or personal taste." It was "a truthful and vast panorama of the recent history" of Argentine literature. The jacket ended by assuring readers (the "researcher, the curious, the lover of pure esthetic enjoyment") that they would find in the book "the most admirable Argentine poems of the twentieth century."

Perhaps it is unfair to quote from a book's jacket, but it is necessary in this case because a vast, unbridgeable gap existed between the claims made by the publisher and those made by Borges in his prologue to the book. He begins by frankly admitting that nothing is more vulnerable to criticism than an anthology of contemporary local writings. Every piece can expect to be discussed by the reader (he emphasizes that he considers himself a reader of the anthology), who will find it too well known, weak in comparison with other poems not included, or superfluous because it is the work of a second-rate poet. Borges proceeds to describe the two basic types of anthology: the encyclopedic, which includes everything and for which the prototype is the mythical one-thousand-and-one-hundred-volume Chinese encyclopedia Borges loves to mention; and the hedonistic, which includes only those pieces the compilers really cherish. In the present anthology, he asserts, the editors decided to exclude their personal preferences: "The index registers all the names that a reasonable curiosity may look for" (*Poesía argentina*, 1941, p. 7). But their personal preferences were not totally excluded. In selecting the poems, they have not followed "the romantic methods of our time"—instead of including those poems which are "more personal, characteristic" of each author, they have chosen "those we believe are better" (ibid., p. 8).

The rest of the prologue is dedicated to explaining the anthology's scope. Borges lists the most important poets included, beginning with Almafuerte, a poet unjustly forgotten, then Lugones, whose work anticipates everything done later by younger poets, and Martínez Estrada, "our best contemporary poet." Three other important writers are mentioned: Enrique Banchs, Evaristo Carriego, and Fernández Moreno. They do not belong to the mainstream (represented by the other three) but are instrumental in defining the new poetry. Borges mocks the old distinctions between rhyme and rhythm, pointing out that today political and religious distinctions are considered more important:

> Endlessly I hear people talk about Marxist, neothomist, nationalist poets. In 1831 Macaulay observed: "To talk about essentially Protestant or essentially Christian governments is like talking about essentially Protestant pastry shops or essentially Christian riding schools." No less demeaning is it to talk about poets of such a sect or party. More important than the subjects the poets treat or their opinions and convictions is the structure of the poem or its prosodic and syntactic effects. (Ibid., pp. 9–10)

The rest of the prologue discusses various ways of classifying poets. Borges prefers a purely literary method of linking writers (for instance, he links Lugones and Güiraldes because they were influenced by the same poet, Jules Laforgue, who also influenced T. S. Eliot). Borges also discusses why he has excluded the popular poetry represented by tango lyrics, which he believes to be inferior to poems in which national feelings are less obvious but are characteristically Argentine. To illustrate, he quotes the sonnets written by Enrique Banchs in a very Spanish style. The last two paragraphs comment on the wealth of Argentine poetry. He affirms that today "no other literary genre practiced by Argentines has attained the merit and diversity of their lyrical poetry" (ibid., p. 11). In concluding, he states his belief that if Argentina has not yet produced a writer of the international magnitude of Emerson, Whitman, Poe, James, or Melville, products of the "barbarous" North Americans, it has produced poets that are in no way inferior to those of other Hispanic countries. As proof he again mentions Lugones, Martínez Estrada, and Banchs.

The anthology was the least successful venture attempted by Borges and the Bioys. Both the anthology and the prologue were criticized for being too personal. Even their most faithful readers rejected

357

it. In her reminiscences for *L'Herne*'s special issue on Borges Victoria Ocampo called the editors (her sister Silvina was one of them) the "accomplices" and justified the expression because "I found them slightly arbitrary. And they think the same of me" (Ocampo, 1964, p. 23).

Today the anthology looks tame and indecisive. It includes too many poets who have not traveled well, too many second-rate writers, too many good friends whose poems the editors loved and could not dismiss. But perhaps the main weakness is the omission of one of Argentina's most important contemporary poets: Jorge Luis Borges. At the time, Borges may have thought that being both one of the compilers and the prologuist barred him from the anthology. He once wrote an acid review of *The Oxford Book of Modern Verse,* edited by W. B. Yeats, in which the "complaisant compiler" had reserved for himself the lion's share: no less than fourteen poems (see *El Hogar,* May 28, 1937, p. 26).

Perhaps Borges' decision to omit his own poems was inspired not by modesty but by a conviction that he was no longer a poet. At the time, he was passing through a crisis. He had come to believe that he would never be a really good poet and had practically ceased to write verses. Perhaps he sincerely believed his poetry was of no consequence.

If Borges seemed unsure about the value of his poetry, he was more confident about his prose writings, and in spite of his show of modesty he knew perfectly well what he was after. At the end of the prologue to the *Anthology of Argentine Poetry,* after praising the quality of contemporary verse, he flatly states:

> The nineteenth century produced an excellent prose, a writing only slightly different from oral language; the twentieth century seems to have forgotten that art, which is still alive in many pages of Sarmiento, López, Mansilla, Eduardo Wilde. Lugones is the first to use a written language, and he cannot always resist the temptations of an oratorical syntax and an excessive vocabulary. . . . An anthology of our contemporary prose would be less diverse than this volume and would include fewer indisputable writers. (Ibid., p. 11)

If the *Anthology of Fantastic Literature* were used as a guide, "Tlön, Uqbar, Orbis Tertius" would have been included among the texts in Borges' hypothetical *Anthology of Argentine Prose.*

One can recognize his confidence in the next volume of his to appear: *The Garden of Forking Paths,* published by *Sur* in 1941 and included later in *Ficciones* (1944). A slim, elegant blue volume of exactly eight short stories, it is perhaps the single most important book of prose fiction written in Spanish in this century. A prologue helps the reader to place the stories. Borges classifies the eight pieces into two categories: the last story, which gives the book its title, is a detective story; the other seven are fantastic. In commenting on each story, Borges (as usual) gives some very perceptive views but leaves many things unsaid. About the title piece he observes only that readers would witness "the execution and all the preliminaries of a crime, a crime whose purpose will not be unknown to them but which they would not understand—it seems to me—until the last paragraph" (*Ficciones*, 1962, p. 15). Borges is right about that. The reader knows, from the very beginning, that the protagonist, a Chinese spy working for the Germans during World War I, has to transmit a message; they know that he has the police on his tracks; they also know that in his flight the spy visits an old Sinologist, leisurely discusses with him the work of one of his ancestors, and finally kills him. What they do not know until the last paragraph is that the message consisted of one word, Albert: both the name of the Sinologist and the name of the Belgian city the Germans had to attack. To communicate the message, the spy had to kill somebody (anybody) with that name. The neat little solution is too neat, of course. Any other writer would have avoided the coincidence of making the spy Chinese and making the victim a Sinologist. For Borges, on the contrary, it is precisely the coincidence that is interesting. To him, in a detective story plots have to be both very neat and mysterious. But if the story is more than an entertainment—to be placed next to Chesterton's, Hitchcock's, and Graham Greene's—it is because Borges (without warning his reader) has woven into it another story.

The title gives the second story away: any garden of forking paths is a labyrinth, and the labyrinth is both the subject and the structure of the story. When the protagonist, Yu Tsun, reaches the house of his future victim, he discovers that its garden is shaped like a labyrinth. In meeting Albert, he learns that he is a Sinologist and has been working on the manuscripts of Ts'ui Pên, one of Yu Tsun's ancestors. Yu Tsun knew that his ancestor was supposed to have attempted two different enterprises: the making of a labyrinth and the writing of an immense novel. At his death (by the hand of an unknown assassin), nobody could find the labyrinth and the unfinished novel seemed absurd. Albert tells Yu Tsun that he has found the solution to the enigma: the novel was the labyrinth his ancestor was building. In the same way, the solution to the enigma postulated by Borges' story is also a labyrinth; it keeps forking (its plot) until the reader is totally lost. There is, as in any labyrinth, one path that leads to the center, and that is the path the first story tells: the detective-story path. But all the other ramifications of the labyrinth are there to provide extra dimensions to the fictional reality. The text proliferates like a labyrinth; the detective-story path proliferates in a multitude of paths that lead to other genres. In the multiple image of the labyrinth (the two labyrinths built by Ts'ui Pên, the labyrinth built by Yu Tsun to trap Albert, the labyrinth built by Borges to trap his reader) one finds the symbol of a new type of narrative. The so-called detective story is much more than that.

In discussing the other stories, those of the fantastic variety, Borges is also tantalizingly elusive. About "The Babylon Lottery" he states only that it is not "innocent of symbolism." A humorous tale about a lottery which begins by distributing prizes and ends up by providing favors and punishments to all the citizens of Babylon, even if they do not possess a ticket, the story is meant to symbolize destiny: the lottery to which all of us are unwitting subscribers. But the story again contains a wealth of hidden allusion and jokes. The lottery system described at the beginning is modeled on the Argentine lottery; there is a reference to "a secret privy called Qaphqa" where "malign or benevolent people deposited accusations" to warn the lottery officers about some delinquencies that ought to be punished or some secret desire that ought to be granted. The name of the privy seems exotic enough, until it is read aloud: then it becomes Kafka. The story is symbolical in the same way Kafka's are. About another Kafkaesque story, "The Library of Babel," Borges notes in the prologue that it was inspired by the writings of Leucipus, Lasswitz, Lewis Carroll, and Aristotle. Not a word, of course, is said about the fact that Borges' own painful experience at the Miguel Cané library is at the root of it.

In commenting on another story, "The Circular Ruins," Borges emphasizes the fact that everything is unreal in that tale of an Indian priest, a worshipper of fire, who decides to dream a son and finally manages to translate his dream into reality. In the prologue Borges does not say a word about the story's epigraph, taken from Carroll's *Through the Looking Glass*—"And if he left off dreaming about you . . ."—which in a sense gives away the plot. But again, the story carries other meanings. The subject of the man created by another the way God has created man and the horror of the final discovery that we are all mere creations of dreams are very closely connected with Borges' (and Georgie's) most primeval fears. In spite of its beautiful prose style, the story is one of the most horrifying of Borges' works. The end is particularly memorable: "He walked toward the sheets of flame. They did not bite his flesh; they caressed him and flooded him without heat or combustion. With relief, with humiliation, with terror, he understood that he also was an illusion, that someone else was dreaming him" (*Ficciones*, 1962, p. 63).

Many years later Borges returned to the subject, this time using a different setting and a different medium. In the poem "The Golem," the Holy Rabbi Löw of Prague creates an artificial man, fit only to sweep the synagogue; this creation is used to explore the mystery of paternity:

> At the anguished hour when the light gets vague
> Upon his Golem his eyes would come to rest.
> Who can tell us the feelings in His breast
> As God gazed on His rabbi there in Prague?
> (*Poems,* 1972, translated by John Hollander, p. 115)

If everything was unreal in "The Circular Ruins," Borges observes that in "Pierre Menard, Author of the *Quixote*" what "is unreal is the destiny imposed upon himself by the protagonist" (*Ficciones,* 1962, p. 15). The observation is correct. In attempting to rewrite *Don Quixote* literally and in its entirety, Menard is embarking on a useless task: the book already exists. But the story, one of Borges' most labyrinthine, is about many other things, especially about the art of reading. Borges says nothing of this in the prologue because the story is explicit enough; the only thing he comments on is Menard's other imaginary productions: "The list of writings I attribute to him is not too amusing but neither is it arbitrary; it constitutes a diagram of his mental history" (ibid., p. 15). Again, the seemingly casual observation contains a valuable hint. There is an anticipation of the insane project in Menard's published work, which consists of essays and poems on subjects such as language, translation, permutations, symbolic logic, metaphysics, and metrical laws. All these activities reveal an obsession with the text as a place where language and the individual mind come together to produce a totally artificial object, be it a poem, a metaphysical treatise on reality, a metrical system, or a new way of playing chess. Literature as a game of permutations would lead Menard to discover reading as another game of permutations.

In the second paragraph of his prologue Borges elucidates one of the basic principles of his narrative work and offers a key to his own peculiar brand of fiction: a mixture of the essay and the tale.

The composition of vast books is a laborious and impoverishing extravagance. To go on for five hundred pages developing an idea whose perfect oral exposition is possible in a few minutes! A better course of procedure is to pretend that these books already exist, and then to offer a résumé, a commentary. Thus proceeded Carlyle in *Sartor Resartus.* Thus Butler in *The Fair Haven.* These are works which suffer the imperfection of being themselves books, and of being no less tautological than the others. More reasonable, more inept, more indolent, I have preferred to write notes upon imaginary books. (Ibid., pp. 15–16)

He then lists the three remaining stories: "Tlön, Uqbar, Orbis Tertius," "An Examination of the Work of Herbert Quain," and "The Approach to al-Mu'tasim." He gives the exact date on which "The Approach to al-Mu'tasim" was written but says nothing about the fact that it had already been included, as an essay, in his book *History of Eternity* (1936). He also compares it to Henry James' novel *The Sacred Fount* (1901), which he read quite recently and whose "general argument is perhaps analogous. The narrator . . . investigates whether or not B is influenced by A or C; in 'The Approach to al-Mu'tasim' the narrator feels a presentiment or divines through B the extremely remote existence of Z, whom B does not know" (ibid., p. 16). Although the connection is interesting, it sheds no light on what makes Borges' story unique: its deliberate use of the format of the book review to tell a tale about a mystical ascension to divinity.

Even more telling is the omission of any specific commentary on "Tlön, Uqbar, Orbis Tertius" and "An Examination of the Work of Herbert Quain," both labyrinths of the most subtle fabrication. "Tlön" is, as has already been shown, a key to Borges' fictions. "Herbert Quain" may seem only a variant of "Pierre Menard" in the sense that it deals with the work of an imaginary writer, but in the discussion of Quain's works Borges anticipates some of the themes and procedures he would use in the near future. Up to a point, Quain is a better mask for Borges than Menard. The first paragraph of the story hints about Borges' attitude toward his own work:

> Quain . . . was not a man who ever considered himself a genius, not even on those extravagant nights of literary conversation in which a man who has already worn out the printing presses inevitably plays at being Monsieur Teste or Doctor Samuel Johnson. . . . He was very clear-headed about the experimental nature of his books; he thought them admirable, perhaps, for their novelty and a certain laconic probity, but not for their passion. "I am like Cowley's Odes," he wrote me from Longford on March 6, 1939. "I do not belong to art, but merely to the history of art." In his mind, there was no discipline inferior to history. (Ibid., p. 73)

Quain's books abound in the kind of games Borges liked to play. One, a detective novel entitled *The God of the Labyrinth,* offers a solution which is accepted by the detective but which is actually false. Borges comments:

> Once the enigma is cleared up, there is a long and retrospective paragraph which contains the following phrase: "Everyone thought that the encounter of the two chess players was accidental." This phrase allows one to understand that the solution is erroneous. The unquiet reader rereads the perti-

nent chapter and discovers *another* solution, the true one. The reader of this singular book is thus forcibly more discerning than the detective. (Ibid., p. 74)

Like Borges, Quain always suggests a second reading which unveils a ✓ second plot.

Another of Quain's novels, *April, March,* anticipates some of Borges' inventions. Borges comments: "In judging this novel, no one would fail to discover that it is a game; it is only fair to remember that the author never considered it anything else" (ibid., p. 75). The novel is written in a "retrograde" fashion, in the same retrograde pattern as its title, which goes from April to March instead of the other way around. Borges even includes a diagram to explain the novel's structure, which is, of course, that of a labyrinth, a garden of forking paths. Quain also wrote a heroic comedy in two acts, *The Secret Mirror,* which again uses a "retrograde" device: the events in the first act are an imaginary transposition of the sordid realities in the life of the protagonist, a poor playwright. At the end of the story Borges tersely admits that he has borrowed from one of Quain's stories "my story 'The Circular Ruins' " (ibid., p. 78).

The real author borrows from his own characters a play that contains both the imaginary and the real life of the protagonists: Borges' Quain is a very Borgesian author. There is also in Quain a touch of the madness shown in Flann O'Brien's *At Swim Two Birds.* In reviewing that novel for *El Hogar* in one of his last long articles for that magazine (June 2, 1939, p. 6), Borges points out the unsettling effect of receding perspective created by a work in which "fiction lives inside fiction." Now he attributes to Quain the same games he himself plays. The importance of the story in making explicit his techniques cannot be overstressed.

The Garden of Forking Paths is a puzzling book, as its first readers discovered. Very few were able to follow its plots or recognize, under the different layers of irony and parody, its truly revolutionary nature. The majority may have reacted as Mother did, asking Borges why he insisted on writing that kind of scary story. One of those who understood what the book had to offer was, of course, Adolfo Bioy Casares. In a review published in *Sur* (May 1942) Bioy stresses the novelty of Borges' fiction: "Like the philosophers of Tlön, he has discovered the literary possibilities of metaphysics. . . . *The Garden of Forking Paths* creates and satisfies the need for a literature about literature and thought" (Bioy Casares, 1942, p. 60). He indicates that Borges' stories are not in the tradition of metaphysical poetry (*De Rerum Natura, Prometheus Unbound,* for instance) but in the best traditions of philosophy and the detective story. In defining the latter, he observes that its chief merit is that it produced not a book but an ideal, "an ideal of invention, rigor, elegance (in the sense used in mathematics) in plots. To underline the importance of structure: that is, perhaps, the meaning of the genre in the history of literature" (ibid., p. 61). He also stresses the fact that Borges' stories are exciting, and he uses the word in English to indicate its exact shade of meaning. Bioy is on less sure ground when he attempts to classify the stories. In his prologue Borges uses a simple distinction, as we have seen. In a footnote to his review Bioy unnecessarily argues that "Tlön" and "al-Mu'tasim" are fantastic stories: that is exactly what Borges has already said.

The rest of the long review evaluates the stories and discusses their importance in the context of Latin American literature. Bioy defends Borges' notion of fiction as a game. Borges has created a new genre, critical fiction, which refuses to indulge in local color and the exaltation of geography or the denunciation of international capitalism. Speaking especially about Argentine literature, Bioy concludes:

> We are on the periphery of the big forests and America's archeological past. I believe, without vanity, that we may be disappointed by our folklore. Our best tradition is that of being a country in the making. Rivadavia, Sarmiento, and all those who organized the Republic believed in that country. . . . For an Argentine, it is normal to think that his literature is the world's best literature. . . . Of that culture . . . and of a possible and perhaps future Argentina that will correspond to it, this book is representative. (Ibid., pp. 64–65)

The review was a landmark in Borges criticism. But the fact that it was written by Borges' closest associate and appeared in a journal owned by the same publishing firm that had published the book made the review suspect. For yet a while the number of Borges readers and admirers did not seem destined to increase.

4.
The Invention of Biorges

The literary collaboration of Borges and Bioy Casares dates back to 1937 when they spent a week in El Pardo, where Bioy's father had a ranch. Speaking about that week in a chronology of his own life and work, Bioy writes: "We plan a story we will never write, which is the germ of *Seis problemas para don Isidro Parodi* [Six Problems for Don Isidro Parodi], about a German philanthropist, Dr. Praetorius, who by hedonistic methods—music, ceaseless games—murders children" (Bioy Casares, 1975, p. 37). Elsewhere, Bioy defines his debt to Borges: "Any collaboration with Borges is the equivalent of one year's work" (Bioy Casares, 1968, p. 140).

Borges has also written about their joint undertakings in his "Autobiographical Essay":

> It is always taken for granted in these cases that the elder man is the master and the younger his disciple. This may have been true at the outset, but several years later, when we began to work together, Bioy was really and secretly the master. He and I attempted many different ventures. We compiled anthologies of Argentine poetry, tales of the fantastic, and detective stories; we wrote articles and forewords; we annotated Sir Thomas Browne and Gracián; we translated short stories by writers like Beerbohm, Kipling, Wells, and Lord Dunsany; we founded a magazine, *Destiempo,* which lasted three issues; we wrote film scripts, which were invariably rejected. Opposing my taste for the pathetic, the sententious, and the baroque, Bioy made me feel that quietness and restraint are more desirable. If I may be allowed a sweeping statement, Bioy led me gradually to classicism. ("Essay," 1970, pp. 245–246)

Borges is probably right, at least in part, about the influence of Bioy Casares' writing on his own. About the invention of Bustos Domecq,

the pseudonym under which Bioy and Borges began writing in collaboration, he has more specific things to say:

> It was at some point in the early forties that we began writing in collabo-
> ration—a feat that up to that time I had thought impossible. I had invented
> what we thought was a quite good plot for a detective story. One rainy
> morning, he told me we ought to give it a try. I reluctantly agreed, and a
> little later that same morning the thing happened. A third man, Honorio
> Bustos Domecq, emerged and took over. (Ibid., p. 246)

In his conversation with Ronald Christ, Borges gives more details. To a question about the method they used, he replies:

BORGES: Well, it's rather queer. When we write together, when we collaborate,
we call ourselves H. Bustos Domecq. Bustos was a great-grandfather of mine
and Domecq was a great-grandfather of his. Now the queer thing is that
when we write, and we write mostly humorous stuff—even if the stories are
tragic, they are told in a humorous way or they are told as if the teller hardly
understood what he was saying—when we write together what comes of the
writing, if we are successful, and sometimes we are—why not? after all I'm
speaking in the plural, no?—when our writing is successful, then what comes
out is something quite different from Bioy Casares' stuff and my stuff; even
the jokes are different. So we have created between us a kind of third person; we have somehow begotten a third person that is quite unlike us.
[CHRIST:] A fantastic author?
BORGES: Yes, a fantastic author with his likes, his dislikes, and a personal style
that is meant to be ridiculous; but still, it is a style of his own, quite different
from the kind of style I write when I try to create a ridiculous character. I
think that's the only way of collaborating. Generally speaking, we go over the
plot together before we set pen to paper—rather I should talk about typewriters, because he has a typewriter. Before we begin writing, we discuss the
whole story; then we go over the details, we change them, of course, we
think of a beginning and then we think the beginning might be the end or
that it might be more striking if somebody said nothing at all or said something quite outside the mark. Once the story is written, if you ask us whether
this adjective or this particular sentence came from Bioy or from me, we
can't tell. . . . I think that's the only way of collaborating, because I have
tried collaborating with other people. Sometimes it works out all right, but
sometimes one feels that the collaborator is a kind of rival. Or, if not—as in
the case of [Manuel] Peyrou—we began collaborating but he is timid and a
very courteous, a very polite kind of person, and consequently if he says anything and you make any objections, he feels hurt and he takes it back. He
says: "Oh, yes, of course, of course, yes, I was quite wrong. It was a blunder."
Or if you propose anything, he says: "Oh, that's wonderful!" Now that kind
of thing can't be done. In the case of me and [Bioy] Casares, we don't feel as
if we are two rivals or even as if we were two men who play chess. There's no

case of winning or losing. What we're thinking of is the story itself, the stuff itself. (Christ, 1967, pp. 145–146)

There is more about Bustos Domecq in the "Autobiographical Essay." Borges seems chiefly interested there in defining Bustos' grip on the collaborators:

> In the long run, he ruled us with a rod of iron and to our amusement, and later to our dismay, he became utterly unlike ourselves, with his own whims, his own puns, and his own very elaborate style of writing. . . . Bustos Domecq's first book was *Six Problems for Don Isidro Parodi* [1942], and during the writing of that volume he never got out of hand. Max Carrados had attempted a blind detective; Bioy and I went one step further and confined our detective to a jail cell. The book was at the same time a satire on the Argentines. For many years, the dual identity of Bustos Domecq was never revealed. When it finally was, people thought that, as Bustos was a joke, his writing could hardly be taken seriously. ("Essay," 1970, p. 246)

Bioy is even blunter. According to his reminiscences, when the first Bustos Domecq book was published, "our friends and the critics [were] not amused" (Bioy Casares, 1975, p. 38). Apparently, the first not to be amused was Victoria Ocampo, whose journal *Sur* published two of the stories and the book as well. The two stories published in *Sur*—"The Twelve Figures of the World" (January 1942) and "The Nights of Goliadkin" (March 1942)—may have puzzled readers. In the first, Parodi has to solve the murder unwillingly committed by the very confused young man who comes to visit him and asks for his help. Full of apocryphal folklore (it takes place in a community of Armenians devoted to astrology), the story follows the Chestertonian pattern of a paradoxical beginning and a series of almost incredible if not miraculous coincidences. A parody of a parody (Chesterton is already a parody of both Poe and Conan Doyle), the story is more memorable for its writing than for its rather cluttered plot. But the real invention occurs in the dialogue. Each character uses colloquial Argentine speech in a way that reveals both his views and his psychology.

The second story is somewhat better. It uses one of the classical loci of detective and spy stories: the express train that runs nonstop from one remote corner of the world to the metropolis. Again, language is master. One of the characters, Gervasio Montenegro, is a successful caricature of the mediocre writer, full of clichés and French bon mots.

The book opens with these two stories, followed by four more. Two items deserve special attention. One is a short biography of H. Bustos Domecq, written in a delightful style, by one Adelia Puglione, a dedicated teacher in a provincial school. Her "silhouette" of Bustos Domecq is almost as comic as the one of Pierre Menard in the story of the same name—the difference being that Menard comes from a French province while Bustos Domecq comes from Santa Fe, Argentina. Even more outrageous is the foreword by Gervasio Montenegro, one of the book's characters. In a sense, Montenegro preempts all criticism because, despite his insufferable pretentiousness, he scores a few good points. After hailing Bustos Domecq, rather excessively, as the first Argentine writer of detective stories (he forgets, among others, Borges himself), he very ably condenses the author's method: to stick to the basic elements of the problem (the enigmatic presentation of facts, the clarifying solution). In commenting on the stories, he selects the three best, in decreasing order of importance: "The victim of Tadeo Limardo," in which the murdered man prepares his own sacrifice, thus disguising what is essentially a suicide; "The Long Search of Tai An," in which the author adds a variation on the problem of the hidden object that Poe and other precursors had postulated; and "San Giácomo's Foresight," in which a cuckold takes the most elaborate and invisible revenge on the bastard offspring his wife had borne. Montenegro also praises, perhaps excessively, the author's ability to draw characters and, in particular, the character of Don Isidro Parodi. He has a few reservations which reveal him to be a true bigot and anti-Semite, much like the obsequious narrator of "Pierre Menard."

What Montenegro does not talk about is what matters most today: the creation of language. Through Bustos Domecq, Borges and Bioy liberated their power of parody. The solemnity of spoken Argentine in all its variations (lower-class slang, the Frenchified speech of pseudo-intellectuals, the thick and obsolete Spanish of Spaniards. Italianate jargon) was exploded through characters who were less narrative figures than figures of speech. For the first time in Argentina a deliberate attempt to create narrative through the parody of narrative form and speech was successful. Although the initial reader reaction was poor, the book's effect on contemporaries was lasting. Both Leopoldo Marechal in his *Adán Buenosayres* and Julio Cortázar in *The Winners* and *Hopscotch* show that they were influenced by Bustos Domecq.

Few people realized that under the outrageous puns and the convoluted plots there were very serious intentions. At one level, the book anticipates some of Borges' most constant preoccupations. "San Giácomo's Foresight," for example, can be read as a draft of "The Dead Man," a tale he would include in his second important book of fantastic fictions, *The Aleph* (1949). Both stories are about a man who, led to believe he is lucky and omnipotent, ends in tragedy. The book is also important at a second level: that of describing Argentine reality. Through parody, the authors hold up a distorted and critical mirror. References to the ineptitude and/or corruption of the Argentine government, to the army and to the European war that was about to engulf the whole world, indicate that both authors were aware that their parodical enterprise had an extra dimension. And as a corrective against the self-satisfied literature of the Argentine establishment, this anarchistic parody was extremely effective. The fact that the detective was himself in jail (convicted of a murder committed by somebody who had very good connections both with the local authorities and the police) added to the satirical nature of the book.

In general, readers were puzzled, outraged, or bored with the book. Talking to Napoléon Murat, Borges recalls:

> When the readers discovered that Bustos Domecq did not exist, they believed all the stories to be jokes and that it was not necessary to read them, that we were poking fun at the reader, which was not the case. I don't know why the idea of a pseudonym made them furious. They said: "Those writers do not exist; there is a name but there is not a writer." Then a general contempt took over, but it was a false reasoning. (Murat, 1964, p. 378)

The readers did not realize that a joke could be serious, and that irony and parody are among the deadliest forms of criticism. The gap between readers and authors was unbridgeable. Not until Bustos Domecq's first book was reissued a quarter of a century later would it be read by readers who could see its point.

One of the first to realize that in Bustos Domecq there was more than met the eye was the Mexican humanist Alfonso Reyes, who reviewed the book in the Mexican magazine *Tiempo* (July 30, 1943), extolling not only its humor and wit but its value as social criticism. Reyes, who had been ambassador to Argentina in the late 1920s and had then formed a long-lasting literary friendship with Borges, observed in his review:

> *Social testimony.* In the meantime, we are transported to strange and baroque places, we visit the most secret corners of Buenos Aires life and in front of our eyes passes a gallery of types of all categories and races in a cauldron of imagination, each one speaking the language that best suits him. To the point that, if one puts aside the interest of the plot, the book has the value of a social testimony, strongly illuminated by poetical lights. Let's make it clear: poetical but not sentimental. There is not the least trace of sentimentality here, which would be contrary to the firm esthetics of Borges. (Reyes, 1943, p. 104)

369

But Reyes' prophetic reading of the book went unheard. That did not deter the co-authors, who continued to collaborate in the same vein. Two more books written or inspired by Bustos Domecq were published in the 1940s. One was *Dos fantasías memorables* (Two Memorable Fantasies), signed Bustos Domecq. The first story in the book, "El testigo" (The Witness), tells about a young girl who has a vision of the Holy Trinity and dies from the shock; the second, "El signo" (The Sign), offers the vision of an interminable procession of food, a glutton's paradise.

The other book, *Un modelo para la muerte* (A Model for Death), was signed by B. Suárez Lynch, a disciple of Bustos Domecq, and pretended to be a detective novel. Borges recalls that the book "was so personal and so full of private jokes that we published it only in an edition that was not for sale. The author of this book we named B. Suárez Lynch. The 'B' stood, I think, for Bioy and Borges, Suárez for another great-grandfather of mine, and Lynch for another great-grandfather of Bioy's" ("Essay," 1970, p. 247). What Borges does not say is that the parody goes further in these two books than in *Six Problems*. Even the publisher's imprint they invented was parodical: Oportet & Haereses alludes in Spanish to port and sherry wines (*oporto* and *jerez*).

The plot of *A Model for Death* is so buried under digressions and puns that it is almost impossible to remember, even after repeated readings. Following the format of *Six Problems,* the book has a preface, by Bustos Domecq, which offers a short literary biography of Suárez Lynch. As a detective novel, the book was a disaster. Even a friendly reviewer such as Carlos Mastronardi in *Sur* (December 1946) pointed out that "the charming and light plot, whose tracing is not easy at all, gets lost and reappears behind the long dialogues and the attractive incidental episodes." Borges and Bioy realized they had gone too far and for a while decided to stop writing as Bustos Domecq or Suárez Lynch. In his conversations with Napoléon Murat, Borges explains how they reached that conclusion:

> . . . We wrote a bit for us, and because this happened in an atmosphere of jokes, the stories became so impossible to unravel and so baroque that it was very difficult to understand them. At the beginning, we made jokes, and then jokes on jokes, it was like in algebra: jokes squared, jokes cubed. . . . Then, we decided to stop writing, because we had come to realize that it was difficult and even impossible to write in another way and that this way was painful, at least for the reader. (Murat, 1964, p. 378)

Bustos Domecq and Suárez Lynch had finally taken over. Borges and Bioy had been replaced by their own creations. A new writer had been born, a writer who ought to be called "Biorges" because he was neither Borges nor Bioy, and because he did not stick to one pseudonym. The only way to cope with his proliferation was to silence him. And that is what Borges and Bioy did in 1946. But they hadn't heard the last of Biorges.

5.
Two Forms of
Reparation

The same year that *Six Problems for Don Isidro Parodi* came out, the Borgeses moved again, to an apartment at 275 Quintana Avenue, near Rodríguez Peña Street, in the same neighborhood where the family had resided since returning from their last trip to Europe in 1924. They stayed there for a few years only, moving in 1944 to a two-bedroom downtown apartment at 994 Maipú Street, which Borges occupies today.

Their everyday life had begun to settle into a routine: Mother stayed at home, busy with household responsibilities (they had only one servant, who functioned as cook and maid) and with her own literary work; Borges went to the Miguel Cané library or also remained at home, writing in a painstaking, minuscule handwriting his articles and reviews, his stories and essays. Mother helped him with his readings and translations. Her English had improved to the point where she began to do some work on her own. Probably her best translation was of a collection of Katherine Mansfield's tales, published by Losada in the same series as Kafka's *The Metamorphosis* and under the title of one of the stories, *The Garden Party*. Borges himself translated William Faulkner's *The Wild Palms* for Sudamericana in 1940 and Henri Michaux's *A Barbarian in Asia* for *Sur* in 1941.

The translation of the Faulkner was significant. Earlier, in *El Hogar,* he had discussed or given favorable mention to Faulkner's novels. Although he never wrote a full-length article about him, he was consistently enthusiastic. He praised Faulkner for being as concerned with the verbal artifices of narrative as with the "passions and works of men" (January 22, 1937, p. 30); he discussed Faulkner's ability to play with time and also to write a straightforward novel, such as *The Un-vanquished,* and he noted that Faulkner's world was "so physical and fleshy" that in comparison Dostoevski's seemed too light (June 24, 1938, p. 30); he came to the conclusion that Faulkner was "the first novelist of our time" (May 5, 1939, p. 62). Of his books, he considered *Light in August* to be "perhaps his most intense work and one of the most memorable of our time" (January 21, 1938, p. 26), but he also had words of praise for *Absalom, Absalom!* and *The Sound and the Fury* (January 22, 1937, p. 30) and for *Sanctuary* (May 5, 1939, p. 62).

He was not so enthusiastic about *The Wild Palms.* In his review of that book for *El Hogar* on May 5, 1939 he observes that while in Faulkner's most important novels new techniques seem necessary and inevitable, in this one they seem "less attractive than inconvenient, less justifiable than exasperating." Discussing the two stories that form the book ("The Wild Palms," about a man "destroyed by the flesh," and "The Old Man," about a man who is given a "useless and atrocious free-dom" by a Mississippi flood), Borges observes that the second is superior. His conclusion—that *The Wild Palms* is not the best introduction to Faulkner—seems paradoxical in view of the fact that this is the Faulkner book he elected to translate.

His translation of *The Wild Palms* has been considered as good as or even better than the original. The style is perhaps tighter than Faulkner's, and the hardness and intensity of the novel's best passages (praised by Borges in his review as "notoriously exceeding the possibil-ities of any other author") indicate how much he put into the transla-tion—in spite of his claims that it was Mother who really did it ("Essay," 1970, p. 207). For the book jacket, Borges wrote a summary of Faulk-ner's work and life which condensed what he had already written in *El Hogar.* Describing *The Wild Palms,* he observes that "there are two dif-ferent plots, which never coincide, but that somehow correspond to each other. The style is passionate, meticulous, hallucinatory."

The importance of this translation for the new Latin American novel was considerable. Although Faulkner's novel *Sanctuary* had al-ready been translated into Spanish by the Cuban novelist Lino Novás Calvo and had been published in Spain in 1934, the translation was mediocre and had been tampered with by the publisher, who was afraid to be too specific about the way Popeye manages to rape Temple Drake. Borges' translation was not only faithful to the original but created in Spanish a writing style that was the equivalent of the origi-nal's English. For many young Latin American novelists who did not know enough English to read the dense original, Borges' tight version meant the discovery of a new kind of narrative writing. They had, in Borges, the best possible guide to Faulkner's dark and intense world.

In spite of so much activity, Borges was still largely unknown in Argentina, and his name was not recognized by the literary establishment. In 1942 his collection of short stories, *The Garden of Forking Paths,* received the second prize in the annual literary competition organized by the city of Buenos Aires. The first prize went to *Ramón Hazaña,* a gaucho novel by Eduardo Acevedo Díaz, Jr., son of one of Uruguay's leading historical novelists. Borges took the matter in stride. A comic reference to the prize appears in his story "The Aleph." There, the pompous poet, Carlos Argentino Daneri, gets second prize in the annual national literary competition. (The first prize is given to a real if second-rate writer, Antonio Aita, who was the secretary of the Argentine PEN Club; the third went to Mario Bonfanti, one of Bustos Domecq's most pitiful characters, borrowed by Borges to underline the inanity of the occasion.)

Although Borges made light of his disappointment, his friends reacted strongly. In July 1942 José Bianco of *Sur* organized a "Reparation to Borges," in which twenty-one writers joined together to praise his work. These included old and new friends—Eduardo Mallea, Patricio Canto, Pedro Henríquez Ureña, Gloria Alcorta, Adolfo Bioy Casares, Carlos Mastronardi, Eduardo González Lanuza, Enrique Amorim, Ernesto Sábato, Manuel Peyrou—as well as people whose points of view were not exactly those of Borges but who nevertheless respected and admired him for his work—Francisco Romero, Luis Emilio Soto, Amado Alonso, Aníbal Sánchez Reulet, Angel Rosenblat, Enrique Anderson Imbert, Bernardo Canal Feijoo. Borges reacted to the homage with amusement. According to Bianco in his reminiscenses:

> I even selected (because I know he does not like green) a bull's blood red cover. As soon as the first copies were out, I sent a couple to his place. The following afternoon, when I went to visit him, he only had jokes about that friendly homage. He seemed happy, of course, but especially astonished that so many writers had taken the trouble to raise their more or less shocked voices because the [city's] Cultural Committee had not paid attention to his extraordinary book. (Bianco, 1964, p. 18)

In spite of the disappointment, Borges continued to write and publish. For Losada he collected his *Poemas* (1922–1943), in a rather slim volume. The cover illustration, by the Italian painter Attilio Rossi, depicted a white angel cutting a brown diamond which was inside a cobweb. Perhaps the illustration was a bit too fanciful for Borges' modest claims as a poet. The book contained his first three books of poems—*Fervor de Buenos Aires* (Adoration of Buenos Aires, 1923), *Luna de enfrente* (Moon Across the Way, 1925), and *Cuaderno San Martín* (San

Martín Copybook, 1929)—plus a section called "Other Poems," which included six new pieces, the only ones he had written in the last fourteen years. The old poems were revised, in some cases drastically. Some pieces were dropped; some added. The sprawling prologue to the first book was condensed into one sentence. If Borges' aim as a young man had been to emulate Whitman, by the 1940s he aspired to be a part-time poet only. A quotation, taken from an English author, helped him to define his attitude. It had already been used in *San Martín Copybook* and belonged to Edward FitzGerald, the urbane translator of Omar Khayyam's *Rubaiyat*. It read: "As to an occasional copy of verses, there are few men who have leisure to read, and are possessed of any music in their souls, who are not capable of versifying on some ten or twelve occasions during their natural lives: at a proper conjunction of the stars. There is no harm in taking advantage of such occasions" (*Poemas,* 1943, p. 119).

If the quotation seemed premature for a book that originally contained twelve poems written in four years, it admirably suited the collected poems of 1943. Three of the more recent poems helped Borges to define some of his metaphysical preoccupations. The second, "Del cielo y del infierno" (On Heaven and Hell), is not memorable in spite of the quasi-Quevedian intonation. The first, on the other hand, is one of his best. Under the title of "La noche cíclica" (The Cyclical Night), it develops a subject that he had already discussed in his essays: the eternal return of man and things. But in the poem it is the anguish of his own flesh, his fears and even terrors, that matter most. One passage is strongly confessional:

> Night after night sets me down in the world
>
> On the outskirts of this city. A remote street
> Which might be either north or west or south,
> But always with a blue-washed wall, the shade
> Of a fig tree, and a sidewalk of broken concrete.
>
> This, here, is Buenos Aires. Time, which brings
> Either love or money to men, hands on to me
> Only this withered rose, this empty tracery
> Of streets with names recurring from the past
>
> In my blood: Laprida, Cabrera, Soler, Suárez . . .
>   (*Poems,* 1972, translated by Alastair Reid, p. 79)

The elegiac mood of the last verse is also visible in the book's last piece, "Poema conjetural" (Conjectural Poem), dedicated to his ancestor Francisco Narciso de Laprida, who was killed in a civil war battle. It is a dramatic monologue, in the style made famous by Browning. In recalling his ancestor's fate (to have his throat cut by the gauchos of Aldao), Borges suggests a subtle contrast with his own fate as an intellectual, living in a country that is slowly reverting to anarchy and barbarism. At the time the poem was published, the signs of the army's increased participation in Argentine political life were all too evident. Colonel Perón was being discussed as a future leader. Borges, who had always hated all forms of government and especially totalitarianism, here comes very close to writing a political poem. Although it is obviously a historical elegy, which may have fooled contemporary readers, if it is placed in the context of its time, the allusions become obvious. It will be sufficient to quote the first strophe:

> Bullets whip the air this last afternoon.
> A wind is up, blowing full of cinders
> as the day and this chaotic battle
> straggle to a close. The gauchos have won:
> victory is theirs, the barbarians'.
> I, Francisco Narciso Laprida,
> who studied both canon law and civil
> and whose voice declared the independence
> of this untamed territory,
> in defeat, my face marked by blood and sweat,
> holding neither hope nor fear, the way lost,
> strike out for the South through the back country.
>   (Ibid., translated by Norman Thomas di Giovanni, p. 83)

The paradox is that Laprida is also able to recognize with joy that he has just come face to face with his South American fate: not the fate of a man of letters but the fate of a man brutally sacrificed for his country. The poem ends vividly, almost erotically:

> My feet tread the shadows of the lances
> that spar for the kill. The taunts of my death,
> the horses, the horsemen, the horses' manes,
> tighten the ring around me. Now the first
> blow, the lance's hard steel ripping my chest,
> and across my throat the intimate knife.
>   (Ibid., p. 85)

In an article on the famous verses that the fifteenth-century Spanish poet Jorge Manrique devoted to the death of his father, Borges observes that they are too rhetorical and do not convey the poet's emotion (the article appears in *El idioma de los argentinos,* published in 1928). In his "Conjectural Poem," in spite of the historical distance, Borges manages to be moving. He himself underlined the political content of the poem by including it at the end of a lecture on gaucho literature that he gave in Montevideo in 1945. Making a pointed reference to the Argentine political situation of the time, he observed that he had come to the realization that "for a second time we had to face darkness and adventure. I thought that the tragic 1820s were back, that the men who had measured themselves against its barbarianism also felt amazement before the face of an unexpected destiny which, nevertheless, they did not flee from" (*Aspectos,* 1950, p. 34). For him, the "Conjectural Poem" was much more than an elegy; it was, in cipher, an image of his own fate. He would later write a story, "The South," which also deals with the destiny of a man torn apart by his double allegiance to European culture and life and to native barbarianism.

In 1943 Borges began his long association with a small publishing house, Emecé Editores, which had recently begun to expand its program by appointing some leading intellectuals (the Spaniard Ricardo Baeza, Eduardo Mallea) as literary editors. Pamphlets of the Chimera was the name given to a series of selected short stories, published singly in elegant little volumes and edited by Mallea; Borges wrote several prologues for it. One prefaced his own translation of Herman Melville's *Bartleby, the Scrivener* (Buenos Aires, 1943). Half of the prologue is devoted to discussing *Moby Dick;* the rest contains a short biography of Melville and a general evaluation of his work. Borges has this to say about *Bartleby:* "Kafka's work projects a curious retrospective light over *Bartleby.* [The story] defines a genre which Kafka would reinvent and deepen toward 1919: one that deals with the fantasies of behavior and feeling that now are wrongly called psychological" (*Prólogos,* 1975, p. 117). He also observes that the beginning of the story is reminiscent of Dickens. After a short bibliography, he concludes: "The vast populations, the high cities, the mistaken and clamorous publicity have conspired to make the great secret man one of America's traditions. Edgar Allan Poe was one of them; Melville, also" (ibid., p. 118).

His second contribution to the Chimera series was a prologue to a translation of Henry James' "The Abasement of the Northmores." In introducing James, Borges stresses his strangeness:

> I have perused part of Eastern literature and several Western literatures; I have compiled an anthology of fantastic literature; I have translated Kafka and Melville, Swedenborg and Bloy; I do not know of a work as strange as that of James. The writers I have just mentioned are, from the very beginning, surprising; the world they present in their works is almost professionally unreal; James, before showing what he is, a resigned and polite inhabitant of hell, risks seeming a mundane novelist, more nondescript than

others. As soon as we begin reading, we are upset by a certain ambiguity, a certain superficiality; after a few pages, we understand that these deliberate neglects have the effect of enhancing the book. (Ibid., p. 101)

After analyzing a few of his favorites among James' stories, Borges concludes with the customary bibliography and a quotation from Graham Greene in which the latter observes that James is as solitary in the history of the novel as Shakespeare is in the history of poetry.

Borges wrote other prologues to volumes edited by Mallea (one on the memoirs of Sarmiento) and to Ricardo Baeza's collection of classics. But his first important contribution to the Emecé list was an anthology called *The Best Detective Stories,* which he compiled in 1943 with Adolfo Bioy Casares. Some of the sixteen stories in the anthology are by obvious names such as Edgar Allan Poe ("The Purloined Letter"), Robert Louis Stevenson (a fragment from *The Master of Ballantrae*), Arthur Conan Doyle (*The Red-Headed League*), Gilbert Keith Chesterton ("The Honor of Israel Gow"), Ellery Queen ("Philately"), and Georges Simenon ("Les sept minutes"); others are by authors not generally associated with the detective genre: Nathaniel Hawthorne ("Mr. Higginbotham's Catastrophe"), Jack London (from *Moon Face*), Guillaume Apollinaire (from *L'Hérésiarque et Cie*), Eden Phillpotts (from *Peacock House*). The anthology also includes stories by Argentine writers such as Carlos Pérez Ruiz, Manuel Peyrou, and Jorge Luis Borges. Although there is no introduction to the volume, the jacket makes some sweeping statements: "Invented in 1841 by the famous poet Edgar Allan Poe, the detective story is the newest of literary genres. It can also be said that it is the literary genre of our time." To validate the statement, the jacket mentions several distinguished readers who favor the genre: André Gide, Keyserling, Victoria Ocampo, Jung, Alfonso Reyes, Aldous Huxley. The aim of the collection is, according to the blurb, to offer a panorama of a significant segment of contemporary literature. To accomplish that purpose, the compilers did not rely exclusively on former anthologies by Dorothy Sayers, Lee Wright, Rhode, Douglas Thompson, and Wrong, or on the studies of Fosca, Haycraft, and Roger Caillois; they used their long and pleasurable association with the original texts, not excluding, of course, the ones produced by Argentines. The blurb also indicates that the chronological order followed in the anthology is designed to help the studious reader to trace the evolution of the genre.

In spite of the jacket's words, the anthology is less the result of scholarship than of love. It reveals the extent to which both Borges and Bioy Casares valued the detective story, the vast knowledge they had of its practitioners, and the independence of their evaluations. In a sense, the anthology complements the one on fantastic literature they compiled in 1940 for Sudamericana. The new anthology had an enormous success and was the foundation of a series of detective novels that Borges and Bioy began to edit for Emecé Editores under the title—suggested by Dante's Inferno—of The Seventh Circle. The first volume to be published was Nicholas Blake's *The Beast Must Die*. On the jacket, unmistakably written by the compilers, the reader is informed that Blake is the pseudonym of the English poet Cecil Day Lewis. The collection later included some masterpieces of the genre (Dickens' *The Mystery of Edwin Drood*, Collins' *The Moonstone* and *The Woman in White*), as well as more contemporary writers such as Eden Phillpotts, Michael Innes, Anthony Berkeley, Vera Caspary, James M. Cain, and Graham Greene, whose *The Ministry of Fear* was hailed by Borges as one of the best novels to come out of the war. The success of The Seventh Circle created a new audience for Borges. It was a toally different audience from the one he had had earlier. Younger, less concerned with high literary standards, slightly iconoclastic, this audience soon moved from the detective stories and novels Borges and Bioy Casares recommended to the ones they themselves wrote. Through a genre generally snubbed by literary intellectuals, Borges came to find a devoted readership. It was a form of reparation.

6.
A New Volume of Stories

World War II was coming to an end. On August 23, 1944, Paris was liberated. Borges, who had always explicitly supported the Allies in an Argentina whose rulers favored the Axis, wrote a short piece for *Sur* (September 1944) that he later collected in *Other Inquisitions* ("A Comment on August 23, 1944," 1952). The article can be seen as a sequel, and perhaps a fit conclusion, to the series of notes and articles about Nazism that he wrote for *Sur* and *El Hogar.* For him, the liberation of Paris was less important than the total defeat of Nazism that he could now foresee. The article begins with a personal statement about August 23:

> That crowded day gave me three heterogeneous surprises: the *physical* happiness I experienced when they told me Paris had been liberated; the discovery that a collective emotion can be noble; the enigmatic and obvious enthusiasm of many who were supporters of Hitler. I know that if I question that enthusiasm I may easily resemble those futile hydrographers who asked why a single ruby was enough to arrest the course of a river; many will accuse me of trying to explain a chimerical occurrence. Still, that was what happened, and thousands of persons in Buenos Aires can bear witness to it. (*Inquisitions,* 1964, p. 134)

The article then tries to unravel the mystery. How was it possible to be on the side of Nazism and at the same time accept, joyously, its defeat? In a roundabout way, after summarizing some of the arguments he had used in previous articles, Borges comes to the conclusion that even Nazi sympathizers did not believe in a Nazi triumph. He quotes a passage from Shaw's *Man and Superman,* "where it is stated that the horror of hell is its unreality," and then tells an anecdote about the day Paris fell into German hands:

> A certain Germanophile, whose name I do not wish to remember, came to my house that day. Standing in the doorway, he announced the dreadful news: the Nazi armies had occupied Paris. I felt a mixture of sadness, disgust, malaise. And then it occurred to me that his insolent joy did not explain the stentorian voice or the abrupt proclamation. He added that the German troops would soon be in London. Any opposition was useless, nothing could prevent their victory. That was when I knew that he too was terrified. (Ibid., p. 135)

The conclusion Borges extracts from his analysis of these two symmetrical episodes is clear:

> Nazism suffers from unreality, like Erigena's hells. It is uninhabitable; men can only die for it, lie for it, kill and wound for it. No one, in the intimate depths of his being, can wish it to triumph. I shall hazard this conjecture: *Hitler wants to be defeated.* Hitler is collaborating blindly with the inevitable armies that will annihilate him, as the metal vultures and the dragon (which must not have been unaware that they were monsters) collaborated, mysteriously, with Hercules. (Ibid., pp. 135–136)

The accuracy of Borges' prophecy was plainly seen a few months later when Hitler died among the ruins of his bunker and of the Third Reich.

In spite of being neglected by the Argentine establishment, Borges continued to receive recognition from a perceptive few. One of the most important was the French critic and sociologist Roger Caillois. Invited by Victoria Ocampo on the eve of the war to come to Argentina to give a few lectures, Caillois remained there for the duration. An extremely imaginative and active man, Caillois could not remain idle while French culture was being destroyed by the German occupation. With the help of Victoria Ocampo, he launched a journal, *Lettres Françaises,* which was printed in Buenos Aires and had on its cover *Sur*'s downward arrow to call attention to the patronage. Some of the best French writers of the time contributed to the journal. In its fourteenth issue, published in October 1944, two of Borges' short stories (under the collective title of "Assyriennes") were translated into French for the first time. The pieces—"The Babylon Lottery" and "The Library of Babel"—were among Borges' most curious. Although the circulation of the journal in metropolitan France was rather limited, the issue came out at the exact moment, after liberation, when France was avidly renewing its contacts with the rest of the world. It would be tempting to date from that moment the beginning of French recognition of Borges, but in fact, Borges (and his promoter Caillois) would have to wait almost sixteen more years for international recognition—until the day in 1961 when the Formentor Prize, given by a group of international publishers, was divided between Samuel Beckett and the unknown Argentine writer.

Caillois' promotion of Borges was not based on a close friendship. As a matter of fact, Borges was ungenerous enough to write a rather catty article in *Sur* (April 1942) reviewing one of Caillois' pamphlets, on the detective novel. Against Caillois' statement that the detective story was born when Joseph Fouché created a well-trained police force in Paris, Borges observes that a literary genre invariably begins with a literary text and points out that the text in question is one of Edgar Allan Poe's stories. An exchange of notes ensued, and the relationship between Borges and Caillois cooled considerably. That did not affect Caillois' admiration for Borges' writings. He continued to promote Borges unflinchingly until he secured for him the Formentor Prize.

Before the end of 1944, *Sur* came out with a new collection of Borges' short stories. Under the title of *Ficciones,* the book included eight stories already collected in *The Garden of Forking Paths* (1941) and added six new ones, under the heading "Artifices." The title of the book and of its second part proved that Borges was adamant: he refused to compromise and follow the realistic line the establishment applauded, or the even staler one of social realism fostered by the Stalinist left. By his very titles, he was proclaiming his belief in a literature that was just that: literature—a fiction that did not pretend to be anything else. A literary text was an artifice, a verbal object; that is, just a text. To introduce the six new pieces, he wrote a short prologue in which he attempted to give clues to three of the stories. He begins with an apologetic statement: "Though less torpidly executed, the pieces in this section are similar to those which form the first part of the book" (*Ficciones,* 1962, p. 105). He proceeds to discuss at some length only two of the stories: "Death and the Compass" and "Funes, the Memorious." He points out that the second is "a long metaphor of insomnia," then moves to elucidate some aspects of the first, which, in spite of

the German or Scandinavian names, occurs in a Buenos Aires of dreams: the twisted Rue de Toulon is the Paseo de Julio; Triste-le-Roy is the hotel where Herbert Ashe received, and probably did not read, the eleventh volume of an illusory encyclopedia. After composing this narrative, I have come to consider the soundness of amplifying the time and space in which it occurs: vengeance could be inherited; the periods of time might be computed in years, perhaps in centuries; the first letter of the Name might be spoken in Iceland; the second, in Mexico; the third, in Hindustan. (Ibid., p. 105)

As a key to understanding both stories, Borges' comments are perhaps too selective. It is true that "Funes" can be seen as a metaphor of insomnia, but that curious tale—in which Borges invented a fantastic being: a man with total recall—contains more than that. In a sense, it is a self-portrait, a view of himself as a man immobilized by memory and insomnia, living in a world that is atrociously lucid, passive, marginal. As a persona, Irineo Funes is another of those characters through whom Borges reveals tantalizing fragments of himself.

The other story, "Death and the Compass," is Borges' second detective story—or perhaps the third, if one also counts "The Approach to al-Mu'tasim." It was written after the invention of Bustos Domecq and the *Six Problems for Don Isidro Parodi.* If the first two detective stories are basically Chestertonian, "Death and the Compass" has some touches of the parodical humor freed by the Bustos stories. It is neatly built around an ingenious, if not original, idea: that the victim the murderer is really trying to trap is the detective. (A similar inversion, the narrator who is the assassin, was used by Agatha Christie in *The Murder of Roger Ackroyd.*) The geometrical plot, which is highly ingenious, and the cool style reveal Borges' handiwork. But some of the atmospheric details (anti-Semitism is the subject of a witty digression) and some peripheral episodes bear the signature of Bustos Domecq—as does the fact emphasized in the prologue to "Artifices," that the geometrical city of the story is really a "Buenos Aires of dreams." Instead of using parody, as in the Bustos Domecq stories, Borges here uses the displacement of nightmares.

There are other levels to the story, which Borges does not attempt to explain. The end contains a double surprise. The obvious one is linked to the plot: the discovery that the fourth intended victim is the detective. But there is another surprise, as elegant as a geometrical problem. When Eric Lönnrot, the detective, realizes that he is going to be shot by Red Scharlach, he understands for the first time the real meaning of the geometrical figure (a rhomb) that the three previous murders in three different parts of the city suggested. He compares the assassin's scheme to a labyrinth:

"In your labyrinth there are three lines too many," he said at last. "I know of a Greek labyrinth which is a single straight line. Along this line so many philosophers have lost themselves that a mere detective might well do so too. Scharlach, when, in some other incarnation, you hunt me, feign to commit (or do commit) a crime at A, then a second crime at B, eight kilometers from

A, then a third crime at C, four kilometers from A and B, halfway en route between the two. Wait for me later at D, two kilometers from A and C, halfway, once again, between both. Kill me at D, as you are now going to kill me at Triste-le-Roy."

"The next time I kill you," said Scharlach, "I promise you the labyrinth made of the single straight line which is invisible and everlasting."

He stepped back a few paces. Then, very carefully, he fired. (*Ficciones,* 1962, p. 141)

The second ending doubly alters the meaning of the story. In the first place, a reversal makes Lönnrot the intellectual victor. He is killed, but first he points out the major flaw in Scharlach's plot: it has too many lines; therefore, it is unnecessarily prolix. In the second place, by referring to the ritual aspect of the killing, Lönnrot introduces the notion of circular time: there will be another time and another meeting and another killing. The concept of eternal return, which Borges had already explored in poems and essays, adds an extra dimension to the story. It changes Scharlach and Lönnrot into characters in a myth: Abel and Cain endlessly pursuing each other and endlessly performing the killing. The story becomes a cosmic charade in which circumstances may vary but the ritual is always the same. Even the fact that the word *red* (for blood) is contained in both protagonists' names adds to the mythical pattern. Borges, of course, gives no clue about that aspect of the tale. In the second edition of *Ficciones* (originally published in 1956), he provides information about the supposed cabalistic background: "Should I add that the Hasidim included saints and that the sacrifice of four lives in order to obtain the four letters imposed by the Name is a fantasy dictated by the form of my story?" (ibid., p. 105). It is a polite way of indicating that the cabala was used only in the story as a diversion.

The second paragraph of the prologue to the new stories in *Ficciones* is terse: "The heterogeneous census of the authors whom I continually reread is made up of Schopenhauer, De Quincey, Stevenson, Mauthner, Shaw, Chesterton, Leon Bloy. I believe I perceive the remote influence of the last-mentioned in the Christological fantasy entitled 'Three Versions of Judas' " (ibid., p. 129). The story postulates the existence of one Nils Runenberg, who devotes part of his existence to obsessively interpreting the real nature of Christ's sacrifice. His final conclusion (the third and most unorthodox of his theories) is that God did not become incarnate in Jesus when He assumed in full the human condition. Rather, "God became a man completely, a man to the point of infamy, a man to the point of being reprehensible—all the way to the abyss. In order to save us, He could have chosen *any* of the destinies which together weave the uncertain web of history; He could have been Alexander, or Pythagoras, or Rurik, or Jesus; He chose an infamous destiny: He was Judas" (ibid., pp. 155–156).

What Borges' prologue does not say is that the same device—the inversion of the functions of martyr and traitor, hero and villain—is also used in two other stories in the book. In "The Shape of the Sword" the protagonist tells the story of a betrayal as if he were the victim, not the betrayer. In "Theme of the Traitor and the Hero" the first becomes the second in a highly dramatic inversion of roles. In both stories, as in "Three Versions of Judas," the mythical and ritualistic view of the world, presented through the pair Abel and Cain, reinforces the double vision of reality. Borges suggests that the hero is as much a villain as the villain is a hero. They are two sides of the same character: man.

Ficciones contains another story that is not dealt with, even by implication, in the prologue. It is entitled "The Secret Miracle" and presents a Jewish playwright who is going to be executed by the Nazis. At the very last second he is saved by a miracle: God gives him a whole year to complete his play. Time is stopped: the executioners freeze while the playwright completes his task; as soon as it is finished, "a quadruple blast" brings him down (ibid., p. 150). This artifice, the playing with time, links the story with some of the experiments attributed to Herbert Quain in the story already included in *The Garden of Forking Paths*. The same interplay between objective, chronological, and subjective time is present here. Borges' love for Berkeleyan idealism is put to use in a fashion that produces an effective narrative. The story is not one of Borges' best and is perhaps a bit too mechanical, but it is one that readers favor. In a sense, it is easier to identify with its protagonist's plight than with Funes' or Nils Runenberg's hallucinatory destinies.

Ficciones was better received than *The Garden of Forking Paths*. A special prize was created to honor the book. At the behest of Enrique Amorim, the Argentine Society of Writers (SADE) awarded the book its first Great Prize of Honor, obviously intended as reparation for the offhand way the city of Buenos Aires had treated *The Garden* in 1942.

For another of Emecé's collections, Borges edited at the beginning of 1945 an anthology called *El compadrito* (The Buenos Aires Hoodlum); this time, the co-editor was not Bioy Casares but a young woman, Silvina Bullrich Palenque, who was beautiful and talented. The subtitle indicated the scope of the small anthology; it attempted to cover the hoodlum's destiny, his neighborhoods, his music. Borges begins the terse prologue by linking the city's hoodlums with the gauchos. He observes that "people believe they admire the gaucho, but essentially they admire the hoodlum" that some gauchos really are. After explaining the scope of the anthology and why the editors have not included either the plays that deal with hoodlums or the tango lyrics that praise them, Borges points out that they have preferred instead descriptions, dialogues, poems, and reports by historians and sociologists. The conclusion expresses the hope that sometime in the future somebody will write a poem that will do for hoodlums what *Martín Fierro* did for gauchos. That was one of Borges' long-cherished projects, of which only the *Evaristo Carriego* biography remains. Yet in 1945, fifteen years after the Carriego book came out, Borges was still dreaming of it.

If the publication of that anthology was, in a sense, a first for Borges—the first time his sole collaborator was a woman—his visit to Montevideo in October of the same year was also a first. He had been invited by the cultural service of the Ministry of Education to give a lecture on gaucho literature at the university. Shy and self-conscious, Borges had never trusted his own voice in public. He generally refused to lecture, and on the rare occasions on which he had been forced to do it he wrote a carefully rehearsed text, then asked a friend to read it for him. That is precisely what he did in Montevideo. While José Pedro Díaz, a young professor of literature, read the long lecture with impeccable diction and a beautiful, sonorous voice, Borges sat behind the podium prompting him, invisibly and inaudibly. It was an uncanny performance, as if he were a ventriloquist controlling his dummy from a distance.

It was there that I met Borges for the first time. I was in charge of the literary pages of *Marcha* (March), a left-wing weekly that was beginning to be known outside Uruguay. Very respectfully, I approached Borges after the lecture and asked him to let me print the complete text of the lecture in *Marcha*'s next issue. Perhaps because I had been introduced to him by two of his favorite cousins, who belonged to the Uruguayan branch of his family and were friends of mine, or perhaps because he was so generous and even careless about what he wrote, he gave me the original of his lecture and authorized me to print it in *Marcha*. I will not attempt to describe my enthusiasm. For years, since I had first discovered his articles and reviews in *El Hogar* in 1936, I had been his fan, collecting all his books, subscribing to the magazines to which he contributed, and imitating him in my own, hopelessly modest, reviews and articles. I was already convinced that he was the best writer the Spanish language had ever produced and was determined to fight to the death anyone who dared to challenge that conviction. In short, I was young and fanatic.

For Borges, that lecture at Montevideo had a different meaning. It was his first attempt to enlarge his audience using a new medium and exploring a new country. His name was known in Uruguay only in the most specialized circles. The lecture, which attracted one of the largest audiences I had ever seen in Montevideo, was a success precisely because it was about a safe subject and Borges handled it with his usual originality. But the lecture had another meaning. It clearly pointed out to him the way to keep contact with a public that was growing and that he had so far neglected. At the time, he did not need to enlarge his audience. He had a regular income from his position as third assistant at the Miguel Cané library and received some extra income from his contributions to journals and magazines. But if he could overcome his shyness and start lecturing, another source of income would be available to him. He was in no hurry. The tortures of having to face an audience were as yet too much for him. Unfortunately (or perhaps, fortunately) in 1946 Argentina would experience a radical political change that would force Borges, in less than a year, to become a lecturer and a teacher. The lecture hall was to be his arena for the rest of his life.

7.
The General and the Chicken Inspector

At the time Borges was lecturing in Montevideo, Argentina was already in the hands of a new leader, Colonel Juan Domingo Perón. His ascent to power was slow but unswerving. Born in 1896, he was a young captain when General Uriburu deposed President Irigoyen in 1930. In spite of joining the senior officers in the coup that overthrew the populist leader, Perón continued to show his independence. He was against Irigoyen, and especially against the palace guard that had isolated the aging leader from his constituency, but he did not subscribe to all the repressive measures the army took to destroy Irigoyen's social and political reforms. Many years later he would speak about the Mole (as Irigoyen was called) as the "first Argentine president to defend the people, the first to challenge the foreign and national interests of the oligarchy to defend his people" (Sanguinetti, 1975, p. 63). But army discipline prevented the young captain from making his criticism public. He accepted a position as private secretary at the Ministry of War (1930–1935) while also teaching at the ministry's high school during the same period. In 1937 he was sent to Chile as a military attaché, and later to Italy during the war. From 1939 to 1940 he joined the Italian army at the Alps and the Abruzzi. He also visited Franco's Spain and was impressed by the devastation that civil war had brought to the country. To some intimate friends he confided that he would always oppose armed conflict in Argentina.

Although practically unknown outside army circles, Perón was already an influential man. The Argentine army was then controlled by men who hated England and admired Italy and were sympathetic to Hitler's crusade for a new world order. Their position is hard to explain in an international context but easy to understand in the River

Plate context. Internationally, England in the early 1940s represented the last bulwark against fascism. It was the hope of democracy, the country of the free. But in Argentina, and to a lesser extent in Uruguay, England was seen merely as the center of imperialism. The economy of the River Plate area was then ruled from London; the chief investors were British: railroads, powerhouses, and even waterworks were in British hands. Only nominally were Argentina and Uruguay independent. To Argentines, British imperialism was intolerable. The army therefore favored fascism and viewed Hitler with sympathetic eyes because it sincerely believed he would help the world to get rid of the British.

Perón shared these views. While in Italy, he was favorably impressed with the way Mussolini had handled the corporate state; he would later borrow freely from his methods. He was not so keen on Hitler, although he admired him as Britain's most powerful enemy. But Perón was also an intuitive politician, a man who had a truly imaginative way of recognizing the popular mood and possessed an uncanny ability to cater to it. He knew he was still too young and unknown to come into the open and lead a coup d'état. Instead, he began by organizing a movement of Young Turks which put pressure on the senior officers and led them into action. The Argentine government of the time was ripe for a fall. Led since 1938 by the totally incompetent President Castillo, it was toppled on June 4, 1943, by a bloodless coup. The army took over openly. The new president was General Farrell, but the real power behind the scenes was Colonel Perón, who had modestly chosen to be appointed vice-president. He was also named minister of war and secretary of work and social protection (actually minister of labor and welfare). As minister of war, he controlled the army; as secretary of work, he was in a position to control the workers and build a power base. Perón realized that there were a large number of workers in Argentina whom the traditional parties had neglected and whom the left-wing parties appealed to only marginally. He began by expanding the Secretariat and increasing its budget. By a series of decrees, he first organized the men who worked in the fields, then began making inroads into the left-wing unions, which controlled local industries. By promoting competing unions (organized directly by the Secretariat) or by bribing the officials of the older unions, he gained in less than two years' time almost complete control over a mass of workers that had so far received no protection from the government and had been poorly represented by their own unions. Perón also learned how to use the state radio station to bring his plans for social reform and his union policy to the attention of all workers, both in the cities and in the fields. His speeches were plain and direct and effectively attuned to the language of his listeners. He was a colonel, but he spoke as one of "us." He also inaugurated a campaign to popularize his image. Very soon, the obscure colonel was recognized—his warm voice, his immense smile, his large, pale face and pomaded black hair—by thousands of people who had up till then felt no interest in the promises of the old-style politicians.

Perón was far less popular with the wealthy ranchers and the political bureaucrats. He was also dangerous to left-wing reformers and entrenched union leaders. They joined together in denouncing his demagoguery, his abuse of power, his bribing and/or terrorizing of his enemies. They called him a Fascist (which he was) and a Nazi (which he was not), a bully (which he was) and a satyr (which he probably was not). His liaison with a young, blonde radio actress, Eva Duarte, was a favorite subject of dirty jokes. The laws that regulated workers' salaries, new pensions, and an improved system of welfare were opposed by the ruling classes. For the first time somebody had dared to challenge their right to pay workers what they pleased. The left-wing parties were in turn furious with a man who was instituting the social reforms they had tried unsuccessfully to achieve for three or four decades. The Church also felt offended by the way he carried on with Evita, as everybody called his mistress. But Perón continued to smile and increase his popularity. Against his enemies, he resorted to torture. It was about this time that the Argentine police imported from Germany and perfected the *picana eléctrica,* a primitive system of electrodes that were generally applied to the genital area to coerce "confessions."

By October 9, 1945, everybody apparently had had enough of Perón. General Farrell was persuaded to ask him to resign all his official positions and retire. Perón agreed and was immediately sent to the Martín García, a small island, close to the Uruguayan coastline, where President Irigoyen had been confined after being deposed. Everybody was convinced that that was the end of Perón. He himself told his friends that he wanted only to marry Evita and retire to a quiet place to write his memoirs. He was then fifty and at the peak of his vitality. Eight days later he was back in Buenos Aires, addressing the biggest crowd so far assembled in that city and reassuring the masses that in next February's election he would be the official candidate for the presidency.

What exactly had happened in those eight days? Legends and myths have grown steadily to the point that it is hard to know exactly what went on behind the scenes. What is known is that hundreds of thousands of Argentines were not only transported to the capital but also fed; they camped in downtown Buenos Aires and refused to move until Perón had been produced and had addressed them, and a "collective orgasm" (to quote one of the most passionate accounts) between the Macho and his people was achieved.

Following these events, the government had to declare a holiday, which the people immediately baptized St. Perón's Day. President Farrell promoted Perón to general. The elections that took place on February 24, 1946, only certified what St. Perón's Day had proclaimed: that he was Argentina's first king.

Before the elections, Perón had married Evita in a discreet civil ceremony, and now she was Señora María Eva Duarte de Perón, Argentina's first lady. For the next ten years, and until her sudden death in 1952, Argentina had a royal couple.

Borges' reaction to the ascent of Perón was not mild. He sincerely believed Perón was a Nazi. Being of British extraction and having followed in detail the transformation of German culture under Hitler, Borges had no love for the new world order the Führer had so brutally attempted to impose on Europe. During the 1930s he used his section in *El Hogar* to discuss political matters, writing with deadly irony about totalitarianism of every kind. He concentrated his fire on Nazism and communism, devoting particular attention to the debasement of German culture by Hitler's propaganda machine and the follies of anti-Semitism. His standing on international matters mirrored his standing on national affairs. He viewed the Argentine situation from the larger perspective of the international fight against fascism.

A statement he made for a Uruguayan newspaper at the time of his lecture on gaucho literature appeared in print exactly fifteen days after Perón's triumphant return to Buenos Aires:

> The [political] situation in Argentina is very serious, so serious that a great number of Argentines are becoming Nazis without being aware of it. Tempted by promises of social reform—in a society that undoubtedly needs a better organization than the one it now has—many people are letting themselves be seduced by an outsized wave of hatred that is sweeping the country. It is a terrible thing, similar to what happened at the beginning of fascism and Nazism [in Europe]. But I must add that Argentine intellectuals are against it and fight it. I believe that the only possible solution is to delegate power to the Supreme Court. Nevertheless, I am pessimistic about a more or less speedy return of the Argentine government to democracy. (*El Plata,* Montevideo, October 31, 1945)

The suggestion that the army ought to delegate power to the Supreme Court before the elections had been one of the demands of the Popular Democratic Union, which opposed Perón's candidacy; but, obviously, Perón refused to relinquish the power he needed to be elected president. In that respect, Borges' skepticism was well justified. Perón used the power and the money of the Secretariat of Work to buy votes, to organize his forces, and to win the election by a bare 51 percent.

If Borges was right about the small chance of a return to democracy, he was wrong in his view that Perón was a Nazi. Perón was a Fascist and a nationalist. By identifying him and his party with the Nazis, Borges and his friends missed precisely what made Perón so attractive to the masses.

Perón's victory made clear to everybody that democracy in Argentina was shelved for the foreseeable future. Borges must have realized how frail his own position was. Although he was already acclaimed locally as one of the leading contemporary writers, he was only a third assistant at the Miguel Cané municipal library; that is, he depended entirely (or almost entirely) for his subsistence on a political appointment. In spite of that, and because he was a proud and free man, he continued to sign the anti-Peronist manifestos that still circulated freely in Buenos Aires. At the beginning, Perón paid little attention to the intellectuals. He was chiefly interested in consolidating his power among the unions, the army, and the industrialists. But after he felt secure, he turned to them and reduced them to silence.

For Borges he invented a truly Macho humiliation. In August 1946 Borges was officially informed that, by decision of city hall, he had been promoted out of the Miguel Cané library to the inspectorship of poultry and rabbits in the public market of Córdoba Street. This is the end of the story in his "Autobiographical Essay": "I went to the City Hall to find out what it was all about. 'Look here,' I said. 'It's rather strange that among so many others at the library I should be singled out as worthy of this new position.' 'Well,' the clerk answered, 'you were on the side of the Allies—what do you expect?' His statement was unanswerable; the next day, I sent in my resignation" ("Essay," 1970, p. 244).

In his account Borges makes no reference to the meaning of that "promotion," but it is obvious that he had been chosen to be the victim of a form of humiliation typical of the River Plate area. Perón and his friends were masters of the art of the *cachada* (to grab, to take somebody unawares). To promote one of the leading Argentine intellectuals to inspector of chickens and rabbits implied a linguistic pun. Chickens and rabbits are in Spanish, as in English, synonymous with cowardice. But Borges decided to ignore the affront and take the promotion as a sign of the regime's vast ignorance of the uses of language. He dutifully resigned but made a public statement in which he recounted the episode with deadpan accuracy. The last paragraph reads:

I don't know if the episode I have just told is a parable. I suspect, neverthe-less, that memory and forgetfulness are gods that know perfectly well what they do. If they have forgotten the rest and if they only preserve this absurd legend, they probably have some justification. I formulate it in these words: dictatorships foment oppression, dictatorships foment subservience, dicta-torships foment cruelty; even more abominable is the fact that they foment stupidity. Buttons which babble slogans, images of leaders, predesignated "hails" and "down withs," walls decorated with names, unanimous ceremo-nies, mere discipline taking the place of lucidity. . . . To fight against those sad monotonies is one of the many duties of writers. Would it be necessary to remind the readers of *Martín Fierro* and *Don Segundo Sombra* that individ-ualism is an old Argentine virtue? ("Dele-Dele," 1946)

Using the same title *Sur* had used at the time *The Garden of Forking Paths* was passed over for the city prize, a group of intellectuals of all persuasions decided to organize a "Reparation to Borges." In the course of the banquet they held, the statement quoted above was read. Among the speeches, the most significant was by the president of the Argentine Society of Writers, Leonidas Barletta, a dedicated Commu-nist and one of the participants in the old Boedo group. Barletta hailed Borges' courage in standing up for his convictions and refusing to be silenced by dictatorship. He recognized in him the true spirit of the resistance each Argentine intellectual ought to show in those "magnifi-cent and terrible" days. His speech, printed with Borges' text in a page of the left-wing journal *Argentina Libre* (Free Argentina, August 15, 1946), was a political manifesto. Borges—the exquisite, apolitical Borges—had suddenly become, and would remain for the next decade, the symbol of Argentina's resistance to totalitarianism. It was an unex-pected role for that shy, ironic man, but he performed it with simplicity and without once flinching. Somehow, Perón had chosen the wrong kind of inspector for his chickens and rabbits.

8.
Living in an Occupied Town

The humiliation Perón and his associates had devised for Borges not only turned him into a popular figure of resistance to the regime; it also forced him to make a momentous literary decision. To resign his modest position as third assistant at the Miguel Cané library threatened to leave him with no regular income at the age of forty-seven. It is true that he had a few literary jobs: regular contributions to *Sur* and *La Nación,* anthologies compiled with friends, prologues and notes to books he edited. But all this activity was marginal and did not constitute a sufficient income. He had to look elsewhere.

The only thing left for him was to lecture. His shyness and a mild stammer that became really uncomfortable when he had to speak in public had prevented him from accepting a regular job as a lecturer or even teacher. But Perón, by promoting him to inspector of chickens and rabbits, had left him with no alternative. It was either starvation or the lecture hall. In anguish, Borges chose the latter.

At first he did not trust his own voice. He had always relied on close friends to read his speeches for him. Even the short text he wrote for the banquet offered by the Argentine Society of Writers was read by the critic Pedro Hendríquez Ureña. But it was unrealistic to believe that he could go on forever asking friends to read his lectures. Little by little he pushed himself into doing it. The account Borges gives of these events in his "Autobiographical Essay" is, as usual, too simplified. After summarizing his dismissal from the Miguel Cané library, he writes:

> I was now out of a job. Several months before, an old English lady had read my tea leaves and foretold that I was soon to travel, to speak, and to take

vast sums of money thereby. On telling my mother about it, we both laughed, for public speaking was far beyond me. At this juncture, a friend came to the rescue, and I was made teacher of English literature at the Asociación Argentina de Cultura Inglesa. I was also asked at the same time to lecture on classic American literature at the Colegio Libre de Estudios Superiores. Since this pair of offers was made three months before classes opened, I accepted, feeling quite safe. As the time grew near, however, I grew sicker and sicker. My series of lectures was to be on Hawthorne, Poe, Thoreau, Emerson, Melville, Whitman, Twain, Henry James, and Veblen. I wrote the first one down. But I had no time to write out the second one. Besides, thinking of the first lecture as Doomsday, I felt that only eternity could come after. The first one went off well enough—miraculously. Two nights before the second lecture, I took my mother for a long walk around Adrogué and had her time me as I rehearsed my talk. She said that she thought it was overlong. "In that case," I said, "I'm safe." My fear had been of running dry. So, at forty-seven, I found a new and exciting life opening up for me. ("Essay," 1970, pp. 244–245)

In spite of Borges' retrospective cheerfulness, things did not go so smoothly. In the first place, the preparation of each lecture took an inordinate amount of time. The first, on Hawthorne (which he later included in his collection *Other Inquisitions,* 1952), was too long and too erudite. It must have taken him the better part of several months to put all the information together and write out the dense text. When he realized that such a method was not suited to a regular course of lectures, he switched to making very precise notes on small pieces of paper. He then memorized these notes so thoroughly that he rarely needed to consult them in the lecture room. To overcome his insecurity, he rehearsed with a friend or with his mother; he also devised an elaborate ritual before each lecture—one that I was able to witness more than once when he came to speak in Montevideo.

The ritual consisted of two parts. The first part was a long walk toward the place where the lecture was to be given. Walking and talking with one or two friends about the subject of the lecture, Borges practiced the sort of peripatetic dialogue that had its roots in ancient Greece, when Aristotle took his disciples for long, learned walks in his garden. The second part of the ritual was perhaps less Aristotelian. When he approached the place where he had to lecture, Borges would go into a café to have a strong drink—generally a *caña* or a *grappa*— which he downed in one gulp and which helped to exorcise his fears.

The lecture had its own ritual. Borges sat very quietly, never looking directly at the audience and focusing his half-blind eyes on a distant spot. While lecturing, he would join his hands in small, precise movements of prayer or discreetly move them around; he would deliver his speech in a rather monotonous, low voice as if he were a priest or a rabbi. His style contrasted radically with the one favored in the River Plate area, where the traditions of Latin oratory were still very much alive. But Borges succeeded precisely because he was so different. His stillness, his precise gestures, the monotone of his voice created an almost incantatory space: a space in which what really mattered was the text, carefully meditated, carefully put together, and always unexpected. The immobility, the low tone, the almost fanatical concentration on the spoken words—all that was the lecture and not the usual histrionics of the orator. Borges had managed to create a spoken style that suited the written style of his work. Audiences, at first puzzled and perhaps slightly alarmed, began to recognize its effectiveness. In less than a few years Borges had become one of the most successful lecturers in the River Plate area.

In his "Autobiographical Essay" he has this to say about his success:

> I traveled up and down Argentina and Uruguay, lecturing on Swedenborg, Blake, the Persian and Chinese mystics, Buddhism, gauchesco poetry, Martin Buber, the Kabbalah, the *Arabian Nights,* T. E. Lawrence, medieval Germanic poetry, the Icelandic sagas, Heine, Dante, expressionism, and Cervantes. I went from town to town, staying overnight in hotels I'd never see again. Sometimes my mother or a friend accompanied me. Not only did I end up making far more money than at the library, but I enjoyed the work and felt that it justified me. ("Essay," 1970, p. 245)

What he fails to convey in his "Essay" is the exact context in which these lectures were given: it is the context of Perón's Argentina. I used to visit him in Buenos Aires during those years. As he came at least once a year to Montevideo, to lecture and see friends and relatives, we repaid his visits as often as we could. Buenos Aires was then literally wallpapered with enormous posters of Perón and his blonde wife, and each poster was covered with aggressive slogans. The city had the look of an occupied town. In that insulted Buenos Aires, Borges walked endlessly. He was then in his late forties, and he still had partial eyesight. He didn't use a cane. His step was nervous, almost brusque. Only when crossing a street would a natural prudence make him hold his companion by the sleeve, rather than the arm, with an imperious gesture that requested but did not beg help. With the same sudden brusqueness, he'd let go on the other side. But verbal communication never stopped.

Borges dimly saw (or guessed) the slogans of the regime, the infinite repetition of Perón's and Evita's names, the calculated humiliation of patrician Buenos Aires. He'd point to each enormous letter, underline each slogan, talk and talk furiously. Gone was the Buenos Aires of his poems and dreams, the suburban neighborhood with its general store and pink corners and local hoodlums wearing white, soft-brimmed hats, its twilight streets open to the invading pampas. Nothing was left of that mythical Buenos Aires of his tales. Now the city was ruled by a regime that proposed to break the back of a powerful oligarchy whose tastes had been formed in London and Paris. Borges was not excessively sorry about the humiliation of a class whose failures and weaknesses he had always satirized, but he hated the demagoguery of this leader who aired social grudges, petty fascist lessons, in a colossal display of mediocrity.

While he walked, Borges' pain was visible in the bitterness of his speech and the brusqueness of his gestures, rather than in the actual words he used. He was like a man skinned alive. Here and there the real Buenos Aires was visible to him. But from his talk a different, more ominous city emerged. It was a city of unrelieved horror, the one that was transcribed phantasmagorically and under European names in "Death and the Compass." Only a thin disguise of chessboard geometry and Chestertonian paradox separated that city where Good and Evil fought, from the real one. The same gray, nightmarish Buenos Aires reappeared in "The Wait," where a man waits in a rented room for his enemies to come to kill him. The ugliness, physical as well as moral, of the Perón capital was the background for some of the more dismal tales of this period.

Listening to Borges, I found it impossible not to feel a sense of rejection mixed with quiet impatience. I did not care if somebody heard us. It is true that the regime set out to persecute the intellectuals, but it did so in a casual, inconsistent manner. These petty persecutions were designed more to humiliate and harass than to frighten. I knew all this, and that is why I felt a sense of rejection: it was not that Borges' words seemed wrong to me; it was that I felt the shame of a person who spies on someone else's nightmares, who involuntarily listens to the cries and private words of a sleeper. Brutally, the passion with which Borges denounced Perón's Buenos Aires brought me into his own labyrinth. Listening to him, sympathizing with him, I wanted nevertheless to say no, to argue that Perón was more than a mediocre tyrant, that he represented something completely different for the workers and the poor, that he had introduced new and necessary social laws, that he was trying (perhaps unsuccessfully) to liberate Argentina from foreign powers. I wanted to tell him that the sinister Buenos Aires of his tales and nightmares hardly existed in reality, that it had another, more bureaucratic mask of informers, petty dealers, and arbitrary policemen. But how can one establish a dialogue with a dreamer?

Borges imposed his nightmare upon me, and I ended up feeling the viscosity of the air, the menace of the walls, the obsessive presence of the endlessly repeated names. His vision had created a labyrinth in this mediocre reality, and I too was lost in it.

As soon as we left the downtown streets and reached Buenos Aires' Southside, Borges' mood would change. The Southside seems (or seemed in the years between 1946 and 1949) like the setting of a Borges tale. He would drag me to see some surviving pink streetcorner; we would step onto patios whose stone pavements recalled another tyrant's times: the Juan Manuel Rosas who reappeared obsessively in his verses. We would cross squares which still held the dampness that had chilled his grandparents. Sometimes, in the evening, we would land in some café such as the Richmond del Sur, where a small band played old-time tangos above the incessant clacking of billiard balls at the back. Then, for a while, Borges would forget Perón and would even laugh. He would tap the table with his hand (somewhat short, with fat fingers) to the rhythms of the tango. I used to think then that Borges was providing me with local color, that he wanted to show the tourist (a Uruguayan is always considered a bit provincial in Buenos Aires) the remains, or perhaps the debris, of a mythical city that still lived in his poems and his biography of Evaristo Carriego. But there was more than that in his mind. Through that tango ritual, Borges managed to escape for a moment from Perón's moral prison, from the loud walls of his own nightmare. The Buenos Aires he loved was still alive in the music of the tango.

We often walked the streets of the Southside and also some quarters of the poorer Northside, which had nothing in common with the fashionable boutiques of Florida Street. I still remember one night when we walked through half of Buenos Aires (he walked to enjoy the quietness of suburban nights) to see a friend who lived in a Jewish neighborhood of sad and dusty streets. On that occasion Perón disappeared from the conversation, which branched off into the labyrinths of English literature that Borges loved so much. Stevenson, Kipling, Chesterton, and James filled the solitary streets with their inventions, brought to life by Borges' words. "Don't you agree?" he never tired of asking with his flawless courtesy. Quoting texts and commenting on them, developing precious hints and pursuing allusions, Borges managed to create, on the borders of the Peronist-made reality, an entire world. From those heady conversations we returned, half dazed, to sinister reality.

It was in March 1946 that he began a new literary venture, as editor of the literary journal *Los Anales de Buenos Aires,* launched by an institution modeled on the Parisian Société des Annales. Like its French counterpart, the Argentine association yearly invited internationally famous intellectuals to come to lecture in Buenos Aires; it also tapped the most brilliant local talent. The first two issues of the journal, which had been edited by the association, presented in a rather arbitrary way lectures given at the institution, pieces by more or less distinguished writers, and assorted texts. Only after Borges began to edit it did it take the shape of a literary magazine. The leading Argentine journal at the time was still *Sur,* although its position had been challenged by *Realidad* (Reality), a magazine whose subtitle, "Review of Ideas," attempted to subtly underline not only its main characteristic but one of *Sur*'s weaknesses. Borges had contributed some articles to *Realidad*—in particular one to the Cervantes issue (September–October 1947)—but he remained loyal to *Sur.* When he agreed to edit *Los Anales,* he continued to contribute to *Sur.* It was obvious to him that Buenos Aires had room for another, and different, monthly.

In a sense, *Los Anales* can be seen as two journals in one. Some of the articles reflected the institution's point of view, sedate and academic. But what gave the journal its distinction was Borges' taste and imagination. He not only included some of his friends' poems, short stories, and articles but went out of his way to find new writers who also favored imagination and had a sophisticated taste. Among the new writers he discovered for the Argentine public was a rather neglected Uruguayan surrealist, Felisberto Hernández, whose story "The Usher" was printed in the June 1946 issue. Another of his finds was Julio Cortázar. At the time, the Argentine novelist was a totally unknown short-story writer. Borges printed several of his stories and a fragment of a rather elaborate version of the myth of Theseus and the Minotaur, a piece called "The Kings" (October–December 1947).

But perhaps the most successful contributions Borges made to *Los Anales* were his own. Under his own name or under several pseudonyms, Borges enhanced the quality of the magazine. Some of his best stories, later collected in *The Aleph* (1949), were originally published in *Los Anales:* "The Immortal" (February 1947); "The Theologians" (April 1947); "The House of Asterion" (May–June 1947); "The Zahir" (July 1947). He also published there some important essays: "Apollinaire's Paradox" (August 1946); "The First Wells" (September 1946); "On Oscar Wilde" (December 1946); "Note on Walt Whitman" (March 1947); "Note on Chesterton" (October–December 1947). The last four were collected in *Other Inquisitions* (1952); the first has never been included in his books.

With the help of Adolfo Bioy Casares and under the pseudonym of B. Lynch Davis (another composite of family names), he edited a section called "Museum." Among many pieces correctly attributed to real authors and works, Borges introduced at least six that were his alone. Not until he published a volume of miscellaneous prose and verse under the title of *El hacedor* (*Dreamtigers,* 1960)—and included in it a section called "Museum"—did he acknowledge the paternity of some of the most brilliant and ironic pieces. Now the map that was so faithful that it had the dimensions and topographical characteristics of the actual country was no longer attributed to the nonexistent Suárez Miranda; the poem about what gets lost in life, and about the limitations and limits of one's own experience, no longer belonged to the 1923 Uruguayan poet Julio Platero Haedo (another combination of family and friends' names). But the most telling admission regarded a piece which had been attributed to Gaspar Camerarius and which consisted of two terse lines:

> I, who have been so many men, have never been
> The one in whose embrace Matilde Urbach swooned.
> > (*Dreamtigers,* 1964, p. 92)

Lost among the witty and strange pieces of *Los Anales'* "Museum," those two lines mean little; included at the end of a book that contained some of Borges' most personal writings, the verses have a completely different meaning. The title of the piece, in French, is "Le regret d'Heraclite" (Heraclitus' Regret). Under the double disguise of a German poet and a poetic persona (Heraclitus), Borges advertises very delicately that he will never have the woman he loves swooning in his arms. A sad, curious way of admitting his erotic powerlessness.

Los Anales de Buenos Aires came to an end at the beginning of 1948. The last issue was devoted to the Spanish poet Juan Ramón Jiménez, who was then visiting Buenos Aires, invited by the association to lecture and read his poetry. It is obvious that Borges had nothing to do with that issue. Although he had been nominally the editor from the third issue onward, the head of the association had retained some power over the journal. She was a rather formidable woman whose literary tastes did not entirely coincide with Borges'. As I was also one of the regular contributors to the journal, I had a chance to meet her. It seemed obvious to me then that she wanted to have Borges' name in the journal but that she was not terribly impressed with the way he edited it. By the end of 1947 she also seemed disappointed with the reception the magazine had. Borges and she parted company without regrets.

By the time Borges was preparing the next to last issue of *Los Anales,* Perón had discovered a new way to humiliate those Argentines who had opposed his regime from the very beginning. This time he (or

400

perhaps Evita) chose a suitable target. On September 8, 1948, a group of ladies gathered together in the afternoon to sing the national anthem on Florida Street and pass around some pamphlets. They attracted the attention of passersby, and in no time a larger group—including two Uruguayan ladies who were buying shoes in one of Florida's boutiques—was formed. As they had no permit to demonstrate in such a way, they were arrested by the police. Among the ladies were Mother and Norah. The magistrate condemned them to one month's imprisonment, but because Mother was an old woman she was confined to her own apartment, with a permanent police guard at the door. In his conversations with Richard Burgin, Borges gives his version of the story:

BORGES: She was in prison in Perón's time. My sister also.
BURGIN: Perón put them in prison?
BORGES: Yes, My sister, well, of course; the case of my mother was different because she was already an old lady—she's ninety-one now—and so her prison was her own home, no? But my sister was sent with some friends of hers to a jail for prostitutes in order to insult her. Then, she somehow smuggled a letter or two to us, I don't know how she managed it, saying that the prison was such a lovely place, that everybody was so kind, that being in prison was so restful, that it had a beautiful patio, black and white like a chessboard. In fact, she worded it so that we thought she was in some awful dungeon, no? Of course, what she really wanted us to feel—well, not to worry so much about her. She kept on saying what nice people there were, and how being in jail was much better than having to go out to cocktails or parties and so on. She was in prison with other ladies, and the other ladies told me that they felt awful about it. But my sister just said the Lord's Prayer. There were eleven in the same room, and my sister said her prayers, then she went to sleep immediately. All the time she was in jail, she didn't know how long a time might pass before she would see her husband, her children, and her mother. And afterward she told me—but this was when she was out of jail—she said that, after all, my grandfather died for this country, my great-grandfather fought the Spaniards. They did all that they could for the country. And I, by the mere fact of being in prison, I was doing something also. So this is as it should be. (Burgin, 1969, pp. 118–119)

In *El grito sagrado* (The Sacred Cry), a book published almost ten years after the event by Adela Grondona, who was imprisoned with Norah, there is a description of Norah making drawings of the inmates and transforming them into angels. She kept finding beautiful objects in prison—a colonnade here, a face there—and kept up her spirits by singing, drawing, and praying. Her letters reflected her own magic vision of life.

The women were kept in prison for a month, but the sentence

401

might have been reduced if they had appealed directly to Mrs. Perón. Borges recalls the incident in his conversations with Burgin:

BORGES: They said, "If you write a letter to the Señora, you'll get out."—"What señora are you talking about?"—"This señora is Señora Perón."—"Well, as we don't know her, and she doesn't know us, it's quite meaningless for us to write to her." But what they really wanted was that those ladies would write a letter, and then they would publish it, no? And the people would say how merciful Perón was, and how we were free now. The whole thing was a kind of trick, it *was* a trick. But they saw through it. That was the kind of thing they had to undergo at the time.

BURGIN: It was a horrible time.

BORGES: Oh, it was. For example, when you have a toothache, when you have to go to the dentist, the first thing that you think about when you wake up is the whole ordeal; but during some ten years, of course, I had my personal grievances too, but in those ten years the first thing I thought about when I was awake was, well, "Perón is in power." (Burgin, 1969, p. 120)

To endure Perón: that was the main problem for Borges during those dark days. Buenos Aires was, to him, an occupied city.

9.
The Writer at Fifty

At the very time when Perón's government seemed more determined than ever to humiliate Borges and his family, his work was reaching full maturity. During those years he produced some of his best fiction and essays, paving the way for the publication of two of his most important books: *The Aleph* (1949) and *Other Inquisitions* (1952). Harassed or ignored by the official and corrupt Argentine press, forced to lecture to make a living, Borges was just then beginning to be acknowledged as Argentina's most distinguished writer and the best prose stylist in the Spanish language. The contrast between his public ignominy and his private distinction helps to explain the new dimension his work acquired. At the time, Borges represented not only an emergent culture; he also represented the dignity of the Latin American writer. He performed the role of writer in the public consciousness. This is what Perón, and his cultural advisers, could not destroy. Undaunted, Borges pursued his quest. It was a specifically literary quest, but in the context of the Argentina of those years it also had the dimensions of a moral quest.

One of the key texts was a slim pamphlet Borges published in 1947 under the title, "A New Refutation of Time." It was printed privately by the apocryphal publishing house Oportet & Haereses, which had also published two Biorges books in 1946. The essay was later included in *Other Inquisitions* (1952). It incorporated ideas about time which had appeared in pieces Borges wrote over the last twenty years. The earliest piece, a sort of autobiographical fantasy, was published in *El idioma de los argentinos* (The Language of the Argentines, 1928). Other treatments of the subject appeared in *Discusión* (1932) and *Historia de la eternidad* (History of Eternity, 1936). The point of departure for this new exploration of time was the writings of the British philosophical idealists. Borges observes: "Berkeley denied that there was an object behind some impressions. David Hume denied that there was a subject behind the perception of changes. Berkeley denied matter; Hume denied the spirit. Berkeley did not wish us to add the metaphysical notion of matter to the succession of impressions, while Hume did not wish us to add the metaphysical notion of a self to the succession of mental states" (*Inquisitions*, 1964, p. 180).

Following these philosophers to their ultimate conclusions, Borges also denies the existence of time: "Nevertheless, having denied matter and spirit, which are continuities, and having denied space also, I do not know with what right we shall retain the continuity that is time. Outside of each perception (actual or conjectural) matter does not exist; outside of each mental state the spirit does not exist; nor will time exist outside of each present instant" (ibid., pp. 183–184). To reinforce his arguments, Borges quotes from Schopenhauer. The German philosopher had observed: "No one has lived in the past, no one will live in the future; the present is the form of all life, it is a possession that no misfortune can take away" (ibid., p. 186). This conviction, which Borges reasons through and finally accepts, was not just the end product of his readings or the final step in an intellectual argument. It had its roots in an experience which might aptly be termed an illumination, if the word could be divorced from its occult connotations—an idea that Borges would flatly reject.

The experience is described in a piece written in 1928, "Sentirse en muerte" (Feeling in Death), later included in *Other Inquisitions*. It happened in the poverty-stricken outskirts of Buenos Aires. One evening, contemplating a simple rose-colored streetcorner, Borges felt that time had come to a halt and that past and present were the same thing. "This is the same as it was thirty years ago," he thought. Out of this uncanny experience, Borges concluded that

> that pure representation of homogeneous facts—clear night, limpid wall, rural scent of honeysuckle, elemental clay—is not merely identical to the scene on that corner so many years ago; it is, without similarities or repetitions, the same. If we can perceive that identity, time is a delusion; the indifference and inseparability of one moment of time's apparent yesterday and another of its apparent today are enough to disintegrate it. (Ibid., pp. 179–180)

The hallucinatory experience of time standing still, of a visible and palpable eternity, which Borges had that night, helped him not only to dispose of time but also to negate his personal identity. Faced with destructible time, Borges felt his identity annihilated: he felt transformed

404

into an "abstract perceiver of the world." What he discovered was the impersonal identity of the perceiver and the object perceived. Time was abolished for him not because he felt eternal or because he believed his art capable of preserving him forever in the eternity of his work—all the feelings romantic poets had exalted—but because he, Borges, was nobody.

Nevertheless—and in spite of that conclusion—the essay on time does not end there. In a somersault that is characteristic of all his work, Borges denies in the last paragraph all that the long essay has tried vainly to prove:

> And yet, and yet—To deny temporal succession, to deny the ego, to deny the astronomical universe, are apparent desperations and secret assuagements. Our destiny (unlike the hell of Swedenborg and the hell of Tibetan mythology) is not horrible because of its unreality; it is horrible because it is irreversible and ironbound. Time is the substance I am made of. Time is a river that carries me away, but I am the river; it is a tiger that mangles me, but I am the tiger; it is a fire that consumes me, but I am the fire. The world, alas, is real; I, alas, am Borges. (Ibid., pp. 186–187)

That is not his only denial. The whole essay lies under the sign of contradiction. In a preface to it Borges emphasizes the pun implicit in its title:

> A word about the title. I am not unaware that it is an example of the monster which logicians have called *contradictio in adjecto,* because to say that a refutation of time is new (or old) is to attribute to it a predicate of a temporal nature, which restores the notion that the subject attempts to destroy. But I shall let it stand, so that this very subtle joke may prove that I do not exaggerate the importance of these word games. Apart from that, our language is so saturated and animated with time that it is very possible that not one line in this book does not somehow demand or invoke it. (Ibid., p. 172)

Neither the irony of the title nor the final rectification succeeds in obliterating his basic intuition of the world's lack of reality, of one man's lack of personal identity. Against the arguments of metaphysics, or logic, or language (the world is real, time exists; Borges, alas, is Borges), the inner vision, the hallucinatory experience, and the literary fiction continue to struggle, offering opposing theses.

The pamphlet was printed in May 1947 and circulated privately among Borges' friends. Even more secret was a piece he wrote with Bioy Casares in November of the same year. It is one of Biorges' stories. Called "La fiesta del monstruo" (The Monster's Celebration), it circulated only in typed copies, among the trusted few. In a grotesque language which is a baroque exaggeration of *lunfardo* (Buenos Aires slang), the protagonist, a Peronist worker from a lower-class district, describes his participation in one of the party's greatest rallies. The story is told in all its comic or sordid details by a witness who is unaware of his own baseness. A satirical description of a type and a class, the story also lampoons the demogoguery of Perón and his friends. The humor is savage and the parody grotesque. But what makes the story unique is its central episode, in which a young intellectual Jew is murdered by the mob for refusing to shout Peronist slogans. The anecdote may seem farfetched today, but episodes of this kind were not uncommon in Buenos Aires at the time Perón was consolidating his power. Among his allies then was a vociferous Nazi group called the Alliance, which made the harassment and beating of Jews one of its specialties. Perón once condemned these practices, but he never ordered the police to interfere with the Alliance.

To publish "The Monster's Celebration" was impossible while Perón was in power. Even the circulation of typed copies was dangerous enough. Perón had made clear that he would not tolerate public opposition. In 1955, after his overthrow, the story was published in the Uruguayan weekly *Marcha,* whose literary section I then edited.

Among the many lectures Borges gave in Montevideo during the Peronist years, one was outstanding. It was dedicated to fantastic literature and was delivered on September 2, 1949. Some of the points of view he presented in that lecture had already been advanced in articles collected in *Discusión,* as far back as 1932, or published in *El Hogar* or *Sur* and *La Nación* during the 1930s and 1940s, especially in the 1940 prologue to *The Invention of Morel,* Bioy Casares' science-fiction novel. Two of the articles published in *La Nación*—"The Flower of Coleridge" (September 23, 1945) and "Partial Enchantments of the *Quixote*" (November 6, 1949)—were instrumental in shaping his views of the genre. They were collected in *Other Inquisitions,* thus preserving the substance of what Borges said so brilliantly in Montevideo.

After stating in his lecture that the literature of fantasy was older than that of realism, Borges outlined four procedures which allow the writer to destroy not only the conventions of realistic fiction but also those of reality. According to Borges, these procedures are the work of art inside the work of art, the contamination of reality by dream, travel through time, and the double. One observation which immediately comes to mind is that, with the exception of the first, these so-called procedures can be seen as subjects more than as technical devices. A work may show thematically how reality is contaminated by a dream; it can include travel in time or present doubles. But Borges was talking specifically about procedures. His implicit perspective was that of a critic who is discussing how to structure a plot. From that point of view (which he did not elucidate but assumed his listeners understood), the contamination of reality by dream, time travel, and the double are not just subjects but procedures used in the structuring of a plot. They belong to the formal and not to the thematic fabric of the story.

With this caveat, it is possible to follow his arguments. He found examples of the first procedure—the work of art inside the work of art—in many famous books: in the second part of the *Quixote* some of the characters have read, and do discuss, the first part; in *Hamlet* the players who visit Elsinore perform, in Act III, a tragedy that bears some similarity to the main one; in the *Aeneid,* the protagonist examines in Carthage a bas relief that depicts the destruction of Troy, and he sees himself among the figures there represented; in the *Iliad* Helen embroiders a double purple gown which represents the story of the poem. The procedure can be recognized in Borges' own stories. In "The Garden of Forking Paths" the labyrinth and the novel described by the Sinologist mirror the story's structure. But Borges has also inverted the procedure: instead of certifying the reality of his stories by introducing one part of them inside their own narrative structure, he has inserted contemporary reality into his strangest fictions. Thus, to avoid any suspicion about the existence of the apocryphal encyclopedia of Tlön, in the story of the same name, he has padded its pages with the names of real persons, from Adolfo Bioy Casares, who starts the quest by a seemingly innocent quotation of a text from Uqbar, to Enrique Amorim, who is with "Borges" at the time one of the magical objects from Tlön is produced. Another variant of the same procedure leads Borges to imagine that the text he is supposed to write has already been written by somebody else, and that his story is a review, or an article, about that book. "The Approach to al-Mu'tasim," "An Examination of the Work of Herbert Quain," and the famous "Pierre Menard" are examples of that procedure.

The second procedure, that of introducing images of a dream which alter reality, is one of the oldest. Borges mentions the folklore of many countries and finds in Coleridge a tantalizing quotation: "If a man could pass through Paradise in a dream, and have a flower presented to him as a pledge that his soul had really been there, and if he found that flower in his hand when he awoke—Ay!—and what then?" In one of his most famous stories, "The Circular Ruins," which has as an epigraph a quotation from another weaver of dreams, Lewis Carroll, Borges plays with the blurred limits between reality and dream: a man who has dreamed another discovers at the end that he is somebody else's dream.

In discussing the third procedure, time travel, Borges notes that it can be combined with Coleridge's flower. As an example, he cites H. G. Wells' novel *The Time Machine,* in which the protagonist, on returning from a trip to the future, brings back a faded flower. In another variation, Henry James once projected and half completed a novel, *The Sense of the Past,* in which the protagonist discovers an eighteenth-century portrait of himself and travels back in time to allow the painter to portray him. Borges observes: "James thus creates an incomparable *regressus in infinitum,* when his hero Ralph Pendrel returns to the eighteenth century because he is fascinated by an old painting, but Pendrel's return to this century is a condition for the existence of the painting. The cause follows the effect, the reason for the journey is one of the consequences of the journey" (*Inquisitions,* 1964, p. 12).

In submitting James' novel to that analysis, Borges clearly shows that he is thinking of travel in time not as a theme but as a procedure, a device to construct a plot in which the consequences engender the cause, and the narrative sequence is completely inverted. This is precisely what he attempted in the story "The Other Death," in which a man who behaved cowardly in a battle when he was very young corrects that cowardice on his deathbed and forces God into performing a miracle: in the memory of those who attended the battle he dies heroically and young. Again, what matters to Borges is not just the subject of the inversion of time but the procedure of inverting the sequence inside the plot: the consequence influences the cause, not the other way around.

The last procedure discussed in Borges' lecture, that of the double, had been used by Poe in "William Wilson" and by James in "The Jolly Corner." Borges' stories are full of doubles. In "Three Versions of Judas" a theologian advances the theory that God is incarnate in the betrayer and not the betrayed; in "Theme of the Traitor and the Hero" one man is successively both; in "The Theologians," in the divinity's eyes, the two antagonists engaged in an endless religious dispute are the same person. But in presenting the theme of the double, Borges has always shown a greater interest in the effects of the theme on the structure of the story than in its value as a subject. The first two stories mentioned are written in such a way that each successive unfolding of the plot implies a new "doubling" of its matter and a new articulation of the whole sequence. In the last example, what really matters to God is the fact that each theological argument used can be inverted to prove its contrary. It is not the opposed and symmetrical destinies of the theologians that make the texture of the story but this constant inversion of the theological arguments: the inversion, in this case, matches the inverted structure of the plot.

At the end of the lecture Borges explicitly states that against the common belief that fantastic literature is an evasion of reality he postulates that fantastic literature helps us to understand reality in a deeper and more complex way. That type of literature is a metaphorical version of reality. The two examples he quotes (Wells' *The Invisible Man* and Kafka's *The Trial*) help him to prove that in both cases the central subject is man's alienation. The same can be said about his own fictions. Under the guise of describing a remote planet, Borges presents a nihilistic view of our planet, the Orbis Tertius of the title; the lottery in Babylon and the library of Babel are metaphors of the labyrinthine fate that governs man and shapes his enigmatic existence. The real world permeates Borges' fantastic fiction to the point where it is almost impossible to draw the line between what is reality and what is fantasy.

10.
The Meeting in a Dream

On June 26, 1949, a new book of short stories by Borges was published by Losada in Buenos Aires. Its title, *The Aleph,* was also the title of the last story. As Borges himself observes in a short epilogue to the book, all the stories except two belong to the "fantastic genre." The two exceptions are "Emma Zunz" and "The Story of the Warrior and the Captive." When "Emma Zunz" was announced in *Sur,* before its publication, it was advertised as "a realistic story." In a sense, it is. The plot (according to the epilogue) had been suggested to Borges by a friend, Cecilia Ingenieros. With his usual modesty, he claims that the plot is "superior to its execution." Perhaps. What is clear is that the plot itself is not terribly realistic. A young woman wants to avenge the death of her father, who committed suicide after being cheated by a business associate. Her revenge takes an odd form: she will accuse the culprit of rape and then murder him for it. To achieve this end, she allows herself to be raped by an unknown sailor; then she goes to visit her father's business associate on a pretext and kills him. When the police come, she can prove that she has been raped.

Borges' terse commentary at the end of the story reveals the mechanism of the revenge: "Actually, the story [she told to the police] *was* incredible, but it impressed everyone because substantially it was true. True was Emma Zunz's tone, true was her shame, true was her hate. True was also the outrage she had suffered: only the circumstances were false, the time, and one or two proper names" (*Labyrinths,* 1962, p. 137). Borges' conclusion underlines the basic "unreality" of the story. Although everything in "Emma Zunz" is realistic, in the sense that it conforms to the principle of verisimilitude, the situation itself is "incredible." From the standpoint of believability, the plot is a failure: a good detective could have proved, by a careful examination of the

410

man's body, that he could not have raped her. But what makes the story basically "unrealistic" is the fact that the whole plot is based on the fantastic behavior of the protagonist. "Emma Zunz" belongs, with Melville's Bartleby and Kafka's characters, to that fictional race of beings whose behavior is strange, "unbelievable."

In his prologue to the Spanish version of *Bartleby, the Scrivener,* Borges discusses this type of fantastic story. The end of his own story is typically Borgesian. It tells us that although Emma Zunz was lying, she was essentially telling the truth. She had been raped; the identity of the rapist (and the fact that she consented willingly) was irrelevant. What matters is the fact that an action committed by one man can be atoned for by another. It is the identity between men, not the differences in their personalities and individual acts, that is the real subject of the story. The so-called realistic story has been deprived of a basic element of realism: a compact between reader and writer, a system of conventions that allows the perfect communication of an accepted, and coded, reading of reality. By altering this compact, by introducing some small details that contradict it, and by finally brazenly declaring that Emma's fictional story "was substantially true," Borges violates the compact and creates a type of fantastic behavior that justifies a fantastic reading of "reality."

The other story which, in Borges' view, interprets reality faithfully is another example of strange and even fantastic behavior. Both the warrior and the captive of the title behave in a way that contradicts the expectations of their societies. The warrior is Droctfult, a barbarian who switches sides and dies defending the cause of Ravenna; the captive is an Englishwoman who is kidnapped by an Indian chieftain and becomes a savage. (The story was told to Georgie by Grandmother Haslam, who actually met the woman.) Their opposite destinies are underlined by Borges:

> A thousand three hundred years and the ocean lie between the destiny of the captive and the destiny of Droctfult. Both of these, now, are equally irrecoverable. The figure of the barbarian who embraced the cause of Ravenna, the figure of the European woman who chose the wasteland, may seem antagonistic. And yet, both were swept away by a secret impulse, an impulse more profound than reason, and both heeded this impulse, which they would not have known how to justify. Perhaps the stories I have related are one single story. The obverse and the reverse of this coin are, for God, the same. (*Labyrinths,* 1962, pp. 130–131)

Again, the characters' individual destinies are telescoped into a single, somehow impersonal destiny. The point of view of God is introduced at the end to abolish personal identity.

411

The same mechanism is used by Borges in another of *The Aleph*'s stories, "The Theologians," in which two men fight each other to prove the validity of their opposed theories only to discover, when both are dead and are facing God, that to the divine mind they are the same person. Borges' commentary on this story in the epilogue to the book is symptomatic: he calls it "a dream, a rather melancholic dream, about personal identity." But the only thing that separates that "dream" from "The Story of the Warrior and the Captive" is the fact that what is presented as a part of the story in "The Theologians" (both men face God in the kingdom of heaven) is presented only as a theoretical argument at the end of "The Story of the Warrior and The Captive." The viewpoint, and the concept of reality it implies, is the same.

The other ten stories in *The Aleph* belong to different levels of the fantastic. The first story, "The Immortal," is about a man who at one time may have been Homer and who is now a twentieth-century antiquary interested in Homer's texts and translations. In his epilogue Borges describes the story as "a draft of an ethics for immortals," but a better description might be that it allegorizes the fate of classical texts, which begin by being read as poetry and end up by being the pasture of scholars. In the narrative Borges parodies the conversion of a poem into a pretext for copious footnotes. The story begins with an almost symbolist reconstruction of the discovery of the City of Immortals by a Roman soldier; after a number of chapters which become more and more clustered with bibiliographic information, Borges concludes with a mere postscript in which the quotations have taken over. The story can thus be read as an allegory of reading.

The next story, "The Dead Man," presents the fate of a young man who joins a group of Uruguayan smugglers and very easily deposes its old chief—taking away his power, his favorite horse, and even his woman—only to discover that he has been allowed to do all that because the old man had, from the very beginning, condemned him to death. The story, set in Uruguay in the 1890s, could be considered realistic except that the old man's behavior is too eccentric and conforms too well to Borges' notion of an irrational fate. In the epilogue to the first edition he observes that the old man is "a rough divinity, a mulatto and barbaric version of Chesterton's incomparable Sunday" (*El Aleph,* 1949, p. 145).

Of the other stories, at least two are variations on existing works. "The Biography of Tadeo Isidoro Cruz (1829–1874)" is a development of a character in Hernández's *Martín Fierro,* but taken from an angle that makes it almost unrecognizable until the very end. Again, it is the story of a man who (like Droctfult and the captive) switches his allegiances at a crucial moment in life to become the opposite of what he was: a police officer ordered to capture the deserter Martín Fierro, he is so impressed by Fierro's courage that he sides with him and becomes an outlaw too.

The other variation on a famous work is more subtle. In "The House of Asterion" Borges retells the myth of the Minotaur from the point of view of the monster, a perspective suggested to him by a Watts painting which showed the Minotaur on a balcony sadly viewing the open country. Borges explains in the epilogue that he owes the story "and the character of its poor protagonist" to Watts' painting. The key word here is the adjective "poor."

A story remotely connected with a famous text is "The Other Death." Borges obviously was inspired by the character of Pier Damiani, whom he discovered in Dante's *Divine Comedy*. But the story itself (about a man who dies twice, first as a coward in bed, then as a valiant soldier in battle) is set in one of the gaucho provinces of Uruguay at the beginning of this century. (Perhaps because the story is located in my home state, Borges gives me a very minor role in the tale: I am supposed to be the person who writes a letter of introduction to one of the main characters.)

Another story, "Deutsches Requiem," was written to interpret the suicidal destiny of Germany. In the epilogue Borges observes: "In the last war, nobody could have wanted more than I that Germany should be defeated; nobody could have felt more than I the tragedy of German destiny; 'Deutsches Requiem' attempts to understand that destiny, which our 'Germanophiles' (who know nothing about Germany) were not able to lament, or to understand" (*ibid.*, p. 146). He also indicates the sources of the last three stories. One, "The God's Script," attributes to a Mayan priest "arguments of a cabalist or a theologian." So much for Borges' respect for accurate scholarship. Both "The Zahir" and "The Aleph" (which deal with a magic object and a magic place respectively) show the influence of one Wells story, "The Crystal Egg."

As usual with Borges, his comments on *The Aleph*'s stories are modest, giving little indication of their real value. This is especially true of "The Zahir" and "The Aleph." Both stories are deceptively simple. In both the protagonist is Borges, or really "Borges": a character who has the same name as the author but is not the author; he is a persona. In "The Zahir" Borges uses the cabalistic superstition of a magical coin to weave the story of a man who becomes obsessed with a twenty-cent Argentine coin he received at a bar. He gets rid of the coin but cannot stop thinking about it and eventually becomes haunted by its image. The fact that he received the coin after coming from the wake of Clementina Villar helps us to understand the erotic meaning of that obsession: the coin is a symbol of Clementina. To be obsessed by it is a way

413

of saying he is obsessed by her—by her beauty, her disdainful character, the unforgettable memory of her. But Borges being Borges, he has to disguise the erotic fixation with his erudite, cabalistic narrative.

A similar situation is explored in "The Aleph." This time the woman's name is Beatriz Viterbo; like Clementina, she is a brilliant society woman who utterly despises the narrator. But "The Aleph" is a much more elaborate story. Beatriz Viterbo's portrait is paralleled by the portrait of her cousin Carlos Argentino Daneri, a pompous poet whose ambition to describe the whole world in a poem is mercilessly satirized by the narrator. And the magical object here is not a coin but a point in Daneri's cellar where the whole world can be seen at once. If in "The Zahir" the erudite allusions distract the reader from the story's secret center ("Borges'" obsession with Clementina Villar), in "The Aleph" the obsession is plainly presented; what is displaced is the model the story is based on. "The Aleph" is really a parodic reduction of the *Divine Comedy*. From that point of view, "Borges" is Dante, Beatriz Viterbo is Beatrice Portinari (as disdainful of the Florentine poet as the Argentine Beatriz is of the author), and Carlos Argentino Daneri is both Dante and Virgil. His name, Daneri, telescopes the Florentine's complete name (*Dante Alighieri*); like Virgil, he is a didactic poet and a guide to the vision of the other world. And the Aleph Borges so beautifully describes in the crucial episode of the story can be seen as a reduction of Dante's vision of the world. There is one major difference: Borges attempts in the short space of two pages to convey what Dante (very wisely) refused to do in the conclusion to his *Comedy:* to describe the ineffable. Using the Whitmanesque device of the anaphora, Borges, in order to describe a point in space which simultaneously contains all points in space and in time, resorts to a dazzling and chaotic enumeration.

The parody is so subtly achieved that many readers of Borges who also are devoted readers of Dante fail to recognize it. But it is plainly there, especially in the comical and ironic allusions to each character's foibles and obsessions. As with all parodical reductions, "The Aleph" is both irreverent and admiring. Even the person to whom Borges dedicates the story, a young Argentine writer named Estela Canto, has the right Dantesque name: Estela (Stella) was the word Dante chose to end each of the three Cantiche of the *Divine Comedy;* Canto was the name of each division in each Cantica. But the name "Estela Canto" also means, in Spanish, "I sing to Estela." At the time Borges wrote the story, he was more than ready to sing to that particular Estela. As homage, he gave her the manuscript, in his own minuscule handwriting, of "The Aleph."

Some critics have attempted to identify Beatriz Viterbo; it is a pointless task. She belongs, with Clementina Villar, to the category of the temptress, the femme fatale, la Belle Dame Sans Merci. She is less a woman than a prototype, and the fact that Borges used the same prototype in two stories that are so basically different proves the pointlessness of any identification. What really mattered to him was that Beatriz Viterbo, or Clementina Villar, belonged to the same category as Dante's Beatrice. Thus the best way to try to find out more about them is to read what Borges has to say about Dante, and Beatrice, in his introduction to a Spanish translation of the *Divine Comedy,* included in a collection of classics (Buenos Aires, Clásicos Jackson, vol. 31) the same year *The Aleph* was published.

In the introduction Borges provides the necessary information for the casual reader: a discussion of the date of composition of the poem and the meaning of its title; a description of the poem's topography, chronology, and symbolic meaning; and a commentary on the best editions, with a strong recommendation to read the text in the original. But the best part of the introduction is the specific analysis of a few episodes: the meetings with Ulysses (*Inferno,* XXVI), Ugolino (*Inferno,* XXXIV), and Beatrice (*Purgatorio,* XXXI). To the centuries of discussion of these famous episodes Borges brings a new and unconventional critical mind. Borges later published his comments on the meeting with Beatrice as a separate essay in *Other Inquisitions* under the title of "The Meeting in a Dream." After describing the episode, and insisting on the way Beatrice scolded and humiliated Dante, he quotes an observation made in 1946 by the German critic Theophil Spoerri: "Undoubtedly Dante himself had imagined that meeting differently. Nothing in the previous pages indicates that the greatest humiliation of his life awaited him there." In an attempt to explain Beatrice's severity, Borges comments:

> To fall in love is to create a religion that has a fallible god. That Dante professed an idolatrous adoration for Beatrice is a truth that does not bear contradicting; that she once ridiculed him and another time rebuffed him are facts recorded by the *Vita nuova.* . . . Dante, when Beatrice was dead, when Beatrice was lost forever, played with the idea of finding her, to mitigate his sorrow. I believe that he erected the triple architecture of his poem simply to insert that encounter. Then what usually happens in dreams happened to him. In adversity we dream of good fortune, and the intimate awareness that we cannot attain it is enough to corrupt our dream, clouding it with sad restraints. That was the case with Dante. Refused forever by Beatrice, he dreamed of Beatrice, but he dreamed her very austere, but he dreamed her inaccessible, but he dreamed her in a chariot drawn by a lion that was a bird and was all bird or all lion when it was reflected in her eyes (*Purgatorio,* XXXI, 121). Those facts can be the prefiguration of a night-

mare, which is set forth and described at length in the following canto. . . . Infinitely Beatrice existed for Dante; Dante existed very little, perhaps not at all, for Beatrice. Our piety, our veneration cause us to forget that pitiful inharmony, which was unforgettable for Dante. I read and reread about the vicissitudes of their illusory encounter, and I think of two lovers who were dreamed by Alighieri in the hurricane of the Second Circle and who are dark emblems, although he perhaps neither knew that nor intended it, of the happiness he did not attain. I think of Francesca and of Paolo, united forever in their Hell. *Questi, che mai da me non fia diviso.* With frightening love, with anxiety, with admiration, with envy, Dante must have formed that line. (*Inquisitions*, 1964, pp. 99–100)

At the beginning of his introduction to the *Divine Comedy* Borges describes an imaginary engraving—Arabic or Chinese—in which everything that ever was or would ever be is represented. Dante's poem (observes Borges) is that engraving. Or, to use a different symbol, Dante's poem is an Aleph. Which brings us back to the story. To read "The Aleph" after reading Borges' introduction to the poem is to realize how much of his interpretation of that meeting between Beatrice and Dante went into the fabric of his story. "Borges" (the character) has his Beatriz Viterbo. Like Dante's, although in a crueler more degrading way, she does not care very much for her devoted lover; like Beatrice, she dies leaving him with no hope of meeting her again except in a dream (a poem or the story); as in Dante, the dream turns into a nightmare. "Borges" comes out of his vision as humiliated as the Florentine. The story is also a microcosm (an Aleph) in the same sense that Dante's poem is. But, of course, in reducing the theological sublimities of the model to the grotesque level of his story, Borges is practicing one of his favorite tricks: the parodic miniaturization of a vast work of art. He had already attempted it with his "Pierre Menard, Author of the *Quixote*" and with "Tlön, Uqbar, Orbis Tertius" (the model here was Thomas More's *Utopia*). But he has never been more successful than in "The Aleph," because the process of miniaturization and the outrageous level on which the parody works are so radical that many readers miss the obvious clues contained in Beatriz Viterbo's name, in Carlos Argentino Daneri's insane poem, and in "Borges" ' quest, which leads him to the vision of the Aleph (Dante's microcosm) in the cellar of an old Buenos Aires house.

In a note Borges wrote for the American edition of *The Aleph* he ambiguously disclaims any parodic intention: "Critics . . . have detected Beatrice Portinari in Beatriz Viterbo, Dante in Daneri, and the descent into hell in the descent into the cellar. I am, of course, duly grateful for these unlooked-for gifts" (*The Aleph*, 1970, p. 264). Borges' modesty is really too much. The coincidences between the two texts are not exclusively the ones he indicates; they are more complex and pro-liferate even further, as we have seen. But Borges always prefers to keep one side of his texts (the best, generally) out of public scrutiny. Nevertheless, in a conclusion to this note he acknowledges that "Beatriz Viterbo really existed and I was very much and hopelessly in love with her. I wrote my story after her death" (ibid., p. 264). The statement, needless to say, enriches the parodical reading of the story.

He also comments in that note that Carlos Argentino Daneri also exists and that he is a good friend of his "who to this day has never suspected he is in the story. The verses are a parody of his verse. Daneri's speech on the other hand is not an exaggeration but a fair rendering. The Argentine Academy of Letters is the habitat of such specimens" (ibid., p. 264). This last observation not only reinforces the assumption of a parodical transposition but shows very clearly another dimension of the story. In satirizing the habits of his compatriots, the vanity of their literary prizes and academic associations, Borges vents his feelings about the humiliation he was subjected to at the time his first collection of fantastic stories, *The Garden of Forking Paths,* came out. "The Aleph" was written and originally published in *Sur* in September 1945, when Borges was still smarting from that snub. But when the story came out in the 1949 volume, Perón's regime had given him a dif-ferent and more grotesque motive for feeling humiliated. Sordid real-ity had taken over from grotesque literary life.

11.
A Useless Debate

At fifty, Borges was on his way to becoming "Borges." He was not the young man who had signed those early poems in Europe or the man whose many volumes of essays, poems, and short stories had been published in Argentina during the 1930s and 1940s. He was beginning to be a persona: a mask behind which the young man and the mature man could hide; a mask which was immediately recognizable because it was a simplified and exalted version of the man. *The Aleph* (1949) and *Other Inquisitions* (1952) helped to define that persona. But it was not until the end of the 1950s that the persona took over, and Borges irrevocably became "Borges."

The "Borges" persona attracted a court of beautiful young women who functioned as erotic (not sexual) companions and/or as secretaries and even collaborators in his many-sided literary output. In the 1930s and early 1940s Borges had been at pains to gather around him a group of faithful young men who were ready to die for him (metaphorically speaking, of course). In the late 1940s and throughout the rest of his literary career Borges was surrounded by a group of young women who were eager to devote their intelligence and sensitivity to help, protect, and thoroughly spoil him.

One of the first of these young women was the beautiful Silvina Bullrich, with whom Borges compiled, in 1945, an anthology on Argentine hoodlums. Deeper and more complex was his relationship with Estela Canto, the young novelist to whom he dedicated "The Aleph." They saw each other regularly, spent some holidays together, and exchanged literary views. When *The Aleph* came out, Estela wrote a perceptive review for *Sur* (October 1949). The following month, to celebrate the twenty-fifth anniversary of the publication of the periodical

Martín Fierro, she published in *Nueva Gaceta* (November 7, 1949) a long interview with Borges. It soon became obvious that they had more than a literary relationship, but apparently Borges could not let himself go emotionally. Their friendship was complicated by his reticence and eventually ended.

Other young women took over. Borges began to be seen as a sort of Argentine Professor Higgins who mesmerized women into becoming, for a while at least, full-scale intellectuals. Like the Shavian Pygmalion, he fell in love with his creations but was too inconstant to pursue the matter to its utmost consequences. This legend was, as usual, based on some reality, but it was a legend nevertheless. In Borges' everyday life, what really mattered was the friendly company, the erotic stimuli produced by the young women; the series of books he produced with their help was less important.

One of the most successful of these books was a manual called *Ancient Germanic Literatures,* which he published in 1951 (Mexico, Fondo de Cultura Económica) with the collaboration of Delia Ingenieros, a sister to that Cecilia who had given him the plot of "Emma Zunz." The book was a restatement of the questions Borges had raised, in 1933, in his article on the metaphors of the ancient Icelandic poets. Borges' knowledge of the subject was insufficient to produce a truly scholarly manual, so in 1966 he published a revised version, *Medieval Germanic Literatures* (Buenos Aires, Falbro Editor), compiled this time with the help of a new Galatea, María Esther Vázquez. Even this second version proved to be faulty. He is still working on a new version of the same book.

In the meantime, between 1951 and 1955, he published four works with the help of various young women: *El "Martín Fierro,"* a rewriting of his essays on gaucho literature, done with Margarita Guerrero (Buenos Aires, Columba, 1953); "The Lost Image," a scenario for a ballet, signed in 1953 with Bettina Edelberg; *Leopoldo Lugones,* a collection of old and new pieces on the Argentine poet, compiled also with the help of Bettina Edelberg (Buenos Aires, Troquel, 1955); and *La hermana de Eloísa,* a collection of short stories by Borges and María Luisa Levinson, one of which was written in collaboration (Buenos Aires, Ene, 1955). None of these ventures was really important or new, and the titles could be omitted from Borges' bibliography without any visible damage; but they expanded Borges' literary empire, adding small, quaint provinces.

Those were years of great productivity. Borges continued his collaboration with Adolfo Bioy Casares. No less than four books came out as a result before the end of 1955: *The Best Detective Stories,* a companion to the 1946 anthology (Buenos Aires, Emecé, 1951); *The Hood-*

lums and *The Paradise of the Believers,* two film scripts which the authors claimed had failed to interest Argentine movie producers (Buenos Aires, Losada, 1955); *Short and Extraordinary Tales,* an idiosyncratic anthology (Buenos Aires, Raigal, 1955); and *Gaucho Poetry,* which in two volumes collected the masterpieces of a genre both compilers adored (Mexico, Fondo de Cultura Económica, 1955).

On his own, Borges published in 1951 a selection of his most popular stories under the title of one of the stories, *Death and the Compass* (Buenos Aires, Emecé). In Paris the same year Roger Caillois published a translation of *Ficciones,* which included as a prologue Néstor Ibarra's essay on Borges. It was the beginning of Borges' following in France. Two years later another collection of stories, *Labyrinths,* was included by Caillois in La Croix du Sud (The Southern Cross), a series on Latin American literature he was then editing. As if to celebrate Borges' new status, Emecé decided to begin printing his complete works in a series of slim gray volumes edited by José Edmundo Clemente. The first volume came out in 1953. It was a reissue of a 1936 book, *History of Eternity.* An expanded edition of Borges' 1943 book of poems and of the 1935 *Universal History of Infamy* were added to the series in 1954. Borges himself was not terribly impressed. The only comment that the publication of his complete works elicits from him in his "Autobiographical Essay" is deprecatory. In talking about his first books of essays, written and published in the 1920s, he says:

> Three of the four essay collections—whose names are best forgotten—I have never allowed to be reprinted. In fact, when in 1953 my present publisher—Emecé—proposed to bring out my "complete writings," the only reason I accepted was that it would allow me to keep those preposterous volumes suppressed. This reminds me of Mark Twain's suggestion that a fine library could be started by leaving out the works of Jane Austen, and that even if that library contained no other books it would still be a fine library, since her books were left out. ("Essay," 1970, pp. 230–231)

Despite his facetiousness, in 1953 the publication of his complete works must have meant something to him. Perón's disdainful and even humiliating treatment had not kept Borges from being recognized as a major Argentine writer. The slim gray volumes reached a new generation of readers, avid young university students or recent graduates who had had till then little opportunity to read Borges' earlier works. They became the avant-garde of a new readership—devoted but also polemical—that turned Borges into Argentina's most controversial and influential writer.

The most important of all the books Borges published during this phase of his career was *Other Inquisitions* (1952). It is a collection of thirty-nine essays which he had selected from among the many he wrote in the late 1930s and 1940s. The title of the volume alludes to Borges' first book of essays, *Inquisitions,* published in 1925. It is as if the writer wants to underline both the continuity of his quest (his inquiring spirit) and the difference in the style of the quest (it was another). In commenting on the collection in an epilogue, Borges makes no attempt to play down its miscellaneous character: "As I corrected the proofs of this volume, I discovered two tendencies in these miscellaneous essays" (*Inquisitions,* 1964, p. 189). At the same time, he subtly indicates the unity behind the plurality of views:

> The first tendency is to evaluate religious or philosophical ideas on the basis of their esthetic worth and even for what is singular and marvelous about them. Perhaps this is an indication of a basic skepticism. The other tendency is to presuppose (and to verify) that the number of fables or metaphors of which men's imagination is capable is limited, but that these few inventions can be all things for all men, like the Apostle. (Ibid., p. 189)

Many of the essays illustrate the first tendency—"Pascal's Sphere," "Time and J. W. Dunne," "The Creation and P. H. Goose," "The Biathanatos," "Pascal," "Avatars of the Tortoise"—but the best example is "A New Refutation of Time," the essay he had anticipated in a 1947 pamphlet. An exposition of his view of reality, the essay also testifies to Borges' skepticism regarding scientific or philosophical explanations of the world.

The second tendency—to recognize behind the variety of fables or metaphors a common unity—is evident in many of the best essays in this book: "The Wall and the Books," "The Flower of Coleridge," "The Dream of Coleridge," "Partial Enchantments of the *Quixote,*" "Kafka and His Precursors," "On the Cult of Books," "Forms of a Legend," "From Allegories to Novels." Relying on a vast library and an even vaster memory, Borges finds the most unexpected connections, showing common points of view in authors whom critics have never put together. Following one idea, one image, one procedure through diverse languages and centuries, Borges can begin with Kafka and end up with Zeno, or start with Coleridge and arrive at Henry James; Benedetto Croce leads him to Chaucer, Buddha to Oscar Wilde, Pope to the Chinese emperor Shih Huang Ti, who ordered the building of the Great Wall. Relentless in his pursuit of the invisible mechanism which controlled the world and writing, Borges is also relentless in his ability to relate and connect, to combine and condense.

What he leaves out in his appraisal of the essays included in *Other Inquisitions* is a third tendency: that of metaphorically condensing the writer's style or approach. The essays on Quevedo, Hawthorne, Whitman, Valéry, Edward FitzGerald, Oscar Wilde, Chesterton, the "first" Wells, and Bernard Shaw, all attempt to discover the actual writer under the mask, or persona, each of these writers had created. In doing so, Borges is not concerned with ferreting out biographical truths. On the contrary, he is interested in discovering the type of literary destiny each particular writer managed to fulfill. In the case of Whitman, he shows the difference between the rather withdrawn and modest Walter Whitman and the emphatic persona Walt Whitman, the Son of Manhattan; in the case of Chesterton, he underlines the contradiction between the ardent believer who joyously proclaimed his Catholic faith and the nightmares in which this same faith is coded. What Borges is after in these literary portraits is the same kind of effect produced by his biographies in *A Universal History of Infamy:* the awareness of the paradoxical nature of all lives, the realization that to portray a man is to reduce the multiplicity of his traits to a composite (and unfaithful) sum of the traits we favor. But in moving from the infamous characters of his early book to the complex characters of these writers, Borges adds a new dimension. Each one of the writers began by creating not only a work but also a persona. And what truly concerned Borges was the creation of that persona.

In compiling the articles for *Other Inquisitions,* Borges was assisted by José Bianco. They worked in Bianco's private library and selected pieces from *Sur, La Nación,* and other well-known sources. According to Bianco, there was no attempt to produce a well-organized volume or to select the "best" essays. On the contrary, they left out (inadvertently or on purpose) some important pieces: the prologue to Bioy Casares' *The Invention of Morel* (1940), in which Borges advances a theory about fantastic literature; the prologue to Herman Melville's *Bartleby, the Scrivener* (1943) and to Henry James' "The Abasement of the Northmores" (1945), which contain important views on both writers; and the prologue to Dante's *Divine Comedy* (1949), of which only one section, on the meeting with Beatrice, is included in the book. Borges being Borges, he was unlikely to take the trouble to put all his most important essays together. Not until 1975 would he consent to the inclusion of these and other important pieces in *Prólogos,* a book of prologues which naturally included a "Prologue of Prologues." But even here, the long essay on Dante is omitted. Probably Borges did not own the copyright on that prologue; or perhaps he was too busy to attempt to save it from the solemn fate its publication in a collection of classics implied.

Following the publication of *Other Inquisitions* in July 1952, María Rosa Lida de Malkiel wrote a learned and witty study for *Sur*

(July–August 1952) entitled "Contribution to the Study of Jorge Luis Borges' Literary Sources." It was the first time that his work was approached with all the armature of serious scholarship. The same year, Enrique Pezzoni published in *Sur* (November–December 1952) a long review of *Other Inquisitions*. Entitled "Approximations to Borges' Latest Book," it is one of the best studies of the book, but it also has a wider intention: to place Borges' work and personality in the larger context of contemporary Argentine literature.

At that time, Borges had become the center of a controversy about the political and cultural role of the Argentine writer. Many of his new readers refused to accept the position that literature was best left to writers, and politics to politicians. In line with Sartre, they were beginning to demand that writers become engaged with their times. They wanted social and political debate to enter academia and assault Parnassus. Borges was, for them, the best example of a writer who could be viewed both as alienated (did he not write about fantastic worlds?) and engaged (was he not one of the most notorious of Perón's opponents?). The debate began in 1948 and continues to the present. But it reached its peak after Borges published *Other Inquisitions*. In a sense, that book, and Pezzoni's article, helped to focus the issues in the debate.

The debate began with a seemingly innocuous piece by one of Argentina's young essayists, H. A. Murena. In an article published in *Sur* (June–July 1948) Murena attacks Borges' poetry on the ground that he uses the symbols of Argentine nationalism but does not share the national feeling these symbols imply. It is obvious that Murena misses Borges' point. Instead of using the symbols of Argentina to emphasize what is unique (and thus parochial) in them, Borges uses them to show what is universal about them. In his poem about the *truco,* what Borges wants to show is not the quaint peculiarities of the popular cardgame but the fact that any game makes us unreal: in following the rules, we repeat the games other men have played before us; for a while, we are these men. In a second and later article, also published in *Sur* (October 1951), Murena advances his argument. This time what he objects to is that Borges represents a culmination of the eclecticism that makes Argentine writers heirs of all cultures. In a sense, Murena seems to resent the fact that Borges is truly cosmopolitan.

In his article Pezzoni reacted strongly to this type of reading. He points out Murena's fallacy in judging Borges' poems not by their texts but in their ethical context within Argentine reality (as Murena saw it). He underlines Borges' right to create his poems out of his own

423

particular vision and craftsmanship. In criticizing the type of analysis Murena attempts, Pezzoni moves toward a more balanced literary and critical approach.

Unfortunately, few people read him. The general trend of the new critics was toward a sociological and political view of literature. Even more unbalanced than Murena's are Jorge Abelardo Ramos' views in his *Crisis and Resurrection of Argentine Literature* (1954). He sees Borges as a representative of the ranchowners' oligarchy and accuses him of writing an alienated, aristocratic, gratuitous kind of literature. The fact that Borges never owned a ranch in his life, and that his point of view (nihilistic if not anarchistic, to say the least) did not at all coincide with the pious, conservative, bourgeois philosophy of the ranchowners, did not bother Ramos at all. A pseudo-Marxist, Ramos believed that Perón was a genuine leader of the workers. For him, Borges, an anti-Peronist, had to represent the enemy.

In a similar vein, younger writers attempted to apply to Borges notions they had scarcely understood in Sartre, Merleau-Ponty, and perhaps even in Lukacs. An example is Adolfo Prieto's small book *Borges and the New Generation* (1954), which had some success. Equally critical of Borges, but less partisan, was a special issue of a new journal, *Ciudad* (no. 2–3, 1955), which was dedicated entirely to Borges. As friends and sympathizers of Prieto, the contributors attempted a balanced view of Borges but generally failed. One of the reasons was that (like Prieto) they lacked complete familiarity with Borges' work. Their ignorance about some of his key writings was embarrassing.

From a certain point of view, the debate was as disorganized and erratic as the colloquium that had been held at *Megáfono* in 1933, when the first edition of *Discusión* was published. Although the vocabulary and the so-called ideology had changed, the objections were pretty much the same: Borges was alienated from national reality; Borges was a foreigner who relished writing about Germans and Arabs, Scandinavians and Jews; Borges was a Byzantine writer, a European. The arguments were repeated, the level of critical inquiry constantly lowered.

Borges himself had answered many of his critics even before they put their ideas to paper. In a lecture he gave in 1951 called "The Argentine Writer and Tradition," later published in *Sur* (January–February 1955), he attacks the kind of literary nationalism which demands that a writer demonstrate he is Argentine or Zulu. He correctly points out that the discussion would be unintelligible to Shakespeare or Racine, who never doubted they had the right to present in their plays a Danish Hamlet or a Greek Andromache, an Egyptian Cleopatra or a Roman Nero. Borges comes to the conclusion that Argentines ought not to be afraid of not being Argentine enough: "Our patrimony is the universe." He adds:

> We should essay all themes. . . . We cannot limit ourselves to purely Argentine subjects in order to be Argentine; for either being Argentine is an inescapable act of fate—and in that case we shall be so in all events—or being Argentine is a mere affectation, a mask. I believe that if we surrender ourselves to that voluntary dream which is artistic creation, we shall be Argentine and we shall also be good or tolerable writers. (*Labyrinths*, 1964, p. 185)

The piece was later included in a new edition of *Discusión*, published as the fourth volume of his complete works in 1956. In a sense, it is a final statement about a subject that had misled and would continue to mislead Argentine criticism for decades.

12.
The End of a Nightmare

The Peronist years were coming to a close. After Evita's death in 1952, the regime seemed to wane in popularity. Opposing forces gathered strength; the Church and a coalition of foreign interests led by England fanned internal divisions in the army and supported the navy's traditional rivalry with Perón. By 1955 it was obvious that only through force could the regime continue. Although Perón threatened to arm the workers and turn them loose on the streets, he was secretly determined not to resort to violence. He was a politician and tried to survive as politicians do: by endlessly playing one force against another. But his room for maneuvering was being reduced by the hour. In September 1955, after the army started an uprising in Córdoba (the fortress of Argentine Catholicism) and the navy supported it, tightly blockading Buenos Aires, Perón accepted defeat and resigned. He was quickly spirited out of the country.

For Borges it was a day of joy. In his "Autobiographical Essay" he has this to say about the great event:

> The long-hoped-for revolution came in September 1955. After a sleepless, anxious night, nearly the whole population came out into the streets, cheering the revolution and shouting the name of Córdoba, where most of the fighting had taken place. We were so carried away that for some time we were quite unaware of the rain that was soaking us to the bone. We were so happy that not a single word was even uttered against the fallen dictator. Perón went into hiding and was later allowed to leave the country. No one knows how much money he got away with. ("Essay," 1970, pp. 248–249)

For Borges it was the end of a nightmare. Despite his increasing recognition as a writer, the Peronist decade had been for him a period of pain and humiliation. Two stories he wrote then echo the feelings of those years. "The South"—originally published in *La Nación* (February 8, 1953) and later included in the second edition of *Ficciones* (1956)—presents an Argentine who, like Borges, is of Nordic ascent. He is challenged to a knife fight by a hoodlum. The protagonist, Juan Dahlmann, accepts the challenge in spite of his lack of skill and goes into the open sure that he is going to be killed. During the Peronist years Borges must have felt like Dahlmann and probably dreamed of a similarly savage ending. The second story, "The Wait," also appeared in *La Nación* (August 27, 1950) and was later included in the second edition of *The Aleph* (1952). In the story a man waits for some hoodlums to come and kill him. Perhaps Borges also waited, or dreamed about waiting, for the police to come and get him.

If the allusions and nightmares in those stories are ambiguous, some poems Borges published during that decade explicitly reveal his hatred and fears. One is called "A Page to Commemorate Colonel Suárez, Victor at Junín" and was originally published in *Sur* (January–February 1945) at the precise time Perón came to power. Superficially it seems to be another of those poems Borges loved to write to celebrate his ancestors' unflinching courage in battle. But the last lines give the game away:

> His great-grandson is writing these lines,
> and a silent voice comes to him out of the past,
> out of the blood:
> "What does my battle at Junín matter if it is only
> a glorious memory, or a date learned by rote
> for an examination, or a place in the atlas?
> The battle is everlasting and can do without
> the pomp of actual armies and of trumpets.
> Junín is two civilians cursing a tyrant
> on a street corner,
> or an unknown man somewhere, dying in prison."
> (*Poems,* 1972, translated by Alastair Reid, p. 91)

By linking his ancestor's epic fight for freedom with civilian resistance to a tyrant, Borges was clearly indicating where the battlefield was located now: in the streets of Buenos Aires.

Another poem is even more explicit, and because of it, more dangerous. It is called "The Dagger" and was rejected by *La Nación*. I published it in *Marcha* (June 25, 1954).

A dagger rests in a drawer.
It was forged in Toledo at the end of the last century. Luis Melián Lafinur gave

it to my father, who brought it from Uruguay. Evaristo Carriego once held it in his hand.

Whoever lays eyes on it has to pick up the dagger and toy with it, as if he had always been on the lookout for it. The hand is quick to grip the waiting hilt, and the powerful obeying blade slides in and out of the sheath with a click.

This is not what the dagger wants.

It is more than a structure of metal; men conceived it and shaped it with a single end in mind. It is, in some eternal way, the dagger that last night knifed a man in Tacuarembó and the daggers that rained on Caesar. It wants to kill, it wants to shed sudden blood.

In a drawer of my writing table, among draft pages and old letters, the dagger dreams over and over its simple tiger's dream. On wielding it, the hand comes alive, sensing itself, each time handled, in touch with the killer for whom it was forged.

At times, I am sorry for it. Such power and single-mindedness, so impassive or innocent its pride, and the years slip by, unheeding.

(Ibid., translated by Norman Thomas di Giovanni, p. 95)

The dagger's obsession was Borges' obsession. It is obvious why *La Nación* was reluctant to print a poem that could have been easily construed as defending the assassination of tyrants. But the fact that not many of his countrymen were ready to follow Borges in his resistance to the regime did not discourage him at all. He went on with his solitary fight. In his "Autobiographical Essay," in recalling the dark days of the Perón regime, he comments on his colleagues' militancy. He had been elected president of the Argentine Society of Writers in 1950, a position he held until 1953. According to Borges, the society "was one of the few strongholds against the dictatorship. This was so evident that many distinguished men of letters did not dare to set foot inside its doors until after the revolution." The society was eventually closed by the regime.

> I remember the last lecture I was allowed to give there. The audience, quite a small one, included a very puzzled policeman who did his clumsy best to set down a few of my remarks on Persian Sufism. During this drab and hopeless period, my mother—then in her seventies—was under house arrest. My sister and one of my nephews spent a month in jail. I myself had a detective on my heels, whom I first took on long, aimless walks and at last made friends with. He admitted that he too hated Perón, but that he was obeying orders. Ernesto Palacio once offered to introduce me to the Unspeakable, but I did not want to meet him. How could I be introduced to a man whose hand I would not shake? ("Essay," 1970, p. 248)

Borges' resistance to Perón was to be recognized publicly by the new military regime. Through the initiative of two of Borges' friends,

428

Esther Zemborain de Torres and Victoria Ocampo, and the public support of the Argentine Society of Writers, he was appointed director of the National Library by the acting president of Argentina, General Eduardo Leonardi. In his "Autobiographical Essay" Borges records the event with pride and subtle self-mockery: "I thought the scheme a wild one, and hoped at most to be given the directorship of some small-town library, preferably to the south of the city." A few days before the appointment was made official,

> my mother and I had walked to the Library . . . to take a look at the building, but, feeling superstitious, I refused to go in. "Not until I get the job," I said. That same week, I was called to come to the Library to take over. My family was present, and I made a speech to the employees, telling them I was actually the Director—the incredible Director. At the same time, José Edmundo Clemente, who a few years before had managed to convince Emecé to bring out an edition of my works, became the Assistant Director. Of course, I felt very important, but we got no pay for the next three months. I don't think my predecessor, who was a Peronista, was ever officially fired. He just never came around to the Library again. They named me to the job but did not take the trouble to unseat him. (Ibid., p. 249)

For Borges, to become director of the National Library was, in a sense, to achieve one of his unacknowledged dreams. It meant reparation not only for the humiliation devised by the Perón regime when he was promoted to inspector of chickens but for the years he had been confined to a modest position in the Miguel Cané municipal library— and perhaps, even further back, for the years when, having returned from Europe, Georgie used to visit the National Library's reference room to read the *Encyclopaedia Britannica.* Too shy to go to the desk and ask for the books he wanted, Georgie kept consulting the only volumes he could borrow without having to ask for them. Now, he could command all the volumes he wanted. The library of Babel was finally his. But there was an even subtler symbolism in his promotion to director of the National Library. The building on Mexico Street where the library was situated had been originally designed to house the national lottery. The symbols of chance which decorated the building did not seem so incongruous after all to a man who had written "The Babylon Lottery." Finally, Borges had found a place where books and chance came harmoniously together.

One of his first decisions as director was to restore the National Library to the position it had had under the directorship of Paul Groussac. He made plans to reissue the journal *La Biblioteca,* which had been founded by Groussac, and asked Clemente to organize a series of lectures at the old building. I was invited in 1956 to lecture on the

Uruguayan short-story writer, Horacio Quiroga, who had lived and worked in Buenos Aires. After the lecture Borges took me to dinner, with some mutual friends, at a restaurant in an old restored warehouse of the Rosas era. The entranceway was through one of the carriage porches which appear in some of his poems. The somber stone-paved patio, the moist plants branching against the dirty whitewashed walls, an old mail coach which perhaps carried Facundo Quiroga to his death in Barranca Yaco (as in Borges' famous poem), comprised the entrance to an enormous room of thin, wooden columns which suggested a stable rather than a restaurant. There we continued to talk about literature, contemporary and old. But Borges was more interested in something else. He never tired of making me see, of looking through my eyes at this relic of Rosas' time. In his memory the ancient hatred for the old tyrant, inherited from grandfathers and great-grandfathers, blended almost perfectly with his hatred for Perón. It was easy to see that Perón and Rosas were one, that both served as a metaphor for Borges' attraction to those cynical men, with their jagged knives or electric-shock treatment, those smiling traitors of Argentine history, whom Borges despises and yet cannot help but admire. Obsessed by the consciousness of not having lived enough, he saw in these men of action the exact counterpart of his meditative self: he was the man of books, they were the men with knives. He denounced them in poems and stories and, at the same time, felt a horrible fascination for them. They were the "other," the dark side of the self. Now that Perón was gone, Borges could go back to Rosas and his times.

Borges was euphoric. He could again breathe in a city freed of demons. He endlessly repeated his loyalty to the new regime which had made him director of the National Library. Once again, I walked with him through the Southside. We visited a Greek church; inside, the still air seemed solid and the light was barely more than a dusky shade. The pale gold ornaments were alive in an atmosphere devoid of human presence. In that setting, like that of so many of his precisely crafted stories, Borges seemed to be in his natural habitat. The darkness of the church was his light.

Yet the complete reality of Borges, of the concrete person Borges is, escaped me until he invited me to tour the National Library the next day. The building over which Groussac had presided was going to seed but still had a certain grandeur. At the time, I didn't know that it had been built to house the national lottery and did not recognize the obvious symbols. Borges took me in hand and led me around, seeing only enough to know where each book he wanted was. He can open a book to the desired page and, without bothering to read—through a feat of memory comparable only to that of his fictional Irineo Funes—quote complete passages. He roams along corridors lined with books; he quickly turns corners and gets into passages which are truly invisible, mere cracks in the walls of books; he rushes down winding staircases which abruptly end in the dark. There is almost no light in the library's corridors and staircases. I try to follow him, tripping, blinder and more handicapped than Borges because my only guides are my eyes. In the dark of the library Borges finds his way with the precarious precision of a tightrope walker. Finally, I come to understand that the space in which we are momentarily inserted is not real: it is a space made of words, signs, symbols. It is another labyrinth. Borges drags me, makes me quickly descend the long, winding staircase, fall exhausted into the center of darkness. Suddenly, there is light at the end of another corridor. Prosaic reality awaits me there. Next to Borges, who smiles like a child who has played a joke on a friend, I recover my eyesight, the real world of light and shadow, the conventions I am trained to recognize. But I come out of the experience like one who emerges from deep water or from a dream, shattered by the (other) reality of that labyrinth of paper.

At that time, Borges was becoming increasingly blind. The doctors had already warned him that unless he stopped reading and writing, he would become totally blind. To save what little eyesight he had, he was forced to renounce one of his greatest pleasures.

He took the news with the usual stoicism. In his "Autobiographical Essay," he bravely attempts to understate it:

> My blindness had been coming on gradually since childhood. There was nothing particularly pathetic or dramatic about it. Beginning in 1927, I had undergone eight eye operations; but since the late 1950s, when I wrote my "Poem of the Gifts," for reading and writing purposes I have been blind. Blindness ran in my family. . . . Blindness also seems to run among the directors of the National Library. Two of my eminent forerunners, José Mármol and Paul Groussac, suffered the same fate. In my poem, I speak of God's splendid irony in granting me at one time 800,000 books and darkness. ("Essay," 1970, p. 250)

The ending of the poem underlines more than fate's irony. It makes visible the tragic condition of that man who, like Groussac, had been denied access to what he most longed for.

> Painfully probing the dark, I grope toward
> The void of the twilight with the point of my faltering
> Cane—I for whom Paradise was always a metaphor,
> An image of libraries.

Something—no need to prattle of chance
Or contingency—presides over these matters;
Long before me, some other man took these books and the dark
In a fading of dusk for his lot.

Astray in meandering galleries,
It comes to me now with a holy, impalable
Dread, that I am that other, the dead man, and walk
With identical steps and identical days to the end.

Which of us two is writing this poem
In the I of the first-person plural, in identical darkness?
What good is the word that speaks for me now in my name,
If the curse of the dark is implacably one and the same?

Groussac or Borges, I watch the delectable
World first disfigure then extinguish itself
In a pallor of ashes, until all that is gone
Seems at one with sleep and at one with oblivion.

(*Poems,* 1972, translated by Ben Belitt, pp. 117–119)

But the blind, groping man was not destined to sleep or oblivion. More gifts were to be bestowed on him till his name would become known to the whole world. At fifty-six, Borges may have felt he had reached a zenith. He was still far from his real goal.

13.
The Birth of
"Borges"

Life changed drastically for Borges because of his blindness. From 1955 onward he became more and more dependent on others for even the simplest task. Unable to read or write, he had to rely on Mother or other members of the family, and even close friends, to help him with a new book or look for a particular quotation from an old one, to take dictation and type his manuscripts. Mother became his secretary and nurse. Others took turns helping him. One of his nephews learned to pronounce German in order to read aloud to him from German texts; Alicia Jurado, a young woman interested in Buddhism, read Oriental literature to him and under his dictation produced a small essay on the subject which would not be published until 1976. With Margarita Guerrero, Borges compiled a *Manual of Fantastic Zoology* (Mexico, 1957), which was later expanded into *The Book of Imaginary Beings* (Buenos Aires, 1967). Its final version appeared in the 1969 English translation done by the author in collaboration with Norman Thomas di Giovanni. Many of the chapters in these books were based on articles from encyclopedias and other sources, but some were solely the fruit of Borges' imagination. Another book he produced in those years of his increasing blindness was an anthology called *The Book of Heaven and Hell* (Buenos Aires, 1960), which he compiled with Bioy Casares.

He was able to write new books with the help of his friends and secretaries, but it became almost impossible for him to compose short stories or elaborate articles. Because he had trained himself to write in such a condensed form, adding pieces bit by bit to a highly complex structure of sentences and paragraphs, the composition of any long prose text was now out of his reach. For more than a decade he

433

stopped writing stories and long articles. His first volume of new stories, *Dr. Brodie's Report,* would not come out until 1970. In compensation, he returned to poetry. Borges recalls:

> One salient consequence of my blindness was my gradual abandonment of free verse in favor of classical metrics. In fact, blindness made me take up the writing of poetry again. Since rough drafts were denied me, I had to fall back on memory. It is obviously easier to remember verse than prose, and to remember regular verse forms rather than free ones. Regular verse is, so to speak, portable. One can walk down the street or be riding the subway while composing and polishing a sonnet, for rhyme and meter have mnemonic virtues. ("Essay," 1970, p. 250)

But he was in no hurry to collect his poems. Not until the middle 1960s would he reissue in a new format his volume of *Poemas* (originally published in 1943 and enlarged in 1954). Called *Obra Poética* (Poetical Works), it came out in 1964 both as a large illustrated volume and as part of the complete works. Poetry written after 1943 makes up two thirds of the book. Borges himself has commented on these new poems:

> I wrote dozens of sonnets and longer poems consisting of eleven-syllable quatrains. I thought I had taken Lugones as my master, but when the verses were written my friends told me that, regrettably, they were quite unlike him. In my later poetry, a narrative thread is always to be found. As a matter of fact, I even think of plots for poems. Perhaps the main difference between Lugones and me is that he held French literature as his model and lived intellectually in a French world, whereas I look to English literature. In this new poetic activity, I never thought of building a sequence of poems, as I always formerly did, but was chiefly interested in each piece for its own sake. In this way, I wrote poems on such different subjects as Emerson and wine, Snorri Sturluson and the hourglass, my grandfather's death, and the beheading of Charles I. I also went in for summing up my literary heroes: Poe, Swedenborg, Whitman, Heine, Camões, Jonathan Edwards, and Cervantes. Due tribute, of course, was also paid to mirrors, the Minotaur, and knives. (Ibid., pp. 250–251)

This double switch, from prose to poetry, and from free verse to regular verse, radically altered Borges' work. He became, in the literal sense of the word, an oral writer; that is, a writer who was forced by blindness to compose his writings orally. He also had to learn how to dictate. Instead of going through endless drafts to refine his sentences and paragraphs, he learned how to compose from memory and how to rely on meter to achieve the effects he had earlier searched for in his minute, spidery handwriting. It was a momentous change. A new

Borges came out of it. No longer was he the master of a complex and subtle style of writing; he was a poet, a bard.

The fact that he was actually blind made him fall easily into another prototype. Instead of an Erasmus, holding a pen and an inkpot in his hands, the new Borges was easily associated with the blind bards—with Milton and with Homer. The blind poet ceased to be a writer and became a seer.

How did blindness affect his everyday life? On many occasions Borges has attempted to debunk the pathetic image of the blind writer. Talking to Richard Burgin, he explains in detail how blindness has changed his habits. To a question about his reading, he answers:

BORGES: I've always been a greater reader than a writer. But, of course, I began to lose my eyesight definitely in 1954, and since then I've done my reading by proxy, no? Well, of course, when one cannot read, then one's mind works in a different way. In fact, it might be said that there is a certain benefit in being unable to read, because you think that time flows in a different way. When I had my eyesight, then if I had to spend say half an hour without doing anything, I would go mad. Because I had to be reading. But now, I can be alone for quite a long time, I don't mind long railroad journeys, I don't mind being alone in a hotel or walking down the street, because, well, I won't say that I am thinking all the time because that would be bragging.

I think I am able to live with a lack of occupation. I don't have to be talking to people or doing things. If somebody had gone out, and I had come here and found the house empty, then I would have been quite content to sit down and let two or three hours pass and go out for a short walk, but I wouldn't feel especially unhappy or lonely. That happens to all people who go blind. (Burgin, 1969, pp. 4–5)

Borges' resignation must have come by degrees. His comments to Burgin in 1967 were the end result of years of preparation, of slowly accepting blindness and settling down to old age. Even in that interview there is a moment in which the pain of adjusting to blindness pierces through the elegant retelling of his experiences. When Burgin asks him specifically what he thinks about when he is alone, he replies very frankly:

BORGES: I could or I might not be thinking about anything, I'd just be living on, no? Letting time flow or perhaps looking back on memories or walking across a bridge and trying to remember favorite passages, but maybe I wouldn't be doing anything, I'd just be living. I never understand why people say they're bored because they have nothing to do. Because sometimes I have nothing whatever to do, and I don't feel bored. Because I'm not doing things all the time, I'm content.

BURGIN: You've never felt bored in your life?
BORGES: I don't think so. Of course, when I had to be ten days lying on my back after an operation, I felt anguish but not boredom. (Ibid., p. 5)

In spite of his brave statement, it was only through a hard and long period of training that Borges came to relish the solitude and emptiness that blindness brought to his life.

The early years of his blindness were crowded with honors. On April 29, 1956, he was given a doctorate honoris causa by the University of Cuyo, one of the oldest in Argentina. It was the first of such doctorates he gathered from universities all over the world. The following year, on June 14, he was appointed professor of English and American literature at the Faculty of Philosophy and Letters at the University of Buenos Aires. He taught there until 1968, when he retired at the age of sixty-eight. But the most important distinction he received came in 1956, when he was awarded the biannual National Prize of Literature. As usual, Borges took the distinction with a grain of salt. Talking to Jean de Milleret ten years later, he commented that it was a bit of a political prize (De Milleret, 1967, p. 82). He was probably right. At the time, the military government wanted to stress the fact that its attitude toward culture was the opposite of Perón's and that it had restored the dignity of Argentine culture. Borges was the most suitable writer to make this restoration visible.

New volumes of his complete works appeared; the fifth was a new edition of *Ficciones* (1956), with three new stories. In a postscript to the prologue to the second section of the book, Borges comments on the additions. He points out that one of the stories, "The End," develops a situation that is implicit in a famous book; his only invention is the character of Recabarren, through whom the story is seen. Although Borges does not reveal which book he is talking about, it is obvious that the model is *Martín Fierro* and that he had ventured to imagine what would have happened if the protagonist had a fight with the brother of one of his victims. In the second story, "The Sect of the Phoenix," Borges attempted the problem of presenting a very common fact in a "vacillating and gradual way which, at the end, became unequivocal." He isn't sure that he has succeeded, he adds. The truth is that many of the readers of that story fail to understand that the Secret of the Sect is the sexual act, which perpetuates and immortalizes men. The third story is one of Borges' most successful and personal. In "The South" Borges allegorizes the fate of a man who, like him, has a double allegiance: to his European roots and to the barbarous country in which he was born. In commenting on the story in the prologue, Borges points out only that it can be "read as a direct narration of novelesque facts and also in a different way." He doesn't say what that "different way" is, but the hint is enough to suggest that the second part of the story is a hallucination and didn't really happen. Juan Dahlmann never fought a knife duel in the pampas; he died under the surgeon's scalpel in a Buenos Aires hospital.

For the sixth volume of his complete works, Borges reissued *Discusión* (1957). It contains six new pieces, among which are two perceptive essays on Flaubert and *Bouvard et Pécuchet* and the lecture on "The Argentine Writer and Tradition," which contains an important statement on the pseudo-literary nationalists. He also took advantage of the new edition to eliminate a 1931 article, "Our Impossibilities," which bitterly satirizes some negative aspects of the national character. At the time it was originally published, Borges was openly critical of the national character, but in 1957, in the context of the so-called Liberating Revolution which had ended Perón's regime, he did not want to sound too harsh a note. The seventh volume was a new edition of *The Aleph* (1957), with four new stories. In a postscript to the epilogue he comments briefly on them. The tone is curiously apologetic, as if he himself is not convinced of the value of some of the stories. But at least one, "The Wait," is very characteristic of that period. In the postscript Borges informs the reader that the story is based on a police report a friend read to him in 1942, at the time he was working in the Miguel Cané library. The real protagonist was a Turk; Borges preferred an Italian in order "to be able to intuit him more easily." What he doesn't say in his comment is that there is an echo of Ernest Hemingway's "The Killers" in the situation of a man who waits for his former associates to come and kill him. Borges also forgets to mention that the waiting is, in a sense, a transposition of his own waiting, during the Perón years, for something terrible to happen to him.

In the 1950s fame began taking different shapes for Borges. Studies and books about him were proliferating. Beginning in 1955, with a monograph by José Luis Ríos Patrón of limited interest, four more books appeared: Marcial Tamayo and Adolfo Ruíz Díaz's *Borges: The Enigma and the Key to It* (1955); César Fernández Moreno's brilliant summary, *A Borges Outline* (1957); Ana María Barrenechea's stylistic examination, *The Expression of Unreality in the Work of Jorge Luis Borges* (1957); and Rafael Gutiérrez Girardot's *Essay of Interpretation* (1959). At the same time, his work was reaching a wider audience. Even before the fall of Perón, the film director Leopoldo Torre Nilsson had made a movie version of "Emma Zunz," under a title borrowed from Carl Theodore Dreyer: *Days of Wrath* (1954). Three years later René Mugica adapted to film the successful "Streetcorner Man." In 1966, in an interview with Jean de Milleret, Borges seemed pleased with the latter film, saying it was better than the original story. But two years later he told Richard Burgin that he found both films wrong and criticized them because they had padded the stories with local color. Yet even if his reactions were contradictory and on the whole negative, the fact was that he had become popular enough to be adapted to the movies.

Borges was sixty when the ninth volume of his complete works came out. (The eighth volume was a 1960 reprint of *Other Inquisitions*.) For the new book, he had thought up the title in English, *The Maker*, and had translated it into Spanish as *El hacedor;* but when the book came out in the United States the American translator preferred to avoid the theological implications and used instead the title of one of the pieces, *Dreamtigers*. According to Borges, the volume was put together almost by accident:

> Around 1954, I began writing short prose pieces—sketches and parables. One day, my friend Carlos Frías, of Emecé, told me he needed a new book for the series of my so-called complete works. I said I had none to give him, but Frías persisted, saying, "Every writer has a book if he only looks for it." Going through drawers at home one idle Sunday, I began ferreting out uncollected poems and prose pieces, some of the latter going back to my days on *Crítica*. These odds and ends, sorted out and ordered and published in 1960, became *El hacedor*. . . . ("Essay," 1970, p. 253)

The pieces that went back to the mid-1930s, when Borges was a regular contributor to *Crítica's Saturday Multicolored Review*, are "Toenails," "Dreamtigers," "Argumentum Ornithologicum," and "The Draped Mirrors." "Dialogue on a Dialogue" was published in *Destiempo* about the same time. But the most interesting pieces were relatively new. As a sort of prologue, Borges wrote a prose poem, "To Leopoldo Lugones," in which he relates a dream he had of visiting Lugones (who had preceded him as director of the National Library) to give him a copy of *El hacedor*. The dream attempts to persuade Borges that Lugones would read the book favorably: "If I am not mistaken, you were not disinclined to me, Lugones, and you would have liked to like some piece of my work. That never happened; but this time you turn the pages and read approvingly a verse here and there—perhaps because you have recognized your own voice in it, perhaps because deficient practice concerns you less than solid theory" (*Dreamtigers*, 1965, p. 21).

The end of the piece is characteristic: Borges realizes that the whole thing is a dream and that Lugones has been dead since 1938:

"My vanity and nostalgia have set up an impossible scene. Perhaps so (I tell myself), but tomorrow I too will have died, and our times will intermingle and chronology will be lost in a sphere of symbols. And then in some way it will be right to claim that I have brought you this book, and that you have accepted it" (ibid., p. 21). As usual, Borges comes to the conclusion that the differences between Lugones and himself are less important than the similarities. By a sleight-of-hand of which he is a master, he and Lugones finally become one.

The "Autobiographical Essay" also insists that in spite of the miscellaneous nature of the pieces collected in *El hacedor* the book has a unique quality:

> Remarkably, this book, which I accumulated rather than wrote, seems to me my most personal work, and to my taste, maybe my best. The explanation is only too easy: the pages of *El hacedor* contain no padding. Each piece was written for its own sake and out of an inner necessity. By the time it was undertaken, I had come to realize that fine writing is a mistake, and a mistake born out of vanity. Good writing, I firmly believe, should be done in an unobtrusive way. ("Essay," 1970, p. 253)

Borges is right about the personal character of the book. He had never been freer to write exclusively about what he liked or what caught his fancy at a given moment. Also, he had never been freer to talk about himself—his foibles and preferences, his manias and dreams—as in the miscellaneous pieces in this book. Two are memorable literary portraits of Borges, as persona and as he really is. One he himself singles out in the "Autobiographical Essay":

> On the closing page of that book, I told of a man who sets out to make a picture of the universe. After many years, he has covered a blank wall with images of ships, towers, horses, weapons, and men, only to find out at the moment of his death that he has drawn a likeness of his own face. This may be the case of all books; it is certainly the case of this particular book. (Ibid., pp. 253–254)

Even more explicitly autobiographical is the other piece, called "Borges and Myself," which became in a sense his final statement on his literary persona. In it, the theme of the double is presented through the opposition between Borges, the private man, and "Borges," the literary character created by the former who, little by little, usurps all of Borges' functions and privileges. The text begins: "It's to the other man, to Borges, that things happen." Everything that Borges now does, or likes, becomes the other's possession, "but in a showy way that turns them into stagy mannerisms." Although Borges admits that he is on

439

good terms with his other self, "I live, I let myself live, so that Borges can weave his tales and poems, and those tales and poems are my justification." The realization does not bring peace to him because he knows that "what is good no longer belongs to anyone—not even the other man—but rather to speech or tradition." He then comes to the sad conclusion that "I am fated to become lost once and for all, and only some moment of myself will survive in the other man." He is bound to leave no trace of himself other than what now belongs to "Borges." The conclusion is masterful:

> Little by little, I have been surrendering everything to him, even though I have evidence of his stubborn habit of falsification and exaggerating. Spinoza held that all things try to keep on being themselves; a stone wants to be a stone and the tiger, a tiger. I shall remain in Borges, not in myself (if it is so that I am someone), but I recognize myself less in his books than in those of others or than in the laborious tuning of a guitar. Years ago, I tried ridding myself of him and I went from myths of the outlying slums of the city to games with time and infinity, but those games are now part of Borges and I will have to turn to other things. And so, my life is a running away, and I lose everything and everything is left to oblivion or to the other man.
>
> Which of us is writing this page I don't know. (*The Aleph,* 1970, pp. 151–152)

By becoming "Borges," Borges had finally obliterated himself. In a sense, he had finally ceased to matter.

A few months after the publication of *El hacedor* a group of international publishers met on Majorca—the same island Georgie had visited as a teenager—and awarded him, jointly with Samuel Beckett, the first Formentor Prize. That prize marked the beginning of his international fame. It was also the beginning of "Borges" ' life and (consequently) the end of Borges' private life. From then on, "Borges" ruled completely. What belonged to Borges were the crumbs, the leftovers, the dregs. From that point on, "Borges" expanded his territory more and more while Borges was reduced to the periphery. It was "Borges" who visited American universities, got literary prize after literary prize, was written about and universally feted, and became a guru for thousands of young people on at least three continents. The other Borges (that is, Borges) slowly receded into nothingness.

Part Five

1.
A Modern
Master

Borges was in his early sixties when the Formentor Prize made him internationally famous. The prize had been established in 1960 by avant-garde publishers from six different Western countries: Librairie Gallimard (France), Giulio Einaudi (Italy), Ernst Rowohlt Verlag (West Germany), Weidenfeld & Nicolson (England), Editorial Seix-Barral (Spain), and Grove Press (United States). It was designed as an "award of $10,000 to an author of any nationality whose existing body of work will, in the view of the jury, have a lasting influence on the development of modern literature." The aim of the prize, "in addition to recognition of exceptional merit," was to "bring the author's work to the attention of the largest possible international audience." The 1961 award was the first to be made, and Borges shared the $10,000 prize with Samuel Beckett. But the loss of half the prize money was worth it. For an obscure Argentine writer to be cited as one of the indisputable masters of twentieth-century literature was distinction enough. At long last, after a career that covered almost four decades, Borges had the fame he deserved.

It took him some time to get used to it. He was dining with Bioy, as he usually did on Sundays, when he heard about the award. His first reaction (he later told Jean de Milleret) was that it had to be a joke. The name Formentor didn't mean a thing to him (De Milleret, 1967, p. 83). In a 1964 interview he claimed that in the citation he had been identified as the "Mexican" writer Jorge Luis Borges. Perhaps some secretary goofed. But it was obvious that the jury knew perfectly well who he was. Recalling the occasion in his "Autobiographical Essay," he generously attributes the award to the efforts of his French translators.

Fame, like my blindness, had been coming gradually to me. I had never expected it, I had never sought it. Néstor Ibarra and Roger Caillois, who in the early 1950s daringly translated me into French, were my first benefactors. I suspect that their pioneer work paved the way for . . . the Formentor Prize . . . , for until I appeared in French I was practically invisible—not only abroad but at home in Buenos Aires. As a consequence of that prize, my books mushroomed overnight throughout the Western world. ("Essay," 1970, p. 254)

Borges' memory is faulty regarding the date of Ibarra's translations of his work into French ("The Babylon Lottery" and "The Library of Babel" came out in *Lettres Françaises* on October 1, 1944), but he is right about the importance of that pioneering effort. Furthermore, Roger Caillois was a member of the jury that awarded him the prize. The immediate consequence of the award was the simultaneous publication of *Ficciones* in six different countries. The Spanish title was kept in the English and American editions, to indicate both the original language in which the book was written and the fact that its meaning was internationally accessible.

The reception of *Ficciones* was extraordinary, and from then on Borges was acknowledged as a modern master. In no time his name began to be linked to those of Kafka and Joyce, Proust and Nabokov. Another windfall from the prize was that Borges was discovered by academia. The first to move was the University of Texas (Austin). Using funds provided by the Edward Laroque Tinker Foundation, the university invited him, in September 1961, to spend a semester as visiting professor. He enthusiastically accepted. For the first time since his last trip to Europe in 1923–1924, he left the River Plate area. He was sixty-two and practically blind, but he was delighted with his new status as the first Latin American writer to be recognized worldwide. In spite of his shyness and his British upbringing, Borges took to fame with an almost childish glee. His time had finally come, and he was not one to let the opportunity pass.

For Mother, Borges' newly acquired status was the fulfillment of her deepest wishes. She had always known that her son was a genius (to use the old-fashioned but, for her, accurate expression), and now it was time to reap the labor of so many years. Since Father's death, Mother had devoted herself completely to Borges, making it her task in life to promote his career. She did not see eye to eye with him in many literary matters, was mistrustful of some of his literary acquaintances, and hated many of the subjects he preferred (hoodlums and slum dwellers, the tango and *Martín Fierro*) as well as those terrifying fantastic stories; but she was entirely loyal to him and fulfilled her duties with the utmost devotion. In a sense, she was more than a mother: she was his eyes and his hands. Borges related to the external world through her; it was as if he had not left the maternal womb. Or, to be more precise, it was as if, by becoming blind, he had returned to it, for good.

It was Mother who accompanied him on his first triumphant visit to the United States. Everywhere people believed her to be his wife, not his mother. At the ripe age of eighty-five, Mother looked sixty. That is, she looked her son's age. And she was proud of it. He was also proud of having such a good-looking mother. The enthusiasm and even childish delight of that first visit can be recognized in the account he gives in the "Autobiographical Essay":

> It was my first physical encounter with America. In a sense, because of my reading, I had always been there, and yet how strange it seemed when in Austin I heard ditch diggers who worked on campus speaking English, a language I had until then always thought of as being denied that class of people. America, in fact, had taken on such mythic proportions in my mind that I was sincerely amazed to find there such commonplace things as weeds, mud, puddles, dirt roads, flies, and stray dogs. Though at times we fell into homesickness, I know now that my mother . . . and I grew to love Texas. She, who always loathed football, even rejoiced over *our* victory when the Longhorns defeated the neighboring Bears. ("Essay," 1970, p. 254)

I saw Borges in Buenos Aires on his return from the United States. In recounting his experiences, he told me an anecdote which, somehow, encapsulated his feeling of nostalgia. One of the members of the Spanish department at the university, a Paraguayan by birth, had once asked him to dinner and, to please him, had put on some tango records, sung by the popular singer Carlos Gardel. Little did he know that Borges hated Gardel's sentimental and (to him) Italianate vocal style. Borges told me that he tried to brace himself for the ordeal and even smiled. But after a few minutes, when Gardel's whining voice had begun to melt the audience, Borges heard, close at hand, sobbing and crying. It took him several seconds to discover that it was he who was so moved by that nostalgic voice.

His seminars on Argentine literature and Leopoldo Lugones' poetry were well attended, but he soon found that his twenty-five to thirty students were more interested in discussing his work than that of his predecessors. He was pleased that North American students, "unlike the run-of-the-mill students in the Argentine," were "far more interested in their subjects than in their grades" (ibid., p. 255). He also took advantage of the long visit (September 1961 to February 1962) to attend seminars on Anglo-Saxon literature, taught by Dr. Rudolph Willard, which helped him to correct some errors in his book *Ancient German Literatures* (1951). From Texas, on his way back to Buenos

Aires, he traveled extensively, lecturing in New Mexico and California, Washington, D.C., New York, Connecticut, and Massachusetts. He visited Columbia, Yale, and Harvard, gave lectures at the Library of Congress and at the Organization of American States in Washington, and was feted everywhere. In the "Essay" he summarizes his visit:

> I found America the friendliest, most forgiving, and most generous nation I have ever visited. We South Americans tend to think in terms of convenience, whereas people in the United States approach things ethically. This—amateur Protestant that I am—I admired above all. It even helped me overlook skyscrapers, paper bags, televisions, plastics, and the unholy jungle of gadgets. (Ibid. p. 255)

He was so enthusiastic about the United States that he even loved the Alamo, which he saw as an example of North American heroism. His views did not go down too well in Mexico, where Texas (and New Mexico and California) are still seen as lost Mexican territory. In spite of that, while Borges was in Texas some Mexican intellectuals broached the idea of inviting him for a visit. But they found strong opposition to him among left-wing intellectuals and others who wanted to pass as such. The cold war was then at its peak, and Castro's triumph in Cuba and his subsequent siding with the Soviets had polarized the Latin American intelligentsia into two irreconcilable factions. From the very beginning, Borges had been outspoken about Castro. He did not like his totalitarian methods—and Castro's association with the Soviet Union did not help at all. In this context, it is easy to understand why Borges' visit to Mexico was canceled even before it was announced.

One of the men behind the cancellation was then editor of the influential *Revista de la Universidad de Mexico;* in its June 1962 issue he published a statement that denounced Borges for "McCarthyism" while praising his literary achievements. In the same issue, the *Revista* included a long interview with Borges by James E. Irby and a short article on Borges' place in Latin American letters by the young Mexican poet José Emilio Pacheco. In a sense, the publication of these two pieces was an apology for the editor's tacit participation in the campaign to deny Borges access to Mexico.

Borges himself seems not to have realized what was going on in Mexico. He continued to praise the Alamo and sing of Texas, apparently unaware of the way his words sounded on the other side of the Rio Grande. His opposition to communism had never been McCarthyite and could not be compared in virulence to the anti-North Americanism so common among Latin American intellectuals. Basically an agnostic and an ideological anarchist, Borges had always criticized any regime, no matter what its ideology, that controlled the individual from womb to tomb. A follower of Spencer's more than of Bakunin's theories, Borges believed in the individual and maintained that the best state was the least visible. But if he was outspoken against communism (as he was then also outspoken against fascism), he was extremely tolerant of his friends' beliefs and politics. In the same way that he had refrained from criticizing Macedonio Fernández's and Leopoldo Lugones' sympathy for fascism, or Leopoldo Marechal's and Xul-Solar's support of Peronism, he abstained from criticizing, for instance, José Bianco's 1961 visit to Cuba. The episode is significant. Bianco was then the editor-in-chief of *Sur,* and when it was announced publicly that he had decided to visit Havana as a member of the Casa de las Américas' literary jury, Victoria Ocampo published a statement in the March–April issue disassociating the magazine from its editor's political allegiances. Bianco immediately resigned. Although Borges was closer politically to Victoria Ocampo than to Bianco, he decided to ignore the incident. In his memoirs, Bianco has this to say:

> We had dinner together a few days after my return. We did not talk about Cuba (he has stated his opposition to Castro's revolution) but he was as friendly as usual. Or even more: as he knew I had to resign my position, he offered me two jobs which later I did not accept. I was deeply hurt and he had the tact to drive away my sadness by leading the conversation toward light, impersonal subjects. . . . His attitude moved me more than he could have foreseen. (Bianco, 1964, p. 17)

The 1961 visit to the United States became the first of many trips Borges took to the principal countries of the Western world—to lecture or read his poems, to receive honors and prizes, to be interviewed and feted. In 1963 he returned to Europe, after an absence of nearly forty years. From January 30 to March 12 he visited Madrid, Paris, Geneva, London, Oxford, Cambridge, and Edinburgh. In all these places he lectured on gaucho poetry and the future of the Spanish language. In his "Autobiographical Essay" he partially summarizes this journey:

> Looking back on this past decade, I seem to have been quite a wanderer. In 1963, thanks to Neil MacKay of the British Council in Buenos Aires, I was able to visit England and Scotland. There, too, again in my mother's company, I made my pilgrimages: to London, so teeming with literary memories; to Lichfield and Dr. Johnson; to Manchester and De Quincey; to Rye and Henry James; to the Lake Country; to Edinburgh. I visited my grandmother's birthplace in Hanley, one of the Five Towns—Arnold Bennett country. Scotland and Yorkshire I think of as among the loveliest places on earth. Sometimes in the Scottish hills and glens I recaptured a strange sense

of loneliness and bleakness that I had known before; it took me some time to trace this feeling back to the far-flung wastes of Patagonia. ("Essay," 1970, p. 256)

Borges' memory, as usual, is highly selective. He forgets Madrid, Paris, and even Geneva, concentrating on the land where some of his ancestors were born.

In Madrid he paid a visit to his old master, Rafael Cansinos-Asséns, and for two days he reminisced in Geneva with his old schoolmates Maurice Abramowicz and Simon Jichlinski. In a sense, it was a return to the past, to the unique cultural experience he had during World War I. Six years later, while sitting on a bench along the Charles River in Cambridge, Massachusetts, Borges would dream a story involving an encounter between his young Genevan self (Georgie) and the old visiting professor (Borges). The story, "The Other," was later included in *El libro de arena* (The Book of Sand, 1975).

The following year an immense volume, the size of a telephone book, entirely dedicated to him, was published in France by *L'Herne*. It contained documents and reminiscences, articles and studies, interviews, a bibliography, and some illustrations. It was homage of a kind seldom given a living writer. Former titles in the same collection had concerned Céline, Ezra Pound, and Joyce. The volume included pieces by the new French critics—Gérard Genette, Jean Ricardou, Claude Ollier—as well as by a handful of specialists in Latin American literature. The importance of the book can be measured by the fact that it established Borges firmly as a writer to be read and studied. More books and special issues of learned journals would follow. The Borges industry was beginning to develop at a truly international level and with relentless speed. "Borges" was anointed a modern master.

2.
The Old Guru

In the spring of 1964 Borges returned to Europe, invited by the Congress for Cultural Freedom to participate in an international congress of writers in West Germany. This time, Mother stayed at home. She was finding these journeys a bit too exhausting for her eighty-eight years. A former student of Borges and a very good friend, María Esther Vázquez, accompanied him. The congress was one of the first to give Latin American literature a place of honor. It was attended by the Brazilian João Guimarães Rosa, author of the novel *The Devil to Pay in the Backlands* (1956), the Guatemalan novelist Miguel Angel Asturias (who received the Nobel Prize in 1967), the Argentine Eduardo Mallea, and the Paraguayan Augusto Roa Bastos. But it was Borges who received the lion's share of publicity. Visiting Paris on his way home, he was invited by UNESCO to participate with Giuseppe Ungaretti in a celebration of Shakespeare's quarter-centenary. Borges delivered in French a short piece, "Shakespeare and Us," which impressed the audience as being one of his most successful improvisations but which (according to María Esther Vázquez) took him the better part of two days to compose. He first dictated it in Spanish, then translated it into French, and finally had María Esther tape the text so he could play it over until he knew it by heart. The "Autobiographical Essay" makes no reference to the West German literary congress or to the UNESCO celebration, but concentrates on personal memories of England and Stockholm.

In England, we stayed with the late Herbert Read in his fine rambling house out on the moors. He took us to Yorkminster, where he showed us some ancient Danish swords in the Viking Yorkshire room of the museum. I later wrote a sonnet to one of the swords, and just before his death Sir Herbert corrected and bettered my original title, suggesting, instead of "To a Sword in York," "To a Sword in Yorkminster." ("Essay," 1970, pp. 256–257)

Again, one can recognize here the return to his British ancestors, to the Anglo-Saxons and the Vikings. The visit to Copenhagen and Stockholm—which he counts "among the most unforgettable cities I have seen, like San Francisco, New York, Edinburgh, Santiago de Compostela, and Geneva" (ibid., p. 257)—at the invitation of his Swedish publisher, Bonnier, must have reinforced his feeling for his Nordic ancestors.

Short trips to different countries in Latin America (Peru, Colombia, and Chile in 1965) helped to increase Borges' popularity across the continent. But he was less impressed by the native cultures of America than he had been by the old cultures of Europe. A visit to the Inca fortress of Machu Picchu—which had inspired one of Pablo Neruda's most extraordinary poems—left Borges curiously unmoved. According to María Esther Vázquez, who was again his companion on that journey, "I have never seen him so politely bored than in his visit to Machu Picchu; the (for him) invisible terraces of the pre-Columbian past failed to move his esthetic passion" (Vázquez, 1977, p. 28).

Borges' second journey to the United States took place in 1967. He was invited by Harvard University to hold the Charles Eliot Norton Chair of Poetry. He gave a lecture ("to well-wishing audiences," as he put it in the "Autobiographical Essay") called "This Craft of Verse"; he also taught a seminar on Argentine writers for the department of Romance languages. It was his first opportunity to live for a while in New England, and he accepted it enthusiastically. As he facetiously remarks in the "Essay," he had a chance to travel all over New England, "where most things American, including the West, seem to have been invented"; he adds that he "made numerous literary pilgrimages—to Hawthorne's haunts in Salem, to Emerson's in Concord, to Melville's in New Bedford, to Emily Dickinson's in Amherst, and to Longfellow's around the corner from where I lived" (ibid., p. 255).

The seven months spent in Cambridge were important for the number of friendships he made, especially with the members of the Spanish department at Harvard (Raimundo Lida, an Argentine scholar, he had met in Buenos Aires in the 1940s, and Juan Marichal, a Spaniard and head of the Latin American studies program). He also became friends with the Spanish poet Jorge Guillén; he lived with his daughter Teresa, who was married to Professor Stephen Gilman of the Spanish department at Harvard. Lastly, at Harvard Borges met two young men to whom he became attached: the Anglo-Argentine John Murchison, who was his secretary during that visit, and Norman Thomas di Giovanni, who for the next eight years served as his secretary, translator, and literary agent.

As on his first visit to the United States, Borges traveled extensively, crisscrossing the American continent from Massachusetts to Iowa ("where I found my native pampas awaiting me"), from Chicago ("recalling Carl Sandburg") to Missouri, Maryland, and Virginia. In his "Essay" he reports that "at the end of my stay, I was greatly honored to have my poems read at the YM-YWHA Poetry Center in New York, with several of my translators reading and a number of poets in the audience" (ibid., p. 256). Borges' pride may be justified on the grounds that his success was so extraordinary he could afford to boast a little. Besides, being professionally skeptical about everything (even reality had always seemed unreal to him), Borges was in the best possible position to be a little vain. If nothing really matters, then fame and success and adulation can be accepted eagerly, as the fictions they actually are. There is no doubt that he enjoyed them and that he took every opportunity to go where he would find applause.

At the beginning of 1969 he visited Israel for the first time, to lecture at the government's invitation. In his "Autobiographical Essay" he gives an enthusiastic account of that visit:

I spent ten very exciting days in Tel Aviv and Jerusalem. I brought home with me the conviction of having been in the oldest and the youngest of nations, of having come from a very living, vigilant land back to a half-asleep nook of the world. Since my Genevan days, I had always been interested in Jewish culture, thinking of it as an integral element of our so-called Western civilization, and during the Israeli-Arab war of a few years back I found myself taking immediate sides. While the outcome was still uncertain, I wrote a poem on the battle. A week later, I wrote another on the victory. Israel was, of course, still an armed camp at the time of my visit. There, along the shores of Galilee, I kept recalling these lines from Shakespeare:

> Over whose acres walk'd those blessed feet,
> Which, fourteen hundred years ago, were nail'd,
> For our advantage, on the bitter cross.
> (Ibid., p. 257)

Borges' deep sympathy for Israel was not shared by Latin America's left-wing intellectuals, who viewed the Palestinians as a dispossessed people and the Israelis as capitalist colonizers. For Borges, the right of the Jewish people to their native land was unquestionable. The poems and the statements he made in those years widened the gap between his view of the Middle East and that favored by the socialist Third World. Once more, Borges (without perhaps being fully aware of it) placed himself on the less popular side of the fence.

That same year, he returned to the United States to attend a "Borges Conference" held at the University of Oklahoma (Norman) on December 5 and 6. He gave some lectures and dutifully attended the elaborate discussion of his texts produced by a handful of specialists. Later, a volume entitled *The Cardinal Points of Borges* was edited by Lowell Dunham and Ivar Ivask with the papers and memorabilia produced by the conference. In his "Autobiographical Essay" Borges calls the editors "my two benefactors," has a nice word to say about his critics, and recalls an anecdote: "Ivask made me a gift of a fish-shaped Finnish dagger—rather alien to the tradition of the old Palermo of my boyhood" (ibid., p. 256). On his return to Argentina, he stopped at Georgetown University in Washington, D.C., to read his poems.

I saw him at the Borges Conference in Oklahoma. It was the first time we had met outside the River Plate area—the first time I had the experience of seeing him not as the almost closet genius who passed unnoticed among the inattentive crowd but as the guru of a new generation of readers (or shall I say listeners?). They were literally spaced out by his words, by the incantatory way in which he delivered them, by his blindness and his almost uncanny face. It was difficult for me to reconcile my many images of Borges—all based on an intimacy with his texts and a friendly, relaxed relationship with the man—with this new Borges. That is, with "Borges." Because by that time "Borges" had taken over almost completely. In spite of all that, I had no trouble finding the old Borges behind the formidable façade of the guru. Sitting with him in the university's cafeteria, I recalled the good old days when he was young and unknown and said something to the effect that we could never have foreseen our meeting in Oklahoma of all places, and on such a solemn occasion. He laughed heartily and observed that we were not that far from doing what we used to do: sitting in a café talking about literature in the middle of nowhere. Oklahoma was to him, mutatis mutandis, another version of the vast expanse of the pampas. I had to agree, especially when I realized that he hadn't lost any of that provocative skepticism and that he took all the tributes and homages in stride, as part of the movable happening his life had become. There was no question that Borges was still very much alive inside "Borges."

On August 22 of the same year he traveled to Brazil to receive the Inter-American Literary Prize awarded by the governor of the state of São Paulo. It consisted of $25,000. He was feted, interviewed, and generally lionized by one of the most sophisticated intellectual communities in Latin America. President Castelo Branco indicated that he

would welcome his visit to Brasilia. On the day appointed, with everything set for the highly complex operation that would take Borges to
the remote capital, he excused himself with the explanation that he had
to return to Buenos Aires. Mother was having a ninety-third birthday
party, and (president or no president) he could not miss it. The Brazilian intellectuals relished that involuntary snub to their president, but
Borges was not trying to make a political point. He was deeply concerned with Mother. He knew she was getting terribly old and he
wanted to be as close to her as possible on that particular occasion.

In 1971 he returned to the United States to receive an honorary doctorate from Columbia University and to participate in a conference attended by Latin American writers and artists, politicians, and
critics of all persuasions. As usual, he became the focus of attention and
was selected as a target of attack by a representative of a group of
Puerto Rican students who wanted to protest the way Columbia was
handling its responsibilities as slum landlord. Instead of criticizing the
university, the student attacked the visitors for associating themselves
with Columbia. In the heat of the discussion the student insulted
Borges, making a remark about his mother's supposed profession and
concluding that Borges had nothing to say about Latin America because he was already dead. Borges' skepticism failed him on that occasion. Instead of realizing that the student, Columbia University, and
the whole world were only part of a larger state of unrest, he became
furious and, banging on the table, challenged the student to settle matters outside. The student must have been barely twenty. Borges (at
seventy-two) was frail, holding his cane in trembling hands. But he
meant every word of his chivalrous invitation. Somehow things quieted
down. At lunchtime I took Borges to the dining room. Awkwardly, I
tried to explain the political situation that had prompted the attack. He
stopped me dead and said that of course he knew the student did not
intend to attack Mother, because if he had thought so, he would have
taken his cane and smashed it over the student's head. He was trembling while he said it and his cane moved uncontrollably.

On that same occasion, he accepted an invitation to go to Yale
University for "An Evening with Jorge Luis Borges." I was then chairman of Yale's Spanish and Portuguese department and of the council
on Latin American studies. We had invited a handful of writers and
critics to talk informally with Borges in front of an audience. We reserved a room for some two hundred people. When we reached the
room, it was overflowing. Somehow, five hundred people had managed
to squeeze inside, but there was no place for Borges. We decided to
search for a larger room. Headed by Borges, a procession formed
slowly and traversed the Yale campus. In no time a police car closed in

on us (it was the days of student unrest and we had no permission to demonstrate). But we were so obviously men of peace that the police let us continue our search. At last we discovered that one of the largest halls was free. When we reached it, it was already jammed: the audience had filled every inch. The janitor (a very firm person when it came to regulations) began to complain loudly that he had not been properly warned and that, besides, the campus police would never allow more than five hundred people in that particular hall. We cajoled and pleaded with him, and finally managed to persuade the police and the janitor to give us the hall. But it took some extra persuasion to convince the audience that it had to clear the podium and the corridors. Finally, after a delay of an hour, the planned intimate conversation on literary matters took place. It was intimate only in the sense that everyone who participated felt very close to Borges. In spite of the crowd and the cavernous size of the hall, intimacy somehow resulted. The members of the audience had invested too much to secure a place, and they were determined to make the evening a success.

Borges began by answering, with his subtlest irony, questions politely put forth by writers and critics. That won them completely. He is one of us, they felt. When the floor was opened to questions, people rushed to ask him about everything that passed through their minds. Borges answered with humor and simplicity, never talking down to them, always comic and gentle. The last question ("Have you ever been in love?") elicited the shortest possible answer: "Yes." It was said with deep feeling, and the final *s* kept sounding for a while. At that the audience roared, and the happening ended.

Earlier, while we were sitting in a small room behind the podium waiting for permission to use the hall, I had asked Borges if he was afraid the audience would become unruly. He said no; besides, he added, he couldn't care less: reality always seemed a bit out of hand to him. Being blind, he was used to not controlling events, to letting reality invade him. At the end of his astonishing performance I understood better what he meant. That shy and extremely sensitive man I had met in Montevideo in 1945—a man who had not dared to read the text of a lecture he knew by heart—had become the grand old man of Latin American letters, the guru to a new generation that came to him not as we used to, to get some crumbs of his literary dinners, but just to see and listen and laugh and be moved by an experience that was not purely literary but belonged to another dimension. Borges could not see his listeners, but he sensed that a rapport existed between him and them; and because he knew it, because he sensed it, he was serene while all of us, who could see, were afraid. He trusted his audience, and it in turn loved him.

454

During the 1970s, Borges continued to visit the United States regularly: in 1972 he inaugurated a chair of Spanish American literature at the University of New Hampshire (Durham), visited Houston, Texas, and received another honorary doctorate, this time from the University of Michigan (East Lansing); in 1975 he returned to the Michigan campus for a short visit; in 1976 he visited the university for a third time, to lecture on Argentine literature. He traveled around, lecturing and reading his poems, and attended a symposium on his work sponsored by the University of Maine (Orono). On that occasion, in a last meeting with a panel of critics and professors, Borges spoke out against a type of criticism that he believed was going too far. He objected to having his stories and poems analyzed to extinction and stated that they were meant to be read simply as entertainment. He also stated firmly that in spite of all his debts to English literature his models were not British or American writers but the Franco-Argentine Paul Groussac and the Mexican Alfonso Reyes. He was right, of course, on the second count; as for the first, since his critics seldom read anything but his own works (as he complained to me later, in an epigram: "Poor things, they only read Borges!"), his comment was ironic.

On his return to Buenos Aires he stopped briefly in New York and, for the second time, had his poetry read at the YM-YWHA Poetry Center. It was again a triumph of the guru. Borges sat on one side of the podium, while Richard Howard and W. S. Merwin, two of his most distinguished translators, and I sat on the opposite side. The poems were read first in Spanish, by me, and then in English, by one of the translators. Borges said a few words on each text. The procedure could have been deadly boring. If it was not, it was because the audience was electrified by that fragile man, whose English sometimes got bogged down by a rather archaic North Country slur or by some mechanical frailties of old age. In spite of that, or perhaps because of that, the old man managed to create an incantatory space. The brusque gestures of his hand, the voice that perversely missed the microphone or plainly stammered, the blind eyes that traveled wildly, were not seen separately but as a single unit: the unit of a magic performance in which it was not what was said or done but what was subliminally communicated that mattered. Borges, like the Cuman sibyl, could never be wrong, or cease to haunt his listeners.

Some of these journeys to the United States included a European extension. In 1971, instead of returning directly to Buenos Aires, Borges flew for the second time to Israel—to receive, on April 19, the Jerusalem Prize of $2,000, an award that had previously been given to Max Frisch, Bertrand Russell, and Ignazio Silone. On his return he stopped in Scotland, went down to Oxford to receive another honorary doctorate, and visited London to lecture at the Institute of Contemporary Arts. In 1973, he made a second trip to Spain, at the invitation of the Franco-sponsored Institute of Hispanic Culture and the Argentine embassy. In December of that year he went to Mexico to receive the Alfonso Reyes Prize. A second trip to Mexico took place in 1976. That same year, he returned to Spain. Everywhere, he was interviewed to distraction, feted and lionized, crowded and almost mobbed with adulation. Everywhere, he lent himself meekly to public worship, stoically suffered bores and illiterate interviewers, polished off one cocktail party after another. Thin, frail, so white that from a distance it was hard to say whether he was standing or floating, Borges seemed to be made of invisible steel: untiring, unbored, undefeatable. He has long accepted the public persona and has resigned himself to being "Borges." What really happens inside that persona is (he firmly believes) nobody's business.

3.
The Art of
Dictating

With blindness, Borges learned how to compose a poem in his mind, polish it, and finally dictate it to Mother or to one of his scores of friends. Short stories and essays presented a greater problem, and for a while he hesitated, looking for the perfect amanuensis. Apart from Bioy Casares (with whom he had a rather symbiotic relationship before his blindness), his collaborators ranged from the merely mechanic—students who had followed his lectures and put them into writing—to the highly creative. Some were too subservient and did not dare to raise their voices, happy to sit at his feet and take down whatever he said. Others were too independent and Borges, after being extremely polite, finally tired of them. One of his regular collaborators, María Esther Vázquez, has described his methods in some detail:

> Borges has a strange way of working. He dictates five or six words, which are the opening of a prose piece or the first verse of a poem, and immediately he has them read back to him. The index finger of his right hand follows the reading on the back of his left hand, as if it were crossing an invisible page. Each phrase is read one, two, three, four, many times until he discovers how to continue and he dictates another five or six words. Then he has all that has been already written read. Since he dictates indicating the signs of punctuation, it is necessary to read all the signs as well. The fragment is read once more, and again he follows it with the movement of his hands until he finds the next phrase. I have read some dozen times a fragment of five lines. Each one of these repetitions is preceded by Borges' apologies, for he somehow torments himself quite a lot over the supposed inconvenience to which he submits his amanuensis. The result is that, after two or three hours of work, one has half a page which no longer needs correction. (Vázquez, 1977, pp. 28–29)

457

In spite of the exquisite slowness of the method, Borges never lacked for an amanuensis, or even distinguished collaborators. For several decades the first and most important was Mother. To her he dictated some of his most significant writings. He told Richard Burgin that while transcribing one of his darkest short stories, "The Intruder," Mother protested. "She thought that the story was a very unpleasant one. She thought it awful" (Burgin, 1969, p. 48). The story tells of two brothers who share the same woman and end up by murdering her. Brotherly love triumphs over heterosexual attachment. In spite of Mother's objections, she not only copied it but contributed a memorable line, which is spoken by the older brother when he invites the younger one to bury the woman. Borges could not find the exact tone, and after a while Mother (who knew how simple old-fashioned Argentines spoke) volunteered: "Let's get busy, brother. In a while the buzzards will take over" (*The Aleph*, 1970, p. 166).

Because Mother was beginning to show her age, Borges had to turn more and more to other people. His literary output was enormous. In 1961 he dictated the prologue to a selection of works by his old master Macedonio Fernández (*Prose and Verse*); compiled an anthology of his own texts, *Personal Anthology;* and wrote the introduction to a selection in Spanish of Gibbon's *Pages of History and Autobiography.* In 1962 it was the turn of another of his favorite Argentine poets, Almafuerte, whose *Prose and Poetry* he prefaced. In 1965 he published two books: a second version of his *Ancient German Literatures,* prepared with the help of María Esther Vázquez, and a collection of poems he wrote to be sung with the guitar, *For the Six Strings.* In 1966 he dictated "The Intruder" to Mother and included it in that year's new edition of *The Aleph;* he also published an enlarged edition of his *Poetic Works* (1923–1966), which came out both in an illustrated edition and as a new edition of the second volume of his complete works. In 1967 he and Bioy Casares published (this time under their own names) the *Chronicles of Bustos Domecq,* a collection of outrageous parodies of Argentine literary and artistic life. The same year, a slim volume based on his lectures came out; called *Introduction to American Literature,* it had been put together with the help of Esther Zemborain de Torres, an old friend. Two more books were added to the canon in 1968: the first was the *New Personal Anthology,* which complemented the one already published in 1961; the second was a new version of his *Manual of Fantastic Zoology,* under the better title of *The Book of Imaginary Beings* and with thirty-four new articles. A completely new volume of poems came out in 1969, *In Praise of Darkness,* as well as the first volume edited by Norman Thomas di Giovanni of the English translation of his work. It was *The Book of Imaginary Beings.*

The original Spanish had been entirely reworded and the result was a new book which contained 120 pieces compared with 82 in the first Spanish edition. Since he had first met Borges at Harvard, in the fall of 1967, Di Giovanni had been spellbound. He had already started publishing translations from the Spanish and had produced a book of Jorge Guillén's poems. But after meeting Borges, he decided to devote all his efforts to translating his writings into English. The task may have seemed easier than it is. The fact that Borges is bilingual and that he has a vast and minute knowledge of both the English language and English literature had undoubtedly influenced his writings in Spanish. But in spite of it, he is a Spanish writer, and very specifically a Spanish American writer, of the River Plate area. He may sound exotic to Spanish readers used to the stiff syntax and vocabulary of Spanish provinces or to the solemn horrors promoted by academies and universities all over the Hispanic world. But to readers of the best prose written in Latin America in the last century (Sarmiento, Groussac, Martí, Alfonso Reyes, Pedro Henríquez Ureña), Borges' writing seems, and is, very Spanish American. Some of his English translators had been too literal and thus had come across insoluble problems. The best example (provided by Borges himself) of the pitfalls of any literal translation can be found in a simple Spanish expression such as "Entró en una habitación oscura." The literal translation would be "He entered into an obscure habitation," which sounds a bit like Sir Thomas Browne. What the phrase means is "He came into a dark room."

Norman Thomas di Giovanni was unhappy with the stiffness and inaccuracies of the existing English versions of Borges, and he decided that the only effective way to translate Borges was to move to Argentina and work in close association with the writer. He managed to get help from the Ingram Merrill Foundation. Borges was delighted. For close to three years Di Giovanni lived in Buenos Aires, working regularly with Borges, doubling as his secretary on some of his journeys (Oklahoma, 1969; Columbia and Yale, 1971), and in general taking care of his rights in England and the United States, helping Borges to earn a substantial income for the first time in his life. In the process, several volumes of stories and poems were translated by Di Giovanni and the author, or by other writers under Di Giovanni's supervision and editorship. An official Borges canon was thus produced in English. Apart from the already mentioned *Book of Imaginary Beings*, the following titles came out of Di Giovanni's industry: *The Aleph and Other Stories: 1933–1969* (1970), a collection of stories not covered by the copyrighted American editions of *Ficciones* and *Labyrinths*; *A Universal History of Infamy* (1972); *Selected Poems: 1923–1967* (1972), with valuable information in the back of the book; *Borges on Writing* (1973), a transcript of Borges' conversations with students enrolled in Columbia University's graduate writing program, edited by Di Giovanni, with the assistance of Daniel Halpern and Frank MacShane; *In Praise of Darkness* (1974), in a bilingual edition; *Chronicles of Bustos Domecq* (1976); and *The Book of Sand* (1977).

Their unique method of translating Borges into English was described in the preface to *The Aleph and Other Stories:*

> Perhaps the chief justification of this book is the translation itself, which we have undertaken in what may be a new way. Working closely together in daily sessions, we have tried to make these stories read as though they had been written in English. We do not consider English and Spanish as compounded of sets of easily interchangeable synonyms; they are two quite different ways of looking at the world, each with a nature of its own. English, for example, is far more physical than Spanish. We have therefore shunned the dictionary as much as possible and done our best to rethink every sentence in English words. This venture does not necessarily mean that we have willfully tampered with the original, though in certain cases we have supplied the American reader with those things—geographical, topographical, and historical—taken for granted by an Argentine. (*The Aleph,* 1970, pp. 9–10)

Di Giovanni helped Borges to write and put together the original Spanish editions as well as English translations of several texts: *In Praise of Darkness* (1969); *Dr. Brodie's Report* (1970); "The Congress" (1971), a short story in which Borges returns to the subject of the secret society he had already explored in "Tlön, Uqbar, Orbis Tertius"; and *The Gold of the Tigers* (1972), a collection of prose and verse. In a foreword to his translation of *Dr. Brodie's Report,* Di Giovanni reiterates what Borges and he had already said in introducing *The Aleph* but adds a significant sentence: "One difference between this volume and the last lies in the fact that the writing and the translation were, except in one case, more or less simultaneous. In this way, our work was easier for us, since, as we were always under the spell of the originals, we stood in no need of trying to recapture past moods. This seems to us the best possible condition under which to practice the craft of translation." (*Brodie,* 1970, p. 7)

This close collaboration between author and translator raised a question neither Borges nor Di Giovanni seems to have faced: by becoming co-author of the translation, Borges had assumed the status of writer in English, a role he had so far avoided. Borges' knowledge of English is indisputable: he uses it as a native, perhaps even better, because he has also studied it as a foreign language. His knowledge of English and American literature is also vast. But all that does not make him an English writer, and especially it does not make him an English writer capable of writing with the freedom, inventiveness, and feeling for words that Borges, the Spanish writer, has. To put it differently, as a translator of his own texts, Borges seems old-fashioned, awkward. His Victorian, bookish handling of the English language does a disservice to the original's truly creative Spanish. On the other hand, Di Giovanni, being a North American and much younger, has a totally different concept of English, both written and spoken. The result, from a literary point of view, is sometimes strange. If their translations cannot be objected to from the point of view of accuracy and scholarship (they are the best one can ask for), they are less than unique from a purely creative point of view.

Borges and Di Giovanni parted company around 1972. But Di Giovanni is still committed to translating some of his older works and continues to receive 50 percent of the income from Borges' English rights. Borges, for his part, has continued to produce new books: his *Obras Completas* (Complete Works), in a bound volume printed on thin paper, was published in 1974. It was immediately sold out. The popularity of the book (extremely expensive by Argentine standards) is such that it is sold at newspaper and magazine stands in Buenos Aires. Borges was not aware of this fact until quite recently—the Argentine writer Ernesto Sábato called it to his attention. Three more titles came out in 1975: *El libro de arena* (The Book of Sand), a collection of thirteen short stories in which he returns to the fantastic genre; *La rosa profunda* (The Unending Rose), thirty-six new poems; and *Prólogos* (Prologues, with a Prologue of Prologues), an important collection of thirty prefaces he had written since 1923, which unfortunately does not include his prologue to the *Divine Comedy*. Three more books came out in 1976: *Libro de sueños* (The Book of Dreams), in which he retells his own and other people's dreams; *La moneda de hierro* (The Iron Coin), a collection of thirty-eight new poems; and *¿Qué es el budismo?* (What Is Buddhism?) a primer compiled with Alicia Jurado.

Of the fifteen-odd new or revised books Borges has published in Spanish in the last fifteen years, only half are truly original. In one of them (*Chronicles of Bustos Domecq*) he had the advantage of collaborating with a close friend and gifted writer. In another, *The Book of Imaginary Beings,* collaboration was less important at the beginning but became decisive as the book took final shape. There, the wit and imagination are totally his, but the painstaking scholarship, the tracing of all the sources half remembered, half invented by Borges, is Di Giovanni's main contribution.

Blindness also brought Borges back to poetry. In the last decade especially, poems seem to flow naturally from him. The old guru is a traditional poet who wisely sticks to the sonnet because it is easy to compose in the mind, who preserves rhyme because it keeps ringing, and who celebrates his discoveries (new places and new readings of old books and authors) but keeps coming back to a handful of trusted subjects: old age, blindness, emptiness (metaphysical and personal), and longing for a reality that has always eluded him. It is conventional in form, but it is made poignant by the intensity with which the poet handles each subject and the underlying pain that tradition and politeness cannot efface. As an old guru, Borges is shamelessly autobiographical. At the same time, decorum never leaves him, and the reader (although offered the chance for an intimate revelation) is finally denied any real exposure.

The short stories have been handled differently by Borges. The battle between the realistic and magic conventions of storytelling has not ceased. In 1966 Borges told César Fernández Moreno that he was tired of labyrinths, tigers, and mirrors, that he had decided to stop making stories about them and was leaving them to his followers: "Now, let them try it and get screwed" (Fernández Moreno, 1967b, p. 25). In the 1969 collection published under the title of *Dr. Brodie's Report,* he aimed at realism. The preface can be read as a manifesto of the old guru against the middle-aged Borges of *Ficciones:*

> I have done my best—I don't know with what success—to write straightforward stories. I do not dare state that they are simple; there isn't anywhere on earth a single page or single word that is, since each thing implies the universe, whose most obvious trait is complexity. . . . Apart from the text that gives this book its title and that obviously derives from Lemuel Gulliver's last voyage, my stories are—to use the term in vogue today—realistic. They follow, I believe, all the conventions of that school, which is as conventional as any other and of which we shall grow tired if we have not already done so. They are rich in the required invention of circumstances. (*Brodie,* 1969, pp. 9–10)

He also insists on the same page that he is not a "committed writer," and that he does not "aspire to be Aesop. My stories, like those of the *One Thousand and One Nights,* try to be entertaining or moving but not persuasive." As an afterthought, he adds that he has always been very open in expressing his political convictions:

> I am a member of the Conservative Party—this in itself is a form of skepticism—and no one has ever branded me a Communist, a nationalist, an anti-Semite, a follower of Billy the Kid or of the dictator Rosas. I believe that someday we will deserve not to have governments. I have never kept my opinions hidden, not even in trying times, but neither have I ever allowed

them to find their way into my literary work, except once when I was buoyed up in exultation over the Six-Day War. (Ibid., p. 10)

Borges' political allusions and his refusal to write "committed" literature have to be read in the context of the Argentine literary situation of the time. The inevitable return of Perón to power had made it virtually impossible for any man of letters to remain uncommitted. Borges seized the occasion offered by the preface to state his belief in a noncommitted literature, thus emphasizing one of the old guru's most provocative traits: to go against the grain, to avoid consensus, to maintain unpopular and even outrageous opinions. But if he was infuriating, he was right about refusing to use his work as a soapbox. He well knew that the author's ideology and the text's ideology rarely coincide. Balzac (whom Marx admired so much) believed in the monarchy, the Catholic Church, and the moral superiority of French women, but his novels presented France as a country run by a pack of capitalistic, greedy, and debauched characters. Dostoevski believed in the czar and the Russian Orthodox Church, was a rabid nationalist, and scorned revolutionaries: his novels tear to pieces the fabric of deceptions and crimes that the institutions he loved had created; his work paved the way for the revolution to come. D'Annunzio in Italy, Pound in the United States, and Céline in France were all in favor of different kinds of fascism, but their writings were not conservative or supportive of the status quo; rather, they dwelled on decadence, madness, and the final absurdity of the human condition.

The man Borges may vote conservative, reject socialism of any kind, and love strong regimes. The text we call Borges does not stoop to that kind of compromise: it is plainly in favor of skepticism, doubts reality has any meaning, and accepts the cruel paradoxes and ironies of the human condition without fear or remorse. Besides, the text is not subject to the infirmities of the flesh and the extravagances of old age. In his preface to *Dr. Brodie's Report,* Borges delivers a final statement: "The art of writing is mysterious, the opinions we hold are ephemeral, and I prefer the Platonic idea of the Muse to that of Poe, who reasoned, or feigned to reason, that the writing of a poem is an act of the intelligence" (ibid., p. 10). Thus it cannot come as a surprise to the reader that these so-called realistic stories are, essentially, similar to the "magic" ones Borges has been writing since he published the original edition of *A Universal History of Infamy* (1935). If the writing seems more terse, less baroque, and the use of circumstantial detail more frequent, the point of view has not changed that much. Not only does the title story, "Dr. Brodie's Report," deal with the uncanny; the other stories also provide examples of strange behavior or offer paradoxical viewpoints. "Pedro Salvadores," for instance, is in a sense a rewriting of Hawthorne's haunting "Wakefield," a story Borges loves. At least two of the remaining stories are frankly fantastic. In "The Meeting" two men fight a duel with knives they do not know how to handle; but because the knives know their job, they fight well. In "The Gospel According to Mark" a rather naïve student reads the Bible to a family of degenerate and illiterate Calvinists only to discover, at the last possible minute, that they take the story of Jesus' crucifixion too literally.

√ Borges' most recent book of original short stories, *The Book of Sand,* is unabashedly fantastic. Instead of a preface, in the Argentine edition it has an epilogue and a signed statement on the back cover. After declaring that it is wrong to discuss in a preface stories the reader has not yet read (but who reads prefaces anyhow?), Borges comments on each story, identifying its nature (fantastic, erotic, autobiographical, historical, and so forth) and insisting on the dreamlike quality throughout. The back cover reiterates, in a slightly different way, some of these arguments, calls the stories "blindman's exercises," and mentions Wells, Poe, and Swift as his models both for style and plot.

The stories (thirteen, a number Borges refuses to view as "magic") repeat some of his literary obsessions: the double ("The Other"), the infinite ("The Book of Sand"), the secret society ("The Congress"), the vagaries of behavior ("Avelino Arredondo"). Only one new topic is added: the splendor of carnal love, which Borges had earlier refused to treat explicitly in his work. Sexual allusions could be found, of course, in poems and even in some stories and essays, but they were always derogatory. Now, the old guru publishes a story about a Norwegian girl who sweetly gives herself to a puzzled and thankful Argentine; and in the labyrinthine narrative "The Congress" he introduces a rather Hemingwayesque version of carnal bliss.

Eroticism was never totally absent in Borges' work. It has always been hidden or disguised, masked or displaced. In his late seventies he has allowed himself finally to admit in print the validity of erotic dreams. Of course, the fact that in "The Congress" (a pun which alludes to copulation) the girl's name is the rather forbidding one of Beatriz Frost may have warned the careful reader about Borges' intentions. The original Beatrice, as is well known, did *not* love Dante and never condescended to anything more intimate than a formal greeting on the streets of Florence. Frost (needless to say) is not easily associated with the heat that love generates. In calling the girl Beatriz Frost, Borges alludes to the tantalizing nature, both warm and chilly, of that dream of carnal ecstasy.

Apart from the books he authored, alone or with the help of friends, Borges has authorized the publication in book form of some long and sometimes repetitive interviews. Three were published in 1967: by Georges Charbonnier, Jean de Milleret, and César Fernández Moreno (included in his book *Reality and Papers* and later condensed in my book *Borges par lui même,* 1970). In 1968 Rita Guibert conducted an extensive interview for *Life en Español* which was later included in her book *Seven Voices* (1973). In 1969 Richard Burgin came out with a volume called *Conversations with Jorge Luis Borges.* Victoria Ocampo's *Dialogues with Borges* came out the same year. In 1977 two more books of conversations were added to the ever increasing canon. The first reproduces a series of meetings between Borges and Ernesto Sábato, the well-known Argentine novelist; the second is the work of María Esther Vázquez and includes not only dialogues with Borges but also the author's own recollections of a long friendship and collaboration.

The number of interviews, of special issues of magazines, of books on any and every aspect of Borges' life and work keeps increasing. Today the Borges industry is at its peak. For better or for worse, Borges has reached a stage in which he no longer belongs to himself: he is public property. Perhaps the extent of his popularity can be measured by the way movies have treated him. Before he became "Borges," a few enthusiastic readers had attempted to translate some of his stories for the Argentine cinema: Leopoldo Torre Nilsson did "Emma Zunz" under the rather Dreyerian title *Days of Wrath* (1953–1954); René Mugica did a rather folkloric version of "Streetcorner Man" (1961–1962). But by the late 1960s and into the 1970s Argentine and European filmmakers began to compete for Borges' themes or subjects: Hugo Santiago made two films from scripts that were partially authored by Borges and Bioy Casares—*Invasion* (Argentina, 1968–1969) and *The Others* (France, 1973–1974); Alain Magrou had a second look at "Emma Zunz" (France, 1969); Bernardo Bertolucci based his *The Spider's Stratagem* (Italy, 1969–1970) on "Theme of the Traitor and the Hero"; Ricardo Luna filmed *The Hoodlums* (Argentina, 1975) from a script Borges had authored with Bioy Casares in 1955; Héctor Olivera adapted "The Dead One" for the screen (Argentina, 1975) with some help from the Uruguayan novelist, Juan Carlos Onetti.

Even more revealing than the existence of these adaptations is the fact that Borges is constantly "quoted" by some of the most sophisticated filmmakers. Jacques Rivette had one of the characters of *Paris Belongs to Us* (1958) read Borges' *Other Inquisitions.* In Jean-Luc Godard's *Alphaville* (1965) the computer which runs that futuristic world quotes some passages from Borges' "A New Refutation of Time." In Nicholas Roeg's *Performance* (1972) one of the characters, a gangster, is seen reading Borges' *Personal Anthology;* even more surprising is the fact that Mick Jagger seems also to have read it: in one scene he quotes lines from it, and in the climax of that movie the photograph of Borges which appears on the cover of the *Personal Anthology* is seen escaping from his head, brutally opened by a shot from James Fox's gun.

Borges, or rather "Borges," has become chic. The old guru has fallen in with fast company. But behind that mask, Borges (the sad, old-fashioned, shy, very Argentine old gentleman) is still very much himself.

4.
A Magic Space

For the last three decades of their life together, Borges and Mother lived in the same two-bedroom apartment on the sixth floor of a house on Maipú Street, in downtown Buenos Aires. From the balcony that runs along the bedrooms, a terrace filled with pots of flowers, one can see the tops of the trees of beautiful San Martín Square. The Borgeses moved to that apartment in 1944, after a rather unsuccessful attempt at sharing lodgings with Norah and her family and a transitional stay at an apartment on Quintana Avenue. The Maipú apartment was to become the final residence for this strangely matched couple.

The first time I went to visit them, in 1946, the apartment was still new (it was probably built in the late 1930s or early 1940s): the entrance hall, the corridors, and the small elevator had the smell of carefully maintained premises. They suggested a relatively affluent middle-class status. The door to their apartment had a small bronze plaque with the surname Borges. Inside, the rather large living room was cluttered with nineteenth-century furniture: in the dining area, a solid table and chairs, a cupboard with some old silver pieces; against the only large window, a small sofa and two chairs. An elegant marquetry cabinet with a marble top and Mother's small writing desk (a present she got on her First Communion) completed the living room area. All the items were good and solid, the mahogany gleamed, the upholstered chairs and sofa looked new in spite of their old-fashioned shape and colors. These pieces were family heirlooms which, in spite of the Borgeses' rather modest financial situation, certified their links with more spacious times. On the walls a few daguerreotypes illustrated the family museum; paintings or drawings by Norah, photographs of Father and Mother when young, of Georgie and his sister, completed the private iconography. A sword, a silver maté gourd, a book beautifully bound: those were the few treasures which they had managed to salvage. In one of the corners of the dining area open shelves contained half of Borges' rather small but select library, carefully put together by Mother's devotion to the books that both Father and Georgie had loved so much. Framing the opposite window, two more shelves contained less elegantly bound books and assorted paperbacks. That day I was not asked to venture any further into the apartment.

I had lunch with Borges and Mother. It was a very simple affair; the table was attended by a middle-aged maid who had been with the Borgeses for quite a long time. I cannot remember what we talked about, but it must have concerned, chiefly, our mutual friends and relations on both sides of the River Plate. Mother had been born in Uruguay, and as I came from there, the subject seemed inevitable. One thing I do remember to this day: when wine was offered (a simple but good Argentine wine), the maid asked Mother, not Borges, if he would also have some wine. Almost at once, Borges and Mother replied in the negative. But what struck me was Mother's way of phrasing her answer. She literally said, "El niño no toma vino," which could be translated as "Master Borges does not drink wine." Master, here, was used in the Victorian sense: male children were always called "Master" by the servants. Borges was then forty-seven, but as he was living in his mother's house and was still unmarried he continued to be addressed as "Master." Although I was then only twenty-five, I was already married. So I was "Mister" and drank wine with Mother.

In a sense, while Mother lived (and she lived to be ninety-nine), Borges never ceased to be a child. Since Father's death in 1938, Borges had, nominally at least, been the head of the house and the principal breadwinner. But at home, in the privileged space of the Maipú apartment, she was Mother and Borges was Georgie. Even the fact that, because of his increasing blindness, Mother doubled as secretary and nurse, and soon had to take on the functions of literary agent and ambassador-at-large, did not alter the basic relationship. She helped him with his literary work, took dictation from him, and read aloud to him in English and French, but it all was done the way a mother helps her child with his homework.

During the next thirty years I visited that apartment many times. To me it seemed like a unique place: a space where Borges and Mother continued to live as if the umbilical cord that once attached them had never been severed. Time passed; they grew old together. New nations emerged in Africa. The Vietnam war—at first a

French colonial enterprise—began to contaminate every corner of the globe. Perón fell, Cuba became socialist, Allende was murdered in Chile, the Uruguayan people were kept in prison by their own army, Perón returned. But the Maipú apartment (and its two incredibly delicate inhabitants) continued there, basically unchanged. Borges' fame did not alter things much. The apartment seemed made of a substance immune to time. It was a magic space, an *omphalós,* the navel or center of a mystical private world. On one of the living room walls a Piranesi engraving which depicts a circular space (an arena or a Roman orchestra) could be seen as an emblem of that apartment.

In due time I was to be casually asked to enter the bedrooms. Mother's was large and sunny: it had a French window which opened onto the balcony. She had kept the furniture she received when she was married at the turn of the century. The room was dominated by a double bed and a big solid chest of drawers, the top literally covered with family photographs. Mother's was the master bedroom. Georgie had the smaller one, reserved for children. It contained a very narrow iron bed with a minuscule night table, a small glass bookcase where he kept the book he was currently working on, a chair, and a narrow chest of drawers with some knick-knacks on top. Everything was very neat and sterile. Over the bed Mother had placed a crucifix. Georgie was indifferent to that symbol of a faith he did not share, but he was careful not to offend Mother.

When it became obvious that Mother was getting too old to take proper care of Georgie, they had to find someone willing to take Mother's place. They used to discuss the matter openly with friends. Both Georgie and Mother were unafraid of their personal deaths and made no bones about the fact that they knew their days were numbered. But the problem was to find somebody to replace Mother. Norah was unsuitable. She could hardly cope with her own family; besides, Borges and she had drifted apart since the fateful day in 1928 when she married Guillermo de Torre. For a while it seemed as if Adolfo Bioy Casares and Silvina could act as surrogate parents. But they traveled a lot and led very leisurely and in a sense separate lives. In spite of their friendship (Borges used to dine with them on Sundays), a certain British formality prevented them from discussing seriously his moving in with them in the event of Mother's death. So the idea of a marriage of convenience for Georgie began to take shape. Unfortunately, Georgie and Mother did not have the same notions about what kind of wife he needed.

In the early 1960s the conflict came into the open. The last trip Mother and Georgie took together (to Europe in 1963) put an enormous strain on her. When, the following year, Borges was invited to go to Germany, Mother decided to stay at home. Borges asked María Esther Vázquez to accompany him. According to her reminiscences, she was seventeen the first time she went to visit Borges at home, in the company of a group of students from the Faculty of Philosophy and Letters of the University of Buenos Aires. Later she began to collaborate regularly with him and became a close friend. Although Mother did not object to their friendship, she objected to Georgie becoming too dependent on her. She was afraid he might decide to ask María Esther to be his wife. Mother wanted Georgie to marry somebody closer to his own age, a mature woman who could also be a nurse. And she believed, rightly, that María Esther—in spite of her friendly attachment to Georgie—was not seriously interested in sharing her whole life with him. But apparently he could not be persuaded, was terribly stubborn and resented what he saw as Mother's interference. Some traces of his irritation can be found in his conversations with Jean de Milleret, taped in 1966, after he had to abandon his plan of marrying María Esther. He was outspoken then and obviously bitter in stressing the ignorance of Mother's branch of the family (De Milleret, 1967, p. 39); in a footnote De Milleret reports how displeased Mother was on seeing Georgie's name coupled with María Esther's on the cover of the book *Ancient German Literatures* (1965), which he authored with her help (ibid., p. 231n). In an even more tantalizing parenthesis De Milleret talks about Borges' despair at not being able to overcome a recent setback in love (ibid., p. 168). It is obvious that he is alluding to Georgie's disappointment at not marrying María Esther. Borges eventually overcame it, and to this day his friendship with her continues.

It is against this background that Georgie's decision to marry Elsa Astete Millán, barely one year after these events, can be better understood. Elsa had been an old if brief flame. They had met around 1927, when he was twenty-seven and she was seventeen. She lived with her family in La Plata, the capital of the province of Buenos Aires and a city whose main claim to distinction is its university. Through Pedro Henríquez Ureña, who was a professor at the university, Georgie met the Astete sisters. One eventually married, and later divorced, one of Georgie's first disciples, Néstor Ibarra; the second, Elsa, attracted Georgie's attention. But she did not seem to be terribly impressed by the young, bashful poet. Their romance (if there ever was one) did not last long. She married Ricardo Albarracín, a young man who was a descendant of Sarmiento, the great nineteenth-century Argentine man of letters. In 1964 Elsa's husband died; three years later, she met Georgie again. If time had changed him for the better (he was now Borges), blindness prevented him from modifying his image of Elsa. They soon decided to marry. Thirty years was a long enough wait. Mother did not like the idea at all. She openly expressed her reservations about the prospective bride. Once she observed, for instance, that Elsa was unsuitable because she did not speak English. From that point of view, Mother was prophetic. Elsa's and Georgie's enjoyment of their journeys to the United States and England were marred by Elsa's unfamiliarity with the English language. But Georgie did not want a repetition of the previous frustration and stubbornly went along with the engagement. On September 21, 1967, they were married. Mother was, of course, present. In a photograph of the occasion published in one of Buenos Aires' largest newspapers, one can see her hand resting on Georgie's. By that time, everything Borges did was public and the press extracted every inch of gossip from the ceremony.

In poems as well as in some documentary movies (such as the one Harold Mantell did in 1969), Georgie records the happiness of his married life. Elsa and he moved to an elegant apartment at 1377 Belgrano Street, not too far from the National Library. Borges soon settled into a routine which included working at the National Library and visiting Mother at her apartment on Maipú Street. In spite of her reservations about his marriage, Mother attempted to present a good face and even shared with Elsa some of Georgie's limelight. On numerous occasions he was photographed between the two women. He seemed to have achieved a long-sought goal.

In 1967 he visited Harvard with Elsa and in 1969 went with her to Israel. At the end of that same year, they returned to the United States to attend the Borges Conference held at the University of Oklahoma. I met Elsa then and she impressed me as a very sociable and energetic person, extremely interested in all the gadgets and amenities that North American technology offered. But she was obviously uncomfortable about the obstacle her unfamiliarity with English represented and was forced to remain aloof when the conversation was not in Spanish. Nevertheless, she tried to put her best foot forward. Borges seemed pleased with her. Less than one year later I found that they had taken the first steps toward divorce. Georgie returned to Mother.

The marriage had lasted some three years. Elsa kept the apartment on Belgrano Street and Georgie, his 1,500-volume library. The Argentine press covered the affair with obvious relish. Georgie managed to avoid being too explicit although he admitted (*Así*, Buenos Aires, September 1970) that the marriage had been a failure. Elsa was more confessional and seemed glad to explain in some detail the causes of that failure (*Confirmado*, Buenos Aires, November 11, 1970, p. 43). She made the obvious observation that Georgie, a confirmed bachelor, had no experience of married life at sixty-seven, while she had been married for some twenty-seven years. Her outspokenness did not endear her to Mother. Many years later, Borges broke his rule of silence and confided to María Esther Vázquez that one of the things he found strange in Elsa was that she did not dream. Being a great dreamer himself, he must have discovered that Elsa's incapacity to dream kept them hopelessly apart.

I visited the Borgeses again the following year, in August 1971. This time I meant to have a good look at the apartment. Everything seemed subtly dilapidated. It was obvious that Mother had long ceased to care for the furniture, the curtains, or the rugs. At ninety-five, she was still going out every afternoon to a nearby church to attend mass. But she was so frail and thin that she seemed more an animated cartoon than a real woman. Georgie was his usual self. He talked endlessly without paying too much attention to people's replies. Since he was becoming increasingly deaf, he tried to cover up that added curse by almost nonstop monologue. But politeness was ingrained in him. Every four or six sentences he would stop to ask his listener, with some hesitation and even urgency, "Don't you think so?"

At the time, the Argentine political situation was very tense. Perón was taking advantage of the general confusion to engineer his return. But literary matters finally had the day. Georgie told me the plot of a story he was then planning to write. It was based on a real event: the birth of a black daughter to a wealthy Argentine family of the last century. It was a practical joke the family genes had played on the proud patricians. To avoid exposure, the parents decided to keep the child upstairs, forever, attended by black servants. Their aim was to create for her a sort of magical world in which the question of color could never be raised. Georgie was very concerned with the ethics of the story (was the girl really happy in her confinement?) and also with the technical problem of how to tell the story. From her point of view? From an ironical observer's? From a member of the family's? I knew that he was less interested in my contribution to the solution of the problem than in the opportunity to rehearse aloud and with a receptive audience the intricacies of the plot. Nevertheless, I volunteered a few suggestions and even recalled a real story, told by André Gide in one of his books, of the woman whose family kept her sequestered in Poitiers for some twenty years. Georgie seemed to have forgotten that incident. The conversation drifted. When Suzanne Jill Levine, who had accompanied me, asked for permission to take a few color photographs to record the visit, Mother suddenly came to life and rushed to her bedroom to get a comb to smooth back Georgie's hair. In his usual manner, he was oblivious to Jill's camera and kept talking, brushing aside Mother's hand as if it were a fly. Later, Georgie invited both of us to take a stroll along Florida Street, one of his familiar hunting grounds. We walked a bit among busy people who suddenly stood still, as if transfixed, when they recognized him. "It's Borges," they would say, pointing their fingers in his direction. Unaware of his own popularity, Georgie went on walking and talking. We ended up in a nearby café, the very British St. James', at the corner of Maipú and Córdoba. A mirror was on the wall next to our table, and Jill could not resist the temptation of having our double images recorded forever.

The following day I returned alone to have a long chat with Mother. Knowing my preferences, she offered me tea, and we talked about her and Georgie's ancestors, about Georgie's schooldays in Geneva, and about many other episodes in their long, fruitful life together. She knew perfectly well that I was engaged in some research for this biography and wanted to help me. I had sent her a copy of an illustrated book on Borges I had published in 1970 in Paris, and she told me that she had liked it very much and had even read it aloud to Georgie. She was pleased with it because I had been thoughtful enough to place at the very end of the book a beautiful photograph of the two of them in New York. I did not tell her that I had put that photograph there because I wanted to make a point.

While we were discussing the family tree, she volunteered to show me one she once had made. She went to the marquetry cabinet, bending down to reach the bottom drawer; when she tried to get up, her legs did not obey her. I rushed to her and helped her to stand. She was so thin and weighed so little, her bones seemed so brittle and her skin so cold, that I shuddered. A few days later, I returned to New Haven. That was the last time I saw her.

Four years later, on July 8, 1975, she died. It had taken her almost two years to do it. The Argentine newspapers recorded the death in great detail and even published some horrid photographs of her lying in bed like a corpse, with Georgie stiffly standing next to her, on the occasion of her ninety-ninth birthday, forty-seven days before her death. The photographs of her funeral did not spare a closeup of Georgie's tears. Two months after she died I visited Buenos Aires again. I went to see Borges at his apartment. There was no point in talking about Mother's death, so I tried to avoid the subject completely, but somehow it came up naturally in the middle of our conversation. Without any warning, he began telling me about her agony, how she pleaded for months with God to be spared the pain; how she addressed her long-deceased mother and father, begging them to ease her out of life; how she also called on Father; how finally she begged the maid to come and throw her into the garbage can. For the last two years her

473

moaning and her cries could be overheard even over the phone. When the end came, she was reduced almost to the bare bones, held together by only a film of parched skin, like a mummified image of herself.

Borges told me all these details, very quietly, in a neutral voice. He went on and on, in the halting, almost asthmatic monotone he generally uses when telling a story. At the end he switched abruptly to a general reflection about the strange things people say when dying, and he illustrated the point with an anecdote about his maternal grandmother. She was a lady of impeccable Victorian decorum. But on dying, she said the first four-letter word in her life: "Carajo, basta de sufrir." ("Fuck, enough of this suffering.") We couldn't stop laughing. It was a hysterical laughter in which repressed emotions found an outlet. The final loss, the cutting of the umbilical cord, was eased by an absurd anecdote.

I was to see him on other occasions, both in Buenos Aires and in the United States. By then he had adjusted to life without Mother. In Buenos Aires he was kept very busy with lectures, interviews, and participation in all kinds of literary events. He also worked regularly on a seminar that was (and still is) held at his home. The project began in the early 1960s. One day a small group of students from his course on English literature came to see him at the National Library, and on his suggestion they started a study of the origins of that literature. According to what Borges later told María Esther Vázquez, he was astonished by their enthusiasm. He tried to warn them that he knew as little as they did about the subject. Nevertheless, the following Saturday they began reading an Anglo-Saxon chronicle. A phrase they found—"Four hundred summers after Troy, the city of the Greek, was devastated"— somehow inspired them. "I don't know why we were so impressed by that phrase; perhaps it was the fact of finding the ancient fable of Troy washed up on the shores of the North Sea. This, and the discovery that Rome was called Romeburg, and the Mediterranean Sea, the Sea of Vandals, made me fall in love with that language" (Vázquez, 1977, p. 151).

After ten years of reading those ancient texts every Saturday and Sunday, Borges has an easy familiarity with the Anglo-Saxon language. To trace its roots, he has studied old Scandinavian writings, especially those of Iceland. He is proud of his small collection of Icelandic literature. On one of my recent visits to Buenos Aires he took me to his bedroom to show me the privileged place they occupy in the glass bookcase. To María Esther Vázquez he once confided that part of his fascination with the study of Scandinavian languages resides in the discovery of words.

BORGES: When one studies a language, one sees words closer. If I am reading Spanish or English, I hear the whole phrase; on the other hand, in a new language—

VÁZQUEZ: One hears word by word.

BORGES: Yes, it's like reading with a magnifying glass. I feel each word more than the native speakers do. This is why there is some prestige in learning foreign languages; there is, also, the prestige of things ancient; that is, to belong to a secret society. . . . (Ibid., p. 61)

Borges has kept the study group small—no more than six students—but he does a certain amount of promoting, even recruiting. I remember once, in January 1962, while we were having lunch in an Italian restaurant in Buenos Aires, he attempted to convince me to drop all my literary and scholarly work (I was then engaged in teaching English and American literature in Montevideo) and move to Buenos Aires to study with him. The invitation was only half-serious. He knew perfectly well that I was totally dependent on my teaching for an income. But I preferred to say no on different grounds. With mock seriousness, I explained to him that to the study of Anglo-Saxon or Scandinavian texts, I preferred the study of Borges' texts. He smiled a Cheshire-cat smile and abruptly changed the subject. Not everybody treated him so firmly. Among the young students who were attracted to the seminar was María Kodama, a young Argentine woman with Japanese ancestors. She became one of his most devoted students and also his part-time secretary. With a special talent for smiling reticence and self-effacement, María is always there when Borges needs her, patiently waits for her cue, and performs all the duties of a sensitive, intelligent, and erudite nurse to a man who is more and more dependent on external aid. In his last trips to the United States, María has been his constant companion.

While in Buenos Aires, she shares her responsibilities with other friends, among whom María Esther Vázquez is one of the most faithful. Now that Borges and Di Giovanni have parted company, María Esther takes care of his daily finances; one of his nephews, Luis de Torre, a lawyer, is responsible for long-range ventures. But the list of people who help Borges and care for him is immense. Not the least of them is Fanny, a solid Argentine woman who acts as housekeeper, cook, and nanny and treats him with the no-nonsense attitude grown-ups have toward children.

Despite all these friends and relatives, Borges is terribly alone. Although he has achieved in Buenos Aires the status of a folk hero (his popularity is second only to that of Carlos Gardel, the tango singer), Borges is totally cut off from the real world by his blindness. In a recent interview in the French magazine *L'Express* (reproduced in

Buenos Aires by *La Opinión*), he confided: "Now that I am blind—and blindness is a form of loneliness—I spend the greatest part of the day alone. Then, not to be bored, I invent stories, and make poems. Later, when somebody comes to see me, I dictate them. I do not have a secretary, and thus my visitors have to put up with my dictation" (*Opinión*, May 15, 1977, p. 28).

Blindness and the absence of Mother have practically abolished time. Borges lives forever inside a magic space, totally empty and gray, in which time does not count or (when it does) is brought about by the sudden invasion of people from the outside, people who still live in time. Protected and isolated by his blindness, in the labyrinth built so solidly by Mother, Borges sits immobile. He doesn't bother to turn on a light. Everything around him is quiet except his imagination. Inside his mind, the empty spaces are filled with stories of murder and wonder, with poems that encompass the whole world of culture, with essays that subtly catalogue the terrors and the painful delights of men. Old, blind, frail, Borges sits finally in the center of the labyrinth.

A Note on
This Book

On many occasions during the last five or six years I had the opportunity to discuss with Borges the project of writing a literary biography of him. Generally, he dislikes discussing his own work, and in this particular case things were made even more difficult because he is very reticent about his private life and finds biography an impossible genre. It is true that in 1930 he had attempted to sketch the life of a popular Argentine poet, Evaristo Carriego, but his book was short and very apologetic. The biographical chapter begins: "That a man would like to arouse in another man memories that only belong to a third is an evident paradox. To carelessly achieve that paradox is the innocent decision behind any biography" (*Carriego*, 1930, p. 31). In spite of this caveat, he *did* write a biographical chapter for that book, and even later wrote many biographical articles (on Hawthorne and Whitman, on Wilde and Edward FitzGerald, on José Hernández and Almafuerte). From 1936 to 1939 he also edited a literary page in *El Hogar,* one of whose features was a capsule biography of a contemporary writer. He has been an avid reader of biographies and, especially, autobiographies.

But in writing biographies, or in praising autobiographies, Borges has always drawn the line at the confessional. On several occasions, he has had good words to say about both Gibbon's and Kipling's autobiographies, never about Rousseau's *Confessions* or Amiel's *Intimate Journal.* What he likes in the former two is their reticence, what they manage to omit or barely suggest. He likes their refusal to surrender to the reader's morbid curiosity. In talking to María Esther Vázquez, he makes that point at least twice (Vázquez, 1977, pp. 155 and 166). In his own "Autobiographical Essay" he has practiced the

477

same restraint. His marriage, for instance, is never explicitly mentioned, although there is one tantalizing reference to it when he discusses a story he hadn't yet made up his mind to write ("The Congress," announced as a work in progress as far back as 1945): "Finally, as I was telling it to my wife, she made me see that no further elaboration was needed" ("Essay," 1970, p. 259). About the happiness and pain of married life, there is not a word.

Because I had read his strictures against biographies and knew his praise of reticence in autobiographies, I was reluctant to discuss my project with him. Finally, one day in 1975 I summoned up enough courage and told him about the kind of biography I wanted to write. It was mainly to be the biography of the literary oeuvre called Borges: how it came to happen, how the experiences of the man (Georgie, Borges, Biorges, and, of course, "Borges") had shaped it, how it had developed inside and outside him, and even in opposition to him. I explained that my main sources would not just be the usual biographical data but the texts themselves: texts authored by Borges alone as well as texts Borges authored with the help of relatives, friends, collaborators, interviewers, critics, and even enemies. I also stressed the fact that I saw my biography of him, my text, as a commentary on and an extension of his "Autobiographical Essay." That is, I aspired to write on the interstices and margins left by his own account. While he had to split into two different personae while writing about himself (the narrator and the protagonist), my task was simpler: I had only to create the perspective of a third literary persona (the reader). My biography, in short, was to be equally concerned with the life of Borges (the *bio* in biography) and with the writing of the life (the *graphy,* of course).

He seemed to like the idea, or at least he was polite enough to let me believe so. From then on, every time we met in Buenos Aires or elsewhere, he was ready to answer my questions and even to offer (voluntarily) here and there, in a very unsystematic way, some nuggets of the unwritten text of his autobiography: personal anecdotes, literary evaluations, short descriptive pieces. There was nothing intimate or confessional in them. He assumed, and I also assumed, that I was to respect the reticence that was so common in old Argentine society and that now, with the growing popularity of psychoanalysis there, is almost unheard of.

By accepting that tacit pact, I did not feel restrained to mention in my book only the public facts of his life. On the contrary, in his own texts and even in some interviews, Borges had communicated tantalizing views of his private life. I felt free to use these texts as well as to read in them as much as I could with the proviso that my readings were exclusively mine and that I, in doing so, was not betraying his confidence. Because our relationship had always avoided the confessional, because I never asked him any intimate questions (as some other critics and interviewers did), I knew I was in no position to betray his confidence. My readings of Borges, as well as of Georgie, were based on what the texts, his or others', said to me.

To be totally free, I did not even ask him to authorize my biography. It was tacitly understood that I would be the only one responsible for it. He himself had trouble understanding what an "authorized biography" was. Discussing another biographical book on him that was in the making, I had to spell out what the author's claims of legitimate biography meant. He was astonished. Believing the reconstruction of a man's life by another practically impossible, he laughed at the idea of an official life. Besides, he was skeptical about some of the claims of scholarship. Once, in writing about Beckford's *Vathek*, he made this remark: "One biography of Poe consists of seven hundred octavo pages. The biographer, fascinated by Poe's changes of residence, barely managed to salvage one parenthesis for the 'Maelstrom' and the cosmogony of 'Eureka' " (*Inquisitions*, 1964, pp. 137–138). Borges' article was originally published in Buenos Aires in 1943. Thirty-three years later he made me promise not to concentrate on his changes of residence and forget all about his books. I solemnly promised to remember them. But in seeing me to the door of his apartment, and while lightly pressing my hand, he went back to one of the anecdotes he had told me about his summer vacations in Uruguay when he was a child, and insisted: "Emir, do not forget to put in that little stream in Paso Molino." He was alluding to a moment in his life when he was extremely happy, swimming in the shaded, cool, and heavy waters of that stream. I promised I would not forget. And I didn't.

E.R.M.

Yale University
March 1978

479

Bibliography

This bibliography includes only the works quoted in the text. The books are first identified by the short titles used in the text references.

I. WORKS BY BORGES

El Aleph, 1949
First Spanish edition: Buenos Aires, Editorial Losada, 1949.

The Aleph, 1970
Complete title: *The Aleph and Other Stories, 1933–1969.* Edited and translated by Norman Thomas di Giovanni in collaboration with the author. New York, Dutton, 1970.

American Literature, 1971
Complete title: *An Introduction to American Literature.* Written in collaboration with Esther Zemborain de Torres. Translated and edited by L. Clark Keating and Robert O. Evans. Lexington, University of Kentucky Press, 1971. First Spanish edition: *Introducción a la literatura norteamericana.* Buenos Aires, Editorial Columba, 1967.

Aspectos, 1950
Spanish edition: *Aspectos de la literatura gauchesca.* Montevideo, Número, 1950.

Brodie, 1971
Doctor Brodie's Report. Translated by Norman Thomas di Giovanni in collaboration with the author. New York, Dutton, 1971. First Spanish edition: *El informe de Brodie.* Buenos Aires, Emecé Editores, 1970.

Carriego, 1930
First Spanish edition: *Evaristo Carriego.* Buenos Aires, Gleizer Editor, 1930.

Carriego, 1955
Second Spanish edition: *Evaristo Carriego.* Buenos Aires, Emecé Editores, 1955.

Dele-dele, 1946
"Dele-dele," in *Argentina Libre,* Buenos Aires, August 15, 1946, p. 5.

Discusión, 1932

480

First Spanish edition: Buenos Aires, Gleizer Editor, 1932.

Dreamtigers, 1964

Translated by Mildred Boyer and Harold Morland. Austin, University of Texas Press, 1964. First Spanish edition: *El hacedor*. Buenos Aires, Emecé Editores, 1960.

Essay, 1970

"An Autobiographical Essay," in *The Aleph and Other Stories, 1933–1969*. New York, Dutton, 1970, pp. 203–260.

Eternidad, 1936

First Spanish edition: *Historia de la eternidad*. Buenos Aires, Viau y Zona, 1936.

Fervor, 1923

First Spanish edition: *Fervor de Buenos Aires*. Buenos Aires, 1923. Privately printed.

Fervor, 1969

A new Spanish edition, thoroughly revised: *Fervor de Buenos Aires*. Buenos Aires, Emecé Editores, 1969.

Ficciones, 1962

Edited and with an introduction by Anthony Kerrigan. New York, Grove Press, 1962. First Spanish edition: Buenos Aires, Editorial Sur, 1944.

Figari, 1930

Spanish edition: Buenos Aires, 1930. Privately printed.

Héroes, 1956

"Estudio preliminar" to his translation of Carlyle's *On Heroes and Hero Worship* and Emerson's *Representative Men*. Buenos Aires, W. M. Jackson, 1956.

Idioma, 1928

Spanish edition: *El idioma de los argentinos*. Buenos Aires, Gleizer Editor, 1928.

Imaginary, 1969

Complete title: *The Book of Imaginary Beings*. Written in collaboration with Margarita Guerrero. Revised, enlarged, and translated by Norman Thomas di Giovanni in collaboration with the author. New York, Dutton, 1969. First Spanish edition: *El libro de los seres imaginarios*. Buenos Aires, Editorial Kier, 1967.

Infamia, 1935

First Spanish edition: *Historia universal de la infamia*. Buenos Aires, Megáfono (Tor), 1935.

Infamy, 1972

Complete title: *A Universal History of Infamy*. Translated by Norman Thomas di Giovanni. New York, Dutton, 1972.

Inquisiciones, 1925

Spanish edition: Buenos Aires, Editorial Proa, 1925.

Inquisitions, 1964

Complete title: *Other Inquisitions, 1937–1952*. Translated by Ruth L. C. Simms. Austin, University of Texas Press, 1964. First Spanish edition: *Otras inquisiciones*. Buenos Aires, Editorial Sur, 1952. (This book should not be confused with *Inquisiciones,* published in 1925, which has never been reprinted.)

Labyrinths, 1964

Complete title: *Labyrinths: Selected Stories and Other Writings*. Edited by Donald A. Yates and James E. Irby. New York, New Directions, 1964.

Lugones, 1955
First Spanish edition: *Leopoldo Lugones*. Written in collaboration with Betina Edelberg. Buenos Aires, Editorial Troquel, 1955.

Luna, 1926
First Spanish edition: *Luna de enfrente*. Buenos Aires, Editorial Proa, 1926.

Modelo, 1946
First Spanish edition: *Un modelo para la muerte*. Written in collaboration with Adolfo Bioy Casares. Buenos Aires, "Oportet & Haereses," 1946. Privately printed.

Morel, 1940
"Prólogo" to Adolfo Bioy Casares' *La invención de Morel*. Buenos Aires, Editorial Losada, 1940. American translation: *The Invention of Morel and Other Stories* (from *La trama celeste*). Translated by Ruth L. C. Simms. Austin, University of Texas Press, 1964.

Obra, 1964
First Spanish edition: *Obra poética, 1923–1964*. Buenos Aires, Emecé Editores, 1964.

Pereda, 1927
"Palabras finales" to Ildefonso Pereda Valdés' *Antología de la moderna poesía uruguaya*. Buenos Aires, El Ateneo, 1927.

Poemas, 1943
First Spanish edition: *Poemas, 1923–1943*. Buenos Aires, Editorial Losada, 1943.

Poems, 1972
Complete title: *Selected Poems, 1923–1967*. Edited, with an introduction and notes, by Norman Thomas di Giovanni. New York, Delacorte Press, 1972.

Poesía argentina, 1941
"Prólogo" to *Antología poética argentina*. Edited by Borges in collaboration with Adolfo Bioy Casares and Silvina Ocampo. Buenos Aires, Editorial Sudamericana, 1941.

Prólogos, 1975
Spanish edition: Buenos Aires, Torres Agüero Editor, 1975.

San Martín, 1929
First Spanish edition: *Cuaderno San Martín*. Buenos Aires, Editorial Proa, 1929.

Sand, 1977
Complete title: *The Book of Sand*. Translated by Norman Thomas di Giovanni. New York, Dutton, 1977. First Spanish edition: *El libro de arena*. Buenos Aires, Emecé Editores, 1975.

Tamaño, 1926
Spanish edition: *El tamaño de mi esperanza*. Buenos Aires, Editorial Proa, 1926.

Tigers, 1977
Complete title: *The Gold of the Tigers: Selected Later Poems*. Translated by Alastair Reid. New York, Dutton, 1977. First Spanish editions: *El oro de los tigres* (Buenos Aires, Emecé Editores, 1972) and *La rosa profunda* (Buenos Aires, Emecé Editores, 1975).

II. INTERVIEWS WITH BORGES

Alcorta, 1964
Alcorta, Gloria: "Entretiens avec Gloria Alcorta," in *L'Herne,* Paris, 1964, pp. 404–408.

Arias, 1971
Arias Usandívaras, Raquel: "Encuentro con Borges," in *Imagen* (no. 90), Caracas, February 1–15, 1971, pp. 2–5.

Burgin, 1969
Burgin, Richard: *Conversations with Jorge Luis Borges.* New York, Holt, Rinehart and Winston, 1969.

Christ, 1967
Christ, Ronald: "The Art of Fiction XXXIX," in *Paris Review* (no. 40), Paris, Winter–Spring 1967, pp. 116–164.

Correa, 1966
Correa, María Angélica: An unpublished interview with Borges. Buenos Aires, September–October 1966.

De Milleret, 1967
De Milleret, Jean: *Entretiens avec Jorge Luis Borges.* Paris, Pierre Belfond, 1967.

Fernández, 1967
Fernández Moreno, César: "Harto de los laberintos," in *Mundo Nuevo* (no. 18), Paris, December 1967, pp. 8–29.

Guibert, 1968
Guibert, Rita: "Jorge Luis Borges," in *Life en Español* (vol. 31, no. 5), New York, March 11, 1968, pp. 48–60.

Guibert, 1973
Guibert, Rita: "Jorge Luis Borges," in *Seven Voices.* New York, Knopf, 1973, pp. 77–117.

Irby, 1962
Irby, James E.: "Entrevista con Borges," in *Revista de la Universidad de México* (vol. 16, no. 10), Mexico City, June 1962, pp. 4–10.

Latitud, 1945
"De la alta ambición en el arte," in *Latitud* (no. 1), Buenos Aires, February 1945, p. 4.

Marx and Simon, 1968
Marx, Patricia, and Simon, John: "An Interview," in *Commonweal* (vol. 84, no. 4), New York, October 25, 1968, pp. 107–110.

Murat, 1964
Murat, Napoléon: "Entretiens avec Napoléon Murat," in *L'Herne,* Paris, 1964, pp. 371–387.

Opinión, 1977
"Las paradojas de Borges contra el castellano y contra sí mismo," in *La Opinión,* Buenos Aires, May 15, 1977, p. 28.

Peralta, 1964
Peralta, Carlos: "L'électricité des mots," in *L'Herne,* Paris, 1964, pp. 409–413.

Plata, 1945

"De novelas y novelistas habló Jorge L. Borges," in *El Plata,* Montevideo, October 31, 1945.

Ribeiro, 1970

Ribeiro, Leo Gilson: "Sou premiado, existo," in *Veja* (no. 103), Rio de Janeiro, August 26, 1970, pp. 3–6.

Simon, 1971

Simon, Herbert: *"Primera Plana* va más lejos con Herbert Simon y Jorge Luis Borges," in *Primera Plana* (no. 414), Buenos Aires, January 5, 1971, pp. 42–45.

Triunfo, 1969

"Habla Jorge Luis Borges," in *Triunfo* (vol. 24, no. 389), Madrid, November 15, 1969, pp. 35–36.

Vázquez, 1977

Vázquez, María Esther: *Borges: Imágenes, Memorias, Diálogos.* Caracas, Monte Avila, 1977.

III. CRITICAL AND BIOGRAPHICAL WORKS

Alén, 1975

Alén Lescano, Luis C.: *La Argentina ilusionada, 1922–1930.* Buenos Aires, Editorial Astrea, 1975.

Anzieu, 1971

Anzieu, Didier: "Le corps et le code dans les contes de J. L. Borges," in *Nouvelle Revue de Psychanalyse,* Paris, July–August 1971, pp. 177–210.

Baudelaire, 1951

Baudelaire, Charles: *Oeuvres complètes.* Paris, Gallimard, 1951.

Bianco, 1964

Bianco, José: "Des souvenirs," in *L'Herne,* Paris, 1964, pp. 33–43.

Bioy, 1940

Bioy Casares, Adolfo: "Prólogo" to *Antología de la literatura fantástica.* Edited in collaboration with Jorge Luis Borges and Silvina Ocampo. Buenos Aires, Editorial Sudamericana, 1940.

Bioy, 1942

Bioy Casares, Adolfo: "Los libros," a review of Borges' *El jardín de senderos que se bifurcan,* in *Sur* (no. 92), Buenos Aires, May 1942, pp. 60–65.

Bioy, 1964

Bioy Casares, Adolfo: *La otra aventura.* Buenos Aires, Editorial Galerna, 1964.

Bioy, 1975

Bioy Casares, Adolfo: "Chronology," in *Review 75* (no. 15), New York, Fall 1975, pp. 35–39.

Borges, 1921

Borges, Jorge (Guillermo): *El caudillo.* Palma (Majorca), 1921. Privately printed.

Britannica, 1911

"The Tichborne Claimant," in *The Encyclopaedia Britannica.* Eleventh edition. New York, Encyclopaedia Britannica Company, 1911. Vol. 26, pp. 932–933.

Chesterton, 1940

Chesterton, G. K.: *The End of the Armistice.* London, Sheed & Ward, 1940.

BIBLIOGRAPHY

Christ, 1969
Christ, Ronald: *The Narrow Act: Borges' Art of Allusion.* New York, New York University Press, 1969.

Clouard, 1947
Clouard, Henri: *Histoire de la littérature française: du symbolisme à nos jours (de 1885 à 1914).* Paris, Albin Michel, 1947.

Corominas, 1967
Corominas, Joan: *Breve diccionario etimológico de la lengua castellana.* Madrid, Gredos, 1967.

Cozarinsky, 1974
Cozarinsky, Edgardo: *Borges y el cine.* Buenos Aires, Editorial Sur, 1974.

De Gourmont, 1912
De Gourmont, Rémy: *Promenades littéraires.* Quatrième série. Paris, Mercure de France, 1912.

De Quincey, 1897
De Quincey, Thomas: *Collected Writings.* Edited by David Masson. London, A. C. Black, 1897. Vol. 3.

De Torre, 1925
De Torre, Guillermo: *Literaturas europeas de vanguardia.* Madrid, Caro Raggio, 1925.

De Torre, 1965
De Torre, Guillermo: *Historia de las literaturas europeas de vanguardia.* Madrid, Guadarrama, 1965.

Fernández, 1967
Fernández Moreno, César: *La realidad y los papeles.* Madrid, Aguilar, 1967.

Genette, 1964
Genette, Gérard: "La littérature selon Borges," in *L'Herne,* Paris, 1964, pp. 323–327.

Gobello, 1953
Gobello, José: *Lunfardía.* Buenos Aires, Argos, 1953.

Grondona, 1957
Grondona, Adela: *El grito sagrado (30 días en la cárcel).* Buenos Aires, 1957. Privately printed.

Ibarra, 1964
Ibarra, Néstor: "Borges et Borges," in *L'Herne,* Paris, 1964, pp. 417–465.

Ibarra, 1969
Ibarra, Néstor: *Borges et Borges.* Paris, L'Herne éditeur, 1969. A revised and enlarged version of the 1964 article.

Irby, 1971
Irby, James E.: "Borges and the Idea of Utopia," in *Books Abroad* (vol. 45, no. 3), Norman (Oklahoma), Summer 1971, pp. 411–419.

Jurado, 1964
Jurado, Alicia: *Genio y figura de Jorge Luis Borges.* Buenos Aires, Editorial Universitaria, 1964.

Klein, 1975
Klein, Melanie: *Love, Guilt, and Reparation and Other Works.* New York, Delta, 1975.

Lacan, 1966
Lacan, Jacques: "Le stade du miroir comme formateur de la fonction du Je," in *Ecrits.* Paris, Editions du Seuil, 1966, pp. 93–100.

Levine, 1973
Levine, Suzanne Jill: "A Universal Tradition: The Fictional Biography," in *Review 73* (no. 8), New York, Spring 1973, pp. 24–28.

Lucio and Revello, 1961
Lucio, Nodier, and Revello, Lydia: "Contribución a la bibliografía de Jorge Luis Borges," in *Bibliografía Argentina de Artes y Letras* (nos. 10–11), Buenos Aires, April–September 1961, pp. 43–112.

Marechal, 1948
Marechal, Leopoldo: *Adán Buenosayres.* Buenos Aires, Editorial Sudamericana, 1948.

Marechal, 1968
Marechal, Leopoldo: "Claves de Adán Buenosayres," in *Cuaderno de navegación.* Buenos Aires, Editorial Sudamericana, 1968, p. 133.

Megáfono, 1933
"Discusión sobre Jorge Luis Borges," in *Megáfono* (no. 11), Buenos Aires, August 1933, pp. 13–33.

Moore, 1929
Moore, Thomas: *The Poetical Works.* Edited by A. D. Godley. Oxford, Clarendon Press, 1929.

Mother, 1964
Acevedo de Borges, Leonor: "Propos," in *L'Herne,* Paris, 1964, pp. 9–11.

Neruda, 1974
Rodríguez-Monegal, Emir: "[Neruda:] The Biographical Background," in *Review 74* (no. 11), New York, Spring 1974, pp. 6–14.

Ocampo, 1961
Ocampo, Victoria: "Saludo a Borges," in *Sur* (no. 272), Buenos Aires, September–October 1961, pp. 76–79.

Ocampo, 1964
Ocampo, Victoria: "Vision de Jorge Luis Borges," in *L'Herne,* Paris, 1964, pp. 19–25.

Ocampo, Silvina, 1964
Ocampo, Silvina: "Image de Borges," in *L'Herne,* Paris, 1964, pp. 26–30.

PEN, 1937
PEN Club de Buenos Aires: *XIV Congreso Internacional de los PEN Clubs.* Buenos Aires, 1937.

Petit de Murat, 1944
Petit de Murat, Ulyses: "Jorge Luis Borges y la revolución literaria de *Martín Fierro,*" in *Correo Literario,* Buenos Aires, January 15, 1944, p. 6.

Pezzoni, 1952
Pezzoni, Enrique: "Aproximación al último libro de Borges," in *Sur* (nos. 217–218), Buenos Aires, November–December 1952, pp. 101–103.

Prose, 1972
Kinzie, Mary, ed.: "Prose for Borges," in *Tri-Quarterly* (no. 25), Evanston (Illinois), Fall 1972.

Reyes, 1943

Reyes, Alfonso: "El argentino Jorge Luis Borges," in *Tiempo,* Mexico City, July 30, 1943, p. 104.

Rivera, 1976

Rivera, Jorge B.: "Los juegos de un tímido," in *Crisis* (no. 38), Buenos Aires, May–June 1976, p. 23.

Rodríguez-Monegal, 1970

Rodríguez-Monegal, Emir: *Borges par lui même.* Paris, Editions du Seuil, 1970.

Sanguinetti, 1975

Sanguinetti, Horacio S.: *La democracia ficta, 1930–1938.* Buenos Aires, Editorial Astrea, 1975.

Videla, 1963

Videla, Gloria: *El ultraísmo.* Madrid, Gredos, 1963.

Vignale, 1927

Vignale, Pedro Juan and Tiempo, César, eds.: *Exposición de la actual poesía argentina, 1922–1927.* Buenos Aires, Editorial Minerva, 1927.

Yates, 1973

Yates, Donald A.: *"Behind 'Borges and I,' "* in *Modern Fiction Studies* (vol. 19, no. 3), West Lafayette (Indiana), Autumn 1973, pp. 317–324.

Zigrosser, 1957

Zigrosser, Carl: *The Expressionists.* London, Thames and Hudson, 1957.

Index

INDEX

INDEX

INDEX

INDEX

INDEX

INDEX

INDEX